"Case in Print" now appears in every chapter. This unique feature demonstrates the correlation between chapter content and actual classroom practice through the use of current newspaper and magazine articles.

CASE *in* PRINT

Middle School Madness

Although it may strike you as odd to think of eleven- and twelve-year-olds as adolescents, developmental psychologists typically apply this term to individuals as young as ten years of age. The reason they do is that the onset of puberty is taken as the primary characteristic that defines the passage from middle childhood to adolescence.

Middle School Rings in a New Level of Parenting for a Mom

DEBRA-LYNN B. HOOK
St. Louis Post-Dispatch 9/24/2000

For almost 12 years now, I have experienced children in the womb, in the high chair, in preschool and K-through-5.

I have lived the good and innocent life surrounded by the likes of Huggies, Gerbers and Mr. Rogers in a home populated by thumb-suckers, diaper-wetters, frogs, insects and little friends whose behavior I could predict and control.

For six of these dozen years, I have waved one to two children off to the neighborhood elementary school. I have blown kisses from the living room window and watched as bouncing backpacks disappear out of view to the school around the corner. I have strolled, any time I've wanted, up to our school, where I have hugged kids on playgrounds, patted teachers on backs and presented dozens of cupcakes on special occasions.

I had become quite comfortable in this baby-powdered mother's role. Too comfortable, some might say. Because one day it had to happen.

Middle School.

One mother told me she put her child on the middle-school bus a little boy, and poof! he turned into a teen-ager.

Middle school, I hear from other mothers, is where formerly clothed girls expose belly buttons when they raise their hands. Middle school is where kids float for years, groundless and unnoticed, between thinking they're supposed to be all grown up and secretly wishing they could sit on the floor and play tiddlywinks, even as they tote 200 pounds of books on their prepubescent backs between classes. Middle school invites a new kind of sleeplessness among parents, who only wish they could retreat to the days when their biggest problem was waking to feed the baby.

Our middle school is big. It has air conditioning. It even smells different. Whereas the grammar school smells of sour milk, pencil erasers and, in the spring, lilac, the middle school smells of new carpet and, I could swear, hormones.

Our middle school has a guidance counselor with a soft voice meant to soothe, and co-opt, skittish parents. During a tour of the school, she assured that the sixth-grade wing is separate from the evil seventh- and eighth-graders'. (As if those devil upper-level girls won't have the opportunity to show my son their belly buttons on the bus.)

She told me our middle school doesn't have a problem with drugs because the drug-sniffing dogs come on a regular basis. (Now that's a nice image.)

The counselor affirmed for me, that yes, middle school represents a difficult time for kids whose ebb-and-flow hormones already have them bewildered. Parents should brace themselves, she said, for their own confusion and imbalance as preadolescent rages begin to shake the house—and parental omnipotence.

On the way home from our tour, I thought about drown-

CASE *in* PRINT

Correcting Gender Bias

Gender bias can affect students in at least three ways: the courses they choose to take, the careers they consider, and the extent to which they participate in class activities and discussions. . . . As you may be aware because of numerous stories in the media, relatively few girls choose careers in science or mathematics. Among high school seniors from Rhode Island, 64 percent of the males who had taken physics and calculus were planning to major in science or engineering in college compared to only 18.6 percent of the females who had taken the same courses. . . . Several factors are thought to influence the choice male and female students make to pursue a career in science or engineering. One is familiarity with and interest in the tools of science.

Girl-Powered

CAROLYN BOWER
St. Louis Post-Dispatch 12/1/2000

Eighteen girls meet once a week at Sappington Elementary School, just west of Grant's Farm in southwest St. Louis County, to discuss binary codes, circuits and computer chips.

The girls, all fifth-graders, come from public and parochial schools throughout the Lindbergh School District. One recent afternoon, they took apart six computers and put them back together, installing CD-ROMs, sound cards and network cards. In a few weeks, they plan to assemble more computers. Then they'll begin to design web pages.

Laurice Badino, a gifted-education teacher at Sappington, 11011 Gravois Road, began the after-school class this fall as a way to interest girls in technology and computer science.

"With such a focus on technology in our world and in schools, you would think girls would continue to pursue this as they get older, but they don't," Badino said.

Federal statistics indicate that women hold only 28 percent of technical jobs, even though the number of women in the work force approaches 50 percent. Less than one in every five people who took Advanced Placement computer science tests last year was a woman. Women also made up less than a third of workers in computer and math jobs, according to the U.S. Bureau of Labor Statistics. Yet information technology jobs are among the fastest-growing occupations.

Badino has taught off and on for twenty years, the past four in the Lindbergh district.

At a recent class, she instructed the girls to hook up power supplies to hard drives. "It only goes in one way, so don't force it," Badino said.

The girls worked in teams of two or three to a computer.

Riley Krus, ten, had come to the class from St. Justin the Martyr School, where she attends fifth grade.

"Two weeks ago, we learned about binary boards and ASCII," she said. "They're both fun."

Students have learned to format hard drives and discs. They also learned about components of circuits, such as microprocessors, capacitors and light-emitting diodes. They learned that an example of a light-emitting diode is when a light signals the use of a computer hard drive.

At the other end of a table from Riley, Ariana Black, ten, a fifth-grader at Truman Elementary School, used a screwdriver and easily installed a CD-ROM in the computer. But Ariana cautioned she was not quite ready to take apart her home computer, which runs Windows 98.

Lindbergh school Superintendent James Sandfort said the girls' focus, concentration and technical skill impressed him.

"We hope that as these girls move up through the grades, they will move toward technical programs rather than away from them," Sandfort said. "When my computer shuts down, I know where to bring it now. These girls have no fear."

Badino would like to see some of her students become CEOs of computer companies some day—or at least be open to taking computer courses in high school and college.

"Now they can tell the boys how things work," Badino said.

Kara Jacquin, eleven, who also attends Truman, said she was intrigued by how the separate parts of a computer flow together.

"I wouldn't mind being smarter than the boys," Kara added.

Psychology Applied to Teaching

TENTH EDITION

Jack Snowman
Southern Illinois University

Robert Biehler

Houghton Mifflin Company Boston New York

Editor in Chief: Patricia A. Coryell
Senior Sponsoring Editor: Sue Pulvermacher-Alt
Senior Development Editor: Lisa Mafrici
Editorial Associate: Sara Hauschildt
Project Editor: Carla Thompson
Editorial Assistant: Kendra Johnson
Senior Production/Design Coordinator: Sarah Ambrose
Manufacturing Manager: Florence Cadran
Marketing Manager: Nicola Poser
Marketing Assistant: Laura McGinn

Cover image: *The Ocean* by Hans Hoffman, © Christie's Images/CORBIS

Text and photo credits appear on pages 587–588, which constitute an extension of the copyright page.

Copyright © 2003 by Houghton Mifflin Company. All rights reserved.

No part of this work may be reproduced or transmitted in any form or by any means, electronic or mechanical, including photocopying and recording, or by any information storage or retrieval system without the prior written permission of Houghton Mifflin Company unless such copying is expressly permitted by federal copyright law. Address inquiries to College Permissions, Houghton Mifflin Company, 222 Berkeley Street, Boston, MA 02116-3764.

Printed in the U.S.A.

Library of Congress Control Number: 2001133350

ISBN: 0-618-19266-2

1 2 3 4 5 6 7 8 9-DOW-06 05 04 03 02

Brief Contents

Contents

Preface to the Tenth Edition

Over thirty years ago, in the first edition of *Psychology Applied to Teaching*, Robert Biehler pioneered many of the student-oriented features still found in the text today. Although he has not been an active contributor to the book for several years, this Tenth Edition continues to show his influence, particularly in its usefulness to teachers. It is written for students enrolled in an introductory educational psychology course and is at once a basic source of information for prospective teachers and a resource for their future use as classroom teachers.

Goals of the Text

As has been the case from the first edition, the Tenth Edition of *Psychology Applied to Teaching* has been written to be used in three ways: (1) as a text that provides basic information, organized and presented so that it will be understood, remembered, and applied; (2) as a source of practical ideas about instructional techniques for student teachers and beginning teachers; and (3) as a means for teachers to improve their effectiveness as they gain experience in the classroom.

Major Features of This Edition

Because of its central role in American society, education is a dynamic enterprise. Tens of thousands of people—including classroom teachers, school administrators, state education officials, politicians, and educational and psychological researchers—are constantly searching for and trying out new ideas to increase student learning and achievement. This is especially true of educational and psychological researchers. Since the last edition of this text, many new developments have occurred in social, emotional, and cognitive development (areas such as memory and cognition); motivation; classroom assessment and management; multicultural education; inclusion of students with disabilities; and especially the use of computer-based technology to support student learning and achievement. The Tenth Edition of *Psychology Applied to Teaching* is extensively revised and updated, incorporating new developments in all its domains. Noteworthy themes of this edition include:

- **Emphasis on educational technology** Each chapter contains at least one section, and sometimes several, on how technology can be used to address the main themes and concepts of that chapter. For example, the reader will find discussions of how such technology tools as multimedia, hypermedia, tutorial programs, simulation programs, telecommunications, and the World Wide Web can be used to foster cognitive development, address individual differences, promote greater multicultural understanding, make learning easier for students with disabilities, promote learning and problem solving for all students, increase motivation for learning, help teachers manage their classroom, and aid in assessment of students. In addition, all chapters provide addresses for World Wide Web sites that contain useful supplementary information and links to other relevant sites. New marginal icons direct readers to the textbook's own web site, which provides connections to extended web resources.

- **Emphasis on classroom applications** *Psychology Applied to Teaching* broke new ground in 1971 as the first educational psychology textbook to provide numerous specific examples and guidelines for applying psychological concepts and research findings to classroom teaching. That orientation not only continues but is augmented by Chapter 10, "Approaches to Instruction," which links the writing of instructional objectives with five approaches to instruction that flow from different conceptions of learning.
- **Emphasis on diverse learners** To help prospective and new teachers understand and cope with the wide range of student diversity they will almost certainly face, we provide extensive treatment of this issue in two chapters: Chapter 4, "Understanding Student Differences," and Chapter 5, "Addressing Cultural and Socioeconomic Diversity." In addition, and where appropriate, we discuss aspects of student diversity in other chapters.
- **Emphasis on real-life contexts** The Case in Print feature offers newspaper articles about actual classrooms, illustrating the relationship between chapter content and real-life classroom practices. Because of this feature's popularity with both students and instructors, we have included it in every chapter of this edition.
- **Tables, graphics, and lists** To help students better understand and compare and contrast theories, concepts, and instructional approaches, and to keep interest and attention at high levels, we have inserted numerous tables, figures, and bulleted lists.
- **Emphasis on educational psychology as an interconnected discipline** Educational psychology, like any other discipline, is composed of an integrated set of theories, principles, concepts, and research findings. That sense of interconnectedness among its elements can easily be lost as students move from one discrete chapter to another. To highlight the interconnected nature of the subject matter that makes up educational psychology, we have made a conscious effort to cross-reference other chapters, both earlier and later, and to point out links among related ideas and approaches.
- **Reflective teaching** The concept of reflective teaching, its importance, and the role that a personal journal can play in helping one become a more reflective teacher are introduced in Chapter 1. This theme is picked up again in Chapter 15, where students learn how to construct a personal journal and how useful this activity is to practicing teachers.

The following lists explain some, though not all, of the major changes made to each chapter

Chapter 1: Applying Psychology to Teaching

- We introduce the topic of the current movement to hold schools accountable for student achievement, a development explored in detail in Chapter 14.
- We have updated sections that comment on the connection between learning about research and applying that knowledge in the classroom.
- To motivate readers to take advantage of the book's pedagogic features (such as key points, summary points, discussion questions, tables, and figures), we summarize a study that underlines the importance of using such learning aids.
- To the technology section we have added not only current statistics and web sites, but also a table illustrating the standards proposed by the International Society for Technology in Education. The section also contains a new discussion of using technology within a learner-centered approach to teaching.

Chapter 2: Theories of Psychosocial and Cognitive Development

- A new section on Vygotsky's theory of cognitive development.
- New material on gender differences in identity formation, adolescents' capabilities for formal operational reasoning, and character education programs.
- A new Case in Print on how multi-age grouping incorporates the ideas of both Piaget and Vygotsky.

Chapter 3: Age-Level Characteristics

- Current research on the development of children's theory of mind and their increasing awareness of cognitive processes and different ways of knowing.
- New material on how the values and practices of middle school teachers affect students' learning.
- Current research on the relationship between parenting styles and adolescent behavior.
- A new Case in Print on the rapid changes that children undergo during the middle school years.

Chapter 4: Understanding Student Differences

- To help students understand the significance of individual differences to teaching, we introduce the concept of differentiated instruction.
- We have updated the discussion of gender differences, intelligence in everyday settings, Gardner's theory of multiple intelligences, and field independence versus field dependence.
- The new Case in Print concerns one school's attempt to interest girls in science and technology.

Chapter 5: Addressing Cultural and Socioeconomic Diversity

- Current statistics on immigration to the United States, birthrate patterns, and the effect of those two forces on the ethnic makeup of the school-age population.
- New research on developmental bilingual programs, peer tutoring, cooperative learning, and the use of technology to help accomplish the goals of multicultural education.

Chapter 6: Accommodating Student Variability

- New and expanded material on inclusion, attention-deficit/hyperactivity disorder, and the use of differentiated instruction with gifted and talented students.
- A new Case in Print that describes a program to help students with learning disabilities improve their social skills.

Chapter 7: Behavioral and Social Learning Theories

- A new section that summarizes research on integrated learning systems and hypermedia programs.
- Enhanced discussion of the computer as both a tutor and a problem-solving tool, as well as suggested web sites that can help teachers evaluate the quality of educational software.
- Current research on the effect of teacher modeling on students' learning of cognitive skills.

Chapter 8: Information-Processing Theory

- Current research on the effect of concreteness and visual imagery on reading comprehension.
- New research on the beneficial effects of mnemonics.
- A new Case in Print on the vagaries of memory.

Chapter 9: Constructivist Learning Theory, Problem Solving, and Transfer

- A new Case in Print that describes the constructivist teaching philosophies and methods of teachers who were named to the All-USA Teacher First Team.
- Updated research on a variety of important topics, including the effect of prior knowledge, the use of worked examples to increase problem-solving skill, and the use of pictures and charts as an aid to problem solving.
- Enhanced discussion of technology's role in constructivist learning, including e-mail exchange programs and the use of computers as tools that support learners' efforts to create integrated knowledge bases and solve problems. The chapter includes recent developments in the CSILE and CoVis projects (and their successors), the Jasper Woodbury series, and the Scientists in Action series.

Chapter 10: Approaches to Instruction

- A new section that discusses recent research relating to humanistic education, especially students' sense of belonging.
- A new section on teachers' adaptations of cooperative learning and the effects of the modifications that many teachers make.
- Updated discussions of intelligent tutoring systems, the Higher Order Thinking Skills (HOTS) program, and the use of technology to support a social constructivist approach.

Chapter 11: Motivation

- A new section about the effect of interest on intrinsic motivation.
- Current research on attribution theory, beliefs about the nature of cognitive ability, and the effect of technology on motivation.
- New suggestions for increasing student motivation.

Chapter 12: Classroom Management

- A new section on the role of interpersonal problem-solving skills in preventing disruptive behavior.
- Additional examples of the use of active listening and I-messages to manage student behavior.
- Expanded and updated discussions of peer mentoring, the Resolving Conflict Creatively Program (RCCP), and the role of technology in classroom management.

Chapter 13: Assessment of Classroom Learning

- A new section on the use of performance tests to assess the knowledge and skills of all students, particularly minority students, more fairly and accurately.
- Expanded discussion of digital portfolios.
- Updated recommendations on technological tools to aid in classroom grading.

Chapter 14: Understanding and Using Standardized Tests

- An extensive new section on high-stakes testing (the use of standardized tests for accountability purposes) and the surrounding controversy.
- A new Case in Print on high-stakes testing.

Chapter 15: Becoming a Better Teacher by Becoming a Reflective Teacher

- New sections on the use of videotaped lessons and a guided reflection protocol to help teachers reflect on the quality of their instruction.
- Guidelines to help teachers construct a professional portfolio.
- Recommendations of technological tools to aid teachers in their professional development.

Special Features of the Text

The pedagogic features introduced in earlier editions have been improved and augmented to make this Tenth Edition more useful and effective than its predecessors.

Key Points At the beginning of each chapter, Key Points are listed under major headings. They also appear in the margins of pages opposite sections in which each point is discussed. The Key Points call attention to sections of the text that are considered to be of special significance to teachers and thus serve as instructional objectives.

Suggestions for Teaching in Your Classroom Most chapters include summaries of research findings and principles relating to a particular topic. These are followed by detailed descriptions of various ways in which the information and concepts might be applied in classrooms. Numerous examples of applications at different grade levels are supplied, and readers are urged to select applications that will fit their own particular personality, style, and teaching situation and record their ideas in a Reflective Journal. The Suggestions for Teaching are intended to be read while the book is used as a text and referred to by future teachers and in-service teachers after they have completed coursework. For ease in reference, these suggestions are surrounded by a colored border. A special index to the Suggestions for Teaching sections appears inside the back cover.

Case in Print This feature, which uses recent news articles to demonstrate how a basic idea or technique in a chapter was applied by educators from the primary grades through high school, has proven to be extremely popular with users. Following each article are several open-ended questions designed to encourage the student to think more deeply about the issue in question. The purpose of the Case in Print feature is to illustrate to preservice teachers that the psychological theory and research that their instructors require them to learn does have real-world relevance. A Case in Print can be found in every chapter.

Journal Entries This feature is intended to help students prepare and use a Reflective Journal when they teach. Readers are urged to use the journal entries, which appear in the margins, to prepare a personal set of guidelines for reference before and during the student teaching experience and during the first years of teaching. A guide for setting up and using a Reflective Journal is included in Chapter 15, "Becoming a Better Teacher by Becoming a Reflective Teacher."

New Links to the Textbook Web Site Because a wealth of material is available on the web site that supplements the text, this edition includes marginal icons to suggest points at which the reader may want to refer to the web site.

Resources for Further Investigation At the end of each chapter, an annotated bibliography is presented, offering sources of information on the major topics covered in the chapter. Internet addresses for World Wide Web sites that provide additional useful information are also listed in this section. Please note that the web sites were active at the time we prepared the text, but we, of course, are not responsible for their continued presence. Readers can access the textbook's web site for live, recently updated links.

Summary A numbered set of summary statements appears after the Resources for Further Investigation. This feature is intended to help students review the main points of a chapter for upcoming examinations or class discussions.

Key Terms Appearing after the Summary is a list of topics that are key aspects of the chapter. Understanding these topics is an essential part of understanding the chapter as a whole. To facilitate use of this feature, the page where each term is initially defined and discussed appears in parentheses.

Discussion Questions This feature appears after the Key Terms. Because understanding and retention of new information are enhanced when learners actively relate it to known ideas and experiences, the Discussion Questions ask the reader to reflect on how previous experiences (or possible future experiences) relate to the chapter material. These questions can serve as the focus for in-class discussion and out-of-class discussion.

Glossary A glossary of key terms and concepts is provided at the back of the book as an aid in reviewing for examinations or classroom discussion.

Instructional Components That Accompany the Text

Study Guide The Study Guide for the Tenth Edition of *Psychology Applied to Teaching* was designed to help students formulate and carry out a strategy for mastering the Key Points. Students are provided general guidelines for analyzing their resources and learning materials, planning a learning strategy, carrying out the strategy, monitoring their progress, and modifying their strategy if they are dissatisfied with the results. As an integral part of the suggested tactics for learning, original concept maps are supplied for each major section of each chapter. These concept maps are schematic representations of how major topics, subtopics, and Key Points of a chapter relate to each other. Also included in the Study Guide are exercises designed to help students enhance memory and understanding of Key Point material and two sets of review questions (multiple-choice and short-answer) to support student efforts at self-monitoring. Feedback is provided following the multiple-choice questions, explaining to students why each choice is either correct or wrong and referring students to specific pages in the text for verification and additional information.

Instructor's Resource Manual This teaching aid provides for each chapter a detailed lecture outline with supplementary teaching suggestions, a specification of new material to aid users of the Tenth Edition of *Psychology Applied to Teaching* in making the transition to the current edition, coverage of Key Points, supplementary discussion topics, student activities, extra references, listings of films, videotapes, software and Internet resources, and "Approaches to Teaching Educational Psychology," a compendium of teaching tactics from professors across the country.

Test Bank The Test Bank has been thoroughly revised by Jack Snowman. It includes test items consisting of multiple-choice items in alternate forms, short-answer questions, and essay questions. Consistent with this text's longstanding emphasis on mastery, each multiple-choice and short-answer question reflects a Key Point and either the Knowledge, Comprehension, Application, or Analysis level of Bloom's taxonomy. Feedback booklets allow instructors to point out misconceptions in students' reasoning.

Computerized Test Bank This component is an interactive computerized version of the Test Bank. It allows users to modify test items and add their own.

Real Deal UpGrade CD-ROM Free with every student text, this CD contains convenient links to sites mentioned in the text, as well as chapter outlines, Key

Points, chapter summaries, a glossary of terms, links to software demos, video clips, and practice tests.

HM Class Prep CD-ROM This product offers resources for instructors, including much of the Instructor's Resource Manual in electronic format for easy customization, PowerPoint slides, test items, and video and web links. Ideas on how to help students overcome potential stumbling blocks in the text and a discussion of student diversity as it relates to each chapter are also included on the CD.

Dedicated Web Site Helping today's instructors and students learn how to use technology meaningfully is a primary strength of new content in this text. As a corollary, a dedicated, interactive web site for this text for both instructors and students is available; it can be accessed from http://education.college.hmco.com.

The site allows instructors and students to locate information and engage in activities in one or more of its four distinct segments: (1) course resources, (2) field experiences, (3) class applications, and (4) student development (for the student side of the site) or web links (for the instructor side). Although the marginal icons in the text remind students to use the web site, there is much more on the site than we can possibly cross-reference in the text. We hope that both instructors and students will explore all the site's offerings.

Houghton Mifflin Teacher Education Web Site Houghton Mifflin's general education web site for students (go to http://education.college.hmco.com/students) provides additional pedagogic support and resources for beginning and experienced professionals in education, including the unique Project-Based Learning Space. This page links to five extended problem-based projects and provides background theory about project-based learning.

Videos Videos are available to course adopters. Instructors can contact their local sales representative for details. In addition, video clips of classroom footage are included on the student CD-ROM.

WebCT and Blackboard Cartridges For instructors using WebCT or Blackboard, modules are available with select content for the Tenth Edition.

Acknowledgments

While the content of a textbook is mostly the product of an author's knowledge, judgment, and communication skill, the suggestions of others play a significant role in shaping its final form. A number of reviewers made constructive suggestions and provided thoughtful reactions at various stages in the development of this edition. Thanks go out to the following individuals for their help:

David J. Ayersman, Mary Washington College
Beate Baltes, National University
Sterling Gerber, Eastern Washington University
Adria Karle, Cumberland University
Andrew Katayama, West Virginia University
Molly Nicaise, Santa Barbara City College
Peggy G. Perkins, University of Nevada, Las Vegas
Lawrence R. Rogien, Boise State University
Cheryl L. Somers, Wayne State University
Lisa Yamagata-Lynch, University of Utah

As we celebrate this Tenth Edition, it is also important to acknowledge the numerous reviewers who have contributed ideas and insights to prior editions. The list is long, and the contributions are many. (To see the full list of reviewers since the First Edition, log onto the book's web site!) In particular, thanks go out to reviewers who have helped shape *Psychology Applied to Teaching* over the past decade (please note that the reviewers' affiliations were those at the time of their review):

Julius Gregg Adams, State University of New York College, Fredonia
Barbara Anderson, Rhode Island College
Tom Boman, University of Minnesota, Duluth
Helen Botnarescue, California State University, Hayward
Lenore S. Brantley, Andrews University
Charles Brochette, Slippery Rock University
Clifford Burgess, Armstrong State College
Richard A. Couch, Clarion University
Richard Craig, Towson State University
Albert C. Ciri, Bridgewater State College
J. Kent Davis, Purdue University
Gail Ditkoff, California University of Pennsylvania
J. B. Engel, Willamette University
Richard English, University of Missouri, Columbia
Paul Erickson, San Diego State University
Lynn Fox, San Francisco State University
Dean Ginther, East Texas State University
Christine Cassatt Givner, Trinity College
William Gnagey, Illinois State University
Mark Grabe, University of North Dakota
Dale Grant, Georgia Southern College
Jerry Gray, Washburn University
Patricia Haensly, Texas A&M University
Richard Heck, Mansfield University
William Herman, Madonna College
Julian Hertzog, William Woods College
William Hopkins, SUNY, Cortland
Mark Isham, Eastern New Mexico University
David Jeffrey, Stephen F. Austin State University
Aileen Johnson, University of Texas, Brownsville
Martha S. Jones, University of Texas, San Antonio
Adria Karle-Weiss, Murray State University
Andrew D. Katayama, Southern Illinois University, Edwardsville
David Larkin, Bemidji State University
George Leddick, Purdue University
G. Sidney Lester, San Jose State University
Adele Levine, San Jose State University
Dov Liberman, University of Houston
Vickie Luttrell, Southwest Missouri State University
Bruce McCormick, Northeast Louisiana University
Thomas McCaig, University of Wisconsin, Stevens Point
Verna Lynn McDonald, National University and CSU, San Marcos
Sharon McNeeley, Northeastern Illinois University
Ethel Migra, National College of Education

Raymond B. Miller, University of Idaho
Anne Nardi, West Virginia University
Molly Nicaise, Santa Barbara City College
Lloyd Noppe, University of Wisconsin at Green Bay
Kenneth R. Romines, San Jose State University
James Rubovits, Rhode Island College
Rolando Santos, California State University, San Bernardino
Naim Sefein, SUNT, Fredonia
Stuart Silverman, University of South Florida
Walter Skinner, Georgia State University
Roy Smith, Long Island University
L. O. Soderberg, University of Rhode Island
Judy Speed, University of California, Davis
Daniel W. Stuempfig, California State University, Chico
Karen Swoope, Washington State University
Mary R. Sudzina, University of Dayton
Carol Takacs, Cleveland State University
Malcolm L. Van Blerkom, University of Pittsburgh at Johnstown
Alice Walker, SUNY, Cortland
Julian Wilder, Adelphi University
Barry Wilson, University of Northern Iowa

I would also like to acknowledge the invaluable contributions and encouragement of the following members of the Houghton Mifflin editorial staff who helped make this text more accurate, readable, useful, and attractive than I could have made it myself: Lisa Mafrici, Carla Thompson, Sarah Ambrose, Sharon Donahue, and Beverly Miller.

J.S.

Psychology Applied to Teaching

Applying Psychology to Teaching

1

As you begin to read this book, you may be asking yourself, "What will this book tell me about teaching that I don't already know?" The answer to that question depends on several factors, including your previous experiences with teaching and the number of psychology courses you have taken. Because you have been actively engaged in the process of formal education for a number of years, you already know a great deal about learning and teaching. You have had abundant opportunities to observe and react to more than one hundred teachers. You have probably read several hundred texts, finished all kinds of assignments, used a variety of software programs, and taken hundreds of examinations. Undoubtedly, you have also established strong likes and dislikes for certain subjects and approaches to teaching.

Yet despite your familiarity with education from the student's point of view, you probably have had limited experience with education from the teacher's point of view. Therefore, a major purpose of this book is to help you take the first steps in what will be a long journey to becoming an expert teacher.

Throughout this book, we will describe many different psychological theories, concepts, and principles and illustrate how you might apply them to teaching. The branch of psychology that specializes in understanding how different factors affect the classroom behavior of both teachers and students is **educational psychology.** In the next several sections, we will briefly describe the nature of this field of study and highlight the different ways that you can use this book to become a more effective teacher. ■

Key Points

These key points will help you learn the important information in this chapter. To help you study, they also appear in the margins of the pages, next to the text where they are discussed.

What Is Educational Psychology?

- Educational psychologists study how students learn in classrooms

How Will Learning About Educational Psychology Help You Be a Better Teacher?

- Teaching is complex work because it requires a wide range of knowledge and skills
- Research in educational psychology offers many useful ideas for improving classroom instruction
- Teachers who have had professional training are generally more effective

The Nature and Values of Science

- Unsystematic observation may lead to false conclusions
- Grade retention policies are influenced by unsystematic observation
- Scientific methods: sampling, control, objectivity, publication, replication

Complicating Factors in the Study of Behavior and Thought Processes

- Research focuses on a few aspects of a problem
- Scholars disagree about the usefulness of different types of research
- Constructivism: Individuals differ in what they perceive and how they form ideas
- Differences of opinion result from selection and interpretation of data
- Accumulated knowledge leads researchers to revise original ideas

Good Teaching Is Partly an Art and Partly a Science

- Teaching as an art: beliefs, emotions, values, flexibility
- Research provides a scientific basis for "artistic" teaching
- Good teachers combine "artistic" and "scientific" characteristics

Reflective Teaching: A Process to Help You Grow from Novice to Expert

- Reflective teachers think about what they do and why
- Reflective teachers have particular attitudes and abilities

What Is Educational Psychology?

Most educational psychologists, us included, would define their field as a scientific discipline that is concerned with understanding and improving how students acquire a variety of capabilities through formal instruction in classroom settings. According to David Berliner (1992a), for example, educational psychology should "study what people think and do as they teach and learn in a particular environment where education and training are intended to take place." This description of educational psychology suggests that to become the most effective teacher possible, you will need to understand such aspects of the learner as physical, social, emotional, and cognitive development; cultural, social, emotional, and intellectual differences; learning and problem-solving processes; self-esteem; motivation; testing; and measurement.

Educational psychologists study how students learn in classrooms

The importance of these topics to classroom learning has been underscored by the American Psychological Association (APA). In November 1997, the APA's Board of Educational Affairs proposed that efforts to improve education be based on a set of fourteen learner-centered psychological principles. These principles, which were derived from decades of research and practice, highlight the importance of learning processes, motivation, development, social processes, individual differences, and instructional practices in classroom learning. These are the same topics and principles that have long been emphasized by *Psychology Applied to Teaching.* A description of and rationale for each principle can be found on the following APA web site: **www.apa.org/ed/lcp.html/**.

This book's web site offers many supplementary resources, such as quick links to web pages mentioned in the text. Go to **http://education.college.hmco.com/students** and select the Snowman textbook site.

We recognize that you may have some doubts right now both about your ability to master all of this material and the necessity to do so. To help you learn as much of this material as possible, we have incorporated into each chapter a number of helpful features that are described at the end of this chapter. But first let's examine why the learning you will do in educational psychology is a worthwhile goal.

How Will Learning About Educational Psychology Help You Be a Better Teacher?

There's no question that knowledge of psychological concepts and their application to educational settings has the potential to help you be a better teacher. Whether that potential is ever fulfilled depends on how willing you are to maintain an open mind and a positive attitude. We say this because many prospective and practicing teachers have anything but a positive attitude when it comes to using psychological knowledge in the classroom. One teacher, for example, notes that "educational psychology and research are relatively useless because they rarely examine learning in authentic classroom contexts" (Burch, 1993). As you read through the next few paragraphs, as well as the subsequent chapters, you will see that criticisms like this are easily rebutted. We will offer a three-pronged argument to explain how educational psychology can help you be a better teacher, whether you plan to teach in an elementary school, a middle school, or a high school.

The information in this book can help you be a better teacher for three reasons: teaching is a complex activity that requires a broad knowledge base; many instructional practices are supported by reasearch; and teachers who are knowledgeable about that research are better teachers.

Teaching Is a Complex Enterprise

The first part of our argument is that teaching is not the simple, straightforward enterprise some people imagine it to be; in fact, it ranks in the top quartile on complexity for all occupations (Rowan, 1994). There are many reasons for this complexity. In increasing ways, teachers have daily responsibility for diverse populations of students with varied and sometimes contradictory needs. But perhaps most fundamental, the complexity of teaching derives from its decision-making nature. Teachers are constantly making decisions—before and after instruction as well as on the spot. To be informed and effective, these decisions should be based on a deep reservoir of knowledge and a wide range of skills.

The view that teaching is a complex activity that requires in-depth knowledge in a number of areas has been recognized by the National Board for Professional Teaching Standards (**www.nbpts.org/**). This is an independent, nonprofit organization of educators, administrators, and political and business leaders whose mission is to establish clear and measurable standards for what accomplished teachers should know and be able to do and to identify those teachers through a voluntary system of certification. The board's standards are based on the following five propositions (National Board for Professional Teaching Standards, 1994):

1. Teachers are committed to students and their learning.
2. Teachers know the subjects they teach and how to teach those subjects to students.
3. Teachers are responsible for managing and monitoring student learning.
4. Teachers think systematically about their practice and learn from experience.
5. Teachers are members of learning communities.

In general, the standards require teachers to be knowledgeable about learning and development, individual differences, motivation, self-concept, assessment, classroom management, and various approaches to instruction, all of which are covered in this textbook. Although the complexity inherent in teaching makes it a difficult profession to master, making progress toward that goal is also one of teaching's greatest rewards.

Teaching is complex work because it requires a wide range of knowledge and skills

To help you prepare to take on such challenges and become an effective teacher, educational psychology offers many useful ideas. It does not, in most cases, provide specific prescriptions about how to handle particular problems; rather, it gives you general principles that you can use in a flexible manner. Fortunately, the research literature contains a wealth of these ideas.

Research That Informs Teachers

The second part of our argument pertains to the potential usefulness of educational psychology research. Contrary to the opinion ventured by the anonymous teacher quoted previously, the research literature contains numerous studies that were conducted under realistic classroom conditions and offer useful ideas for improving instruction. There is consistent classroom-based support for the following instructional practices (Berliner & Casanova, 1993; Cruickshank, 1990; Porter & Brophy, 1988), all of which are discussed in later chapters of this text:

Research in educational psychology offers many useful ideas for improving classroom instruction

1. Using more advanced students to tutor less advanced students
2. Giving positive reinforcement to students whose performance meets or exceeds the teacher's objectives and giving corrective feedback to students whose performance falls short of the teacher's objectives

3. Communicating to students what is expected of them and why
4. Requiring students to respond to higher-order questions
5. Providing students with cues about the nature of upcoming tasks by giving them introductory information and telling them what constitutes satisfactory performance
6. Teaching students how to monitor and improve their own learning efforts and offering them structured opportunities to practice independent learning activities
7. Knowing the misconceptions that students bring to the classroom that will likely interfere with their learning of a particular subject matter
8. Creating learning situations in which students are expected to organize information in new ways and formulate problems for themselves
9. Accepting responsibility for student outcomes rather than seeing students as solely responsible for what they learn and how they behave
10. Showing students how to work in small cooperative learning groups

Coursework and Competence

The third part of our argument that educational psychology can help you be a better teacher concerns the courses you are currently taking, particularly this educational psychology course. Many researchers have asked, "How do the courses teachers take as students relate to how capable they perceive themselves to be as teachers?" One means that researchers have used to determine the answer has been to ask beginning teachers to rate how prepared they feel to handle a variety of classroom tasks.

On the plus side, a study by Yona Leyser, Laura Frankiewicz, and Rebecca Vaughn (1992) found that most of the beginning teachers surveyed believed they were adequately or well prepared to deal with such tasks as understanding early adolescent development, assessing student achievement, understanding and responding to individual differences in ability, and promoting the social growth of students. On the negative side, many teachers have reported that they feel uncomfortable in areas such as motivating students to learn, working with culturally diverse students, teaching exceptional students, managing the classroom, and teaching students how to use computers (e.g., Houston & Williamson, 1992–1993; Leyser et al., 1992; Queen & Gretes, 1982; Scales, 1993). In fact, a recent survey conducted for the U.S. Department of Education's National Center for Education Statistics found that only 20 to 30 percent of teachers felt very well prepared to meet the needs of students with disabilities, use performance assessment techniques, and integrate educational technology into classroom instruction (Lewis, Parsad, Carey, Bartafi, Farris, & Smerdon, 1999). This textbook will address all of these issues, with special emphasis on most of those about which teachers have reported discomfort. Our belief is that this course and this book will be one important means for helping you feel prepared to enter your first classroom.

Another way to gauge the value of teacher-education coursework is to look at the relationship between the courses teachers took as students and how effective they are as teachers. Patrick Ferguson and Sid Womack (1993) found that for students majoring in secondary education, the grades they received in their education courses were a better predictor of their subsequent effectiveness as teachers than either their grade-point average in their major (such as history, biology, math, English) or their specific knowledge (as measured by the specialty score on the National Teacher Examination).

Teachers who have had professional training are generally more effective

Finally, there are the cases of individuals who make dramatic improvements in teaching effectiveness as a result of specific courses in a teacher-education program. Linda Valli (1993) describes one student who stopped working on his bachelor's degree in mathematics to teach full time at a parochial high school. After one year of teaching, in which he described his classes as "basically out of control," he quit teaching, returned to college, and completed a teacher-education program in high school mathematics. Recalling the contributions of his educational psychology course, he judged his next teaching job as much more successful than his first.

The Nature and Values of Science

For the most part, this book summarizes information produced by people who were trained as psychologists. In addition, the observations of individuals not classified as psychologists will sometimes be mentioned. Indeed, people with many different kinds of backgrounds have taken an interest in education, and their ideas will occasionally be noted in the chapters that follow.

The primary purpose of this book, however, is to offer suggestions on how psychology (the scientific study of behavior and mental processes) might be applied to teaching. This text is based on the premise that information reported by scientists can be especially useful for those who plan to teach. Some of the reasons for this conviction become apparent when the characteristics of science are examined and compared with the limitations of casual observation.

Limitations of Unsystematic Observation

Unsystematic observation may lead to false conclusions

Those who make unsystematic observations of human behavior may be easily misled into drawing false conclusions. For instance, they may treat the first plausible explanation that comes to mind as the only possible explanation. Or they may mistakenly apply a generalization about a single episode to superficially similar situations. In the process, they may fail to realize that an individual's reactions in a given situation are due primarily to unrecognized idiosyncratic factors that may never occur again or that the behavior of one person under certain circumstances may not resemble that of other persons in the same circumstances. In short, unsystematic observers are especially prone to noting only evidence that fits their expectations and ignoring evidence that does not.

Grade retention policies are influenced by unsystematic observation

A clear example of the limitations of unsystematic observation is the practice of retaining children for a second year in a given grade because of poor achievement. Grade retention has long been used as a way of dealing with individual differences in learning rate, emotional development, and socialization skills. Retention rates between kindergarten and eighth grade in the United States are estimated to be as high as 20 percent (Roderick, 1995). In some school districts, the retention rate for a given grade level has been reported to be as high as 50 percent (Schultz, 1989). These rates may increase in the near future as states enact laws designed to hold schools accountable for student achievement. A number of states have considered passing laws that would require school districts to retain children who do not meet some predetermined standard. Such laws could specify, for example, that students who read more than one grade level below their current grade must automatically be retained.

The constructivist view of learning holds that individual differences in such factors as age, gender, race, and ethnic background lead to differences in what people perceive and how they form ideas.

Selection and Interpretation of Data

The amount of scientific information available on behavior and mental processes is so extensive that no individual could examine or interpret all of it. Accordingly, researchers learn to be highly selective in their reading. In addition, conclusions about the meaning of scientific results vary from one researcher to another. As you read this book, you will discover that there are differences of opinion among psychologists regarding certain aspects of development, motivation, and intelligence. Opposing views may be based on equally scientific evidence, but the way in which the evidence is selected and interpreted will vary. The fact that a topic is studied scientifically does not necessarily mean that opinions about interpretations of the data will be unanimous.

Differences of opinion result from selection and interpretation of data

New Findings Mean Revised Ideas

Scientific information is not only voluminous and subject to different interpretations; it is also constantly being revised. A series of experiments may lead to the development of a new concept or pedagogical technique that is highly successful when it is first tried out. Subsequent studies, however, may reveal that the original research was incomplete, or repeated applications of a technique may show that it is less effective once the novelty has worn off. But frequent shifts of emphasis in education also reflect the basic nature of science. A quality of science that sets it apart from other intellectual processes is that the discoveries by one generation of scientists set the stage for more complete and far-reaching discoveries by the next. More researchers are studying aspects of psychology and education now than at any previous time in history. And thousands of reports of scientific research are published every month.

Accumulated knowledge leads researchers to revise original ideas

As our knowledge accumulates, it is inevitable that interpretations of how children learn and how we should teach will continue to change. We know more about development, learning, and teaching today than ever before, but because of the nature of some of the factors just discussed and the complexity of human behavior, our answers are tentative and incomplete.

You should be aware, of course, that fads occur in education (just as they occur in other fields). Occasionally, national or international events cause changes in our political and social climate that often result in pressures on education to "do something." And when large numbers of educators embrace a new practice without waiting for or paying attention to research findings, fads develop (see Slavin, 1989, for an example). One of our objectives in writing this text is to demonstrate the importance of basing your practices on principles that have some research support. If you do so, you can avoid contributing to fads.

Over the past few pages, we have asked you to consider some of the values of science, the strengths of scientific observation, and a few of the factors that complicate the scientific study of behavior and lead to frequent changes of emphasis in teaching techniques. These considerations help explain why this book stresses how psychology might be applied to teaching; they also support the position that information reported by scientists can be especially valuable for those who plan to teach. At the same time, our intention has been to acquaint you with a few of the limitations and sometimes unsettling by-products of science.

The science of psychology has much to offer educators, but a scientific approach to teaching does have its limits. Because teaching is a dynamic *decision-making process,* you will be greatly aided by a systematic, objective framework for making your decisions. Research on teaching and learning can give you that framework. But for the reasons just cited, research cannot give you a prescription or a set of rules that specify how you should handle every situation. Often you will have to make on-the-spot, subjective decisions about how to present a lesson, explain a concept, handle mass boredom, or reprimand a student. This contrast between an objective, systematic approach to planning instruction and the need to make immediate (yet appropriate) applications and modifications of those plans calls attention to a question that has been debated for years: Is teaching primarily an art or a science—or a combination of both?

Good Teaching Is Partly an Art and Partly a Science

Some educators have argued that teaching is an art that cannot be practiced or even studied in an objective or scientific manner because of its inherent unpredictability (Dawe, 1984; Flinders, 1989; Hansgen, 1991; Rubin, 1985). Selma Wasserman (1999), who taught public school and college for many years, recounts how her teacher-education program prepared her for her first day as a public school teacher:

> Learning the "correct answers" not only had *not* equipped me for the complex and confusing world of the classroom but, even worse, had led me down the garden path. Implicit in what I had learned was that teaching was merely a matter of stockpiling certain pieces of information *about* teaching. If I only knew what the answers were,

Teaching Can Be a Rewarding Experience

Good teaching is as much the result of one's beliefs, values, and emotions as of one's formal knowledge. A few examples of beliefs that support good teaching are that teaching is one of society's most valuable and rewarding activities, that teaching must be done as well as possible every day, that it is important to get students excited about learning, and that there is no such thing as an unteachable student.

Special Young Teacher Wins a $1,500 Apple

CAROLYN BOWER

St. Louis Post-Dispatch, 9/7/96

Lisa Shipley will try almost anything to get her students' attention.

Macaroni for punctuation. Mr. Potato Head for a lesson in poetry personification. Popcorn for bribes.

"I always look at a lesson and say, 'Would that make me sleep?'" said Shipley, 24. "If it would, I would not do that to children."

Shipley, now in her second year as a seventh-grade teacher at A. B. Green Middle School in the Maplewood–Richmond Heights School District, is one of 51 teachers across the country selected recently to receive the Sallie Mae First Class Teacher Award.

The award, sponsored by the Student Loan Marketing Association, carries a $1,500 prize and an all-expense-paid trip to Washington Sept. 20. The award, in its 12th year, recognizes first-year teachers who have shown outstanding performance. In Illinois, the award will go to Sarah Drake, a history teacher at Naperville High School in Naperville, near Chicago.

The principal at A. B. Green, Arline Kalishman, recommended Shipley for the award. "This girl is such a winner," said Kalishman, whose school has won a national blue ribbon for excellence.

Kalishman gave these examples:

- Before Shipley's first teaching day a year ago, she compiled five notebooks, one for every seventh-grade teacher, to use in teaching novels. The books contained questions about novels, background information and suggested activities.
- Shipley helped train students for oratorical contests. Some students took first place.
- She sponsored the yearbook and got businesses to donate 10 cameras to students and to process their film for free.
- She oversaw the production of two plays.
- Shipley had her students decorate potatoes to teach the idea of inanimate objects taking on human characteristics.
- She had students redesign Frosty the Snowman in a simulated ad campaign to learn descriptive writing, persuasive writing and propaganda techniques.
- She compiled her own textbooks, such as an 80-page collection of poetry and a 50-page collection of short stories. The books discuss topics such as point of view, character and narrator.

Shipley gets some ideas from the Internet; others are her own creations. Raw test scores show Shipley's students performed as well or better than students in previous years, Kalishman said.

Shipley, who grew up in south St. Louis County, said she picked A. B. Green over 14 other job offers and $12,000 more pay in a wealthier district because "they needed me here." She likes to work with students from less-affluent homes, who appreciate what she does. She liked the freedom school officials offer to take risks with her 120 students.

Katie Mallon, 12, said, "She tries to make learning more fun."

Shipley said she was delighted but surprised to get the award.

"I don't feel I'm doing anything outstanding," she said. "I give the best I can every day so the kids will give their best. It's something everyone should do."

Questions and Activities

1. Lisa Shipley, the first-year teacher in this story, is obviously internally motivated, creative, and not shy about taking initiative. Do you think these are characteristics that people are born with or that develop with experience? If you think such characteristics are at least partly learnable and if you think you might be lacking in one or more of these areas, what can you do to improve your levels of motivation, creativity, and leadership?
2. Good teachers spend a considerable amount of time preparing for class so that, as Lisa Shipley pointed out, students are not bored or turned off. In this chapter and in the final chapter, we describe how to create a Reflective Journal as a way to help you plan, revise, and refine your instruction. If you would like to be as dynamic and effective as the teacher in this story, resolve to begin a Reflective Journal this semester and to add to it in the coming years.
3. This story illustrates that good teachers are internally motivated and committed to all aspects of their role. One way to start down the road to being this kind of teacher is to make a list of the special knowledge and talents you possess and then to think about the various school-related activities in which you could participate that would allow you to use those capabilities.

> I would be prepared to face the overwhelming and exhausting human dilemmas that make up life in classrooms. Unfortunately, I had been swindled. My training in learning the answers was as useless as yesterday's pizza. I was entering a profession in which there are few, if any, clear-cut answers, a profession riddled with ambiguity and moral dilemmas that would make Solomon weep. Even more of a handicap was that I became desperate in my search for the answers—certain that they were out there, somewhere, if only I could find them. (p. 466)

Wasserman's account suggests that there are no authoritative sources that will provide teachers with fail-safe prescriptions for the myriad problems they will face. Good teaching is as much the result of one's beliefs, values, and emotions as of one's formal knowledge. A few examples of beliefs that support good teaching are that teaching is one of society's most valuable and rewarding activities, that teaching must be done as well as possible every day, that it is important to get students excited about learning, and that there is no such thing as an unteachable student. The Case in Print tells the story of a first-year teacher who obviously subscribes to these beliefs.

When Wasserman states that teaching is not a matter of clear-cut answers, she is urging teachers to be flexible. Flexibility, which can be thought of as a "feel" for doing the right thing at the right time, can take many forms. First, it means being able to choose from among all the techniques and information at your disposal to formulate effective lesson plans that take the diverse needs and interests of all your students into consideration. It means knowing, for example, when to present a formal lesson and when to let students discover things for themselves, when to be demanding and when to make few demands, when and to whom to give direct help and when and to whom to give indirect help.

Second, flexibility entails the communication of emotions and interest in a variety of ways. David Flinders (1989) describes a teacher who, when talking to students, would lean or step in their direction and maintain eye contact. At various times, she would raise her eyebrows, nod her head, smile, and bring the index finger of her right hand to her lips, indicating serious consideration of the student's comments. In their book *Acting Lessons for Teachers: Using Performance Skills in the Classroom* (1994), Robert Tauber and Cathy Sargent Mester describe the importance for successful teaching of such acting skills as voice animation (variations in pitch, volume, voice quality, and rate), body animation (facial expressions, gestures), and use of classroom space.

Part of the art of teaching is knowing when to introduce an unusual assignment or activity that captures students' interest.

Third, flexibility includes the ability to improvise. When a lesson plan falls flat, the flexible teacher immediately thinks of an alternative presentation that recaptures the students' interest. Expert teachers actually plan improvisation into their lessons. Instead of writing out what they intend to do in great detail, they formulate general mental plans and wait to see how the students react before filling in such details as pacing, timing, and number of examples (Livingston & Borko, 1989; Westerman, 1991). Obviously, this type of high-wire act requires a great deal of experience and confidence. A nice example of capturing students' attention by the unorthodox use of space can be seen in the 1989 film *Dead Poets Society* when the teacher (played by Robin Williams) stands on his desk to lecture.

Fourth, flexibility involves the willingness and resourcefulness to work around impediments. Teaching does not always occur under ideal circumstances, and teachers must sometimes cope with inadequate facilities, insufficient materials, interruptions, and other difficulties. Thus, **teaching as an art** involves beliefs, emotions, values, and flexibility. Because these characteristics are intangible, they can be very difficult, if not impossible, to teach. Teachers must find these qualities within themselves.

Teaching as an art: beliefs, emotions, values, flexibility

The argument for **teaching as a science** is equally persuasive. Scholars such as Paul Woodring (1957), Nathaniel Gage (1984), David Berliner (1986), and Lee Shulman (1986) agree that the science of teaching, as such, does not exist. But they contend that it is possible and desirable to have a scientific basis for the art of teaching. By drawing on established research findings, both prospective and practicing teachers can be taught many of the prerequisites that make artistic teaching possible. Also, as Robert Slavin (1989) persuasively argues, working from a scientific basis helps teachers avoid the pitfall of subscribing to the latest fad.

Research provides a scientific basis for "artistic" teaching

This argument rests on the existence of a usable body of research findings, which educational psychologists believe does exist. As evidence, you might consult "Toward a Knowledge Base for School Learning" (Wang, Haertel, & Walberg, 1993) and "Productive Thinking and Instruction: Assessing the Knowledge Base" (Walberg, 1990). The authors of both articles identify dozens of research-validated instructional practices that have been shown to improve achievement. For example, twenty-four of twenty-five studies found that giving teachers more instructional time—that is, giving students more time to learn—leads to higher achievement. (This finding is often used to support proposals for a longer school year.) Other studies have demonstrated the benefits of alerting students to important material through the use of objectives and pretests, engaging students in a task through the use of questions and homework, and providing corrective feedback and reinforcement with written comments, verbal explanations, and praise.

Another example of usable research is analysis of the characteristics of expert teachers. One reason some teachers are experts is that they can quickly and accurately recall relevant knowledge from two large areas: subject-matter knowledge and knowledge of classroom organization and management (Berliner, 1986; Sternberg & Horvath, 1995). From the research being done in this area, we are learning how expert teachers acquire this knowledge, recall it, and use it appropriately.

Look back at the heading of this section. Notice that it reads "Good Teaching Is Partly an Art and Partly a Science," not "Teaching as an Art Versus Teaching as a Science." Our choice of wording indicates our belief that good teaching is a skillful blend of artistic and scientific elements. The teacher who attempts to base every action on scientific evidence is likely to come across as rigid and mechanical—perhaps even indecisive (when the scientific evidence is lacking or unclear). The teacher who ignores scientific knowledge about teaching and learning and makes arbitrary decisions runs the risk of using methods that are ineffective.

Good teachers combine "artistic" and "scientific" characteristics

Reflective Teaching: A Process to Help You Grow from Novice to Expert

The blending of artistic and scientific elements can be seen in discussions of what is called **reflective teaching** (see, for example, Eby, 1998; Hatton & Smith, 1995; Ross, Bondy, & Kyle, 1993; and Schön, 1987). Reflective teachers are constantly engaged in thoughtful observation and analysis of their actions in the classroom before, during, and after interactions with their students.

Reflective teachers think about what they do and why

Prior to instruction, reflective teachers may think about such things as the types of knowledge and skills students in a democratic society need to learn, the kind of classroom atmosphere and teaching techniques that are most likely to produce this learning, and the kinds of assessments that will provide clear evidence that these goals are being accomplished (a topic that we discuss at some length in the chapters on assessment and testing). Jere Brophy and Janet Alleman (1991) illustrate the importance of thinking about long-range goals by pointing out how the choice of goals affects content coverage and how content coverage affects teachers' choice of classroom activities. If, for example, one goal is for students to acquire problem-solving skills, students would likely be engaged in activities that call for inquiring, reasoning, and decision making. Debates, simulations, and laboratory experiments are just three examples of activities that might be used to meet such a goal. If the goal is for students to memorize facts and information, students will likely be given activities that call for isolated memorization and recall. Worksheets and drill-and-practice exercises are typically used to meet this type of goal. The point here is that effective teachers are reflective: they think about these issues as a basis for drawing up lesson plans.

Reflective teachers set aside time to think about what they do in class, why they do it, and how their methods affect student performance.

As they interact with students, reflective teachers are highly aware of how students are responding to what they are doing and are prepared to make minor but significant changes to keep a lesson moving toward its predetermined goal. Consider an elementary school classroom in which some students are having difficulty understanding the relationship between the orbits of the planets around the sun and their position in the night sky. The teacher knows there is a problem: some students have a puzzled expression on their faces, and others cannot describe this phenomenon in their own words. Realizing that some students think in more concrete terms than others, the teacher decides to push the desks to the sides of the room and have the students simulate the planets by walking through their orbits. All in the moment, this teacher engages in thoughtful observation, spontaneous analysis, and flexible, resourceful problem solving.

For events that cannot be handled on the spot, some period of after-school time should be set aside for reflection. This is the time to assess how well a particular lesson met its objective, to wonder why some students rarely participate in class discussions, to ponder the pros and cons of grouping students by ability, and to formulate plans for dealing with these concerns.

Reflective teachers have particular attitudes and abilities

To become a reflective teacher, you will need to acquire several attitudes and abilities. Three of the most important attitudes are an introspective orientation, an open-minded but questioning attitude about educational theories and practices, and the willingness to take responsibility for your decisions and actions. These attitudes need to be combined with the ability to view situations from the perspectives of others (students, parents, principal, other teachers), the ability to find information that allows an alternative explanation of classroom events and produces more effective instructional methods, and the ability to use compelling evidence in support of a decision (Eby, 1998; Ross et al., 1993). We hasten to add that although reflection is largely a solitary activity, you should discuss your concerns with colleagues, friends, students, and parents to get different perspectives on the nature of a problem and possible alternative courses of action.

As you can probably see from this brief discussion, the reflection process is likely to work well when teachers have command of a wide range of knowledge about the nature of students, the learning process, and the instructional process. By mastering much of the content of this text, you will be that much more prepared than your less knowledgeable peers to make productive use of the time you devote to reflection.

Another factor that has been shown to contribute to teacher reflectivity is journal writing. Keeping a written journal forces you to express with some clarity your thoughts and beliefs about the causes of classroom events, how you feel about those events, and what you might do about them (Bolin, 1990; Han, 1995). Thus, one potentially helpful way you might begin developing this reflective capacity is to follow our suggestion for compiling a Reflective Journal. In the final chapter of this book, we describe how you might set up this journal.

Uses of This Book

This book has been written so that it can be used in three ways. First, it is a text for a course in educational psychology intended to help you master an organized sampling of scientific knowledge about development, learning, objectives, motivation, evaluation, and classroom management. Second, it is a source of practical ideas and suggestions for use during your time as a student teacher and your first years of teaching. Third, it is a resource to help you reflect on and analyze your own teaching when used in conjunction with the compilation of a Reflective Journal.

Using This Book to Acquire Scientific Information

A substantial amount of scientific knowledge is of potential value to teachers. This book offers a selection of information from this pool of knowledge, organized so that you can learn and remember what you read as easily and effectively as possible. Chances are that your instructor will present lectures, organize discussions, provide videotapes and software programs, and perhaps arrange field trips that will tie in with what is discussed in assigned chapters of this text. The first way you can use this book, then, is to become well acquainted with an organized body of scientific information in the field of educational psychology.

For study aids, see the web site sections called Study Strategy Links, ACE Self-Testing, Chapter Themes, and Thought Questions. Go to this book's web site at **http://education.college.hmco.com/students**.

To help you learn and accurately recall as much of this information as possible (because in all likelihood, you will have to take exams), we have included in each chapter such features as key points, bold and italicized items, headings and subheadings, tables and figures, summary points, and discussion questions. While you may have every intention at this point of using these features to learn the information in each chapter and pass your exams, such personal resolutions are often easier to make than to keep. To drive this point home, and perhaps motivate you to do a better job of learning than most other students, consider the findings of a recent study (Winne & Jamieson-Noel, 2001). Several dozen college students who read and were tested on an unfamiliar reading passage made very infrequent use of such study tactics as trying to learn terms in boldface or italics, attending to headings, comparing one figure to another, and comparing text explanations with figures. Furthermore, as they encountered objectives that ranged from those that required less cognitive effort (for example, describing important concepts) to those that required more cognitive effort (such as explaining cause-and-effect relations, applying principles, and generating and evaluating alternative answers), they used fewer, rather than more, of the above study tactics.

Using This Book as a Source of Practical Ideas

The Field Experiences section on the textbook web site can help you in your student teaching; see **http://education.college.hmco.com/students**.

The second way this book can be used is as a source of practical ideas on how to teach in diverse, demanding, and often technologically sophisticated classrooms. To that end, you should think of specific ways in which you might apply what you learn from this text.

Sooner or later, you will engage in student teaching. You may be student teaching at the same time you are taking educational psychology, in fact. Your performance as a student teacher will probably be one of the most important factors considered when you apply for a teaching position. Furthermore, once you secure a

This book contains much scientific information and several features, such as suggestions for teaching, uses of technology, and suggestions for constructing a Reflective Journal, that will help you become and effective teacher during the early and later stages of your career.

job, your performance in the classroom will determine whether you will be offered a contract for a second year. Therefore, you will be eager to function as a prepared, confident, resourceful student teacher and first-year teacher. This book has been designed to help you get ready for your first teaching experiences and serve as a resource for finding solutions to problems as they arise.

Using This Book to Become a Reflective Teacher

As you gain experience in the classroom, you should begin to observe your own teaching and reflect daily on what you feel is working and what is not. Because you cannot anticipate all the problems you will encounter in any classroom, you will need to continually make adjustments and engage in a process of trial and error. Thus, the third way you can use this book (especially in conjunction with the compilation of your own Reflective Journal) is to analyze specific facets of your instructional techniques and plan how to correct errors and improve successes.

Special Features of This Book

This book has several distinctive features that are intended to be used in rather specialized ways: Key Points, Suggestions for Teaching in Your Classroom, Case in Print, one or more sections of every chapter that are devoted to discussing applications of technology to teaching, references to numerous Web sites that relate to various aspects of teaching and learning, Resources for Further Investigation, and Journal Entries. In addition, your compilation of a separate component to accompany this book—the Reflective Journal—is recommended. This journal makes use of the text's Journal Entries and the Suggestions for Teaching.

Key Points

At the beginning of each chapter, you will find a list of *Key Points*. The Key Points also appear within the body of the chapter, printed in small type in the margins. These points have been selected to help you learn and remember sections of each chapter that are of special significance to teachers. (These sections may be stressed on exams, but they were originally selected because they are important, not because they can serve as the basis for test items.) To grasp the nature of the Key Points, turn back to the opening page of this chapter, which lists points stressed under the chapter's major headings. Then flip through the chapter to see how the appearance of the Key Points in the margins calls attention to significant sections of the text.

Suggestions for Teaching in Your Classroom

In most of the chapters, you will find summaries of research that serve as the basis for related principles or conclusions. These sets of principles or conclusions are the foundation for *Suggestions for Teaching in Your Classroom*. Suggestions are usually followed by examples illustrating how they might be applied. In most cases, examples are provided for both elementary and secondary grades because there usually are differences in the way a principle might be applied in dealing with younger and with older students. To help you find information relating to particular aspects of teaching, an index to the Suggestions for Teaching in Your Classroom is printed inside the back cover.

Many research articles and textbooks provide only vague guidelines for classroom use and no concrete examples. But when new research-based ideas are presented in a concrete and usable form, teachers are much more likely to try them out (Gersten & Brengelman, 1996). This is why *Psychology Applied to Teaching* places so much emphasis on concrete suggestions for teaching. But as useful as our suggestions might be, you cannot use them as prescriptions. Every school building and every group of students is different. You have to learn how to adapt the suggestions in this book and any other books that you will read to the particular dynamics of each class. This is the essence of being a reflective teacher.

Case in Print

This feature presents a recent newspaper article that either elaborates on an idea or technique described in the chapter or shows how public school educators applied an idea.

The Role of Technology in Learning and Instruction

Go to the Web Sources section at **http://education.college.hmco.com/students** for links to important web pages. To explore educational technology, check the Technology Demos section.

The use of computer-based technology in education grew so rapidly during the last half of the 1990s that it is now almost commonplace. In 1994, only 35 percent of elementary and secondary schools and 3 percent of classrooms had access to the Internet. By 1999, those figures had exploded to 95 percent of schools and 63 percent of classrooms (U.S. Department of Education, 2000). In addition, teachers can use the **World Wide Web** (a global system of interconnected computers) for professional development. As a teacher in the new millennium, you will undoubtedly want to be knowledgeable about the many ways technology can contribute to learning and instruction.

A good place to begin your exploration of what the web has to offer is the we page Teacher Resources for a Global Community of Learners (**www.cheneysd.org/websites.htm**). Here you will find links to web sites that will aid your professional development, arranged in five categories (K–12 Reference Sites, K–8 Curriculum Sites, 9–12 Curriculum Sites, Free Pictures and Clip Art, and Assessment and Essential Academic Learning Requirements). Some sites provide materials and ideas for lessons, and others make it possible for you to exchange teaching tips with and solicit opinions from other teachers about how to solve various instructional and classroom management problems. In the final chapter, we provide our own list of web sites that have discussion forums or chatrooms for preservice and practicing teachers.

We believe that it is important for prospective teachers to understand how to integrate technology in the curriculum regardless of the content area or student age level. In fact, *Psychology Applied to Teaching* is the first educational psychology textbook that discusses technology possibilities for teaching and learning in every chapter. Throughout the book, we will explore an assortment of educational technologies, including simulations, tutorials, word processors, hypermedia, multimedia, and online learning tools, and point out how they can have a significant impact on classroom learning. All references to software and other forms of computer technology in this book will be highlighted by a blue vertical bar, such as the one appearing here.

As with any other instructional method, material, or medium that has been enthusiastically received, you should strive to keep things in proper perspective. There is no doubt about the computer's ability to help students analyze, sort, transform, and present information in a variety of formats or about the ability of the World Wide Web to connect students to other individuals and information sources. But as Richard Mayer, a leading educational psychology researcher, has noted, educational technology is simply a medium of instruction, not a method of instruction. It is Mayer's belief, and ours, that teachers should embed technology within a learner-centered approach to teaching (Suomala & Shaughnessy, 2000)—that is, within an approach based on an understanding of how students develop and learn.

As you examine the technology resources and ideas mentioned in this book, you should be thinking about the ways in which they might enhance the learning environment of your classroom. To help you do this, we encourage you to examine the standards and competencies that have been proposed for four grade levels by the International Society for Technology in Education (ISTE, 1998). For each grade level, Table 1.1 lists two of the six standards and their respective competencies. The complete list of technology standards and competencies for students as well as standards for teachers and administrators can be found on the ISTE web site (**http://www.cnets.org/**).

RESOURCES FOR FURTHER INVESTIGATION

Despite this book's attempt to provide at least partial solutions to the most common difficulties that teachers face, you are bound, sooner or later, to become aware of problems that are not discussed in these pages. You may want additional data on some aspects of teaching, either while you are taking this course or afterward. For this reason, we provide an annotated bibliography at the end of each chapter. *Resources for Further Investigation* lists articles, books, and online (Internet) sources you might consult.

For additional resources keyed to each chapter, use the Web Sources section at **http://education.college.hmco.com/students**.

Two important points should be mentioned regarding Internet sources of information. First, all the databases and resources listed or described throughout this book have been checked for accuracy as of the book's publication date. The world of online information, however, is in constant flux: databases are updated, moved, renamed, or deleted from the Internet network every day. If you are unable to find one of the resources mentioned, we recommend that you consult your school's com-

Table 1.1 Examples of Technology Standards and Competencies for Students

Grade Level	Standards	Competencies
PreK–2	Basic Operations and Concepts	Use input devices (e.g., mouse, keyboard, remote control) and output devices (e.g., monitor, printer) to successfully operate computers, VCRs, audiotapes, and other technologies.
	Technology Communication Tools	Gather information and communicate with others using telecommunications, with support from teachers, family members, or student partners.
3–5	Social, Ethical, and Human Issues	Discuss common uses of technology in daily life and the advantages and disadvantages those uses provide.
	Technology Problem-Solving and Decision-Making Tools	Evaluate the accuracy, relevance, appropriateness, comprehensiveness, and bias of electronic information sources.
6–8	Technology Productivity Tools	Use content-specific tools, software, and simulations (e.g., environmental probes, graphing calculators, exploratory environments, Web tools) to support learning and research.
	Technology Research Tools	Select and use appropriate tools and technology resources to accomplish a variety of tasks and solve problems.
9–12	Social, Ethical, and Human Issues	Identify capabilities and limitations of contemporary and emerging technology resources and assess the potential of these systems and services to address personal, lifelong learning, and workplace needs.
	Technology Productivity Tools	Investigate and apply expert systems, intelligent agents, and simulations in real-world situations.

International Society for Technology in Education (1998).

puter support person or your colleagues (because the most current information is often passed by word of mouth).

This brings up the second important point about online information: it is no more reliable (and in some cases is definitely less reliable) than what you may find in print. In particular, newsgroups and discussion groups are notorious for participants' distribution of incorrect, incomplete, or misleading advice or information. Our recommendation to you is to treat online information as you would print: try to stay with publishers or databases that are maintained by reputable sources, such as education or psychology departments of universities, major educational associations, and the U.S. government. Double-check the information you gather online. Never assume that because it appears on a computer it is accurate! And remember that participating in a newsgroup discussion is most useful for generating new ideas or potential directions that you can pursue further on your own or with a group of classmates.

JOURNAL ENTRIES

Within the margins of each chapter, you will find numerous instances of the phrase *Journal Entry.* These marginal headings are related to the material just opposite in the text. They are intended to serve as suggested wordings for the headings of pages in a Reflective Journal that we strongly encourage you to keep. In the final chapter, we describe the beneficial effects of reflection and journal writing on teaching, and we describe how you can use the suggested journal entries to organize your first Reflective Journal. If you do not have time to begin your journal while taking the course, we hope you will go through the book a second time, after you finish this course, for the purpose of developing a custom-designed journal.

For additional journal topics, check the Reflective Journal Questions at **http://education.college.hmco.com/students**.

RESOURCES FOR FURTHER INVESTIGATION

■ The Art and Science of Teaching

Louis J. Rubin examines teaching as art and teaching as theater in *Artistry in Teaching* (1985). In *Acting Lessons for Teachers: Using Performance Skills in the Classroom* (1994), Robert Tauber and Cathy Sargent Mester provide additional insights into the art of teaching. They discuss how such theatrical skills as gesture, body movement, voice pitch, role playing, use of props, and suspense contribute to teacher enthusiasm and student achievement. Don't overlook Appendix II, which contains testimonials from eighteen award-winning college professors about the value of acting skills in the classroom.

Borrowing from the writings of ancient Greek philosophers and the early twentieth-century philosopher John Dewey, James Garrison describes teaching as a creative calling that involves such factors as emotions, intuition, values, and practical wisdom in *Dewey and Eros: Wisdom and Desire in the Art of Teaching* (1997). In Chapter 1 of *Researching the Art of Teaching: Ethnography for Educational Use* (1996), Peter Woods summarizes the various arguments that have been made for teaching as an art, as a science, and as an activity that combines both art and science. Using a letter format, Vito Perrone covers such topics as deciding what to teach, engaging students, valuing differences, empowering teachers, and refining the craft of teaching in *A Letter to Teachers: Reflections on Schooling and the Art of Teaching* (1991).

To learn about the scientific knowledge base that underlies teaching, you might want to look at *Putting Research to Work in Your School* (1993), by David Berliner and Ursula Casanova. In each of six sections (teaching, instructional strategies, learning, motivation, school and society, and testing), they point out how a research study has shed light on such relevant issues as how to make cross-age tutoring work, teaching memory skills to students, and motivating students through project-based learning.

Several handbooks provide excellent analyses of research on various aspects of teaching. Part 2 of the *Handbook of Research on Teaching* (3d ed., 1986), edited by Merlin Wittrock, contains articles on teachers' thought processes, students' thought processes, teacher behavior and student achievement, and teaching functions. Part V of the *Handbook of Research on Teacher Education* (2d ed., 1996), edited by John Sikula, discusses the problems of beginning teachers, among other topics. Part IV of the *Handbook of Educational Psychology* (1996), edited by David C. Berliner and Robert C. Calfee, contains seven chapters that deal with such issues as learning to teach, the beliefs and knowledge base of teachers, and teaching and learning in a classroom context. Section I, Part A of the *Handbook of Education and Human Development* (1996), edited by David R. Olson and Nancy Torrance, deals with the psychological foundations of teaching.

■ Reflective Teaching

Several books explain what it means to be a reflective teacher and describe the benefits that this approach to teaching can produce. The briefest of these books, at seventy-eight pages, is *Reflective Teaching: An Introduction* (1996), by Kenneth M. Zeichner and Daniel P. Liston. Christopher M. Clark adds an interesting dimension to reflective teaching in his book *Thoughtful Teaching* (1995). In addition to the common conception of a reflective teacher as one who solves problems and makes decisions, Clark's reflective teacher is also considerate of the feelings and viewpoints of students and colleagues. Two other books on reflective teaching are *Reflective Teaching for Student Empowerment* (1993), by Dorene D. Ross, Elizabeth Bondy, and Diane W. Kyle, and *Reflective Planning, Teaching, and Evaluation: K–12* (2nd ed., 1998), by Judith W. Eby.

Summary

1. Educational psychology is a scientific discipline that seeks to understand and improve how students learn from instruction in classroom settings.
2. Learning about the research findings and principles of educational psychology can help you be a better teacher because (a) teaching is complex work that requires a wide range of knowledge and skills, (b) the research literature contains numerous useful ideas for improving your instruction, and (c) teachers who have had professional training are often more effective than those who have not had such training.
3. Unsystematic observations of students may lead teachers to draw false conclusions because of limited cases, unrecognized or unusual factors, and a tendency to ignore contrary evidence. As an example, although scientific evidence does not support the practice of grade retention, it remains popular among teachers and parents because of unsystematic observations about its effectiveness.
4. Scientifically gathered evidence is more trustworthy than casual observation because it involves sampling, control, objectivity, publication, and replication.
5. The scientific study of education is complicated by the limited focus of research, debates about which type of research is most useful, individual differences in perception and thinking, the inability of researchers to keep up with all published research, different interpretations of findings, and the ongoing accumulation of new knowledge.
6. Research on teaching and learning provides a systematic, objective basis for making instructional decisions, but it cannot specify how to handle every classroom situation. Many classroom decisions must be made on the spot. This contrast represents the science and the art of teaching.
7. Those who argue that teaching is an art point to communication of emotions, values and beliefs, and flexibility as qualities that good teachers must possess but that are not easily taught. In contrast, other scholars contend that there is a scientific basis for teaching that can be learned.
8. Good teachers strike a balance between the art and the science of teaching.
9. Reflective teachers constantly think about such issues as the goals they are trying to achieve, the types of teaching methods they use and how effective those methods are, and the extent to which their methods and goals are supported by scientific evidence.

Key Terms

educational psychology *(1)*
teaching as an art *(12)*
teaching as a science *(12)*
reflective teaching *(13)*
World Wide Web *(17)*

Discussion Questions

1. Imagine that you are a second-grade teacher at the end of the school year. You have just finished telling your principal about a student who performed so poorly during the year that you question whether the student is adequately prepared for third grade. The principal suggests that the child repeat second grade next year. Given what you know about the research on retention, how would you respond to the principal's suggestion?
2. Think of or identify a popular instructional practice. Would you classify that practice as a fad or as the outgrowth of accumulated scientific knowledge? Why? How can you tell the difference between the two?
3. The effective teacher as artist displays enthusiasm and believes that the content and teaching methods are worthwhile. At some point, however, you may be asked to teach a grade level or a subject for which you have little enthusiasm, or you may grow bored teaching the same grade level or subject in the same way year after year. How will you fulfill the role of teacher-artist if faced with these conditions?
4. This chapter made the point that good teachers strike a balance between the art and the science of teaching. How do they do so? Are they born with the right type of personality? Are they the products of good teacher-education programs? Or is some combination of these elements at work? If you believe that both factors play a role, which do you feel is more important?
5. The reflective teacher sets aside regular blocks of time to think about teaching activities and to make new plans. Most teachers complain about having insufficient time to reflect and plan. What would you do to make more time available?

Student Characteristics

Part I

2 Theories of Psychosocial and Cognitive Development

In the opening chapter, we pointed out that individuals vary in how they perceive and think about the world around them. This commonplace observation implies that you need to be aware of the major ways in which students differ from one another in order to design potentially effective lessons. What may work well for one part of your class may not work quite so well for another part. The lesson that was a huge success with last year's class may be a disaster with this year's group if you fail to take into account critical differences between the two classes. The five chapters in this part of the book will introduce you to how students may differ from one another in psychosocial development, cognitive development, age, mental ability, thinking style, achievement, ethnic background, and social class. You will also discover how those differences affect classroom learning.

Human development is a complex topic to discuss because, in addition to analyzing many different forms of behavior, one must trace the way each type of behavior changes as a child matures. Authors of books on development have adopted different strategies for coping with this problem.

Key Points

These key points will help you learn the important information in this chapter. To help you study, they also appear in the margins of the pages, next to the text where they are discussed.

Erikson: Psychosocial Development

- Erikson's theory encompasses the life span, highlights the role of the person and culture in development
- Personality development based on epigenetic principle
- Personality grows out of successful resolution of psychosocial crises
- 2 to 3 years: autonomy vs. shame and doubt
- 4 to 5 years: initiative vs. guilt
- 6 to 11 years: industry vs. inferiority
- 12 to 18 years: identity vs. role confusion
- Role confusion: uncertainty as to what behaviors others will react to favorably
- Students' sense of industry hampered by unhealthy competition for grades
- Identity: accepting one's body, having goals, getting recognition
- Psychosocial moratorium delays commitment
- Adolescents exhibit a particular process, called an identity status, for establishing an identity
- Individuals in identity diffusion avoid thinking about jobs, roles, values
- Individuals in foreclosure unquestioningly endorse parents' goals and values
- Individuals in moratorium uncertain about identity
- Individuals who have reached identity achievement status have made their own commitments

Piaget: Cognitive Development

- Organization: tendency to systematize processes
- Scheme: organized pattern of behavior or thought
- Adaptation: tendency to adjust to environment
- Assimilation: new experience is fitted into existing scheme
- Accommodation: scheme is created or revised to fit new experience
- Equilibration: tendency to organize schemes to allow better understanding of experiences
- Sensorimotor stage: schemes reflect sensory and motor experiences
- Preoperational stage: child forms many new schemes but does not think logically
- Perceptual centration, irreversibility, egocentrism: barriers to logical thought
- Egocentrism: assumption that others see things the same way
- Concrete operational stage: child is capable of mentally reversing actions but generalizes only from concrete experiences

Some have described theories that outline stages in the emergence of particular forms of behavior. Others have summarized significant types of behavior at successive age levels. Still others have examined specific types of behavior, noting age changes for every topic. Each approach has advantages and disadvantages.

Developmental theories call attention to the overall sequence, continuity, and interrelatedness of aspects of development, but they typically account for only limited facets of behavior. Texts organized in terms of age levels make readers aware of varied aspects of children's behavior at a given age but sometimes tend to obscure how particular types of behavior emerge and change. And although texts organized according to types of behavior do not have the limitation of the age-level approach, they may make it difficult for the reader to grasp the overall pattern of behavior at a particular stage of development.

In an effort to profit from the advantages and to minimize the disadvantages of each approach, this chapter and the next present discussions of development that combine all three. This chapter focuses on Erik Erikson's psychosocial stages, Jean Piaget's cognitive stages, and Lev Vygotsky's views on the role of social interaction. It also describes Piaget's ideas about moral development, Lawrence Kohlberg's extension of Piaget's work, and Carol Gilligan's criticism and modification of Kohlberg's theory. The next chapter describes age-level characteristics of students at five levels: preschool, primary school, elementary school, middle school, and high school. Discussion at each age level focuses on four types of behavior: physical, social, emotional, and cognitive. The information in these chapters will help you adapt teaching techniques to the students who are in the age range that you expect to teach. The patterns of behavior described in these chapters are ones exhibited by typical children and adolescents.

The following three chapters are devoted to individual differences and how to deal with them. The chapter "Understanding Student Differences"

- Formal operational stage: child is able to deal with abstractions, form hypotheses, engage in mental manipulations
- Adolescent egocentrism: one's thoughts and actions are assumed to be as central to others as to oneself
- Piaget: cognitive development more strongly influenced by peers than by adults
- Instruction can accelerate development of schemes that have begun to form
- Piaget's theory underestimates children's abilities
- Most adolescents are not formal operational thinkers
- Sequence of stages uniform across cultures but rate of development varies

Vygotsky: Cognitive Development

- How we think influenced by current social forces and historical cultural forces
- Psychological tools aid and change thought processes
- Cognitive development strongly influenced by those more intellectually advanced
- Teachers should help students learn how to use psychological tools
- Cognitive development promoted by instruction in zone of proximal development
- Scaffolding techniques support student learning

Using Technology to Promote Cognitive Development

- Computer-based simulations promote exploration and visual representations of abstract ideas, and correct misconceptions
- Computer programs can act as expert collaborative partners

Piaget, Kohlberg, and Gilligan: Moral Development

- Morality of constraint (moral realism): rules are sacred, consequences determine guilt
- Morality of cooperation (moral relativism): rules are flexible, intent important in determining guilt
- Preconventional morality: avoid punishment, receive benefits in return
- Conventional morality: impress others, respect authority
- Postconventional morality: mutual agreements, consistent principles
- Moral education programs may produce modest acceleration in moral development
- Males and females may use different approaches to resolve real-life moral dilemmas
- Moral knowledge does not always result in moral behavior

discusses the nature of variability and how students vary with respect to gender, mental ability, and cognitive style. The chapter titled "Addressing Cultural and Socioeconomic Diversity" describes the characteristics of students from different ethnic and social-class backgrounds. And the chapter "Accommodating Student Variability" describes types of students who vary from their classmates to such an extent that they may require special kinds of education. ■

Erikson: Psychosocial Development

Of all the developmental theories that we could have chosen to discuss, why did we decide to open this chapter with Erik Erikson's theory of psychosocial development? There are several reasons for this choice. First, Erikson described psychological growth from infancy through old age. Thus, one can draw out instructional implications for every level of education from preschool through adult education. Second, Erikson's theory portrays people as playing an active role in their own psychological development through their attempts to understand, organize, and integrate their everyday experiences. Third, this theory highlights the important role that cultural goals, aspirations, expectations, requirements, and opportunities play in personal growth (a theme we will discuss in the chapter "Understanding Student Differences") (Newman & Newman, 1991).

To preview this chapter's basic concepts, read the Chapter Themes on the Snowman textbook site at **http://education.college.hmco.com/students**.

Erikson's theory encompasses the life span, highlights the role of the person and culture in development

Although Erikson (1902–1994) studied with Sigmund Freud, he concluded that Freud's tendency to stay in Vienna and interact with only a small and very select group of individuals had prevented the founder of psychoanalysis from fully appreciating how social and cultural factors (for example, values, attitudes, beliefs, and customs) influence behavior, perception, and thinking. Erikson decided to formulate a theory of development based on psychoanalytic principles but taking into account such influences.

Basic Principles of Erikson's Theory

Epigenetic Principle Erikson based his description of personality development on **the epigenetic principle,** which states that in fetal development, certain organs of the body appear at certain specified times and eventually "combine" to form a child. Erikson hypothesized that just as the parts of the body develop in interrelated ways in a human fetus, so the personality of an individual forms as the ego progresses through a series of interrelated stages. All of these ego stages exist in some form from the very beginning, but each has a critical period of development.

Personality development based on epigenetic principle

Psychosocial Crisis In Erikson's view, personality development occurs as one successfully resolves a series of turning points, or psychosocial crises. Although the word *crisis* typically refers to an extraordinary event that threatens our well-being, Erikson had a more benign meaning in mind. Crises occur when people feel compelled to adjust to the normal guidelines and expectations that society has for them but are not altogether certain that they are prepared to carry out these demands fully. For example, Western societies expect children of elementary and middle school age (roughly ages six to eleven years) to develop a basic sense of industry, mostly through success in school. Adolescents are expected to come to terms with

Personality grows out of successful resolution of psychosocial crises

such questions as, "Who am I?" and "Where am I going?" (Newman & Newman, 1991).

As you will see in the next section, Erikson described these crises in terms of opposing qualities that individuals typically develop. For each crisis, there is a desirable quality that can emerge and a corresponding unfavorable characteristic. Yet Erikson did not mean to imply that a healthy individual develops only the positive qualities. He emphasized that people are best able to adapt to their world when they possess both the positive and negative qualities of a particular stage, provided the positive quality is significantly stronger than the negative quality. In the first stage, for example, it is important that the child learn trust, but a person who never experienced a bit of mistrust would struggle to understand the world. In Erikson's view, difficulties in development and adjustment arise only when the negative quality outweighs the positive for any given stage or when the outcome for most stages is negative (Newman & Newman, 1991).

As you read through the following brief descriptions of the stages of psychosocial development, keep in mind that a positive resolution of the issue for each stage depends on how well the issue of the previous stage was resolved. An adolescent who at the end of the industry versus inferiority stage strongly doubts her own capabilities and devalues the quality of her work, for example, may have trouble making the occupational commitments required for identity development (Marcia, 1991).

Stages of Psychosocial Development

The following designations, age ranges, and essential characteristics of the stages of personality development are proposed by Erikson in *Childhood and Society* (1963).[1]

Trust Versus Mistrust (Birth to One Year) The basic psychosocial attitude for infants to learn is that they can trust their world. Trust is fostered by "consistency, continuity, and sameness of experience" in the satisfaction by the parents of the infant's basic needs. Such an environment will permit children to think of their world as safe and dependable. Conversely, children whose care is inadequate, inconsistent, or negative will approach the world with fear and suspicion.

2 to 3 years: autonomy vs. shame and doubt

Autonomy Versus Shame and Doubt (Two to Three Years; Preschool) Just when children have learned to trust (or mistrust) their parents, they must exert a degree of independence. If toddlers are permitted and encouraged to do what they are capable of doing at their own pace and in their own way—and with judicious supervision by parents and teachers—they will develop a sense of autonomy. But if parents and teachers are impatient and do too many things for young children or shame young children for unacceptable behavior, these children will develop feelings of self-doubt.

4 to 5 years: initiative vs. guilt

Initiative Versus Guilt (Four to Five Years; Preschool to Kindergarten) The ability to participate in many physical activities and to use language sets the stage for initiative, which "adds to autonomy the quality of undertaking, planning, and 'attacking' a task for the sake of being active and on the move." If four- and five-year-olds are given freedom to explore and experiment and if parents and teachers take time to answer questions, tendencies toward initiative will be encouraged. Conversely, if children of this age are restricted and made to feel that their activities and

[1] All quotations in "Stages of Psychosocial Development" are drawn from Chapter 7 of *Childhood and Society.*

questions have no point or are a nuisance to adults and older siblings, they will feel guilty about acting on their own.

Industry Versus Inferiority (Six to Eleven Years; Elementary to Middle School) A child entering school is at a point in development when behavior is dominated by intellectual curiosity and performance. "He now learns to win recognition by producing things. . . . He develops a sense of industry." If the child is encouraged to make and do things well, helped to persevere, allowed to finish tasks, and praised for trying, industry results. If the child's efforts are unsuccessful or if he is derided or treated as bothersome, a feeling of inferiority results. Children who feel inferior may never learn to enjoy intellectual work and take pride in doing at least one kind of thing really well. At worst, they may believe they will never excel at anything.

6 to 11 years: industry vs. inferiority

Identity Versus Role Confusion (Twelve to Eighteen Years; Middle Through High School) The goal at this stage is development of the roles and skills that will prepare adolescents eventually to take a meaningful place in adult society. The danger at this stage is **role confusion:** having no clear conception of appropriate types of behavior that others will react to favorably. If adolescents succeed (as reflected by the reactions of others) in integrating roles in different situations to the point of experiencing continuity in their perception of self, identity develops. In common terms, they know who they are. If they are unable to establish a sense of stability in various aspects of their lives, role confusion results.

12 to 18 years: identity vs. role confusion

Role confusion: uncertainty as to what behaviors others will react to favorably

Intimacy Versus Isolation (Young Adulthood) To experience satisfying development at this stage, the young adult needs to establish close and committed intimate relationships and partnerships with other people. The hallmark of intimacy is the "ethical strength to abide by such commitments, even though they may call for significant sacrifices and compromises." Failure to do so will lead to a sense of isolation.

Generativity Versus Stagnation (Middle Age) "Generativity . . . is primarily the concern of establishing and guiding the next generation." Erikson's use of the term *generativity* is purposely broad. It refers, of course, to having children and raising them. In addition, it refers to the productive and creative efforts in which adults take part (for example, teaching) that have a positive effect on younger generations. Those unable or unwilling to "establish" and "guide" the next generation become victims of stagnation and self-absorption.

Integrity Versus Despair (Old Age) Integrity is "the acceptance of one's one and only life cycle as something that had to be and that, by necessity, permitted of no substitutions. . . . Despair expresses the feeling that the time is now short, too short for the attempt to start another life and to try out alternate roads to integrity."

Of Erikson's eight stages, the two you should pay particular attention to are industry versus inferiority and identity versus role confusion, because they are the primary psychosocial issues that students must resolve during their elementary, middle school, and high school years. If you are committed to helping students learn as much as possible, you need to have a basic understanding of these two stages so that your lesson plans and instructional approaches help students achieve a strong sense of industry and identity. The next two sections will briefly describe the major factors that contribute to students' sense of industry and their grasp of who they are and what they might become.

Helping Students Develop a Sense of Industry

Between kindergarten and sixth grade, most children are eager to demonstrate that they can learn new skills and successfully accomplish assigned tasks. One factor that has long been known to have a detrimental effect on one's sense of industry is competition for a limited number of rewards. If you have ever taken a class where the teacher graded exams or projects "on a curve," you are familiar with the most common form that such competition takes in schools. What the teacher does is compare each student's score with the score of every other student in that class. The few students who achieve the highest scores receive the top grade, regardless of the actual level of their scores. Then a predetermined number of B's, C's, D's, and F's are awarded. Because the resulting distribution of grades looks something like the outline of a bell, it is often referred to as a "bell-shaped curve" (which explains the origin of the term "grading on the curve").

Students' sense of industry hampered by unhealthy competition for grades

There are at least two reasons that this practice may damage a student's sense of industry:

1. Grading on the curve limits the top rewards to a relatively small number of students regardless of each student's actual level of performance. If the quality of instruction is good and students learn most of what has been assigned, the range of scores will be relatively small. Consider the impact to your sense of industry if you respond correctly to 85 percent of the questions on an exam but earn only a grade of C. The same problem exists when, for whatever reasons, all students perform poorly. How much pride can you have in a grade of A or B when you know it is based on a low success rate? The senior author of this book endured a college chemistry class in which the top grade on an exam went to a student who answered only 48 percent of the questions correctly.
2. Curve grading also guarantees that some students have to receive failing grades regardless of their actual level of performance. Students who are forced into this unhealthy type of competition (there are acceptable forms of competition, which we describe in the chapter titled "Approaches to Instruction") may develop a sense of inadequacy and inferiority that will hamper them for the rest of their school career.

The solution to this problem is to base grades on realistic and attainable standards that are worked out ahead of time and communicated to the students. In our chapter on standardized testing, we describe how to do this. Also, in the chapter "Approaches to Instruction," we describe several instructional approaches that will likely have a beneficial impact on students' sense of industry because they all promote learning and a sense of accomplishment. In general, they involve establishing a classroom atmosphere in which students feel accepted for who they are and understand that the teacher is as interested in their success as they are. These goals are accomplished by providing clear expectations as to what students should be able to do after a unit of instruction, designing lessons that are logical and meaningful, and using teaching methods that support effective learning processes.

Helping Students Formulate an Identity

Identity: accepting one's body, having goals, getting recognition

The most complex of Erikson's stages is identity versus role confusion; he wrote more extensively about this stage than any other. Because this stage is often misunderstood, let's use Erikson's own words to describe the concept of **identity:** "An optimal sense of identity . . . is experienced merely as a sense of psychosocial well-being. Its most obvious concomitants are a feeling of being at home in one's body, a sense of 'knowing where one is going' and an inner assuredness of anticipated recognition from those who count" (1968, p. 165). As you may know from your own experience or the experiences of others, the process of identity formation is not always smooth, and it does not always follow the same path. But by being aware of the problems and uncertainties that adolescents may experience as they try to develop a sense of who they are, you can help them positively resolve this major developmental milestone.

Taking a Psychosocial Moratorium For individuals who are unprepared to make a career choice, Erikson suggested the possibility of a **psychosocial moratorium.** This is a period marked by a delay of commitment. Such a postponement occurred in Erikson's own life: after leaving high school, he spent several years wandering around Europe without making any firm decision about the sort of job he would seek. Under ideal circumstances, a psychosocial moratorium should be a period of adventure and exploration, having a positive, or at least neutral, impact on the individual and society.

Psychosocial moratorium delays commitment

ADOLESCENT IDENTITY STATUSES

Erikson's observations on identity formation have been usefully extended by James Marcia's notion of **identity statuses** (1966, 1980, 1991). Identity statuses, of which there are four, are styles or processes "for handling the psychosocial task of establishing a sense of identity" (Waterman & Archer, 1990, p. 35). Marcia (1980) developed this idea as a way to test scientifically the validity of Erikson's notions about identity.

Adolescents exhibit a particular process, called an identity status, for establishing an identity

Marcia established the four identity statuses after he had conducted semistructured interviews with a selected sample of male youths. The interviewees were asked their thoughts about a career, their personal value system, their sexual attitudes, and their religious beliefs. Marcia proposed that the criteria for the attainment of a mature identity are based on two variables: crisis and commitment. "Crisis refers to times during adolescence when the individual seems to be actively involved in choosing among alternative occupations and beliefs. Commitment refers to the degree of personal investment the individual expresses in an occupation or belief" (1967, p. 119).

After analyzing interview records with these two criteria in mind, Marcia established four identity statuses, described in Table 2.1, that vary in their degree of crisis and commitment:

- Identity diffusion
- Foreclosure
- Moratorium
- Identity achievement

The moratorium and identity achievement statuses are generally thought to be more developmentally mature than the foreclosure and identity diffusion statuses because individuals exhibiting moratorium and identity achievement have either evaluated alternatives and made a commitment or are actively involved in obtaining and evaluating information in preparation for a commitment (Archer, 1982). Support for the hypothesized superiority of the identity achievement status was provided by Anne Wallace-Broscious, Felicisima Serafica, and Samuel Osipow (1994). They found that high school students who had attained the identity achievement status scored higher on measures of career planning and career certainty than did students in the moratorium or diffusion statuses.

As you read the brief descriptions of each identity type in Table 2.1, keep a few

Individuals in identity diffusion avoid thinking about jobs, roles, values

Individuals in foreclosure unquestioningly endorse parents' goals and values

Individuals in moratorium uncertain about identity

Individuals who have reached identity achievement status have made their own commitments

Table 2.1 James Marcia's Identity Statuses

Identity Status	Crisis	Commitment	Characteristics
Diffusion	Not yet experienced. Little serious thought given to occupation, gender roles, values.	Weak. Ideas about occupation, gender roles, values are easily changed as a result of positive and negative feedback.	Not self-directed; disorganized, impulsive, low self-esteem, alienated from parents; avoids getting involved in school work and interpersonal relationships.
Foreclosure	Not experienced. May never suffer doubts about identity issues.	Strong. Has accepted and endorsed the values of his or her parents.	Close-minded, authoritarian, low in anxiety; has difficulty solving problems under stress; feels superior to peers; more dependent on parents and other authority figures for guidance and approval than in other statuses.
Moratorium	Partially experienced. Has given some thought to identity-related questions.	Weak. Has not achieved satisfactory answers.	Anxious, dissatisfied with school; changes major often, daydreams, engages in intense but short-lived relationships; may temporarily reject parental and societal values.
Achievement	Fully experienced. Has considered and explored alternative positions regarding occupation, gender roles, values.	Strong. Has made self-chosen commitments to at least some aspects of identity.	Introspective; more planful, rational, and logical in decision making than in other identity statuses; high self-esteem; works effectively under stress; likely to form close interpersonal relationships. Usually the last identity status to emerge.

SOURCES: Bilsker & Marcia (1991); Blustein & Palladino (1991); Frank, Pirsch, & Wright (1990); Kroger (1996); Vondracek, Schulenberg, Skorikov, Gillespie, & Walheim (1995).

points in mind. First, the more mature identity statuses are slow to evolve. Among sixth graders, only about 11 percent are likely to show any evidence of either an identity achievement or a moratorium status. By twelfth grade, only about 20 percent will have attained either status (Archer, 1982). Second, an identity status is not a once-and-for-all accomplishment. If an ego-shattering event (loss of a job, divorce) occurs later in life, individuals who have reached identity achievement, for example, may find themselves uncertain about old values and behavior patterns and once again in crisis. But for most individuals, a new view of oneself is eventually created. This cycling

Identity, as Erikson defines it, involves acceptance of one's body, knowing where one is going, and recognition from those who count. A high school graduate who is pleased with his or her appearance, who has already decided on a college major, and who is admired by parents, relatives, and friends is likely to experience a sense of psychosocial well-being.

between certainty and doubt as to who one is and where one fits in society may well occur in each of the last three of Erikson's stages (Stephen, Fraser, & Marcia, 1992).

Finally, because identity is an amalgam of commitments from a number of different domains, only a small percentage (about 20 percent) of adolescents will experience a triumphant sense of having "put it all together." To cite just one example, an adolescent is more likely to have made a firm occupational choice than to be decisive about gender role or religious values (Waterman, 1988).

Although the foreclosure status is the historical norm for adolescents in Western societies, things can and do change. For example, individuals in moratorium were more numerous during the 1960s and 1970s than during the 1980s. This was a time of great social and cultural upheaval (opposition to the war in Vietnam, civil rights demonstrations, the women's movement), and many adolescents reacted to the uncertainty produced by these changes by not making a commitment to occupational, sexual, and political values (Scarr, Weinberg, & Levine, 1986; Waterman, 1988). Also, recent evidence indicates that African-American adolescents are now more likely to be in a moratorium status or an identity achievement status, or in transition between these two statuses, than in the foreclosure status common to earlier generations (Watson & Protinsky, 1991).

Gender differences in identity status are most apparent in the areas of political ideology, family and career priorities, and sexuality. With respect to political beliefs, males are more likely to exhibit a foreclosure process and females a diffusion process. With respect to family and career priorities and sexuality, males are likely to be foreclosed or diffuse, whereas females are likely to express an identity achievement or a moratorium status. These findings indicate that female adolescents are more likely than males to make developmentally advanced decisions in the areas of family and career roles and sexuality. A likely explanation has to do with how the female sex role has and has not changed over the past twenty years. Although most females now work outside the home, they are still expected to have primary responsibility for child rearing (Archer, 1991).

A relevant question to ask about Marcia's identity statuses, particularly if you plan to teach in a foreign country or to instruct students with different cultural backgrounds, is whether these identity statuses occur only in the United States. The answer appears to be no. Researchers in such diverse countries as Korea, India, Nigeria, Japan, Denmark, and Holland report finding the same patterns (Scarr et al., 1986).

Criticisms of Erikson's Theory

Erikson's theory has been described as somewhat vague and difficult to test. As a result, researchers are not sure how best to measure such complex qualities as initiative and integrity or which kinds of experiences should be studied to discover how people cope with and successfully resolve psychosocial conflicts (Ochse & Plug, 1986; Sigelman & Shaffer, 1991).

Although Erikson occasionally carried out research investigations, most of his conclusions are based on personal and subjective interpretations that have been only partly substantiated by controlled investigations of the type that American psychologists value. As a result, there have been only limited checks on Erikson's tendency to generalize from limited experiences. Some of his observations on identity, for example, reflect his own indecision about occupational choice.

Some critics, such as Carol Gilligan (1982, 1988), argue that Erikson's stages reflect the personality development of males more accurately than that of females. Gilligan believes that the process and timing of identity formation are different for each gender. Marcia (as cited in Scarr et al., 1986) contends that beginning in about fourth grade (the industry versus inferiority stage), girls are as concerned with the nature of interpersonal relationships as they are with achievement, whereas boys focus mainly on achievement. And during adolescence, many young women seem to work through the crises of identity *and* intimacy simultaneously, whereas most young men follow the sequence that Erikson described: identity versus role confusion, then intimacy versus isolation (Gilligan, 1982; Ochse & Plug, 1986; Scarr et al., 1986).

A final criticism is that Erikson's early stages—those covering ages two through eleven—seem to stress the same basic qualities. Autonomy, initiative, and industry all emphasize the desirability of permitting and encouraging children to do things on their own. Doubt, guilt, and inferiority all focus on the need for parents and teachers to provide sympathetic support (Kroger, 1996).

If you keep these reservations in mind, you are likely to discover that Erikson's observations (as well as the identity statuses that Marcia described) will clarify important aspects of development. Suggestions for Teaching that draw on Erikson's observations follow. (These suggestions might also serve as the nucleus of a section in your Reflective Journal. Possible journal entries are indicated in the margins, and more can be found on the book's web site.)

Piaget: Cognitive Development

Basic Principles of Piaget's Theory

Jean Piaget's conception of intellectual development reflected his basic interest in biology and knowledge. Piaget (1896–1980) postulated that human beings inherit two basic tendencies: **organization** (the tendency to systematize and combine

SUGGESTIONS FOR TEACHING IN YOUR CLASSROOM

Applying Erikson's Theory of Psychosocial Development

1 Keep in mind that certain types of behaviors and relationships may be of special significance at different age levels.

2 With younger preschool children, allow plenty of opportunities for free play and experimentation to encourage the development of autonomy, but provide guidance to reduce the possibility that children will experience doubt. Also avoid shaming children for unacceptable behavior.

Journal Entry
Ways to Apply Erikson's Theory (Preschool and Kindergarten)

3 With older preschool children, encourage activities that permit the use of initiative and provide a sense of accomplishment. Avoid making children feel guilty about well-motivated but inconvenient (to you) questions or actions.

4 During the elementary and middle school years, help children experience a sense of industry by presenting tasks that they can complete successfully.

Journal Entry
Ways to Apply Erikson's Theory (Elementary Grades)

Arrange such tasks so that students will know they have been successful. To limit feelings of inferiority, play down comparisons and encourage cooperation and self-competition. Also try to help jealous children gain satisfaction from their own behavior. (Specific ways to accomplish these goals will be described in several later chapters.)

Journal Entry
Ways to Apply Erikson's Theory (Secondary Grades)

5 At the secondary school level, keep in mind the significance of each student's search for a sense of identity.

The components of identity that Erikson stressed are acceptance of one's appearance, recognition from those who count, and knowledge about where one is going. Role confusion is most frequently caused by failure to formulate clear ideas about gender roles and by indecision about occupational choice.

The American school system, particularly at the high school level, has been described as a place where individual differences are either ignored or discouraged and where negative feedback greatly outweighs positive feedback (Boyer, 1983; Csikszentmihalyi & Larson, 1984; Friedenberg, 1963; Murphy, 1987). When John Murphy (1987), a professor of education at Brooklyn College, asked his students to recall positive learning experiences from high school, few were able to do so. Because you are important to your students, you can contribute to their sense of positive identity by recognizing them as individuals and praising them for their accomplishments. If you become aware that particular students lack recognition from peers because of abrasive qualities or ineptness and if you have the time and opportunity, you might also attempt to encourage social skills.

You might be able to reduce identity problems resulting from indecisiveness about gender roles by having class discussions (for example, in social science courses) centering on changes in attitudes regarding masculinity, femininity, and family responsibilities. Following the suggestions of Jeanne Block (1973), you can encourage boys to become more sensitive to the needs of others and girls to be more achievement oriented. This approach to sex-role development that combines traditional "masculine" and "feminine" behaviors is called **psychological androgyny.**

Another forum for such discussion is an on-line bulletin board or class web site. On-line writing can be conducive to explorations of sensitive issues because it provides a slightly slower, more thoughtful pace and also allows an equal voice to male and female students, even those who feel shy about speaking out loud in class. An on-line discussion that is carefully moderated by an experienced teacher can both model and explore the territory of psychological androgyny.

Working with your school counselor, you may in some cases be able to help students make decisions about occupational choice by providing them with information (gleaned from classroom performance and standardized test results) about their intellectual capabilities, personality traits, interests, and values (Lambert & Mounce, 1987). Or you may be able to help students decide whether to apply for admission to college instead of entering the job market after high school graduation.

For additional ideas about best teaching practices, go to the Field Experiences section on this book's Web site at **http://education.college.hmco.com/students**.

6 Remember that the aimlessness of some students may be evidence that they are engaging in a psychosocial moratorium. If possible, encourage such individuals to focus on short-term goals while they continue to search for long-term goals.

There are many ways to enable students to work toward short-term goals, particularly in your classroom. These will be described in detail in later chapters that deal with approaches to instruction and motivation.

7 Remain aware that adolescents may exhibit characteristics of different identity status types.

Some may drift aimlessly; others may be distressed because they realize they lack goals and values. A few high school students may have arrived at self-chosen commitments; others may have accepted the goals and values of their parents.

If you become aware that certain students seem depressed or bothered because they are unable to develop a satisfactory set of personal values, consult your school psychologist or counselor. In addition, you might use the techniques just summarized to help these students experience at least a degree of identity achievement. Perhaps the main value of the identity status concept is that it calls attention to individual differences in the formation of identity. Because students in the foreclosure status will pose few, if any, classroom problems, you must keep in mind that foreclosure is not necessarily desirable for the individual student. Those experiencing identity diffusion or moratorium may be so bothered by role confusion that they are unwilling to carry out even simple assignments—unless you supply support and incentives.

STAGES OF COGNITIVE DEVELOPMENT

Organization and adaptation are what Piaget called *invariant functions.* This means that these thought processes function the same way for infants, children, adolescents, and adults. Schemes, however, are not invariant. They undergo systematic change at particular points in time. As a result, there are real differences between the ways younger children and older children think and between the ways children and adults think. The schemes of infants and toddlers, for example, are sensory and motor in nature. They are often referred to as *habits* or *reflexes.* In early childhood, schemes gradually become more mental in nature; during this period, they are called *concepts* or *categories.* Finally, by late adolescence or early adulthood, schemes are very complex and result in what we call *strategic* or *planful* behavior.

Go to **http://education.college.hmco.com/students** to explore current uses of Piaget's stages in the Web Sources section.

On the basis of his studies, Piaget concluded that schemes evolve through four stages. The *rate* at which a particular child proceeds through these stages varies, but Piaget believed the *sequence* is the same in all children.

Piaget's four stages are described in the following sections. To help you grasp the sequence of these stages, Table 2.2 briefly outlines the range of ages to which they generally apply and their distinguishing characteristics.

Although Piaget used this "stage" or stair-step metaphor to describe the pattern of cognitive development, don't be misled into thinking that children "jump" from one stage to the next. In trying to understand certain concepts or solve certain problems, children may on some occasions use a more advanced kind of thinking but on other occasions revert to an earlier, less sophisticated form. Over time, the more advanced concepts and strategies supplant the less sophisticated ones. Because of this variability in how children think, some developmental psychologists (e.g., Siegler, 1996) prefer to use the metaphor of overlapping waves rather than stages to characterize the nature of cognitive development. But because Piaget spoke in terms of stages, we will as well.

Table 2.2 Piaget's Stages of Cognitive Development

Stage	Age Range	Characteristics
Sensorimotor	Birth to two years	Develops schemes primarily through sense and motor activities. Recognizes permanence of objects not seen.
Preoperational	Two to seven years	Gradually acquires ability to conserve and decenter but not capable of operations and unable to mentally reverse actions.
Concrete operational	Seven to eleven years	Capable of operations but solves problems by generalizing from concrete experiences. Not able to manipulate conditions mentally unless they have been experienced.
Formal operational	Eleven years	Able to deal with abstractions, form hypotheses, solve problems systematically, engage in mental manipulations.

Sensorimotor stage: schemes reflect sensory and motor experiences

Sensorimotor Stage (Infants and Toddlers) Up to the age of two, children acquire understanding primarily through sensory impressions and motor activities. Therefore, Piaget called this the *sensorimotor stage.* Because infants are unable to move around much on their own during the first months of postnatal existence, they develop schemes primarily by exploring their own bodies and senses. After toddlers learn to walk and manipulate things, however, they get into everything and build up a sizable repertoire of schemes involving external objects and situations.

An important cognitive development milestone, *object permanence,* occurs between the fourth and eighth months of this stage. Prior to this point, the phrase "out of sight, out of mind" is literally true. Infants treat objects that leave their field of vision as if they no longer exist. When they drop an object from their hands or when an object at which they are looking is covered, for example, they do not search for it. As object permanence develops, children's intentional search behaviors become increasingly apparent.

Most children under age two are able to use schemes they have mastered to engage in mental as well as physical trial-and-error behavior. By age two, toddlers' schemes have become more mental in nature. You can see this in the way toddlers imitate the behavior of others. They imitate people they have not previously observed, they imitate the behavior of animals, and, most important, they imitate even when the model is no longer present (this is called *deferred imitation*). These types of imitative behaviors show toddlers' increasing ability to think in terms of symbols.

Preoperational stage: child forms many new schemes but does not think logically

Preoperational Stage (Preschool and Primary Grades) The thinking of preschool and primary grade children (roughly two to seven years old) centers on mastery of symbols (such as words), which permits them to benefit much more from past experiences. Piaget believed that many symbols are derived from mental imitation and involve both visual images and bodily sensations (notice how the schemes of this stage incorporate and build on the schemes of the previous stage). Although the thinking at this stage is much more sophisticated than that of one- and two-year-olds, preschool children are limited in their ability to use their new symbol-oriented schemes. From an adult perspective, their thinking and behavior are illogical.

Perceptual centration, irreversibility, egocentrism: barriers to logical thought

When Piaget used the term *operation,* he meant an action carried out through logical thinking. *Preoperational,* then, means prelogical. The main impediments to logical thinking that preschoolers have to overcome are *perceptual centration, irreversibility,* and *egocentrism.* You can see these impediments at work most clearly when children attempt to solve **conservation** problems—those that test their ability to recognize that certain properties stay the same despite a change in appearance or position.

One of the best-known conservation problems is conservation of continuous quantity. A child is taken to a quiet place by an experimenter, who then pours water (or juice or beans or whatever else) into identical short glasses until the child agrees that each contains an equal amount. Then the water is poured from one of these glasses into a tall, thin glass. At that point the child is asked, "Is there more water in this glass [the experimenter points to the tall glass] or this one [the short glass]?" Immediately after the child answers, the experimenter asks, "Why do you think so?" If the child's response is evasive or vague, the experimenter continues to probe until the child's underlying thought processes become clear.

In carrying out this experiment (and many others similar to it) with children of different ages, Piaget discovered that children below the age of six or so maintain that there is more water in the tall, thin glass than in the short, squat glass. Although they agree at the beginning of the experiment that the water in the two identical glasses is equal, young children stoutly insist that after the water has been poured, the taller glass contains more. When asked, "Why do you think so?" many preschool children immediately and confidently reply, "Because it's taller." Children over the age of six or so, by contrast, are more likely to reply, "Well, it *looks* as if there's more water in this one because it's taller, but they're really the same."

One reason preoperational stage children have difficulty solving conservation problems (as well as other problems that require logical thinking) is **perceptual centration.** This is the very strong tendency to focus attention on only one characteristic of an object or aspect of a problem or event at a time. The young child focuses only on the height of the water in the two containers and ignores the differences in width and volume. Another way to put this is to say that the child has not yet mastered **decentration**—the ability to think of more than one quality at a time—and is therefore not inclined to contemplate alternatives.

The second impediment to logical thinking is **irreversibility.** This means that young children cannot mentally pour the water from the tall, thin glass back into the short, squat one (thereby proving to themselves that the glasses contain the same amount of water). For the same reason, these youngsters do not understand the logic behind simple mathematical reversals ($4 + 5 = 9$; $9 - 5 = 4$).

Egocentrism: assumption that others see things the same way

The third major impediment is **egocentrism.** When applied to preschool children, *egocentric* does not mean selfish or conceited. It means that youngsters find it difficult, if not impossible, to take another person's point of view. In their conversations and in experimental situations in which they are asked to describe how something would look if viewed by someone else, preschool children reveal that they often have difficulty seeing things from another person's perspective (Piaget & Inhelder, 1956). They seem to assume that others see things the same way they see them. As a result, attempts to explain the logic behind conservation are usually met with quizzical looks and the insistence (some would mistakenly call it stubbornness) that the tall, thin glass contains more water.

Concrete operational stage: child is capable of mentally reversing actions but generalizes only from concrete experiences

Concrete Operational Stage (Elementary to Early Middle School) Through formal instruction, informal experiences, social contact, and maturation, children over the age of seven gradually become less influenced by perceptual centration, irreversibility, and egocentrism (DeVries, 1997). Schemes are developing that allow a greater understanding of such logic-based tasks as conservation (matter is neither created nor destroyed but simply changes shape or form or position), class inclusion (the construction of hierarchical relationships among related classes of items), and seriation (the arrangement of items in a particular order).

But operational thinking is limited to objects that are actually present or that children have experienced concretely and directly. For this reason, Piaget described the stage from approximately seven to eleven years as that of *concrete operations.* The nature of the concrete operational stage can be illustrated by the child's mastery of different kinds of conservation.

By the age of seven, most children are able to explain correctly that water poured from a short, squat glass into a tall, thin glass is still the same amount of water. Being able to solve the water-pouring problem, however, does not guarantee that a seven-year-old will be able to solve a similar problem involving two balls of clay. A child who has just explained why a tall glass of water contains the same amount as a short one may inconsistently maintain a few moments later that rolling one of two equally sized balls of clay into an elongated shape causes the rolled one to appear as if it contains more clay.

Children in the primary and early elementary grades tend to react to each situation in terms of concrete experiences. The tendency to solve problems by generalizing from one situation to a similar situation does not occur with any degree of consistency until the end of the elementary school years.

Nevertheless, children in the concrete operational stage are often more capable of learning advanced concepts than most people realize. Kathleen Metz (1995) argues that Piaget's theory has been improperly interpreted as suggesting that formal science education should be delayed until children have started to demonstrate the capacity for formal operational reasoning. She provides evidence in support of the view that such abstract concepts as *theory*, *evidence*, and *hypothesis* begin to emerge during the elementary school years and are sufficiently understood by children that they should be included in science education programs.

Because most elementary grade students are in the concrete operational stage of development, science educators have concluded that children cannot think in hypothetical-deductive terms (e.g., "What if . . ." and "If I do such and such, then such and such should occur") but are limited to hands-on activities and to such descriptive forms of reasoning as observation, assigning objects to categories (class inclusion), and arranging objects in serial order (seriation). Metz cites evidence that preschool children begin to think in terms of simple categories and that most sixth graders can distinguish between theory and evidence. She also argues that Piaget's work with elementary school children indicates that although their thinking is based on concrete objects, they can construct from these experiences simple forms of such abstract concepts as time, speed, and probability. Consequently, she believes that elementary grade children can understand and carry out, in a simplified form, such advanced elements of scientific inquiry as posing questions, gathering and interpreting data, and revising one's theory on the basis of the data.

Although some Piagetian scholars (e.g., Kuhn, 1997) agree with Metz that children have the potential to design and carry out scientific inquiries, they caution that most elementary grade children will be unable truly to understand the nature of scientific inquiry (such as changing one's beliefs in the light of contradictory evidence, drawing only conclusions that are supported by existing evidence, recalling and accurately summarizing the evidence that support one's conclusions, using the same methods and logic from one inquiry to another) and use this understanding to regulate their subsequent behavior. If, for example, you told a student at the concrete operational stage to assume that a feather could break a piece of glass and then asked him whether the deduction "If one hits the glass with a feather, then the glass will break" is true or false, he would likely respond that it is false because in his experience, feathers do not break glass (Overton & Byrnes, 1991).

The science education standards for students in grades K–4 that have been proposed by the National Research Council (1996) reflect the conclusions of both Metz (1995) and Kuhn (1997). The standards state:

> In elementary grades, students begin to develop the physical and intellectual capabilities of scientific inquiry. They can design investigations to try things to see what happens—they tend to focus on concrete results of tests and will entertain the idea of a "fair" test (a test in which only one variable at a time is changed). However, children in K–4 have difficulty with experimentation as a process of testing ideas and the logic of using evidence to formulate explanations. (p. 122)

Formal operational stage: child is able to deal with abstractions, form hypotheses, engage in mental manipulations

Formal Operational Stage (Middle School, High School, and Beyond) When children *do* reach the point of being able to generalize and to engage in mental trial and error by thinking up hypotheses and testing them in their heads, they are at the stage of *formal operations,* according to Piaget. The term *formal* reflects the ability to respond to the *form* of a problem rather than its content and to *form* hypotheses. For example, the formal operational thinker can read the analogies "5 is to 15 as 1 is to

Students who are within Piaget's formal operational stage of cognitive development are capable of solving problems by systematically using abstract symbols to represent real objects.

3" and "penny is to dollar as year is to century" and realize that despite the different content, the form of the two problems is identical (both analogies are based on ratios). In the same way, the formal thinker can understand and use complex language forms: proverbs ("Strike while the iron is hot"), metaphor ("Procrastination is the thief of time"), sarcasm, and satire.

We can see the nature of formal operational thinking and how it differs from concrete operational thinking by looking at a simplified version of Piaget's rod-bending experiment. Adolescents are given a basin filled with water, a set of metal rods of varying lengths, and a set of weights. The rods are attached to the edge of the basin and the weights to the ends of the rods. The subject's task is to figure out how much weight is required to bend a rod just enough to touch the water. Let's say that our hypothetical subject picks out the longest rod in the set (which is 9 inches long), attaches it to the edge of the basin, and puts just enough weight on the end of it to get it to touch the water. This observation is then recorded. Successively shorter rods are selected, and the same procedure is carried out. At some point, the subject comes to the 4-inch rod. This rod does not touch the water even when all of the weights have been attached to it. There are, however, three more rods, all of which are shorter than the last one tested.

This is where the formal and concrete operators part company. The formal operational thinker reasons that if all of the available weights are not sufficient to bend the 4-inch rod enough to touch the water, the same will be true of the remaining rods. In essence, the rest of the experiment is done mentally and symbolically. The concrete operational thinker, however, continues trying out each rod and recording each observation independent of the others. Although both subjects reach the same conclusion, the formal operator does so through a more powerful and efficient process.

But remember that new schemes develop gradually. Although adolescents can sometimes deal with mental abstractions representing concrete objects, most twelve-year-olds solve problems haphazardly, using trial and error. It is not until the end of the high school years that adolescents are likely to attack a problem by forming hypotheses, mentally sorting out solutions, and systematically testing the most promising leads.

Some interpreters of Piaget (e.g., Ginsburg & Opper, 1988) note that a significant aspect of formal thought is that it causes the adolescent to concentrate more on possibilities than on realities. This is the ability that Erikson and others (e.g., Kalbaugh & Haviland, 1991) suggest is instrumental in the emergence of the identity crisis. At the point when older adolescents can become aware of all the factors that have to be considered in choosing a career and can imagine what it might be like to be employed, some may feel so threatened and confused that they postpone the final choice. Yet the same capability can also help resolve the identity crisis because adolescents can reason about possibilities in a logical manner. An adolescent girl, for example, may consider working as a pediatrician, teacher, or child psychologist in an underprivileged environment because she has always enjoyed and sought out activities that allowed her to interact with children and has also been concerned with the effects of deprivation on development.

Although mastery of formal thought equips the older adolescent with impressive intellectual skills, it may also lead to a tendency for the burgeoning formal thinker to become preoccupied with abstract and theoretical matters. Herbert Ginsburg and Sylvia Opper (1988) interpret some of Piaget's observations on this point in the following way:

> In the intellectual sphere, the adolescent has a tendency to become involved in abstract and theoretical matters, constructing elaborate political theories or inventing complex philosophical doctrines. The adolescent may develop plans for the complete reorganization of society or indulge in metaphysical speculation. After discovering capabilities for abstract thought, he then proceeds to exercise them without restraint. Indeed, in the process of exploring these new abilities the adolescent sometimes loses touch with reality and feels that he can accomplish everything by thought alone. In the emotional sphere the adolescent now becomes capable of directing emotions at abstract ideals and not just toward people. Whereas earlier the adolescent could love his mother or hate a peer, now he can love freedom or hate exploitation. The adolescent has developed a new mode of life: the possible and the ideal captivate both mind and feeling. (pp. 202–203)

David Elkind (1968) suggests that unrestrained theorizing about ideals without complete understanding of realities tends to make the young adolescent a militant rebel with little patience for parents or other adults who fail to find quick solutions to personal, social, and other problems. Only when the older adolescent begins to grasp the complexities of interpersonal relationships and of social and economic problems does more tempered understanding appear.

Elkind also suggests that the egocentrism of early childhood reappears in a different form as **adolescent egocentrism.** This occurs when high school students turn their new powers of thought on themselves and become introspective. The strong tendency to analyze self is projected on others. This helps explain why adolescents are so self-conscious: they assume their thoughts and actions are as central to others as to themselves. The major difference between the egocentrism of childhood and that of adolescence is summed up in Elkind's observation: "The child is egocentric in the sense that he is unable to take another person's point of view. The adolescent, on the other hand, takes the other person's point of view to an extreme degree" (1968, p. 153).

Adolescent egocentrism: one's thoughts and actions are assumed to be as central to others as to oneself

Elkind believes that adolescent egocentrism also explains why the peer group becomes such a potent force in high school:

> Adolescent egocentrism . . . accounts, in part, for the power of the peer group during this period. The adolescent is so concerned with the reactions of others toward him, particularly his peers, that he is willing to do many things which are opposed to all of his previous training and to his own best interests. At the same time, this egocentric impression that he is always on stage may help to account for the many and varied adolescent attention-getting maneuvers. (1968, p. 154)

Toward the end of adolescence, this form of exploitative egocentrism gradually declines. The young person comes to realize that other people are much more concerned with themselves and their problems than they are with him and his problems.

The Role of Social Interaction and Instruction in Cognitive Development

How Social Interaction Affects Cognitive Development When it comes to social experiences, Piaget clearly believed that peer interactions do more to spur cognitive development than do interactions with adults. The reason is that children are more likely to discuss, analyze, and debate the merits of another child's view of some issue (such as who should have which toy or what the rules of a game should be) than they are to take serious issue with an adult. The balance of power between children and adults is simply too unequal. Not only are most children quickly taught that adults know more and use superior reasoning, but also the adult always gets to have the last word: argue too long, and it's off to bed with no dessert. But when children interact with one another, the outcome is more dependent on how well each child uses her wits.

Piaget: cognitive development more strongly influenced by peers than by adults

It is the need to understand the ideas of a peer or playmate in order to formulate responses to those ideas that leads to less egocentrism and the development of new, more complex mental schemes. Put another way, a strongly felt sense of cognitive conflict automatically impels the child to strive for a higher level of equilibrium. Formal instruction by an adult expert simply does not have the same impact regardless of how well designed it might be. That is why parents and teachers are often surprised to find children agreeing on some issue after having rejected an adult's explanation of the very same thing. Thus, educational programs that are patterned after Piaget's ideas usually provide many opportunities for children to interact socially and to discover through these interactions basic ideas about how the world works (Crain, 1992; Rogoff, 1990; Tudge & Winterhoff, 1993). As proof of the feasibility of this approach, William Damon and Erin Phelps (1991) describe a study they conducted in which fourth graders who worked collaboratively were more successful than similar students who did not work collaboratively at solving mathematical, spatial reasoning, and balance scale problems.

How Instruction Affects Cognitive Development Although Piaget believed that formal instruction by expert adults will not significantly stimulate cognitive development, not all American psychologists have been willing to accept this conclusion at face value. Over the past twenty-five years, dozens of experiments have been conducted to determine whether it is possible to teach preoperational stage children to understand and use concrete operational schemes or to teach students in the concrete operational stage to grasp formal operational reasoning.

The main conclusion of psychologists who have analyzed and evaluated this body of research is, unfortunately, one of uncertainty (see, e.g., Case, 1975; Good & Brophy, 1995; Nagy & Griffiths, 1982; Sprinthall, Sprinthall, & Oja, 1998). Because of shortcomings in the way some studies were carried out and disagreements about what constitutes evidence of true concrete operational thinking or formal operational thinking, a decisive answer to this question is simply not available.

Nevertheless, something of value can be gleaned from the research on cognitive acceleration. Two recent analyses of this literature (Sigelman & Shaffer, 1991; Sprinthall et al., 1998) conclude that children who are in the process of developing the schemes that will govern the next stage of cognitive functioning can, with good-quality instruction, be helped to refine those schemes a bit faster than would normally be the case. For example, teachers can teach the principle of conservation by using simple explanations and concrete materials and by allowing children to manipulate the materials. This means that teachers should nurture the process of cognitive growth at any particular stage by presenting lessons in a form that is consistent with but slightly more advanced than the students' existing schemes. The objective here is to help students assimilate and accommodate new and different experiences as efficiently as possible.

Instruction can accelerate development of schemes that have begun to form

Criticisms of Piaget's Theory

Underestimating Children's Capabilities Among the thousands of articles that have been published in response to Piaget's findings are many that offer critiques of his work. Some psychologists argue that Piaget underestimated children's abilities not only because he imposed stringent criteria for inferring the presence of particular cognitive abilities, but also because the tasks he used were often complex and far removed from children's real-life experiences. The term *preoperational,* for instance, stresses what is absent rather than what is present. Over the past two decades, researchers have focused more on what preoperational children *can* do. The results (summarized by Gelman & Baillargeon, 1983; Kamii, 2000; Siegler, 1998) suggest that preschoolers' cognitive abilities are more advanced in some areas than Piaget's work suggests.

Piaget's theory underestimates children's abilities

Overestimating Adolescents' Capabilities Other evidence suggests that Piaget may have overestimated the formal thinking capabilities of adolescents. Research summarized by Constance Kamii (1984) revealed that only 20 to 25 percent of college freshmen were able to use formal operational reasoning consistently. Herman Epstein (1980) found that among a group of ninth graders, 32 percent were just beginning the concrete operational stage, 43 percent were well within the concrete operational stage, 15 percent were just entering the formal operational stage, and only 9 percent were mature formal operators. In addition, Norman Sprinthall and Richard Sprinthall (1987) reported that only 33 percent of a group of high school seniors could apply formal operational reasoning to scientific problem solving. According to these studies, formal reasoning seems to be the exception, not the rule, throughout adolescence.

Most adolescents are not formal operational thinkers

A more recent study of French adolescents (Flieller, 1999) reported similar percentages but also sought to determine if the pattern has changed in recent years. Of a group of ten- to twelve-year-olds who were tested on formal operational tasks in 1972, only 9 percent were at the beginning of that stage and only 1 percent were mature formal operators. The percentages for a group of ten- to twelve-year-olds tested in 1993 were just slightly higher, at 13 percent and 3 percent, respectively. Significantly larger differences were noted, however, between two groups of thirteen- to fifteen-year-olds. Among those tested in 1967, 26 percent were early formal operators and 9 percent were mature formal operators. But among those tested in 1996, 40 percent were early formal operators and 15 percent were mature formal operators. The author of this study suggested that the increase in formal operational thinking among thirteen- to fifteen-year-olds may be attributable in part to teaching practices (such as creating tables to display information and using tree diagrams to clarify grammatical structure) that foster the development of formal operational schemes.

Vague Explanations for Cognitive Growth Piaget's theory has also been criticized for its vagueness in specifying the factors that are responsible for cognitive growth. Why, for example, do children give up conserving responses in favor of non-conserving responses at a particular age?

On the basis of recent research, Robert Siegler (1996) has suggested an explanation. He believes that variability in children's thinking plays an influential role. For example, it is not uncommon to hear children use on successive occasions different forms of a given verb, as in "I ate it," "I eated it," and "I ated it." Similar variability has been found in the use of memory strategies (five-year-old and eight-year-old children do not always rehearse information they want to remember), addition rules, time-telling rules, and block-building tasks. Siegler's explanation is that variability gives the child a range of plausible options about how to deal with a particular problem. The child then tries them out in an attempt to see which one produces the best adaptation. Note the use of the qualifying word *plausible.* Most children do not try out any and all possible solutions to a problem. Instead, they stick to possibilities that are consistent with the underlying principles of a problem.

Sequence of stages uniform across cultures but rate of development varies

Cultural Differences Questions have also been raised as to whether children from different cultures develop intellectually in the manner Piaget described. The answer at this point is both yes and no. The sequence of stages appears to be universal, but the rate of development may vary from one culture to another (Dasen & Heron, 1981; Hughes & Noppe, 1991; Leadbeater, 1991; Rogoff & Chavajay, 1995).

The average Eskimo child acquires the spatial concept of horizontalness faster than the average West African child. But many West African children (around the age of twelve or thirteen) understand conservation of quantity, weight, and volume sooner than Eskimo children do (Dasen & Heron, 1981). Although children in Western, industrialized societies (like ours) usually are not given baby-sitting responsibilities until they are at least ten years old because their high level of egocentrism prevents them from considering the needs of the other child, Mayan children in Mexican villages as young as age five play this role because their culture stresses the development of cooperative behavior (Sameroff & McDonough, 1994).

Research conducted during the 1970s found that individuals living in non-Western cultures who had little formal education did not engage in formal operational thinking. Although these same people used concrete operational schemes when tested with the kinds of tasks Piaget used, they usually did so at a later age than the Swiss children Piaget originally studied. This result was attributed to their lack of schooling, which left them unfamiliar with the language and conventions of formal testing. When concrete operational tasks were conducted with materials that were part of these people's everyday lives (such as asking children from Zambia to reproduce a pattern with strips of wire rather than with paper and pencil), they performed as well as Western children who drew the patterns on paper (Rogoff & Chavajay, 1995).

Now that you are familiar with Piaget's theory of cognitive development, you can formulate specific classroom applications. You might use the Suggestions for Teaching for the grade level you expect to teach as the basis for a section in your journal.

SUGGESTIONS FOR TEACHING IN YOUR CLASSROOM

Applying Piaget's Theory of Cognitive Development

GENERAL GUIDELINES

1 Focus on what children at each stage can do and avoid what they cannot meaningfully understand.

This implication must be interpreted carefully, as recent research has shown that children at the preoperational and concrete operational levels can do more than Piaget believes. In general, however, it is safe to say that since preoperational stage children (preschoolers, kindergartners, most first and some second graders) can use language and other symbols to stand for objects, they should be given many opportunities to describe and explain things through the use of speech, artwork, body movement, role play, and musical performance. Although the concepts of conservation, seriation, class inclusion, time, space, and number can be introduced, attempts at mastering them should probably be postponed until children are in the concrete operational stage.

Concrete operational stage children (grades 3–6) can be given opportunities to master such mental processes as ordering, seriating, classifying, reversing, multiplying, dividing, subtracting, and adding by manipulating concrete objects or symbols. Although a few fifth and sixth graders may be capable of dealing with abstractions, most exercises that involve theorizing, hypothesizing, or generalizing should be done with concrete objects or symbols.

Formal operational stage children (grades 7 through high school) can be given activities that require hypothetical-deductive reasoning, reflective thinking, analysis, synthesis, and evaluation.

2 Because individuals differ in their rates of intellectual growth, gear instructional materials and activities to each student's developmental level.

3 Because intellectual growth occurs when individuals attempt to eliminate a disequilibrium, instructional lessons and materials that introduce new concepts should provoke interest and curiosity and be moderately challenging in order to maximize assimilation and accommodation.

4 Although information (facts, concepts, procedures) can be efficiently transmitted from teacher to student through direct instruction, knowledge (rules and hypotheses) is best created by each student through the mental and physical manipulation of information.

Accordingly, lesson plans should include opportunities for activity, manipulation, exploration, discussion, and application of information. Small-group science projects are one example of how to implement this goal.

5 Because students' schemes at any given time are an outgrowth of earlier schemes, point out to them how new ideas relate to their old ideas and extend their understanding. Memorization of information for its own sake should be avoided.

Jean Piaget believes that children's schemes develop more quickly when children interact with one another than when they interact with adults. But Lev Vygotsky believes that children learn more from the instructional interactions they have with those who are more intellectually advanced, particularly if the instruction is designed to fall within the child's zone of proximal development.

that way? Because they are the product of a culture that prizes the ability of its members to think at the most abstract levels (which is why Piaget saw formal operations as the most advanced stage of thinking).

Typically, then, parents and schools will shape children's thought processes to reflect that which the culture values. So even when individuals are by themselves, what they think and do is the result of cultural values and practices, some of which may stretch back over hundreds or thousands of years, as well as recent social contacts (Wertsch & Tulviste, 1996).

The Importance of Psychological Tools Vygotsky believed that the most important things a culture passes on to its members (and their descendants) are what he called *psychological tools.* These are the cognitive devices and procedures with which we communicate and explore the world around us. They both aid and change our mental functioning. Speech, writing, gestures, diagrams, numbers, chemical formulas, musical notation, rules, and memory techniques are some examples of common psychological tools.

Psychological tools aid and change thought processes

Early explorers, for example, created maps to help them represent where they had been, communicate that knowledge to others, and plan future trips. Today we use the same type of tool to navigate efficiently over long distances or within relatively compact but complex environments (like large cities). Another example is the use of multiplication. If asked to solve the multiplication problem 343 × 822, you would, in all likelihood, quickly and easily come up with the answer, 281,946, by using the following procedure:

```
     343
   × 822
     686
    686
  2744
 281,946
```

But you could have produced the same answer by adding 343 to itself 821 times. Why would you automatically opt for the first procedure? Because the culture in which you operate has, through the medium of formal instruction, provided you with a psychological tool called multiplication as a means of more efficiently and accurately solving certain types of complex mathematical problems (Wertsch, 1998). Children are first introduced to a culture's major psychological tools through social interactions with their parents and later through more formal interactions with classroom teachers.

How Social Interaction Affects Cognitive Development

The difference between Vygotsky's views on the origin and development of cognitive processes and those of other cognitive developmental psychologists is something like the old question, "Which came first: the chicken or the egg?" Influenced by Piaget, many developmental psychologists argue that as children overcome cognitive conflict through the internal processes of assimilation, accommodation, and equilibration, they become more capable of higher-level thinking, and so come to understand better the nature of the world in which they live and their place in it. In other words, cognitive development makes social development possible (see our discussion of Robert Selman's work on the social development of children in the next chapter).

Vygotsky, however, believed that just the opposite was true. He saw social interaction as the primary cause of cognitive development. Unlike Piaget, Vygotsky believed that children gain significantly from the knowledge and conceptual tools handed down to them by those who are more intellectually advanced, whether they are same-age peers, older children, or adults.

Cognitive development strongly influenced by those more intellectually advanced

Consider, for example, a simple concept like grandmother. In the absence of formal instruction, a primary grade child's concept of grandmother is likely to be very narrow in scope because it is based on personal experience ("My grandmother is seventy years old, has gray hair, wears glasses, and makes the best apple pie"). But when children are helped to understand the basic nature of the concept with such instructional tools as family tree diagrams, they understand the notion of grandmother (and other types of relatives) on a broader and more general basis. They can then use this concept to compare family structures with friends and, later, to do genealogical research (Tappan, 1998).

In order for social interactions to produce advances in cognitive development, Vygotsky argued, they have to contain a process called *mediation*. Mediation occurs when a more knowledgeable individual interprets a child's behavior and helps transform it into an internal and symbolic representation that means the same thing to the child as to others (Rogoff, 1990; Tudge & Winterhoff, 1993; Wertsch & Tulviste, 1966). Perhaps the following example will help clarify this point: Imagine a child who reaches out to grasp an object that is beyond her reach. A nearby parent thinks

Multi-Age Grouping: Applying the Ideas of Piaget and Vygotsky

When it comes to social experiences, Piaget clearly believed that peer interactions do more to spur cognitive development than do interactions with adults. It is the need to understand the ideas of a peer or playmate in order to formulate responses to those ideas that leads to less egocentrism and the development of new, more complex mental schemes.

Unlike Piaget, Vygotsky believed that children gain significantly from the knowledge and conceptual tools handed down to them by those who are more intellectually advanced, be they same-age peers, older children, or adults.

Return of the One-Room Schoolhouse?

RENEE STOVSKY

St. Louis Post-Dispatch 10/15/96

It's 9:30 A.M. at Glenridge Elementary School in Clayton, and Kathryn Mitchell Pierce's class is engaged in small-group activities.

Four first-graders practice penmanship at a common table. Two second-graders huddle over a computer, composing a report on vertebrates, based on a recent field trip to the zoo. Several third-graders complete a unit on simple machines, such as pulleys, and how they work. Another group, involved in a study of the human body, experiments with how their lungs function by inflating and deflating plastic bags with straws. For anyone familiar with free choice time in the primary grades, there's nothing inherently unusual about this scene, except one thing—the diversity of pupils, age-wise, grouped together. These first-, second- and third-graders share the same classroom and teacher throughout the day.

To the uninitiated, multi-age classrooms—one of the newer wrinkles in elementary education—may seem like a throwback to the one-room schoolhouse. Grouping children of different ages together is seen as a way to not only accommodate pupils of various abilities and backgrounds, but also nurture cooperative learning and build character.

"Every teacher knows that no two children show up on Sept. 5 with the same basic skills to progress through a curriculum," says Marian Scheer, principal of Pierremont Elementary School in the Parkway School District. Four multi-age classrooms have been in operation there since 1993.

Barbara Geno puts it more bluntly: "Children are not born in litters, like puppies. Why do we think we need to educate them that way?" Geno is a director of Clayton Academy, a private elementary school that features all multi-age classrooms.

Children of different ages can learn from each other, Geno says. Mixing age groups provides powerful opportunities to not only model academic achievement, but to refine more intangible skills like teamwork and tolerance. Multi-age classes naturally stress cooperation rather than comparison, say experts like Suzi Nall, professor of early childhood education at Southern Illinois University at Edwardsville.

Though so far there are only a handful of public schools in the St. Louis area that offer multi-age classes—besides Glenridge and Pierremont, others include Captain Elementary School in Clayton, Holman Accelerated Elementary School in Ferguson-Florissant and Tillman Elementary School in Kirkwood—interest nationally in the concept is high. Kentucky has mandated multi-age classrooms in primary grades as part of a statewide school reform program; Columbus, Ohio, and Portland, Ore., are employing them heavily as well.

While it's easy to visualize multi-age classrooms functioning well in terms of individual or small-group study, it's harder to imagine the logistics of an entire class project. Here's how it worked during a recent whole language activity in Diana Wichman's kindergarten-first grade class at Pierremont:

Each pupil was expected to create a book called "My Favorite Sport." Seated in a semicircle around the blackboard, the children listened as Wichman demonstrated how to get started by drawing a "web" that illustrated appropriate information to include. The entire class brainstormed possible details of where the sport could be played, what kind of equipment was needed.

"Youngers"—kindergartners—were to make their books three pages long. Since many were just beginning to learn about the different parts of a book, as well as the differences between letters, words and sentences, their "writing" consisted of dictating stories and then illustrating them on their own.

"Olders"—first graders—were to produce 5-page books, and many could actually "write" on their own. But if kindergartners were able to "write" on their own, they were encouraged to do so. And those first-graders who were struggling a bit were coached along with the "youngers." Neither was considered beyond the parameters of normalcy.

That's one of the reasons Jean Beel, another multi-age teacher at Pierremont, is sold on the idea. "It fosters strong comfort levels for the children. And that, in turn, creates a wonderful, risk-free environment for learning," she says.

Experts say there are other benefits to multi-age classrooms as well. Because most children stay in the same class for more than one year, they often experience being a follower as well as a leader. That's much more difficult in a regular classroom, where the same children tend to be leaders or followers year after year.

And since most kids "loop" up with the same teacher, time isn't wasted at the beginning of each school year getting to know a child, as well as his or her academic strengths and weaknesses.

Pierce, of Glenridge, finds that a plus for two reasons. "First, it allows the teacher to measure big areas of real individual growth over time," she says. "Second, it forces everyone—children, teachers and parents—to work harder at social relations.

"I tell parents it's like comparing a blind date to a marriage. A kid can 'put up' with a bad classroom situation for a year, just like an adult can 'put up' with a bad companion for an evening. Long-term relationships take more commitment."

The opportunity to remain with the same teacher over time appealed strongly to Rhea Oelbaum, whose son, Seth, 10, spent three years in Pierce's multi-age class.

"Transitions have never been Seth's strong point, so this kind of continuity was a good alternative for him," she says. "I also appreciated the hands-on approach to learning and the emphasis on group projects. There just seemed to be so much more flexibility with this approach. It made it OK to be 'different.'"

Though Oelbaum initially worried about how her son would function in a regular fourth-grade class, she says he has had "zero trouble" adjusting this year. And she thinks he entered with some strong organizational and research skills that he may not have honed in a more traditional setting.

In fact, studies show that students educated in multi-age classrooms that have the same pupil diversity and follow the same curriculum as the rest of the school do at least as well, if not slightly better, on standardized tests than those students in single-grade settings.

And multi-age educators are convinced they come away with important extras. Chief among them: High self-esteem.

"By mixing age levels, you can teach to low-, middle- and high-achievers without anyone feeling singled out for extra attention—either remediation or enrichment," says Geno. "When kids feel good about themselves and they enjoy the classroom environment, academic excellence follows. School success then further boosts self-esteem; it becomes a self-perpetuating cycle."

Sue Heick, a Pierremont multi-age teacher, says she sees concrete evidence that her kids go on to make good use of the group dynamics skills they learn. A disproportionate number of them run for student council or take on other leadership roles. "They are self-confident as well as compassionate," she says.

Despite such testimonials, multi-age education is not without its critics. Among them are those who worry that the movement is driven by the need to "dumb down" curricula and address the problems of economically disadvantaged and/or slower learners at the expense of brighter students.

Reform-minded educators disagree. "Instead of being the more traditional 'sage on stage,' this approach can help teachers to become the 'guide on the side,'" says Rick Burns, associate principal in charge of curriculum and instruction at Kirkwood High School. "It encourages kids to become more active learners. That's beneficial for all students; gifted pupils can solidify their mastery of knowledge by reteaching it to others."

Pro or con, all educators agree on one major disadvantage of multi-age classrooms: the amount of preparation and support its teachers need.

"This involves a tremendous commitment on the part of staff members—planning materials, creating interdisciplinary projects and so forth. You can have the most wonderful facilities, the most cooperative parents, the best curriculum—but the linchpin is the human element. You've got to have excellent, enthusiastic teachers," says Nall.

One way to nurture that enthusiasm is to offer multi-age classes as a choice, instead of a mandate, to both teachers and parents. "It's not for everyone," Nall says.

Still, most teachers who have gotten the necessary support, training and experience to lead a multi-age class say they would never go back to a "straight-age" situation.

"Horace Mann based our system of graded classrooms on 19th-century industrialist philosophy," says Beel, the Pierremont teacher. "But running a factory is not the same as operating a school. This is so much more developmentally appropriate. It takes more effort, but the rewards are much greater—for me as well as the children."

Questions and Activities

1. Is the multi-age classroom described in this article more consistent with Piaget's theory or Vygotsky's theory, or does it reflect aspects of both theories? Why do you think so?
2. According to Suzi Nall, a professor of early childhood education who was interviewed for this article, multi-age classrooms naturally stress cooperation rather than competition. Do you agree? If so, what is it about multi-age classrooms that leads Professor Nall to make that observation?
3. The article describes several ways in which multi-age grouping benefits students. What benefits are there for the teacher?

the child is pointing at the object and says, "Oh, you want the box of crayons," and retrieves the item for the child. Over time, what began as a grasping action becomes transformed, through the mediation of an adult, into an internalized sign ("I want you to give that object to me") that means the same thing to the child as it does to the adult (Driscoll, 2000). Thus, a child's potential level of mental development can be brought about only by introducing the more advanced thought processes of another person. The Case in Print illustrates how multiage grouping can be used to implement Piaget's and Vygotsky's ideas.

How Instruction Affects Cognitive Development

Vygotsky drew a distinction between the type of information that preschool children learn and the type of information that children who attend school learn (or should learn). During early childhood, children acquire what Vygotsky called **spontaneous concepts.** That is, they learn various facts and concepts and rules (such as how to speak one's native language and how to classify objects in one's environment), but they do so for the most part as a by-product of such other activities as engaging in play and communicating with parents and playmates. This kind of knowledge is unsystematic, unconscious, and directed at the child's everyday concrete experiences. Hence, Vygotsky's use of the term *spontaneous*.

To delve further into Vygotsky's ideas, go to the Web Sources section at **http://education.college.hmco.com/students**.

Schooling, however, should be directed to the learning of what Vygotsky called **scientific concepts.** Scientific concepts are the psychological tools mentioned earlier that allow us to manipulate our environment consciously and systematically. Vygotsky believed that the proper development of a child's mind depended on learning how to use these psychological tools, and this would occur only if classroom instruction was properly designed. This meant providing students with explicit and clear verbal definitions as a first step. The basic purpose of instruction, then, is not simply to add one piece of knowledge to another like pennies in a piggy bank but to stimulate and guide cognitive development (Crain, 2000; Rogoff, 1990).

Teachers should help students learn how to use psychological tools

Contemporary Russian psychologists have extended Vygotsky's notions of spontaneous and scientific concepts. They use the term **empirical learning** to refer to the way in which young children acquire spontaneous concepts. The hallmark of empirical learning is that the most observable characteristics of objects and events are noticed and used as a basis for forming general concepts. The main limitation of this approach is that salient characteristics are not necessarily critical or defining characteristics, and it is the latter that form the basis of correct concept formation. For example, in the absence of formal instruction, children come to believe that any utterance that has two or more words is a sentence, that whales are fish, and that bamboo is not a type of grass.

Theoretical learning, on the other hand, involves using psychological tools to learn scientific concepts. As these general tools are used repeatedly with a variety of problems, they are gradually internalized and generalized to a wide variety of settings and problem types. Good-quality instruction, in this view, is aimed at helping children move from the very practical empirical learning to the more general theoretical learning and from using psychological tools overtly, with the aid of an adult, to using these tools mentally, without outside assistance (Karpov & Bransford, 1995).

Here's an example that compares the efficacy of the empirical and theoretical approaches: Two groups of six-year-old children were taught how to write the twenty-two letters of the Russian alphabet. Group 1 was taught using the empirical approach. The teacher gave the students a model of each letter, showed them how to write each one, and also gave a verbal explanation of how to write each letter. The students then copied each letter under the teacher's supervision. When they produced an acceptable copy of a letter, they were taught the next letter. Group 2 was taught using the theoretical approach. First, students were taught to analyze the shape of each letter so they could identify where the direction of the contour of each line changed. Then they were to place dots in those locations outlining the change in contour. Finally, they were to reproduce the pattern of dots on another part of the page and connect the dots with a pencil.

The speed with which the children in each group learned to produce the letters of the alphabet accurately differed by quite a large margin. The average student in the empirical group needed about 170 trials to learn the first letter and about 20 trials to write the last letter. The number of trials taken to learn all twenty-two letters was about 1,230. The average student in the theoretical group required only about fourteen trials to learn how to write the first letter correctly, and from the eighth letter on needed only one trial per letter. The number of trials needed to learn all twenty-two letters for the second group was about 60. Furthermore, these students were able to use the general method they were taught to help them learn to write the letters of the Latin and Arabic alphabets (Karpov & Bransford, 1995).

Instruction and the Zone of Proximal Development This discussion of empirical and theoretical learning illustrates Vygotsky's belief that well-designed instruction is like a magnet. If it is aimed slightly ahead of what children know and can do at the present time, it will pull them along, helping them master things they cannot learn on their own. We can illustrate this idea with an experiment that Vygotsky (1986) described. He gave two eight-year-olds of average ability problems that were a bit too difficult for them to solve on their own. (Although Vygotsky did not specify what types of problems they were, imagine that they were math problems.) He then tried to help the children solve the problems by giving them leading questions and hints. With this aid, he found that one child was able to solve problems designed for twelve-year-olds, whereas the other child could reach only a nine-year-old level.

Cognitive development promoted by instruction in zone of proximal development

Vygotsky referred to the difference between what a child can do on his own and what can be accomplished with some assistance as the **zone of proximal development (ZPD).** The size of the first eight-year-old's zone is 4 (that is, the eight-year-old could, with help, solve the problem designed for a child four years older), whereas the second child has a zone of 1 (he could solve the problem designed for a child one year older). According to Vygotsky, students with wider zones are likely to experience greater cognitive development when instruction is pitched just above the lower limit of their ZPD than will students with narrower zones because the former are in a better position to capitalize on the instruction. The ZPD, then, encompasses those abilities, attitudes, and patterns of thinking that are in the process of maturing and can be refined only with assistance (Tappan, 1998).

Scaffolding techniques support student learning

Helping students answer difficult questions or solve problems by giving them hints or asking leading questions is an example of a technique called **scaffolding.** Just as construction workers use external scaffolding to support their building efforts, Vygotsky recommended that teachers similarly support learning in its early phases. The purpose of scaffolding is to help students acquire knowledge and skills they would not have learned on their own. As the student demonstrates mastery over the content in question, the learning aids are faded and removed. Scaffolding techniques that are likely to help students traverse their ZPD include prompts, suggestions, checklists, modeling, rewards, feedback, cognitive structuring (using such devices as theories, categories, labels, and rules for helping students organize and understand ideas), and questioning (Gallimore & Tharp, 1990; Ratner, 1991). As students approach the upper limit of their ZPD, their behavior becomes smoother, more internalized, and more automatized. Any assistance offered at this level they are likely to perceive as disruptive and irritating.

Mark Tappan (1998) has proposed the following four-component model that teachers can use to optimize the effects of their scaffolding efforts and help students move through their ZPD:

1. ***Model desired academic behaviors.*** Children can imitate many behaviors that they do not have the capability to exhibit independently, and such experiences stimulate students to act this way on their own.
2. ***Create a dialogue with the student.*** A child's understanding of concepts, procedures, and principles becomes more systematic and organized as a result of the exchange of questions, explanations, and feedback between teacher and child within the child's ZPD. As with modeling, the effectiveness of this dialogue is determined, at least in part, by the extent to which the teacher and student are committed to creating and maintaining a relationship in which each makes an honest effort to satisfy the needs of the other.
3. ***Practice.*** Practice speeds up the internalizing of thinking skills that students observe and discuss with others.
4. ***Confirmation.*** To confirm others is to bring out the best in them by focusing on what they can do with some assistance, and this process helps create a trusting and mutually supportive relationship between teacher and student. For example, you might say to a student, "I know this assignment seems difficult right now and that you have had some problems in the past with similar assignments, but with the help I'm willing to offer, I'm certain you'll do good-quality work."

Vygotsky's notion of producing cognitive development by embedding instruction within a student's ZPD is an attractive one and has many implications for instruction. In the chapter on information-processing theory, for example, we will describe how this notion was used to improve the reading comprehension skills of low-achieving seventh graders.

Using Technology to Promote Cognitive Development

Piaget and Vygotsky believed that people use physical, mental, and social experiences to construct personal conceptions (schemes) of what the world is like. Al-

Computer-based technology can be used to promote cognitive development in ways that are consistent with both Piaget's and Vygotsky's views.

though there are numerous opportunities throughout the course of each day to watch what other people do, try out ideas, and interact with others, we are normally limited to the physical and social stimuli that make up our immediate environment. Factors such as distance, time, and cost keep us from wider-ranging interactions. Technology, however, greatly reduces these limitations and thus has the potential to expand the range of our experiences.

For instance, there are electronic tools for **computer conferencing** (also known as *Web-based conferencing* or *on-line discussion forums*), **videoconferencing,** group brainstorming, expert feedback, **real-time chatting,** peer debating, and polling student opinions (Grabe & Grabe, 2001). Computer conferencing occurs when individuals at different locations log onto a computer site, voice their views on a particular subject, and respond to the views of others. Videoconferencing involves a real-time visual communication with one or more individuals in other locations. Real-time chatting is similar to videoconferencing except that the conversations occur on a computer network and are written. With all of these new instructional tools, technology is bringing new learning forums and opportunities into our schools. But how do these technological advances relate to theories of cognitive development?

Technology Applied to Piaget

There are at least two main ways in which technology can be used in schools to support Piaget's original ideas about the cognitive development of young children: (1) as a simulation tool, or microworld, for displaying knowledge and repairing misconceptions and errors in thinking, and (2) as a source for same-age peers to debate issues, thereby fostering cognitive conflict and disequilibrium.

Computers provide many routes to knowledge and can help restructure common student misconceptions (for example, that the seasons are caused by the closeness of the earth to the sun or that electrical current is equal in all parts of a circuit).

One way technology can overcome such misconceptions is to create explorable **microworlds,** or simulated learning environments, that allow students to get a sense of how things work in the real world (Grabe & Grabe, 2001; Nickerson, 1995). One such microworld, the Geometric Supposer, provides students with an electronic drawing board to test mathematical hypotheses while constructing, measuring, and investigating figures such as triangles, quadrilaterals, and circles (Lampert, 1995, Schwartz, 1995). Microworlds foster cognitive development by encouraging student exploration, student control, and visual representation of abstract ideas.

Computer-based simulations promote exploration and visual representations of abstract ideas, and correct misconceptions

A **microcomputer-based laboratory (MBL)** can also be used to build on existing knowledge and correct misconceptions. In an MBL, one or more sensors are attached to a microcomputer to generate graphs of physical reactions. The following anecdote illustrates how helpful an MBL can be. When seventh- and eighth-grade students were asked to draw a graph depicting how fast a bicyclist travels uphill, downhill, and on flat stretches, their products represented the hills and valleys rather than the bicyclist's speed. That is, they drew an ascending line to represent the bicyclist's speed going uphill without realizing that such a line represented the downhill portion of the journey since it indicated increasing speed. In effect, they drew pictures that represented the exact opposite of what they were asked to represent. The students' graph-interpretation skills were significantly improved by having them work with an MBL. As the student applied a source of energy to one of the sensors—heating up and allowing to cool down a beaker of water, for example—a corresponding graphic representation was instantly created on the computer's screen (Kozma, 1991).

To explore microworlds and MBLs, follow the links on the textbook Web site at **http://education.college.hmco.com/students**.

MBL sensors and probes have been developed since the late 1970s for such variables as temperature, heat, force, brain waves, heart rate, voltage, and humidity to help clarify confusing laws of nature (Ruopp, Gal, Drayton, & Pfister, 1993). In a review of twenty MBL studies, Mary Nakhleh (1994) found that MBL applications show promise in altering or restructuring students' faulty understandings of key science concepts. Evidently, MBLs foster important cognitive changes by representing information in multiple ways and graphing information quickly enough for students to make connections between symbolic representations and the real world.

A second way to put Piaget's ideas into practice is to use technology to promote cognitive conflict. Remember that, according to Piaget, cognitive development is contingent on students' confronting others who have contradictory thoughts and claims, thereby creating internal tension and conflict. When students notice a discrepancy or a contradiction of what they believe, they are motivated to find more information and move back to a state of equilibrium. One way to accomplish this goal is to have students debate with peers over a computer network. Curt Bonk and Jack Cummings (1998), for example, discuss how World Wide Web–based debates can be used to get students to reflect on the different positions people take on controversial issues. Students are also encouraged to consult the original source material that their opponents use. Such a technique, Bonk and Cummings argue, enhances the quality of student rebuttals and reaction papers. The advantage of a computer network is that the peers one debates can be students in the class down the hall, students in another school district, students in another state, or even students in another country. This kind of easy access to others greatly increases the probability that students will encounter people who hold truly divergent views on issues.

Technology Applied to Vygotsky

As with Piaget, there are at least two ways to link educational technology with the ideas of Vygotsky: (1) using the computer as an expert peer or collaborative partner to support skills and strategies that can be internalized by the learner and (2) using the computer as a tool to link learners to more knowledgeable peers and experts, who establish a master-novice apprenticeship and scaffold the student's learning.

As you'll recall, Vygotsky believed that children gain significantly from the knowledge and conceptual tools handed down to them by those who are more intellectually advanced. Roy Pea (1985) and Gavriel Salomon (1988) were among the first to suggest that the computer might play the same role as more capable tutors with such tasks as writing an essay and reading a book. Basically, the computer is programmed to provide prompts and expert guidance during reading and writing tasks. These supports, or scaffolds, are gradually faded as students become more competent at regulating their own behavior. According to some researchers (Bereiter & Scardamalia, 1987), such support is vital in writing, because young children often lack the cognitive resources and skills to move beyond simple knowledge telling in their compositions. Salomon, who helped develop both the Reading Partner and Writing Partner software tools, found that they improved children's reading comprehension, essay writing, effort, and awareness of useful self-questioning strategies (Salomon, Globerson, & Guterman, 1989; Zellermayer, Salomon, Globerson, & Givon, 1991). Other studies, however, have not always reported such positive results (Bonk & Reynolds, 1992; Daiute, 1985; Reynolds & Bonk, 1996).

Computer programs can act as expert collaborative partners

The second technology-based technique that has been derived from Vygotsky's view of cognitive development is the **cognitive apprenticeship** (Bonk & Cunningham, 1998; Brown, Collins, & Duguid, 1989). Like the traditional master-apprentice relationship in the skilled crafts and trades, a mentor works closely with a learner to develop the learner's cognitive skills. Also like the traditional apprenticeship, mentors provide students with real-life tasks to perform under realistic conditions. The learner moves from newcomer to expert by first observing the mentor and then participating in some tasks. Gradually, there is a shift in responsibility for solving the task from the expert or teacher to the student as the student moves from the fringes of the community to a more central role within it. As that happens, new skills are tested and, it is hoped, internalized.

When this master-apprentice relationship occurs on a computer network, it is called a **teleapprenticeship** (Levin, Kim, & Riel, 1990; Teles, 1993). The education and technology literature is filled with examples of teleapprenticeships in K–12 education (Schrum & Berenfeld, 1997). For instance, international weather projects such as the Kids as Global Scientists project (Songer, 1998), the Collaborative Visualization project (Edelson, Pea, & Gomez, 1996), and the Global Learning and Observations to Benefit the Environment program (Singletary & Jordan, 1996) all involve students in genuine scientific data collection and reporting. The collaborative relationships that students establish with peers and mentors create in students a strong sense of participation in what is called a community of practice.

Richard Ruopp et al. (1993) documented how an electronic community of physics teachers, in a project called Labnet, was able to use MBLs to get students to share and compare their experimental findings across sites, while simultaneously providing a vehicle for teacher pooling of talents and discussion of lesson plans. Such a project is a prime example of two-tiered scaffolding (Gaffney & Anderson, 1991): consultants and experts scaffolded teachers, who in turn scaffolded students. With the rise in telecommunications and collaborative technologies for the Internet, the possibilities for working on-line with specialists, practitioners, or content experts continue to increase.

Piaget, Kohlberg, and Gilligan: Moral Development

PIAGET'S ANALYSIS OF THE MORAL JUDGMENT OF THE CHILD

Because he was intrigued by all aspects of children's thinking, Piaget became interested in moral development. He began his study of morality by observing how children played marbles. (He first learned the game himself, so that he would be able to understand the subtleties of the conception.) Piaget discovered that interpretations of rules followed by participants in marble games changed with age.

Age Changes in Interpretation of Rules Four- to seven-year-olds just learning the game seemed to view rules as interesting examples of the social behavior of older children. They did not understand the rules but tried to go along with them. Seven- to ten-year-olds regarded rules as sacred pronouncements handed down by older children or adults. At about the age of eleven or twelve, children began to see rules as agreements reached by mutual consent. Piaget concluded that younger children see rules as absolute and external.

Although children ranging from the age of four to about ten do not question rules, they may frequently break them because they do not understand rules completely. After the age of eleven or so, children become increasingly capable of grasping why rules are necessary. At that point, Piaget concluded, they tend to lose interest in adult-imposed regulations and take delight in formulating their own variations of rules to fit a particular situation. Piaget illustrated this point by describing how a group of ten- and eleven-year-old boys prepared for a snowball fight (1965, p. 50). They divided themselves into teams, elected officers, decided on rules to govern the distances from which the snowballs could be thrown, and agreed on a system of punishments for those who violated the rules. Although they spent a substantial amount of playtime engaging in such preliminary discussions, they seemed to thoroughly enjoy their newly discovered ability to make up rules to supplant those that previously had been imposed on them by their elders.

Moral Realism Versus Moral Relativism The way children of different ages responded to rules so intrigued Piaget that he decided to use the interview method to obtain more systematic information about moral development. He made up pairs of stories and asked children of different ages to discuss them. Here is a typical pair of stories:

> A: There was a little boy called Julian. His father had gone out and Julian thought it would be fun to play with father's ink-pot. First he played with the pen, and then he made a little blot on the table cloth.
>
> B: A little boy who was called Augustus once noticed that his father's ink-pot was empty. One day that his father was away he thought of filling the ink-pot so as to help his father, and so that he should find it full when he came home. But while he was opening the ink-bottle he made a big blot on the table cloth. (1965, p. 122)

After reading these stories, Piaget asked, "Are these children equally guilty? Which of the two is naughtiest, and why?" As was the case with interpretations of rules,

Piaget found that younger children reacted to these stories differently from older children. The younger children maintained that Augustus was more guilty than Julian because he had made a bigger inkblot on the tablecloth. They took no account of the fact that Julian was misbehaving and that Augustus was trying to help his father. Older children, however, were more likely to base their judgment of guilt on the intent of each child.

Morality of constraint (moral realism): rules are sacred, consequences determine guilt

Morality of cooperation (moral relativism): rules are flexible, intent important in determining guilt

Piaget referred to the moral thinking of children up to the age of ten or so as the **morality of constraint,** but he also called it *moral realism.* (Remember our definition of *decentration* in the earlier discussion of Piaget's theory. How do you think the young child's lack of decentration might affect her moral reasoning?) The thinking of children of eleven or older Piaget called the **morality of cooperation.** He also occasionally used the term *moral relativism.* Piaget concluded that the two basic types of moral reasoning differ in several ways. We summarize these differences in Table 2.3.

Table 2.3 Morality of Constraint Versus Morality of Cooperation

Morality of Constraint (Typical of Six-Year-Olds)	Morality of Cooperation (Typical of Twelve-Year-Olds)
Holds single, absolute moral perspective (behavior is right or wrong)	Is aware of different viewpoints regarding rules
Believes rules are unchangeable	Believes rules are flexible
Determines extent of guilt by amount of damage	Considers the wrongdoers' intentions when evaluating guilt
Defines moral wrongness in terms of what is forbidden or punished	Defines moral wrongness in terms of violation of spirit of cooperation
(Notice that these first four differences call attention to the tendency for children below the age of ten or so to think of rules as sacred pronouncements handed down by external authority.)	
Believes punishment should stress atonement and does not need to "fit the crime"	Believes punishment should involve either restitution or suffering the same fate as one's victim
Believes peer aggression should be punished by an external authority	Believes peer aggression should be punished by retaliatory behavior on the part of the victim*
Believes children should obey rules because they are established by those in authority	Believes children should obey rules because of mutual concerns for rights of others
(Notice how these last three differences call attention to the tendency for children above the age of ten or so to see rules as mutual agreements among equals.)	

*Beyond the age of twelve, adolescents increasingly affirm that reciprocal reactions, or "getting back," should be a response to good behavior, not bad.

SOURCES: Freely adapted from interpretations of Piaget (1932) by Kohlberg (1969) and Lickona (1976).

Kohlberg's Description of Moral Development

Just as James Marcia elaborated Erikson's concept of identity formation, Lawrence Kohlberg elaborated Piaget's ideas on moral thinking. Kohlberg believed that (1) moral reasoning proceeds through fixed stages, and (2) moral development can be accelerated through instruction.

Kohlberg's Use of Moral Dilemmas As a graduate student at the University of Chicago in the 1950s, Lawrence Kohlberg became fascinated by Piaget's studies of moral development. He decided to expand on Piaget's original research by making up stories involving moral dilemmas that would be more appropriate for older children. Here is the story that is most often mentioned in discussions of his work:

> In Europe a woman was near death from cancer. One drug might save her, a form of radium that a druggist in the same town had recently discovered. The druggist was charging $2,000, ten times what the drug cost him to make. The sick woman's husband, Heinz, went to everyone he knew to borrow the money, but he could only get together about half of what it cost. He told the druggist that his wife was dying and asked him to sell it cheaper or let him pay later, but the druggist said "No." The husband got desperate and broke into the man's store to steal the drug for his wife. Should the husband have done that? Why? (1969, p. 376)

Kohlberg's Six Stages of Moral Reasoning After analyzing the responses of ten- to sixteen-year-olds to this and similar moral dilemmas, Kohlberg (1963) eventually developed a description of six stages of moral reasoning. Be forewarned, however, that Kohlberg later revised some of his original stage designations and that descriptions of the stages have also been modified since he first proposed them. In different discussions of his stages, therefore, you may encounter varying descriptions. The outline presented in Table 2.4 is a composite summary of the sequence of moral development as described by Kohlberg, but you should expect to find differences if you read other accounts of his theory.

The scoring system Kohlberg developed to evaluate a response to a moral dilemma is extremely complex. Furthermore, the responses of subjects are lengthy and may feature arguments about a particular decision. To help you understand a bit more about each Kohlberg stage, the following list offers simplified examples of responses to a dilemma such as that faced by Heinz. For maximum clarity, only brief typical responses to the question "Why shouldn't you steal from a store?" are mentioned.

Preconventional morality: avoid punishment, receive benefits in return

Stage 1: punishment-obedience orientation. "You might get caught." (The physical consequences of an action determine goodness or badness.)

Stage 2: instrumental relativist orientation. "You shouldn't steal something from a store, and the store owner shouldn't steal things that belong to you." (Obedience to laws should involve an even exchange.)

Conventional morality: impress others, respect authority

Stage 3: good boy–nice girl orientation. "Your parents will be proud of you if you are honest." (The right action is one that will impress others.)

Stage 4: law-and-order orientation. "It's against the law, and if we don't obey laws, our whole society might fall apart." (To maintain the social order, fixed rules must be obeyed.)

Stage 5: social contract orientation. "Under certain circumstances laws may have to be disregarded—if a person's life depends on breaking a law, for instance."

Table 2.4 Kohlberg's Stages of Moral Reasoning

LEVEL 1: PRECONVENTIONAL MORALITY. (Typical of children up to the age of nine. Called *preconventional* because young children do not really understand the conventional or rules of a society.)

Stage 1 Punishment-obedience orientation. The physical consequences of an action determine goodness or badness. Those in authority have superior power and should be obeyed. Punishment should be avoided by staying out of trouble.

Stage 2 Instrumental relativist orientation. An action is judged to be right if it is instrumental in satisfying one's own needs or involves an even exchange. Obeying rules should bring some sort of benefit in return.

LEVEL 2: CONVENTIONAL MORALITY. (Typical of nine- to twenty-year-olds. Called *conventional* since most nine- to twenty-year-olds conform to the conventions of society because they *are* the rules of a society.)

Stage 3 Good boy–nice girl orientation. The right action is one that would be carried out by someone whose behavior is likely to please or impress others.

Stage 4 Law-and-order orientation. To maintain the social order, fixed rules must be established and obeyed. It is essential to respect authority.

LEVEL 3: POSTCONVENTIONAL MORALITY. (Usually reached only after the age of twenty and only by a small proportion of adults. Called *postconventional* because the moral principles that underlie the conventions of a society are understood.)

Stage 5 Social contract orientation. Rules needed to maintain the social order should be based not on blind obedience to authority but on mutual agreement. At the same time, the rights of the individual should be protected.

Stage 6 Universal ethical principle orientation. Moral decisions should be made in terms of self-chosen ethical principles. Once principles are chosen, they should be applied in consistent ways.*

*In an article published in 1978, several years after Kohlberg had originally described the six stages, he described the last stage as an essentially theoretical ideal that is rarely encounterd in real life.

SOURCE: Based on descriptions in Kohlberg (1969, 1976, 1978).

Postconventional morality: mutual agreements, consistent principles

(Rules should involve mutual agreements; the rights of the individual should be protected.)

Stage 6: universal ethical principle orientation. "You need to weigh all the factors and then try to make the most appropriate decision in a given situation. Sometimes it would be morally wrong *not* to steal." (Moral decisions should be based on consistent applications of self-chosen ethical principles.)

Criticisms and Evaluations of Kohlberg's Theory Is Kohlberg's contention that moral reasoning proceeds through a fixed universal sequence of stages accurate? Based on analysis of research on moral development, Martin Hoffman (1980) believes that although Kohlberg's sequence of stages may not be true of every individual in every culture, it may provide a useful general description of how moral reasoning develops in American society. Carol Gilligan (1979), whose position we will discuss in detail later, has proposed two somewhat different sequences that reflect differences in male and female socialization.

What about Kohlberg's view that moral development can be accelerated through direct instruction? Is this another "mission impossible," as some critics contend? Research on this question has produced some limited but moderately positive results. Most of these studies have used a teaching method known as *direct discussion* or *dilemma discussion*. After reading a set of moral dilemmas (like the one about Heinz and the cancer drug) and identifying those issues that could help resolve the dilemma, students, under the teacher's guidance, discuss the different ways each of them would choose to resolve the dilemma. This process can involve challenging one another's thinking, reexamining assumptions, building lines of argument, and responding to counterarguments.

Alan Lockwood (1978), after summarizing the findings of almost a dozen studies on acceleration of moral reasoning, concludes that the strongest effects (about half a stage increase in reasoning) occurred among individuals whose reasoning reflected stages 2 and 3. The effect of the instruction varied considerably from one subject to another. Some individuals showed substantial increases in reasoning; others showed no change. A comprehensive review of research on this topic by Andre Schlaefli, James Rest, and Stephen Thoma (1985) revealed similar conclusions. The authors found that moral education programs produced modest positive effects. They also found that the strongest effects were obtained with adult subjects.

Moral education programs may produce modest acceleration in moral development

Paul Vitz (1990) criticizes Kohlberg's use of moral dilemmas on the grounds that they are too far removed from the kinds of everyday social interactions in which children and adolescents engage. He prefers instead the use of narrative stories, both fictional and real accounts of others, because they portray such basic moral values as honesty, compassion, fairness, and hard work in an understandable context. Others (e.g., Rest, Narvaez, Bebeau, & Thoma, 1999) have criticized the fact that Kohlberg relied on the ability of his participants to explain clearly how they solved such hypothetical dilemmas as Heinz's. Individuals not adept at self-reflection or without the vocabulary to express their thoughts clearly either would not be recruited into such studies or would have little to contribute.

The final criticism we will mention concerns the type of moral issue that most interested Kohlberg. Kohlberg's theory deals primarily with what are called macromoral issues, such as civil rights, free speech, the women's movement, and wilderness preservation. The focus is on how the behavior of individuals affects the structure of society and public policy. At this level, a moral person is one who attempts to influence laws and regulations because of a deeply held principle. For some psychologists (for example, Rest, Narvaez, Bebeau, & Thoma, 1999), a limitation of Kohlberg's theory is that it does not adequately address micromoral issues. Micromoral issues concern personal interactions in everyday situations, examples of which include courtesy (not interrupting someone before that person has finished speaking), helpfulness (giving up your seat on a crowded bus or train to an elderly person), remembering significant events of friends and family, and being punctual for appointments. For micromoral issues, a moral person is one who is loyal, dedicated, and cares about particular people.

Educational Implications of Kohlberg's Theory Carol Harding and Kenneth Snyder (1991) believe that teachers can make productive use of contemporary films to illustrate moral dilemmas. Film is an attractive medium to students, and several types of moral dilemmas are often portrayed in the space of about two hours. To highlight the dilemma of the rights of the individual versus the rights of others in a community, Harding and Snyder recommend the films *Platoon* and *Wall Street*. *Platoon* is a story about the Vietnam War and contains scenes of American soldiers burning villages and abusing villagers who are suspected of having ties to or of being the enemy. In response to such scenes, students can be asked such questions as, "Should the enemy in war be granted certain rights, or is personal survival more important?" *Wall Street* is a story about a corporate raider who uses borrowed money to take control of public companies and then sells off the assets (thereby eliminating people's jobs) to enrich himself.

The Tom Snyder educational software company offers a series of computer-based programs titled Decisions, Decisions, in which students identify and discuss moral dilemmas such as protecting the environment or using drugs. Students discuss each situation and as a group choose a response. Each response is stored by the program and in turn affects the development and outcome of the following situations to illustrate that events do not occur in isolation and that all decisions have consequences.

If films or computer programs are not available but you occasionally wish to engage your students in a discussion of moral dilemmas, the daily newspaper is an excellent source of material. Biology teachers, for example, can point to stories of the conflicts produced by machines that keep comatose patients alive or by medical practices based on genetic engineering. Other science teachers might bring in articles that describe the moral dilemma produced by the debate over nuclear power versus fossil fuel. Civics or government teachers could use news items that reflect the dilemma that arises when freedom of speech conflicts with the need to curtail racism.

Gilligan's View of Identity and Moral Development

Carol Gilligan (1982, 1988) argues that Erikson's view of identity development and Kohlberg's view of moral development more accurately describe what occurs with adolescent males than with adolescent females. In her view, Erikson's and Kohlberg's ideas emphasize separation from parental authority and societal conventions. Instead of remaining loyal to adult authority, individuals as they mature shift their loyalty to

Carol Gilligan believes that Erikson's theory of identity development and Kohlberg's theory of moral development do not accurately describe the course of identity formation and moral reasoning in females. She believes that adolescent females place a higher value on caring, understanding, and sharing of experiences than they do on independence, self-reliance, and justice.

abstract principles (for example, self-reliance, independence, justice, and fairness). This process of detachment allows adolescents to assume a more equal status with adults. It's almost as if adolescents are saying, "You have your life, and I have mine; you don't intrude on mine, and I won't intrude on yours."

But, Gilligan argues, many adolescent females have a different primary concern. They care less about separation and independence and more about remaining loyal to others through expressions of caring, understanding, and sharing of experiences. Detachment for these female adolescents is a moral problem rather than a sought-after developmental milestone. The problem for them is how to become autonomous while also being caring and connected.

Given this view, Gilligan believes that adolescent females are more likely to resolve Erikson's identity versus role confusion and intimacy versus isolation crises concurrently rather than consecutively. The results of at least one study (Ochse & Plug, 1986) support this view. With respect to Kohlberg's theory, Gilligan argues that because females are socialized to value more highly the qualities of understanding, helping, and cooperation with others than that of preserving individual rights, and because this latter orientation is reflected most strongly in Kohlberg's two conventional stages, females are more likely to be judged to be at a lower level of moral development than males.

Stephen Thoma (1986) has offered a partial answer to Gilligan's criticism. After reviewing more than fifty studies on gender differences in moral development, he drew three conclusions. First, the effect of gender on scores from the Defining Issues Test (the DIT is a device that uses responses to moral dilemmas to determine level of moral reasoning) was very small. Less than one-half of 1 percent of the differences in DIT scores was due to gender differences. Second, females almost always scored higher. This slight superiority for females appeared in every age group studied (middle school, high school, college, adults). Third, differences in DIT scores were strongly associated with differences in age and level of education. That is, individuals who were older and who had graduated from college were more likely to score at the postconventional level than those who were younger and had less education. Thoma's findings suggest that females are just as likely as males to use justice and fairness concepts in their reasoning about *hypothetical* moral dilemmas.

Males and females may use different approaches to resolve real-life moral dilemmas

But there is one aspect of Gilligan's criticism that cannot be answered by Thoma's analysis of existing research. She argues that when females are faced with their own real-life moral dilemmas (abortion, civil rights, environmental pollution) rather than hypothetical ones, they are more likely to favor a caring-helping-cooperation orientation than a justice-fairness-individual rights orientation. Perhaps the best approach that educators can take when they involve students in discussions of moral issues is to emphasize the utility of *both* orientations.

DOES MORAL THINKING LEAD TO MORAL BEHAVIOR?

The Hartshorne and May Studies Hugh Hartshorne and Mark May (1929, 1930a, 1930b) observed thousands of children at different age levels reacting in situations that revealed their actual moral behavior. The researchers also asked the children to respond to questions about hypothetical situations to reveal how much they understood about right and wrong behavior. Elementary school children, for example, were allowed to correct their own papers or record their own scores on measures of athletic skill without being aware that accurate measures were being made independently by adult observers. The children were also asked what they *thought* was the right thing to do in similar situations.

Moral knowledge does not always result in moral behavior

A comparison of the two sets of data made it possible to determine, among other things, whether children practiced what they preached. What Hartshorne and May discovered was that many children who were able to describe right kinds of behavior in hypothetical situations indulged in wrong behavior in real-life situations. Children reacted in specific, rather than consistent, ways to situations that called for moral judgment. Even a child who was rated as among the most honest in a group would behave in a dishonest way under certain circumstances. A boy who was an excellent student but an indifferent athlete, for example, would not cheat when asked to correct his own paper, but he *would* inflate scores on sports skills.

Another significant, and dismaying, discovery that Hartshorne and May made was that children who went to Sunday school or who belonged to such organizations as the Boy Scouts or Girl Scouts were just as dishonest as children who were not exposed to the kind of moral instruction provided by such organizations. Hartshorne and May concluded that one explanation for the ineffectiveness of moral instruction in the 1920s was that too much stress was placed on having children memorize values such as the Ten Commandments or the Boy Scout oath and law. The two researchers suggested that it would be more effective to invite children to discuss real-life moral situations as they occurred. Instead of having children chant, "Honesty is the best policy," for example, Hartshorne and May urged teachers to call attention to the positive consequences of honest acts. If a student in a school reported that she had found money belonging to someone else, the teacher might praise the child and ask everyone in the class to think about how relieved the person who had lost the money would be to get it back.

Research on Character Education Programs Many parents, educators, and political leaders believe that today's students lack the moral values possessed by previous generations. Concerned adults cite statistics such as the following (Bebeau, Rest, & Narvaez, 1999):

- Homicides committed by youths doubled from 1970 to 1980, then doubled again by 1987, then doubled yet again by 1992. (Notice that the time span for each period was shorter than the previous one.)
- On any given day, over 130,000 school children bring a gun to school.
- More unmarried teenagers in the United States become pregnant than in any other industrialized country.
- More teenagers in the United States abuse drugs than in any other industrialized country.

One commonly voiced solution to these problems is for the schools to institute moral education programs (also called character education programs). After reviewing the research on the effectiveness of character education programs, James Leming (1993) drew the following conclusions:

- Telling students what they should or should not do, through either slogans ("Just say no") or conduct codes, is unlikely to have significant or lasting effects on character.
- Helping students think about how to resolve moral dilemmas in higher-level ways does not automatically result in increases in morally acceptable behavior.
- An individual's social environment plays an important role in the learning and exhibiting of virtuous behavior. When students have clear rules with which to guide their behavior, when they accept those rules as appropriate and worthwhile, and when they are rewarded for complying with those rules, they are more likely to exhibit morally acceptable behavior.

Ms. Kittle: You mean if other 12-year-old kids had to pay the full price for their tickets, then it's not fair for Mark and Steven to get in cheaper?

Troy: Right. (Lickona, 1998)

4 Create a classroom atmosphere that will enhance open discussion. For example, arrange face-to-face groupings, be an accepting model, foster listening and communication skills, and encourage student-to-student interaction.

Richard Hersh, Diana Paolitto, and Joseph Reimer (1979) offer the following specific suggestions for supervising classroom discussions:

- *Highlight the moral issue to be discussed.* Example: Describe a specific real or hypothetical moral dilemma.
- *Ask "why?" questions.* Example: After asking students what they would do if they were faced with the moral dilemma under discussion, ask them to explain why they would act that way.
- *Complicate the circumstances.* Example: After students have responded to the original dilemma, mention a factor that might complicate matters—for example, the involvement of a best friend in the dilemma.
- *Use personal and naturalistic examples.* Example: Invite students to put themselves in the position of individuals who are confronted by moral dilemmas described in newspapers or depicted on television.

Before you use any techniques of moral education in your classes, it is wise to check with your principal. In some communities, parents have insisted that they, not teachers, should take the responsibility for moral instruction.

To solidify your understanding of this chapter, use the Thought Questions and ACE Self-Testing on the Snowman web site at **http://education.college.hmco.com/students**.

Resources for Further Investigation

Erikson's Description of Development

Erik Erikson's books are of considerable significance for their speculations about development and education. In the first six chapters of *Childhood and Society* (2d ed., 1963), he describes how studying Native Americans and observing patients in treatment led him to develop the Eight Ages of Man (described in Chapter 7 of the book). In the final chapters of this book, Erikson uses his conception of development to analyze the lives of Hitler and Maxim Gorky (a Russian novelist of the late 1800s and early 1900s). *Identity: Youth and Crisis* (1968) features a revised description of the eight stages of development, with emphasis on identity and role confusion. Erikson comments on many aspects of his work in an interview with Richard Evans, published as *Dialogue with Erik Erikson* (1967). And James Marcia reviews research on identity statuses in "Identity in Adolescence," in *Handbook of Adolescent Psychology* (1980), edited by Joseph Adelson.

Piaget's Theory of Cognitive Development

Jean Piaget has probably exerted more influence on theoretical discussions of development and on educational practices than any other contemporary psychologist. Of his own books, you might wish to consult *The Language and Thought of the Child* (1952a), *The Origins of Intelligence in Children* (1952b), and *The Psychology of the Child* (1969), the last of which was written in collaboration with Barbel Inhelder. Howard Gruber and Jacques Vonèche have edited *The Essential Piaget: An Interpretive Reference and Guide* (1977), which Piaget describes in the foreword as "the best and most complete of all anthologies of my work." An inexpensive paperback that provides a biography of Piaget and an analysis of his work is *Piaget's Theory of Intellectual Development* (3d ed., 1988), by Herbert Ginsburg and Sylvia Opper. Other books about Piaget are *Piaget for Teachers* (1970), by Hans Furth; *Piaget's Theory of Cognitive and Affective Development* (5th ed., 1996), by Barry Wadsworth; *Theories of Developmental Psychology* (3d ed., 1993), by Patricia Miller; and *Piaget's Theory: Prospects and Possibilities* (1992), edited by Harry Beilin and Peter Pufall.

An online source of information and relevant publications for Piaget is the Jean Piaget Society database, located at **www.piaget.org/**. It contains electronic journals and conference information and is dedicated to "the presentation and discussion of scholarly work on issues related to human knowledge and its development."

Vygotsky's Theory of Cognitive Development

Comprehensive descriptions and analyses of Lev Vygotsky's ideas about cognitive development can be found in *Vygotsky and Education: Instructional Implications and Applications of Sociohistorical Psychology* (1990), edited by Luis Moll; *Vygotsky's Sociohistorical Psychology and Its Contemporary Application* (1991), by Carl Ratner; and *Lev Vygotsky: Revolutionary* (1993), by Fred Newman and Lois Holzman. The web site of Best Practices in Education devotes a page to Vygotsky (**www.bestpraceduc.org/people/LevVygotsky.html**) that contains a brief biographical sketch, examples of teaching practices based on Vygotsky's theory, and a list of several web sites that discuss Vygotsky and his work.

Piaget's Description of Moral Development

Piaget describes his observations on moral development in *The Moral Judgment of the Child* (1965). Thomas Lickona summarizes research investigations stimulated by Piaget's conclusions in "Research on Piaget's Theory of Moral Development," in *Moral Development and Behavior: Theory, Research, and Social Issues* (1976), an excellent compilation of articles on all aspects of morality, which Lickona edited.

Kohlberg's Stages of Moral Development

If you would like to read Kohlberg's own account of the stages of moral development, examine "Moral Stages and Moralization: The Cognitive-Developmental Approach," in *Moral Development and Behavior: Theory, Research, and Social Issues* (1976), edited by Thomas Lickona. Kohlberg discusses changes in his theory in "Revisions in the Theory and Practice of Moral Development," in *New Directions for Child Development: Moral Development* (1978), edited by William Damon. Techniques for encouraging moral development by taking account of Kohlberg's stages are described in *Promoting Moral Growth: From Piaget to Kohlberg* (1979), by Richard Hersh, Diana Paolitto, and Joseph Reimer. A discussion of research on moral development can be found in *Approaches to Moral Development: New Research and Emerging Themes* (1993), edited by Andrew Garrod.

Gilligan's Analysis of Adolescent Development

If you would like to know more about the basis of Carol Gilligan's critique of Erikson's and Kohlberg's theories and her arguments for a broader view of adolescent development, start with her widely cited book *In a Different Voice: Psychological Theory and Women's Development* (1982). Briefer and more recent analyses of this issue are "Adolescent Development Reconsidered," a chapter in *Adolescent Social Behavior and Health* (1987), edited by Charles Irwin, Jr.; and "Exit Voice Dilemmas in Adolescent Development," a chapter in *Mapping the Moral Domain: A Contribution of Women's Thinking to Psychological Theory and Education* (1988), edited by Carol Gilligan, Janie Ward, Jill Taylor, and Betty Bardige.

Character Education Programs

The Character Education Partnership (CEP) is a coalition of organizations and individuals who are dedicated to the implementation of character education programs in schools. Its web site (**www.character.org/**) contains a discussion of eleven principles that schools can use to design and evaluate their own character education programs (CEP, 2000).

Summary

1. Erikson's theory of psychosocial development is notable because it covers the life span, describes people as playing an active role in their own psychological development as opposed to passively responding to external forces, and emphasizes the role played by cultural norms and goals.

2. Erikson's theory is based on the epigenetic principle of biology. Just as certain parts of the fetus are formed at certain times and combine to produce a biologically whole individual at birth, certain aspects of personality develop at certain times and combine to form a psychologically whole individual.

3. Erikson's theory describes eight stages, from birth through old age. The stages that deal with the personality development of school-age children are initiative versus guilt (four to five years), industry versus inferiority (six to eleven years), and identity versus role confusion (twelve to eighteen years).

4. Forcing students to compete with one another for grades is likely to have a negative effect on their sense of industry.

5. Individuals with a strong sense of identity are comfortable with their physical selves, have a sense of purpose and direction, and know they will be recognized by others.

3 Age-Level Characteristics

The theories described in the preceding chapter call attention to the course of psychosocial, cognitive, and moral development. Although these types of behavior are important, they represent only a small part of the behavior repertoire of a child or adolescent. This chapter, which is organized by age and grade levels, will present an overview of types of behavior that are not directly related to any particular theory. In selecting points for emphasis, we used one basic criterion: Does this information about development have potential significance for teachers?

To organize the points to be discussed, we have divided the developmental span into five levels, corresponding to common grade groupings in schools:

Key Points

These key points will help you learn the important information in this chapter. To help you study, they also appear in the margins of the pages, next to the text where they are discussed.

Preschool and Kindergarten

- Large-muscle control better established than small-muscle control and eye-hand coordination
- Play patterns vary as a function of social class, gender, and age
- Gender differences in toy preferences and play activities noticeable by kindergarten
- By age four, children have a theory of mind: aware of own mental processes and that others may think differently
- Young children stick to own language rules

Primary Grades

- Primary grade children have difficulty focusing on small print
- Accident rate peaks in third grade because of confidence in physical skills
- Rigid interpretation of rules in primary grades
- To encourage industry, use praise, avoid criticism
- Awareness of cognitive processes begins to emerge

Elementary Grades

- Boys slightly better at sports-related motor skills; girls better at flexibility, balance, rhythmic motor skills
- Peer group norms for behavior begin to replace adult norms
- Self-concept becomes more generalized and stable; is based primarily on comparisons with peers
- Delinquents have few friends, are easily distracted, are not interested in schoolwork, lack basic skills
- Elementary grade students reason logically but concretely
- Self-efficacy beliefs for academic and social tasks become strong influences on behavior

Middle School

- Girls' growth spurt occurs earlier, and so they look older than boys of same age
- After growth spurt, boys have greater strength and endurance
- Early-maturing boys likely to draw favorable responses
- Late-maturing boys may seek attention
- Late-maturing girls likely to be popular and carefree
- Average age of puberty: girls, eleven; boys, fourteen
- Discussion of controversial issues may be difficult because of strong desire to conform to peer norms
- Teenagers experience different degrees of emotional turmoil
- Environment of middle schools does not meet needs of adolescents, leading to lower levels of learning

High School

- Sexual activity among male, female teens due to different factors
- Adolescents likely to be confused about appropriateness of premarital sex
- Parents influence values, plans; peers influence immediate status
- Girls more likely than boys to experience anxiety about friendships
- Depression most common among females, teens from poor families
- Depression may be caused by negative cognitive set, learned helplessness, sense of loss
- Depression and unstable family situation place adolescents at risk for suicide
- Political thinking becomes more abstract, less authoritarian, more knowledgeable

Preschool and kindergarten. Ages three through five
Primary grades. Grades 1 through 3; ages six through eight
Elementary grades. Grades 4 and 5; ages nine and ten
Middle school. Grades 6 through 8; ages eleven through thirteen
High school. Grades 9 through 12; ages fourteen through seventeen

Because the way grades are grouped varies, you may find yourself teaching in a school system where the arrangement described in this chapter is not followed. In that case, simply refer to the appropriate age-level designations and, if necessary, concentrate on two levels rather than one.

You should read all of the chapter with care. Even though you now anticipate that you will teach a particular grade level, you may at some point teach younger or older students. You may also gain awareness of continuities of development and come to realize how some aspects of the behavior of older children were influenced by their earlier experiences. Indeed, although a particular type of behavior is discussed at a level where it is considered to be of special significance, that behavior may be important at any age level.

At each of the five levels, behaviors are discussed under four headings: physical, social, emotional, and cognitive characteristics. Following each characteristic are implications for teachers. To help you establish a general conception of what children are like at each level, brief summaries of the types of behavior stressed by the theorists discussed in the preceding chapter are listed in a table near the beginning of each section (Tables 3.1, 3.2, 3.3, 3.4, and 3.7). ■

Preschool and Kindergarten (Three, Four, and Five Years)

Physical Characteristics: Preschool and Kindergarten

Journal Entry
Active Games

1. *Preschool children are extremely active. They have good control of their bodies and enjoy activity for its own sake.* Provide plenty of opportunities for the children to run, climb, and jump. Arrange these activities, as much as possible, so that they are under your control. If you follow a policy of complete freedom, you may discover that thirty improvising three- to five-year-olds can be a frightening thing. In your Reflective Journal, you might note some specific games and activities that you could use to achieve semicontrolled play.

Journal Entry
Riot-Stopping Signals and Activities

2. *Because of an inclination toward bursts of activity, kindergartners need frequent rest periods. They themselves often don't recognize the need to slow down.* Schedule quiet activities after strenuous ones. Have rest time. Realize that excitement may build up to a riot level if the attention of "catalytic agents" and their followers is not diverted. In your journal, you might list some signals for calling a halt to a melee (for example, playing the opening chords of Beethoven's Fifth Symphony on the piano) or for diverting wild action into more or less controlled activity (marching around the room to a brisk rendition of "Stars and Stripes Forever").

Journal Entry
Allowing for Large-Muscle Control

3. *Preschoolers' large muscles are more developed than those that control fingers and hands. Therefore, preschoolers may be quite clumsy at, or physically incapable of, such skills as tying shoes and buttoning coats.* Avoid too many small-motor activities, such as pasting paper chains. Provide big brushes, crayons, and tools. In your journal, you

Table 3.1 Applying Stage Theories of Development to the Preschool and Kindergarten Years

Stage of psychosocial development: initiative vs. guilt. Children need opportunities for free play and experimentation as well as experiences that give them a sense of accomplishment.

Stage of cognitive development: preoperational thought. Children gradually acquire the ability to conserve and decenter but are not capable of operational thinking and are unable to mentally reverse operations.

Stage of moral development: morality of constraint, preconventional. Rules are viewed as unchangeable edicts handed down by those in authority. Punishment-obedience orientation focuses on physical consequences rather than on intentions.

General factors to keep in mind: Children are having their first experiences with school routine and interactions with more than a few peers and are preparing for initial academic experiences in group settings. They need to learn to follow directions and get along with others.

might note other activities or items of king-sized equipment that would be appropriate for the children's level of muscular development.

Large-muscle control better established than small-muscle control and eye-hand coordination

4. *Young children find it difficult to focus their eyes on small objects. Therefore, their eye-hand coordination may be imperfect.* If possible, minimize the necessity for the children to look at small things. (Incomplete eye development is the reason for large print in children's books.) This is also important to keep in mind if you are planning to use computers or software programs; highly graphic programs requiring a simple point-and-click response are most appropriate for very young students.

5. *Although children's bodies are flexible and resilient, the bones that protect the brain are still soft.* Be extremely wary of blows to the head in games or fights between children. If you notice an activity involving such a blow, intervene immediately; warn the class that this is dangerous and explain why.

6. *Although boys are bigger, girls are ahead of boys in practically all other areas of development, especially in fine motor skills, so don't be surprised if boys are clumsier at manipulating small objects.* Because of this gender difference in motor-skill development, boy-girl comparisons or competition involving such skills should be avoided.

Social Characteristics: Preschool and Kindergarten

1. *Most children have one or two best friends, but these friendships may change rapidly. Preschoolers tend to be quite flexible socially; they are usually willing and able to play with most of the other children in the class. Favorite friends tend to be of the same gender, but many friendships between boys and girls develop.* Young children are quite adept at figuring out which social and linguistic skills elicit responses from playmates. Typical gambits include inviting a peer to engage in rough-and-tumble play, offering an object to a playmate, offering to exchange objects with a playmate, sticking to the topic of a conversation, moving close to the person to whom one is speaking, and asking a question or giving a command (Guralnick, 1986). You might make a habit of noticing whether some children seem to lack the ability or confidence to join others. In some cases, a child may prefer to be an observer. But if you sense that a child really wants to get to know others, you might provide some assistance.

Young children engage in a variety of types of play. These play patterns may vary as a function of social class and gender.

Journal Entry
How Much Control Is Necessary?

2. *Play groups tend to be small and not too highly organized; hence, they change rapidly.* You should not be concerned if children flit constantly from one activity to another. Such behavior is normal for this age group, although it may be a bit disconcerting. You might think about how much control you will want to exert over your students, particularly during free-play periods. At what point is insistence on silence and sedentary activities justifiable? Should you insist that students stick with self-selected activities for a specified period of time?

3. *Younger children exhibit different types of play behavior.* Mildred Parten (1932) observed the free play of children in a preschool and noted the types of social behavior they engaged in. Eventually, she was able to write quite precise descriptions of six types of **play behavior:**

Unoccupied behavior. Children do not really play at all. They either stand around and look at others for a time or engage in aimless activities.

Solitary play. Children play alone with toys that are different from those used by other children within speaking distance of them. They make no attempt to interact with others.

Onlooker behavior. Children spend most of their time watching others. They may kibitz and make comments about the play of others, but they do not attempt to join in.

Parallel play. Children play beside but not really with other children. They use the same toys in close proximity to others but in an independent way.

Associative play. Children engage in rather disorganized play with other children. There is no assignment of activities or roles; individual children play in their own ways.

Cooperative play. Children engage in an organized form of play in which leadership and other roles are assigned. The members of the group may cooperate in creating some project, dramatize some situation, or engage in some sort of coordinated enterprise.

4. *Play patterns may vary as a function of social class and gender.* Kenneth Rubin, Terence Maioni, and Margaret Hornung (1976) observed and classified the free play

of preschoolers according to their level of social and cognitive participation. The four levels of social participation they observed (solitary, parallel, associative, and cooperative) were taken from the work of Parten. The four levels of cognitive participation they observed were taken from the work of Sara Smilansky (1968), who based them on Piaget's work, and are as follows:

Functional play. Making simple, repetitive muscle movements with or without objects
Constructive play. Manipulating objects to construct or create something
Dramatic play. Using an imaginary situation
Games with rules. Using prearranged rules to play a game

Play patterns vary as a function of social class, gender, and age

The Parten and Rubin et al. studies found that children of lower socioeconomic status engaged in more parallel and functional play than their middle-class peers, whereas middle-class children displayed more associative, cooperative, and constructive play. Girls engaged in more solitary- and parallel-constructive play and in less dramatic play than did the boys. Boys engaged in more solitary-functional and associative-dramatic play than did girls.

These studies call attention to the variety of play activities common to preschool children. This knowledge may help you determine if a child *prefers* solitary play or plays alone because of shyness or lack of skills for joining in associative or cooperative play.

5. *Quarrels are frequent, but they tend to be of short duration and are quickly forgotten.* When thirty children are thrown together for the first time in a restricted environment with a limited number of objects to be shared, disputes over property rights and similar matters are inevitable. Do not be surprised if you find that the majority of quarrels and aggressive acts involve two or more boys. Research has shown that males are more likely than females to behave aggressively. The gender difference in aggression is greatest among preschoolers and least noticeable among college students (Hyde, 1986). Whenever possible, let the children settle these differences on their own; intervene only if a quarrel gets out of hand. If you do have to intervene, you might try one of two tactics: suggest that one or both children engage in another equally attractive activity, or impose a turn-taking rule. (Other methods of classroom control will be discussed later in the book.)

Gender differences in toy preferences and play activities noticeable by kindergarten

6. *Awareness of gender roles and gender typing is evident.* By the time children enter kindergarten, most of them have developed an awareness of gender differences and of masculine and feminine roles (Wynn & Fletcher, 1987). This awareness of **gender roles** shows up very clearly in the toys and activities that boys and girls prefer. Boys are more likely than girls to play outdoors, to engage in rough-and-tumble play, and to behave aggressively. Boys play with toy vehicles and construction toys, and they engage in action games (such as football). Girls prefer art activities, doll play, and dancing (Carter, 1987). Gender role differences are often reinforced by the way parents behave: they encourage boys to be active and independent and girls to be more docile and dependent. Peers may reinforce these tendencies. A boy or girl may notice that other children are more willing to play when he or she selects a gender-appropriate toy.

Journal Entry
Encouraging Girls to Achieve, Boys to Be Sensitive

Therefore, if you teach preschool children, you may have to guard against a tendency to respond too soon when little girls ask for help. If they *need* assistance, of course you should supply it; but if preschool girls can carry out tasks on their own, you should urge them to do so. You might also remind yourself that girls need to be encouraged to become more achievement oriented and boys to become more sensitive to the needs of others.

EMOTIONAL CHARACTERISTICS: PRESCHOOL AND KINDERGARTEN

1. *Kindergarten children tend to express their emotions freely and openly. Anger outbursts are frequent.* It is probably desirable to let children at this age level express their feelings openly, at least within broad limits, so that they can recognize and face their emotions. In *Between Parent and Child* (1965) and *Teacher and Child* (1972), Haim Ginott offers some specific suggestions on how a parent or teacher can help children develop awareness of their feelings. His books may help you work out your own philosophy and techniques for dealing with emotional outbursts.

Suppose, for example, that a boy who was wildly waving his hand to be called on during share-and-tell time later knocks down a block tower built by a girl who monopolized sharing time with a spellbinding story of a kitten rescued by firefighters. When you go over to break up the incipient fight, the boy angrily pushes you away. In such a situation, Ginott suggests you take the boy to a quiet corner and engage in a dialogue such as this:

You: It looks as if you are unhappy about something, Connor.

Boy: Yes, I am.

You: Are you angry about something that happened this morning?

Boy: Yes.

You: Tell me about it.

Boy: I wanted to tell the class about something at sharing time, and Lily talked for three hours, and you wouldn't let me say anything.

You: And that made you mad at Lily and at me?

Boy: Yes.

You: Well, I can understand why you are disappointed and angry. But Lily had an exciting story to tell, and we didn't have time for anyone else to tell what they had to say. You can be the very first one to share something tomorrow morning. Now how about doing an easel painting? You always do such interesting paintings.

Journal Entry
Helping Students Understand Anger

Ginott suggests that when children are encouraged to analyze their own behavior, they are more likely to become aware of the causes of their feelings. This awareness, in turn, may help them learn to accept and control their feelings and find more acceptable means of expressing them. But because these children are likely to be in Piaget's preoperational stage of intellectual development, bear in mind that this approach may not be successful with all of them. The egocentric orientation of four- to five-year-olds makes it difficult for them to reflect on the thoughts of self or others. Anger outbursts are more likely to occur when children are tired, hungry, or exposed to too much adult interference. If you take such conditions into account and try to alleviate them (by providing a nap or a snack, for example), temper tantrums may be minimized.

Journal Entry
Ways to Avoid Playing Favorites

2. *Jealousy among classmates is likely to be fairly common at this age since kindergarten children have much affection for the teacher and actively seek approval. When there are thirty individuals competing for the affection and attention of just one teacher, some jealousy is inevitable.* Try to spread your attention around as equitably as possible, and when you praise particular children, do it in a private or casual way. If one child is given lavish public recognition, it is only natural for the other children to feel resentful. Think back to how you felt about teachers' pets during your own school

Finally, **rejecting-neglecting parents** do not make demands on their children or respond to their emotional needs. They do not structure the home environment, are not supportive of their children's goals and activities, and may actively reject or neglect their child-rearing responsibilities. Children of rejecting-neglecting parents are the least socially and intellectually competent of the four types.

You might refer to these observations not only when you plan how to encourage competence but also when you think about the kind of classroom atmosphere you hope to establish.

Primary Grades (1, 2, and 3; Six, Seven, and Eight Years)

PHYSICAL CHARACTERISTICS: PRIMARY GRADES

1. *Primary grade children are still extremely active. Because they are frequently required to participate in sedentary pursuits, energy is often released in the form of nervous habits—for example, pencil chewing, fingernail biting, and general fidgeting.* You will have to decide what noise and activity level should prevail during work periods. A few teachers insist on absolute quiet, but such a rule can make children work so hard at remaining quiet that they cannot devote much effort to their lessons. The majority of teachers allow a certain amount of moving about and talking. Whatever you decide, be on the alert for the point of diminishing returns—whether from too much or too little restriction.

For interactive Netlabs on child development, go to the textbook site at **http://education.college.hmco.com/students**.

To minimize fidgeting, avoid situations in which your students must stay glued to their desks for long periods. Have frequent breaks, and try to work activity (such as bringing papers to your desk) into the lessons themselves. When children use

Journal Entry
Building Activity into Classwork

Table 3.2 Applying Stage Theories of Development to the Primary Grade Years

Stage of psychosocial development: industry vs. inferiority. Students need to experience a sense of industry through successful completion of tasks. Try to minimize and correct failures to prevent development of feelings of inferiority.

Stage of cognitive development: transition from preoperational to concrete operational stage. Students gradually acquire the ability to solve problems by generalizing from concrete experiences.

Stage of moral development: morality of constraint, preconventional. Rules are viewed as edicts handed down by authority. Focus is on physical consequences, meaning that obeying rules should bring benefit in return.

General factors to keep in mind: Students are having first experiences with school learning, are eager to learn how to read and write, and are likely to be upset by lack of progress. Initial attitudes toward schooling are being established. Initial roles in a group are being formed, roles that may establish a lasting pattern (for example, leader, follower, loner, athlete, or underachiever).

computer software that contains sound effects, distribute headphones to ensure that they concentrate on their own work and minimize distractions from others.

2. *Children at these grade levels still need rest periods; they become fatigued easily as a result of physical and mental exertion.* Schedule quiet activities after strenuous ones (story time after recess, for example) and relaxing activities after periods of mental concentration (art after spelling or math).

3. *Large-muscle control is still superior to fine coordination. Many children, especially boys, have difficulty manipulating a pencil.* Try not to schedule too much writing at one time. If drill periods are too long, skill may deteriorate, and children may develop a negative attitude toward writing or toward school in general.

Primary grade children have difficulty focusing on small print

4. *Many primary grade students may have difficulty focusing on small print or objects. Quite a few children may be farsighted because of the shallow shape of the eye.* Try not to require too much reading at one stretch. Be on the alert for rubbing the eyes or blinking, signs of eye fatigue. When you are preparing class handouts, be sure to print in large letters or use a primary grade typewriter. Until the lens of the eye can be easily focused, young children have trouble looking back and forth from near to far objects.

Another vision problem that preschool and primary grade children encounter is amblyopia, or "lazy eye." In normal vision, the muscles of the two eyes work together to fuse their two images into one. If the eye muscles are not coordinated, however, children may experience double vision. In their efforts to cope with this problem, children may try to eliminate one image by closing one eye, tilting their heads, or blinking or rubbing their eyes. You should watch for signs of amblyopia, and let the parents know if you detect any.

Although many children at this age have had extensive exposure to computer games and video games and therefore have begun to develop greater eye-hand coordination with images on-screen, it's still appropriate to select software programs that incorporate easy-to-see graphics and easy-to-click buttons to avoid frustration.

Accident rate peaks in third grade because of confidence in physical skills

Journal Entry
Safe But Strenuous Games

5. *At this age children tend to be extreme in their physical activities. They have excellent control of their bodies and develop considerable confidence in their skills. As a result, they often underestimate the danger involved in their more daring exploits. The accident rate is at a peak in the third grade.* You might check on school procedures for handling injuries, but also try to prevent reckless play. During recess, for example, encourage class participation in "wild" but essentially safe games (such as relay races involving stunts) to help the children get devil-may-care tendencies out of their systems. In your journal, you might list other games to use for this purpose.

6. *Bone growth is not yet complete. Therefore, bones and ligaments can't stand heavy pressure.* If you notice students indulging in strenuous tests of strength (punching each other on the arm until one person can't retaliate, for example), you might suggest that they switch to competition involving coordinated skills. During team games, rotate players in especially tiring positions (for example, the pitcher in baseball).

Social Characteristics: Primary Grades

The characteristics noted here are typical of both primary and elementary grade students and underlie the elementary-level characteristics described in the next section.

1. *Children become somewhat more selective in their choice of friends and are likely to have a more or less permanent best friend.* Friendships are typically same-sex relation-

difficult or unfamiliar material and may need to be prompted to think about how well they are understanding what they read. By the primary grades, this awareness and monitoring of one's learning processes, called metacognition, begins to emerge. We will return to the subject in the chapter on information-processing theory.

3. *Because of continuing neurological development and limited experience with formal learning tasks, primary grade children do not learn as efficiently as older children do.* Therefore, you should assign primary grade children relatively short tasks and switch periodically from cognitively demanding activities to less demanding ones. Providing youngsters with periodic breaks, such as recess, increases their ability to attend to and perform well on subsequent classroom tasks. The nature of the recess activity does not seem to be important. It can be physical activity in a schoolyard or playing games in class (Pellegrini & Bjorklund, 1997).

Journal Entry
Assigning Short and Varied Tasks

4. *Because of the literal interpretation of rules associated with this stage of development, primary grade children may tend to be tattletales.* Sometimes telling the teacher that someone has broken a school or class rule is due to a child's level of moral development, sometimes it is due to jealousy or malice, and sometimes it is simply a way to get attention or curry favor. If a child calls your attention to the misbehavior of others and you respond by saying, "Don't be a tattletale," the child may be hurt and confused. If you thank the child too enthusiastically and then proceed to punish the culprit, you may encourage members of the class to inform on each other. Perhaps the best policy is to tell an informant that you already are aware of the errant behavior and that you intend to do something about it. Then you might follow up by talking to the offending parties.

Journal Entry
Ways to Handle Tattletales

Elementary Grades (4 and 5; Nine and Ten Years)

PHYSICAL CHARACTERISTICS: ELEMENTARY GRADES

1. *Both boys and girls become leaner and stronger.* In general, there is a decrease in the growth of fatty tissue and an increase in bone and muscle development, although this process occurs more rapidly in boys. In a year's time, the average child of this age will grow about 2 inches and gain about 5 pounds. As a result, children often have a lean and gangly look. Beginning at about age nine and lasting until about age fourteen, girls are slightly heavier and taller than boys. Because secondary sex characteristics have not yet appeared, boys and girls can be mistaken for one another. This is particularly likely to happen when girls have close-cropped hair, boys have very long hair, and both genders wear gender-neutral clothing (Hetherington & Parke, 1993; LeFrançois, 1995; Mitchell, 1990).

2. *Obesity can become a problem for some children of this age group.* Because nine- and ten-year-olds have more control over their eating habits than younger children do, there is a greater tendency for them to overeat, particularly junk food (foods high in calories and fat but low in nutritional value). When this eating pattern is coupled with a relatively low level of physical activity (mainly because of television watching) and a genetic predisposition toward obesity, children become mildly to severely overweight. Not only do overweight children put themselves at risk for cardiovas-

Elementary grade boys tend to be better than girls on motor skill tasks that involve large muscle movement, while elementary grade girls tend to perform better than boys on motor skill tasks that involve muscular flexibility, balance, and rhythmic movements.

cular problems later in life, but they also become targets for ridicule and ostracism in the present from peers (Hetherington & Parke, 1993; Mitchell, 1990).

Boys slightly better at sports-related motor skills; girls better at flexibility, balance, rhythmic motor skills

3. *Although small in magnitude, gender differences in motor skill performance are apparent.* Boys tend to outperform girls on tasks that involve kicking, throwing, catching, running, broad jumping, and batting. Girls surpass boys on tasks that require muscular flexibility, balance, and rhythmic movements. These differences may be due in part to gender role stereotyping. That is, because of socialization differences,

Table 3.3 Applying Stage Theories of Development to the Elementary Grade Years

Stage of psychosocial development: industry vs. inferiority. Keep students constructively busy; try to play down comparisons between best and worse learners.

Stage of cognitive development: concrete operational. Except for the most intellectually advanced students, most will need to generalize from concrete experiences.

Stage of moral development: morality of constraint; transition from preconventional to conventional. A shift to viewing rules as mutual agreements is occurring, but "official" rules are obeyed out of respect for authority or out of a desire to impress others.

General factors to keep in mind: Initial enthusiasm for learning may fade as the novelty wears off and as the process of perfecting skills becomes more difficult. Differences in knowledge and skills of fastest and slowest learners become more noticeable. "Automatic" respect for teachers tends to diminish. Peer group influences become strong.

girls are more likely to play hopscotch and jump rope, whereas boys are more likely to play baseball and basketball.

Journal Entry
Minimizing Gender Differences in Motor Skill Performance

One benefit of attaining mastery over large and small muscles is a relatively orderly classroom. Fourth and fifth graders can sit quietly for extended periods and concentrate on whatever intellectual task is at hand (Hetherington & Parke, 1993; Mitchell, 1990). Another benefit is that children enjoy arts and crafts and musical activities.

4. *This is a period of relative calm and predictability in physical development.* Growth in height and weight tends to be consistent and moderate, hormonal imbalances are absent, disease occurs less frequently than at any other period, and bodily coordination is relatively stable (Hetherington & Parke, 1993; Mitchell, 1990).

Social Characteristics: Elementary Grades

Peer group norms for behavior begin to replace adult norms

1. *The peer group becomes powerful and begins to replace adults as the major source of behavior standards and recognition of achievement.* During the early school years, parents and teachers set standards of conduct, and most children try to live up to them. But by grades 4 and 5, children are more interested in getting along with one another without adult supervision. Consequently, children come to realize that the rules for behavior within the peer group are not quite the same as the rules for behavior within the family or the classroom.

Journal Entry
Moderating the Power of Peer Group Norms

This newfound freedom can have a down side. Because children of this age typically want to be accepted by their peers, have a relatively naive view of right and wrong, and do not have enough self-assurance to oppose group norms, they may engage in behaviors (shoplifting, fighting, prejudice against outsiders) that they would not exhibit at home or in the classroom (Mitchell, 1990).

2. *Friendships become more selective and gender based.* Elementary grade children become even more discriminating than primary grade children in the selection of friends and playmates. Most children choose a best friend, usually of the same gender. These relationships, based usually on common ideas, outlooks, and impressions of the world, may last through adolescence. Although children of this age will rarely refuse to interact with members of the opposite sex when directed to do so by parents and teachers, they will avoid the opposite sex when left to their own devices (Mitchell, 1990).

Emotional Characteristics: Elementary Grades

1. *During this period, children develop a global and moderately stable self-image.* Susan Harter (1988, 1990) and William Damon (1988) have made extensive studies of how children formulate their **self-image.** According to both researchers, the overall picture upper elementary grade children have of themselves, a mental self-portrait, so to speak, is made up of two components: a description of their physical, social, emotional, and cognitive attributes (normally referred to as **self-concept**) and the evaluative judgments they make about those attributes (normally referred to as **self-esteem**). They may, for example, describe themselves as being taller but clumsier than most others or as having a lot of friends because of superior social skills.

Self-concept becomes more generalized and stable; is based primarily on comparisons with peers

There are several important facts to keep in mind about the formulation of a child's self-portrait. First, it is more generalized than is the case for primary grade children because it is based on information gained over time, tasks, and settings. A child may think of herself as socially adept not just because she is popular at school but because she has always been well liked and gets along well with adults as well as peers in a variety of situations. It is this generalized quality that helps make self-portraits relatively stable.

Second, comparison with others is the fundamental basis of a self-portrait during the elementary grades. This orientation is due in part to the fact that children are not as egocentric as they were a few years earlier and are developing the capability to think in terms of multiple categories. It is also due to the fact that competition and individualism are highly prized values in many Western cultures. Consequently, children will naturally compare themselves to one another ("I'm taller than my friend") as well as to broad-based norms ("I'm tall for my age") in an effort to determine who they are. But as William Damon and Daniel Hart (1988) point out, comparison is a less important basis for building a self-image in cultures where competition and individualism are downplayed.

Journal Entry
Ways to Improve Students' Self-Concept

Third, the self is described for the first time in terms of emotions (pride, shame, worry, anger, happiness) and how well they can be controlled. Fourth, a child's sense of self is influenced by the information and attitudes that are communicated by such significant others as parents, teachers, and friends and by how competent the child feels in areas where success is important. The implications of this fact will be discussed in many of the remaining chapters of the text.

Because major developmental changes usually do not occur during the elementary grades, a child's self-image will remain fairly stable for a few years if there are no major changes in the child's home or social environment. But as you will see later in this chapter, the developmental changes that typically occur during the middle school and high school grades often produce dramatic changes in the sense of self.

2. *Disruptive family relationships, social rejection, and school failure may lead to delinquent behavior.* Gerald Patterson, Barbara DeBarsyshe, and Elizabeth Ramsey (1989) marshal a wide array of evidence to support their belief that delinquent behavior is the result of a causal chain of events that originates with dysfunctional parent-child relationships. In their view, poor parent-child relationships lead to behavior problems, which lead to peer rejection and academic failure, which lead to identification with a deviant peer group, which results in delinquent behavior. Parents of such children administer harsh and inconsistent punishment, provide little positive reinforcement, and do little monitoring and supervising of each child's activities.

Delinquents have few friends, are easily distracted, are not interested in schoolwork, lack basic skills

Because these children have not learned to follow adult rules and regulations but have learned how to satisfy their needs through coercive behavior, they are rejected by their peers, are easily distracted when doing schoolwork, show little interest in the subjects they study, and do not master many of the basic academic skills necessary for subsequent achievement. Attempts at short-circuiting this chain of events stand a greater chance of success if they begin early and are multifaceted. In addition to counseling and parent training, mastery of basic academic skills is important.

Cognitive Characteristics: Elementary Grades

Elementary grade students reason logically but concretely

1. *The elementary grade child can think logically, although such thinking is constrained and inconsistent.* In terms of Piaget's stages, upper elementary grade children are concrete operational stage thinkers. Most will have attained enough mastery of logical schemes that they can understand and solve tasks that involve such processes as class inclusion (understanding the superordinate-subordinate relationships that make up hierarchies), seriation, conservation, and symbolic representation (reading maps, for example), provided that the content of the task refers to real, tangible ideas that the

Although elementary grade children understand the logical basis for tasks such as classification, seriation, and conservation, they can solve such tasks only if they are based on concrete objects and ideas.

child has either experienced or can imagine. But general and abstract ideas often escape the elementary-age child. For example, sarcasm, metaphor, and allegory are usually lost on concrete stage thinkers.

The knowledge base of fourth- and fifth-grade children contains many misconceptions, and they may behave illogically. To prove a point or win a debate with a classmate or playmate, the upper elementary child may reel off a string of facts, some of which reflect authoritative sources, some of which are exaggerations, and some of which are invented on the spot. A ten-year-old may believe, for example, that people can live for several months without eating and that vacant houses are haunted. As John Mitchell (1990) humorously put it, "Many kids possess a gift for compressing the largest number of words into the smallest amount of thought" (p. 213).

2. *On tasks that call for simple memory skills, elementary grade children often perform about as well as adolescents or adults. But on tasks that require more complex memory skills, their performance is more limited.* When tasks call for recognizing previously learned information, such as vocabulary words or facts about a person or event, or for rehearsing several items for immediate use, elementary grade children can perform about as well as older students. Relatively simple memory processes like recognition or rote repetition approach their maximum levels by this point in cognitive development. But the same is not true for tasks that require such advanced memory processes as elaboration and organization. When asked to sort a set of pictures into categories, for example, elementary grade children create fewer and more idiosyncratic categories (which are generally less effective for later recall of the items in the category) than do older children or adults. Similarly, fewer than half of a group of ten-year-olds in one study devised a way to help them remember to take a batch of cupcakes out of an oven after thirty minutes had elapsed, whereas 75 percent of a group of fourteen-year-olds did (Kail, 1990).

Middle School (Grades 6, 7, and 8; Eleven, Twelve, and Thirteen Years)

In this section, we use the term *adolescent* for the first time. Although it may strike you as odd to think of eleven- and twelve-year-olds as adolescents, developmental psychologists typically apply this term to individuals as young as ten years of age. The reason they do is that the onset of puberty is taken as the primary characteristic that defines the passage from middle childhood to adolescence (Allen, Splittgerber, & Manning, 1993; Balk, 1995). This transition, and how it affected the mother of a middle school age child, is humorously described in the Case in Print. Although a variety of terms are used to denote the initial period of change that marks the adolescent years (ages ten to fourteen), we use two of the more popular: *early adolescent* and *emerging adolescent*.

Physical Characteristics: Middle School

Girls' growth spurt occurs earlier, and so they look older than boys of same age

1. *Physical growth tends to be both rapid and uneven.* During the middle school years, the average child will grow 2 to 4 inches per year and gain 8 to 10 pounds per

Table 3.4 Applying Stage Theories of Development to the Middle School Years

Stage of psychosocial development: transition from industry vs. inferiority to identity vs. role confusion. Growing independence leads to initial thoughts about identity. There is greater concern about appearance and gender roles than about occupational choice.

Stage of cognitive development: beginning of formal operational thought for some. There is increasing ability to engage in mental manipulations and test hypotheses.

Stage of moral development: transition to morality of cooperation, conventional level. There is increasing willingness to think of rules as flexible mutual agreements; "official" rules are still likely to be obeyed out of respect for authority or out of a desire to impress others.

General factors to keep in mind: Growth spurt and puberty influence many aspects of behavior. An abrupt switch occurs (for sixth graders) from being the oldest, biggest, most sophisticated students in elementary school to being the youngest, smallest least knowledgeable students in middle school. Acceptance by peers is extremely important. Students who do poor schoolwork begin to feel bitter, resentful, and restless. Awareness grows of a need to make personal value decisions regarding dress, premarital sex, and code of ethics.

Middle School Madness

Although it may strike you as odd to think of eleven- and twelve-year-olds as adolescents, developmental psychologists typically apply this term to individuals as young as ten years of age. The reason they do is that the onset of puberty is taken as the primary characteristic that defines the passage from middle childhood to adolescence.

Middle School Rings in a New Level of Parenting for a Mom

DEBRA-LYNN B. HOOK
St. Louis Post-Dispatch 9/24/2000

For almost 12 years now, I have experienced children in the womb, in the high chair, in preschool and K-through-5.

I have lived the good and innocent life surrounded by the likes of Huggies, Gerbers and Mr. Rogers in a home populated by thumb-suckers, diaper-wetters, frogs, insects and little friends whose behavior I could predict and control.

For six of these dozen years, I have waved one to two children off to the neighborhood elementary school. I have blown kisses from the living room window and watched as bouncing backpacks disappear out of view to the school around the corner. I have strolled, any time I've wanted, up to our school, where I have hugged kids on playgrounds, patted teachers on backs and presented dozens of cupcakes on special occasions.

I had become quite comfortable in this baby-powdered mother's role. Too comfortable, some might say. Because one day it had to happen.

Middle School.

One mother told me she put her child on the middle-school bus a little boy, and poof! he turned into a teen-ager.

Middle school, I hear from other mothers, is where formerly clothed girls expose belly buttons when they raise their hands. Middle school is where kids float for years, groundless and unnoticed, between thinking they're supposed to be all grown up and secretly wishing they could sit on the floor and play tiddlywinks, even as they tote 200 pounds of books on their prepubescent backs between classes. Middle school invites a new kind of sleeplessness among parents, who only wish they could retreat to the days when their biggest problem was waking to feed the baby.

Our middle school is big. It has air conditioning. It even smells different. Whereas the grammar school smells of sour milk, pencil erasers and, in the spring, lilac, the middle school smells of new carpet and, I could swear, hormones.

Our middle school has a guidance counselor with a soft voice meant to soothe, and co-opt, skittish parents. During a tour of the school, she assured that the sixth-grade wing is separate from the evil seventh- and eighth-graders'. (As if those devil upper-level girls won't have the opportunity to show my son their belly buttons on the bus.)

She told me our middle school doesn't have a problem with drugs because the drug-sniffing dogs come on a regular basis. (Now that's a nice image.)

The counselor affirmed for me, that yes, middle school represents a difficult time for kids whose ebb-and-flow hormones already have them bewildered. Parents should brace themselves, she said, for their own confusion and imbalance as preadolescent rages begin to shake the house—and parental omnipotence.

On the way home from our tour, I thought about drowning out the entire experience with a rousing rendition of the "I love you" Barney theme song. I instead turned to my son.

"I hope you know you can still be a kid," I began in rapid-fire to the baseball cap in the passenger seat. "Just because you're going to middle school doesn't mean you have to be all grown up. You think everybody wants you to be all grown up? Well, ha, they don't. Of course, that doesn't mean you can't grow up! Or shouldn't! Growing up is good. I tell you what, whatever you need this year, I'm right here. You just ask away."

It was the first of many bumbling speeches I will likely make in the coming year, prompting what is likely to be one of many puzzled responses.

"No offense, Mom," my son replied. "But what are you talking about?"

I love you. You love me. We're a happy fa-mi-ly. With a great big hug and a kiss from me to you. Won't you say you love me, too?

Questions and Activities

1. The author of this article describes the middle school years as a difficult time for students and parents. The counselor of the middle school that the author's children attend said that parents should "brace themselves for their own confusion and imbalance as preadolescent rages begin to shake the house—and parental omnipotence." Do you think this description is accurate or exaggerated? Explain your answer.
2. If the middle school years are especially challenging for eleven- to thirteen-year-olds and their parents, then they certainly will be for teachers as well. What characteristics of this age group should you keep uppermost in mind, and what general approaches to instruction should you seek to implement?
3. To find out for yourself what middle school students are like, arrange to visit several middle school classrooms and then interview some students and teachers.

year. But some parts of the body, particularly the hands and feet, grow faster than others. Consequently, middle school children tend to look gangly and clumsy (Ames & Miller, 1994). Because girls mature more rapidly than boys, their **growth spurt** begins at about age ten and a half, reaches a peak at about age twelve, and is generally complete by age fourteen. The growth spurt for boys begins on average at about age twelve and a half, peaks at about age fourteen, and is generally complete by age sixteen (Dusek, 1996).

The result of this timing difference in the growth spurt is that many middle school girls look considerably older than boys of the same age. After the growth spurt, however, the muscles in the average boy's body are larger, as are the heart and lungs. Furthermore, the body of the mature male has a greater capacity than that of the female for carrying oxygen in the blood and for neutralizing the chemical products of muscular exercise, such as lactic acid. Thus, the average male has greater strength and endurance than the average female (Tanner, 1972).

After growth spurt, boys have greater strength and endurance

If you notice that students are upset about sudden growth (or lack of it), you might try to help them accept the situation by explaining that things will eventually even out. To reduce the unhappiness that arises from conflicts between physical attributes and gender roles, you might try to persuade students that being male or female should not in itself determine what a person does.

Journal Entry
Helping Students Adjust to the Growth Spurt

After reviewing research on early and later maturation, Norman Livson and Harvey Peskin (1980) conclude that differences in physical maturation are likely to produce specific differences in later behavior (see Table 3.5). The **early-maturing boy** is likely to draw favorable responses from adults (because of his adult appearance), which promotes confidence and poise (thus contributing to leadership and popularity with peers). The **late-maturing boy,** by contrast, may feel inferior and attempt to compensate for his physical and social frustration by engaging in bossy and attention-getting behavior. The very success of the early-maturing boy in high school, however, may cause him to develop an inflexible conception of himself, leading to problems when he must deal with new or negative situations later in life. The need for the late-maturing boy to cope with difficult adjustment situations in high school may equip him to adapt to adversity and change later in life.

Early-maturing boys likely to draw favorable responses

Late-maturing boys may seek attention

Livson and Peskin observe that the late-maturing boy is psychologically and socially out of step with peers, and the same applies to the **early-maturing girl.** The **late-maturing girl,** whose growth is less abrupt and whose size and appearance are likely to reflect the petiteness featured in stereotyped views of femininity, shares many of the characteristics (poise, popularity, leadership tendencies) of the early-maturing boy. The advantages enjoyed by the late-maturing girl are not permanent,

Late-maturing girls likely to be popular and carefree

Table 3.5 The Impact of Early and Late Maturation

Maturational Stage	Characteristics as Adolescents	Characteristics as Adults
Early-maturing boys	Self-confident, high in self-esteem, likely to be chosen as leaders (but leadership tendencies more likely in low-SES boys than in middle-class boys)	Self-confident, responsible, cooperative, sociable. But also rigid, moralistic, humorless, and conforming
Late-maturing boys	Energetic, bouncy, given to attention-getting behavior, not popular, lower aspirations for educational achievement	Impulsive and assertive. But also insightful, perceptive, creatively playful, able to cope with new situations
Early-maturing girls	Not popular or likely to be leaders, indifferent in social situations, lacking in poise (but middle-class girls more confident than those from low-SES groups), more likely to date, smoke, and drink earlier	Self-possessed, self-directed, able to cope, likely to score high in ratings of psychological health
Late-maturing girls	Confident, outgoing, assured, popular, likely to be chosen as leaders	Likely to experience difficulty adapting to stress, likely to score low in ratings of overall psychological health

SOURCES: Clausen (1975); Hetherington & Parke (1993); Jones (1957, 1965); Livson & Peskin (1980); Mussen & Jones (1957); Peterson & Taylor (1980).

however. Livson and Peskin report that "the stress-ridden early-maturing girl in adulthood has become clearly a more coping, self-possessed, and self-directed person than the late-maturing female in the cognitive and social as well as emotional sectors. . . . It is the late-maturing female, carefree and unchallenged in adolescence, who faces adversity maladroitly in adulthood" (1980, p. 72).

If late-maturing boys in your classes appear driven to seek attention or inclined to brood about their immaturity, you might try to give them extra opportunities to gain status and self-confidence by succeeding in schoolwork or other nonathletic activities. If you notice that early-maturing girls seem insecure, you might try to bolster their self-esteem by giving them extra attention and by recognizing their achievements.

Journal Entry
Helping Early and Late Maturers Cope

2. *Pubertal development is evident in practically all girls and in many boys.* From ages eleven through thirteen, most girls develop sparse pubic and underarm hair and exhibit breast enlargement. In boys, the testes and scrotum begin to grow, and lightly pigmented pubic hair appears (Hetherington & Parke, 1993).

Average age of puberty: girls, eleven; boys, fourteen

3. *Concern and curiosity about sex are almost universal, especially among girls.* The average age of puberty for girls in the United States is eleven years (Dusek, 1996);

the range is from eight to eighteen years. For boys, the average age of puberty is fourteen years; the range is from ten to eighteen years. Since sexual maturation involves drastic biological and psychological adjustments, children are concerned and curious. It seems obvious that accurate, unemotional answers to questions about sex are desirable. However, for your own protection, you should find out about the sex education policy at your school. Many school districts have formal programs approved by community representatives and led by designated educators. Informal spur-of-the-moment class discussions may create more problems than they solve.

Social Characteristics: Middle School

1. *The development of interpersonal reasoning leads to greater understanding of the feelings of others.* Robert L. Selman (1980) has studied the development of **interpersonal reasoning** in children. Interpersonal reasoning is the ability to understand the relationship between motives and behavior among a group of people. The results of Selman's research are summarized in Table 3.6. The stages outlined there reveal that during the elementary school years, children gradually grasp the fact that a person's overt actions or words do not always reflect inner feelings. They also come to comprehend that a person's reaction to a distressing situation can have many facets. Toward the end of the elementary school years and increasingly during adolescence, children become capable of taking a somewhat detached and analytical view of their own behavior as well as the behavior of others.

Not surprisingly, a child's interpersonal sensitivity and maturity seem to have an impact on relationships with others. Selman (1980) compared the responses of seven- to twelve-year-old boys who were attending schools for children with learning and interpersonal problems with the responses of a matched group of boys attending regular schools. The boys attending special schools were below average for their age in understanding the feelings of others.

Because of the importance of peer group values, middle school students often dress and behave similarly.

2. *As a result of the continued influence of egocentric thought, middle school students are typically self-conscious and self-centered.* Because emerging adolescents are acutely aware of the physical and emotional changes that are taking place within them, they assume that everyone else is just as interested in, and is constantly evaluating, their appearance, feelings, and behavior. Consequently, they are deeply concerned about such matters as what type of clothing to wear for special occasions, with whom they should and should not be seen in public (they should never be seen with their parents at the mall, for example), and how they greet and talk with various people.

Another manifestation of adolescent egocentrism is the assumption that adults do not, indeed cannot, understand the thoughts and feelings of early adolescence. It's as if the early adolescent believes she is experiencing things no one else has ever experienced before. Hence, a teen or preteen will likely say to a parent, "You just don't know what it feels like to be in love" (Wiles & Bondi, 2001).

Cognitive Characteristics: Middle School

1. *Because of the psychological demands of early adolescence, middle school students need a classroom environment that is open, supportive, and intellectually stimulating.* Early adolescence is an unsettling time for students because of changes in their physical development, social roles, cognitive development, and sexuality. Another source of stress is coping with the transition from the elementary grades to a middle school (which often begins in sixth grade) or junior high (which typically begins in seventh grade). Partly because of these personal and environmental stresses, the self-concept, academic motivation, and achievement levels of adolescents decline, sometimes drastically. Are schools at all to blame for these problems? Perhaps they are. Jacquelynne Eccles and her associates (1993) provide persuasive evidence that these negative changes are due in part, perhaps in large part, to the fact that the typical school environment does not meet the needs of developing adolescents.

Their argument is based on an analysis of the psychological needs of early ado-

Early adolescents are faced with several developmental challenges. Consequently, middle school teachers should make a special effort to establish a supportive classroom atmosphere in which students can meet their social, emotional, and cognitive needs.

lescence and the kinds of changes that take place in classroom organization, instruction, and climate as one moves from the last of the elementary grades to the first of the middle school or junior high grades. Early adolescent development is characterized by an increased need for autonomy, a focus on oneself (resulting in an acute self-consciousness), the importance of peer acceptance, concerns about identity, and the capacity for abstract thought. The typical middle school environment, however, is largely incompatible with the needs of the typical adolescent:

Environment of middle schools does not meet needs of adolescents, leading to lower levels of learning

- Instead of providing students with opportunities to make decisions about such things as classroom rules, seating arrangements, homework assignments, and time spent on various tasks, teachers impose most of the requirements and limit the choices students can make.
- Students perceive their relationships with their teachers as being less friendly, supportive, and caring than those in earlier grades.
- Competition and social comparisons among students are increased as a result of such practices as whole-class instruction, ability grouping, normative grading also called grading on the curve, a practice we discuss in our chapter on classroom assessment), and public evaluations of one's work. Small-group instruction is infrequent, and individualized instruction almost never occurs.
- In a comparison of seventh-grade middle school and junior high teachers with sixth-grade elementary school teachers, the former rated themselves as being less effective with students, particularly in mathematics. This attitude seemed to affect the students, for by the end of their first year in middle school, they rated themselves less capable in math, had lower expectations for success in math, and saw it as being a more difficult subject to master than they did in sixth grade.
- Finally, many classroom tasks in middle school or junior high involve low-level seatwork, verbatim recall of information, and little opportunity for discussion or group work. In one study of eleven junior high school science classes, the most frequent activity was copying information from the board or textbook onto worksheets.

Because of the work of Eccles and others and the support provided by such groups as the Carnegie Task Force on Education of Young Adolescents, the Illinois Middle Grades Network, and the National Forum to Accelerate Middle-Grades Reform, improvements have been made in providing the type of emotionally responsive and caring atmosphere in middle schools that is consistent with early adolescent development. But similar improvements in providing an intellectually stimulating environment appear to be lagging at this point. Part of the problem concerns the type of achievement goal that the school environment encourages students to adopt.

Motivation theorists like Carol Dweck describe achievement goals as being either mastery or performance in nature. Students who subscribe to a mastery goal are primarily interested in understanding ideas and their interrelationships, acquiring new skills, and refining them over time. Students who subscribe to a performance goal are primarily interested in demonstrating their ability to finish first (however that is defined) and avoiding situations where a relative lack of ability would be apparent. Mastery goals have been associated with positive feelings about one's ability, potential, the subject matter, and school, and with the use of effective learning strategies (which we describe in the chapter on information-processing theory).

The most recent evidence suggests that as students move from the elementary grades to the middle grades, there is a shift in their values and practices that leads to more of an emphasis on performance goals. For example, middle grade teachers are more inclined to post papers and exams with the highest scores, grade on a curve, accord special privileges to high achievers, and remind students of the importance of getting high grades and producing mistake-free papers. Such an environment tells students that meaningful learning is not necessarily expected and that support of learning will not be provided (Midgley & Edelin, 1998).

2. *Self-efficacy becomes an important influence on intellectual and social behavior.* As we mentioned in point 1 of social characteristics, middle school children become capable of analyzing both their own view of an interpersonal interaction and that of the other person. This newfound analytic ability is also turned inward, resulting in evaluations of one's intellectual and social capabilities. Albert Bandura (1986), a learning theorist whom we will discuss later in the book, coined the term **self-efficacy** to refer to how capable people believe they are at dealing with one type of task or another. Thus, a student may have a very strong sense of self-efficacy for math ("I know I can solve most any algebraic equation"), a moderate degree of self-efficacy for certain athletic activities ("I think I play baseball and basketball about as well as most other kids my age"), and a low sense of self-efficacy for interpersonal relationships ("I'm just no good at making friends").

These self-evaluative beliefs influence what activities students choose and for how long they will persist at a given task, particularly when progress becomes difficult. Students with a moderate to strong sense of self-efficacy will persist at a task long enough to obtain the success or corrective feedback that leads to expectations of future success. Students with a low sense of self-efficacy, however, tend to abandon tasks at the first sign of difficulty, thereby establishing a pattern of failure, low expectations of future success, and task avoidance. Because self-efficacy beliefs grow out of personal performance, observation of other people doing the same thing, and verbal persuasion, you can help students develop strong feelings of self-efficacy by following the suggestions we will make in later chapters about modeling and imitation, learning strategies, and effective forms of instruction.

Self-efficacy beliefs for academic and social tasks become strong influences on behavior

High School (Grades 9, 10, 11, and 12; Fourteen, Fifteen, Sixteen, and Seventeen Years)

PHYSICAL CHARACTERISTICS: HIGH SCHOOL

1. *Most students reach physical maturity, and virtually all attain puberty.* Although almost all girls reach their ultimate height, some boys may continue to grow even after graduation from high school. Tremendous variation exists in height and weight and in rate of maturation. As noted earlier, late-maturing boys seem to have considerable difficulty adjusting to their slower rate of growth. There is still concern about appearance, although it may not be as strong as during the middle school years. Glandular changes leading to acne may be a source of worry and self-consciousness to some students. The most significant glandular change accompanying puberty is arousal of the sex drive.

2. *Many adolescents become sexually active but experience confusion regarding sexual relationships.* Surveys as of 1995 reveal that 68 percent of males and 49 percent of females had engaged in sexual intercourse at least once by age nineteen. The per-

Many adolescents may experience confusion about sexual relationships. They are expected to be interested in sex, but at the same time attitudes toward sex are often imbued with strong moral overtones.

centages for African American, Hispanic American, and white males are 80 percent, 61 percent, and 50 percent, respectively. For African American, Hispanic American, and white females, the percentages are 59 percent, 53 percent, and 49 percent, respectively (Abma & Sonenstein, 2001).

For a group of eleven hundred adolescents, J. Richard Udrey (1990) found that initiation of sexual intercourse in white males was strongly related to hormone production and was only weakly related to the discouraging or encouraging efforts of parents, schools, friends, and the media. It was not unusual for adolescent males to

Table 3.7 Applying Stage Theories of Development to the High School Years

Stage of psychosocial development: identity vs. role confusion. Concerns arise about gender roles and occupational choice. Different identity statuses become apparent.

Stage of cognitive development: formal operational thought for many students. There is increasing ability to engage in mental manipulations, understand abstractions, and test hypotheses.

Stage of moral development: morality of cooperation, conventional level. There is increasing willingness to think of rules as mutual agreements and to allow for intentions and extenuating circumstances.

General factors to keep in mind: Achievement of sexual maturity has a profound effect on many aspects of behavior. Peer group and reactions of friends are extremely important. There is concern about what will happen after graduation, particularly for students who do not intend to continue their education. Awareness grows of the significance of academic ability and importance of grades for certain career patterns. There is a need to make personal value decisions regarding use of drugs, premarital sex, and code of ethics.

week, and seventeen-year-olds worked 18 hours per week (U.S. Department of Labor, 2000).

The pros and cons of after-school employment have been vigorously debated. On the positive side, it is thought to enhance self-discipline, a sense of responsibility, self-confidence, and attitudes toward work. On the negative side, part-time employment leaves less time for homework, participation in extracurricular activities, and development of friendships; it may also lead to increased stress, lower grades, and lower career aspirations. Most experts agree that students who work more than 20 hours per week are likely to have lower grades than students who work less or not at all (Steinberg, 1999).

EMOTIONAL CHARACTERISTICS: HIGH SCHOOL

1. *Many psychiatric disorders either appear or become prominent during adolescence. Included among these are eating disorders, substance abuse, schizophrenia, depression, and suicide.* Eating disorders are much more common in females than in males. *Anorexia nervosa* is an eating disorder characterized by a preoccupation with body weight and food, behavior directed toward losing weight, peculiar patterns of handling food, weight loss, intense fear of gaining weight, and a distorted perception of one's body. This disorder occurs predominantly in females (more than 90 percent of the cases) and usually appears between the ages of fourteen and seventeen (APA, 1994).

Bulimia nervosa is a disorder in which binge eating (uncontrolled rapid eating of large quantities of food over a short period of time), followed by self-induced vomiting, is the predominant behavior. Binges are typically followed by feelings of guilt, depression, self-disgust, and fasting. As with anorexia, over 90 percent of individuals with bulimia are female (APA, 1994).

Adolescents who engage in *substance abuse* (tobacco, alcohol, and controlled substances such as marijuana and cocaine) not only jeopardize their physical and

Many high school students, girls in particular, experience periods of depression, loneliness, and anxiety. Because severe depression often precedes a suicide attempt, teachers should refer students they believe to be depressed to the school counselor.

emotional health but increase their risk of doing poorly in school or of dropping out of school. A 1999 survey of high school students found that:

- More than one-third reported smoking on one or more of the previous thirty days, and about 17 percent reported smoking on twenty or more of the previous thirty days.
- About one-half reported drinking in the previous thirty days. Twenty-eight percent of female students and 35 percent of male students engaged in binge drinking.
- Forty-seven percent had used marijuana at least once during their lifetime, and 27 percent had used marijuana one or more times in the past thirty days.
- Ten percent reported using some form of cocaine at least once during their lifetime, and 4 percent reported using cocaine in the past thirty days (Mackay et al., 2000).

Although *schizophrenia* (a thinking disorder characterized by illogical and unrealistic thinking, delusions, and hallucinations) is relatively rare among adolescents, it is the most frequently occurring psychotic disorder, and the number of cases diagnosed between the ages of twelve and eighteen is steadily increasing. Early symptoms include odd, unpredictable behavior; difficulty communicating with others; social withdrawal; and rejection by peers (Beiser, Erickson, Fleming, & Iacono, 1993; Conger & Galambos, 1997).

I
m
ta

2. *The most common type of emotional disorder during adolescence is depression.* Estimates of **depression** among high school youths range from 7 to 28 percent, depending on the level of depression being examined and the criteria being used to measure it. The most common forms of depression, from least to most serious, are *depressed mood, depressive syndrome,* and *clinical depression.* The most common form of depression among adolescents is depressed mood. This state is primarily characterized by feelings of sadness or unhappiness, although emotions such as anxiety, fear, guilt, anger, and contempt are frequently present as well. According to parents' reports, 10 to 20 percent of boys and 15 to 20 percent of girls were in a depressed mood in the past six months. But if you ask adolescents themselves, the percentages are higher. About 20 to 35 percent of boys and 25 to 40 percent of girls report having been in a depressed mood (Peterson et al., 1993).

Depression most common among females, teens from poor families

Individuals from low-income families are typically the most depressed. Depression in adolescents often precedes substance abuse (MacKay et al., 2000). Prior to puberty, twice as many boys as girls exhibit depressive syndromes; after puberty, the ratio is just the opposite (Cicchetti & Toth, 1998; Conger & Galambos, 1997). Females may exhibit greater tendencies than males to feel depressed, but this does not mean that such reactions occur only in high school girls. Extreme feelings of depression are the most common reason that teenagers of both sexes are referred to psychiatric clinics.

Common symptoms of depression include feelings of worthlessness, crying spells, and suicidal thoughts, threats, and attempts. Additional symptoms are moodiness, social isolation, fatigue, hypochondria, and difficulty in concentrating (Cicchetti & Toth, 1998; Peterson et al., 1993). High school students who experience such symptoms typically try to ward off their depression through restless activity or flight to or from others. They may also engage in problem behavior or delinquent acts carried out in ways that make it clear they are appealing for help. (A depressed fifteen-year-old boy may carry out an act of vandalism, for instance, at a time when a school authority or police officer is sure to observe the incident.)

Selecting Technologies for Different Age Levels

As this chapter and the preceding one indicate, your teaching approaches will be influenced by the developmental level of your students. Your incorporation of educational technology will be no different. For kindergarten and primary grade teachers, tools to enhance student literacy are likely to be a priority. Elementary, middle school, and high school teachers will be more interested in tools that promote thinking, problem solving, and communication.

Technology and Literacy

Technology and literacy have always been intertwined. In most societies, spoken language resulted in the development of various media (stone, wood, and paper, for example) with which to record, store, and transmit ideas. As written information became more widely available and as societies became more technological, the need for increasing numbers of literate people grew. With the availability of word processors today, ideas can be swiftly recorded, rearranged, modified, and copied. Writing technologies have emerged during the past two decades to help young children prewrite and rewrite their text, publish their stories, write reactions to stories they have read, and store data banks of words they are learning (Rowland & Scott, 1992). In addition, voice synthesis or feedback allows students to hear how their stories sound, thereby building their phonemic awareness and assisting in the transition from listening and speaking to reading and writing (MacArthur, 1998a, 1998b; Scrase, 1997). There are also numerous software tools to help children learn such vital reading skills as differentiating phonics sounds and letter blends, sounding out words, and recognizing rhyming patterns.

One of the more controversial early literacy tools, IBM's Writing to Read program (now called Writing to Read 2000), has been used with kindergarten and first-grade students since 1983. In Writing to Read (WTR), students rotate among five workstations, where they work on phonics skills, electronically type their stories, listen to recorded stories, write stories using pen and paper, and practice making letter sounds and words. At the heart of this program is a speech synthesizer that helps students learn forty-two phoneme, or letter-sound, combinations presented in ten instructional cycles (Labbo, Murray, & Phillips, 1995–1996). To extend these efforts, IBM developed Writing to Write (WTW), a literature-based approach for second, third, and fourth graders that includes both partner and individual activities such as paired editing, cooperative learning groups, and journal writing (Keeler, 1996).

Go to this text's web site at **http://education.college.hmco.com/students**. You can access demos of literacy-related software.

Evaluations of WTR claim that the program promotes an environment that is rich in student conversation and successful writing (Casey & Martin, 1994). Some studies have also determined that it produces higher levels of reading and writing and more positive student attitudes than traditional classes (Casey & Martin, 1994; Gredler, 1997).

Despite these positive reports, WTR does have its limits. Research shows that the positive results found during kindergarten are not always maintained in first grade (Gredler, 1997), and the system is costly (Slavin, 1990a). WTR classrooms have also been described as inflexible, fragmented, discouraging of student creativity, allowing few choices, too focused on discrete activities and time requirements,

For quick links to featured web sites, go to **http://education.college.hmco.com/students** and select this textbook site.

and lacking links back to regular classroom activities (Huenecke, 1992). In its latest version of the software and teacher-support materials, IBM has attempted to improve the integration with the rest of the curriculum. For information on the current version, see the company's web site, **www.can.ibm.com/k12/software.html.**

Another computer program for developing literacy skills of young children, Bubble Dialogue, provides an environment resembling a cartoon strip in which young students can create a dialogue between characters (Jones & Selby, 1997). Bubble Dialogue supports dialogue and role play between pairs of students by using "thought" and "speech" bubbles to foster student expression of ideas and interaction. Students work on their writing skills by inserting text into the empty comic strip balloons. The theoretical basis of this tool is Vygotsky's belief, mentioned in the last chapter, that language development needs to take place first in the social world so as to provide a meaningful basis for internalizing the rules of language use. Research by Charoula Angeli and Donald Cunningham (1998) indicates that Bubble Dialogue promotes student articulation of ideas, development of thought processes and word meanings, and acquisition of sentence structure awareness.

Because there is a natural distancing effect in Bubble Dialogue (characters rather than the child do the talking and thinking), this tool is useful for exploring controversial topics and sensitive issues (Eakin, 1997). For instance, it can be used as a therapeutic tool for adopted or foster children as well as those suffering from abuse (Jones & Selby, 1997).

Using Technology to Reduce Egocentrism

As we pointed out in the preceding chapter, primary to elementary grade children are limited by egocentrism in their ability to think logically. Egocentrism, as you may recall, is the inability to understand the world from any perspective but your own. According to Jean Piaget, who first proposed the concept, the main factor that contributes to the decline of egocentrism is exposure to different points of view through social interaction. Because these interactions do not have to be face-to-face, it is quite possible that sharing experiences and points of view by computer may produce the same result.

Judi Harris (1997) notes that World Wide Web networking activities can be structured to foster six different types of interpersonal exchanges:

1. *Keypals.* Students from two or more locations are matched as e-mail pals.
2. *Global classrooms.* Two or more classrooms anywhere in the world study a common topic together.
3. *Electronic "appearances."* Famous people interact with students over a web site, or electronic commemorations of important historical events are staged on the Web.
4. *Telementoring.* In **telementoring,** subject matter experts use e-mail or the Web to help learners understand a concept or complete a task.
5. *Question-and-answer services.* Web sites such as Ask-a-Geologist provide answers to students' questions.
6. *Impersonation projects.* Participants communicate as someone else, often a famous historical figure.

EFFECT OF TECHNOLOGY ON COGNITIVE AND INTERPERSONAL REASONING

Electronic conferencing, by allowing students to assume roles, can promote the development of interpersonal reasoning. For instance, middle school and high school students who assume the role of famous historical characters on sensitive environmental issues exhibit higher levels of dialogue and interpersonal reasoning than would be expected by Selman's (1980) developmental scheme (Bonk & Sugar, 1998).

Another type of program that allows students to interact electronically with experts and explorers around the world is **adventure learning.** For instance, students from various schools might get together for virtual field trips to places like the Statue of Liberty for insights on immigration policies or the Civil War battlefield at Gettysburg for demonstrations of military tactics (Siegel & Kirkley, 1998). They also might communicate electronically with explorers traversing the Arctic tundra or the Amazon rain forest. While on virtual field trips, students are electronically transported to the actual site to view historical reenactments, listen to experts, ask questions, and electronically correspond with peers across the nation. Adventure-learning explorations can be incorporated into the project-based learning (PBL) approach, a technique that promotes formal operational thought by emphasizing real-world problem solving. We discuss PBL in our chapter on approaches to instruction. Two adventure-learning web sites that you might want to take a look at are the Global Online Adventure Learning Site at **www.goals.com/** and ThinkQuest's Ocean AdVENTure site at **library.thinkquest.org/18828/.**

To review this chapter, see the ACE Self-Testing section on this book's site at **http://education.college.hmco.com/students**.

RESOURCES FOR FURTHER INVESTIGATION

How Children Develop

Helen Bee describes how children develop physically, socially, emotionally, and cognitively in *The Developing Child* (9th ed., 2000). Robert V. Kail does the same in *Children and Their Development* (1998).

Children's Play Behavior

In *Children, Play, and Development* (1991), Fergus Hughes discusses the history of play in the Western world; different theories of play; cultural differences in play behaviors; patterns of play among toddlers, preschoolers, school-age children, and adolescents; gender differences in play; and the play behaviors of children with disabilities. Sandra Heidemann and Deborah Hewitt (1992), in *Pathways to Play,* describe the play categories of Mildred Parten and the proper conditions for children's play (such as time, space, and props), give a checklist for observing play behaviors, and explain how to use the results of the checklist for teaching children different play skills.

Cognitive Development

Henry Wellman and Susan Gelman (1992) describe what three- to five-year-olds understand about the workings of their own mind and those of others in "Cognitive Development: Foundational Theories of Core Domains," in volume 43 of the *Annual Review of Psychology.* Discussions of the biological, social, and school factors that influence cognitive development can be found in *Directors of Development: Influences on the Development of Children's Thinking* (1991), edited by Lynn Okagaki and Robert Sternberg.

Teaching the Middle School Grades

Turning Points 2000: Educating Adolescents in the 21st Century (2000), by Anthony W. Jackson and Gayle A. Davis, provides a comprehensive, research-based discussion of the type of school atmosphere and instruction that leads to high-quality outcomes. In *Changing Middle Schools: How to Make Schools Work for Young Adolescents* (1994), Nancy Ames and Edward Miller describe the experiences of four urban Indiana middle schools that were part of a restructuring program called the Middle Grades Improvement Program.

Several foundations and organizations are committed to helping educators make education in the middle grades more consistent with what is known about the characteristics of early adolescence. For example, the web site of the National Forum to Accelerate Middle-Grades Reform (**www.mgforum.org/**) contains a Schools to Watch page that specifies a set of criteria that middle schools must meet if they are to be judged as having an exemplary program. The page also describes four award-winning schools that were judged to have met those criteria.

The home page of MiddleWeb (**www.middleweb.com/**) includes the latest news and updates on middle school reform, as well as an index that will take you to documents and links about such topics as assessment and evaluation, curriculum and instruction, parents and the public, student and school life, teacher professional development, and teachers at work.

Characteristics of Adolescence

For a good overall treatment of the major developmental changes that occur during adolescence—biological, cognitive, moral reasoning, self-concept and self-esteem, identity, gender role socialization, sexuality, vocational choice—consult the third edition of *Adolescent Development and Behavior* (1996), by Jerome Dusek.

If you expect to be teaching adolescents, you should read *Puberty, Sexuality, and the Self: Boys and Girls at Adolescence* (1996) by Karin A. Martin. Based on extensive interviews with teenage boys and girls, this highly readable narrative describes the role of puberty and sexuality in teens' self-concept and behavior. In addition to the author's analysis, each chapter contains many interesting and revealing quotes from the interviewees.

In *Adolescent Stress* (1991), edited by Mary Ellen Colten and Susan Gore, fourteen authors discuss such sources of adolescent stress as negative emotions, conflicts with parents, drug use, pregnancy, and abuse at home and how adolescents try to cope with them. Robert D. Ketterlinus and Michael E. Lamb (1994), in *Adolescent Problem Behaviors: Issues and Research*, describe how such factors as sexual behavior, delinquency, risk taking, and childhood victimization give rise to troublesome behaviors among adolescents.

Summary

1. Preschool and kindergarten children are quite active and enjoy physical activity. Their incomplete muscle and motor development limits what they can accomplish on tasks that require fine motor skills, eye-hand coordination, and visual focusing.
2. The social behavior of preschool and kindergarten children is marked by rapidly changing friendships and play groups, a variety of types of play, short quarrels, and a growing awareness of gender roles.
3. Kindergartners openly display their emotions. Anger and jealousy are common.
4. By age four, children are aware of their own mental activity and the fact that others may think about the world differently.
5. Kindergartners like to talk and are reasonably skilled at using language. Preschoolers tend to apply their own rules of grammar. An authoritative approach by parents is more likely to produce competent preschoolers than is an authoritarian, or permissive, or rejecting-neglecting approach.
6. Primary grade children exhibit many of the same physical characteristics as preschool and kindergarten children (high activity level, incomplete muscle and motor development, frequent periods of fatigue). Most accidents occur among third graders because they overestimate their physical skills and underestimate the dangers in their activities.
7. Primary grade children's friendships are typically same sex and are made on a more selective basis than young children do. Quarrels among peers typically involve verbal arguments, although boys may engage in punching, wrestling, and shoving.
8. Primary grade students are becoming more emotionally sensitive. As a result, they are more easily hurt by criticism, respond strongly to praise, and are more likely to hurt another child's feelings during a quarrel.
9. Primary grade children recognize that fact-based explanations are superior to theory-based explanations and are beginning to realize that their cognitive processes are under their control. They learn best when tasks are relatively short and when less cognitively demanding tasks occasionally follow more cognitively demanding tasks.
10. Elementary grade boys and girls become leaner and stronger and tend to have a gangly look. But some run the risk of becoming overweight because of poor eating habits and lack of exercise. Boys usually outperform girls on such sports-related motor skills as kicking, throwing, catching, running, and jumping, whereas girls often surpass boys on such play-related motor skills as flexibility, balance, and rhythm.
11. The peer group becomes a strong influence on the norms that govern the behavior of elementary grade children.
12. Friendships in the elementary grades become even more selective and gender based than they were in the primary grades.
13. A child's self-image (self-concept plus self-esteem) becomes more stable and generalized during the elementary grades. As a result of the decline of egocentric thought and the competitive nature of American society, self-image is based primarily on comparisons with peers.

14. Delinquency occurs more frequently among elementary grade children than at earlier ages and is associated with dysfunctional parent-child relationships and academic failure.

15. The thinking of elementary grade children, although more logical, can be wildly inconsistent and is constrained by the limitations of Piaget's concrete operational stage.

16. Although most children grow rapidly during the middle school years, girls grow more quickly and begin puberty earlier than boys. Early versus late maturation in boys and girls may affect subsequent personality development.

17. The social behavior of middle school children is increasingly influenced by peer group norms and the development of interpersonal reasoning. Children are now capable of understanding why they behave as they do toward others and vice versa.

18. Because the peer group is the primary source for rules of acceptable behavior, conformity and concern about what peers think reach a peak during the middle school years.

19. Although anxiety, worry, and concern about self-esteem, physical appearance, academic success, and acceptance by peers are prominent emotions among many adolescents, some cope with these emotions better than others.

20. Although middle schools are doing a better job of meeting the social and emotional needs of early adolescents than they did in the past, the intellectual needs of these youngsters are still largely unmet.

21. Self-efficacy beliefs, or how competent one feels at carrying out a particular task, begin to stabilize during the middle school years and influence the willingness of students to take on and persist at various academic and social tasks.

22. Physical development during the high school years is marked by physical maturity for most students and by puberty for virtually all. Sexual activity increases.

23. The long-range goals, beliefs, and values of adolescents are likely to be influenced by parents, whereas immediate status is likely to be influenced by peers. Many teens have part-time, after-school employment.

24. Eating disorders, substance abuse, schizophrenia, depression, and suicide are prominent emotional disorders among adolescents. Depression is the most common emotional disorder during adolescence. Depression coupled with an unstable family situation places adolescents at risk for suicide.

25. Cognitively, high school students become increasingly capable of formal operational thought, although they may function at the concrete operational level a good deal of the time. The influence of formal operational reasoning can be seen in political thinking, which becomes more abstract and knowledgeable.

26. Technologies that aid student learning and development are available for every age level, ranging from beginning reading and writing programs for primary and elementary grade children to complex problem-solving and collaborative programs for high school students.

KEY TERMS

play behavior *(77)*
gender roles *(78)*
theory of mind *(80)*
early language development *(80)*
authoritative parents *(81)*
authoritarian parents *(81)*
permissive parents *(81)*
rejecting-neglecting parents *(83)*
self-image *(88)*
self-concept *(88)*
self-esteem *(88)*
growth spurt *(93)*
early-maturing boy *(93)*
late-maturing boy *(93)*
early-maturing girl *(93)*
late-maturing girl *(93)*
interpersonal reasoning *(95)*
self-efficacy *(100)*
sexually transmitted diseases (STDs) *(102)*
depression *(105)*
telementoring *(109)*
adventure learning *(110)*

DISCUSSION QUESTIONS

1. Given the physical, social, emotional, and cognitive characteristics of preschool and kindergarten children, what type of classroom atmosphere and instructional tactics would you use to foster learning and enjoyment of school?

2. The primary and elementary years correspond to Erikson's stage of industry versus inferiority. The implication of this stage is that educators should do whatever is necessary to encourage a sense of industry and competence in each student. On a scale of 1 to 10, where 1 is the low end of the scale, how well do you think schools accomplish this goal? If your rating was lower than 10, what is it that schools do (or fail to do) that prevented you from assigning a perfect rating?

3. During the middle school years, the peer group becomes the general source for rules of behavior. Why? What advantages and disadvantages are associated with a situation in which the peer group establishes the norms for behavior?

4. Given the high rates of sexually transmitted diseases among high school students, you could persuasively argue that adolescents should receive more sex education than they do. What are the advantages and disadvantages of providing this education in the school instead of in the home? For help in formulating your answer, visit the web sites of the National Campaign to Prevent Teen Pregnancy (**www.teenpregnancy.org/**) and the Sexuality Information and Education Council of the United States (**www.siecus.org/**).

4 Understanding Student Differences

Sit back for a few minutes, and think about some of your friends and classmates over the past twelve years. Make a list of their physical characteristics (height, weight, visual acuity, and athletic skill, for example), social characteristics (outgoing, reserved, cooperative, sensitive to the needs of others, assertive), emotional characteristics (self-assured, optimistic, pessimistic, egotistical), and intellectual characteristics (methodical, creative, impulsive, good with numbers, terrible at organizing ideas). Now analyze your descriptions in terms of similarities and differences. In all likelihood, they point to many ways in which your friends and classmates have been alike, but to even more ways in which they have differed from one another. Indeed, although human beings share many important characteristics, they also differ from one another in significant ways (and we tend to notice the differences more readily than the similarities).

Now imagine yourself a few years from now, when your job as a teacher is to help every student learn as much as possible despite all the ways in

Key Points

These key points will help you learn the important information in this chapter. To help you study, they also appear in the margins of the pages, next to the text where they are discussed.

The Nature and Measurement of Intelligence

- Intelligence test scores most closely related to school success, not job success, marital happiness, or life happiness
- IQ scores can change with experience, training
- Intelligence involves more than what intelligence tests measure
- Triarchic theory: part of intelligence is ability to achieve personal goals
- Multiple intelligences theory: intelligence composed of eight distinct forms of intelligence
- Individuals with a high level of a particular intelligence may use it in different ways
- Factors other than high levels of a particular intelligence influence interests, college major, career choice
- Triarchic theory suggests that instruction and assessment should emphasize all types of ability
- Various technology tools may strengthen different intelligences

Learning Styles

- Learning styles are preferences for dealing with intellectual tasks in a particular way
- Impulsive students prefer quick action; reflective students prefer to collect and analyze information before acting
- Field-independent students prefer their own structure; field-dependent students prefer to work within existing structure
- Legislative style prefers to create and plan; executive style prefers to follow explicit rules; judicial style prefers to evaluate and judge
- Teachers should use various instructional methods to engage all styles of learning at one time or another
- Teachers should use various test formats to measure accurately what students with various styles have learned

Gender Differences and Gender Bias

- Boys score higher on tests of visual spatial ability, math reasoning; girls score higher on tests of memory, language skills
- Gender bias: responding differently to male and female students without having sound educational reasons for doing so
- Gender bias can affect course selection, career choice, and class participation of male and female students
- Academic success, encouragement, models influence women to choose careers in science, math
- Loss of voice: students suppress true beliefs about various topics in the presence of parents, teachers, and classmates of opposite sex
- Females and males have equal access to computers, but females use them more for school-related purposes

which students differ from one another. By fourth grade, for example, the range of achievement in some classes is greater than four grade levels. Some children's reading or math skills may be at the second-grade level, while other children may be functioning at the sixth-grade level. By sixth grade, about one-third of all children will be working one grade level or more below the average student in class (Biemiller, 1993).

The variability among any group of students is one reason that teaching is both interesting and challenging. Richard Snow, who has written extensively about individual differences in education, has summarized this challenge as follows:

> At the outset of instruction in any topic, students of any age and in any culture will differ from one another in various intellectual and psychomotor abilities and skills, in both general and specialized prior knowledge, in interests and motives, and in personal styles of thought and work during learning. These differences, in turn, appear directly related to differences in the students' learning progress. (1986, p. 1029)

Although it usually will be essential for you to plan lessons, assignments, and teaching techniques by taking into account typical characteristics, you will also have to expect and make allowances for differences among students. The practice of using different learning materials, instructional tactics, and learning activities with students who vary along such dimensions as intelligence, learning style, gender, ethnicity, and social class is commonly referred to as *differentiated instruction* (see, e.g., Tomlinson, 1999). The aim is for all students to meet the same goals.

Over the next two chapters, we examine five broad characteristics that distinguish one group of students from another and have a demonstrated effect on learning. In this chapter, we focus on differences in mental ability (usually referred to as *intelligence*), learning styles, and gender. In the next chapter, we explore two related characteristics that are becoming more important every year: cultural and socioeconomic background. Teachers and researchers have demonstrated a strong interest in all five characteristics in recent years, and much has been written about them. ■

The Nature and Measurement of Intelligence

The Origin of Intelligence Testing

To preview this chapter's basic concepts, read the Chapter Themes on the Snowman textbook site at **http://education.college.hmco.com/students**.

The form and content of contemporary intelligence tests owe much to the pioneering work of French psychologist Alfred Binet. In 1904, Binet was appointed to a commission of experts charged by the minister of public instruction for the Paris school system with figuring out an accurate and objective way of distinguishing between children who could profit from normal classroom instruction and those who required special education. Since the point of this project was to predict degree of future academic success, Binet created a set of questions and tasks that reflected the same cognitive processes as those demanded by everyday classroom activities. Thus, Binet's first scale measured such processes as memory, attention, comprehension, discrimination, and reasoning.

In 1916, Lewis Terman of Stanford University published an extensive revision of Binet's test. This revision, which came to be known as the Stanford-Binet, proved to be extremely popular. One reason for its popularity was that Terman, following the 1912 suggestion of a German psychologist named William Stern, expressed a child's level of performance as a global figure called an intelligence quotient (IQ). Stern's original formula divided a child's mental age, which was determined by performance on the test, by the child's chronological age and multiplied the resulting figure by 100 to eliminate fractional values (Seagoe, 1975).

We have provided this abbreviated history lesson to illustrate two important points:

1. The form and function of contemporary intelligence tests have been directly influenced by the task Binet was given a century ago. Intelligence test items are still selected on the basis of their relationship to school success. Thus, predictions about job success, marital bliss, happiness in life, or anything else made on the basis of an IQ score are attempts to make the test do something for which it was not designed. As some psychologists have pointed out, this type of test might better have been called a test of scholastic aptitude or school ability rather than a test of intelligence.
2. Stern and Terman's use of the IQ as a quantitative summary of a child's performance was not endorsed by Binet, who worried that educators would use a summary score as an excuse to ignore or get rid of uninterested or troublesome students. Binet's intent was "to identify in order to help and improve, not to label in order to limit" (Gould, 1981, p. 152).

Intelligence test scores most closely related to school success, not job success, marital happiness, or life happiness

Later in this section, we will see that Binet's concern was well placed. First, however, we will turn to a more detailed consideration of what intelligence tests do and do not measure.

What Traditional Intelligence Tests Measure

In 1904, British psychologist Charles Spearman noticed that children given a battery of intellectual tests (such as the memory, reasoning, and comprehension tests that Binet and Terman used) showed a strong tendency to rank consistently from test to test: children who scored high (or average or below average) on memory tests tended to score high (or average or below average) on reasoning and comprehension tests. Our use of the words *tendency* and *tended* indicates, of course, that the rankings were not identical. Some children scored well on some tests but performed more poorly on others.

Spearman explained this pattern by saying that intelligence is made up of two types of factors: a general factor (abbreviated as *g*) that affected performance on all intellectual tests and a set of specific factors (abbreviated as *s*) that affected performance on only specific intellectual tests. Spearman ascribed to the *g* factor the tendency for score rankings to remain constant over tests. That the rankings varied somewhat from test to test, he said, resulted from individual differences in specific factors. Not surprisingly, Spearman's explanation is called the *two-factor theory of intelligence.*

When you examine such contemporary intelligence tests as the Stanford-Binet, the Wechsler Intelligence Scale for Children–III, and the Wechsler Adult Intelligence Scale–Revised (1981), you will notice that the items in the various subtests differ greatly from one another. They may involve performing mental arithmetic, explaining the meanings of words, describing how two things are alike, indicating what part is missing from a pictured object, reproducing a pictured geometric design with blocks, or tracing a path through a maze. These varied items are included because, despite their apparent differences, they relate strongly to one another and to per-

Do you want to take a sample intelligence test? Go to **http://education.college.hmco.com/students** and see the Netlabs on this book's site.

Individually administered intelligence tests (such as the one shown here) are usually given to determine eligibility for a special class because they were designed to predict, and are moderately good predictors of, academic performance.

formance in the classroom. In other words, intelligence tests still reflect Binet's original goal and Spearman's two-factor theory. In practice, the examiner can combine the scores from each subtest into a global index (the IQ score), offer a prediction about the tested individual's degree of academic success for the next year or so, and make some judgments about specific strengths and weaknesses.

Limitations of Intelligence Tests

So where does all this leave us in terms of trying to decide what traditional intelligence tests do and do not measure? Four points seem to be in order:

1. The appraisal of intelligence is limited by the fact that it cannot be measured directly. Our efforts are confined to measuring the overt manifestations (responses to test items) of what is ultimately based on brain function and experience.
2. The intelligence we test is a sample of intellectual capabilities that relate to classroom achievement better than they relate to anything else. That is why, as stated earlier, many psychologists prefer the terms *test of scholastic aptitude* or *test of school ability.*
3. Since current research demonstrates that the cognitive abilities measured by intelligence tests can be improved with systematic instruction (Sternberg, 1998), intelligence test scores should not be viewed as absolute measures of ability. Many people—parents, especially—fail to grasp this fact. An IQ score is not a once-and-for-all judgment of how bright a child is. It is merely an estimate of how successful a child is in handling certain kinds of problems at a particular time on a particular test as compared with other children of the same age.
4. Since IQ tests are designed to predict academic success, anything that enhances classroom performance (such as a wider range of factual information or more effective learning skills) will likely have a positive effect on intelligence test performance. This means that IQ scores are not necessarily permanent. Research on the stability of IQ scores shows that although they do not change significantly for most people, they can change dramatically for given individuals, and changes are most likely to occur among individuals who were first tested as preschoolers (Brody, 1992). This last point is often used to support early intervention programs like Head Start and Follow-Through.

IQ scores can change with experience, training

Because traditional theories of intelligence and their associated IQ tests view intelligence as being composed of a relatively small set of cognitive skills that relate best to academic success, and because the results of such tests are used primarily to place students in special programs, contemporary theorists have proposed broader conceptions of intelligence that have more useful implications for classroom instruction.

Contemporary Views of Intelligence

David Wechsler's Global Capacity View As David Wechsler (1975) persuasively points out, intelligence is not simply the sum of one's tested abilities. Wechsler defines **intelligence** as the global capacity of the individual to act purposefully, think rationally, and deal effectively with the environment. Given this definition, which many psychologists endorse, an IQ score reflects just one facet of a person's global capacity: the ability to act purposefully, rationally, and effectively on academic tasks in a *classroom* environment. However, people display intelligent behavior in other settings (at work, home, and play, for example), and other characteristics contribute

Intelligence involves more than what intelligence tests measure

to intelligent behavior (such as persistence, realistic goal setting, the productive use of corrective feedback, creativity, and moral and aesthetic values). A true assessment of intelligence would take into account behavior related to these other settings and characteristics. In fact, recent research (Perkins, Tishman, Ritchhart, Donis, & Andrade, 2000) has shown that in everyday settings, intelligent behavior is related to the ability to recognize occasions that call for various capabilities and the motivation actually to use those capabilities. For example, in a situation that had the potential to become confrontational and hostile, intelligence might involve being open-minded and using a sense of humor.

Assessment of intelligence in everyday settings would be highly subjective and take a great deal of time. That is one reason current intelligence tests assess only a small sample of cognitive abilities. But if recent formulations of intelligence by psychologists Robert Sternberg (1985) and Howard Gardner (1983) become widely accepted, future intelligence tests may be broader in scope than those in use today. Even before such tests are devised, these theories serve a useful purpose by reminding us that intelligence is multifaceted and can be expressed in many ways.

Robert Sternberg's Triarchic Theory Like David Wechsler, Robert Sternberg (1985, 1996a) believes that most of the research evidence supports the view that intelligence has many facets, or dimensions, and that traditional mental ability tests measure just a few of these facets. Sternberg's **triarchic theory of intelligence** has, as its name suggests, three main parts: practical ability, creative ability, and analytical ability (see Figure 4.1). Sternberg's work is a break with tradition in two respects. First, it includes an aspect of intelligence that has been—and still is—largely overlooked: how people use practical intelligence to adapt to their environment. Second, Sternberg believes that each of these abilities can be improved through instruction and that students learn best when all three are called into play.

Figure 4.1 **The Three Components of Sternberg's Triarchic Theory**

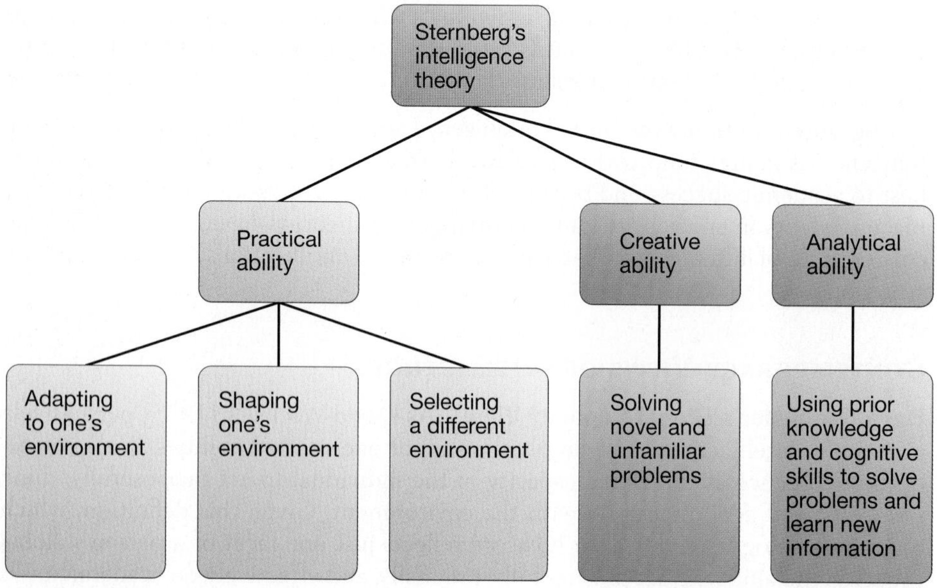

SOURCE: Adapted from Sternberg (1985): Sternberg, Ferrari, Clinkenbeard, & Grigorenko (1996).

Triarchic theory: part of intelligence is ability to achieve personal goals

In describing the nature of practical intelligence, Sternberg argues that part of what makes an individual intelligent is the ability to achieve personal goals (for example, graduating from high school or college with honors, working for a particular company in a particular capacity, or having a successful marriage). One way to accomplish personal goals is to understand and adapt to the values that govern behavior in a particular setting. For example, if most teachers in a particular school (or executives in a particular company) place a high value on conformity and cooperation, the person who persistently challenges authority, suggests new ideas without being asked, or operates without consulting others will, in all likelihood, receive fewer rewards than those who are more willing to conform and cooperate. According to Sternberg's theory, this person would be less intelligent.

Where a mismatch exists and the individual cannot adapt to the values of the majority, the intelligent person explores ways to make the values of others more consistent with his own values and skills. An enterprising student may try to convince her teacher, for example, that short-answer questions are better measures of achievement than essay questions or that effort and classroom participation should count just as much toward a grade as test scores. Finally, where all attempts at adapting or attempting to change the views of others fail, the intelligent person seeks out a setting where his behaviors are more consistent with those of others. For instance, many gifted and talented students will seek out private alternative schools where their particular abilities are more highly prized.

Sternberg's basic point is that intelligence should be viewed as a broad characteristic of people that is evidenced not only by how well they answer a particular set of test questions but also by how well they function in different settings. The individual with average test scores who knows how to get people to do what she wants is, in this view, at least as intelligent as the person who scores at the ninety-ninth percentile of a science test.

In an evaluation of the triarchic model (Sternberg, Ferrari, Clinkenbeard, & Grigorenko, 1996), 225 high school students who were considered by their school

A unique aspect of Robert Sternberg's triarchic theory of intelligence is practical ability, which is defined as the ability to either adapt to one's environment, shape one's environment, or select an alternative environment.

to be gifted were administered the Sternberg Triarchic Abilities Test and, on the basis of their scores, admitted to the Yale Summer Psychology Program. Five groups of students were identified: high in analytical ability, high in creative ability, high in practical ability, high in all three abilities, and low in all three abilities (those who scored below the mean of this group). All the students then took a one-month summer course in college-level psychology that called for the use of memory, analysis, creativity, and practical abilities in the morning and then split into groups that emphasized only one of those four abilities in the afternoon. Students in the analytical section, for example, analyzed the validity of theories, compared the relative merits of theories, and criticized experiments. Students in the creative section focused on generating new theories and experiments. Students in the practical section mostly worked on applying psychological concepts to everyday life. A memory-oriented condition was included as a traditional form of instruction against which the other three could be compared because many classrooms emphasize memorization of factual information.

Students' abilities to recall factual information, analyze concepts and theories, create new ideas, and apply psychological principles to everyday life were measured through homework assignments, a midterm and final examination (multiple-choice and essay items), and an independent project. The multiple-choice questions primarily measured recall. The homework assignments, essay questions, and course project were used to measure analytical, creative, and practical abilities. For example, the essay questions from the midterm asked students to discuss the advantages and disadvantages of having armed guards at school (analysis), describe what their ideal school would be like (creativity), and describe some problem they have been facing in their life and then give a practical solution (practicality).

There were two very interesting findings:

- Students who were taught and tested in a way that matched their abilities performed significantly better than students who were mismatched.
- Most of the high-analytic students were white and from middle- to upper-middle-class homes, whereas most of the high-creative and high-practical groups were more racially, ethnically, and socioeconomically diverse.

A similar study (Sternberg, Torff, & Grigorenko, 1998) was done with third graders and eighth graders. Students in the experimental group received instruction that emphasized memory of facts as well as the triarchic skills of analytical, creative, and practical thinking. A second group of students received only analytical thinking instruction, and a third group received only memory-based instruction. Both age groups were tested with multiple-choice questions that measured recall of facts and open-ended questions that measured analytical, creative, and practical thinking skills. For example, the creative assessment for the third graders asked them to imagine a place where no one followed the rules at school or in the community and then write a story about a visit to this town. The practical assessment for the eighth graders asked them to describe how they would use psychological theory (which they had studied) to help someone quit smoking. On average, third-grade and eighth-grade students who received triarchically based instruction outscored the other two groups on all four measures.

Howard Gardner's Multiple Intelligences Theory Howard Gardner's (1983) conception of intelligence, like Sternberg's, is broader than traditional conceptions. It is different from Sternberg's, however, in that it describes eight separate types of intelligence. Accordingly, Gardner's work is referred to as the **theory of multiple in-**

Multiple intelligences theory: intelligence composed of eight distinct forms of intelligence

telligences (or MI theory). The intelligences that Gardner described are logical-mathematical, linguistic, musical, spatial, bodily-kinesthetic, interpersonal (understanding of others), intrapersonal (understanding of self), and naturalist (the ability to notice the characteristics that distinguish one plant, mineral, or animal from another and to create useful classification schemes called taxonomies) (Gardner, 1999). Table 4.1 describes each of these intelligences and provides examples of the kind of person who best represents each one.

Because these intelligences are presumed to be independent of one another, an individual would likely exhibit different levels of skill in each of these domains. One student, for example, may show evidence of becoming an outstanding trial lawyer, novelist, or journalist because his linguistic intelligence produces a facility for vividly describing, explaining, or persuading. Another student may be able to manipulate as-

Table 4.1 Gardner's Eight Intelligences

Intelligence	Core Components	End States
Logical-mathematical	Sensitivity to, and capacity to discern, logical or numerical patterns; ability to handle long chains of reasoning	Scientist Mathematician
Linguistic	Sensitivity to the sounds, rhythms, and meanings of words; sensitivity to the different functions of language	Poet Journalist
Musical	Abilities to produce and appreciate rhythm, pitch, and timbre; appreciation of the forms of musical expression	Violinist Composer
Spatial	Capacities to perceive the visual-spatial world accurately and to perform transformations on one's initial perceptions	Sculptor Navigator
Bodily-kinesthetic	Abilities to control one's body movements and handle objects skillfully	Dancer Athlete
Interpersonal	Capacities to discern and respond appropriately to the moods, temperaments, motivations, and desires of other people	Therapist Salesperson
Intrapersonal	Access to one's own feelings and the ability to discriminate among them and draw on them to guide behavior; knowledge of one's own strengths, weaknesses, desires, and intelligences	Person with detailed, accurate self-knowledge
Naturalist	Ability to recognize and classify the numerous plants and animals of one's environment and their relationships on a logical, justifiable basis; talent of caring for, taming, and interacting with various living creatures	Botanist Entomologist

SOURCE: Gardner (1999); Gardner & Hatch (1989).

pects of sound (such as pitch, rhythm, and timbre) to produce musical experiences that people find highly pleasing. And the student who is adept at understanding her own and others' feelings and how those feelings relate to behavior would be exhibiting high intrapersonal and interpersonal intelligence. Like Sternberg's work, Gardner's theory cautions us against focusing on the results of IQ tests to the exclusion of other worthwhile behaviors.

Gardner's MI theory has become extremely popular among educators. As usually happens with such ideas, they are often misinterpreted. A number of misconceptions have arisen:

1. *Misconception: A person who has a strength in a particular intelligence will excel on all tasks within that domain.* Not so. A student with a high level of linguistic intelligence may be quite good at writing insightful essays on various topics but be unable to produce a good poem. Another student may excel at the kind of direct, fact-oriented style of writing that characterizes good newspaper reporting but be limited in her ability to write a long, highly analytical essay.

Individuals with a high level of a particular intelligence may use it in different ways

Instead of focusing on how much intelligence students have, we need to attend to the different ways in which students make the most of their intelligences. For example, Thomas Hatch (1997), an associate of Gardner, describes how three children, all of whom were judged to have a high level of interpersonal intelligence, used that ability in different ways. One child was very adept at organizing the classroom activities of his classmates. The second was able to resolve conflicts among his classmates far better than anybody else in that class. The third child shunned leadership and was sometimes excluded from group activities, but excelled at forming friendships among his peers. He was so good at this that he was able to make friends with one of the least popular students in class.

2. *Misconception: Ability is destiny.* If a child exhibits a high level of linguistic intelligence, she will not necessarily choose to major in English or journalism or seek a job as a writer. Not only do intelligences change over time in how they are used, but decisions about a college major and career are influenced by many other factors. The student who wrote such interesting stories as a child may grow up to be a college professor who excels at writing journal articles and textbooks or a noted politician or a successful business leader (Hatch, 1997).
3. *Misconception: Every child should be taught every subject in eight different ways in order to develop all of the intelligences.* MI theory does not indicate or even suggest that such a step is necessary in order for learning to occur. In fact, it may be counterproductive if students are turned off by lessons that appear forced and contrived. And as a practical matter, there simply isn't enough time in the day to teach every lesson eight ways (Gardner, 1999; Hatch, 1997).

Factors other than high levels of a particular intelligence influence interests, college major, career choice

Gardner and his colleagues are in the process of trying to validate the theory of multiple intelligences. In one program, Arts PROPEL, junior and senior high school students in the Pittsburgh public schools were assessed for growth in the areas of music, creative writing, and the visual arts. In a second project, all students in an Indianapolis elementary school were exposed to special classes and enrichment activities designed to enhance the various intelligences. A third effort, Project Spectrum, is aimed at preschool and kindergarten children. Spectrum classrooms are equipped with a variety of materials that invite children to use one or another intelligence. For example, household objects that can be taken apart and reassembled afford children the opportunity to exercise spatial intelligence. In these programs, Gardner and his associates measure intelligence by observing and evaluating what students do as they

Contemporary theories typically view intelligence as being composed of several types of capabilities. Howard Gardner's theory of multiple intelligences, for example, describes several different ways of expressing intelligent behavior.

work through a variety of everyday tasks and projects. A preliminary assessment of Project Spectrum children provided partial support for Gardner's theory (Blythe & Gardner, 1990; Gardner & Hatch, 1989).

Using the New Views of Intelligence to Guide Instruction

The various theories of intelligence that were formulated during the first half of the twentieth century are of limited value to educators because they do not allow teachers to match instructional approaches and learning assessments to abilities. For example, because traditional intelligence tests, like the Stanford-Binet or the Wechsler Intelligence Scale for Children–III, are designed to rank students according to how they score rather than to assess how they think, their basic educational use is to determine eligibility for programs for the gifted and talented, learning disabled, and mentally disabled. What sets the theories of Sternberg and Gardner apart is their belief in a broad view of intelligence that can inform instructional practice and improve student performance. As we have shown, the preliminary evidence suggests that these beliefs have merit. What follows are a few illustrations of how you can use their ideas in your classroom.

Sternberg's Triarchic Theory Based on his triarchic theory, Sternberg proposes a teaching and assessment model (Sternberg, 1996b, 1997a; Sternberg, Ferrari, et al., 1996). He suggests that for any grade level and for any subject, teaching and testing can be designed to emphasize the three abilities in his triarchic theory—analytical, creative, and practical—as well as memory. (As we pointed out, although memory is not an explicit part of Sternberg's theory, some memorization of factual information is necessary in any classroom.) To take into account individual differences, instruction and testing should involve all four abilities. At some point, each student has an opportunity to excel because the task and related test match the student's ability. Table 4.2 shows how language arts, mathematics, social studies, and science can be taught so as to emphasize all four of these abilities. Notice that Sternberg does not

Triarchic theory suggests that instruction and assessment should emphasize all types of ability

Table 4.2 Teaching Different Subjects from a Triarchic Perspective

	Memory	Analysis	Creativity	Practicality
Language arts	Remember the name of Tom Sawyer's aunt.	Compare the personality of Tom Sawyer to that of Huckleberry Finn.	Write a very short story with Tom Sawyer as a character.	Describe how you could use Tom Sawyer's power of persuasion.
Mathematics	Remember the mathematical formula Distance = Rate × Time.	Solve a mathematical word problem using the $D = R \times T$ formula.	Create your own mathematical word problem using the $D = R \times T$ formula.	Show how to use the $D = R \times T$ formula to estimate driving time from one city to another.
Social studies	Remember a list of factors that led up to the U.S. Civil War.	Compare, contrast, and evaluate the arguments of those who supported slavery versus those who opposed it.	Write a page of a journal from the viewpoint of either a Confederate or a Union soldier.	Discuss the applicability of the lessons of the Civil War to countries today.
Science	Name the main types of bacteria.	Analyze the means the immune system uses to fight bacterial infections.	Suggest ways to cope with the increasing immunity bacteria are showing to antibiotic drugs.	Suggest three steps that individuals might take to reduce the chances of bacterial infection.

SOURCE: Adapted from Sternberg (1997a).

suggest that *all* instruction and assessment match a student's dominant ability. Some attempts need to be made to strengthen abilities that are relatively weak.

Gardner's Multiple Intelligences Theory Gardner's general recommendation for applying MI theory in the classroom is essentially the same as Sternberg's. He believes that teachers should use MI theory as a framework for devising alternative ways to teach subject matter. Some children learn a subject best when it is presented in a particular format or emphasizes a particular type of ability, whereas other children learn well when the subject is taught under different conditions (Checkley, 1997).

MI theory should lead to increased transfer of learning to out-of-school settings. Because MI theory helps students mentally represent ideas in multiple ways, they are likely to develop a better understanding of the topic and be able to use that knowledge in everyday life.

Because MI theory stresses different ways of learning and expressing one's understanding, it fits well with the current emphasis on performance assessment (described in the later chapters on assessment and testing). For example, instead of using just multiple-choice questions to measure linguistic competence, teachers can ask students to play the role of newspaper editor and write an editorial in response to a current issue.

As we mentioned earlier, it is a mistake to think that every lesson has to be designed to involve all eight intelligences. But with a little thought, many lessons can be designed to include two or three. For example, a high school algebra teacher combined kinesthetic and logical-mathematical abilities to teach a lesson on graphing. Instead of using in-class paper-and-pencil exercises, this teacher took the students outside to the school's courtyard. Using the large cement pavement squares as a grid and the grooves between the squares as X and Y coordinates, she had the students stand at various junctures and plot their own location. Similarly, as part of a primary grade lesson on birds and their nesting habits, students designed and built birdhouses and then noted whether the birds used them, thereby using spatial, bodily-kinesthetic, and logical-mathematical abilities (Campbell, 1997).

Using Technology to Develop Intelligence

Because contemporary theories view intelligence as being made up of modifiable cognitive skills, you shouldn't be overly surprised that there are technology implications for the development of intelligence. In fact, Robert Sternberg (1997c), author of the triarchic theory, recently stated, "Technology can enable people to better develop their intelligence—no question about it" (p. 13). How can technology play this role? Consider the following possibilities.

For demos of multimedia and hypermedia software packages, see the Technology Demos section of this book's web site at **http://education.college.hmco.com/students**.

Multimedia (a communication format integrating several types of media such as text, graphics, animation, sound, images, and video) and **hypertext** (a system of linking text in a nonlinear way, thereby enabling users to jump from one section of text to another section of the same document or to other documents, often through highlighted words) are two forms of technology that can have a positive impact on the analytical and creative abilities that make up most of Sternberg's theory of intelligence. **Hypermedia** involves a marriage of multimedia and hypertext in which the learner can explore facts, concepts, or knowledge domains and immediately traverse to interesting links or appealing presentation formats. Most web sites use hypermedia, and so do computerized encyclopedias and many other types of educational software.

For instance, a fourth-grade child interested in President John F. Kennedy could use a hypermedia encyclopedia to read information about his life, peruse a bibliography list, view photographs of the president with foreign dignitaries, hear selected pieces from his famous inaugural address and perhaps even watch some original video footage of the address, read related articles, explore a knowledge tree relating Kennedy to other political leaders, and connect to information about his family as well as his political adversaries. Since hypermedia encourages the rapid movement from one information resource to another (Grabe & Grabe, 2001), users can also view historical timelines and discover key events in history that occurred at the same time as Kennedy's presidency.

Various technology tools may strengthen different intelligences

According to Hilary McLellan (1996a), technology holds great promise in addressing the multiple intelligences theory promoted by Gardner. For instance, electronic role play and web-based conferencing might promote students' interpersonal intelligence (McLellan, 1996a). Intrapersonal intelligence might be aided by computer prompts, style checkers, and journal aids. Programs that make it easy to do concept mapping, flowcharting, and three-dimensional imaging are closely tied to visual-spatial intelligence (Anderson-Inman, Knox-Quinn, & Horney, 1996). Idea generation and prewriting software tools, like IdeaFisher and Inspiration, can assist verbal intelligence (Kellogg, 1989). Computer programming with tools like LOGO might help students' problem solving and logical-mathematical intelligence (Keller, 1990; Yusuf, 1995). Other software addresses musical intelligence (for instance, by enabling students to see musical scores as the notes are played) and bodily-kinesthetic intelligence (by offering a visual breakdown of an athletic skill such as a tennis swing). Clearly, there are technology tools for all the aspects of intelligence that Sternberg and Gardner described.

As a teacher, these tools allow you a great deal of flexibility. With the many options that hypermedia applications offer, you can allow students to choose ways of learning that match their own strongest abilities, or you can have students use software that helps them improve in areas where they are weak.

Learning Styles

Whether one conceives of intelligence as having one major component or several, psychologists agree that it is an *ability*. Typically it is better to have more of an ability than less of it. In recent years, psychologists have also studied how students use their abilities, and this line of research has led to the concept of a learning style. Unlike abilities, styles are value neutral—that is, all styles are adaptive under the right circumstances.

A **learning style** can be defined as a consistent preference over time and subject matter for perceiving, thinking about, and organizing information in a particular way. Some students, for example, prefer to think about the nature of a task, collect relevant information, and formulate a detailed plan before taking any action, while others prefer to run with the first idea they have and see where it leads. Some students prefer to work on several aspects of a task simultaneously, while others prefer to work on one aspect at a time in a logical sequence.

Learning styles are preferences for dealing with intellectual tasks in a particular way

Notice that styles are referred to as *preferences*. They are not fixed modes of behavior that we are locked into. When the situation warrants, we can, at least temporarily, adopt different styles, although some people are better than others at switching styles.

In the psychological literature on styles, a distinction is drawn between cognitive styles and learning styles. Because learning style is considered to be the more inclusive concept and because the implications for instruction are the same, we will use the term *learning style* throughout this section. Among the many learning style dimensions that have been investigated, we will examine three. Two of these (reflectivity-impulsivity and field dependence-field independence) were formulated over forty years ago and have a long history of research. The third (mental self-government) is more recent in origin and contains some original elements, but also includes styles that have been the subject of much research.

Reflectivity and Impulsivity

One of the first learning style dimensions to be investigated was reflectivity-impulsivity. During the early 1960s, Jerome Kagan (1964a, 1964b) found that some students seem to be characteristically **impulsive,** whereas others are characteristically **reflective.** Impulsive students are said to have a fast conceptual tempo. When faced with a task for which there is no ready solution or a question for which the answer is uncertain, the impulsive student responds more quickly than students who are more reflective. In problem-solving situations, the impulsive student collects less information, does so less systematically, and gives less thought to various solutions than do more reflective students. Reflective students, in contrast, prefer to spend more time

Impulsive students prefer quick action; reflective students prefer to collect and analyze information before acting

During the elementary years it becomes very apparent that students approach tasks in different ways. This preference for doing things in a particular way is often referred to as a cognitive style. Some students, for example, are impulsive thinkers who tend to react quickly when asked a question; other students are reflective thinkers who prefer to mull over things before answering.

collecting information (which means searching one's memory as well as external sources) and analyzing its relevance to the solution before offering a response (Morgan, 1997).

Kagan discovered that when tests of reading and inductive reasoning were administered in the first and second grades, impulsive students made more errors than reflective students did. He also found that impulsiveness is a general trait; it appears early in a person's life and is consistently revealed in a great variety of situations.

Field Dependence and Field Independence

Field-independent students prefer their own structure; field-dependent students prefer to work within existing structure

Another very popular learning style dimension, known as field dependence–field independence, was proposed by Herbert Witkin (Witkin, Moore, Goodenough, & Cox, 1977) and refers to the extent to which a person's perception and thinking about a particular piece of information are influenced by the surrounding context. For example, when some individuals are shown a set of simple geometric figures and asked to locate each one (by outlining it with a pencil) within a larger and more complex display of intersecting lines, those with a **field-dependent style** take significantly longer to respond and identify fewer of the figures than individuals with a **field-independent style.** The former are labeled field dependent because their perception is strongly influenced by the prevailing field. The latter are called field independent because they are more successful in isolating target information despite the fact that it is embedded within a larger and more complex context. As one practical example, individuals who are field independent will probably be better than field-dependent individuals at locating insects that have the same coloration as the surrounding branches and leaves on which they sit.

When we talk about individuals who have a field-dependent style and compare them to individuals who have a field-independent style, we do not mean to imply that there are two distinctly different types of individuals. That is like saying that people are either tall or short. Just as people's heights range over a measured span, students can vary in the extent to which they are field dependent or field independent. In fact, relatively few individuals exhibit a pure field-dependent or field-independent style (Morgan, 1997).

In school, the notes that field-dependent students take are more likely to reflect the structure and sequence of ideas as presented by the teacher or textbook author, whereas the notes of field-independent students are more likely to reflect their own ideas about structure and sequence. When reading, field-independent students are more likely than field-dependent students to analyze the structure of the story. The significance of this difference in approach is clearly seen with materials and tasks that are poorly structured. Field-independent students usually perform better in these situations because of their willingness to create a more meaningful structure.

The positive effect of field independence on achievement is particularly noticeable in the sciences because of their emphasis on analyzing objects and ideas into their component parts, reorganizing ideas into new configurations, and identifying potential new uses of that information. Biology students, for example, need to be able to identify tissues, organs, and systems that are difficult to see at first glance because they are embedded in the surrounding tissue of an organism.

In social situations, field-dependent people, in comparison to field-independent people, spend more time looking directly at the faces of others; are more aware of prevailing attitudes, values, and behaviors; prefer to be in the company of other people; and are generally thought of as more tactful, considerate, socially outgoing, and affectionate than field-independent individuals (Fehrenbach, 1994; Morgan, 1997; Witkin et al., 1977).

MENTAL SELF-GOVERNMENT STYLES

Robert Sternberg (1994), whose ideas on intelligence we discussed earlier in this chapter, has proposed an interesting learning style theory that is roughly modeled on the different functions and forms of civil government. Sternberg's **styles of mental self-government** theory describes thirteen styles that fall into one of five categories (functions, forms, levels, scope, and leaning). There are legislative, executive, and judicial functions; monarchic, hierarchic, oligarchic, and anarchic forms; global and local levels; internal and external scopes; and liberal and conservative leanings. Most individuals have a preference for one style within each category. In Table 4.3 we briefly describe the main characteristics of each style and suggest an instructional activity consistent with it. If you are wondering how to identify these styles, Sternberg offers a simple solution: Teachers can simply note the type of instruction that various students prefer and the test types on which they perform best.

Legislative style prefers to create and plan; executive style prefers to follow explicit rules; judicial style prefers to evaluate and judge

USING AWARENESS OF LEARNING STYLES TO GUIDE INSTRUCTION

Because the typical classroom contains two dozen or more students who collectively exhibit several styles, teachers must be flexible and learn to use a variety of teaching and assessment methods so that at some point, every student's style is addressed (recall our discussion of the teacher-as-artist earlier in the book). An impulsive boy, for example, may disrupt a class discussion by blurting out the first thing that pops into his head, thereby upstaging the reflective types, who are still in the process of

Teachers should use various instructional methods to engage all styles of learning at one time or another

Table 4.3 Matching Instructional Activities to Sternberg's Mental Self-Government Styles

Styles	Characteristics	Instructional Activities
Legislative	Prefers to formulate rules and plans, imagine possibilities, and create ideas and products.	Require students to design science projects, write stories, imagine how historical figures might have done things differently, organize work groups.
Executive	Prefers to follow rules and guidelines.	Present well-organized lectures, require students to prepare book reports, work out answers to problems.
Judicial	Prefers to compare things and make evaluations about quality, worth, effectiveness.	Require students to compare literary characters, critique an article, evaluate effectiveness of a program.
Monarchic	Prefers to work on one task at a time or to use a particular approach to tasks.	Assign one project, reading assignment, or homework assignment at a time. Allow ample time to complete all aspects of the assignment before assigning another.
Hierarchic	Prefers to have several tasks to work on, deciding which one to do first, second, and so on, and for how long.	Assign several tasks that vary in length, difficulty, and point value and are due at various times over several weeks.
Oligarchic	Prefers to have several tasks to work on, all of which are treated equally.	Assign several tasks that are equivalent in length, difficulty, and point value.
Anarchic	Prefers an unstructured, random approach to learning that is devoid of rules, procedures, or guidelines.	Assign tasks and problems that require nonconventional thinking and methods, self-directed form of study.
Global	Prefers to have an overall view of a task before beginning work.	Require students to scan a reading assignment to identify major topics, create an outline before writing, formulate a plan before beginning a complex task.
Local	Prefers to identify and work on the details of a particular part of a task before moving to another part.	Present a detailed outline or overview of a lecture or project. Require students to identify and interrelate particular details of each part of a reading assignment.
Internal	Prefers to work alone.	Require seatwork, projects, and assignments that do not depend on others for completion.
External	Prefers to work with others.	Assign group projects or reports, encourage study groups, create discussion groups.
Liberal	Prefers to work out own solution to problems.	Assign projects for which students must work out solution procedures. For example, identify and report on proposed legislation that concerns the environment.
Conservative	Prefers to do things according to established procedures.	Assign homework or projects that specify the steps, procedures, or rules for accomplishing the task.

SOURCE: Adapted from Sternberg (1994).

formulating more searching answers. To minimize this possibility, you may want to have an informal rotation scheme for recitation or sometimes require that everyone sit and think about a question for two or three minutes before answering. To give the impulsive style its place in the sun, you might schedule speed drills or question-and-answer sessions covering previously learned basic material.

To motivate students with a legislative style, have them describe what might have happened if a famous historical figure had acted differently than he or she did. For example, how might World War II have ended if President Harry Truman had decided *not* to drop the atomic bomb on Japan? To motivate students with a judicial style, have them compare and contrast the literary characters Tom Sawyer (from Mark Twain's novel of the same name) and Holden Caulfield (from J. D. Salinger's novel *Catcher in the Rye*).

To expand your thinking about teaching for various learning styles, see the Site-Based Cases section on this textbook site at **http://education.college.hmco.com/students**.

When you design your classroom assessments, keep in mind that multiple-choice tests, for example, match up nicely with the executive and conservative styles, while students with a legislative style are more likely to perform better on projects and performances. Try to use a variety of assessment methods on each test and across all the tests given during a term. You may also want to consider letting students choose the type of assessment they prefer. Another reason for using various teaching techniques and testing formats is that it may stimulate students to expand their own repertoire of learning styles (Sternberg, 1994). You might want to peruse Table 4.3 again to review which methods of instruction are most likely to fit which styles.

Teachers should use various test formats to measure accurately what students with various styles have learned

USING TECHNOLOGY TO ACCOMMODATE LEARNING STYLES

Just as technology can be used to strengthen different forms of intelligence, so can it target different learning styles. Certainly, simulations and **virtual reality** (computer-generated environments that mimic real-life situations) tools have the potential to make key concepts and principles more concrete, and multimedia technology can help students who prefer text communication, interactive visual displays, or auditory cues.

W. Patrick Dickson (1985) points out how visualizing mathematical equations and statistics allows visual learners to understand the material better and lets all learners move between different ways of representing information. By immediately presenting visual summaries of physical events, the microcomputer-based laboratory mentioned earlier in this book is a prime example of how technology might take advantage of multiple modalities. No longer are students left simply with masses of data; they can now see the data displayed visually or hear them. When this occurs, students are freer to process information in a way that is consistent with their learning style.

In a series of three studies, Roy Clariana (1997) found that computer-assisted learning environments shifted both early adolescent and adult learners toward preferring more active and concrete learning experiences—the types of experiences that many educators believe lead to more meaningful learning.

Gender Differences and Gender Bias

At the beginning of this chapter, we asked you to think about the ways in which friends and classmates over the past twelve or so years may have differed from one another. In all likelihood, you thought about how those people differed cognitively, socially, and emotionally. And with good reason. As we have seen so far in this chapter and in preceding ones, students' academic performance is strongly influenced by their cognitive, social, and emotional characteristics. But there is another major characteristic you may have ignored: gender. Although it may not be obvious, there are noticeable differences in the achievement patterns of males and females and in how they are taught. As Myra Sadker and David Sadker (1994) point out, "Sitting in the same classroom, reading the same textbook, listening to the same teacher, boys and girls receive very different educations" (p. 1). Just how different is the subject of the next few sections.

Gender Differences in Cognition and Achievement

Although there are reliable gender differences in cognitive functioning and achievement, they do not always favor one sex. On some tests, boys outscore girls, and on other tests girls have the upper hand (Halpern & LeMay, 2000; Marsh & Yeung, 1998). Although these differences are statistically significant (meaning they are probably not due to chance), they tend to be modest in size—about 10 to 15 percentile ranks.

Males outscore females on the following tests:

Boys score higher on tests of visual spatial ability, math reasoning; girls score higher on tests of memory, language skills

- *Visual-spatial ability.* This category includes tests of spatial perception, mental rotation, spatial visualization, and generation and maintenance of a spatial image. Male superiority in visual-spatial ability appears during the preschool years and persists throughout the life span.
- *Mathematical reasoning.* This difference may be related to males' superior visual-spatial skill.
- *College entrance.* Tests like the Scholastic Achievement Test (SAT) are designed to predict grade-point average after the freshman year of college. The superiority of males in this category may be related to differences in mathematical reasoning.

Females outscore males on the following tests:

- *Memory.* This is a broad category that includes memory for words from word lists, working memory (the number of pieces of information that one is aware of and that are available for immediate use), name-face associations, first-last name associations, memory for spatial locations, and episodic memory (memories for the events in one's own life). This difference appears to persist throughout the life span.
- *Language use.* This is another broad category that encompasses tests of spelling, reading comprehension, writing, onset of speech, and rate of vocabulary growth. Gender differences in language use appear anywhere between one and five years of age and grow larger over time. For example, the average difference in the size of males' and females' vocabulary at sixteen, twenty, and twenty-four months of age is 13, 51, and 115 words, respectively. On tests of reading comprehension, the gender gap also grows larger over time. By the senior year of high school, girls outscore boys by almost 10 percentile ranks. The superior scores that girls get on tests of writing are due in large part to the fact that their essays are better organized, more grammatically correct, and more logical. It is worth noting that although these writing skills would strike most people as being reflective of intelligence, they are not part of standardized tests of intelligence.

A 1999 study of mathematics achievement among eighth graders in thirty-eight countries concluded that most of the participating countries, including the United States, were making progress toward gender equity in mathematics education (Mullis et al., 2001). Among the major findings from this study were the following:

- In most countries, the mathematics achievement differences between boys and girls were statistically nonsignificant.
- Boys significantly outscored girls in only four countries: Israel, Czech Republic, Iran, and Tunisia.
- There was a modest overall significant difference in favor of boys.
- A slightly higher percentage of boys had scores above the median (the midpoint of a distribution) and above the 75th percentile.

Why do gender differences in cognition and achievement exist? No one knows for sure, although hormonal differences, differences in brain structure, and socialization differences are all thought to play a role. Despite increased awareness of how society reinforces gender-role stereotyping and measures taken to ensure greater gender equity, girls and boys continue to receive different messages about what is considered to be appropriate behavior. One source of influence that is being intensively studied is the peer group. During the middle childhood years (roughly ages six through nine), boys and girls are often under more pressure from their peers to exhibit gender-typed behaviors, in order to maintain the group's identity, than they are from their parents. But these observations do not answer the question of causation. Are gender differences the result of social pressures to participate in some activities and not others, or are socialization patterns the result of biological differences, or do both factors play a role? We simply do not know yet.

Although you should be aware of gender differences in cognitive functioning and should take steps to try to reduce them, you should also keep the following points in mind. First, there are many tasks for which differences do not exist. Second, some differences do not appear until later in development. For example, boys and girls have similar scores on tests of mathematical problem solving until adolescence, when boys begin to pull ahead. Third, what is true in general is not true of all individuals. Some boys score higher than most girls on tests of language use, and some girls score higher than most boys on tests of mathematical reasoning. Finally, as Robert Sternberg and Howard Gardner have argued, virtually all cognitive skills can be improved to some degree with the aid of well-designed instruction (Halpern, 1997).

Gender Bias

If you asked your class a question and some students answered without waiting to be called on, how do you think you would react? Do you think you would react differently to male students than to female students? Do not be so sure that you would not. Studies have found that teachers are more willing to listen to and accept the spontaneous answers of male students than female students. Female students are often reminded that they are to raise their hand and be recognized by the teacher before answering. Boys also receive more extensive feedback than do girls, but are punished more severely than girls for the same infraction. These consistent differences in response to male and female students when there is no sound educational reason for doing so are the essence of **gender bias.**

Gender bias: responding differently to male and female students without having sound educational reasons for doing so

Why do teachers react so differently to males and females? Probably because they are operating from traditional gender-role stereotypes: they expect boys to be more impulsive and unruly and girls to be more orderly and obedient (Matthews, Binkley, Crisp, & Gregg, 1998; Wellesley College Center for Research on Women, 1992).

Exposure to gender bias apparently begins early in a child's school life. Most preschool programs stress the importance of following directions and rules (impulse control) and contain many activities that facilitate small-muscle development and language skills. Because girls are typically better than boys in these areas before they go to preschool, the typical preschool experience does not help girls acquire new academically related skills and attitudes. For example, preschool-age girls are usually not as competent as boys at large-motor activities (such as jumping, climbing, throwing, and digging) or investigatory activities (such as turning over rocks or pieces of wood to see what is under them). Lest you think that climbing, digging, and investigating one's environment are trivial behaviors, bear in mind that they are critical to the work of scientists who do field research (for example, botanists, geologists, anthropologists, and oceanographers), occupations in which women are significantly underrepresented. Perhaps the designers of preschool curricula should make a greater effort to include these more male-oriented activities (Wellesley College Center for Research on Women, 1992).

Other students can be the source of gender bias as easily as the teacher can be. The authors of one study (Matthews et al., 1998) observed a fifth-grade classroom for four months and made the following observations:

- The class was divided into six small groups to work on ideas for a drug prevention program. Five of the groups chose a boy to deliver their report.
- On another occasion, the students worked in groups to create a machine that would produce both sounds and action. After each group demonstrated its machine, they called on other students to provide a name for it. Boys were called on thirty-one times, while girls were called on thirty times.
- After a science lab, a girl complained that the boys said that the way in which the girls were weighing items and comparing the weights was wrong. Another girl remarked that the boys did not want the girls to touch any of the equipment. On hearing this, one of the boys said that he thought the girls might drop or damage something.
- Boys were more likely than girls to name a boy as the best student in mathematics and science, while the girls usually named a girl as the best in English.
- Boys usually named another boy as the one who contributed most to class discussions, while girls named both boys and girls.

How Gender Bias Affects Students

Gender bias can affect course selection, career choice, and class participation of male and female students

Gender bias can affect students in at least three ways: the courses they choose to take, the careers they consider, and the extent to which they participate in class activities and discussions.

Course Selection There are modest but noticeable differences in the percentage of high school boys and girls who take math and science courses. In 1998, a larger percentage of girls than boys took algebra II (63.7 versus 59.8 percent) and trigonometry (9.7 versus 8.2 percent). Although there was no difference in the percentages of boys and girls who took geometry and precalculus, slightly more boys than girls took calculus (11.2 versus 10.6 percent). The pattern for science courses was similar. A larger percentage of girls than boys took biology (94.1 versus 91.4 percent), Advanced Placement or honors biology (18 versus 14.5 percent), and chemistry (63.5 versus 57.1 percent), while more boys than girls took physics (31.7 versus 26.2 percent) and engineering (7.1 versus 6.5 percent) (Bae, Choy, Geddes, Sable, & Snyder, 2000).

Women who choose a career in math or science are likely to be those who do well in science classes, are encouraged to pursue math or science careers by parents or teachers, and have respected models available to emulate.

Career Choice As you may be aware because of numerous stories in the media, relatively few girls choose careers in science or mathematics. For the 1996–97 academic year, more males than females earned bachelor's degrees in the biological sciences (5.7 versus 5.3 percent), computer and information sciences (3.5 versus 1.3 percent), physical sciences (2.3 versus 1.1 percent), engineering (12.0 versus 1.9 percent), and mathematics (1.3 versus 0.9 percent) (Bae *et al.*, 2000).

Several factors are thought to influence the choice male and female students make to pursue a career in science or engineering. One is familiarity with and interest in the tools of science. One study found that 51 percent of third-grade boys had used a microscope and 49 percent of eleventh-grade boys had used an electricity meter. The corresponding percentages for females were 37 percent and 17 percent, respectively (Wellesley College Center for Research on Women, 1992). In another study of middle school science classes that emphasized hands-on experiences by instructors who were committed to increasing girls' active participation, gender differences were noted. Boys spent more time than girls manipulating the equipment, thereby forcing girls to participate in more passive ways (Jovanovic & King, 1998).

A second factor is perceived self-efficacy (how confident one feels in being able to meet the demands of a task). In the middle school science classes just mentioned (Jovanovic & King, 1998), even though end-of-year science grades were equal for girls and boys, only girls showed a significant decrease in their perception of their science ability over the school year. A 1996 survey found that although fourth-grade boys and girls were equally confident about their math abilities, by twelfth grade only 47 percent of girls were confident about their math skills as compared to 59 percent of the boys (Bae et al., 2000).

A third factor is encouragement from parents and teachers. Girls who major in science in college cite the encouragement of teachers as an important factor in their decision (Wellesley College Center for Research on Women, 1992). The Case in Print describes how one school district is trying to interest more girls in computer science and related careers.

Supporting evidence for the roles of accomplishment, self-efficacy, and encouragement from others in pursuing a career in math or science comes from a recent study of fifteen women with established careers in math, science, or technology. Because there have always been women who have successfully carved out careers in math or science, Amy Zeldin and Frank Pajares (2000) wanted to know what sets them apart from equally qualified women who choose other fields. Zeldin and Pajares found that these fifteen women had very high levels of self-efficacy for math and science that could be traced to three sources: (1) early and consistent academic success, (2) encouragement to pursue math and science careers from such influential others as parents and teachers, and (3) the availability of respected models (both male and female) whom they could observe and model themselves after. All three sources working in concert appear necessary to persuade women to consider a career in math, science, or technology.

Academic success, encouragement, models influence women to choose careers in science, math

Class Participation As we pointed out earlier, many children tend to adopt the gender role that society portrays as the more appropriate and acceptable. Through the influence of parenting practices, advertising, peer norms, textbooks, and teaching practices, girls are reinforced for being polite, helpful, obedient, nonassertive, quiet, and aware of and responsive to the needs of others. Boys are reinforced for being assertive, independent, aggressive, competitive, intellectually curious, and achievement oriented. When females look at the world around them, they see relatively few women in positions of power and influence, relatively few women interviewed by the media for their opinion or expertise on various issues, and boys either ignoring or not taking seriously the suggestions and opinions offered by girls. The result, according to Carol Gilligan and others, is that adolescent girls learn to suppress their true personality and beliefs. Instead of saying what they really think about a topic, they say either that they have no opinion or what they think others want to hear. Gilligan refers to this behavior as **loss of voice** (Harter, Waters, & Whitesell, 1997).

Loss of voice: students suppress true beliefs about various topics in the presence of parents, teachers, and classmates of opposite sex

To measure the extent of loss of voice in different contexts, Susan Harter, Patricia Waters, and Nancy Whitesell gave questionnaires to several hundred students of both genders in grades 6 through 12. The questionnaire items asked students to rate how honestly they voiced their ideas when they were in the presence of teachers, male classmates, female classmates, parents, and close friends. Their main findings were:

- Males and females are most likely to speak their mind when they are with close friends and classmates of the same gender and are less likely to do so when they are in the presence of members of the opposite gender, parents, and teachers.
- Loss of voice did not increase between grades 6 and 12.
- Equal numbers of males and females reported suppressing their true thoughts in certain circumstances.
- Girls who strongly identified with the stereotypical female gender role were more likely than androgynous females (those who exhibit behaviors that are characteristic of both gender roles) to suppress their true thoughts when interacting with their teachers and male classmates. This difference between feminine and androgynous females disappeared with close friends and parents.
- Androgynous males and females who said they were frequently encouraged and supported by teachers for expressing their views were most likely to speak their mind in classroom and other settings.

These findings have major implications for the way in which teachers address female students, particularly those who have adopted a strong feminine gender role, and for the use of constructivist approaches to teaching (discussed in detail in the chapter "Approaches to Instruction"). Because constructivism relies heavily on free and open discussion to produce its effects, teachers need to monitor carefully the verbal exchanges that occur among students and to intervene when necessary to ensure that all students feel that their opinions are getting a fair and respectful hearing.

Working Toward Gender Equity in the Classroom

Although much of the literature on gender bias highlights the classroom obstacles that make it difficult for girls to take full advantage of their talents, gender equity is about producing an educational experience that will be equally meaningful for students of both genders. Susan McGee Bailey (1996), who has written extensively about gender issues in education, suggests the following three techniques to benefit both genders.

1. Use work arrangements and reward systems that will encourage all students to value a thorough understanding of a subject or task and that emphasize group success as well as individual accomplishment. In the chapter "Approaches to Instruction," we will describe how a technique called cooperative learning does just this.

Correcting Gender Bias

Gender bias can affect students in at least three ways: the courses they choose to take, the careers they consider, and the extent to which they participate in class activities and discussions. . . . As you may be aware because of numerous stories in the media, relatively few girls choose careers in science or mathematics. Among high school seniors from Rhode Island, 64 percent of the males who had taken physics and calculus were planning to major in science or engineering in college compared to only 18.6 percent of the females who had taken the same courses. . . . Several factors are thought to influence the choice male and female students make to pursue a career in science or engineering. One is familiarity with and interest in the tools of science.

Girl-Powered

CAROLYN BOWER

St. Louis Post-Dispatch 12/1/2000

Eighteen girls meet once a week at Sappington Elementary School, just west of Grant's Farm in southwest St. Louis County, to discuss binary codes, circuits and computer chips.

The girls, all fifth-graders, come from public and parochial schools throughout the Lindbergh School District. One recent afternoon, they took apart six computers and put them back together, installing CD-ROMs, sound cards and network cards. In a few weeks, they plan to assemble more computers. Then they'll begin to design web pages.

Laurice Badino, a gifted-education teacher at Sappington, 11011 Gravois Road, began the after-school class this fall as a way to interest girls in technology and computer science.

"With such a focus on technology in our world and in schools, you would think girls would continue to pursue this as they get older, but they don't," Badino said.

Federal statistics indicate that women hold only 28 percent of technical jobs, even though the number of women in the work force approaches 50 percent. Less than one in every five people who took Advanced Placement computer science tests last year was a woman. Women also made up less than a third of workers in computer and math jobs, according to the U.S. Bureau of Labor Statistics. Yet information technology jobs are among the fastest-growing occupations.

Badino has taught off and on for twenty years, the past four in the Lindbergh district.

At a recent class, she instructed the girls to hook up power supplies to hard drives. "It only goes in one way, so don't force it," Badino said.

The girls worked in teams of two or three to a computer.

Riley Krus, ten, had come to the class from St. Justin the Martyr School, where she attends fifth grade.

"Two weeks ago, we learned about binary boards and ASCII," she said. "They're both fun."

Students have learned to format hard drives and discs. They also learned about components of circuits, such as microprocessors, capacitors and light-emitting diodes. They learned that an example of a light-emitting diode is when a light signals the use of a computer hard drive.

At the other end of a table from Riley, Ariana Black, ten, a fifth-grader at Truman Elementary School, used a screwdriver and easily installed a CD-ROM in the computer. But Ariana cautioned she was not quite ready to take apart her home computer, which runs Windows 98.

Lindbergh school Superintendent James Sandfort said the girls' focus, concentration and technical skill impressed him.

"We hope that as these girls move up through the grades, they will move toward technical programs rather than away from them," Sandfort said. "When my computer shuts down, I know where to bring it now. These girls have no fear."

Badino would like to see some of her students become CEOs of computer companies some day—or at least be open to taking computer courses in high school and college.

"Now they can tell the boys how things work," Badino said.

Kara Jacquin, eleven, who also attends Truman, said she was intrigued by how the separate parts of a computer flow together.

"I wouldn't mind being smarter than the boys," Kara added.

Questions and Activities

1. This article describes several environmental influences on learning and classroom behavior and at least one innate factor. List these various influences and factors. Then describe how they might interact with one another to affect your students' learning differently depending on their gender. Is your description consistent with your own experience as a student? Why or why not?
2. The program described in this article indicates that girls can be successful at and enjoy science and technology activities if certain classroom conditions are established. Is a girls-only program the only way to meet this goal? If not, is it the best way? On what evidence or experience (or both) do you base your conclusion?
3. Kara Jacquin, the eleven-year-old girl quoted at the end of the article, said that she "wouldn't mind being smarter than the boys." Why do you think she, and presumably many of the other girls in her class, believe that boys are smarter than girls with respect to computer science? In addition to programs like the one described in this article, what other ideas can you come up with to ensure that girls think of themselves as equal in ability to boys in math and science?

2. Emphasize materials that highlight the accomplishments and characteristics of women (such as Hillary Rodham Clinton, Oprah Winfrey, and Sandra Day O'Connor) and women's groups.
3. Talk about the practical, everyday applications of math and science. Although girls seem more interested in science when they understand how such knowledge transfers to everyday life, so do many boys. Nobody suffers when the curriculum is made more meaningful and relevant.

Charles Rop (1998) describes how Anna Kasov, a veteran high school teacher, teaches introductory chemistry. In high school and college, Kasov found science to be a male-dominated profession that did not go out of its way to make women students feel comfortable or accepted. Consequently, her goal as a teacher is to combat the message that chemistry is not women's work and that interesting women are not scientists by creating a supportive atmosphere in her classroom. To accomplish her goal, Kasov (1) models how scientists think (formulate hypotheses about chemical processes, conduct experiments, use that evidence to support your hypotheses) and encourages students to do the same, (2) requires that students treat each others' ideas with respect, and (3) attends to how frequently girls and boys contribute to class discussions and to the nature of the contributions.

As Kasov and others have pointed out, science becomes more interesting for all students, but for girls in particular, when they understand its relevance. The following quotation from Kasov about her own college experience is instructive:

> One of the things that I vividly remember is sitting in this lecture going through these biochemical cycles. I wondered where this happens—in the cell, in the nucleus, in the mitochondria? The guy didn't even bother to tell us. We were counting ATPs somewhere and I thought, "This is so stupid. I have no idea what this has to do with anything." (p. 60)

Consequently, Kasov recommends giving girls opportunities to manipulate technology, deemphasizing competition in favor of collaborative problem solving, showing how the products of chemical research affect the everyday lives of people, and integrating chemical concepts with other subjects, such as history, literature, and the arts.

GENDER DIFFERENCES AND TECHNOLOGY: OVERCOMING THE GAP

In the 1980s, when desktop computers first started appearing in classrooms, surveys showed that females were less likely than males to use a computer at both school and home. That difference has all but disappeared among primary and elementary grade students. A national survey of kindergarten through sixth-grade students in 1997 found that about 75 percent of males and females reported using a computer at school and about 40 percent of both sexes reported using a computer at home (Bae et al., 2000).

Gender differences still exist, however, for the ways in which computers are used. More females than males use computers for such school-related activities as word processing (28 versus 22 percent), graphics and design (17.4 versus 14.3 percent), and educational programs (50.4 versus 48 percent). The largest difference in favor of the males was for the category of playing games (90.5 of males versus 88.7 percent of females) (Bae et al., 2000).

Females and males have equal access to computers, but females use them more for school-related purposes

The picture at the middle and high school levels is both similar and different. There was no difference in the percentage of eighth and eleventh graders in 1996 who reported using a computer every day at school, but there was a gender difference in frequency of use. At both grade levels, males used computers more often than females did (Bae et al., 2000). A 1998 national survey of eighth, tenth, and twelfth graders found that just as with younger students, females were more likely than males to use a computer for school-related activities, with the largest difference (32 percent of females versus 23 percent of males) occurring among twelfth graders (Libsch & Breslow, 2000).

Significant gender differences have also been found in student preferences for such computer-based environments as the Internet, CD-ROMs, web-based conferencing, videoconferencing, and teleconferencing. Female students favor more traditional methods of instruction and have less favorable perceptions of computer-based technology than do male students (Proost, Elen, & Lowyck, 1997). Such gender differences certainly strip away a tremendous number of learning opportunities for the female population. As Joella Gipson (1997) notes, these women will be less prepared to contribute to and profit from our increasingly technological society.

Although this computer technology gap often does not appear until the teenage years (Martin, Heller, & Mahmoud, 1992), gender differences do appear at lower grade levels. A recent study revealed that boys as young as first grade are often more aggressive and rude to girls in criticizing their computing choices and products, thereby shaking young girls' confidence (Nicholson, Gelpi, Young, & Sulzby, 1998). Not surprisingly, females perform better when using computers with females nearby than with a male audience (Corston & Colman, 1996).

What can be done to reduce the gender gap? Several steps have been recommended (Gipson, 1997; Koch, 1994; Nicholson et al., 1998; Sanders, 1985):

- Because the research literature indicates that early positive experiences with computers are central to later success, teachers' attitudes and actions must demonstrate that the computer is equally important to both genders.
- As computer technology expands in schools, teachers and administrators should try to embed it in reading, writing, history, and literature curricula, not just in math and science.
- Girls need more role models of female computer users in their schools and the workplace.

- Parents may need training in raising their mathematical and technological expectations of their female children, as well as advice on the role of computer technology in the home.
- Some scholars recommend computer camps, programs, and classes just for girls to interest them in science and technology careers.
- Because males tend to dominate open computer workstations during free choice time, teachers might increase access time or require turn-taking practices on the computer.
- Schools and teachers need to establish policies on software, thereby avoiding purchase of the more violent and insulting or demeaning products. They might choose to select new software games with female main characters and computer tools that appeal to girls.

The Suggestions for Teaching that follow will help you better respond to differences in intelligence, learning styles, and gender.

Suggestions for Teaching in Your Classroom

Addressing Student Differences

1 Design lessons and test items that call for memory, analytical, creative, and practical abilities.

Robert Sternberg (1997a) has pointed out that many teachers tend to emphasize memory and analytical abilities, which is fine for students who are good at memorizing facts or breaking things down into their component parts and explaining how the parts relate to each other. But students whose abilities are in the creative or practical areas may appear to be less capable than they really are. You can get a better idea of each student's strengths and weaknesses and how well students have learned the subject matter you just taught by using a variety of instructional cues and test items.

To emphasize students' memory abilities when you teach and test, use prompts such as:

"Who said . . . ?"
"Summarize the ideas of . . ."
"Who did . . . ?"
"When did . . . ?"
"How did . . . ?"
"Describe . . ."

To emphasize students' analytical abilities, use prompts like:

"Why in your judgment . . . ?"
"Explain why . . ."
"Explain what caused . . ."
"Critique . . ."

To emphasize creative abilities, use prompts like:

"Imagine . . ."
"Design . . ."

Figure 5.1 Projected Change in Percentage of School-Age Children for Four Ethnic Groups Between 2001 and 2020

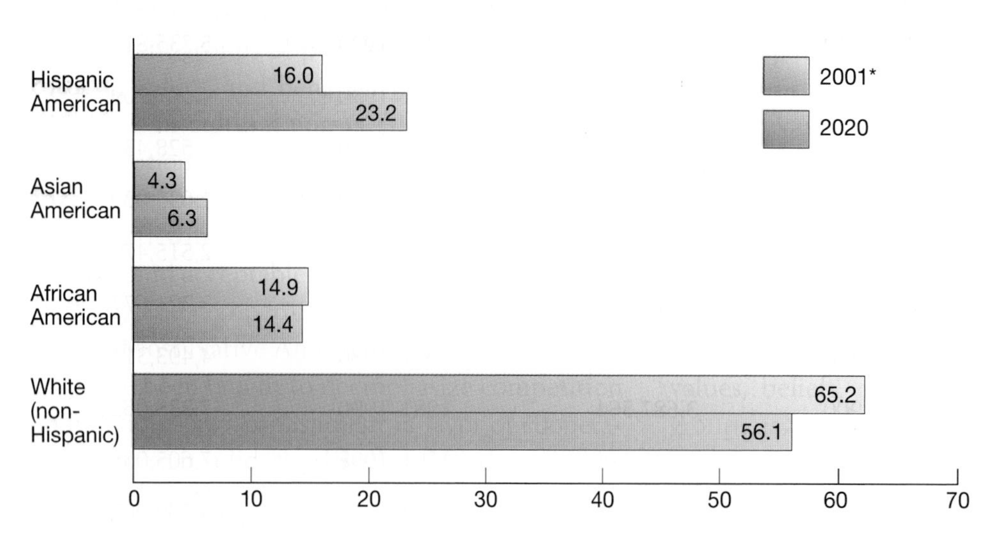

SOURCE: U. S. Bureau of the Census (2000b).

*Because of rounding errors, percentages for 2001 do not add up to exactly 100 percent.

fact that immigrant mothers have a higher birthrate than native-born mothers. As of 1998, native-born women averaged 59 births per 1,000, while foreign-born women averaged 72.8 per 1,000 (U.S. Bureau of the Census, 2000a).

These immigration and birthrate patterns are expected to have a significant effect over the next two decades on the makeup of the school-age population (see Figure 5.1). According to Census Bureau projections, the populations of Hispanic American and Asian American school children will increase rapidly, raising their combined percentage of the school-age population to about 30 percent. African American school-age children will also increase in numbers, although their proportion of the overall school population will remain at 14 to 15 percent. The proportion of white non-Hispanic school children will fall from 65 percent to 56 percent. As these figures make clear, the United States is rapidly on its way to becoming an even more ethnically diverse nation than ever before.

U.S. becoming more culturally diverse because of changes in immigration, birthrates

Taking Account of Your Students' Cultural Differences

As we pointed out in the opening paragraphs of this chapter, culture refers to the way in which a group of people perceives, thinks about, and interacts with the world. It provides a set of norms that guide what we say and how we say it, what we

Culture: how a group of people perceives, believes, thinks, behaves

feel, and what we do in various situations. Two significant factors that most readily distinguish one culture from another are ethnicity and social class.

Because of the demographic changes occurring in the United States, teachers must be familiar with the similarities and differences of students from different ethnic groups and social classes. But for you and your students to benefit from your knowledge of cultural diversity, you must view it in the proper perspective. The perspective we encourage you to adopt has three aspects.

1. *You should recognize that differences are not necessarily deficits.* Students who subscribe to different value systems and exhibit different communication patterns, time orientations, learning modes, motives, and aspirations should not be viewed as incapable. Looking on ethnic and social class differences as deficits usually stems from an attitude called *ethnocentrism*. This is the tendency of people to think of their own culture as superior to the culture of other groups. You may be able to moderate your ethnocentric tendencies and motivate your students to learn by consciously using instructional tactics that are congruent with the different cultural backgrounds of your students.

Ethnocentrism: belief that one's own culture is superior to other cultures

2. *You need to recognize that the groups we and others describe with a general label are frequently made up of subgroups with somewhat different characteristics.* These subgroups, in fact, may use different labels to refer to themselves. Among Native Americans, for example, Navajos differ from the Hopi in physical appearance, dress, and hairstyle. Individuals who are called *Hispanic* often refer to themselves as either *Chicano, Latino, Mexicano, of Mexican descent,* or *of Spanish descent* (Losey, 1995).

3. *Although our descriptions of various ethnic groups may accurately portray some general tendencies of a large group of people, they may apply only partly or not at all to given individuals.* One must always be careful in applying general knowledge to particular cases. The Mexican American high school student who vehemently opposes abortion, for example, may do so more because of his Roman Catholic faith than because of cultural values concerning family relationships (Chinn & Plata, 1987–1988).

The Effect of Ethnicity on Learning

An **ethnic group** is a collection of people who identify with one another on the basis of one or more of the following characteristics: country from which one's ancestors came, race, religion, language, values, political interests, economic interests, and behavior patterns (Banks, 2001; Gollnick & Chinn, 1998). Viewed separately, the ethnic groups in the United States, particularly those of color, are numerical minorities; collectively, however, they constitute a considerable portion of American society (Banks, 2001). Most Americans identify with some ethnic group (Irish Americans, German Americans, Italian Americans, African Americans, Chinese Americans, and Hispanic Americans, to name but a few). As a teacher, you need to know how your students' ethnicity can affect student-teacher relationships.

Christine Bennett (1999) identifies five aspects of ethnicity that are potential sources of student-student and student-teacher misunderstanding: verbal communication, nonverbal communication, time orientation, social values, and instructional formats and learning processes.

Verbal Communication Patterns Problems with verbal communication can occur in a number of ways. Verbal exchanges in the classroom typically take the following form: the teacher elicits a comment from a student by either making a to determine if there is any truth to the common perception that Japanese students tend to be literal learners who emphasize memorizing at the expense of their own views and interpretations. People who believe this description attribute it to the emphasis in Japanese culture on subordination of individual viewpoints to the group's perceptions and goals.

Purdie and Hattie found that the Japanese students they interviewed chose memorizing as their preferred learning process, while a similar group of Australian students gave it a very low preference rating (eighteenth out of twenty-four options). A group of Japanese students who had been living in Australia for almost three years at the time of the study were in between these two extremes.

These findings suggest that although cultural background does influence choice of learning activity, the effects of culture seem to diminish as one becomes more accustomed to and comfortable with the values and practices of another culture.

The Effect of Social Class on Learning

The social class from which a student comes plays an influential role in behavior. **Social class** is an indicator of an individual's or a family's relative standing in society. It is determined by such factors as annual income, occupation, amount of education, place of residence, types of organizations to which family members belong, manner of dress, and material possessions. The first three factors are used by the federal government to determine the closely related concept of **socioeconomic status (SES).** The influence of social class is such that the members of working-class Hispanic American and Irish American families may have more in common than the members of an upper-middle-class Hispanic American family and those of a working-class Hispanic American family (Gollnick & Chinn, 1998).

Because of the severe and long-lasting historic pattern of discrimination experienced by ethnic groups of color in the United States, many members of these groups have fewer years of education, a less prestigious occupation, and a lower income than the average white person. Significantly, more African American, Hispanic American, and Native American adolescents drop out of high school than do whites, thereby shortening their years of education. And because they have less education, people of color are more likely to be unemployed or working in such low-paying occupations as office clerk, private house cleaner, and manual laborer.

Poverty rates higher for ethnic families of color than for whites

In 1999, 16.9 percent of American children under age eighteen lived in families with incomes below the poverty level. Although most such children are white (meaning of European ancestry), Figure 5.2 shows that the poverty rates among African American, Native American, and Hispanic American families are usually about three times higher than that for white children (U.S. Bureau of the Census, 2000c).

Many low-SES students are what might be called educationally disadvantaged or educationally at risk because they are continually exposed to various adverse factors that inhibit physical, social, emotional, and intellectual development. Before you read about some of these factors in the following paragraphs, we caution you to keep in mind that these differences appear to be largely due to environmental causes. On tests of cognitive development comparing low-SES children with those from more advantaged homes, significant score differences do not appear until after two years of age (Sanders-Phillips, 1989).

1. *Many low-SES Americans do not receive satisfactory health care.* For example, African American women have a high level of such pregnancy complications as toxemia, hemorrhage, hypertension, heart disease, infection, and diabetes. In addition, inadequate diets during pregnancy are common (Sanders-Phillips, 1989). As a con-

Figure 5.2 Percentage of Families Within Ethnic Groups Living Below Poverty Level in 1999

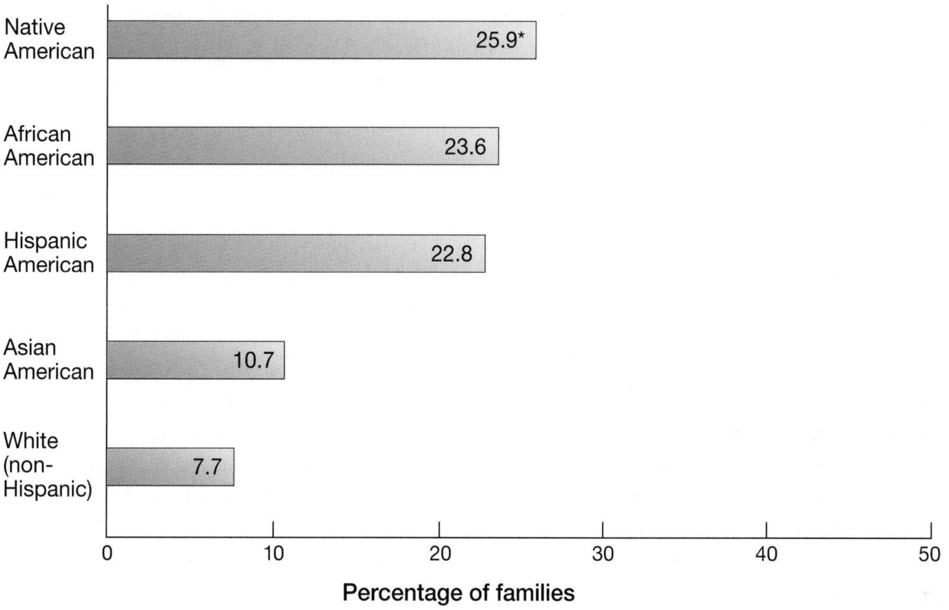

	Percentage of families
Native American	25.9*
African American	23.6
Hispanic American	22.8
Asian American	10.7
White (non-Hispanic)	7.7

0 10 20 30 40 50

Percentage of families

SOURCE: U.S. Bureau of Census (2000c).

*The average from 1997 to 1999.

sequence, there is a greater incidence of premature births, birth defects, and infant mortality among low-SES children as compared to middle-class children (as consistently revealed by National Institutes of Health statistics). Because poor children do not receive medical or dental care regularly, accurate statistics on general health are difficult to compile. It seems reasonable to assume, however, that the same inadequate nutrition and health care that leads to elevated infant mortality rates probably also leads to higher rates of illness in later years. In other words, low-SES children probably continue to suffer from untreated illnesses at a rate that may be at least twice that of middle-class children (Sanders-Phillips, 1989).

Another health-related factor in the development and intellectual performance of low-SES children is lead poisoning. Because many of these children live in homes that were painted prior to the discontinuation of lead-based paint, their ingestion of paint dust and chips leads to elevated levels of lead in the blood. Exposure to lead, even in small amounts, is associated with low standardized test scores, attention deficits, and disruptive behavior in children. Almost 37 percent of African American children and 17 percent of Mexican American children between the ages of one and five have lead levels in their blood that are associated with cognitive impairments and behavioral problems. These impairments need not be permanent, however: medication can reduce the level of lead in the blood, leading to an improvement in the children's academic performance (Jackson, 1999).

2. *Educationally disadvantaged students are more likely than middle-class students to grow up in one-parent families (the father usually being the missing parent).* Like many other risk factors, the effect of a one-parent family on the academic performance of a child is not straightforward. It depends on such factors as the duration and cause of the separation, the age and sex of the child, and the type of interactions the child has with the remaining parent. But although one-parent families may not negatively affect a child's performance in school, two-parent families are likely to be more effective because both parents have the potential to exert a positive influence (Levine & Levine, 1996).

Low-SES children more likely to live in stressful environment that interferes with studying

3. *Many low-SES students, especially those in urban areas, live in relatively small, and sometimes overcrowded, apartments.* Adequate study space is often nonexistent, and parental supervision is spotty or absent. In their neighborhoods, street crime is a constant threat (Levine & Levine, 1996).

4. *Educationally disadvantaged children typically have not been exposed to a wide variety of experiences.* Compared with the parents of low-SES children, the parents of middle-class children in the United States tend to buy their children more books, educational toys, and games and take them on more trips that expand their knowledge of the world. These experiences accumulate and make school learning more familiar and easy than it would otherwise be. A child who has not had such experiences is likely to be at a disadvantage when placed in competitive academic situations (Levine & Levine, 1996). Furthermore, there has been increasing concern about the development of a technological underclass of children whose families cannot afford to provide access to computers and online services at home.

5. *The interactions that occur between low-SES parents and their children tend to lack the characteristic of mediation* (a concept we introduced earlier in the book in connection with Vygotsky's theory of cognitive development). When mediation occurs, someone who is more intellectually advanced than the learner presents, explains, and interprets stimuli in a way that produces a more meaningful understanding than the learner could have obtained working alone. A parent or older sibling, for example, may mediate by discussing objects, ideas, or events that are separated in time or space and pointing out their similarities and differences; presenting a set of seemingly different objects and explaining how they all belong to the same category; and providing some sort of context for an idea that allows the child to connect that idea to his or her life.

To illustrate this process, imagine a child walking alone through a hands-on science museum looking at the various exhibits, occasionally pushing the buttons of interactive displays, and listening to some of the prerecorded messages. What the child learns from this experience is likely to be a haphazard collection of isolated fragments of information that are not meaningful. Now imagine another child of the same age looking at and interacting with the same exhibits but accompanied by a parent or older sibling who wants this to be a meaningful learning experience. The parent or sibling points out specific aspects of the displays, names them, describes their purpose, and explains how they work. This child is more likely than the first child to construct a set of cohesive, interrelated, and meaningful knowledge structures (Ben-Hur, 1998).

Educationally disadvantaged children often have low motivation to achieve

6. *Many low-SES students may not be strongly motivated to do well in school because of lower levels of a characteristic called* need for achievement. A need for achievement (which is discussed more fully in our chapter on motivation) is a drive to accomplish tasks and is thought to be one of the main reasons that people vary in their willingness to invest time and energy in the achievement of a goal. Recent research suggests that low-SES African American students score lower than comparable groups of white students on tests of need for achievement, but this racial difference is considerably smaller among middle-class samples (Cooper & Dorr, 1995).

Low-SES males often place a low value on academic achievement

7. *Many low-SES students, particularly African American males, do not place a high value on academic achievement.* Sandra Graham (1997) found that African American middle school female students admired, respected, and wanted to be like their female classmates who got good grades and followed school rules, indicating that these girls valued effort and achievement. But the responses of the boys were quite different. They were least likely to nominate their high-achieving classmates as individuals whom they admired, respected, and wanted to emulate. This gender difference appears to be valid; Graham has replicated it in two other samples of African American adolescents. Graham notes that data from other studies indicate that African American males recognize the importance of working hard and fulfilling one's potential. But for reasons that are not yet understood, many of them adopt an indifferent attitude toward high levels of school achievement. (The views of Marc Elrich's sixth-grade students, which we will discuss in a moment, provide a possible explanation.)

8. *Educationally disadvantaged students may have no definite career plans after leaving school and may be limited to low-paying, dead-end jobs, resulting in low self-esteem (Pollard, 1993).* But a perceived scarcity of attractive employment opportunities does not automatically lead to low self-esteem. Recent evidence (van Laar, 2000) shows that many African American high school and college students score as high on measures of self-esteem as do whites even though the African American students had lower levels of achievement. This seeming paradox results from minority students' believing that because of discrimination, they will not have available to them the same opportunities for employment and career advancement that are available to white students. Being able to blame the environment rather than oneself allows one to maintain a healthy sense of self-esteem. This perception may also play a role in minorities' lower need for achievement scores (mentioned in point 5).

A clear and chilling example of the last three characteristics is offered by Marc Elrich (1994), a sixth-grade teacher in a Maryland school district just outside Washington, D.C. His class of twenty-nine students was composed almost entirely of African American and Hispanic American low-SES youths who saw no value in education and who exhibited low self-esteem and low expectations. To prompt a discussion of self-esteem, he showed them a film based on a Langston Hughes story about an African American youth who attempts to steal the purse of an elderly African American woman. He fails, and the woman takes him into her home, where she tries to change his attitudes and behavior. The message of the film is that with love, we all learn that we have it within ourselves to be better people. When Elrich asked for reactions to the film, this exchange occurred:

Student: As soon as you see a black boy, you know he's gonna do something bad.

Teacher: Just because he's black, he's bad?

Student: Everybody knows that black people are bad. That's the way we are. (p. 12)

When Elrich asked who else agreed with that assessment, twenty-four students raised their hands. Further discussion revealed that most of the students agreed with the following statements:

- Blacks are poor and stay poor because they're dumber than whites (and Asians).
- Black people don't like to work hard.
- Black men make women pregnant and leave.
- Black boys expect to die young and unnaturally.
- White people are smart and have money.
- Asians are smart and have money.
- Asians don't like blacks or Hispanics.

- Hispanics are more like blacks than whites. They can't be white so they try to be black.
- Hispanics are poor and don't try hard because, like blacks, they know it doesn't matter. They will be like blacks because when you're poor, you have to be bad to survive. (p. 13)

According to Elrich (1994), his students' view of the world was that

> hard work does not equal success in their world; instead, it means that parents are gone and children take care of children, they told us. The people who have the material goods that reflect the good life get their money through guns and drugs. Wimps die young and live in fear. Tough guys die young but are proud. Bosses are white and workers are black, and black people don't do important things, except in school books. In their world, few aspire to be doctors, scientists, or lawyers. (p. 14)

During the course of the year, Elrich prompted discussions of slavery, racism, and class. In an attempt to help his students understand that the effects of bigotry and racism are not necessarily permanent, he pointed out that two hundred years ago, life for most whites was harsh and not terribly free, especially in Europe, and that ideas about race and class were taught and promoted in the interest of a few—primarily very wealthy and privileged—white men. But over time and with persistent effort, many of these barriers to personal advancement were either eliminated or drastically reduced. Therefore, his students could influence what they became if they worked at doing so.

The Effect of Ethnicity and Social Class on Teachers' Expectations

So far we have described how students' ethnic and social class backgrounds influence their approach to and success with various learning tasks. Now we would like to tell you how those and other characteristics often affect (consciously and unconsciously) the expectations that teachers have for student performance and how those expectations affect the quantity and quality of work that students exhibit. This phenomenon has been extensively studied since 1968 and is known variously as the *Pygmalion effect*, the *self-fulfilling prophecy*, and the **teacher expectancy effect.** By becoming aware of the major factors that influence teachers' perceptions of and actions toward students, you may be able to reduce subjectivity to a minimum, particularly with students whose cultural backgrounds are very different from your own.

Teacher expectancy (Pygmalion) effect: impact of teacher expectations leads to self-fulfilling prophecy

The teacher expectancy effect basically works as follows:

1. On the basis of such characteristics as race, SES, ethnic background, dress, speech pattern, and test scores, teachers form expectancies about how various students will perform in class.
2. They subtly communicate those expectancies to the students in a variety of ways.
3. Students come to behave in a way that is consistent with what the teacher expects.

This phenomenon was first proposed by Robert Rosenthal and Lenore Jacobson in their 1968 book, *Pygmalion in the Classroom*. They described an experiment in which first- through sixth-grade teachers were led to believe that certain children had untapped potential and were "likely to show unusual intellectual gains in the year ahead" because of their scores on a new kind of ability test. In fact, the test was composed of standard items, and the designated students were chosen at random. Nevertheless, Rosenthal and Jacobson reported that the students who were labeled potential achievers showed significant gains in intelligence quotient (IQ) and that the reason for these gains was that their teachers expected more of these students. The authors referred to this phenomenon as the Pygmalion effect because they felt that teacher expectations had influenced the students to become intelligent in the same way that the expectations of the mythical Greek sculptor Pygmalion caused a statue he had carved to come to life.

Research on the Effects of Teachers' Expectancies Given the obvious implications of the teacher expectancy effect for shaping student behavior, researchers wasted no time investigating its validity and limits. Despite the dramatic results that Rosenthal and Jacobson reported, subsequent research showed that the effect of teacher expectancy on IQ scores was essentially limited to first- and second-grade students, was moderate in strength at those grade levels, and occurred only when it was induced within the first two weeks of the school year (Raudenbush, 1984). Apparently, once teachers have had an opportunity to observe and interact with their students, they view these experiences as more credible and informative than the results of a mental ability test.

Limited effect of teacher expectancy on IQ scores

But research that has investigated the effect of teacher expectancy on classroom achievement and participation has generally found sizable positive *and* negative effects (for example, Braun, 1976; Brophy, 1983; Cooper, 1979; Rosenthal, 1985). In addition, it appears that teacher expectations are more likely to maintain already existing tendencies than to alter well-established behaviors drastically. For example, primary grade teachers react differently to students in the fast-track reading group than to students in the slow-track group. When working with the more proficient readers, teachers tend to smile, lean toward the students, and establish eye contact more often, and they tend to give criticism in friendlier, gentler tones than they use in the slow-track group. They often overlook the oral reading errors of proficient readers, and when they give corrections, they do so at the end of the sentence or other meaningful unit rather than in the middle of such units. And they ask comprehension questions more often than factual questions as a means of monitoring students' attention to the reading selection.

Strong effect of teacher expectancy on achievement, participation

In contrast, teachers correct less proficient readers more often and in places that interrupt meaningful processing of the text, give these students less time to decode difficult words or to correct themselves, and ask low-level factual questions as a way of checking on students' attention. Teachers' body posture is often characterized by frowning, pursing the lips, shaking the head, pointing a finger, and sitting erect. In sum, through a variety of subtle ways, teachers communicate to students that they expect them to perform well or poorly and then create a situation that is consistent with the expectation. As a result, initial differences between good and poor readers either remain or widen over the course of the school career (Wuthrick, 1990).

Factors That Help Create Expectancies In addition to documenting the existence of teacher expectancy effects and the conditions under which they occur, researchers have sought to identify the factors that might create high or low teacher expectations. Here are some important factors taken from analyses by Carl Braun (1976), Gloria Ladson-Billings (1994), Vonnie McLoyd (1998), and Sonia Nieto (2000):

Teacher expectancies influenced by social class, ethnic background, achievement, attractiveness, gender

- Middle-class students are expected to receive higher grades than low-SES students, even when their IQ scores and achievement test scores are similar.
- African American students are given less attention and are expected to learn less than white students, even when both groups have the same ability.
- Teachers tend to perceive children from poor homes as less mature, less capable of following directions, and less capable of working independently than children from more advantaged homes.

In order for children to understand and appreciate different cultural values and experiences, those values and experiences have to be integrated into the curriculum and rewarded by the teacher.

Culture: What ethnic elements (for example, values, customs, perspectives) are present in the group's culture today? How is the group's culture reflected in its music, literature, and art?

Identity: To what extent does the group see itself as separate and apart from other groups in society because of its unique history?

Perspectives: To what extent do most members of the group hold the same view on an issue of importance to it?

Ethnic institutions: What educational, commercial, religious, and social organizations were formed by members of the group to help satisfy its needs?

Demographic, social, political, and economic status: How can the current status of the group be described in terms of numbers, political influence, and income?

Racism and discrimination: In what ways has this group been subjected to racism and discrimination?

Intraethnic diversity: How do members of the group differ from each other in terms of such major characteristics as geographical location, social class, religion, and political affiliation?

Acculturation: To what extent has the group influenced and been influenced by the mainstream society?

Characteristics of Effective Multicultural Teachers

Although Banks's ideas about how to structure multicultural education programs are well conceived, they require the efforts of effective teachers for their potential benefits to be realized. Eugene García (1999), on the basis of his own research and that of others, identifies several characteristics that contribute to the success some teachers have in teaching students from culturally diverse backgrounds. Briefly stated, the effective multicultural teacher:

Advocates of multicultural education believe that ethnic minority students learn more effectively when some of their learning materials and assignments contain ethnically related content.

Interested in the experiences of actual teachers in culturally diverse classrooms? See the Site-Based Cases section on the textbook site at **http://education.college.hmco.com/students**.

1. Provides students with clear objectives.
2. Continuously communicates high expectations to the student.
3. Monitors student progress and provides immediate feedback.
4. Has several years of experience in teaching culturally diverse students.
5. Can clearly explain why she uses specific instructional techniques (like the ones described in the next section).
6. Strives to embed instruction in a meaningful context. For example, a topic from one subject, such as controlling crop-damaging insects with insecticide, could be extended to other subjects (examining the effects of insecticide on human health, graphing crop yields sprayed with various types and amounts of insecticides).
7. Provides opportunities for active learning through small-group work and hands-on activities. One teacher, for example, created writing workshops in which students wrote, revised, edited, and published their products for others to read.
8. Exhibits a high level of dedication. Effective multicultural teachers are among the first to arrive at school and among the last to leave, work weekends, buy supplies with their own money, and are constantly looking for opportunities to improve their instructional practices.
9. Enhances students' self-esteem by having classroom materials and practices reflect students' cultural and linguistic backgrounds.
10. Has a strong affinity for the students. Effective multicultural teachers describe their culturally diverse students in such terms as "I love these children like my own" and "We are a family here."

Instructional Goals, Methods, and Materials

Teachers whose classes have a high percentage of children from ethnic minority and low-SES backgrounds often assume that they need to emphasize mastery of basic skills (such as computation, spelling, grammar, and word decoding) because minority and low-SES students are often deficient in those skills. Although this approach does improve children's performance on tests of basic skills, some educators argue

Computer-based technology helps students learn more about other cultures and social classes by providing access to various reference sources and individuals from almost anywhere in the world.

Seattle did (Golub, 1994)? What an incredible opportunity for students to gain access to new information, analyze and evaluate it, and communicate their own insights and ideas.

The 4Directions Project is another significant example. Developed by a consortium of nineteen Native American schools in ten states and eleven public and private universities and organizations, the project allows isolated far-flung members of Native American schools to share local customs and values with other Native American tribes around the country. The students display their projects and achievements and participate in virtual communities through Internet teleconferencing. Although the 4Directions web site (**http://4directions.org/**) was created to facilitate communication among Native American communities, the project welcomes other schools to participate in the project or use its resources (Allen et al., 1999).

Earlier in this chapter, we indicated that many students from low-SES homes are considered to be at risk for educational failure because of adverse conditions surrounding their physical, social, emotional, and cognitive development. Creative technology products may be able to reduce the numbers of at-risk students who perform at low levels or drop out of school altogether. One multimedia environment, MOST (Multimedia Environments That Organize and Support Learning Through Technology), was designed to engage at-risk middle school and high school students in authentic tasks that develop their literacy skills (Bransford et al., 1996; Cognition and Technology Group at Vanderbilt, 1994). Students create interesting multimedia products that teach their parents, teachers, peers, and others about important life concepts and issues such as drug abuse, AIDS, and driving safety, all while working on their literacy skills. Technological supports, or scaffolds, are embedded in MOST environments to foster student reading comprehension, listening, communication, and information-generation skills. Besides engaging students in a meaningful learning context, MOST environments attempt to build on student strengths and connect to out-of-school experiences.

MOST environments have three common components. First, they involve a videodisk and animated tutor that helps students in word recognition and decoding as well as text passage comprehension. Brief video clips are linked to readings to enrich student comprehension. Word fluency is fostered through a speaker-dependent voice-recognition system that students train to identify their voice. Second, students can use the Multimedia Producer to create their own multimedia productions, incorporating text, digital sound, and video. Completed student work can be displayed, thereby allowing students who are developmentally behind their peers to make noteworthy classroom contributions. Third, the use of two-way videoconferencing brings students into contact with content-area specialists, designers, other schools, and the surrounding community.

Now that you are familiar with the nature and goals of multicultural education programs and some of the instructional tools that are available to you, the following Suggestions for Teaching should help you get started.

Suggestions for Teaching in Your Classroom

Promoting Multicultural Understanding and Classroom Achievement

1 Use every possible means for motivating educationally disadvantaged students to do well in school.

Perhaps the major reason many educationally disadvantaged students do poorly in school is not lack of ability but lack of interest in learning. As the account of Marc Elrich (1994), the sixth-grade teacher whose experiences we summarized earlier, makes clear, a number of circumstances may conspire to prevent such students from acquiring a desire to do well in school: lack of encouragement from parents, the absence of role models in the form of parents and siblings who have benefited from schooling, a level of aspiration set low to avoid possible failure, and lack of success leading to a low need for achievement.

Support for this argument comes from a recent study of factors that contributed to African American seventh, eighth, and ninth graders' staying in school (Connell, Halpern-Felsher, Clifford, Crichlow, & Usinger, 1995). These researchers found that support from parents at home and from teachers at school contributed to feelings of academic competence, autonomy (schoolwork is related to important personal goals or is intrinsically interesting), and relatedness to others at school. Students with high levels of competence, autonomy, and relatedness were more likely to be successful in school and to stay in school than were students with low levels of these characteristics.

2 Use a variety of instructional techniques to help educationally disadvantaged students master both basic and higher-order knowledge and skills.

Web resources for bilingual education are also expanding rapidly. For example, the web site La Clase Mágica (**communication.ucsd.edu/LCM/**) is written partly in English and partly in Spanish and contains an electronic wizard (el Maga) that survives by eating the words in the messages that children type to el Maga. The web site Science Fair Assistant (**www.iteachilearn.com/teach/tech/science.htm**), written in both English and Spanish, is designed to help children in grades K–8 find experiments and ideas for a science project.

To review this chapter, go to the Thought Questions and ACE Self-Testing sections on this book's site at **http://education.college.hmco.com/students**.

RESOURCES FOR FURTHER INVESTIGATION

■ Multicultural Education: Theory and Practice

James Banks offers a brief (seven chapters, 121 pages) introduction to multicultural education in *An Introduction to Multicultural Education* (1999). A more detailed discussion can be found in his *Teaching Strategies for Ethnic Studies* (1997). Part 1 discusses goals for multicultural programs, key concepts, and planning a multicultural curriculum. Parts 2 through 5 provide background information about ten ethnic groups and strategies for teaching about each group. Part 6 provides an example of a multicultural unit and an evaluation strategy. The book concludes with such useful appendixes as a list of videotapes and films on U.S. ethnic groups, a bibliography of books about women of color, and a chronology of key events concerning ethnic groups in U.S. history.

Another practical book is *Comprehensive Multicultural Education: Theory and Practice* (1999), by Christine Bennett. Part 1 of this book (Chapters 1 to 5) presents the case for multicultural education. Part 2 (Chapters 6 and 7) describes culturally based individual differences that affect teaching and learning. Part 3 (Chapters 8 and 9) presents a model for multicultural curriculum development, guidelines for instruction, and a set of twenty-eight illustrative lessons written by classroom teachers. The lessons include statements of goals and objectives, a description of the instructional sequence, a list of needed materials, and a means for evaluating how well the objectives were met.

Cultural Diversity in Schools: From Rhetoric to Practice (1994), edited by Robert DeVillar, Christian Faltis, and James Cummins, contains chapters on the use of cooperative learning in culturally diverse classrooms, the promotion of positive cross-cultural attitudes, the management of behavior in the culturally diverse classroom, and the use of computer technology in culturally diverse and bilingual classrooms.

A large number of multicultural resources are available on the Internet. Several good starting points include:

Multicultural Education Resources:

www.education.gsw.edu/johnson/MulticulturalEducation.htm
www.brevard.cc.fl.us/multicultural/links.html

National Association for Multicultural Education:
www.nameorg.org/

Center for Multicultural Education:
depts.washington.edu/centerme/

Intercultural E-Mail Classroom Connections:
www.teaching.com/iecc/

■ Ethnic Minority Groups

American Indian Leaders: Studies in Diversity (1980), edited by R. David Edmunds, contains chapters on twelve Native American leaders from the mid-1700s to the twentieth century. For information on how to obtain books, films, and reports about African Americans, Asian Americans, Hispanic Americans, and Native Americans, consult *Guide to Multicultural Resources* (1993–1994), edited by Charles A. Taylor. *Sourcebook of Hispanic Culture in the United States* (1982), edited by David Foster, contains several chapters on the history, anthropology, sociology, literature, and art of Hispanic American groups living in the United States. Angela Carrasquillo provides a comprehensive discussion of Hispanic American children and youths in the United States in *Hispanic Children and Youth in the United States: A Resource Guide* (1991). For information about various aspects of development among African-American adolescents, see *Black Adolescence: Current Issues and Annotated Bibliography* (1990), by the Consortium for Research on Black Adolescence.

An Internet search using the names of particular cultural groups or names of individuals may be the best way to find specific resources online.

■ Bilingual Education

Judith Lessow-Hurley offers a readable introduction to bilingual education in *The Foundations of Dual Language Instruction* (2000). The political issues that often surround bilingual education as well as various programmatic and instructional issues are discussed in *Bilingual Education: Politics, Practice, and Research* (1993), edited by Beatriz Arias and Ursula Casanova.

Teaching English as a Second Language: A Resource Guide

(1994), by Angela Carrasquillo, contains eleven chapters that discuss such topics as language acquisition, individual differences in language learning, different types of ESL programs, and characteristics of ESL programs at different grade levels. An excellent online directory of bilingual education resources is maintained at the University of Texas, Austin. Its address is **www.edb.utexas.edu/coe/depts/CI/bilingue/resources.html.**

Kathryn Lindholm and Halford Fairchild describe the evaluation of a bilingual-immersion program in a southern California school district in Chapter 8 of *Bilingual Education: Issues and Strategies* (1990, edited by Amado Padilla, Halford Fairchild, and Concepción Valadez).

SUMMARY

1. Culture refers to the perceptions, emotions, beliefs, ideas, experiences, and behavior patterns that a group of people have in common.
2. Beginning in the 1960s, the notion of the United States as a cultural melting pot became less popular, and the concept of cultural diversity, or cultural pluralism, increased in popularity. As the latter became more widely accepted, calls were made for the establishment of multicultural education programs in American public schools.
3. The concept of cultural pluralism assumes that every culture has its own internal coherence and logic, that no culture is inherently inferior or superior to another, and that all people are somewhat culture bound.
4. Because of immigration patterns and high birthrates in some ethnic groups, the United States is becoming an increasingly diverse country.
5. Two important factors that distinguish one culture from another are ethnicity and social class.
6. People of the same ethnic group typically share many of the following characteristics: ancestral country of origin, race, religion, values, political interests, economic interests, and behavior patterns.
7. Ethnic differences in communication patterns and preferences, time orientation, values, and thinking styles can lead to misunderstandings among students and between students and teachers.
8. Social class indicates an individual's or a family's relative position in society in terms of such factors as income, occupation, level of education, place of residence, and material possessions.
9. Educationally disadvantaged students often receive irregular health care, experience a lack of mediation in their interactions with their parents, are not exposed to a wide variety of experiences, are not motivated to do well in school, and have low career aspirations.
10. The teacher expectancy effect, also known as the self-fulfilling prophecy or the Pygmalion effect, occurs when teachers communicate a particular expectation about how a student will perform and the student's behavior changes so as to be consistent with that expectation.
11. Although the effect of teacher expectancy on IQ scores originally reported by Rosenthal and Jacobson has never been fully replicated, research has demonstrated that teacher expectancy strongly affects classroom achievement and participation in both positive and negative ways.
12. Factors that seem to play a strong role in producing a teacher expectancy effect are a student's social class, ethnic background, gender, achievement, and attractiveness.
13. Multicultural education programs assume that minority students will learn more and have a stronger self-concept if teachers understand, accept, and reward the thinking and behavior patterns characteristic of the students' culture.
14. Effective multicultural teachers use such proven instructional techniques as providing clear objectives, communicating high expectations, monitoring progress, providing immediate feedback, and making lessons meaningful. In addition, they have experience in teaching culturally diverse classes, exhibit a high level of dedication, and have a strong affinity for their students.
15. Peer tutoring, cooperative learning, and mastery learning are three generally effective instructional tactics that are particularly well suited to multicultural education programs.
16. Calls for multicultural education were stimulated by changing immigration and birthrate patterns, low levels of school achievement by many ethnic minority children, and students' need to work productively with members of other cultures.
17. For students who live in culturally homogeneous communities, an increased understanding of the characteristics of students from different cultural backgrounds and the problems they face can be gained by using such technological tools as videoconferencing and electronic communities.
18. Most bilingual education programs reflect either a transition goal or a maintenance goal. Transition programs

teach students in their native language only until they speak and understand English well enough to be placed in a regular classroom. Maintenance programs try to maintain or improve students' native-language skills.

19. Developmental bilingual education programs, in which subject matter instruction is provided in both the minority and majority languages are growing in popularity.

KEY TERMS

culture *(145–146)*
multicultural education *(146)*
melting pot *(146)*
cultural pluralism *(147)*
ethnic group *(149)*
social class *(152)*
socioeconomic status (SES) *(152)*
teacher expectancy effect *(156)*
peer tutoring *(162)*
cooperative learning *(163–164)*
mastery learning *(164–165)*
developmental bilingual education (DBE) *(178)*

DISCUSSION QUESTIONS

1. Culture refers to the way in which a group of people views the world; formulates beliefs; evaluates objects, ideas, and experiences; and behaves. Ethnocentrism often causes people to view the cultural beliefs and practices of others as deficits. How can you use the concept of constructivism (discussed earlier in this book) to help students overcome any ethnocentrism they may have and understand the beliefs and practices of other cultures?

2. The school dropout rate for African American, Hispanic American, and Native American students is much higher than the rate for white students. A likely contributing factor is the sense of alienation from school that grows out of low teacher expectations, expressions of racial or ethnic group prejudice, and discrimination. What steps might you take to reduce or eliminate this sense of alienation in students?

3. How have your experiences with members of ethnic or racial minority groups been similar to or different from what you have heard and read about those groups?

4. In this chapter, we briefly described four approaches to multicultural education: contributions, ethnic additive, transformation, and decision making and social action. What advantages and disadvantages do you see for each approach? Which approach would you use? Why?

5. In the section on multicultural education under the heading "Basic Approaches and Concepts," we described a set of key concepts proposed by James Banks around which multicultural lessons and units can be organized. Why are these concepts so important that Banks labels them *key* concepts?

Accommodating Student Variability

6

Prior to the twentieth century, few educators had to deal with the challenge of teaching extremely diverse groups of students. Most communities were fairly small, and students in a given school tended to come from similar backgrounds. Many children, especially those of low socioeconomic status (SES), attended school irregularly or not at all. In 1900, for example, only 8.5 percent of eligible students attended high school (Boyer, 1983), and these students were almost entirely from the upper and middle classes (Gutek, 1992). In addition, children with mental, emotional,

Key Points

These key points will help you learn the important information in this chapter. To help you study, they also appear in the margins of the pages, next to the text where they are discussed.

Ability Grouping

- Ability grouping assumes intelligence is inherited, reflected by IQ, unchangeable, and instruction will be superior
- No research support for between-class ability grouping
- Joplin Plan and within-class ability grouping for math and science produce moderate increases in learning
- Between-class ability grouping negatively influences teaching goals and methods
- Joplin Plan and within-class ability grouping may allow for better-quality instruction

The Individuals with Disabilities Education Act (IDEA)

- Before placement, student must be given complete, valid, and appropriate evaluation
- IEP must include objectives, services to be provided, criteria for determining achievement
- Students with disabilities must be educated in least restrictive environment
- Mainstreaming: policy of placing students with disabilities in regular classes
- Procedural safeguards intended to protect rights of students and parents
- Inclusion policy aims to keep students with disabilities in regular classroom for entire day
- Students who are learning disabled, speech impaired, mentally retarded, or emotionally disturbed most likely to be served under IDEA
- Multidisciplinary assessment team determines if student needs special services
- Classroom teacher, parents, several specialists prepare IEP

Students with Mental Retardation

- Students with mild retardation may frustrate easily, lack confidence and self-esteem
- Students with mild retardation tend to oversimplify, have difficulty generalizing
- Give students with mild retardation short assignments that can be completed quickly

Students with Learning Disabilities

- Learning disabilities: disorders in basic processes that lead to learning problems not due to other causes
- Students with learning disabilities have problems with perception, attention, memory, metacognition
- Symptoms of ADHD include inattention, hyperactivity, and impulsivity
- Help students with learning disabilities to reduce distractions, attend to important information

Students with Emotional Disturbance

- Emotional disturbance: poor relationships, inappropriate behavior, depression, fears
- Term *behavior disorder* focuses on behavior that needs to be changed, objective assessment
- Students with behavior disorders tend to be either aggressive or withdrawn
- Foster interpersonal contact among withdrawn students
- Use techniques to forestall aggressive or antisocial behavior

Gifted and Talented Students

- Gifted and talented students show high performance in one or more areas
- Minorities underrepresented in gifted classes because of overreliance on test scores
- Gifted and talented students differ from their nongifted peers intellectually and emotionally
- Separate classes for gifted and talented students aid achievement but may lower academic self-concept of some students

Using Technology to Assist Exceptional Students

- Federal legislation has led to the development of various assistive technologies or physical disabilities were sent to special schools, educated at home, or not educated at all. In comparison with today's schools, earlier student populations were considerably less diverse.

In the preceding chapter, you read about the varieties of cultural and socioeconomic diversity among today's students. This chapter focuses on another dimension of diversity: the twin (but often somewhat fuzzy) concepts of ability and disability. Before explaining how educators attempt to meet the needs of diverse students, we take a brief look at historical developments that helped shape current educational practices. ■

Historical Developments

The Growth of Public Education and Age-Graded Classrooms

By 1920, public education in the United States was no longer a small-scale and optional enterprise, largely because of three developments. First, by 1918, all states had passed compulsory attendance laws. Second, child labor laws had been enacted by many states, as well as by Congress in 1916, to eliminate the hiring of children and adolescents in mines and factories. Third, large numbers of immigrant children arrived in the United States from 1901 through 1920. The result was a vast increase in the number and diversity of children attending elementary and high school.

For a preview of this chapter's main concepts, see the Chapter Themes on the Snowman textbook site at **http://education.college.hmco.com/students**.

Educators initially dealt with this growth in student variability by forming age-graded classrooms. Introduced in the Quincy, Massachusetts, schools in the mid-1800s, these classrooms grouped all students of a particular age together each year to master a certain portion of the school's curriculum (Gutek, 1992). The main assumptions behind this approach were that teachers could be more effective in helping students learn and that students would have more positive attitudes toward themselves and school when classrooms were more homogeneous than heterogeneous (Oakes, 1985; Peltier, 1991). Regardless of whether these assumptions were well founded (an issue we will address shortly), they were (and still are) so widely held by educators that two additional approaches to creating even more homogeneous groups were eventually implemented: ability grouping and special class placement.

Ability-Grouped Classrooms

Ability grouping involved the use of standardized mental ability or achievement tests to create groups of students who were considered very similar to each other in learning ability. In elementary and middle schools, students typically were (and frequently still are) placed in low-, average-, or high-ability groups. At the high school level, students were placed into different tracks that were geared toward such different post–high school goals as college, secretarial work, and vocational school.

Ability grouping was another means for school authorities to deal with the large influx of immigrant students. Because many of these children were not fluent in English and had had limited amounts of education in their native countries, they scored low on standardized tests when compared to American test norms. In addition, many of these children came from poor homes and were in poor health. At the time, their assignment to a low-ability group seemed both logical and appropriate (Wheelock, 1994).

In the first major part of this chapter, we will look at current applications of ability grouping, which now takes several forms and is still used to reduce the normal range of variability in cognitive ability and achievement found in the typical classroom.

Special Education

For more or less normal children, age grading and ability testing were seen as workable approaches to creating more homogeneous classes. But compulsory attendance laws also brought to school many children with mild to severe mental and physical disabilities. These students were deemed incapable of profiting from any type of normal classroom instruction and so were assigned to special schools. Unfortunately, as Alfred Binet feared, the labeling of a student as mentally retarded or physically disabled often resulted in a vastly inferior education. Early in this century, special schools served as convenient dumping grounds for all kinds of children who could not adapt to the regular classroom (Vallecorsa, deBettencourt, & Zigmond, 2000).

In the latter two-thirds of this chapter, we will detail the varied types and degrees of special class placement for children whose intellectual, social, emotional, or physical development falls outside (above as well as below) the range of normal variation. In discussing this approach, we pay particular attention to Public Law (PL) 101-476, the Individuals with Disabilities Education Act (IDEA), which was enacted to counter past excesses of special class placement and to encourage the placement of children with disabilities in regular classes.

Ability Grouping

Ability grouping is a widespread practice (for example, Brewer, Rees, & Argys, 1995; Loveless, 1998; Wheelock, 1994). In the elementary grades, virtually all teachers form separate groups within their classrooms for instruction in reading, and many do so for mathematics as well. At the middle school level, approximately two-thirds to three-fourths of schools assign students to different self-contained classes in one or more subjects on the basis of standardized test scores. This proportion rises to about 85 percent at the high school level. In this section, we will describe the most common ways in which teachers group students by ability, examine the assumptions that provide the rationale for this practice, summarize research findings on the effectiveness of ability grouping, and look at alternative courses of action.

Types of Ability Groups

Four approaches to ability grouping are popular among educators today: between-class ability grouping, regrouping, the Joplin Plan, and within-class grouping. You may be able to recall a few classes in which one or another of these techniques was used. If not, you will no doubt encounter at least one of them during your first year of teaching.

In ability grouping, students are selected and placed in homogeneous groups with other students who are considered to have very similar learning abilities.

Between-Class Ability Grouping The goal of **between-class ability grouping** is for each class to be made up of students who are homogeneous in standardized intelligence or achievement test scores. Three levels of classes are usually formed: high, average, and low. Students in one ability group typically have little or no contact with students in others during the school day. Although each group covers the same subjects, a higher group does so in greater depth and breadth than lower groups. At the high school level, this approach is often called *tracking.* Traditionally, high school tracks have been labeled academic (or college preparatory), vocational, and general. These terms have been increasingly replaced by such designations as advanced (or honors), regular, and basic (Hallinan, 1994).

Regrouping The groups formed under a **regrouping** plan are more flexible in assignments and narrower in scope than between-class groups. Students of the same age, ability, and grade but from different classrooms come together for instruction in a specific subject, usually reading or mathematics. If a student begins to outperform the other members of the group significantly, a change of group assignment is easier since it involves just that particular subject. Regrouping has two major disadvantages, however. First, it requires a certain degree of planning and cooperation among the teachers involved. They must agree, for example, to schedule reading and arithmetic during the same periods. Second, many teachers are uncomfortable working with children whom they see only once a day for an hour or so.

Joplin Plan The **Joplin Plan** is a variation of regrouping. The main difference is that regroupings take place across grade levels. For example, all third, fourth, and fifth graders whose grade-equivalent scores in reading are 4.6 (fourth grade, sixth month) would come together for reading instruction. The same would be done for mathematics. The Joplin Plan has the same advantages and disadvantages as simple regrouping.

Within-Class Ability Grouping The most popular form of ability grouping, occurring in almost all elementary school classes, **within-class ability grouping** involves the division of a single class of students into two or three groups for reading and math instruction. Like regrouping and the Joplin Plan, within-class ability grouping has the advantages of being flexible in terms of group assignments and being restricted to one or two subjects. In addition, it eliminates the need for cooperative scheduling. One disadvantage of this approach is that the teacher needs to be skilled at keeping the other students in the class productively occupied while working with a particular group.

Assumptions Underlying Ability Grouping

Ability grouping assumes intelligence is inherited, reflected by IQ, unchangeable, and instruction will be superior

When ability grouping was initiated early in the twentieth century, much less was known about the various factors that affect classroom learning. Consequently, educators simply assumed certain things to be true. One of those assumptions was that intelligence, which affects the capacity to learn, was a fixed, inherited trait and that little could be done to change the learning capacity of individuals. A second assumption was that intelligence was adequately reflected by an intelligence quotient (IQ) score. A third assumption was that all students would learn best when grouped with those of similar ability (Hallinan, 1994; Marsh & Raywid, 1994; Oakes & Lipton, 1992). Although many educators still believe these assumptions are true, the research evidence summarized here and elsewhere in this book casts doubt on their validity.

Evaluations of Ability Grouping

Because ability grouping occurs in virtually all school districts, its effects have been intensively studied (for example, Hoffer, 1992; Kulik & Kulik, 1991; Lloyd, 1999; Lou et al., 1996; Marsh & Raywid, 1994; Raudenbush, Rowan, & Cheong, 1993; Slavin, 1990b). The main findings of these analyses are as follows:

No research support for between-class ability grouping

1. There is little to no support for between-class ability grouping. Students assigned to low-ability classes generally performed worse than comparable students in heterogeneous classes. Students assigned to average-ability classes performed at about the same level as their nongrouped peers. High-ability students sometimes performed slightly better in homogeneous classes than in heterogeneous classes. The Task Force on the Education of Young Adolescents (1989) has characterized between-class ability grouping as "one of the most divisive and damaging school practices in existence. Time and time again, young people placed in lower academic tracks or classes, often during middle grades, are locked into dull, repetitive instructional programs leading at best to minimum competencies" (pp. 49–50).
2. Research on the effect of regrouping for reading or mathematics is inconclusive. Some of the relatively few studies that have been done on this form of ability grouping suggest that it can be effective if the instructional pace and level of the text match the student's actual achievement level rather than the student's nominal grade level. In other words, a fifth grader who scores at the fourth-grade level on a reading test should be reading out of a fourth-grade reading book.

Joplin Plan and within-class ability grouping for math and science produce moderate increases in learning

3. The Joplin Plan yields moderately positive effects compared with instruction in heterogeneous classes.
4. Within-class ability grouping in mathematics and science in grades 1 through 12 produced modestly positive results (about eight percentile ranks) compared with whole-class instruction and an even smaller positive effect (about four percentile ranks) when compared with mixed-ability groups. Average-achieving

students benefit most from being placed in homogeneous-ability groups, while low-achieving students benefit most from being placed in mixed-ability groups. Because within-class ability grouping for reading is an almost universal practice at every grade level, researchers have not had the opportunity to compare its effectiveness with whole-class reading instruction. Nevertheless, it would be reasonable to expect much the same results for reading as were found for mathematics and science.

5. Students in homogeneously grouped classes scored the same as students in heterogeneously grouped classes on measures of self-esteem.
6. Students in high-ability classes had more positive attitudes about school and higher educational aspirations than did students in low-ability classrooms.
7. Between-class ability grouping affected the quality of instruction received by students.

Between-class ability grouping negatively influences teaching goals and methods

   a. The best teachers were often assigned to teach the highest tracks, whereas the least experienced or weakest teachers were assigned to teach the lowest tracks.
   b. Teachers of high-ability classes stressed critical thinking, self-direction, creativity, and active participation, whereas teachers of low-ability classes stressed working quietly, following rules, and getting along with classmates. This effect was particularly noticeable in math and science.
   c. Teachers of low-ability groups covered less material and simpler material than did teachers of high-ability groups.
   d. Teachers of low-ability students expected and demanded less of them than did teachers of high-ability students.

To Group or Not to Group?

The findings just summarized suggest three courses of action. The first course is to discontinue the use of full-day, between-class ability groups. Despite the fact that most middle and high schools continue to use this form of ability grouping, students do not learn more or feel more positively about themselves and school. This is a case in which even widely held beliefs must be modified or eliminated when the weight of evidence goes against them.

The second course of action is to use only those forms of ability grouping that produce positive results: within-class grouping and the Joplin Plan, especially for reading and mathematics. We do not know why these forms of ability grouping work. It is assumed that the increase in group homogeneity allows for more appropriate and potent forms of instruction (for example, greater effort by the teacher to bring lower-achieving groups up to the level of higher-achieving groups). If this assumption is correct, within-class ability grouping and the Joplin Plan must be carried out in such a way that homogeneous groups are guaranteed to result. The best way to achieve similarity in cognitive ability among students is to group them on the basis of past classroom performance, standardized achievement test scores, or both. The least desirable (but most frequently used) approach is to base the assignments solely on IQ scores.

Joplin Plan and within-class ability grouping may allow for better-quality instruction

The third course of action is to dispense with all forms of ability grouping. But bear in mind that unless teachers make a concerted effort to meet the educational needs of all students, detracking (the term often used to denote the elimination of ability groups, particularly at the middle school and high school levels) may lead to slightly lower performance of average and above-average students (Loveless, 1999).

In keeping with the concept of differentiated instruction mentioned earlier in the book, teachers can use a variety of organizational and instructional techniques that will allow them to cope with a heterogeneous class, or they can use these same techniques in conjunction with the Joplin Plan or within-class grouping. For instance, you might use with all students instructional techniques that are associated with high achievement. These would include making clear presentations, displaying a high level of enthusiasm, reinforcing students for correct responses, providing sufficient time for students to formulate answers to questions, prompting correct responses, providing detailed feedback about the accuracy of responses, requiring a high level of work and effort, and organizing students into small, heterogeneous learning groups (a technique known as cooperative learning, which we will discuss in detail in the chapter on approaches to instruction). Other ideas include optional honors activities, pullout (meaning programs that occur outside the classroom) challenge classes that are available to all students, study skills classes for low-achieving students, and small-group projects (Oakes & Wells, 1998).

The Individuals with Disabilities Education Act (IDEA)

Many of the criticisms and arguments marshaled against ability grouping have come to be applied as well to special classes for students with disabilities. In addition, the elimination of racially segregated schools by the U.S. Supreme Court in the case of *Brown v. Board of Education* (1954) established a precedent for providing students with disabilities an equal opportunity for a free and appropriate education (Ornstein & Levine, 2000). As a result, influential members of Congress were persuaded in the early 1970s that it was time for the federal government to take steps to correct the perceived inequities and deficiencies in our educational system. The result was a landmark piece of legislation, Public Law 94-142, the Education for All Handicapped Children Act of 1975. This law was revised and expanded in 1986 as the Handicapped Children's Protection Act (PL 99-457) and again in 1990 as the Individuals with Disabilities Education Act (IDEA, PL 101-476).

IDEA was then amended in 1997 to broaden and clarify a number of its provisions. The 1990 version of IDEA, for example, said nothing about the participation of children with disabilities in standardized testing programs. The 1997 amendment, however, states that children with disabilities must be provided with whatever modifications are necessary (for instance, large print for children who have visual impairments, extended time limits for children with a learning disability) to allow them to take part in state- and district-wide assessments. If a child with a disability does not participate in a standardized assessment, school district officials must explain why they feel such an assessment is inappropriate and how that child will be assessed (Ysseldyke, Algozzine, & Thurlow, 2000).

Major Provisions of IDEA

A Free and Appropriate Public Education The basic purpose of IDEA is to ensure that all individuals from birth through age twenty-one who have an identifiable disability, regardless of how severe, receive at public expense supervised special education and related services that meet their unique educational needs. These services can be delivered in a classroom, at home, in a hospital, or in a specialized institution and may include physical education and vocational education, as well as instruction in the typical academic subjects (Office of the Federal Register, 1994).

Preplacement Evaluation Before a child with a disability can be placed in a program that provides special education services, "a full and individual evaluation of the child's educational needs" must be conducted. Such an evaluation must conform to the following rules:

Before placement, student must be given complete, valid, and appropriate evaluation

1. Tests must be administered in the child's native language.
2. A test must be valid for the specific purpose for which it is used.
3. Tests must be administered by trained individuals according to the instructions provided by the test publisher.
4. Tests administered to students who have impaired sensory, manual, or speaking skills must reflect aptitude or achievement rather than the impairment.
5. No single procedure (such as an IQ test) can be the sole basis for determining an appropriate educational program. Data should be collected from such nontest sources as observations by other professionals (such as the classroom teacher), medical records, and parental interviews.
6. Evaluations must be made by a multidisciplinary team that contains at least one teacher or other specialist with knowledge in the area of the suspected disability.
7. The child must be assessed in all areas related to the suspected disability (Office of the Federal Register, 1994).

When you deal with students whose first language is not English, it is important to realize that standardized tests are designed to reflect cultural experiences common to the United States and that English words and phrases may not mean quite the same thing when translated. Therefore, these tests may not be measuring what they were developed to measure. In other words, they may not be valid. The results of such assessments should therefore be interpreted very cautiously (Kubiszyn & Borich, 2000).

Individualized Education Program Every child who is identified as having a disability and who receives special education services must have an **individualized education program (IEP)** prepared. The IEP is a written statement that describes the educational program that has been designed to meet the child's unique needs. The IEP must include the following elements:

1. A statement of the child's existing levels of educational performance
2. A statement of annual goals, including short-term instructional objectives
3. A statement of the specific special education and related services to be provided to the child and the extent to which the child will be able to participate in regular educational programs
4. The projected dates for initiation of services and the anticipated duration of the services
5. Appropriate objective criteria and evaluation procedures and schedules for determining, on at least an annual basis, whether short-term objectives are being achieved (Office of the Federal Register, 1994)

IEP must include objectives, services to be provided, criteria for determining achievement

The IEP is to be planned by a multidisciplinary team composed of the student's classroom teacher in collaboration with a person qualified in special education, one or both of the student's parents, the student (when appropriate), and other individuals at the discretion of the parents or school. (An example of an IEP is depicted later in this chapter in Figure 6.1.)

Students with disabilities must be educated in least restrictive environment

Least Restrictive Environment According to the 1994 Code of Federal Regulations that governs the implementation of IDEA, educational services must be provided to children with disabilities in the **least restrictive environment** that their disability will allow. A school district must identify a continuum of increasingly restrictive placements (instruction in regular classes, special classes, home instruction, instruction in hospitals and institutions) and, on the basis of the multidisciplinary team's evaluation, select the least restrictive setting that will best meet the student's special educational needs. This provision is often referred to as **mainstreaming** because the goal of the law is to have as many children with disabilities as possible, regardless of the severity of the disability, enter the mainstream of education by attending regular classes with nondisabled students. In recent years, mainstreaming has frequently evolved into *inclusion*, a practice we discuss later in this chapter.

Mainstreaming: policy of placing students with disabilities in regular classes

Procedural safeguards intended to protect rights of students and parents

Procedural Safeguards The basic purpose of the various procedural safeguards that were written into IDEA is to make sure that parents are fully informed about the actions a school district intends to take to classify their child as having a disability, protect the legal rights of parents and their child, and provide a way to resolve disputes about any aspect of the process. Among other rights, parents have the right to inspect their child's education records; obtain an independent assessment of their child; obtain written prior notice of identification, assessment, and placement procedures; request a due process hearing; appeal the results of a due process hearing;

The least restrictive environment provision of IDEA has led to mainstreaming—the policy that children with disabilities should attend regular classes to the maximum extent possible. Some special education proponents argue that full-time regular classroom placement should be the only option for such students.

or file a lawsuit in state or federal court. A due process hearing is a fact-finding procedure that is intended to resolve disagreements between the school district and the parents of a child with a disability. Such hearings include a hearing officer, the parents of the disabled child, school district personnel (such as the classroom teacher, the principal, and the school psychologist), and attorneys for the parents and the school district.

THE POLICY OF INCLUSION

Although IDEA calls for children with disabilities to be placed in the least restrictive environment, the law clearly allows for more restrictive placements than those of the regular classroom "when the nature or severity of the disability is such that education in regular classes with the use of supplementary aids and services cannot be achieved satisfactorily" (Office of the Federal Register, 1994, p. 54). Nevertheless, there has been a movement in recent years to eliminate this option. Known as **inclusion** or **full inclusion,** this extension of the mainstreaming provision has become one of the most controversial outgrowths of IDEA (see also MacMillan, Gresham, & Forness, 1996).

As most proponents use the term, *inclusion* means keeping special education students in regular classrooms and bringing support services to the children rather than the other way around. *Full inclusion* refers to the practice of eliminating all pullout programs *and* special education teachers and of providing regular classroom teachers with training in teaching special-needs students so that they can teach these students in the regular classroom (Rogers, 1993; Smelter, Rasch, & Yudewitz, 1994; Staub & Peck, 1994–1995).

Inclusion policy aims to keep students with disabilities in regular classroom for entire day

The Debate About Inclusion The proponents of inclusion and full inclusion often raise three arguments to support their position:

1. Research suggests that special-needs students who are segregated from regular students perform more poorly academically and socially than comparable students who are mainstreamed (McLeskey & Waldron, 1996).
2. Given the substantial body of evidence demonstrating the propensity of children to observe and imitate more competent children (see, for example, Schunk, 1987), it can be assumed that students with disabilities will learn more by interacting with nondisabled students than by attending homogeneous classes (Sapon-Shevin, 1996).
3. The Supreme Court in *Brown v. Board of Education* declared the doctrine of separate but equal to be unconstitutional. Therefore, pullout programs are a violation of the civil rights of children with special needs because these programs segregate them from their nondisabled peers in programs that are assumed to be separate but equal (Sapon-Shevin, 1996; Skrtic, Sailor, & Gee, 1996; Staub & Peck, 1994–1995).

The opponents of inclusion often cite cases of students who fail to learn basic skills, students whose disabilities interrupt the normal flow of instruction, or teachers who are ill prepared to adequately assist the various special-needs students who are placed in their classes (for example, Fox & Ysseldyke, 1997; Kauffman, Lloyd, Baker, & Reidel, 1995; MacMillan et al., 1996; McLeskey & Waldron, 1996).

Research Findings The evidence that bears on the inclusion issue is a combination of anecdotes (reports about individual cases) and experiments that compare inclusive to noninclusive practices for special-needs students. It seems to indicate, at least for now, that inclusion works well for some students but produces modest or no benefits for others. On the basis of this evidence (for example, Baker, Wang, & Walberg, 1994–1995; MacMillan et al., 1996; Raison, Hanson, Hall, & Reynolds, 1995; Staub & Peck, 1994–1995; Stevens & Slavin, 1995; Zigmond et al., 1995), three conclusions seem warranted:

1. Inclusion may not be an appropriate course of action for every child with a disability.
2. Inclusion will likely work best when the presence of a disabled student stimulates the teacher to improve the general quality of classroom instruction and well-trained support staff, such as teacher aides and inclusion facilitators, are available (see, for example, Choate, 2000; Ruder, 2000).
3. For students who are mainstreamed, IEPs should be written so as to reflect better what a given student probably can and cannot accomplish.

What IDEA Means to Regular Classroom Teachers

By the time you begin your teaching career, the original legislation governing the delivery of educational services to the disabled, PL 94-142, will have been in effect for a quarter-century or more. Each state was required to have established laws and policies for implementing the various provisions by 1978. The first guiding principle to follow, therefore, is, *find out what the local ground rules are.* You will probably be told during orientation meetings about the ways IDEA is being put into effect in your state and local school district. But if such a presentation is not given or is incomplete, it would be wise to ask about guidelines you should follow. Your second guiding principle, then, should be, *when in doubt, ask.* With these two caveats in mind, consider some questions you may be asking yourself about the impact of IDEA as you approach your first teaching job.

What Kinds of Disabling Conditions Are Included Under IDEA? According to the U.S. Department of Education (2000), during the 1998–1999 academic year, 5.25 million children and youths from ages six through seventeen (about 11 percent of the total number of individuals in this age group) received special education services under IDEA.

IDEA recognizes thirteen categories of students with disabilities. Many states use the same categories. Others use fewer, more inclusive classification schemes. The thirteen categories described in the legislation are listed as follows in alphabetical order, with brief definitions of each type:

Autism. Significant difficulty in verbal and nonverbal communication and social interaction that adversely affects educational performance.

Deaf-blindness. Impairments of both hearing and vision, the combination of which causes severe communication, developmental, and educational problems. The combination of these impairments is such that a child's educational and physical needs cannot be adequately met by programs designed for only deaf children or only blind children.

Deafness. Hearing impairment so severe that even with hearing aids, a child has problems processing speech.

Hearing impairment. Permanent or fluctuating difficulty in understanding speech that adversely affects educational performance and is not included under the definition of deafness.

Mental retardation. Significant subaverage general intellectual functioning accompanied by deficits in adaptive behavior (how well a person functions in social environments).

Multiple disabilities. Two or more impairments (such as mental retardation—blindness and mental retardation-orthopedic, but not deaf-blindness) that cause such severe educational problems that a child's needs cannot be adequately met by programs designed solely for one of the impairments.

Orthopedic impairments. Impairment in a child's ability to use arms, legs, hands, or feet that significantly affects that child's educational performance.

Other health impairments. Conditions such as asthma, hemophilia, sickle cell anemia, epilepsy, heart disease, and diabetes that so limit the strength, vitality, or alertness of a child that educational performance is significantly affected.

Serious emotional disturbance. Personal and social problems exhibited in an extreme degree over a period of time that adversely affect a child's ability to learn and get along with others.

Specific learning disability. A disorder in one or more of the basic psychological processes involved in understanding or using language that leads to learning problems not traceable to physical disabilities, mental retardation, emotional disturbance, or cultural-economic disadvantage.

Speech or language impairment. A communication disorder such as stuttering, impaired articulation, or a language or voice impairment that adversely affects educational performance.

Table 6.1 Students Receiving Special Education Services, 1998–1999

Disabling Condition	Percentage of Total School Enrollment[a]	Percentage of Students with Disabilities Served
Specific learning disabilities	5.68	50.8
Speech or language impairments	2.28	20.3
Mental retardation	1.16	10.3
Serious emotional disturbance	0.93	8.3
Other health impairments	0.45	4.0
Multiple disabilities	0.20	1.8
Hearing impairments	0.14	1.2
Orthopedic impairments	0.14	1.2
Autism	0.11	0.9
Visual impairments	0.05	0.4
Traumatic brain injury	0.02	0.2
Deaf-blindness	0.00	0.0
Total	11.16	99.4[b]

[a]Percentages are based on children with disabilities ages 6–17 as a percentage of total school enrollment for kindergarten through twelfth grade.

[b]Percentages do not add to 100 percent because of rounding.

SOURCE: U.S. Department of Education (2000a).

Traumatic brain injury. A brain injury due to an accident that causes cognitive or psychosocial impairments that adversely affect a child's educational performance.

Visual impairment including blindness. A visual impairment so severe that even with corrective lenses, a child's educational performance is adversely affected.

Students who are learning disabled, speech impaired, mentally retarded, or emotionally disturbed most likely to be served under IDEA

The percentages of each type of student who received special educational services during the 1998–1999 school year are indicated in Table 6.1. As you can see, the most common types of children with disabilities receiving services (89.7 percent of the total) were those classified as having a specific learning disability, a speech or language impairment, mental retardation, or a serious emotional disturbance.

What Are the Regular Classroom Teacher's Responsibilities Under IDEA?

Regular classroom teachers may be involved in activities required directly or indirectly by IDEA in four possible ways: referral, assessment, preparation of the IEP, and implementation and evaluation of the IEP.

Referral Most referrals for assessment and possible special instruction are made by a child's teacher or his or her parents because they are the ones most familiar with the quality of the child's daily work and progress as compared to other children.

Multidisciplinary assessment team determines if student needs special services

Assessment The initial assessment procedures, which must be approved by the child's parents, are usually carried out by school psychologists who are certified to administer tests. If the initial conclusions of the school psychologist support the teacher's or parents' perception that the student needs special services, the **multidisciplinary assessment team** required under IDEA will be formed. Because the 1997 amendment of IDEA requires that classroom teachers be part of the multidisciplinary assessment team, you should be prepared to provide such information as the quality of the child's homework and test scores, ability to understand and use language, ability to perform various motor functions, alertness at different times of the day, and interpersonal relationships with classmates (Kubiszyn & Borich, 2000; Smith, 2001).

The decision as to whether a child qualifies for special education services under IDEA is made largely on the basis of information supplied by the multidisciplinary assessment team. Classroom teachers typically contribute information about the child's academic and social behavior.

Figure 6.1 Example of an Individualized Education Program (IEP)

INDIVIDUAL EDUCATIONAL PLAN 11/2000
DATE

STUDENT: Last Name | First | Middle
School of Attendance | Home School | 5.3 Grade Level | 8 - 4 - 89 Birthdate/Age
School Address | School Telephone Number

Child Study Team Members

Name	Title	Case Manager	LD Teacher
Name	Homeroom (Title)	Name	Parents (Title)
Name	Facilitator (Title)	Name	Title
Name	Speech (Title)	Name	Title

Summary of Assessment results

IDENTIFIED STUDENT NEEDS: Reading from last half of DISTAR II - present performance level

LONG TERM GOALS: To improve reading achievement level by at least one year's gain. To improve math achievement to grade level. To improve language skills by one year's gain.

SHORT TERM GOALS: Master Level 4 vocabulary and reading skills. Master math skills in basic curriculum. Master spelling words from Level 3 list. Complete units 1-9 from Level 3 curriculum.

MAINSTREAM MODIFICATIONS:

White Copy—Cumulative Folder
Pink Copy—Special Teacher
Goldenrod Copy—Case Manager
Yellow Copy—Parent

Description of Services to Be Provided

Type of Service	Teacher	Starting Date	Amt. of time per day	OBJECTIVES AND CRITERIA FOR ATTAINMENT
SLD level III	LD Teacher	11 - 11 - 96	2 1/2 hrs	Reading: will know all vocabulary through the "Honeycomb" level. Will master skills as presented through Distar II Will know 1 2 3 second - symbols presented in "Sound Way to Reading." Math: will pass all tests at Basic 4 level. Spelling: 5 words each week from level 3 lists Language: will complete Units 1 - 9 of the 4th grade language program. Will also complete supplemental units from "Language Step by Step."

Mainstream Classes	Teacher	Amt. of time per day	OBJECTIVES AND CRITERIA FOR ATTAINMENT
		3 1/2 hrs	Out of seat behavior: Sit attentively and listen during mainstream class discussions. A simple management plan will be implemented if he does not meet this expectation. Mainstream modifications of Social Studies: will keep a folder in which he expresses through drawing the topics his class will cover. Modified district Social Studies curriculum. No formal testing will be made.

The following equipment and other changes in personnel, transportation, curriculum methods, and educational services will be provided: Distar II Reading Program, Spelling Level 3, "Sound Way to Reading" Program, Vocabulary tapes

Substantiation of least restrictive alternatives: The planning team has determined academic needs are best met with direct SLD support in reading, math, language, and spelling

ANTICIPATED LENGTH OF PLAN 1 yr. The next periodic review will be held: May 2001
DATE/TIME/PLACE

☐ I approve this program placement and the above IEP
☐ I do not approve this placement and/or the IEP
☐ I request a conciliation conference

PARENT/GUARDIAN

Form 2011

Principal or Designee

Preparation of the IEP At least some, if not all, of the members of the assessment team work with the teacher (and the parents) in preparing the IEP. The necessary components of an IEP were described earlier, and they are illustrated in Figure 6.1.

Classroom teacher, parents, several specialists prepare IEP

Implementation and Evaluation of the IEP Depending on the nature and severity of the disability, the student may spend part or all of the school day in a regular classroom or be placed in a separate class or school. If the student stays in a regular classroom, the teacher will be expected to put into practice the various instructional techniques listed in the IEP. Because the IEP is planned by a multidisciplinary team, you will be given direction and support in providing regular class instruction for students who have a disabling condition as defined under IDEA. The classroom teacher may also be expected to determine if the listed objectives are being met and to furnish evidence of attainment. Various techniques of instruction as well as approaches to evaluation that stress student mastery of individualized assignments will be discussed in several of the chapters that follow.

The types of atypical students you will sometimes be expected to teach in your classroom will vary. Some will be special education students who are being mainstreamed for part of the school day. Others, although different from typical students in some noticeable respect, will not qualify for special education services under IDEA. The remainder of this chapter will describe students from both categories and techniques for teaching them. Students with mental retardation, learning disabilities, and emotional disturbance often require special forms of instruction, and we will focus on these categories in the remainder of this chapter. In addition, though not mentioned in IDEA, students who are gifted and talented require special forms of instruction, as we will also discuss.

Students with Mental Retardation

Classification of Children with Mental Retardation

Despite the trend away from the rigid use of classification schemes in American education, the American Association on Mental Retardation (AAMR) believes that children with mental retardation need to be classified in order to plan and finance special education for them. The AAMR applies the term **mental retardation** to individuals who have IQ scores of 67 and below and who have concurrent problems functioning in social environments. The AAMR uses the following classifications:

Mild retardation: IQ score between 67 and 52
Moderate retardation: IQ score between 51 and 36
Severe retardation: IQ score between 35 and 20
Profound retardation: IQ score of 19 and below

As a result of legal challenges to IQ testing and special class placement, as well as to the trend toward mainstreaming, students classified as mildly retarded who were once separated are more likely now to be placed in regular classes. You probably will not encounter a great many mainstreamed children classified as moderately or severely retarded because of the specialized forms of care and instruction they need. You may, however, be asked to teach one or more of the higher-scoring children with mild retardation for at least part of the day.

Characteristics of Children with Mild Retardation

Students who have below-average IQ scores follow the same general developmental pattern as their peers with higher IQ scores, but they differ in the rate and degree of development.[1] Accordingly, students with low IQ scores may possess characteristics typical of students with average IQ scores who are younger than they are. One general characteristic of such students, therefore, is that they often appear immature compared with their age-mates. Immature students are likely to experience frustration frequently when they find they are unable to do things their classmates can do, and many students with mild retardation tend to have a low tolerance for frustration

Students with mild retardation may frustrate easily, lack confidence and self-esteem

[1]Many of the points in this section are based on a discussion of characteristics of mentally retarded children in *Exceptional Children and Youth* (1999), by Nancy Hunt and Kathleen Marshall; *Exceptional Children: An Introduction to Special Education* (2000), by William L. Heward; *Educating Exceptional Children* (2000), by Samuel Kirk, James Gallagher, and Nicholas Anastasiow; and *Introduction to Special Education* (2001), by Deborah Deutsch Smith.

and a tendency toward low self-esteem, low confidence, and low motivation. These feelings, in conjunction with the cognitive deficits outlined in the next paragraph, sometimes make it difficult for the child with mild retardation to make friends and get along with peers of average ability.

Students with mild retardation tend to oversimplify, have difficulty generalizing

The cognitive characteristics of children with mild retardation include a limited amount of knowledge about how one learns and the factors that affect learning (this concept is known as *metacognition* and will be discussed more fully in the chapter on information-processing theory), a tendency to oversimplify concepts, limited ability to generalize, smaller memory capacity, shorter attention span, the inclination to concentrate on only one aspect of a learning situation and to ignore other relevant features, the inability to formulate learning strategies that fit particular situations, and delayed language development.

Several of these cognitive deficits often operate in concert to produce or contribute to the learning problems of students with mild retardation. Consider, for example, the problem of generalization (also known as transfer). This refers to the ability of a learner to take something that has been learned in one context, such as paper-and-pencil arithmetic skills, and use it to deal with a similar but different task, such as knowing whether one has received the correct change after making a purchase at a store. Students with mild mental retardation may not spontaneously exhibit transfer because (1) their metacognitive deficits limit their tendency to look for signs of similarity between two tasks, (2) their relatively short attention span prevents them from noticing similarities, and (3) their limited memory capacity and skills lessen their ability to recall relevant knowledge.

These characteristics can be understood more completely if they are related to Jean Piaget's description of cognitive development. Middle and high school students with mild retardation may never move beyond the level of concrete operations. They may be able to deal with concrete situations but find it difficult to grasp abstractions, generalize from one situation to another, or state and test hypotheses. Younger children with retardation tend to classify things in terms of a single feature.

The following Suggestions for Teaching take into account the characteristics just described, as well as points made by Nancy Hunt and Kathleen Marshall (1999, pp. 129–132); William L. Heward (2000, pp. 222–233); Samuel Kirk, James Gallagher, and Nicholas Anastasiow (2000, pp. 200–205); and Deborah Deutsch Smith (2001, pp. 253–258).

SUGGESTIONS FOR TEACHING IN YOUR CLASSROOM

Instructing Students with Mild Retardation

1 As much as possible, try to avoid placing students with mild retardation in situations that are likely to lead to their frustration. When, despite your efforts, such students indicate that they are close to their limit of frustration tolerance, encourage them to engage in relaxing change-of-pace pursuits or in physical activities.

Journal Entry
Helping Students with Mild Retardation Deal with Frustration

Because children with retardation are more likely to experience frustration than their more capable peers, try to minimize the frequency of such experiences in the classroom. Probably the most effective way to do this is to give students with mild retardation individual assignments so that they are not placed in situations where their work is compared with that of others. No matter how hard you try, however, you will not be able to eliminate frustrating experiences, partly because you will have to schedule some all-class activities and partly because even individual assignments may be difficult for a child with mild retardation to handle. If you notice that such a student appears to be getting more and more bothered by an inability to complete a task, you might try to divert attention to a less demanding form of activity or allow the student to take a short break by sharpening pencils or going for a drink of water.

2 Do everything possible to encourage a sense of self-esteem.

Children with mild retardation are prone to devalue themselves because they are aware that they are less capable than their classmates at doing many things. One way to combat this tendency toward self-devaluation is to make a point of showing that you have positive feelings about less capable students. You might, for example, say something like "I'm so glad you're here today. You make the classroom a nicer place to be in." If you indicate that you have positive feelings about an individual, that person is likely to acquire similar feelings about herself.

Journal Entry
Combating the Tendency to Communicate Low Expectations

As you saw in the preceding chapter, many teachers, usually inadvertently, tend to communicate low expectations to some of their students. To avoid committing the same error, you might do one or more of the following: make it clear that you will allow plenty of time for all students to come up with an answer to a question, repeat the question and give a clue before asking a different question, remind yourself to give frequent personal attention to students with mild retardation, or try to convey to these students the expectation that they *can* learn. Perhaps the best overall strategy to use in building self-esteem is to help children with retardation successfully complete learning tasks. Suggestions 3 through 5 offer ideas you might use.

Journal Entry
Giving Students with Mild Retardation Simple Assignments

3 Present learning tasks that contain a small number of elements, at least some of them familiar to students, and that can be completed in a short period of time.

Because students with retardation tend to oversimplify concepts, try to provide learning tasks that contain only a few elements, at least some of which they have previously learned. For example, you might ask middle or secondary school social studies students with mild retardation to prepare a report on the work of a single police officer, as opposed to preparing an analysis of law enforcement agencies (which might be an appropriate topic for the most capable student in the class). Also, because students with retardation tend to have a short attention span, short assignments are preferable to long ones.

Give students with mild retardation short assignments that can be completed quickly

4 Try to arrange what is to be learned into a series of small steps, each of which leads to immediate feedback.

Again because of their short attention span, students with retardation may become distracted or discouraged if they are asked to concentrate on demanding tasks that lead to a delayed payoff. Therefore, it is better to give a series of short activities that produce immediate feedback than to use any sort of contract approach or the equivalent in which the student is expected to engage in self-directed effort leading to a remote goal.

Students who lack confidence, tend to think of one thing at a time, are unable to generalize, and have a short memory and attention span usually respond quite positively to programmed instruction and certain forms of computer-assisted instruction (described more completely in the chapter on behavioral and social learning theories).

Some computer programs offer a systematic step-by-step procedure that emphasizes only one specific idea per step or frame. They also offer immediate feedback. These characteristics closely fit the needs of children who are mildly retarded. You might look for computer programs in the subject or subjects you teach or develop your own materials, perhaps in the form of a workbook of some kind.

5 Teach simple techniques for improving memory, and consistently point out how use of these techniques leads to more accurate recall.

In our chapter on information-processing theory, we will describe a set of memory aids called mnemonic devices. Used for thousands of years by scholars and teachers in different countries, most are fairly simple devices that help a learner organize information, encode it meaningfully, and generate cues that allow it to be retrieved from memory when needed. The simplest mnemonic devices are rhymes, first-letter mnemonics (also known as acronyms), and sentence mnemonics. For example, a first-letter mnemonic or acronym for the Great Lakes is *HOMES: H*uron, *O*ntario, *M*ichigan, *E*rie, *S*uperior.

6 Devise and use record-keeping techniques that make it clear that students have completed assignments successfully and are making progress.

Students who are experiencing difficulties in learning are especially in need of tangible proof of progress. When, for instance, they correctly fill in blanks in a programmed workbook and discover that their answers are correct, they are encouraged to go on to the next question. You might use the same basic approach in more general ways by having students with retardation keep their own records showing their progress. (This technique might be used with all students in a class.) For example, you could make individual charts for primary grade students. As they successfully complete assignments, have them color in marked-off sections, paste on gold stars or the equivalent, or trace the movement of animal figures, rockets, or something else toward a destination.

Journal Entry
Giving Students with Mild Retardation Proof of Progress

Students with Learning Disabilities

By far the greatest number of students who qualify for special education under IDEA are those classified as learning disabled. According to Department of Education (2000) figures, the number of students identified as learning disabled increased from approximately 800,000 in 1976–1977 to 2,669,852 in 1998–1999. In the 1976–1977 school year, students with learning disabilities accounted for about 24 percent of the disabled population. By the 1998–1999 school year, that estimate had grown to almost 51 percent. Especially because so many students are now classified as learning disabled, it is important to define and explore the characteristics of students with **learning disabilities.**

CHARACTERISTICS OF STUDENTS WITH LEARNING DISABILITIES

In the early 1960s, groups of concerned parents called attention to a problem in American education: a significant number of students in public schools were expe-

Students with a learning disability learn more slowly than other students because of deficits in perception, attention, and memory.

riencing difficulties in learning but were not eligible for special classes or remedial instruction programs. These children were not mentally retarded, deaf, blind, or otherwise disabled, but they were unable to respond to aspects of the curriculum presented in regular classrooms. In 1963, parents of such children formed the Association for Children with Learning Disabilities to call attention to the scope of these problems. Their efforts were rewarded in 1968 when the National Advisory Committee on the Handicapped of the U.S. Office of Education developed a definition of specific learning disabilities, which Congress used the following year in the Learning Disability Act of 1969. That definition was revised and inserted in PL 94-142 (the predecessor of IDEA). It stresses the following basic points:

Learning disabilities: disorders in basic processes that lead to learning problems not due to other causes

1. The individual has a *disorder in one or more of the basic psychological processes.* These processes refer to intrinsic prerequisite abilities such as memory, auditory perception, visual perception, and oral language.
2. The individual has *difficulty in learning,* specifically in the areas of speaking, listening, writing, reading (word recognition skills and comprehension), and mathematics (calculation and reasoning).
3. A *severe discrepancy exists between the student's apparent potential for learning and low level of achievement.*
4. The problem is *not due primarily to other causes,* such as visual or hearing impairments, motor disabilities, mental retardation, emotional disturbance, or economic, environmental, or cultural disadvantage.

In addition to these problems with cognitive processing and learning, many students with a learning disability (as well as students with mild mental retardation and students with emotional disturbance) have more poorly developed social skills than their nondisabled peers. Such students are more likely to ignore the teacher's directions, cheat, use profane language, disturb other students, disrupt group activities, and start fights. As the Case in Print illustrates, they are often rejected by the rest of the class, which contributes to lowered self-esteem and poor academic performance (Gresham & MacMillan, 1997).

Some people dismiss the notion of a learning disability as a fiction because, they

Learning Disabled Often Means Socially Disabled as Well

In addition to . . . problems with cognitive processing and learning, many students with a learning disability (as well as students with mild mental retardation and students with emotional disturbance) have more poorly developed social skills than their nondisabled peers. Such students are more likely to ignore the teacher's directions, cheat, use profane language, disturb other students, disrupt group activities, and start fights. [As a result,] they are often rejected by the rest of the class, which contributes to lowered self-esteem and poor academic performance. (p. 201)

Helping Kids Gain Social Skills

RENEE STOVSKY

St. Louis Post-Dispatch 9/25/96

For Chad Altwies, the problem began early in elementary school.

Like many kids with learning disabilities, Chad spent a portion of his day in a resource room. There, he received tutoring to help him keep up academically with peers and to compensate for attention deficit disorder and auditory and visual processing problems.

But the special help brought special, unwanted attention along with it. Kids teased Chad about being different. Bullies found him to be an easy target for intimidation. Chad—once eager to make friends—began to withdraw.

In high school, Chad blossomed academically. But despite the fact that he participated on sports teams, was involved in church youth groups and received counseling from a variety of therapists, his social skills did not improve.

"Chad never had a group of friends. And he never went to any dance, homecoming or prom," his mother, Terry Altwies, recalled. "He was immature. He had trouble understanding quick wit or humor. He was a poor conversationalist and listener."

For Chad—now a student at St. Louis Community College at Meramec—the experience, while not a happy one, was not devastating. For his mother, a teacher, it was "the most frustrating experience of my lifetime."

"Chad used to ask me why kids never called, never invited him anywhere," she says. "But he didn't seem to require a great deal of social stimulation, either.

"It was heartbreaking for me, though. I could find tutors to help Chad with reading or higher level math. I spent summers driving him to a 'fun' job with other kids at Six Flags. I enrolled him in an Outward Bound program in Colorado, where he could learn to be part of a team. But there just wasn't much progress. It's so hard to teach someone how to make friends."

The Altwieses' experience is certainly not unique. Though kids can have social difficulties for a myriad of reasons—anything from being shy or depressed to obese or gifted—a significant portion of the learning disabled population struggles with what nationally known special educator Richard Lavoie describes as the "last one picked, first one picked on" syndrome.

As awareness of the problem grows psychologists, social workers and educators are seeking ways to address it.

[According to] Harvard psychiatrist Edward Hallowell . . . one of the reasons children with learning disabilities often appear to be socially inept is that many of them have difficulty "reading" social cues, both verbal and nonverbal. Others—especially those with ADD—have trouble with impulsivity.

That doesn't mean that such children cannot be taught to be more successful in the social arena. The key, Hallowell says, is acceptance first, and then coaching.

"So many parents put a premium these days on having an outgoing child . . . yet the image of a kid who gets invited to every birthday party is unrealistic," he says. "There isn't a parent alive who wants his or her child to be ridiculed. But popularity does not necessarily mean success in life. Thoreau was not exactly Joe Congenial."

Parents, says Hallowell, need to first "know their child's brain" and then accept and love that child, not the child they wish they might have had. "The goal is to make a child feel good about himself—unafraid socially, academically and physically."

Next, it is up to the adult world to teach children to be accepting of one another, regardless of differences. In a classroom situation, that means teaching and interacting without the use of shame, humiliation or ridicule. Outside of school, it means things like putting an emphasis on team success rather than individual performance.

And there are certainly steps that can be taken to teach all kids—but especially kids with learning differences—to be more effective at peer relations. Because learning disabled children tend to be "concrete" thinkers, they need more guidance to be able to abstract others' intent, or realize the impact of their own actions on others.

At home, it may mean family dinner discussions about the day's events, games to help encourage a child to relate to others, "magic back rubs" at bedtime to help heal a psychological wound, says Hallowell. In individual or group therapy, it might consist of role playing or conducting what Lavoie calls "autopsies"—examinations of social errors (rather than punishment for them) to discover the cause and prevent recurrences.

Marie Ferzacca, a partner at Learning Consultants in Clayton, which specializes in individual and group social skills training for preschool to college-aged kids, says 65 percent of her clients have a different learning profile—and what makes or breaks them is their ability to believe in themselves.

"The problem with most learning disabled kids is that they are bright and they know they are different," she says. "If they can keep their self-esteem intact through adolescence, the adult world is usually much more tolerant of those differences.

"I see the kids that wind up making the world a good place to be—they can be so humorous, so creative. If Robin Williams were a kid today, he would definitely be in one of our groups—he's so out-of-bounds, so impulsive and socially disinhibited," she says. "And think how much joy he has brought to the world."

Questions and Activities

1. Students with poorly developed social skills, like many of those with learning disabilities, are either shunned by others or are the targets of teasing and bullying. In order to prevent this problem, one first has to have some insight about its cause. Why do you think some children tease or bully classmates with disabilities?
2. What steps can you take to prevent the teasing and bullying of students with poorly developed social skills and to encourage others to include them in activities? You might interview a few local teachers to learn how they deal with this problem.
3. Edward Hallowell, the psychiatrist interviewed in this article, stated that it is the responsibility of the adult world to teach children to be accepting of one another, regardless of differences. Make a list of ten ways you can accomplish this goal in a classroom setting.

say, everyone at one time or another has misread numbers, letters, and words; confused pronunciations of words and letters; and suffered embarrassing lapses of attention and memory. But students with learning disabilities really are different from others—mostly in degree rather than in kind. Although the nondisabled individual may occasionally exhibit lapses in basic information processing, the learning disabled individual does so consistently and with little hope of self-correction. The important point to keep in mind is that you need to know what a student with a learning disability (as well as a low-achieving non–learning disabled student) can and cannot do so that you can effectively remediate those weaknesses (Spear-Swerling & Sternberg, 1998).

Problems with Basic Psychological Processes

The fundamental problem that underlies a learning disability is, as the law states, "a disorder in one or more basic psychological processes." Although this phrase is somewhat vague, it generally refers to problems with how students receive information, process it, and express what they have learned. Specifically, many students with learning disabilities have deficits in perception, attention, memory encoding and storage, and metacognition.

Students with learning disabilities have problems with perception, attention, memory, metacognition

Some students with learning disabilities have great difficulty perceiving the difference between certain sounds (*f* and *v*, *m* and *n*, for example) or letters (*m* and *n*, *b*, *p*, and *d*, for example). As a result, words that begin with one letter (such as *v*ase) are sometimes perceived and pronounced as if they begin with another letter (as in *f*ase). As you can no doubt appreciate from this simple example, this type of deficit makes learning to read and reading with comprehension long and frustrating for some students.

Many students with learning disabilities also have difficulty with attention and impulse control: focusing on a task, noticing important cues and ideas, and staying with the task until it is completed. The source of the distraction may be objects and activities in the classroom, or it may be unrelated thoughts. In either case, the student misses much of what the teacher says or what is on a page of text or misinterprets directions.

Because so many students with learning disabilities have problems with perception and attention, they also have problems with accurate recall of information. Accurate recall is heavily dependent on what gets stored in memory in the first place and where in memory information is stored (Hunt & Marshall, 1999), so students who encode partial, incorrect, or unimportant information have memory problems.

Like students with mild retardation, many students with learning disabilities have a deficit in metacognitive skills (Hunt & Marshall, 1999). As a result, their learning activities are chaotic, like those of young children. For example, they may begin a task before they have thought through all of the steps.

Students with learning disabilities tend to be characterized as passive and disorganized: passive in the sense that they take few active steps to attend to relevant information, store it effectively in memory, and retrieve it when needed; and disorganized in the sense that their learning activities are often unplanned and subject to whatever happens to capture their attention at the moment.

Attention-Deficit/Hyperactivity Disorder Children with extreme deficits in attention or unusually high levels of activity and impulsiveness, or both, may be diagnosed as having **attention-deficit/hyperactivity disorder (ADHD).** For a student to be judged as having ADHD, the symptoms have to appear before the age of seven; they have to be displayed in several settings, such as at home, at school, and at play; and they have to persist over time. The main symptoms of ADHD are inattention, hyperactivity, and impulsivity.

Symptoms of ADHD include inattention, hyperactivity, and impulsivity

The American Psychiatric Association recognizes three types of ADHD: children who are predominantly inattentive, children who are predominantly hyperactive and impulsive, and children who exhibit a combination of all three behaviors. It is estimated that 3 to 5 percent of all children have ADHD, with boys outnumbering girls by six to one (American Psychiatric Association, 1994). Services for children with ADHD can be funded under the "specific learning disabilities" category, the "seriously emotionally disturbed" category, or the "other health impaired" category of IDEA (Lerner, Lowenthal, & Lerner, 1995).

ADHD is usually treated with a combination of drug and behavioral therapies. The most popular class of drug prescribed for children who have been diagnosed with ADHD is amphetamines (such as Ritalin and Dexedrine). The effect of such medications is highly specific. Some children do better on Ritalin, others on Dexedrine, and still others show no improvement with either. As an adjunct to medica-

How would you respond to a child with ADHD? Read about an actual teacher's experiences in the Site-Based Cases section on this book's web site at **http://education.college.hmco.com/students**.

tion, children should also receive daily report cards, frequent positive reinforcement, social skills training, and individual therapy (Schlozman & Schlozman, 2000).

The following Suggestions for Teaching will give you some ideas about how to help students with learning disabilities and ADHD improve their learning skills and feel better about themselves.

Suggestions for Teaching in Your Classroom

Instructing Students with Learning Disabilities

1 Structure learning tasks to help students with learning disabilities and ADHD compensate for weaknesses in psychological processes.

Journal Entry
Helping Students with Learning Disabilities Improve Basic Learning Processes

Because of their weaknesses in basic psychological processes, students with learning disabilities and ADHD are often distractible, impulsive, forgetful, disorganized, poor at comprehension, and unaware of the factors that affect learning. Research findings indicate that the most effective instructional approach in such cases is one that combines direct instruction with strategy instruction (both methods are described in the chapter "Approaches to Instruction"). This combined approach has produced substantial improvements in reading comprehension, vocabulary, word recognition, memory, writing, cognitive processing, and self-concept (Swanson & Hoskyn, 1998).

The following examples are consistent with an instructional approach that is based on both direct instruction and strategy instruction.

Examples

- For students who have difficulty distinguishing between similar-looking or -sounding stimuli (such as letters, words, or phrases), point out and highlight their distinguishing characteristics. For example, highlight the circular part of the letters *b, p,* and *d* and place a directional arrow at the end of the straight segment to emphasize that they have the same shape but differ in their spatial orientation. Or highlight the letters *t* and *r* in the words *though, thought,* and *through* to emphasize that they differ from each other by the absence or presence of one letter.

Help students with learning disabilities to reduce distractions, attend to important information

- For students who are easily distracted, instruct them to place only the materials being used on top of the desk or within sight.
- For students who seem unable to attend to important stimuli such as significant sections of a text page, show them how to underline or outline in an effort to distinguish between important and unimportant material. Or suggest that they use a ruler or pointing device under each line as they read so that they can evaluate one sentence at a time. To help them attend to important parts of directions, highlight or write key words and phrases in all capitals. For especially important tasks, you might want to ask students to paraphrase or repeat directions verbatim.
- For students who have a short attention span, give brief assignments, and divide complex material into smaller segments. After each short lesson segment, provide both immediate positive feedback and tangible evidence of progress. (Many sets of published materials prepared for use with students with learning disabilities are designed in this way.)
- To improve students' memory and comprehension of information, teach memorization skills and how to relate new information to existing knowledge schemes to improve long-term storage and retrieval. Also, make frequent use of simple, concrete

analogies and examples to explain and illustrate complex, abstract ideas. (We will describe several techniques for enhancing memory and comprehension in the chapter on information-processing theory.)

- To improve organization, suggest that students use a notebook to keep a record of homework assignments, a checklist of materials needed for class, and a list of books and materials they need to take home for studying and homework.
- To improve general awareness of the learning process, emphasize the importance of thinking about the factors that could affect one's performance on a particular task, of forming a plan before actually starting to work, and of monitoring the effectiveness of learning activities.
- Consider the variety of learning environments available through multimedia software programs. Some students with learning disabilities may respond better to a combination of visual and auditory information, while others may learn best in a hands-on setting. Multimedia programs provide options to address these different styles and also allow the student to control the direction and pace of learning. Some excellent examples for young children are the Living Books series (The Learning Company).

2 Capitalize on the resources in your classroom to help students with learning disabilities improve academically, socially, and emotionally.

Although you and the resource teacher will be the main sources of instruction and support for mainstreamed students, recognize that other sources of classroom support are almost always available. The other students in your class, for example, can supplement your instructional efforts. As we pointed out in the previous chapter, peer tutoring typically produces gains in achievement and improvements in interpersonal relationships and attitudes toward subject matter. These effects have been documented for students with a learning disability as well as low-achieving students without a learning disability (Fuchs, Fuchs, Mathes, & Simmons, 1997). And do not overlook the benefits of having students with learning disabilities play the role of tutor. Giving students with disabilities the opportunity to tutor either a low-achieving classmate in a subject that is not affected by the student's disability or a younger student in a lower grade can produce a noticeable increase in self-esteem.

For more ideas for your journal, see the Reflective Journal Questions at **http://education.college.hmco.com/students**.

Another way to make use of the other students in your class is through cooperative learning. This technique was described in the last chapter and is explored in more detail in the chapter on approaches to instruction. Like peer tutoring, which it incorporates, it also produces gains in achievement, interpersonal relationships, and self-esteem.

Finally, make use of the various ways in which information can be presented to students and in which students can respond. In addition to text material and lecturing, you can use films, computer-based presentations, picture charts, diagrams, and demonstrations. In addition to having students demonstrate what they have learned through paper-and-pencil tests and other written products, you can have them make oral presentations, produce pictorial products, create an actual product, or give a performance. Hands-on activities are particularly useful for students with ADHD.

Students with Emotional Disturbance

Estimates of Emotional Disturbance

In the 2000 report to Congress on the implementation of IDEA, the Department of Education noted that 436,845 students between the ages of six and seventeen were classified as seriously emotionally disturbed for the 1998–1999 school year. This figure accounted for 8.3 percent of all schoolchildren classified as disabled and slightly less than 1 percent of the general school-age population. Not everyone agrees that these figures accurately reflect the scope of the problem. Other estimates of the extent of serious emotional disturbances in the general school-age population range from 1 percent to 20 percent (Kirk et al., 2000).

Frank Wood and Robert Zabel (1978) offer an explanation for these differences between estimates and classifications by suggesting that most identification procedures ask teachers to rate children in their classes at a particular point in time. Some identification procedures, however, stress recurrent problems. It seems possible, therefore, that although perhaps one out of five students attending public schools may sometimes exhibit emotional problems, only two or three out of one hundred will display severe, persistent problems.

Definitions of Emotional Disturbance

Two other reasons that estimates of **emotional disturbance** vary are the lack of clear descriptions of such forms of behavior and different interpretations of the descriptions that do exist. Children with *serious emotional disturbance* are defined in IDEA in this way:

Emotional disturbance: poor relationships, inappropriate behavior, depression, fears

(I) The term means a condition exhibiting one or more of the following characteristics over a long period of time and to a marked degree that adversely affects a child's educational performance:

  (A) An inability to learn that cannot be explained by intellectual, sensory, or health factors;
  (B) An inability to build or maintain satisfactory interpersonal relationships with peers and teachers;
  (C) Inappropriate types of behavior or feelings under normal circumstances;
  (D) A general pervasive mood of unhappiness or depression; or
  (E) A tendency to develop physical symptoms or fears associated with personal or school problems.

(II) The term includes schizophrenia. The term does not apply to children who are socially maladjusted, unless it is determined that they have a serious emotional disturbance. (Office of the Federal Register, 1994, pp. 13–14)

Several special education scholars (for example, Kirk et al., 2000, pp. 260–263; Heward, 2000, pp. 290–291; Smith, 2001, pp. 343–350) point out the difficulties caused by vague terminology in distinguishing between students who have emotional disturbance and students who are normal. The phrase *a long period of time,* for example, is not defined in the law (although many special education experts use six months as a rough rule of thumb). Indicators such as *satisfactory interpersonal relationships, a general pervasive mood,* and *inappropriate types of behavior or feelings under normal circumstances* are difficult to measure objectively and can often be observed in normal individuals. Because long-term observation of behavior is often critical in making a correct diagnosis of emotional disturbance, you can aid the multidisciplinary assessment team in this task by keeping a behavioral log of a child you suspect may have this disorder.

That many educators and psychologists use such terms as *emotionally disturbed*, *socially maladjusted*, and *behavior disordered* synonymously makes matters even more confusing. The term **behavior disorder** has many adherents and has been adopted by several states for two basic reasons. One reason is that it calls attention to the actual behavior that is disordered and needs to be changed. The second reason is that behaviors can be directly and objectively assessed. Although there are subtle differences between the terms *emotionally disturbed* and *behavior disorder*, they are essentially interchangeable, and you can probably assume that those who use them are referring to children who share similar characteristics. Because of the nature of bureaucracies, however, it may be necessary for anyone hoping to obtain special assistance for a child with what many contemporary psychologists would call a behavior disorder to refer to that child as *seriously emotionally disturbed* since that is the label used in IDEA.

Term *behavior disorder* focuses on behavior that needs to be changed, objective assessment

Characteristics of Students with a Serious Emotional Disturbance

Several classifications of emotional disturbance (or behavior disorders) have been made (see, for example, Quay, 1986; Wicks-Nelson & Israel, 2000). Most psychologists who have attempted to classify such forms of behavior describe two basic patterns: externalizing and internalizing.

Students who have an emotional disturbance tend to be either aggressive or withdrawn. Because aggressive students disrupt classroom routines, teachers need to focus on classroom design features and employ behavior management techniques to reduce the probability of such behaviors.

Students with behavior disorders tend to be either aggressive or withdrawn

- Externalizing students are often aggressive, uncooperative, restless, and negativistic. They tend to lie and steal, defy teachers, and be hostile to authority figures. Sometimes they are cruel and malicious.
- Internalizing students, by contrast, are typically shy, timid, anxious, and fearful. They are often depressed and lack self-confidence.

Teachers tend to be more aware of students who display aggressive disorders because their behavior often stimulates or forces reactions. The withdrawn student, however, may be more likely to develop serious emotional problems such as depression and may even be at risk of suicide during the adolescent years. The following Suggestions for Teaching will help you teach both the withdrawn student and the aggressive student.

SUGGESTIONS FOR TEACHING IN YOUR CLASSROOM

Instructing Students with Emotional Disturbance

1 Design the classroom environment and formulate lesson plans to encourage social interaction and cooperation.[2]

Foster interpersonal contact among withdrawn students

Students whose emotional disturbance manifests itself as social withdrawal may stay away from others on purpose (perhaps because they find social contacts threatening), or they may find that others stay away from them (perhaps because they have poorly developed social skills). Regardless of the cause, the classroom environment and your instructional activities can be designed to foster appropriate interpersonal contact.

Journal Entry
Activities and Materials That Encourage Cooperation

Examples

- Preschool and elementary school teachers can use toys and materials as well as organized games and sports that encourage cooperative play and have a reduced focus on individual performance. Activities might include dress-up games or puppet plays; games might include soccer, variations of It (such as tag), and kickball or softball modified such that everyone on the team gets a turn to kick or bat before the team plays in the field.
- Elementary and middle school teachers can use one or more of several team-oriented learning activities. *Cooperative Learning* (2d ed., 1995), by Robert Slavin, provides details on using such activities as student teams–achievement divisions, jigsaw, and team-accelerated instruction.

2 Prompt and reinforce appropriate social interactions.

Prompting and positive reinforcement are basic learning principles that will be discussed in the chapter on behavioral learning theory. Essentially, a prompt is a stimulus that draws out a desired response, and positive reinforcement involves giving the student a positive reinforcer (something the student wants) immediately after a desired behavior. The aim is to get the student to behave that way again. Typical reinforcers are verbal praise, stickers (with pictures of gold stars and smiley faces, for instance), and small prizes (such as a pencil with the child's name printed on it).

---

[2]Most of these suggestions were derived from points made in Chapters 6 and 8 of *Strategies for Managing Behavior Problems in the Classroom* (1998), by Mary Margaret Kerr and C. Michael Nelson.

Example

- You can set up a cooperative task or activity: "Marc, I would like you to help Carol and Raquel paint the scenery for next week's play. You can paint the trees and flowers, Carol will paint the grass, and Raquel will do the people." After several minutes, say something like, "That's good work. I am really pleased at how well the three of you are working together." Similar comments can be made at intervals as the interaction continues.

3 Train other students to initiate social interaction.

In all likelihood, you will have too many classroom responsibilities to spend a great deal of time working directly with a withdrawn child. It may be possible, however, using the steps that follow, to train other students to initiate contact with withdrawn students.

Example

- First, choose a student as a helper who interacts freely and well, can follow your instructions, and can concentrate on the training task for at least ten minutes. Second, explain that the goal is to get the withdrawn child to work or play with the helping student but that the helper should expect rejection, particularly at first. Role-play the actions of a withdrawn child so that the helper understands what you mean by rejection. Emphasize the importance of making periodic attempts at interaction. Third, instruct the helper to suggest games or activities that appeal to the withdrawn student. Fourth, reinforce the helper's attempts to interact with the withdrawn child.

Journal Entry
Getting Students to Initiate Interaction with a Withdrawn Child

4 Design the classroom environment to reduce the probability of disruptive behavior.

Use techniques to forestall aggressive or antisocial behavior

The best way to deal with aggressive or antisocial behavior is to nip it in the bud. This strategy has at least three related benefits. One benefit of fewer disruptions is that you can better accomplish what you had planned for the day. A second benefit is that you are likely to be in a more positive frame of mind than if you spend half the day acting as a referee. A third benefit is that because of fewer disruptions and a more positive attitude, you may be less inclined to resort to permissible or even impermissible forms of physical punishment (which often produces undesirable side effects).

Examples

- With student input, formulate rules for classroom behavior and penalties for infractions of rules. Remind all students of the penalties, particularly when a disruptive incident seems about to occur, and consistently apply the penalties when the rules are broken.
- Place valued objects and materials out of reach when they are not needed or in use.
- Minimize the aggressive student's frustration with learning by using some of the same techniques you would use for a child with mild retardation: break tasks down into small, easy-to-manage pieces; provide clear directions; and reinforce correct responses.

5 Reinforce appropriate behavior, and, if necessary, punish inappropriate behavior.

In suggestion 2, we described the use of positive reinforcement to encourage desired behavior. Reinforcement has the dual effect of teaching the aggressive student which behavior is appropriate and reducing the frequency of inappropriate behavior as it is replaced by desired behavior. Disruptive behavior will still occur, however. Three effective techniques for suppressing it while reinforcing desired behaviors are contingency contracts, token economies and fines, and time-out. Each of these techniques will be described in the chapter on behavioral and social learning theories.

6 Use group contingency-management techniques.

Up to now, we have suggested methods that focus on aggressive students. In addition, you may want to reward the entire class when the aggressive student behaves appropriately for a certain period of time. Such rewards, which may be free time, special classroom events, or certain privileges, should make the aggressive student the hero and foster better peer relationships.

Gifted and Talented Students

Students who learn at a significantly faster rate than their peers or who possess superior talent in one or more areas also need to be taught in special ways if they are to make the most of their abilities. Unlike students with mental retardation, learning disabilities, and emotional disturbance, however, students with superior capabilities are not covered by IDEA. Instead, the federal government provides technical assistance to states and local school districts for establishing programs for superior students. Although most states have such programs, some experts in special education (for example, Horowitz & O'Brien, 1986) feel that they are not given the resources they need to meet the needs of all gifted and talented students adequately. The Suggestions for Teaching that follow a bit later reflect this situation. All of the suggestions are inexpensive to implement and require few additional personnel.

A definition of the term **gifted and talented** was part of a bill passed by Congress in 1988:

Gifted and talented students show high performance in one or more areas

> The term *gifted and talented children and youth* means children and youth who give evidence of high performance capability in areas such as intellectual, creative, artistic, or leadership capacity, or in specific academic fields, and who require services or activities not ordinarily provided by the school in order to fully develop such capabilities. (Title IV-H.R.5, 1988, pp. 227–228)

Identification of Gifted and Talented Students

Eligibility for gifted and talented programs has traditionally been based on standardized test scores, particularly IQ tests. It was not uncommon in years past for students to have to achieve an IQ score of at least 130 to be admitted to such programs. But criticisms about the narrow range of skills covered by such tests (mainly Gardner's linguistic and logical-mathematical intelligences and Sternberg's analytical ability) have led most states to eliminate the use of a numerical cutoff score for identification (Cassidy & Johnson, 1986).

Although this is seen as a step in the right direction, critical weaknesses in the identification of gifted and talented children remain, particularly gifted children from minority cultures:

Minorities underrepresented in gifted classes because of overreliance on test scores

- Achievement and mental ability, especially IQ, are still often looked to as indicators of giftedness at the expense of such other relevant characteristics as motivation, creativity, leadership, and critical thinking ability (Feldhusen, 1998).
- Many educators are unfamiliar with ways of measuring human characteristics other than by standardized tests. Checklists, rating scales, and nominations by peers and adults can also be used (Richert, 1997).
- There is a general ignorance of characteristics that are more highly valued by a minority culture than by the majority culture. Some Native American tribes, for example, deemphasize the concept of giftedness because it runs counter to their belief that the welfare and cohesion of the group are more important than celebrating and nurturing the talents of any individual. The members of other tribes may place as much value on a child's knowledge of tribal traditions, storytelling ability, and artistic ability as they do on problem-solving ability and scientific reasoning (Callahan & McIntire, 1994). A child's giftedness may therefore be evident only when examined from the perspective of a particular culture. This may explain why only 2 percent of Native Americans can be found in classes for the gifted and talented (Winner, 1997).

CHARACTERISTICS OF GIFTED AND TALENTED STUDENTS

In one sense, gifted and talented students are like any other group of students. Some are healthy and well coordinated, whereas others are not. Some are extremely popular and well liked, but others are not. Some are well adjusted; others are not (Heward, 2000). But as a group, gifted and talented students are often noticeably different (see, for example, discussions by Dai, Moon, & Feldhusen, 1998; Piechowski, 1997; and Winner, 1997). Here are some of the main characteristics that many gifted and talented students share:

Gifted and talented students differ from their nongifted peers intellectually and emotionally

- They excel on tasks that involve language, abstract logical thinking, and mathematics.
- They are faster at encoding information and retrieving it from memory.
- They are highly aware of how they learn and the various conditions that affect their learning. As a result, they excel at transferring previously learned information and skills to new problems and settings.
- They exhibit such high levels of motivation and task persistence that the phrase "rage to master" is sometimes used to describe their behavior. Their motivation to learn is partly due to high levels of self-efficacy and appropriate attributions. That is, they believe they have the capability to master those tasks and subject matters they choose to tackle and that their success is the result of both high ability and hard work.
- They tend to be more solitary and introverted than average children.
- They tend to have very intense emotional lives. They react with intense feelings, such as joy, regret, or sorrow, to a story, a piece of music, or a social encounter. They also tend to be emotionally sensitive and sometimes surpass adults in their ability to notice and identify with the feelings of others.

For the most part, gifted and talented students see themselves as they were just described. In comparison to intellectually average students, they have a moderately

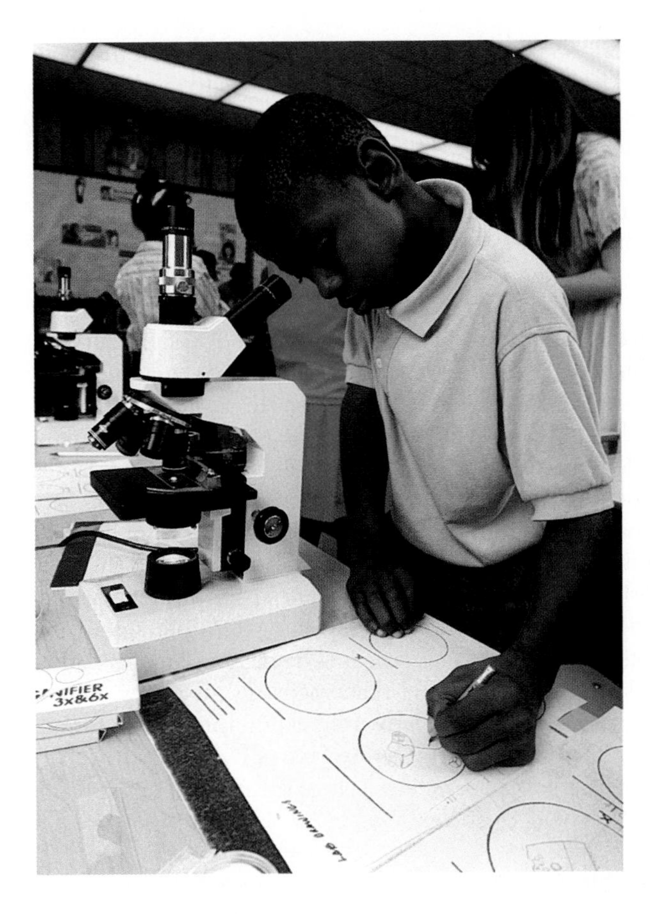

Because gifted and talented students understand and integrate abstract ideas more quickly than do their non-gifted classmates, they are capable of successfully completing tasks that older students routinely carry out.

stronger academic self-concept but score at about the same level on measures of physical and social self-concepts (Hoge & Renzulli, 1993).

Instructional Options

For the story of one teacher's response to a gifted child, see the Site-Based Cases section on this book's web site at **http://education.college.hmco.com/students**.

Gifted and talented students constantly challenge a teacher's skill, ingenuity, and classroom resources. While trying to instruct the class as a whole, the teacher is faced with the need to provide more and more interesting and challenging materials and ideas to gifted students. In this section, we will examine three possible ways to engage these students.

Accelerated Instruction Accelerated instruction is often suggested as one way to meet the academic needs of gifted and talented students. For many people, the phrase *accelerated instruction* means allowing the student to skip one or more grades, which, while not as common as in years past, does occasionally occur. But there are at least three other ways of accomplishing the same goal: (1) the curriculum can be compressed, allowing gifted and talented students to complete the work for more than one grade during the regular school year; (2) the school year can be extended by the use of summer sessions; and (3) students can take college courses while still in high school.

Whatever the form of accelerated instruction, this is always a hotly debated topic, with pros and cons on each side. Two often quoted advantages for giving gifted students the opportunity to work on complex tasks are that it keeps them from becoming bored with school, and it produces more positive attitudes toward learning. On the negative side, two frequent arguments are that a gifted student may have trouble with the social and emotional demands of acceleration, and acceleration produces an undesirable sense of elitism among gifted students (Benbow, 1991; Kulik & Kulik, 1984). As with all other informed educational decisions, the unique needs of the individual and the situation must be considered before the best course of action can be determined.

Gifted and Talented Classes and Schools Some public school districts offer separate classes for gifted and talented students as either an alternative to accelerated instruction or something that follows accelerated instruction. In addition, so-called magnet schools are composed of students whose average level of ability is higher than that found in a typical elementary, middle, or high school. Finally, many states sponsor high-ability high schools, particularly in mathematics and science.

Separate classes for gifted and talented students aid achievement but may lower academic self-concept of some students

Recent findings suggest that such placements do not produce uniformly positive results and should be made only after the characteristics of the student and the program have been carefully considered. In terms of achievement, the typical gifted student can expect to score moderately higher (at about the sixty-third percentile) on tests than comparable students who remain in heterogeneous classes (Kulik & Kulik, 1991). But the effects of separate class or school placement on measures of academic self-concept have been inconsistent; some researchers find them to be higher than those of students who remain in heterogeneous classes, whereas other researchers have found either no differences or declines (Hoge & Renzulli, 1993; Kulik & Kulik, 1991; Marsh, Chessor, Craven, & Roche, 1995).

Enrichment and Differentiated Instruction Because of the potential negative effects of grade skipping, the limited availability of special classes and schools, and the fact that such classes and schools are not good options for some gifted and talented students, teachers may find themselves with one or two gifted and talented students in a regular classroom. A solution for meeting the special needs of these students (as well as those with disabilities) is a practice often referred to as *differentiated instruction*, a technique we have mentioned earlier. Basically, this means using different learning materials, instructional methods, assignments, and tests for different groups of students (Page, 2000; Winebrenner, 2000).

One scheme for delivering differentiated instruction to gifted and talented learners can be found in two books by Joseph Renzulli and Sally Reis (Reis & Renzulli, 1985; Renzulli & Reis, 1985). Renzulli and Reis describe three levels of curriculum enrichment for gifted and talented learners:

Type I enrichment: Exploratory activities that are designed to expose students to topics, events, books, people, and places not ordinarily covered in the regular curriculum. The basic purpose of these activities is to stimulate new interests. Among the many suggestions Renzulli and Reis offer are having students view and write reports on films and videocassettes (such as *The Eagle Has Landed: The Flight of Apollo 11*) and having local residents make presentations on their occupation or hobby.

Type II enrichment: Instructional methods and materials aimed at the development of such thinking and feeling processes as thinking creatively, classifying and analyzing data, solving problems, appreciating, and valuing.

Type III enrichment: Activities in which students investigate and collect data about a real topic or problem. For example, a student may decide to document the history of her school, focusing on such issues as changes in size, instructional materials and methods, and curriculum.

Numerous sites on the Internet are devoted to long-distance education, enrichment, and tutoring. You might explore the Global Network Academy (**www.gnacademy.org/**), which offers online courses in a wide range of areas. The International Tutoring Foundation (**edie.cprost.sfu.ca/it/programs.html**), a nonprofit organization based at the University of Toronto, provides tutoring for all age and grade levels, including special programs for gifted students (as well as for students with disabilities). The following Suggestions for Teaching provide further ideas for working with gifted and talented students.

Suggestions for Teaching in Your Classroom

Instructing Gifted and Talented Students

1 Consult with gifted and talented students regarding individual study projects, perhaps involving a learning contract.

Journal Entry
Individual Study for Students Who Are Gifted and Talented

One of the most effective ways to deal with gifted students is to assign individual study projects. These may involve a contract approach, in which you consult with students on an individual basis and agree on a personal assignment that is to be completed by a certain date.

Such assignments should probably be related to some part of the curriculum. If you are studying Mexico, for example, a gifted student could devote free time to a special report on some aspect of Mexican life that intrigues him. In making these assignments, you should remember that even very bright students may not be able to absorb, organize, and apply abstract concepts until they become formal thinkers. Thus, until early middle school years, it may be preferable to keep these assignments brief rather than comprehensive.

To provide another variation of the individual study project, you could ask the gifted student to act as a research specialist and report on questions that puzzle the class. Still another individual study project is the creation of an open-ended, personal yearbook. Any time a gifted student finishes the assigned work, she might be allowed to write stories or do drawings for such a journal.

When possible, unobtrusive projects are preferable. Perhaps you can recall a teacher who rewarded the fast workers by letting them work on a mural (or the equivalent) covering the side board. If you were an average student, you can probably attest that the sight of the class "brains" having the time of their lives was not conducive to diligent effort on the part of the have-nots sweating away at their workbooks. Reward assignments should probably be restricted to individual work on unostentatious projects.

2 Encourage supplementary reading and writing.

Journal Entry
Providing Gifted and Talented Students with Opportunities for Additional Reading and Writing

Encourage students to spend extra time reading and writing. A logical method of combining both skills is the preparation of book reports. It is perhaps less threatening to call them book *reviews* and emphasize that you are interested in personal reaction, not a précis or an abstract. Some specialists in the education of the gifted have suggested that such students be urged to read biographies and autobiographies.

The line of reasoning here is that potential leaders might be inspired to emulate the exploits of a famous person. Even if such inspiration does not result, you could recommend life stories simply because they are usually interesting.

Other possibilities for writing are e-mail exchanges with other students, siblings at college, or friends in different areas. Or a student may write a review of a World Wide Web site that she has discovered. If the appropriate software and support are available, students could be encouraged to create home pages or web sites for themselves, either on a topic mutually selected with the teacher or on their personal interests (the latter would be much like a yearbook entry).

3 Have gifted students act as tutors.

Depending on the grade, subject, and personalities of those involved, gifted students might be asked to act occasionally as tutors, lab assistants, or the equivalent. Some bright students will welcome such opportunities and are capable of providing instruction in such a way that their peers do not feel self-conscious or humiliated. Others may resent being asked to spend school time helping classmates or may lack skills in interpersonal relationships. If you do decide to ask a gifted student to function as a tutor, it would be wise to proceed tentatively and cautiously.

Using Technology to Assist Exceptional Students

There is perhaps no other place in education today where technology is making as significant an impact as in the field of special education. Interpretations of least restrictive environments and other legislation have expanded the scope of technological services that schools are required to provide for disabled students (Parette, Dunn, & Hoge, 1995). For instance, the Education of the Handicapped Act Amendments of 1980 (PL 99-457) mandate the provision of adapted technology for any need related to the learning or development of a child (Snider & Badgett, 1995).

Federal legislation has led to the development of various assistive technologies

As the laws related to the disabled have expanded, there has been a simultaneous proliferation in assistive technologies to help students with special learning needs succeed academically. **Assistive technology** refers to "any item, device, or piece of equipment that is used to increase, maintain, or improve the functional abilities of persons with disabilities" (PL 100-407, Technology Related Assistance for Individuals with Disabilities Act of 1988, 29 U.S.C. 2202, Section 3[2]; Holder-Brown & Parette, 1992). Such tools may range from less expensive low-tech equipment such as adapted spoons, joysticks, taped stories, adaptive switches, head-pointing devices, and communication boards (message display devices that contain vocabulary choices from which the child can select an answer) to commercially developed high-tech devices such as screen magnifiers, speech synthesizers and digitizers, voice-recognition devices, touch screens, and alternative computer keyboards (Blackhurst, 1997; Messerer, 1997; Snider & Badgett, 1995).

What kinds of assistive technology are available? Check the links in the Technology Demos section at **http://education.college.hmco.com/students**.

Advances in technology to assist visually and hearing-impaired students, provide powered mobility for the physically impaired, and offer augmented communication tools to those who lack the ability to communicate their needs to others are occurring worldwide (Howell, 1996; Parette, Hourcade, & VanBiervliet, 1993).

TECHNOLOGY FOR STUDENTS WITH HEARING IMPAIRMENTS

Hearing-impaired students can be assisted with technology tools in a number of ways, including closed captioning, multimedia technologies, and electronic networking. Recent laws have required television sets in the United States to be equipped with internal decoding circuitry for captioning of text on the screen so that it can be read, while placing pressure on educators to provide captioning within educational videotapes and television programs (Elwell, Reeve, & Hofmeister, 1992).

Multimedia programs and other technologies are emerging to help hearing-impaired students develop their sign language and lip-reading skills, vocabulary and reading comprehension, and spoken and written communication skills (Aedo, Miranda, Panetsos, Torra, & Martin, 1994). One highly visible electronic network–based classroom known as ENFI (Electronic Networks for Interaction) (Bruce, Peyton, & Batson, 1993) was developed in 1985 at Gallaudet University, a well-known school for the deaf in Washington, D.C. Collaborative writing tools like Realtime Writer are included within ENFI to teach writing to hearing-impaired students by conducting all class discussion and interaction in electronic writing. Here, students and the teacher sit at computer terminals and compose messages at the bottom of their computer screens. Student work can be transmitted to all computer screens in the class, or it can be read by and discussed privately with the teacher.

For links to the web sites mentioned in this section, plus other important web resources, go to **http://education.college.hmco.com/students**.

The web site for Gallaudet University includes a page that describes its Technology Access Program (**http://tap.gallaudet.edu/**). This program examines technologies and services that eliminate communication barriers traditionally faced by the deaf and hard of hearing. It describes, for example, the current state of speech-to-text software (also known as speech recognition software). Another part of the Gallaudet web site is Software to Go (**http://clerccenter2.gallaudet.edu/stg/**), a clearinghouse for software evaluation.

TECHNOLOGY FOR STUDENTS WITH VISUAL IMPAIRMENTS

Closed captioning and web-based conferencing tools are popular among deaf students; speech synthesizers and speech recognition devices offer similar liberating assistance to those who are visually impaired (Messerer, 1997; Scrase, 1997). With speech synthesis, the user can select a word, sentence, or chunk of information from any written or scanned text and hear it pronounced by a speech synthesizer. For example, DECTalk is a speech synthesis program that analyzes, synthesizes, and converts plain text into high-quality speech that is nearly as comprehensible as recorded speech. Using seven built-in voices, the DECTalk system provides online reading and computerized speech support (Leong, 1995). Speech recognition allows the visually impaired student to access computer files and different options by talking.

In addition, software programs called screen readers (such as Job Access with Speech, Windows-Eyes, WinVision, and ScreenPower) allow individuals with visual impairments to have the contents of a screen read to them by a speech synthesis program. The web sites of the National Federation of the Blind (**www.nfb.org/**) and the American Printing House for the Blind (**www.aph.org/**) describe screen readers and other software and hardware devices that are available for individuals with visual impairments.

Technology for Students with Orthopedic Impairments

For students who have physical limitations, pointing devices held in the mouth or attached to the head may provide the needed device control. Students with more limited fields of motion but acceptable fine motor skill may also benefit from condensed or mini keyboards that position the keys more closely together and require less strength to use (Snider & Badgett, 1995). For students with less fine motor control, touch-sensitive expanded keyboards offer more space between keys and are often programmed to accept overlay plastic sheets for different applications or user needs. Free programs (called freeware) and inexpensive ones (called shareware) for helping individuals with physical and other disabilities more effectively use computers can be found at the Virtual Assistive Technology Center web site (**www.at-center.com/**) These programs are available for the Mac, Windows, and DOS operating systems.

Technology for Students with Speech or Language Impairments

Technology can also help individuals with communication impairments. Using computer software with a speech synthesizer and expanded keyboard, Teris Schery and Lisa O'Connor (1997) demonstrated positive effects of computer training in vocabulary, early grammar skills, and social communication among toddlers with Down syndrome as well as young children with severe language and behavioral disabilities. In a small pilot study, they later discovered that parent volunteers briefly trained in using this software can be more effective than a professional speech pathologist. Computer programs designed to help students with speech or language impairments acquire language and communication skills can be found on the web sites of Apple Computer (**www.apple.com/disability/language/**) and the International Society for Augmentative and Alternative Communication (**www.isaac-online.org/**).

Technology for Students with Learning Disabilities

Whereas assistive technology is intended to compensate for or circumvent a disability, some instructional technologies are meant to help students with learning disabilities remediate their difficulties (Raskind, 1993). Many new technology tools can help learning disabled (LD) students spend less time concentrating on such surface-level task demands as the spelling and formatting of papers and more time analyzing problems, interpreting information, and reflecting on answers. According to David Kumar and Cynthia Wilson (1997), a variety of tools are now available for LD students to reduce the cognitive demands of a task by serving as external memory aids. For instance, talking calculators provide auditory feedback or confirmation of basic mathematical operations.

In the area of reading, some software programs can help young LD readers focus on basic phoneme identification and segmentation (Torgesen & Barker, 1995), and hypertext applications can help younger children develop prereading skills (Boone, Higgins, Notari, & Stump, 1996). For high school students, hypertext can create multiple ways to interact with text material and learn new information (Higgins, Boone, & Lovitt, 1996). For instance, Charles MacArthur and Jacqueline Haynes (1995) found that the reading comprehension of LD high school students was enhanced when the computer system included such features as speech synthesis, an online glossary, links between questions raised and the text, computer highlighting of main ideas, and supplemental summaries and explanations.

In the area of writing, Charles MacArthur (1996) notes that there are many tools for students with learning disabilities that can help them—and other students—with basic sentence generation, transcription, and revision. As indicated earlier, spelling, style, and grammar checkers can help raise student focus from the mechanical demands and surface-level concerns about task length requirements to higher-level text cohesion and integration issues. However, MacArthur (1994) cautions that technology by itself does not improve middle school LD student writing. Instead, he has found that sound instructional practices such as peer tutoring on the word-processed text raise the quality and number of student revisions and overall quality of their writing.

There are also tools for LD students to set writing goals, generate content, and plan and evaluate their writing (MacArthur, 1996). Personal data managers, for instance, might help LD students record writing deadlines, remember important due dates, and plan their writing schedules (Raskind, 1993). Computerized sticky notes, outlining aids, and semantic webbing tools can also facilitate organization of their ideas prior to writing (Raskind, 1993). In addition, computer prompting programs can help students brainstorm and organize ideas and reflect on audience needs (Bonk & Reynolds, 1992). Finally, electronic dictionaries, thesauruses, and encyclopedias open up new vistas in LD student written communication (Skinner, Gillespie, & Balkam, 1997).

Additional information about resources and teaching strategies for students with learning disabilities can be found on the web sites for LD Online (**www.ldonline.org/**) and the Council for Learning Disabilities (**www.cec.sped.org/**). The former contains two potentially useful features. One is called Ask Dr. Silver, in which Larry Silver, a child and adolescent psychiatrist who specializes in treating children with LD or ADHD, answers questions. The other is Mentor Teacher of the Month (found on the Teacher's Home Page, **http://www.ldonline.org/teaching/index.html**), in which an experienced teacher shares ideas and strategies for teaching students with learning disabilities.

Technology for Gifted and Talented Students

Gifted students can also benefit from advances in instructional technology, such as distance education. Stanford University, for instance, has been experimenting with providing year-round accelerated instruction in mathematics, physics, English, and computer science to gifted high school students through the Education Program for Gifted Youth (EPGY) (Ravaglia, Suppes, Stillinger, & Alper, 1995). In addition to digitized lectures and online quizzes, students in EPGY can contact the instructors using e-mail, telephone project staff, attend discussion sessions at Stanford, and try out various physics experiments at home. Given all these supports, it is not surprising that students have done exceedingly well in this program. The web site for EPGY can be found at **www-epgy.stanford.edu/**.

An online enrichment activity that can be used for any student, including the gifted and talented, is a web quest. This is an inquiry-oriented activity in which most or all of the information that students need is drawn from the Web. An excellent source of web quests is the WebQuest Page of San Diego State University (**http://edweb.sdsu.edu/webquest/webquest.html/**). Here you will find dozens of activities arranged by grade level and by subject matter within each grade level. For example, one of the English–language arts activities at the middle school level is, "Was It Murder? The Death of King Tutankhamun: The Boy King." A team of five students is given the following task and questions to answer:

SUMMARY

1. Three early attempts at dealing with student variability were age-graded classrooms, ability grouping, and special class placement. Age-graded classrooms grouped students who were roughly the same age. Ability grouping sorted normal students into separate classes according to mental ability test scores. Special class placement was used to separate normal students from those with mental and physical disabilities.

2. Virtually all elementary schools and most middle and high schools use some form of ability grouping.

3. The four currently popular approaches to ability grouping are between-class ability grouping, regrouping, the Joplin Plan, and within-class ability grouping. Within-class ability grouping is most frequently used in the elementary grades, while between-class ability grouping is most frequently used in the high school grades.

4. Ability grouping is based on the assumptions that intelligence is genetically determined, is reflected by an IQ score, and is unchangeable and that instruction is more effective with homogeneous groups of students.

5. There is no research support for between-class ability grouping and limited support for regrouping. Moderately positive results have been found for the Joplin Plan, as well as within-class ability grouping.

6. Students in low-ability groups often receive lower-quality instruction.

7. In the light of research findings on ability grouping, educators may choose to discontinue the use of between-class ability grouping, use only within-class grouping and the Joplin Plan, or discontinue all forms of ability grouping.

8. The Education for All Handicapped Children Act (Public Law 94-142) was enacted in 1975 to ensure that students with disabling conditions receive the same free and appropriate education as nondisabled students. Since then, the law has been revised and expanded, and it is now known as the Individuals with Disabilities Education Act (IDEA).

9. Major provisions of IDEA include the right to a free and appropriate public education, an appropriate and valid preplacement evaluation, the development of an individualized education program (IEP), the education of students with disabilities in the least restrictive environment (also known as mainstreaming), and procedural safeguards.

10. In some school districts, mainstreaming has been extended to the point where students with disabilities are taught only in regular classrooms by regular and special education teachers. This practice is known as inclusion, or full inclusion.

11. The evidence on inclusion, although somewhat limited and inconsistent, indicates that the practice produces at least moderate benefits for some students with disabilities but has little beneficial effect on others.

12. Inclusion is likely to work best for students with disabilities for whom the regular classroom is an appropriate setting and in classrooms where the teacher uses instructional methods that are proven to be effective with a wide variety of learners.

13. The regular classroom teacher's responsibilities under IDEA may include participation in referral, assessment, preparation of the IEP, and implementation of the IEP.

14. Children with mild mental retardation are likely to be mainstreamed for some part of the school day and week. They are likely to have a low tolerance for frustration, lack confidence and self-esteem, oversimplify matters, and have difficulty generalizing from one situation to another.

15. Students with learning disabilities account for more than half of all students with disabilities. They have a disorder in one or more of such basic psychological processes as perception, attention, memory, and metacognition, which leads to learning problems not attributable to other causes.

16. Children with attention-deficit/hyperactivity disorder (ADHD) may be inattentive, hyperactive, and impulsive, or all three, over an extended period of time and in such different settings as home, school, and at play.

17. The actual number of schoolchildren with serious emotional disturbance is unknown because of variation in identification procedures, vague definitions of emotional disturbance, and differences in interpretation of definitions.

18. Most classifications of disturbed behavior focus on aggressive behavior or withdrawn behavior.

19. Students who are gifted and talented excel in performing tasks that require intellectual, creative, artistic, or leadership ability.

20. Minorities are underrepresented in gifted and talented classes because standardized test scores are emphasized at the expense of other indexes such as motivation, creativity, leadership, and critical thinking ability.

21. The academic needs of students who are gifted and talented are usually met through accelerated instruction, placement in classes or schools for the gifted and talented, or classroom enrichment activities. Special classes and schools typically produce moderate achievement benefits but can also produce declines in academic self-concept.

22. A variety of adaptive technologies exist to help students with special needs. These include closed captioning, word processing within networked computers, speech synthesis, voice recognition, screen magnifiers, special keyboards, writing tools, and distance education.

Key Terms

between-class ability grouping *(186)*
regrouping *(186)*
Joplin Plan *(186)*
within-class ability grouping *(186)*
individualized education program (IEP) *(190)*
least restrictive environment *(191)*
mainstreaming *(191)*
inclusion *(192)*
full inclusion *(192)*
multidisciplinary assessment team *(195)*
mental retardation *(197)*
learning disabilities *(200)*
attention-deficit/hyperactivity disorder (ADHD) *(204)*
emotional disturbance *(207)*
behavior disorder *(208)*
gifted and talented *(211)*
assistive technology *(216)*

Discussion Questions

1. You probably experienced ability grouping in one form or another at the elementary and secondary levels. Try to recall the ability grouping used in your schools. Think about whether it might have been between-class grouping, regrouping, the Joplin Plan, or within-class grouping. Could you tell which group you were in? Did you have feelings about being in that group? How did you feel about classmates who were in other groups? Do you think this practice aided or hindered your educational progress? Why? Given your own experiences as a student and what you have learned from this chapter, would you advocate or employ some form of ability grouping for your own students someday?

2. Many regular classroom teachers say that although they agree with the philosophy behind IDEA, they feel that their training has not adequately prepared them for meeting the needs of students with disabling conditions. Would you say the same about your teacher education program? Why? If you feel that your training is not adequately equipping you to teach students who are mentally retarded, learning disabled, or emotionally disturbed, what might you do to prepare yourself better?

3. Relatively little money is spent on programs for the gifted and talented compared to the amounts made available for the disabled. Defenders of this arrangement sometimes argue that because money for educational programs is always short and because gifted students have a built-in advantage rather than a disability, we *should* invest most of our resources in programs and services for the disabled. Do you agree or disagree? Explain why.

Learning and Instruction

Part II

7 Behavioral and Social Learning Theories

Now that you are familiar with how students develop from preschool through high school, some of the major ways in which students differ from one another, and the main ways in which schools try to address student variability, it is time to examine what is perhaps the most fundamental and important aspect of schooling: the learning process. Because the primary reason that we have schools is to help children acquire the knowledge and skills that adults consider necessary for successful functioning in society, the instructional and curricular decisions that teachers make should be based on an understanding of how people learn. But as with most of the other topics in this

KEY POINTS

These key points will help you learn the important information in this chapter. To help you study, they also appear in the margins of the pages, next to the text where they are discussed.

Operant Conditioning

- Operant conditioning: voluntary response strengthened or weakened by consequences that follow
- Positive reinforcement: strengthen a target behavior by presenting a positive reinforcer after the behavior occurs
- Negative reinforcement: strengthen a target behavior by removing an aversive stimulus after the behavior occurs
- Punishment: weaken a target behavior by presenting an aversive stimulus after the behavior occurs
- Time-out: weaken a target behavior by temporarily removing a positive reinforcer after the behavior occurs
- Extinction: weaken a target behavior by ignoring it
- Spontaneous recovery: extinguished behaviors may reappear spontaneously
- Generalization: responding in similar ways to similar stimuli
- Discrimination: responding in different ways to similar stimuli
- Complex behaviors are shaped by reinforcing closer approximations to terminal behavior
- Fixed interval schedules: reinforce after regular time intervals
- Variable interval schedules: reinforce after random time intervals
- Fixed ratio schedules: reinforce after a set number of responses
- Variable ratio schedules: reinforce after a different number of responses each time

Educational Applications of Operant Conditioning Principles

- Programmed instruction: arrange material in small steps; reinforce correct responses
- Types of CAI programs include drill and practice, simulations, tutorials
- CAI-taught students learn more with simulation programs than with drill-and-practice programs
- CAI works best for elementary grade students, low achievers, urban students
- ILS: comprehensive, self-paced learning system
- Behavior modification: shape behavior by ignoring undesirable responses, reinforcing desirable responses
- Premack principle: required work first, then chosen reward
- Token economy is a flexible reinforcement system
- Contingency contracting: reinforcement supplied after student completes mutually agreed-on assignment
- Time-out works best with disruptive, aggressive children
- Punishment is likely to be ineffective because of temporary impact, side effects

Social Learning Theory

- People learn to inhibit or make responses by observing others
- Processes of observational learning: attention, retention, production, motivation
- Imitation is strengthened through direct reinforcement, vicarious reinforcement, self-reinforcement
- Self-efficacy: how capable one feels to handle particular kinds of tasks
- Self-efficacy influenced by past performance, persuasion, emotional reactions, observation of models
- Self-efficacy affects one's goals, thought processes, persistence, emotions
- Cognitive skills can be learned by observation of models

Using Computer-Assisted Instruction in Your Classroom

- Computers in school used mostly for word processing, drill, and as reference source
- Need to make informed choices of software
- CAI no substitute for high-quality teaching

text, learning is a complex phenomenon that has been studied from different perspectives.

Since 1879, when the first laboratory devoted to the scientific study of human behavior was opened in Leipzig, Germany, by Wilhelm Wundt, learning has been studied more extensively by more psychologists than any other aspect of human behavior. As a result, there are varied, seemingly conflicting opinions about how teachers should arrange learning activities in classrooms. Such differences of opinion are not necessarily a problem because different theories and the approaches to teaching that flow from them complement, rather than compete with, one another. Think of these different theories as something like a jigsaw puzzle. To see the entire picture, you need to have all the pieces, and you need to know how to put them together. We hope that you will have some sense of how to do that by the end of Part II.

This chapter is devoted to two theories of learning: a type of behavioral learning theory known as operant conditioning and social learning theory. Although different, they share certain assumptions about principles of learning. We begin with operant conditioning because it was the earlier of the two theories and because it helps lay the groundwork for understanding social learning theory. ■

Operant Conditioning

In 1913, with the publication of an article titled "Psychology as the Behaviorist Views It," the influential American psychologist John Watson argued that psychology would quickly lose credibility as a science if it focused on internal mental and emotional states that could not be directly observed or accurately measured. The solution was to study what could be directly observed and objectively and accurately measured: the external stimuli that people experienced and what people did in response—in a word, behavior.

From this point until the late 1960s, behavioral theories of one sort or another dominated the psychology of learning. Although they are less popular today, they still offer many useful ideas for classroom teachers.

For a preview of this chapter's key ideas, see the Chapter Themes on the Snowman textbook site at **http://education.college.hmco.com/students**.

Basic Nature and Assumptions

Operant conditioning: voluntary response strengthened or weakened by consequences that follow

Behavioral learning theories culminated in the work of B. F. Skinner. Skinner put together a theory that not only successfully combines many different ideas but also serves as the basis for a variety of applications to human behavior. Skinner's theory, **operant conditioning,** takes as its starting point that many of the voluntary responses of animals and humans are strengthened when they are reinforced (followed by a desirable consequence) and weakened when they are either ignored or punished. In this way, organisms learn new behaviors and when to exhibit them and "unlearn" existing behaviors. The term *operant conditioning* refers to the fact that organisms learn to "operate" on their environment (make a particular response) in order to obtain or avoid a particular consequence. Some psychologists use the term *instrumental* because the behavior is instrumental in bringing about the consequence.

Most of the experiments on which the principles of operant conditioning are based involved an ingenious apparatus that Skinner invented and is appropriately referred to as a Skinner box. This is a small enclosure that contains only a bar (or lever) and a small tray. Outside the box is a hopper holding a supply of food pellets that are dropped into the tray when the bar is pressed under certain conditions.

A hungry rat is placed in the box, and when in the course of exploring its new environment, the rat approaches and then presses the bar, it is rewarded with a food pellet. The rat then presses the bar more frequently than it did before being rewarded. If food pellets are supplied under some conditions when the bar is pushed down—for example, when a tone is sounded—but not under others, the rat learns to discriminate one situation from the other, and the rate of bar pressing drops noticeably when the tone is not sounded. If a tone is sounded that is very close in frequency to the original tone, the rat generalizes (treats the two tones as equivalent) and presses the bar at the same rate for both. But if the food pellets are not given after the rat presses the bar, that behavior stops, or is extinguished.

The Skinner box's prominent role in operant conditioning experiments reflects Skinner's view of psychology as a natural science. Several important assumptions underlie this view:

- *Assumption 1.* Underlying all natural sciences is the assumption that natural phenomena (such as weather patterns, earthquakes, and human behavior) may appear on the surface to be random but really operate according to set laws. What psychology needed, in Skinner's view, was the means by which a researcher could control the environment to observe the lawful and hence predictable influence of environmental factors on behavior.
- *Assumption 2.* A science develops most effectively when scientists study some phenomenon at its simplest, most fundamental level. What is learned at this level can then be used to understand more complex processes.
- *Assumption 3.* Principles of learning that arise from experiments with animals *should* apply to humans. Note the conditional phrasing of this sentence. Although Skinner accepted the usefulness of animal research, he was always careful to point out that such principles needed to be tested again at the human level.
- *Assumption 4.* A change in an organism's behavior pattern is the only basis for concluding that learning has occurred. Although admitting the existence of such internal processes as thoughts, motives, and emotions, Skinner had two objections to including them in his theoretical system. First, such processes have no place in the scientific study of learning because they cannot be directly observed or measured. Second, he believed that his experiments with rats in the Skinner box show that learning is caused not by internal processes but by the environmental consequences that follow behavior.

Basic Principles of Operant Conditioning

To repeat the basic idea behind operant conditioning: all behaviors are accompanied by certain consequences, and these consequences strongly influence (some might say determine) whether these behaviors are repeated and at what level of intensity. In general, the consequences that follow behavior are either pleasant and desirable or unpleasant and aversive. Depending on conditions that we will discuss shortly, these consequences either increase (strengthen) or decrease (weaken) the likelihood that the preceding behavior will recur under the same or similar circumstances.

When consequences strengthen a preceding behavior, *reinforcement* has taken place. When consequences weaken a preceding behavior, *punishment* and *extinction* have occurred. There are two forms of reinforcement and two forms of punishment. This section describes both forms of reinforcement, both forms of punishment, extinction, and several related principles that can be applied to aspects of human learning.

Positive reinforcement: strengthen a target behavior by presenting a positive reinforcer after the behavior occurs

Positive Reinforcement Although the term *positive reinforcement* may be unfamiliar to you, the idea behind it probably is not. If you can recall spending more time studying for a certain subject because of a compliment from the teacher or a high grade on an examination, you have experienced positive reinforcement. Specifically, **positive reinforcement** involves strengthening a target behavior—that is, increasing and maintaining the probability that a particular behavior will be repeated—by presenting a stimulus (called a *positive reinforcer*) immediately after the behavior has occurred. Praise, recognition, and the opportunity for free play are positive reinforcers for many (but not all) students.

The term *positive* as Skinner used it refers to the act of presenting a stimulus (think of positive as *adding* here); it does not refer to the pleasant nature of the stimulus itself. You will understand better why this distinction is very important as we consider the other form of reinforcement.

Negative reinforcement: strengthen a target behavior by removing an aversive stimulus after the behavior occurs

Negative Reinforcement People frequently have difficulty understanding the concept of negative reinforcement, most often confusing it with punishment, so we will examine it carefully here. The goal of **negative reinforcement** is the same as positive reinforcement: to *increase* the strength of a particular behavior. The method, however, is different. Instead of supplying a desirable stimulus, *one removes an unpleasant and aversive stimulus* whenever a target behavior is exhibited. As you study this definition, pay special attention to the removing action. Just as positive refers to adding, negative refers to the act of *removing* a stimulus. By removing something unwanted, you encourage the student to learn new behaviors.

In everyday life, negative reinforcement occurs quite frequently. A child picks up his clothes or toys to stop his parents' nagging. A driver uses a seat belt to stop the annoying buzzer sound. Later in the chapter, we will describe how educators use negative reinforcement. We will also discuss its desirability relative to positive reinforcement.

Punishment: weaken a target behavior by presenting an aversive stimulus after the behavior occurs

Punishment There are three procedures that reduce the likelihood that a particular behavior will be repeated. The first is **punishment,** also known as Type I

Students are likely to be motivated to learn if they are positively reinforced for completing a project or task. Awards and praise from the teacher and one's peers are strong positive reinforcers for many students.

punishment or presentation punishment. Punishment is defined by operant psychologists as the presentation of an aversive stimulus (such as scolding, paddling, ridiculing, or making a student write five hundred times "I will not chew gum in class") that reduces the frequency of a target behavior. From an operant perspective, you can claim to have punished someone else only if the target behavior is actually reduced in frequency. (Note that whether these methods of punishment do achieve their goal and are effective and whether they are ethical are other issues—ones that we will discuss later in this chapter.)

How well do you understand reinforcement? Try the Netlabs at **http://education.college.hmco.com/students**.

Many people confuse negative reinforcement with punishment. Both involve the use of an aversive stimulus, but the effects of each are opposite. Remember that negative reinforcement strengthens a target behavior, whereas punishment weakens or eliminates a behavior.

Time-Out The second procedure that decreases the frequency of or eliminates a target behavior is another form of punishment, **time-out.** But instead of presenting an aversive stimulus, time-out *temporarily removes the opportunity to receive positive reinforcement.* (Time-out is sometimes called Type II punishment, or removal punishment.) For instance, a student who frequently disrupts classroom routine to get attention may be sent to sit in an empty room for five minutes. Removal from a reinforcing environment (as well as the angry tone of voice and facial expression that normally accompany the order to leave the classroom) is usually looked on as an aversive consequence by the individual being removed. An athlete who is suspended from competition is another example of this form of punishment.

Time-out: weaken a target behavior by temporarily removing a positive reinforcer after the behavior occurs

Extinction A third consequence that weakens undesired behavior is extinction. **Extinction** occurs when a previously reinforced behavior decreases in frequency, and eventually ceases altogether, because reinforcement is withheld. Examples of extinction include a mother's ignoring a whining child or a teacher's ignoring a student who spontaneously answers a question without waiting to be called on. Both extinction and time-out are most effective when combined with other consequences, such as positive reinforcement. To help yourself define and remember the distinguishing characteristics of positive reinforcement, negative reinforcement, punishment, and extinction, study Table 7.1.

Extinction: weaken a target behavior by ignoring it

Spontaneous Recovery When used alone, extinction is sometimes a slow and difficult means of decreasing the frequency of undesired behavior because extin-

Spontaneous recovery: extinguished behaviors may reappear spontaneously

Table 7.1 Conditions That Define Reinforcement, Punishment, and Extinction

Type of Stimulus	+	Action	+	Effect on Behavior	=	Result
Desirable		Present		Strengthen		Positive reinforcement
Aversive		Remove		Strengthen		Negative reinforcement
Aversive		Present		Weaken		Type I punishment
Desirable		Remove		Weaken		Type II punishment (also called time-out)
Desirable		Withhold		Weaken		Extinction

guished behaviors occasionally reappear without having been reinforced, an occurrence known as **spontaneous recovery**. Under normal circumstances, however, the time between spontaneous recoveries lengthens, and the intensity of the recurring behavior becomes progressively weaker. If the behavior undergoing extinction is not terribly disruptive and if the teacher (or parent, counselor, or supervisor) is willing to persevere, these episodes can sometimes be tolerated on the way to more complete extinction.

Generalization: responding in similar ways to similar stimuli

Discrimination: responding in different ways to similar stimuli

Generalization When an individual learns to make a particular response to a particular stimulus and then makes the same or a similar response in a slightly different situation, **generalization** has occurred. For example, students who were positively reinforced for using effective study skills in history go on to use those same skills in chemistry, social studies, algebra, and other subjects. Or, to use a less encouraging illustration, students ignore or question a teacher's every request and direction because they have been reinforced for responding that way to their parents at home. The less similar the new stimulus is to the original, however, the less similar the response is likely to be.

The time-out procedure recommended by behavior modification enthusiasts involves weakening an undesirable form of behavior (such as shoving on the playground) by temporarily removing positive reinforcement (by having the misbehaving student remain in a corner of the classroom for five minutes while the rest of the class continues to enjoy another activity).

Discrimination When inappropriate generalizations occur, as in the preceding example, they can be essentially extinguished through discrimination training. In **discrimination** individuals learn to notice the unique aspects of seemingly similar situations (for example, that teachers are not parents, although both are adults) and to respond differently to each situation. Teachers can encourage this process by reinforcing only the desired behaviors (for instance, attention, obedience, and cooperation) and withholding reinforcement following undesired behaviors (such as inattention or disobedience).

Shaping Up to now, we have not distinguished relatively simple learned behaviors from more complex ones. A bit of reflection, however, should enable you to realize that many of the behaviors human beings learn (such as playing a sport or writing a term paper) are complex and are acquired gradually. The principle of **shaping** best explains how complex responses are learned.

In shaping, actions that move progressively closer to the desired *terminal behavior* (to use Skinner's term) are reinforced. Actions that do not represent closer approximations of the terminal behavior are ignored. The key to success is to take one step at a time. The movements must be gradual enough so that the person or animal becomes aware that each step in the sequence is essential. This process is typically called *reinforcing successive approximations to the terminal behavior.*

At least three factors can undermine the effectiveness of shaping. First, too much positive reinforcement for early, crude responses may reduce the learner's willingness to attempt a more complex response. Second, an expectation of too much progress too soon may decrease the likelihood of an appropriate response. If this results in a long period of nonreinforcement, what has been learned up to that point may be extinguished. For example, expecting a student to work industriously on a homework assignment for ninety minutes just after you have shaped forty-five minutes of appropriate homework behavior is probably too big a jump. If it is, the student may revert to her original level of performance owing to the lack of reinforcement. Third, delay in the reinforcement of the terminal behavior allows time for additional, unrelated behaviors to occur. When the reinforcement eventually occurs, it may strengthen one or more of the more recent behaviors rather than the terminal behavior.

Schedules of Reinforcement If you have been reading this section on basic principles carefully, you may have begun to wonder if the use of operant conditioning principles, particularly positive reinforcement, requires you as the teacher to be present every time a desired response happens. If so, you might have some justifiable reservations about the practicality of this theory. The answer is yes, up to a point, but after that, no. As we have pointed out, when you are trying to get a new behavior established, especially if it is a complex behavior that requires shaping, learning proceeds best when every desired response is positively reinforced and every undesired response is ignored. This is known as a *continuous reinforcement* schedule.

Complex behaviors are shaped by reinforcing closer approximations to terminal behavior

Once the behavior has been learned, however, positive reinforcement can be employed on a noncontinuous, or intermittent, basis to perpetuate that behavior. There are four basic *intermittent reinforcement* schedules: fixed interval (FI), variable interval (VI), fixed ratio (FR), and variable ratio (VR). Each schedule produces a different pattern of behavior.

Fixed Interval Schedule In this schedule, a learner is reinforced for the first desired response that occurs after a predetermined amount of time has elapsed (for example, five minutes, one hour, or seven days). Once the response has occurred and been reinforced, the next interval begins. Any desired behaviors that are made during an interval are ignored. The reinforced behavior occurs at a lower level during the early part of the interval and gradually rises as the time for reinforcement draws closer. Once the reinforcer is delivered, the relevant behavior declines in frequency and gradually rises toward the end of the next interval.

Fixed interval schedules: reinforce after regular time intervals

FI schedules of reinforcement occur in education when teachers schedule exams or projects at regular intervals. The grade or score is considered to be a reinforcer. As you are certainly aware, it is not unusual to see little studying or progress occur during the early part of the interval. However, several days before an exam or due date, the pace quickens considerably.

Variable Interval Schedule If you would like to see a more consistent pattern of behavior, you might consider using a variable interval schedule. With a VI schedule, the length of time between reinforcements is essentially random but averages out to a predetermined interval. Thus, four successive reinforcements may occur at the following intervals: one week, four weeks, two weeks, five weeks. The average interval is three weeks. Teachers who give surprise quizzes or call on students to answer oral questions on the average of once every third day are invoking a variable interval schedule.

Variable interval schedules: reinforce after random time intervals

Fixed Ratio Schedule Within this schedule, reinforcement is provided whenever a predetermined number of responses are made. A rat in a Skinner box may be reinforced with a food pellet whenever it presses a lever fifty times. A factory worker may earn $20 each time he assembles five electronic circuit boards. A teacher may reinforce a student with praise for every ten arithmetic problems correctly completed. FR schedules tend to produce high response rates since the faster the learner responds, the sooner the reinforcement is delivered. However, a relatively brief period of no or few responses occurs immediately after the reinforcer is delivered.

Fixed ratio schedules: reinforce after a set number of responses

Variable Ratio Schedule Like a variable interval schedule, this schedule tends to eliminate irregularities in response rate, thereby producing a more consistent rate. This is accomplished through reinforcement after a different number of responses from one time to the next according to a predetermined average. If you decided to

Variable ratio schedules: reinforce after a different number of responses each time

use a VR fifteen schedule, you might reinforce a desired behavior after twelve, seven, twenty-three, and eighteen occurrences, respectively (that is, after the twelfth, nineteenth, forty-second, and sixtieth desired behaviors). Because the occurrence of reinforcement is so unpredictable, learners tend to respond fairly rapidly for long periods of time. If you need proof, just watch people play the slot machines in gambling casinos.

Educational Applications of Operant Conditioning Principles

In the late 1940s when Skinner's daughter was in elementary school, he observed a number of instructional weaknesses that concerned him. These included the excessive use of aversive consequences to shape behavior (students studying to avoid a low grade or embarrassment in the classroom), an overly long interval between students taking tests or handing in homework and getting corrective feedback, and poorly organized lessons and workbooks that did not lead to specific goals. Skinner became convinced that if the principles of operant conditioning were systematically applied to education, all such weaknesses could be reduced or eliminated.

That belief, which he then reiterated consistently until his death in 1990 (see, for example, Skinner, 1984), is based on four prescriptions that come straight from his laboratory research on operant conditioning:

1. Be clear about what is to be taught.
2. Teach first things first.
3. Allow students to learn at their own rate.
4. Program the subject matter.

This straightforward formulation became the basis for two educational applications: an approach to teaching that we now call computer-assisted instruction and a set of procedures for helping students learn appropriate classroom behaviors referred to as behavior modification. The next few sections will describe the nature of these applications and assess the extent to which they improve classroom learning.

Computer-Assisted Instruction

The Precursor: Skinner's Programmed Instruction The key idea behind Skinner's approach to teaching is that learning should be shaped. Programs of stimuli (material to be learned) and consequences should be designed to lead students step by step to a predetermined end result. In the mid-1950s, Skinner turned this shaping approach into an innovation called **programmed instruction.**

When programmed materials were first made commercially available during the mid-1950s, they were designed to be presented to students in one of two ways: in book form or as part of teaching machines. The earliest teaching machines were simple mechanical devices. A program on a roll of paper was inserted in the machine, and the first statement or question was "framed" in a viewing window. (That is why the individual steps of a program are referred to as **frames.**) Today, programmed instruction in book format is very uncommon, and the early mechanical teaching machines have been almost totally supplanted by the personal computer because computers can do everything the books or the machine could do—and far more.

Programmers begin developing a program by defining precisely what is to be learned (the terminal behavior). They then arrange facts, concepts, and principles in a logical sequence so that students will be adequately prepared for each frame, or numbered problem, when they reach it. *Prompts* are periodically provided to draw out the desired response, and the step size (the knowledge needed to go from frame to frame) is made small enough so that reinforcement occurs with optimal frequency. Feedback about the correctness of the response is given immediately, and students work through the program at their own pace.

Programmed instruction: arrange material in small steps; reinforce correct responses

According to Skinner (1968, 1986), when programmed materials are well designed and appropriately used, they produce the following effects:

1. Reinforcement for the right answer is immediate.
2. The teacher can monitor each student's progress more closely.
3. Each student learns at his own rate, completing as many problems as possible within the allotted time.
4. Motivation stays high because of the high success level designed into the program.
5. Students can easily stop and begin at almost any point.
6. Learning a complex repertoire of knowledge proceeds efficiently.

Does Computer-Based Technology Aid Learning? When desktop computers and the instructional programs that were created for them were introduced into public schools in the early 1980s, many educators and psychologists believed that students would learn significantly more through this medium than through traditional teacher-led, text-based instruction. This new approach to instruction was referred to as either **computer-assisted instruction (CAI)** or **computer-based instruction (CBI)**.

Computer-assisted instruction can help teachers shape new capabilities in students through the use of good quality drill-and-practice, tutorial, and simulation programs.

Instructional programs designed for desktop computers generally fall into one of three categories:

Types of CAI programs include drill-and-practice, simulations, tutorials

- **Drill-and-practice programs:** Students practice knowledge and skills learned earlier.
- **Simulation programs:** These artificial environments mimic the real world in which students have to use previously learned knowledge to solve problems.
- **Tutorial programs:** Students learn new information and skills.

The research that has been done on the effectiveness of these varieties of CAI paints an interesting picture.

Research on Early Versions of CAI CAI research results have been summarized over such major variables as students of different ages and abilities, different types of computer programs, and various subject matters. In general, CAI-taught students have scored at about the sixtieth percentile on classroom achievement tests, while their conventionally taught (lecture, discussion, worksheets) peers have scored at the fiftieth percentile (Christmann, Badgett, & Lucking, 1997; Fletcher-Flinn & Gravatt, 1995). Researchers consider a difference of this magnitude to be relatively small.

CAI-taught students learn more with simulation programs than with drill-and-practice programs

CAI works best for elementary grade students, low achievers, urban students

The picture brightens considerably, however, when a more finely grained analysis of the research is done. Compared to conventional instruction, CAI produces stronger effects for simulation programs than for drill-and-practice programs (Khalili & Shashaani, 1994); for elementary grade students than for middle school or high school students (Bangert-Drowns, Kulik, & Kulik, 1985; Kulik, Kulik, & Bangert-Drowns, 1985); for low-achieving students than for high-achieving students (Kulik et al., 1985; Bangert-Drowns et al., 1985); for learning such complex cognitive skills as planning, problem solving, and reasoning than for learning subject matter (Liao, 1992); and for students who live in urban settings than for students who live in rural or suburban settings (Christmann et al., 1997). For these comparisons, the advantage ranges from 18 to 28 percentile ranks.

ILS: comprehensive, self-paced learning system

Newer Computer-Based Applications In recent years, some software packages have combined tutorial programs based on operant conditioning principles with programs that keep track over time of student performance and provide feedback to both the student and the teacher. These packages are called **integrated learning systems (ILS)** (Underwood, Cavendish, Dowling, Fogelman, & Lawson, 1996). Technology experts estimate that integrated learning systems may be used by as many as 25 percent of all school districts and, because of their high cost ($60,000 and up), account for about 50 percent of all technology-related expenditures by schools (Brush, Armstrong, Barbrow, & Ulintz, 1999).

Such systems present information in a more sequenced and comprehensive fashion than traditional CAI programs. Integrated learning systems can, in fact, cover the content for an entire K–8 mathematics curriculum. They also allow students to go through tutorials at their own pace, administer tests, track student progress across grade levels, and present students with appropriate remediation or enrichment activities.

Research on the effectiveness of ILS has produced mixed results. A study conducted in England found that elementary grade students who used an ILS outscored non-ILS students in mathematics by 9 percent and that high school students outscored their non-ILS counterparts by 4.5 percent. There were no differences, however, in reading (Underwood et al., 1996). A large-scale study (over fifty schools) of third-grade students in Indiana found no differences between ILS and non-ILS groups on tests of mathematics, reading, and language arts (Estep, McInerney,

Vockell, & Kosmoski, 1999–2000). A report issued by the North Central Regional Educational Laboratory (1999) noted that ILS users usually score better than non-ILS users on tests of the knowledge and skills taught by the program, but they do no better than non-ILS users on tests of transfer of learning to another context. Finally, a study of the impact of an ILS on the mathematics achievement of fifth graders produced more favorable results for concept learning than for computations and applications. This is an especially interesting finding, since CAI programs have been criticized for some time for not teaching concepts (Clariana, 1996).

Other recent developments include more elaborate versions of simulation and tutorial programs and new ways of using computer-based technology. For example, hypermedia, as we mentioned in earlier chapters, is a program format that combines hypertext (a system of links that allow users to jump from one section of text to another or from one document to another in whatever order they desire) and multimedia (the combination of several forms of media, such as text, graphics, animation, sound, pictures, and video).

Although hypermedia programs were expected to boost student learning greatly, their effects to date have been more modest. They appear to have no effect on student comprehension of information, and lower-ability students tend to be overwhelmed by the decision making such programs call for and by the need to keep track of which links one has visited. Hypermedia does, however, help higher-ability students to search through lengthy and multiple information sources rapidly in order to locate target information (Dillon & Gabbard, 1998).

Because of the growth of the World Wide Web and the number of classrooms now connected to it, telecommunication exchange projects are also becoming increasingly popular. We will consider them in the chapter on constructivist theories of learning.

Evaluation of Computer-Based Instruction How can we sum up the varieties of computer-based or computer-assisted instruction that have evolved from operant conditioning principles? Overall, the research findings suggest that CAI, when properly designed and used, can effectively supplement a teacher's attempts to present, explain, apply, and reinforce knowledge and skills. The relatively high degree of structure inherent in traditional CAI seems to be particularly helpful to low-achieving and younger students.

These findings also reaffirm what we suggested in the opening chapter about good teaching being partly an art and partly a science. Whenever you as a teacher apply any psychological principle in your classroom, you will need to ask yourself: For whom is this instructional technique likely to be beneficial? With what materials? For what outcome? We will return to the issue of using computer-based instruction in your classroom at the end of this chapter.

Behavior Modification

Although applied in many ways, the term **behavior modification** basically refers to the use of operant conditioning techniques to (as the phrase indicates) modify behavior. Because those who use such techniques attempt to manage behavior by making rewards contingent on certain actions, the term *contingency management* is also sometimes used.

After Skinner and his followers had perfected techniques of operant conditioning in modifying the behavior of animals, they concluded that similar techniques could be used with humans. We will briefly discuss several techniques in this section that teachers may use to strengthen or weaken specific behaviors. Techniques applied in education to strengthen behaviors include shaping, token economies, and contingency contracts. Techniques that aim to weaken behaviors include extinction and punishment.

Behavior modification: shape behavior by ignoring undesirable responses, reinforcing desirable responses

Shaping You may want to take a few minutes now to review our earlier explanation of shaping. Most attempts at shaping important classroom behaviors should include at least the following steps (Walker & Shea, 1999):

1. Select the target behavior.
2. Obtain reliable baseline data (that is, determine how often the target behavior occurs in the normal course of events).
3. Select potential reinforcers.
4. Reinforce successive approximations of the target behavior each time they occur.
5. Reinforce the newly established target behavior each time it occurs.
6. Reinforce the target behavior on a variable reinforcement schedule.

To illustrate how shaping might be used, imagine that you are a third-grade teacher (or a middle or high school teacher) with a chronic problem: one of your students rarely completes more than a small percentage of the arithmetic (or algebra) problems on the worksheets you distribute in class, even though you know the student possesses the necessary skills. To begin, you decide that a reasonable goal would be for the student to complete at least 85 percent of the problems on a given worksheet. Next, you review the student's work for the past several weeks and determine that, on average, he completed only 25 percent of the problems per worksheet. Your next step is to select positive reinforcers that you know or suspect will work.

Reinforcers come in a variety of forms. Most elementary school teachers typically use such things as stickers, verbal praise, smiles, and classroom privileges (for example, feed the gerbil, clean the erasers). Middle school and high school teachers can use letter or numerical grades, material incentives (such as board games and computer games, as long as school policy and your financial resources allow it), and privately given verbal praise.

With certain reservations, public forms of recognition can also be used. The reservations include the following:

- Any public display of student work or presentation of awards should be made to several students at the same time (to avoid possible embarrassment among adolescents) (Emmer, Evertson, Clements, & Worsham, 2000).
- Awards should be made without letter grades.
- Awards should be given with an awareness that public displays of recognition are not appropriate or comfortable for all cultures.

One popular shaping technique that has stood the test of time involves having students list favorite activities on a card. Then they are told that they will be able to indulge in one of those activities for a stated period of time after they have completed a set of instructional objectives. This technique is sometimes called the **Premack principle** after psychologist David Premack (1959), who first proposed it. It is also called *Grandma's rule* since it is a variation of a technique that grandmothers have used for hundreds of years ("Finish your peas, and you can have dessert").

Premack principle: required work first, then chosen reward

Once you have decided on a sequence of objectives and a method of reinforcement, you are ready to shape the target behavior. For example, you can start by reinforcing the student for completing five problems (25 percent) each day for several consecutive days. Then you reinforce the student for completing five problems and starting a sixth (a fixed ratio schedule). Then you reinforce the student for six completed problems and so on. Once the student consistently completes at least 85 percent of the problems, you provide reinforcement after every fifth worksheet on the average (a variable ratio schedule).

Although you control the classroom environment while students are in school, this accounts for only about half of their waking hours. Accordingly, parents might supplement your efforts at shaping behavior. The first step in a home-based reinforcement program is obtaining the parents' and student's formal agreement to participate. Then you typically send home a brief note or form on a regular basis (daily, weekly) indicating whether the student exhibited the desired behaviors. For example, in response to the items "Was prepared for class" and "Handed in homework," you would circle "yes" or "no." In response to a homework grade or test grade, you would circle the appropriate letter or percentage correct designation. The parents are then responsible for providing the appropriate reinforcement or punishment (temporary loss of a privilege, for example). This procedure has been successful in both reducing disruptive classroom behavior and increasing academic performance (longer time on tasks and higher test scores, for example). Some studies suggest that it may not be necessary to target both areas, as improved academic performance often results in decreased disruptiveness (Kelley & Carper, 1988).

Token Economies A second technique used to strengthen behavior in the classroom, the **token economy,** was introduced first with people who had been hospitalized for emotional disturbances and then with students in special education classes. A token is something that has little or no inherent value but can be used to "purchase" things that do have inherent value. In society, money is our most ubiquitous token. Its value lies not in what it is made of but in what it can purchase—a car, a house, or a college education. By the same token (if you will excuse the pun), students can accumulate check marks, gold stars, or happy faces and "cash them in" at some later date for any of the reinforcers already mentioned.

Token economy is a flexible reinforcement system

One reason for the development of the token economy approach was the limited flexibility of more commonly used reinforcers. Candies and cookies, for instance, tend to lose their reinforcing value fairly quickly when supplied continually. It is not always convenient to award free time or the opportunity to engage in a highly preferred activity immediately after a desired response. And social rewards may or may not be sufficiently reinforcing for some individuals. Tokens, however, can always be given immediately after a desirable behavior, can be awarded according to one of the four schedules mentioned earlier, and can be redeemed for reinforcers that have high reinforcing value.

Token economies are effective in reducing such disruptive classroom behaviors as talking out of turn, being out of one's seat, fighting, and being off task. They are also effective in improving academic performance in a variety of subject areas (Naughton & McLaughlin, 1995; Shook, LaBrie, Vallies, McLaughlin, & Williams, 1990). Token economies have been used successfully with individual students, groups of students, entire classrooms, and even entire schools.

Some studies have shown that awarding tokens for group efforts is at least as effective as and possibly more effective than awarding them to individuals (McLaughlin & Williams, 1988). Accordingly, token economies can be easily used in conjunction with the cooperative learning technique that was briefly mentioned earlier in the book and that will be described in detail in the chapter on instructional approaches. The Case in Print illustrates one token economy in action in a school system.

For real-life classroom examples, see the Site-Based Cases section on the textbook web site at **http://education.college.hmco.com/students**.

One useful method for positively reinforcing desired behavior is a token economy—supplying students with objects that have no inherent value but that can be accumulated and redeemed for more meaningful reinforcers.

Contingency Contracting A third technique teachers use to strengthen behavior is **contingency contracting.** A contingency contract is simply a more formal method of specifying desirable behaviors and consequent reinforcement. The contract, which can be written or verbal, is an agreement worked out by two people (teacher and student, parent and child, counselor and client) in which one person (student, child, client) agrees to behave in a mutually acceptable way, and the other person (teacher, parent, counselor) agrees to provide a mutually acceptable form of reinforcement. For example, a student may contract to sit quietly and work on a social studies assignment for thirty minutes. When the student is done, the teacher may reinforce the child with ten minutes of free time, a token, or a small toy.

Contingency contracting: reinforcement supplied after student completes mutually agreed-on assignment

Contracts can be drawn up with all members of a class individually, with selected individual class members, or with the class as a whole. As with most other contracts, provisions can be made for renegotiating the terms. Moreover, the technique is flexible enough to incorporate the techniques of token economies and shaping. It is possible, for example, to draw up a contract that provides tokens for successive approximations to some target behavior (Bushrod, Williams, & McLaughlin, 1995).

Extinction, Time-Out, and Response Cost The primary goal of behavior modification is to strengthen desired behaviors. Toward that end, techniques such as shaping, token economies, and contingency contracts are likely to be very useful. There will be times, however, when you have to weaken or eliminate undesired behaviors because they interfere with instruction and learning. For these occasions, you might consider some form of extinction.

The most straightforward approach is to ignore the undesired response. If a student bids for your attention by clowning around, for instance, you may discourage repetition of that sort of behavior by ignoring it. It is possible, however, that

Learning Is a Rewarding Experience for Some Students

Token economies are effective in reducing such disruptive classroom behaviors as talking out of turn, being out of one's seat, fighting, and being off task. They are also effective in improving academic performance in a variety of subject areas. Token economies have been used successfully with individual students, groups of students, entire classrooms, and even entire schools. (p. 238)

Studying's Rewards

SACHA PFEIFFER
Boston Globe 1/3/96

NEWTON—Life, David Morris will tell you, is all about incentive.

Give him a scenario, be it the classroom or in the workplace, and the 18-year-old Newton North High School senior will give you an example of a society motivated by the prospect of gain—a better school, a better job, a better income.

Now, in a program designed by Morris, honor roll students at Newton North have an additional enticement: a coupon book containing more than $300 worth of gifts tailored to the teen-age appetite.

The book offers more than mere discounts and buy-one, get-one-free offers. Bearers are entitled to such things as free pizzas, ice cream, bagels, car washes, movie rentals, beeper services, health club visits and limousine rentals.

"All around us, there are different types of incentives, whether they are varsity letters or merit scholarships," said Morris, who, perhaps not surprisingly, is bound for the University of Pennsylvania's Wharton School of Business next fall. "So why not reward those students who think academics are important?"

The ultimate reward of the program, dubbed the Newton North High School Honor Roll Card Coupon Book, is a scholarship fund for college-bound seniors created by a $200 mandatory contribution from participating businesses.

The dual membership requirement for merchants presented a tough challenge to Morris and his small but growing sales staff.

"Most stores would immediately say, 'Wait, you want me to give money and a discount?' " recalled junior Noam Schimmel, who will run the program next year. "Their usual response was, 'Hi, thanks for calling, but that's a lot of money.' "

But hard work pays off, as the program's motto proclaims, and 50 merchants from Newton and beyond eventually agreed to participate. Collectively, those businesses made a $10,000 infusion to the fund last year—more than half of which was given to academically eligible, financially needy students.

The program, now entering its fourth grading period, weathered its share of criticism before getting off the ground.

"We had to ask ourselves if we were selling grades," said high school principal V. James Marini, echoing the concerns of educators who believe academic achievement should not be a material pursuit.

But recalling a discussion he had with Morris, Marini said the entrepreneurial student countered that young people are always told hard work will yield rewards. "How can you argue with that?" the principal said.

By the accounts of students, teachers and administrators, the program has been a roaring success, and may be a factor motivating some of Newton North's 1,800 high schoolers to study that extra hour. The school experienced a 37 percent jump in the number of seniors named to the honor roll last grading period, and a 21 percent increase among juniors.

The coupon book "definitely entices kids to want to succeed," said junior Daniel Steinberg. "If you give kids the book and say, 'Here, take this as a sign of your accomplishment,' you give them a better reason to feel better about themselves."

Even senior Josh Newman, who says he was skeptical that the book would catch on among students, now calls himself a coupon convert.

"I never thought it would work and I didn't think kids would even come pick the books up," admitted Newman, who said he has friends who raised their grades to become part of the program. "But the free stuff is great . . . and a larger amount of kids are trying harder in school because of it."

And, Morris boasts, not a penny of school or scholarship money was spent to run the program. All goods and services, from display easels to adhesive tapes, were donated. . . .

Student Schimmel says he is confident the program will continue with the same success when he takes it over next year.

"This program is a community-wide acknowledgment of academic achievement and educational excellence," said Schimmel. "It's an innovative way of saying, 'Thank you, good job.' And kids realize that beyond the little slice of pizza they got, there's something to perseverance and working hard."

Questions and Activities

1. Although the coupon book program had been in operation for only three grading periods at the time the article was written, it appeared to be quite successful. Do you think reinforcement programs like this one are likely to be successful over an extended period of time? Why or why not?

2. Students are typically given reinforcers by teachers in school-based token economies. Is there any reason that the behavior of teachers and administrators should not be reinforced by students when the occasion warrants? What might be the advantages (and disadvantages) of a token economy that runs in both directions?

3. The principal in this article is portrayed as being initially hesitant to implement the coupon book incentive program as it might have been perceived by some as the equivalent of bribing students to learn. But the student who created the program argued that it should be tried since adults constantly tell young people that if they work hard and succeed, they will be rewarded by society. These two views suggest that the token economy has potential advantages and disadvantages as a way to motivate students to learn. Based on the material in the chapter and your own experiences, write down as many advantages and disadvantages as you can think of.

classmates will not ignore the behavior but laugh at it. Such response-strengthening reactions from classmates will likely counteract your lack of reinforcement. Accordingly, you need to observe what happens when you try to extinguish behavior by not responding.

If other students are reinforcing a youngster's undesired behavior, you may want to apply the time-out procedure. Suppose a physically active third-grade boy seems unable to keep himself from shoving classmates during recess. If verbal requests, reminders, or warnings fail to limit shoving, the boy can be required to take a five-minute time-out period immediately after he shoves a classmate. He must sit alone in the classroom for that period of time while the rest of the class remains out on the playground. Time-out appears to be most effective when it is used with aggressive, group-oriented children who want the attention of the teacher and their peers (Walker & Shea, 1999). The rules for the procedure should be clearly explained, and after being sentenced to time-out (which should last no more than five minutes), a child should be given reinforcement for agreeable, helpful behavior—for example, "Thank you for collecting all the playground balls so nicely, Tommy."

Time-out works best with disruptive, aggressive children

Another technique, **response cost,** is similar to time-out in that it involves the removal of a stimulus. It is often used with a token economy. With this procedure, a certain amount of positive reinforcement (for example, 5 percent of previously earned tokens) is withdrawn every time a child makes an undesired response. Anyone who has been caught exceeding the speed limit and been fined at least $50 can probably attest to the power of response cost as a modifier of behavior.

Punishment Punishment is one of the most common behavior modification techniques, particularly when it takes the form of corporal punishment. It is also one of the most controversial. As of this writing, corporal punishment has been banned in twenty-seven states by either state law or state department of education regulation (National Coalition to Abolish Corporal Punishment in Schools, 2001). The remaining twenty-three states either explicitly permit schools to punish students physically or are silent on the matter. In states that allow corporal punishment, local school districts may regulate, but not prohibit, its use. Where states have not addressed the issue, local districts may regulate the use of corporal punishment or ban it altogether.

Although corporal punishment is actually fairly widely used in classrooms where it is permitted, considerable laboratory evidence, collected from human and animal subjects, suggests that it is likely to be ineffective in modifying behavior. The following reasons are typically cited:

Punishment is likely to be ineffective because of temporary impact, side effects

- Mild punishment (which is the kind usually applied) does not permanently eliminate undesirable behaviors. At best, it suppresses them temporarily.
- Punished behaviors may continue to occur when the punisher is not present.
- Punishment may actually increase the strength of undesirable behavior. Many teachers assume that a public reprimand is aversive. But for some students, teacher and peer attention, regardless of the form it takes, acts as a positive reinforcer and thus tends to increase behaviors the teacher seeks to eliminate.
- Punishment may produce undesirable emotional side effects. Just as a shocked rat comes to fear a Skinner box, punished children may perceive the teacher and the school as objects to fear and avoid. The result is truancy, tardiness, and high levels of anxiety, all of which impair the ability to learn.
- Punishers model a type of behavior (physical aggression) that they do not want students to exhibit.
- To be effective, punishment must often be severe and must occur immediately after an undesirable response. Legal, ethical, and moral restrictions do not allow severe punishment.

Should You Use Behavior Modification? This may seem a strange question to ask given the number of pages we have just spent covering behavior modification methods. Obviously, we feel that the results of decades of research on these techniques justify their use by teachers. Nevertheless, there are criticisms of behavior modification that are not adequately addressed by research findings and that you should carefully consider.

One criticism is that many students, including those in the primary grades, will eventually catch on to the fact that they get reinforced only when they do what the teacher wants them to do. Some may resent this and misbehave out of spite. Others may weigh the amount of effort required to earn a favorable comment or a privilege and decide the reinforcer is not worth the trouble. Still others may develop a "What's in it for me?" attitude. That is, some students may come to think of learning as something they do only to earn an immediate reinforcer. The potential danger of using behavior modification over an extended period of time is that learning may come to an abrupt halt when no one is around to supply reinforcement (Kohn, 1993). (This point will be addressed by the next theory to be examined, social learning theory.)

A second major criticism is that behavior modification methods, because of their potential power, may lend themselves to inappropriate or even unethical uses. For example, teachers may shape students to be quiet and obedient because it makes their job easier, even though such behaviors do not always produce optimum conditions for learning.

In response to these criticisms, Skinner and other behavioral scientists (see Chance, 1993, for example) argue that if we do not systematically use what we know about the effects of stimuli and consequences on behavior, we will leave things to chance. In an uncontrolled situation, some fortunate individuals will have a favorable chain of experiences that will equip them with desirable attitudes and skills, but others will suffer an unfortunate series of experiences that will lead to difficulties and disappointment. In a controlled situation, it may be possible to arrange experiences so that almost everyone acquires desirable traits and abilities. What behavioral psychologists seem to be saying is that educators could be accused of being unethical for not making use of an effective learning tool. The challenge, of course, is to use it wisely.

Despite the popularity of operant conditioning among many American psychologists, a number of researchers, beginning in the 1940s, were eager to study types of human behavior that could not be readily explained in terms of principles of operant conditioning. They shared the desire of Skinner and his followers to study behavior as objectively as possible, but they wanted to analyze human behavior in social settings to see how children acquire acceptable forms of social behavior (or become socialized). Together, these researchers contributed to the development of a set of ideas about human learning that borrowed from operant conditioning but was different from it as well. These ideas came to be called social learning theory.

Social Learning Theory

Albert Bandura, the acknowledged spokesperson for the social learning theory point of view, presents what is generally considered to be the definitive exposition of this theory in *Social Foundations of Thought and Action: A Social Cognitive Theory* (1986). In essence, **social learning theory** deemphasizes the role of reinforcement in learning by attributing initial changes in behavior to the observation and imitation of a model (which explains why social learning is also called **observational learning**).

In the sections that follow, we will discuss some of the main features of Bandura's social learning theory and examine some of the research it has spawned. First, we will describe the various ways in which observational learning occurs: inhibition, disinhibition, facilitation, and true observational learning. Following this, we will describe the four processes that underlie observational learning: attention, retention, production, and motivation.

Social learning theory holds that many behaviors are learned not by direct reinforcement but by observing and imitating a model with whom one identifies.

Types of Observational Learning Effects

Inhibition In many instances, we learn not to do something that we already know how to do because a model we are observing refrains from behaving in that way, is punished for behaving in that way, or does something different from what we intended to do. Consider the following example: a ten-year-old is taken to her first symphony concert by her parents. After the first movement of Beethoven's Fifth Symphony, she is about to applaud but notices that her parents are sitting quietly with their hands in their laps. She does the same.

People learn to inhibit or make responses by observing others

Disinhibition On occasion, we learn to exhibit a behavior that is usually disapproved of by most people because a model does the same without being punished. For example, a student attends his school's final football game of the season. As time expires, thousands of students run onto the field and begin tearing up pieces of turf to take home as a souvenir. Noticing that the police do nothing, the student joins in.

Facilitation This effect occurs whenever we are prompted to do something that we do not ordinarily do because of insufficient motivation rather than social disapproval. For example, a college student attends a lecture on reforming the American education system. Impressed by the lecturer's enthusiasm and ideas, the student vigorously applauds at the end of the presentation. As several members of the audience stand and applaud, so does the student.

True Observational Learning This effect occurs when we learn a new behavior pattern by watching and imitating the performance of someone else. A teenage girl learning how to hit a topspin forehand in tennis by watching her instructor do the same is an example of observational learning. The four processes that make this form of learning possible will be discussed next.

Processes in Observational Learning

Attention Clearly, if learning is observational, paying attention to a model's behavior is a critical first step. Among the factors that affect the willingness of a child to observe and mimic the behavior of a model, the most important seems to be the degree of similarity between the model and the observer. On the basis of an extensive review and analysis of previous research, Dale Schunk (1987) drew the following conclusions about the effect of observer-model similarity on observational learning:

Processes of observational learning: attention, retention, production, motivation

- When children are concerned about the appropriateness of a behavior or have self-doubts about their capabilities, they are more likely to model a peer than an older child or adult.
- Age similarity seems less important for the learning of skills, rules, and novel responses than does the competence of the model. When children question the competence of peers, they tend to model the behavior of adults.
- Children learn academic skills from models of either sex, but they are more likely to perform behaviors displayed by models whom they believe are good examples of their gender role.
- Children who have a negative self-concept or have had learning problems in the past are more likely to imitate a peer who exhibits some initial learning difficulties and overcomes them (a coping model) than a peer who performs flawlessly

(a mastery model). Improvements in self-concept and achievement are more likely to occur in response to coping models than to master models.

Retention Once we have noticed a model's behavior with the intention of imitating it, we must encode that behavior in memory. Encoding may encompass just the observed behaviors, or it may also include an explanation of why, how, and when something is done. In the case of behavior, the encoding may be visual (that is, mental pictures) or verbal (or both). In the case of behavioral rules, the encoding will likely be in terms of verbal propositions. The benefit of encoding behavioral rules is the ability to generalize the response.

Modeled behaviors may be unitary, terminal behaviors (for example, working on a problem until it is solved), or they may be components of a complex behavior (such as striking a golf ball with a golf club). Once the behavior has been modeled, the observer should have several opportunities to engage in overt and covert rehearsal.

Production Bandura divides production into (1) selecting and organizing the response elements and (2) refining the response on the basis of informative feedback. The smooth operation of the production process is based on the assumption that the necessary response elements have been previously acquired (for example, gripping a golf club, addressing the ball, executing the swing, following through).

Motivation Like Skinner, Bandura acknowledges the motivational value of reinforcement and incorporates it into his theory. Unlike Skinner, however, Bandura thinks of reinforcement in broader terms. As a result, he talks about direct reinforcement, vicarious reinforcement, and self-reinforcement.

Imitation is strengthened through direct reinforcement, vicarious reinforcement, self-reinforcement

As part of observational learning, **direct reinforcement** occurs when an individual watches a model perform, imitates that behavior, and is reinforced (or punished) by the model or some other individual. A primary grade student, for example, may be told by the teacher to observe how a fellow student cleans up his desk at the end of the day. If that behavior is imitated, the teacher will praise the child.

Vicarious reinforcement refers to a situation in which the observer anticipates receiving a reward for behaving in a given way because someone else has been so rewarded. A middle school student who observes that a classmate is praised by the teacher for completing an assignment promptly may strive to work quickly and diligently on the next assignment in anticipation of receiving similar praise.

Self-reinforcement refers to a situation in which the individual strives to meet personal standards and does not depend on or care about the reactions of others. A high school student may strive to become as skillful as a classmate at word processing primarily because of an internal desire to prove that she can master that skill.

The Effect of Self-Efficacy on Observational Learning and Behavior

Self-efficacy: how capable one feels to handle particular kinds of tasks

Unlike self-concept, which we described in the chapter on age-level characteristics as the *overall*, or *global*, picture that people have of themselves, *self-efficacy* refers to how capable or prepared we believe we are for handling *particular* kinds of tasks (Bandura 1982, 1986, 1989). For example, a student may have a high level of self-efficacy for mathematical reasoning—a feeling that she can master any math task that she might encounter in a particular course—but have a low level of self-efficacy for critical analysis of English literature. There are at least two reasons for Bandura's interest (and for general interest as well) in this phenomenon: (1) an individual's level of self-efficacy can be influenced by several factors, one of which is observing the behavior of a model, and (2) self-efficacy appears to strongly affect a variety of behaviors.

Factors That Affect Self-Efficacy One obvious way in which we develop a sense of what we can and cannot do in various areas is by thinking about how well we have performed in the past on a given task or a set of closely related tasks. If, for example, my friends are always reluctant to have me on their team for neighborhood baseball games and if I strike out or ground out far more often than I hit safely, I will probably conclude that I just do not have whatever skills it takes to be a competitive baseball player. Conversely, if my personal history of performance in school is one of mostly grades of A and of consistently being among the top ten students, my sense of academic self-efficacy is likely to be quite high.

Self-efficacy influenced by past performance, persuasion, emotional reactions, observation of models

A second source of influence that Bandura mentioned—verbal persuasion—is also fairly obvious. We frequently try to convince a child, student, relative, spouse, friend, or coworker that he has the ability to perform some task at a creditable level, and he in turn frequently tries to convince us of the same thing. Perhaps you can recall feeling somewhat more confident about your ability to handle some task (like college classes) after having several family members and friends express their confidence in your ability.

A third source of influence is more subtle. It is the emotions we feel as we prepare to engage in a task. Individuals with low self-efficacy for science may become anxious, fearful, or restless prior to attending chemistry class or taking an exam in physics. Those with high self-efficacy may feel assured, comfortable, and eager to display what they have learned. Some individuals are acutely aware of these emotional states and infer from them high or low capabilities for performing specific tasks.

Finally, our sense of self-efficacy may be influenced by observing the successes and failures of individuals with whom we identify—what Bandura refers to as *vicarious experience.* If I take note of the fact that a sibling or neighborhood friend who is like me in many respects but is a year older has successfully adjusted to high school, I may feel more optimistic about my own adjustment the following year.

Types of Behaviors That Are Affected by Self-Efficacy Bandura has identified four types of behaviors that are at least partly influenced by an individual's level of self-efficacy: the goals and activities in which the person chooses to engage, the kind of thought processes she uses, how hard and how long she strives to achieve a goal, and the kinds of emotional reactions she experiences when she takes on certain tasks.

Self-efficacy affects one's goals, thought processes, persistence, emotions

Individuals with a strong sense of self-efficacy, particularly if it extends over several areas, are more likely than others to consider a variety of goals and participate in a variety of activities. They may, for example, think about a wide range of career options, explore several majors while in college, take a variety of courses, participate in different sporting activities, engage in different types of social activities, and have a wide circle of friends.

One way in which the thinking of high-self-efficacy individuals differs from that of their low-self-efficacy peers is in their tendency to use higher-level thought processes (such as analysis, synthesis, and evaluation) to solve complex problems.

Thus, in preparing a classroom report or a paper, low-self-efficacy students may do little more than repeat a set of facts they found in various sources (because of their belief that they are not capable of more), whereas high-self-efficacy individuals discuss similarities and differences, inconsistencies and contradictions, and make evaluations about the validity and usefulness of the information they have found. Another difference is that high-self-efficacy people are more likely to visualize themselves being successful at some challenging task, whereas low-self-efficacy individuals are more likely to imagine disaster. This leads to differences in the next category of behaviors: motivation.

Those who rate their capabilities as higher than average can be expected to work harder and longer to achieve a goal than those who feel less capable. This difference should be particularly noticeable when individuals experience frustrations (poor-quality instruction, for example), problems (coursework being more difficult than anticipated), and setbacks (a serious illness).

Finally, when faced with a challenging task, the high-self-efficacy individual is more likely to experience excitement, curiosity, and an eagerness to get started rather than the sense of anxiety, depression, and impending disaster that many low-self-efficacy individuals feel.

Research on Social Learning Theory

The research that has been stimulated by social learning theory supports Bandura's basic view that we can and do learn many types of behaviors by watching what other people do and the consequences they experience. In this section, we will summarize several studies that, taken together, illustrate the wide range of this form of learning.

Effects of Modeling on Aggression The essential principles of social learning theory that Bandura described can be illustrated by a series of three classic experiments he carried out in the 1960s. In the first experiment (Bandura, Ross, & Ross, 1961), a child was seated at a table and encouraged to play with a toy. The model sat at a nearby table and either played quietly with Tinker Toys for ten minutes or played with the Tinker Toys for a minute and then played aggressively with an inflatable clown "Bobo" doll for several minutes, punching, kicking, and sitting on it and hitting it with a hammer. In a subsequent structured play situation, children who did not observe a model as well as those who observed a nonaggressive model displayed little aggression. By contrast, children exposed to the aggressive model behaved with considerably more aggression toward the Bobo doll and other toys.

The second study (Bandura, Ross, & Ross, 1963a) obtained similar results in response to children viewing a film of either an adult or an adult dressed as a cartoon character engaging in aggressive behavior. The third study (Bandura, Ross, & Ross, 1963b) attempted to determine how rewarding the model for aggressive behavior would affect children's imitative behavior. In general, children were more aggressive after they saw an aggressive model positively rewarded than when the model was punished. These studies, as you may have realized, illustrate the disinhibition effect described earlier.

These three studies stimulated hundreds of other investigations of the same type, particularly because of the implication that viewing aggressive behavior in a film or television program would lead to violence. Reviews of this research, such as those by T. H. A. van der Voort (1986), have found that exposure to repeated scenes of violence *can* engender violent behavior if the right set of conditions is in place.

These conditions include the nature of the television program being watched (if the violent behavior is realistic and appears to be justified by the circumstances), the characteristics of the individual child (some children are more aggressive than others), the child's family, the child's neighborhood, and the reactions of others who are watching the program with the child.

Cognitive skills can be learned by observation of models

Effects of Teacher Modeling on the Learning of Cognitive Skills Because the main focus of classroom life is the learning of various cognitive skills, researchers interested in social learning theory began to wonder if cognitive skills could be learned through modeling and if such modeling would produce higher levels of achievement. Numerous studies have supported this hypothesis. In one (Schunk, 1981), the researcher arranged for nine-, ten-, and eleven-year-old children who had done poorly in math to receive one of two types of instruction. Children in the modeling condition received written materials that explained how to solve long-division problems, and they observed an adult model. While solving a series of problems, the model verbalized the underlying cognitive operations (such as estimating the quotient and multiplying the quotient by the divisor). The children then practiced what they had observed, with the researchers providing corrective modeling for any operations the youngsters failed to grasp. Children in the nonmodeling condition received the same written materials, which they studied on their own. When comprehension problems arose, these children were told to review the relevant section of the written instructions.

In comparison to pretest scores, both treatments enhanced persistence, self-confidence, and accuracy of performance. The modeling condition, however, produced greater gains in accuracy than did the nonmodeling condition. (For more about how modeling aids the learning of cognitive skills, see Schunk & Zimmerman, 1997.)

A second illustration of how students learn what their teachers model (and do not learn what they do not model) was offered by Diane Miller (1993). She described a middle school math teacher who was upset because his students did not use such terms as *numerator* and *denominator* in their writings about fractions. Instead, they substituted the phrases *the number on the top* and *the number on the bottom*. But when the teacher was observed reviewing a unit on fractions, he never used the terms *numerator* and *denominator*. When asked after class why he had avoided using these two terms, he said that he thought he had used them and was quite surprised to learn otherwise.

In a third example (Pressley, Rankin, & Yokoi, 1996), researchers found that a sample of primary grade teachers who were judged as being highly effective at teaching reading and writing used modeling on a daily basis. These teachers demonstrated what they meant by reading, comprehension strategies, and writing skills.

The last study we will mention (Mariage, 1995) illustrates that modeling is an effective instructional technique even among those with no professional training or teaching experience. The researcher examined the teaching behaviors of two groups of college seniors who volunteered to teach a reading comprehension strategy to primary and elementary grade students with learning disabilities. The strategy was called POSSE, which stood for predict what ideas are in the story, organize one's thoughts, search for the structure, summarize the main idea, and evaluate the result. On the basis of how many ideas students recalled from a story they read, the teachers were divided into low-gain and high-gain groups. The low-gain teachers made far fewer modeling statements of the POSSE strategy (about 15 percent of all instructional statements) than did the high-gain teachers (about 35 percent of all instructional statements).

Effects of Modeling on Self-Efficacy Dale Schunk and Antoinette Hanson (1989) confirmed Bandura's contention that an individual's self-efficacy can be enhanced by watching a competent model. Nine- to twelve-year-old children whose math achievement was below the thirty-fifth percentile on a standardized test watched a videotape of a similar child receiving instruction in how to do subtraction-with-regrouping problems (i.e., borrowing) and then solving similar problems. In comparison to a group of similar children who saw a videotape of a teacher solving subtraction-with-regrouping problems and a group that did not see a model, those who saw a peer model had significantly higher self-efficacy ratings.

Now that you are familiar with operant conditioning and social learning theory, it is time to examine several Suggestions for Teaching derived from the principles and research findings that have just been discussed.

Suggestions for Teaching in Your Classroom

Applying Behavioral Learning Theory and Social Learning Theory in the Classroom

1 Remain aware that behavior is the result of particular conditions.

Journal Entry
Checking on Causes of Behavior

Unlike the controlled environment of a Skinner box, many causes of behavior in a real-life classroom may not be observable or traceable. You might as well accept the fact, therefore, that quite often you are going to be a haphazard shaper of behavior. Nevertheless, there will be times when you and your students may benefit if you say to yourself, "Now, there have to be some causes for that behavior. Can I figure out what they are and do something about changing things for the better? Am I doing something that is leading to types of behavior that are making life difficult for some or all of us in the room?" When you are engaging in such speculations, keep in mind that reinforcement strengthens behavior. And check to see if you are inadvertently rewarding students for misbehavior (by calling attention to them, for example, or failing to reinforce those who engage in desirable forms of behavior).

Examples

- If you become aware that it takes a long time for your students to settle down at the beginning of a period and that you are reacting by addressing critical remarks specifically to those who dawdle the longest, ignore the dawdlers, and respond positively to those who are ready to get to work.
- Let's say that you have given students thirty minutes to finish an assignment. To your dismay, few of them get to work until almost the end of the period, and you find that you have to do a lot of nagging to hold down gossip and horseplay. When you later analyze why this happened, you conclude that you actually encouraged the time-killing behavior because of the way you set up the lesson. The next time you give a similar assignment, tell the students that as soon as they complete it, they can have class time to work on homework, a term project, or the equivalent and that you will be available to give help or advice to those who want it.

2 Use reinforcement, and use it appropriately to strengthen behaviors you want to encourage.

Why would we remind you to do something as obvious as reinforce behaviors you want students to acquire and exhibit in the future? Wouldn't you do that almost automatically? Well, we certainly hope so, but statistics suggest otherwise. A large team of researchers headed by Jon Goodlad (1984) observed the classroom behavior of 1,350 teachers and 17,163 students in thirty-eight schools from seven sections of the country. What they found may surprise you. Teachers' praise of student work occurred about 2 percent of the observed time in the primary grades and about 1 percent of the time in high school.

Journal Entry
Ways to Supply Reinforcement

Once you have resolved to reinforce desired behavior systematically, you need to be sure that you do it appropriately. Although reinforcement is a simple principle that can be readily understood at an intuitive level, it has to be used in the right way to produce desired results. Paul Chance (1992) offers seven guidelines for the effective use of positive reinforcement:

- Use the weakest reward available to strengthen a behavior. In other words, do not use material rewards when you know that praise will be just as effective a reinforcer. Save the material rewards for that special behavior for which praise or other reinforcers may not be effective.
- When possible, avoid using rewards as incentives. What Chance means is not to get into the habit of automatically telling the student that if she does what you want, you will provide a specific reward. Instead, sometimes ask the student to do something (like work quietly or help another student), and then provide the reinforcer.
- Reward at a high rate in the early stages of learning, and reduce the frequency of rewards as learning progresses.
- Reward only the behavior you want repeated. Although you may not realize it, students are often very sensitive to what is and is not being reinforced. If you decide that one way to encourage students to be more creative in their writing is to tell them not to worry about spelling and grammar errors, then do not be sur-

One of the basic principles of instruction derived from operant conditioning experiments is that teachers should provide elementary grade students with immediate reinforcement for correct responses.

prised to see many misspelled words and poorly constructed sentences. Or if you decide to reward only the three highest scorers on a test, reasoning that competition brings out the best in people, be prepared to deal with the fact that competition also brings out some of the worst in people (like cheating and refusing to help others).

- Remember that what is an effective reinforcer for one student may not be for another. For some students, comments such as "Very interesting point," "That's right," or "That was a big help" will strengthen the target behavior. But for others, something less overt, such as smiling encouragingly, may be just right.
- Set standards so that success is a realistic possibility for each student. Because classrooms are becoming increasingly diverse, you may have students whose English proficiency is limited or who have disabilities related to learning and intellectual functioning. One way to deal with such diversity is to reward students for making steady progress from whatever their baseline level of performance was at the beginning of the term.
- An often-mentioned goal of teachers is to have students become intrinsically motivated or to take personal pride and satisfaction in simply doing something well. You can use natural instructional opportunities to point this out—for example, explore with students how satisfying it is to write a clear and interesting story as they are writing.

3 Take advantage of knowledge about the impact of different reinforcement schedules to encourage persistent and permanent learning.

a. When students first attempt a new kind of learning, supply frequent reinforcement. Then supply rewards less often.

When students first try a new skill or type of learning, praise almost any genuine attempt, even though it may be inept. As they become more skillful, reserve your praise for especially good performances. Avoid a set pattern of commenting on student work. Make favorable remarks at unpredictable intervals.

b. If you want to encourage periodic spurts of activity, use a fixed interval schedule of reinforcement.

Occasionally, you will want to encourage students to engage in spurts of activity since steady output might be too demanding or fatiguing. In such cases, supply reinforcement at specified periods of time. For example, when students are engaging in strenuous or concentrated activity, circulate and provide praise and encouragement by following a set pattern that will bring you in contact with each student at predictable intervals.

4 Give students opportunities to make overt responses, and provide prompt feedback.

a. Require students to make frequent, overt, and relevant responses.

The tendency of teachers is to talk, and for large chunks of time. Those who advocate a programmed approach to teaching recommend that teachers limit the amount of information and explanation they give to students and substitute opportunities for students to respond overtly. In addition, the responses should be directly related to the objectives. If your objectives emphasize the application of concepts and principles, then most of the responses students are asked to make should be about applications. The reason for this suggestion is that the delivery of corrective feedback and other forms of positive reinforcement can be increased when students make frequent responses, thereby accelerating the process of shaping.

Examples

- Instead of lecturing for twenty to thirty minutes at a time about the development of science and technology in the twentieth century, present information in smaller chunks, perhaps eight to ten minutes at a time, and then ask students to describe how an everyday product or service grew out of a particular scientific principle.
- Periodically ask students to summarize the main points of the material you presented over the past several minutes.

b. Provide feedback so that correct responses will be reinforced and students will become aware of and correct errors.

Research clearly shows that students who study material about a topic, answer a set of questions about that material, and are then told whether their responses are correct and why score significantly higher on a subsequent test of that material than do students who receive no feedback. The difference was about three-fourths of a standard deviation, meaning that the average student who received no feedback scored at the fiftieth percentile, whereas the average student who received feedback scored at the seventy-seventh percentile. Here are a couple of examples of how you can provide timely and useful feedback to students (Bangert-Drowns, Kulik, Kulik, & Morgan, 1991).

Journal Entry
Ways to Supply Immediate Feedback

Examples

- Immediately after students read a chapter in a text, give them an informal quiz on the key points you listed. Then have them pair off, exchange quizzes, and correct and discuss them.
- As soon as you complete a lecture or demonstration, ask individual students to volunteer to read to the rest of the class what they wrote about the points they were told to look for. Indicate whether the answer is correct; if it is incorrect or incomplete, ask (in a relaxed and nonthreatening way) for additional comments. Direct students to amend and revise their notes as they listen to the responses.

5 When students must struggle to concentrate on material that is not intrinsically interesting, use special forms of reinforcement to motivate them to persevere.

For a variety of reasons, some students may have an extraordinarily difficult time concentrating on almost anything. And, as we all know, to master almost any skill or subject, we have to engage in a certain amount of tedious effort. Accordingly, you may sometimes find it essential to use techniques of behavior modification to help students stick to a task. If and when that time comes, you might follow these procedures.

Journal Entry
Ways to Encourage Perseverance

a. Select, with student assistance, a variety of reinforcers.

A behavior modification approach to motivation appears to work most successfully when students are aware of and eager to earn a payoff. Because students react differently to rewards and because any reward is likely to lose effectiveness if used to excess, it is desirable to list several kinds of rewards and permit students to choose. Some behavior modification enthusiasts (for example, Walker & Shea, 1999) even recommend that you make up a *reinforcement preference list* for each student. If you allow your students to prepare individual reinforcement menus themselves, they should be instructed to list school activities they really enjoy doing. It would be wise, however, to stress that the student's lists must be approved by you so that they will not conflict with school regulations or interfere with the rights of others. A student's reward menu might include activities such as read a book of one's choice, work on an art or craft project, or view a videotape in another room.

A reinforcement menu can be used in conjunction with Grandma's rule (the Premack principle). Set up learning situations, particularly those that are not intrinsically appealing, by telling students that as soon as they finish their broccoli (for example, doing a series of multiplication problems), they can have a chocolate sundae (an item from their reinforcement menu).

b. Establish, in consultation with individual students, an initial contract of work to be performed to earn a particular reward.

Once you have established a list of payoffs, you might consult with students (on an individual basis, if possible) to establish a certain amount of work that must be completed for students to obtain a reward selected from the menu. Refer to our chapter on instructional approaches for Robert Mager's suggestions for preparing specific objectives. To ensure that students will earn the reward, the first contract should not be too demanding. For example, it might be something as simple as, "Successfully spell at least seven out of ten words on a list of previously misspelled words," or "Correctly answer at least six out of ten questions about the content of a textbook chapter."

c. Once the initial reward is earned, establish a series of short contracts leading to frequent, immediate rewards.

The results of many operant conditioning experiments suggest that the frequency of reinforcement is of greater significance than the amount of reinforcement. Therefore, having students work on brief contracts that lead to frequent payoffs immediately after the task is completed is preferable to having them work toward a delayed, king-sized award.

6 Remember the basic processes of observational learning: make effective use of modeling and imitation.

You can enhance learning of skills and promote desirable kinds of behavior if you take into account the four basic processes of observational learning: attention, retention, production, and motivation. If you plan to demonstrate the correct way to perform some skill or process, first make sure you have the attention of everyone in the class. (Techniques for securing attention will be discussed in the chapter on information-processing theory.) Then, after explaining what you are going to do (perhaps noting particular points students should look for), demonstrate. Immediately after you demonstrate, have all the students in the class try out the new skill to foster retention. For complex skills, have them write down the steps to follow before they try the activity on their own. Finally, arrange for all the students to get feedback and experience satisfaction and reinforcement immediately after they imitate your behavior by proving to themselves that they can carry out the activity on their own.

Journal Entry
Modeling Desirable Behaviors

The importance of modeling various behaviors, especially those thought processes that are normally hidden from observation, was noted by Margaret Metzger (1998), a high school English teacher. To help students better understand the process of literary interpretation and criticism, she recommended a procedure in which she led some students through a discussion of a story while the other students observed and took notes on the process.

Examples

- Show primary grade students how to solve multiplication problems by first placing a large, colorful poster on a bulletin board with a diagram of the process. Explain the diagram, and then demonstrate how to solve some simple problems. As soon as you finish, hand out a worksheet containing several simple problems similar to those you just demonstrated.
- Have students work on the problems for a specified period of time. Then secure their attention once again, and demonstrate on the board the correct procedure for solving each problem. Have students correct their own papers as you demonstrate, point out that they now know how to do multiplication problems, and praise them for learning the skill so rapidly.
- In a high school business class, follow a similar procedure when showing students how to set up a word processor to type a form letter. Make sure everyone is paying attention. Demonstrate the correct procedure. Have students write down the steps they should follow to imitate your actions and then study the steps before setting up their own word processor. Have them reproduce the letter. Provide reinforcement to supplement their own satisfaction in having completed the task successfully.
- Select low-achieving students who have mastered a skill to demonstrate the skill to other low-achieving students.
- A final point to remember about observational learning is that in the lower grades particularly, you will be an admired model your students will be inclined to imitate. If you are well organized and businesslike, but also thoughtful and considerate, your students may act that way themselves.

To gather more ideas for your journal, check the Reflective Journal Questions at **http://education.college.hmco.com/students**.

Using Computer-Assisted Instruction in Your Classroom

We mentioned earlier that under the right conditions, computers can effectively supplement classroom instruction. If you are now thinking that you might like to use CAI in your own classroom, you should consider the multiple ways computers can be used and how you can get the most out of them for your own students.

Uses of Computers

Computer use in schools falls into one of three categories. The first use—the type you have read about in this chapter—is often called "the computer as tutor." In this mode, students consolidate information learned earlier through drill-and-practice programs, acquire new information and skills through tutorial programs, and solve problems through simulations and games (Table 7.2 notes the purpose and main features of these types of programs). For most drill-and-practice programs and some tutorial programs, this approach is consistent with behavioral theory because it presents information in a structured, step-by-step fashion with consistent feedback. The Center for Programmed Instruction maintains a web site (**www.centerforpi.com/**)

Table 7.2 Major Types of CAI Programs

Type of Program	Purpose	Main Features*
Drill and practice	Practice knowledge and skills learned earlier to produce fast and accurate responses	• Presents many problems, questions, and exercises. • Checks answers and provides feedback. • Provides cues when student is not sure of correct responses. • Keeps track of errors. • Adjusts difficulty level of problems and questions to the proficiency level of the student.
Tutorial	Teach new information (e.g., facts, definitions, concepts) and skills	• New material presented in linear or branching format. • Linear programs require all students to begin with first frame and work through subsequent frames in given sequence. Incorrect responses minimized by brief answers, small steps, and frequent prompts. • Branching programs allow students to respond to different sets of frames depending on correctness of responses. For incorrect responses, program provides supplementary material that attempts to reteach. • Dialogue programs mimic teacher-student interactions by presenting material, evaluating responses, and adjusting subsequent instruction by presenting either more difficult or easier material.
Problem-solving programs: Simulations and games	Teach new information and skills and provide an opportunity to apply what was learned in a meaningful context that would otherwise be unavailable because of cost, physical danger, and time constraints	• Student uses newly learned and existing information to solve a realistic problem. • Settings may be realistic (e.g., piloting a plane), historical/adventure (e.g., guiding a wagon train across the Oregon Trail), or imaginary (e.g., colonizing a new world). • Students practice creating and testing hypotheses on effects of different variables on achieving a goal.

*Not all programs contain all of the listed features.

SOURCES: Grabe & Grabe (2001); Neill & Neill (1993).

that teaches you how to create tutorials and training programs through a series of self-paced, on-line tutorials.

A second way in which computers are used is as a learning and problem-solving tool. Typical applications in this category include word processing, data analysis, production of graphic material, information organization, and searching the Web for information. This "computer as a learning tool" approach is more typical of the cognitive approaches to learning that are covered in following chapters.

The third use involves learning how to program computers to perform one type of activity or another (Grabe & Grabe, 2001).

Computers in school used mostly for word processing, drill, and as reference source

There are both similarities and differences in the types of applications favored by elementary, middle school, and high school teachers. At all grade levels, word processing is the most frequently used application. For elementary teachers, drill-and-practice games for mathematics and language arts are the second most frequently used application. For middle and high school teachers, having students use the computer as a reference source is the most common use after word processing. Middle school teachers do this more often with CD-ROM software than with the World Wide Web, whereas the opposite pattern prevails among high school teachers (Becker, Ravitz, & Wong, 1999).

Getting the Most Out of Computer-Based Instruction

We would like to make two points about how you can optimize your use of computer-based instruction. First, recognize that out of the thousands of instructional programs that are on the market, most have such significant shortcomings in their design that they are not worth using. Thus, you will have to be an informed consumer either by conducting your own evaluations of instructional software (not as difficult a job as you might think) or consulting sources whose evaluations can be trusted. Here are the names and addresses of several web sites to help get you started:

Need to make informed choices of software

Educational Products Information Exchange Institute: **www.epie.org/**
California Learning Resource Network: **http://clrn.org/home/**
The School House Review: **www.worldvillage.com/wv/school/html/scholrev.htm**
Learning Resources and Technology: **http://lrt.ednet.ns.ca/demo.htm**
Software Evaluation Form: **http://kathyschrock.net/1computer/page4.htm**

For quick links to web sites, go to **http://education.college.hmco.com/students**.

Second, as enthusiastic as you and others may be about the potential of CAI, recognize that it cannot substitute for high-quality classroom teaching. There is a set of skills all teachers need to master in order to integrate computers successfully in a classroom. As we noted early in this text and as Larry Cuban (1986) points out in a provocative book about the relationship between teachers and machines, successful teaching often depends on the ability of a live teacher to establish a positive emotional climate (by communicating interest, excitement, expectations, and caring), to monitor student actions and reactions (by "reading" students' verbal and nonverbal communications), and to orchestrate the sequence and pace of instructional events (by making additions, deletions, and modifications in lesson plans). If one thinks of the computer as simply another tool to work with, then each type of computer program—drills, tutorials, simulations, integrated learning systems—requires teachers to plan learning activities, interact with students, provide encouragement and feedback, and design assessments. Although acquiring these skills may be a challenge, many teachers feel that being able to give their students meaningful access to such powerful learning tools is a significant reward (Grabe & Grabe, 2001).

CAI no substitute for high-quality teaching

To review this chapter, see the Thought Questions and ACE Self-Testing sections on the textbook web site at **http://education.college.hmco.com/students**.

Resources for Further Investigation

B. F. Skinner

In three highly readable volumes—*Particulars of My Life* (1976), *The Shaping of a Behaviorist* (1979), and *A Matter of Consequences* (1983)—B. F. Skinner describes his interests, aspirations, triumphs, and failures; the people and events that led him into psychology; and the forces that led him to devise operant conditioning. *The Technology of Teaching* (1968) is Skinner's most concise and application-oriented discussion of operant conditioning techniques related to pedagogy.

A highly readable summary and critical analysis of Skinner's brand of operant conditioning can be found in Robert Nye, *What Is B. F. Skinner Really Saying?* (1979). According to Nye, "Two major thoughts accompanied the writing of this book: a growing sense of the importance of Skinner's work and the awareness that his ideas are often misjudged" (p. 4).

In *Walden Two* (1948), Skinner describes his conception of a utopia based on the application of science to human behavior. To get the full impact of the novel and of Skinner's ideas, you should read the entire book. However, if you cannot read the whole book at this time, Chapters 12 through 17, which describe the approach to child rearing and education at Walden Two, may be of special interest to you as a future teacher.

Behavior Modification

If the possibilities of behavior modification seem attractive, you may wish to examine issues of the journals *Behavior Modification*, *Behavior Research and Therapy*, *Child Behavior Therapy*, *Journal of Applied Behavior Analysis*, and *Journal of Behavioral Education*. If you browse through the education and psychology sections of your college bookstore, you are likely to find a number of books on behavior modification. Or you might look for these titles in the library: *Classroom Management for Elementary Teachers* (2000), by Carolyn Evertson, Edmund Emmer, Barbara Clements, and Murray Worsham; *Classroom Management for Secondary Teachers* (2000), by Edmund Emmer, Carolyn Evertson, Barbara Clements, and Murray Worsham; and *Behavior Modification: What It Is and How to Do It* (1999), by Garry Martin and Joseph Pear. And, as the title suggests, *Beyond Behavior Modification: A Cognitive-Behavioral Approach to Behavior Management in the School* (1995), by Joseph Kaplan, goes beyond the typical behavior modification book. It includes chapters on assessing the classroom and school environment and teaching students how to use self-management, social, and stress-management skills.

Social Learning Theory

A good introduction to Bandura's social learning theory can be found in *Learning Theories: An Educational Perspective* (2000), by Dale Schunk. Another source of information and materials relating to social learning is the Oregon Social Learning Center, which can be found at **www.oslc.org:80/.**

Software Programs to Explore

The following are a few software programs whose excellence is generally recognized. They cover the range of drills, tutorials, simulations, and games:

Operation: Frog (Scholastic): allows students to simulate the dissection of a frog, complete with full graphics and video. Students can also "rebuild" the frog to practice locating its organs.

MathMagic (MindPlay Educational Software): offers an addition and subtraction drill program with an arcade game format, appropriate for elementary school students.

Oregon Trail (The Learning Company): enables students to experience the journey from Independence, Missouri, to Oregon as the pioneers did in 1865. Students are responsible for stocking a wagon, avoiding obstacles on the trail, making decisions about how to cross rivers and catch food, and so forth.

SimCity, SimCoaster, and SimThemePark (Electronic Arts): allow students to control a large number of variables in complex simulations. The simulations are challenging, but the extensive tutorials and touch of humor in the programs reduce the risk of frustration. Excellent for group work.

Where in the World Is Carmen Sandiego? (The Learning Company): requires students to interpret clues, put new or known facts (such as the location of cities) to use, and problem-solve creatively.

Summary

1. Operant conditioning is a theory of learning devised by B. F. Skinner. It focuses on how voluntary behaviors are strengthened (made more likely to occur in the future) or weakened by the consequences that follow them.

2. Operant conditioning assumes that human behavior is a natural phenomenon that can be explained by a set of general laws, that the best way to understand complex behaviors is to analyze and study the components that make them up, that the results of animal learning studies are potentially useful in understanding human learning, and that learning is the ability to exhibit a new behavior pattern.

3. Basic learning principles that derive from Skinner's work are positive reinforcement, negative reinforcement, punishment (Type I, or presentation punishment), time-out (Type II, or removal punishment), extinction, spontaneous recovery, generalization, and discrimination.

4. Positive reinforcement and negative reinforcement strengthen behaviors. Punishment, time-out, and extinction weaken target behaviors.

5. Complex behaviors can be learned by the reinforcement of successive approximations to the terminal (final) behavior and by the ignoring of nonapproximate behaviors, a process called shaping.

6. Once a new behavior is well established, it can be maintained at that level by the supplying of reinforcement on an intermittent schedule. The four basic schedules are fixed interval, variable interval, fixed ratio, and variable ratio.

7. One of the first educational applications of operant conditioning principles was programmed instruction. It involves presenting written material in small steps according to a predetermined sequence, prompting the

correct response, and presenting positive reinforcement in the form of knowledge of results.

8. The early efforts in programmed instruction gave rise to computer-assisted instruction (CAI). The varieties of CAI include drill-and-practice programs, simulations, tutorials, and integrated learning systems.

9. CAI has its strongest effect on simulation programs, elementary grade students, low-achieving students, urban students, and learning complex cognitive skills.

10. CAI can be an effective supplement to regular classroom instruction when it is used appropriately.

11. Another application of operant conditioning principles is behavior modification. The goal of behavior modification is for the teacher to help students learn desirable behaviors by ignoring or punishing undesired behaviors and reinforcing desired ones. Techniques for achieving this goal include shaping, token economies, contingency contracts, extinction, and punishment.

12. Social learning theory, which was devised largely by Albert Bandura, explains how individuals learn by observing a model (who may or may not be reinforced for the behavior involved) and imitating the model's behavior.

13. The processes involved in social learning (also called observational learning) are attention, retention, production, and motivation (reinforcement). The reinforcement can come from observing someone else (direct), anticipating that one will be treated as the model was (vicarious), or meeting personal standards (self-reinforcement).

14. Self-efficacy refers to how capable people believe they are for handling a particular task.

15. An individual's sense of self-efficacy is likely to be affected by a combination of past performance, persuasive comments from others, emotional reactions about an imminent task, and observation of the behavior of models judged to be similar to the individual.

16. Self-efficacy can affect an individual's choice of goals and activities, thought processes, willingness to persist at difficult tasks, and emotional reactions.

17. Research suggests that many social behaviors, such as aggression, may be learned by imitation of a model. Many academic-related behaviors, such as persistence, self-confidence, cognitive skills, and self-efficacy, can also be learned by observing and imitating a model.

18. Of the three main ways in which computers are used in schools—using the computer as a tutor, using the computer as a learning and problem-solving tool, and learning how to program computers—the first is most closely allied with the principles of operant conditioning.

19. To get the most out of computer-based instruction, teachers need to select good-quality programs and integrate their use of technology with effective teaching techniques.

KEY TERMS

operant conditioning *(227)*
positive reinforcement *(229)*
negative reinforcement *(229)*
punishment *(229)*
time-out *(230)*
extinction *(230)*
spontaneous recovery *(231)*
generalization *(231)*
discrimination *(231)*
shaping *(231)*
programmed instruction *(233)*
frames *(233)*
computer-assisted instruction (CAI) *(232)*
computer-based instruction *(CBI)* *(232)*
drill-and-practice programs *(235)*
simulation programs *(235)*
tutorial programs *(235)*
integrated learning systems (ILS) *(235)*
behavior modification *(236)*
Premack principle *(237)*
token economy *(238)*
contingency contracting *(239)*
response cost *(241)*
social learning theory *(243)*
observational learning *(243)*
direct reinforcement *(245)*
vicarious reinforcement *(245)*
self-reinforcement *(245)*

DISCUSSION QUESTIONS

1. The theory of operant conditioning holds that we learn to respond or not respond to certain stimuli because our responses are followed by desirable or aversive consequences. How many of your own behaviors can you explain in this fashion? Why, for example, are you reading this book and answering these questions?

2. Many educators have a negative attitude toward operant conditioning because they feel it presents a cold, dehumanizing picture of human learning and ignores the role of such factors as free will, motives, and creativity. Did you feel this way as you read through the chapter? Do you think positive attributes of operant conditioning balance out possible negative aspects of the theory?

3. Skinner has argued that society too frequently uses aversive means to shape desired behavior (particularly punishment) rather than the more effective positive reinforcement. As you think about how your behavior has been shaped by your parents, teachers, friends, supervisors at work, law enforcement officials, and others, would you agree or disagree with Skinner's observation? Can you think of some possible reasons we tend to use punishment more frequently than positive reinforcement?

4. Can you recall a teacher whom you admired so much that you imitated some aspects of her behavior (if not immediately, then sometime later)? What was it about this teacher that caused you to behave in the same way? How might you have the same effect on your students?

8 Information-Processing Theory

In the chapter on behavioral learning theories, we noted that operant conditioning emphasizes the role of external factors in learning. Behavioral psychologists focus on the nature of a stimulus to which a student is exposed, the response that the student makes, and the consequences that follow the response. They see no reason to speculate about what takes place in the student's mind before and after the response. The extensive Suggestions for Teaching in Your Classroom presented in the chapter on behavioral learning theories serve as evidence that conclusions and principles based on

Key Points

These key points will help you learn the important information in this chapter. To help you study, they also appear in the margins of the pages, next to the text where they are discussed.

The Information-Processing View of Learning

- Information processing: how humans attend to, recognize, transform, store, retrieve information

A Model of Information Processing

- Sensory register: stimuli held briefly for possible processing
- Recognition: noting key features and relating them to stored information
- Attention: focusing on a portion of currently available information
- Information in long-term memory influences what we attend to
- Short-term memory: about seven bits of information held for about twenty seconds
- Maintenance rehearsal: hold information for immediate use
- Elaborative rehearsal: use stored information to aid learning
- Organizing material reduces number of chunks, provides recall cues
- Meaningful learning occurs when organized material is associated with stored knowledge
- Long-term memory: permanent storehouse of unlimited capacity
- Information in long-term memory organized as schemata
- Students remember much of what they learn in school, especially if mastery and active learning are emphasized

Metacognition

- Metacognition: our own knowledge of how we think
- Insight into one's learning processes improves with age

Helping Students Become Strategic Learners

- Strategy: plan to achieve a long-term goal
- Tactic: specific technique that helps achieve immediate objective
- Rote rehearsal not a very effective memory tactic
- Acronym: word made from first letters of items to be learned
- Acrostic: sentence made up of words derived from first letters of items to be learned
- Loci method: visualize items to be learned stored in specific locations
- Keyword method: visually link pronunciation of foreign word to English translation
- Mnemonic devices meaningfully organize information, provide retrieval cues
- Self-questioning improves comprehension, knowledge integration
- Taking notes and reviewing notes aid retention and comprehension
- Learning strategy components: metacognition, analysis, planning, implementation, monitoring, modification
- Reciprocal teaching: students learn comprehension skills by demonstrating them to peers

Suggestions for Teaching in Your Classroom

- Unpredictable changes in environment usually command attention
- Attention span can be increased with practice
- Distributed practice: short study periods at frequent intervals
- Serial position effect: tendency to remember items at beginning and end of a long list
- Concrete analogies can make abstract information meaningful

Technology as an Information-Processing Tool

- Computer-based technology helps students organize and represent ideas and comprehend text
- Hypermedia and multimedia tools produce both positive and negative results

analyses of external stimuli, observable responses, and observable consequences can be of considerable value to teachers.

But cognitive psychologists, meaning those who study how the mind works and influences behavior, are convinced that it is possible to study nonobservable behavior, such as thought processes, in a scientific manner. Some cognitive psychologists focus on how people use what they know to solve different kinds of problems in different settings; their work will be discussed in the chapter on constructivist learning theory and problem solving. Many cognitive psychologists are especially interested in an area of study known as **information-processing theory,** which seeks to understand how people acquire new information, how they store information and recall it from memory, and how what they already know guides and determines what and how they will learn.

Information-processing theory became a popular approach to the study of learning because it provided psychologists with a framework for investigating the role of a variable that behaviorism had ignored: the nature of the learner. Instead of being viewed as relatively passive organisms that respond in fairly predictable ways to environmental stimuli, learners were now seen as highly active interpreters and manipulators of environmental stimuli. The stage was set for psychology to study learning from a broader and more complicated perspective—namely, as an *interaction* between the learner and the environment. ■

The Information-Processing View of Learning

Information-processing theory rests on a set of assumptions of which three are worth noting.

Information processing: how humans attend to, recognize, transform, store, retrieve information

1. Information is processed in steps, or stages. The major steps typically are attending to a stimulus, recognizing it, transforming it into some type of mental representation, comparing it with information already stored in memory, assigning meaning to it, and acting on it in some fashion (Searleman & Herrmann, 1994). At an early processing stage, human beings *encode* information (represent it in thought) in somewhat superficial ways (as when they represent visual and auditory stimuli as true-to-life pictures and sounds) and at later stages in more meaningful ways (as when they grasp the gist of an idea or its relationship to other ideas).
2. There are limits on how much information can be processed at each stage. Although the absolute amount of information human beings can learn appears to be limitless, it must be acquired gradually.
3. The human information-processing system is interactive. Information already stored in memory influences and is influenced by perception and attention. We see what our prior experiences direct us to see, and, in turn, what we see affects what we know.

To preview this chapter's key ideas about information processing, see the Chapter Themes on the Snowman textbook site at **http://education.college.hmco.com/students**.

Thus, according to the information-processing view, learning results from an interaction between an environmental stimulus (the *information* that is to be learned) and a learner (the one who *processes*, or transforms, the information). What an information-processing psychologist wants to know, for instance, is what goes on in a student's mind as a teacher demonstrates how to calculate the area of a triangle or as the student reads twenty pages of a social studies text or responds to test questions. In the sense that contemporary information processing emphasizes the use of existing knowledge schemes to interpret new information and build new knowledge structures, it can be considered a *constructivist* view of learning (Mayer, 1996). (See the chapter on constructivism for a full description of the nature of the theory and the viewpoints most associated with it.)

We believe that you ought to read this chapter very carefully because the information-processing decisions you make affect when you learn, how much you learn, how well you learn—indeed, whether you learn at all. To give you an appreciation of the information-processing approach to learning and how it can help teachers and students do their jobs, the next section will describe several basic cognitive processes and their role in how people store and retrieve information. The section following that will describe research on selected learning tactics and discuss the nature of strategic learning.

A Model of Information Processing

Information-processing psychologists assume that people process new information in stages, that there are limits on how much information can be processed at each stage, and that previously learned information affects how and what people currently learn. Consequently, many psychologists think of information as being held in and transferred among three memory stores: a sensory register, a short-term store, and a long-term store. Each store varies as to the processes required to move information into and out of it, how much information it can hold, and for how long it can hold information. A symbolic representation of these memory stores and their associated processes appears in Figure 8.1. Called a *multi-store* model, it is based on the work of several theorists (for example, Atkinson & Shiffrin, 1968; Norman & Rumelhart, 1970). Note that our use of the term *memory stores* is not meant to suggest specific locations in the brain where information is held; it is simply a metaphorical device for classifying different memory phenomena.

Shortly after the introduction of multi-store models, information-processing theorists divided themselves into two groups. In one camp are those who believe that a multi-store model is the best way to explain a variety of memory phenomena. In the other camp are those who favor a theoretically leaner, single memory system. Although this debate has yet to be firmly resolved, the multi-store model is seen as having enough validity that it can be productively used to organize and present much of what is known about how humans store, process, and retrieve information from memory (Searleman & Herrmann, 1994; Spear & Riccio, 1994).

As shown in Figure 8.1, *control processes* govern both the manner in which information is encoded and its flow between memory stores. These processes include *recognition, attention, maintenance rehearsal, elaborative rehearsal* (also called *elaborative encoding*), and retrieval. Each control process is associated primarily with a particular memory store.

The control processes are an important aspect of the information-processing system for two reasons. First, they determine the quantity and quality of information that the learner stores in and retrieves from memory. Second, it is the learner who decides whether, when, and how to employ them. That the control processes are under our direct, conscious control will take on added importance when we discuss

Figure 8.1 An Information-Processing Model of Learning

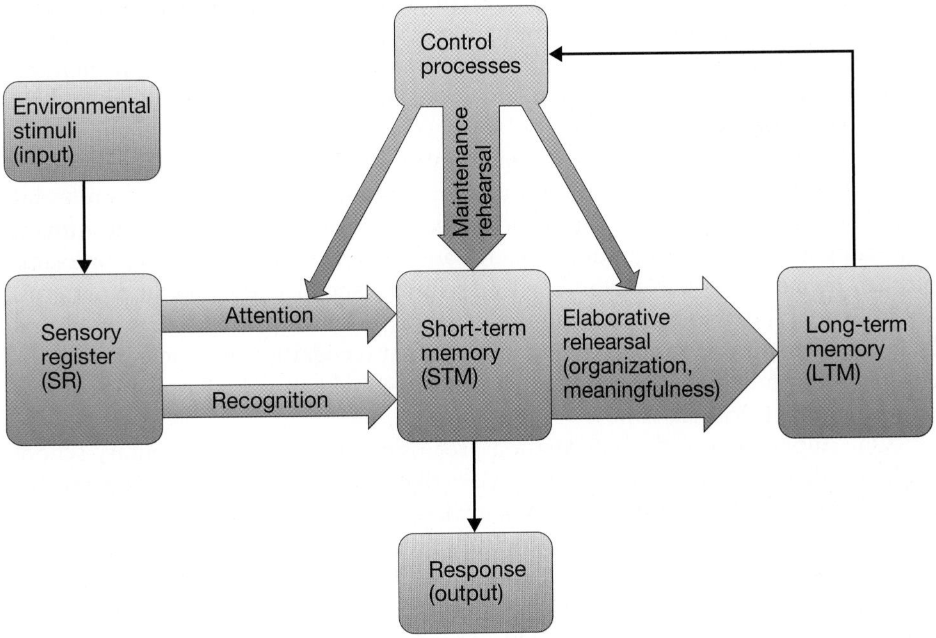

educational applications a bit later. Before we get to applications, however, we need to make you more familiar with the three memory stores and the control processes specifically associated with each of them.

The Sensory Register and Its Control Processes

The Sensory Register A description of how human learners process information typically begins with environmental stimuli. Our sense receptors are constantly stimulated by visual, auditory, tactile, olfactory, and gustatory stimuli. These experiences are initially recorded in the **sensory register (SR),** the first memory store. It is called the sensory register because the information it stores is thought to be encoded in the same form in which it is originally perceived—that is, as raw sensory data.

Sensory register: stimuli held briefly for possible processing

The purpose of the SR is to hold information just long enough (about one to three seconds) for us to decide if we want to attend to it further. Information not selectively attended to and recognized decays or disappears from the system. At the moment you are reading these words, for example, you are being exposed to the appearance of letters printed on paper, sounds in the place where you are reading, and many other stimuli. The sensory register might be compared to an unending series of instant-camera snapshots or videotape segments, each lasting from one to three seconds before fading away. If you recognize and attend to one of the snapshots, it will be "processed" and transferred to short-term memory.

The Nature of Recognition The process of **recognition** involves noting key features of a stimulus and relating them to already stored information. This process is interactive in that it depends partly on information extracted from the stimulus itself and partly on information stored in long-term memory. The ability to recognize a dog, for example, involves noticing those physical features of the animal that give it "dogness" (for example, height, length, number of feet, type of coat) and combining the results of that analysis with relevant information from long-term memory (such as that dogs are household pets, are walked on a leash by their owners, and are used to guard property).

Recognition: noting key features and relating them to stored information

To the degree that an object's defining features are ambiguous (as when one observes an unfamiliar breed of dog from a great distance) or a learner lacks relevant prior knowledge (as many young children do), recognition and more meaningful processing will suffer. Recognition of words and sentences during reading, for example, can be aided by such factors as clear printing, knowledge of spelling patterns, knowledge of letter sounds, and the frequency with which words appear in natural language. The important point to remember is that recognition and meaningful processing of information are most effective when we make use of all available sources of information (Driscoll, 2000).

One implication of this information-processing view is that elementary school students need more structured learning tasks than middle school or high school students. Because of their limited store of knowledge in long-term memory and narrow ability to relate what they do know logically to the task at hand, younger students should be provided with clear, complete, explicit directions and learning materials (see, for example, Doyle, 1983).

The Impact of Attention The environment usually provides us with more information than we can deal with at one time. From the multitude of sights, sounds, smells, and other stimuli impinging on us at a given moment, we notice and record in the sensory register only a fraction. At this point, yet another reduction typically occurs. We may process only one-third of the already-selected information recorded in the SR. We continually focus on one thing at the expense of something else. This selective focusing on a portion of the information currently stored in the sensory register is what we call **attention.**

Attention: focusing on a portion of currently available information

As with any other human characteristic, there are individual differences in attention. Some people can concentrate on a task while they are surrounded by a variety of sights and sounds. Others need to isolate themselves in a private study area. Still others have difficulty attending under any conditions. What explains these differences? Again, information from long-term memory plays an influential role. According to Ulric Neisser, "Perceivers pick up only what they have schemata for, and willy-nilly ignore the rest" (1976, p. 79). In other words, we choose what we will see (or hear) by using our prior knowledge and experiences (i.e., schemata) to anticipate the nature of incoming information. Students daydream, doodle, and write letters rather than listen to a lecture because they anticipate hearing little of value. (In other words, the familiar statement, "I'll believe it when I see it," becomes "I'll see it when I believe it" from the perspective of information-processing theory.)

Information in long-term memory influences what we attend to

Moreover, these anticipatory schemata are likely to have long-lasting effects. If someone asked you now to read a book about English grammar, you might recall having been bored by diagramming sentences and memorizing grammatical rules in elementary school. If that was the case, you might not read the grammar text very carefully. A basic challenge for teachers is to convince students that a learning task will be useful, enjoyable, informative, and meaningful. Later in this chapter, we will present some ideas as to how this might be accomplished.

Short-Term Memory and Its Control Processes

Short-term memory: about seven bits of information held for about twenty seconds

Short-Term Memory Once information has been attended to, it is transferred to **short-term memory (STM),** the second memory store. Short-term memory can hold about seven unrelated bits of information for approximately twenty seconds. Although this brief time span may seem surprising, it can be easily demonstrated. Imagine that you look up and dial an unfamiliar phone number and receive a busy signal. If you are then distracted by something or someone else for fifteen to twenty seconds, chances are you will forget the number. Short-term memory is often referred to as *working memory* since it holds information we are currently aware of at any given moment and is the place where various encoding, organizational, and retrieval processes occur.

Working memory is increasingly being viewed as a critical component in our information-processing system. In the view of one researcher, working memory capacity may be equivalent to Spearman's *g* factor (intelligence as a general mental capability) and "is more highly related to learning, both short-term and long-term, than is any other cognitive factor" (Kyllonen, 1996, p. 73).

Rehearsal A severe limitation of short-term memory is how quickly information disappears or is forgotten in the absence of further processing. This problem can be dealt with through *rehearsal.* Most people think of rehearsal as repeating something over and over either in silence or out loud. The usual purpose for such behavior is to memorize information for later use, although occasionally we simply want to hold material in short-term memory for immediate use (for example, to redial a phone number after getting a busy signal). Rehearsal can serve both purposes, but not in the same way. Accordingly, cognitive psychologists have found it necessary and useful to distinguish two types of rehearsal: maintenance and elaborative.

Maintenance rehearsal: hold information for immediate use

Maintenance rehearsal (also called *rote rehearsal* or *repetition*) has a mechanical quality. Its only purpose is to use mental and verbal repetition to hold information

To help students encode information, teach them how to group objects and ideas according to some shared feature.

in short-term memory for some immediate purpose. Although this is a useful and often-used capability (as in the telephone example), it has no effect on long-term memory storage.

Elaborative rehearsal (also called *elaborative encoding*) consciously relates new information to knowledge already stored in long-term memory. Elaboration occurs when we use information stored in long-term memory to add details to new information, clarify the meaning of a new idea, make inferences, construct visual images, and create analogies (King, 1992b). In these ways, we facilitate both the transfer of information to long-term memory and its maintenance in short-term memory. For example, if you wanted to learn the lines for a part in a play, you might try to relate the dialogue and behavior of your character to similar personal experiences you remember. As you strive to memorize the lines and actions, your mental "elaborations" will help you store your part in long-term memory so that you can retrieve it later.

Elaborative rehearsal: use stored information to aid learning

Elaborative rehearsal, whereby information from long-term memory is used in learning new information, is the rule rather than the exception. Mature learners don't often employ maintenance rehearsal by itself. The decision to use one or the other, however, depends on the demands you expect the environment to make on you. If you need to remember things for future use, use elaborative rehearsal; if you want to keep something in consciousness just for the moment, use rote rehearsal.

It is important for you to keep in mind that younger children may not use rehearsal processes in the same way as more mature learners. Kindergarten students rarely engage in spontaneous rehearsal. By the age of seven, however, children typically use simple rehearsal strategies. When presented with a list of items, the average seven-year-old rehearses each word by itself several times. From the age of ten, rehearsal becomes more like that of an adult. Several items may be grouped together and rehearsed as a set.

So far, we have explained the effect of elaborative rehearsal in terms of relating new information to information already stored in long-term memory. That's fine as a very general explanation. But to be more precise, we need to point out that elaborative rehearsal is based on *organization* (as in the preceding example, where several items were grouped together on some basis and rehearsed as a set) and *meaningfulness* (as in the earlier example, where lines in a play were related to similar personal experiences).

Organization Quite often the information we want to learn is complex and interrelated. We can simplify the task by organizing multiple pieces of information into a few "clumps," or "chunks," of information, particularly when each part of a chunk helps us remember other parts. The value of organizing material was illustrated by an experiment (Bower, Clark, Lesgold, & Winzenz, 1969) in which two groups of subjects were asked to learn 112 words in four successive lists but under different conditions. One group was given each of the four lists for four trials in the hierarchical arrangement displayed in Figure 8.2. The other group was given the same lists and the same hierarchical tree arrangement, but the words from each list were randomly arranged over the four levels of the hierarchy.

As you can see, through the first three trials, the first group recalled more than twice as many words as the second and achieved perfect recall scores for the last two trials. The organized material was much easier to learn not only because there were fewer chunks to memorize but also because each item in a group served as a cue for the other items. When you decide to store pertinent material from this chapter in your long-term memory in preparation for an exam, you will find the job much easier if you organize what you are studying. To learn the various parts of the

Organizing material reduces number of chunks, provides recall cues

Figure 8.2 **Hierarchical Arrangement of Words Produces Superior Recall**

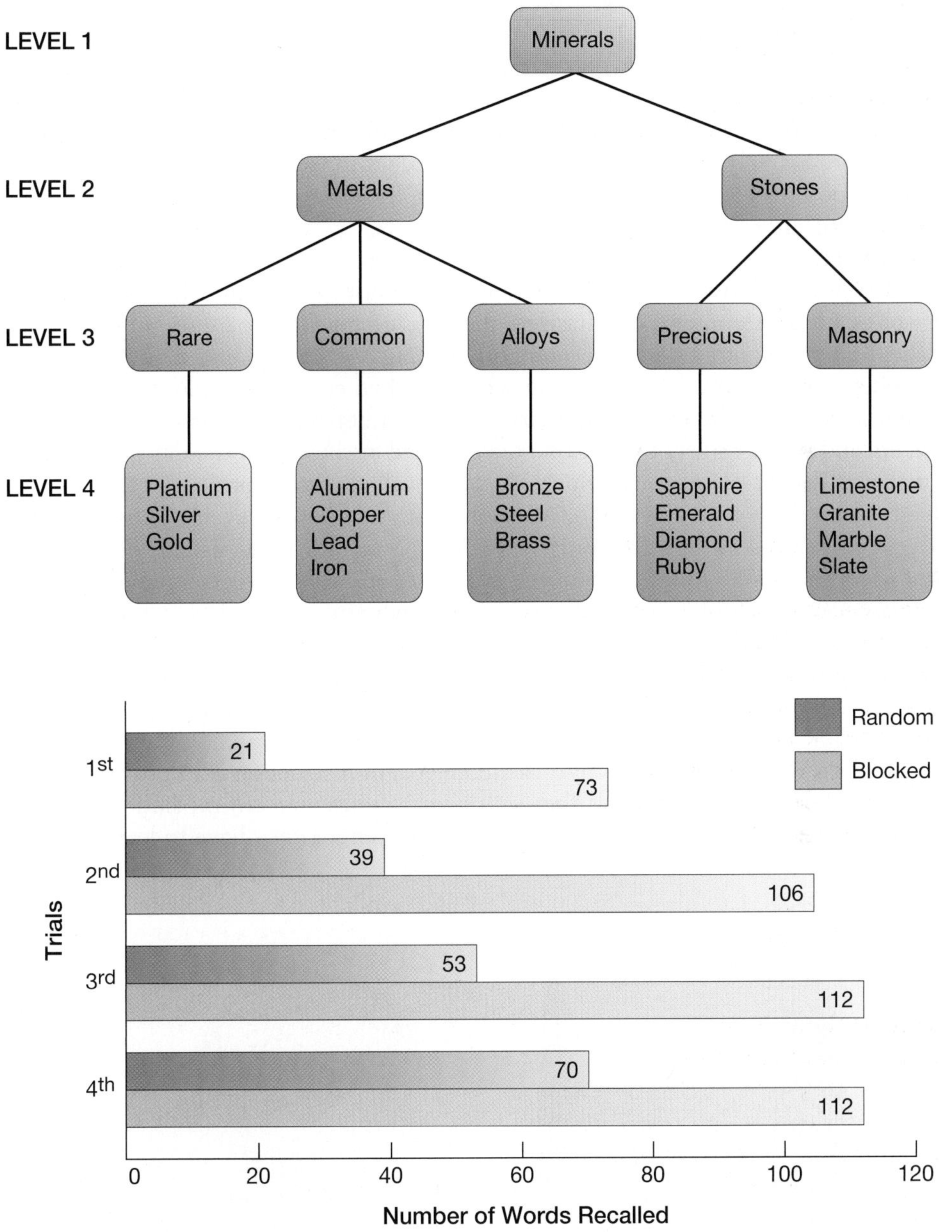

SOURCE: Bower et al. (1969).

information-processing model under discussion, for instance, you might group the ideas being described under the various headings used in this chapter (as we do in the *Study Guide*).

Meaningfulness The meaningfulness of new information that one is about to learn has been characterized as "potentially the most powerful variable for explaining the learning of complex verbal discourse" (Johnson, 1975, pp. 425–426). According to David Ausubel (Ausubel, Novak, & Hanesian, 1978), **meaningful learning** occurs when a learner encounters clear, logically organized material and consciously tries to relate the new material to ideas and experiences stored in long-term memory. You might, for example, imagine yourself using learning theory principles to teach a lesson to a group of students. Or you might modify a previously constructed flowchart on the basis of new information. The basic idea behind meaningful learning is that the learner actively attempts to associate new ideas to existing ones. The questions that we pose to you at the end of each chapter, for example, are designed to foster meaningful encoding by getting you to relate text information to relevant prior experience.

Meaningful learning occurs when organized material is associated with stored knowledge

Lev Vygotsky, the Russian psychologist we mentioned in the chapter on stage theories of development, emphasized the role of teachers, parents, siblings, and other kinds of expert tutors in meaningful learning. Vygotsky pointed out that some of what we learn about the world in which we live comes from direct, unfiltered contact with stimuli. Touch a hot stove, and you get burned. Insult or ridicule a friend, and you are likely to have one fewer friend at the end of the day. The limitation of this kind of learning, which Vygotsky called *direct* learning, is that one is likely to miss the general lesson or principle that underlies the event. Consequently, Vygotsky favored *mediated* learning. A mediator is an individual, usually older, more knowledgeable, and skilled, who selects stimuli to attend to, directs attention to certain aspects of the chosen stimulus, and explains why things are the way they are and why things are done in a certain way. Thus, parents explain to their children why it is not acceptable to hit or tease playmates, and teachers explain to students why it is necessary for them to learn how to use the concepts and rules of English grammar, plane geometry, and the like (Kozulin & Presseisen, 1995).

From a Vygotskian perspective, the main goal of instruction is to provide learners with the psychological tools they will need to engage in *self*-mediation. If individuals are to function effectively once they leave school, they have to learn how to

According to Russian psychologist Lev Vygotsky, meaningful learning is most likely to occur when a more knowledgeable and skilled individual explains to a less knowledgeable individual why things are the way they are, as when one points out the reasons behind various rules and procedures, the causes of different events, and the motives for people's behaviors.

look beyond the immediate situation and see how they can use new knowledge and skills in future situations. Psychologists refer to this process as transfer of learning; we will discuss it at length in the chapter on constructivism and problem solving.

This brief description of meaningfulness and its role in learning contains a strong implication for teaching in culturally diverse classrooms. You can foster meaningful learning for students from other cultures by pointing out similarities between ideas presented in class and students' culture-specific knowledge. For example, you might point out that September 16 has the same significance to people of Mexican origin as July 4 has to U.S. citizens since the former date commemorates Mexico's revolution against and independence from Spain.

Visual Imagery Encoding Generating mental images of objects, ideas, and actions is a particularly powerful form of elaborative encoding. Like pictures, images can be said to be worth a thousand words because they contain a wealth of information in a compact, organized, and meaningful format. Such notable individuals as Albert Einstein (physics), Michael Faraday (physics), Sir Francis Galton (anthropology and genetics), James D. Watson (biochemistry), and Joan Didion (literature) have described how mental imagery played a significant role in their thinking and problem-solving efforts (Shepard, 1978).

Research has consistently shown that directing students to generate visual images as they read lists of words or sentences, several paragraphs of text, or lengthy text passages produces higher levels of comprehension and recall as compared to students who are not so instructed. Also, text passages that contain many concrete words and phrases are more easily understood and more accurately recalled than passages that contain more abstract than concrete ideas (Clark & Paivio, 1991). In one study (Sadoski, Goetz, & Rodriguez, 2000), the beneficial effect of concreteness was obtained for several passage types (such as expository text, persuasive text, stories, and narratives). The more concrete the passage was, the more it was rated comprehensible by students, and students who read concrete passages recalled 1.7 times as much information as students who read abstract passages. As we will see later in the chapter, concreteness and visual imagery are an integral part of several effective study skills.

The theory that these findings support is Allan Paivio's dual coding theory (Clark & Paivio, 1991). According to the **dual coding theory,** concrete material (such as pictures of familiar objects) and concrete words (such as *horse, bottle, water*) are remembered better than abstract words (such as *deduction, justice, theory*) because the former can be encoded in two ways—as images and as verbal labels—whereas abstract words are encoded only verbally. This makes retrieval easier since a twice-coded item provides more potential retrieval cues than information that exists in only one form.

Long-Term Memory

Long-term memory: permanent storehouse of unlimited capacity

We have already referred in a general way to the third memory store, **long-term memory (LTM),** which is perhaps the most interesting of all. On the basis of neurological, experimental, and clinical evidence, most cognitive psychologists believe that the storage capacity of LTM is unlimited and that it contains a permanent record of everything an individual has learned, although some doubt exists about the latter point (see, for example, Loftus & Loftus, 1980).

The neurological evidence comes from the work of Wilder Penfield (1969), a Canadian neurosurgeon who operated on more than one thousand patients who experienced epileptic seizures. To determine the source of the seizures, Penfield electrically stimulated various parts of the brain's surface. During this procedure, many patients reported vivid images of long-dormant events from their past. It was as if a neurological videotape had been turned on.

The experimental evidence, although less dramatic, is just as interesting. In a typical memory study (such as Tulving & Pearlstone, 1966), subjects receive a list of nouns to learn. After giving subjects ample opportunity to recall as many of the words as possible, researchers provide retrieval cues—for instance, category labels such as "clothing," "food," or "animals." In many cases cued subjects quickly recall additional items. Experiments on how well people recognize previously seen pictures have produced some startling findings. Thirty-six hours after viewing over 2,500 pictures, a group of college students correctly identified an average of about 2,250, or 90 percent (Standing, Conezio, & Haber, 1970). In fact, it has been estimated that if 1 million pictures could be shown, recognition memory would still be 90 percent or better (Standing, 1973). Finally, psychiatrists and psychotherapists have reported many case histories of individuals who have been helped to recall seemingly forgotten events through hypnosis and other techniques (Erdelyi & Goldberg, 1979).

How Information Is Organized in Long-Term Memory As you have seen, long-term memory plays an influential role throughout the information-processing system. The interests, attitudes, skills, and knowledge of the world that reside there influence what we perceive, how we interpret our perceptions, and whether we process information for short-term or long-term storage. In most instances, retrieval of information from long-term memory is extremely rapid and accurate, like finding a book in a well-run library. Accordingly, we can conclude that information in long-term memory must be organized. The nature of this organization is a key area in the study of memory. The insights it provides help to illuminate the encoding and retrieval processes associated with long-term memory.

Many cognitive psychologists believe that our store of knowledge in long-term

Because people interpret new information and experience on the basis of existing memory schemes, and because no two people's schemes are identical, each person is likely to represent the same idea or experience in a unique fashion.

Information in long-term memory organized as schemata

memory is organized in terms of **schemata** (which is plural for *schema* and is related in meaning to Jean Piaget's *scheme*). Richard Anderson (1984) defines a schema as an abstract structure of information. It is abstract because it summarizes information about many different cases or examples of something, and it is structured because it represents how its own informational components are interrelated. Schemata give us expectations about objects and events (dogs bark, birds fly, students listen to their teachers and study industriously). When our schemata are well formed and a specific event is consistent with our expectation, comprehension occurs. When schemata are poorly structured or absent, learning is slow and uncertain. The following example should make this notion of schemata more understandable.

For almost everyone raised in the United States, the word *classroom* typically calls to mind a scene that includes certain people (teacher, students), objects (desks, chalkboard, books, pencils), rules (attend to the teacher's instructions, stay in the classroom unless given permission to leave), and events (reading, listening, writing, talking, drawing). This is a generalized representation, and some classrooms may contain fewer or more of these characteristics. However, as long as students and teachers share the same basic classroom schema, each will generally know what to expect and how to behave in any classroom. It is when people do not possess an appropriate schema that comprehension, memory, and behavior problems arise.

This notion was first investigated during the early 1930s by Sir Frederick Bartlett (1932), an English psychologist. In one experiment, Bartlett had subjects read and recall a brief story, entitled "The War of the Ghosts," that was based on North American Indian folklore. Since Bartlett's subjects had little knowledge of Native American culture, they had difficulty accurately recalling the story; they omitted certain details and distorted others. The distortions were particularly interesting because they reflected an attempt to interpret the story in terms of the logic and beliefs of Western culture. Similar studies, conducted more recently with other kinds of reading materials, have reported similar results (diSibio, 1982). The conclusion that Bartlett and other researchers have drawn is that remembering is not simply a matter of retrieving a true-to-life record of information. People often remember their *interpretations* or *constructions* of something read, seen, or heard. In addition, when they experience crucial gaps in memory, they tend to fill in these blanks with logical reconstructions of what they think must have been. People then report these reconstructions as memories of actual events (diSibio, 1982).

Interested in finding out about your own memory? Go to the Netlabs section of this text's web site at **http://education.college.hmco.com/students**.

These experiments and the Case in Print vividly demonstrate the interactive nature of memory. What we know influences what we perceive and how we interpret and store those perceptions. And because our memories of specific events or experiences are assembled, constructed, and sometimes reassembled by the brain over time, accurate and complete recall of information we once stored is not always possible. As a teacher, then, you should pay deliberate attention to how your students use their background knowledge, helping them to use it as accurately and completely as possible to process new information.

How Well Do We Remember What We Learn in School? Conventional wisdom (which is often wrong, by the way) holds that much of the information that we learn in school is forgotten soon after a unit of instruction or course has ended. You may have felt the same way yourself on more than one occasion. But is this belief true? To answer this question, George Semb and John Ellis (1994) reviewed the results of fifty-six research articles published between 1930 and 1993. Their main findings are very consistent with the information-processing principles that you have read about and should at least partially reassure you that you haven't been wasting your time all these years:

"Remembering" Things That Never Were

People often remember their interpretations or constructions of something read, seen, or heard. In addition, when they experience crucial gaps in memory, people tend to fill in these blanks with logical reconstructions of what they think must have been. People then report these reconstructions as memories of actual events. (p. 271)

"Memory" Can Play Tricks, Researchers Discover Here

JOHN G. CARLTON
St. Louis Post-Dispatch 11/8/1998

A college student's smiling face flashed upon the giant screen inside Washington University's May Auditorium on Saturday afternoon.

She had just been telling an interviewer about the time she got lost in a large department store. It was back when she was 5 years old, the student had said, retelling the tale with remarkable detail and clarity.

But there was something she left out—an important fact that even the student didn't know until informed by a memory researcher.

It never really happened.

The smile slowly drained from the student's face. And as it did, a room full of scientists and psychotherapists sat riveted to the screen.

Like members of two sometimes-warring tribes, they gathered in St. Louis on Saturday searching for common ground in a rapidly shifting landscape.

The occasion was a conference sponsored by the St. Louis Psychoanalytic Institute and Washington University's department of psychology and school of social work.

It comes at a time when research has begun calling into question widely held assumptions about how memories are constructed.

Scientists at the University of Washington in Seattle, who made the videotape shown Saturday, and their colleagues around the world have demonstrated how easy it is to create "memories" of events that never actually occurred.

Others have shown that the way children are interviewed can drastically alter what they claim to remember and how much confidence they have in those memories.

Even more unsettling, they have shown that it can be nearly impossible to differentiate so-called false memories from recollections of actual events.

It may sound dry and academic, but the work—some of it done by participants at Saturday's conference—has enormous implications.

During the late 1980s and early 1990s, for example, teachers and day care providers were charged with sexually abusing children in a half-dozen high-profile cases around the country.

Prosecutors in those cases often relied heavily on testimony from children as young as 4 and 5 years old, whom jurors believed to be too young to lie.

That's what made one videotape so shocking.

Maggie Bruck, a professor of psychology at McGill University in Montreal, showed a videotape Saturday of a doctor examining a girl. After he completed his examination, the doctor measured the girl's wrist with a ribbon and tickled her foot with a stick.

The next day, the girl was asked to show on an anatomically correct doll how she had been examined. Her videotaped response: The doctor strangled her with the ribbon and inserted the stick into her genitals.

Bruck also played tapes of children subjected to repeated, suggestive questioning. After first answering an interviewer's questions truthfully, the tapes showed child after child changing their answers.

And it isn't only children who can be made to believe "memories" of events that never actually occurred.

Using suggestive interviewing techniques favored by some therapists, Elizabeth F. Loftus, a professor of psychology and law at the University of Washington, found she could make students "remember" things like getting lost in a department store.

Over time, students become more and more convinced that the events—which had been fabricated by researchers with the help of students' family members—had actually occurred.

In the same way, some patients have become convinced that they were sexually abused as children after being treated by therapists who used techniques such as hypnosis.

None of that research disputes the terrible reality of child sexual abuse, Loftus and other presenters said. Such abuse occurs, and it is often corroborated when children speak out.

But the new research may prompt a re-examination of how abuse is investigated, and how certain interviewing techniques can result in innocent people being accused. It also underlines the fact that some memories of childhood abuse recovered by adults are inaccurate or unreliable.

Questions and Activities

1. Because people interpret experiences on the basis of their long-term memory schemes and, on occasion, add extraneous information to create a more meaningful and logical recollection, it is not surprising that disagreements occur about the details of an event. Teachers sometimes find themselves in such situations as, for example, when parents confront a teacher and demand to know why the teacher embarrassed their child in front of the rest of the class. The teacher is dumbfounded by the accusation and replies that she did no such thing. What might you do to avoid such confrontations by ensuring that you and your students have a common understanding of important or sensitive events?
2. What kinds of classroom situations are most likely to be interpreted differently and hence remembered differently by teachers and students?
3. If you plan to have students view a film or videotape as part of a lesson, you may be able to demonstrate the phenomenon of false memory. Two weeks after students have viewed the film or tape and without prior warning, announce that a prize will be awarded to the student who recalls the most information from the film. Have students write down as much as they can recall of what they saw and heard. Then give them a list of all the ideas that actually occurred in the film. Have them compare both lists and make a tally of both how many actual ideas they recalled and how many ideas they recalled that had never appeared.

- More than seven out of ten studies reported less than a 20 percent loss of what was learned when measured with a recognition task. Half of the studies reported less than a 20 percent loss of what was learned when measured with free recall.
- Subject matter that had a higher-than-average level of unfamiliar facts and associations (such as zoology, anatomy, and medical terminology) and for which students would have little relevant prior knowledge (such as electricity, mechanics, and linguistics) was associated with increased levels of forgetting.
- Most of the forgetting of information occurred within four weeks after the end of a unit of instruction. Additional declines in recall occurred more slowly.
- Less forgetting occurred among students who learned the material to a high level either by being required to achieve a high score on an exam before moving on to the next unit of instruction, having to teach it to less knowledgeable students, or taking advanced courses.
- Less forgetting occurred in classes where students were more actively involved in learning (as in a geography field trip where students had to observe, sketch, record, and answer questions).

Students remember much of what they learn in school, especially if mastery and active learning are emphasized

The instructional implications that flow from these findings include an emphasis on mastery learning, peer tutoring, frequent testing with corrective feedback, and forms of instruction that actively involve students in learning.

Metacognition

The discussion up to this point has focused on a general explanation of how people attend to, encode, store, and retrieve information. In a word, we have described some of the major aspects of thinking. During the past few decades, researchers have inquired into how much knowledge individuals have about their own thought processes and what significance this knowledge has for learning. The term that was coined to refer to how much we know of our own thought processes is metacognition. As we will see, it plays a very important role in learning.

THE NATURE AND IMPORTANCE OF METACOGNITION

The notion of metacognition was proposed by developmental psychologist John Flavell (1976) to explain why children of different ages deal with learning tasks in different ways. For example, when seven-year-olds are taught how to remember pairs of nouns using both a less effective technique (simply repeating the words) and a more effective technique (imagining the members of each pair doing something together), most of these children will use the less effective technique when given a new set of pairs to learn. Most ten-year-olds, however, will opt to use the more effective method (Kail, 1990). The explanation for this finding is that the seven-year-old has not had enough learning experiences to recognize that some problem-solving methods are better than others. To the younger child, one means is as good as another. This lack of metacognitive knowledge makes true strategic learning impossible for young children.

One way to grasp the essence of metacognition is to contrast it with cognition. The term *cognition* is used to describe the ways in which information is processed—that is, the ways it is attended to, recognized, encoded, stored in memory for various lengths of time, retrieved from storage, and used for one purpose or another. **Metacognition** refers to our knowledge about those operations and how they might best be used to achieve a learning goal. As Flavell put it:

Metacognition refers to the knowledge we have about how we learn. It is a key component of our ability to regulate our learning processes.

Metacognition: our own knowledge of how we think

> I am engaging in metacognition . . . if I notice that I am having more trouble learning A than B; if it strikes me that I should double-check C before accepting it as a fact; if it occurs to me that I had better scrutinize each and every alternative in any multiple-choice type task situation before deciding which is the best one; if I become aware that I am not sure what the experimenter really wants me to do; if I sense that I had better make a note of D because I may forget it; if I think to ask someone about E to see if I have it right. Such examples could be multiplied endlessly. (1976, p. 232)

Metacognition is obviously a very broad concept. It covers everything an individual can know that relates to how information is processed. To get a better grasp of this concept, you may want to use the three-part classification scheme that Flavell (1987) proposed: knowledge-of-person variables, task variables, and strategy variables. An example of knowledge-of-person variables is that one is good at learning verbal material but poor at learning mathematical material. Another example is knowing that information not rehearsed or encoded is quickly forgotten. An example of knowledge of task variables is that passages with long sentences and unfamiliar words are usually harder to understand than passages that are more simply written. An example of knowledge-of-strategy variables is knowing that one should skim through a text passage before reading it to determine its length and difficulty level.

Lev Vygotsky believed that children acquire metacognitive knowledge and skills most effectively through direct instruction, imitation, and social collaboration in the following way:

1. Children are told by more experienced and knowledgeable individuals what is true and what is false, what is right and what is wrong, how various things should and should not be done, and why. ("Jason, don't touch that stove. It's hot and will give you a painful burn if you touch it.")
2. As opportunities arise, children use this knowledge to regulate their own behavior (saying out loud, "Hot stove. Don't touch.") as well as the behavior of others. If you have ever seen young children play "House" or "School" and faithfully mimic the dictates of their parents or teacher, then you have seen this process at work.
3. Children regulate their own behavior through the use of inner speech.

Vygotsky's analysis strongly suggests that providing children with opportunities to regulate their own and others' behavior, as in peer tutoring, is an excellent way to help them increase their metacognitive knowledge and skills and to improve the quality of their learning. Later in this chapter, we describe one such program, reciprocal teaching. Programs like reciprocal teaching have produced high levels of learning, motivation, and transfer (Karpov & Haywood, 1998).

Recent research indicates significant differences in what younger and older children know about metacognition. What follows is a discussion of some of these differences.

Age Trends in Metacognition

Two reviews of research on metacognition (Duell, 1986; Kail, 1990) examined how students of different ages use memorization techniques and how well they understand what they are doing. Following are some of the key conclusions of the reviews:

- In terms of diagnosing task difficulty, most six-year-olds know that more familiar items are easier to remember than less familiar items and that a small set of items is easier to recall than a large set of items. What six-year-olds do not yet realize is that the amount of information they can recall immediately after they study it is limited.

- Similar findings have been obtained for reading tasks. Most second graders know that interest, familiarity, and story length influence comprehension and recall. However, they are relatively unaware of the effect of how ideas are sequenced, the introductory and summary qualities of first and last paragraphs, and the relationship between reading goals and tactics. Sixth graders, by contrast, are much more aware of the effects of these variables on comprehension and recall.
- Most young children know very little about the role their own capabilities play in learning. For example, not until about nine years of age do most children realize that their recall right after they study something is limited. Consequently, children through the third grade usually overestimate how much they can store in and retrieve from short-term memory. One likely reason for this developmental difference is that younger children base their prediction on irrelevant personal characteristics (such as, "I'm pretty smart"), whereas older children focus more on relevant task characteristics.
- There are clear developmental differences in how well students understand the need to tailor learning tactics to task demands. For example, four- and six-year-old children in one study cited by Robert Kail (1990) did not alter how much time they spent studying a set of pictures when they were told that a recognition test would follow either three minutes later, one day later, or one week later. Eight-year-olds did use that information to allocate less or more study time to the task.
- In terms of monitoring the progress of learning, most children younger than seven or eight are not very proficient at determining when they know something well enough to pass a memory test. Also, most first graders typically don't know what they don't know. When given multiple opportunities to study and recall a lengthy set of pictures, six-year-olds chose to study pictures they had previously seen and recalled as well as ones they hadn't. Third graders, by contrast, focused on previously unseen pictures.

The general conclusion that emerges from these findings is that the youngest school-age children have only limited knowledge of how their cognitive processes work and when to use them. Consequently, primary grade children do not systematically analyze learning tasks, formulate plans for learning, use appropriate techniques of enhancing memory and comprehension, or monitor their progress because they do not (some would say cannot) understand the benefits of doing these things. But as children develop and gain more experience with increasingly complex academic tasks, they acquire a greater awareness of metacognitive knowledge and its relationship to classroom learning. In this process, teachers can assist their students and guide them toward maximum use of their metacognitive knowledge. To help you understand how, the next section will discuss learning tactics and strategies.

Insight into one's learning processes improves with age

Helping Students Become Strategic Learners

With some effort and planning, a teacher can make logically organized and relevant lessons. However, this is only half the battle because students must then attend to the information, encode it into long-term memory, and retrieve it when needed. Getting students to use the attention, encoding, and retrieval processes discussed in the previous sections is not always easy. The sad fact is that most children and adults are inefficient learners (as evidenced, for example, by Bond, Miller, & Kennon, 1987; Brown, Campione, & Day, 1981; Covington, 1985; Davies, 1984; Selmes, 1987; Simpson, 1984; Winne & Jamieson-Noel, 2001). Their attempts at encoding rarely go beyond rote rehearsal (for example, rereading a textbook chapter), simple organizational schemes (outlining), and various cueing devices (underlining or highlighting). And although evidence exists that some students use different learning skills for different tasks (Hadwin, Winne, Stockley, Nesbit, & Woszczyna, 2001), most do not do so consistently or systematically.

One reason for this state of affairs is that students are rarely taught how to make the most of their cognitive capabilities. In one study, sixty-nine kindergarten through sixth-grade teachers gave strategy instruction only 9.5 percent of the time they were observed. Rationales for strategy use were given less than 1 percent of the time, and 10 percent of the teachers gave no strategy instructions at all. Moreover, the older the students were, the less likely they were to receive strategy instruction (Moely et al., 1992). A similar study of eleven middle school teachers eight years later produced the same findings. Teaching behaviors that reflected strategy instruction occurred only 9 percent of the time (Hamman, Berthelot, Saia, & Crowley, 2000).

Findings such as these are surprising, not to mention disappointing, since it is widely recognized that the amount of independent learning expected of students increases consistently from elementary school through high school and into college. The rest of this chapter will try to convince you that it need not be this way, at least for your students.

The Nature of Learning Tactics and Strategies

Strategy: plan to achieve a long-term goal

Tactic: specific technique that helps achieve immediate objective

A **learning strategy** is a general *plan* that a learner formulates for achieving a somewhat distant academic goal (like getting an A on the next exam). Like all other strategies, it specifies what will be done to achieve the goal, where it will be done, and when it will be done. A **learning tactic** is a specific *technique* (like a memory aid or a form of note taking) that a learner uses to accomplish an immediate objective (such as to understand the concepts in a textbook chapter and how they relate to one another).

As you can see, tactics have an integral connection to strategies. They are the learning tools that move you closer to your goal. Thus, they have to be chosen so as to be consistent with the goals of a strategy. If you had to recall verbatim the Preamble to the U.S. Constitution, for example, would you use a learning tactic that would help you understand the gist of each stanza or one that would allow for accurate and complete recall? It is surprising how often students fail to consider this point. Because understanding the different types and roles of tactics will help you better understand the process of strategy formulation, we will discuss tactics first.

Types of Tactics

Most learning tactics can be placed in one of two categories based on the tactic's primary purpose:

- *Memory-directed tactics,* which contain techniques that help produce accurate storage and retrieval of information
- *Comprehension-directed tactics,* which contain techniques that aid in understanding the meaning of ideas and their interrelationships (Levin, 1982)

Because of space limitations, we cannot discuss all the tactics in each category. Instead, we have chosen to discuss a few briefly that are either very popular with students or have been shown to be reasonably effective. The first two, rehearsal and mnemonic devices, are memory-directed tactics. Both can take several forms and are used by students of almost every age. The last two, self-questioning and note taking, are comprehension-directed tactics and are used frequently by students from the upper elementary grades through college.

Rehearsal The simplest form of rehearsal—rote rehearsal—is one of the earliest tactics to appear during childhood, and almost everyone uses it on occasion. It is not a particularly effective tactic for long-term storage and recall because it does not produce distinct encoding or good retrieval cues (although, as discussed earlier, it is a useful tactic for purposes of short-term memory). According to research reviewed by Kail (1990), most five- and six-year-olds do not rehearse at all. Seven-year-olds sometimes use the simplest form of rehearsal. By eight years of age, youngsters start to rehearse several items together as a set instead of rehearsing single pieces of information one at a time. A slightly more advanced version, *cumulative rehearsal*, involves rehearsing a small set of items for several repetitions, dropping the item at the top of the list and adding a new one, giving the set several repetitions, dropping the item at the head of the set and adding a new one, rehearsing the set, and so on.

Rote rehearsal not a very effective memory tactic

By early adolescence, rehearsal reflects the learner's growing awareness of the organizational properties of information. When given a list of randomly arranged words from familiar categories, thirteen-year-olds will group items by category to form rehearsal sets. This version of rehearsal is likely to be the most effective because of the implicit association between the category members and the more general category label. If at the time of recall the learner is given the category label or can generate it spontaneously, the probability of accurate recall of the category members increases significantly.

Mnemonic Devices A **mnemonic device** is a memory-directed tactic that helps a learner transform or organize information to enhance its retrievability. Such devices can be used to learn and remember individual items of information (a name, a fact, a date), sets of information (a list of names, a list of vocabulary definitions, a sequence of events), and ideas expressed in text. These devices range from simple, easy-to-learn techniques to somewhat complex systems that require a fair amount of practice. Because they incorporate visual and verbal forms of elaborative encoding, their effectiveness is due to the same factors that make imagery and category clustering successful: organization and meaningfulness.

Although mnemonic devices have been described and practiced for over two thousand years, they were rarely made the object of scientific study until the 1960s (see Yates, 1966, for a detailed discussion of the history of mnemonics). Since that time, mnemonics have been frequently and intensively studied by researchers, and there are several reviews of mnemonics research (for example, Bellezza, 1981; Higbee, 1979; Pressley, Levin, & Delaney, 1982; Snowman, 1986). Table 8.1 provides descriptions, examples, and uses of five mnemonic devices: rhymes, acronyms, acrostics, the loci method, and the keyword method.

Acronym: word made from first letters of items to be learned

Acrostic: sentence made up of words derived from first letters of items to be learned

Loci method: visualize items to be learned stored in specific locations

Keyword method: visually link pronunciation of foreign word to English translation

Why Mnemonic Devices Are Effective Mnemonic devices work so well because they enhance the encodability and retrievability of information. First, they provide a context (such as acronyms, sentences, mental walks) in which apparently unrelated items can be organized. Second, the meaningfulness of material to be learned is

Table 8.1 Five Types of Mnemonic Devices

Mnemonic	Description	Example	Uses
Rhyme	The items of information that one wants to recall are embedded in a rhyme that may range from one to several lines. A rhyme for recalling the names of the first 40 U.S. presidents, for example, contains 14 lines.	• Thirty days hath September, April, June, and November • Fiddlededum, fiddlededee, a ring around the moon is $\pi \times d$, If a hole in your sock you want repaired, Use the formula π r squared (to recall the formulas for circumference and area)	Recalling specific items of factual information
Acronym	The first letter from each to-be-remembered item is used to make a word. Often called the *first-letter mnemonic.*	• HOMES (for the names of the Great Lakes—Huron, Ontario, Michigan, Erie, Superior)	Recalling a short set of items, particularly abstract items, in random or serial order
Acrostic	The first letter from each to-be-remembered item is used to create a series of words that forms a sentence. The first letter of each word in the sentence corresponds to the first letters of the to-be-remembered items.	• Men Very Easily Make Jugs Serve Useful New Purposes (for the names of the 9 planets in our solar system—Mercury Venus, Earth, Mars, Jupiter, Saturn, Uranus, Neptune, Pluto) • A Rat In The House May Eat The Ice Cream (to recall the spelling of the word *arithmetic*)	Recalling items, particularly abstract ones, in random or serial order
Method of loci	Generate visual images of and memorize a set of well-known locations that form a natural series (such as the furniture in and the architectural features of the rooms of one's house). Second, generate images of the to-be-learned items (objects, events, or ideas), and place each in a separate location. Third, mentally walk through each location, retrieve each image from where it was placed, and decode into a written or spoken message. *Loci* (pronounced *low-sigh*) is the plural of *locus,* which means "place."	• To recall the four stages of Piaget's theory: For sensorimotor stage, picture a car engine with eyes, ears, nose, and a mouth. Place this image in your first location (fireplace mantel). For preoperational stage, picture Piaget dressed in a surgical gown scrubbing up before an operation. Place this image in your second location (bookshelf). For concrete-operational stage, picture Piaget as a surgeon cutting open a piece of concrete. Place this image in your third location (chair). For formal-operational stage, picture Piaget as an operating room surgeon dressed in a tuxedo. Place this image in your fourth location (sofa).	Can be used by children, college students, and the elderly to recall lists of discrete items or ideas from text passages. Works equally well for free recall and serial recall, abstract and concrete items.
Keyword	Created to aid the learning of foreign language vocabulary, but is applicable to any task in which one piece of information has to be associated with another. First, isolate some part of the foreign word that, when spoken, sounds like a meaningful English word. This is the keyword. Then create a visual image of the keyword. Finally, form a compound visual image between the keyword and the translation of the foreign word.	• Spanish word *pato* (pronounced pot-o) means "duck" in English. Keyword is *pot.* Imagine a duck with a pot over its head or a duck simmering in a pot. • English psychologist Charles Spearman proposed that intelligence was composed of two factors—*g* and *s.* Keyword is "spear." Imagine a spear being thrown at a gas (for *g* and *s*) can.	For kindergarten through fourth grade, works best when children are given keywords and pictures. Can be used to recall cities and their products, states and their capitals, medical definitions, and famous people's accomplishments.

SOURCES: Atkinson (1975); Atkinson & Raugh (1975); Bellezza (1981); Carney, Levin, & Levin (1994); Raugh & Atkinson (1975); Yates (1966).

enhanced through associations with more familiar meaningful information (for example, memory pegs or loci). Third, they provide distinctive retrieval cues that must be encoded with the material to be learned. Fourth, they force the learner to be an active participant in the learning process (Morris, 1977).

Mnemonic devices meaningfully organize information, provide retrieval cues

One example of these mnemonic benefits can be seen in a study by Russell Carney and Joel Levin (2000). They had college students use a variation of the keyword mnemonic to associate the names of twenty-four artists with a characteristic feature of each artist's style. The work of Georges Rouault, for example, is characterized by dark, heavy strokes. To help the students associate Rouault's name with his painting style, Carney and Levin supplied them with a copy of one of Rouault's paintings, a keyword (*ruler*) to help them store and recall Rouault's name, and the following direction: "Imagine making the heavy, dark lines of this painting with a *ruler* (Rouault) dipped in black paint." In comparison to a group of students who used their own methods, the mnemonic-trained students performed better on a test where they had to match the names of each artist with the paintings they had studied (82.1 percent correct versus 97.4 percent correct, respectively) as well as on a test where they had to match the names of each artist with a new painting by that artist (56.7 percent correct versus 85.1 percent correct, respectively).

A second example comes from a study done in a fourth-grade classroom with five special education students (Mastropieri, Sweda, & Scruggs, 2000). Four of these students had a learning disability with speech or language impairment, and one had a learning disability with emotional disturbance. The teacher taught all the students in the class a variation of the keyword mnemonic to help them learn social studies facts and concepts (for instance, the meaning of the concept "charter" or the name of the continent from which explorers traveled to the New World). Although the students without disabilities performed well on a unit test (88.9 percent correct for information that was taught mnemonically versus 83.3 percent for information that was not taught mnemonically), the five students with disabilities benefited even more (75 percent correct versus 36.7 percent correct).

Why You Should Teach Students How to Use Mnemonic Devices Despite the demonstrated effectiveness of mnemonic devices, many people argue against teaching them to students. They feel that students should learn the skills of critical thinking and problem solving rather than ways to recall isolated bits of verbatim information reliably. When factual information is needed, one can always turn to a reference source. Although we agree with the importance of teaching students to be critical thinkers and problem solvers, we feel this view is shortsighted for three reasons. First, it is very time-consuming to be constantly looking things up in reference books. Second, it ignores the fact that effective problem solving depends on ready access to a well-organized and meaningful knowledge base. Indeed, people who are judged to be expert in a particular field have an impressive array of factual material at their fingertips. Third, it focuses only on the "little idea" that mnemonic usage aids verbatim recall of bits of information. The "big idea" is that students come to realize that the ability to learn and remember large amounts of information is an acquired capability. Too often students (and adults) assume that an effective memory is innate and requires high intelligence. Once they realize that learning is a skill, students may be more inclined to learn how to use other tactics and how to formulate broad-based strategies.

Self- and Peer Questioning Because students are expected to demonstrate much of what they know by answering written test questions, self-questioning can be a valuable learning tactic. The key to using questions profitably is to recognize that different types of questions make different cognitive demands. Some questions require little more than verbatim recall or recognition of simple facts and details. If an exam is to stress factual recall, then it may be helpful for a student to generate such questions while studying. Other questions, however, assess comprehension, application, or synthesis of main ideas or other high-level information.

To ensure that students fully understood how to write comprehension-aiding questions, Alison King (1992b) created a set of question stems (see Table 8.2) that were intended to help students identify main ideas and think about how those ideas related to each other and to what the student already knew. When high school and college students used these question stems, they scored significantly better on tests of recall and comprehension of lecture material than did students who simply reviewed the same material. King (1994, 1998) also demonstrated that pairs of fourth- and fifth-grade students who were taught how to ask each other high-level questions and respond with elaborated explanations outperformed untrained students on tests that measured both comprehension and the ability to integrate text information with prior knowledge.

Self-questioning improves comprehension, knowledge integration

Self-questioning is a highly recommended learning tactic because it has a two-pronged beneficial effect:

- It helps students to understand better what they read. In order to answer the kinds of question stems King suggested, students have to engage in such higher-level thinking processes as translating ideas into their own words (What is the

Table 8.2 Self-Questioning Stems

What is a new example of . . . ?
How would you use . . . to . . . ?
What would happen if . . . ?
What are the strengths and weaknesses of . . . ?
What do we already know about . . . ?
How does . . . tie in with what we learned before?
Explain why . . .
Explain how . . .
How does . . . affect . . . ?
What is the meaning of . . . ?
Why is . . . important?
What is the difference between . . . and . . . ?
How are . . . and . . . similar?
What is the best . . . , and why?
What are some possible solutions to the problem of . . . ?
Compare . . . and . . . with regard to . . .
How does . . . cause . . . ?
What do you think causes . . . ?

SOURCE: From King, A. (1992b). "Facilitating Elaborative Learning Through Guided Student Generated Questioning," *Educational Psychologist, 27* (1), 111–126. Reprinted by permission of Lawrence Erlbaum Associates, Inc.

meaning of . . . ? Explain why . . .), looking for similarities and differences (What is the difference between . . . and . . . ? How are . . . and . . . similar?), thinking about how ideas relate to one another (Compare . . . and . . . with regard to . . .) and to previously learned information (How does . . . tie in with what we learned before?), and evaluating the quality of ideas (What are the strengths and weaknesses of . . . ?). In short, answering high-level question stems leads to deeper processing of the reading material.
- It helps students to monitor their comprehension. If too many questions cannot be answered or if the answers appear to be too superficial, this provides clear evidence that the student has not achieved an adequate understanding of the passage.

Studies that have examined the effect of responding to question stems report very strong effects. The average student who responded to question stems while reading a passage scored at the eighty-seventh percentile on a subsequent teacher-made test, while the average student who did not answer questions scored only at the fiftieth percentile. Differences of this magnitude do not appear in research studies very often and, in this case, argue strongly for providing students with question stems and teaching them how to construct their own questions and answers (Rosenshine, Meister, & Chapman, 1996). Discussion of the conditions that underlie effective self-questioning instruction can be found in articles by Bernice Wong (1985) and Zemira Mevarech and Ziva Susak (1993).

Note Taking As a learning tactic, note taking comes with good news and bad. The good news is that note taking can benefit a student in two ways. First, the process of taking notes while listening to a lecture or reading a text leads to better retention and comprehension of the noted information than just listening or reading does. For example, Andrew Katayama and Daniel Robinson (2000) found that college students who were given a set of partially completed notes for a text passage and told to fill in the blank spaces scored higher on a test of application than students who were given a complete set of notes. Second, the process of reviewing notes produces additional chances to recall and comprehend the noted material. The bad news is that we know very little about the specific conditions that make note taking an effective tactic.

Taking notes and reviewing notes aid retention and comprehension

This uncertainty as to what constitutes a good set of notes probably explains the results Alison King (1992a) obtained in a comparison of self-questioning, summarizing, and note taking. One group of students was given a set of question stems, shown how to generate good questions with them, and allowed to practice. A second group was given a set of rules for creating a good summary (identify a main idea or subtopic and related ideas, and link them together in one sentence), shown how to use them to create good summaries, and allowed to practice. A third group, however, was told simply to take notes as group members normally would in class. Both the self-questioning and summarizing groups scored significantly higher on an immediate and one-week-delayed retention test.

Conclusions Regarding Learning Tactics On the basis of this brief review, we would like to draw two conclusions. One is that students need to be systematically taught how to use learning tactics to make connections among ideas contained in text and lecture, as well as between new and previously learned information. No one expects students to teach themselves to read, write, and compute. So why should they be expected to teach themselves how to use a variety of learning tactics?

The second conclusion is that learning tactics should not be taught as isolated techniques, particularly to high school students. If tactics are taught that way, most students probably will not keep using them for very long or recognize that as the situation changes, so should the tactic. Therefore, as we implied earlier, students should be taught how to use tactics as part of a broader learning strategy.

Using Learning Strategies Effectively

Learning strategy components: metacognition, analysis, planning, implementation, monitoring, modification

The Components of a Learning Strategy As noted, a learning strategy is a plan for accomplishing a learning goal. It consists of six components: metacognition, analysis, planning, implementation of the plan, monitoring of progress, and modification. To give you a better idea of how to formulate a learning strategy of your own, here is a detailed description of each of these components (Snowman, 1986, 1987):

1. *Metacognition.* In the absence of some minimal awareness of how we think and how our thought processes affect our academic performance, a strategic approach to learning is simply not possible. At the very least, we need to know that effective learning requires an analysis of the learning situation, formulation of a learning plan, skillful implementation of appropriate tactics, periodic monitoring of our progress, and modification of things that go wrong. In addition, we need to know why each of these steps is necessary, when each step should be carried out, and how well prepared we are to perform each step. Without this knowledge, students who are taught one or more of the learning tactics mentioned earlier do not keep up their use for very long, nor do they apply the tactics to relevant tasks.
2. *Analysis.* To analyze the task and obtain relevant information, the strategic learner can play the role of an investigative journalist, asking questions that pertain to what, when, where, why, who, and how. In this way, the learner can identify important aspects of the material to be learned (what, when, where), understand the nature of the test that will be given (why), recognize relevant personal learner characteristics (who), and identify potentially useful learning activities or tactics (how).

To discover how actual teachers have aided students' information processing, see the Site-Based Cases section on the textbook web site at **http://education.college.hmco.com/students**.

Students can formulate strategic learning plans that identify and analyze the important aspects of a task. Then they can tailor these plans to their own strengths and weaknesses as learners.

3. *Planning.* Once satisfactory answers have been gained from the analysis phase, the strategic learner then formulates a learning plan by hypothesizing something like the following: "I know something about the material to be learned (I have to read and comprehend five chapters of my music appreciation text within the next three weeks), the nature of the test criterion (I will have to compare and contrast the musical structure of symphonies that were written by Beethoven, Schubert, and Brahms), my strengths and weaknesses as a learner (I am good at tasks that involve identifying similarities and differences, but I have difficulty concentrating for long periods of time), and the nature of various learning activities (skimming is a good way to get a general sense of the structure of a chapter; mnemonic devices make memorizing important details easier and more reliable; note taking and self-questioning are more effective ways to enhance comprehension than simple rereading). Based on this knowledge, I should divide each chapter into several smaller units that will take no longer than thirty minutes to read, take notes as I read, answer self-generated compare-and-contrast questions, use the loci mnemonic to memorize details, and repeat this sequence several times over the course of each week."
4. *Implementation of the plan.* Once the learner has formulated a plan, each of its elements must be implemented *skillfully.* A careful analysis and a well-conceived plan will not work if tactics are carried out poorly. Of course, a poorly executed plan may not be entirely attributable to a learner's tactical skill deficiencies. Part of the problem may be a general lack of knowledge about what conditions make for effective use of tactics (as is the case with note taking).
5. *Monitoring of progress.* Once the learning process is under way, the strategic learner assesses how well the chosen tactics are working. Possible monitoring techniques include writing out a summary, giving an oral presentation, working practice problems, and answering questions.
6. *Modification.* If the monitoring assessment is positive, the learner may decide that no changes are needed. If, however, attempts to memorize or understand the learning material seem to be producing unsatisfactory results, the learner will need to reevaluate and modify the analysis. This will cause changes in both the plan and the implementation.

There are two points we would like to emphasize about the nature of a learning strategy. The first is that learning conditions constantly change. Subject matters have different types of information and structures, teachers use different instructional methods and have different styles, exams differ in the kinds of demands they make, and the interests, motives, and capabilities of students change over time. Accordingly, strategies must be *formulated* or constructed anew as one moves from task to task rather than *selected* from a bank of previously formulated strategies. The true strategist, in other words, exhibits a characteristic that is referred to as *mindfulness* (Alexander, Graham, & Harris, 1998). A mindful learner is aware of the need to be strategic, attends to the various elements that make up a learning task, and thinks about how to use the leaning skills he or she possesses to greatest effect.

The second point is that the concept of a learning strategy is obviously complex and requires a certain level of intellectual maturity. Thus, you may be tempted to conclude that although *you* could do it, learning to be strategic is beyond the reach of most elementary and high school students. Research evidence suggests otherwise, however. A study of high school students in Scotland, for example, found that some students are sensitive to contextual differences among school tasks and vary their approach to studying accordingly (Selmes, 1987). Furthermore, as we are about to show, research in the United States suggests that elementary school youngsters can be trained to use many of the strategy components just mentioned.

Research on Learning Strategy Training Research clearly shows that training students to use various tactics and strategies is a worthwhile use of the teacher's time. Students who were trained to use a single mnemonic technique outperformed nontrained students by a wide margin on subsequent tests of memory (eighty-sixth percentile versus fiftieth percentile, respectively). The effect was particularly noticeable among primary grade and low-achieving students. A similar advantage was found for students who had been taught to use a variety of tactics and were tested for memory and low-level comprehension (seventy-fifth percentile versus the control group's fiftieth percentile). Although the weakest effect was found in studies where students were taught general strategy rather than specific tactics, these students nevertheless performed significantly better than students who were left to their own devices (seventieth percentile versus fiftieth percentile, respectively) (Hattie, Biggs, & Purdie, 1996).

Reciprocal teaching: students learn comprehension skills by demonstrating them to peers

A particularly effective strategy training program, as we mentioned earlier, is the *reciprocal teaching* (RT) program of Annemarie Palincsar and Ann Brown (1984). As the title of this program indicates, students learn certain comprehension skills by demonstrating them to each other. Palincsar and Brown trained a small group of seventh graders whose reading comprehension scores were at least two years below grade level to use the techniques of summarizing, self-questioning, clarifying, and predicting to improve their reading comprehension. They chose these four methods because students can use them to improve *and* monitor comprehension.

During the early training sessions, the teacher explained and demonstrated the four methods while reading various passages. The students were then given gradually increasing responsibility for demonstrating these techniques to their peers, with the teacher supplying prompts and corrective feedback as needed. Eventually, each student was expected to offer a good summary of a passage, pose questions about important ideas, clarify ambiguous words or phrases, and predict upcoming events, all to be done with little or no intervention by the teacher. (This approach to strategy instruction is based on Vygotsky's zone of proximal development concept that we mentioned previously in the book.)

Palincsar and Brown found that the RT program produced two general beneficial effects. First, the quality of students' summaries, questions, clarifications, and predictions improved. Early in the program, students produced overly detailed summaries and many unclear questions. But in later sessions, concise summaries and questions dealing explicitly with main ideas were the rule. For example, questions on main ideas increased from 54 percent to 70 percent. In addition, the questions were increasingly stated in paraphrase form rather than as verbatim statements from the passage. Second, the RT-trained students, who had begun the sessions well below grade level, scored as high as a group of average readers on tests of comprehension (about 75 percent correct for both groups) and much better than a group taught how to locate information that might show up in a test question (75 percent correct versus 45 percent correct). Most impressive, these levels of performance held up for at least eight weeks after the study ended (no measures were taken after that point) and generalized to tests of social studies and science (20 percent correct prior to training versus 60 percent correct after training).

Subsequent research on the effectiveness of RT under both controlled and realistic conditions has continued to produce positive findings across a broad age spectrum (fourth grade through college). On the average, RT students have scored at the sixty-second percentile on standardized reading comprehension tests (compared to the fiftieth percentile for the average control student) and at the eighty-first percentile rank on reading comprehension tests that were created by the experimenters (Alfassi, 1998; Carter, 1997; Rosenshine & Meister, 1994a).

The message of strategy training programs like reciprocal teaching is that knowledge of the learning process and the conditions that affect it should be as much a part of the curriculum as learning to read, write, and compute. Proponents have argued persuasively that mastery of traditional basic skills is influenced by the nontraditional but even more basic skills of strategic reasoning (see, for example, Bracey, 1983). Accordingly, children should gradually be made aware of the general relationship between cognitive means and academic ends, the potential range of application of various learning tactics, how to determine if learning is proceeding as planned, and what to do if it is not.

In the following section, we offer several Suggestions for Teaching that will help your students become more strategic and efficient learners.

SUGGESTIONS FOR TEACHING IN YOUR CLASSROOM

Helping Your Students Become Efficient Information Processors

1 Develop and use a variety of techniques to attract and hold attention, and give your students opportunities to practice and refine their skills in maintaining attention.

a. Be aware of what will capture your students' attention.

The ability to capture your students' attention is affected by characteristics of the information itself and the learners' related past experiences. Learners are more likely to attend to things they expect to find interesting or meaningful. It is also true that human beings are sensitive to abrupt, sudden changes in their environment. Thus, anything that stands out, breaks a rhythm, or is unpredictable is almost certain to command students' attention.

Journal Entry
Techniques for Capturing Attention

Unpredictable changes in environment usually command attention

Examples

- Print key words or ideas in extra-large letters on the board.
- Use colored chalk to emphasize important points written on the board.
- When you come to a particularly important part of a lesson, say, "Now really concentrate on this. It's especially important." Then present the idea with intensity and emphasis.
- Start off a lesson with unexpected remarks, such as, "Imagine that you have just inherited a million dollars and . . ."

b. To maintain attention, emphasize the possible utility of learning new ideas.

Although it is possible to overdo attempts at making the curriculum relevant, it never hurts to think of possible ways of relating school learning to the present and future lives of students. When students realize that the basic purpose of school is to help them adapt to their environment, they are more likely to pay close attention to what you are trying to do.

Journal Entry
Techniques for Maintaining Attention

Example

- Teach basic skills—such as arithmetic computation, arithmetic reasoning, spelling, writing, and reading—as part of class projects that relate to students' natural interests (for example, keeping records of money for newspaper deliveries; measuring rainfall, temperature, and wind speed; writing letters to local television stations to express opinions on or request information about television shows).

c. Teach students how to increase their span of attention.

Journal Entry
Techniques for Increasing Attention Span

Remember that paying attention is a skill that many students have not had an opportunity to refine. Give your students plenty of opportunities to practice and improve their ability to maintain attention.

Examples

Attention span can be increased with practice

- Institute games that depend on maintaining attention, such as playing Simon Says, keeping track of an object hidden under one of several boxes (the old shell game), or determining whether two pictures are identical or different. At first, positively reinforce students for all correct responses. Then reinforce only for improvements in performance. Remind students that their success is a direct result of how well they pay attention.
- Read a short magazine or newspaper story, and ask students to report who, what, where, when, and why.

2 Point out and encourage students to recognize that certain bits of information are important and can be related to what they already know.

Attention is one control process for the sensory register; the other is recognition. Sometimes the two processes can be used together to induce students to focus on important parts of material to be learned. Sometimes you can urge your students to recognize key features or familiar relationships on their own.

Examples

- Have students practice grouping numbers, letters, or classroom items according to some shared feature, such as odd numbers, multiples of five, letters with circles, or things made of wood.
- Say, "This math problem is very similar to one you solved last week. Does anyone recognize something familiar about this problem?"
- Say, "In this chapter, the same basic point is made in several different ways. As you read, try to recognize and write down as many variations on that basic theme as you can."

3 Use appropriate rehearsal techniques, including an emphasis on meaning and chunking.

Journal Entry
Ways to Use Chunking to Facilitate Learning

The power of chunking information into meaningful units was demonstrated in a study conducted with a single college student of average memory ability and intelligence (Ericsson, Chase, & Faloon, 1980). Over twenty months, he was able to improve his memory for digits from seven to almost eighty. Being a track and field buff, he categorized three- and four-digit groups as running times for imaginary races. Thus, 3,492 became "3 minutes and 49.2 seconds, near world record time." Number groups that could not be encoded as running times were encoded as ages. These two chunking techniques accounted for almost 90 percent of his associations.

The main purpose of chunking is to enhance learning by breaking tasks into small, easy-to-manage pieces. To a large degree, students who are ten and older can learn to do this for themselves if you show them how chunking works. In addition, you can help by not requiring students to learn more than they can reasonably handle at one time. If you have a list of fifty spelling words to be learned, it is far better to present ten words a day, five days in a row, during short study periods than to give all fifty at once. This method of presentation is called **distributed practice.** A description of the positive effect of distributed practice on classroom learning and an explanation of why educators do not make greater use of it have been offered by Frank Dempster (1988).

Distributed practice: short study periods at frequent intervals

In distributed practice, it is usually necessary to divide the material into small parts, which seems to be the best way for students to learn and retain unrelated material (for example, spelling words). This approach makes use of the **serial position effect,** which is people's tendency to learn and remember the words at the beginning and end of a long list more easily than those in the middle. By using short lists, you in effect eliminate the hard-to-memorize middle ground.

Serial position effect: tendency to remember items at beginning and end of a long list

Distributed practice may not be desirable for all learning tasks. If you ask students to learn roles in a play, short rehearsals might not be effective because students may have a difficult time grasping the entire plot. If you allow enough rehearsal time to run through a whole act, your students will be able to relate one speech to another and comprehend the overall structure of the play. When students learn by way of a few rather long study periods, spaced infrequently, psychologists call it **massed practice.**

You might also tell your students about the relative merits of distributed versus massed practice. Robert Bjork (1979) has pointed out that most students not only are unaware of the benefits of distributed study periods but also go to considerable lengths to block or mass the study time devoted to a particular subject, even when that tactic is a hindrance rather than a help.

4 Organize what you ask your students to learn, and urge older students to organize material on their own.

At least some items in most sets of information that you ask your students to learn will be related to other items, and you will find it desirable to call attention to interrelationships. The Bower et al. (1969) experiment described earlier in which one group of students was given a randomly arranged set of items to learn and another group was presented the same items in logically ordered groups illustrates the value of organization. By placing related items in groups, you reduce the number of chunks to be learned and also make it possible for students to benefit from cues supplied by the interrelationships between items in any given set. And by placing items in logical order, you help students grasp how information at the beginning of a chapter or lesson makes it easier to learn information that is presented later.

Journal Entry
Organizing Information into Related Categories

Examples

- If students are to learn how to identify trees, birds, rocks, or the equivalent, group items that are related (for example, deciduous and evergreen trees). Call attention to distinctive features and organizational schemes that have been developed.
- Print an outline of a chapter on the board, or give students a duplicated outline, and have them record notes under the various headings. Whenever you give a lecture or demonstration, print an outline on the board. Call attention to the sequence of topics, and demonstrate how various points emerge from or are related to other points.

5 As much as possible, stress meaningfulness.

When you present material to be learned, emphasize the logic behind it, and urge students to look for meaning on their own. Concrete analogies offer one effective

Journal Entry
Ways to Stress Meaningfulness

Concrete analogies can make abstract information meaningful

way to add meaning to material. Consider someone who has no knowledge of basic physics but is trying to understand a passage about the flow of electricity through metal. For this person, statements about crystalline lattice arrays, free-floating electrons, and the effects of impurities will mean very little. However, such abstract ideas can be explained in more familiar terms. You might compare the molecular structure of a metal bar to a Tinker Toy arrangement, for example, or liken the effect of impurities to placing a book in the middle of a row of falling dominoes. Such analogies increase recall and comprehension (Royer & Cable, 1975, 1976).

Examples

- Give students opportunities to express ideas in their own words and relate new knowledge to previous learning.
- When you explain or demonstrate, express complex and abstract ideas in several different ways. Be sure to provide plenty of examples.
- Construct essay tests and homework assignments that emphasize comprehension and application. Give credit for thoughtful answers even though they do not exactly match the answer you would have given.
- For topics that are somewhat controversial (for example, nuclear energy, genetic engineering, pesticide use), require students to present both pro and con arguments.

6 Demonstrate a variety of learning tactics, and allow students to practice them.

a. Teach students how to use various forms of rehearsal and mnemonic devices.

Journal Entry
Ways to Teach Memory Tactics

At least two reasons recommend the teaching of rehearsal. One is that maintenance rehearsal is a useful tactic for keeping a relatively small amount of information active in short-term memory. The other is that maintenance rehearsal is one of a few tactics that young children can learn to use. If you do decide to teach rehearsal, we have two suggestions. First, remind young children that rehearsal is something that learners consciously decide to do when they want to remember things. Second, remind students to rehearse no more than seven items (or chunks) at a time.

Upper elementary grade students (fourth, fifth, and sixth graders) can be taught advanced forms of maintenance rehearsal, such as cumulative rehearsal, and forms of elaborative rehearsal, such as rehearsing sets of items that form homogeneous categories. As with younger students, provide several opportunities each week to practice these skills.

As you prepare class presentations or encounter bits of information that students seem to have difficulty learning, ask yourself if a mnemonic device would be useful. You might write up a list of the devices discussed earlier and refer to it often. Part of the value of mnemonic devices is that they make learning easier. They are also fun to make up and use. Moreover, rhymes, acronyms, and acrostics can be constructed rather quickly. You might consider setting aside about thirty minutes two or three times a week to teach mnemonics. First, explain how rhyme, acronym, and acrostic mnemonics work, and then provide examples of each (see Table 8.1). Once students understand how the mnemonic is supposed to work, have them construct mnemonics to learn various facts and concepts. You might offer a prize for the most ingenious mnemonic.

b. Teach students how to formulate comprehension questions.

We concluded earlier that self-questioning could be an effective comprehension tactic if students were trained to write good comprehension questions and given opportunities to practice the technique. We suggest you try the following instructional sequence:

Journal Entry
Ways to Teach Comprehension Tactics

1. Discuss the purpose of student-generated questions.
2. Point out the differences between knowledge-level questions and different types of comprehension-level questions (such as analysis, synthesis, and evaluation). An excellent discussion of these types can be found in the *Taxonomy of Educational Objectives, Handbook I: Cognitive Domain* (Bloom, Englehart, Furst, Hill, & Krathwohl, 1956).
3. Explain and illustrate the kinds of responses that should be given to different types of comprehension-level questions.
4. Provide students with a sample paragraph and a set of high-level question stems. Have students formulate questions and responses either individually or in pairs.
5. Provide corrective feedback.
6. Give students short passages from which to practice.
7. Provide corrective feedback (André & Anderson, 1978–1979, King, 1994).

c. Teach students how to take notes.

Despite the limitations of research on note taking, mentioned earlier, three suggestions should lead to more effective note taking. First, provide students with clear, detailed objectives for every reading assignment. The objectives should indicate what parts of the assignment to focus on and how that material should be processed (whether memorized verbatim, reorganized and paraphrased, or integrated with earlier reading assignments). Second, inform students that note taking is an effective comprehension tactic when used appropriately. Think, for example, about a reading passage that is long and for which test items will demand analysis and synthesis of broad concepts (as in

Journal Entry
Teaching Students How to Take Notes

Research findings demonstrate that note taking in one form or another is an effective tactic for improving comprehension of text and lecture material. Consequently, students should be taught the basic principles that support effective note taking.

"Compare and contrast the economic, social, and political causes of World War I with those of World War II"). Tell students to concentrate on identifying main ideas and supporting details, paraphrase this information, and record similarities and differences. Third, provide students with practice and corrective feedback in answering questions that are similar to those on the criterion test.

7 Encourage students to develop their metacognitive knowledge and skills by thinking about the various conditions that affect how they learn and remember.

The very youngest students (through third grade) should be told periodically that such cognitive behaviors as describing, recalling, guessing, and understanding mean different things, produce different results, and vary in how well they fit a task's demands. For older elementary school and middle school students, explain the learning process, and focus on the circumstances in which different learning tactics are likely to be useful. Then have students keep a diary or log in which they note when they use learning tactics, which ones, and with what success. Look for cases where good performance corresponds to frequent reported use of tactics, and positively reinforce those individuals. Encourage greater use of tactics among students whose performance and reported use of them are below average.

Although this same technique can be used with high school and college students, they should also be made aware of the other elements that make up strategic learning. Discuss the meaning of and necessity for analyzing a learning task, developing a learning plan, using appropriate tactics, monitoring the effectiveness of the plan, and implementing whatever corrective measures might be called for.

To develop further ideas for your journal, check the Reflective Journal Questions at **http://education.college.hmco.com/students**.

The next section describes several ways that you can use computer-based technology to improve your students' information-processing skills.

Technology as an Information-Processing Tool

Although computer-based technology may have had its roots in behavioral learning theory, as you saw in the chapter on that subject, current technology is more likely to reflect an information-processing perspective. The programs and devices described in this section influence how we access, filter, represent, and evaluate knowledge. As the limitations of human memory and the difficulty of creating learning strategies have been clarified, computer-based technology has been called on to help overcome these constraints and reduce the cognitive processing burden of complex tasks. For instance, technology might help someone better grasp an idea for a musical composition, see the structure of her writing plans, or watch chemical molecules react.

In this section, we will examine technological tools that help students formulate and represent knowledge, acquire important knowledge and skills from different subject areas, provide multiple representations of knowledge, and regulate their own thinking.

Tools to Represent Knowledge

One of the first knowledge representation tools, the Learning Tool, was developed in the 1980s (Kozma, 1987). This program was designed to help students organize, chunk, link, and use knowledge gathered from a variety of sources. Tools for outlining and mapping out one's ideas as well as taking notes are available in the Learning Tool to augment the limitations of human working memory. Knowledge representation tools are designed to help students represent knowledge in multiple formats, organize and restructure knowledge, activate relevant prior knowledge, and efficiently retrieve information.

Computer-based technology helps students organize and represent ideas and comprehend text

A current program that performs these functions is Inspiration (**www.inspiration.com/**). Inspiration allows learners to specify ideas in a variety of formats (outline, narrative text, pictorial, symbolic) and arrange and rearrange them in spatial displays known as *concept maps*. Considerable research documents the positive effect of concept mapping on students' recall and comprehension (see, for example, Novak, 1990, 1998; Romance & Vitale, 1999).

Go to the Technology Demos section at this book's web site at **http://education.college.hmco.com/students** for demos of important software.

TECHNOLOGY TOOLS FOR WRITING

In his review of more than thirty studies examining the effects of word processing on writing, Robert Bangert-Drowns (1993) concluded that word processing without instructor guidance or relevant instructional activities may simply cause writers to write longer documents but not necessarily enhance the quality of their text. Students need more instructional guidance when using writing tools. Fortunately, tools like Writer's Workbench have proven effective at improving student editing and revising practices, while others, like Writer's Helper, use subprograms to force students to attend to prewriting, drafting, and revising. According to Mike Reed (1996), this division of writing into stages is helpful because studies show that good writers spend about 85 percent of their time prewriting and only 2 percent drafting their work, while average and less effective writers devote 98 percent of their time to drafting and nearly no time prewriting.

In addition to the tools just mentioned, there are prewriting tools such as IdeaFisher as well as notecards, outlining aids, journal writing supports, idea processors, and mind mapping or semantic webbing software (Kellogg, 1989; MacArthur, 1996). For revision, the major word processors now contain text analysis software that checks and corrects one's writing style and format (for example, Grammatik, included in WordPerfect), and there are also computer prompting and metacognitive questioning tools to help one reflect on a written draft (Bonk & Reynolds, 1992; Zellermayer, Salomon, Globerson, & Givon, 1991). Appropriate prompts can provide less skilled and young writers with procedural support or strategic assistance for higher-level writing activities, such as creating paragraph transitions or checking for bias in one's writing. Research, in fact, reveals that computer prompts effectively move student concerns from lower-level spelling and grammar issues to higher-level idea generation and revision practices (Reynolds & Bonk, 1996; Zellermayer et al., 1991).

The World Wide Web offers myriad opportunities for collaborative writing and the facilitation of audience awareness with interactive debate forums, peer mentor commenting windows, and online mentoring. And when students respond to such comments, their thinking processes become visible to the instructor (Neuwirth & Wojahn, 1996). Two web sites that provide opportunities for collaborative writing projects are Kidforum (**www.kidlink.org/KIDFORUM/collaborative_writing.htm**) and Through Our Eyes (**www.kidlink.org/KIDPROJ/eyes01/**). Other electronic writing tools exist to add layers of comments, arrows to signify text movements, and annotations that allow multiple users to make suggestions without directly affecting the underlying document. Even common word processing programs allow users to

Use the Web Sources at **http://education.college.hmco.com/students** for quick links to web sites.

annotate text, highlight changes, and keep track of multiple versions, offering many possibilities for collaboration and commentary by teachers and students.

Technology Tools for Reading

As with writing, electronic support systems have been used to increase student reading comprehension and metacognitive skill (Salomon, Globerson, & Guterman, 1989). A videodisk-based story or popular book (for example, *Jurassic Park*) can be segmented, replayed, debated, and compared to the original text version. Research on such tools indicates that student vocabulary can be enriched by anchoring student learning in these realistic and motivating contexts (Xin, Glaser, & Rieth, 1996). As indicated in previous chapters, with the emergence of voice recognition and speech synthesis, computers might highlight words being spoken or read them back to a writer, thereby increasing reading fluency.

Technology Tools for Science and Math

In mathematics and science, Marcia Linn (1992) and other prominent researchers have argued that students should spend less time manually calculating and plotting data and more time using technology to summarize and interpret data, look for trends, and predict relationships. Based on over ten years of research, Linn (1997) created the Knowledge Integration Environment (KIE) to help middle school and high school students locate information on the World Wide Web, record and organize their findings and ideas in an electronic notebook, and participate in online discussions to make collaborative decisions about science. Like the writing tools mentioned earlier, the KIE notebook tool allows science students to organize and analyze evidence. Procedural guidance and hints are provided in the system to help students think critically and evaluate the evidence they gather. Although the KIE web site (**www.kie.berkeley.edu/KIE.html**) was still operational as this chapter was being written, it has been succeeded by a similar project, the Web-based Integrated Science Environment (WISE) Project (**http://wise.berkeley.edu/**). The goals of the WISE project are essentially the same as those of the KIE Project, but the software is now completely web based.

As with the microcomputer-based laboratory equipment mentioned previously in the book, computer sensors and data logging devices connected to computers can quickly create graphs that help convey complex scientific information visually. Computer tools also exist for electronically dissecting animals and performing operations, exploring laws of physics, and conducting chemistry experiments (Snir, Smith, & Grosslight, 1993). CD-ROM resources can supply captivating animations of abstract microscopic events, video depictions of various chemical reactions, text information about potential hazards of these experiments, sample demonstrations and laboratory activities, and encyclopedias of teaching suggestions (Brooks & Brooks, 1996). In effect, with CD-ROMs and other technology, safety is no longer the overriding concern in a chemistry class. CD-ROMs might also be used to study such large-scale phenomena as hurricanes or winter storm patterns.

For mathematics and physics, the Calculator-Based Laboratory (CBL) from Texas Instruments provides "a data-collection system that uses probes, such as temperature, light, and voltage probes, to gather data into a graphing calculator" (Nicol, 1997, p. 86). The current version is the CBL 2. CBLs convert information from sensors and probes into data that can be understood and graphed by the calculator. Students taking a math class might use this tool to represent and manipulate quadratic equations in algebra, visualize statistics and other information in geometry classes, and better understand derivatives and inequalities in calculus (Engebretsen, 1997; Ferrini-Mundy & Lauten, 1994). In addition, there are computer tools that can be used to create sales forecast models and spreadsheets to track inventories for a local company, design truss structures in a physics class, or generate mathematical models of sports activities such as shooting a free throw (Murdick, 1996). This visualization and manipulation of data help students investigate problems, tie the information together, perceive different aspects of problems, test real-life data and problems, and gain a sense of ownership over the learning process.

Technology Tools for Art and Music

As you may be aware, computer tools are also being used in the fine and performing arts. Art education, for instance, benefits from electronic tools that quickly erase or alter ideas. For instance, Jane Chia and Birnie Duthie (1993) provide examples of how electronic sketchpads, draw palettes, and paint packages can enhance the generation of elementary student visual imagery. For the music classroom, there are tools such as digital oscilloscopes that help students understand relationships between pitch and wavelength, as well as software like KidsNotes (now included in a package called KidsTime) that can emulate an electronic keyboard to help students develop pitch discrimination (Magnusson, 1996). In addition, CD technology can be used to present graphical representations of notes as they are played, sections of which can saved and compared to other verses of the same song or to other songs, thereby helping students understand themes and patterns in music. There are also a number of musical microworld tools that encourage students to construct and play their own music. Moreover, computer tools such as Musical Instrument Digital Interface (MIDI) (Reese, 1995) allow students to play a musical instrument and record it on a computer. Students can explore concepts of pitch, duration, sound combination, repetition, and melody and engage in the process of musical thinking.

Multimedia Tools

As mentioned in previous chapters, multimedia encyclopedias, databases, and libraries provide students with a wide variety of information resources. Multimedia tools offer multiple views (text, photographs, digitized video, animation, sound) on difficult concepts that can enrich student understanding of the topic (Toomey & Ketterer, 1995). The use of multimedia tools is related to such information-processing concepts as meaningful learning, the dual coding of information (Clark & Paivio, 1991), the use of visual imagery, and elaborative rehearsal. Like the mind, multimedia tools provide more than one way to retrieve or visit information; the richer or more dense the network or web of connections, the more likely one will comprehend the meaning.

Hypermedia Tools

Hypermedia technology exists when multimedia information can be nonsequentially accessed, examined, and constructed by users, thereby enabling them to move from one information resource to another while controlling which options to take (Grabe & Grabe, 2001). Dispersed information fragments (called "nodes") are associated in hypermedia through links that reference one another or help organize the resource. There are clear advantages to hypermedia, such as the richness of the network of ideas, the compact storage of information, the rapid nonlinear access to information, the flexible use of information, and learner control over the system. Not surprisingly, it has been suggested that hypermedia tools radically alter the way people read, write, compute, and perhaps even think (Nelson & Palumbo, 1992).

For such subjects as English literature, history, or teacher education, hypermedia tools can encourage the learner to see problems from multiple perspectives and develop more flexible knowledge structures (Spiro, Feltovich, Jacobson, & Coulson, 1991). Rand Spiro and his colleagues have used this concept to develop an instructional technique called "criss-crossing" the landscape. From this perspective, because there are multiple correct answers or plausible solutions that need to be explored by the learner from many directions, hypertexts can build "cognitive flexibility" (Spiro et al. 1991, p. 22) in the learner, while developing both cognitive processing skills and content knowledge. For instance, in your teacher education programs, you might be given multiple case situations that are tailored around a common theme (such as how to help to develop student self-concept).

Hypermedia tools in mathematics might include a video presentation, simple diagrams, digitized images of real-life phenomena, dynamic video clips or computer animation of problem sequences, definitions of terms, and computer prompts to go back and read the problem.

One science hypermedia tool, a CD-ROM called Microsoft Dinosaurs, contains an atlas that provides vital information about the location and movement of dinosaurs, a timeline that depicts changes in life forms over time, dinosaur movies that provide animations of dinosaur behavior, an index to search for topics, vocabulary tools, and a guided tour to learn how to use the hypermedia components of the tool (Shepardson & Britsch, 1996). In addition to being able to explore this information, the user of Microsoft Dinosaurs can try out various games, such as dinosaur mystery episodes that contain currently debated questions about dinosaurs. A review of Microsoft Dinosaurs can be found on the following web site: **www.upei.ca/~fac_ed/tlit/darcy/dare.htm.**

As multimedia and hypermedia technology spreads, it is likely that your students will be making such search and selection decisions at least daily. For instance, CD's and videodisks now provide text, still photographs, motion video, and games for children to dynamically explore newly discovered Mayan ruins, create multimedia presentations of zoo animals, confront life-and-death moral decisions, and better learn foreign languages (Kozma, 1991; Meskill, 1996). In terms of foreign or second language learning, Carla Meskill points out that students can control the rate and style of presentation to suit their own needs. For instance, a student learning the Russian language by watching a television show from Moscow in a multimedia format might not only be able to view the broadcast but can have a copy of the verbatim text, an online Russian-English dictionary, links to related news stories and events, the capability to revisit earlier episodes, and a menu of other programs and commercials.

Research on Multimedia and Hypermedia Technology Do multimedia and hypermedia technology improve learning? David Ayersman's (1996) review of the initial research on hypermedia-based learning indicates that this tool has resulted in a number of positive outcomes, including a greater sense of control and personal freedom, increased intrinsic motivation, better recall of information and enhanced student listening comprehension, more effective study skills and strategies, greater individualization of learning, improved knowledge and skills, and more positive attitudes. But such preliminary findings have not been consistent across studies, as students' previous learning experiences in linear formats have not always been easy to overcome, nor are all commercially developed hypermedia software packages of high quality. A review of hypermedia research we summarized in a previous chapter (Dillon & Gabbard, 1998) also reported mixed results. The technology appeared to have minimal effects on comprehension but helped higher-ability students to search rapidly through lengthy and multiple information sources in order to locate target information.

Other research indicates that multimedia environments can address individual learning preferences and expand the ways in which students can express themselves. Not surprisingly, student comprehension of hypermedia documents is positively affected when they use learning tactics such as comprehension monitoring, elaboration, and rehearsal (Davidson-Shivers, Rasmussen, & Bratton-Jeffery, 1997). One study has shown that students working on multimedia compositions in realistic environments can experience significant knowledge gains (Bonk, Hay, & Fischler, 1996).

Hypermedia and multimedia tools produce both positive and negative results

On the negative side, students with poorly developed organizational skills can be distracted by multimedia environments that provide readily accessible graphics, animation, and sound. And although students can gain vital knowledge from information-rich hypermedia and multimedia tools, the research to date also clearly shows that they can end up disoriented, lacking in self-confidence, anxious, frustrated, overwhelmed, and confused (Morrell, Marchionini, & Neuman, 1993). Such research indicates that it is the pedagogical strategies and teacher guidance that often determine the difference between sophisticated student learning or casual browsing within these systems. Furthermore, Daniel Shepardson and Susan Britsch (1996) caution that the hypermedia environment lacks the ability to negotiate meaning with the learner or involve him or her in a community of learners. Unfortunately, this is true of most multimedia and hypermedia learning tools.

EFFECTS OF TECHNOLOGY ON METACOGNITION

When students select search topics and associated terms and then evaluate search results, they are making decisions about what information to read, thinking about knowledge interrelationships, and engaging in extensive self-questioning and note taking (Kozma, 1991). When they create databases of related ideas or link information in multiple formats, they are making decisions and elaboratively encoding the information. These are important skills. But can computer-based instructional technology help students develop their metacognitive skills in addition to helping them learn content?

To answer this question, tools such as LOGO have been extensively explored for what they can offer in terms of student planning, error detection, comprehension monitoring, and other metacognitive skills. LOGO is a simple computer programming language that was designed to foster children's higher-order thinking and mathematical reasoning skills. Although initial studies were inconclusive, more research has found increases in metacognitive performance among elementary students when instructors mediate the learning environment (Lehrer, Lee & Jeong, 1999) or when students work in pairs or small groups (Clements & Nastasi, 1999). One recent study shows that simply having computers in the home or having access to them can promote metacognitive changes in the minds of preschool children (Fletcher-Flinn & Suddendorf, 1996). However, it is starting to become clear that computer environments *combined with* teacher guidance and explicit metacognitive training to plan, monitor, and evaluate learning seem to be the most effective means of developing children's self-regulatory skills and problem solving strategies.

To review this chapter, see the Thought Questions and ACE Self-Testing sections on this book's web site at **http://education.college.hmco.com/students**.

Resources for Further Investigation

■ The Nature of Information-Processing Theory

For more on how information-processing theory relates to teaching and learning, read Chapter 1 of *Cognitive Classroom Learning* (1986). Written by Thomas André and Gary Phye and titled "Cognition, Learning, and Education," the chapter compares information processing with behavioral learning theory, describes the nature of memory stores and control processes, and discusses the value of an information-processing perspective for educational practice.

Another source of information is *The Cognitive Psychology of School Learning* (1993), by Ellen Gagné, Carol Walker Yekovich, and Frank Yekovich. The goal of these authors is to help educators use information-processing theory and research to answer the questions, "What shall we teach?" and "How shall we teach?" Chapters 12 through 15 describe how to use this knowledge base to teach reading, writing, mathematics, and science, respectively.

■ Memory Structures and Processes

Norman Spear and David Riccio describe various aspects of memory structures and processes in *Memory: Phenomena and Principles* (1994). As the title suggests, Alan Searleman and Douglas Herrmann cover the same ground, plus such additional topics as the role of social factors in memory, individual differences in memory, and changes in memory ability, in *Memory from a Broader Perspective* (1994). Alan Baddeley provides a detailed account of memory phenomena in *Human Memory: Theory and Practice* (1998).

■ Metacognition

If you would like to know more about the nature of metacognition and its role in memory, eyewitness testimony, and problem solving; its development in adulthood and old age; and the neuropsychology of metacognition, take a look at *Metacognition: Knowing About Knowing* (1994), edited by Janet Metcalfe and Arthur Shimamura. If teaching reading is going to be one of your future responsibilities, you may glean some useful ideas from Ruth Garner, *Metacognition and Reading Comprehension* (1987).

■ Learning Tactics and Strategies

One of the most popular (and useful) memory improvement books available is *The Memory Book* (1974), by Harry Lorayne and Jerry Lucas. They explain why and how you should think up ridiculous associations, offer suggestions for using substitute words, provide techniques for learning foreign and English vocabulary, and describe ways to remember names and faces.

Meredith Gall, Joyce Gall, Dennis Jacobsen, and Terry Bullock summarize underlying theories of information processing and motivation, outline why it is important to teach students study skills, and describe how a school or district can implement a study skills program in *Tools for Learning: A Guide to Teaching Study Skills* (1990).

Although written principally for college students and their instructors, *Learning to Learn: Making the Transition from Student to Life-Long Learner* (1998), by Kenneth A. Kiewra and Nelson F. DuBois, offers much of value to high school students and their teachers.

■ Individual Differences in Memory

One of the most striking accounts of supernormal memory is provided by Alexander Luria, *The Mind of a Mnemonist: A Little Book About a Vast Memory* (1968). Luria describes his experiments and experiences over a period of almost thirty years with the man he refers to as S, who could recall nonsense material he had not seen for fifteen years. Charles Thompson, Thaddeus Cowan, and Jerome Frieman describe in *Memory Search by a Memorist* (1993) a series of studies done with Rajan Mahadevan, who earned a place in the *Guinness Book of World Records* by memorizing the first 31,811 digits of pi. Additional articles about people with unusually proficient memory capability can be found in *Memory Observed* (1982), edited by Ulric Neisser.

Robert Kail describes memory differences among normal children, as well as differences between normal and mentally retarded children in *The Development of Memory in Children* (1990). Also briefly discussed is the phenomenon of the idiot savants—individuals who are below average on all measures of ability except one, in which they far surpass almost all other individuals—and the reliability of children's eyewitness testimony. Leon Miller describes musical savants, individuals with mental retardation, who can perfectly reproduce musical passages on an instrument after one hearing, in *Musical Savants: Exceptional Skill in the Mentally Retarded* (1989).

Summary

1. Information-processing theory attempts to explain how individuals acquire, store, recall, and use information.
2. A popular model of information processing is composed of three memory stores and a set of control processes that determine the flow of information from one memory store to another. The memory stores are the sensory register, short-term memory, and long-term memory. The control processes are recognition, attention, maintenance rehearsal, elaborative rehearsal, and retrieval.

3. The sensory register holds information in its original form for one to three seconds, during which time we may recognize and attend to it further.

4. Recognition involves noticing key features of a stimulus and integrating those features with relevant information from long-term memory.

5. Attention is a selective focusing on a portion of the information in the sensory register. Information from long-term memory influences what we focus on.

6. Short-term memory holds about seven bits of information for about twenty seconds (in the absence of rehearsal). It is often called working memory because it is where various encoding, organizational, and retrieval processes occur.

7. Information can be held in short-term memory indefinitely through the use of maintenance rehearsal, which is rote repetition of information.

8. Information is transferred from short-term memory to long-term memory by the linking of the new information to related information in long-term memory. This process is called elaborative rehearsal.

9. Elaborative rehearsal is based partly on organization. This involves grouping together, or chunking, items of information that share some important characteristic.

10. Elaborative rehearsal is also based on meaningfulness. Meaningful learning occurs when new information that is clearly written and logically organized is consciously related to information the learner currently has stored in long-term memory.

11. Long-term memory is thought by some psychologists to be an unlimited storehouse of information from which nothing is ever lost.

12. Many psychologists believe the information in long-term memory is organized in the form of schemata. A schema is a generalized abstract structure of information. When schemata are absent or crudely formed, learning and recall problems occur.

13. Contrary to popular belief, students remember much of the information they learn in school, especially if it was well learned to start with and if it was learned in a meaningful fashion.

14. Metacognition refers to any knowledge an individual has about how humans think and how those processes can be used to achieve learning goals.

15. Metacognition increases gradually with experience. This helps explain why junior high and high school students are more flexible and effective learners than primary grade students.

16. A learning strategy is a general plan that specifies the resources one will use, when they will be used, and how one will use them to achieve a learning goal.

17. A learning tactic is a specific technique one uses to help accomplish an immediate task-related objective.

18. Most teachers provide little or no direct instruction to students in the formulation and use of strategies and tactics.

19. Learning tactics can be classified as memory directed or comprehension directed. The former are used when accurate storage and retrieval of information are important. The latter are used when comprehension of ideas is important.

20. Two types of memory-directed tactics are rehearsal and mnemonic devices. Because most forms of rehearsal involve little or no encoding of information, they are not very effective memory tactics. Because mnemonic devices organize information and provide built-in retrieval cues, they are effective memory tactics.

21. Popular mnemonic devices include rhymes, acronyms, acrostics, the loci method, and the keyword method.

22. Two effective comprehension tactics are self-questioning and note taking.

23. The components of a learning strategy are metacognition, analysis, planning, implementation, monitoring, and modification.

24. Learning strategy training raises the reading comprehension scores of both average and below-average readers.

25. Contemporary computer-based technology supports information processing by helping students to organize and mentally represent ideas, write more clearly, better comprehend text, interpret scientific and mathematical data, and understand musical patterns.

KEY TERMS

information-processing theory *(261)*
sensory register (SR) *(263)*
recognition *(263)*
attention *(264)*
short-term memory (STM) *(265)*
maintenance rehearsal *(265)*
elaborative rehearsal *(266)*
meaningful learning *(268)*
dual coding theory *(269)*
long-term memory (LTM) *(269)*
schemata *(271)*
metacognition *(274)*
learning strategy *(277)*
learning tactic *(277)*
mnemonic device *(278)*
distributed practice *(288)*
serial position effect *(288)*
massed practice *(288)*

Discussion Questions

1. Can you think of any personal, everyday experiences that illustrate the nature of one or more of the three memory stores? Have you recently, for instance, retrieved a long-dormant memory because of a chance encounter with an associated word, sound, or smell?

2. Information-processing psychologists have expressed disappointment that the results of their research on memory stores and processes, learning tactics, and learning strategies have not been widely implemented by teachers. Is this complaint consistent with your experience? Can you recall any instances when you were taught how to use a variety of learning tactics to formulate different strategies? How about out of school? Did you acquire any such skills without the help of a classroom teacher?

3. Many teachers have said that they would like to teach their students more about the nature and use of learning processes but that they don't have time because of the amount of subject material they must cover. What can you do as a teacher to avoid this pitfall?

4. A major problem in training students to use learning strategies and tactics is getting the youngsters to spend the time and effort required to master these skills. Suppose some students expressed their lack of interest, saying their own methods would be just as effective (although you know full well they would not be). How would you convince these students otherwise?

9 Constructivist Learning Theory, Problem Solving, and Transfer

When you begin to teach, you may devote a substantial amount of class time to having students learn information discovered by others. But the acquisition of a storehouse of facts, concepts, and principles is only part of what constitutes an appropriate education. Students must also learn how to *find*, *evaluate*, and *use* what they need to know to accomplish whatever goals they set for themselves. In other words, students need to learn how to be effective problem solvers.

One justification for teaching problem-solving skills in *addition* to ensuring mastery of factual information is that life in technologically oriented countries is marked by speedy change. New products, services, and social conventions are rapidly introduced and integrated into our lifestyles. Microcomputers, the Internet, cellular telephones, anticancer drugs, and in vitro fertilization, to name just a few examples, are relatively recent innovations that significantly affect the lives of many people.

Key Points

These key points will help you learn the important information in this chapter. To help you study, they also appear in the margins of the pages, next to the text where they are discussed.

Meaningful Learning within a Constructivist Framework

- Constructivism: creating a personal interpretation of external ideas and experiences
- Bruner: discover how ideas relate to each other and to existing knowledge
- Construction of ideas strongly influenced by student's prior knowledge
- Construction of ideas aided by discussion and debate
- Cognitive constructivism emphasizes role of cognitive processes in meaningful learning
- Social constructivism emphasizes role of culture and social interaction in meaningful learning
- Scaffolding: provide student with enough help to complete a task; gradually decrease help as student becomes able to work independently
- Constructivism aided by cognitive apprenticeship, realistic tasks, multiple perspectives
- Constructivist-oriented teaching encourages creating new views; uses scaffolding, realistic tasks, and class discussion

The Nature of Problem Solving

- Well-structured problems: clearly stated, known solution procedures, known evaluation standards
- Ill-structured problems: vaguely stated, unclear solution procedures, vague evaluation standards
- Issues: ill-structured problems that arouse strong feelings
- Problem finding depends on curiosity, dissatisfaction with status quo
- Problem framing depends on knowledge of subject matter, familiarity with problem types
- Inert knowledge due to learning isolated facts under limited conditions
- Studying worked examples is an effective solution strategy
- Solve simpler version of problem first; then transfer process to harder problem
- Break complex problems into manageable parts
- Work backward when goal is clear but beginning state is not
- Solve a similar problem and then apply the same method
- Create an external representation of the problem
- Evaluate solutions to well-structured problems by estimating or checking

Suggestions for Teaching in Your Classroom

- Comprehension of subject matter critical to problem solving

Transfer of Learning

- Early view of transfer based on degree of similarity between two tasks
- Positive transfer: previous learning makes later learning easier
- Negative transfer: previous learning interferes with later learning
- Specific transfer due to specific similarities between two tasks
- General transfer due to use of same cognitive strategies
- Low-road transfer: previously learned skill automatically applied to similar current task
- High-road transfer: formulate rule from one task and apply to related task
- Low-road and high-road transfer produced by varied practice at applying skills, rules, memory retrieval cues

Technology Tools for Knowledge Construction and Problem Solving

- Technology tools are available to help students construct knowledge, become better problem solvers

But change, particularly rapid change, can be a mixed blessing. Although new products and services such as those just mentioned can make life more convenient, efficient, and enjoyable, they can also make life more complicated and problematic. The use of robots to perform certain jobs, for example, promises increased efficiency and productivity (which contribute to our standard of living), but it also threatens the job security of thousands of workers. Advances in medical care promise healthier and longer lives, but they introduce a host of moral, ethical, legal, and economic problems.

The educational implication that flows from these observations is clear: if we are to benefit from our ability to produce rapid and sometimes dramatic change, our schools need to invest more time, money, and effort in teaching students how to be effective problem solvers. As Lauren Resnick, a past president of the American Educational Research Association, argues:

> We need to identify and closely examine the aspects of education that are most likely to produce ability to adapt in the face of transitions and breakdowns. Rather than training people for particular jobs—a task better left to revised forms of on-the-job training—school should focus its efforts on preparing people to be good *adaptive learners*, so that they can perform effectively when situations are unpredictable and task demands change. (1987, p. 18)

Resnick's argument, which echoes many others, is not without some justification. A recent survey by the American Management Association (Greenberg, Canzoneri, & Joe, 2000) found that 38 percent of job applicants in 1999 lacked sufficient skills for the positions they sought. Nevertheless, the authors note that "the sharp increase in the deficiency rate from the 1997 level of 22.8% is not evidence of a 'dumbing down' of the incoming workforce. Instead, it testifies to the higher skills required in today's workplace" (p. 2).

Good problem solvers share two general characteristics: a well-organized, meaningful fund of knowledge and a systematic set of problem-solving skills. Historically, cognitive learning theories have been particularly useful sources of ideas for imparting both. In this chapter, then, we will examine the issue of meaningful learning from the perspective of a cognitive theory that we introduced previously in the book: constructivism. We will then go on to describe the nature of the problem-solving process and what you can do to help your students become better problem solvers. We will conclude by describing the circumstances under which learned capabilities are applied to new tasks, a process known as transfer of learning. ■

Meaningful Learning Within a Constructivist Framework

Constructivism: creating a personal interpretation of external ideas and experiences

To preview this chapter's key ideas, see the Chapter Themes on the Snowman textbook site at **http://education.college.hmco.com/students**.

Constructivism, as you may recall, holds that meaningful learning occurs when people actively try to make sense of the world—when they construct an interpretation of how and why things are—by filtering new ideas and experiences through existing knowledge structures (referred to in previous chapters as schemes). For example, an individual who lives in a country that provides, for little or no cost, such social services as medical care, counseling, education, job placement and training, and several weeks of paid vacation a year is likely to have constructed a rather different view of the role of government in people's lives from someone who lives in a country with a more market-oriented economy. To put it another way, meaningful learning is the active creation of knowledge structures (such as concepts, rules, hypotheses, and associations) from personal experience. In this section, we'll take a brief look at an early constructivist-oriented approach to learning, examine the nature of the constructivist model, and then put it all in perspective by considering the limits as well as the advantages of the constructivist perspective.

JEROME BRUNER AND DISCOVERY LEARNING: AN EARLY CONSTRUCTIVIST PERSPECTIVE

Constructivist explanations of learning are not new. Over the past seventy-five years, they have been promoted by such notable scholars as John Dewey, Jean Piaget, Lev Vygotsky, and Jerome Bruner. The constructivist perspective enjoyed a rebirth during the 1960s as a result of the Soviet Union's becoming the first country to put a satellite (called *Sputnik*) in orbit around the earth in 1957. In an effort to catch up with and pass the Soviets in space technology, a renewed emphasis was placed on alternative approaches to classroom learning and instruction, particularly in the areas of mathematics and science. Among the many ideas proposed in the 1960s for improving school learning was the **discovery learning** view of psychologist Jerome Bruner.

One of Bruner's major points was that too much school learning takes the form of step-by-step study of verbal or numerical statements or formulas that students can reproduce on cue but are unable to use outside the classroom. When students are presented with such highly structured materials as worksheets and other types of drill-and-practice exercises, Bruner argues, they become too dependent on other people. Furthermore, they are likely to think of learning as something done only to earn a reward.

Instead of using techniques that feature preselected and prearranged materials, Bruner believes teachers should confront children with problems and help them seek solutions either independently or by engaging in group discussion. True learning, says Bruner, involves "figuring out how to use what you already know in order to go beyond what you already think" (1983, p. 183). Like Piaget, Bruner argues that conceptions that children arrive at on their own are usually more meaningful than those proposed by others and that students do not need to be rewarded when they seek to make sense of things that puzzle them. Bruner maintains, in addition, that when children are given a substantial amount of practice in finding their own solutions to problems, they not only develop problem-solving skills but also acquire confidence in their own learning abilities, as well as a propensity to function later in life as problem solvers. They learn *how* to learn *as* they learn.

Bruner: discover how ideas relate to each other and to existing knowledge

Bruner does not suggest that students should discover every fact or principle or formula they may need to know. Discovery is simply too inefficient a process to be used that widely, and learning from others can be as meaningful as personal discovery. Rather, Bruner argues that certain types of outcomes—understanding the ways in which ideas connect with one another, the possibility of solving problems on our own, and how what we already know is relevant to what we are trying to learn—are the essence of education and can best be achieved through personal discovery.

As an example of this discovery approach, Bruner describes his approach to teaching geography in the elementary grades. Instead of having a group of fifth graders memorize a set of geography facts, he gave them blank outline maps that showed the location of rivers, lakes, mountains, valleys, plains, and so on. Their task was to figure out where the major cities, railways, and highways might be located. The students were not permitted to consult books or other maps; they had to figure out locations on their own by drawing on their prior knowledge and reasoning ability (Bruner, 1960).

Discovery learning is increasingly being done now with computer simulation programs and for the purpose of learning science concepts and skills: for instance, designing and conducting genetics experiments, creating graphs from experimental data, or determining the cause of the spread of an influenza epidemic. The effect of such programs has been inconsistent, probably because many students are not prepared to cope with the demands of discovery learning. For the effects of simulations to be more uniformly beneficial in helping students discover science concepts, students need to have first learned how to generate hypotheses from gathered data, design experiments that allow for a valid test of one's hypotheses (learners have a tendency to design experiments that will confirm rather than disconfirm a hypothesis), interpret experimental data, and monitor the adequacy of their own reasoning processes (de Jong & van Joolingen, 1998).

Constructivism Today

Contemporary constructivist theory has several variations, two of which we will describe shortly. But despite their differences, all the variations incorporate the following four facets.

Facets of Constructivism As we mentioned earlier, one facet of constructivism is that meaningful learning is the active creation of knowledge structures from personal experience. Each learner builds a personal view of the world by using existing knowledge, interests, attitudes, goals, and the like to select and interpret currently available information (Brooks & Brooks, 1999a; Perkins, 1999). As Rochel Gelman (1994) points out, this assumption highlights the importance of what educational psychologists call *entering behavior*—the previously learned knowledge and skill that students bring to the classroom.

Construction of ideas strongly influenced by student's prior knowledge

The knowledge that learners bring with them to a learning task has long been suspected of having a powerful effect on subsequent performance. In 1978, David Ausubel wrote on the flyleaf of his textbook, *Educational Psychology: A Cognitive View*, "If I had to reduce all of educational psychology to just one principle, I would say this: the most important single factor influencing learning is what the learner already knows. Ascertain this and teach him accordingly" (Ausubel, Novak, & Hanesian, 1978). Research findings appear to have borne out Ausubel's contention. A review of 183 studies (Dochy, Segers, & Buehl, 1999) concluded that a strong relationship exists between prior knowledge and performance. Almost all of the studies (91 percent) reported a positive effect of prior knowledge on performance, and in some circumstances most of the variation (60 percent) in students' scores on a test was a function of what learners knew about the topic prior to instruction.

A second facet of constructivism is that the essence of one person's knowledge can never be *totally* transferred to another person because knowledge is the result of a personal interpretation of experience, which is influenced by such factors as the learner's age, gender, race, ethnic background, and knowledge base. When knowledge is transferred from one person to another, some aspects of it are invariably "lost in translation." The area of musical performance provides an apt illustration of this aspect of constructivism. Although a piano teacher can tell a student volumes about how and why a piece should be performed in a particular way, the teacher cannot tell the student everything. The interpretation of a composition is constructed from such factors as the performer's knowledge of the composer's personality and motives, the nature of the instrument or instruments for which the composition was written, and the nature of the music itself. Because performers assign different meanings to such knowledge, different (yet equally valid) interpretations of the same composition result. Think, for example, of the many different ways in which you have heard "The Star-Spangled Banner" sung. Although listeners may prefer one version over another, there is no one correct way to sing this song.

The third facet follows directly from the second. Does constructivism necessarily mean that everyone walks around with a personal, idiosyncratic view of the world and that consensus is impossible? A few minutes of reflection should tell you that the answer is no. And if you recall what you read in the chapter on cultural and socioeconomic diversity, you will recognize that the cultures and societies to which people belong channel and place limits on the views people have of the world around them. Consequently, individuals make observations, test hypotheses, and draw conclusions that are largely consistent with one another (Cognition and Technology Group at Vanderbilt, 1991; Duffy & Cunningham, 1996). Of course, there are many instances when people cannot reconcile their views and so agree to disagree. For example, in 1995 the world observed the fiftieth anniversary of the atomic bombing of Hiroshima. Although everyone agreed on the basic facts of the event, there was sharp disagreement about why the bomb was dropped, whether it was necessary, and what exactly the anniversary should be observing. In matters such as these, truth is where it always is for the constructivist: in the mind of the beholder.

The fourth and final facet of constructivism that we will discuss has to do with the formation and changing of knowledge structures. Additions to, deletions from, or modifications of these interpretations come mainly from the sharing of multiple perspectives. Systematic, open-minded discussions and debates are instrumental in helping individuals create personal views (Cobb & Bowers, 1999; Cunningham, 1991). As we have seen in previous chapters, scholars form and reform their positions on aspects of theory or research as a result of years of discussion and debate with colleagues. The debate between the Piagetians and the Vygotskians (discussed in the chapter on stage theories of development) is a good example of this facet. Consequently, students need to be provided with conditions that allow them to share and discuss multiple perspectives on information and experiences.

Construction of ideas aided by discussion and debate

Two Variations on a Constructivist Theme One view of meaningful learning that we have described, Jean Piaget's, holds that it is the natural result of an intrinsic drive to resolve inconsistencies and contradictions—that is, always to have a view of the world that makes sense in the light of what we currently know. One contemporary variation of constructivism, **cognitive constructivism,** is an outgrowth of Piaget's ideas because it focuses on the cognitive processes that take place within individuals. In other words, an individual's conception of the truth of some matter (for example, both birds and airplanes can fly because they use the same aeronautical principles; high interest rates are bad because they discourage companies from borrowing money and expanding their businesses; high interest rates are good because they provide more money to people who have investments in interest-bearing securities) is based on her ability, with teacher guidance, to assimilate information effectively into existing schemes and develop new schemes and operations (the process Piaget called accommodation) in response to novel or discrepant ideas (Duffy & Cunningham, 1996; Fosnot, 1996).

Cognitive constructivism emphasizes role of cognitive processes in meaningful learning

The constructivist variation that is known as **social constructivism** holds that meaningful learning occurs when people are explicitly taught how to use the psychological tools of their culture (like language, mathematics, diagrams, and approaches to problem solving) and are then given the opportunity to use these tools to create a common, or shared, understanding of some phenomenon. Students are

Social constructivism emphasizes role of culture and social interaction in meaningful learning

Most constructivist theories take one of two forms: cognitive constructivism or social constructivism. The former emphasizes the effect of one's cognitive processes on meaningful learning while the latter emphasizes the effect of other people's arguments and points of view on meaningful learning.

encouraged to engage in open-ended discussion with peers and the teacher about such things as the meaning of terms and procedures, the relationships among ideas, and the applicability of knowledge to specific contexts. This process is often referred to by social constructivists as *negotiating meaning*. This view has its roots in the writings of such individuals as the psychologist Lev Vygotsky and the educational philosopher John Dewey (Duffy & Cunningham, 1996; Perkins, 1999; Scheurman, 1998).

Although the cognitive and social constructivist perspectives emphasize different aspects of learning, they are not incompatible. The cognitive approach does not deny the value of learning in group activities, and the social approach does not deny the value of working independently of others. For example, people who play musical instruments in an orchestra practice both in a group and by themselves because there are some things that are best learned either in isolation (aspects of technique, such as breathing, fingering, or bowing) or as part of the orchestra (watching the conductor, listening to one's colleagues). In athletics, too, certain skills are practiced alone while others are practiced with others (Anderson, Greeno, Reder, & Simon, 2000). Both perspectives also subscribe to the belief that "learning is an active process that is student-centered in the sense that, *with the teacher's help* [italics in the original], learners select and transform information, construct hypotheses, and make decisions" (Chrenka, 2001, p. 694).

Table 9.1 summarizes the characteristics of cognitive and social constructivism and the basic instructional approaches that flow from each of these variations. The main conditions that support an individual's attempt to construct personally meaningful knowledge are detailed in the next section.

Conditions That Foster Constructivism The fostering conditions that constructivists typically mention include a cognitive apprenticeship between student and teacher, a use of realistic problems and conditions, and an emphasis on multiple perspectives (Bednar, Cunningham, Duffy, & Perry, 1991).

Scaffolding: provide student with enough help to complete a task; gradually decrease help as student becomes able to work independently

Cognitive Apprenticeship The first condition, that of a cognitive apprenticeship, was illustrated in the chapter on information-processing theory when we described the reciprocal teaching program of Annemarie Palincsar and Ann Brown (1984). Its main feature is that the teacher models a cognitive process that students are to learn and then gradually turns responsibility for executing the process over to students as they become more skilled. As you may recall from our earlier discussions, providing

Table 9.1 Cognitive and Social Constructivist Approaches to Learning and Teaching

Approach	Basic Characteristics	Instructional Implications
Cognitive constructivism	• Existing knowledge schemes and operations are modified by the addition (assimilation) of new ideas that are judged to be related. New knowledge schemes and operations are created (accommodation) to adapt to ideas and procedures that are inconsistent with existing schemes. • Assimilation and accommodation processes assumed to be innate and supported by opportunities to interact with peers and the physical environment.	• Teacher challenges students' current conceptions by presenting new ideas that do not quite fit (inducing disequilibrium). • Students work individually and together to construct new, more effective schemes. • Emphasis is on constructing personal meaning by developing new schemes.
Social constructivism	• Learning initially occurs in the presence of and is influenced by more knowledgeable others. • The knowledge and skills that are acquired through the guidance of others are connected to existing schemes and gradually internalized, allowing the learner to become increasingly self-regulated and independent.	• Teacher helps students through scaffolded instruction to construct ideas using realistic, open-ended tasks. • Under teacher guidance, students work collaboratively to construct new conceptions. • Emphasis is on constructing and internalizing shared meaning.

such environmental supports as modeling, hints, leading questions, and suggestions, and then gradually removing them as the learner demonstrates increased competence is called *scaffolding.* Cognitive apprenticeships also occur in less formal circumstances, as when a child joins an existing peer group (like a play group), at first mostly watches what the other children do, and then gradually, with little explicit direction from the others, participates in one or more aspects of the task.

Situated Learning The second condition, often called **situated learning** (or situated cognition), is that students be given learning tasks set in realistic contexts. A realistic context is one in which students must solve a meaningful problem by using a variety of skills and information. The rationale for this condition is twofold:

1. Learning is more likely to be meaningful (related to previously learned knowledge and skills) when it is embedded in a realistic context (Duffy & Cunningham, 1996).
2. Traditional forms of classroom learning and instruction, which are largely decontextualized in the sense that what students learn is relevant only to taking tests and performing other classroom tasks, leads to a condition that has been re-

ferred to as **inert knowledge.** That is, students fail to use what they learned earlier (such as mathematical procedures) to solve either real-life problems (such as calculating the square footage of the walls of a room in order to know how many rolls of wallpaper to buy) or other school-related problems because they don't see any relationship between the two (Perkins, 1999). (We discuss the issue of inert knowledge and its relationship to transfer of learning later in this chapter.)

An example of situated learning would be to use the game of baseball as a vehicle for middle school or high school students to apply aspects of science, mathematics, and sociology. Students could be asked to use their knowledge of physics to explain how pitchers are able to make the ball curve left or right or drop down as it approaches home plate. They could be asked to use their mathematical skills to figure out how far home runs travel. They could also be asked to read about the Negro Leagues and Jackie Robinson and discuss why it took until the early 1950s for major league baseball to begin integration. The Case in Print provides real-life examples of how teachers have put the concept of situated learning into practice.

Constructivism aided by cognitive apprenticeship, realistic tasks, multiple perspectives

Multiple Perspectives The third condition fostering constructivism is that students should view ideas and problems from multiple perspectives. The rationale, again, is twofold: most of life's problems are multifaceted, and the knowledge base of experts is a network of interrelated ideas. The complex process of becoming an effective teacher is a good example of the need for multiple perspectives. As we mentioned at the beginning of the book, being an effective teacher requires the mastery of many skills and disciplines so that classroom problems (such as why a particular student does not perform up to expectations) can be analyzed and attacked from several perspectives.

The following section provides an example of a constructivist-oriented teaching lesson.

Constructivist-oriented teaching encourages creating new views; uses scaffolding, realistic tasks, and class discussion

An Example of Constructivist Teaching A first-grade teacher who wanted her students to understand the importance of using a standardized instrument, like a ruler, to make measurements decided to have them measure the size of the *Mayflower*, the boat that the English Pilgrims sailed in to the New World. After outlining the shape of the *Mayflower* in masking tape on the classroom floor, she began the lesson by saying, "Well, what should we do? Who has an idea?" By using probing questions to responses ("Why do you think the boat is three feet long?"), allowing for painful periods of silence, and pointing out dead ends (when the largest boy in class measured the boat the same way they measure the height of horses, in hands, the teacher suggested that the smallest girl in class do the same), this teacher subtly helped them construct the concept of a standard unit of measure and understand its importance (Schifter, 1996).

The essence of a constructivist-oriented lesson is to provide students with realistic problems that cannot be solved with their current level of understanding and, by allowing them to interact mainly among themselves, to work out new understandings. It's important to emphasize the social nature of this approach. The experiences and ideas of others become springboards for further experimentation and discussion. This approach also emphasizes the role of the teacher as artist. Because a teacher does not know beforehand what questions students will ask or what solutions they will propose, the teacher's questions and suggestions cannot be scripted in advance. They have to be generated on the spot, and they have to further the point of the lesson most of the time.

Constructing Real Learning Experiences

The fostering conditions that constructivists typically mention include a cognitive apprenticeship between student and teacher, a use of realistic problems and conditions, and an emphasis on multiple perspectives. . . . The second condition, often called ***situated learning*** *(or situated cognition), is that students be given learning tasks set in realistic contexts. A realistic context is one in which students must solve a meaningful problem by using a variety of skills and information. (p. 306)*

All-USA Teacher Team: Changing Lives One Class at a Time

TRACEY WONG BRIGGS
USA Today 10/14/99

In rural Alaska, science teacher Steven Jacquier's high school students feed alcohol to pregnant mice.

After the students see the deformed fetuses that develop, they hold clinics to spread the message in their Eskimo villages, where fetal alcohol syndrome is a major problem.

In Walnut, Calif., Suzanne Middle School teacher Alan Haskvitz had his social studies students rewrite voting instructions because they couldn't understand them. Their changes were used by Los Angeles County.

And in Newnan, Ga., seventh- and eighth-graders who have arrived at Fairmont Alternative School through the juvenile court system can experience the other side of the bench as judges, lawyers, bailiffs and jurors through a school judicial system Carmella Williams Scott created to turn criminal thinkers into critical thinkers.

For their success at unlocking student minds and making a difference in their lives, Jacquier, Haskvitz and Scott, along with 13 other individual teachers and four teaching teams, have been named to USA TODAY's All-USA Teacher First Team as representatives of all outstanding teachers. . . .

"These stellar teachers inspire their students to be the best they can be, academically. They also teach lessons of empowerment, responsibility and community," says Tom Curley, president and publisher of USA Today "By honoring them, we recognize what they're doing is building a better future."

The teachers unlock minds in a variety of situations, from Jacquier, who travels to three remote Eskimo villages in western Alaska each year to teach science in 12-week modules; to Suzanne Taffet-Romano, who transforms Long Island children with autism from non-communicators to students who read and tell jokes.

Among the 20 First Team members, 10 teach elementary school, two teach middle school and six teach high school. Scott teaches at an alternative middle/high school, and Taffet-Romano teaches at the Rosemary Kennedy School for students with cognitive disorders in Wantagh, N.Y.

Science of Discovery

The First Team represents a diversity of outstanding teaching, but there is also a strong scientific bent. Nearly half either teach science or are noted for how well they incorporate science into the curriculum:

- Myron Blosser's molecular genetics students not only design original research but also order their supplies and maintain thousands of dollars' worth of lab equipment at Harrisonburg (Va.) High. That's real science—and real life, Blosser says.
- Edna Waller led school and community efforts to establish two wetland areas and nature trails on the grounds of Magnolia Park Elementary School, bordering Gulf Islands National Seashore in Ocean Springs, Miss. The outdoor labs draw students not just into the science of the wetlands but also into the history and economics of Ocean Springs, which relies on the shrimping industry. "It makes a connection to them to real life," Waller says.
- Sylvia Dee Shore trains her Clubview Elementary third-graders to monitor water quality and work on water conservation in Columbus, Ga. In five years, Shore's River Kids Network has spread to 17 schools and more than 1,000 students statewide. "They truly believe they're making a difference, and they are," Shore says.
- Susan Roberts Bradburn has fourth- to sixth-graders research science exhibits to present to other classes and finds they work harder to finish their schoolwork correctly so they have more time for their mobile museum projects. "It's like I've just found this secret," says Bradburn, who teaches at West Marion (N.C.) Elementary School.
- Tina Cross has involved students in writing $179,000 worth of grants for Carver High in Columbus, Ga. "I don't

think there's a student in the magnet program who hasn't been involved in a grant," says senior Phillip Moore, 17.

The process teaches students larger lessons about going after what they want, Cross says. "They know where the equipment comes from and what it takes to get it."

Teamwork

Four of the 20 First Team slots this year went to teams of teachers who collaborate:

- In Bio/Geo, a biology/geometry course dubbed "math and science get wet and muddy," Sandra Duck Eidson and Lela Whelchel's students at West Hall High in Oakwood, Ga., teamed up to build DNA models and monitor creek water quality.

  "It taught me to think about getting other people's opinions instead of just my own," says Justin Woodsmall, 17.
- Craig Yager and Lise Blumenthal tap parent and grandparent volunteers, student teachers, professors and others to help teach the Fifth Grade Flock at Whittier Elementary School in Boulder, Colo.
- The "Zoo School" faculty in Lincoln, Neb., encourages students to pursue their own interests and share their expertise. "We are a community of learners," science teacher Sara Leroy-Toren says.
- And the four-member Tiger Team at Andrew Jackson Middle School in Cross Lanes, W. Va., builds interdisciplinary units around subjects such as the Native American experience and World War II that help eighth-graders understand the dangers of intolerance.

"When the World War II unit is done, student behavior changes. They become more tolerant and see hate and prejudice in a different light," math teacher Karen McNeer says.

First Teamers run student-centered classrooms that foster individual and community growth in ways not found in any textbook:

- Jody Solmonson introduces her fifth-graders at Bear Valley Elementary in Anchorage to Shakespeare, atomic structure and the physics of energy loss, often through activities that encourage them to forge their own way. True accomplishment is the only path to self-esteem, Solmonson says: "You can't give it. You can only earn it. You set up challenges that they can overcome."
- Linda Chelman welcomes students with special needs in to her second-grade class at Jefferson Elementary in Franklin, Mass. Beyond designing activities using different talents to reinforce the same concept, she uses inclusion to build a sense of community. Twice a week, Chelman gathers her students in a circle to talk about problem-solving strategies and how to include other students. "Students have to realize that we're all different, but we're all alike," she says.
- And Spanish teacher Maria Garcia-Rameau opens up the entire Latin world to students at Scarborough High in Houston, many of whom don't think beyond Mexico, say former student Brett Millican, 30. Millican credits his high school Spanish with opening the door to his Coast Guard career, in which he has served on cutters off Florida and Puerto Rico.

Questions and Activities

1. What principles of constructivist learning theory are reflected in the instructional activities of those teachers who were named to *USA Today*'s All-USA First Team?
2. What other field-based projects can you think of that would accomplish the same objectives as the projects described in this story? Describe where you would take students, what you would have them do, and what you would hope to accomplish.
3. Some of the projects described in this story required students to visit such field sites as wetlands, rivers, and creek and to conduct projects that benefited such other groups as municipal governments. How would you respond to a parent who believed that students were learning less because of decreased classroom time?

Putting Constructivism in Perspective Although constructivism has much to offer teachers, like any other theory, it does have its limitations. Here are a few you should keep in mind:

- Because of constructivism's emphasis on guiding rather than telling, accepting different perspectives on issues and solutions to problems, modifying previous conceptions in the light of new information, and creating an atmosphere that encourages active participation, it is almost impossible to create highly detailed lesson plans. Much of what teachers do depends on how students respond. Teaching from this perspective will place a premium on your teacher-as-artist abilities.
- Teaching from a constructivist perspective is more time-consuming and places higher demands on learners as compared to a typical lecture format (de Jong & van Joolingen, 1998; Perkins, 1999).
- Recognize that students construct their own interpretations of things regardless of whether you teach from a constructivist perspective. You can provide students with a clear description of what you want them to learn, provide expert scaffolded instruction, and provide realistic tasks to which students can relate, and still find some students who have developed a very different idea of the purpose of the lesson.
- Constructivism is not the only orientation to learning and teaching that you will ever need (nor is any other theory, for that matter). You need to know which theory or approach best fits which purposes and circumstances. Sometimes memorization of factual information is essential, and sometimes an instructional objective can be accomplished more efficiently (and just as effectively) with a clear and well-organized lecture (Airasian & Walsh, 1997).

There are many techniques you can use to foster meaningful learning within a constructivist framework. Several computer-based approaches are described at the end of this chapter. One that does not rely on computer technology but is particularly well suited to developing, comparing, and understanding different points of view is the classroom discussion (Rabow, Charness, Kipperman, & Radcliffe-Vasile, 1994; Schiever, 1991). Because this format also allows students to deal with realistic problems and to exercise cognitive skills taught by the teacher, it is an excellent general-purpose method for helping students construct a meaningful knowledge base. Let's turn our attention to some specific Suggestions for Teaching that describe how to use discussion to emphasize meaningful learning in your classroom.

SUGGESTIONS FOR TEACHING IN YOUR CLASSROOM

Using a Constructivist Approach to Meaningful Learning

1 Arrange the learning situation so that students are exposed to different perspectives on a problem or an issue.

This is the crux of the discovery approach and the constructivist view of learning. The basic idea is to *arrange* the elements of a learning task and *guide* student actions so that students discover, or construct, a personally meaningful conception of a problem or issue. In some cases, you may present a topic that is a matter of opinion or that all students are sure to know something about. In other cases, you might structure the discussion by exposing all participants to the same background information.

Journal Entry
Ways to Arrange for Discovery to Take Place

a. Ask students to discuss familiar topics or those that are matters of opinion.

Examples

- "What are some of the techniques that advertising agencies use in television commercials to persuade us to buy certain products?"
- "What do you think is the best book you ever read, and why do you think so?"

b. Provide necessary background information by asking all students to read all or part of a book, take notes on a lecture, view a film, conduct library research, or conduct research on the Internet.

Examples

- After the class has read *Great Expectations,* ask, "What do you think Dickens was trying to convey when he wrote this novel? Was he just trying to tell a good story, or was he also trying to get us to think about certain kinds of relationships between people?"
- "After I explain some of the principles of electrical currents, I'm going to ask you to suggest rules for connecting batteries in series and in parallel. Then we'll see how well your rules work."

2 Structure discussions by posing a specific question, presenting a provocative topic-related issue, or asking students to choose topics or subtopics.

Journal Entry
Questions That Are Likely to Stimulate Productive Classroom Discussion

It is important to structure a discovery session by giving students something reasonably specific to discuss; otherwise, they may simply engage in a disorganized and desultory bull session. You might supply direction in the following ways:

a. In some cases, encourage students to arrive at conclusions already reached by others.

Thousands of books provide detailed answers to such questions as, "What is human about human beings? How did they get that way? How can they be made more so?" But constructivists believe that answers mean more when they are constructed by the individual, not supplied ready-made by others. As you look over lesson plans, therefore, you might try to put together some questions for students to answer by engaging in discussion rather than by reading or listening to what others have already discovered. In searching for such topics, you might take into account the techniques that Bruner described. Here is a list of those techniques, together with an example of each one. In your Reflective Journal you might describe similar applications that you could use when you begin to teach. Keep in mind that students often acquire a deeper understanding of ideas and issues when they have had appropriate previous experience:

- *Emphasize contrast.* In an elementary school social studies unit on cultural diversity, say, "When you watch this film on Mexico, look for customs and ways of living that differ from ours. Then we'll talk about what these differences are and why they may have developed."
- *Stimulate informed guessing.* In a middle school unit on natural science, you might say, "Suppose we wanted to figure out some kind of system to classify trees so that we could later find information about particular types. What would be the best way to do it?" After students have developed a classification scheme, show them schemes that specialists have developed.
- *Encourage participation.* In a high school political science class, illustrate the jury system by staging a mock trial. (Note that the use of a simulation satisfies the constructivist criterion of realistic tasks and contexts.)

themselves and each other. Jacob Kounin (1970) points out that when a teacher first names a student and then asks a question, the rest of the class may tend to turn its attention to other things. The same tendency to tune out may occur if a teacher follows a set pattern of calling on students (for example, by going around a circle). To keep all the students on their toes, you might ask questions first and then, in an unpredictable sequence, call on those who volunteer to recite, frequently switching from one part of the room to another. As you look around the room before selecting a volunteer, remember Skinner's criticism that a few students may make all the discoveries. Guard against the temptation to call primarily on students you expect to give good or provocative answers. Repeatedly ignoring students who may be a bit inarticulate or unimaginative may cause them and their classmates to conclude that you think they are incompetent. These students may then lose interest in and totally ignore what is taking place.

4 If abundant time is available and if a controversial or subdivided topic is to be discussed, divide the class into groups of five or so, and arrange for each member of each group to have eye contact with every other group member.

A major limitation of any kind of discussion is that only one person can talk at a time. You can reduce this difficulty by dividing the class into smaller groups before asking them to exchange ideas. A group of about five seems to work best. If only two or three students are interacting with each other, the exchange of ideas may be limited. If there are more than five, not all members will be able to contribute at frequent intervals.

Journal Entry
Techniques for Arranging Small-Group Discussions

One way to form groups, particularly if students have suggested subtopics, is to ask them to list in order their first three subject preferences. (Mention at the start that it is unlikely that all the students in the class will get their first choice.) Then you can divide by referring to the lists. One advantage of this technique is that students embark on a discovery session with the feeling that they have chosen to do so. Another advantage is that you can arrange group membership to a certain extent since students won't know how many of their classmates listed a particular topic as first choice. You might break up potentially disruptive pairings and also spread around talkative, creative, and thoughtful students.

Another way to divide the class, particularly if all groups are to discuss the same topic, is to ask all students in a row to form a group. Or have the class count off from one to five. After all students have counted off, ask all "ones" to move to one part of the room, "twos" to another part, and so on. You can manage to achieve different assortments of students by having the class count off in different ways each time.

The Nature of Problem Solving

As with most of the other topics covered in this book, an extensive amount of theorizing and research on problem solving has been conducted over the years. We will focus our discussion on the types of problems that students are typically required to deal with, the cognitive processes that play a central role in problem solving, and various approaches to teaching problem solving in the classroom.

Let's begin by asking what we mean by the terms *problem* and *problem solving.* Most, if not all, psychologists would agree that "a problem is said to exist when one has a goal and has not yet identified a means for reaching that goal" (Gagné, Yekovich, & Yekovich, 1993, p. 211). **Problem solving,** then, is the identification and application of knowledge and skills that result in goal attainment (Martinez, 1998). Although this definition encompasses a wide range of problem types, we will focus on three types that students frequently encounter both in school and out.

Three Common Types of Problems

Well-structured problems: clearly stated, known solution procedures, known evaluation standards

In the first category are the well-structured problems of mathematics and science—the type of problems that students from kindergarten through middle school are typically required to solve. **Well-structured problems** are clearly formulated, can be solved by recall and application of a specific procedure (called an *algorithm*), and result in a solution that can be evaluated against a well-known, agreed-on standard (Hamilton & Ghatala, 1994)—for example:

$5 + 8 =$
$732 - 485 =$
$8 + 3x = 40 - 5x$

What constitutes a problem to be solved varies with the age and experience of the learner and the nature of the problem itself (Martinez, 1998). The second of the mathematical examples is likely to be a genuine problem for some first or second graders who are used to seeing subtraction exercises arrayed vertically (minuend on top, subtrahend beneath, horizontal line under the subtrahend). Fifth graders, however, who have had experience with arithmetic assignments in a variety of formats, would be able to retrieve and use the correct algorithm automatically. Because the fifth graders know the means to reach their goal, they do not face a problem-solving task according to our definition, but just a type of exercise or practice.

Well-structured problems have a clear structure, can be solved by using a standard procedure, and produce solutions that can be evaluated against an agreed-on standard. They are the type of problem that students are asked to solve most frequently.

In the second category are the ill-structured problems often encountered in everyday life and in disciplines such as economics or psychology. **Ill-structured problems** are more complex, provide few cues pointing to solution procedures, and have less definite criteria for determining when the problem has been solved (Hamilton & Ghatala, 1994). Examples of ill-structured problems are how to identify and reward good teachers, how to improve access to public buildings and facilities for persons with physical disabilities, and how to increase voter turnout for primary and general elections.

Ill-structured problems: vaguely stated, unclear solution procedures, vague evaluation standards

The third category includes problems that are also ill structured but differ from the examples just mentioned in two respects. First, these problems tend to divide people into opposing camps because of the emotions they arouse. Second, the primary goal, at least initially, is not to determine a course of action but to identify the most reasonable position. These problems are often referred to as **issues** (Ruggiero, 1988, 2001). Examples of issues are capital punishment, gun control, and nondenominational prayer in classrooms. Beginning with the freshman year in high school, students usually receive more opportunities to deal with ill-structured problems and issues.

Issues: ill-structured problems that arouse strong feelings

Helping Students Become Good Problem Solvers

Despite the differences that exist among well-structured problems, ill-structured problems, and issues, recent theory and research suggest that good problem solvers employ the same general approach when solving one or another of these problem types (see, for example, Bransford & Stein, 1993; Gagné et al., 1993; Gick, 1986; Krulik & Rudnick, 1993; Nickerson, 1994; Ruggiero, 1988, 2001). When used to solve ill-structured problems or to analyze issues, this approach consists of five steps or processes (although the solution of well-structured problems may call only for the implementation of steps 2, 4, and 5):

1. Realize that a problem exists.
2. Understand the nature of the problem.
3. Compile relevant information.
4. Formulate and carry out a solution.
5. Evaluate the solution.

We will discuss each of these steps in the next few pages, along with some specific techniques that you can use to help your students become good problem solvers.

Step 1: Realize That a Problem Exists Most people assume that if a problem is worth solving, they won't have to seek it out; it will make itself known. Like most other assumptions, this one is only partly true. Well-structured problems are often thrust on us by teachers, in the form of in-class exercises or homework, or by supervisors at work. Ill-structured problems and issues, however, often remain hidden from most people. It is a characteristic of good problem solvers that they are more sensitive to the existence of problems than most of their peers (Okagaki & Sternberg, 1990).

The keys to problem recognition, or *problem finding* as it is sometimes called, are curiosity and dissatisfaction. You need to question why a rule, procedure, or product is the way it is or to feel frustrated or irritated because something does not work as well as it might. The organization known as Mothers Against Drunk Driving, for example, was begun by a woman who, because her daughter had been killed in a traf-

Problem finding depends on curiosity, dissatisfaction with status quo

fic accident by a drunk driver, was dissatisfied with current, ineffective laws. This organization has been instrumental in getting state legislatures to pass laws against drunk driving that mandate more severe penalties. As another example, John Bransford and Barry Stein (1993) mention a business that was able to eliminate the generation of 120 tons of paper per year by taking a critical look at its record-keeping procedure.

Problem finding does not come readily to most people, possibly because schools emphasize solving well-structured problems and possibly because most people have a natural tendency to assume that things work as well as they can. Like any other cognitive process, however, problem recognition can improve with instruction and practice. Students can be sensitized in a number of ways to the absence or flaws and shortcomings of products, procedures, rules, or whatever else. We will make some specific suggestions about improving problem recognition and the other problem-solving processes a bit later in Suggestions for Teaching in Your Classroom.

Step 2: Understand the Nature of the Problem The second step in the problem-solving process is perhaps the most critical. The problem solver has to construct an *optimal* representation, or understanding, of the nature of a problem or issue. The preceding sentence stresses the word *optimal* for two reasons. First, most problems can be expressed in a number of ways. Written problems, for example, can be recast as pictures, equations, graphs, charts, or diagrams. Second, because the way we represent the problem determines the amount and type of solution-relevant information we recall from long-term memory, some representations are better than others. For obvious reasons, problem-solving researchers often refer to this process as **problem representation** or **problem framing.**

Problem framing depends on knowledge of subject matter, familiarity with problem types

To achieve an optimal understanding of a problem, an individual needs two things: a high degree of knowledge of the subject matter (facts, concepts, and principles) on which the problem is based and familiarity with that particular type of problem. This background will allow the person to recognize important elements (words, phrases, and numbers) in the problem statement and patterns of relationships among the problem elements. This recognition will activate one or more solution-relevant schemes from long-term memory. It is this level of knowledge of subject matter and problem types that distinguishes the high-quality problem representations of the expert problem solver from the low-quality representations of the novice. Experts typically represent problems in terms of one or more basic patterns or underlying principles, whereas novices focus on limited or superficial surface features of problems.

To give you a clearer idea of the nature and power of an optimal problem representation, consider the following situation. When novices are given a set of physics problems to solve, they sort them into categories on the basis of some noticeable feature. For example, they group together all problems that involve the use of an inclined plane, or all the ones that involve the use of pulleys, or all those that involve friction. Then novices search their memory for previously learned information. The drawback to this approach is that although two or three problems may involve the use of an inclined plane, their solutions may depend on the application of different laws of physics. Experts, in contrast, draw on their extensive and well-organized knowledge base to represent groups of problems according to a common underlying principle, such as conservation of energy or Newton's third law (Gagné et al., 1993; Gick, 1986).

An important aspect of the problem-solving process is the ability to activate relevant schemes (organized collections of facts, concepts, principles, and procedures) from long-term memory when they are needed. The more relevant and powerful the activated scheme is, the more likely it is that an effective problem solution will be achieved. But as many observers of education have pointed out, acquiring this ability is often easier said than done. John Bransford argues that standard educational practices produce knowledge that is *inert*. As mentioned earlier in the chapter, inert knowledge can be accessed only under conditions that closely mimic the original learning context (Bransford, Sherwood, Vye, & Rieser, 1986). Richard Feynman, a Nobel Prize–winning physicist, made the same observation in describing how his classmates at the Massachusetts Institute of Technology failed to recognize the application of a previously learned mathematical formula: "They didn't put two and two together. They didn't even know what they 'knew.' I don't know what's the matter with people: they don't learn by understanding; they learn by some other way—by rote, or something. Their knowledge is so fragile!" (1985, p. 36). To overcome this limitation of inert and fragile knowledge, teachers need to present subject matter in a highly organized fashion, and students need to learn more about the various conditions under which their knowledge applies.

Inert knowledge due to learning isolated facts under limited conditions

Step 3: Compile Relevant Information For well-structured problems that are relatively simple and familiar (such as arithmetic drill problems), this step in the problem-solving process occurs simultaneously with problem representation. In the process of defining a problem, we very quickly and easily recall from long-term memory all the information needed to achieve a solution. As problems and issues become more complex, however, we run into two difficulties: the amount of information relevant to the solution becomes too great to keep track of mentally, and there is an increasing chance that we may not possess all the relevant information. As a result, we are forced to compile what we know in the form of lists, tables, pictures, graphs and diagrams, and so on and to seek additional information from other sources.

The key to using oneself as an information source is the ability to accurately retrieve from long-term memory information that will aid in the solution of the problem. We need to think back over what we have learned in other somewhat similar situations, make a list of some other form of representation of those ideas, and make a judgment as to how helpful that knowledge might be. Techniques for ensuring accurate and reliable recall were discussed in the chapter on information-processing theory.

In addition to relying on our own knowledge and experience to solve problems, we can draw on the knowledge and experience of friends, colleagues, and experts. According to Vincent Ruggiero, "Investigating other people's views calls for little talking and a lot of careful listening. We do well, in such cases, to ask questions rather than make statements" (1988, p. 39). The main purpose of soliciting the views of others about solutions to problems and positions on issues is to identify the reasons and evidence those people offer in support of their positions. This skill of asking questions and analyzing responses is quite useful in debates and classroom discussions of controversial issues.

Step 4: Formulate and Carry Out a Solution When you feel you understand the nature of a problem or issue and possess sufficient relevant information, you are ready to attempt a solution. The first step is to consider which of several alternative approaches is likely to be most effective. The literature on problem solving mentions quite a few solution strategies. Because these solution strategies are very

In order to become proficient at carrying out a proposed solution to a problem or evaluating the adequacy of a solution, students need many opportunities to practice these skills.

general in nature—they can apply to different kinds of problems in different content areas and offer only a general approach to solving a problem—they are referred to as heuristics (Martinez, 1998). We will discuss six **heuristics** that we think are particularly useful.

Studying worked examples is an effective solution strategy

- *Study worked examples.* This approach may strike you as so obvious that it hardly merits attention, but it is worth mentioning for two reasons. First, obvious solution strategies are the ones that are most often overlooked. Second, it is a very effective solution strategy. Mary Gick (1986) cites almost a dozen studies in which learners improved their ability to solve a variety of problems by studying similar problems whose solutions had already been worked out. The beneficial effect is thought to be due to the learners' acquisition of a general problem schema. To get the most out of this heuristic, use multiple examples and different formats for each problem type and encourage learners to explain to themselves the problem-solving strategy illustrated by the examples (Atkinson, Derry, Renkl, & Wortham, 2000).

  There is one circumstance, however, in which providing worked examples is likely to be less effective than usual. Individuals who have a moderate to extensive amount of prior knowledge about the subject matter are likely to do better on problem-solving tests when they are given problem-solving instruction and practice than when they are given worked examples to study (Kalyuga, Chandler, Tuovinen, & Sweller, 2001).

Solve simpler version of problem first; then transfer process to harder problem

- *Work on a simpler version of the problem.* This is another common and very effective approach. Geometry offers a particularly clear example of working on a simpler problem. If you are having difficulty solving a problem of solid geometry (which involves three dimensions), work out a similar problem in plane geometry (two dimensions) and then apply the solution to the three-dimensional example (Nickerson, 1994; Polya, 1957). Architects and engineers employ this approach when they construct scaled-down models of bridges, buildings, experimental aircraft, and the like. Scientists do the same thing by creating laboratory simulations of real-world phenomena.

- *Break the problem into parts.* The key to this approach is to make sure you break the problem into manageable parts. Whether you can do this will depend largely on how much subject-matter knowledge you have. The more you know about the domain from which the problem comes, the easier it is to know how to break a problem into logical, easy-to-handle parts.

  At least two benefits result from breaking a problem into parts: it reduces the amount of information you have to keep in short-term memory to a manageable level, and the method used to solve one part of the problem can often be used to solve another part. Bransford and Stein (1993) use the following example to illustrate how this approach works.

  Problem: What day follows the day before yesterday if two days from now will be Sunday?

  1. What is today if two days from now will be Sunday? (Friday)
  2. If today is Friday, what is the day before yesterday? (Wednesday)
  3. What day follows Wednesday? (Thursday)

Break complex problems into manageable parts

- *Work backward.* This is a particularly good solution strategy to use whenever the goal is clear but the beginning state is not. Bransford and Stein (1993) offer the following example. Suppose you arranged to meet someone at a restaurant across town at noon. When should you leave your office to be sure of arriving on time? By working backward from your destination and arrival time (it takes about ten minutes to find a parking spot and walk to the restaurant; it takes about thirty minutes to drive to the area where you would park; it takes about five minutes to walk from your office to your car), you would more quickly and easily determine when to leave your office (about 11:15) than if you had worked the problem forward.

Work backward when goal is clear but beginning state is not

- *Solve an analogous problem.* If you are having difficulty solving a problem, possibly because your knowledge of the subject matter is incomplete, it may be useful to think of a similar problem about a subject in which you are more knowledgeable. Solve the analogous problem, and then use the same method to solve the first problem. In essence, this is a way of making the unfamiliar familiar.

  Although solving analogous problems is a very powerful solution strategy, it can be difficult to employ, especially for novices. In our previous discussion of understanding the problem, we made the point that novices represent problems on the basis of superficial features, whereas experts operate from knowledge of underlying concepts and principles. The same is true of analogies. Novices are more likely than experts to use superficial analogies (Gick, 1986).

Solve a similar problem and then apply the same method

- *Create an external representation of the problem.* This heuristic is doubly useful because it also aids in problem framing (quickly review what we said about problem framing in the first paragraph of "Understand the Nature of the Problem"). Many problems can be represented as pictures, equations, graphs, flowcharts, and the like. The figures in the next Suggestions for Teaching section illustrate how a pictorial or symbolic form of representation can help one both understand and solve the problem (Martinez, 1998).

Create an external representation of the problem

Step 5: Evaluate the Solution The last step in the problem-solving process is to evaluate the adequacy of the solution. For relatively simple, well-structured problems where the emphasis is on producing a correct response, two levels of evaluation are available:

Evaluate solutions to well-structured problems by estimating or checking

- The problem solver can ask whether, given the problem statement, the answer makes sense. For example, if the problem reads 75 × 5 = ? and the response is 80, a little voice inside the problem solver's head should say that the answer cannot possibly be right. This signal should prompt a reevaluation of the way the problem was represented and the solution procedure that was used (for example, "I misread the times sign as a plus sign and added when I should have multiplied").
- The problem solver can use an alternative algorithm (a fixed procedure used to solve a problem) to check the accuracy of the solution. This is necessary because an error in carrying out an algorithm can produce an incorrect response that is in the ballpark. For example, a common error in multiple-column subtraction problems is to subtract a smaller digit from a larger one regardless of whether the small number is in the minuend (top row) or the subtrahend (bottom row) (Mayer, 1987), as in

$$\begin{array}{r} 522 \\ -\ 418 \\ \hline 116 \end{array}$$

  Since this answer is off by only 12 units, it "looks right." The flaw can be discovered, however, by adding the answer to the subtrahend to produce the minuend.

The evaluation of solutions to ill-structured problems is likely to be more complicated and time-consuming for at least two reasons. First, the evaluation should occur both before and after the solution is implemented. Although many flaws and omissions can be identified and corrected beforehand, some will slip through. There is much to be learned by observing the effects of our solutions. Second, because these problems are complex, often involving a dozen or more variables, some sort of systematic framework should guide the evaluation. Vincent Ruggiero suggests a four-step procedure (1988, pp. 44–46):

1. Ask and answer a set of basic questions. Imagine, for example, that you have proposed a classroom incentive system (a token economy, perhaps) to enhance student motivation. You might ask such questions as, How will this program be implemented? By whom? When? Where? With what materials? How will the materials be obtained?
2. Identify imperfections and complications. Is this idea, for example, safe, convenient, efficient, economical, and compatible with existing policies and practices?
3. Anticipate possible negative reactions from other people. For instance, might parents or the school principal object?
4. Devise improvements.

The next section contains guidelines and examples that will help you improve the problem-solving skills of your students.

- Properly interpreting factual data (for example, recognizing that an increase in a state's income tax rate from 4 to 6 percent is an increase not of 2 percent but of 50 percent).
- Testing the credibility of hypotheses. On the basis of existing data, hypotheses can range from highly improbable to highly probable.
- Making important distinctions (for instance, between preference and judgment, emotion and content, appearance and reality).
- Recognizing unstated assumptions (for example, that because two events occur close together in time, one causes the other; that what is clear to us will be clear to others; that if the majority believes something, it must be true).
- Evaluating the validity and truthfulness of one's arguments (by, for example, checking that conclusions logically follow from premises and that conclusions have not been influenced by such reasoning flaws as either-or thinking, overgeneralizing, or oversimplifying).
- Recognizing when evidence is insufficient.

All of these ten skills can be modeled and taught in your classroom.

For more help in applying this chapter's ideas to your own teaching, see the Field Experiences section on this book's web site at **http://education.college.hmco.com/students**.

Transfer of Learning

Throughout this chapter and preceding ones, we have indicated that classroom instruction should be arranged in such a way that students independently apply the knowledge and problem-solving skills they learn in school to similar but new situations. This capability is the main goal of problem-solving instruction and is typically valued very highly by educators (Halpern, 1998; Haskell, 2001). Referred to as **transfer of learning,** it is the essence of being an autonomous learner and problem solver. In this section, we will examine the nature of transfer and discuss ways in which you can help bring it about.

THE NATURE AND SIGNIFICANCE OF TRANSFER OF LEARNING

The Theory of Identical Elements During the early 1900s, it was common practice for high school students and colleges to require that students take such subjects as Latin, Greek, and geometry. Because they were considered difficult topics to learn, mastery of them was expected to improve a student's ability to memorize, think, and reason. These enhanced abilities were then expected to facilitate the learning of less difficult subjects. The rationale behind this practice was that the human mind, much like any muscle in the body, could be exercised and made stronger. A strong mind, then, would learn things that a weak mind would not. This practice, known as the *doctrine of formal discipline,* constituted an early (and incorrect) explanation of transfer.

Early view of transfer based on degree of similarity between two tasks

In 1901, Edward Thorndike and Robert Woodworth proposed an alternative explanation of how transfer occurs. They argued that the degree to which knowledge and skills acquired in learning one task can help someone learn another task depends on how similar the two tasks are (if we assume that the learner recognizes the similarities). The greater the degree of similarity is between the tasks' stimulus and response elements (as in riding a bicycle and riding a motorcycle), the greater the

If teachers want students to apply what they learn in the classroom in other settings in the future, they should create tasks and conditions that are similar to those that students will encounter later.

amount of transfer will be. This idea became known as the **theory of identical elements** (Cox, 1997).

Positive, Negative, and Zero Transfer In time, however, other psychologists (among them Ellis, 1965; Osgood, 1949) identified different types of transfer and the conditions under which each type prevailed. A useful distinction was made among positive transfer, negative transfer, and zero transfer (Ormrod, 1999).

Positive transfer: previous learning makes later learning easier

The discussion up to this point has been alluding to **positive transfer,** defined as a situation in which prior learning aids subsequent learning. According to Thorndike's analysis, positive transfer occurs when a new learning task calls for essentially the same response that was made to a similar, earlier-learned task. The accomplished accordion player, for instance, probably will become a proficient pianist faster than someone who knows how to play the drums or someone who plays no musical instrument at all, all other things being equal. Similarly, the native English speaker who is also fluent in French is likely to have an easier time learning Spanish than is someone who speaks no foreign language.

Negative transfer: previous learning interferes with later learning

Negative transfer is defined as a situation in which prior learning interferes with subsequent learning. It occurs when two tasks are highly similar but require different responses. A tennis player learning how to play racquetball, for example, may encounter problems at first because of a tendency to swing the racquetball racket as if it were a tennis racket. Primary grade children often experience negative transfer when they encounter words that are spelled alike but pronounced differently (as in "I will *read* this story now since I *read* that story last week").

Zero transfer is defined as a situation in which prior learning has no effect on new learning. It can be expected when two tasks have different stimuli and different responses. Learning to conjugate Latin verbs, for example, is not likely to have any effect on learning how to find the area of a rectangle.

Specific and General Transfer The preceding description of positive transfer, although useful, is somewhat limiting because it is unclear whether transfer from one task to another is due to specific similarities or to general or nonspecific similarities. Psychologists (as described by Ellis, 1978) decide whether transfer is due to specific or general factors by setting up learning tasks such as the following for three different but equivalent groups of learners.

	Initial Task	Transfer Task
Group 1	Learn French	Learn Spanish
Group 2	Learn Chinese	Learn Spanish
Group 3	Learn Spanish	

If on a Spanish test, group 1 scores higher than group 2, the difference is attributed **to specific transfer** of similarities between French and Spanish (such as vocabulary, verb conjugations, and sentence structure). If groups 1 and 2 score the same but both outscore group 3, the difference is attributed to nonspecific transfer, or **general transfer,** of similarities between the two tasks since Chinese shares no apparent specific characteristics with French or Spanish. In this case, it is possible that learners use cognitive strategies—such as imagery, verbal elaboration, and mnemonic devices—when learning a foreign language and that these transfer to the learning of other foreign languages. Such nonspecific transfer effects have also been demonstrated for other classroom tasks, such as problem solving and learning from text (Ellis, 1978; Royer, 1979).

Specific transfer due to specific similarities between two tasks

General transfer due to use of same cognitive strategies

Contemporary Views of Specific and General Transfer

Gavriel Salomon and David Perkins (1989) offer a treatment of specific and general transfer under the labels *low-road transfer* and *high-road transfer,* respectively.

Low-Road Transfer **Low-road transfer** refers to a situation in which a previously learned skill or idea is almost automatically retrieved from memory and applied to a highly similar current task. For example, a student who has mastered the skill of two-column addition and correctly completes three-column and four-column addition problems with no prompting or instruction is exhibiting low-road transfer. Another example is a student who learns how to tune up car engines in an auto shop class and then almost effortlessly and automatically carries out the same task as an employee of an auto repair business. As you may have suspected, low-road transfer is basically a contemporary version of Thorndike and Woodworth's identical elements theory (Cox, 1997).

Low-road transfer: previously learned skill automatically applied to similar current task

Two conditions need to be present for low-road transfer to occur:

1. Students have to be given ample opportunities to practice using the target skill.
2. Practice has to occur with different materials and in different settings. The more varied the practice is, the greater is the range of tasks to which the skill can be applied.

If, for example, you want students to be good note takers, give them instruction and ample practice at taking notes from their biology, health, and English textbooks. Once they become accomplished note takers in these subjects, they will likely apply this skill to other subjects in an almost automatic fashion. The auto mechanic who has learned to change the spark plugs in a Chrysler, a Toyota, and a Mercedes-Benz should be able to do the same job as efficiently in a Ford, a Buick, or a Nissan.

In essence, what we are describing is the behavioral principle of generalization. Because the transfer task is similar in one or more respects to the practice task, this type of transfer is also called *near transfer.* To understand how people transfer prior knowledge and skills to new situations that look rather different from the original task, we will need to explore the nature of high-road transfer.

High-road transfer: formulate rule from one task and apply to related task

High-Road Transfer High-road **transfer** involves the conscious, controlled, somewhat effortful formulation of an "abstraction" (that is, a rule, a schema, a strategy, or an analogy) that allows a connection to be made between two tasks. For example, an individual who learns to set aside a certain number of hours every day to complete homework assignments and study for upcoming exams formulates the principle that the most efficient way to accomplish a task is to break it down into small pieces and work at each piece according to a set schedule. As an adult, the individual uses this principle to deal successfully with complex tasks at work and at home.

As another example, imagine a student who, after much observation and thought, has finally developed a good sense of what school is and how one is supposed to behave there. This student has developed a school schema. Such a schema would probably be made up of actors (teachers and students), objects (desks, chalkboards, books, pencils), and events (reading, listening, writing, talking, drawing). Because this is an idealized abstraction, actual classrooms may contain fewer or greater numbers of these characteristics in varying proportions. Even so, with this schema, a student could walk into any instructional setting (another school classroom, a training seminar, or a press briefing, for example) and readily understand what was going on, why it was going on, and how one should behave. Of course, with repeated applications of schemata, rules, strategies, and the like, the behaviors become less conscious and more automatic. What was once a reflection of high-road transfer becomes low-road transfer.

Gavriel Salomon and David Perkins (1989) refer to this deliberate, conscious, effortful formulating of a general principle or schema that can be applied to a variety of different-looking but fundamentally similar tasks as *mindful abstraction.* The *mindful* part of the phrase indicates that the abstraction must be thought about and fully understood for high-road transfer to occur. That is, people must be aware of what they are doing and why they are doing it. This is essentially training in metacognition. Recall our earlier discussion in this chapter of inert knowledge and Richard Feynman's observations of how his classmates at the Massachusetts Institute of Technology failed to recognize the application of a previously learned mathematical formula because it was initially learned for use only in that course.

Teaching for Low-Road and High-Road Transfer As we noted at the beginning of this section, transfer of previously learned knowledge and skill to new tasks and settings is a goal that is high on almost every teacher's list. Yet one study of classroom activity found that only 7 percent of tasks required students to use information they had learned previously (Bennett, Desforges, Cockburn, & Wilkinson, 1984). Perhaps most teachers feel they simply don't know how to teach for transfer. That need not be your fate. The following guidelines should produce greater levels of both low-road and high-road transfer:

Low-road and high-road transfer produced by varied practice at applying skills, rules, memory retrieval cues

1. Provide students with multiple opportunities for varied practice to help them develop a rich web of interrelated concepts.
2. Give students opportunities to solve problems that are similar to those they will eventually have to solve.
3. Teach students how to formulate for a variety of tasks general rules, strategies, or schemes that they can use in the future with a variety of similar problems.
4. Give students cues that will allow them to retrieve from memory earlier-learned information that can be used to make current learning easier.

5. Teach students to focus on the beneficial effects of creating and using rules and strategies to solve particular kinds of problems (Anderson, Reder, & Simon, 1996; Cox, 1997; Halpern, 1998; Salomon & Perkins, 1989).

If there is one thing we hope you have learned from this discussion of transfer of learning, it is this: *if you want transfer, teach for transfer.* As you can see, students have to be carefully prepared and coached to use the information and skills they learn in school. If you expect transfer, whether low road or high road, to occur on its own, you will be disappointed most of the time.

Technology Tools for Knowledge Construction and Problem Solving

Previously in the book, we noted that one way in which computers are used in schools is as learning and problem-solving tools. This use of computer-based technology supports a constructivist approach to learning and is often called learning *with* computers (Jonassen, 2000). Students learn with computers when computers support knowledge construction, exploration, learning by doing, learning by conversing, and learning by reflecting.

Technology tools are available to help students construct knowledge, become better problem solvers

David Jonassen (2000) uses the term *mindtools* to refer to computer applications that lend themselves to these types of activities. Mindtools include databases, semantic networks (concept mapping programs), spreadsheets, expert systems (artificial intelligence), microworlds, search engines, visualization tools, hypermedia, and computer conferencing. Rather than using computer programs just to present and represent information, which is what drill and tutorial programs do, mindtools allow learners to construct, share, and revise knowledge in more open-ended environments. In effect, learners become producers, designers, and "authors of knowledge" (Lehrer, 1993). In the sections that follow, we briefly examine applications of computer-based technology that support the constructivist view of learning.

HyperAuthor

Richard Lehrer (1993) has developed an interesting tool for knowledge construction called HyperAuthor. The rationale for HyperAuthor is based partly on John Dewey's progressive education idea to have students develop and design rather than receive knowledge (Lehrer, Erickson, & Connell, 1994). In HyperAuthor, there are tools for students to construct hypermedia design projects, such as web pages and other presentations. Students can create and label their links, draw pictures, design graphs or animations, and generate text. Lehrer (1993) points out that, as with the composing process, a hypermedia design project fosters the problem-solving skills of planning, finding and selecting information, organizing and representing that information, and, finally, evaluating and revising the design. In effect, students using HyperAuthor are constantly making decisions about what is important information, how to segment it, and how to organize and link it.

In one study (Lehrer, 1993), eighth-grade students used HyperAuthor to design hypermedia presentations during a six-week unit on the Civil War. Rather than attending a traditional class and relying on textbooks, HyperAuthor students designed their own electronic information about the Civil War. One result was that many students selected somewhat unusual topics, such as women or photographers of the Civil War, instead of the more traditional famous generals and battles. Another positive outcome was that enthusiasm for the project was so high that students were requesting access to the computers during study hall, after school, and on weekends. By the end of the project, these students had developed an elaborate and deep understanding of the Civil War and came to view history as more of an interpretation than a collection of facts. Tests a year later indicated that these gains had been maintained compared to students taught in a traditional fashion.

In a follow-up study, ninth-grade students used HyperAuthor to design American history presentations. Once again, Lehrer et al. (1994) observed high student interest, task focus, planning, and concerted mental effort. The result was innovative and complex hypermedia documents about various aspects of American history. Long-term studies of HyperAuthor have revealed that, over time, students develop the ability to create and link hypermedia documents in ways that are useful for such other audiences as classmates, friends, and parents (Erickson & Lehrer, 1998).

Computer-Supported Intentional Learning Environments

Marlene Scardamalia and Carl Bereiter (1996, p. 10) ask us to "imagine a network of networks—people from schools, universities, cultural institutions, service organizations, businesses—simultaneously building knowledge within their primary groups while advancing the knowledge of others. We might call such a community network a knowledge-building society." Since the 1980s, these researchers have developed and tested aspects of such a network with the Computer-Supported Intentional Learning Environments (CSILE) project (Scardamali & Bereiter, 1991).

The CSILE project is built around the concept of intentional learning (Scardamalia, Bereiter, McLean, Swallow, & Woodruff, 1989). In an intentional learning environment, students learn how to set goals, generate and interrelate new ideas, link new knowledge to old, negotiate meaning with peers, and relate what they learned to other tasks. The product of these activities, like the product of any scientific inquiry, is then made available to other students.

The CSILE project allows students to create informational links, or "notes," in several ways (for example, text notes, drawings, graphs, pictures, timelines, and maps). CSILE also contains designated "cooperation" icons that encourage students to reflect on how their work links to others, as well as idea browsing and linking tools for marking notes that involve or intend cooperation. Using this database system, students comment on the work of others, read responses to their hypotheses, or search for information posted by their peers under a particular topic title. For instance, a search for the word *whales* would call up all the work of students who assigned that word as a keyword in their CSILE contributions. In such a decentralized, free-flowing environment, no longer must the teacher initiate all discussion and coordinate turn taking (Scardamalia & Bereiter, 1991, 1996).

Studies show that students who use CSILE perform better on standardized language and reading tests, ask deeper questions, are more elaborate and coherent in their commentaries, demonstrate more mature beliefs about learning, and engage in discussions that are more committed to scientific progress (Scardamalia & Bereiter, 1996). The availability of a cooperation icon seems to foster greater peer commenting and cooperative efforts (Scardamalia & Bereiter, 1991), and students who make more conceptual progress with CSILE tend to be more problem- than fact-oriented (Oshima, Scardamalia, & Bereiter, 1996).

A new version of CSILE for the Web, called Knowledge Forum 3, is now available. The goal of Knowledge Forum is to have students mimic the collaborative knowledge-building process that characterizes the work of expert learners. Consequently, students must label their contribution to a communal database topic prior to posting it by using such labels as *My Theory, I Need to Understand, New Information, This Theory Cannot Explain, A Much Better Theory,* and *Putting Our Knowledge Together.* So, if in the course of helping to build a knowledge base about human vision, a student wrote, "I need to understand why we have two eyes instead of one or three," another member of this community could post a New Information note that discussed the relationship between binocular vision and depth perception. The resulting knowledge base would then be subject to modifications and additions from others. Like the CoVis project mentioned next, the Web version of CSILE also encourages experts, parents, and community members to participate in the project. As such, it moves students from writing individual notes to jointly writing ideas to shared problems using discussion notes. You can obtain more information about Knowledge Forum 3 at **www.learn.motion.com/lim/kf/KF0.html.**

To explore CSILE and other technology projects, go to **http://education.college.hmco.com/students** and check the Technology Project Example Web Links in the Technology Demos section.

Learning Through Collaborative Visualization

As indicated in previous chapters, the emergence of computer networks has fostered global scientific data collection and sharing. Now, less skilled young learners can be apprenticed into fields like meteorology and environmental science through social interaction with experts and peers in a learning community. Many science projects illustrate how to embed learning in real-world contexts by having students collect such data as rainfall, wind speed, and environmental pollutants, and share findings with peers. Such projects exemplify both the situated learning and social constructivist ideas outlined earlier in this chapter.

One such project was called Learning Through Collaborative Visualization (CoVis). One of the primary goals of CoVis was to foster project-based science learning, or "collaboratories" (Edelson, Pea, & Gomez, 1996, p. 158), which use computer networks so that students can access practicing environmental scientists and scientific tools. The belief was that science is learned through participation and "learning-in-doing," not through preparation by someone else. The project included e-mail, news group discussions, listservs (Internet sites where individuals exchange information and ask questions about a specific topic), remote screen sharing, and communication with peers and scientists using both video and audio conferencing. Students' collaborative investigations might include such topics as weather forecasting, ozone depletion trends, global warming, and severe storms. Unlike conventional instruction, CoVis used computer visualization tools to represent real-time data (for example, temperature as color, wind as vectors, and atmospheric pressure as contours).

CoVis researchers also developed the Collaboratory Notebook, which served as the key vehicle for students from different high schools to engage in scientific inquiries. Using this tool, students noted their questions, plans, and hypotheses regarding their investigation. And as with the CSILE projects, CoVis students labeled their individual contributions to the inquiry (for example, *Information, Commentary, Question, Conjecture, Evidence for, Evidence against, Plan,* and *Step in the Plan*).

From 1992 to 1998, the CoVis project involved over one hundred teachers and three thousand students in innovative telecommunications projects meant to enhance science education. Research on CoVis revealed mixed success with the telecommunications tools, as some were easier and more practical to use than others (Gomez, Fishman, & Pea, 1998). This research also indicated that teachers need assistance in developing assessment devices for student work, and students may need some help adapting to this new type of learning environment. Case studies also found dramatic differences in adaptation and inventive use of CoVis between low- and high-socioeconomic schools (Shrader, Lento, Gomez, & Pea, 1997).

Although the CoVis program ended in 1998, its web site (**www.covis.nwu.edu/**) serves as an archive for CoVis materials. Research ideas spawned by CoVis are now being conducted by the Center for Learning Technologies in Urban Schools (**www.letus.org/**). You can download a visualization program called WorldWatcher from the web site of the WorldWatcher Project (**www.worldwatcher.nwu.edu/**), which grew out of CoVis.

E-mail Exchange Programs

Even without participating in programs like CSILE and CoVis, students in two or more classrooms that are hundreds or thousands of miles apart, and who may reflect different cultures, can use e-mail and web sites to work collaboratively on projects that are arranged by the students' teachers. In some cases, an exchange service (for instance, Apple Computer's Global Education Network or the International Education and Resource Network) arranges for communication between students and scientists who are doing research in the field.

These electronic exchange programs are expected to improve the quality of students' writing for at least three reasons:

1. The prospect of having to communicate effectively to an authentic distant audience should motivate students to write more naturally. Writing for the teacher, it is argued, leads to more formal and stilted prose because the teacher's primary role is to evaluate the quality of the students' writing.
2. The relatively quick responses that are characteristic of e-mail exchanges will provide timely feedback about how clear, informative, and persuasive one has been.
3. Students will experience a smoother flow of ideas as they write because they will be less concerned with detecting and correcting errors than if they write only for the teacher's eyes.

As persuasive as these hypotheses may be, there simply hasn't been enough research yet to know if they are true. We don't know, for example, if students pay less attention to the mechanics of writing (such as spelling and punctuation) and write less clearly because no one is formally evaluating their writing, whether some students benefit from electronic exchange projects but others do not, how much and what type of assistance teachers should provide, and at what age such projects are likely to be beneficial to students (Fabos & Young, 1999).

Jasper Woodbury and Anchored Instruction

Another project that attempts to foster constructivist principles while overcoming the inert knowledge problem mentioned already in the chapter comes from a group of researchers at Vanderbilt University called the Cognition and Technology Group at Vanderbilt (CTGV). For more than a decade, CTGV researchers have devised and tested an interesting set of instructional materials that incorporate constructivist principles based on ideas of anchored instruction. **Anchored instruction** involves creating tasks that situate and focus student learning in interesting real-world contexts with many subproblems or issues (for example, making a business plan for the dunking booth at a school's fun fair; Barron et al., 1995). Anchoring problems in a larger context helps students gain a meaningful understanding of the problems and perceive both critical aspects of problems and different points of view (CTGV, 1990).

The Adventures of Jasper Woodbury is a videodisk-based series designed to promote mathematical problem solving, reasoning, and effective communication among middle school students using anchored instruction. There are three stories for each of four topics (complex trip planning, statistics and business plans, geometry, and algebra) in the series. Each story is a fifteen- to twenty-minute adventure that involves Jasper Woodbury and other characters. At the end of each story, the characters are faced with a problem that students must solve before they are allowed to see how the characters in the video solved the problem. The basic design principles of such an approach are the video-based presentation, generative learning format, relevant and irrelevant data embedded within the problems, sufficient problem complexity, analogous problems to promote transfer and generalization, links across the curriculum to multiple content areas, and episodes designed to be consistent with the learning standards recommended by the National Council of Teachers of Mathematics (CTGV, 1993). The ability to replay video scenes on demand is also important.

In the course of solving the problem posed in the video, students become involved in activities such as generating subgoals, identifying relevant information, cooperating with others, discussing the advantages and disadvantages of possible solutions, and comparing perspectives (CTGV, 1992a, 1992b). Information about the twelve adventures, the theory behind the Jasper series, research findings, and how the video disks can be ordered can be found on the Jasper Woodbury web site (**www.peabody.vanderbilt.edu/projects/funded/jasper/**).

Despite the complexity of these problems and the fact that Jasper students received less direct basic math instruction than control students, they performed quite well on standardized tests. On tests of basic math concepts such as units of time or distance, area, decimals, and fractions, both groups improved at the same rate. However, Jasper students scored significantly higher than the control students on word problems, tests of planning, and attitudes toward math, and they better appreciated complex challenges (CTGV, 1992a, 1992b). It has also been shown that the beneficial effects of the Jasper experience can be increased by exposing students to related material and experiences prior to their working on the problems. Before students in a sixth-grade class watched the "Rescue at Boone's Meadow" story (about an attempt to rescue an injured eagle from a remote area), two members of the local Audubon Society brought a wounded bald eagle to class and discussed the habitat, way of life, and locations of eagles. This was followed by two days of related activities on eagles. In comparison to a group of sixth graders who engaged in an unrelated activity for those three days, the students in the experimental group recalled more information from the story and were more likely to consider alternative rescue options (Arthurs, DeFranco, & Young, 1999). Despite these positive findings, students do not always formulate effective solutions to problems. The most frequent error students made in solving Jasper problems is overlooking such important solution elements as expenses, amount of time needed to carry out the plan, and the degree of risk incurred by the plan. If you use the Jasper series, you should be prepared to model for students how to analyze such complex problems and formulate an appropriate solution plan (Vye, Goldman, Voss, Hmelo, Williams, & Cognition and Technology Group at Vanderbilt, 1997).

The CTGV researchers have extended their anchored instruction research to create a videodisk-based Scientists in Action series meant to help students experience and better understand actual science work (Sherwood, Petrosino, Lin, and Cognition and Technology Group at Vanderbilt, 1998). This series differs from the Jasper Woodbury series in several ways:

- Challenges are posed at several points during the course of the story rather than at the end. When the video resumes, students can compare their solutions to what the scientists on the video actually did.
- While some of the information needed to solve the problem is presented in the video, much of it is available in ancillary materials (such as topographic maps and actual data from experiments on water quality) that the characters in the video refer to.
- There are links to other curriculum areas, especially social issues related to science.
- The stories are designed so that the hypothesis most students are expected to generate will be wrong (such as the source of river pollution). The video then provides additional data that allows students to revise their original hypothesis. This procedure is used to mimic more closely the way science is done in the real world.

For more information on the four episodes that make up this series, visit the Scientists in Action web site (**peabody.vanderbilt.edu/projects/funded/sia/**).

A third project by this group, the Little Planet Literacy Series, is a multimedia program that also uses anchored instruction to support children's decoding, writing, and recording of their own books (Secules, Cottom, Bray, & Miller, 1997); additional information about the Little Planet series is available at **www.littleplanetliteracy.com/**.

Use the Web Sources at **http://education.college.hmco.com/students** for convenient links to web sites mentioned in this section.

Constructivist-Oriented Web Sites

Dozens of web sites provide constructivist-oriented inquiry and problem-solving activities for students of all ages. In this section, we briefly describe four of them to give you an idea of what is available.

National Geographic offers an Xpeditions web site (**www.nationalgeographic.com/xpeditions/**) that has numerous resources and activities to help students learn about geographic concepts and issues. In "A Reason for the Season," students are given basic information about the rotation of the earth around the sun, the tilt in the earth's axis, the summer and winter solstices, and the autumnal and vernal equinoxes, and they are then challenged to figure out why the seasons change. The site includes teacher-tested lesson plans sorted by geography standard and grade level.

ThinkQuest (**www.thinkquest.org/**) is an international academic competition for students aged twelve to nineteen (there is a ThinkQuest Junior for younger students). Students work in teams to research a topic in science, mathematics, literature, the social sciences, or the arts, and publish their findings as a web site that teachers and students around the world can use.

Educational Web Adventures (**www.eduweb.com/adventures.html**) offers adventures that deal with the topics of art and art history, science and nature, and history and geography. For example, the game "Loyalty or Liberty?" is designed to help students in grades five and up understand some of the issues surrounding the American Revolution. Students gather secrets for both Loyalists and Patriots in revolutionary Virginia, and then decide where their loyalties lie.

The TryScience web site (**http://tryscience.org/**) contains content contributed by science centers and museums from around the world. It allows students to take virtual field trips (with video camera clips and accompanying narration), have an outer space adventure, or conduct experiments (either online or at home).

For help in reviewing this chapter, see the Thought Questions and ACE Self-Testing sections on this book's web site **http://education.college.hmco.com/students**.

KEY TERMS

discovery learning *(302)*
cognitive constructivism *(304)*
social constructivism *(304)*
situated learning *(306)*
situated learning *(308)*
inert knowledge *(307)*
problem solving *(315)*
well-structured problems *(315)*
ill-structured problems *(316)*
issues *(316)*
problem representation, problem framing *(317)*
heuristics *(319)*
transfer of learning *(326)*
theory of identical elements *(327)*
positive transfer *(327)*
negative transfer *(327)*
zero transfer *(327)*
specific transfer *(328)*
general transfer *(328)*
low-road transfer *(328)*
high-road transfer *(329)*
anchored instruction *(333)*

DISCUSSION QUESTIONS

1. According to constructivist theory, meaningful learning occurs when students are encouraged to think about how the basic ideas of a subject relate to one another and to what students already know, when learning is set in realistic contexts, and when students can work together to figure out the meaning of ideas. Can you recall a class in which the instructor made use of constructivist techniques? What did the instructor do? How did you react? Was the learning outcome more meaningful than for other classes? How could you tell? How might you use constructivist-oriented teaching techniques?

2. Critics of American education argue that contemporary students are poor problem solvers because they receive little systematic instruction in problem-solving processes. How would you rate the quantity and quality of the instruction you received in problem solving? In terms of the five steps discussed in this chapter, which ones were you taught? What can you do to ensure that your students become good problem solvers?

3. Educational psychologists who have studied transfer have said to teachers that if they want transfer, they should teach for transfer. What do you think this statement means? Go to the Adventures of Jasper Woodbury web site at **peabody.vanderbilt.edu/projects/funded/jasper/** and read the summaries of the adventures for any of the four subject areas. Are these materials likely to produce transfer? Why?

Approaches to Instruction

10

This chapter is concerned with helping you answer two questions: What are my objectives? (or, What do I want students to know and be able to do after I complete a unit of instruction?) and How can I help students achieve those objectives? The ordering of these two questions is not arbitrary. Instructional planning should always begin with a description of what you want students to know and be able to do some weeks, or even months, after the beginning of an instructional unit.

To appreciate why, suppose that you follow the common practice of many teachers and prepare lesson plans by examining texts and other curriculum materials in order to devise an instructional sequence. Probably your first inclination is to concentrate on what is going to happen tomorrow and to put off thinking about what is going to happen

Key Points

These key points will help you learn the important information in this chapter. To help you study, they also appear in the margins of the pages, next to the text where they are discussed.

Devising and Using Objectives

- Goals are broad, general statements of desired educational outcomes
- Instructional objectives specify observable, measurable student behaviors
- Taxonomy: categories arranged in hierarchical order
- Cognitive taxonomy: knowledge, comprehension, application, analysis, synthesis, evaluation
- Taxonomy of affective objectives stresses attitudes and values
- Psychomotor taxonomy outlines steps that lead to skilled performance
- Most test questions stress knowledge, ignore higher levels of cognitive taxonomy
- Mager: state specific objectives that identify act, define conditions, state criteria
- Gronlund: state general objectives, list sample of specific learning outcomes
- Objectives work best when students are aware of them

The Behavioral Approach to Teaching: Direct Instruction

- Direct instruction: focus on learning basic skills, teacher makes all decisions, keep students on task, emphasize positive reinforcement
- Direct instruction involves structured, guided, and independent practice
- Direct instruction helps students learn basic skills

The Cognitive Approach to Teaching: Facilitating Meaningful and Self-Directed Learning

- Information-processing approach: design lessons around principles of meaningful learning, teach students how to learn more effectively
- Tell students what you want them to learn, why, and how they will be tested
- Present organized and meaningful lessons
- Present new information in small chunks
- Constructivist approach: students discover how to be autonomous, self-directed learners
- Meaningful learning aided by exposure to multiple points of view
- Technology supports a cognitive approach to instruction by helping students code, store, and retrieve information

The Humanistic Approach to Teaching: Student-Centered Instruction

- Maslow: help students develop their potential by satisfying their needs
- Rogers: establish conditions that allow self-directed learning
- Humanistic approach addresses needs, values, motives, self-perceptions
- Japanese classrooms marked by humanistic orientation, high scores on international math and science test

The Social Approach to Teaching: Teaching Students How to Learn from Each Other

- Competitive reward structures may decrease motivation to learn
- Cooperative learning characterized by heterogeneous groups, positive interdependence, promotive interaction, individual accountability
- Cooperative learning effects likely due to stimulation of motivation, cognitive development, meaningful learning
- Students in mixed ability groups outperform students in homogeneous groups on problem-solving tests
- Successful technology applications are embedded in an active social environment

two weeks or a month ahead when the time comes to evaluate what students have learned. You might reason that there is no point in thinking about tests until it is time to prepare tests. Quite a few teachers operate in such a one-thing-at-a-time way, and you are probably familiar with the results: disorganized lessons, lectures, and assignments, followed by exams that may not have much to do with what you think you were supposed to have learned.

You can avoid falling into that common trap by concentrating at the very beginning on what you want your students to be able to do at the end of a unit of study. If you decide in advance what you want your students to achieve, you can prepare lessons that logically lead to a particular result and also use evaluation techniques efficiently designed to determine what level of achievement has occurred.

Once you have a clear idea of what you are trying to accomplish with your students, you can consider how you are going to help get them there. Here is where you can use your knowledge of learning and motivation. After all, if the goal of teaching is to help students acquire and use a variety of knowledge and skills, what better way to do that than to use approaches and techniques that are consistent with what is known about how people learn and the conditions under which they learn best?

The theories that underlie the approaches to instruction described in this chapter emphasize different aspects of the learning process, and each has been supported by research. Thus, no one theory is sufficiently comprehensive and powerful that you can rely exclusively on it as a guide for designing classroom instruction. To work effectively with the diversity of students you will almost certainly encounter, you will need to use a variety of instructional approaches and techniques. For some objectives and students, you may want to use a highly structured approach that is consistent with the principles of behavioral and social learning theories. For other objectives, you may want to focus on helping students develop more effective learning and problem-solving skills. You may also want students to work productively in groups and respond to you and to learning in positive ways and develop positive feelings about themselves as students. And you will probably also want to integrate computer-based technology with one or more of these approaches.

In the next section, we will introduce you to the concept of instructional objectives. We will distinguish between goals and objectives, describe organizational schemes called taxonomies that help you decide what you want your students to learn, and describe methods for preparing and using objectives. ■

Devising and Using Objectives

CONTRASTING OBJECTIVES WITH EDUCATIONAL GOALS

One way to help you understand the nature of instructional objectives is to contrast them with something with which they are often confused: educational goals. Goals are relatively broad statements of what political and educational leaders would like to see schools accomplish. Perhaps the best-known set of educational goals were those in the U.S. government's Goals 2000 program. Signed into law in 1994, Goals 2000 listed eight goals that the government hoped to achieve by the year 2000. (The current status of the Goals 2000 program is described on a web site maintained by the U.S. Department of Education. It can be found at **www.ed.gov/G2K/**.) Although a few of the goals were stated in measurable terms ("At least 90 percent of all students will graduate from high school"), others were much vaguer in their wording, such as these:

Goals are broad, general statements of desired educational outcomes

To preview this chapter's central concepts, see the Chapter Themes on the Snowman textbook site at **http://education.college.hmco.com/students**.

- Students will acquire the thinking skills that will allow them to become responsible citizens, independent learners, and productive workers.
- All adults will be sufficiently literate, knowledgeable, and skilled to compete in a global economy and behave as responsible citizens.

Unfortunately, statements of this sort do not provide very useful guidelines for teachers charged with the responsibility for achieving the goals. What exactly is meant by "thinking skills" or being "sufficiently literate, knowledgeable, and skilled"? And will these terms mean the same thing to every teacher? Thinking skills, for example, could be interpreted to mean everything from memorization to problem solving.

Instructional objectives specify observable, measurable student behaviors

Instructional objectives, in contrast to these broad educational goals, specify the kinds of observable and measurable student behaviors that make it possible for the underlying goals to be achieved. To give teachers both a common vocabulary and a system for writing different kinds of objectives, psychologists have created organizational schemes called taxonomies.

Taxonomies of Objectives

Awareness of the vagueness of educational goals stimulated a group of psychologists who specialized in testing to seek a better way to describe educational objectives. After experimenting with various ways to prepare lists of objectives that would be more useful to teachers than vaguely worded sets of goals, the test specialists decided to develop taxonomies of educational objectives.

Taxonomy: categories arranged in hierarchical order

A **taxonomy** is a classification scheme with categories arranged in hierarchical order. Because goals of education are extremely diverse, the decision was made to prepare taxonomies in three areas, or *domains:* cognitive, affective, and psychomotor. The taxonomy for the **cognitive domain** stresses knowledge and intellectual skills; the taxonomy for the **affective domain** concentrates on attitudes and values; and that for the **psychomotor domain** focuses on physical abilities and skills.

Taxonomy for the Cognitive Domain The taxonomy for the cognitive domain was prepared by Benjamin S. Bloom, Max D. Englehart, Edward J. Furst, Walker H. Hill, and David R. Krathwohl (1956). It consists of six hierarchically ordered levels of instructional outcomes: knowledge, comprehension, application, analysis, synthesis, and evaluation. The taxonomy is described as a hierarchy because it was reasoned that comprehension relies on prior mastery of knowledge or facts, application depends on comprehension of relevant ideas, and so on through the remaining levels. An abridged outline of the taxonomy for the cognitive domain follows:

Cognitive taxonomy: knowledge, comprehension, application, analysis, synthesis, evaluation

Taxonomy of Educational Objectives: Cognitive Domain

1.00 *Knowledge.* Remembering previously learned information, such as facts, terms, procedures, and principles.

2.00 *Comprehension.* Grasping the meaning of information by putting it into one's own words, drawing conclusions, or stating implications.

3.00 *Application.* Applying knowledge to actual situations as in taking principles learned in math and applying them to laying out a baseball diamond or applying principles of civil liberties to current events.

4.00 *Analysis.* Breaking down objects or ideas into simpler parts and seeing how the parts relate and are organized. For example, discussing how the public and the private sectors differ or detecting logical fallacies in an argument.

The taxonomy of objectives for the cognitive domain calls attention to the fact that instructional outcomes can range from such basic capabilities as verbatim recall and comprehension to such higher-level capabilities as application of knowledge and skill, analysis of complex ideas into their component parts, synthesis of different ideas into an integrated whole, and evaluation of the quality of ideas.

5.00 *Synthesis.* Rearranging component ideas into a new whole. For example, planning a panel discussion or writing a comprehensive term paper.

6.00 *Evaluation.* Making judgments based on internal evidence or external criteria. For example, evaluating a work of art, editing a term paper, or detecting inconsistencies in the speech of a politician.

Taxonomy for the Affective Domain In addition to arranging instructional experiences to help students achieve cognitive objectives, virtually all teachers are interested in encouraging the development of attitudes and values. To clarify the nature of such objectives, a taxonomy for the affective domain was prepared (Krathwohl, Bloom, & Masia, 1964). Affective objectives are more difficult to define, evaluate, or encourage than cognitive objectives because they are often demonstrated in subtle or indirect ways. Furthermore, certain aspects of value development are sometimes considered to be more the responsibility of parents than of teachers. Finally, because values and attitudes involve a significant element of personal choice, they are often expressed more clearly out of school than in the classroom. The complete taxonomy for the affective domain stresses out-of-school values as much as, if not more than, in-school values.

Taxonomy of affective objectives stresses attitudes and values

The following abridgment concentrates on the kinds of affective objectives you are most likely to be concerned with as a teacher. You will probably recognize, though, that there is not much you can do to influence substantially the kinds of objectives described in the higher levels of the taxonomy because they represent a crystallization of values formed by experiences over an extended period of time.

Taxonomy of Educational Objectives: Affective Domain

1.0 *Receiving (attending).* Willingness to receive or attend.

2.0 *Responding.* Active participation indicating positive response or acceptance of an idea or policy.

3.0 *Valuing.* Expressing a belief or attitude about the value or worth of something.

4.0 *Organization.* Organizing various values into an internalized system.
5.0 *Characterization by a value or value complex.* The value system becomes a way of life.

Taxonomy for the Psychomotor Domain Cognitive and affective objectives are important at all grade levels, but so are psychomotor objectives. Regardless of the grade level or subject you teach, at some point you are likely to want to help your students acquire physical skills of various kinds. In the primary grades, for example, you will want your students to learn how to print legibly. And in many subjects in middle school and high school, psychomotor skills (for example, driving a car, playing a violin, adjusting a microscope, manipulating a computer keyboard, operating a power saw, throwing a pot) may be essential. Recognition of the importance of physical skills prompted Elizabeth Simpson (1972) to prepare a taxonomy for the psychomotor domain. An abridged version of the taxonomy follows:

Taxonomy of Educational Objectives: Psychomotor Domain

Psychomotor taxonomy outlines steps that lead to skilled performance

1.0 *Perception.* Using sense organs to obtain cues needed to guide motor activity.
2.0 *Set.* Being ready to perform a particular action.
3.0 *Guided response.* Performing under the guidance of a model.
4.0 *Mechanism.* Being able to perform a task habitually with some degree of confidence and proficiency. For example, demonstrating the ability to get the first serve in the service area 70 percent of the time.
5.0 *Complex or overt response.* Performing a task with a high degree of proficiency and skill. For example, typing all kinds of business letters and forms quickly with no errors.
6.0 *Adaptation.* Using previously learned skills to perform new but related tasks. For example, using skills developed while using a word processor to do desktop publishing.
7.0 *Origination.* Creating new performances after having developed skills. For example, creating a new form of modern dance.

Why Use Taxonomies? Using these taxonomies will help you avoid two common instructional failings: ignoring entire classes of outcomes (usually affective and psychomotor) and overemphasizing the lowest level of the cognitive domain. According to Benjamin S. Bloom, organizer and driving force of the team that prepared the first taxonomy,

Most test questions stress knowledge, ignore higher levels of cognitive taxonomy

> After the sale of over one million copies of the *Taxonomy of Educational Objectives—Cognitive Domain* [Bloom et al., 1956] and over a quarter of a century of use of this domain in preservice and in-service teacher training, it is estimated that over 90% of test questions that U.S. public school students are *now* expected to answer deal with little more than information. Our instructional material, our classroom teaching methods, and our testing methods rarely rise above the lowest category of the Taxonomy—knowledge. (1984, p. 13)

The next section describes how you can write and profitably use objectives.

Ways to State and Use Objectives

Many psychologists have offered suggestions for writing and using objectives, but the following discussion is limited to recommendations made by two of the most influential writers on the subject: Robert F. Mager and Norman E. Gronlund.

Mager's Recommendations for Use of Specific Objectives With the publication of a provocative and unorthodox little treatise titled *Preparing Instructional Objectives* (1962, 1997), Mager sparked considerable interest in the use of objectives. Mager emphasizes the importance of objectives by pointing out that

> if you don't know where you're going, the best-made maps won't help you get there. . . . Without a way to communicate your instructional objectives to others:
>
> - You wouldn't be able to decide which instructional content and procedures would help you to accomplish your objectives.
> - You wouldn't be able to create measuring instruments (tests) that tell you whether your students had become competent enough to move on.
> - And your students wouldn't be able to decide for themselves when to stop practicing. (1997, p. vi)

Mager then offers these suggestions for writing **specific objectives** of instruction:

Mager: state specific objectives that identify act, define conditions, state criteria

1. Describe what you want learners to be doing when demonstrating achievement, and indicate how you will know they are doing it.
2. In your description, identify and name the behavioral act that indicates achievement, define the conditions under which the behavior is to occur, and state the criterion of acceptable performance.
3. Write a separate objective for each learning performance.

Here are some examples of the types of objectives Mager recommends:

Correctly solve at least seven addition problems consisting of three two-digit numbers within a period of three minutes.

Correctly answer at least four of the five questions on the last page of story booklet 16 in the Reading Comprehension series of booklets.

Given pictures of ten trees, correctly identify at least eight as either deciduous or evergreen.

Mager recommends that teachers use objectives that identify the behavioral act that indicates achievement, define conditions under which the behavior is to occur, and state the criterion of acceptable performance.

Correctly spell at least 90 percent of the words on the list handed out last week.
Given a computer and word processing program, set it up to type a business letter (according to the specifications provided) within two minutes.

Note that the criterion of acceptable performance can be stated as a time limit, a minimum number of correct responses, or a proportion of correct responses.

Mager's proposals were widely endorsed immediately after the publication of *Preparing Instructional Objectives*, but in time it became apparent that the very specific kinds of objectives he recommended were most useful in situations where students were asked to acquire knowledge of factual information or to learn simple skills. Norman E. Gronlund concluded that a different type of objective was more appropriate for more complex and advanced kinds of learning.

Gronlund's Recommendations for Use of General Objectives Gronlund (2000) has developed a two-step procedure for writing a more general type of objective:

1. Examine what is to be learned with reference to lists of objectives such as those included in the three taxonomies. Use such lists to formulate **general objectives** of instruction that describe types of behavior students should exhibit in order to demonstrate what they have learned.
2. Under each general instructional objective, list up to five *specific learning outcomes* that begin with an *action verb* and indicate specific, observable responses. These sets of specific learning outcomes should provide a representative sample of what students should be able to do when they have achieved the general objective.

Gronlund: state general objectives, list sample of specific learning outcomes

If you were teaching an educational psychology course and you wanted to write a Gronlund-type objective that reflected an understanding of the four stages of Piaget's theory of cognitive development, it might look like this:

1. The student will understand the characteristics of Piaget's four stages of cognitive development.
   - 1.1 Describe in his or her own words the type of thinking in which students at each stage can and cannot engage.
   - 1.2 Predict behaviors of students of different ages.
   - 1.3 Explain why certain teaching techniques would or would not be successful with students of different ages.

If you wanted to cover the same outcome with a list of Mager-type objectives, it might look like this:

1. Given a list of the names of each of Piaget's four stages of cognitive development, the student, within twenty minutes, will describe in his or her own words two problems that students at each stage should and should not be able to solve.
2. Given a videotape of kindergarten students presented with a conservation-of-volume problem, the student will predict the response of 90 percent of the students.
3. Given a videotape of fifth-grade students presented with a class inclusion problem, the student will predict the response of 90 percent of the students.
4. Given eight descriptions of instructional lessons, two at each of Piaget's four stages, the student will be able to explain in each case why the lesson would or would not succeed.

Gronlund gives several reasons for beginning with general objectives. First, most learning activities are too complex to be described in terms of a specific objective for every learning outcome, as Mager proposed. Second, the kind of specific objective Mager advocated may tend to cause instructors and students to concentrate on memorizing facts and mastering simple skills. As indicated earlier, these types of behaviors are at the lowest levels of the taxonomies of objectives. Third, specific objectives can restrict the flexibility of the teacher. Gronlund's objectives allow performance criteria to be kept separate from the objective so a teacher can revise performance standards as needed without having to rewrite the objective. This feature is useful if the same behavior is to be evaluated several times over the course of a unit of instruction, with successively higher levels of performance required. A fourth and final reason is that general objectives help keep you aware that the main target of your instructional efforts is the general outcome (such as comprehension, application, or analysis).

Need guidance in preparing lesson plans? Go to Class Applications on this book's site at **http://education.college.hmco.com/students**.

To illustrate the differences between general objectives and specific outcomes, Gronlund has prepared lists of phrases and verbs that can be used in writing each type of objective for each of the levels of all three taxonomies of educational objectives. These lists can be found in Appendix B of Gronlund's *How to Write and Use Instructional Objectives* (2000) and in Appendix G of Linn and Gronlund's *Measurement and Assessment in Teaching* (2000).

Aligning Assessment with Objectives and Instruction

Deciding in advance what you want your students to achieve by drawing from the various levels of the taxonomies and formulating instructional methods to help them master those objectives will be a largely wasted effort if you fail to recognize that the tests you create must also fit those objectives and methods.

As we discuss in the chapter on assessment, there are several types of classroom assessment methods, each of which is most useful for measuring only *certain* outcomes. Multiple-choice, short-answer, and true-false tests are useful for measuring mastery of basic factual knowledge. For objectives that emphasize the comprehension, analysis, and synthesis levels of Bloom's Taxonomy, essay questions that call for students to summarize, compare, and contrast would be more useful. For objectives that reflect a constructivist orientation, paper-and-pencil tests are likely to be much less useful than requiring students to solve a complex problem, create a product over an extended period of time, or work productively with a small group of peers on a project. (This type of testing, called performance assessment, is discussed in the chapters on assessment and testing.)

Here's a small example of how things can go wrong if you don't align your tests with both your objectives and your instructional methods. If you tell students that you want them to organize information into logical structures, integrate ideas into broad themes, and make connections with knowledge learned elsewhere, and then teach them how to think along those lines but load your tests with short-answer and multiple-choice items that require rote memorization, don't be surprised when students simply memorize facts. From their perspective, the content and level of the test items are the real objectives.

One final comment about alignment. In the first paragraph, we referred to the tests you *create* rather than the tests you *use*. These two terms imply a subtle but important distinction. The best way to ensure alignment of objectives, teaching approach, and assessment is for you to be the creator of the assessment. If you use a test that somebody else has designed, such as a standardized test, it is almost a certainty that some of the items will not match your objectives or instructional approach.

Evaluations of the Effectiveness of Objectives

Do students learn more when their teachers provide them with clearly written objectives? The answer is yes, but only under certain conditions. Reviews of research on the effectiveness of objectives (for example, Faw & Waller, 1976; Klauer, 1984; Melton, 1978) lead to the following conclusions:

Objectives work best when students are aware of them

1. Objectives seem to work best when students are aware of them, treat them as directions to learn specific sections of material, and feel they will aid learning.
2. Objectives seem to work best when they are clearly written and the learning task is neither too difficult nor too easy.
3. Students of average ability seem to profit more from being given objectives than do students of higher or lower ability.
4. Objectives lead to an improvement in intentional learning (what is stressed as important) but to a decline in incidental learning (not emphasized by the teacher). General objectives of the type that Gronlund recommended seem to lead to more incidental learning than do specific objectives of the type that Mager recommended.

As we mentioned at the beginning of the chapter, once you have decided what it is you want your students to learn, you need to decide which approaches you will use to help them achieve those objectives. Our use of the term *approaches* is deliberate. To repeat what we said at the beginning of the chapter, different approaches to instruction are based on different theories of learning and motivation, and given the complexity of the learning process and the diversity of learners in most classrooms, no one theory can be used for all instructional purposes and for all students. So as you read through the next several sections, try to imagine how you might use each approach over the course of a school year.

The Behavioral Approach to Teaching: Direct Instruction

For behavioral psychologists, learning means acquiring new behaviors, and new behaviors are learned because of the role that external stimuli play. Thus, a behavioral approach to teaching involves arranging and implementing those conditions that make it highly likely that a desired response will occur in the presence of a particular stimulus (such as reading a sentence fluently, accurately using the correct mathematical operations when faced with a long-division problem, and giving the correct English translation to a paragraph written in Spanish). Perhaps the most popular approach to teaching that is based on behavioral theory is direct instruction (although the label *explicit teaching* is sometimes used).

The Nature of Direct Instruction

The underlying philosophy of **direct instruction** is that if the student has not learned, the teacher has not effectively taught. This approach calls for the teacher to keep students consistently engaged in learning basic skills and knowledge through the design of effective lessons, corrective feedback, and opportunities for practice.

It is most frequently used in the teaching of basic skills (for example, reading, mathematical computation, writing) and subject matter (for example, science, social studies, foreign language vocabulary) in the primary and elementary grades but is also used to teach remedial classes at the middle school and high school levels. It is felt to be most useful for young learners, slow learners, and all learners when the material is new and difficult to grasp at first. Although there are several variations of direct instruction, the following represents a synthesis of descriptions offered by George Adams and Sigfried Engelmann (1996), Bruce Joyce and Marsha Weil (2000), Barak Rosenshine (1987), and Barak Rosenshine and Carla Meister (1994b).

The main characteristics of direct instruction include:

1. Focusing almost all classroom activity on learning basic academic knowledge and skills. Affective and social objectives, such as improved self-esteem and learning to get along with others, are either deemphasized or ignored.
2. Having the teacher make all instructional decisions, such as how much material will be covered at one time, whether students work individually or in groups, and whether students work on mathematics during the morning and social studies during the afternoon.
3. Keeping students working productively toward learning new academic knowledge and skills (usually called being on task) as much as possible.
4. Maintaining a positive classroom climate by emphasizing positive reinforcement and avoiding the use of aversive consequences.

Direct instruction: focus on learning basic skills, teacher makes all decisions, keep students on task, emphasize positive reinforcement

The goal of direct instruction is to have students master basic skills because students who mislearn information require substantially more time and effort to relearn concepts than would have been the case had they learned them correctly in the first place.

For obvious reasons, direct instruction is a highly structured approach to teaching and is often referred to as *teacher-directed* or *teacher-led instruction*.

The Components of Direct Instruction

Bruce Joyce and Marsha Weil (2000) identify five general components, or phases, that make up direct instruction: orientation, presentation, structured practice,

Teachers who subscribe to direct instruction emphasize efficient learning of basic skills through the use of structured lessons, positive reinforcement, and extensive practice.

Journal Entry
Using a Direct Instruction Approach

guided practice, and independent practice. These components are not derived just from theory. They reflect the techniques that effective teachers at all grade levels have been observed to use.

Orientation During the orientation phase, the teacher provides an overview of the lesson, explains why students need to learn the upcoming material, relates the new subject either to material learned during earlier lessons or to their life experience, tells students what they will need to do to learn the material, and tells students what level of performance they will be expected to exhibit.

Presentation The presentation phase initially involves explaining, illustrating, and demonstrating the new material. As with all other forms of instruction based on operant conditioning, the lesson is broken down into small, easy-to-learn steps to ensure mastery of each step in the lesson sequence. Numerous examples of new concepts and skills are provided, and, consistent with social learning theory, the teacher demonstrates the kind of response students should strive for (such as a particular pronunciation of foreign vocabulary, a reading of a poem or story, the steps in mathematical operations, or how to analyze a novel for theme, character, or setting). To assist comprehension, and where appropriate, material can be presented pictorially (for example, slides, videotapes, videodisks, on computer) or graphically (as a concept map, or a timeline, or in table form). At the first sign of difficulty, the teacher gives additional explanations.

The last step of the presentation phase is to evaluate students' understanding. This is typically done through a question-and-answer session in which the questions call for specific answers as well as explanations of how students formulated their answers. Some sort of system is used to ensure that all students receive an equal opportunity to respond to questions. Throughout the lesson, efforts are made to stay on task and avoid nonproductive digressions.

Structured, Guided, and Independent Practice The last three phases of the direct instruction model all focus on practice, although with successively lower levels of assistance. Joyce and Weil (2000) refer to these three phases as *structured practice, guided practice,* and *independent practice.* Because the level of teacher assistance is gradually withdrawn, you may recognize this progression as an attempt to apply the behavioral principle of shaping. You may also recognize it as the constructivist principle of scaffolding.

Direct instruction involves structured, guided, and independent practice

Structured practice involves the greatest degree of teacher assistance. The teacher leads the entire class through each step in a problem or lesson so as to minimize incorrect responses. Visual displays, such as overhead transparencies, are commonly used during structured practice as a way to illustrate and help students recall the components of a lesson. As the students respond, the teacher reinforces correct responses and corrects errors.

During guided practice, students work at their own desks on problems of the type explained and demonstrated by the teacher. The teacher circulates among the students, checking for and correcting any errors.

When students can correctly solve at least 85 percent of the problems given to them during guided practice, they are deemed ready for independent practice. At this point, students are encouraged to practice on their own either in class or at home. Although the teacher continues to assess the accuracy of the students' work and provide feedback, it is done on a more delayed basis.

Getting the Most Out of Practice

Joyce and Weil (2000) offer the following suggestions to help make practice effective:

1. Shape student learning by systematically moving students from structured practice to guided practice to independent practice.
2. Schedule several relatively short but intense practice sessions, which typically produces more learning than fewer but longer sessions. For primary grade students, several five- to ten-minute sessions scattered over the day are likely to produce better results than the one or two thirty- to forty-minute sessions that middle school or high school students can tolerate.
3. Carefully monitor the accuracy of students' responses during structured practice to reinforce correct responses and correct unacceptable responses. The reason for this suggestion comes straight out of operant conditioning research. As you may recall from the chapter on behavioral learning theory, Skinner found that new behaviors are learned most rapidly when correct responses are immediately reinforced and incorrect responses are eliminated. When a learner makes incorrect responses that are not corrected, they become part of the learner's behavioral repertoire and impede the progress of subsequent learning.
4. To ensure the high degree of success that results in mastery of basic skills, students should not engage in independent practice until they can respond correctly to at least 85 percent of the examples presented to them during structured and guided practice.
5. Practice sessions for any lesson should be spread over several months. The habit of some teachers of not reviewing a topic once that part of the curriculum has been covered usually leads to a lower quality of learning. Once again, distributed practice produces better learning than massed practice.
6. Space practice sessions close together during structured practice but further and further apart for guided practice and independent practice.

Effectiveness of Direct Instruction

George Adams and Sigfried Engelmann (1996) conducted a review of thirty-seven studies of direct instruction and reported strong effects. On average, direct instruction students scored at the eighty-first percentile on an end-of-unit exam, whereas their conventionally taught peers scored at the fiftieth percentile. Positive effects for direct instruction have also been found for teaching reading comprehension and writing strategies to students with learning disabilities (Gleason, 1995), for teaching phonemic awareness skills (the ability to identify letter sounds, blends, and sequences of letters in words) to young children (Spector, 1995), for producing high levels of on-task behavior and low levels of disruptive behavior among third graders with behavior disorders (Nelson, 1996), and for increasing standardized achievement test scores among ethnic and racial minority second-grade students (Brent & DiObilda, 1993).

Direct instruction helps students learn basic skills

Using Technology to Support Behavioral Approaches to Instruction

The computer-based approach to instruction that uses behavioral learning principles emphasizes specific performance objectives, breaking learning down into small steps, shaping student success, using immediate feedback and consistent rewards, and predefining assessment techniques. Learning is viewed much like an industrial assembly line: information is transferred efficiently from a computer program to a waiting student.

Most of the drill-and-practice computer-assisted instruction tools and integrated learning systems mentioned in the chapter on behavioral learning theory fit within this framework (Van Dusen & Worthen, 1995), as would multimedia technology if used simply to embellish a lecture with new pictures or sounds. Although this approach to the use of technology in instruction may be perceived as rote, boring, and dehumanizing, it can prove valuable if you are interested in accurate and efficient learning of basic facts and skills.

The Cognitive Approach to Teaching: Facilitating Meaningful and Self-Directed Learning

The focus of cognitive learning theories is the mind and how it works. Hence, cognitive psychologists are primarily interested in studying those mental processes that expand our knowledge base and allow us to understand and respond to the world differently. In this section, we will lay out two approaches to instruction that are based on different forms of cognitive theory: information processing and constructivism. The information-processing approach to teaching involves implementing those conditions that help students effectively transfer information from the "outside" (a text or lecture, for example) to the "inside" (the mind), while the constructivist approach focuses on providing students opportunities to create their own meaningful view of reality.

The Nature and Elements of an Information-Processing Approach

As we noted previously in the book, information-processing theory focuses on how human beings interpret and mentally manipulate the information they encounter. In most instances, we attend to some things (or parts of things) and not others, we mentally change the form and organizational properties of information, we integrate information into existing bodies of knowledge, we retrieve certain aspects of stored information, and we use that information to solve a variety of everyday problems. The research evidence that has been generated over the past forty to forty-five years in this field supports the following view of learning:

1. Information moves through a series of mental storehouses that vary in the way in which information is stored and for how long.
2. Learning occurs gradually because of limits on how much information we can attend to and think about at any point in time.
3. What we know strongly influences what we learn.
4. We can exert a great deal of control over the cognitive processes that result in learning.

In sum, for information to be meaningfully learned, it must be attended to, its critical features must be noticed, and it must be coded in an organized and meaningful way so as to make its retrieval more likely (Corno, 1986; Marx & Winne, 1987; Pressley, Woloshyn, & Associates, 1995).

The approach to teaching that flows from information-processing theory has two main parts. First, design lessons and gear teaching behaviors to capitalize on what is known about the learning process. As you will see, this part of the information-processing approach has much in common with the behavioral approach that we just covered. Both approaches direct you to structure the classroom environment in a certain way (and to use some of the same tactics) to improve the effectiveness and efficiency of learning. Second—and this is what makes the information-processing approach unique—make students aware of how they learn and how they can use those processes to improve their classroom performance. Following are several suggestions for helping students become more effective processors of classroom instruction.

Information-processing approach: design lessons around principles of meaningful learning, teach students how to learn more effectively

Communicate Clear Goals In previous chapters, we pointed out that motivation for learning is highest when students can relate new information to what they already know and to out-of-school experiences. The ability to make these links is what makes learning in general, and school learning in particular, meaningful. The first question that students ask themselves when they take a new course, encounter a new topic, or are asked to learn a new skill is, "Why do I have to learn this?"

Journal Entry
Using an Information-Processing Approach to Instruction

Unfortunately, many teachers seem unaware of the need to explain clearly to students the immediate and larger purposes of learning most of a school's curriculum. Seymour Sarason (1993), who has written extensively and persuasively about the problems of education (including teacher education) and the need for reform, notes that "although that kind of question occurs to every child, I have never heard a student ask that question out loud, just as I have never observed a teacher address the issue" (p. 224). But some teachers do recognize the value of communicating clear goals. Margaret Metzger (1996), a veteran high school teacher, notes that teachers have to convince students that what they learn in school is important and relevant to their lives outside school, both now and in the future.

At the beginning of each lesson, tell students what you want them to accomplish, why you think it's important that they learn this knowledge or skill, and how you are going to assess their learning. If you intend to use paper-and-pencil tests, tell them what content areas will be covered, what kinds of questions you will include (in terms of the levels of Bloom's Taxonomy), and how many of each type of question will be on the test. Without this information, students will be unable to formulate a rational approach to learning and studying since they will be forced to guess about these features. They may, for example, take your general directive to "learn this material for the test" as a cue to memorize, when you expected them to be able to explain ideas in their own words. If you intend to use performance measures, tell students the conditions under which they will have to perform and what criteria you will use to judge their performance.

Tell students what you want them to learn, why, and how they will be tested

Use Attention-Getting Devices Information-processing theory holds that material not attended to is not processed, and material that is not processed is not stored in memory. Consequently, you should use (but not overuse) a variety of attention-getting devices. The suggestion we just made to explain the purpose of a lesson, what students will be held accountable for learning, and how student learning will be assessed will likely capture the attention of some students. But once you are into a lesson, you may need to gain and maintain students' attention repeatedly.

One implication of the information processing approach to instruction is to use attention-getting devices since information not attended to will not be learned.

The Suggestions for Teaching in Your Classroom in the chapter on information-processing theory mentioned a few devices for capturing students' attention. Here are several more:

- Orally emphasize certain words or phrases by raising or lowering your voice.
- Use dramatic gestures.
- Underline key words and phrases that you write on a chalkboard or whiteboard.
- When discussing the work of important people, whether in science, math, social studies, or history, dress up to look like the person and speak as you think the person might have spoken.

Present organized and meaningful lessons

Emphasize Organization and Meaningfulness Research studies have repeatedly found that students learn and recall more information when it is presented in an organized format and a meaningful context. Information is organized when the components that make it up are linked together in some rational way. If you teach high school physics, you can organize material according to major theories or basic principles or key discoveries, depending on your purpose. For history, you can identify main ideas and their supporting details or describe events as a chain of causes and effects. Just about any form of organization would be better than having students memorize names, dates, places, and other facts as isolated fragments of information.

A popular method for organizing and spatially representing the relationships among a set of ideas is *concept mapping*. This technique involves specifying the ideas that make up a topic and indicating with lines how they relate to one another.

Figure 10.1 Two Concept Maps Constructed from Identical Concepts

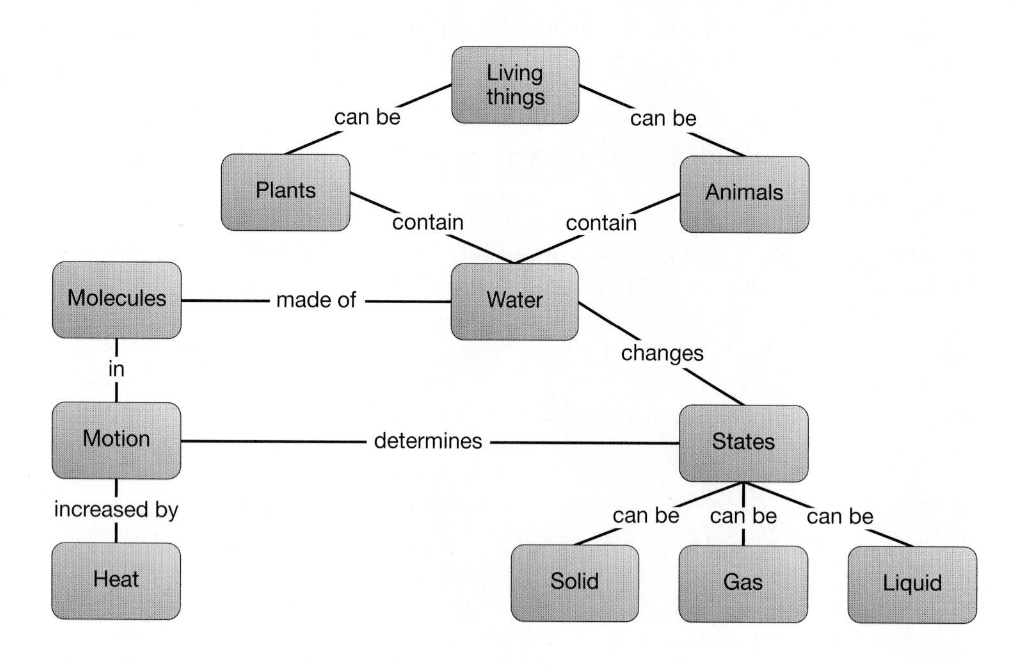

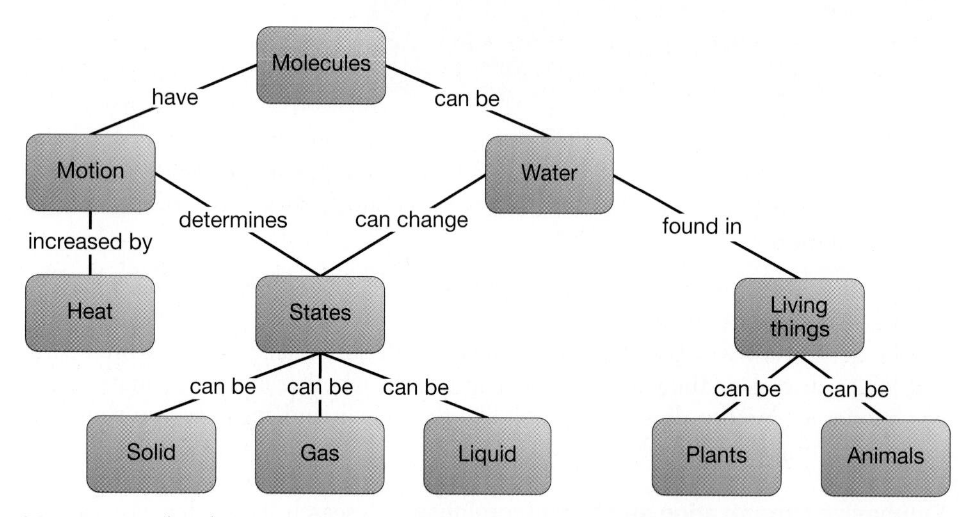

SOURCE: Novak and Gowin (1984).

Figure 10.1 is a particularly interesting example of both organized knowledge and a constructivist view of learning. (We will take a further look at this latter angle when we discuss constructivist approaches.)

As we pointed out in the chapter on information-processing theory, meaningful learning results in richer and more stable memory representations and occurs more readily when information can be related to familiar ideas and experiences. Several techniques are known to facilitate meaningful learning:

- Using some form of overview or introduction that provides a meaningful context for new material
- Using concrete examples and analogies to illustrate otherwise abstract ideas
- Using visually based methods of representing information, such as maps, graphs, three-dimensional models, and illustrations
- Stressing practical applications and relationships to other subjects (you may recall from a previous chapter that this tactic is used to help adolescent girls remain interested in science)

Present Information in Learnable Amounts and over Realistic Time Periods When students struggle to master the information they are expected to learn, the problem sometimes arises simply from an excess of information being presented to them at once—that is, from too great an external demand. At other times, the student's working (short-term) memory is strained because of the nature of the task itself: for instance, if the task has several components that all have to be monitored. By taking the nature of the task into consideration, you can judge how much information to expect your students to learn in a given time.

For tasks where a set of discrete elements must be learned in a one-at-a-time fashion, such as learning foreign language vocabulary or the symbols of chemical elements, the demand on working memory and comprehension is low because the elements are independent. Learning the meaning of one word or symbol has no effect on learning any of the others. As long as the external load on working memory is kept reasonable by limiting the number of words or symbols that students have to learn at any time, learning problems should be minimal.

Other tasks make greater demands on working memory because their elements interact. Learning to produce and recognize grammatically correct utterances ("The cat climbed up the tree" versus "Tree the climbed cat up the") is a task that places a higher demand on working memory because the meaning of all the words must be considered simultaneously in order to determine if the sentence makes sense. For such tasks, keeping the amount of information that students are required to learn at a low level is critically important because it leaves the student with sufficient working memory to engage in schema construction (Sweller, van Merrienboer, & Paas, 1998).

Present new information in small chunks

One instructional recommendation that flows from this analysis is the same as one of the recommendations for direct instruction: break lessons into small, manageable parts and don't introduce new topics until you have evidence that students have learned the presented material. A second recommendation is to build into lessons opportunities for students to write about, discuss, and use the ideas they are learning. By monitoring the accuracy of their responses, you will also have the information you need to judge whether it is time to introduce new ideas. Finally, arrange for relatively short practice sessions spread over several weeks rather than one or two long practice sessions because distributed practice leads to better learning than massed practice.

Facilitate Encoding of Information into Long-Term Memory High-quality learning rarely occurs when students adopt a relatively passive orientation. As we pointed out in the chapter on information-processing theory, many students do little more than read assigned material and record ideas in verbatim form. They spend little time thinking about how ideas within topics and between topics relate to one another or to concepts they have already learned. One reason is that many students simply do not know what else to do with information. Another reason is that teachers do little to support the kind of encoding that results in more meaningful forms of learning. Recall the study we mentioned that found that primary grade through middle school teachers provided students with suggestions for processing information less than 10 percent of the time and explanations for the suggestions they did give less than 1 percent of the time. To help your students encode information for more effective storage in and retrieval from long-term memory, incorporate the following techniques into your classroom instruction:

- Present information through such different media as pictures, videotape, audiotape, live models, and manipulation of physical objects.
- Use lots of examples and analogies (to foster elaboration).
- Prompt students to elaborate by asking them to put ideas in their own words, relate new ideas to personal experience, and create their own analogies.

Practice What You Preach As we pointed out in discussing social learning theory, a great deal of learning takes place by observing and imitating a model. Because teachers are generally perceived by students as being competent, in a high-status occupation, and having power, their behaviors are likely to be noticed and imitated. This is especially true when the behaviors that teachers model are important to a student's classroom success. If you are convinced that how students process information plays a major role in how well they learn that information, then you should clearly and explicitly demonstrate how to analyze a task, formulate a learning plan, use a variety of learning tactics (such as mnemonics, summarizing, self-questioning, note taking, concept mapping), monitor the effectiveness of those tactics, and make changes when the results are unsatisfactory.

THE NATURE AND ELEMENTS OF A CONSTRUCTIVIST APPROACH

In previous chapters, we noted that the essence of constructivist theory is that people learn best by creating their own understanding of reality. Using such characteristics as existing knowledge, attitudes, values, and experiences as filters, people interpret current experience in a way that seems to make sense to them at the time. As Figure 10.1 demonstrates, by constructing two different concept maps from an identical set of concepts, knowledge can be organized in any number of ways, and the scheme one creates will reflect one's purpose or focal point. Thus, some students understand that the Jane Austen novel *Sense and Sensibility* is as much a satire of the paternalistic class system of 1800s England as it is a love story, while other students see it only as a love story, and a boring one at that. The goal of constructivist-oriented teaching, then, is to provide a set of conditions that will lead students to construct a view of reality that both makes sense to them and addresses the essence of your objectives.

A brief description of four of the more prominent elements that help define a constructivist-oriented classroom follows. Although two of these elements reflect a social constructivist orientation, bear in mind that the goal of both cognitive and social constructivism is the same: to help students become more effective thinkers and problem solvers by helping them construct richer and more meaningful schemes. A social constructivist orientation simply gives greater weight to the role of social interaction in this process.

Provide Scaffolded Instruction Within the Zone of Proximal Development To review quickly what we said previously in the book, the zone of proximal develop-

Journal Entry
Using a Constructivist Approach to Instruction

ment is the difference between what a learner can accomplish without assistance and what can be accomplished with assistance. As an example, consider the case of a youngster who has been given her first bicycle. Because the child has no experience with balancing herself on a two-wheeled bike, her parents know she will fall quite a few times before learning how to balance, steer, and pedal at the same time. To avoid injury and loss of motivation, one parent holds the bike upright and helps the child steer in a straight line while she figures out how to monitor her balance and make the necessary adjustments. This is done initially at very low speeds with the parent firmly holding the frame of the bike. Gradually, the child is allowed to pedal faster and the parent loosens his grip on the bike. Eventually, the parent does little more than run alongside the bike, and then he withdraws altogether.

This common example illustrates two related points about teaching from a constructivist (particularly a social constructivist) perspective: instruction should demand more than what a student is capable of doing independently and, because of these demands, instruction should be scaffolded. That is, teachers should provide just enough support, through such devices as explanations, modeling, prompting, offering clarifications, and verifying the accuracy of responses, that the learner can successfully complete the task. As students indicate that they have begun to internalize the basic ideas and procedures of the lesson, the scaffolding is gradually withdrawn (Roehler & Cantlon, 1997).

Constructivist approach: students discover how to be autonomous, self-directed learners

Provide Opportunities for Learning by Discovery By its very nature, constructivism implies the need to let students discover things for themselves. But what things? According to Jerome Bruner, whose pioneering work we mentioned in the chapter on constructivist learning theory, the process of discovery should be reserved for those outcomes that allow learners to be autonomous and self-directed. These include understanding how ideas connect with one another, knowing how to analyze and frame problems, asking appropriate questions, recognizing when what we already know is relevant to what we are trying to learn, and evaluating the effectiveness of our strategies. The case we cited in the previous chapter of the first-grade teacher who wanted her students to understand the importance of using a standardized measuring instrument is a good example of how these outcomes can be learned by guided discovery.

Meaningful learning aided by exposure to multiple points of view

Foster Multiple Viewpoints Given the basic constructivist premise that all meaningful learning is constructed and that everyone uses a slightly different set of filters with which to build his or her view of reality, what we refer to as knowledge is actually a consensus of slightly different points of view. Thus, another element of a constructivist approach to teaching is to help students understand that different views of the same phenomena exist and that they can often be reconciled to produce a broader understanding.

In the chapter on constructivism, we described how classroom discussions can be used for this purpose. Computer-based technology, such as e-mail, as well as regular mail, can be used to increase both the number and the diversity of individuals with whom students can interact. In one elementary classroom, students from a small town in Indiana exchanged stories, letters, and photographs with a similar classroom of students from Northern Ireland. This exchange awakened students to differences between them that ranged from the trivial (dates are written differently in Europe) to the significant (differences in car ownership by families and the constant presence of army patrols carrying loaded weapons) (Duffy & Cunningham, 1996).

The technique of cooperative learning is another way to expose students to peers who may have different views about the "right" way to do something or the "truth" of some matter and help them forge a broader understanding that is acceptable to all members of the group. Consider, for example, a group of college students who, as part of a science methods course, were asked to figure out how to generate electricity for a home using windmills, with the condition that batteries could not be used. Some members of the group were stumped because they couldn't figure out how to supply the house with a constant supply of electricity in the absence of a battery (which is just a particular type of energy-storage device). Their inability to solve this problem was due to their narrow conception of an energy storage device—the kinds of batteries that are used to power such things as toys, flashlights, and cars. But other members of the group maintained that the function of a battery could be performed by any device that stored energy, such as a spring or a tank of hot water, thereby helping the rest of the group to see a different and broader truth (Brooks & Brooks, 1999b). In the last major section of this chapter, we describe cooperative learning in considerable detail.

How do teachers apply constructivist principles in the classroom? For real-life examples, see the Site-Based Cases section at **http://education.college.hmco.com/students**.

Emphasize Relevant Problems and Tasks Can you recall completing a class assignment or reading a chapter out of a textbook that had no apparent relevance to anything that concerned you? Not very interesting or exciting, was it? Unfortunately, too many students perceive too much of schooling in that light. One constructivist remedy is to create interest and relevance by posing problems or assigning tasks that are both challenging and realistic. A basic purpose for emphasizing problems and tasks that are relevant to the lives of students is to overcome the problem of inert knowledge, mentioned in our chapter on constructivism. Constructivists believe that the best way to prepare students to function effectively in real-life contexts is to embed tasks in contexts that come as close as possible to those of real life (Duffy & Cunningham, 1996).

Problems can be challenging either because the correct answer is not immediately apparent or because there is no correct answer. The ill-structured problems and issues that we described previously are, by their nature, challenging and realistic and do not have solutions that everyone perceives as being appropriate and useful. But if you assign students an ill-structured task to investigate, pose it in such a way that they will see its relevance. For example, instead of asking high school students to debate the general pros and cons of laws that restrict personal freedoms, have them interview their community's mayor, chief of police, business owners, and peers about the pros and cons of laws that specify curfews for individuals under a certain age and that prohibit such activities as loitering and the purchase of alcohol and tobacco. Because many adolescents consider themselves mature enough to regulate their own behavior, analyzing and debating laws that are intended to restrict certain adolescent behaviors is likely to produce a fair amount of disequilibrium.

The technology section that follows presents some additional ideas for embedding learning in realistic settings.

USING TECHNOLOGY TO SUPPORT COGNITIVE APPROACHES TO INSTRUCTION

As educators begin to understand and address cognitive learning theories, the focus of computer technology is shifting from remediating learner skill deficiencies and rehearsing basic skills to finding ways to help the learner build, extend, and amplify new knowledge (Pea, 1985).

Technology supports a cognitive approach to instruction by helping students code, store, and retrieve information

Helping Students Process Information An information-processing approach to instruction uses technology to minimize the cognitive demands of a task; help learners form schemas, or patterns, of information; extend or augment thinking in new directions; and supply information overviews and memory cues (Kozma, 1987). The programs for outlining and note taking mentioned in the chapter on information-processing theory are consistent with this approach, as are electronic encyclopedias (for example, Grolier's Multimedia Encyclopedia) and hypermedia databases that contain conceptual resources like timelines, information maps, and overviews. Concept mapping software like Inspiration helps students organize their knowledge and ideas.

Intelligent Tutoring Systems The cognitive approach has been taken a step further by **intelligent tutoring systems,** computer tools that provide individualized guidance by comparing the problem-solving history of the user with models of expert performance. Ken Koedinger and John Anderson (1993), for instance, have developed the Geometry Tutor to help students understand the process of solving geometry problems. This program can help students visually represent the problem, generate goal statements, and search through the problem for the "given" information. Instead of simply providing feedback about whether an answer or step is "right" or "wrong," these tools build up elaborate cognitive models of the user that map out his or her problem-solving decisions and compare the decisions to those of experts (Cognition and Technology Group at Vanderbilt, 1996). Such information is used to determine the learner's level of conceptual development and make decisions about the timing, content, and order of hints that the system provides to help the student solve the problem.

Intelligent tutoring systems have been created for a college-level course on solid state electronics (Callear, 1999), a multimedia simulation in which students construct a playground within space and budget constraints (Johnson & O'Neill-Jones, 1999), helping students reflect on what aspects of a hypermedia environment they explore and why (Kashihara, Uji'i, & Toyoda, 1999), and helping students solve algebra problems assigned for homework (Lee & Heyworth, 2000). Although the concept of intelligent tutors is an interesting one, the benefits of such systems have not been as strong as expected, possibly because they make few provisions for collaboration among students (Siemer-Matravers, 1999). As we point out later in the chapter, students who work together on computer-based projects engage in more task-related conversation than do students who work on other types of activities.

Discovery and Exploratory Environments Computers are not just tools to transmit or represent information for the learner; they also provide environments that allow for discoveries and insights. In such an **exploratory environment,** students might explore exciting information resources on the Web (see the Case in Print about online expeditions), enter simulations or microworlds like LEGO-LOGO, browse and rotate objects in a hypermedia or Web database, and use imaging technologies to explore inaccessible places (for example, underwater canyons or planet surfaces; Woolsey & Bellamy, 1997). For instance, the Geometric Supposer, mentioned in a previous chapter, is an exploratory tool that students can use to construct, manipulate, and measure different geometric figures and relationships. Such simulated environments, or microworlds, allow students the chance to explore relationships among variables or concepts and build personal models of how things work.

Microcomputer-based laboratory (MBL) equipment, also mentioned previously, allows students to make predictions, test hypotheses, and interpret the results. MBLs and other devices that create exploratory environments enable students to try out many potential solution paths and problem-solving strategies without fear of being wrong, while learning how to solve problems. There are now, for example, exploratory modeling programs for learning key principles of economics, solving difficult physics problems, exploring the behavior of ant colonies, and analyzing molecular models of proteins and DNA (Alessi & Pena, 1999; Barowy & Laserna, 1997; Doerr, 1996.)

Guided Learning Although students can use modeling programs and simulations to plan experiments, take measurements, analyze data, and graph findings, there is still a need for teacher scaffolding and guidance in support of the learning process (de Jong & van Joolingen, 1998). In fact, most educational experts emphasize teacher-guided approaches when using technology (Toomey & Ketterer, 1995). In these **guided learning** environments, teachers might help students set goals, ask questions, encourage discussions, and provide models of problem-solving processes. In technology environments for social studies, for instance, Lee Ehman and his colleagues found that the teachers who were most successful at fostering problem solving provided a sense of structure, or metacognitive guidance, for their students (Ehman, Glenn, Johnson, & White, 1992). Such teachers provided a clear road map of the unit at the beginning, clear expectations and sequencing of activities, continued reinforcement and guidance, teacher modeling, opportunities for students to practice problem-solving steps, reflection on learning, and regular checking and sharing of student progress. (Note how this approach combines elements of the behavioral and information-processing approaches.)

One guided learning environment, the Higher Order Thinking Skills program (HOTS), focuses on higher-order thinking skills among at-risk youth in grades 4 through 8 (Pogrow, 1990, 1999). HOTS was designed around active learning, Socratic questioning, and reflection activities in using computers. Instead of the rote computer-based drills that these students would normally receive, they are prompted to reflect on their decision-making process while using computer tools. Teachers do not give away the answers but instead draw out key concepts by questioning students or telling them to go back and read the information on the computer screen. The developer of HOTS, Stanley Pogrow, calls this "controlled floundering," or leading students into frustration so that they have to reflect on the information on the screen to solve a problem. In effect, the learning dialogues and conversations between the teacher and student are the keys to learning here, not student use of the computer, since small-group discussion allows students to compare strategies and reflect on those that work.

Pogrow (1999) reports that students in the HOTS program record year-to-year gains that are twice those of the national average on standardized tests of reading and math and three times those of control groups on tests of reading comprehension. Approximately 15 percent of HOTS students make the honor roll of their school. Gains in self-concept, as well as in thinking skills, have also been reported (Eisenman & Payne, 1997). Additional information on the HOTS program can be found at **www.hots.org/**.

For direct links to the HOTS site and others mentioned in this chapter, go to the Web Sources section of this book's web site at **http://education.college.hmco.com/students**.

Problem- and Project-Based Learning Another way to implement constructivist trends in education is to use technology for problem-based learning (PBL), an instructional method that requires learners to develop solutions to real-life problems (Cognition and Technology Group at Vanderbilt, 1996). When using PBL with technology, students can plan and organize their own research while working collaboratively with others. In contrast to case-based learning, which is often used to test student knowledge after presenting information, PBL is used to help students

Technology can be used to support a learner-centered, problem-based approach to learning in which students create knowledge by designing and carrying out experiments and projects.

learn the material by developing their own positions on the material rather than hearing about someone else's position.

Although PBL has its roots in medical and business school settings, the emergence of technologies for student exploration and knowledge construction has made this approach feasible with K–12 populations. John Savery and Thomas Duffy (1996) point to eight constructivist principles that can guide those interested in using PBL: (1) anchoring learning in larger tasks or problems, (2) supporting the learner in developing ownership of the overall problem or task, (3) designing authentic tasks at students' developmental level, (4) providing sufficient task complexity, (5) allowing student ownership of the process used to develop a solution, (6) encouraging teacher questioning and other challenges, (7) testing ideas in a learning community, and (8) providing opportunities for reflection. Students can be given a problem (for example, What caused the flooding in the Midwest in 1993, and what should be done to prevent floods in the future?), or they can generate questions as a class or small group. In either case, the problem must be perceived as real and not simplified into a prespecified set of readings or objectives.

In addition to PBL, science educators are advocating the use of technology within project-based learning in schools. Project-based learning provides structure by giving students a project or a problem, along with project goals and deadlines. Ronald Marx, Phyllis Blumenfeld, Joseph Krajcik, and Elliot Soloway (1997) identified the following key components of project-based science:

- Driving questions (for example, instead of asking what the atmosphere of Mars is like, one should ask, "What kinds of environments could be built on Mars for humans to survive?")
- Feasible real-world investigations (for example, "Is this lake dying?")
- Tangible products (such as multimedia documents, posters, and group presentations)
- Group collaboration (for example, sharing and negotiating ideas, drawing on expertise of others, and extending the thinking of group members)

Making Learning a (Virtual) Adventure

Computers are not just tools to transmit or represent information for the learner; they also provide environments that allow for discoveries and insights. In such an exploratory environment, students might explore exciting information resources on the Web. (p. 359)

Teachers Spin a World Wide Web of Virtual Voyages

CHRISTINA PINO-MARINA
USA Today 9/29/98

For the 52.7 million students who started school this fall, an adventurous field trip could be just a mouse-click away.

Kids connected to the Internet can watch a team of AfricaQuest researchers climb Mount Kilimanjaro.

They can follow five explorers of GlobaLearn.com as they document a 4,000-mile drive across the USA. Students can research rain forests, oceans and wildlife while interacting with scientists taking part in expeditions run by The Jason Project, Scholastic and SitesALIVE!

Such on-line odysseys took shape in the early '90s and are playing an increasing role in public, private and home-school curricula across the nation.

Fourth-grade teacher Cynthia Thomas says these virtual field trips have changed her academic approach after 22 years in her profession.

"It just made me fall in love with teaching again," says Thomas, of Oak Hill Elementary in Austin, Texas. The school of 820 students has one Internet connection. Students there will focus on AfricaQuest this year. "It is so exciting for me to take these kids to different places," she says.

There are a host of educational Web sites, but teachers say that K–12 students get excited by the interactive nature of on-line expeditions.

"A textbook is two-dimensional," says Linda Hiller, a technology specialist at Long Branch Elementary School in Arlington, Va. "When you are following somebody on the Internet, you can go where they go and discover with them. It makes a powerful impact on the students." The 435 K–5 students at Hiller's school follow GlobaLearn.com.

Educational projects like those run by GlobaLearn, AfricaQuest, The Jason Project, Scholastic and SitesALIVE! will offer several social and scientific courses of study throughout the school year.

The subject matter varies on each Web site, but the projects are linked in their mission to engage and educate students through technology.

"We're providing teachers with a multimedia toolbox, not only to excite students but to help teachers become more involved in the classroom," says Tim Armour, executive director of The Jason Project, which focuses on the study of rain forests in 1998.

Kids can learn about remote places and communicate with explorers, researchers and scientists during on-line chats or satellite broadcasts. The credentials these experts bring to the on-line odysseys are part of the appeal for students.

Oceanographer Robert Ballard's location of the sunken Titanic in 1985 sparked the interest of young students before the advent of the World Wide Web and creation of The Jason Project.

AfricaQuest team leader Dan Buettner is famous for having set world records while biking across three continents. Rich Wilson, founder of SitesALIVE! producer Ocean Challenge, captivated students when he broke a 140-year-old sailing record in 1993, rounding Cape Horn in 69 days and 20 hours in a great clipper ship.

But qualifications of on-line experts aside, some critics still question the educational value of the Internet and President Clinton's goal of having the nation's classrooms wired to the information superhighway by 2000.

David Gelernter, a computer science professor at Yale University, says the Internet is a distraction that encourages children to develop short attention spans.

"We have schools that are already failing miserably," says Gelernter. "It is more important for children to learn the basics—to read, to understand math, to use the library."

Gelernter says that, while the Internet has encouraged a resurgence of written communication, teachers should steer clear of the "escape hatch into cyberspace" that will never replace the value of well-written textbooks.

A recent study by Market Data Retrieval, an independent research firm, supports Gelernter's belief that the Internet does not necessarily help students. A random survey of 6,000 teachers, librarians and computer coordinators found that 86.6% believe that Internet use by kids in grades 3–12 does not improve classroom performance.

In 1998, the Federal Communications Commission will allocate $1.275 billion for school Internet connections, a 43% cut from the proposed $2.25 billion.

Nevertheless, many teachers will continue to use educational expeditions to motivate students. "Whether we like it or not, this is a technological world," Hiller says.

At M. V. Leckie Elementary School in Washington, D.C., teacher Hilda Taylor helps her students make connections to the world of technology.

Last year's fifth grade class was introduced to the study of sea plankton through The Jason Project. Afterward, Taylor took her students on a field trip to Echo Hill, Md., where they did science projects on marsh life.

"Before seeing The Jason Project, I didn't even know there was such a thing as plankton," says 11-year-old Jamal Hansberry, who observed the tiny animals and plants in a test tube during the field trip. Jamal says he was inspired as he watched a live broadcast—which he called "better than TV."

Schoolmate Joshua Franklin, 13, agrees. "You get to ask scientists a lot of questions," he says. And unlike TV, "No one will tell you to turn it off."

Questions and Activities

1. David Gelernter, the computer science professor from Yale mentioned in the article, was highly critical of the Internet. He called it "a distraction that encourages children to develop short attention spans." Why do you think he holds this belief? Do you think his conclusion is valid?

2. Assume that Professor Gelernter's assertion is correct. Is this a fault of the technology or the way in which it is used? Why do you think so? (Before answering, you might want to read the chapter's section on guided learning.)

3. The article notes that almost 87 percent of six thousand teachers, librarians, and computer coordinators do not believe that Internet use leads to improved classroom performance. Criticisms like these are often based on observations of a few cases and anecdotal evidence offered by others (whose weaknesses we discussed early in this book). Before accepting such conclusions at face value, you should search several research literature databases (like ERIC and PsycINFO) to see what researchers have found about the effects of technology on student learning.

- The use of technology tools (to visualize dynamic relationships like cloud cover at night, collect data on a stream or lake, or publish student work on the Web)

However, Marx et al. (1997) also admit that there are concerns and problems with these projects, such as the time required for deep exploration of ideas, meeting existing curriculum standards, balancing classroom management concerns with student exploration, designing proper assessments, and a lack of teacher training on how to scaffold instruction and effectively use technology tools.

Situated Learning As you may recall from the chapter on constructivism, situated learning, or situated cognition, is the concept that knowledge is closely linked to the environment in which it is acquired. The more true to life the task is, the more meaningful the learning will be. Technology can play a key role in providing access to a wide variety of real-world learning situations (Derry & Lesgold, 1996).

For instance, computer-based instructional technology can apprentice students into real work settings by providing access to authentic data and the tools to manipulate that data. According to Sasha Barab, Ken Hay, and Thomas Duffy (1998), tools like the videos in the Jasper Woodbury project mentioned in the constructivism chapter, as well as the simulations discussed in this chapter, illustrate how technology can influence instructional practices using situated cognition. Simulations like the

Chelsea Bank simulation project (Hawley & Duffy, 1997) situate students in real-life events by placing them in certain defined roles (for example, bank teller, bank manager) and giving them problems to solve with various pieces of information (for example, bank manuals, account information, and materials submitted by the customer). With rich multimedia stories or episodes to draw on, student recall is enhanced and the chance that students will simply acquire inert knowledge is lessened.

The Humanistic Approach to Teaching: Student-Centered Instruction

The **humanistic approach** pays particular attention to the role of noncognitive variables in learning, specifically, students' needs, emotions, values, and self-perceptions. It assumes that students will be highly motivated to learn when the learning material is personally meaningful, understand the reasons for their own behavior, and believe that the classroom environment supports their efforts to learn, even when they struggle. Consequently, a humanistic approach to teaching strives to help students better understand themselves and create a supportive classroom atmosphere that activates the inherent desire all human beings have to learn and fulfill their potential (Groeben, 1994; Maslow, 1987; Rogers, 1983).

The relevance of a humanistic approach to teaching may not be immediately apparent to everyone, but it is easy to support. First, we've known for some time that learning is as much influenced by how students feel about themselves as by the cognitive skills they possess. When students conclude that the demands of a task are beyond their current level of knowledge and skill (what we referred to in a previous chapter as a low sense of self-efficacy), they are likely to experience such debilitating emotions as anxiety and fear. Once these negative self-perceptions and emotions are created, the student has to divert time and energy from the task at hand to figuring out how to deal with them. And the solutions that students formulate are not always appropriate. Some may, for instance, decide to reduce their efforts and settle for whatever passing grade they can get. Others may give up entirely by cutting class, not completing homework assignments, and not studying for tests. A considerable amount of research from the health field has shown that people are more likely to use positive methods of coping with the stress of illness and disease when they perceive their environment to be *socially supportive.* The small amount of comparable research that exists on classroom learning suggests a similar outcome (Boekarts, 1993).

Second, this approach has the implicit support of teachers and parents. High on their list of desired educational outcomes is for students to develop positive feelings about themselves and about learning and to perceive school as a place where they will be supported in their efforts to develop new knowledge and skills.

PIONEERS OF THE HUMANISTIC APPROACH

The humanistic approach to teaching was proposed during the 1960s principally by Abraham Maslow, Carl Rogers, and Arthur Combs.

Maslow: Let Children Grow Abraham Maslow's approach to the study of human behavior was unique for its time (1960s). While most of his colleagues studied the psychological processes of people who were having problems dealing with the demands and stresses of everyday life (as Sigmund Freud had done), Maslow decided that more could be learned by studying the behavior of especially well-adjusted people, whom he referred to as *self-actualizers*. Self-actualizers, be they children, adolescents, or adults, have an inherent need for experiences that will help them fulfill their potential.

In Chapter 15 of *Toward a Psychology of Being* (1968), Maslow describes forty-three basic propositions that summarize his views (a more detailed outline of Maslow's view is presented in the chapter on motivation). Some of the most significant of these propositions are as follows:

Maslow: help students develop their potential by satisfying their needs

- Each individual is born with an essential inner nature.
- This inner nature is shaped by experiences and unconscious thoughts and feelings, but it is not *dominated* by such forces. Individuals control much of their own behavior.
- Children should be allowed to make many choices about their own development.
- Parents and teachers play a significant role in preparing children to make wise choices by satisfying their physiological, safety, love, belonging, and esteem needs, but they should do this by helping and letting children grow, not by attempting to shape or control the way they grow.

Rogers: Learner-Centered Education Carl Rogers was a psychotherapist who pioneered a new approach to helping people cope more effectively with their problems. He called it *client-centered* (or *nondirective*) therapy, to stress the fact that the client, rather than the therapist, should be the central figure and that the therapist was not to tell the patient what was wrong and what should be done about it.

As he practiced this person-centered approach, Rogers came to the conclusion that he was most successful when he did not attempt to put up a false front of any kind; established a warm, positive, acceptant attitude toward his clients; and was able to sense their thoughts and feelings. Rogers concluded that these conditions set the stage for successful experiences with therapy because clients became more self-accepting and aware of themselves. Once individuals acquired these qualities, they were inclined and equipped to solve personal problems without seeking the aid of a therapist (1967).

Rogers: establish conditions that allow self-directed learning

In addition to functioning as a therapist, Rogers served as a professor. Upon analyzing his experiences as an instructor, he concluded that the person-centered approach to therapy could be applied just as successfully to teaching. He thus proposed the idea of **learner-centered education:** that teachers should try to establish the same conditions as do person-centered therapists. Rogers argues (1980) that the results of learner-centered teaching are similar to those of person-centered therapy: students become capable of educating themselves without the aid of direct instruction from teachers.

Combs: The Teacher as Facilitator Arthur Combs assumed that "all behavior of a person is the direct result of his field of perceptions at the moment of his behaving" (1965, p. 12). From this assumption, it follows that the way a person perceives herself or himself is of paramount importance and that a basic purpose of teaching is to help each student develop a positive self-concept. He observed, "The task of the teacher is not one of prescribing, making, molding, forcing, coercing, coaxing, or cajoling; it is one of ministering to a process already in being. The role required of the teacher is that of facilitator, encourager, helper, assister, colleague, and friend of his students" (1965, p. 16).

Combs elaborated on these points by listing six characteristics of good teachers: (1) they are well informed about their subject; (2) they are sensitive to the feelings of students and colleagues; (3) they believe that students can learn; (4) they have a positive self-concept; (5) they believe in helping all students do their best; and (6) they use many different methods of instruction (1965, pp. 20–23).

Taken together, the observations of Maslow, Rogers, and Combs lead to a conception of education in which teachers trust pupils enough to permit them to make many choices about their own learning. At the same time, teachers should be sensitive to the social and emotional needs of students, empathize with them, and respond positively to them. Finally, teachers should be sincere, willing to show that they too have needs and experience positive feelings about themselves and what they are doing.

Teaching from a Humanistic Orientation

Humanistic approach addresses needs, values, motives, self-perceptions

Teachers who adopt a humanistic orientation seek to create a classroom atmosphere in which students believe that the teacher's primary goal is to understand the student's needs, values, motives, and self-perceptions and to help the student learn. This atmosphere is established primarily by the teacher's expressing genuine interest in and acceptance of the student. The teacher avoids giving the impression that he or she would like the student better if only the student dressed more appropriately, had a more positive attitude toward learning, associated with a different group of peers, and so on. In this kind of setting, students will be more inclined to discuss openly their feelings about and problems with learning and related issues. The teacher is then in a position to help students figure out better approaches to their schoolwork and relationships with others. The teacher does not tell students what to do but guides them to the correct action. Because the students' perceptions and decisions are the central focus, this approach is often referred to as either *student-directed* or *nondirective* (Joyce & Weil, 2000).

To illustrate this approach, consider the case of a student who is unhappy about a poor grade on a test. The instinctive reaction of most teachers would be to explain how to study and prepare for the next test. The humanistically oriented teacher instead asks the student to describe his interest in the subject matter, how capable a learner the student feels himself to be, how well the student understands the subject, under what conditions the student studies, whether the student feels the teacher's instruction to be clear and well organized, and so on. To help students understand their feelings and the role they play in learning, the teacher may disclose some of her own feelings. For example, the teacher may tell this hypothetical student, "When I've had a bad day and feel as if I've let my students down, I sometimes question my ability as a teacher. Is that how you feel?" Once these self-perceptions have been raised and clarified, the teacher encourages the student to suggest a solution to the problem (Joyce & Weil, 2000).

The Humanistic Model

According to Bruce Joyce and Marsha Weil (2000), the nondirective model is made up of the following components:

Journal Entry
Using a Humanistic Approach to Instruction

1. *Defining the helping situation.* The topic that the student wants to discuss is identified, and the student is told that he or she is free to express any and all feelings that relate to the topic.
2. *Exploring the problem.* If the teacher has been able to establish the atmosphere of trust just described, it is assumed that students will be willing to describe the problem and any associated feelings. The teacher does not attempt to diagnose the student's problem but seeks to understand the situation as the student experiences it and then reflects this understanding back to the student. The teacher functions more as a resource, facilitator, and guide than as a director.
3. *Developing insight.* The student uses the information gained from exploring the problem to understand how various perceptions, emotions, beliefs, and behaviors cause various effects (such as a belief that one lacks ability, leading to incomplete homework assignments and lack of interest in the subject, or a need for affiliation leading to more socializing than studying).
4. *Planning and decision making.* The teacher helps the student identify alternative behaviors and how they will be carried out.
5. *Integration.* The student reports on actions taken, their effects, and plans for future actions.

Research on Aspects of Humanistic Education

As we noted previously, Maslow believed that children's academic and personal growth is enhanced when various needs are met. One of those needs, belonging, has been the subject of considerable research. Belonging, which is also referred to as relatedness and sense of community, means the desire to get support from and be accepted by teachers and classmates and to have opportunities to participate in classroom planning, goal setting, and decision making.

According to some motivational theorists, belonging is one of three basic psychological needs (autonomy and competence are the other two) essential to human growth and development. Yet the need to belong receives less attention from educators than autonomy or competence does. One possible reason for this discrepancy is the belief that students' emotional needs are best met at home and in other out-of-school groups. This attitude does a disservice to students for two reasons: teachers play an important role in helping to satisfy the need to belong (a point we elaborate on below), and research has uncovered positive relationships between satisfaction of the need to belong and the following school-related outcomes (Osterman, 2000):

- Increased intrinsic motivation to learn
- A strong sense of competence
- A heightened sense of autonomy
- A stronger sense of identity
- The willingness to conform to classroom rules and norms
- Positive attitudes toward school, class work, and teachers
- Higher expectations of success
- Lower levels of anxiety
- Being supportive of others

Feelings of rejection or exclusion from the group are associated with the following negative outcomes (Osterman, 2000):

- Behavior problems in school
- Lower interest in school

- Lower achievement
- Dropping out of school

Teachers affect students' sense of belonging by the instructional methods they use, the type of support they give, and the type of authority relationship they establish.

Two instructional techniques that relate to students' sense of belonging are cooperative learning and classroom discussion, topics we have visited in previous chapters. We will describe the characteristics and effects of cooperative learning in some detail in the next section. For now, all we need say is that cooperative learning reinforces the belief among its participants that one is personally liked, that other students care about how much each member of the group learns, and that other students want to help each member of the group learn. Classroom discussion, as suggested by the writings of Dewey and Vygotsky and by the social constructivist view of learning, not only provides students with a fuller view of problems and issues, but helps students develop a better appreciation of others and gives them the sense of being part of a community. Unfortunately, students at all grade levels get relatively few opportunities to engage in meaningful classroom discussion. In one study of high school classes, group discussion averaged fifteen seconds per fifty-minute period (Osterman, 2000).

Teachers can promote a sense of community in the classroom by giving all students the opportunity to exercise autonomy, work collaboratively with others, and participate in group problem-solving and decision-making activities. But in many instances, only some students receive teacher support for such activities. Those who do (as we pointed out in the chapter on cultural and socioeconomic diversity) typically conform to a teacher's unconscious profile of an ideal student with respect to ability, race, gender, social class, and appearance. Others receive treatment that says (whether the message is intended or not) that they are not as highly valued members of the classroom community (Osterman, 2000).

In the chapter on age-level characteristics, we noted that parents who use an authoritative style of interaction tend to have children who are more autonomous than children whose parents use an authoritarian style. That is, children who experience an authoritative style are able to set standards for themselves and understand why certain procedures should be followed. They stand up for what they believe, yet are able to work productively with others. Similarly, teachers whose style is authoritative produce students who are more autonomous than students who experience an authoritarian style, and autonomy has been consistently and strongly linked with developing a sense of belonging or community (Osterman, 2000).

A study that reinforces these findings comes from an unusual source: an analysis of why Japanese students outscore U.S. students after fourth grade on an internationally normed standardized test of mathematics and science (the Third International Mathematics and Science Study). After observing ten science lessons taught in five Japanese public schools, Marcia Linn, Catherine Lewis, Ineko Tsuchida, and Nancy Butler Songer (2000) attributed the difference in part to a classroom atmosphere that Abraham Maslow and Carl Rogers would have endorsed.

Japanese classrooms marked by humanistic orientation, high scores on international math and science test

In addition to emphasizing cognitive development, elementary education in Japan also places a high value on children's social and ethical development. This is done by such tactics as (1) giving children various classroom responsibilities so they feel a valued part of the school, (2) emphasizing such qualities as friendliness, responsibility, and persistence, and (3) communicating to students that teachers value their presence in the classroom and the contributions they make. By fourth grade, Japanese children have been steeped in a school culture that emphasizes responsibility to the group, collaboration, and kindness. In addition, Linn et al. found that almost every lesson began with an activity that was designed to spark the students' interest in the topic by connecting it to either their personal experiences or to previous lessons. The positive emotional attachment to school and the commitment to the values of hard work and cooperation that this approach produces are thought to play a strong role in how well students learn mathematics and science lessons.

Using Technology to Support Humanistic Approaches to Instruction

Using technology to support a humanistic approach to teaching may seem like a contradiction in terms. But educational technology is becoming more learner centered in both its design and its use. As we move from the relatively passive and predetermined approach of computer-assisted instruction of the 1960s and 1970s, learning with technology is now best viewed as a learner-centered process involving peers, teachers, experts, and other learning resources (Bonk, Hay, & Fischler, 1996; Sandholtz, Ringstaff, & Dwyer, 1997).

The learner-centered psychological principles from the American Psychological Association (American Psychological Association, 1997), mentioned early in this book, focus on helping learners meaningfully construct and represent their knowledge, creating challenging and novel learning environments that help students link new information to old, achieving complex learning goals, and building thinking and reasoning strategies. They also emphasize fostering curiosity and intrinsic motivation, nurturing social interaction and interpersonal relationships, recognizing individual differences in learning, and setting appropriately high and challenging learning standards and goals. Technology can help achieve all of these goals.

Learner-centered technology tools can link concepts to everyday experiences, guide students in the problem-solving process, encourage learners to think more deeply, facilitate unique knowledge construction, and provide opportunities for social interaction and dialogue. For example, graphing calculators, hand-held computers, and microcomputer laboratory equipment allow students to depict data collected from a polluted stream or pond. Prompts embedded in a word processing program encourage reflection on one's report about that environmental problem. Finally, computer conferencing on the Web allows these same students to engage in discussions about their findings with same-age peers far beyond their own classroom. A key strength of emerging technology environments is that they place the responsibility for learning in the hands of learners, thereby enabling them to ask personally relevant questions, pursue needed knowledge, and generally be more self-directed.

The Social Approach to Teaching: Teaching Students How to Learn from Each Other

Classroom tasks can be structured so that students are forced to compete with one another, work individually, or cooperate with one another to obtain the rewards that teachers make available for successfully completing these tasks. Traditionally, competitive arrangements have been assumed to be superior to the other two in increasing motivation and learning. But reviews of the research literature by David Johnson and Roger Johnson (Johnson & Johnson, 1995; Johnson, Johnson, & Smith, 1995) found cooperative arrangements to be far superior in producing these benefits. In this section, we will describe cooperative, competitive, and individual learning arrangements; identify the elements that make up the major approaches to cooperative learning; and examine the effect of cooperative learning on motivation, achievement, and interpersonal relationships. We would also like to point out that cooperative learning methods are fully consistent with social constructivism because they encourage inquiry, perspective sharing, and conflict resolution.

TYPES OF CLASSROOM REWARD STRUCTURES

Competitive Structures Competitive goal structures are those in which one's grade is determined by how well everyone else in the group performs (a reward structure that is typically referred to as *norm referenced*). The traditional practice of grading on the curve predetermines the percentage of A, B, C, D, and F grades regardless of the actual distribution of test scores. Because only a small percentage of students in any group can achieve the highest rewards and because this accomplishment must come at some other students' expense, competitive goal structures are characterized by negative interdependence. Students try to outdo one another, view classmates' failures as an advantage, and come to believe that the winners deserve their rewards because they are inherently better (Johnson, Johnson, & Holubec, 1994; Johnson et al., 1995).

Some researchers have argued that competitive reward structures lead students to focus on ability as the primary basis for motivation. This orientation is reflected in the question, "Am I smart enough to accomplish this task?" When ability is the basis for motivation, competing successfully in the classroom may be seen as relevant to self-esteem (since nobody loves a loser), difficult to accomplish (since only a few can succeed), and uncertain (success depends on how everyone else does). These perceptions may cause some students to avoid challenging subjects or tasks, give up in the face of difficulty, reward themselves only if they win a competition, and believe that their own successes are due to ability, whereas the successes of others are due to luck (Ames & Ames, 1984; Dweck, 1986).

Competitive reward structures may decrease motivation to learn

Individualistic Structures Individualistic goal structures are characterized by students working alone and earning rewards solely on the quality of their own efforts. The success or failure of other students is irrelevant. All that matters is whether the student meets the standards for a particular task (Johnson et al., 1994, 1995). For example, thirty students working by themselves at computer terminals are functioning in an individual reward structure. According to Carole Ames and Russell Ames (1984), individual structures lead students to focus on task effort as the primary basis for motivation (as in "I can do this if I try"). Whether a student perceives a task as difficult depends on how successful she has been with that type of task in the past.

Cooperative Structures Cooperative goal structures are characterized by students working together to accomplish shared goals. What is beneficial for the other students in the group is beneficial for the individual and vice versa. Because students in cooperative groups can obtain a desired reward (such as a high grade or a feeling of satisfaction for a job well done) only if the other students in the group also obtain the

Cooperative reward structures are more likely to motivate almost all students in a class to study and develop positive attitudes toward learning than are competitive or individualistic arrangements.

same reward, cooperative goal structures are characterized by positive interdependence. Also, all groups may receive the same rewards, provided they meet the teacher's criteria for mastery. For example, a teacher might present a lesson on map reading, then give each group its own map and a question-answering exercise. Students then work with each other to ensure that all know how to interpret maps. Each student then takes a quiz on map reading. All teams whose average quiz scores meet a preset standard receive special recognition (Johnson et al., 1994, 1995; Slavin, 1995).

Cooperative structures lead students to focus on effort and cooperation as the primary basis of motivation. This orientation is reflected in the statement, "We can do this if we try hard and work together." In a cooperative atmosphere, students are motivated out of a sense of obligation: one ought to try, contribute, and help satisfy group norms (Ames & Ames, 1984). William Glasser points out that student motivation and performance tend to be highest for such activities as band, drama club, athletics, the school newspaper, and the yearbook, all of which require a team effort (Gough, 1987).

Elements of Cooperative Learning

Over the past thirty years, different approaches to cooperative learning have been proposed by different individuals. The three most popular are those of David Johnson and Roger Johnson (Johnson et al., 1994), Robert Slavin (1994, 1995), and Shlomo Sharan and Yael Sharan (Sharan, 1995; Sharan & Sharan, 1994). To give you a general sense of what cooperative learning is like and to avoid limiting you to any one individual's approach, the following discussion is a synthesis of the main features of each approach.

Group Heterogeneity The size of cooperative-learning groups is relatively small and as heterogeneous as circumstances allow. The recommended size is usually four to five students. At the very least, groups should contain both males and females and students of different ability levels. If possible, different ethnic backgrounds and social classes should be represented as well.

Group Goals/Positive Interdependence A specific goal, such as a grade or a certificate of recognition, is identified for the group to attain. Students are told that they will have to support one another because the group goal can be achieved only if each member learns the material being taught (in the case of a task that culminates in an exam) or makes a specific contribution to the group's effort (in the case of a task that culminates in a presentation or a project).

Promotive Interaction This element is made necessary by the existence of positive interdependence. Students are shown how to help one another overcome problems and complete whatever task has been assigned. This may involve episodes of peer tutoring, temporary assistance, exchanges of information and material, challenging of one another's reasoning, feedback, and encouragement to keep one another highly motivated.

Cooperative learning characterized by heterogeneous groups, positive interdependence, promotive interaction, individual accountability

Individual Accountability This feature stipulates that each member of a group has to make a significant contribution to achieving the group's goal. This may be satisfied by achieving a minimal score on a test, having the group's test score be the sum or average of each student's quiz scores, or having each member be responsible for a particular part of a project (such as doing the research and writing for a particular part of a history report).

Interpersonal Skills Positive interdependence and promotive interaction are not likely to occur if students do not know how to make the most of their face-to-face interactions. And you can safely assume that the interpersonal skills most students possess are probably not highly developed. As a result, they have to be taught such basic skills as leadership, decision making, trust building, clear communication, and conflict management. The conflict that arises over differences of opinion, for example, can be constructive if it is used as a stimulus to search for more information or to rethink one's conclusions. But it can destroy group cohesion and productivity if it results in students' stubbornly clinging to a position or referring to one another as "stubborn," "dumb," or "nerdy."

Equal Opportunities for Success Because cooperative groups are heterogeneous with respect to ability and their success depends on positive interdependence, promotive interaction, and individual accountability, it is important that steps be taken to ensure that all students have an opportunity to contribute to their team. You can do this by awarding points for degree of improvement over previous test scores, having students compete against comparable members of other teams in a game- or tournament-like atmosphere, or giving students learning assignments (such as math problems) that are geared to their current level of skill.

Team Competition This may seem to be an odd entry in a list of cooperative-learning components, especially in the light of the comments we already made about the ineffectiveness of competition as a spur to motivation and learning. But we're not being contradictory. The main problem with competition is that it is rarely used appropriately. When competition occurs between well-matched teams, is done in the absence of a norm-referenced grading system, and is not used too frequently, it can be an effective way to motivate students to cooperate with each other.

Does Cooperative Learning Work?

The short answer to this question is yes. In the vast majority of studies, forms of cooperative learning have been shown to be more effective than noncooperative reward structures in raising the levels of variables that contribute to motivation, raising achievement, and producing positive social outcomes.

Effect on Motivation Because a student's sense of self-esteem can have a strong effect on motivation, this variable has been examined in several cooperative-learning studies. The results are encouraging yet confusing. Slavin (1995) found that in eleven of fifteen studies, cooperative learning produced bigger increases in some aspect of self-esteem (general self-esteem, academic self-esteem, social self-esteem) than the noncooperative method with which it was compared. But these effects were not consistent across studies. Some researchers reported increases in academic self-esteem or social self-esteem, but others found no effect. Adding to the confusion is the conclusion that Johnson and Johnson (1995) drew that cooperative learning consistently produces higher self-efficacy scores than do competitive or individualistic conditions.

Such inconsistencies may reflect weaknesses in the self-esteem instruments that were used (self-ratings are not always accurate), weaknesses in the designs of the studies (many cooperative-learning studies last anywhere from a few days to a few weeks, yet changes in self-esteem happen slowly), or differences in specific cooperative-learning programs. Perhaps future research will clarify this issue.

Another way in which cooperative learning contributes to high levels of motivation is in the proacademic attitudes that it fosters among group members. Slavin (1995) cites several studies in which students in cooperative-learning groups felt more strongly than did other students that their groupmates wanted them to come to school every day and work hard in class.

Probably because of such features as promotive interaction and equal opportunities for success, cooperative learning has been shown to have a positive effect on motivation-inducing attributions. That is, students in cooperative-learning groups were more likely to attribute success to hard work and ability than to luck (Slavin, 1995).

A strong indicator of motivation is the actual amount of time students spend working on a task. Most studies have found that cooperative-learning students spend significantly more time on task than do control students (Johnson et al., 1995; Slavin, 1995).

Effect on Achievement Slavin (1995) examined several dozen studies that lasted four or more weeks and used a variety of cooperative-learning methods. Overall, students in cooperative-learning groups scored about one-fourth of a standard deviation higher on achievement tests than did students taught conventionally. This translates to an advantage of ten percentile ranks (sixtieth percentile for the average cooperative-learning student versus fiftieth percentile for the average conventionally taught student). But the beneficial effect of cooperative learning varied widely as a function of the particular method used. The best performances occurred with two techniques called Student Teams–Achievement Divisions and Teams-Games-Tournaments. (Both are described in the chapter on motivation.) The cooperative-learning features that seem to be most responsible for learning gains are group goals and individual accountability.

David Johnson, Roger Johnson, and Karl Smith (1995) also reviewed much of the cooperative-learning literature but drew a somewhat different conclusion. They found that the test scores of students in the cooperative-learning groups were about two-thirds of a standard deviation higher than the test scores of students in competitive or individualistic situations. This translates to an advantage of twenty-five percentile ranks (seventy-fifth versus fiftieth). It's not clear why Slavin's analysis produced a somewhat lower estimate of the size of the advantage produced by cooperative learning. It may be due in part to differences in the studies that each cited; Slavin focused on studies lasting at least four weeks. It may also be due to differences in the cooperative techniques that various researchers used.

In addition to achievement outcomes, researchers have also assessed the impact of cooperative learning on problem solving. Given the complex nature of problem solving and the multiple resources that a cooperative group has at its disposal, one would logically expect cooperative learning to have a positive effect on this outcome as well. This hypothesis was confirmed by Zhining Qin, David Johnson, and Roger Johnson (1995). After reviewing forty-six studies, they concluded that students of all age levels (elementary, secondary, college, adult) who worked cooperatively outscored students who worked competitively. The average student in a cooperative group solved more problems correctly than 71 percent of the students who worked competitively.

Effect on Social Relationships In most studies, students exposed to cooperative learning were more likely than students who learned under competitive or individualistic conditions to name a classmate from a different race, ethnic group, or social class as a friend or to label such individuals as "nice" or "smart." In some studies, the friendships that were formed were deemed to be quite strong. A similar positive effect was found for students with mental disabilities who were mainstreamed. Furthermore, the cooperation skills that students learn apparently transfer. Cooperative-learning students were more likely than other students to use the cooperative behaviors they were taught when they worked with new classmates (Johnson & Johnson, 1995; Slavin, 1995).

Students who learn cooperatively tend to be more highly motivated to learn because of increased self-esteem, the proacademic attitudes of groupmates, appropriate attributions for success and failure, and greater on-task behavior. They also score higher on tests of achievement and problem solving and tend to get along better with classmates of different racial, ethnic, and social class backgrounds. This last outcome should be of particular interest if you expect to teach in an area marked by cultural diversity.

WHY DOES COOPERATIVE LEARNING WORK?

When researchers attempt to explain the widespread positive effects that are typically found among studies of cooperative learning, they usually cite one or more of the following explanations (Slavin, 1995).

Cooperative learning effects likely due to stimulation of motivation, cognitive development, meaningful learning

Motivational Effect The various features of cooperative learning, particularly positive interdependence, are highly motivating because they encourage such achievement-oriented behaviors as trying hard, attending class regularly, praising the efforts of others, and receiving help from one's groupmates. Learning is seen as an obligation and a valued activity because the group's success is based on it and one's groupmates will reward it.

Cognitive-Developmental Effect According to Lev Vygotsky, collaboration promotes cognitive growth because students model for each other more advanced ways of thinking than any would demonstrate individually. According to Jean Piaget, collaboration among peers hastens the decline of egocentrism and allows the development of more advanced ways of understanding and dealing with the world.

Cognitive Elaboration Effect As we saw in the previous discussion of information-processing theory, new information that is elaborated (restructured and related to existing knowledge) is more easily retrieved from memory than is information that is not elaborated. A particularly effective means of elaboration is explaining something to someone else.

Teachers' Use of Cooperative Learning

Journal Entry
Using a Social Approach to Instruction

As we have seen, cooperative learning is a topic about which much has been written and much research has been done. But until recently, no one had tried to assess the extent to which teachers actually use it and in what form. To fill that gap in the literature, Laurence Antil, Joseph Jenkins, Susan Wayne, and Patricia Vadasy (1998) interviewed twenty-one teachers from six elementary schools to assess the extent to which they used cooperative learning methods. All of the teachers claimed they were familiar with cooperative learning through preservice learning, student teaching, graduate classes, workshops, or other teachers. Seventeen of the teachers said they used it every day in a typical week. Most reported being attracted to cooperative learning because it enabled them to address both academic and social learning goals within a single approach. But just because teachers say they use cooperative learning, they aren't necessarily using it as it was intended.

Antil et al. argued that for an instructional approach to merit the label *cooperative learning,* it must include at least the conditions of positive interdependence and individual accountability. A more stringent definition would call for the inclusion of promotive interaction, group heterogeneity, and the development of interpersonal skills. Only five of the twenty-one teachers met the two-feature criterion, and only one reported using all five features. For example, instead of creating heterogeneous groups by putting students of different ability levels together, some teachers used random assignment, allowed students to select their teammates, or allowed students who sat near one another to form groups.

Why do teachers follow the spirit but not the letter of the cooperative learning model? Antil et al. offer several possibilities:

As you reflect on your own teaching practices, see the Reflective Journal Questions at **http://education.college.hmco.com/students**.

- Perhaps teachers find the models too complicated and difficult to put into practice. For example, in Slavin's model, individual accountability involves keeping a running log of students' weekly test scores, computing individual averages and improvement scores, totaling scores for each team based on members' improvement scores, and assigning group rewards.
- Teachers don't really believe the researchers' claims that certain elements of cooperative learning are essential for improved learning, perhaps because their classroom experience has led them to believe otherwise.
- Teachers interpret the research as providing suggestions or guidelines rather than prescriptions that must be followed, leaving them free to construct personal adaptations.
- Researchers rarely explicitly state that the demonstrated benefits of cooperative learning will occur only when certain conditions are met.

Do teachers' adaptations of the cooperative learning approaches advocated by researchers lead to inferior outcomes? Unfortunately, that's a question that has no definitive answer at this point, since there is little research on how effective cooperative learning is when some of its defining elements are omitted. But the following study, which looked at the effects of group heterogeneity on problem solving, suggests that you should stay as close as circumstances permit to the original features of cooperative learning.

Noreen Webb, Kariane Nemer, Alexander Chizhik, and Brenda Sugrue (1998) looked at seventh- and eighth-grade students who had been given three weeks of instruction on electricity concepts (such as voltage, resistance, and current) and electric circuits and who were judged as being either low ability, low-medium ability, medium-high ability, or high ability. These students were assigned to either homogeneous or heterogeneous groups and then allowed to work collaboratively to solve a hands-on physics test (create a circuit by using batteries, bulbs, wires, and resis-

Table 10.1 Behavioral, Cognitive, Humanistic, and Social Approaches to Instruction

Behavioral (direct instruction)	Teacher presents information efficiently. Student accepts all information transmitted by teacher and textbook as accurate and potentially useful. Emphasis is on acquiring information in small units through clear presentations, practice, and corrective feedback and gradually synthesizing the pieces into larger bodies of knowledge.
Cognitive (information) processing)	Teacher presents and helps students to process information meaningfully. Student accepts all information transmitted by teacher and textbook as accurate and potentially useful. Emphasis is on understanding relationships among ideas, relationships between ideas and prior knowledge, and on learning how to control one's cognitive processes effectively.
Cognitive (constructivist)	Teacher helps students to construct meaningful and adaptive knowledge structures by requiring them to engage in higher levels of thinking such as classification, analysis, synthesis, and evaluation; providing scaffolded instruction within the zone of proximal development; embedding tasks in realistic contexts; posing problems and tasks that cause uncertainty, doubt, and curiosity; exposing students to multiple points of view; and allowing students the time to formulate a consensus solution to a task or problem.
Humanistic	Teacher creates a classtoom environment that addresses students' needs, helps students understand their attitudes toward learning, promotes a positive self-concept in students, and communicates the belief that all students have value and can learn. Goal is to activate the students' inherent desire to learn and grow.
Social	Teacher assigns students to small, heterogeneous groups and teaches them how to accomplish goals by working together. Each student is accountable for making a significant contribution to the achievement of the group goal. Because of its emphasis on peer collaboration, this approach is consistent with a social constructivist view of learning.

Students in mixed ability groups outperform students in homogeneous groups on problem-solving tests

tors). Low-ability and low-medium-ability students who worked in heterogeneous groups (that is, groups that included either a medium-high or high-ability student) outscored their peers in homogeneous groups on both the hands-on test and a subsequent paper-and-pencil test that students took individually. The difference was attributed to the active involvement of the lower-ability students in the problem-solving process. They made and defended suggestions, asked questions, and paraphrased other students' suggestions.

Now that you have read about the behavioral, cognitive, humanistic, and social approaches to instruction, you should take a few minutes to study Table 10.1. It summarizes the basic emphases of each approach and allows you to compare them for similarities and differences.

Using Technology to Support Social Approaches to Instruction

Social Constructivist Learning While the cognitive constructivist looks to find tools to help the child's mind actively construct relationships and ideas, the social constructivist looks as well for tools that help children negotiate ideas and findings in a community of peers. For instance, some point out that it is not just the quality of a computer simulation or microworld that determines the degree to which students will become more like expert scientists; rather, the social activities and talk between students and teachers in that environment are also central to student learning (Roschelle, 1996).

Successful technology applications are embedded in an active social environment

Research indicates not only that students who work together on computer-based tasks interact more than students who work on other types of classroom activities, but that the nature of the interactions is different. Eight-year-old students who worked with a peer on a computer-based task exhibited two to three times as many interactions per minute as did students who worked together on other activities (6.8 interactions per minute for computer tasks, 2.9 interactions per minute for creative activities, and 2.1 interactions per minute for other school activities). For the students who worked on a computer-based task, 89 percent of their interactions were about how to do the task, while 9 percent of their comments were emotional statements (most of which were positive, as in, "That's a nice drawing!"). For the students who worked on creative and other school activities, about 60 percent of their comments were task related, and about 10 percent were emotional statements. Most of the rest of the comments for both groups were not school related (Svensson, 2000). This study suggests that working with classmates on computer-based tasks produces a very high level of on-task behavior. As a teacher, you might attempt to foster rich conversations and collaborations among your students by incorporating computer networks, online information services, e-mail, discussion groups, bulletin boards, chat lines, collaborative web sites and pages, or electronic newsletters and journals.

Cooperative and Collaborative Learning Cooperative learning is fairly well structured, with assigned roles, tasks, and procedures to help students learn material covered in a classroom setting; a related concept, **collaborative learning,** allows the students themselves to decide on their roles and use their individual areas of expertise to help investigate problems (Marx et al., 1997). As noted throughout this book, with the emergence of the World Wide Web and telecommunications technologies that enable students to publish and share their work internationally, there is no shortage of cooperative and collaborative learning opportunities (Harasim, Hiltz, Teles, & Turoff, 1995). Networking technologies can be used for many cooperative and collaborative tasks—for example:

- Collecting data for group science projects (Marx et al., 1997)
- Sharing video and text messages and ideas with peers and experts in a multimedia bulletin board (Woolsey & Bellamy, 1997)
- Asking questions of explorers as students explore the environment (Bonk & Sugar, 1998)
- Explaining theories and findings from excavations of simulated archaeological or geological sites (Woolsey & Bellamy, 1997)
- Engaging in global peace projects and simulations to build students' appreciation and knowledge of world events and problems (Rottier, 1995)
- Gathering and sharing data on current events in one's community (for example, the weather; Bonk, Hay, & Fischler, 1996; Dede, 1996)
- Creating plays with sister schools (Sauer, 1994)
- Designing hypermedia "metastacks" that visually depict how all student hypermedia projects relate to one another (Scholten & Whitmer, 1996)
- Practicing reading and writing in a foreign language (Meagher, 1995)
- Giving peer feedback on writing assignments and reports (Hirtle, 1996)
- Cross-age mentoring (Dede, 1996)
- Communicating with electronic pen pals in other countries (Bradsher, 1996)
- Sharing artwork with students from schools around the world (Copen, 1995)

As noted in previous chapters, the emergence of computer networking technologies is creating many interesting opportunities for students to enter into virtual communities with peers from other schools and countries and share and discuss various data and ideas. The National Geographic Kids Network, for instance, involves research teams of ten or more classes from the United States and over forty other countries collecting real-world data (for example, acid rain samples). With the collection of raw data, each participant is actually making a vital contribution to project success. In some global projects, students not only see how their peers in troubled parts of the world are affected by international events, but they can actually make an impact on their lives (Copen, 1995; Meagher, 1995).

Of course, success requires finding suitable partners, sharing background information, establishing clear goals and roles, coordinating schedules, tracking participation, having technology access across sites, facilitating group interaction, establishing a division of labor, building trust between sites, sustaining student progress and momentum with encouraging feedback, determining how credit is divided, and perhaps even changing one's teaching approach (Kimball, 1995). Given these constraints, it is important for teachers to reflect on the purpose and scope of a collaborative technology project before deciding to initiate one (Hirtle, 1996).

As you review this chapter, check the Thought Questions and ACE Self-Testing sections on the textbook web site at **http://education.college.hmco.com/students**.

RESOURCES FOR FURTHER INVESTIGATION

Mager and Gronlund on Objectives

If you would like to read Robert Mager's complete description of his recommendations for writing specific objectives, peruse his brief paperback *Preparing Instructional Objectives* (1997). Norman Gronlund explains his approach to using objectives in *How to Write and Use Instructional Objectives* (2000) and in *Measurement and Assessment in Teaching* (2000), which he coauthored with Robert Linn.

Direct Instruction

In *Research on Direct Instruction: 25 Years Beyond DISTAR* (1996), Gary Adams and Siegfried Engelmann cover the origins of Direct Instruction (by capitalizing the term *Direct Instruction*, Adams and Engelmann seek to distinguish the original and highly structured approach that Engelmann devised in 1964 from the more generic approach we described in this chapter), its features, myths about its nature, and a review of research results on its effects. Appendix A provides a list of Direct Instruction programs for reading, language arts, writing, spelling, mathematics, and science.

The Cognitive Approach to Instruction

In *Cognitive Strategy Instruction That Really Improves Children's Academic Performance* (1995), Michael Pressley, Vera Woloshyn, and others describe how to use information-processing principles to design cognitive strategy instruction for beginning reading, reading comprehension, vocabulary, spelling, writing, mathematics, science, and learning facts.

Scaffolding Student Learning: Instructional Approaches and Issues (1997), edited by Kathleen Hogan and Michael Pressley, contains five chapters that describe and illustrate with actual classroom examples how to use scaffolding for a variety of instructional outcomes.

The Humanistic Approach to Instruction

William W. Purkey and John M. Novak describe a humanistic approach to teaching called "invitational learning" in *Inviting School Success: A Self-Concept Approach to Teaching, Learning, and Democratic Practice* (1996). If you would like to sample a variety of descriptions and interpretations of humanistic education, examine *Readings in Values Clarification* (1973), edited by Howard Kirschenbaum and Sidney B. Simon, or *Humanistic Education Sourcebook* (1975), edited by Donald A. Read and Sidney B. Simon.

Cooperative Learning

The New Circles of Learning: Cooperation in the Classroom and School (1994), by David W. Johnson, Roger T. Johnson, and Edythe Johnson Holubec, is a brief (105 pages) and readable description of the basic elements of the authors' version of cooperative learning. In *Cooperative Learning* (1995), Robert E. Slavin describes the cooperative learning techniques that he favors, analyzes the research evidence that supports their use, and provides detailed directions on how to use them. Lynda Baloche provides numerous examples of how to use cooperative learning techniques in *The Cooperative Classroom: Empowering Learning* (1998).

Cooperative learning is sufficiently flexible that it can be used at all levels of education. Four books that describe how to use cooperative methods for specific grade levels are: *Cooperative Learning in the Early Childhood Classroom* (1991), by Harvey C. Foyle, Lawrence Lyman, and Sandra A. Thies; *Cooperative Learning in the Elementary Classroom* (1993), by Lawrence Lyman, Harvey C. Foyle, and Tara S. Azwell; *Cooperative Learning in Middle-Level Schools* (1991), by Jerry Rottier and Beverly J. Ogan; and *Secondary Schools and Cooperative Learning* (1995), edited by Jon E. Pedersen and Annette D. Digby.

SUMMARY

1. Goals are broad, general statements of desired educational outcomes. Because of their general language, they mean different things to different people and cannot be precisely measured.

2. The vagueness of such goals stimulated psychologists to specify educational outcomes as specific, clearly stated objectives and to organize objectives as taxonomies in each of three domains: cognitive, affective, and psychomotor.

3. The taxonomy for the cognitive domain that Bloom and several associates prepared is composed of six levels: knowledge, comprehension, application, analysis, synthesis, and evaluation.

4. The taxonomy for the affective domain that Krathwohl and several associates prepared is composed of five levels: receiving, responding, valuing, organization, and characterization by a value or value complex.

5. The taxonomy for the psychomotor domain that Simpson prepared is composed of seven levels: perception, set, guided response, mechanism, complex or overt response, adaptation, and origination.

6. Most teachers use test questions that measure knowledge-level objectives, largely ignoring higher-level cognitive outcomes.

7. Mager states that well-written objectives should specify what behaviors the learner will exhibit to indicate mastery, the conditions under which the behavior will be exhibited, and the criteria of acceptable performance.

8. Gronlund believes that complex and advanced kinds of learning do not lend themselves to Mager-type objectives. Complex outcomes are so broad in scope that it is impractical to ask students to demonstrate everything they have learned. Instead, Gronlund suggests that teachers first state a general objective and then specify a sample of related specific outcomes.

9. Objectives must be consistent with the instructional approach one uses and the types of tests one creates.

10. Objectives work best when students are aware of them and understand their intent, they are clearly written, and they are provided to average students for tasks of average difficulty. Objectives often increase intentional learning but may decrease incidental learning.

11. Direct instruction is an approach derived from behavioral learning theory. Lessons are broken down into small steps, the teacher models the desired behavior, material is presented in a variety of formats, students are given extensive opportunities to practice, and feedback is given consistently.

12. An information-processing approach to teaching is based on knowledge of how information is meaningfully processed and attempts to teach students how to be self-directed learners. Teachers should communicate their

goals clearly, use attention-getting devices, present information in organized and meaningful ways, present information in relatively small chunks over realistic time periods, use instructional techniques that facilitate encoding of information in long-term memory, and model effective learning processes.

13. A constructivist approach to teaching is based on the view that meaningful learning occurs when students are encouraged and helped to create the knowledge schemes that produce a broad understanding of ideas and lead to self-directed learning. Key elements of the constructivist approach include scaffolded instruction within a student's zone of proximal development, learning by discovery, exposure to multiple points of view, and use of relevant and realistic problems and tasks.

14. A humanistic approach to teaching assumes all students will be motivated to learn if the classroom environment satisfies their basic needs, strengthens their self-concept, provides assistance in learning new ideas and skills, and allows them to direct their learning experiences.

15. A social approach to learning focuses on teaching students how to learn from one another in a cooperative environment. For students to be able to work together successfully, the following conditions are necessary: heterogeneous groups, achievement of group goals by having students help one another to achieve individual goals, holding each student responsible for making a significant contribution to the group goal, development of interpersonal skills, giving each student an opportunity to succeed, and allowing for competition among teams. Cooperative learning is successful because it raises the motivation levels of students, promotes cognitive growth, and encourages meaningful learning.

16. Research on the effects on problem solving of homogeneous versus mixed-ability groups suggests that teachers should implement all the defining features of cooperative learning rather than just one or two.

17. Technology tools can be used to support behavioral, information-processing, learner-centered, and social approaches to instruction.

KEY TERMS

instructional objectives *(341)*
taxonomy *(341)*
cognitive domain *(341)*
affective domain *(341)*
psychomotor domain *(341)*
specific objectives *(344)*
general objectives *(345)*
direct instruction *(347)*
intelligent tutoring systems *(359)*
exploratory environments *(359)*
guided learning *(360)*
humanistic approach *(364)*
learner-centered education *(365)*
collaborative learning *(377)*

DISCUSSION QUESTIONS

1. Based on the content of this chapter and your own experiences as a student, do you agree that writing objectives and providing them to students are worthwhile expenditures of a teacher's time and effort? If so, then what steps will you take to ensure that you will make writing objectives a standard part of your professional behavior?

2. One criticism of writing objectives is that it limits the artistic side of teaching. That is, objectives lock teachers into a predetermined plan of instruction and eliminate the ability to pursue unplanned topics or interests. Can you respond to this criticism by recalling a teacher who provided you and your classmates with objectives but was still enthusiastic, flexible, spontaneous, and inventive?

3. In the chapter on information-processing theory, we cited research indicating that instruction in how to process information effectively is rarely provided to students by elementary grade teachers, despite its demonstrated effectiveness in study after study. One reason is that teacher education programs typically provide little or no coursework on information-processing and learning strategy instruction. Is this true of your program? Why? What can you do when you teach to make full use of information-processing principles?

4. Can you recall any teachers who practiced the humanistic techniques that Maslow, Rogers, and Combs suggested? Did you like these teachers? Did you feel as if you learned as much from them as from other teachers? Would you model yourself after such teachers?

5. Have you ever experienced a competitive reward structure in school? Were your reactions to it positive or negative? Why? Would you use it in your own classroom? For what purpose and under what circumstances?

6. Have you ever experienced a cooperative reward structure in school? Were your reactions to it positive or negative? Why? Would you use it in your own classroom? For what purpose and under what circumstances?

Creating a Positive Learning Environment

Part III

11 Motivation

Teaching is very much like putting together a puzzle. You first have to identify the pieces and then figure out how to construct them into a meaningful whole. This book is designed to help you identify the relevant pieces that make up the effective teaching puzzle and give you some ideas for using them in a coordinated fashion. In Part I, for example, you learned the importance of understanding how students develop socially, emotionally, and cognitively; what students are like at different ages; and how they differ from one another. In Part II, you were introduced to those pieces of the puzzle that pertain to the learning process and how different views of learning can be used to guide

Key Points

These key points will help you learn the important information in this chapter. To help you study, they also appear in the margins of the pages, next to the text where they are discussed.

Behavioral Views of Motivation

- Behavioral view of motivation: reinforce desired behavior
- Social learning view of motivation: observation, imitation, vicarious reinforcement
- Extrinsic motivation occurs when learner does something to earn external reward
- Intrinsic motivation occurs when learner does something to experience inherently satisfying results
- Excessive use of external rewards may lead to temporary behavior change, materialistic attitudes, decreased intrinsic motivation
- Intrinsic motivation undermined by rewarding students merely for engaging in an activity
- Intrinsic motivation enhanced when reward is given according to predetermined standard or is consistent with individual's level of skill
- Give rewards sparingly, especially on tasks of natural interest

Cognitive Views of Motivation

- Cognitive development view of motivation: strive for equilibration; master the environment
- Need for achievement revealed by desire to attain goals that require skilled performance
- High-need achievers prefer moderately challenging tasks
- Low-need achievers prefer very easy or very hard tasks
- Unsuccessful students attribute success to luck, easy tasks; failure, to lack of ability
- Successful students attribute success to effort, ability; failure, to lack of effort
- Students with entity beliefs tend to have performance goals and are motivated to get high grades, avoid failure
- Students with incremental beliefs tend to have mastery goals and are motivated to meaningfully learn, improve skills
- High interest in a subject can lead to mastery goals and intrinsic motivation, or mastery goals can lead to high interest and motivation
- Interest in a subject can be influenced by individual or situational factors
- Often difficult to arouse cognitive disequilibrium
- Need for achievement difficult to assess on basis of short-term observations
- Faulty attributions difficult to change

The Humanistic View of Motivation

- People are motivated to satisfy deficiency needs only when those needs are unmet
- Self-actualization depends on satisfaction of lower needs, belief in certain values
- When deficiency needs are not satisfied, person likely to make bad choices
- Encourage growth choices by enhancing attractions, minimizing dangers
- Teachers may be able to satisfy some deficiency needs but not others

The Role of Self-Perceptions in Motivation

- Self-concept is description of self; self-esteem is value we place on that description
- High self-esteem due to being competent at valued tasks, reinforcement from others
- Self-esteem declines when students move from elementary grades to middle school and from middle school to high school
- Self-efficacy affects choice of goals, expectations of success, attributions for success and failure
- Raise self-esteem by helping students become better learners

Motivating Students with Technology

- Technology can be used to support both extrinsic and intrinsic motivation
- Technology increases intrinsic motivation by making learning more interesting and meaningful

the type of instruction you provide. The puzzle pieces in this part deal with the importance of establishing a classroom environment that will motivate students to learn and of maintaining that positive atmosphere over time.

Previous chapters provided you with several explanations of how people learn and suggested related approaches for helping students achieve objectives. In this chapter, we address the question of why students strive (or don't strive) for academic achievement—that is, what motivates students? The importance of motivation was vividly pointed out by Larry Cuban, a Stanford University professor of education who returned to teach a high school class for one semester after a sixteen-year absence. Of this experience, he says, "If I wanted those students to be engaged intellectually, then every day—and I *do* mean *every* day—I had to figure out an angle, a way of making connections between whatever we were studying and their daily lives in school, in the community, or in the nation" (1990, pp. 480–481).

Cuban's comment about the importance of motivating students is as applicable to the elementary and middle school teacher as it is to the high school teacher. Researchers have consistently found that interest in school in general decreases the most between fourth and fifth grades, while interest in specific subjects decreases the most between sixth and seventh grades. Declines in motivation have also been found among girls when they move from a kindergarten through eighth-grade school to a traditional high school setting (Anderman & Maehr, 1994).

Motivation is typically defined as the forces that account for the selection, persistence, intensity, and continuation of behavior. In practical terms, motivation is simply the willingness to expend a certain amount of effort to achieve a particular goal. Nevertheless, many teachers have at least two major misconceptions about motivation that prevent them from using this concept with maximum effectiveness. One misconception is that some students are unmotivated. Strictly speaking, that is not an accurate statement. As long as a student chooses goals and expends a certain amount of effort to achieve them, he is, by definition, motivated. What teachers really mean is that students are not motivated to behave in the way teachers would like them to behave. The second misconception is that one person can directly motivate another. This view is inaccurate because motivation comes from within a person. What you *can* do, with the help of the various motivation theories discussed in this chapter, is create the circumstances that *influence* students to do what you want them to do (Maehr & Meyer, 1997).

Many factors determine whether the students in your classes will be motivated or not motivated to learn. You should not be surprised to discover that no single theoretical interpretation of motivation explains all aspects of student interest or lack of it. Different theoretical interpretations do, however, shed light on why some students in a given learning situation are more likely to want to learn than others. Furthermore, each theoretical interpretation can serve as the basis for the development of techniques for motivating students in the classroom. Several theoretical interpretations of motivation—some of which are derived from discussions of learning presented earlier—will now be summarized. ■

Behavioral Views of Motivation

Earlier in the text we noted that some psychologists explain learning from a theoretical perspective that focuses exclusively on the effects of observable stimuli, responses, and consequences on our propensity to exhibit particular behaviors. This approach is called operant conditioning. Other psychologists explain learning from a theoretical perspective that includes the effects of both observable external events and the effects of unobservable internal processes on our propensity to imitate the behavior of others. This approach is called social learning theory. Both approaches have, as we will see in this section, also been applied to the issue of motivation.

OPERANT CONDITIONING AND SOCIAL LEARNING THEORY

The Effect of Reinforcement In the chapter on behavioral learning theory, we discussed Skinner's emphasis on the role of reinforcement in learning. After demonstrating that organisms tend to repeat actions that are reinforced and that behavior can be shaped by reinforcement, Skinner developed the technique of programmed instruction to make it possible for students to be reinforced for every correct response. Supplying the correct answer—and being informed by the program that it *is* the correct answer—motivates the student to go on to the next frame, and as the student works through the program, the desired terminal behavior is progressively shaped.

To preview this chapter's main ideas, see the Chapter Themes on this book's Web site at **http://education.college.hmco.com/students**.

Following Skinner's lead, many behavioral learning theorists devised techniques of behavior modification. Students are motivated to complete a task by being promised a reward of some kind. Many times, the reward takes the form of praise or a grade. Sometimes it is a token that can be traded in for some desired object, and at other times the reward may be the privilege of engaging in a self-selected activity.

Behavioral view of motivation: reinforce desired behavior

Operant conditioning interpretations of learning help reveal why some students react favorably to particular subjects and dislike others. For instance, some students may enter a required math class with a feeling of delight, while others may feel that they have been sentenced to prison. Skinner suggests that such differences can be traced to past experiences. He would argue that the student who loves math has been shaped to respond that way by a series of positive experiences with math. The math hater, in contrast, may have suffered a series of negative experiences.

The Power of Persuasive Models Social learning theorists, such as Albert Bandura, call attention to the importance of observation, imitation, and vicarious reinforcement (expecting to receive the same reinforcer that we see someone else get

Social learning view of motivation: observation, imitation, vicarious reinforcement

When students admire and identify with classmates who are positively reinforced for their behavior, the observing students are often motivated to exhibit the same behavior.

for exhibiting a particular behavior). A student who identifies with and admires a teacher of a particular subject may work hard partly to please the admired individual and partly to try becoming like that individual. A student who observes an older brother or sister reaping benefits from earning high grades may strive to do the same with the expectation of experiencing the same or similar benefits. A student who notices that a classmate receives praise from the teacher after acting in a certain way may decide to imitate such behavior to win similar rewards. As we pointed out in discussing social learning theory in an earlier chapter, both vicarious reinforcement and direct reinforcement can raise an individual's sense of self-efficacy for a particular task, which, in turn, leads to higher levels of motivation.

Limitations of the Behavioral View

Extrinsic motivation occurs when learner does something to earn external reward

Intrinsic motivation occurs when learner does something to experience inherently satisfying results

Although approaches to motivation based on positive reinforcement are often useful, you should be aware of the disadvantages that can come from overuse or misuse of such techniques. Most of the criticisms of the use of reinforcement as a motivational incentive stem from the fact that it represents **extrinsic motivation**. That is, the learner decides to engage in an activity (such as participate in class, do homework, study for exams) to earn a reward that is not inherently related to the activity (such as receive praise from the teacher, earn a high grade, or enjoy the privilege of doing something different). By contrast, students under the influence of **intrinsic motivation** study a subject or acquire a skill because it produces such inherently positive consequences as becoming more knowledgeable, competent, and independent.

Although extrinsic motivation is widespread in society (individuals are motivated to engage in many activities because they hope to win certificates, badges, medals, public recognition, prizes, or admiration from others), this approach has at least three potential dangers:

Excessive use of external rewards may lead to temporary behavior change, materialistic attitudes, decreased intrinsic motivation

1. Changes in behavior may be temporary. As soon as the extrinsic reward has been obtained, the student may revert to such earlier behaviors as studying inconsistently, turning in poor-quality homework, and disrupting class with irrelevant comments and behaviors.
2. Students may develop a materialistic attitude toward learning. They may think (or say), "What tangible reward will I get if I agree to learn this information?" If the answer is "none," they may decide to make little or no effort to learn it.
3. Giving students extrinsic rewards for completing a task may lessen whatever intrinsic motivation they may have for that activity (Kohn, 1993).

Intrinsic motivation undermined by rewarding students merely for engaging in an activity

This last disadvantage, which is referred to as the *undermining effect*, has been extensively investigated by researchers. It appears that giving students rewards may indeed decrease their intrinsic motivation for a task, but only when (1) initial interest in the activity is very high, (2) the rewards used are not reinforcers (meaning they do not increase the desired behavior), (3) the rewards are held out in advance as incentives, and, most important, (4) the rewards are given simply for engaging in an activity (Cameron & Pierce, 1994; Eisenberger & Cameron, 1996; Ryan & Deci, 1996).

Intrinsic motivation enhanced when reward is given according to predetermined standard or is consistent with individual's level of skill

However, there are two instances in which external rewards may enhance intrinsic motivation. First, when rewards are given according to some predetermined standard of excellence, when the task is moderately challenging, and when the reward is relatively large, intrinsic interest in the task is likely to increase. Second, intrinsic motivation can be enhanced when the task is moderately challenging and the size of the reward is consistent with the individual's perceived level of skill. If a student wins first prize in a science fair, for example, and believes that her project was truly superior to those of the other participants, a large reward may cause her to maintain a strong interest in science (Pintrich & Schunk, 1996).

Taken as a whole, these results strongly suggest that teachers should avoid the indiscriminate use of rewards for influencing classroom behavior, particularly when an activity seems to be naturally interesting to students. Instead, rewards should be used to provide students with information about their level of competence on tasks they have not yet mastered (Lepper, Keavney, & Drake, 1996; Pintrich & Schunk, 1996).

Give rewards sparingly, especially on tasks of natural interest

Cognitive Views of Motivation

Cognitive views stress that human behavior is influenced by the way people think about themselves and their environment. The views of motivation described in this section emphasize how the following five characteristics affect students' intrinsic motivation to learn: the inherent need to construct an organized and logically consistent knowledge base, one's expectations for successfully completing a task, the factors that one believes account for success and failure, one's beliefs about the nature of cognitive ability, and one's interests.

You should also be aware that intrinsic motivation for school learning is fairly well developed by about nine years of age (fourth grade) and becomes increasingly stable through late adolescence. Thus, it is important to develop intrinsic motivation in students in the primary grades as well as to identify students with low levels of academic motivation (Gottfried, Fleming, & Gottfried, 2000).

Cognitive Development and the Need for Conceptual Organization

The cognitive development view is based on Jean Piaget's principles of equilibration, assimilation, accommodation, and schema formation, which we discussed in the chapter on stage theories of development. Piaget proposes that children possess an inherent desire to maintain a sense of organization and balance in their conception of the world (equilibration). A sense of equilibration may be experienced if a child assimilates a new experience by relating it to an existing scheme, or the child may accommodate by modifying an existing scheme if the new experience is too different.

In addition, individuals will repeatedly use new schemes because of an inherent desire to master their environment. This explains why young children can, with no loss of enthusiasm, sing the same song, tell the same story, and play the same game over and over and why they repeatedly open and shut doors to rooms and cupboards with no apparent purpose. It also explains why older children take great delight in collecting and organizing almost everything they can get their hands on and why adolescents who have begun to attain formal operational thinking will argue incessantly about all the unfairness in the world and how it can be eliminated (Stipek, 1998).

Cognitive development view of motivation: strive for equilibration; master the environment

The Need for Achievement

Have you ever decided to take on a moderately difficult task (like take a course on astronomy even though you are a history major and have only a limited background in science) and then found that you had somewhat conflicting feelings about it? On the one hand, you felt eager to start the course, confident that you would be pleased with your performance. But on the other hand, you also felt a bit of anxiety because of the small possibility of failure. Now try to imagine the opposite situation. In reaction to a suggestion to take a course outside your major, you refuse because the probability of failure seems great, while the probability of success seems quite small.

In the early 1960s, John Atkinson (1964) proposed that such differences in achievement behavior are due to differences in something called the *need for achievement*. Atkinson described this need as a global, generalized desire to attain goals that require some degree of competence. He saw this need as being partly innate and partly the result of experience. Individuals with a high need for achievement have a stronger expectation of success than they do a fear of failure for most tasks and therefore anticipate a feeling of pride in accomplishment. When given a choice, high-need achievers seek out moderately challenging tasks because they offer an optimal balance between challenge and expected success. By contrast, individuals with a low need for achievement avoid such tasks because their fear of failure greatly outweighs their expectation of success, and they therefore anticipate feelings of shame. When faced with a choice, they typically choose either relatively easy tasks because the probability of success is high or very difficult tasks because there is no shame in failing to achieve a lofty goal.

Need for achievement revealed by desire to attain goals that require skilled performance

High-need achievers prefer moderately challenging tasks

Low-need achievers prefer very easy or very hard tasks

Atkinson's point about taking fear of failure into account in arranging learning experiences has been made by William Glasser in *Control Theory in the Classroom* (1986) and *The Quality School* (1990). Glasser argues that for people to succeed at life in general, they must first experience success in one important aspect of their lives. For most children, that one important part should be school. But the traditional approach to evaluating learning, which emphasizes comparative grading (commonly called "grading on the curve"), allows only a minority of students to achieve A's and B's and feel successful. The self-worth of the remaining students (who may be quite capable) suffers, which depresses their motivation to achieve on subsequent classroom tasks (Covington, 1985).

Explanations of Success and Failure: Attribution Theory

Some interesting aspects of success and failure are revealed when students are asked to explain why they did or did not do well on some task. The four reasons most commonly given stress are ability, effort, task difficulty, and luck. To explain a low score on a math test, for example, different students might make the following statements:

"I just have a poor head for numbers." (lack of ability)
"I didn't really study for the exam." (lack of effort)
"That test was the toughest I've ever taken." (task difficulty)
"I guessed wrong about which sections of the book to study." (luck)

Because students *attribute* success or failure to the factors just listed, research of this type contributes to what is referred to as **attribution theory**.

Unsuccessful students attribute success to luck, easy tasks; failure, to lack of ability

Students with long histories of academic failure and a weak need for achievement typically attribute their success to easy questions or luck and their failures to lack of ability. Ability is a stable attribution (that is, people expect its effect on achievement to be pretty much the same from one task to another), while task difficulty and luck are both external attributions (in other words, people feel they have little control over their occurrence). Research has shown that stable attributions, particularly ability, lead to expectations of future success or failure, whereas internal attributions (those under personal control) lead to pride in achievement or to shame

Students who attribute success to effort and failure to insufficient effort are more motivated to continue learning than are students who cite task difficulty and luck to explain their successes and failures.

following failure. Because low-achieving students attribute failure to low ability, they see future failure as more likely than future success. In addition, ascribing success to factors beyond one's control diminishes the possibility of taking pride in achievement and placing a high value on rewards. Consequently, satisfactory achievement and reward may have little effect on the failure-avoiding strategies that poor students have developed over the years.

Successful students attribute success to effort, ability; failure, to lack of effort

Success-oriented students (high-need achievers), in contrast, typically attribute success to ability and effort and failure to insufficient effort. Consequently, failure does not diminish expectancy of success, feelings of competence, or reward attractiveness for these students. They simply resolve to work harder in the future (Graham & Weiner, 1993). This attribution pattern holds even for academically gifted students who might be expected to focus on ability because they excel at most tasks and are well aware of their superior capabilities. Citing effort as a factor in their success or failure is thought to be more motivating than citing just ability because effort is a modifiable factor that allows one to feel in control of one's destiny (Dai, Moon, & Feldhusen, 1998).

The typical attribution pattern of high-achieving students highlights an important point: both effort and ability should be credited with contributing to one's success. Students who attribute their success mostly to effort may conclude that they have a low level of ability because they have to work harder to achieve the same level of performance as others (Tollefson, 2000).

Beliefs About the Nature of Cognitive Ability

Throughout the primary and elementary grades, most children believe that academic ability is closely related to effort; those who work hard succeed and become "smarter." But as these same children reach the middle school and high school grades, many of them adopt a different view. Cognitive ability now comes to be seen as a trait—a fixed, stable part of a person that basically cannot be changed. It is not uncommon, for example, to hear older children and adolescents talk about peers who do or do not have "it" (Anderman & Maehr, 1994). Why this change occurs, and why it occurs in some individuals but not others, is not entirely known, but the increased emphasis on norm-referenced grading procedures (meaning that the performance of every student in class is compared to the performance of every other student in that class to determine who gets which grades, a practice we will discuss further in later chapters) is suspected of playing a major role. One casualty of this belief is motivation for learning.

Carol Dweck, who has done extensive research on this topic (see, for example, Cain & Dweck, 1995; Henderson & Dweck, 1990), has found that students can be placed into one of two categories based on their beliefs about the nature of cognitive ability. On the one hand are students who subscribe to what Dweck calls an *entity theory* because they talk about intelligence (another term for cognitive ability) as if it were a thing, or an entity, that has fixed characteristics. On the other hand are students who believe that intelligence can be improved through the use of new thinking skills. Dweck describes these students as subscribing to an *incremental theory* to reflect their belief that intelligence can be improved gradually by degrees or increments.

Students with entity beliefs tend to have performance goals and are motivated to get high grades, avoid failure

Students who believe that intelligence is an unchangeable entity are primarily motivated to prove their ability by getting high grades and praise and by avoiding low grades, criticism, and shame. Such students are said to have *performance goals*. When confronted with a new task, their initial thought is likely to be, "Am I smart enough to do this?" They may forgo opportunities to learn new ideas and skills if they think they will become confused and make mistakes (Mueller & Dweck, 1998).

Among students who subscribe to the entity theory, there is a difference between those with high confidence in their ability and those with low confidence. High-confidence entity theorists are likely to demonstrate such mastery-oriented behaviors as seeking challenges and persisting in the face of difficulty. Those with low confidence, in contrast, may be more interested in avoiding failure and criticism—even after achieving initial success—than in continuing to be positively reinforced for outperforming others. Because of their anxiety over the possibility of failure, these low-confidence entity theorists are less likely than students who have an incremental view of ability to exhibit subsequent motivation for a task (Rawsthorne & Elliot, 1999). If avoidance is not possible, they become discouraged at the first sign of difficulty. This, in turn, produces anxiety, ineffective problem solving, and withdrawal from the task (as a way to avoid concluding that one lacks ability and thereby maintain some self-esteem). According to attribution theory, entity theorists should continue this pattern since success is not attributed to effort, but failure is attributed to low ability.

Students with incremental beliefs tend to have mastery goals and are motivated to meaningfully learn, improve skills

Students with incremental beliefs tend to be motivated to acquire new and more effective cognitive skills and are said to have *mastery goals*. They seek challenging tasks and do not give up easily because they see obstacles as a natural part of the learning process. They often tell themselves what adults have told them for years: "Think carefully," "Pay attention," and "Try to recall useful information that you learned earlier." They seem to focus on the questions, "How do you do this?" and "What can I learn from this?" Errors are seen as opportunities for useful feedback.

The Effect of Interest on Intrinsic Motivation

Interest can be described as a psychological state that involves focused attention, increased cognitive functioning, persistence, and emotional involvement (Hidi, 2000).

The level of interest a student brings to a subject or activity has been shown to affect intrinsic motivation for that task. Such individuals pay greater attention to the task, stay with it for a longer period of time, learn more from it, and enjoy their involvement to a greater degree.

This view of interest may seem obvious. But interest can also grow out of a task situation and produce the same effect on motivation. Consider, for example, a high school student who knows nothing of how information is stored in and retrieved from memory but learns about it when she has to read a chapter on memory in her psychology textbook. Fascinated with the description of various forms of encoding and retrieval cues because of her own problems with being able to recall information for tests accurately, she searches for additional books and articles on the topic and even thinks about majoring in psychology in college.

Students' interest in and level of motivation for a task is also related to whether they adopt mastery goals or performance goals. Students who are highly interested in a task are more likely than those who are less interested to adopt mastery goals and exhibit high motivation. But it can also be the case that students who bring mastery goals to a learning task may be more likely to become interested in the topic than students who have performance goals.

High interest in a subject can lead to mastery goals and intrinsic motivation, or mastery goals can lead to high interest and motivation

Given that some students may develop a strong interest in a topic as a result of a classroom activity or assignment and that this initial interest may grow into a personal interest and the adoption of mastery goals, a general recommendation is for teachers to do what constructivist learning theory implies: involve students in a variety of subject matters and meaningful activities (Hidi & Harackiewicz, 2000).

Factors That Influence Interest A person's interest in a particular subject or activity is typically influenced by a number of factors that fall into one of two categories: individual or situational (Bergin, 1999)—for example:

Interest in a subject can be influenced by individual or situational factors

- *Ideas and activities that are valued by one's culture or ethnic group.* As we discussed in the chapter on cultural diversity, culture is the filter through which groups of people interpret the world and assign values to objects, ideas, and activities. Thus, inner-city male youths are likely to be strongly interested in playing basketball and following the exploits of professional basketball players, whereas a rural midwestern male of the same age is likely to be interested in fishing and hunting.
- *The emotions that are aroused by the subject or activity.* Students who experience extreme math anxiety, for example, are less likely to develop a strong interest in math-related activities than those who experience more positive emotions.
- *The degree of competence one attains in a subject or activity.* People typically spend more time pursuing activities that they are good at than activities at which they do not excel.
- *The degree to which a subject or activity is perceived to be relevant to achieving a goal.* As noted in the chapter on approaches to instruction, many students fail to perceive such relevance, partly because teachers rarely take the time to explain how a topic or lesson may affect students' lives.
- *Level of prior knowledge.* People are often more interested in topics they already know something about than in topics they know nothing about.
- *A perceived hole in a topic that the person already knows a good deal about.* A person who considers himself to be well informed about the music of Mozart would likely be highly interested in reading the score of a newly discovered composition by Mozart.

The situational factors that influence interest include:

- *The opportunity to engage in hands-on activities.*
- A *state of cognitive conflict or disequilibrium.* Teachers can sometimes spark students' interest in a topic by showing or telling them something that is discrepant with a current belief. Consider, for example, a high school class on government. The teacher has a lesson planned on government spending and wants to avoid the usual lack of interest that this topic produces. One tactic would be to ask students if they believe that the money they contribute to social security from their part-time jobs (or the full-time jobs they will eventually have) is placed in an account with their name on it, where it remains until they become eligible for benefits in their mid-sixties. Most will probably believe something like that. The teacher could then tell them that the contributions they make today are actually used to pay the benefits of current retirees and that their social security benefits will come from the social security taxes levied on a future generation of workers.
- *The opportunity to work on a task with others.* As we saw earlier in the book, cooperative arrangements are highly motivating and produce high levels of learning.
- *The opportunity to observe influential models.*
- *The teacher's use of novel stimuli.*
- *The teacher's use of games and puzzles.*

These findings, particularly the ones about individual factors, have several instructional implications. First, find out what your students' interests are, and design as many in-class and out-of-class assignments as possible around those interests. Second, try to associate subjects and assignments with pleasurable rather than painful experiences by using such techniques as cooperative learning, constructivist approaches to teaching, and humanistic approaches to teaching, as well as providing students with the information-processing tools they need to master your objectives. Third, link new topics to information students are already likely to have or provide relevant background knowledge in creative yet understandable ways. Suggestions about how to capitalize on situational factors appear in item 7 of the Suggestions for Teaching in Your Classroom section.

Limitations of Cognitive Views

Often difficult to arouse cognitive disequilibrium

Cognitive Development Although cognitive development theory, with its emphasis on people's need for a well-organized conception of the world, can be useful as a means for motivating students, it has a major limitation: it is not always easy or even possible to induce students to experience a cognitive disequilibrium sufficient to stimulate them to seek answers. This is particularly true if an answer can be found only after comparatively dull and unrewarding information and skills are mastered. (How many elementary school students, for example, might be expected to experience a self-impelled urge to learn English grammar or acquire skill in mathematics?) You are likely to gain some firsthand experience with the difficulty of arousing cognitive disequilibrium the first time you ask students to respond to what you hope will be a provocative question for class discussion. Some students may experience a feeling of intellectual curiosity and be eager to clarify their thinking, but others may stare out the window or surreptitiously do homework for another class.

Need for Achievement Perhaps the major problem that teachers have in using Atkinson's theory of need for achievement is the lack of efficient and objective instruments for measuring its strength. Although you could probably draw reasonably accurate conclusions about whether a student has a high or low need for achievement by watching that student's behavior over time and in a variety of situations, you may not be in a position to make extensive observations. And the problem with short-term observations is that a student's achievement orientation may be affected by more or less chance circumstances.

Need for achievement difficult to assess on basis of short-term observations

A student might do well on a first exam in a course, for example, because the teacher gave in-class time for study and happened to offer advice at a crucial point during the study period. The high score on that test might inspire the student to work for an A in that class. But if that exam happened to be scheduled the day after a two-week bout with the flu, the student might not be well prepared and could end up with a C or D grade. Such a poor performance might cause the student to forget about the A and concentrate instead on obtaining a C.

Attribution Theory and Beliefs About Ability The major implication of the idea that faulty attributions are at least partly responsible for sabotaging students' motivation for learning is to teach students to make more appropriate attributions. But this is likely to be a substantial undertaking requiring a concerted, coordinated effort. One part of the problem in working with students who attribute failure to lack of ability is that ability tends to be seen as a stable factor that is relatively impervious to change. The other part of the problem is that the same students often attribute their success to task difficulty and luck, two factors that cannot be predicted or controlled because they are external and random. Ideas about how to teach students to make more appropriate attributions for success and failure can be found in *Enhancing Motivation: Change in the Classroom* (1976), by Richard deCharms.

Faulty attributions difficult to change

An additional limitation is that attribution training is not likely to be fully effective with elementary school children. For them, two individuals who learn the same amount of material are equally smart despite the fact that one person has to work twice as long to achieve that goal. Older children and adolescents, however, have a better grasp of the concept of efficiency; they see ability as something that influences the amount and effectiveness of effort (Stipek, 1998).

The Humanistic View of Motivation

Abraham Maslow earned his Ph.D. in a psychology department that supported the behaviorist position. After he graduated, however, he came into contact with Gestalt psychologists (a group of German psychologists whose work during the 1920s and 1930s laid the foundation for the cognitive theories of the 1960s and 1970s), prepared for a career as a psychoanalyst, and became interested in anthropology. As a result of these various influences, he came to the conclusion that American psychologists who endorsed the behaviorist position had become so preoccupied with overt behavior and objectivity that they were ignoring other important aspects of human existence (hence, the term *humanistic* to describe his views). When Maslow observed the behavior of especially well-adjusted persons—or *self-actualizers,* as he called them—he concluded that healthy individuals are motivated to seek fulfilling experiences.

For interactive Netlabs on motivation, go to this book's web site at **http://education.college.hmco.com/students**.

Maslow's Theory of Growth Motivation

Maslow describes seventeen propositions, discussed in Chapter 1 of *Motivation and Personality* (1987), that he believes would have to be incorporated into any sound theory of *growth motivation* (or *need gratification*). Referring to need gratification as the most important single principle underlying all development, he adds that "the single, holistic principle that binds together the multiplicity of human motives is the tendency for a new and higher need to emerge as the lower need fulfills itself by being sufficiently gratified" (1968, p. 55).

Maslow elaborates on this basic principle by proposing a five-level hierarchy of needs. *Physiological* needs are at the bottom of the hierarchy, followed in ascending order by *safety, belongingness and love, esteem,* and *self-actualization* needs (see Figure 11.1). This order reflects differences in the relative strength of each need. The lower a need is in the hierarchy, the greater is its strength, because when a lower-level need is activated (as in the case of extreme hunger or fear for one's physical safety), people will stop trying to satisfy a higher-level need (such as esteem or self-actualization) and focus on satisfying the currently active lower-level need (Maslow, 1987).

People are motivated to satisfy deficiency needs only when those needs are unmet

The first four needs (physiological, safety, belongingness and love, and esteem) are often referred to as **deficiency needs** because they motivate people to act only when they are unmet to some degree. Self-actualization, by contrast, is often called a **growth need** because people constantly strive to satisfy it. Basically, **self-actualization** refers to the need for self-fulfillment—the need to develop all of one's potential talents and capabilities. For example, an individual who felt she had the capability to write novels, teach, practice medicine, and raise children would not feel self-actualized until she had accomplished all of these goals to some minimal degree. Because it is at the top of the hierarchy and addresses the potential of the whole person, self-actualization is discussed more frequently than the other needs.

Figure 11.1 Maslow's Hierarchy of Needs

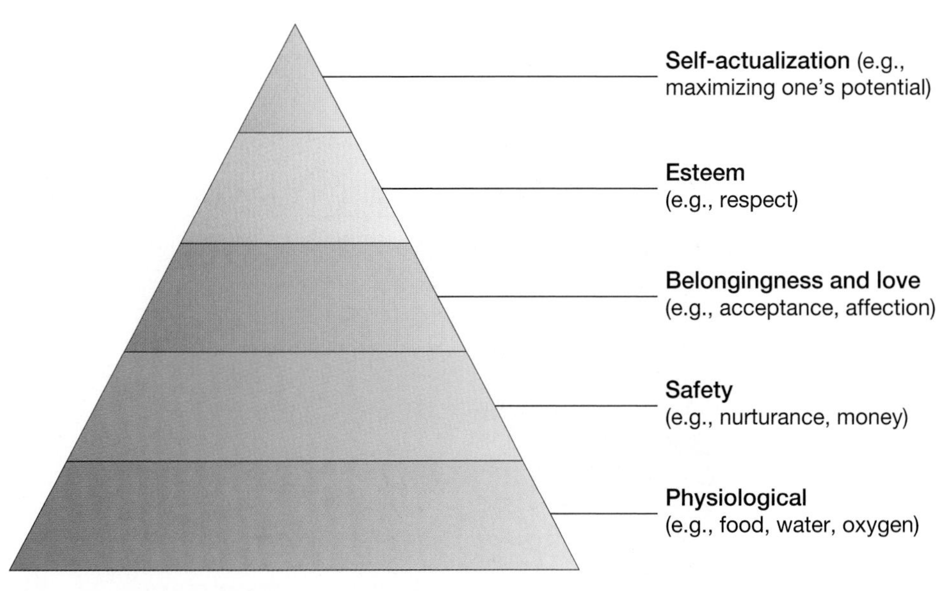

SOURCE: Maslow (1943).

Maslow originally felt that self-actualization needs would automatically be activated as soon as esteem needs were met, but he changed his mind when he encountered individuals whose behavior did not fit this pattern. He concluded that individuals whose self-actualization needs became activated and met held in high regard such values as truth, goodness, beauty, justice, autonomy, and humor (Feist & Feist, 2001).

Self-actualization depends on satisfaction of lower needs, belief in certain values

In addition to the five basic needs that compose the hierarchy, Maslow describes cognitive needs (such as the needs to know and to understand) and aesthetic needs (such as the needs for order, symmetry, or harmony). Although not part of the basic hierarchy, these two classes of needs play a critical role in the satisfaction of basic needs. Maslow maintains that such conditions as the freedom to investigate and learn, fairness, honesty, and orderliness in interpersonal relationships are critical because their absence makes satisfaction of the five basic needs impossible. (Imagine, for example, trying to satisfy your belongingness and love needs or your esteem needs in an atmosphere characterized by dishonesty, unfair punishment, and restrictions on freedom of speech.)

Implications of Maslow's Theory

The implications of Maslow's theory of motivation for teaching are provocative. One down-to-earth implication is that a teacher should do everything possible to see that the lower-level needs of students are satisfied so that students are more likely to function at the higher levels. Students are more likely to be primed to seek satisfaction of the esteem and self-actualization needs, for example, if they are physically comfortable, feel safe and relaxed, have a sense of belonging, and experience self-esteem.

When deficiency needs are not satisfied, person likely to make bad choices

Only when the need for self-actualization is activated is a person likely to choose wisely when given the opportunity. Maslow emphasizes this point by making a distinction between *bad choosers* and *good choosers.* When some people are allowed freedom to choose, they seem to make wise choices consistently. Most people, however, frequently make self-destructive choices. An insecure student, for example, may choose to attend a particular college more on the basis of how close it is to home than on the quality of its academic programs.

Growth, as Maslow sees it, is the result of a never-ending series of situations

Theorists like Abraham Maslow, who argue that deficiency needs such as belongingness and self-esteem must be satisfied before students will be motivated to learn, call attention to the importance of positive teacher-student relationships in the classroom.

offering a free choice between the attractions and dangers of safety and those of growth. If a person is functioning at the level of growth needs, the choice will ordinarily be a progressive one. Maslow adds, however, that "the environment (parents, therapists, teachers) . . . can help by making the growth choice positively attractive and less dangerous, and by making the regressive choice less attractive and more costly" (1968, pp. 58–59). This point can be clarified by a simple diagram Maslow uses to illustrate a situation involving choice (1968, p. 47).

Enhance the dangers		Enhance the attraction
Safety	← **Person** →	**Growth**
Minimize the attractions		Minimize the dangers

This diagram emphasizes that if you set up learning situations that impress students as dangerous, threatening, or of little value, they are likely to play it safe, make little effort to respond, or even try to avoid learning. If, however, you make learning appear appealing, minimize pressure, and reduce possibilities for failure or embarrassment, your students are likely to be willing, if not eager, to do an assigned task.

Encourage growth choices by enhancing attractions, minimizing dangers

Limitations of Maslow's Theory

Although Maslow's speculations are thought provoking, they are also sometimes frustrating. You may conclude, for instance, that awareness of his hierarchy of needs will make it possible for you to do an excellent job of motivating your students, only to discover that you don't know exactly how to apply what you have learned. Quite often, for example, you may not be able to determine precisely which of a student's needs are unsatisfied. Even if you *are* quite sure that a student lacks interest in learning because he feels unloved or insecure, you may not be able to do much about it. A girl who feels that her parents do not love her or that her peers do not accept her may not respond to your efforts. And if her needs for love, belonging, and esteem are not satisfied, she is less likely to be in the mood to learn.

Teachers may be able to satisfy some deficiency needs but not others

Then again, there will be times when you can be quite instrumental in helping to satisfy certain deficiency needs. The development of self-esteem, for example, is closely tied to successful classroom achievement for almost all students. Although you may not be able to feed students when they are hungry or protect them from physical danger, you can always take steps to help them learn more effectively.

The Role of Self-Perceptions in Motivation

Current interest in the effects of self-perceptions on school motivation and achievement runs high and seems to have been prompted by such developments as a better understanding of the nature of self-concept and self-esteem, Albert Bandura's introduction of the self-efficacy concept, advances in the measurement of self-perceptions, and the consistent finding of a positive relationship among self-perceptions, motivation, and school achievement. Much of this interest can be traced to ideas published during the 1960s and 1970s by psychologists such as Abraham Maslow, Carl Rogers, and Arthur Combs. These individuals stressed that how students see and judge themselves and others play an important part in determining how motivated they are and how much they learn.

Table 11.1 Comparing Self-Concept, Self-Esteem, and Self-Efficacy

Type of Self-Perception	Characteristics	Examples
Self-concept	• The nonevaluative picture people have of themselves. • Made up of components that are hierarchically arranged—for example, academic self-concept = verbal self-concept + mathematical self-concept + science self-concept, etc.	• "I am a sixth grader." • "I am five feet one inch tall." • "My favorite subject is history."
Self-esteem	• The evaluative judgments we make of the various components of our self-concept. • Self-concept describes who you are; self-esteem indicates how you feel about that identity.	• "I'm pretty smart at math." • "I'm not attractive because my nose is too big for my face." • "I'm disappointed that most people don't like me." • "I'm satisfied with how well I speak and understand a foreign language."
Self-efficacy	• The evaluative judgments we make of how capable we think we are at organizing and carrying out a specific course of action.	• "I believe I can learn how to use a computer program." • "I'll never be able to figure out how to solve quadratic equations."

SOURCES: Bandura (1986); Beane (1994); Harter (1988); Marsh, Byrne, & Shavelson (1992); Pajares (1996); Schunk (1995).

Self-concept is description of self; self-esteem is value we place on that description

Previously in the book, we discussed the notions of self-concept, self-esteem, and self-efficacy as important aspects of children's emotional and cognitive development. We review each of these concepts in Table 11.1 because of their relationship to motivation.

For a classroom example of self-efficacy and motivation, see the Site-Based Cases at **http://education.college.hmco.com/students**.

The Role of Self-Concept and Self-Esteem in Motivation and Learning

Over the years, researchers have consistently found a moderately positive relationship (called a correlation) between measures of self-esteem and school achievement. Students who score relatively high on measures of self-esteem tend to have higher-than-average grades. But correlation does not imply causation. The fact that students with high self-esteem scores tend to have high grades is not sufficient grounds for concluding that high self-esteem causes high achievement. It is just as plausible that high achievement causes increased self-esteem or that increases in both variables are due to the influence of a third variable. Recent work on the antecedents and consequences of self-esteem has begun to shed some light on what causes what.

Figure 11.2 **Causes and Consequences of Academic Self-Esteem**

Competence in domains where success is important → Self-Esteem
Support, positive feedback from significant others → Self-Esteem
Self-Esteem → Mood → Motivation

SOURCE: Adapted from Harter (1988).

High self-esteem due to being competent at valued tasks, reinforcement from others

Susan Harter (1988), on the basis of her own research and that of others, proposes the causal explanation depicted in Figure 11.2. Harter believes that achieving an acceptable level of competence in school, valuing academic success (which most students do), and being given support and positive feedback for one's academic accomplishments by parents, teachers, and friends are the primary determinants of high self-esteem. High self-esteem contributes, in turn, to feeling satisfied and pleased about one's accomplishments, which contributes to the development of intrinsic motivation. Such students are likely to be curious about many things, to find schoolwork interesting, and to prefer moderately challenging tasks. This motivational orientation leads to high levels of achievement, which maintain high levels of self-esteem, and so on.

Students who have a positive self-concept tend to be intrinsically motivated. They have a high level of curiosity, are interested in schoolwork, and prefer moderately challenging tasks.

difficult as it might seem. Some researchers use a relatively small set of questions ("How good are you at math?" "If you were to rank all the students in your math class from the worst to the best, where would you put yourself?" "Compared to your other school subjects, how good are you at math?") and ask students to rate themselves on a 7-point scale that may range from "not at all good" to "very good" (Stipek, 1998).

Another problem is that whatever success you may have in changing the sense of self-esteem and self-efficacy of students is likely to be slow in coming. This conclusion follows from two others. One is that changes in self-perception are best made by helping students become more effective learners than by constantly telling them they should feel good about themselves. The second conclusion is that learning how to use the cognitive skills that result in meaningful learning takes time because of their complexity and the doubts that some students will have about their ability to master these skills.

Motivating Students with Technology

Extrinsic Versus Intrinsic Motivation

Previously in this chapter, we contrasted the behavioral, or extrinsic, approach to motivation with various cognitive, or intrinsic, approaches. Our goal was not to demonstrate that one approach is inherently superior to the other but to point out how and when both approaches can profitably be used to support classroom learning. A parallel situation exists with regard to the motivating effects of technology. Behavioral psychologists, for example, argue that students who work on computer-based drill-and-practice programs are motivated by the immediate feedback they receive and the steady progress they make. Cognitive psychologists argue that involving students in fantasy environments or authentic tasks that are directed to audiences beside the teacher is intrinsically motivating because such programs and tasks give students a sense of confidence, personal responsibility, and control over their own learning (Collins, 1996).

Despite the differences in these two approaches to motivation, they are not mutually exclusive. Some of the most innovative and effective technological aids to learning combine both approaches. For example, the Jasper Woodbury series, which we mentioned in the chapter on constructivist learning theory, tries to engage intrinsic motivation by giving students control over and responsibility for how they collect, analyze, and use the data presented by the program and by embedding the task in a realistic context. The accompanying extrinsic rewards include class announcements of accomplishments, student demonstrations of problem-solving strategies, teacher praise for correct problem solutions, and feedback and encouragement from peers in other schools about one's problem solutions (Barron et al., 1995; Cognition and Technology Group at Vanderbilt, 1996). Other types of extrinsic rewards that can be used in conjunction with other technology-based approaches to learning include membership in multimedia clubs, special computer events and fairs for parents or the community, and certificates of recognition.

Technology can be used to support both extrinsic and intrinsic motivation

Can Technology Increase Motivation to Learn?

Now that we've established that computer-based technology can accommodate extrinsic and intrinsic approaches to motivation, we can look at whether it does, in fact, increase students' motivation to learn.

Critics of computer-based learning argue that any observed increases in student motivation are likely to be short term and due largely to the novelty of the medium. But several studies have demonstrated that the use of computer-based instruction increases students' intrinsic motivation and performance. Diana Cordova and Mark Lepper (1996) found that rich fantasy contexts, personalization, and provision for student choice within children's software not only foster intrinsic motivation and deeper engagement in learning but also boost the amount that students learn, their perceived level of competence, and their levels of aspiration. Another study looked at Malaysian middle school students who were considered to be at risk because of low self-efficacy and motivation. These students were taught how to use CD-ROMs and the Internet to locate information for various subjects. They then became the "technology experts" for projects that were assigned to their respective cooperative learning group. Over the school year, these students became more interested in their school work, were more willing to work on class assignments, and increased their participation in class discussions (Gan, 1999).

A collaborative research and development program among public schools, universities, research agencies and the Apple Computer Corporation, called Apple Classrooms of Tomorrow (ACOT), was created in 1985 to study the effects of technology on teaching and learning. A decade-long evaluation of the ACOT project by Judith Haymore Sandholtz, Cathy Ringstaff, and David Dwyer (1997) revealed that once the novelty factor has worn off, at least five factors affect student engagement with technology:

1. Motivation remains high when technology use is appropriate for the assignment and when teachers treat educational technology as one of many possible instructional tools.
2. Technology must be integrated, or immersed, into the curriculum, not treated as a separate subject.
3. Students are more engaged when using the computer as a tool than when the computer is mostly used as a drill-and-practice tutor.
4. Teachers must adjust their use of technology to student ability levels; tasks that are too hard are likely to be frustrating, and tasks that are too simple are likely to be boring.
5. Teachers must be willing to allow students more control over their own learning by using projects and interdisciplinary forms of learning.

More information on ACOT can be found on the Apple web site at **www.apple.com/education/k12/leadership/acot/**.

Go to the Web Sources section of this book's web site at **http://education.college.hmco.com/students** for direct links to ACOT materials and other important web pages.

Using Multimedia and Hypermedia to Increase Motivation

As we indicated previously, the images, text, sound, video, and animation of multimedia and hypermedia can help gain student attention and make learning more relevant, thereby fostering a sense of learner control and intrinsic motivation (Becker & Dwyer, 1994).

Research shows that multimedia presentations are more motivating than print

CASE *in* PRINT

Helping Teachers Develop Students' Self-Efficacy, Self-Esteem, and Motivation

Achieving an acceptable level of competence in school, valuing academic success . . . and being given support and positive feedback for one's academic accomplishments by parents, teachers, and friends are the primary determinants of high [academic] self-esteem. High self-esteem contributes, in turn, to feeling satisfied and pleased about one's accomplishments, which contributes to the development of intrinsic motivation. (p. 396–397)

Instituting Efficacy: Self-Esteem Principles May Be Tested at Burke High

ESTHER SHEIN

Boston Sunday Globe 6/18/95

One of the first calls Steven Leonard made when he was named headmaster of Boston's Jeremiah E. Burke High School was to the Lexington-based Efficacy Institute. Leonard, who earlier this month was given the formidable task of helping the Burke regain its accreditation, has trained at the institute himself, and he was confident it could help his teachers.

His confidence is based not just on his own experience. Since it was founded 10 years ago, the Efficacy Institute has trained some 20,000 teachers in 64 school districts across the state. Its teaching is based on the principle that intelligence is a developmental process, not something a person is born with. It tries to instill the notion in teachers that all students have the ability to learn when teachers believe in the students' capabilities and the students are given confidence.

If he can come up with the $300 per-person training fee for the institute's four-day training sessions, Leonard said, Efficacy training will be a requirement for all teachers who remain at the Burke next fall.

"Efficacy is part of the solution," he said in a recent interview. "After you eliminate . . . the staff people that can't perform or don't want to perform in ways that are essential to educating children, you get to the realization that, in many, if not most, cases, teachers have been left in the lurch as far as professional development in teaching the contemporary child."

Efficacy founder Jeff Howard said he will work closely with Leonard to train the Burke's teachers. But he said the city, in turn, needs to make an investment in the school building to show the students it cares about their welfare.

"The City of Boston ought to be ashamed of how it's treated that building," said Howard, a Harvard-educated social psychologist, "and the deplorable conditions the faculty has had to work under."

Another hurdle, Howard said, is helping teachers overcome a high level of frustration. They have become demoralized, he said, because society no longer views the teaching profession as prestigious.

"It's a terrible state for teachers to be in," he said. "They desperately want to be great teachers again—everybody wants to be effective in their work—and our secret weapon is that we help them feel effective again."

Another burden placed on teachers, Howard said, is the notion that there's an "unequal distribution of intelligence, and that the kinds of kids that go to inner-city schools . . . don't have a lot of intelligence."

That, he said, puts teachers "in a tough situation. They're given these kids that nobody thinks can learn much, and then they're given the mandate that they have to teach them."

Efficacy's role, according to Howard, is to "explode that bind. The underlying premise is all wrong." All students can learn, he said, if they are perceived to have the right attitude. But before that can happen, he said, the teachers' own attitude has to change.

"They have the capacity to be some of the best professionals in American society," Howard said of the teachers. "They have potential to be creative, disciplined, highly skilled, lifelong learners, but they have to believe in themselves and the kids. American society makes that hard; we make it easy."

Mia Roberts, director of community services for the institute, said much of the frustration lies in the fact that "kids come into school now with lots of other needs," including emotional and health issues.

Consequently, she said, the teachers become "educators, counselors, psychologists and moms and dads all rolled into one . . . and that can be very overwhelming."

Efficacy stresses, she said, that "all people are capable of brilliance and no one has limits. Human capabilities . . . can be developed throughout life."

That idea has become almost a religious belief for Jesse Solomon, a math teacher at Brighton High School who first learned about the institute while doing a college internship there.

"Having someone unconditionally believe in your intelligence can only be a positive thing," he said. "It turns kids around at best, and allows them small successes at worst."

Solomon believes he has always had a positive attitude toward his students, but he said Efficacy helped him translate that into action.

"Everything you see in your classroom sends a million messages a day," Solomon said, including messages about high expectations. But if those messages come from someone who believes in them, he said, the students are more likely to perform effectively.

Solomon recalled a middle-school student he taught for two years. For no particular reason, Solomon said, the student did poorly his first year.

"Showing him that I had a belief in him that wasn't going to go away . . . caused him to put in hard work," Solomon said. "He came to school every day, and he graduated as a competent and confident student, more so than when I first met him."

Solomon attributes the turnaround to the student's increased motivation level and the desire to "make himself get smarter. The work has to be well-designed and supported, but I think that's the only way to get smarter."

Solomon said Efficacy also taught him the importance of creating networks with other teachers.

"No change or reform is going to come without those networks," he said. Calling teaching "a very isolated profession," Solomon said it would be cathartic for teachers to meet once a week after school to discuss issues such as dealing with students, developing curricula together or even reading articles about education.

"Often," he said, "there's no built-in time to share what you do professionally or no time to discuss their craft."

. . . The new headmaster said his challenge is to change the misperception that "some kids make it and some kids don't, and those who flunk are dumb . . . and the kids who make it are smart."

Leonard said Efficacy helps teachers understand that, many times, what's perceived as their failure is really "the failure of school systems and the university community to prepare teachers to do the job of urban education in 1995."

Even the best teachers will be deemed ineffective if they're asked to perform at levels that "exhaust their physical or mental resources, and right now that's what's being asked of many teachers—especially in urban environments—where issues of poverty are becoming more demanding and resources are decreasing."

Questions and Activities

1. The philosophy of the Efficacy Institute is that students' intellectual capabilities can be improved through systematic efforts that combine high-quality instruction and positive feedback from teachers about students' competence. This is the same idea as Dweck's incremental theory of intelligence. Do you share that belief? If so, what evidence can you cite in support of it? If you don't share that belief, can you explain why not?

2. Mia Roberts, the director of community services for the Efficacy Institute, noted that one of the challenges for teachers is that "kids come into school now with lots of other needs," and that these needs include emotional and health issues. As we pointed out in this chapter, Maslow's theory suggests that as long as a person's deficiency needs are unmet, growth needs will not be activated. One implication of this analysis is that teachers need to be aware of students' unmet deficiency needs. What steps can you take to increase the likelihood that you will notice and attend to a student's physiological, safety, belongingness, and esteem needs?

3. If you have the opportunity to work with a low-achieving student, systematically provide the type of positive feedback described in the article and note any subsequent changes in the student's behavior. Ask the student whether his or her self-efficacy and beliefs about intelligence changed as a function of your comments.

materials for middle school and high school students. In one study (Woodul, Vitale, & Scott, 2000), a group of eighth graders who were judged to be candidates for dropping out of school because of academic and social problems received two weeks of instruction on the Bill of Rights. For the following week, some of these students put together a multimedia project on the Bill of Rights and its influence on the life of Dr. Martin Luther King, Jr., while the remaining students were exposed to a combination of lecture, review, and classroom projects on the same topic. After a one-week delay, the multimedia group displayed their project to other eighth-grade students in the school, while the traditional group was given a short review of the material. The multimedia group significantly outscored the traditional group on a subsequent test on the Bill of Rights, as well as on measures of attitude toward social studies learning, attitude toward school, and self-confidence in school learning. In another study (Marr, 2000), high school seniors working in cooperative learning groups created PowerPoint presentations on the themes of poets of the Romantic period (PowerPoint is a software program from Microsoft that allows users to create slide shows that combine text, graphics, motion, sounds, and video). Compared to previous classes, this group showed a much higher level of motivation for learning about this subject matter.

Technology increases intrinsic motivation by making learning more interesting and meaningful

One form of multimedia, CD-ROM storybooks, allows young children a chance to pursue topics of interest and learn at their own pace and with their personal learning style (Glasgow, 1997). Since a CD-ROM can store 500,000 pages of text, large collections of literature can be contained on a single disk. With some of these tools, children not only read or listen to a story, but can even create their own storybook presentations or songs, complete with pictures, words, and sound. Such activities encourage active involvement in learning and the development of children's imaginations.

For slightly older children, CD-ROMs like Where in the World Is Carmen Sandiego? can teach research and geography skills as students track a gang of thieves who have stolen some of the world's greatest treasures from across the globe (Carroll, Knight, & Hutchinson, 1995). Motivators here include the humorous format, the challenge of following clues as a detective would in order to issue a warrant and complete an arrest, and amassing the points awarded for correct capture. Math Heads is a CD-ROM designed for students who need help with math reasoning; relationships with fractions, decimals, and percentages; solving word problems; and developing estimating skills. Students begin by creating a character. All the characters then become contestants on "Math Head TV," where they compete to solve math problems and earn points (Allen, 1997).

Using Constructivist-Oriented Technology to Increase Motivation

Common computer application tools—word processors, databases, simulations, telecommunications, spreadsheets, outlining tools, three-dimensional charts and graphs, and presentation tools—can also be used to motivate students. Databases might inspire students to search and sort through information while creating reports and knowledge bases, and simulations offer various gamelike features and immediate feedback. Such tools can be combined for enhancing student motivation through multimedia project presentations or interactive exhibits placed in local museums (Carver, 1995). Some students in one Nevada school were so motivated by their semester-long multimedia project on water use in their state that they came to school as early as 6 A.M. to work on it and stayed after 4 P.M. Students also conducted additional field studies to verify their work and spent weekends checking out possible sites for videotaping (Ebert & Strudler, 1996).

As mentioned in previous chapters, the Geometric Supposer software can motivate students to learn mathematics by allowing them to invent, explore, and question various geometric properties and relationships (Schwartz, 1995). Similarly, a program called Cocoa (which can be downloaded from the Kids Domain web site at **www.kidsdomain.com/games/cocoa/download.html**) allows children to build their own simulations by designing objects and then creating and combining rules for the behavior of those objects on the screen (Woolsey & Bellamy, 1997). For instance, a student might draw a school of fish on the screen and then make decisions about the way they swim, the food they eat, and what they do if any of them runs into a wall or another fish. Research on such constructivist tools, in particular LOGO, demonstrates that they can increase student **locus of control**, which is the perception that positive and negative events are under one's control (Bernhard & Siegel, 1994), as well as student willingness to accept challenges (Tyler & Vasu, 1995). These tools can also increase student motivation and perceived competence (Nastasi & Clements, 1994).

As mentioned in previous chapters, web-based conferencing, e-mail, online chats, and electronic discussion forums increase motivation to learn since they provide students access to information and communities that previously were beyond the boundaries of their classrooms and offer unique opportunities to collect meaningful, real-life data.

E-mail is often used to heighten student interest and motivation through pen pal projects that link students in different countries or locales or to coordinate interschool projects. Celeste Oakes (1996) described how she used e-mail with her first-grade class in Nevada to correspond with students in Alaska, ask questions of space shuttle astronauts, collaboratively write stories with students from other schools, and write letters to Santa Claus. Rebecca Sipe (2000) described a project in which her preservice teacher education undergraduates corresponded with tenth-grade English students, who helped the preservice students formulate realistic classroom beliefs and practices. Dean Blase (2000) arranged for his middle school class in Cincinnati to exchange e-mail messages about the meaning of a novel with students from Vermont, Massachusetts, and Texas. Carole Duff (2000) described how female high school students use e-mail to get career advice, academic guidance, and personal support from a professional woman mentor. In any of these projects, it is critical to have icebreaking activities, goals that relate to key objectives, and ground rules for collaboration (for example, time length, targeted deadlines, final project guidelines, and plans for culminating activities).

Now that you are familiar with the various theories about and approaches to motivation, it is time to consider the Suggestions for Teaching in Your Classroom that follow and show how these ideas can be converted into classroom practice.

SUGGESTIONS FOR TEACHING IN YOUR CLASSROOM

Motivating Students to Learn

1 Use behavioral techniques to help students exert themselves and work toward remote goals.

Journal Entry
Using Behavior Modification Techniques to Motivate

Maslow's hierarchy of needs calls attention to the reasons that few students come to school bursting with eagerness to learn. Only students with all their deficiency needs satisfied are likely to experience a desire to know and understand. But even growth-motivated students may not fully appreciate the need to master certain basic skills before they can engage in more exciting and rewarding kinds of learning. And as we noted already, the information that appropriately administered reinforcement provides about one's level of competence contributes to high levels of self-esteem. Accordingly, you may often need to give your students incentives to learn. Techniques you might use for this purpose were described in the chapter on behavioral and social learning theories. They include verbal praise, shaping, modeling, symbolic reinforcers (smile faces, stars, and the like), and contingency contracting.

a. Give positive reinforcement, but do so effectively.

Think about the times when you've been praised for a job well done, particularly when you weren't sure about the quality of your work. In all likelihood, it had a strong, maybe even dramatic, effect on your motivation. That being the case, you might think that effective positive reinforcement in the form of verbal praise is a common occurrence in the classroom. But you would be wrong. Extensive observations of classroom life reveal that verbal praise is rarely given (Goodlad, 1984) and is often given in ways that limit its effectiveness (Brophy, 1981). Jere Brophy recommends that teachers use praise in the following ways:

- As a spontaneous expression of surprise or admiration. ("Why, Juan! This report is really excellent!")
- As compensation for criticism or as vindication of a prediction. ("After your last report, Lily, I said I knew you could do better. Well, you have done better. This is really excellent.")
- As an attempt to impress all members of a class. ("I like the way Nguyen just put his books away so promptly.")
- As a transition ritual to verify that an assignment has been completed. ("Yes, Maya, that's very good. You can work on your project now.")
- As a consolation prize or as encouragement to students who are less capable than others. ("Well, Josh, you kept at it, and you got it finished. Good for you!")

In an effort to help teachers administer praise more effectively, Brophy drew up the guidelines for effective praise listed in Table 11.2.

b. Use other forms of positive reinforcement.

In addition to verbal praise, you can make use of such other forms of positive reinforcement as modeling, symbolic reinforcers, and contingency contracts.

EXAMPLES

- Arrange for students to observe that classmates who persevere and complete a task receive a reinforcer of some kind. (But let this occur more or less naturally. Also, don't permit students

Table 11.2 Guidelines for Effective Praise

Effective Praise	Ineffective Praise
1. Is delivered contingently	1. Is delivered randomly or unsystematically
2. Specifies the particulars of the accomplishment.	2. Is restricted to global positive reactions
3. Shows spontaneity, variety, and other signs of credibility; suggests clear attention to the student's accomplishment	3. Shows a bland uniformity, which suggests a conditional response made with minimal attention
4. Rewards attainment of specified performance criteria (which can include effort criteria, however)	4. Rewards mere participation, without consideration of performance process or outcomes
5. Provides information to students about their competence or the value of their accomplishments	5. Provides no information at all or gives students information about their status
6. Orients students toward better appreciation of their own task-related behavior and thinking about problem solving	6. Orients students toward comparing themselves with others and thinking about competing
7. Uses students' own prior accomplishments as the context for describing new accomplishments	7. Uses the accomplishments of peers as the context for describing students' present accomplishments
8. Is given in recognition of noteworthy effort or success at tasks that are difficult (for *this* student)	8. Is given without regard to the effort expended or the meaning of the accomplishment (for *this* student)
9. Attributes success to effort and ability, implying that similar successes can be expected in the future	9. Attributes success to ability alone or to external factors such as luck or easy task
10. Leads students to expend effort on the task because they enjoy the task or want to develop task-relevant skills	10. Leads students to expend effort on the task for external reasons—to please the teacher, win a competition or reward, etc.
11. Focuses students' attention on their own task-relevant behavior	11. Focuses students' attention on the teacher as an external authority figure who is manipulating them
12. Fosters appreciation of and desirable attributions about task-relevant behavior after the process is completed	12. Intrudes into the ongoing proccess, distracting attention from task-relevant behavior.

SOURCE: Brophy (1981).

who have finished an assignment to engage in attention-getting or obviously enjoyable self-chosen activities; those who are still working on the assignment may become a bit resentful and therefore less inclined to work on the task at hand.)

- Draw happy faces on primary grade students' papers, give check marks as students complete assignments, write personal comments acknowledging good work, and assign bonus points.
- Develop an individual reward menu, or contract, with each student based on the Premack principle (Grandma's rule), which we discussed earlier in the book. After passing a spelling

12 Classroom Management

By now you have no doubt begun to realize what we pointed out at the beginning of the book: teaching is a complex enterprise. It is complex for the following reasons:

- Students vary in their physical, social, emotional, cognitive, and cultural characteristics.
- Learning occurs gradually and only with extensive and varied practice.
- Different students learn at different rates.
- Systematic preparations have to be made to ensure that students master the objectives that teachers lay out.
- Students are motivated to learn (or not learn) by different factors.
- Learning can be measured and evaluated in a variety of ways.

If not managed properly, an endeavor as complex as teaching can easily become chaotic. When that happens, students are likely to become confused, bored, uninterested, restless, and perhaps even disruptive. But a well-managed classroom is not what many people think: students working silently at their desks (or in front of their computers), speaking only when spoken to, and providing verbatim

Key Points

These key points will help you learn the important information in this chapter. To help you study, they also appear in the margins of the pages, next to the text where they are discussed.

Authoritarian, Permissive, and Authoritative Approaches to Classroom Management

- Authoritative approach to classroom management superior to permissive and authoritarian approaches

Preventing Problems: Techniques of Classroom Management

- Ripple effect: group response to a reprimand directed at an individual
- Teachers who show they are "with it" head off discipline problems
- Being able to handle overlapping activities helps maintain classroom control
- Teachers who continually interrupt activities have discipline problems
- Keeping entire class involved and alert minimizes misbehavior
- Identify misbehavers; firmly specify constructive behavior
- Well-managed classroom: students complete clear assignments in busy but pleasant atmosphere
- Effective teachers plan how to handle classroom routines
- During first weeks, have students complete clear assignments under your direction
- Manage behavior of adolescents by making and communicating clear rules and procedures

Suggestions for Teaching in Your Classroom: Techniques of Classroom Management

- Establish, call attention to, and explain class rules the first day
- Establish a businesslike but supportive classroom atmosphere

Techniques for Dealing with Behavior Problems

- Use supportive reactions to help students develop self-control
- Give criticism privately; then offer encouragement
- I-message: tell how you feel about an unacceptable situation
- Determine who owns a problem before deciding on course of action
- No-lose method: come to mutual agreement about a solution to a problem

Suggestions for Teaching in Your Classroom: Handling Problem Behavior

- Be prompt, consistent, reasonable when dealing with misbehavior

Violence in American Schools

- Incidents of crime and serious violence occur relatively infrequently in public schools
- Male aggressiveness due to biological and cultural factors
- Middle school boys with low grades may feel trapped
- Misbehavior of high school students may reveal lack of positive identity
- School violence can be reduced by improving student achievement levels
- Violence less likely when students invited to participate in making decisions

recitations of what the teacher and textbook said. Such a classroom is incompatible with the contemporary views of learning and motivation described in the preceding chapters. If some of your goals are for students to acquire a meaningful knowledge base, become proficient problem solvers, and learn how to work productively with others, then you have to accept the idea that these goals are best met in classrooms that are characterized by a fair amount of autonomy, physical movement, and social interaction (McCaslin & Good, 1992).

To help you accomplish these goals *and* keep student behavior within manageable bounds, we describe in this chapter a general approach to classroom management that is related to an effective parenting style, various techniques that you can use to prevent behavior problems from occurring, and a set of techniques for dealing with misbehavior once it has occurred. In addition, we analyze the issue of school violence and summarize approaches to reducing its frequency. ■

Authoritarian, Permissive, and Authoritative Approaches to Classroom Management

To preview this chapter's key ideas, see the Chapter Themes on the Snowman textbook site at **http://education.college.hmco.com/students**.

You may recall from the chapter on age-level characteristics that Diana Baumrind (1971, 1991a) found that parents tend to exhibit one of four styles in managing the behavior of their children: authoritarian, permissive, authoritative, or rejecting-neglecting. The first three of these styles have been applied to a teacher's actions in the classroom. We will quickly review Baumrind's categories and then take a brief look at how teachers' approaches to management can be characterized by these styles too.

Authoritarian parents establish rules for their children's behavior and expect them to be blindly obeyed. Explanations of why a particular rule is necessary are almost never given. Instead, rewards and punishments are given for following or not following rules. *Permissive* parents represent the other extreme. They impose few controls. They allow their children to make many basic decisions (such as what to eat, what to wear, when to go to bed) and provide advice or assistance only when asked. *Authoritative* parents provide rules but discuss the reasons for them, teach their children how to meet them, and reward children for exhibiting self-control. Authoritative parents also cede more responsibility for self-governance to their children as the children demonstrate increased self-regulation skills. This style, more so than the other two, leads to children's internalizing the parents' norms and maintaining intrinsic motivation for following them in the future.

You can probably see the parallel between Baumrind's work and classroom management. Teachers who adopt an authoritarian style tend to have student compliance as their main goal ("Do what I say because I say so") and make heavy use of rewards and punishments to produce that compliance. Teachers who adopt a permissive style rely heavily on students' identifying with and respecting them as their main approach to classroom management ("Do what I say because you like me and respect my judgment"). Teachers who adopt an authoritative style have as their main goal students who can eventually regulate their own behavior. By explaining the rationale for classroom rules and adjusting those rules as students demonstrate the ability to govern themselves appropriately, authoritative teachers hope to convince students that adopting the teacher's norms for classroom behavior as their own will lead to the achievement of valued academic goals ("Do what I say because doing so will help you learn more"). The students of authoritative teachers better understand the need for classroom rules and tend to operate within them most of the time (McCaslin & Good, 1992).

Authoritative approach to classroom management superior to permissive and authoritarian approaches

The next part of this chapter will describe guidelines you might follow to establish and maintain an effective learning environment.

Preventing Problems: Techniques of Classroom Management

Kounin's Observations on Group Management

Interest in the significance of classroom management was kindled when Jacob Kounin wrote a book titled *Discipline and Group Management in Classrooms* (1970). Kounin noted that he first became interested in group management when he reprimanded a college student for blatantly reading a newspaper in class. Kounin was struck by the extent to which the entire class responded to a reprimand directed at only one person, and he subsequently dubbed this the **ripple effect**. Chances are you can recall a situation when you were diligently working away in a classroom and the teacher suddenly became quite angry at a disruptive classmate. If you felt a bit tense after the incident (even though your behavior was blameless) and tried to give the impression that you were a paragon of student virtue, you have had personal experience with the ripple effect.

Ripple effect: group response to a reprimand directed at an individual

Once his interest in classroom behavior was aroused, Kounin supervised a series of observational and experimental studies of student reactions to techniques of teacher control. In analyzing the results of these various studies, he came to the con-

Jacob Kounin found that teachers who were "with it" could deal with overlapping situations, maintained smoothness and momentum in class activities, used a variety of activities, kept the whole class involved, and had few discipline problems.

clusion that the following classroom management techniques appear to be most effective.

Teachers who show they are "with it" head off discipline problems

1. *Show your students that you are "with it."* Kounin coined the term **withitness** to emphasize that teachers who prove to their students that they know what is going on in a classroom usually have fewer behavior problems than teachers who appear to be unaware of incipient disruptions. An expert at classroom management will nip trouble in the bud by commenting on potentially disruptive behavior before it gains momentum. An ineffective teacher may not notice such behavior until it begins to spread and then perhaps hopes that it will simply go away.

   At first glance Kounin's suggestion that you show that you are with it might seem to be in conflict with operant conditioning's prediction that nonreinforced behavior will disappear. If the teacher's reaction is the only source of reinforcement in a classroom, ignoring behavior may cause it to disappear. In many cases, however, a misbehaving student gets reinforced by the reactions of classmates. Therefore, ignoring behavior is much less likely to lead to extinction of a response in a classroom than in controlled experimental situations.

Journal Entry
Learning to Deal with Overlapping Situations

2. *Learn to cope with overlapping situations.* When he analyzed videotapes of actual classroom interactions, Kounin found that some teachers seemed to have one-track minds. They were inclined to deal with only one thing at a time, and this way of proceeding caused frequent interruptions in classroom routine. One primary grade teacher whom Kounin observed, for example, was working with a reading group when she noticed two boys on the other side of the room poking each other. She abruptly got up, walked over to the boys, berated them at length, and then returned to the reading group. By the time she returned, however, the children in the reading group had become bored and listless and were tempted to engage in mischief of their own.

   Being able to handle overlapping activities helps maintain classroom control

   Kounin concluded that withitness and skill in handling overlapping activities seemed to be related. An expert classroom manager who is talking to children in a reading group, for example, might notice two boys at the far side of the room who are beginning to scuffle with each other. Such a teacher might in mid-sentence tell the boys to stop and make the point so adroitly that the attention of the children in the reading group does not waver.

Journal Entry
Learning to Handle Momentum

3. *Strive to maintain smoothness and momentum in class activities.* This point is related to the previous one. Kounin found that some teachers caused problems for themselves by constantly interrupting activities without thinking about what they were doing. Some teachers whose activities were recorded on videotape failed to maintain the thrust of a lesson because they seemed unaware of the rhythm of student behavior (that is, they did not take into account the degree of student inattention and restlessness but instead moved ahead in an almost mechanical way). Others flip-flopped from one activity to another. Still others would interrupt one activity (for example, a reading lesson) to comment on an unrelated aspect of classroom functioning ("Someone left a lunch bag on the floor"). There were also some who wasted time dwelling on a trivial incident (making a big fuss because a boy lost his pencil). And a few teachers delivered individual, instead of group, instruction ("All right, Charlie, you go to the board. Fine. Now, Rebecca, you go to the board"). All of these types of teacher behavior tended to interfere with the flow of learning activities.

   Teachers who continually interrupt activities have discipline problems

4. *Try to keep the whole class involved, even when you are dealing with individual students.* Kounin found that some well-meaning teachers had fallen into a pattern of calling on students in a predictable order and in such a way that the rest of the class served as a passive audience. Unless you stop to think about what you are doing during group recitation periods, you might easily fall into the same trap. If you do, the "audience" is almost certain to become bored and may be tempted to engage in troublemaking activities just to keep occupied.

   Some teachers, for example, call on students to recite by going around a circle, or going up and down rows, or following alphabetical order. Others call on a child first and then ask a question. Still others ask one child to recite at length (read an entire page, for example). All of these techniques tend to spotlight one child in predictable order and cause the rest of the class members to tune out until their turn comes. You are more likely to maintain interest and limit mischief caused by boredom if you use techniques such as the following:

   - Ask a question, and after pausing a few seconds to let everyone think about it, pick out someone to answer it. With subsequent questions, call on students in an unpredictable order so that no one knows when he or she will be asked to recite. (If you feel that some students in a class are very apprehensive about being called on, even under relaxing circumstances, you can either ask them extremely easy questions or avoid calling on them at all.)
   - If you single out one child to go to the board to do a problem, ask all other students to do the same problem at their desks, and then choose one or two at random to compare their work with the answers on the board.
   - When dealing with lengthy or complex material, call on several students in quick succession (and in unpredictable order) and ask each to handle one section. In a primary grade reading group, for example, have one child read a sentence; then pick someone at the other side of the group to read the next sentence and so on.
   - Use props in the form of flashcards, mimeographed sheets, or workbook pages to induce all students to respond to questions simultaneously. Then ask students to compare answers. One ingenious elementary school teacher whom Kounin observed had each student print the ten digits on cards that could be inserted in a slotted piece of cardboard. She would ask a question such as "How much is 8 and 4?" and then pause a moment while the students arranged their answers in the slots and then say, "All show!")

Journal Entry
Ways to Keep the Whole Class Involved

Keeping entire class involved and alert minimizes misbehavior

5. *Introduce variety, and be enthusiastic, particularly with younger students.* After viewing videotapes of different teachers, Kounin and his associates concluded that some teachers seemed to fall into a deadly routine much more readily than others. They followed the same procedure day after day and responded with the same, almost reflexive comments. At the other end of the scale were teachers who introduced variety, responded with enthusiasm and interest, and moved quickly to new activities when they sensed that students either had mastered or were satiated by a particular lesson. It seems logical to assume that students will be less inclined to sleep, daydream, or engage in disruptive activities if they are exposed to an enthusiastic teacher who varies the pace and type of classroom activities.

6. *Be aware of the ripple effect.* When criticizing student behavior, be clear and firm, focus on behavior rather than on personalities, and try to avoid angry outbursts.

If you take into account the suggestions just made, you may be able to reduce the amount of student misbehavior in your classes. Even so, some behavior problems are certain to occur. When you deal with these, you can benefit from Kounin's research on the ripple effect. On the basis of observations, questionnaires, and experimental evidence, he concluded that "innocent" students in a class are more likely to be positively impressed by the way the teacher handles a misbehavior if the following conditions exist:

Identify misbehavers; firmly specify constructive behavior

- The teacher identifies the misbehaver and states what the unacceptable behavior is. ("Jorge! Don't flip that computer disk at Jamal.")
- The teacher specifies a more constructive behavior. ("Please put the computer disk back in the storage box.")
- The teacher explains why the deviant behavior should cease. ("If the computer disk gets broken or dirty, no one else will be able to use it, and we'll have to try to get a new one.")
- The teacher is firm and authoritative and conveys a no-nonsense attitude. ("All infractions of classroom rules will result in an appropriate punishment—no ifs, ands, or buts.")
- The teacher does not resort to anger, humiliation, or extreme punishment. Kounin concluded that extreme reactions did not seem to make children behave better. Instead, anger and severe reprimands upset them and made them feel tense and nervous. ("Roger, I am deeply disappointed that you used obscene language in your argument with Michael. Such behavior is simply unacceptable in my classroom.")
- The teacher focuses on behavior, not on personality. (Say, "Ramona, staring out the window instead of reading your textbook is unacceptable behavior in my classroom" rather than "Ramona, you're the laziest student I have ever had in class.")

University of Texas Studies of Group Management

Stimulated by Kounin's observations, members of the Research and Development Center for Teacher Education at the University of Texas at Austin instituted a series of studies on classroom management. The basic procedure followed in most studies was to first identify very effective and less effective teachers by using a variety of criteria (often stressing student achievement) and then analyze in detail classroom management techniques that very effective teachers used. In some studies (for example, Brophy, 1979; Good, 1982), basic characteristics of well-managed classrooms were described. They can be summarized as follows:

Well-managed classroom: students complete clear assignments in busy but pleasant atmosphere

1. Students know what they are expected to do and generally experience the feeling that they are successful doing it.
2. Students are kept busy engaging in teacher-led instructional activities.
3. There is little wasted time, confusion, or disruption.
4. A no-nonsense, work-oriented tone prevails, but at the same time there is a relaxed and pleasant atmosphere.

These conclusions can be related to information presented in earlier chapters. The first point can be interpreted as supporting the use of instructional objectives that are stated in such a way that students know when they have achieved them. The next three points stress student productivity under teacher guidance and a no-nonsense, work-oriented atmosphere. These outcomes are more likely when teachers use procedures that behavioral and cognitive psychologists have recommended.

Another set of studies carried out by the Texas researchers led to two recent books on group management—one for elementary school teachers (Evertson,

Emmer, Clements, & Worsham, 2000) and the other for secondary school teachers (Emmer, Evertson, Clements, & Worsham, 2000). You may wish to examine the appropriate book for your grade level (complete titles and names of authors are given in Resources for Further Information at the end of this chapter), but for now we will provide the following summary of basic keys to management success stressed in both volumes.

1. On the first day with a new class, very effective teachers clearly demonstrate that they have thought about classroom procedures ahead of time. They have planned first-day activities that make it possible for classroom routine to be handled with a minimum of confusion. They also make sure students understand why the procedures are necessary and how they are to be followed.
2. A short list of basic classroom rules is posted or announced (or both), and students are told about the penalties they will incur in the event of misbehavior.
3. During the first weeks with a new group of students, effective teachers have students engage in whole-group activities under teacher direction. Such activities are selected to make students feel comfortable and successful in their new classroom.
4. After the initial shakedown period is over, effective teachers maintain control by using the sorts of techniques that Kounin described: they show they are with it, cope with overlapping situations, maintain smoothness and momentum, and avoid ignoring the rest of the class when dealing with individual students.
5. Effective teachers give clear directions, hold students accountable for completing assignments, and give frequent feedback.

Effective teachers plan how to handle classroom routines

During first weeks, have students complete clear assignments under your direction

Managing the Middle, Junior High, and High School Classroom

Most of the classroom management techniques and suggestions we have discussed so far are sufficiently general that they can be used in a variety of classroom settings and with primary through secondary grade students. Nevertheless, teaching preadolescents and adolescents is sufficiently different from teaching younger students that the management of the middle school, junior high, and high school classroom requires a slightly different emphasis and a few unique practices.

Classroom management has to be approached somewhat differently in the secondary grades (and in those middle schools where students change classes several times a day) because of the segmented nature of education for these grades. Instead of being in charge of the same twenty-five to thirty students all day, most junior high or high school teachers (and some middle school teachers) are responsible for as many as five different groups of twenty-five to thirty students for about fifty minutes each. This arrangement results in a wider range of individual differences, a greater likelihood that these teachers will see a wide range of behavior problems, and a greater concern with efficient use of class time.

Because of the special nature of adolescence, relatively short class times, and consecutive classes with different students, middle school, junior high, and high school teachers must concentrate their efforts on preventing misbehavior. Edmund Emmer, Carolyn Evertson, Barbara Clements, and Murray Worsham (2000), in *Classroom Management for Secondary Teachers*, discuss how teachers can prevent misbehavior by carefully organizing the classroom environment, establishing clear rules and procedures, and delivering effective instruction.

According to Emmer and his associates, the physical features of the classroom should be arranged to optimize teaching and learning. They suggest an environment

Because middle school, junior high, and high school students move from one teacher to another every 50 minutes or so, it is important to establish a common set of rules that govern various activities and prodedures and to clearly communicate the reasons for those rules.

in which (1) the arrangement of the seating, materials, and equipment is consistent with the kinds of instructional activities the teacher favors; (2) high-traffic areas, such as the teacher's desk and the pencil sharpener, are kept free of congestion; (3) the teacher can easily see all students; (4) frequently used teaching materials and student supplies are readily available; and (5) students can easily see instructional presentations and displays.

In too many instances, teachers spend a significant amount of class time dealing with misbehavior rather than with teaching and learning, either because students are never told what is expected of them or because rules and procedures are not communicated clearly. Accordingly, Emmer and associates suggest that classroom rules be specifically stated, discussed with students on the first day of class, and, for seventh, eighth, and ninth grades, posted in a prominent place. Sophomores, juniors, and seniors should be given a handout on which the rules are listed. A set of five to eight basic rules should be sufficient. Some examples of these basic rules follow:

Bring all needed materials to class.
Be in your seat and ready to work when the bell rings.
Respect and be polite to all people.
Do not talk or leave your desk when someone else is talking.
Respect other people's property.
Obey all school rules.

You may also want to allow some degree of student participation in rule setting. You can ask students to suggest rules, arrange for students to discuss why certain classroom rules are necessary, and perhaps allow students to select a few rules. This last suggestion should be taken up cautiously, however. Because middle school and secondary teachers teach different sets of students, having a different set of rules for each class is bound to cause confusion for you and hard feelings among some students. You may find yourself admonishing a student for breaking a rule that applies to a different class, and some students will naturally want to know why they cannot do something that is allowed in another class.

In addition to rules, various procedures need to be formulated and communicated. Procedures differ from rules in that they apply to a specific activity and are usually directed at completing a task rather than completing a behavior. To produce a well-run classroom, you will need to formulate efficient procedures for beginning-of-the-period tasks (such as taking attendance and allowing students to leave the classroom), use of materials and equipment (such as the encyclopedia, dictionary, and pencil sharpener), learning activities (such as discussions, seatwork, and group work), and end-of-the-period tasks (such as handing in seatwork assignments, returning materials and equipment, and making announcements).

Manage behavior of adolescents by making and communicating clear rules and procedures

Much of what Jacob Kounin, Carolyn Evertson, and Edmund Emmer mention in relation to the characteristics of effective instruction has been described in previous chapters. For example, they recommend that short-term (daily, weekly) and long-term (semester, annual) lesson plans be formulated and coordinated, that instructions and standards for assignments be clear and given in a timely manner, that feedback be given at regular intervals, and that the grading system be clear and fairly applied. As the next section illustrates, technology can help you carry out these tasks efficiently and effectively.

Technology Tools for Classroom Management

A large part of classroom management involves such routine tasks as taking attendance, completing forms, maintaining student records, tracking student progress, and settling disputes. Although effectively carrying out such tasks is part of what makes a classroom well managed, they can be both tedious and time-consuming. Fortunately, technology tools now exist to help teachers keep records of student progress, organize teaching notes, create lesson plans and timelines, send individualized notes to students, update attendance records, and generate electronic study guides (Allen, 1996; McNally & Etchison, 2000). Computer technology can help teachers create test question banks and individual tests (including alternate forms), as well as record, calculate, and graph student grades. Moreover, teachers can employ database, word processing, and spreadsheet files to maintain class rosters, develop seating charts, create professional-looking handouts and worksheets, and note missing student work. Still other classroom management tools can aid teachers in rethinking and redesigning basic classroom layouts and space utilization (Holzberg, 1995).

More information about how to use technology for classroom management purposes can be found on the web site of the SouthEast Initiatives Regional Technology in Education Consortium (**www.seirtec.org/k12/management.html**). The web site of Myschoolonline.com (**www.myschoolonline.com/golocal/**) allows you to access the web sites of school districts around the country and their ideas about technology use and classroom management. You can also create your own electronic web-based gradebook and access it from any computer that is connected to the Internet.

For direct links to sites mentioned here, go to the Web Sources section of this book's web site at **http://education.college.hmco.com/students**.

Teachers can rely on samples of prior student work posted to a classroom's or school's web site to lessen anxiety or confusion about how an assignment should be carried out. To avoid more significant behavioral problems, teachers might use software packages that teach anger control, conflict resolution, and better peer relationships (Allen, 1996).

In addition to using computer technology to assist in classroom activities and overall organization, teachers can use it to monitor and assess student progress. For instance, through the use of local area networks, a teacher can monitor student progress from his or her workstation without interrupting student work. Second, individual keypad systems can immediately and anonymously tally and graph student responses to teacher or class questions (Fischer, 1996). Third, in "smart lectern" systems, a teacher can remotely control technology presentation equipment, thereby allowing him or her additional mobility within the classroom in order to check on student work.

Centralized Information Systems The tools mentioned so far are designed for a single teacher's use in a single classroom. Centralized student information systems are designed to be used by all teachers in a school (O'Lone, 1997). With such systems, teachers can take attendance for their own records and have that information simultaneously transferred to a central administration computing system. In return, teachers have automatic access to this information as well as that related to student special needs, test results, and pertinent family data. Centralized information systems allow teachers and administrators more efficiently to access records of infractions and action taken, and any notes, photos, or other information that might aid them with difficult decisions regarding student behavioral problems (O'Lone, 1997).

Integrated Learning Systems As mentioned in the chapter on behavioral learning theory, an integrated learning system adjusts the difficulty of the instructional activity according to student ability level, while offering teachers a great deal of detail about student academic progress and performance. Developers of these systems also claim that they individualize instruction, continually monitor student activities, provide useful instructional feedback, accurately summarize student performance, and accelerate student learning.

As with most other instructional tools, integrated learning systems have their advantages and disadvantages. On the positive side, they have been found to increase student engaged time by nearly 20 percent over traditional forms of instruction, they allow teachers to create user-friendly and informative reports, and they reduce the need for teacher-scored assignments (Van Dusen & Worthen, 1995). On the negative side, such systems can effectively shift instructional decision making from the instructor to the developers of the system, thereby lowering the status of teachers from instructional experts to managers of a fairly rigid system (Callister & Dunne, 1992). As some have argued (Van Dusen & Worthen, 1995, for example), instead of allowing technology to disempower teachers, teachers need to think about how this technology, or any other technology for that matter, fits into their plans for student instruction and assessment and how it might help them shift their role from dispenser of information to student coach or learning guide.

New Classroom Roles for Teachers What happens to the classroom management duties of teachers when schools adopt technology? Carolyn Keeler's (1996) study of thirteen elementary classrooms engaged in a schoolwide computer implementation project revealed that students were more on-task, self-managed, and engaged than before. As technology tools provided greater insight into student thought processes, the teachers became more interested in individual students and their progress. Given the perceived improvements in student motivation and behavior, as well as increases in student responsibility for their own learning, these teachers stated that they would most likely not return to the instructional techniques that they used prior to project implementation. In effect, technology significantly changed the teaching-learning environment of this school.

John Mergendoller (1996) argues that although many technology tools and ideas simplify everyday tasks, they also create new and more difficult managerial and instructional roles for teachers. "American teachers," he wrote, "will need to become experts in the management of complex classroom social interactions and the noted by Redl and Wattenberg; some are based on the ideas of Walker and Shea; some are the results of reports by students and teachers; some are based on personal experience. You might use the Journal Entries to pick out or devise techniques that seem most appropriate for your grade level or that you feel comfortable about.

The value of these techniques is that they appeal to self-control and imply trust and confidence on the part of the teacher. However, they may become ineffective if they are used too often, and that is why we describe so many different techniques. The larger your repertoire is, the less frequently you will have to repeat your various gambits and ploys.

Signals such as staring at a misbehaving student or putting a finger to one's lips are examples of the influence techniques suggested by Redl and Wattenberg.

Planned Ignoring As we pointed out in the chapter on behavioral learning theory, you might be able to extinguish inappropriate attention-seeking behaviors by merely ignoring them. Such behaviors include finger snapping, body movements, book dropping, hand waving, and whistling. If you plan to use this technique, make sure the student is aware that he is engaging in the behavior and that the behavior does not interfere with the efforts of other students.

Example

- Carl has recently gotten into the habit of tapping his pencil on his desk as he works on an assignment as a way to engage you in a conversation that is unrelated to the work. The next several times Carl does this, do not look at him or comment on his behavior.

Signals In some cases, a subtle signal can put an end to budding misbehavior. The signal, if successful, will stimulate the student to control herself. (Note, however, that this technique should not be used too often and that it is effective only in the early stages of misbehavior.)

Journal Entry
Signals to Use to Nip Trouble in the Bud

Examples

- Clear your throat.
- Stare at the offender.
- Stop what you are saying in midsentence and stare.
- Shake your head (to indicate no).
- Say, "Someone is making it hard for the rest of us to concentrate" (or the equivalent).

Proximity and Touch Control Place yourself close to the misbehaving student. This makes a signal a bit more apparent.

Examples

- Walk over and stand near the student.
- With an elementary grade student, it sometimes helps if you place a gentle hand on a shoulder or arm.

Use supportive reactions to help students develop self-control

Interest Boosting If the student seems to be losing interest in a lesson or assignment, pay some additional attention to the student and the student's work.

Example

- Ask the student a question, preferably related to what is being discussed. (Questions such as, "Ariel, are you paying attention?" or "Don't you agree, Ariel?" invite wisecracks. *Genuine* questions are preferable.) Go over and examine some work the student is doing. It often helps if you point out something good about it and urge continued effort.

Humor Humor is an excellent all-around influence technique, especially in tense situations. However, remember that it should be *good*-humored humor—gentle and benign rather than derisive. Avoid irony and sarcasm.

Example

- "Shawn, for goodness sake, let that poor pencil sharpener alone. I heard it groan when you used it just now."

Perhaps you have heard someone say, "We're not laughing at you; we're laughing *with* you." Before you say this to one of your students, you might take note that one second grader who was treated to that comment unhinged the teacher by replying, "I'm not laughing."

Helping over Hurdles Some misbehavior undoubtedly occurs because students do not understand what they are to do or lack the ability to carry out an assignment.

Examples

- Try to make sure your students know what they are supposed to do.
- Arrange for students to have something to do at appropriate levels of difficulty.
- Have a variety of activities available.

Journal Entry
Using Alternative Activities to Keep Students on Task

Program Restructuring At the beginning of this book, we noted that teaching is an art because lessons do not always proceed as planned and must occasionally be changed in midstream. The essence of this technique is to recognize when a lesson or activity is going poorly and to try something else.

Examples

- "Well, class, I can see that many of you are bored with this discussion of the pros and cons of congressional term limits. Let's turn it into a class debate instead, with the winning team getting 50 points toward its final grade."
- "I had hoped to complete this math unit before the Christmas break, but I can see that most of you are too excited to give it your best effort. Since today is the last day before the break, I'll postpone the lesson until school resumes in January. Let's do an art project instead."

Antiseptic Bouncing Sometimes a student will get carried away by restlessness, uncontrollable giggling, or the like. If you feel that this is nonmalicious behavior and due simply to lack of self-control, ask the student to leave the room. (You may have recognized that antiseptic bouncing is virtually identical to the *time-out* procedure described by behavior modification enthusiasts.)

Examples

- "Nancy, please go down to the principal's office and sit on that bench outside the door until you feel you have yourself under control."
- Some high schools have "quiet rooms": supervised study halls that take extra students any time during a period, no questions asked.

Physical Restraint Students who lose control of themselves to the point of endangering other members of the class may have to be physically restrained. Such restraint should be protective, not punitive, that is, don't shake or hit. This technique is most effective with younger children; such control is usually not appropriate at the secondary level.

Example

- If a boy completely loses his temper and starts to hit another child, lead him gently but firmly away from the other students, or sit him in a chair, and keep a restraining hand on his shoulder.

Direct Appeals When appropriate, point out the connection between conduct and its consequences. This technique is most effective if done concisely and infrequently.

Examples

- "We have a rule that there is to be no running in the halls. Scott forgot the rule, and now he's down in the nurse's office having his bloody nose taken care of. It's too bad Mr. Harris opened his door just as Scott went by. If Scott had been walking, he would have been able to stop in time."
- "If everyone would stop shouting, we'd be able to get this finished and go out to recess."

Criticism and Encouragement On those occasions when it is necessary to criticize a particular student, do so in private if possible. When public criticism is the only possibility, do your best to avoid ridiculing or humiliating the student. Public humiliation may cause the child to resent you or hate school, to counterattack, or to withdraw. Because of the ripple effect, it may also have a negative impact on innocent students (although nonhumiliating public criticism has the advantage of setting an example for other students). One way to minimize the negative after-effects of criticism is to tack on some encouragement in the form of a suggestion as to how the backsliding can be replaced by more positive behavior.

Give criticism privately; then offer encouragement

Examples

- If a student doesn't take subtle hints (such as stares), you might say, "LeVar, you're disturbing the class. We all need to concentrate on this." It sometimes adds punch if you make this remark while you are writing on the board or helping some other student.
- Act completely flabbergasted, as though the misbehavior seems so inappropriate that you can't comprehend it. A kindergarten teacher used this technique to perfection. She would say, "Adam! Is that you?" (Adam has been belting Lucy with a shovel.) "I can't believe my eyes. I wonder if you would help me over here." Obviously, this gambit can't be used too often, and the language and degree of exaggeration have to be altered a bit for older students. But indicating that you expect good behavior and providing an immediate opportunity for the backslider to substitute good deeds can be very effective.

Defining Limits In learning about rules and regulations, children go through a process of testing the limits. Two year olds particularly, when they have learned how to walk and talk and manipulate things, feel the urge to assert their independence. In addition, they need to find out exactly what the house rules are. (Does Mommy *really* mean it when she says, "Don't take the pots out of the cupboard"? Does Daddy *really* mean it when he says, "Don't play with that hammer"?) Older children do the same thing, especially with new teachers and in new situations. The technique of defining limits includes not only establishing rules (as noted earlier) but also enforcing them.

Examples

- Establish class rules, with or without the assistance of students, and make sure the rules are understood.
- When someone tests the rules, show that they are genuine and that there *are* limits.

Postsituational Follow-Up Classroom discipline occasionally has to be applied in a tense, emotion-packed atmosphere. When this happens, it often helps to have a postsituational discussion—in private if an individual is involved, with the whole class if it was a groupwide situation.

Examples

- In a private conference: "Leila, I'm sorry I had to ask you to leave the room, but you were getting kind of carried away."
- "Well, everybody, things got a bit wild during those group work sessions. I want you to enjoy yourselves, but we practically had a riot going, didn't we? And that's why I had to ask you to stop. Let's try to hold it down to a dull roar tomorrow."

Marginal Use of Interpretation Analysis of behavior can sometimes be made while it is occurring rather than afterward. The purpose here is to help students become aware of potential trouble and make efforts to control it.

Example

- To a restless and cranky prelunch class, you might say, "I know that you're getting hungry and that you're restless and tired, but let's give it all we've got for ten minutes more. I'll give you the last five minutes for some free visiting time."

I-Messages

Journal Entry
Using I-Messages

I-message: tell how you feel about an unacceptable situation

In *Teacher and Child*, Haim Ginott offers a cardinal principle of communication: "Talk to the situation, not to the personality and character" (1972, p. 84). Instead of making derogatory remarks about the personalities of two boys who have just thrown bread at each other, Ginott suggests that as a teacher you deliver an **I-message** explaining how you feel. Don't say, "You are a couple of pigs"; say, "I get angry when I see bread thrown around. This room needs cleaning." According to Ginott, guilty students who are told why a teacher is angry will realize the teacher is a real person, and this realization will cause them to strive to mend their ways.

Ginott offers several examples of this cardinal principle of communication in Chapter 4 of *Teacher and Child*. And in Chapter 6 he offers some observations on discipline:

- Seek alternatives to punishment.
- Try not to diminish a misbehaving student's self-esteem.
- Try to provide face-saving exits.

Despite the fact that Ginott's work is over thirty years old, its usefulness is demonstrated by the fact that his ideas appear regularly in recent books on classroom management (for instance, Cangelosi, 2000; DiGiulio, 2000).

Problem Ownership and Active Listening

Determine who owns a problem before deciding on course of action

In *TET: Teacher Effectiveness Training* (1974), Thomas Gordon suggests that teachers try to determine who owns a problem before they decide how to handle that problem. If a student's misbehavior (such as disrupting the smooth flow of instruction with inappropriate comments or joking remarks) results in the teacher's feeling annoyed, frustrated, or angry at not being able to complete a planned lesson, the teacher owns the problem and must respond by doing something to stop the disruptive behavior. But if a student expresses anger or disappointment about some classroom incident (getting a low grade on an exam), that student owns the problem.

Journal Entry
Speculating About Problem Ownership

Gordon suggests that failure to identify problem ownership may cause teachers to intensify difficulties unwittingly, even as they make well-intended efforts to diminish them. If a student is finding it difficult to concentrate on schoolwork because her needs are not satisfied, the situation will not be ameliorated if the teacher orders, moralizes, or criticizes. According to Gordon, such responses act as roadblocks to finding solutions to student-owned problems because they tend to make the student feel resentful and misunderstood.

The preferred way to deal with a student who owns a problem is to use what Gordon calls **active listening**. The listener is *active* in the sense that interest is shown and the talker is encouraged to continue expressing feelings; the listener does *not* actively participate by interpreting, explaining, or directing. The listener *does* respond, however, by recognizing and acknowledging what the student says.

For teacher-owned problems—those that involve misbehavior that is destructive or in violation of school regulations—Gordon agrees with Ginott that I-messages are appropriate. Instead of ordering, threatening, moralizing, using logic, offering solutions, or commenting on personal characteristics, teachers should explain why they are upset. Proof of the effectiveness of I-messages takes the form of anecdotes reported in *TET* and provided by teachers who used the technique successfully. A principal of a continuation school for dropouts, for example, reported that a group of tough boys responded very favorably when he told them how upset he became when he saw them break some bottles against the school wall.

Active listening and I-messages are popular tactics for helping students understand and manage the emotional reactions that are a part of disagreements and conflicts. A high school assistant principal, for example, arranged a series of five large posters on one wall of her office and named it the "Conflict Wall." The first poster provided a definition of conflict. The second poster listed steps that can be taken to reduce or eliminate one's anger. Poster three encouraged the use of I-messages. Poster four listed typical behaviors that escalate a conflict. The last poster described the use of active listening techniques (Phillips, 1997). Active listening was one of several components of a conflict resolution program that was made part of all subject matter instruction in the K–12 curriculum of the Montgomery County (Maryland) school system. For example, seventh-grade language arts students were asked to show how active listening on the part of the characters of a short story might have changed the story's outcome (Jeweler & Barnes-Robinson, 1999).

No-Lose Method

Thomas Gordon (1974) urges teachers to try resolving conflicts in the classroom by using the **no-lose method**. If either person in a conflict loses, there is bound to be resentment. If you tell a girl who is fooling around during a work period that she must settle down or stay after school, *she* loses. If you make a halfhearted and unsuccessful effort to control her and then try to cover up your failure by ignoring her and working with others, *you* lose. In Gordon's method, the preferred procedure is to talk over the problem and come up with a mutually agreeable compromise solution. He offers this six-step procedure for coming up with no-lose solutions, a procedure that is similar to the one we described in our chapter on constructivist learning theory and problem solving:

No-lose method: come to mutual agreement about a solution to a problem

1. Define the problem.
2. Generate possible solutions.
3. Evaluate the solutions.
4. Decide which solution is best.
5. Determine how to implement the solution.
6. Assess how well the solution solved the problem. (1974, p. 228)

Journal Entry
Trying the No-Lose Method

To put this procedure into practice with an individual, you might approach a boy who is disruptive during a work period and engage in a dialogue something like this:

You: You're making such a ruckus over here by talking loudly and shoving others that I can't hear the group I'm working with.

Student: I think this workbook junk is stupid. I already know how to do these problems. I'd rather work on my science project.

You: Well, suppose we try this. You do one page of problems. If you get them all correct, we'll both know you can do them, and you should be free to work on your science project. If you make some mistakes, that means you need more practice. Suppose you do a page and then ask me to check it. Then we can take it from there. How does that sound?

Some general guidelines you might consider when you find it necessary to resort to disciplinary techniques appear in Suggestions for Teaching in Your Classroom.

Suggestions for Teaching in Your Classroom

Handling Problem Behavior

1 Have a variety of influence techniques planned in advance.

You may save yourself a great deal of trouble, embarrassment, and strain if you plan ahead. When first-year teachers are asked which aspects of teaching bother them most, classroom control is almost invariably near the top of the list. Perhaps a major reason is that problems of control frequently erupt unexpectedly, and they often demand equally sudden solutions. If you lack experience, your shoot-from-the-hip reactions may be ineffective. Initial attempts at control that are ineffective tend to reinforce misbehavior, and you will find yourself trapped in a vicious circle. You can avoid this sort of trap if you devise specific techniques ahead of time. Being familiar with several of the techniques mentioned in the preceding section will prepare you for the inevitable difficulties that arise.

If you find yourself forced to use prepared techniques too often, some self-analysis is called for. How can you prevent so many problems from developing?

Violence in American Schools

HOW SAFE ARE OUR SCHOOLS?

You have probably read or heard reports about the frequency of crime in the United States, particularly among juveniles. According to figures compiled by the Office of Juvenile Justice and Delinquency Prevention (2000), juveniles (those under the age of eighteen) accounted for 17 percent of all arrests and 16 percent of all violent crime arrests in 1999. The good news about these figures is that they were at their lowest levels since the late 1980s.

Since the kinds of behaviors one observes in schools tend to reflect trends in society at large, it is natural that a certain amount of violent behavior occurs on school grounds and during school hours. However, schools are still relatively safe places. One basis for that claim is that the most common types of school-based conflicts fall into a few time-honored categories: verbal harassment (name calling, insults, teasing), verbal arguments, and physical fights (hitting, kicking, scratching, and pushing). Most of the fights do not involve serious injury or violations of law (Johnson & Johnson, 1996). Second, a recent government report found relatively low levels of violence and crime (Kaufman et al., 2000). Here are the main findings from that report.

Incidents of crime and serious violence occur relatively infrequently in public schools

- In 1996–1997, 10 percent of all public schools reported at least one serious violent crime. Another 47 percent reported at least one less serious violent or nonviolent crime (such as physical attack, theft, vandalism). The remaining 43 percent of schools did not report any of these crimes to police.
- Violence and crime are more likely to occur in middle and high schools than in elementary schools and are more likely to involve males than females.
- The number of school-age students (ages five through nineteen) murdered at school from July 1997 through June 1998, as compared to the number of students murdered outside school, was 35 versus 2,717, or 1.3 percent.
- The percentage of students ages twelve through eighteen who were victims of nonfatal crimes while at school (crimes such as rape, sexual assault, robbery, aggravated assault) decreased from 10 percent in 1995 to 8 percent in 1999.
- The percentage of high school students who were threatened or injured with a weapon within a twelve-month period between 1993 and 1997 remained constant at about 8 percent.
- The percentage of students ages twelve through eighteen who reported avoiding one or more places at school for their own safety decreased between 1995 and 1999 from 9 percent to 5 percent.
- From 1994 through 1998, 1.8 percent of elementary school teachers were victims of violent crimes (mostly simple assault). The rates for middle school and high school teachers were 6 percent and 3.8 percent, respectively.

These findings suggest that crime rates in schools are decreasing, that students feel increasingly safe at school, and that most teachers and students are likely to be physically safe in their own classrooms and school buildings. Nevertheless, school violence can occur in any school and at any time. Accordingly, you should be aware of the various explanations of school violence and the steps that can be taken to reduce its frequency.

Analyzing Reasons for Violence

Male aggressiveness due to biological and cultural factors

Biological Factors The research just cited noted that the level of violence was highest in middle and high schools and among male students. One of the clear-cut gender differences that has been repeatedly supported by consistent evidence is that males are more aggressive than females (Gropper & Froschl, 2000; Paquette & Underwood, 1999). Although the cause of this difference cannot be traced precisely, it is likely due in part to neurological and hormonal factors, as well as cultural factors. In the face of an immediate perceived threat or an opportunity for need gratification, two brain structures, the amygdala and the hypothalamus, prime individuals for assertive responses. So when faced with what we perceive to be an immediate threat, we are inclined to act first and think later. In addition, elevated levels of the male sex hormone testosterone and depressed levels of the neurotransmitter serotonin can transform assertive behavior into aggressive behavior (Sylwester, 1999). Moreover, because of long-established cultural expectancies, males in our society are encouraged to assert themselves in physical ways. As a result, tendencies toward high energy and activity levels aroused by male sex hormones may be expressed in the form of aggressiveness against others.

Gender-Related Cultural Influences As noted in the discussion of age-level characteristics in an earlier chapter, there is evidence that young girls in our society are encouraged to be dependent and to be eager to please adults, while young boys are encouraged to assert their independence (Block, 1973; Fagot, 1978). Furthermore, it appears that boys are more likely than girls to be reinforced for assertive and illegal forms of behavior. Martin Gold and Richard Petronio (1980) speculate that delinquency in our society seems to have a masculine character. They suggest that the range of delinquent behavior that will be admired by peers is narrower for females than for males and that boys are more likely than girls to achieve recognition by engaging in illegal acts.

The same reasoning may well apply to disruptive behavior in the classroom. A boy who talks back to the teacher or shoves another boy in a skirmish in the cafeteria is probably more likely to draw a favorable response from peers than is a girl who exhibits the same behavior. This cultural difference adds to the physiological factors that predispose boys to express frustration and hostility in physical and assertive ways.

Academic Skills and Performance Boys also seem more likely than girls to experience feelings of frustration and hostility in school. For a variety of reasons (more rapid maturity, desire to please adults, superiority in verbal skills), girls earn higher grades, on the average, than boys do. A low grade almost inevitably arouses feelings of resentment and anger. In fact, any kind of negative evaluation is a very direct threat to a student's self-esteem. Thus, a middle school, junior high, or high school boy who has received an unbroken succession of low grades and is unlikely to graduate may experience extreme frustration and anger. Even poor students are likely to be aware that their chances of getting a decent job are severely limited by the absence of a high school diploma.

Middle school and junior high boys with low grades may feel trapped

Older high school boys can escape further humiliation by dropping out of school, but middle school and junior high boys cannot legally resort to the same solution, which may partially explain why violent acts are twice as frequent in seventh, eighth, and ninth grades as in the upper grades.

Interpersonal Cognitive Problem-Solving Skills Children who get along reasonably well with their peers do so in part because they are able to formulate realistic plans to satisfy their social goals and can think of several possible solutions to interpersonal problems. The former skill is referred to as *means-ends thinking*, and the latter is called *alternative solution thinking.* Students who are deficient in these two interpersonal cognitive problem-solving skills are more likely than others to show an inability to delay gratification, have difficulty making friends, have emotional blowups when frustrated, show less sympathy to others in distress, and exhibit verbal and physical aggression (Shure, 1999).

Psychosocial Factors Other explanations of disruptive classroom behavior are supplied by Erik Erikson's observations on identity, which we discussed in the chapter on stage theories of development. A teenager who has failed to make a clear occupational choice, is confused about gender roles, or does not experience acceptance "by those who count" may decide to establish what Erikson called a negative identity. Instead of striving to behave in ways that parents and teachers respond to positively, negative-identity teenagers may deliberately engage in opposite forms of behavior (Lowry, Sleet, Duncan, Powell, & Kolbe, 1995).

Misbehavior of high school students may reveal lack of positive identity

James Marcia's identity status concept (1980, 1991), also discussed previously, may help you understand why certain students cause problems in class. Individuals in foreclosure who have accepted parental values may well be model students. Those in a moratorium state who are experiencing identity crises of different kinds may feel impelled to release frustration and anger. But even students who are not experiencing identity problems, either because they are too young to be concerned or because they have resolved their identity conflicts, may misbehave because they need to release frustration and tension.

School Environment So far we have mentioned the role of biological, gender-related cultural, academic, cognitive, and psychosocial factors in school violence. Each of these explanations places the responsibility for violent behavior largely or entirely on the individual. Other explanations focus instead on schools that are poorly designed and do not meet the needs of their students. Violent behavior, in this view, is seen as a natural (though unacceptable) response to schools that are too large, impersonal, and competitive; that do not enforce rules fairly or consistently; that use punitive ways of resolving conflict; and that impose an unimaginative, meaningless curriculum on students (Lowry et al., 1995).

Dona Kagan (1990) reports that students who are at risk of dropping out of school believe that their teachers neither care about them nor consider them capable of academic success. Ironically, the self-esteem and motivation of a large proportion of these students improve after they leave school to the extent that they enroll in general equivalency diploma or job training programs. Similar observations on the characteristics of schools that have low levels of violence are stressed by Eugene Howard, an authority on school climate and discipline, who writes:

> Schools with positive climates are places where people care, respect, and trust one another; and where the school as an institution cares, respects, and trusts people. In such a school people feel a high sense of pride and ownership which comes from each individual having a role in making the school a better place. . . . Schools with positive climates are characterized by people-centered belief and value systems, procedures, rules, regulations, and policies. (1981, p. 8)

One example of the kind of climate that Howard described is Crystal City High School in Crystal City, Missouri. Because of a peer mentoring program, this high school has been successful in meeting the safety, belongingness, and esteem needs of

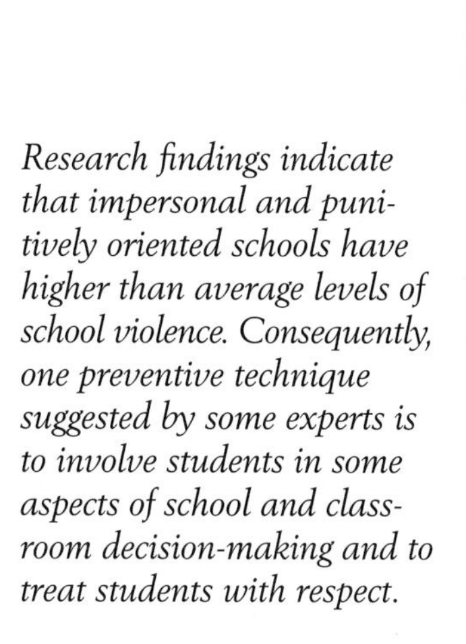
Research findings indicate that impersonal and punitively oriented schools have higher than average levels of school violence. Consequently, one preventive technique suggested by some experts is to involve students in some aspects of school and classroom decision-making and to treat students with respect.

Maslow's theory that we discussed in previous chapters. Junior and senior students who meet the school's criteria for grade-point average, attendance, citizenship, and trustworthiness are eligible to volunteer to mentor one or two freshmen. Mentors participate in discussions of issues facing young high school teens, are trained in team-building and basic counseling skills, and are told when it is appropriate to involve the school counselor. Meetings between mentors and mentees take place about once every three weeks and cover such topics as participation in classroom discussions, study skills, problems with students or teachers, and problems at home. Mentors also provide tutoring and help with homework.

The effect of this program on the overall school climate was quite noticeable to the faculty. Previously, as in many other high schools, there was constant tension between individual students and groups of students. Suspensions were a common occurrence. After the mentor program had been in effect for several years, an atmosphere of cooperation, friendliness, and being at ease became the norm. Between 1994–1995 and 1998–1999, out-of-school suspensions decreased by 40 percent, the dropout rate declined to 3 percent, and average daily attendance improved to 93 percent. As older students became concerned about the welfare of their mentees, the hazing of freshmen became rare. The popularity of the program is such that over 95 percent of freshmen participate and over 60 percent of juniors and seniors apply to be mentors. Of those who become mentors, 100 percent said they would volunteer to do it again (Stader & Gagnepain, 2000).

Reducing School Violence

School violence can be reduced by improving student achievement levels

Classroom Tactics Several analyses of school violence (for example, Howard, 1981; Kagan, 1990; Zwier & Vaughan, 1984) suggest that academic achievement and school atmosphere can play a significant role in reducing school violence. To foster respectable levels of achievement by as many students as possible, teachers can make effective use of carefully selected objectives, help students establish at least short-term goals, use efficient instructional techniques (such as those advocated by behavioral theorists), teach students how to use learning strategies, and implement a mastery approach. If you show that students who do not do well on the first try at an assignment will receive your help and encouragement to improve their performance, you may be able to convert at least some resentment into a desire to achieve.

At the same time, it appears that students should be invited to participate in making at least some decisions about what is to be studied and about school and classroom rules. Constructivist techniques and contingency contracts, for example, permit some self-direction by students. Such tactics may ease students' fears that schooling is impersonal and that they have no control over what happens to them. As humanistic psychologists have argued, students seem to respond more positively to schooling when they are treated as individuals, when their feelings and opinions are taken into account, and when they are invited to participate in making decisions about how the school and the classroom function.

Programs to Reduce Violence and Improve Discipline Several states and many school districts have initiated programs to make schools safer places for students and teachers. One such program is the *just community*. An outgrowth of Lawrence Kohlberg's work on moral development (which we discussed in the chapter on stage theories), the goal of a just community is to prevent conflicts. It does this in two ways: (1) by letting students help establish a school's policy for misbehavior, and (2) by helping students take responsibility for reducing undesirable behaviors (such as petty bickering among students, the development of cliques, and graffiti on restroom walls) and for promoting more desirable actions (such as cooperative learning, cleanup activities, and the organization of fund-raising events) (Michlowski, 1999; Murphy, 1988).

Violence less likely when students invited to participate in making decisions

A somewhat different approach to decreasing physical violence, particularly between students, is the Resolving Conflict Creatively Program (RCCP), created by Linda Lantieri in 1985. The goal of the program is to teach students how to use nonviolent conflict resolution techniques in place of their more normal and more violent methods. Students are trained by teachers to monitor the school environment (such as the playground, the cafeteria, and hallways) for imminent or actual physical confrontations between students. For example, picture two students who are arguing about a comment that struck one as an insult. As the accusations and counter accusations escalate, one student threatens to hit the other. At that moment, one or two other students who are wearing T-shirts with the word *mediator* printed across the front and back intervene and ask if the two students would like help in resolving their problem. The mediating students may suggest that they all move to a quieter area where they can talk. The mediators then establish certain ground rules, such as each student gets a turn to talk without being interrupted and name calling is not allowed.

RCCP was designed as a primary prevention program. This means that all students, even those not prone to violence, are taught how to prevent disagreements from becoming violent confrontations. In schools where the program has been implemented, teachers have noted less physical violence in their classrooms, fewer insults and verbal put-downs, and greater spontaneous use of conflict resolution skills (Lantieri, 1995).

Nevertheless, educators noticed that the program did not produce desirable re-

One approach to reducing school violence is to train students to mediate disputes between other students.

sults with all students. So during the 1997–1998 school year, an intervention component was added for children who exhibit behaviors that are associated with violent behavior in later years. School counselors and RCCP-trained teachers, working with groups of fifteen to twenty children, engaged the students in activities that were designed to increase a sense of social responsibility (caring and cooperative behaviors, for example) and develop such interpersonal skills as active listening. The capstone of this thirty-week program is the social action project. The group has to decide on and implement a community service project, such as fixing dinner for a family in need of assistance, making Easter baskets for the mentally disabled residents of a nearby center, or collecting books and art materials for a children's hospital. An evaluation of this new component reported improvements in listening skills, anger management skills, ability to share with others, relationships with teachers and students, self-esteem, and attitudes towards school (Lantieri, 1999).

Additional information about RCCP, the states and school districts in which it has been implemented, and whom to contact can be found on the following web site: **www.esrnational.org/about-rccp.html**.

A general review of research on various types of conflict resolution programs concluded that students who have not been trained in how to settle conflicts among themselves appropriately tend to leave their conflicts unresolved by ignoring the other student, suppressing an aggressive response, or coercing the other student to behave in a desired manner ("If you don't stop spreading rumors about me, I'll see to it that nobody has anything to do with you."). After training, students are more likely to resolve conflicts through the use of discussion and negotiation procedures that produce mutually acceptable agreements. In comparison to untrained students, students who use conflict resolution procedures tend to have a more positive attitude toward school, increased self-esteem, and fewer discipline problems and suspensions (Johnson & Johnson, 1996).

Another innovative approach to reducing school violence by modifying the school environment is being tried by a large high school in Baltimore, Maryland. Patterson High School used to be a typical large (two thousand students) urban high school, with numerous instances of vandalism, fighting, gambling, cutting classes, and verbal abuse directed at teachers. On some days, the attendance rate was as low as 50 percent. But a dramatic change occurred after the school was reorganized into six self-contained units. One part of the building is devoted to the ninth-grade Success Academy in which teachers and students work in small groups. The rest of the building houses five Career Academies that combine a college-oriented curriculum with career interests. Each academy has about three hundred students, its own entrance, its own administrator, and its own guidance counselor and is separated from the other academies by walls and doors.

Students who would normally be suspended or transferred for discipline problems have to attend an after-hours program at Patterson High called the Twilight School. Students are placed in small classes and receive help from teachers and counselors in resolving their academic and behavioral problems.

Daily average attendance rose to 80 percent, the promotion rate to ninth grade increased from 35 percent to 80 percent, transfer requests from teachers declined to almost zero, the school was graffiti free, and most faculty described the school environment as being like a big family and conducive to learning (McPartland, Jordan, Legters, & Balfanz, 1997).

A description of how conflict resolution and other violence reduction programs are being implemented in the schools is presented in the Case in Print.

Fighting Violence with Nonviolence

Violent behavior, in this view, is seen as a natural (though unacceptable) response to schools that are too large, impersonal, and competitive; that do not enforce rules fairly or consistently; that use punitive ways of resolving conflict; and that impose an unimaginative, meaningless curriculum on students. . . . Several states and many school districts have initiated programs to make schools safer places for students and teachers. (pp. 442,444)

Pathways to Peace

MICKEY BACA

Merrimack Valley Sunday 3/5/95

At the Kelley Elementary School in Newburyport [Massachusetts], a fourth grader who flares up in anger is moved to a separate area of the room surrounded by restful scenes and posters. He is given drawing materials and earphones to listen to relaxation tapes until he cools off enough to discuss what sent him up the anger "escalator."

At Triton Regional School in Salisbury, two eighth graders involved in a shoving match in the hall sit down with a pair of student mediators to analyze what led to the scuffle. After nearly two hours, they emerge with a written agreement on how to avoid future strife.

At Newburyport's Nock Middle School, a couple of fifth graders who sometimes clash because one's mother buys her clothes at K-Mart rather than the more trendy Gap find themselves working together to solve a burglary case in a group lesson designed to build cooperation and understanding.

Like their counterparts around the country, local schools are turning to a variety of techniques to try to combat intolerance and violence in their students. . . .

. . . "There's a real culture in our society that reinforces violence," says Susan Fallon, health coordinator at Triton. "We're trying to create a culture that reinforces nonviolence."

For the past three years, the Triton School District—which includes Salisbury, Rowley and Newbury—has been training its staff and passing on to its students the latest techniques in violence prevention. Teachers have attended seminars on something called "conflict resolution skills"—methods to resolve disputes through nonviolent means such as better communication, collaboration and compromise. The idea, according to former state Rep. Barbara Hildt of Amesbury, who works in violence prevention and is participating in the Partnership effort, is to give students strategies to better manage anger, listen more, "talk about problems, not people," offer choices and work with others on problem solving.

Triton also has a peer mediation program in which students are trained to act as impartial middlemen in student conflicts to root out and hopefully defuse their causes. . . .

"They provide a neutral way to clarify what the problem is," says Fallon. "And to help each side understand the other's point of view." . . .

Under peer mediation at Triton, school staff advising the mediators take referrals about fights between students or even about conflicts that could lead to fights eventually. The referrals can come from a teacher, parent, bus driver, hallway monitor or a student who is either being picked on or perhaps has a friend facing conflict, according to Fallon. Mediation augments, but doesn't replace, regular school disciplinary consequences to violence. . . .

Staff advisors decide what's appropriate for mediation. Some things—like harassment cases or any kind of dating violence—are not, Fallon says. . . .

Fallon says one indication she sees that Triton's commitment to anti-violence training is paying off is the kids' willingness to use the relatively new peer mediation option. She and other educators say kids like the idea of sitting down with their peers rather than with adults to resolve their differences.

What's more, Fallon says, the results of mediation sessions are encouraging. "It can be truly moving. You can see some tough kids becoming choked up."

Over in Newburyport, where anti-violence training is less developed in the schools, officials have mixed reactions to the training trend.

Doug Lay, principal at the Nock Middle School, says some schools seem to have a positive track record with such training, but it's hard to say how effective things like conflict resolution training will be in the long run in changing middle school kids' views towards violence.

"I don't see that it's ever going to resolve all of the conflicts," he says.

What it will do, Lay says, is build a common vocabulary for nonviolent problem-solving and spell out ways to break down conflicts more objectively.

Given that framework, kids are willing to work at solving conflicts, Lay finds, and have also shown more of a willingness to seek the help of an adult when facing problems.

. . . [Newburyport High School] Principal Mary Lanard . . . sees a clear need for it at the high school, she says, particularly in the area of teaching kids to tolerate diversity.

"We're looking at ways we can make it easier for kids who are coming from other schools or who are different," Lanard says. "I think we're trying to make the school more humane."

At the elementary school level, Chris Morton, a fourth grade teacher at the Kelley School, a strong proponent of violence prevention training, says her students have been quick to pick up the conflict resolution lessons they've been getting since last year.

"I think we know it works when we begin seeing kids solve problems without violence," she says, noting that she does hear her students using the terminology of conflict resolution.

Morton says Newburyport elementary schools have also begun a unique "time out" process that really seems to help students better manage their anger. An area of the classroom is set up away from the rest of the class where angry students go to cool off and get in control by listening to relaxation tapes. The area also features posters that remind kids to do things like count backwards from 10 when they feel themselves getting angry.

For the most part, she says, kids are able to calm down in 15 or 20 minutes and are then ready to talk about the problem. . . .

One program that Lay says has been effective in promoting understanding and stemming conflicts at his school is an effort started last year, called Prime Time. Under that program, the school's student population is divided up into groups of roughly 16 that meet three mornings a week for 45 minutes.

Group advisors, including teachers and Lay himself, lead the groups in exercises that emphasize group cohesiveness, encourage students to share their thoughts and feelings and look at issues like peer pressure and conflict.

Like other area school officials, Lay doesn't see racial or cultural differences as a source of conflict among his students. His school population, and the population through Essex County, is pretty homogeneous in that respect.

What he does see is economic prejudices and stereotypes fueling conflict, Lay notes.

"Kids making fun of each other's clothing. Do you buy at the Gap or do you buy at K-Mart? You end up with a potentially polarized population."

The most important thing Lay believes school programs should teach kids is tolerance and respect of diversity. . . .

After only a year, Prime Time seems to be working. Lay says there's a lot more cohesiveness and a lot less tension and conflict among students this year.

Questions and Activities

1. According to two educators interviewed in this article, student-based conflict resolution strategies are not appropriate for dealing with certain types of problems and may not effectively resolve other types of conflicts. Do you agree with this view? If you do agree, what types of problems should student mediators not try to resolve? Why? Where peer mediation is appropriate, with which types of conflicts is it likely to be unsuccessful? Why? If you do not agree that peer mediation has its limits, explain why.

2. Although peer mediation is an attractive method for helping students peacefully resolve conflicts, it may not work effectively below a certain grade level. Review the discussion of Piaget's theory of cognitive development in the chapter on stage theories, note the lowest grade level below which you would not institute this type of program, and explain why.

3. Relate what you have learned in this book about teaching in a culturally diverse classroom to the comments about diversity in this article. Do you agree with the educator who says that the most important things school programs can teach are tolerance and respect for diversity? Why or why not? As a classroom teacher with an awareness of issues related to cultural or economic diversity, how could you augment some of the strategies and policies described in this article?

4. To test the feasibility of peer mediation, try acting as a go-between the next time two friends or family members have a disagreement (with their permission, of course). Ask each party to describe the source of the conflict, why the two parties have different views, what their feelings are, and what ideas they might have for resolving it.

USING TECHNOLOGY TO KEEP STUDENTS IN SCHOOL

As we pointed out previously, students who exhibit poor academic performance and believe that their teachers don't care about them are prone to engage in disruptive and violent behavior. They are also at risk for dropping out of school. In 1999, 11.2 percent of sixteen to twenty-four year olds were classified as dropouts (were out of school and had not earned a diploma or alternative credential). The percentages for white, black, and Hispanic youth were 7.3 percent, 12.6 percent, and 28.6 percent, respectively (U.S. Department of Education, 2001). Although these dropout rates have steadily fallen over the past twenty-five years, some believe that creative uses of technology may cause them to fall even faster. Here are a few examples of how some schools have used technology to reduce student absenteeism and the dropout rate:

- The Carrollton City School System in rural western Georgia reduced its dropout rate from 19 percent to 6 percent in just a few years while increasing student use of library media and motivation to learn. The types of technology used by the Carrollton City Schools included self-paced instructional modules, a graphics art laboratory, a TV studio, a career center, a computer-aided design laboratory, increased computer networking, desktop videoconferencing, televisions, videocassette recorders, and overhead projectors (Mitchell, 1996).
- The Hueneme School District in Hueneme, California, created a "smart classroom" to help retain students who are at risk of dropping out. Students in this program got experience in computerized robotics, computer-aided manufacturing, desktop publishing, and aeronautics and pneumatic technology. Average daily attendance for this program was close to 100 percent (Cardon & Christensen, 1998).
- The Azusa Unified School District in Azusa, California, made extensive use of an integrated learning system to encourage student attendance and retention. Students spent four class periods each day working at their computer terminals on English, reading, social studies, mathematics, and science. By the end of the program's second year, the average daily attendance was 96 percent, and 93 percent of students remained in the program from one year to the next (Cardon & Christensen, 1998).
- Virtual high schools (high school courses and entire four-year programs that are available on the Web) are a recent development that may help students with high absentee rates—such as the children of migrant workers, students whose school districts don't offer desired courses, and students who are home-schooled—to take courses and complete their schooling. Three such programs are the Virtual High School, the Virginia Internet High School, and Cyberschool (Barker, 2000; Roblyer & Elbaum, 1999–2000; Rutkowski, 1999).

Although computer-based technology can be used in a number of creative ways to combat the problems of low achievement, disruptive behavior, absenteeism, and dropping out of school, we don't want to leave you with the impression that these are relatively simple problems for which technology is an all-purpose solution. We have, after all, spent this entire book showing you that school learning and instruction are complex phenomena. Technology is but a tool. And as with any other tool, its effectiveness is largely determined by how well educators understand its strengths and its limitations and how it can best be used in combination with other resources to serve various purposes.

To review this chapter, see the Thought Questions and ACE Self-Testing sections at **http://education.college.hmco.com/students**.

Resources for Further Investigation

Classroom Management

Although the second edition of *Mental Hygiene in Teaching,* by Fritz Redl and William Wattenberg, was published in 1959, its clear, concise, and well-organized analysis of influence techniques remains useful. Many of the techniques it describes have been used by teachers for years and will continue to be used as long as an instructor is asked to supervise a group of students. Recent textbooks that mention some of Redl and Wattenberg's ideas include *Elementary Classroom Management: Lessons from Research and Practice* (1997), by Carol Weinstein and Andrew Mignano, Jr.; *Behavior Management: A Practical Approach for Educators* (1999), by James Walker and Thomas Shea; and *Principles of Classroom Management: A Professional Decision-Making Model* (2000), by James Levin and James F. Nolan.

Other recent analyses of classroom control techniques can be found in *Positive Classroom Management* (2000), by Robert DiGiulio; *Classroom Management for Elementary Teachers* (2000), by Carolyn Evertson, Edmund Emmer, Barbara Clements, and Murray Worsham; and *Classroom Management for Secondary Teachers* (2000), by Edmund Emmer, Carolyn Evertson, Barbara Clements, and Murray Worsham.

Discussions of classroom management that emphasize particular approaches or techniques can also be found. For instance, James Cangelosi emphasizes the use of methods that foster student cooperation in *Classroom Management Strategies: Gaining and Maintaining Students' Cooperation* (2000); and William Purkey and David Strahan emphasize the use of invitational learning in *Positive Discipline: A Pocketful of Ideas* (1986).

Online resources for classroom management include Teacher Talk, a web site maintained by the Indiana University Center for Adolescent Studies at **http://education.indiana.edu/cas/tt/tthmpg.html**. The site is a journal with articles on many topics, including coverage of classroom management. In particular, it includes a self-survey to help you determine your classroom management style. The survey can be found at **www.education.indiana.edu/cas/tt/v1i2/what.html**.

Teachnet.com (**www.teachnet.com/**) is another resource with tips for classroom management. Use the site's T2T Boards area to find information on classroom management techniques.

Teachers Helping Teachers provides postings by teachers about particular topics, including classroom management. Many of these first-person comments are insightful and relevant to most beginning teachers. The site can be found at **www.pacificnet.net/~mandel/ClassroomManagement.html**.

The AskERIC online database contains a large number of resources for classroom management. The searchable database is found at **http://ericir.sunsite.syr.edu/**. It can be searched for articles, ERIC digests, postings from newsgroups and classroom-related listservs, and so forth.

School Violence

A comprehensive approach to school violence interventions can be found in *School Violence Intervention: A Practical Handbook* (1997), edited by Arnold P. Goldstein and Jane Close Conoley. Eleven of its twenty chapters discuss student-oriented interventions, school-oriented interventions, and system-oriented interventions.

A number of online resources are dedicated to educating educators, parents, and students about violence and its effects. One unusual site is Danger High, a simulation in which students are confronted with somewhat realistic situations and must solve problems. Developed by the Metro Nashville Police Department on a National Institute of Justice grant, it can be found at **www.telalink.net/~police/dangerhi/**.

Summary

1. Just as parents adopt an authoritarian, permissive, authoritative, or rejecting-neglecting approach to raising children, teachers adopt approaches to managing the behavior of students. The authoritative approach, which revolves around explaining the rationale for classroom rules and adjusting those rules as students demonstrate the ability for self-governance, produces the highest level of desirable student behavior.

2. Kounin, one of the early writers on classroom management, identified several effective classroom management techniques. He emphasized being aware of the ripple effect, cultivating withitness, coping with overlapping activities, maintaining the momentum of a lesson, keeping the whole class involved in a lesson, using a variety of instructional techniques enthusiastically, focusing on the misbehavior of students rather than on their personalities, and suggesting alternative constructive behaviors.

3. Researchers at the University of Texas found that in well-managed classrooms, students know what they are expected to do and do it successfully, are kept busy with teacher-designated activities, and exhibit little confusion or disruptive behavior. Such classrooms are marked by a work-oriented yet relaxed and pleasant atmosphere.

4. Classroom management can be made easier by using technology tools to carry out such tasks as test construction, record keeping, developing seating arrangements, analyzing space utilization, and monitoring student work. Software programs exist that teach students how to resolve conflicts nonviolently.

5. Redl and Wattenberg proposed a set of behavior management methods in 1959 called influence techniques that were designed to help teachers deal with classroom misbehavior.

6. Ginott suggests that teachers use I-messages when responding to misbehavior. These are statements that indicate to students how the teacher feels when misbehavior occurs. The aim is to comment on the situation rather than on the personality and character of the student.

7. Gordon recommends that teachers determine who owns a problem, use active listening when the student owns the problem, and resolve conflicts by using the no-lose method. The no-lose method involves discussing problem behaviors with the misbehaving student and formulating a mutually agreeable compromise solution.

8. Despite reports in the media about school-based crime and violence, classrooms and school buildings are relatively safe environments. Close to half of all schools report no or few instances of crime, and only 10 percent of schools report one or more instances of serious violent crime.

9. Possible explanations for misbehavior and violence, particularly among boys at the middle school, junior high, and high school levels, include brain structures that prime individuals for assertive responses, high levels of the male sex hormone testosterone, a culture that encourages male aggression and independence, feelings of resentment and frustration over low levels of achievement, lack of interpersonal problem-solving skills, and difficulty in establishing a positive identity.

10. Other explanations for school violence focus on the characteristics and atmosphere of schools that are so large that they seem impersonal, emphasize competition, do not enforce rules fairly or consistently, use punishment as a primary means of resolving conflict, and offer a curriculum perceived as unimaginative and meaningless.

11. Steps that classroom teachers can take to reduce school violence include providing students with well-conceived objectives, helping students set short-term goals, using instructional techniques derived from behavioral learning theories, teaching students how to use learning strategies, using a mastery approach, and allowing students to make some decisions about classroom rules and what is to be studied.

12. Schoolwide programs that may reduce violence and improve behavior are the just community, in which students are given responsibility for reducing undesirable behavior and increasing the frequency of desirable behavior; the Resolving Conflict Creatively Program, in which students mediate disputes between other students to prevent physical violence; and dividing large, impersonal high schools into relatively small, self-contained units.

13. Some school districts have been able to reduce their absenteeism and dropout rates by getting students interested in using technological aids to learning.

KEY TERMS

ripple effect *(420)*
withitness *(421)*
I-message *(435)*
active listening *(436)*
no-lose method *(436)*

DISCUSSION QUESTIONS

1. Can you recall any classes in which you experienced Kounin's ripple effect? Because this phenomenon simultaneously affects the behavior of several students, would you consider using it deliberately? Why?

2. Haim Ginott and Thomas Gordon recommend that when responding to misbehavior, teachers speak to the behavior and not the character of the student. How often have you seen this done? If it strikes you as a good approach that is not practiced often enough, what steps will you take to use it as often as possible with your own students?

3. Do you agree with the argument raised earlier that school violence can be caused by a nonmeaningful, unimaginative curriculum? If so, what can you do to make the subjects you teach lively, interesting, and useful?

Assessment of Students

Part IV

13 Assessment of Classroom Learning

Earlier parts of this book discuss three major aspects of the teacher's role: understanding student differences and how to address them properly, understanding the learning process and how to use that knowledge to formulate effective approaches to instruction, and establishing a positive learning environment by influencing motivation to learn and creating an orderly classroom. This last part, assessing performance, is as significant an aspect of the teacher's role as the first three. Virtually everyone connected with public schools, from students to teachers and administrators to state education officials to members of the U.S. Congress, is keenly interested in knowing how much and how well students have learned. In this and the next chapter, we describe a twofold process for assessing

Key Points

These key points will help you learn the important information in this chapter. To help you study, they also appear in the margins of the pages, next to the text where they are discussed.

The Role of Assessment in Teaching

- Measurement: assigning numbers to things according to rules to create a ranking
- Evaluation: making judgments about the value of a measure
- Summative evaluation: measure achievement; assign grades
- Formative evaluation: monitor progress; plan remedial instruction
- Tests can positively affect many aspects of students' learning
- Moderate testing produces more learning than no testing or infrequent testing

Ways to Measure Student Learning

- Written tests measure degree of knowledge about a subject
- Selected-response tests objectively scored and efficient but usually measure lower levels of learning
- Short-answer tests easy to write but measure lower levels of learning
- Essay tests measure higher levels of learning but are hard to grade consistently
- Performance tests measure ability to use knowledge and skills to solve realistic problems, create products
- Performance tests may vary in degree of realism
- Reliability and validity of performance tests not yet firmly established

Ways to Evaluate Student Learning

- Norm-referenced grading: compare one student to others
- Norm-referenced grading based on absence of external criteria
- Norm-referenced grading can be used to evaluate advanced levels of learning
- Criterion-referenced grading: compare individual performance to stated criteria
- Criterion-referenced grades provide information about strengths and weaknesses
- Mastery approach: give students multiple opportunities to master goals at own pace

Improving Your Grading Methods: Assessment Practices to Avoid

- Be aware of and avoid faulty measurement and grading practices

Technology for Classroom Assessment

- Digital portfolio: collection of work that is stored and illustrated electronically
- Special rubrics needed to assess digital portfolios and presentations

Suggestions for Teaching in Your Classroom: Effective Assessment Techniques

- Necessary to obtain a representative sample of behavior when testing
- Table of specifications helps ensure an adequate sample of content, behavior
- Elementary grade students tested as much for diagnostic, formative evaluation purposes as for summative purposes
- Rating scales and checklists make evaluations of performance more systematic
- Item analysis tells about difficulty, discriminating power of multiple-choice items

student learning: using teacher-made tests to assess mastery of the teacher's specific objectives and using professionally prepared standardized tests to measure the extent of a student's general knowledge base and aptitudes. Although the items that make up teacher-made and standardized tests can be very similar, if not identical, these two types of tests differ significantly in their construction, the conditions under which they are administered, and the purposes for which they are used. ■

The Role of Assessment in Teaching

To preview this chapter's main ideas, see the Chapter Themes on this book's web site at **http://education.college.hmco.com/students**.

Assessing student learning is something that every teacher has to do, and usually quite frequently. Written tests, book reports, research papers, homework exercises, oral presentations, question-and-answer sessions, science projects, and artwork of various sorts are just some of the ways in which teachers measure student learning, with written tests accounting for about 45 percent of a typical student's course grade (Green & Stager, 1986–1987). One elementary teacher estimated that on average, students take a written test once every twelve days (Barksdale-Ladd & Thomas, 2000). It is no surprise, then, that the typical teacher can spend about one-third of class time engaged in one or another type of assessment activity (McTighe & Ferrara, 1998). Assessing student learning is a task that most teachers dislike and few do well. One reason is that many have little or no in-depth knowledge of assessment principles (Crooks, 1988; Hills, 1991). Another reason is that the role of assessor is seen as being inconsistent with the role of teacher (or helper). Because teachers with more training in assessment use more appropriate assessment practices than do teachers with less training (Green & Stager, 1986–1987), a basic goal of this chapter is to help you understand how to use such knowledge to reinforce, rather than work against, your role as teacher. Toward that end, we will begin by defining what we mean by the term *assessment* and by two key elements of this process: *measurement* and *evaluation*.

What Is Assessment?

Broadly conceived, classroom assessment involves two major types of activities: collecting information about how much knowledge and skill students have learned (measurement) and making judgments about the adequacy or acceptability of each student's level of learning (evaluation). Both aspects of classroom assessment can be accomplished in a number of ways. The most common way that teachers determine how much learning has occurred is to have students take exams, respond to oral questions, do homework exercises, write papers, solve problems, create products, and make oral presentations. Teachers can then evaluate the scores from those activities by comparing them either to one another or to an absolute standard (such as an A equals 90 percent correct). In this chapter, we will explain and illustrate the various ways in which you can measure and evaluate student learning with assessments that you create and administer regularly (Airasian, 2001).

Measurement: assigning numbers to things according to rules to create a ranking

Measurement **Measurement** is the assignment of numbers to certain attributes of objects, events, or people according to a rule-governed system. For our purposes, we will limit the discussion to attributes of people. For example, we can measure someone's level of typing proficiency by counting the number of words the person accurately types per minute or someone's level of mathematical reasoning by counting the number of problems correctly solved. In a classroom or other group situation, the rules that are used to assign the numbers ordinarily create a ranking that reflects how much of the attribute different people possess (Airasian, 2001).

Evaluation **Evaluation** involves using a rule-governed system to make judgments about the value or worth of a set of measures (Airasian, 2001). What does it mean, for example, to say that a student answered eighty out of one hundred earth science questions correctly? Depending on the rules that are used, it could mean that the student has learned that body of knowledge exceedingly well and is ready to progress to the next unit of instruction or, conversely, that the student has significant knowledge gaps and requires additional instruction.

Evaluation: making judgments about the value of a measure

Why Should We Assess Students' Learning?

This question has several answers. We will use this section to address four of the most common reasons for assessment: to provide summaries of learning and information on learning progress, diagnose specific strengths and weaknesses in an individual's learning, and motivate further learning.

Summative Evaluation The first, and probably most obvious, reason for assessment is to provide to all interested parties a clear, meaningful, and useful summary or accounting of how well a student has met the teacher's objectives. When testing is done for the purpose of assigning a letter or numerical grade, it is often called **summative evaluation** since its primary purpose is to sum up how well a student has performed over time and at a variety of tasks.

Summative evaluation: measure achievement; assign grades

Classroom assessments serve several purposes. They provide information about the extent to which students have acquired the knowledge and skills that have recently been taught, they indicate whether students are understanding and keeping up with the pace of instruction, they may identify the particular cause of a student's learning difficulties, and they help students effectively regulate their study efforts.

Formative evaluation: monitor progress; plan remedial instruction

Formative Evaluation A second reason for assessing students is to monitor their progress. The main things that teachers want to know from time to time are whether students are keeping up with the pace of instruction and are understanding all of the material that has been covered so far. For students whose pace of learning is either slower or faster than average or whose understanding of certain ideas is faulty, you can introduce supplementary instruction (a workbook or a computer-based tutorial program), remedial instruction (which may also be computer based), or within-class ability grouping (recall that we discussed the benefits of this arrangement in the chapter "Accommodating Student Variability"). Because the purpose of such assessment is to facilitate, or form, learning and not to assign a grade, it is usually called **formative evaluation**.

One way to accomplish formative evaluation is to engage in a process called *dynamic assessment*, based on Vygotsky's zone of proximal development. The goal of dynamic assessment is to determine what a student is capable of doing independently and with expert guidance. With this type of assessment, teachers are allowed to provide everything from hints about how a question should be answered or a problem solved to partial explanations or demonstrations of a task (Shepard, 2000).

Diagnosis A third reason follows from the second. If you discover a student who is having difficulty keeping up with the rest of the class, you will probably want to know why in order to determine the most appropriate course of action. This purpose may lead you to construct an assessment (or to look for one that has already been made up) that will provide you with specific diagnostic information.

Tests can positively affect many aspects of students' learning

Effects on Learning A fourth reason for assessment of student performance is that it has potentially positive effects on various aspects of learning and instruction. As Terence Crooks (1988) points out, classroom assessment guides students' "judgment of what is important to learn, affects their motivation and self-perceptions of competence, structures their approaches to and timing of personal study (e.g., spaced practice), consolidates learning, and affects the development of enduring learning strategies and skills. It appears to be one of the most potent forces influencing education" (p. 467).

Proof of Crooks's contention that classroom testing helps students consolidate their learning (despite students' arguments to the contrary) was examined by Robert Bangert-Drowns, James Kulik, and Chen-Lin Kulik (1991). They analyzed the results of forty studies conducted in actual classrooms and drew the following conclusions:

Moderate testing produces more learning than no testing or infrequent testing

- Students who were tested more frequently (six or seven tests over the course of a semester) scored about one-fourth of a standard deviation higher on a final exam than did students who were tested less frequently. (See the chapter on standardized tests for a discussion of standard deviations.) This translated to an advantage of 9 percentile ranks for the more frequently tested students.
- The advantage was even larger (20 percentile ranks) when students who were tested several times were compared to students who were never tested.
- As students took more tests over the course of a semester, they generally scored higher on a final exam, but the increases became successively smaller for each additional test. The benefit of taking multiple tests seemed to peak by the sixth or seventh test.

Ways to Measure Student Learning

Just as measurement can play several roles in the classroom, teachers have several ways to measure what students have learned. Which type of measure you choose will depend, of course, on the objectives you have stated. For the purposes of this discussion, objectives can be classified in terms of two broad categories: knowing *about* something (for example, that knots are used to secure objects, that dance is a form of social expression, that microscopes are used to study things too small to be seen by the naked eye) and knowing *how to do* something (for example, tie a square knot, dance the waltz, operate a microscope). Measures that attempt to assess the range and accuracy of someone's knowledge are usually called *written tests*. And measures that attempt to assess how well somebody can do something are often referred to as *performance tests*. Keep in mind that both types have a legitimate place in a teacher's assessment arsenal. Which type is used, and to what extent, will depend on the purpose or purposes you have for assessing students. In the next two sections, we will briefly examine the nature of both types.

WRITTEN TESTS

As we indicated at the beginning of this chapter, teachers spend a substantial part of each day assessing student learning, and much of this assessment activity involves giving and scoring some type of written test. Most written tests are composed of one or more of the following categories and item types: *selected response* (multiple-choice, true-false, and matching, for example) and *constructed response* (short-answer and essay). They are designed to measure how much people know about a particular subject. In all likelihood, you have taken hundreds of these types of tests in your school career thus far.

Written tests measure degree of knowledge about a subject

Most of the tests that students take are written tests composed of multiple-choice and short-answer items. Written tests are efficient in that many items can be asked in a short space of time and they can be quickly and reliably scored. But they tend to be used to measure the lowest level of Bloom's taxonomy.

In the next couple of pages, we will briefly describe the main features, advantages, and disadvantages of each test. As you read, bear in mind that what we said about the usefulness of both written and performance tests applies here as well. No one type of written test will be equally useful for all purposes. You are more likely to draw correct inferences about students' capabilities by using a variety of selected- and constructed-response items.

Selected-Response Tests Selected-response tests are so named because the student reads a relatively brief opening statement (called a stem) and selects one of the provided alternatives as the correct answer. Selected-response tests are typically made up of multiple-choice, true-false, or matching items. Quite often all three item types are used in a single test.

Characteristics Selected-response tests are sometimes called "objective" tests because they have a simple and set scoring system. If alternative b of a multiple-choice item is keyed as the correct response and the student chose alternative d, the student is marked wrong regardless of how much the teacher wanted the student to be right. Selected-response tests are typically used when the primary goal is to assess what might be called *foundational knowledge*. This is the basic factual information and cognitive skills that students need in order to do such high-level tasks as solve problems and create products (Stiggins,2001).

Advantages A major advantage of selected-response tests is efficiency: a teacher can ask many questions in a short period of time. Another advantage is ease and reliability of scoring. With the aid of a scoring template (such as a multiple-choice answer sheet that has holes punched out where the correct answer is located), many tests can be quickly and uniformly scored. Moreover, there is some evidence that selected-response tests, when well written, can measure higher-level cognitive skills as effectively as constructed-response tests (Martinez, 1999).

Selected-response tests objectively scored and efficient but usually measure lower levels of learning

Disadvantages Because items that reflect the lowest level of Bloom's Taxonomy (verbatim knowledge) are the easiest to write, most teacher-made tests (and many standardized tests as well) are composed almost entirely of knowledge-level items (a point we made initially in the chapter "Approaches to Instruction"). As a result, students focus on verbatim memorization rather than on meaningful learning (Martinez, 1999). Another disadvantage is that although we get some indication of what students know, such tests reveal nothing about what students can do with that knowledge.

Short-Answer Tests As their name implies, short-answer tests require a brief written response from the student.

Characteristics Instead of *selecting* from one or more alternatives, the student is asked to *supply* from memory a brief answer consisting of a name, word, phrase, or symbol. Like selected-response tests, short-answer tests can be scored quickly, accurately, and consistently, thereby giving them an aura of objectivity. They are primarily used for measuring foundational knowledge.

Advantages Short-answer items are relatively easy to write, so a test, or part of one, can be constructed fairly quickly. They allow for either broad or in-depth assessment of foundational knowledge since students can respond to many items within a short space of time. Because students have to supply an answer, they have to recall, rather than recognize, information.

Disadvantages Short-answer tests have the same basic disadvantages as selected-response tests. Because short-answer items ask only for short verbatim answers, students are likely to limit their processing to that level, and these items provide no information about how well students can use what they have learned. In addition, unexpected but plausible answers may be difficult to score.

Short-answer tests easy to write but measure lower levels of learning

Essay Tests Essay items require students to organize a set of ideas and write a somewhat lengthy response to a broad question.

Characteristics The student is given a somewhat general directive to discuss one or more related ideas according to certain criteria. An example of an essay question is, "Compare operant conditioning theory and information-processing theory in terms of basic assumptions, typical research findings, and classroom applications."

Advantages Essay tests reveal how well students can recall, organize, and clearly communicate previously learned information. When well written, essay tests call on such higher-level abilities as analysis, synthesis, and evaluation. Because of these demands, students are more likely to try to meaningfully learn the material on which they are tested (Martinez, 1999).

Disadvantages Consistency of grading is likely to be a problem. Two students may have essentially similar responses yet receive different letter or numerical grades because of differences in vocabulary, grammar, and style (Martinez, 1999). These test items are also very time-consuming to grade. And because it takes time for students to formulate and write responses, only a few questions at most can be given.

Essay tests measure higher levels of learning but are hard to grade consistently

PERFORMANCE TESTS

In recent years, many teachers, learning theorists, and measurement experts have argued that the typical written test should be used far less often than it is because it reveals little or nothing of the depth of students' knowledge and how students use their knowledge to work through questions, problems, and tasks. These individuals argue that because we are living in a more complex and rapidly changing world than was the case a generation ago, schools can no longer be content to hold students accountable just for how well they can learn, store, and retrieve information in more or less verbatim form. Instead, we need to teach and assess students for such capabilities as how well they can frame problems, formulate and carry out plans, generate hypotheses, find information that is relevant to the solution to a problem, and work cooperatively with others because those are the types of skills that are necessary to cope successfully with the demands of life after school in the twenty-first century (Cunningham, 2001; Eisner, 1999).

In addition, the learning standards of such professional groups as the National Council of Teachers of Mathematics (**www.standards.nctm.org/**), the National Council for the Social Studies (**www.socialstudies.org/standards/**), the National Council of Teachers of English (**www.ncte.org/standards/**), and the National Research Council (**www.nap.edu/catalog/4962.html**) call for students to develop a sufficiently deep understanding of subject matter that they can demonstrate their knowledge in socially relevant ways.

For direct links to these and other web sites, go to the Web Sources section of this book's web site at **http://education.college.hmco.com/students**.

Performance tests assess how well students complete a task under realistic conditions.

One way to address these concerns is to use one or more of what are called performance tests.

Performance tests measure ability to use knowledge and skills to solve realistic problems, create products

What Are Performance Tests? **Performance tests** require students to use a wide range of knowledge and skills over an extended period of time to complete a task or solve a problem under more or less realistic conditions. At the low end of the realism spectrum, students may be asked to construct a map, interpret a graph, or write an essay under highly standardized conditions. Everyone in the class completes the same task in the same amount of time and under the same conditions. At the high end of the spectrum, students may be asked to conduct a science experiment, produce a painting, or write an essay under conditions that are similar to those of real life. For example, students may be told to produce a compare-and-contrast essay on a particular topic by a certain date, but the resources students choose to use, the number of revisions they make, and when they work on the essay are left unspecified. When performance testing is conducted under such realistic conditions, it is also called **authentic assessment** (Baker, O'Neil, & Linn, 1993; Meyer, 1992).

Perhaps the clearest way to distinguish between traditional paper-and-pencil tests (like multiple-choice tests) and performance tests is to say that the former measure how much students know, whereas the latter measure what students can do with what they know. In the sections that follow, we will first define four different types of performance tests and then look at their most important characteristics.

Types of Performance Tests There are four ways in which the performance capabilities of students are typically assessed: direct writing assessments, portfolios, exhibitions, and demonstrations.

Direct Writing Assessments These tests ask students to write about a specific topic ("Describe the person whom you admire the most, and explain why you admire that person.") under a standard set of conditions. Each essay is then scored by two or more people according to a set of defined criteria.

Portfolios A **portfolio** contains one or more pieces of a student's work, some of which demonstrate different stages of completion. For example, a student's writing portfolio may contain business letters; pieces of fiction; poetry; and an outline, rough draft, and final draft of a research paper. Through the inclusion of various stages of a research paper, both the process and the end product can be assessed. Portfolios can also be constructed for math and science, as well as for projects that combine two or more subject areas.

Either the student alone or the student in consultation with the teacher decides what is to be included in the portfolio. The portfolio is sometimes used as a showcase to illustrate exemplary pieces, but it also works well as a collection of pieces that represent a student's typical performances. In its best and truest sense, the portfolio functions not just as a housing for these performances but also as a means of self-expression, self-reflection, and self-analysis for an individual student (Hebert, 1998; LaBoskey, 2000).

Exhibitions Exhibitions involve just what the label suggests: a showing of such products as paintings, drawings, photographs, sculptures, videotapes, and models. As with direct writing assessments and portfolios, the products a student chooses to exhibit are evaluated according to a predetermined set of criteria.

Demonstrations In this type of performance testing, students are required to show how well they can use previously learned knowledge or skills to solve a somewhat unique problem (such as conducting a scientific inquiry to answer a question, interpreting a graph, or diagnosing the cause of a malfunctioning engine and describing the best procedure for fixing it) or perform a task (such as reciting a poem, performing a dance, or playing a piece of music). Figure 13.1 shows a performance item for graph interpretation, the partially correct response of a student, and the corrective feedback offered by two classmates.

Characteristics of Performance Tests Performance tests are different from traditional written tests in that they require the student to make an active response, are more like everyday tasks, contain problems that involve many variables, are closely related to earlier instructional activities, use scoring guides that clearly specify the criteria against which responses will be evaluated, emphasize formative evaluation, and are probably more responsive to cultural diversity.

Emphasis on Active Responding As we pointed out previously, the goal of performance testing is to gain some insight into how competently students can carry out various tasks. Consequently, such tests focus on processes (that is, the underlying skills that go into a performance), products (an observable outcome such as a speech or a painting), or both. For example, a speech teacher may be interested in assessing how well students use gestures, pauses, and changes in voice pitch and volume; the accuracy and comprehensiveness of the content of their speeches; or both (Linn & Gronlund, 2000). A science teacher may want to know if students can use their knowledge of electric circuitry to determine the types of electrical elements that are inside a set of boxes (Shavelson & Baxter, 1992).

Performance tests may vary in degree of realism

Degree of Realism Although performance tests strive to approximate everyday tasks, not every test needs to be or can be done under the most realistic circumstances. How realistic the conditions should be depends on such factors as time, cost,

Figure 13.1 Example of a Performance Assessment: Interpreting a Graph

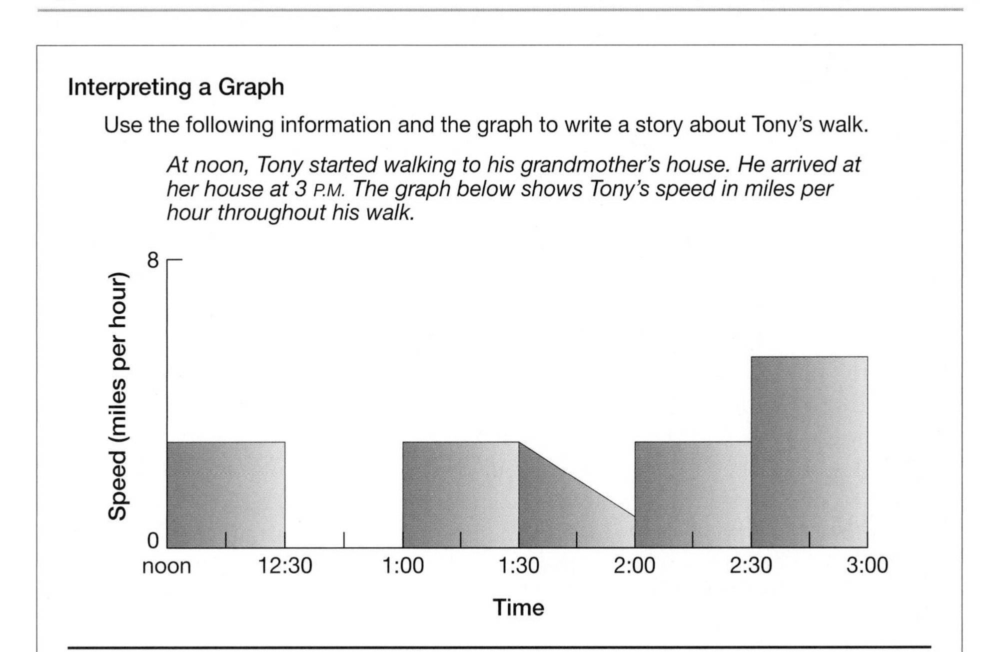

Write a story about Tony's walk. In your story, describe what Tony might have been doing at the different times.

> *Tony left his grandmother's house at noon. He made a stop at 12:30 to get a bite to eat Taco Bell. From 12:30 to 1:00 he stopped to rest on a bench at the park. From 1:00 to 1:30 he continued his walk. So Tony decided to stop at a friend house from 1:30 to 2:00. From 2:00 to 2:30 he continued his walk. Finally he arrived back at his grandmothers.*

Students critique the response:

> *Because while he was at a friends house he was going 3 miles per hour. Also he didn't say when he sped up they didn't say.*

> *Watch the chart when you write and put in minor details as well. Plus you can watch your speed.*

SOURCE: Parke and Lane (1997).

availability of equipment, and the nature of the skill being measured. Imagine, for example, that you are a third-grade teacher and one of your objectives is that students will be able to determine how much change they should receive after making a purchase in a store. If this is a relatively minor objective or if you do not have a lot of props available, you might simply demonstrate the situation with actual money and ask the students to judge whether the amount of change received was correct. If, however, you consider this to be a major objective and you have the props available, you might set up a mock store and have each student make a purchase using real money (Gronlund, 1998).

Emphasis on Complex Problems To assess how well students can use foundational knowledge and skills in a productive way, the questions and problems they are given should be sufficiently open-ended and ill structured (Wiggins, 1993). The problems contained in The Adventures of Jasper Woodbury program that we described in earlier chapters are good examples of complex and somewhat ill-structured tasks. They have several interrelated parts, provide few cues as to how the problem might be solved, and contain some uncertainty about what constitutes an appropriate solution.

Close Relationship Between Teaching and Testing All too often students walk out of an exam in a state of high frustration (if not anger) because the content and format of the test seemed to have little in common with what was covered in class and the way in which it was taught. It's the old story of teaching for one thing and testing for something else. Performance testing strives for a closer match between teaching and testing.

For example, if in giving an oral book report, a student is expected to speak loudly and clearly enough for everyone to hear, speak in complete sentences, stay on the topic, and use pictures or other materials to make the presentation interesting, the student needs to be informed of these criteria, and classroom instruction should be organized around them. One proponent of performance testing cited the old farm adage, "You don't fatten the cattle by weighing them," to make this point. He then went on to note, "If we expect students to improve their performance on these new, more authentic measures, we need to engage in 'performance-based instruction' on a regular basis" (McTighe, 1996–1997, p. 7). By the same token, the assessment of students' performances should be limited to just the criteria emphasized during instruction (Egeland, 1996–1997; McTighe, 1996–1997). One reason that proponents of performance testing push for this feature is that it has always been a standard part of successful programs in sports, the arts, and vocational education. Football coaches, for example, have long recognized that if they want their quarterback to know when during a game (the equivalent of a final exam) to attempt a pass and when not to, they must provide him with realistic opportunities to practice making this particular type of decision. Perhaps you recall our mentioning in the chapter on constructivist learning theory that realistic and varied practice are essential if students are to transfer what they learn in an instructional setting to an applied setting.

Use of Scoring Rubrics A **rubric** is a scoring guide that specifies the capabilities students should exhibit (also known as content standards), describes the qualitative levels or categories into which the responses will be sorted (also known as performance standards), and specifies how the responses will be scored (as separate elements or holistically). For writing tasks, which are probably the most common performance measures, some commonly used criteria are clarity of purpose, organization, grammatical usage, spelling, and use of supporting detail (Mabry, 1999). An example of a scoring rubric for an oral report is provided in Table 13.1.

Creating and using scoring rubrics is highly desirable for at least three reasons:

1. They increase the objectivity, consistency, and efficiency of scoring.
2. They help teachers match their instructional activities to the demands of the performance measure, the goal we discussed in the previous section.
3. By providing students with verbal descriptions and examples of the desired performance or product, teachers clearly communicate to students the types of behaviors that represent the range from unacceptable to exceptional performance (Goodrich, 1996–1997; Wiggins 1993).

As we noted in the chapter on information-processing theory, planning and monitoring are two components of strategic learning. Thus, if you want to help students be strategic learners, provide them with the measurement conditions that

Table 13.1 Scoring Rubric for a Group Oral Presentation

Level	Content	Audiovisual Components	Group Members	Audience Members
Excellent	Accurate, specific, research based, retold in own words	Unique, add to presentation quality of materials used, are neat, present clear message	Each member is equally involved in presentation and is well informed about the topic	Maintain eye contact with presenters, ask many questions
Good	Less detailed, lacking depth, limited number of sources used	Support topic but do not enhance presentation; some attempts at originality, clear message	Most members are active; most members are informed about the topic	Some members of the audience not attending; questions are limited or off the topic
Minimal	Limited information, general, strays from topic, not presented in own words	Inappropriate, no originality, detract from presentation, message is confusing	One or two members dominate; some members do not seem well prepared or well informed	Audience is not attending; no questions asked or questions are off the topic

SOURCE: Montgomery (2000).

make that behavior possible. Although this type of preparation is unfortunately not a common part of everyday classroom testing, it is typically used in the performing arts, the studio arts, athletics, and vocational education.

Bear in mind, however, that scoring rubrics have their limitations. Although the rubrics used by two teachers to score writing samples may have some of the same content standards (such as clarity of purpose, organization, and grammar), they may differ as well (for instance, in the presence or absence of idea development, use of detail, and figurative use of language) because there are different ways to define good writing. Thus, any one rubric is not likely to represent the domain of writing fully and may provide few or no opportunities for scorers to reward certain desirable writing skills (Mabry, 1999).

Use of Formative Evaluation Earlier, we pointed out that tests can be used as a source of feedback to help students improve the quality of their learning efforts. Because many real-life performances and products are the result of several feedback and revision cycles, performance testing often includes this feature as well. As anyone who has ever done any substantial amount of writing can tell you (and we are no exception), a satisfactory essay, story, or even personal letter is not produced in one attempt. Usually, there are critical comments from oneself and others and subsequent attempts at another draft. If we believe that the ability to write well, even among people who do it for a living, is partly defined by the ability to use feedback profitably, why should this be any different for students (Wiggins, 1993)? Some specific forms of formative assessment are dress rehearsals, practice tests, reviews of writing drafts, and peer response groups (McTighe, 1996–1997).

Responsiveness to Cultural Diversity Traditional written tests have been criticized over the years for being culturally biased. That is, they are thought to underestimate the capabilities of many ethnic minority and low-SES students because they rely on a narrow range of item types (mainly selected response) and on content that mostly reflects the experiences of the majority culture. This criticism is based in large part on the constructivist view of learning: that meaningful learning occurs within a cultural context with which one is familiar and comfortable. If this is so, say the critics, then tests should be more consistent with the cultural context in which learning occurs. Performance tests have been promoted as a way to assess more fairly and accurately the knowledge and skills of all students, and particularly minority students, because of their realism (including group problem solving) and closer relationship between instruction and assessment (Hood, 1998; Lee, 1998).

Much research on this issue remains to be done, but there is some evidence to support the arguments of the critics. In one study (Supovitz & Brennan, 1997), white, black, and Hispanic first- and second-grade students either took a standardized test of language arts or constructed a language arts portfolio. While the white students significantly outscored the black and Hispanic students on the standardized test, the gap for the portfolio assessment was smaller by about half. In another study (Supovitz, 1998), white, black, and Hispanic fourth graders took either an open-ended paper-and-pencil science test or a science performance test. Although the score of the white students on the paper-and-pencil exam was higher than the scores of the black and Hispanic students, there was no difference among the three groups on the performance assessment. Within groups, white students performed better on the paper-and-pencil measures than on the performance measures, and the black and Hispanic students scored higher on the performance measures.

Some Concerns About Performance Assessment There is no question that alternative assessment methods have excited educators and will be used with increasing frequency. But some of the same features that make these new assessment methods attractive also create problems that may or may not be solvable. For example, creating and evaluating portfolios, exhibits, and demonstrations is time-consuming, labor intensive, and expensive, and it cuts into the amount of time available for instruction. In addition, there are questions about the reliability (consistency of performance) and validity (how accurately the test measures its target) of such measures. It is difficult to obtain reliable and valid measures of some characteristics by judging the quality of portfolios, performances, and exhibitions because there is as yet no consensus as to what a portfolio should include, how large a portfolio should be, what standards should be used to judge products and performances, and whether all students should be assessed under precisely the same conditions (Madaus & O'Dwyer, 1999; Terwilliger, 1997; Wiggins, 1993; Worthen, 1993).

Reliability and validity of performance tests not yet firmly established

The few research findings currently available suggest that the proponents of performance assessment have their work cut out for them. Richard Shavelson and Gail Baxter (1992) investigated the reliability and validity of different kinds of science assessments for fifth and sixth graders. The good news was that several raters had little problem agreeing on the quality of students' performances as they worked through three science investigations (a form of reliability known as *interrater reliability*). The troubling news was that students' scores were very inconsistent from task to task (thereby producing a relatively low level of a form of reliability known as *internal consistency*). Thus, to get a clear picture of whether a student understands the use of basic scientific principles, understands how to do scientific projects of a particular type, or can complete only the particular science project that is contained in the assessment, a number of tasks may be needed. This calls the feasibility of performance assessment into question since it becomes even more expensive and time-consuming.

John Herman, Maryl Gearhart, and Eva Baker (1993) found that the writing portfolios of first-, third-, and fourth-grade children could be consistently scored by trained raters and that the same rating scale could be used to score different types of writing products. But they also reported two troubling findings. One was that the pieces students wrote in class for inclusion in their portfolios were scored higher than a narrative they wrote in thirty minutes under standardized conditions (an example of a direct writing assessment). The researchers could not determine which writing sample was a better estimate of students' writing ability. The second problem was that overall portfolio scores were substantially higher than the aggregate scores of the individual items that made up the portfolio, truly a case of the whole being greater than the sum of its parts. Whatever the cause of this effect, it suggests that those who are selected to rate portfolios need to be given rational, clear, and comprehensive directions.

To see how actual teachers apply assessment methods, read the Site-Based Cases in the text web site at **http://education.college.hmco.com/students**.

Finally, we have a word about keeping things in perspective. Like most other new ideas, performance assessment has been vigorously debated as *the* solution to the shortcomings and distortions of traditional tests. The truth, of course, is almost always somewhere in between. As we have pointed out in previous chapters and in numerous ways, *nothing works for everyone all the time or under all circumstances.* Writing portfolios, for example, do not engage all students. As one middle school student rather dramatically put it: "I would rather shovel coal in hell than put together another one of these portfolios" (Spalding, 2000, p. 762).

Despite these problems, the Case in Print illustrates why performance tests have become so popular among educators, including primary grade teachers.

Ways to Evaluate Student Learning

Once you have collected all the measures you intend to collect—for example, test scores, quiz scores, homework assignments, special projects, and laboratory experiments—you will have to give the numbers some sort of value (the essence of evaluation). As you probably know, this is most often done by using an A to F grading scale. There are two general ways to approach this task. One approach is comparisons among students. Such forms of evaluation are called norm-referenced since students are identified as average (or normal), above average, or below average. An alternative approach is called criterion-referenced because performance is interpreted in terms of defined criteria. Although both approaches can be used, we favor criterion-referenced grading for reasons we will mention shortly.

Norm-Referenced Grading

A **norm-referenced grading** system assumes that classroom achievement will naturally vary among a group of heterogeneous students because of differences in such characteristics as prior knowledge, learning skills, motivation, and aptitude (to be discussed in the chapter on standardized tests). Under ideal circumstances (hundreds of scores from a diverse group of students), this variation produces a bell-shaped, or "normal," distribution of scores that ranges from low to high, has few tied scores, and has only a very few low scores and only a very few high scores. For this reason, norm-referenced grading procedures are also referred to as "grading on the curve."

Those Who Can, Perform

In recent years many teachers, learning theorists, and measurement experts have argued that the typical written test should be used far less often because it reveals little or nothing of the depth of students' knowledge and how students use their knowledge to work through questions, problems, and tasks. One way to address these concerns is to use one or more of what are called performance tests. *(p. 458)*

Teachers Look for New Ways to Measure Learning

DALE SINGER

St. Louis Post-Dispatch 1/26/98

Congratulations! You've been invited to Joe's birthday party along with Stephanie and Andrea and will get some of those terrific chocolate-chunk cookies baked by his grandmother.

But there's one problem: You have 15 cookies for four partygoers. What is the best way to share?

In the past, second-graders faced with this question on a test would be able to choose the right answer from a set of possibilities. As tests move away from multiple choice in favor of judging how well students can solve problems—and describe how they came up with their answers—cooking up the proper response is more difficult.

As teachers discovered in a recent workshop, devising properly phrased questions—ones that fairly and accurately test what they are designed to test—isn't so easy either.

"I left that meeting feeling kind of frustrated," said Melanie Avery, a teacher at Robinson School in Kirkwood, who came up with the cookie question along with Judith Joerding, a second-grade teacher at Airport School in the Ferguson-Florissant district. "I felt we needed to go back and really rethink that question and make sure we are addressing the higher-level thinking that performance assessment is supposed to address."

"When Melanie and I got together and designed the task," Joerding added, "we wanted the children to use problem-solving skills. The world they're going to live in won't necessarily have one correct answer. They're going to need different ways and strategies to solve a problem."

Cookies, Clay and Marshmallows

Before such thinking became popular, anyone faced with the cookie dilemma probably would have had choices like this:

(a) 3 cookies each.
(b) 4 cookies each.
(c) 5 cookies each.
(d) 3¾ cookies each.

Students who came up with the right answer—in this case (d), if the goal was to make sure each person had an equal cookie ration—didn't necessarily know how to divide 15 by four. They could have guessed or used real-life substitutes like clay or marshmallows to eliminate some wrong options.

As new tests are born, students in Missouri will have to do more than simply fill in a correct answer. They'll have to explain how they got there and why they think their choice is right. The change is designed to show how they can turn the basic knowledge they have into real problem-solving skills instead of simply the ability to take tests.

"You could really psych out the test," said Bill Foster about the multiple-choice variety. Foster is director of professional development schools at the School of Education of the University of Missouri at St. Louis. "If you'd memorized a lot, you could easily pick out the answer. It's like bench engineers who are surprised by new graduates who don't know how to approach a problem and come up with a creative solution. They know a lot of facts and theories, but they don't know how to use them."

Foster and Mike Fulton, an assistant to the superintendent of the Pattonville School District for planning and assessment, are helping develop the techniques needed to test such skills. Their Show-Me Classroom Performance Assessment Project brings together teachers from across Missouri, under a grant from the Department of Elementary and Secondary Education, to devise ways to determine how well students are learning what the state's education standards demand.

"We want them to think in ways so that if they can do these kind of activities," Fulton said, "they should be able to do well on the test."

Bake More Cookies

That's where Joe and his birthday cookies come in. Avery, Joerding and other teachers met on a recent Saturday at Holman Middle School, 11055 St. Charles Rock Road in St. Ann, to go over questions they had devised earlier and the answers their students had given in the classroom. Responses didn't always match expectations.

For example, the cookie question was phrased this way: "Now you will need to figure out a way to share the cookies among the FOUR of you."

Even though they knew elementary division, few students used precision to give each child 3¾ cookies. Most used more creative solutions, like giving Joe extra cookies because he was the guest of honor; or letting Joe's mother share the feast, giving each person three cookies; or baking more cookies so that the bigger batch would let everyone share equally.

Such answers may be resourceful, but the teachers had to determine whether they really responded to the question. They also had to determine what grade to give each response, based on a four-point scale, with each level responding to certain criteria.

Matching each answer to a grade was slippery work, but for such tests to be meaningful when they are given to a large group of students, both the questions and the grading scale must be uniformly understood.

"You have to make sure you come up with tasks where the question you ask is not phrased in a way that will allow confusion," said Foster. "It's not fair to students to have them guessing what you want. It should be clear to them the kind of thing you are looking for."

Creativity Within Limits

Teachers also wanted to make sure students had room to use their imaginations to come up with different ways to reach their conclusion, within the proper limits. Creativity doesn't mean anything goes; there may not be just one right answer, but students' responses have to fit what the question is asking and what skills the test is trying to assess.

Questions and Activities

1. Performance-based assessment has the advantage of requiring students to demonstrate both their understanding of information and their ability to use it to solve problems. But what are the disadvantages of this testing format? Can they be reduced or overcome? How?

2. For students to do well on a performance-based test, they have to be able to recognize that previously learned information is relevant to the problem they are working on and to retrieve that information accurately from memory or a reference source. This is essentially a problem of transfer of learning (which we discussed in the chapter on constructivist learning theory and problem solving). What should teachers do to maximize the probability that transfer will occur when students take performance-based tests?

3. The teachers mentioned in this article discovered that writing good performance-based assessment items is not necessarily an easy task. Because some amount of specialized knowledge about assessment is necessary to write good test items and because you will be responsible some day for creating both paper-and-pencil and performance tests, you might think about how you will acquire the knowledge and skill that helps one produce good tests. If your program offers a classroom measurement course that is not required, you would be wise to consider adding it to your electives.

Norm-referenced grading: compare one student to others

The Nature of Norm-Referenced Grading Course grades, like standardized test scores, are determined through a comparison of each student's level of performance to the normal, or average, level of other, similar students in order to reflect the assumed differences in amount of learned material. The comparison may be to all other members of the student's class that year, or it may be to the average performance of several classes stretching back over several years. It is probably better for teachers to use a broad base of typical student performance made up of several classes as grounds for comparison than to rely on the current class of students. Doing so avoids two severe distorting effects: when a single class contains many weak students, those with more well-developed abilities will more easily obtain the highest grades; and when the class has many capable students, the relatively weaker students are virtually predestined to receive low or failing grades (Gronlund, 1998; Kubiszyn & Borich, 2000).

The basic procedure for assigning grades on a norm-referenced basis involves just a few steps:

1. Determine what percentage of students will receive which grades. If, for example, you intend to award the full range of grades, you may decide to give A's to the top 15 percent, B's to the next 25 percent, C's to the middle 35 percent, D's to the next 15 percent, and F's to the bottom 10 percent.
2. Arrange the scores from highest to lowest.
3. Calculate which scores fall in which category, and assign the grades accordingly.

Many other arrangements are also possible. How large or small you decide to make the percentages for each category will depend on such factors as the nature of the students in your class, the difficulty of your exams and assignments, and your own sense of what constitutes appropriate standards. Furthermore, a norm-referenced approach does not necessarily mean that each class will have a normal distribution of grades or that anyone will automatically fail. For example, it is possible for equal numbers of students to receive A's, B's, and C's if you decide to limit your grading system to just those three categories and award equal numbers of each grade. A norm-referenced approach simply means that the grading symbols being used indicate one student's level of achievement relative to other students.

Norm-referenced grading based on absence of external criteria

Proponents of norm-referenced grading typically point to the absence of acceptable external criteria for use as a standard for evaluating and grading student performance. In other words, there is no good way to determine externally how much learning is too little, just enough, or more than enough for some subject. And if there is no amount of knowledge or set of behaviors that all students must master, then grades may be awarded on the basis of relative performance among a group of students (Gronlund, 1998).

Strengths and Weaknesses of Norm-Referenced Grading There are at least two circumstances under which it may be appropriate to use norm-referenced measurement and evaluation procedures:

Norm-referenced grading can be used to evaluate advanced levels of learning

1. *Evaluating advanced levels of learning.* You might, for example, wish to formulate a two-stage instructional plan in which the first stage involves helping all students master a basic level of knowledge and skill in a particular subject. Performance at this stage would be measured and evaluated against a predetermined standard (such as 80 percent correct on an exam). Once this has been accomplished, you could supply advanced instruction and encourage students to learn as much of the additional material as possible. Because the amount of learning during the second stage is not tied to a predetermined standard and it will likely vary because of differences in motivation and learning skills, a norm-referenced approach to grading can be used at this stage. This situation also fits certain guidelines for the use of competitive reward structures (discussed in the chapter "Approaches to Instruction") since everyone starts from the same level of basic knowledge.
2. *Selection for limited-enrollment programs.* Norm-referenced measurement and evaluation are also applicable in cases where students with the best chances for success are selected for a limited-enrollment program from among a large pool of candidates. One example is the selection of students for honors programs who have the highest test scores and grade-point averages (Gronlund, 1998).

The main weakness of the norm-referenced approach to grading is that there are few situations in which the typical public school teacher can appropriately use it. Ei-

Norm-referenced grading systems should rarely, if ever, be used in schools since there are few circumstances that warrant their use and they are likely to depress the motivation of all but the highest scoring students.

ther the goal is not appropriate (as in mastery of certain material and skills by all students or diagnosis of an individual student's specific strengths and weaknesses), or the basic conditions cannot be met (classes are too small or homogeneous, or both). When a norm-referenced approach is used in spite of these weaknesses, communication and motivation problems are often created.

Consider the example of a group of high school sophomores having a great deal of difficulty mastering German vocabulary and grammar. The students may have been underprepared, the teacher may be doing a poor job of organizing and explaining the material, or both factors may be at work. The top student averages 48 percent correct on all of the exams, quizzes, and oral recitations administered during the term. That student and a few others with averages in the high 40s will receive the A's. Although these fortunate few may realize their knowledge and skills are incomplete, others are likely to conclude falsely that these students learned quite a bit about the German language since a grade of A is generally taken to mean superior performance.

At the other extreme, we have the example of a social studies class in which most of the students are doing well. Because the students were well prepared by previous teachers, used effective study skills, were exposed to high-quality instruction, and were strongly motivated by the enthusiasm of their teacher, the final test averages ranged from 94 to 98 percent correct. And yet the teacher who uses a norm-referenced scheme would assign at least A's, B's, and C's to this group. Not only does this practice seriously damage the motivation of students who worked hard and performed well, but it also miscommunicates to others the performance of students who received B's and C's (Airasian,2001).

Criterion-Referenced Grading

A **criterion-referenced grading** system permits students to benefit from mistakes and improve their level of understanding and performance. Furthermore, it establishes an individual (and sometimes cooperative) reward structure, which fosters motivation to learn to a greater extent than other systems.

Criterion-referenced grading: compare individual performance to stated criteria

The Nature of Criterion-Referenced Grading Under a criterion-referenced system, grades are determined through comparison of the extent to which each student has attained a defined standard (or criterion) of achievement or performance. Whether the rest of the students in the class are successful or unsuccessful in meeting that criterion is irrelevant. Thus, any distribution of grades is possible. Every student may get an A or an F, or no student may receive these grades. For reasons we will discuss shortly, very low or failing grades may occur less frequently under a criterion-referenced system.

A common version of criterion-referenced grading assigns letter grades on the basis of the percentage of test items answered correctly. For example, you may decide to award an A to anyone who correctly answers at least 85 percent of a set of test questions, a B to anyone who correctly answers 75 to 84 percent, and so on down to the lowest grade. To use this type of grading system fairly, which means specifying realistic criterion levels, you would need to have some prior knowledge of the levels at which students typically perform. You would thus be using normative information to establish absolute, or fixed, standards of performance. However, although both norm-referenced and criterion-referenced grading systems spring from a normative database (that is, from comparisons among students), only the former system uses those comparisons to directly determine grades.

Strengths and Weaknesses of Criterion-Referenced Grading Criterion-referenced grading systems (and criterion-referenced tests) have become increasingly popular in recent years primarily because of the following advantages:

Criterion-referenced grades provide information about strengths and weaknesses

- Criterion-referenced tests and grading systems provide more specific and useful information about student strengths and weaknesses than do norm-referenced grading systems. Parents and teachers are more interested in knowing that a student received an A on an earth science test because she mastered 92 percent of the objectives for that unit than they are in knowing that she received an A on a test of the same material because she outscored 92 percent of her classmates.
- Criterion-referenced grading systems promote motivation to learn because they hold out the promise that all students who have sufficiently well-developed learning skills and receive good-quality instruction can master most of a teacher's objectives (Gronlund, 1998). The motivating effect of criterion-referenced grading systems is likely to be particularly noticeable among students who adopt mastery goals (which we will discuss in a moment) since they tend to use grades as feedback for further improvement (Covington, 1999).

One weakness of the criterion-referenced approach to grading is that the performance standards one specifies (such as a grade of A for 90 percent correct) are arbitrary and may be difficult to justify to parents and colleagues. (Why not 87 percent correct for an A? Or 92 percent?) A second weakness is that although a teacher's standards may appear to be stable from one test to another (90 percent correct for an A for all tests), they may in reality fluctuate as a result of unnoticed variation in the difficulty of each test and the quality of instruction (Gronlund, 1998).

Finally, we would like to alert you to a characteristic of criterion-referenced evaluation that is not a weakness but is an unfortunate fact of educational life that you may have to address. In a variety of subtle and sometimes not so subtle ways, teachers are discouraged from using a criterion-referenced approach to grading because it tends to produce higher test scores and grades than a norm-referenced approach does. The reason for the higher scores is obvious and quite justified. When test items are based solely on the specific instructional objectives that teachers write and when those objectives are clear and provided to students, students know what they need to learn and what they need to do to meet the teacher's objectives. Also, because students' grades depend only on how well they perform, not how well their classmates perform, motivation for learning tends to be higher. The result is that students tend to learn more and score higher on classroom tests. So why should this happy outcome be a cause for concern? Because individuals who are not well versed in classroom measurement and evaluation may believe that the only reason large numbers of students achieve high grades is that the teacher has lower standards than other teachers. Consequently, you may find yourself in a position of having to defend the criteria you use to assign grades. As Tom Kubiszyn and Gary Borich point out, "It is a curious fact of life that everyone presses for excellence in education, but many balk at marking systems that make attainment of excellence within everyone's reach" (2000, p. 206).

A particular criterion-referenced approach to grading is often referred to as a mastery approach because it allows students multiple opportunities to learn and demonstrate their mastery of instructional objectives. This approach stems in large part from the work of John Carroll (1963) and Benjamin Bloom (1968, 1976) on the concept of *mastery learning.* The basic idea behind mastery learning is that most students can master most objectives if they are given good-quality instruction and sufficient time to learn and are motivated to continue learning.

Journal Entry
Trying a Mastery Approach to Grading

Elements of a Mastery Approach to Grading The following suggestions can be adapted for use at any grade level and any subject area.

1. Go through a unit of study, a chapter of a text, or an outline of a lecture, and pick out what you consider to be the most important points—that is, the points you wish to stress because they are most likely to have later value or are basic to later learning.
2. List these points in the form of a goal card (a list of the major concepts and skills that should be acquired by the end of an instructional unit), instructional objectives (as described by Robert Mager, 1997, or Robert Linn and Norman Gronlund, 2000), key points, or the equivalent. If appropriate, arrange the objectives in some sort of organized framework, perhaps with reference to the relevant taxonomy of educational objectives (see the chapter "Approaches to Instruction").
3. Distribute the list of objectives at the beginning of a unit. Tell your students that they should concentrate on learning those points and that they will be tested on them.
4. Consider making up a study guide in which you provide specific questions relating to the objectives and a format that students can use to organize their notes.
5. Use a variety of instructional methods and materials to explain and illustrate objectives-related ideas.
6. Make up exam questions based on the objectives and the study guide questions. Try to write several questions for each objective.
7. Arrange these questions into at least two (preferably three) alternate exams for each unit of study.
8. Make up tentative criteria for grade levels for each exam and for the entire unit or report period (for example, A for not more than one question missed on any exam; B for not more than two questions missed on any exam; C for not more than four questions missed on any exam).

Mastery approach: give students multiple opportunities to master goals at own pace

9. Test students either when they come to you and indicate they are ready or when you determine they have all had ample opportunity to learn the material. Announce all exam dates in advance, and remind students that the questions will be based only on the objectives you have mentioned. Indicate the criteria for different grade levels, and emphasize that any student who fails to meet a desired criterion on the first try will have a chance to take an alternate form of the exam.
10. Grade and return the exams as promptly as possible, go over questions briefly in class (particularly those that caused problems for more than a few students), and offer to go over exams individually with students. Allow for individual interpretations, and give credit for answers you judge to be logical and plausible, even if they differ from the answers you expected.
11. Schedule alternate exams, and make yourself available for consultation and tutoring the day before. (While you are giving alternate exams, you can administer the original exam to students who were absent.)
12. If students improve their score on the second exam but still fall below the desired criterion, consider a safety valve option: invite them to provide you with a completed study guide (or the equivalent) when they take an exam the second time, or give them an open-book exam on the objectives they missed to see whether they can explain them in terms other than those of a written examination. If a student fulfills either of these options satisfactorily, give credit for one extra answer on the second exam.

13. To supplement exams, assign book reports, oral reports, papers, or some other kind of individual work that will provide maximum opportunity for student choice. Establish and explain the criteria you will use to evaluate these assignments, but stress that you want to encourage freedom of choice and expression. (Some students will thrive on free choice; others are likely to feel threatened by open-ended assignments. To allow for such differences, provide specific directions for those who need them and general hints or a simple request that "original" projects be cleared in advance for the more independent thinkers.) Grade all reports Pass or Do Over, and supply constructive criticism on those you consider unsatisfactory. Announce that all Do Over papers can be reworked and resubmitted within a certain period of time. Have the reports count toward the final grade—for example, three reports for an A, two for a B, one for a C. (In addition, students should pass each exam at the designated level.) You might also invite students to prepare extra papers to earn bonus points to be added to exam totals.

This basic technique will permit you to work within a traditional A to F framework, but in such a way that you should be able, without lowering standards, to increase the proportion of students who do acceptable work. An example of a mastery-oriented, criterion-referenced approach to grading appears in Figure 13.2.

Improving Your Grading Methods: Assessment Practices to Avoid

Earlier in this chapter, we noted that the typical teacher has little systematic knowledge of assessment principles and as a result may engage in a variety of inappropriate testing and grading practices. We hope that the information in this chapter will help you become more proficient at these tasks. (In addition, we strongly encourage you to take a course in classroom assessment if you have not already done so.) To reinforce what you have learned here, we will describe some of the more common inappropriate testing and grading practices that teachers commit. The following list is based largely on the observations of Thomas Haladyna (1999), Robert Lynn Canady and Phyllis Riley Hotchkiss (1989), and John Hills (1991).

Be aware of and avoid faulty measurement and grading practices

1. *Worshiping averages.* Some teachers mechanically average all scores and automatically assign the corresponding grade, even when they know an unusually low score was due to an extenuating circumstance. Allowances can be made for physical illness, emotional upset, and the like; students' lowest grade can be dropped, or they can repeat the test on which they performed most poorly. Although objectivity in grading is a laudatory goal, it should not be practiced to the extent that it prevents you from altering your normal procedures when your professional judgment indicates an exception is warranted.

   Another shortcoming of this practice is that it ignores measurement error. No one can construct the perfect test, and no person's score is a true indicator of knowledge and skill. Test scores represent estimates of these characteristics. Accordingly, giving a student with an average of 74.67 a grade of D when 75 is the minimum needed for a C pretends the test is more accurate than it really is. This is why it is so important to conduct an item analysis of your tests. If you

Figure 13.2 Page from a Teacher's Grade Book and Instructions to Students: Mastery Approach Featuring + or – Grading

	1st Exam		2nd Exam		3rd Exam		Exam	Projects			Extra Project	Grade
	1st Try	2nd Try	1st Try	2nd Try	1st Try	2nd Try	Total Points	1	2	3		
Adams, Ann	16	18	17	18	18			P	P	P		
Baker, Charles	13	14	14		10	14		P				
Cohen, Matthew	14	16	15	16	17			P	P			
Davis, Rebecca	19		19		20			P	P	P		
Evans, Deborah	16	18	17	18	16	18		P	P	P		
Ford, Harold	15	16	17		15			P	P			
Grayson, Lee	10	13	12	14	12	15		P				
Hood, Barbara	16		17		15			P	P			
Ingalls, Robert	16	18	16		15			P	P			
Jones, Thomas	11	14	12	16	15			P				
Kim, David	18		19		19			P	P	P		
Lapine, Craig	14	16	18		16			P	P			
Moore, James	17		17		17			P	P			
Nguyen, Tuan	17	18	19		16	17		P	P	P		
Orton, John	10	10	11		9							
Peck, Nancy	14		15		14			P				
Quist, Ann	16	18	17	18	18			P	P	P		
Richards, Mary	16		17		15			P	P			
Santos, Maria	13		15		14			P				
Thomas, Eric	15	16	15	17	15			P	P			
Wong, Yuen	14		15		16			P				
Vernon, Joan	11	14	13	14	12	14		P				
Zacharias, Saul	16	18	17		16	19		P	P	P		

Instructions for Determining Your Grade in Social Studies

Your grade in social studies this report period will be based on three exams (worth 20 points each) and satisfactory completion of up to three projects.

Here are the standards for different grades:

A—Average of 18 or more on three exams, plus three projects at Pass level
B—Average of 16 or 17 on three exams, plus two projects at Pass level
C—Average of 14 or 15 on three exams, plus one project at Pass level
D—Average of 10 to 13 on three exams
F—Average of 9 or less on three exams

Another way to figure your grade is to add together points as you take exams. This may be the best procedure to follow as we get close to the end of the report period. Use this description of standards as a guide:

A—At least 54 points, plus three projects at Pass level
B—48 to 53 points, plus two projects at Pass level
C—42 to 47 points, plus one project at Pass level
D—30 to 41 points
F—29 points or less

If you are not satisfied with the score you earn on any exam, you may take a different exam on the same material in an effort to improve your score. (Some of the questions on the alternate exam will be the same as those on the original exam; some will be different.) Projects will be graded P (Pass) or DO (Do Over). If you receive a DO on a project, you may work to improve it and hand it in again. You may also submit an *extra* project, which may earn up to 3 points of bonus credit (and can help if your exam scores fall just below a cutoff point). As you take each exam and receive a Pass for each project, record your progress on this chart.

First Exam		Second Exam		Third Exam		Project 1	Project 2	Project 3	Extra Project	Grade
1st Try	2nd Try	1st Try	2nd Try	1st Try	2nd Try					

discover several items that are unusually difficult, you may want to make allowances for students who are a point or two from the next highest grade (and modify the items if you intend to use them again). We describe a simple procedure for analyzing your test items in the next Suggestions for Teaching section.

2. *Using zeros indiscriminately.* The sole purpose of grades is to communicate to others how much of the curriculum a student has mastered. When teachers also use grades to reflect their appraisal of a student's work habits or character, the validity of the grades is lessened. This occurs most dramatically when students receive zeros for assignments that are late (but are otherwise of good quality), incomplete, or not completed according to directions and for exams on which they are suspected of cheating. This is a flawed practice for two reasons. First, and to repeat what we said in point 1, there may be good reasons that projects and homework assignments are late, incomplete, or different from what was expected. You should try to uncover such circumstances and take them into account. The second reason for not automatically giving zeros is that they cause communication problems. If a student who earns grades in the low 90s for most of the grading period is given two zeros for one or more of the reasons just mentioned, that student could easily receive a D or an F. Such a grade is not an accurate reflection of what was learned. If penalties are to be given for work that is late, incomplete, or not done according to directions and for which there are no extenuating circumstances, they should be clearly spelled out far in advance of the due date, and they should not seriously distort the meaning of the grade. For students suspected of cheating, for example, a different form of the exam can be given.
3. *Providing insufficient instruction before testing.* For a variety of reasons, teachers occasionally spend more time than they had planned on certain topics. In an effort to "cover the curriculum" prior to a scheduled exam, they may significantly increase the pace of instruction or simply tell students to read the remaining material on their own. The low grades that typically result from this practice will unfortunately be read by outsiders (and this includes parents) as a deficiency in students' learning ability when in fact they more accurately indicate a deficiency in instructional quality.
4. *Teaching for one thing but testing for another.* This practice takes several forms. For instance, teachers may provide considerable supplementary material in class through lecture, thereby encouraging students to take notes and study them extensively, but base test questions almost entirely on text material. Or if teachers emphasize the text material during class discussion, they may take a significant number of questions from footnotes and less important parts of the text. A third form of this flawed practice is to provide students with simple problems or practice questions in class that reflect the knowledge level of Bloom's Taxonomy but to give complex problems and higher-level questions on a test. Remember what we said earlier in this book: if you want transfer, then teach for transfer.
5. *Using pop quizzes to motivate students.* If you recall our discussion of reinforcement schedules, you will recognize that surprise tests represent a variable interval schedule and that such schedules produce a consistent pattern of behavior in humans under certain circumstances. Being a student in a classroom is not one of those circumstances. Surprise tests produce an undesirable level of anxiety in many students and cause others simply to give up. If you sense that students are not sufficiently motivated to read and study more consistently, consult the chapter "Motivation" for better ideas on how to accomplish this goal.

6. *Keeping the nature and content of the test a secret.* Many teachers scrupulously avoid giving students any meaningful information about the type of questions that will be on a test or what the test items will cover. The assumption that underlies this practice is that if students have been paying attention in class, have been diligently doing their homework, and have been studying at regular intervals, they will do just fine on a test. But they usually don't—and the main reason can be seen in our description of a learning strategy (see the chapter on information-processing theory). A good learning strategist first analyzes all of the available information that bears on attaining a goal. But if certain critical information about the goal is not available, the rest of the strategy (planning, implementing, monitoring, and modifying) will suffer.
7. *Keeping the criteria for assignments a secret.* This practice is closely related to the previous one. Students may be told, for example, to write an essay on what the world would be like if all diseases were eliminated and to give their imagination free rein in order to come up with many original ideas. But when the papers are graded, equal weight is given to spelling, punctuation, and grammatical usage. If these aspects of writing are also important to you and you intend to hold students accountable for them, make sure you clearly communicate that fact to them.
8. *Shifting criteria.* Teachers are sometimes disappointed in the quality of students' tests and assignments and decide to change the grading criteria as a way to shock students into more appropriate learning behaviors. For example, a teacher may have told students that mechanics will count for one-third of the grade on a writing assignment. But when the teacher discovers that most of the papers contain numerous spelling, punctuation, and grammatical errors, she may decide to let mechanics determine half of the grade. As we indicated before, grades should not be used as a motivational device or as a way to make up for instructional oversights. There are far better ways to accomplish these goals.

A number of technological formats and products have been developed to make the task of classroom assessment easier, more informative, and less prone to error. The next section describes several of these formats and products.

Technology for Classroom Assessment

At the beginning of this chapter, we mentioned that assessment activities can account for about one-third of a teacher's time. This large investment in time is partly due to the importance of assessment in both teaching and learning, but it is also related to the fact that many assessment activities involve time-consuming methods of creating, administering, and scoring tests and analyzing and recording scores. Fortunately, computer-based technology now allows for the efficient creation of test-item banks, assembling of examinations, maintaining of student records, and generation of reports (Baker & O'Neil, 1995; Kumar & Helgeson, 1995). Test-item banks are large collections of test items that publishers often supply with particular textbooks or that teachers can construct themselves using the database programs in Microsoft Works or AppleWorks. They can store information regarding date of entry, author, references, type of item (for example, true-false), cognitive skill addressed, and item difficulty; thus, they are an efficient way to generate one or more forms of a classroom test.

Assessment technology also makes it possible for teachers to record student interviews and observations in portable and hand-held computers, scan student work into portfolios, diagnose student misconceptions, track student solutions, and generate multidimensional displays or profiles of students' progress (Altschuld, 1995).

ELECTRONIC GRADEBOOKS

Electronic gradebooks can store records of student test performance, compute test averages and cumulative averages, weight scores, note students with particular scores or characteristics, and print grade reports with standard as well as specific student comments (Vockell & Fiore, 1993). Edward Vockell and Douglas Fiore (1993) found that speed, accuracy, customizability, and organization are the key advantages of these systems. However, they also admit that there can be distinct disadvantages to electronic gradebooks, such as incorrect data entry, system impersonality, and inflexibility with absent students and special situations. Three electronic gradebooks that you may want to examine are Gradebook (**www.gradebook.com/**), GradeStar (**www.shelltech.com/**), and Grade Busters (**www.gradebusters.com/**). For more flexibility in electronic record keeping, you may want to consider regular database and spreadsheet programs, which will allow you to tailor assessment records to your specific needs (Vockell & Fiore, 1993).

Go to the Web Sources section at **http://education.college.hmco.com/students** for convenient links to recommended web sites.

As online instructional activities and courses proliferate, teachers increasingly will need to know how to use grading mechanisms designed for both World Wide Web and videoconferencing courses. Fortunately, there are systems on the Web that can grade student tests and offer feedback, recommend remediation, show Web references for information related to missed items, and keep the student from progressing to new lessons until mastery has been achieved (Dickinson, 1997). Additionally, these Web test systems can be password protected and date and time restricted to prevent unauthorized access and cheating. A web site that will help you create online tests is FunBrain (**www.funbrain.com/**). Ken Cardwell (2000), a Redmond, Oregon, teacher who has described his experiences in creating and using online tests, recommends this site for accessing ready-made tests or making your own.

TECHNOLOGY-BASED PERFORMANCE ASSESSMENT

As you may recall from our earlier discussion, performance assessments give students the opportunity to demonstrate how well they can use the knowledge and skills that were the focus of an instructional unit to carry out realistic and meaningful tasks. Computer-based technology is an excellent vehicle for this purpose. You can require students to use computer programs and web-based resources to carry out such tasks as preparing documentaries on weather-related issues, determining energy use in taking a shower or cooking a meal, and determining the impact of a recycling plan on landfill use (Okey, 1995). Clearly, no matter what subject you will teach, you will have numerous performance assessment options.

Computer-based simulation is another potentially useful form of technology-based performance assessment. While simulations help students grasp the complexity of such real-life tasks as developing buildings or cities, operating a nuclear reactor, or running a factory, they can also be used to assess how well students have grasped such important issues as time, safety, and complexity (Kumar & Helgeson, 1995). Computer-based simulations also maintain full records of student performance and reveal approaches to solutions that may not have been apparent in more traditional forms of assessment (Baker & O'Neil, 1995; Shavelson & Baxter, 1992).

Technology tools like hypermedia, with text, audio, video, and graphics components, also offer opportunities for students to demonstrate their ability to solve real-world problems in a number of content areas. Ivan Baugh (1994), for instance, notes that students investigating concepts such as biomes and ecosystems could (1) construct hypermedia stacks such as encyclopedias and pictorial atlases on CD-ROM, (2) record narrative voice-overs for such segments, (3) use telecommunications to exchange information with people living near those environments, (4) use videodisks to provide illustrations of food chains in action, (5) digitize videotape taken from the local environment, (6) type environmental reports, newspapers, and brochures in a word processor, and (7) create brief replayable movies about the different locales that link to other hypermedia or word processing documents.

Digital Portfolios

What Is a Digital Portfolio? Terry Wiedmer (1998, p. 586) defines a **digital portfolio** as "a purposeful collection of work, captured by electronic means, that serves as an exhibit of individual efforts, progress, and achievements in one or more areas." In their digital portfolios, students can create, store, and manage various products and processes that they want to document and perhaps showcase.

Digital portfolio: collection of work that is stored and illustrated electronically

Digital portfolios are similar in purpose to the more traditional portfolios, but they extend beyond paper versions because they can include sound effects, audio and video testimonials, voice-over explanations of a student's thinking process as a project is worked on, special visual effects such as animation, movies of how the student used recently learned knowledge to produce a product (such as using mathematical principles to help build a homeless shelter), and diagrams and drawings to indicate growth over a period of time (Wiedmer, 1998).

The Components and Contents of Digital Portfolios Because the purposes for having students construct a digital portfolio (such as to assign grades, assess students' strengths and weaknesses, evaluate a program or curriculum) are not always the same, the portfolio structure will vary somewhat across teachers and school districts. But some components, such as those in the list that follows, are frequently recommended (for instance, Barrett, 1998; Niguidula, 1997; Tuttle, 1997) and should always be seriously considered for inclusion:

- The goals the student was attempting to achieve
- The guidelines that were used to select the included material
- Work samples
- Teacher feedback
- Student self-reflection
- The criteria that were used to evaluate each entry
- Examples of good-quality work

Just as the general components of a digital portfolio may vary, so may the particular media that are used. Following are some specific examples of the types of media a student may use and information that would be represented by each medium (Moersch & Fisher, 1995; Mohnsen & Mendon, 1997; O'Lone, 1997; Tuttle, 1997):

- *Digitized pictures and scanned images*: photos of the student and/or objects he or she has created, artwork, models, science experiments over time, fax exchanges with scientists, spelling tests, math work, self-assessment checklists

- *Documents*: electronic copies of student writing, reflection journals, publications, copies of web pages created, and teacher notes and observations
- *Audio recordings*: persuasive speeches, poetry readings, rehearsals of foreign language vocabulary, readings of select passages, self-evaluations, interviews or voice notes regarding the rationale for work included
- *Videotapes*: student or teams of students engaged in science experiments and explaining their steps, student performances in physical education or the performing arts
- *Multimedia presentations*: QuickTime movies of interdisciplinary projects

Creating Digital Portfolios Portfolios can be created by using one of two types of software programs. One option is to purchase generic portfolio templates such as the Grady Profile (**www.aurbach.com/**). The second option is to purchase authoring programs such as HyperCard (**www.apple.com/hypercard/**), HyperStudio (**www.hyperstudio.com/**), K–6 Multimedia (**www.apple.com/education/learningseries/als/k6multi.html**), and Macromedia Authorware (**www.macromedia.com/software/authorware/**), which give students total freedom to design their own portfolios.

Advantages and Disadvantages of Digital Portfolios The main advantage of a digital portfolio is the ability of students to explain in text and narration why they gave their portfolio its particular content and form. It is very important that each student portfolio submission be linked to self-reflections about why the item was selected, since "without time for reflection, the digital portfolio might be no different from a paper portfolio filed away in a locked cabinet" (Niguidula, 1997, p. 28). Using this opportunity for self-reflection, students can demonstrate what they know, how they came to know it, how their knowledge increased and evolved, and what they have accomplished with that knowledge. David Berliner (1992b) points out that portfolios, in contrast to other forms of assessment, are more representative of the range of learning experiences and curriculum activities that students are exposed to during a year or a unit.

Another advantage of digital portfolios is the ability to store a considerable amount of information in a very compact space. The format most commonly recommended is the compact disk in either recordable (CD-R) or rewritable (CD-RW) form. Such disks are physically small (4 1/2 inches in diameter), have a large capacity (about 600 megabytes), are not expensive (less than $1 apiece when purchased in bulk), are easily stored and transported, hold information in multiple media (such as photographs, video, audio, and text), and can be played on any computer with a CD-ROM drive (Barrett, 1998; Georgi & Crowe, 1998).

However, many of the same disadvantages that occur when computers are used for other purposes apply to the creation and use of digital portfolios. Because portfolios are personal documents, access to them needs to be restricted. This is typically done with passwords, which, as you probably know, are easily forgotten. Second, portfolios that are stored on a school's server (basically a large-capacity computer) can be altered or destroyed by hackers. Third, work that is not saved while working on a portfolio can be lost if the computer crashes. Finally, if your school's computers are not relatively new, they will probably lack the capability to create (or "burn") a CD. In that case, separate CD-RW machines (called "burners") will have to be purchased at anywhere from $100 to $300 apiece.

Rubrics for Digital Portfolios and Presentations With all the information a digital portfolio might contain, how can a classroom teacher fairly and efficiently assess

Special rubrics needed to assess digital portfolios and presentations

student learning? First, electronic writing, just like paper-based compositions, can be assessed holistically in a general impression rating. It can also be analyzed with specific criteria such as whether the work is insightful, well organized, clear, focused, relevant, sequentially flowing, persuasive, inspirational, and original (see Bonk & Cummings, 1998). In terms of the process of electronic research, Rich Lehrer (1993) suggests assessing student ability to use electronic databases, locate and select information, segment information into useful categories, and interpret and summarize information from multiple sources. For hypermedia or multimedia designs, he recommends evaluating the structure of student presentations, the rationale for including different information, the use of multiple ways of representing information, any consideration of audience, the division of labor within a group, and product changes in response to previous evaluations. There are also rubrics for analyzing the mechanics of student hypermedia presentations (for example, the ability to explain the project, amount of eye contact with the audience, voice, use of examples, text and screen clarity, organization, and visual aids; see Pate, Homestead, & McGinnis, 1993).

Performance and Portfolio Assessment Problems

We would be remiss not to point out the problems often associated with technology-based performance and portfolio assessment. High-quality performance assessments require extensive time, electronic equipment, careful planning, and continued modification (O'Neil, 1992; Shavelson & Baxter, 1992). Student performance in these assessments varies widely, thereby requiring a substantial number of tasks to estimate a student's achievement. Electronic portfolios can become large, complex, and time-consuming to grade fairly and thus can overload teachers with work (Moersch & Fisher, 1995).

Staff development and teacher training are additional barriers to effective use of performance assessment and digital portfolios. But with proper training, teachers may begin to ask whether technology-based school and classroom assessment plans are practical, cost-effective, and qualitatively better than traditional assessments.

The following Suggestions for Teaching should help you properly implement the assessment concepts and research findings presented in this chapter.

Suggestions for Teaching in Your Classroom

Effective Assessment Techniques

1 As early as possible in a report period, decide when and how often to give tests and other assignments that will count toward a grade, and announce tests and assignments well in advance.

If you follow the suggestions for formulating objectives presented in the chapter "Approaches to Instruction," you should be able to develop a reasonably complete master plan that will permit you to devise a course outline even though you have only limited experience with teaching or with a particular text or unit of study. In doing so, you will have not only a good sense of the objectives you want your students to achieve but also the means by which achievement will be assessed.

Journal Entry
Announcing Exams and Assignments

Before the term starts is a good time to block out the number of tests you will give in that term. Recall that research cited earlier has shown that students who take six or seven tests per term (two or three per grading period) learn more than students who are tested less frequently or not at all. Don't assume, however, that if giving three tests per grading period is good, then giving five or six tests is better. A point of diminishing returns is quickly reached after the fourth test.

If you announce at the beginning of a report period when you intend to give exams or set due dates for assignments, you not only give students a clear idea of what they will be expected to do, but you also give yourself guidelines for arranging lesson plans and devising, administering, and scoring tests. (If you will be teaching elementary students, it will be better to announce exams and assignments for a week at a time rather than providing a long-range schedule.)

In order for students to effectively plan how they will master your objectives, they need to know as early as possible how many tests they will have to take, when the tests will occur, what types of items each test will contain, and what content they will be tested on.

For the most part, it is preferable to announce tests well in advance. Pop quizzes tend to increase anxiety and tension and force students to cram on isolated sections of a book on a day-by-day and catch-as-catch-can basis. Simple homework assignments or the equivalent are more likely to encourage more careful and consistent study than pop quizzes. When tests are announced, it is useful to students to know exactly what material they will be held responsible for, what kinds of questions will be asked, and how much tests will count toward the final grade. Research indicates that students who are told to expect (and who receive) an essay test or a multiple-choice test score slightly higher on an exam than students who do not know what to expect or who are led to expect one type of test but are given another type (Lundeberg & Fox, 1991).

For term papers or other written work, list your criteria for grading the papers (for example, how much emphasis will be placed on style, spelling and punctuation, research, individuality of expression). In laboratory courses, most students prefer a list of experiments or projects and some description of how they will be evaluated (for example, ten experiments in chemistry, fifteen drawings in drafting, five paintings in art, judged according to posted criteria).

2 Prepare a content outline or a table of specifications of the objectives to be covered on each exam, or otherwise take care to obtain a systematic sample of the knowledge and skill acquired by your students.

The more precisely and completely goals are described at the beginning of a unit, the easier and more efficient assessment (and teaching) will be. The use of a clear outline will help ensure an adequate sample of the most significant kinds of behavior.

Necessary to obtain a representative sample of behavior when testing

When the time comes to assess the abilities of your students, you can't possibly observe and evaluate all relevant behavior. You can't listen to more than a few pages of reading by each first grader, for example, or ask high school seniors to answer questions on everything discussed in several chapters of a text. Because of the limitations imposed by large numbers of students and small amounts of time, your evaluation will have to be based on a sample of behavior—a three- or four-minute reading performance and questions covering points made in only a few sections of text material assigned for an exam. It is therefore important to try to obtain a representative, accurate sample.

Psychologists who have studied measurement and evaluation often recommend that as teachers prepare exams, they use a **table of specifications** to note the types and numbers of test items to be included so as to ensure thorough and systematic coverage. You can draw up a table of specifications by first listing along the left-hand margin of a piece of lined paper the important topics that have been covered. Then insert appropriate headings from the taxonomy of objectives for the cognitive domain (or for the affective or psychomotor domain, if appropriate) across the top of the page.

Figure 13.3 Example of a Table of Specifications for Material Covered in This Chapter

Topic	Objectives					
	Knows	Comprehends	Applies	Analyzes	Synthesizes	Evaluates
Nature of measurement and evaluation						
Purposes of measurement and evaluation						
Types of written tests						
Nature of performance tests						

An example of such a table of specifications for the information discussed so far in this chapter is provided in Figure 13.3. A computer spreadsheet program such as Microsoft Excel is an ideal tool for creating a table of specifications. Doing your work on the computer gives you the ability to save and modify it for future use.

Table of specifications helps ensure an adequate sample of content, behavior

Test specialists often recommend that you insert in the boxes of a table of specifications the percentage of test items that you intend to write for each topic and each type of objective. This practice forces you to think about both the number and the relative importance of your objectives before you start teaching or writing test items. Thus, if some objectives are more important to you than others, you will have a way of ensuring that these are tested more thoroughly. If, however, a test is going to be brief and emphasize all objectives more or less equally, you may wish to put a check mark in each box as you write questions. If you discover that you are overloading some boxes and that others are empty, you can take steps to remedy the situation. The important point is that by taking steps to ensure that your tests cover what you want your students to know, you will be increasing the tests' validity.

For reasons to be discussed shortly, you may choose not to list all of the categories in the taxonomy for all subjects or at all grade levels. Tables of specifications that you draw up for your own use therefore may contain fewer headings across the top of the page than those in the table illustrated in Figure 13.3.

3 Consider the purpose of each test or measurement exercise in the light of the developmental characteristics of the students in your classes and the nature of the curriculum for your grade level.

In addition to considering different uses of tests and other forms of measurement when you plan assessment strategies, you should think about the developmental characteristics of the students you plan to teach and the nature of the curriculum at

way to speed up the grading of short-essay exams (so that you can evaluate up to thirty tests in a single session of forty minutes or so) is to use plus or minus grading. If you use a point scale to grade short-essay answers, you will spend an agonizing amount of time deciding just how much a given answer is worth. But with practice, you should be able to write short-essay questions and answers (on your key) that can be graded plus or minus.

To develop skill in writing such questions, make up a few formative quizzes that will not count toward a grade. Experiment with phrasing questions that require students to reveal that they either know or don't know the answer. Prepare your key as you write the questions. When the time comes to grade papers, simply make a yes or no decision about the correctness of each answer. With a felt-tip pen, make a bold check over each satisfactory answer on an exam, and tally the number of checks when you have read all the answers. (Counting up to eight or ten is obviously a lot quicker and easier than adding together various numbers of points for eight or ten answers.) Once you have developed skill in writing and evaluating short-essay questions that can be graded plus or minus, prepare and use summative exams. If you decide to use this type of exam, guard against the temptation to write items that measure only knowledge. Use a table of specifications, or otherwise take steps to write at least some questions that measure skills at the higher levels of the taxonomy for the cognitive domain.

b. Be willing and prepared to defend the evaluations you make.

You will probably get few complaints if you have a detailed key and can explain to the class when exams are returned how each answer was graded. To a direct challenge about a specific answer to an essay or short-essay question, you might respond by showing complainers an answer that received full credit and inviting them to compare it with their own.

Perhaps the best way to provide feedback about responses to multiple-choice questions is to prepare a feedback booklet (see the Study Guide that accompanies this text for an example). As you write each multiple-choice question, also write a brief explanation as to why you feel the answer is correct and why the distracters are incorrect. If you follow this policy (which takes less time than you might expect), you can often improve the questions as you write your defense of the answer. If you go a step further (described in the next point), you can obtain information to use in improving questions after they have been answered. This is a good policy to follow with any exam, multiple choice or otherwise.

6 During and after the grading process, analyze questions and answers in order to improve future exams.

If you prepare sufficient copies of feedback booklets for multiple-choice exams, you can supply them to all students when you hand back scored answer sheets (and copies of the question booklets). After students have checked their papers and identified and examined questions that were marked wrong, invite them to select up to three questions that they wish to challenge. Even after they read your explanation in the feedback booklet, many students are likely to feel that they selected a different answer than you did for logical and defensible reasons. Permit them to write out a description of the reasoning behind their choices. If an explanation seems plausible, give credit for the answer. If several students chose the same questions for comment, you have evidence that the item needs to be revised. (It's also possible that the in-

Journal Entry
Analyzing Test Items

For more journal ideas, see the Reflective Journal Questions at **http://education.college.hmco.com/students**.

formation reflected in the item was not directly related to your objectives or was poorly taught.)

If you follow the procedure of supplying feedback booklets, it is almost essential to prepare at least two forms of every exam. After writing the questions, arrange them into two tests. Make perhaps half of the questions the same and half unique to each exam. (If you have enough questions, you might prepare three forms.) If you teach multiple sections, give the first form to period 1, the next form to period 2, and thereafter use the forms in random order. This procedure will reduce the possibility that some students in later classes will have advance information about most of the questions on the test. (Having two or more forms also equips you to use a mastery approach.)

If you find that you do not have time to prepare feedback booklets, you might invite students to select three answers to defend as they record their choices when taking multiple-choice exams. This will supply you with information about ambiguous questions, even though it will not provide feedback to students. It may also provide you with useful information about how well the items were written.

Item analysis tells about difficulty, discriminating power of multiple-choice items

Turning back to multiple-choice questions, you may also want to use simple versions of item-analysis techniques that measurement specialists use to analyze and improve this type of item. These techniques will allow you to estimate the difficulty level and discriminating power of each item. Discriminating power is the ability of a test item to distinguish students who have learned that piece of information from students who have not. To do so, try the following steps suggested by Norman Gronlund (1998):

1. Rank the test papers from highest score to lowest score.
2. Select approximately the top one-third, and call this the upper group. Select approximately the bottom one-third, and call this the lower group. Set the middle group of papers aside.
3. For each item, record the number of students in the upper group and in the lower group who selected the correct answer and each distracter as follows (the correct answer has an asterisk next to it):

Item 1 Alternatives	**A**	**B***	**C**	**D**	**E**
Upper group	0	6	3	1	0
Lower group	3	2	2	3	0

4. Estimate the item difficulty by calculating the percentage of students who answered the item correctly. The difficulty index for the preceding item is 40 percent ($8/20 \times 100$). Note that the smaller the percentage is, the more difficult the item is.
5. Estimate the item discriminating power by subtracting the number in the lower group who answered the item correctly from the number in the upper group, and divide by one-half of the total number of students included in the item analysis. For the preceding example, the discrimination index is 0.40 ($6 - 2 \div 10$). When the index is positive, as it is here, it indicates that more students in the upper group than in the lower group answered the item correctly. A negative value indicates just the opposite.

As you can see, this type of item analysis is not difficult to do, nor is it likely to be very time-consuming. It is important to remember, however, that the benefits of item analysis can quickly be lost if you ignore certain limitations. One is that you will be working with relatively small numbers of students. Therefore, the results of item analysis are likely to vary as you go from class to class or from test to test with the same class. Because of this variation, you should retain items that a measurement specialist would discard or revise. In general, you should retain multiple-choice items whose difficulty index lies between 50 and 90 percent and whose discrimination index is positive (Gronlund, 1998). Another limitation is that you may have objectives that everyone must master. If you do an effective job of teaching these objectives, the corresponding test items are likely to be answered correctly by nearly every student. These items should be retained rather than revised to meet arbitrary criteria of difficulty and discrimination.

To review this chapter, see the Thought Questions and ACE Self-Testing on the Snowman web site at **http://education.college.hmco.com/students**.

RESOURCES FOR FURTHER INVESTIGATION

Suggestions for Constructing Written and Performance Tests

For specific suggestions on ways to write different types of items for paper-and-pencil tests of knowledge and on methods for constructing and using rating scales and checklists to measure products, performances, and procedures, consult one or more of the following books: *Measurement and Evaluation in Teaching* (2000), by Robert Linn and Norman Gronlund; *Assessment of Student Achievement* (1998), by Norman Gronlund; *Classroom Assessment: What Teachers Need to Know* (2002), by W. James Popham; *Student-Involved Classroom Assessment* (2001), by Richard Stiggins; and *Classroom Assessment* (4th ed.), by Peter Airasian.

Two books that are devoted exclusively to performance assessment are *Principles and Practices of Performance Assessment* (1998), by Nidhi Khattri, Alison L. Reeve, and Michael B. Kane; and *Authentic Assessment in Action* (1995), by Linda Darling-Hammond, Jacqueline Ancess, and Beverly Falk. The latter book describes the effect that performance-based assessments had on teachers and students in five schools.

Middle school and high school mathematics teachers may want to take a look at *A Collection of Performance Tasks and Rubrics: Middle School Mathematics* (1997), by Charlotte Danielson, and *A Collection of Performance Tasks and Rubrics: High School Mathematics* (1998), by Charlotte Danielson and Elizabeth Marquez. Both books describe how to construct scoring rubrics for performance tasks and provide numerous examples of scoring rubrics.

The most extensive online database of assessment information is the ERIC/AE Test Locator, which is found at **ericae.net/testcol.htm**. It includes numerous topics, reviews of tests, suggestions and digests relating to alternative assessment, and standards and policymaking information concerning the evaluation and assessment of students.

The web site of the organization Relearning by Design (**www.relearning.org/**) contains a Resources page on which you can either view or download a variety of materials and references on classroom assessment, curriculum design, and grading. Another part of the site, the UbD Exchange, allows you to search, download, and adapt curriculum units designed by educators around the country. Relearning by Design is headed by Grant Wiggins, a noted scholar on assessment.

Writing Higher-Level Questions

As Benjamin Bloom and others point out, teachers have a disappointing tendency to write test items that reflect the lowest level of the taxonomy: knowledge. To avoid this failing, carefully read Part 2 of *Taxonomy of Educational Objectives: The Classification of Educational Goals, Handbook I: Cognitive Domain* (1956), edited by Benjamin Bloom, Max Englehart, Edward Furst, Walker Hill, and David Krathwohl. Each level of the taxonomy is clearly explained and followed by several pages of illustrative test items.

Analyzing Test Items

Norman Gronlund briefly discusses item-analysis procedures for norm-referenced and criterion-referenced tests in Chapter 7 of *Assessment of Student Achievement* (1998). For norm-referenced multiple-choice tests, these include procedures for assessing the difficulty and discriminating power of each item and the effectiveness of each alternative answer. For criterion-referenced tests, they include a measure for assessing the effects of instruction. More detailed discussions of item-analysis procedures can be found in Chapter 8 of *Educational Testing and Measurement: Classroom Application and Practice* (2000), by Tom Kubiszyn and Gary Borich.

Question Mark Computing, based in Great Britain, produces a software program that can help teachers generate high-quality test items. Information on the software can be found at **www.qmark.com** or by calling the U.S. distributor at 800-863-3950.

Classroom Grading

For detailed information on how to construct an accurate and fair grading system, examine *A Complete Guide to Student Grading* (1999), by Thomas Haladyna, and *Transforming Classroom Grading* (2000), by Robert J. Marzano.

Summary

1. Classroom assessment, which involves the measurement and evaluation of student learning, accounts for about one-third of a teacher's class time.
2. Measurement involves ranking individuals according to how much of a particular characteristic they possess. Evaluation involves making judgments about the value or worth of a set of measures.
3. Teachers give tests and assign grades to communicate to others how well students have mastered the teacher's objectives, find out if students are keeping up with and understanding the learning material, diagnose students' strengths and weaknesses, and positively affect students' approaches to studying.
4. Research indicates that students who take four to six exams a term learn more than students who take fewer or no exams.
5. Written tests are used to measure how much knowledge people have about some topic. Test items can be classified as selected response (multiple choice, true-false, matching), and constructed response (short answer and essay).
6. Selected-response tests are efficient to administer and score but tend to reflect the lowest level of the cognitive domain taxonomy and provide no information about what students can do with the knowledge they have learned.
7. Short-answer tests measure recall, rather than recognition, of information and allow for comprehensive coverage of a topic, but they have the same disadvantages as selected-response tests.
8. Essay tests measure such high-level skills as analysis, synthesis, and evaluation but are difficult to grade consistently, are time-consuming to grade, and allow only limited coverage of material.
9. Performance tests measure how well students use basic knowledge to perform a particular skill or produce a particular product under somewhat realistic conditions.
10. Performance tests are characterized by active responding, realistic conditions, complex problems, a close relationship between teaching and testing, use of scoring rubrics, and use of test results for formative evaluation purposes.
11. It has not yet been demonstrated that student performances and products can be measured reliably (consistently) and validly (accurately).
12. When grades are determined according to a norm-referenced system, each student's level of performance is compared to the performance of a group of similar students. A norm-referenced scheme is used by those who feel that external criteria for determining the adequacy of performance are unavailable.
13. In a criterion-referenced grading system, each student's level of performance is compared to a predetermined standard.
14. A mastery approach to criterion-referenced measurement and evaluation, which is based on the concept of mastery learning, allows students multiple opportunities to pass tests.
15. The potential benefits of measurement and evaluation activities can be undermined by any one of several inappropriate testing and grading practices.
16. Classroom assessment can be made easier through the use of such technological products and formats as test-item banks, electronic gradebooks, simulation programs, hypermedia, videodisks, telecommunications, and digital portfolios.
17. To be sure that the number of various types of items on a test is consistent with your instructional objectives, prepare a table of specifications.
18. For primary and elementary grade students, the formative evaluation purpose of tests should be emphasized at least as much as the summative purpose.
19. Item-analysis procedures exist to determine the difficulty and discriminating power of multiple-choice items.

Key Terms

measurement *(453)*
evaluation *(454)*
summative evaluation *(454)*
formative evaluation *(455)*
performance tests *(459)*
authentic assessment *(459)*
portfolio *(460)*
rubric *(462)*
norm-referenced grading *(465)*
criterion-referenced grading *(469)*
digital portfolio *(477)*
table of specifications *(480)*

DISCUSSION QUESTIONS

1. Because students in American schools feel considerable pressure to obtain high grades, a significant number of them feel driven to cheat. Knowing that you will almost certainly have to give tests and assign grades on one basis or another, what might you do to reduce your students' tendency to cheat?

2. Although performance assessment is a relatively new development in education, it has been used for some years in the fine arts, athletics, and vocational education. Have you ever taken any kind of performance assessment as a student? Did you feel that it accurately reflected what you had learned? To what extent would you use performance measures for such academic subjects as writing, math, science, and social studies? Why?

3. Over the past ten to twelve years, you have taken probably hundreds of classroom tests. What types of tests best reflected what you learned? Why?

4. A norm-referenced approach to grading is often called grading on the curve. Have you ever taken a class in which grades were determined in this fashion? Did you feel that your grade accurately reflected how much you had learned? If not, explain why the grade was too low or too high.

Understanding and Using Standardized Tests

14

Because standardized assessment of scholastic aptitude and achievement is such a popular practice in the United States (as well as in many other countries), this chapter will focus on the nature of standardized tests, how they are used to assess student variability, and how these test results can be employed in putting together effective instructional programs for students. As we will see, the use of standardized tests is truly a double-edged sword: it has the potential to harm students as well as help them. ■

KEY POINTS

These key points will help you learn the important information in this chapter. To help you study, they also appear in the margins of the pages, next to the text where they are discussed.

Standardized Tests

- Standardized tests: items presented and scored in standard fashion; results reported with reference to standards
- Basic purpose of standardized test is to obtain accurate, representative sample of some aspect of a person
- Standardized test scores used to identify strengths and weaknesses, plan instruction, select students for programs
- Reliability: similarity between two rankings of test scores obtained from the same individual
- Validity: how accurately a test measures what users want it to measure
- Content validity: how well test items cover a body of knowledge and skill
- Predictive validity: how well a test score predicts later performance
- Construct validity: how accurately a test measures a theoretical attribute
- Meaningfulness of standardized test scores depends on representativeness of norm group
- Formal testing of young children is inappropriate because of rapid developmental changes
- Achievement tests measure how much of a subject or skill has been learned
- Diagnostic achievement tests designed to identify specific strengths and weaknesses
- Competency tests determine if potential graduates possess basic skills
- Aptitude tests measure predisposition to develop advanced capabilities in specific areas
- Norm-referenced tests compare one student with others
- Criterion-referenced tests indicate degree of mastery of objectives
- Percentile rank: percentage of scores at or below a given point
- Standard deviation: degree of deviation from the mean of a distribution
- z score: how far a raw score is from the mean in standard deviation units
- T score: raw score translated to a scale of 1–100 with a mean of 50
- Stanine score: student performance indicated with reference to a 9-point scale based on normal curve

Using Standardized Tests for Accountability Purposes: High-Stakes Testing

- High-stakes testing: using test results to hold students and educators accountable for achievement
- All states have high-stakes testing programs
- High-stakes testing programs have many problems
- Some states use performance-based assessment methods

Standardized Testing and Technology

- Clarity of test standards aided by putting examples on CD-ROM, computer files, videotape
- Computer-adaptive testing: computers determine sequence and difficulty level of test items

Standardized Tests

NATURE OF STANDARDIZED TESTS

The kinds of assessment instruments described in this chapter are typically referred to as **standardized tests**, although the term *published tests* is sometimes used (because they are prepared, distributed, and scored by publishing companies or independent test services). You have almost certainly taken several of these tests during your academic career, and so you are probably familiar with their appearance and general characteristics. They are called standardized tests for the following reasons:

For a preview of this chapter's basic concepts, see the Chapter Themes on this book's web site at **http://education.college.hmco.com/students**.

- They are designed by people with specialized knowledge and training in test construction.
- Every person who takes the test responds to the same items under the same conditions.
- The answers are evaluated according to the same scoring standards.
- The scores are interpreted through comparison to the scores obtained from a group (called a norm group) that took the same test under the same conditions or (in the case of some achievement tests) through comparison to a predetermined standard.

Standardized tests: items presented and scored in standard fashion; results reported with reference to standards

The basic purpose of giving a standardized test is to obtain an *accurate and representative sample* of how much of some characteristic a person possesses (such as knowledge of a particular set of mathematical concepts and operations). The benefit of getting an accurate measure from a test is obvious. When standardized tests are well designed, they are likely to be more accurate measures of a particular characteristic than nonstandardized tests. Standardized tests measure a *sample* of the characteristic since a comprehensive measure would be too expensive, time-consuming, and cumbersome to administer (Walsh & Betz, 2001).

Basic purpose of standardized test is to obtain accurate, representative sample of some aspect of a person

PREVALENCE OF STANDARDIZED TESTING

No one knows for certain how many students are tested in a given year or how many tests the typical student takes because comprehensive and unambiguous data are not available. (If a student takes an achievement battery that covers four subjects, does that count as one test or four?) Richard Phelps (1997) estimates that 36 million district-wide and statewide tests are given each year in the United States. Peter Sacks (1997) cites estimates of 127 million standardized tests of all types being given in a year. Walter Haney, George Madaus, and Robert Lyons (1993) provide low and high estimates on the basis of data from the late 1980s for four kinds of testing: state-mandated testing programs, school district testing programs, testing of special populations, and college admissions testing. On the low end, they estimate that slightly more than 143 million students a year were tested and that the average child took 2.7 tests per year. On the high end, they estimate that just over 395 million students a year were tested and that the average child took 5.4 tests per year. In any case, it seems accurate to say that American schools engage in a substantial amount of standardized testing.

Uses of Standardized Tests

Standardized test scores used to identify strengths and weaknesses, plan instruction, select students for programs

Historically, educators have used standardized test scores, particularly achievement tests, for a variety of instructionally related purposes. Teachers, guidance counselors, and principals have used test data to identify general strengths and weaknesses in student achievement, inform parents of their child's general level of achievement, plan instructional lessons, group students for instruction, and recommend students for placement in special programs. To cite just one example, when a child moves to a different neighborhood within a city or a different city within a state or a different part of the country, it is highly desirable for those in the child's new school to have some idea as to what he or she knows about basic subjects. Standardized achievement tests do an effective job of providing information about the mastery of general subject matter and skills and thus can be used for planning, grouping, placement, and instructional purposes.

When you read the test profiles that report how students in your classes have performed on standardized tests, you will get a general idea of some of your students' strengths and weaknesses. If certain students are weak in particular skill areas and you want to help them overcome those weaknesses, test results *may* give you *some* insights into possible ways to provide remedial instruction. If most of your students score below average in certain segments of the curriculum, you will know that you should devote more time and effort to presenting those topics and skills to the entire class. You can and should, of course, supplement what you learn from standardized test results with your own tests and observations in order to design potentially effective forms of remedial or advanced instruction.

Criteria for Evaluating Standardized Tests

Like most other things, standardized tests vary in quality. To use test scores wisely, you need to be an informed consumer—to know what characteristics distinguish well-constructed from poorly constructed tests. Four criteria are widely used to

When properly used, standardized test scores can keep parents, students, and educators aware of a student's general level of achievement, and they can help teachers and administrators make decisions about placing students in special programs.

evaluate standardized tests: reliability, validity, normed excellence, and examinee appropriateness. Each of these criteria will be explained individually.

Reliability A basic assumption that psychologists make about human characteristics (such as intelligence and achievement) is that they are relatively stable, at least over short periods of time. For most people, this assumption seems to be true. Thus, you should be able to count on a test's results being consistent, just as you might count on a reliable worker's doing a consistent job time after time. This stability in test performance is known as **reliability**. It is one of the most important characteristics of standardized tests and can be assessed in a number of ways.

To illustrate the importance of reliability, imagine that you wish to form cooperative learning groups for mathematics. Because these types of groups should be composed of five to six students who differ on a number of characteristics, including achievement, you use the students' most recent scores from a standardized mathematics test to assign two high, medium, and low achievers to each group. One month later, the children are retested, and you now find that many of those who scored at the top initially (and whom you thought were very knowledgeable about mathematics) now score in the middle or at the bottom. Conversely, many students who initially scored low now have average or above-average scores. What does that do to your confidence in being able to form heterogeneous groups based on scores from this test? If you want to be able to differentiate among individuals consistently, you need to use an instrument that performs consistently.

Reliability: similarity between two rankings of test scores obtained from the same individual

Psychologists who specialize in constructing standardized tests assess reliability in a variety of ways. One method is to administer the same test to the same people on two occasions and measure the extent to which the rankings change over time. This approach results in *test-retest reliability*. Another method is to administer two equivalent forms of a test to the same group of students at the same time. This approach results in *alternate-form reliability*. A third approach is to administer a single test to a group of students, create two scores by dividing the test in half, and measure the extent to which the rankings change from one half to the other. This method results in *split-half reliability* and measures the internal consistency of a test.

Regardless of which method is used to assess reliability, the goal is to create two rankings of scores and see how similar the rankings are. This degree of consistency is expressed as a correlation coefficient (abbreviated with a lowercase r) that ranges from 0 to 1. Well-constructed standardized tests should have correlation coefficients of about 0.95 for split-half reliability, 0.90 for test-retest reliability, and 0.85 for alternate-form reliability (Kubiszyn & Borich, 2000). Bear in mind, however, that a particular test may not report all three forms of reliability and that reliabilities for subtests and for younger age groups (kindergarten through second grade) are likely to be lower than these overall figures.

Validity A second important characteristic of a test is that it accurately measures what it claims to measure. A reading comprehension test should measure just that—nothing more, nothing less. Whenever we speak of a test's accuracy, we are referring to its **validity**. Because most of the characteristics we are interested in knowing something about (such as arithmetic skills, spatial aptitude, intelligence, and knowledge of the American Civil War) are internal and hence not directly observable, tests are indirect measures of those attributes. Therefore, any test-based conclusions we may draw about how much of a characteristic a person possesses, or any predictions we may make about how well a person will perform in the future (on other types of tests, in a job, or in a specialized academic program, for example), are properly referred to as *inferences*. So when we inquire about the validity of a test by asking,

Validity: how accurately a test measures what users want it to measure

A standardized test that is considered to be valid measures what it claims to measure and allows educators to make reasonably accurate predictions about how well students perform academically in the near future.

"Does this test measure what it claims to measure?" we are really asking, "How accurate are the inferences that I wish to draw about the test taker?" (See, for example, Messick, 1989.)

The degree to which these inferences can be judged accurate, or valid, depends on the type and quality of the supporting evidence that we can muster. Three kinds of evidence that underlie test-based inferences are content validity evidence, predictive validity evidence, and construct validity evidence.

Content validity: how well test items cover a body of knowledge and skill

Content Validity Evidence This kind of evidence rests on a set of judgments about how well a test's items reflect the particular body of knowledge and skill (called a *domain* by measurement specialists) about which we want to draw inferences. If a test on the American Civil War, for example, contained no items on the war's causes, its great battles, or the years it encompassed, some users might be hesitant to call someone who had achieved a high score knowledgeable about this topic. Then again, other users might not be nearly so disturbed by these omissions (and the inference that would be drawn from the test score) if they considered such information to be relatively unimportant.

Predictive validity: how well a test score predicts later performance

Predictive Validity Evidence This evidence allows us to make probabilistic statements about how well students will behave in the future ("Based on his test scores, there is a strong likelihood that Yusef will do well in the creative writing program next year"). Many colleges, for example, require students to take the American College Testing Program (ACT) or the Scholastic Assessment Test (SAT) and then use the results (along with other information) to predict each prospective student's grade-point average at the end of the first year. All other things being equal, students with higher test scores are expected to have higher grade-point averages than students with lower test scores and thus stand a better chance of being admitted.

Construct validity: how accurately a test measures a theoretical attribute

Construct Validity Evidence This evidence indicates how accurately a test measures a theoretical description of some internal attribute of a person. Such attributes—for

with academic demands), like the familiar SAT, and many specific tests of aptitude, such as tests of musical aptitude, mechanical aptitude, and spatial relations.

However, Richard Snow (1992) argues for a broader conception of aptitude that also includes affective and motivational predispositions. In his scheme, which we find attractive, such characteristics of people as extroversion, conformity, independence, production of mental images, attention span, beliefs, and fear of failure would also be considered aptitudes because they are fairly broad and stable predispositions to respond to tasks in certain ways.

Further, some contemporary psychologists argue that we should stop trying to distinguish between aptitude (or ability) and achievement and should abandon the view that one's ability is the cause of one's achievement. Robert Sternberg (1998), for example, notes that the items that appear in various mental ability tests (such as vocabulary, reading comprehension, verbal analogies, arithmetic problem solving, and determining similarities) are often the focus of classroom instruction and are the same types of items that appear on many achievement tests. Second, he notes that achievement test scores are as good predictors of ability test scores as ability test scores are predictors of achievement test scores. Rather than thinking of such aptitudes as verbal reasoning, mathematical reasoning, spatial orientation, and musical aptitude as largely inherited capabilities that are responsible for the level of expertise one develops in a particular area, he prefers to think of aptitudes as various forms of *developing* expertise.

Norm-referenced tests compare one student with others

Norm-Referenced Tests Most of the achievement and aptitude tests just described are referred to as **norm-referenced tests** since performance is evaluated with reference to norms—the performance of others—established when the final form of the test was administered to the sample of students who made up the standardization group. After taking an achievement battery in the elementary grades, for example, you were probably told that you had performed as well on reading comprehension questions as 80 percent (or whatever) of all of the students who took the test. If you take the Graduate Record Exam (GRE), you will be told how far from the average score of 500 you are (in terms of a score to be described shortly). Thus, you will learn just where you stand in a distribution of scores arranged from lowest to highest. Tests that are constructed according to norm-referenced criteria tend to cover a broad range of knowledge and skill but have relatively few items for each topic or skill tested. But in the last twenty-five years or so, an alternative approach to reporting achievement scores has been developed: the criterion-referenced method.

Criterion-referenced tests indicate degree of mastery of objectives

Criterion-Referenced Tests A different approach to reporting achievement test scores is used by **criterion-referenced tests**. When a test is scored in this manner, an individual's performance is not compared with the performance of others. Instead, students are evaluated according to how well they have mastered specific objectives in various well-defined skill areas. Because of this feature, you may find criterion-referenced tests more useful than norm-referenced tests in determining who needs how much additional instruction in what areas (provided, of course, that the test's objectives closely match your own).

The criterion-referenced approach is intended to reduce overtones of competition and emphasize mastery of objectives at a rate commensurate with students' abilities. Tests that have criterion-referenced scoring systems tend to cover less ground than norm-referenced tests but contain more items for the objectives they do assess. Because norm-referenced and criterion-referenced scoring systems provide different types of information about student achievement, many testing companies provide both types of scores.

A relatively new development in criterion-referenced testing has occurred in several states. In an attempt to counter some of the disadvantages of traditional norm-referenced standardized testing, states such as Vermont and Kentucky have begun to rely partly or entirely on performance-based measures in their statewide assessment systems. We will look at these new tests in greater detail later in this chapter.

Interpreting Standardized Test Scores

Scores on the most widely used standardized tests are typically reported on student profile forms that summarize and explain the results. Although most profiles contain sufficient information to make it possible to interpret scores without additional background, you should know in advance about the kinds of scores you may encounter, particularly since you may be asked to explain scores to students as well as to their parents.

Grade Equivalent Scores The **grade equivalent score** interprets test performance in terms of grade levels. A student who makes a grade equivalent score of 4.7 on an achievement test, for example, got the same number of items right on this test as the average fourth grader in the standardization group achieved by the seventh month of the school year.

The grade equivalent score was once widely used at the elementary level, but because it may lead to misinterpretations, it is not as popular as it once was. One problem with grade equivalent scores is the tendency to misinterpret a score above a student's actual grade level as an indication that the student is capable of consistently working at that level. This kind of assumption might lead parents or perhaps teachers themselves to consider accelerated promotion. Remember that although such scores may show that a student did somewhat better on the test than the average student a grade or two above her, they do not mean that the student tested has acquired knowledge of all the skills covered in the grade that she would miss if she skipped a grade.

Percentile rank: percentage of scores at or below a given point

Percentile Ranks Probably the most widely used score for standardized tests is the **percentile rank**. This score indicates the percentage of students who are at and below a given student's score. It provides specific information about relative position.

Students earning a percentile rank of 87 did as well as or better than 87 percent of the students in the particular normative group being used. They did not get 87 percent of the questions right—unless by coincidence—and this is the point parents are most likely to misunderstand. Parents may have been brought up on the percentages grading system, in which 90 or above was A, 80 to 90 was B, and so on down the line. If you report that a son or daughter has a percentile rank of 50, some parents are horror-struck or outraged, not understanding that the child's score on this test is average, not a failure. In such cases, the best approach is to emphasize that the percentile rank tells the percentage of cases at or below the child's score. You might also talk in terms of a hypothetical group of 100; for example, a child with a percentile rank of 78 did as well as or better than 78 out of every 100 students who took the test.

Although the percentile rank gives simple and direct information on relative position, it has a major disadvantage: the difference in achievement among students clustered around the middle of the distribution is often considerably less than the difference among those at the extremes. The reason is that *most* scores are clustered around the middle of most distributions of large groups of students. The difference in raw score (number of items answered correctly) between students at percentile ranks 50 and 51 may be 1 point. But the difference in raw score between the student ranked 98 and one ranked 97 may be 10 or 15 points because the best (and worst) students scatter toward the extremes. This quality of percentile ranks means that ranks on different tests cannot be averaged. To get around that difficulty, standard scores are often used.

Standard deviation: degree of deviation from the mean of a distribution

Standard Scores Standard scores are expressed in terms of a common unit: the **standard deviation**. This statistic indicates the degree to which scores in a group of tests (a distribution) differ from the average, or mean. (The *mean* is the arithmetical average of a distribution and is calculated by adding all scores and dividing the total by the number of scores.) The standard deviation is most valuable when it can be related to the normal probability curve. Figure 14.1 shows a normal probability curve indicating the percentage of cases to be found within 3 standard deviations above and below the mean. The horizontal axis indicates the score, ranging from low on the left to high on the right; the vertical axis represents the number of cases corresponding to each score. Notice, for example, that more than 68 percent of the cases fall between +1 SD (one standard deviation above the mean) and –1 SD (one standard deviation below the mean).

The normal probability curve, or **normal curve** as it is usually known, is a mathematical concept that depicts a hypothetical bell-shaped distribution of scores. Such a perfectly symmetrical distribution rarely, if ever, occurs in real life. However, since many distributions of human characteristics and performance closely *resemble* the normal distribution, it is often assumed that such distributions are typical enough to be treated as "normal." Thus, information that mathematicians derive for the hypothetical normal distribution can be applied to the approximately normal distributions that are found when human attributes are measured. When very large numbers

Figure 14.1 **Normal Probability Curve**

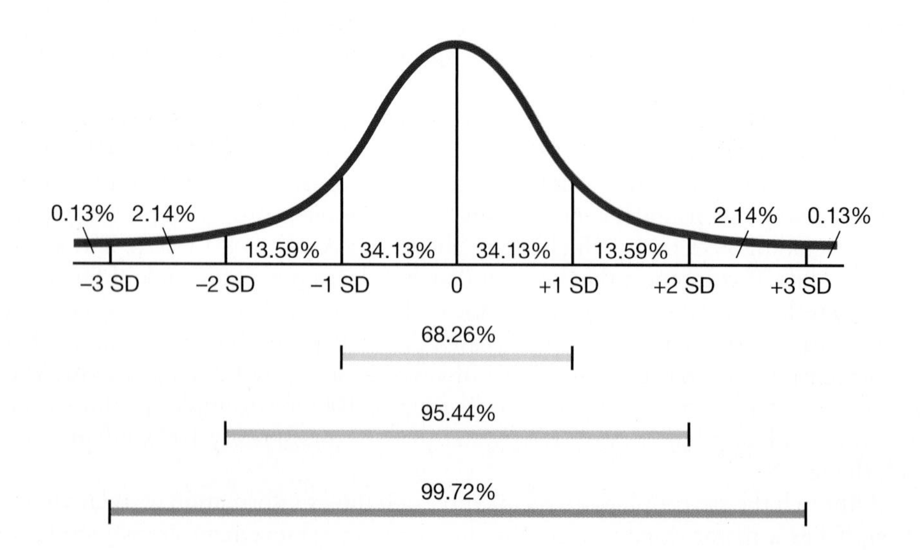

of students are asked to take tests designed by specialists who go to great lengths to cancel out the impact of selective factors, it may be appropriate to interpret the students' scores on such tests with reference to the normal curve.

For purposes of discussion, and for purposes of acquiring familiarity with test scores, it will be sufficient for you to know about two of the standard scores that are derived from standard deviations. One, called a **z score**, tells how far a given raw score is from the mean in standard deviation units. A z score of –1.5, for example, would mean that the student was 1.5 standard deviation units below the mean. Because some z scores (such as the one in the example just given) are negative and involve decimals, **T scores** are often used instead. T scores range from 0 to 100 and use a preselected mean of 50 to get away from negative values. Most standardized tests that use T scores offer detailed explanations, either in the test booklet or on the student profile of scores, of how they should be interpreted. In fact, many test profiles adopt the form of a narrative report when explaining the meaning of all scores used.

z score: how far a raw score is from the mean in standard deviation units

T score: raw score translated to a scale of 1–100 with a mean of 50

To grasp the relationship among z scores, T scores, and percentile ranks, examine Figure 14.2. The diagram shows each scale marked off below a normal curve. It supplies information about the interrelationships of these various scores, provided that the distribution you are working with is essentially normal. In a normal distribution, for example, a z score of +1 is the same as a T score of 60 or a percentile rank of 84; a z score of –2 is the same as a T score of 30 or a percentile rank of about 2. (In addition, notice that the distance between the percentile ranks clustered around the middle is only a small fraction of the distance between the percentile ranks at the ends of the distribution.)

Stanine Scores During World War II, U.S. Air Force psychologists developed a statistic called the **stanine score** (an abbreviation of "standard nine-point scale"),

Figure 14.2 Relationship Among z Scores, T Scores, and Percentile Ranks

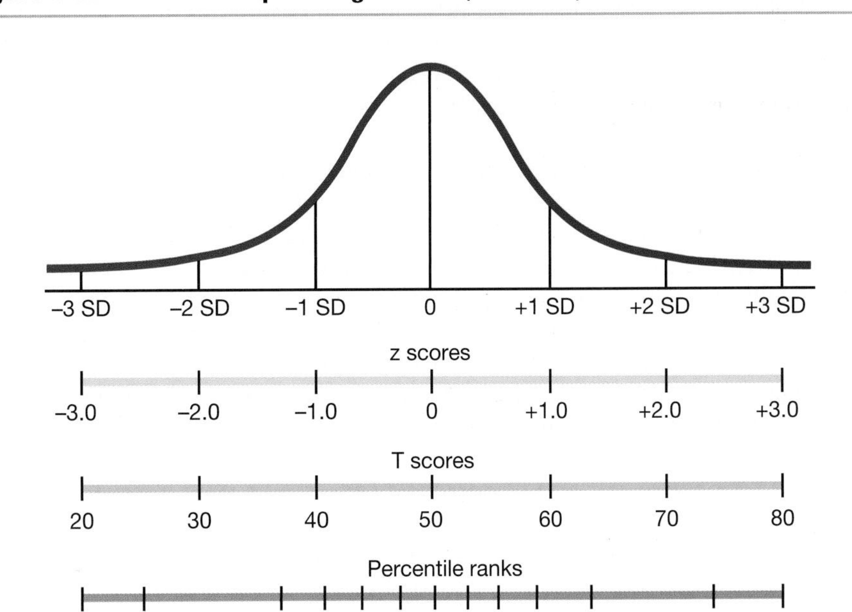

Figure 14.3 Percentage of Cases in Each Stanine (with Standard Deviation Units Indicated)

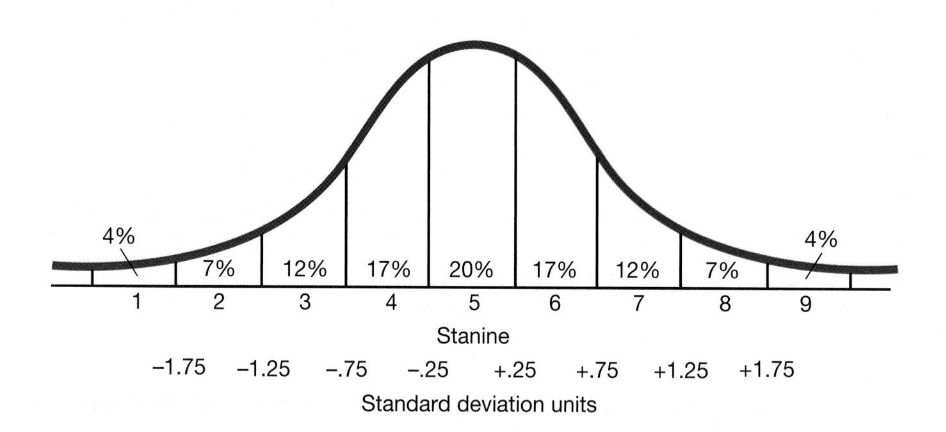

reflecting the fact that it is a type of standard score and divides a population into nine groups. Each stanine is one-half of a standard deviation unit, as indicated in Figure 14.3.

Stanine score: student performance indicated with reference to a 9-point scale based on normal curve

When stanines were introduced on test profiles reporting the performance of public school children on standardized tests, they were often used to group students. (Students in stanines 1, 2, and 3 would be placed in one class; those in 4, 5, and 6 in another class; and so on.) For the reasons given in the chapter "Accommodating Student Variability" and later in this chapter, such ability grouping has become a highly controversial issue in American schools. Consequently, stanine scores are now used to indicate relative standing. They are easier to understand than z scores or T scores since any child or parent can understand that stanines represent a 9-point scale with 1 as the lowest, 5 as the average, and 9 as the highest. Furthermore, unlike percentile ranks, stanine scores can be averaged. When it is desirable to have more precise information about relative standing, however, percentile ranks may be more useful, even though they cannot be averaged.

Local and National Norms Percentile ranks and stanines are often used when local norms are prepared. As noted in our earlier description of how standardized tests are developed, the norms used to determine a student's level of performance are established by asking a representative sample of students to take the final form of the test. Inevitably, there will be differences between school systems (in texts used and the time during a school year or years when certain topics are covered, for instance). Accordingly, some test publishers report scores in terms of local as well as national norms. Each student's performance is thus compared not only with the performance of the members of the standardization group but also with the performance of all students in the same school system.

Earlier, we pointed out that standardized tests can be used in several ways to support the instructional goals of a school and a teacher. When teachers fully understand the characteristic being measured; reliable, valid, and well-normed tests are readily available; and teachers know how to interpret test results appropriately, this strategy for assessing individual differences can work quite well, particularly when it is supplemented with teacher observations and informal assessments. Effective remedial reading and math programs, for example, are based to a large extent on scores from diagnostic reading and math tests. But when tests are used for purposes other than those for which they were designed, misuses occur, and inappropriate decisions and controversy often result. In the next section, we'll take a look at the widespread and controversial practice of high-stakes testing: using standardized test scores to hold students, teachers, and administrators accountable for academic achievement.

Using Standardized Tests for Accountability Purposes: High-Stakes Testing

The Push for Accountability in Education

The current preoccupation with holding educators accountable for student achievement can be traced to 1983, when the National Commission on Excellence in Education published its report *A Nation at Risk: The Imperative for Educational Reform.* The report painted a bleak picture of the quality of education in the United States. It noted, for example, that about 13 percent of all seventeen-year-olds were judged to be functionally illiterate, that standardized test scores had generally fallen below levels achieved twenty-five years earlier, and that many seventeen-year-olds were judged as being deficient in such higher-order thinking skills as drawing inferences from written material and writing a persuasive essay. To justify the amount of money being spent on education and to improve student outcomes, the report called for standardized tests to be used as a way of documenting students' achievement and bringing about changes in the content and methods of instruction.

Subsequent standardized test data, such as scores from the National Assessment of Educational Progress and the Third International Mathematics and Science Study,

To hold students accountable for achieving learning standards and to improve the quality of education, all states administer annually a battery of standardized achievement tests.

and reports on the numbers of students who were being promoted from grade to grade despite poor reading, writing, and math skills, reinforced the perception that American students were poorly educated and had fallen behind students in many other countries. (For alternative interpretations of these findings, see Bracey, 2000, and Berliner & Biddle, 1995.) State legislatures or state departments of education have responded by mandating the establishment of learning standards, the administration of standardized tests to determine how well those standards are being met, and, in some cases, mechanisms for rewarding or punishing students, teachers, and administrators for acceptable or unacceptable scores.

There is virtually no research on whether the adoption of content and performance standards leads to higher levels of student achievement. The authors of one article (Nave, Miech, & Mosteller, 2000) were able to locate only one small-scale study (of one high school teacher teaching earth science to three classes of students in one school). The results of this study plus other anecdotal evidence suggest that content and performance standards, when used constructively, can have beneficial effects on student achievement. But we will have to await the results of several large-scale tests of the standards-achievement link before drawing even a tentative conclusion.

The lack of research evidence supporting statewide standards has not prevented their adoption, nor has it hindered the use, of tests designed to measure student performance in relation to the standards. Because standardized test scores, either by themselves or in conjunction with other data, are being used to determine whether students get promoted to the next grade or graduate from high school, whether teachers and administrators receive financial rewards or demotions, and whether school districts receive additional state funds or lose their accreditation, this practice is commonly referred to as **high-stakes testing**, and it has swept the nation (see the Case in Print for an example in two midwestern states).

High-stakes testing: using test results to hold students and educators accountable for achievement

Proponents believe that high-stakes testing, keyed to statewide standards, will spur schools and teachers to improve. Critics, however, see the likely effects as more negative than positive. The next section summarizes the current status of the high-stakes testing movement.

CURRENT STATUS OF HIGH-STAKES TESTING

In December 2001, the U.S. Congress passed legislation proposed by President George W. Bush to implement testing of students in reading and mathematics in all public schools that receive federal funds. Tests will be given annually in grades 3 through 8 and once during the high school years. Schools whose students do not improve will receive financial aid to help raise scores. If scores in a particular school do not improve after two years, students can transfer to other public schools. If there is no improvement after three years, the school's staff and curriculum may be replaced.

Despite this federal initiative, most of the developments in high-stakes testing have occurred at the state level. All fifty states now conduct an annual standardized assessment of student achievement. Forty-seven states have content standards in the core subjects of English, math, science, and social studies; two states have standards in some of those core areas (Education Week on the Web, 2001).

All states have high-stakes testing programs

Type of Test Used Forty states report using criterion-referenced tests in English. Thirty-four states report using such tests in math. The remaining states use norm-referenced tests in these subjects (Education Week on the Web, 2001).

Use of Test Scores States are using the test scores for various purposes:

- Eleven states hold schools accountable for student learning solely on the basis of students' test scores, either by rating all schools or by identifying low-performing schools and releasing the ratings to the public. Although sixteen states include other measures in their rating system (such as attendance and dropout rates), test scores carry significantly greater weight (Education Week on the Web, 2001).
- Twenty states provide financial rewards to schools whose students perform at what is considered to be an acceptable level. Fourteen states can close, restaff, or overhaul schools in which a large percentage of students score poorly (Education Week on the Web, 2001).
- Eighteen states require students to pass a state-mandated test in order to be granted a high school diploma. Six more plan to implement this requirement in the near future. Of these eighteen states, fifteen require that students who fail the test be given additional help, but only nine provide the funds for school districts to do so (Education Week on the Web, 2001).
- Three states require students in certain grades to pass a state-mandated test to be promoted. One of these three states does not provide funds for remedial instruction for students who fail the test. Four more states plan to have a similar requirement by 2003 (Education Week on the Web, 2001).

Problems with High-Stakes Testing Programs

Whether high-stakes testing programs produce any beneficial effects will depend on how well they adhere to a rigorous set of conditions like those promoted by the American Educational Research Association (2000). Some of the twelve conditions mentioned in AERA's position statement include not relying solely on test scores to make educational decisions, limiting inferences only to those that are supported by research, aligning a test's content with a school's curriculum, providing evidence for the validity of performance standards (such as "passing," "proficient," "needs improvement"), and providing opportunities for meaningful remediation to students who do not achieve a passing score. As the following sections illustrate, the claimed advantages of high-stakes testing programs may be a long time in coming because few, if any, states seem to have met all the conditions required of such a program.

High-stakes testing programs have many problems

The Place of Tests in Educational Reform Ideally, education reform should start with informed discussions and decisions about goals, scope, and sequencing of curriculum, classroom and school organization, and instructional methods. Only then should tests be developed, and they should be aligned with the curriculum and instruction that students actually experience. In many states, unfortunately, this sequence has been stood on its head. Tests are mandated and developed first, causing educators to adapt their curriculum and methods to the test's content (Merrow, 2001; Thompson, 2001).

Characteristics of Standardized Tests Some problems in the current wave of high-stakes testing stem from the characteristics of standardized tests themselves:

- Standardized tests are typically narrow in scope. To avoid overly long test-taking sessions, tests sample the knowledge and skills in a content domain with a relatively small set of forty to fifty items. Consequently, the results from a

The States Raise the Stakes

Because standardized test scores, either by themselves or in conjunction with other data, are being used to determine whether students get promoted to the next grade or graduate from high school, whether teachers and administrators receive financial rewards or demotions, and whether school districts receive additional state funds or lose their accreditation, this practice is commonly referred to as high-stakes testing. (p. 502)

Students Await Standardized Tests

HOLLY K. HACKER

St. Louis Post-Dispatch 4/2/2001

Get those No. 2 pencils sharpened. For children on both sides of the Mississippi River, it's time for a new round of state tests.

Testing season officially opens today in Illinois public schools with the Illinois Standards Achievement Tests [ISAT]. They cover five subjects. Missouri public schools still have a week to prepare for the Missouri Assessment Program. Starting April 9, children will be tested in five subjects, with a local option for six.

Both states spread the tests over several grades, so a child is not tested in every subject. Illinois will test about 750,000 students and Missouri about 400,000.

In many states, testing used to be a ho-hum affair—if state testing happened at all. Typically, a school with poor scores faced few or no consequences. Standardized tests now carry more weight than ever because legislators, policymakers and others want to know how well schools and students are doing.

In Missouri, test scores heavily influence a school district's state accreditation status. Districts that fail to boost test scores risk state takeover. Illinois is developing its own system for evaluating school districts, and ISAT results will be a major factor. Districts in both states may consider test scores and other measures in deciding whether to send children to summer school or hold them back a year.

Given the new emphasis on testing, many local districts go all-out to encourage students to do their best on the exams.

Lemasters Elementary School in north St. Louis County installed a giant scoreboard in the cafeteria that shows the days, hours, minutes and seconds remaining until the MAP tests begin.

The Normandy School District, also in north St. Louis County, will hold a ceremony Tuesday honoring students who scored well on last year's state exams.

Throughout the school year, many districts test children to track academic progress.

Teachers also help students become familiar with the format of standardized tests.

Unlike the old multiple-choice exams, Missouri and Illinois tests also require students to write essays and show how they arrived at answers.

"Anyone who says they're not doing some review work in preparation for the ISAT is probably not being truthful," said James Rosborg, superintendent of the Belleville School District.

"I know all of our teachers are doing some review work with the children to make sure the children have a comfort level with the material we've covered over the year."

State testing has drawn its share of criticism. For instance, some educators say test scores don't reflect the fact some schools have lots of children who move frequently or live in poverty. Those children tend to score lower.

In Illinois, some educators complain that the testing system seems to change every year. Three years ago, the state introduced the ISAT and started phasing out older tests. For the past two years, 10th-graders have taken the ISAT, but later this month they'll take a new test called the Prairie State Achievement Exam. And this year, the ISAT testing window moved to this month from February.

All of those changes make it difficult to accurately track test scores over time, educators say.

"We're tired of jumping around. We want to be able to look at data and make meaningful improvements to our schools and our curriculum," said Karen Perry, an assistant superintendent in the Collinsville School District. Because Collinsville's spring break starts April 9, the district took advantage of a state provision and started testing last week.

Rosborg said testing needs to be based on good research, not politics and emotion. "It's impossible to look at historical test data because of the constant changes," he said. Both states expect to have test results back in early fall.

Questions and Activities

1. As we mentioned in the text and as this newspaper article notes, "Standardized tests now carry more weight than ever because legislators, policymakers and others want to know how well schools and students are doing." Yet measurement experts have been highly critical of using standardized tests for this purpose because of insufficient validity. What kinds of content, predictive, and construct validity evidence would a test have to have in order to support the inference that high (or low) test scores largely reflect the efforts of the teachers and administrators in helping students learn?
2. State-mandated assessments are often referred to as high-stakes testing because the scores are frequently used to reward or punish the students, teachers, and administrators of a school district. Using standardized test scores for this purpose leads many teachers to gear their instruction to the content of the test, a process known as teaching to the test. What are the pros and cons of allowing the content of tests to influence classroom instruction? (*Hint:* Think about the points we made in the chapter "Approaches to Instruction" about the role of objectives.)
3. Interview several teachers at different grade levels to learn what they think of high-stakes testing programs. Make a note of the techniques they use to address the demands of such testing programs.

particular test cannot be generalized to other tests of the same material, resulting in misleading inferences about what students do and do not know (Popham, 1999; Smith & Fey, 2000). In one study (Linn, 2000), scores on a statewide assessment increased almost every year for seven years in reading and math. In the eighth year, a new test of similar reading and math skills was introduced. Scores in both areas fell dramatically and then rose in subsequent years. This phenomenon is sometimes referred to as WYTIWYG: what you test is what you get.

- Tests that are norm-referenced are designed to produce a spread of scores. The job of a norm-referenced standardized test is to allow for comparisons among students, schools, districts, and states. To accomplish this goal, most items on a standardized test are designed to be answered correctly by 40 to 60 percent of students. Items that are much below or above those levels are considered to be too difficult and too easy, respectively, and are usually not included in the

Because norm-referenced standardized tests are designed to produce a spread of scores, measurement experts argue that they should not be used in state-mandated assessment programs, which ought to focus instead on whether students meet a certain standard.

published version. But some of the so-called easy items may reflect knowledge and skills that most teachers consider important and spend much time making sure students learn (Bracey, 2000; Popham, 1999).

- Many factors that affect learning, such as the physical facilities and general climate of a school, students' values about learning, students' level of interest in a subject, students' home environment, and the quality of instruction that teachers deliver, are not assessed by standardized tests. Consequently, linking such high-stakes decisions as retention, promotion, financial rewards, and accreditation solely to standardized test scores is wholly inappropriate because the tests have no validity for those purposes (Heubert & Hauser, 1999; Popham, 1999; Smith & Fey, 2000; Thompson, 2000).

Relationship of Tests to State Standards Although the current high-stakes tests are intended to measure students' progress in relation to state standards, that connection is often less than compelling, for the following reasons:

- Most tests do not adequately reflect their state standards in two ways: not every standard is assessed, and many standards are assessed with multiple-choice tests that reflect only knowledge and comprehension—which, as you will recall from the chapter "Approaches to Instruction," are the lowest levels of Bloom's Taxonomy. In one state, 57 percent of eighth-grade math standards did not appear on the state test (Bracey, 2000; Education Week on the Web, 2001).
- Many states list more standards than can be realistically addressed, and some standards are not clearly written (Education Week on the Web, 2001).
- Many states set performance standards that are unrealistically high because the standards are divorced from data about students' historical levels of performance (Education Week on the Web, 2001).
- Many states, instead of evaluating schools on the basis of improvement, require all students to achieve the same level of performance regardless of the socioeconomic makeup of the districts (Education Week on the Web, 2001).

Breadth of Assessment The ways in which students' competencies are assessed are extremely narrow. Only seven states require students to write essays or engage in some sort of performance task in subjects other than English. Only two states, Kentucky and Vermont, use portfolios as part of their state assessment (Education Week on the Web, 2001).

Use of Test Results to Support Remediation Only four states provide feedback to teachers as to how their students performed on each item. Only nine states provide teachers with their students' scored work on essay questions (Education Week on the Web, 2001). Some states provide no funds to help school districts provide remedial instruction to students who have failed an exam (Education Week on the Web, 2001).

Use of Test Results to Support Improvements in Instruction Most states are not providing funds to help teachers improve the quality of their instruction through professional development activities (such as workshops and conferences), but are relying almost solely on the rewards and punishments associated with test performance (Education Week on the Web, 2001).

Impact on Curriculum and Instructional Methods Sixty-six percent of a national sample of over a thousand public school teachers said that state tests caused

To read about standardized testing in actual classrooms—and some of the problems that arise—see the Site-Based Cases at this book's web site at **http://education.college.hmco.com/students**.

them to concentrate on topics covered by the test at the expense of other important topics, a practice known as *teaching to the test*. A middle school teacher, for example, eliminated a popular math and science unit on sharks because it wasn't covered by the state assessment (Education Week on the Web, 2001). Other teachers have increased their use of drill-and-practice and test preparation activities and either curtailed or decreased their use of techniques like silent reading, collaborative writing, science experiments, classroom dramas, creative activities, math and reading games, and field trips (Barksdale-Ladd & Thomas, 2000). Eighty percent of a group of 236 North Carolina teachers reported spending more than 20 percent of their instructional time practicing for the state test, and almost one-third (28 percent) reported spending more than 60 percent of their instructional time preparing for the test. Thus, what is referred to as standards-based reform is, in reality, test-based reform (McColskey & McMunn, 2000).

Effects on Students A sample of teachers and parents in one study did not notice any positive effects on children as a function of test preparation and test taking. They did notice, however, such negative reactions as excessive worrying, crying, loss of self-confidence, and decreased interest in school (Barksdale-Ladd & Thomas, 2000).

Standardized Test Scores and High-Stakes Decisions

Now that you are familiar with the scope of high-stakes testing and the problems involved in it, we can ask, Why have policymakers and the general public embraced standardized testing as the solution to school accountability and reform? Why haven't alternative solutions, such as equalizing school funding, providing professional development opportunities for teachers, lowering class size, and instituting universal preschool, been proposed? There appear to be four principal reasons:

1. In comparison to the alternative solutions just mentioned, testing programs can be implemented quickly and inexpensively.
2. Uniform testing programs can be imposed on all school districts by state legislatures and state departments of education.
3. It is widely assumed that the lure of rewards and the threat of punishment for high and low scores will lead to improved learning and instruction.
4. Test scores provide what seems to be a standard and objective way to hold educators accountable for student achievement (Linn, 2000; Smith & Fey, 2000; Thompson, 2001).

Although some of the problems we have mentioned may be resolved as states refine their testing programs, many educators are highly critical of how testing programs are designed and carried out and how the scores are used. They are particularly disturbed that such high-stakes decisions as promotion or retention, graduation, and additional school financing are often made on the basis of a single test score despite the universal admonition by measurement experts never to make such decisions on this basis. The intensity of the critics' discontent can be seen in the titles of some of their articles: "Burnt at the High Stakes" (Kohn, 2000), "News from the Test Resistance Trail" (Ohanian, 2001), "Why Standardized Tests Don't Measure Educational Quality" (Popham, 1999), and "High Stakes Are for Tomatoes" (Schrag, 2000). Another measure of the discontent is the disappointment, frustration, and anger expressed in many of the articles. Here, for example, are, respectively, the sentiments of a teacher, a prominent measurement expert, and a television producer of programs about education:

> All these years, I believed we were supposed to teach the child at the child's level, at the zone of proximal development. I took courses and studied . . . but now the state tells me that I was wasting my time because their standards are the name of the game, not the children. (Barksdale-Ladd & Thomas, 2000, p. 389)

> As someone who has spent his entire career doing research, writing, and thinking about educational testing and assessment issues, I would like to conclude by summarizing a compelling case showing that the major uses of tests for student and school accountability during the past 50 years have improved education and student learning in dramatic ways. Unfortunately, this is not my conclusion. Instead, I am led to conclude in most cases that instruments and technology have not been up to the demands that have been placed on them by high-stakes accountability. . . . The unintended negative effects of the high-stakes accountability uses often outweigh the intended positive effects. (Linn, 2000, p. 14)

> I believe that high-stakes tests are a serious threat to excellence and national standards. Unchecked, they will choke the life out of many excellent schools and drive gifted teachers out of classrooms. Furthermore, they will lead to debased and unnecessarily low standards, undermining the very cause for which they were instituted in the first place. Bad tests, used to make high-stakes decisions, are the enemy of good (i.e., high) standards. (Merrow, 2001, p. 653)

Performance-Based Assessment and High-Stakes Testing

In spite of the many difficulties with state standards and high-stakes testing, there have been some positive developments. As we mentioned in the preceding chapter, because of the limitations of traditional selected-response tests (those composed of multiple-choice, matching, and true-false items), teachers are increasingly turning to performance tests to measure students' mastery of classroom objectives. For the same reason,

Because traditional standardized tests provide little or no information on how well students can use the knowledge they have acquired in school, some states have included performance-based tests in their assessment program. The most popular types of performance tests include writing portfolios and math and science problem solving.

Figure 14.4 Example of a Performance-Based Item

1. Bus Ride – A friend of yours, who just moved to the United States, must ride the bus to and from school each day. The bus ride costs 50 cents. Your friend must have exact change and must use only nickels, dimes, and quarters. Your friend has a problem because she does not yet understand our money, and she does not know how to count our money.

   Help your friend find the right coins to give to the bus driver. Draw and write something on a whole sheet of paper that can help her. She needs a sheet of paper that can show which combinations of coins can be used to pay for the 50-cent bus ride.

Sample Student Answer 1

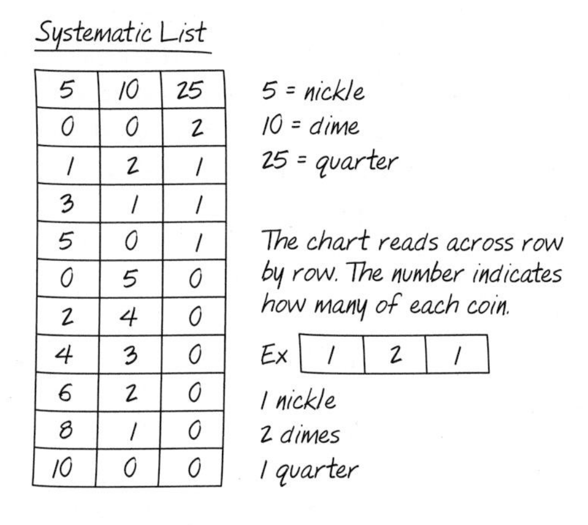
Systematic List

5	10	25
0	0	2
1	2	1
3	1	1
5	0	1
0	5	0
2	4	0
4	3	0
6	2	0
8	1	0
10	0	0

Sample Student Answer 2

10 + 10 + 10 + 10 + 10 = 50¢

25
+ 25
50¢

1 3 1
25 | 5 | 10 | 50

SOURCE: Shepard & Bliem (1995).

some state-mandated testing programs include performance-based learning standards and assessment methods, along with the more traditional multiple-choice items.

Some states use performance-based assessment methods

Vermont's assessment program, for example, includes mathematics problem solving and writing portfolios (Vermont Department of Education, 2000). Kentucky's program includes writing portfolios and open-ended items that require students to explain the reasoning behind their answers in reading, science, social studies, mathematics, and arts and humanities (Kentucky Department of Education, 2000). Maryland's program incorporates performance assessments of writing, science, and mathematics (Maryland State Department of Education, 2001). If more states include similar assessment measures in their testing programs, such disadvantages of high-stakes testing as narrowing the curriculum to low-level cognitive outcomes may be minimized. Figure 14.4 provides an example of a performance-based item that measures ability to use arithmetic knowledge to solve a realistic problem.

In the next section we describe how recent developments in technology are making it easier to prepare students for standardized assessments, administer the tests, and score students' responses.

Standardized Testing and Technology

Given the prevalence of standardized testing and the large amount of money that schools spend on testing programs, it is not too surprising that technology tools exist for a wide range of assessment formats, including the standard true-false, multiple-choice, and fill-in-the-blank questions, as well as alternative assessments such as essay writing, debate forums, simulations, and electronic exhibitions of student work. As we discuss in this section, technology can be used in all phases of testing, including preparing students for standardized tests, administering tests, and scoring students' responses.

To explore web sites relevant to standardized testing, go to the Web Sources section at **http://education.college.hmco.com/students**.

Using Technology to Prepare Students for Assessments

For students to perform well on standardized tests, they need to have a clear understanding of the standards that will be used to evaluate their responses, and they need to be adequately prepared to meet those standards. As national educational standards are developed for disciplines such as mathematics, science, reading, writing, and even physical education, the role of technology in the preparation and assessment of students is steadily increasing.

Clarity of test standards aided by putting examples on CD-ROM, computer files, videotape

In physical education, for instance, standards related to demonstrating competency in many movement forms and applying what one has learned to improve motor skills in an area could be addressed by: (1) using CD-ROM videos to model proper tennis techniques, (2) employing heart monitors to assess and graph targeted heart rates in an aerobics class, (3) comparing printouts from one's performance on fitness equipment to fitness goals as well as to previous accomplishments, and (4) videotaping athletic performances of peers and presenting hypermedia summaries and suggestions of what individual students learned (Baugh, 1994; Mohnsen, 1997).

Another way professional organizations, states, school districts, and teachers in any discipline electronically communicate their standards and student performance goals is through the use of electronic exemplars (Lavigne & Lajoie, 1996). For instance, weak and strong examples of a skill might be posted to the Web to make performance criteria visible and provide a model for students to discuss and debate. And with the rise of technology on the Web for condensing and replaying audio and video files, segments from videotapes of expert or targeted performances can be digitized and placed into a library of electronic performance standards. In addition, many state departments of education have made available on their web sites either practice tests or sample items from past state assessments.

Using Technology to Assess Mastery of Standards

In addition to using technology to model standards, technology can be used to assess whether certain standards have been met. For instance, ACT test developers have created a computerized writing assessment, piloted with more than thirteen thousand students, that asks examinees to edit several 225-word passages on a computer screen (Davey, Godwin, & Mittelholtz, 1997). Instead of merely flagging errors for students and giving them lists of alternative corrections, this system requires the examinee to determine if a writing problem exists. In selecting from four alternative ways of rewriting each passage segment, the test taker must move the cursor to the section of text that he or she thinks needs to be changed and select from alternatives related to grammar, organization, or style of that section. Such problem-finding tests will add another dimension to both standardized and classroom testing and perhaps speed up college or even high school placement decisions.

National testing services are also interested in using technology to grade essay exam questions since human judgment on national tests is fairly subjective, costly, and cursory. Ellis Page (1994) has developed a technology tool, Project Essay Grade (PEG), to show that computers can rate student essays as well as or better than humans. According to Page and Nancy Petersen (1995), this tool evaluates such complex and important writing variables as content, organization, style, and creativity, in addition to mechanics and document length. In one experiment, Page took hundreds of twelfth-grade student writing samples from the 1988 and 1990 National Assessment of Writing Progress to show that computer scoring is superior to human scoring, even when there are multiple human raters on each essay. Computer scoring is not only quicker and more economical, but apparently it is more accurate and statistically informative than human ratings (Page & Petersen, 1995). Although programs like PEG are used mostly at the college and graduate school levels, they are also being tried out at the middle school and high school levels (McCollum, 1998). Given the millions of essays rated each year by the Educational Testing Service alone and the growing reliance on essay writing in future SATs and GREs, computer-rated essays may soon become commonplace in standardized testing.

Computer Adaptive Testing

Computer adaptive testing: computers determine sequence and difficulty level of test items

Technology has also changed the very nature of some tests. Instead of subjecting every student to the same sequence of test items, **computer adaptive testing (CAT)** adjusts item difficulty and sequence to the ability level and responses of the examinee (Meijer & Nering, 1999; Olson, 2000). With immediate feedback and developmentally appropriate assistance, the student can recover from erroneous steps and get back on track to solve the problem, thereby exhibiting knowledge that ordinarily would remain hidden (Singley & Taft, 1995).

As followers of Vygotsky would propose, such diagnostic tests can reveal both the current level of a student's performance and his or her potential with a bit of support. And the more diagnostic information one has about student conceptual and skill deficiencies, the greater the chance is for teachers to differentiate student zones of development and determine how to work successfully with each student (Zehavi, 1997). In addition to the immediate feedback and individualization provided by CAT, it is highly flexible, avoids human error in rating, reduces the number of examination proctors, awards partial credit, follows a student's pace or rhythm, and takes less time to complete (Singley & Taft, 1995; Trentin, 1997). In effect, computer technology can help create personalized tests that would be too time-consuming and complex for a human to develop. On the downside, these complex testing systems are available only for certain types of cognitive skills (for example, memory tasks) and are often limited by computer hardware availability (Trentin, 1997).

In the next section we offer several Suggestions for Teaching that will help you and your students appropriately use standardized test scores.

personal wealth as an analogy to illustrate this last point. Whether someone is considered poor, financially comfortable, or wealthy depends on how much money everyone else in that person's reference group possesses. A net worth of $100,000 is considered wealthy in some circles and barely adequate in others.

If you are discussing achievement test scores, make sure you understand the differences among diagnostic tests, norm-referenced tests, and criterion-referenced tests:

- Scores from a diagnostic achievement test can be used to discuss a student's strengths and weaknesses in such skills as reading, math, and spelling.
- Scores from a norm-referenced achievement test can be used to discuss general strengths and weaknesses in one or more content areas. For achievement tests that provide multiple sets of norms, start your interpretation at the most local level (school norms, ideally) since they are likely to be the most meaningful to parents, and then move to a more broad-based interpretation (district, state, or national norms).
- Scores from a criterion-referenced achievement test can be used to discuss how well a student has mastered the objectives on which the test is based. If there is a close correspondence between the test's objectives and those of the teacher, the test score can be used as an indicator of how much the student has learned in class.

The instructional decisions you make in the classroom will be *guided* but not dictated by the test scores. Many parents fear that if their child obtains a low score on a test, she will be labeled a slow learner by the teacher and receive less attention than higher-scoring students do. This is a good opportunity to lay such a fear to rest in two ways. First, note that test scores are but *one* source of information about students. You will also take into account how well they perform on classroom tests, homework assignments, and special projects, as well as in classroom discussions. Second, emphasize that you are committed to using test scores not to classify students but to help them learn.

To review this chapter, see the Thought Questions and ACE Self-Testing sections at **http://education.college.hmco.com/students**.

Resources for Further Investigation

Technical and Specialized Aspects of Testing

For more information about standardized tests and how to use the information they provide appropriately, consult one or more of these books: *Psychological Testing* (1997), by Anne Anastasi and Susan Urbina; *Measurement and Assessment in Teaching* (2000), by Robert Linn and Norman Gronlund; and *Tests and Assessment* (2001), by W. Bruce Walsh and Nancy Betz.

For information about issues surrounding the testing of minority students, examine *Assessment and Instruction of Culturally and Linguistically Diverse Students with or At-Risk of Learning Problems: From Research to Practice* (1997), by Virginia Gonzalez, Rita Brusca-Vega, and Thomas Yawkey; *Multicultural Assessment Perspectives for Professional Psychology* (1993), by Richard Dana; and *Assessment and Placement of Minority Students* (1991), by Ronald Samuda, Siu Kong, Jim Cummins, Juan Pascual-Leone, and John Lewis.

References for Evaluating Standardized Tests

To obtain the information necessary for evaluating standardized tests, examine *The Thirteenth Mental Measurements Yearbook* (1998), edited by James Impara and Barbara Plake; and Volume 10 of *Test Critiques* (1994), edited by Daniel Keyser and Richard Sweetland. You may have to check earlier editions of *Mental Measurements Yearbook* and *Test Critiques* for information on a specific test since there are far too many tests available for either publication to review in a single edition.

Some additional online resources for you to explore include the ERIC Clearinghouse on Assessment and Evaluation at **http://ericae.net/**. This site includes a test locator, links to other assessment-oriented web sites, an online assessment library, and an assessment-oriented listserv.

The American Psychological Association provides a Code of Fair Testing Practices at **www.apa.org/science/fairtestcode.html**. The Code is also available from the ERIC Clearinghouse on Assessment and Evaluation at **ericae.net/code.htm**.

The National Center for Fair and Open Testing (more commonly known as FairTest) is an advocacy group whose goal is the development of fair, open, and educationally sound standardized tests. Its home page can be found at **www.fairtest.org/**. Under a menu titled "Our Programs" you will find a "K–12 Testing" page with several links to fact sheets and publications.

High-Stakes Testing

An excellent analysis of the high-stakes testing issue can be found in *High Stakes: Testing for Tracking, Promotion, and Graduation* (1999) by Jay Heubert and Robert Hauser.

Summary

1. Standardized tests are designed by people with specialized training in test construction, are given to everyone under the same conditions, are scored the same for everyone, and are interpreted with reference to either a norm group or a set of predetermined standards.
2. The purpose of giving a standardized test is to obtain an accurate and representative sample of some characteristic of a person, since it is impractical to measure that characteristic comprehensively.
3. Standardized tests are typically used to identify students' strengths and weaknesses, inform parents of their child's general level of achievement, plan instructional lessons, and place students in special groups or programs.
4. One of the most important characteristics of a standardized test is its reliability—the similarity between two rankings of test scores obtained from the same individuals.
5. Another important characteristic of standardized tests is validity. A valid test accurately measures what its users intend it to measure and allows us to draw appropriate inferences about how much of some characteristic the test taker possesses. Three types of evidence that contribute to accurate inferences are content validity evidence, predictive validity evidence, and construct validity evidence.
6. A third important characteristic of a standardized test is its norm group—a sample of students specially chosen and tested so as to reflect the population of students for whom the test is intended. The norm group's performance becomes the standard against which scores are compared.
7. Standardized achievement tests measure how much has been learned about a particular subject. The major types of achievement tests are single subject, batteries, diagnostic, competency, and special purpose.
8. Diagnostic tests identify specific strengths and weaknesses in basic learning skills.
9. Competency tests measure how well high school students have acquired such basic skills as reading, writing, and computation.
10. Aptitude tests estimate an individual's predisposition to acquire additional knowledge and skill in specific areas with the aid of effective instruction.
11. Tests that use a norm-referenced scoring system compare an individual's score to the performance of a norm group.
12. Tests that use a criterion-referenced scoring system judge scores in terms of mastery of a set of objectives.
13. Percentile rank indicates the percentage of scores that are at or below a person's score.
14. A z score is a standard score that indicates how far in standard deviation units a raw score is from the mean.
15. A T score is a standard score based on a scale of 1 to 100, with a mean of 50.
16. A stanine score indicates in which of nine normal-curve segments a person's performance falls.
17. Perceived deficiencies and lack of accountability in education during the 1980s led to the development of statewide testing programs.
18. The practice of using standardized test scores to determine promotion to the next grade, graduation from high school, additional state funding, job security for teachers and administrators, and school accreditation is called high-stakes testing. Although high-stakes tests are given in every state and are related to learning standards, little is known about their effects on student achievement.
19. High-stakes testing programs are popular because they can be implemented quickly and inexpensively, can be imposed on all school districts by legislative or bureaucratic fiat, are assumed to produce higher-quality instruction when they are associated with rewards and punishments, and appear to be an objective way to hold educators accountable for student achievement. But many high-stakes testing programs have numerous shortcomings and flaws and produce negative effects on teachers and students.
20. Performance-based tests are part of several states' testing programs.
21. Technology can aid in preparing students for standardized tests and in administering and scoring the tests.

KEY TERMS

standardized tests *(490)*
reliability *(492)*
validity *(492)*
norm group *(494)*
single-subject achievement test *(495)*
achievement battery *(495)*
diagnostic test *(495)*
competency test *(495)*
special-purpose achievement test *(495)*
aptitude test *(495)*
scholastic aptitude *(495)*
norm-referenced test *(496)*
criterion-referenced test *(496)*
grade equivalent score *(497)*
percentile rank *(497)*
standard deviation *(498)*
normal curve *(498)*
z score *(499)*
T score *(499)*
stanine score *(499)*
high-stakes testing *(502)*
computer adaptive testing (CAT) *(511)*

DISCUSSION QUESTIONS

1. If you are like most other people, you took a variety of standardized tests throughout your elementary and high school years. The results of those tests were probably used to help determine what you would be taught and how. Do you think that those tests adequately reflected what you had learned and were capable of learning and therefore were always used in your best interest? What can you do to increase the chances you will use test scores to help *your* students fulfill their potential?

2. Think about norm-referenced tests and criterion-referenced tests. Which do you think you prefer? Why? Can you describe a set of circumstances in which a norm-referenced test would be clearly preferable to a criterion-referenced test, and vice versa?

3. If you had to tell parents about the results of a standardized test, which type of score could you explain most clearly: raw score, percentile rank, z score, T score, or stanine score? Which do you think would be most informative for parents? For you as a teacher? If you do not understand completely the one that you think is most informative, what can you do about this situation?

4. Instead of accepting high-stakes testing as a fact of life, critics suggest that teachers try to persuade policymakers either to eliminate or modify the worst aspects of such programs. Among their recommendations are to attend and speak out at school board meetings that deal with education policies, organize a letter-writing campaign to school board members and legislators expressing concern that test preparation is squeezing out more important aspects of the curriculum, organize a delegation of parents and educators to visit state legislators, write letters to the editor of the local newspaper, and organize a workshop or panel discussion on the abuses of high-stakes testing. How many of these activities would you be willing to engage in? Why?

Becoming a Better Teacher by Becoming a Reflective Teacher

15

As you know from personal experience, some teachers are much more effective than others. Take a moment, and think back to as many teachers as you can remember. How many of them were really outstanding in the sense that they established a favorable classroom atmosphere, were sensitive to the needs of students, and used a variety of techniques to help you learn? How many of them did an adequate job but left you bored or indifferent most of the time? How many of them made you dread entering their classrooms because they were either ineffective teachers or insensitive or even cruel in dealing with you and your classmates?

Chances are you remember just a few outstanding teachers and had at least one who was incompetent or tyrannical (and perhaps several of them). You probably know from your experiences as a student that ineffective or vindictive teachers are often dissatisfied with themselves and with their jobs. It seems logical to assume a circular relationship in such cases: unhappy teachers often do a poor job of instruction; teachers who do a poor job of instruction are likely to be unhappy.

If you hope to be an effective teacher who enjoys life in the classroom (most of the time), you must be well prepared and willing to work. You will need a wide variety of skills, sensitivity to the needs of your students, and awareness of many instructional techniques. Each chapter in this book was written to help you acquire these various skills, sensitivities, and techniques. In addition, you will need to develop the reflective attitudes and abilities that help you formulate thoughtful instructional goals and plans, implement those plans, observe their effects, and judge whether your goals were met. This chapter offers some suggestions you might use to enhance such attitudes and abilities. ■

Improving Your Teaching and Reflection Skills

To aid your professional development, go to this textbook's web site at **http://education.college.hmco.com/students** and explore the many resources among the Professional Links in the Web Sources section.

Scholars who study instructional processes often liken the role of the classroom teacher to that of an orchestra conductor. Jere Brophy and Carolyn Evertson, for example, note that "effective teaching involves *orchestration* of a large number of factors, continually shifting teaching behavior to respond to continually shifting needs" (1976, p. 139). They also note that "the most successful teachers looked upon themselves as diagnosticians and problem solvers" (p. 45). Taken together, these two comments emphasize the point that to be consistently effective, you will need to observe and analyze what you do in the classroom and use different approaches with different groups of students.

This recommendation holds even when you are using programs that have been developed by others and for which considerable positive research exists. One such program that you may eventually come into contact with is *Success for All*. Designed by researchers at Johns Hopkins University (Slavin, Madden, Karweit, Dolan, & Wasik, 1992; Slavin, Madden, Dolan, & Wasik, 1996) to prevent the development of reading deficiencies among at-risk elementary grade students, the program provides teachers with very specific training, materials, and guidelines (for instance, spending a certain amount of time on particular lessons). Nevertheless, studies of schools that have adopted Success for All have shown that virtually all teachers, even those who strongly support the program, make some adaptations to it to fit their own philosophies, teaching styles, and classroom circumstances (Datnow & Castellano, 2000). The one caveat we would offer (as we did when discussing teachers' use of cooperative learning) is to avoid making changes of such magnitude that you create something entirely different from what the developers had envisioned and what the research literature supports.

As you strive to become a more reflective and effective teacher, a number of methods can help you analyze what you do and adapt it to new circumstances. You might ask for students' evaluations or suggestions, employ peer or self-assessment techniques, or use a Reflective Journal both to troubleshoot your teaching and systematically analyze your goals and techniques. Each of these will be discussed separately.

Student Evaluations and Suggestions

In many respects, students are in a better position to evaluate teachers than anyone else. They may not always be able to analyze *why* what a teacher does is effective or ineffective (even an experienced expert observer might have difficulty doing so), but they know, better than anyone else, whether they are responding and learning. Furthermore, students form their impressions after interacting with a teacher for hundreds or thousands of hours. Most principals or other adult observers may watch a teacher in action for only a few minutes at a time. It therefore makes sense to pay attention to and solicit opinions from students.

As a matter of fact, it will be virtually impossible for you to ignore student reactions. Every minute that school is in session, you will receive student feedback in the form of attentiveness (or lack of it), facial expressions, restlessness, yawns, sleeping, disruptive behavior, and the like. If a particular lesson arouses either a neutral or a negative reaction, this should signal to you that you need to seek a better way to present the same material in the future. If you find that you seem to be spending much of your time disciplining students, it will be worth your while to evaluate why and to find other methods.

In addition to analyzing the minute-by-minute reactions of your students, you may find it helpful to request more formal feedback. After completing a unit, you might say, "I'd like you to tell me what you liked and disliked about the way this unit was arranged and give me suggestions for improving it if I teach it again next year."

A more comprehensive and systematic approach is to distribute a questionnaire or evaluation form and ask students to record their reactions anonymously. You might use a published form or devise your own. In either case, a common format is to list a series of statements and ask students to rate them on a 5-point scale. Some of the published forms use special answer sheets that make it possible to tally the results electronically. One disadvantage of many rating-scale evaluation forms is that responses may not be very informative unless you can compare your ratings to those of colleagues. If you get an overall rating of 3.5 on "makes the subject matter interesting," for example, you won't know whether you need to work on that aspect of your teaching until you discover that the average rating of other teachers of the same grade or subject was 4.2. Another disadvantage is that published evaluation forms may not be very helpful unless all other teachers use the same rating scale. Fortunately, this may be possible in school districts that use a standard scale to obtain evidence for use in making decisions about retention, tenure, and promotion.

Another disadvantage of many rating scales is indicated by the phrase *leniency problem*. Students tend to give most teachers somewhat above-average ratings on most traits. Although leniency may soothe a teacher's ego, wishy-washy responses do not provide the information needed to improve pedagogical effectiveness. To get around the leniency problem and to induce students to give more informative reactions, forced-choice ratings are often used. Figure 15.1 shows a forced-choice rating form, the Descriptive Ranking Form for Teachers, developed by Don Cosgrove (1959). This form is designed to let teachers know how students perceive their skill in four areas of performance: (1) knowledge and organization of subject matter, (2) adequacy of relations with students in class, (3) adequacy of plans and procedures in class, and (4) enthusiasm in working with students. If you decide to use this form, omit the numbers in brackets that follow each statement when you prepare copies for distribution to students. On your own copy of the form, write in those numbers, and use them to prepare your score in each of the four categories.

First, direct your students to rank the phrases in each set from 1 ("most like you") to 4 ("least like you"). Then calculate your index of effectiveness in each category of the Descriptive Ranking Form for Teachers by assigning a score of 4 to the phrase in each group that is ranked 1, a score of 3 to the phrase marked 2, and so on. Add together the scores for all phrases identified by the parenthetical number 1, and do the same for the other sets of phrases. The cluster of phrases that yields the highest score is perceived by your students to be your strongest area of teaching; the cluster that yields the lowest score is considered to be your weakest. A total of 30 points for all phrases indicated by the parenthetical number 1, for example, means that you ranked high in category 1 (knowledge and organization of subject matter). If, however, you get only 12 points for phrases identified by the parenthetical number 4, you will need to work harder at being enthusiastic when working with students.

Do you wonder how you might use an evaluation form in primary grades? See the Site-Based Cases at this book's web site at **http://education.college.hmco.com/students**.

Quite often, a homemade form that covers specific points regarding your personal approach to teaching will provide useful information. You might ask a series of questions about specific points (Were there enough exams? Did you think too much homework was assigned?). Or you can ask students to list the three things they liked best, the three things they liked least, and what they would suggest you do to improve the way a particular unit is taught. When you ask students to respond to questions like these, not only do you usually get feedback about teaching techniques, but you also get ideas you might use to improve your teaching skill. (If you are rated below average on an item such as "Examinations are too difficult" On a rating scale, you may not know *why* you were rated low or what you might do to change things for the better.)

Peer and Self-Assessment Techniques

Observation Schedules Although your students can supply quite a bit of information that can help you improve your teaching, they cannot always tell you about technical flaws in your instructional technique. This is especially true with younger students. Accordingly, you may wish to submit to a detailed analysis of your approach

Figure 15.1 Descriptive Ranking Form for Teachers

Set a
- ——— Always on time for class [3]
- ——— Pleasant in class [2]
- ——— Very sincere when talking with students [4]
- ——— Well-read [1]

Set b
- ——— Contagious enthusiasm for subject [4]
- ——— Did not fill up time with trivial material [3]
- ——— Gave everyone an equal chance [2]
- ——— Made clear what was expected of students [1]

Set c
- ——— Classes always orderly [3]
- ——— Enjoyed teaching class [4]
- ——— Friendliness did not seem forced [2]
- ——— Logical in thinking [1]

Set d
- ——— Encouraged creativity [4]
- ——— Kept course material up to date [1]
- ——— Never deliberately forced own decisions on class [2]
- ——— Procedures well thought out [3]

Set e
- ——— Authority on own subject [1]
- ——— Friendly attitude toward students [4]
- ——— Marked tests very fairly [3]
- ——— Never criticized in a destructive way [2]

Set f
- ——— Good sense of humor [4]
- ——— Spaced assignments evenly [3]
- ——— Students never afraid to ask questions in class [2]
- ——— Well-organized course [1]

Set g
- ——— Accepted students' viewpoints with open mind [2]
- ——— Increased students' vocabulary by own excellent usage [1]
- ——— Students always knew what was coming up next day [3]
- ——— Students willingly worked for teacher [4]

Set h
- ——— Always knew what he or she was doing [3]
- ——— Appreciated accomplishment [4]
- ——— Did not ridicule wrong answers [2]
- ——— Well informed in all related fields [1]

Set i
- ——— Always had class material ready [3]
- ——— Covered subject well [1]
- ——— Encouraged students to think out answers [4]
- ——— Rules and regulations fair [2]

Set j
- ——— Always managed to get things done on time [3]
- ——— Course had continuity [1]
- ——— Made material significant [4]
- ——— Understood problems of students [2]

SOURCE: Cosgrove (1959).

to teaching. Several observation schedules have been developed for this purpose. The Flanders Interaction Analysis Categories (Flanders, 1970) is perhaps the most widely used teacher behavior schedule, but ninety-eight others are described in *Mirrors for Behavior III: An Anthology of Observation Instruments* (1974), edited by Anita Simon and E. Gil Boyer.

Soliciting comments about the effectiveness of one's teaching methods from students and colleagues and reflecting on these comments is an excellent way to become a better teacher.

As the title of the Flanders schedule indicates, it stresses verbal interactions between teacher and students. The following ten categories are listed on a record blank:

- Accepts feelings
- Praises or encourages
- Uses student ideas
- Asks questions
- Lectures
- Gives directions
- Criticizes
- Pupil talk—response
- Pupil talk—initiation
- Silence or confusion

A trained observer puts a check mark opposite one of these categories every three seconds during a period when teacher and students are interacting verbally. Once the observation is completed, it is a simple matter to tally checks and determine the percentage of time devoted to each activity. Then, if a teacher discovers that a substantial amount of time was spent in silence or confusion and only a tiny fraction of interactions involved praise or encouragement, she can make a deliberate effort to change for the better.

Perhaps the biggest problem with such observational approaches is the need for a trained observer. But it would be possible to team up with another teacher and act as reciprocal observers if you feel that a detailed analysis of your teaching style would be helpful.

Audiotaped Lessons If it is not possible for you to team up with a colleague, you might consider trying to accomplish the same goal through the use of audiotape. Your first step should be to decide which classes or parts of classes you want to record, for how long, and on what day of the week. The goal should be to create a representative sample of the circumstances under which you teach. Then you should inform your students that you intend to tape-record a sample of your lessons over a period of several weeks to study and improve your instructional methods and that you will protect their confidentiality by not allowing anyone else but you to listen to the tapes. Then you can analyze the tapes according to the same categories that make up the Flanders instrument and any others that might be of interest.

When this method was used with ten secondary student teachers, significant improvements were achieved in such behaviors as the amount of time used for bringing a lesson to closure, waiting for students to formulate answers to questions (commonly referred to as wait time), and making positive statements. The impact of listening to yourself as an outsider can be appreciated from the following comment by one student teacher: "Now I'm just so much more aware of waiting. Before, I would address all questions to the class and whoever wanted could blurt out the answer. Whereas, now, I'm much more conscious of calling a name and waiting for a response from that person" (Anderson & Freiberg, 1995, p. 83).

Videotaped Lessons Allowing yourself to be videotaped as you teach and then analyzing your actions later can be a valuable learning experience because it often reveals (even more clearly than audiotape) discrepancies between the instructional beliefs you espouse and how you put those beliefs into practice. Think of it as putting into practice the old saying, "Actions speak louder than words." The potential of videotaped lessons to reveal these discrepancies and produce major shifts in teaching behavior was illustrated in a study (Wedman, Espinosa, & Laffey, 1999) of eleven individuals whose teaching experience ranged from none to twenty-two years. The participant with twenty-two years of experience, a primary grade teacher who had never had her teaching observed, claimed to have a student-centered philosophy. She believed that teachers should provide students with opportunities to explore and experiment. But her videotaped lessons revealed a strong teacher-directed, teacher-centered approach. She selected all the material and activities for the students and provided few opportunities for student expression, exploration, or questioning. As a result of reviewing and discussing her videotaped lessons, she began to look for ways to be more student centered and to emphasize inquiry rather than information dissemination as her approach to student learning.

Because videotaping is more intrusive than audiotaping, teachers are often concerned that the natural flow of classroom events will be disrupted. Experience has shown, however, that both students and teachers quickly lose their self-consciousness and treat the camera as just part of the background. As with audiotaped lessons, make sure your students are informed of what will occur and why and how you will keep the results confidential (Lonoff, 1997).

Reflective Lesson Plans You may want to try something called reflective lesson plans (Ho, 1995). To do so, follow these four steps:

1. Divide a sheet of paper in half. Label the left-hand side "Lesson Plan." Label the right-hand side "Reflective Notes."
2. On the lesson plan side, note relevant identifying information (fourth period English, January 23, 9:00 A.M.; honors algebra; fourth-grade social studies), the objectives of the lesson, the tasks that are to be carried out in chronological order, the materials and equipment that are to be used, and how much time has been allotted for this lesson.
3. On the reflective notes side, write your thoughts about the worth of the objective that underlies the lesson, the adequacy of the materials, and how well

you performed the basic mechanics of teaching as soon as possible after the lesson.

4. Make changes to the lesson plan based on your analysis of the reflective notes.

Guided Reflection Protocol A technique that is somewhat less structured than the reflective lesson plan is the guided reflection protocol (Hole & McEntee, 1999). After choosing one or more teaching episodes that you would like to examine, ask and try to answer as honestly as possible the following four questions:

1. *What happened?* The main requirement of this step is simply to describe the incident as fully as possible. Note, for instance, when and where the incident occurred, who was involved, and what occurred just prior to, during, and immediately after the incident. Avoid analysis and interpretation.
2. *Why did it happen?* If you've provided enough context in answering the first question, you should be able to identify the events that produced the incident.
3. *What might it mean?* Note the conditional wording of this question. Using the word *might* instead of *does* is intended to help you realize that there are usually several possible interpretations of the meaning of an incident. A teacher who reprimands a class for not finishing an assignment on time may, for example, need to examine the clarity of her objectives, the amount of time she budgets for the completion of assignments, the ability of students to use their time productively, or her ability to cope with administrative pressure to cover the curriculum in time for an upcoming high-stakes test.
4. *What are the implications for my practice?* Consider what you might do differently in a similar situation in the light of how you answered the first three questions.

Developing a Reflective Journal

Seymour Sarason (1993), who has written extensively about schooling and school reform, points out what may seem obvious but is often missed in practice: every teacher should be an expert in both subject matter and how children learn in classrooms. The goal, and the challenge, is to figure out how to present the subject matter so that students understand it, remember it, and use it. To do that, you must constantly prepare, observe, and reflect on the results of your actions. The Reflective Journal that we mentioned at the beginning of the book and is described in this section is intended to help you begin that process in a systematic way.

We recommend that you develop a Reflective Journal for two basic purposes: (1) to serve as a repository of instructional ideas and techniques that you have either created from your own experiences or gleaned from other sources and (2) to give yourself a format for recording your observations and reflections on teaching. These two purposes can be separate from each other or, if you choose, related to each other in a cycle of reflectivity that we will describe. As you read this section, refer to Figure 15.2 for an illustration of how a journal page might look.

All of this book's marginal Journal Entries and others are grouped for handy reference at **http://education.college.hmco.com/students**.

The form your Reflective Journal takes will probably change over the years to reflect your experiences and changing needs. But to begin, we suggest that you organize your first journal around the marginal notes in each chapter that are labeled "Journal Entry." Use the Journal Entries as just what their name implies: page headings in your Reflective Journal. To allow room for both the expansion of your teaching ideas and the inclusion of your ongoing reflections, you might purchase a three-ring binder so that you can add and drop pages. Alternatively, if you have regular access to a computer, you might want to create your Reflective Journal as

Figure 15.2 Sample Page for Your Reflective Journal

Journal Entry: *Ways to Teach Comprehension Tactics*
Source: *"Information-Processing Theory"*

Ideas for Instruction

Note: All the ideas you list here will pertain to the particular journal entry/instructional goal for this journal page.

- *Customized suggestions for teaching—those points, principles, activities, and examples taken from the text and the Suggestions for Teaching that are most relevant to your own situation.*
- *Ideas generated from past experiences as a student.*
- *Ideas provided by professional colleagues.*
- *Ideas collected from student-teaching experiences.*
- *Ideas gathered from methods textbooks.*

Reflections: Questions and "Restarter" Suggestions for Instruction

Reflective Question (to focus observation of my teaching and my students' learning): *Do my students have difficulty understanding the meaning of what they read or of what I present in class?*

(Record your ongoing reflections, observations, and analytic notes about your instruction and your students' learning of this topic here. If necessary, you may need to "jump-start" or reorient your instruction. One possible idea follows.)

Suggested Action: *Schedule a series of sessions on how to study. Explain the purpose of various comprehension tactics, and provide opportunities for students to practice these skills on material they have been assigned to read. Give corrective feedback.*

electronic files, which would give you unlimited capacity for interaction and expansion.

Under each heading, you can develop a two-part page or multipage entry. As illustrated in the top half of Figure 15.2, the first part should contain your own teaching ideas, custom-tailored from the Suggestions for Teaching sections of the chapters of this book and from personal experience and other sources to fit the grade level and subjects you expect to teach.

To illustrate, let's use a Journal Entry from the chapter on information-processing theory, "Ways to Teach Comprehension Tactics." First, search your memory for techniques that your past teachers used. Did your fifth-grade teacher, for instance, have a clever way of relating new information to ideas that you had learned earlier in order to make the new information easier to understand? Describe the technique so you will remember to try it yourself. Did a high school teacher have an ingenious way of displaying the similarities and differences among a set of ideas? Exactly how did she or he do it? After you exhaust your own recollections, ask roommates or

Research has shown that keeping a personal journal about one's teaching activities and outcomes helps teachers improve their effectiveness because it forces them to focus on what they do, why they do it, and what kinds of results are typically obtained.

classmates if they can remember any successful ways that their teachers made learning easier.

Next, examine the examples opposite the Journal Entry. Which ones seem most appropriate for the grade level and subject you will be teaching? Jot them down. Do any of the examples suggest variations you can think of on your own? Write them down before you forget them.

Finally, add ideas that you pick up in methods classes or during your student-teaching experience. If you see a film in a methods class that shows how a teacher helps students understand a particular point, describe it in your journal. If your master teacher uses a successful technique to clarify difficult-to-understand material, record it. If you follow some or all of these suggestions for using the Journal Entries, you will have a rich source of ideas to turn to when you discover that your students seem confused and anxious because of poor comprehension and you find yourself wondering if there is anything you can do about it.

With this part of the journal under way, you should feel reasonably well prepared when you first take charge of a class. But given the complexity of classroom teaching, lessons or techniques that looked good on paper do not always produce the intended effect. This is the point at which you need to reflect on and analyze what you are doing and how you might bring about improvements. On the bottom half of your journal page, write in question form what the nature of the problem seems to be. Then try to identify the cause (or causes) of the problem and at least one possible solution. You can use this suggestion to get restarted or headed in a new direction with your teaching. If, for example, some of your students still have difficulty comprehending what they read despite the comprehension-enhancing techniques that you embedded into your lessons, you might reread the chapter on information-processing theory, as well as other articles and books on information processing, and decide that your students really need systematic instruction in how to use various comprehension-directed learning tactics.

Are Reflection and Journal Writing Effective? Recent research found that student teachers who were given questions as reflective prompts (for example, Why was this event significant? How did you react to this event? Why did you react that way? What did you learn from this event?) were more likely to note the reasons for their actions and to make judgments about the adequacy of their efforts than were those who were not given such prompts. According to one student teacher:

> After your lesson, you may say, "It's over," and you may not think about it again. But with the reflective logs, you are forced to sit down and really think about what was something significant about the class and what did you do about it? So, I think it is important. Because if this assignment wasn't there, I probably would just go on and forget about the lesson, and this is not a good thing to do. (Tsangaridou & O'Sullivan, 1994, p. 23)

If we haven't yet convinced you of the value of keeping a Reflective Journal, perhaps the experiences of a veteran teacher will. Lynne Streib, who has taught kindergarten and first and second grades for the Philadelphia, Pennsylvania, schools for over twenty years, had this to say about journal writing:

> Keeping a journal has been a realistic way for me to learn about, inquire into, collect data about, and enhance my practice as well as to learn about and plan for the children. Although writing in my journal each day takes time, it is economical and is the genre most compatible with my style of writing, my way of teaching, and my way of thinking.

> Since 1980, I have kept some kind of journal. . . . I continue to keep a journal for a variety of reasons. First and most important, it helps me with my teaching. When used in certain ways, the journal allows me to look closely at the curriculum. As I teach, I wonder how my thinking and my students' thinking evolve over time. I wonder what I have valued and what the children are interested in and value. Lesson plans don't tell me this, but the journal does. My journal is a place for planning, for raising questions, for figuring things out, and for thinking. (Streib, 1993, pp. 121–122)

Using a Portfolio with Your Journal Middle school teacher Linda Van Wagenen used a personal portfolio along with a Reflective Journal to analyze and improve the quality of her instruction (Van Wagenen & Hibbard, 1998). She compiled a portfolio of her efforts to achieve certain teaching goals and used that to examine her effectiveness. She judged her first two efforts at analysis to be unsatisfactory because they were largely descriptive; they emphasized what she had done and ignored what effects those efforts had on her students (self-assessment), what she thought about the quality of her own instruction (self-evaluation), or what she planned to do next (self-regulation). Her third attempt focused on ways to motivate students to improve their performance in persuasive and expository writing. She identified a set of steps that would help her understand the problem and produce improvements. Evidence of her successes and failures made up the portfolio. In addition, she kept a Reflective Journal because she felt it would help her stay focused on finding a solution to the problem and would stimulate attempts at self-evaluation and self-regulation. The result of this third attempt was judged to be much more useful than either of her first two efforts. In addition to addressing the question, "What did I do?" she also addressed the questions, "What did I learn?" and "Now what will I do?"

The Case in Print describes a portfolio-type of Reflective Journal that some teacher education programs require their students to compile and that students are using to demonstrate to potential employers their readiness to teach. In thinking about the contents of your own portfolio, you might want to start with the following list of items:

1. A table of contents
2. A résumé
3. A statement of your educational philosophy, which may include the reasons that you chose teaching as a career
4. A statement of your teaching goals
5. Official documents (transcripts, teaching certificates, test scores, lesson plans, teaching activities)
6. Letters of recommendation
7. Teaching evaluations
8. Photographs and videotapes
9. Samples of college work
10. Samples of students' work
11. Examples of learning activities (especially those that contain innovative ideas)
12. An autobiography
13. Reflections about how teaching (or student teaching) has contributed to your growth as a person and a teacher (Hurst, Wilson, & Cramer, 1998; Lyons, 1999)

Using Technology for Reflection

Throughout this book, we have described how you can use various technology tools to help your students become more effective learners. Now it's time to consider how you can use such technologies as the World Wide Web, videotape, and multimedia and hypermedia programs to help you think about and improve your own teaching skills.

Discussion Forums and Chatrooms

A major source of frustration for teachers is the limited intellectual and social contact they have with one another (Sarason, 1993). Certainly during school hours, there are few opportunities for teachers to engage in meaningful discussions about teaching and learning. And after school, many teachers are either busy grading papers and making lesson plans or are at home with their families. Computer-based technologies can help break down this sense of isolation by providing forums for teachers to discuss instructional ideas and problems from any location and at any time. You can begin that process now by using the World Wide Web to discuss ideas and field experiences with peers in this country and others. (Bonk, Malikowski, Angeli, & East, 1998; Thurston, Secaras, & Levin, 1997). Later, when you have a full-time teaching position, you can use the Web to discuss such issues as teaching philosophy and common classroom problems and their solutions and to explore relevant resources. Numerous web sites have been designed for K–12 teachers and contain discussion forums or chatrooms (or both). Here are five you might consider using:

- The Connect page of ALPS, Harvard's Teacher Lab (**learnweb.harvard.edu/alps/bigideas/q5.cfm**)
- The New Teachers On-Line page of Teachers Network.org (**www.teachnet.org/docs/ntol/**)
- The Interactive Forums page of the International Education and Resource Network (**foro.iearn.org/**)
- The Teacher2Teacher page of Teachnet.com (**www.teachnet.com/t2t/**)
- The Teachers Helping Teachers Guestbook page of Teachers Helping Teachers (**www.pacificnet.net/~mandel/guestbook.html**)

For direct links to these and other web sites, use the Web Sources at this book's web site at **http://education.college.hmco.com/students**.

Multimedia Case-Based Instruction

In addition to online conferencing, educational researchers and teacher education programs are using multimedia and hypermedia programs that feature case-based learning formats that encourage new models of teaching, learning, and assessment among both preservice and practicing teachers (Abell, Bryan, & Anderson, 1998; Baker, 2000; Hughes, Packard, & Pearson, 2000; Stephens, Leavell, & Fabris, 1999).

These materials contain video-based stories to provide a context or situation for teacher reflection and introduce a more constructivist teaching orientation. Tools are provided for selecting and displaying problem cases and situations, recording preliminary case solutions, browsing through expert commentary and supplemental case information, exploring library materials for case solutions and alternative cases, and provoking student reflection. And with technology's replay capabilities, a preservice teacher like you could use these multimedia cases to identify key instructional

Starting a Reflective Journal Now Pays Off in the Future

Seymour Sarason (1993), who has written extensively about schooling and school reform, points out what may seem obvious but is often missed in practice: every teacher should be an expert in both subject matter and how children learn in classrooms. The goal, and the challenge, is to figure out how to present the subject matter so that students understand it, remember it, and use it. To do that, you must constantly prepare, observe, and reflect on the results of your actions. The Reflective Journal . . . that is described in this section is intended to help you begin that process in a systematic way. (p. 523)

Portfolios Give Prospective Teachers an Edge When They Interview for Jobs

VALERIE SCHREMP

St. Louis Post-Dispatch 12/14/97

Katherine Karoby, professor of education at Webster University, often tells a story about a student who showed up to a job interview with a teaching portfolio in her lap. The principal asked, "How would you teach reading in the second grade?"

"I would tell you," said the student, "But I would like to show you." She pulled a videotape from her portfolio, pulled in a VCR cart, popped in the tape, pressed play and got the job.

Karoby and the employed teacher are not alone in their testimony. Colleges, student teachers and even the Missouri Department of Elementary and Secondary Education are also praising portfolios. Teacher portfolios may contain videotapes, photos of bulletin boards and sample lesson plans.

The portfolios accomplish three things: they show the state Board of Education that a school is producing worthy teachers; they give students a record of growth over their college careers; and they show what a teacher can do.

Starting in fall 1998, Missouri will require education colleges to start portfolio programs. Every five years, to ensure the quality of an education program, the state will examine randomly selected portfolios from at least 10 percent of a program's students.

"Before, we focused on things like making sure institutions offered appropriate courses and hours," said Mike Lucas, head of certification for the Missouri Department of Elementary and Secondary Education. "Just because a student takes courses for x number of hours doesn't mean the individual has the competency to teach."

Several of Missouri's 34 teacher-educating colleges have already launched portfolio programs. So have Illinois colleges, though the state board does not require them.

Fontbonne College required this year's freshmen education students to begin portfolios. It even sells oversized, three-ring binders in its school bookstore as "start-up kits." Webster University wants to put portfolios on CD-ROM.

The University of Missouri at St. Louis, which placed 450 student teachers last year, uses portfolios to help grade students in education classes. Kathie Heywood, associate dean for academic affairs, said the education professors at first doubted the value of the portfolios. They feared students would put only their best pieces in them, presenting a false picture.

So they encourage students to include examples from the science lesson gone awry, or the behavior management plan that just didn't cut it in a high school class. That way, professors can help students correct their work or advise them not to go into teaching.

When students start looking for jobs, they can put together a professional portfolio, full of their best pieces to show off on interviews.

Principals notice. Phillip Silsby, principal of Belleville West High School, has seen just a few portfolios but called them effective. This year, he hired a counselor who had a portfolio of newspaper clips about a career education program she started at another school.

Jim Schwab, principal of Carollton Oaks Elementary in the Pattonville School District, says about one out of three applicants comes into an interview with a portfolio. "I look through them more out of courtesy than anything," he said. "But if two people come in with equal interviewing skills and equal credentials, a portfolio would certainly give them an edge."

One teacher interviewed at the school a couple of years ago, toting what Schwab called an impressive portfolio, full of creative ideas and projects. "That definitely put her over the top," he said. He hired her to teach third grade.

Questions and Activities

1. This article describes how prospective teachers are using portfolios to demonstrate their teaching skills to prospective employers. If this technique impresses you, start now to create your own portfolio. Save assignments from different classes, particularly those that required several steps to complete. As this article indicates, you can include videotapes, photographs, and newspaper articles, as well as the traditional written format.

2. In addition to using portfolios as a job-seeking technique, you can use them to practice reflective teaching. Think about how you can combine the Reflective Journal described in this chapter with a portfolio.

decisions in planning or conducting a lesson. After watching a video sequence a second or third time for critical teaching decisions, you might post some reflection notes or compare that situation to another. Perhaps more important, such tools are not only useful for individual exploration; they also promote rich conversations among teachers.

One set of such materials (Baker, 2000) focuses on the reading and writing of an elementary grade student over the course of a school year. Each videotape segment shows the student either reading or writing with classmates or the teacher. The book that the student reads from and the students' written products can be easily read from the videotape. The video segments can be arranged in such a way that one can track the student's performance either over time or across subject matter areas.

One study (Abell et al., 1998) focused on science education undergraduates who viewed videodisk cases of first graders learning about eggs and seeds. The experience produced significant changes in the future teachers' beliefs about the capabilities of six-year-olds. According to one undergraduate:

> My expectations for a first grade science lesson have really changed after viewing the Seeds and Eggs lesson. The first graders are able to handle hands-on a lot better than I thought they would. I thought the teacher would mainly do all of the talking and experimenting. I saw these students, even though they are young, being able to conduct and observe experiments on their own. I thought they would misbehave if there was not a lot of supervision. This class really surprised me at how well behaved and under control they were. (p. 505)

How will you use reflective teaching in your own career? To prompt your thinking, read the Thought Questions at **http://education.college.hmco.com/students**.

Resources for Further Investigation

Reflective Teaching

Among the many recently published books on reflection in teaching, you might take a look at *Interwoven Conversations: Learning and Teaching Through Critical Reflection* (1991), by Judith Newman. Written in an interesting narrative form, this book describes the author's inquiry into her own pedagogical assumptions, teaching practices, and contradictions between beliefs and practices. Another book is *Teachers and Teaching: From Classroom to Reflection* (1992), edited by Tom Russell and Hugh Munby. The four topics covered by this book are "Reflection in Teaching," "Reflection in Cases in Teaching," "Narrative in Reflection," and "Reflection in the Context of Teacher Education."

Chapter 1 of *Reflective Teaching for Student Empowerment* (1993), by Dorene Ross, Elizabeth Bondy, and Diane Kyle, describes the essence of reflective teaching, explains why reflection is essential in teaching, and describes the knowledge and skills one must learn in order to teach reflectively. Judy Eby notes that her book, *Reflective Planning, Teaching, and Evaluation: K–12* (1998), is intended to help beginning and practicing teachers improve their performance through a process of self-discovery. The first five chapters of *Becoming a*

competency test A test to determine a student's ability to handle basic subjects.

computer adaptive testing (CAT) A testing technique in which a computer program adapts the difficulty of questions to the ability level of the examinee based on his or her responses, thereby resulting in a reduction in test length and greater efficiency.

computer-assisted instruction (CAI) Teaching methods that use interactive software as an aid to learning.

computer-based instruction (CBI) (*See* **computer-assisted instruction**)

computer conferencing An online discussion group, typically organized by topic, that can provide students with access to information, viewpoints, and communities beyond the boundaries of their classrooms.

concept mapping A technique for identifying and visually representing on paper the ideas that comprise a section of text and the ways in which they relate to each other.

conservation The recognition that certain properties stay the same despite a change in appearance or position.

constructivism The view that meaningful learning is the active creation of knowledge structures rather than a mere transferring of objective knowledge from one person to another.

contingency contracting A behavior-strengthening technique that specifies desirable behaviors and consequent reinforcement.

cooperative learning An approach that uses small heterogeneous groups for purposes of mutual help in the mastery of specific tasks.

criterion-referenced grading A system in which grades are determined on the basis of whether each student has attained a defined standard of achievement or performance.

criterion-referenced tests Tests in which students are evaluated according to how well they have mastered specific objectives in various well-defined skill areas.

cultural pluralism A set of tenets based on three principles: (1) every culture has its own internal coherence, integrity, and logic; (2) no culture is inherently better or worse than another; and (3) all persons are to some extent culture-bound.

culture A description of the ways a group of people perceives the world; formulates beliefs; evaluates objects, ideas, and experiences; and behaves.

decentration The ability to think of more than one quality of an object or problem at a time. (*See* **perceptual centration**)

deficiency needs The first four levels (physiological, safety, belongingness or love, and esteem) in Maslow's hierarchy of needs, so called because these needs cause people to act only when they are unmet to some degree.

depression An emotional disorder characterized by self-deprecation, crying spells, and suicidal thoughts, afflicting between 7 and 28 percent of all adolescents.

developmental bilingual education (DBE) An approach to bilingual education in which instruction is provided to all students in both the minority language and the majority language. Also called *bilingual immersion* or *dual language*.

diagnostic test A single-subject achievement test intended to identify the source of a problem in basic subjects and perhaps in study skills. (*See* **single-subject achievement test**)

digital portfolio A multimedia collection of student work that documents individual expertise, achievement, accomplishments, and growth in one or more areas over extended periods of time. Also called *electronic portfolio*.

direct instruction An approach to instruction that emphasizes the efficient acquisition of basic skills and subject matter through lectures and demonstrations, extensive practice, and corrective feedback.

direct reinforcement A situation in which an individual watches a model perform, imitates the behavior, and is reinforced by the model or some other individual.

discovery learning A teaching strategy that encourages children to seek solutions to problems either on their own or in group discussion.

discrimination A process in which individuals learn to notice the unique aspects of seemingly similar situations and thus learn different ways of responding.

distributed practice The practice of breaking up learning tasks into small, easy-to-manage pieces that are learned over several relatively brief sessions.

drill-and-practice programs Computer programs that help students practice skills and learn factual information.

dual coding theory A theory of elaboration that states that concrete objects and words are remembered better than abstract information because they are coded in memory as both visual images and verbal labels, whereas abstract words are only encoded verbally.

early language development The phase of language learning in which children tend to stick to their own rules, despite efforts to correct them.

early-maturing boy A boy whose early physical maturation typically draws favorable adult responses and promotes confidence and poise, thus contributing to leadership and popularity with peers. (*See* **late-maturing boy**)

early-maturing girl A girl whose early physical maturation typically makes her socially out of step with her peers. (*See* **late-maturing girl**)

educational psychology The branch of psychology that specializes in understanding how different factors affect the classroom behavior of both teachers and students.

egocentrism Difficulty in taking another person's point of view, a characteristic typical of young children.

elaborative rehearsal A process that consciously relates new information to knowledge already stored in long-term memory. Also called *elaborative encoding.* (*See* **long-term memory**)

electronic portfolio (*See* **digital portfolio**)

emotional disturbance An emotional condition in which inappropriate aggressive or withdrawal behaviors are exhibited over a long period of time and to a marked degree, adversely affecting a child's educational performance.

empirical learning The use of noticeable characteristics of objects and events to form spontaneous concepts; a form of learning typical of young children.

epigenetic principle The notion that a child's personality develops as the ego progresses through a series of interrelated stages, much as the human body takes shape during its fetal development.

equilibration The tendency to organize schemes to allow better understanding of experiences. (*See* **scheme**)

ethnic group A collection of people who identify with one another on the basis of such characteristics as ancestral origin, race, religion, language, values, political or economic interests, and behavior patterns.

evaluation In assessment, the use of a rule-governed system to make judgments about the value or worth of a set of measures.

exploratory environments Electronic environments that provide students with materials and resources to discover interesting phenomena and construct new insights; for example, computer simulations. Also called *discovery environments*. (*See* **discovery learning**)

extinction The weakening of a target behavior by ignoring it.

extrinsic motivation A form of incentive based on a system of rewards not inherent in a particular activity. (*See* **intrinsic motivation**)

field-dependent style A learning style in which a person's perception of and thinking about a task or problem are strongly influenced by such contextual factors as additional information and other people's behavior.

field-independent style A learning style in which a person's perception of and thinking about a task or problem are influenced more by the person's knowledge base than by the presence of additional information or other people's behavior.

foreclosure status An adolescent identity status marked by the unquestioning endorsement of parents' goals and values.

formative evaluation A type of assessment that monitors a student's progress in order to facilitate learning rather than assign a grade.

frames The individual steps in a teaching program. (*See* **programmed instruction**)

full inclusion The practice of eliminating pullout programs (those outside the classroom) and providing regular teachers with special training so as to keep special needs students in regular classrooms. Also called *inclusion*.

gender bias The tendency of teachers to respond differently to male and female students when there is no educationally sound reason for doing so.

gender roles Sets of behaviors typically identified with either males or females in a society; young children's awareness of these roles shows up clearly in the different toys and activities that boys and girls prefer.

generalization The learned ability to respond in similar ways to similar stimuli.

general objectives Objectives that use the three taxonomies (cognitive, affective, and psychomotor) to describe types of behavior that would demonstrate a student's learning. (*See* **affective domain taxonomy; cognitive domain taxonomy; psychomotor domain taxonomy**)

general transfer A situation in which prior learning aids subsequent learning due to the use of similar cognitive strategies.

gifted and talented student A student who shows unusual ability in any of a variety of ways and who may require services not ordinarily provided by his or her school.

grade equivalent score A measurement that interprets test performance in terms of grade levels.

growth need A yearning for personal fulfillment that people constantly strive to satisfy. (*See* **self-actualization**)

growth spurt The rapid and uneven physical growth that besets adolescents during the middle school years.

guided learning Environments where teachers, experts, or more knowledgeable peers support student inquiry by helping students set plans and goals, ask questions, discuss issues, solve problems, and reflect on strategies and solutions. Also called *guided discovery learning*. (*See* **cognitive apprenticeship; constructivism**)

heuristics General approaches to solving problems, such as studying worked examples and breaking problems into parts, that can be applied to different subject areas.

high-road transfer A situation involving the conscious, controlled, somewhat effortful formulation of an "abstraction" (that is, a rule, a schema, a strategy, or an analogy) that allows a connection to be made between two tasks.

high-stakes testing The use of standardized test results to make such significant decisions as whether students get promoted to the next grade or graduate from high school, whether teachers and administrators receive financial rewards or demotions, and whether school districts receive additional state funds or lose their accreditation.

humanistic approach An approach to instruction that emphasizes the effect of student needs, values, motives, and self-perceptions on learning.

hypermedia A technology that combines multimedia and hypertext so that the learner can nonsequentially access and explore interesting and important information resources. (*See* **hypertext; multimedia**)

hypertext A system of linking text in a nonlinear way, thereby enabling users to jump from one section of text to another section of the same document or to other documents, often through pressing highlighted or "hot" words.

IDEA Acronym for the Individuals with Disabilities Education Act (originally called the Education for All Handicapped Children Act), the principal federal law governing the education of children with disabilities.

identity A relatively stable conception of where and how one fits into a society that is strongly influenced by the perception of one's physical appearance, the goals one establishes and achieves, and recognition from significant others in the environment.

identity achievement status An adolescent identity status marked by self-chosen commitments with respect to at least some aspects of identity.

identity diffusion status An adolescent identity status marked by the avoidance of choices pertaining to jobs, roles, or values and the readiness to change one's position in response to negative or positive feedback.

identity status A style or approach that adolescents adopt to deal with such identity-related issues as career goal, gender-role orientation, and religious beliefs. James Marcia identified four identity statuses: identity diffusion, moratorium, foreclosure, and identity achievement.

ill-structured problems Vaguely stated problems with unclear solution procedures and vague evaluation standards. (*See* **well-structured problems**)

I-message A first-person statement by a teacher that emphasizes the teacher's feelings about a situation rather than his or her feelings about the students.

impulsive A learning style in which students respond relatively quickly to questions or tasks for which there is no obvious correct answer or solution.

inclusion An extension of the least restrictive environment provision of IDEA in which students with disabilities are placed in regular classrooms for the entire school day and receive some instruction and support from a special education teacher. (*See also* **full inclusion**)

individualized education program (IEP) A written statement describing an educational program designed to meet the unique needs of a child with a particular disability.

inert knowledge Information, typically memorized verbatim, that is unconnected, lacking in context, and not readily accessible for application to real-world tasks. (*See* **anchored instruction; drill-and-practice programs; meaningful learning; situated learning**)

information-processing theory An area of study that seeks to understand how people acquire, store, and recall information and how their current knowledge guides and determines what and how they will learn.

instructional objectives Statements written by teachers that specify the knowledge and skills students should be able to exhibit after a unit of instruction.

integrated learning systems (ILS) Computer-based instructional systems that provide sequenced and self-paced learning activities to students in many different content areas as well as appropriate remediation or enrichment activities.

intelligence The ability of an individual to use a variety of cognitive and noncognitive capabilities to formulate goals, logically work toward achieving those goals, and adapt to the demands of the environment.

intelligent tutoring systems Computer tools that attempt to provide timely and individualized guidance by comparing the problem-solving histories of the user with models of expert performance in that domain.

Internet *See* **World Wide Web**.

interpersonal reasoning The ability to understand the relationship between motives and behavior among a group of people.

intrinsic motivation A form of incentive inherent in a particular activity, such as the positive consequence of becoming more competent or knowledgeable. (*See* **extrinsic motivation**)

irreversibility The inability of a young child to mentally reverse physical or mental processes, such as pouring water from a tall, thin glass back into a short, squat one.

issues Ill-structured problems that arouse strong feelings. (*See* **ill-structured problems**)

Joplin Plan An ability grouping technique that combines students of different grade levels according to their standardized test scores. (*See* **regrouping**)

late-maturing boy A boy whose delayed physical maturation typically causes inferiority feelings and leads to bossy and attention-getting behavior. (*See* **early-maturing boy**)

late-maturing girl A girl whose delayed physical maturation typically makes her more poised than others her age and elicits praise from elders, thus conferring leadership tendencies. (*See* **early-maturing girl**)

learner-centered education An educational philosophy in which the teacher helps guide students to construct knowledge meaningfully and monitor their own learning by emphasizing student choice, responsibility, challenge, intrinsic motivation, and ownership of the learning process.

learning disabilities Problems in otherwise mentally fit students who are unable to respond to certain aspects of the curriculum presented in regular classrooms because of disorders in one or more basic psychological processes.

learning strategy A general plan that a learner formulates for achieving a somewhat distant academic goal.

learning style A consistent tendency or preference to respond to a variety of intellectual tasks and problems in a particular fashion.

learning tactic A specific technique that a learner uses to accomplish an immediate learning objective.

least restrictive environment A requirement (under the 1994 Code of Federal Regulations governing the implementation of IDEA) that disabled children be provided with education in the least restrictive setting possible, usually by including them in regular classrooms. (*See* **mainstreaming**)

locus of control The tendency to perceive positive and negative events as being either under one's control (that is, internal) or due to outside factors and circumstances (that is, external).

long-term memory (LTM) Storehouse of permanently recorded information in an individual's memory.

loss of voice The tendency of adolescent females to suppress their true beliefs about issues and either claim that they have no opinion or state what they think others want to hear because of socialization practices.

low-road transfer A situation in which a previously learned skill or idea is almost automatically retrieved from memory and applied to a highly similar current task. (*See* **high-road transfer**)

mainstreaming The policy of placing students with disabilities in regular classes.

maintenance rehearsal A rather mechanical process that uses mental and verbal repetition to hold information in short-term memory for some immediate purpose. Also called *rote rehearsal* or *repetition*. (*See* **short-term memory**)

massed practice An approach to learning that emphasizes a few long, infrequently spaced study periods.

mastery learning An approach that assumes most students can master the curriculum if certain conditions are established: (1) sufficient aptitude, (2) sufficient ability to understand instruction, (3) a willingness to persevere, (4) sufficient time, and (5) good-quality instruction.

meaningful learning Learning that occurs when new information or activities are made relevant by relating them to personal interests and prior experiences or knowledge.

measurement The assignment of numbers to certain attributes of objects, events, or people according to a rule-governed system.

melting pot A term referring to the assimilation of diverse ethnic groups into one national mainstream.

mental retardation A condition in which learning proceeds at a significantly slow rate, is limited to concrete experiences, and is accompanied by difficulty functioning in social environments.

metacognition Knowledge about the operations of cognition and how to use them to achieve a learning goal.

microcomputer-based laboratory (MBL) A microcomputer with attached sensors and probes that can quickly represent such data as temperature or speed in multiple ways in order to help students explore concepts, test hypotheses, and repair scientific misconceptions.

microworld A computer scenario intended to foster cognitive development and overcome misconceptions by allowing students the chance to explore relationships among variables or concepts and build personal models of how things work.

mnemonic device A memory-directed tactic that helps a learner transform or organize information to enhance its retrievability.

morality of constraint Piaget's term for the moral thinking of children up to age ten or so, in which they hold sacred rules that permit no exceptions and make no allowance for intentions. Also called *moral realism*.

morality of cooperation Piaget's term for the moral thinking of children age eleven or older, based on flexible rules and considerations of intent. Also called *moral relativism*.

moratorium status An adolescent identity status marked by various kinds of identity crises, often involving experimentation and restless searching.

multicultural education An approach to learning and teaching that seeks to foster an understanding of and mutual respect for the values, beliefs, and practices of different cultural groups.

multidisciplinary assessment team A group of people involved in determining the nature of a child's disability, typically consisting of a school psychologist, guidance counselor, classroom teacher, school social worker, school nurse, learning disability specialist, physician, and psychiatrist.

multimedia The combination of several forms of media such as text, graphics, animation, sound, images, and video that teachers can use to enrich student understanding and address various student learning styles, preferences, and impairments. (*See* **dual coding theory; hypermedia**)

negative reinforcement A way of strengthening a target behavior by removing an aversive stimulus after a particular behavior is exhibited. (*See* **positive reinforcement**)

negative transfer A situation in which one's prior learning interferes with subsequent learning. (*See* **positive transfer**)

no-lose method A conflict-resolving procedure that involves discussing problems and coming up with a mutually agreeable compromise.

normal curve The bell-shaped distribution of scores that tends to occur when a particular characteristic is measured in thousands of people.

norm group A sample of individuals carefully chosen to reflect the larger population of students for whom a test is intended.

norm-referenced grading A system of grading that assumes classroom achievement will vary among a group of heterogeneous students because of such differences as prior knowledge, learning skills, motivation, and aptitude, and so compares the score of each student to the scores of other students in order to determine grades.

norm-referenced test A test in which individual performance is evaluated with reference to the performance of a norm group.

observational learning (*See* **social learning theory**)

operant conditioning The theory of behavior developed by B. F. Skinner, based on the fact that organisms respond to their environments in particular ways to obtain or avoid particular consequences.

organization The tendency to systematize and combine processes into coherent general systems.

peer tutoring An approach to learning that involves the teaching of one student by another, based on evidence that a child's cognitive growth benefits from exposure to alternative cognitive schemes.

percentile rank A score that indicates the percentage of students who are at or below a given student's achievement level, providing specific information about relative position.

perceptual centration The tendency to focus attention on only one characteristic of an object or aspect of a problem or event at a time.

performance tests Assessment devices that attempt to gauge how well students can use basic knowledge and skill to perform complex tasks or solve problems under more or less realistic conditions. Also called *performance-based assessment* and *authentic assessment*.

permissive parents Parents who make few demands on their children and fail to discourage immature behavior, thus reflecting their own tendency to be disorganized, inconsistent, and lacking in confidence.

play behavior Kinds of free play observed in preschool children and described by Mildred Parten as consisting of six types: unoccupied, solitary, onlooker, parallel, associative, and cooperative.

portfolio A collection of one or more pieces of a person's work, some of which typically demonstrate different stages of completion.

positive reinforcement A way of strengthening a target behavior (increasing and maintaining the probability that a particular behavior will be repeated) by supplying a positive stimulus immediately after a desired response. (*See* **negative reinforcement**)

positive transfer A situation in which prior learning aids subsequent learning, when, for example, a new learning task calls for essentially the same response that was made to a similar earlier-learned task. (*See* **negative transfer**)

Premack principle A shaping technique that allows students to indulge in a favorite activity after completing a set of instructional objectives. Also called *Grandma's rule*. (*See* **shaping**)

problem-based learning (PBL) An instructional method that requires learners to develop solutions to authentic and complex problems through problem analysis, hypothesis generation, collaboration, reflection, and extensive teacher coaching and facilitation.

problem representation/framing The process of finding ways to express a problem so as to recall the optimal amount of solution-relevant information from long-term memory. (*See* **long-term memory**)

problem solving The identification and application of knowledge and skills that result in goal attainment.

programmed instruction A method of instruction developed by B. F. Skinner that presents specially designed written material to students in a predetermined sequence.

project-based learning An approach to teaching and learning that attempts to motivate students through collaborative investigations of real-world problems that result in tangible products.

psychological androgyny An acquired sense of gender that combines traditional masculine and feminine traits.

psychomotor domain taxonomy A classification of instructional outcomes that focuses on physical abilities and skills.

psychosocial moratorium A period of identity development marked by a delay of commitment, ideally a time of adventure and exploration having a positive, or at least neutral, impact on the individual and society.

punishment A method of weakening a target behavior by presenting an aversive stimulus after the behavior occurs.

real-time chatting The sending and receiving of synchronous or real-time messages in a public or private area on a computer network.

recognition A cognitive process that involves noting key features of a stimulus and relating them to previously stored information in an interactive manner.

reflective A learning style in which students collect and analyze information before offering an answer to a question or a solution to a problem.

reflective teaching A way of teaching that blends artistic and scientific elements through thoughtful analysis of classroom activity.

regrouping A form of ability grouping that brings together students of the same age, ability, and grade but from different classrooms, for instruction in a specific subject, usually reading or mathematics.

rejecting-neglecting parents Parents who make no demands on their children, provide no structure at home, and do not support their children's goals, activities, and emotional needs.

reliability Consistency in test results, related to the assumption that human characteristics are relatively stable over short periods of time.

response cost The withdrawal of previously earned positive reinforcers as a consequence of undesirable behavior, often used with a token economy. (*See* **token economy**)

ripple effect The extent to which an entire class responds to a reprimand directed at only one student.

role confusion Uncertainty as to what behaviors will elicit a favorable reaction from others.

rubric A scoring guide used in performance assessment that helps define and clarify levels of student performance from poor to exemplary.

scaffolding Supporting learning during its early phases through such techniques as demonstrating how tasks should be accomplished, giving hints to the correct solution to a problem or answer to a question, and providing leading questions. As students become more capable of working independently, these supports are withdrawn.

schema An abstract information structure by which our store of knowledge is organized in long-term memory. The plural is *schemas* or *schemata*. (*See* **long-term memory**)

scheme An organized pattern of behavior or thought that children formulate as they interact with their environment, parents, teachers, and agemates.

scholastic aptitude The cognitive skills that most directly relate to and best predict the ability to cope with academic demands. Often used as a synonym for *intelligence*.

scientific concepts A term coined by Russian psychologist Lev Vygotsky to denote such psychological tools as language, formulas, rules, and symbols that are learned mostly with the aid of formal instruction.

self-actualization The movement toward full development of a person's potential talents and capabilities.

self-concept A self-description of one's physical, social, emotional, and cognitive attributes. (*See* **self-esteem; self-image**)

self-efficacy The degree to which people believe they are capable or prepared to handle particular tasks.

self-esteem The evaluative judgments made about self-attributed qualities. (*See* **self-concept; self-image**)

self-fulfilling prophecy The tendency of students to achieve the levels expected of them by their teachers. Also called the *Pygmalion effect* (*See* **teacher expectancy effect)**

self-image A mental self-portrait composed of self-concept and self-esteem elements. (*See* **self-concept; self-esteem**)

self-reinforcement A situation in which the individual strives to meet personal standards and does not depend on or care about the reactions of others.

sensory register (SR) The primary memory store that records temporarily (for one to three seconds) an incoming flow of data from the sense receptors.

serial position effect The tendency to learn and remember words at the beginning and end of a list more easily than those in the middle.

sexually transmitted diseases (STDs) Contagious diseases, such as HIV/AIDS, gonorrhea, and herpes, that are spread by sexual contact.

shaping Promoting the learning of complex behaviors by reinforcing successive approximations to the terminal behavior.

short-term memory (STM) The second temporary memory store, which holds about seven bits of information for about twenty seconds. (Also called *working memory*)

simulation programs Highly individualized and flexible programs that allow learners to test hypotheses, display knowledge, repair errors in thinking, and solve problems in an artificial environment that imitates the real world.

single-subject achievement test A test designed to assess learning or achievement in a particular basic school subject, such as reading or mathematics.

situated learning The idea that problem-solving skills, cognitive strategies, and knowledge are closely linked to the specific context or environment in which they are acquired; hence, the more authentic, or true to life, the task, the more meaningful the learning. Also called *situated cognition*. (*See* **cognitive apprenticeship; inert knowledge; teleapprenticeship**)

social class An individual's or a family's relative standing in society, determined by such factors as income, occupation, education, place of residence, types of associations, manner of dress, and material possessions.

social constructivism A form of constructivist learning theory that emphasizes how people use such cultural tools as language, mathematics, and approaches to problem solving in social settings to construct a common or shared understanding of the world in which they live. (*See* **constructivism**)

social learning theory A theory, exemplified in the work of Albert Bandura, that deemphasizes the role of reinforcement in learning by attributing initial changes in behavior to the observation and imitation of a model. Also called *observational learning*.

socioeconomic status (SES) A quantifiable level of social standing, determined by the federal government on the basis of a person's income, occupation, and education. (*See* **social class**)

special-purpose achievement test A test to determine specific qualifications, such as the College-Level Examination Program or the National Teacher Examination.

specific objectives Objectives that specify the behavior to be learned, the conditions under which it will be exhibited, and the criterion for acceptable performance.

specific transfer A situation in which prior learning aids subsequent learning because of specific similarities between two tasks.

spontaneous concepts A term coined by Russian psychologist Lev Vygotsky to denote the facts, concepts, and rules that young children acquire as a natural consequence of engaging in everyday activities.

spontaneous recovery The reappearance of a seemingly extinguished behavior. (*See* **extinction**)

standard deviation A statistic that indicates the degree to which scores in a group of tests differ from the average or mean.

standardized tests Assessment tools designed by people with specialized knowledge and applied to all students under the same conditions.

stanine score A statistic reflecting a division of a score distribution into nine groups, with each stanine being one-half of a standard deviation unit.

styles of mental self-government theory A theory of learning style formulated by Robert Sternberg that is based on the different functions and forms of civil government. The theory describes thirteen styles that can vary in terms of function, form, level, scope, and learning.

summative evaluation Testing done for the purpose of assigning a letter or numerical grade to sum up a student's performance at a variety of tasks over time.

table of specifications A table used in exam preparation that notes types and numbers of included test items, ensuring systematic coverage of the subject matter.

taxonomy A classification scheme with categories arranged in hierarchical order.

teacher expectancy effect The tendency of students to behave in ways they think the teacher expects them to behave. Also called *self-fulfilling prophecy*; *Pygmalion effect*.

teaching as an art A way of teaching that involves intangibles such as emotions, values, and flexibility.

teaching as a science A way of teaching based on scientific methods such as sampling, control, objectivity, publication, and replication.

teleapprenticeship The use of networking technologies by experts, mentors, instructors, and peers to demonstrate ideas, pose questions, offer insights, and provide relevant information that can help learners build new knowledge and effectively participate in a learning community. (*See* **cognitive apprenticeship**)

telementoring The use of technology by experts, instructors, and peers to provide various forms of support or assistance (for example, hints, questions, explanations, simplifications, examples.) to help the learner understand a concept or complete a task that may ordinarily be out of reach. (*See* **teleapprenticeship**)

theoretical learning Learning how to use psychological tools across a range of settings and problem types to acquire new knowledge and skills.

theory of identical elements The theory that a similarity between the stimulus and response elements in two different tasks accounts for transfer of learning from one task to the other. (*See* **transfer of learning**)

theory of mind The ability, typically developed by children around the age of four, to be aware of the difference between thinking about something and experiencing that same thing and to predict the thoughts of others.

theory of multiple intelligences A theory formulated by Howard Gardner that describes intelligence as being composed of eight, mostly independent capabilities.

time-out A procedure that weakens a target behavior by temporarily removing the opportunity for the behavior to be rewarded.

token economy A behavior-strengthening technique that uses items of no inherent value to "purchase" other items perceived to be valuable.

transfer of learning A student's ability to apply knowledge and problem-solving skills learned in school to similar but new situations.

triarchic theory of intelligence A theory formulated by Robert Sternberg that describes intelligence as being composed of practical, creative, and analytical components.

T score A standardized test score that ranges from 0 to 100 and uses a preselected mean of 50 to avoid negative values. (*See* **z score**)

tutorial programs Programs that attempt to teach facts, definitions, concepts, and other new material to students in either a step-by-step or a more individualized, branching approach.

validity The extent to which a test measures what it claims to measure.

vicarious reinforcement A situation in which the observer anticipates receiving a reward for behaving in a given way because someone else has been so rewarded.

videoconferencing Real-time communications between two or more locations where participants can see and hear each other and share ideas, opinions, and points of view across time zones and geographic distances.

virtual reality A technology to contextualize a student's experience by immersing him or her in a highly interactive, computer-generated, three-dimensional environment that responds in real time to participant movements using special glasses, body suits, headgear, and/or data gloves.

well-structured problems Clearly formulated problems with known solution procedures and known evaluation standards. (*See* **ill-structured problems**)

within-class ability grouping A form of ability grouping that involves the division of a single class of students into two or three groups for reading and math instruction.

withitness An attribute of teachers who prove to their students that they know what is going on in a classroom and as a result have fewer discipline problems than teachers who lack this characteristic.

World Wide Web A global system of interconnected computers that provides access to a wide variety of data in different formats. Also called *the Internet; the Web; WWW*)

zero transfer A situation in which prior learning has no effect on new learning.

zone of proximal development (ZPD) Vygotsky's term for the difference between what a child can do on his or her own and what can be accomplished with some assistance.

z score A standardized test score that tells how far a given raw score differs from the mean in standard deviation units. (*See* **T score**)

References

Abell, S. K., Bryan, L. A., & Anderson, M. A. (1998). Investigating preservice elementary science teacher reflective thinking using integrated media case-based instruction in elementary science teacher preparation. *Science Education, 82*(4), 491–510.

Abma, J. C., & Sonenstein, F. L. (2001). *Sexual activity and contraceptive practices among teenagers in the United States, 1988 and 1995*. Hyattsville, MD: National Center for Health Statistics. Retrieved January 2, 2002, from www.cdc.gov/nchs/data/series/sr_23/sr23_21.pdf

Achenbach, T. M., & Edelbrock, C. S. (1983). *Manual for the child behavior checklist and revised child behavior profile*. Burlington, VT: University of Vermont.

Adams, G. L., & Engelmann, S. (1996). *Research on direct instruction: 25 years beyond DISTAR*. Seattle, WA: Educational Achievement Systems.

Adelson, J. (1972). The political imagination of the young adolescent. In J. Kagan & R. Coles (Eds.), *Twelve to sixteen: Early adolescence*. New York: Norton.

Adelson, J. (Ed.). (1980). *Handbook of adolescent psychology*. New York: Wiley.

Adelson, J. (1986). *Inventing adolescence: The political psychology of everyday schooling*. New Brunswick, NJ: Transaction Books.

Aedo, I., Miranda, P., Panetsos, F., Torra, N., & Martin, M. (1994). A teaching methodology for the hearing impaired using hypermedia and computer animation. *Journal of Computing in Childhood Education, 5*(3/4), 353–369.

Ainsworth, M. D. S., & Wittig, B. A. (1972). Attachment and exploratory behavior of one-year-olds in a strange situation. In B. M. Foss (Ed.), *Determinants of infant behavior* (Vol. 4). New York: Wiley.

Airasian, P. W. (2001). *Classroom assessment* (4th ed.). Boston: McGraw-Hill.

Airasian, P. W., & Walsh, M. E. (1997). Constructivist cautions. *Phi Delta Kappan, 78*(6), 444–449.

Alessi, S. M., & Pena, C. M. (1999). Promoting a qualitative understanding of physics. *Journal of Computers in Mathematics and Science Teaching, 18*(4), 439–457.

Alexander, P. A., Graham, S., & Harris, K. R. (1998). A perspective on strategy research: Progress and prospects. *Educational Psychology Review, 10*(2), 129–154.

Alfassi, M. (1998). Reading for meaning: The efficacy of reciprocal teaching in fostering reading comprehension in high school students in remedial reading classes. *American Educational Research Journal, 35*(2), 309–332.

Allen, D. (1996). Problem-solving strategies. *Teaching PreK–8, 27*(3), 14–16.

Allen, D. (1997). Math & science motivators. *Teaching PreK–8, 27*(4), 16–18.

Allen, H. A., Splittgerber, F. L., & Manning, M. L. (1993). *Teaching and learning in the middle school*. New York: Merrill.

Allen, N., Christal, M., Perrot, D., Wilson, C., Grote, B., & Earley, M. A. (1999). Native American schools move into the new millennium. *Educational Leadership, 56*(7), 71–74.

Almy, M. C., Chittenden, E., & Miller, P. (1966). *Young children's thinking*. New York: Columbia University, Teacher's College.

Altschuld, J. W. (1995). Evaluating the use of computers in science assessment: Considerations and recommendations. *Journal of Science Education and Technology, 4*(1), 57–64.

American Educational Research Association. (2000). AERA position statement concerning high-stakes testing in preK–12 education. Retrieved January 2, 2002, from www.aera.net/about/policy/stakes.htm

American Psychiatric Association. (1994). *Diagnostic and statistical manual of mental disorders* (4th ed.). Washington, DC: Author.

American Psychological Association. (1997). *Learner-centered psychological principles: A framework for school redesign and reform*. Retrieved January 2, 2002, from www.apa.org/ed/lcp.html

Ames, C., & Ames, R. (1984). Systems of student and teacher motivation: Toward a qualitative definition. *Journal of Educational Psychology, 76*(4), 535–556.

Ames, N. L., & Miller, E. (1994). *Changing middle schools: How to make schools work for young adolescents*. San Francisco: Jossey-Bass.

Amiram, R., Bar-Tal, D., Alona, R., & Peleg, D. (1990). Perception of epistemic authorities by children and adolescents. *Journal of Youth and Adolescence, 19*(5), 495–510.

Anastasi, A., & Urbina, S. (1997). *Psychological testing* (7th ed.). Upper Saddle River, NJ: Prentice Hall.

Anderman, E. M., & Maehr, M. L. (1994). Motivation and schooling in the middle grades. *Review of Educational Research, 64*(2), 287–309.

Anderson, J. B., & Freiberg, H. J. (1995). Using self-assessment as a reflective tool to enhance the student teaching experience. *Teacher Education Quarterly, 22*(1), 77–91.

Anderson, J. R., Greeno, J. G., Reder, L. M., & Simon, H. A. (2000). Perspectives on learning, thinking, and activity. *Educational Researcher, 29*(4), 11–13.

Anderson, J. R., Reder, L. M., & Simon, H. A. (1996). Situated learning and education. *Educational Researcher, 25*(4), 5–11.

Anderson, R. C. (1984). Some reflections on the acquisition of knowledge. *Educational Researcher, 13*(9), 5–10.

Anderson-Inman, L., Knox-Quinn, C., & Horney, M. A. (1996). Computer-based study strategies for students with learning disabilities: Individual differences associated with adoption level. *Journal of Learning Disabilities, 29*(5), 461–484.

André, M. E. D. A., & Anderson, T. H. (1978–1979). The development and evaluation of a self-questioning study technique. *Reading Research Quarterly, 14*(4), 605–623.

Andre, T., & Phye, G. D. (1986). Cognition, learning, and education. In G. D. Phye & T. Andre (Eds.), *Cognitive classroom learning*. Orlando, FL: Academic Press.

Angeli, C., & Cunningham, D. J. (1998). Bubble Dialogue: Tools for supporting literacy and mind. In C. J. Bonk & K. S. King (Eds.), *Electronic collaborators: Learner-centered technologies for literacy, apprenticeship, and discourse* (pp. 81–101). Mahwah, NJ: Erlbaum.

Antil, L. R., Jenkins, J. R., Wayne, S. K., & Vadasy, P. F. (1998). Cooperative learning: Prevalence, conceptualizations, and the relation between research and practice. *Review of Educational Research, 35*(3), 419–454.

Appleton, N. (1983). *Cultural pluralism in education*. New York: Longman.

Archer, S. L. (1982). The lower age boundaries of identity development. *Child Development, 53*(6), 1551–1556.

Archer, S. L. (1991). Identity development, gender differences in. In R. M. Lerner, A. C. Peterson, & J. Brooks-Gunn (Eds.), *Encyclopedia of adolescence*. New York: Garland.

Bonk, C. J., Malikowski, S., Angeli, C., & East, J. (1998). Web-based case conferencing for preservice teacher education: Electronic discourse from the field. *Journal of Educational Computing Research, 19*(3), 267–304.

Bonk, C. J., & Reynolds, T. H. (1992). Early adolescent composing within a generative-evaluative computerized prompting framework. *Computers in Human Behavior, 8*(1), 39–62.

Bonk, C. J., & Sugar, W. A. (1998). Student role play in the World Forum: Analyses of an arctic adventure learning apprenticeship. *Interactive Learning Environments, 6*(1–2), 1–29.

Boone, R., Higgins, K., Notari, A., & Stump, C. S. (1996). Hypermedia pre-reading lessons: Learner-centered software for kindergarten. *Journal of Computing in Childhood Education, 7*(2), 36–69.

Bower, G. H., Clark, M. C., Lesgold, A. M., & Winzenz, D. (1969). Hierarchical retrieval schemes in recall of categorized word lists. *Journal of Verbal Learning and Verbal Behavior, 8*(3), 323–343.

Bowman, B. T. (1989). Educating language-minority children: Challenges and opportunities. *Phi Delta Kappan, 71*(2), 118–120.

Boyer, E. L. (1983). *High school.* New York: Harper & Row.

Bracey, G. W. (1983). On the compelling need to go beyond minimum competency. *Phi Delta Kappan, 64*(10), 717–721.

Bracey, G. W. (2000). The 10th Bracey report on the condition of public education. *Phi Delta Kappan, 82*(2), 133–144.

Bradsher, M. (1996). Making friends in the global village: Tips on international collaborations. *Learning and Leading with Technology, 23*(6), 58–61.

Bransford, J. D., Sherwood, R., Vye, N., & Rieser, J. (1986). Teaching thinking and problem solving: Research foundations. *American Psychologist, 41*(10), 1078–1089.

Bransford, J. D., Sharp, D. M., Vye, N. J., Goldman, S. R., Hasselbring, T. S., Goin, L., O'Banion, K., Liverois, J., Saul, E., & the Cognition and Technology Group at Vanderbilt. (1996). MOST environments for accelerating literacy development. In S. Vosniadou, E. De Corte, R. Glaser, & H. Mandl (Eds.), *International perspectives on the design of technology-supported learning environments* (pp. 223–255). Hillside, NJ: Erlbaum.

Bransford, J. D., & Stein, B. S. (1993). *The ideal problem solver* (2nd ed.). New York: Freeman.

Braun, C. (1976). Teacher expectations: Sociopsychological dynamics. *Review of Educational Research, 46*(2), 185–213.

Brent, G., & DiObilda, N. (1993). Effects of curriculum alignment versus direct instruction of urban children. *Journal of Educational Research, 86*(6), 333–338.

Brewer, D. J., Rees, D. I., & Argys, L. M. (1995). Detracking America's schools: The reform without cost? *Phi Delta Kappan, 77*(3), 210–215.

Brittain, C. V. (1967). An exploration of the bases of peer compliance and parent-compliance in adolescence. *Adolescence, 2*(8), 445–458.

Brody, N. (1992). *Intelligence* (2nd ed.). San Diego, CA: Academic Press.

Brooks, H. B., & Brooks, D. W. (1996). The emerging role of CD-ROMs in teaching chemistry. *Journal of Science Education and Technology, 5*(3), 203–215.

Brooks, M. G., & Brooks, J. G. (1999a). The courage to be constructivist. *Educational Leadership, 57*(3), 18–24.

Brooks, J. G., & Brooks, M G. (1999b). *In search of understanding: The case for constructivist classrooms* (rev. ed.). Alexandria, VA: Association for Supervision and Curriculum Development.

Brophy, J. E. (1979). Teacher behavior and its effects. *Journal of Educational Psychology, 71*(6), 733–750.

Brophy, J. E. (1981). Teacher praise: A functional analysis. *Review of Educational Research, 51*(1), 5–32.

Brophy, J. E. (1983). Research on the self-fulfilling prophecy and teacher expectations. *Journal of Educational Psychology, 75*(5), 631–661.

Brophy, J. E., & Alleman, J. (1991). Activities as instructional tools: A framework for analysis and evaluation. *Educational Researcher, 20*(4), 9–23.

Brophy, J. E., & Evertson, C. M. (1976). *Learning from teaching.* Boston: Allyn & Bacon.

Brown, A. L., Campione, J. C., & Day, J. D. (1981). Learning to learn: On training students to learn from text. *Educational Researcher, 10*(2), 14–24.

Brown, J. S., Collins, A., & Duguid, P. (1989). Situated cognition and the culture of learning. *Educational Researcher, 18*(1), 32–42.

Brown, R. (1973). *A first language: The early stages.* Cambridge, MA: Harvard University Press.

Brown, S. M., & Walberg, H. J. (1993). Motivational effects on test scores of elementary students. *Journal of Educational Research, 86*(3), 133–136.

Bruce, B., Peyton, J. K., & Batson, T. (Eds.). (1993). *Network-based classrooms: Realities and promises.* New York: Cambridge University Press.

Bruner, J. S. (1960). *The process of education.* New York: Vintage Books.

Bruner, J. S. (1983). *In search of mind: Essays in autobiography.* New York: Harper & Row.

Brush, T. A., Armstrong, J., Barbrow, D., & Ulintz, L. (1999). Design and delivery of integrated learning systems: Their impact on student achievement and attitudes. *Journal of Educational Computing Research, 21*(4), 475–486.

Burch, C. B. (1993). Teachers vs. professors: The university's side. *Educational Leadership, 51*(2), 68–76.

Burden, P. R. (2000). *Powerful classroom management strategies: Motivating students to learn.* Thousand Oaks, CA: Corwin.

Bushrod, G., Williams, R. L., & McLaughlin, T. F. (1995). An evaluation of a simplified daily report system with two kindergarten pupils. *B. C. Journal of Special Education, 19* (1), 35–43.

Cain, K. M., & Dweck, C. S. (1995). The relation between motivational patterns and achievement cognitions through the elementary school years. *Merrill-Palmer Quarterly, 41*(1), 25–52.

Callahan, C. M., & McIntire, J. A. (1994). *Identifying outstanding talent in American Indian and Alaska native students.* Washington, DC: U. S. Department of Education, Office of Educational Research and Improvement.

Callear, D. (1999). Intelligent tutoring environments as teacher substitutes: Use and feasibility. *Educational Technology, 39*(5), 6–8.

Callister, T. A., & Dunne, F. (1992). The computer as doorstop: Technology as disempowerment. *Phi Delta Kappan, 74*(4), 324–326.

Cameron, J., & Pierce, W. D. (1994). Reinforcement, reward, and intrinsic motivation: A meta-analysis. *Review of Educational Research, 64*(3), 363–423.

Campbell, L. (1997). How teachers interpret MI theory. *Educational Leadership, 55*(1), 14–19.

Canady, R. L., & Hotchkiss, P. R. (1989). It's a good score! Just a bad grade. *Phi Delta Kappan, 71*(1), 68–71.

Cangelosi, J. S. (2000). *Classroom management strategies: Gaining and maintaining students' cooperation* (4th ed.). New York: Wiley.

Cardon, P. L., & Christensen, K. W. (1998). Technology-based programs for drop-out prevention. *Journal of Technology Studies, 24*(1), 50–54.

Cardwell, K. (2000). Electronic assessment. *Learning and Leading with Technology, 27*(7), 22–26.

Carney, R. N., & Levin, J. R. (2000). Mnemonic instruction, with a focus on transfer. *Journal of Educational Psychology, 92*(4), 783–790.

Carney, R. N., Levin, J. R., & Levin, M. E. (1994). Enhancing the psychology of memory by enhancing memory of psychology. *Teaching of Psychology, 21*(3), 171–174.

Carrasquillo, A. L. (1991). *Hispanic children and youth in the United States: A resource guide*. New York: Garland.

Carrasquillo, A. L. (1994). *Teaching English as a second language: A resource guide*. New York: Garland.

Carroll, J. B. (1963). A model of school learning. *Teachers College Record, 64*, 723–733.

Carroll, T., Knight, C., & Hutchinson, E. (1995). Carmen Sandiego: Crime can pay when it comes to learning. *Social Education, 59*(3), 165–169.

Carter, C. J. (1997). Why reciprocal teaching? *Educational Leadership, 54*(6), 64–68.

Carter, D. B. (1987) The role of peers in sex role socialization. In D. B. Carter (Ed.), *Current Conceptions of Sex Roles and Sex Typing.* New York: Praeger.

Carver, S. M. (1995). Cognitive apprenticeships: Putting theory into practice on a large scale. In C. A. Hedley, P. Antonacci, & M. Rabinowitz (Eds.), *Thinking and literacy: The mind at work* (pp. 203–228). Hillsdale, NJ: Erlbaum.

Case, R. (1975). Gearing the demands of instruction to the developmental capacities of the learner. *Review of Educational Research, 45*(1), 59–88.

Casey, J., & Martin, L. (1994). Literacy instruction in an integrated curriculum. *Computing Teacher, 21*(5), 33–34, 36–37.

Cassidy, J., & Johnson, N. (1986). Federal and state definitions of giftedness: Then and now. *Gifted Child Today, 9*(6), 15–21.

Chaillé, C., & Britain, L. (1991). *The young child as scientist: A constructivist approach to early childhood science education* (2nd ed.). New York: Longman.

Chance, P. (1992). The rewards of learning. *Phi Delta Kappan, 74*(3), 200–207.

Chance, P. (1993). Sticking up for rewards. *Phi Delta Kappan, 74*(10), 787–790.

Character Education Partnership. (2000). *Eleven principles of effective character education.* Retrieved January 2, 2002, from www.character.org/

Checkley, K. (1997). The first seven . . . . and the eighth: A conversation with Howard Gardner. *Educational Leadership, 55*(1), 8–13.

Chia, J., & Duthie, B.(1993). Primary children and computer-based art work. *Art Education, 46*(6), 23–26, 35–41.

Chinn, P. C., & Plata, M. (1987/1988). Multicultural education: Beyond ethnic studies. *Teacher Education and Practice, 4*(2), 7–10.

Choate, J. S. (Ed.).(2000). *Successful inclusive teaching: Proven ways to detect and correct special needs* (3rd ed.). Boston: Allyn & Bacon.

Chrenka, Lynn. (2001). Misconstructing constructivism. *Phi Delta Kappan, 82*(9), 694–695.

Christmann, E. P., Badgett, J. L., & Lucking, R. A. (1997). Progressive comparison of the effects of computer-assisted instruction on the academic achievements of secondary students. *Journal of Research on Computing in Education, 29*(4), 325–337.

Christmann, E. P., Lucking, R. A., & Badgett, J. L. (1997). The effectiveness of computer-assisted instruction on the academic achievement of secondary students: A meta-analytic comparison between urban, suburban, and rural educational settings. *Computer in the Schools, 13*(3/4), 31–40.

Cicchetti, D., & Toth, S. L. (1998). The development of depression in children and adolescents. *American Psychologist, 53*(2), 221–241.

Clariana, R. B. (1996). Differential achievement gains for mathematics computation, concepts, and applications with an integrated learning system. *Journal of Computers in Mathematics and Science Teaching, 15*(3), 203–215.

Clariana, R. B. (1997). Considering learning style in computer-assisted learning. *British Journal of Educational Technology, 28*(1), 66–68.

Clark, C. M. (1995). *Thoughtful teaching.* New York: Teachers College Press.

Clark, J. M., & Paivio, A. (1991). Dual coding theory and education. *Educational Psychology Review, 3*(3), 149–210.

Clausen, J. (1975). The social meaning of differential physical and sexual maturation. In S. Dragastin & G. H. Elder, Jr. (Eds.), *Adolescence in the life cycle.* New York: Wiley.

Clements, D. H., & Nastasi, B. K. (1999). Metacognition, learning, and educational computer environments. *Information Technology in Childhood Education Annual,* 5–38.

Cobb, P., & Bowers, J. (1999). Cognitive and situated learning perspectives in theory and practice. *Educational Researcher, 28*(2), 4–15.

Cognition and Technology Group at Vanderbilt. (1990). Anchored instruction and its relationship to situated cognition. *Educational Researcher, 19*(6), 2–10.

Cognition and Technology Group at Vanderbilt. (1991). Some thoughts about constructivism and instructional design. *Educational Technology, 31*(9), 16–18.

Cognition and Technology Group at Vanderbilt. (1992a). The Jasper series: A generative approach to improving mathematical thinking. In K. Sheingold, L. G. Roberts, & S. M. Malcolm (Eds.), *This year in school science 1991: Technology for teaching and learning.* Washington, DC: American Association for the Advancement of Science.

Cognition and Technology Group at Vanderbilt. (1992b). The Jasper series as an example of anchored instruction: Theory, program description, and assessment data. *Educational Psychologist, 27*(3), 291–315.

Cognition and Technology Group at Vanderbilt. (1993). Anchored instruction and situated cognition revisited. *Educational Technology, 33* (3), 52–70.

Cognition and Technology Group at Vanderbilt. (1994). Multimedia environments for developing literacy for at-risk students. In B. Means (Ed.), *Technology and educational reform: The reality behind the promise* (pp. 23–56). San Francisco, CA: Jossey-Bass.

Cognition and Technology Group at Vanderbilt. (1996). Looking at technology in context: A framework for understanding technology and education research. In D. C. Berliner & R. C. Calfee (Eds.), *Handbook of educational psychology* (pp. 807–840). New York: Simon & Schuster.

Colangelo, N., & Davis, G. A. (Eds.).(1997). *Handbook of gifted education* (2d ed.). Boston: Allyn & Bacon.

Coleman, J. C. (1980). Friendship and the peer group in adolescence. In J. Adelson (Ed.), *Handbook of adolescent psychology.* New York: Wiley.

Collier, C. (1999). Project-based student technology competencies. *Learning and Leading with Technology, 27*(3), 50–53.

Collins, A. (1996). Design issues for learning environments. In S. Vosniadou, E. De Corte, R. Glaser, & H. Mandl (Eds.), *International perspectives on the design of technology-supported learning environments* (pp. 347–361). Mahwah, NJ: Erlbaum.

Colten, M. E., & Gore, S. (Eds.).(1991). *Adolescent stress.* New York: Aldine de Gruyter.

Combs, A. W. (1965). *The professional education of teachers.* Boston: Allyn and Bacon.

Conger, J. J., & Galambos, N. L. (1997). *Adolescence and youth* (5th ed.). New York: Longman.

Connell, J. P., Halpern-Felsher, B. L., Clifford, E. L., Crichlow, W., & Usinger, P. (1995). Hanging in there: Behavioral, psychological, and contextual factors affecting whether African American adolescents stay in school. *Journal of Adolescent Research, 10*(1), 41–63.

Consortium for Research on Black Adolescence. (1990). *Black adolescence: Current issues and annotated bibliography*. Boston: G. K. Hall.

Cooper, H. M. (1979). Pygmalion grows up: A model for teacher expectation, communication, and performance influence. *Review of Educational Research, 49*(3), 389–410.

Cooper, H., & Dorr, N. (1995). Race comparisons on need for achievement: A meta-analytic alternative to Graham's narrative review. *Review of Educational Research, 65*(4), 438–508.

Copen, P. (1995). Connecting classrooms through telecommunications. *Educational Leadership, 53*(2), 44–47.

Cordova, D. I., & Lepper, M. R. (1996). Intrinsic motivation and the process of learning: Beneficial effects of contextualization, personalization, and choice. *Journal of Educational Psychology, 88*(4), 715–730.

Corno, L. (1986). Teaching and self-regulated learning. In D. C. Berliner & B. V. Rosenshine (Eds.), *Talks to teachers*. New York: Random House.

Corston, R., & Colman, A. (1996). Gender and social facilitation effects on computer competence and attitudes toward computers. *Journal of Educational Computing Research, 14*(2), 171–183.

Cosgrove, D. J. (1959). Diagnostic ratings of teacher performance. *Journal of Educational Psychology, 50*(5), 200–204.

Covington, M. V. (1985). Strategic thinking and the fear of failure. In J. W. Segal, S. F. Chipman, & R. Glaser (Eds.), *Thinking and learning skills* (Vol. 1). Hillsdale, NJ: Erlbaum.

Covington, M. V. (1999). Caring about learning: The nature and nurturing of subject-matter appreciation. *Educational Psychologist, 34*(2), 127–136.

Cox, B. D. (1997). The rediscovery of the active learner in adaptive contexts: A developmental-historical analysis of transfer of training. *Educational Psychologist, 32*(1), 41–55.

Crain, W. (2000). *Theories of development: Concepts and applications* (4th ed.). Upper Saddle River, NJ: Prentice-Hall.

Crooks, T. J. (1988). The impact of classroom evaluation practices on students. *Review of Educational Research, 58*(4), 438–481.

Cruickshank, D. R. (1990). *Research that informs teachers and teacher educators*. Bloomington, IN: Phi Delta Kappa Educational Foundation.

Csikszentmihalyi, M., & Larson, R. (1984). *Being adolescent*. New York: Basic Books.

Cuban, L. (1986). *Teachers and machines: The classroom use of technology since 1920*. New York: Teachers College Press.

Cuban, L. (1990). What I learned from what I had forgotten about teaching: Notes from a professor. *Phi Delta Kappan, 71*(6), 479–482.

Cummins, J. (1999). Alternative paradigms in bilingual education research. *Educational Researcher, 28*(7), 26–32, 41.

Cunningham, D. J. (1991). In defense of extremism. *Educational Technology, 31*(9), 26–27.

Cunningham, D. J. (2001, April). *Fear and loathing in the information age.* Paper presented at the annual meeting of the American Educational Research Association, Seattle, WA.

Dai, D. Y., Moon, S. M., & Feldhusen, J. F. (1998). Achievement motivation and gifted students: A social cognitive perspective. *Educational Psychologist, 33*(2/3), 45–63.

Daiute, C. (1985). Issues in using computers to socialize the writing process. *Educational Communication and Technology, 33*(1), 41–50.

Damon, W. (1988). *The moral child.* New York: Free Press.

Damon, W., & Hart, D. (1988). *Self-understanding in childhood and adolescence*. New York: Cambridge University Press.

Damon, W., & Phelps, E. (1991). Peer collaboration as a context for cognitive growth. In L. T. Landsmann (Ed.), *Culture, schooling, and psychological development.* Norwood, NJ: Ablex.

Dana, R. H. (1993). *Multicultural assessment perspectives for professional psychology*. Boston: Allyn & Bacon.

Danielson, C. (1997). *A collection of performance tasks and rubrics: Middle school mathematics*. Larchmont, NY: Eye on Education.

Danielson, C., & Marquez, E. (1998). *A collection of performance tasks and rubrics: High school mathematics*. Larchmont, NY: Eye on Education.

Darling-Hammond, L., Ancess, J., & Falk, B. (1995). *Authentic assessment in action*. New York: Teachers College Press.

Darling-Hammond, L., & Falk, B. (1997). Using standards and assessments to support student learning. *Phi Delta Kappan, 79*(3), 190–199.

Dasen, P., & Heron, A. (1981). Cross-cultural tests of Piaget's theory. In H. C. Triandis & A. Heron (Eds.),*Handbook of cross-cultural psychology, developmental psychology* (Vol. 4). Boston: Allyn & Bacon.

Datnow, A., & Castellano, M. (2000). Teachers' responses to Success for All: How beliefs, experiences, and adaptations shape implementations. *American Educational Research Journal, 37*(3), 775–799.

Davey, T., Godwin, J., & Mittelholtz, D. (1997). Developing and scoring an innovative computerized writing assessment. *Journal of Educational Measurement, 34*(1), 21–41.

Davidson-Shivers, G. V., Rasmussen, K. L., & Bratton-Jeffery, M. F. (1997). Investigating learning strategies generation in a hypermedia environment using qualitative methods. *Journal of Computing in Childhood Education, 8*(2/3), 247–261.

Davies, L. J. (1984). Teaching university students how to learn. *Improving University and College Teaching, 31*(4), 160–165.

Dawe, H. A. (1984). Teaching: A performing art. *Phi Delta Kappan, 65*(8), 548–552.

deCharms, R. (1976). *Enhancing motivation: Change in the classroom*. New York: Irvington.

de Jong, T., & van Joolingen, W. R. (1998). Scientific discovery learning with computer simulations of conceptual domains. *Review of Educational Research, 68*(2), 179–201.

Dede, C. (1996). The evolution of distance education: Emerging technologies and distributed learning. *American Journal of Distance Education, 10*(2), 4–36.

Dempster, F. N. (1988). The spacing effect: A case study in the failure to apply the results of psychological research. *American Psychologist, 43*(8), 627–634.

Derry, S., & Lesgold, A. (1996). Toward a situated social practice model for instructional design. In D. C. Berliner & R. C. Calfee (Eds.), *Handbook of educational psychology* (pp. 787–806). New York: Simon & Schuster.

DeVillar, R. A., Faltis, C. J., & Cummins, J. P. (Eds.).(1994). *Cultural diversity in schools: From rhetoric to practice*. Albany, NY: State University of New York Press.

DeVries, R. (1997). Piaget's social theory. *Educational Researcher, 26*(2), 4–17.

Dickinson, K. (1997). Distance learning on the Internet: Testing students using web forms and the computer gateway interface. *TechTrends, 42*(2), 38–42.

Dickson, W. P. (1985). Thought-provoking software: Juxtaposing symbol systems. *Educational Researcher, 14*(5), 30–38.

DiGiulio, R. (2000). *Positive classroom management* (2nd ed.). Thousand Oaks, CA: Corwin.

Dill, E. M., & Boykin, A. W. (2000). The comparative influence of individual, peer tutoring, and communal learning contexts of the text recall of African American children. *Journal of Black Psychology, 26*(1), 65–78.

Dillon, A., & Gabbard, R. (1998). Hypermedia as an educational technology: A review of the quantitative research literature on learner comprehension, control,

and style. *Review of Educational Research, 68*(3), 322–349.
diSibio, M. (1982). Memory for connected discourse: A constructivist view. *Review of Educational Research, 52*(2), 149–174.
Dochy, F., Segers, M., & Buehl, M. M. (1999). The relation between assessment practices and outcomes of studies: The case of research on prior knowledge. *Review of Educational Research, 69*(2), 145–186.
Doerr, H. M. (1996). Integrating the study of trigonometry, vectors, and force through modeling. *School Science and Mathematics, 96*(8), 407–418.
Donahue, P. L., Finnegan, R. J., Lutkus, A. D., Allen, N. L., & Campbell, J. R. (2001). *The nation's report card: Fourth-grade reading 2000*. Washington, DC: National Center for Educational Statistics. Retrieved January 2, 2002, from nces.ed.gov/nationsreportcard/pubs/main2000/2001499.asp
Doyle, W. (1983). Academic work. *Review of Educational Research, 53*(2), 159–200.
Driscoll, M. P. (2000). *Psychology of learning and instruction* (2nd ed.). Boston: Allyn & Bacon.
Duell, O. K. (1986). Metacognitive skills. In G. D. Phye & T. Andre (Eds.), *Cognitive classroom learning*. Orlando, FL: Academic Press.
Duff, C. (2000). Online mentoring. *Educational Leadership, 58*(2), 49–52.
Duffy, T. M., & Cunningham, D. J. (1996). Constructivism: Implications for the design and delivery of instruction. In D. Jonassen (Ed.), *Handbook of research for educational communications and technology* (pp. 170–198). New York: Macmillan Library Reference.
Dunn, R., & Dunn, K. (1992). *Teaching elementary students through their individual learning styles*. Boston: Allyn & Bacon.
Dunn, R., & Dunn, K. (1993). *Teaching secondary students through their individual learning styles*. Boston: Allyn & Bacon.
Dusek, J. B. (1996). *Adolescent development and behavior* (3rd ed.). Upper Saddle River, NJ: Prentice-Hall.
Dweck, C. S. (1986). Motivational processes affecting learning. *American Psychologist, 41*(10), 1040–1048.
Eakin, S. S. (1997). Educators on the edge: Spreading the wise use of technology. *Technos, 6*(3), 15–22.
Ebert, E., & Strudler, N. (1996). Improving science learning using low-cost multimedia. *Learning and Leading with Technology, 24*(1), 23–26.
Eby, J. W. (1994). *Reflective planning, teaching, and evaluation: K–12*. New York: Merrill.
Eccles, J. S., Midgley, C., Wigfield, A., Buchanan, C. M., Reuman, D., Flanagan, C., & Mac Iver, D. (1993). Development during adolescence: The impact of stage-environment fit on young adolescents' experiences in schools and families. *American Psychologist, 48*(2), 90–101.
Edelson, D. C., Pea, R. D., & Gomez, L. (1996). Constructivism in the collaboratory. In B. G. Wilson (Ed.), *Constructivist learning environments: Case studies in instructional design* (pp. 151–164). Englewood Cliffs, NJ: Educational Technology Publications.
Edmunds, R. D. (Ed.). (1980). *American Indian leaders: Studies in diversity*. Lincoln, NE: University of Nebraska Press.
Education Week on the Web. (2001). Quality counts 2001: A better balance. Retrieved January 2, 2002, from www.edweek.org/sreports/qc01/
Egeland, P. (1996/1997). Pulleys, planes, and student performance. *Educational Leadership, 54*(4), 41–45.
Ehman, L. H., Glenn, A. D., Johnson, V., & White, C. S. (1992). Using computer databases in student problem solving: A study of eight social studies teachers' classrooms. *Theory and Research in Social Education, 20*(2), 179–206.
Eisenberger, R., & Cameron, J. (1996). Detrimental effects of reward: Reality or myth? *American Psychologist, 51*(11), 1153–1166.
Eisenman, G., & Payne, B. D. (1997). Effects of the higher order thinking skills program on at-risk young adolescents' self-concept, reading achievement, and thinking skills. *Research in Middle Level Education Quarterly, 20*(3), 1–25.
Eisner, E. W. (1999). The uses and limits of performance assessment. *Phi Delta Kappan, 80*(9), 658–660.
Elkind, D. (1968). Cognitive development in adolescence. In J. F. Adams (Ed.), *Understanding adolescence*. Boston: Allyn & Bacon.
Elkind, D. (1989). Developmentally appropriate practice: Philosophical and practical implications. *Phi Delta Kappan, 71*(2), 113–117.
Ellis, H. C. (1965). *The transfer of learning*. New York: Macmillan.
Ellis, H. C. (1978). *Fundamentals of human learning, memory, and cognition* (2d ed.). Dubuque, IA: William. C. Brown.
Elrich, M. (1994). The stereotype within. *Educational Leadership, 51*(8), 12–15.
Elwell, C. C., Reeve, K., & Hofmeister, A. (1992). Captioning instructional video. *Educational Technology, 32*(8), 45–50.
Emmer, E. T., Evertson, C. M., Clements, B. S., & Worsham, M. E. (2000). *Classroom management for secondary teachers* (5th ed.). Boston: Allyn and Bacon.
Engebretsen, A. (1997). Visualizing least-square lines of best fit. *Mathematics Teacher, 90*(5), 405–408.
Epstein, H. T. (1980). Brain growth and cognitive functioning. In D. R. Steer (Ed.), *The emerging adolescent: Characteristics and educational implications*. Columbus, OH: National Middle School Association.
Erdelyi, M. H., & Goldberg, B. (1979). Let's now sweep repression under the rug: Towards a cognitive psychology of repression. In J. Kihlstrom & F. Evans (Eds.), *Functional disorders of memory*. Hillsdale, NJ: Erlbaum.
Erickson, J., & Lehrer, R. (1998). The evolution of critical standards as students design hypermedia documents. *Journal of the Learning Sciences, 7*(3 & 4), 351–386.
Ericsson, K. A., Chase, W. G., & Faloon, S. (1980). Acquisition of a memory skill. *Science, 208*(4448), 1181–1182.
Erikson, E. H. (1963). *Childhood and society* (2d ed.). New York: Norton.
Erikson, E. H. (1968). *Identity: Youth and crisis*. New York: Norton.
Estep, S. G., McInerney, W. D., Vockell, E., & Kosmoski, G. (1999–2000). An investigation of the relationship between integrated learning systems and academic achievement. *Journal of Educational Technology Systems, 28*(1), 5–19.
Evans, R. I. (1967). *Dialogue with Erik Erikson*. New York: Harper & Row.
Evertson, C. M., Emmer, E. T., Clements, B. S., & Worsham, M. E. (2000). *Classroom management for elementary teachers* (5th ed.). Boston: Allyn and Bacon.
Fabos, B., & Young, M. D. (1999). Telecommunication in the classroom: Rhetoric versus reality. *Review of Educational Research, 69*(3), 217–259.
Fabris, M. E. (1992–1993). Using multimedia in the multicultural classroom. *Journal of Educational Technology Systems, 21*(2), 163–171.
Fagot, B. I. (1978). The influence of sex of child on parental reactions to toddler children. *Child Development, 49*(2), 459–465.
FairTest. (1990). *Standardized tests and our children: A guide to testing reform*. Cambridge, MA: National Center for Fair and Open Testing.
Fantuzzo, J. W., Polite, K., & Grayson, N. (1990). An evaluation of reciprocal peer tutoring across elementary school settings. *Journal of School Psychology, 28*(4), 309–323.
Fantuzzo, J. W., Riggio, R. E., Connelly, S., & Dimeff, L. A. (1989). Effects of reciprocal peer tutoring on academic achievement and psychological adjustment: A component analysis. *Journal of Educational Psychology, 81*(2), 173–177.

Faw, H. W., & Waller, T. G. (1976). Mathemagenic behaviors and efficiency in learning from prose materials. *Review of Educational Research, 46,* 691–720.

Fehrenbach, C. R. (1994). Cognitive styles of gifted and average readers. *Roeper Review, 16*(4), 290–292.

Feist, J., & Feist, G. J. (2001). *Theories of personality* (5th ed.). Dubuque, IA: McGraw-Hill.

Feldhusen, J. F. (1998). Programs for the gifted few or talent development for the many? *Phi Delta Kappan, 79*(10), 735–738.

Ferguson, P., & Womack, S. T. (1993). The impact of subject matter and education coursework on teaching performance. *Journal of Teacher Education, 44*(1), 55–63.

Ferrini-Mundy, J., & Lauten, D. (1994). Learning about calculus learning. *Mathematics Teacher, 87*(2), 115–121.

Feynman, R. P. (1985). *"Surely you're joking, Mr. Feynman."* New York: Norton.

Fischer, C. (1999/2000) An effective (and affordable) intervention model for at-risk high school readers. *Journal of Adolescent and Adult Literacy, 43*(4) 326–335.

Fischer, M. J. (1996). Integrated learning systems: An application linking technology with human factors and pedagogical principles. *Educational Technology Research and Development, 44*(3), 65–72.

Fitzgerald, J. (1995). English-as-a-second-language learners' cognitive reading processes: A review of the research in the United States. *Review of Educational Research, 65*(2), 145–190.

Flanders, N. A. (1970). *Analyzing teacher behavior.* Reading, MA: Addison-Wesley.

Flavell, J. H. (1976). Metacognitive aspects of problem solving. In L. B. Resnick (Ed.), *The nature of intelligence.* Hillsdale, NJ: Erlbaum.

Flavell, J. H. (1987). Speculations about the nature and development of metacognition. In F. E. Weinert & R. H. Kluwe (Eds.), *Metacognition, motivation, and understanding.* Hillsdale, NJ: Erlbaum.

Fletcher-Flinn, C. M., & Gravatt, B. (1995). The efficacy of computer assisted instruction (CAI): A meta-analysis. *Journal of Educational Computing Research, 12*(3), 219–242.

Fletcher-Flinn, C. M., & Suddendorf, T. (1996). Do computers affect "the mind"? *Journal of Educational Computing Research, 15*(2), 97–112.

Flieller, A. (1999). Comparison of the development of formal thought in adolescent cohorts aged 10 to 15 years (1967–1996 and 1972–1993). *Developmental Psychology, 35*(4), 1048–1058.

Flinders, D. J. (1989). Does the "art of teaching" have a future? *Educational Leadership, 46*(8), 16–20.

Foot, H. C., Shute, R. H., & Morgan, M. J. (1990). Theoretical issues in peer tutoring. In H. C. Foot, M. J. Morgan, & R. H. Shute (Eds.), *Children helping children.* New York: Wiley.

Fosnot, C. T. (1996). Constructivism: A psychological theory of learning. In C. T. Fosnot (Ed.), *Constructivism: Theory, perspectives, and practice.* New York: Teachers College Press.

Foster, D. W. (1982). *Sourcebook of Hispanic culture in the United States.* Chicago: American Library Association.

Fox, N. E., & Ysseldyke, J. E. (1997). Implementing inclusion at the middle school level: Lessons from a negative example. *Exceptional Children, 64*(1), 81–98.

Foyle, H. C., Lyman, L., & Thies, S. A. (1991). *Cooperative learning in the early childhood classroom.* Washington, DC: National Education Association.

Frank, S. J., Pirsch, L. A., & Wright, V. C. (1990). Late adolescents' perceptions of their relationships with their parents: Relationships among deidealization, autonomy, relatedness, and insecurity and implications for adolescent adjustment and ego identity status. *Journal of Youth and Adolescence, 19*(6), 571–588.

Freedman, K., & Liu, M. (1996). The importance of computer experience, learning processes, and communication patterns in multicultural networking. *Educational Technology Research and Development, 44*(1), 1042–1629.

Friedenberg, E. Z. (1963). *Coming of age in America: Growth and acquiescence.* New York: Vintage Books.

Fuchs, D., Fuchs, L. S., Mathes, P. G., & Simmons, D. C. (1997). Peer-assisted learning strategies: Making classrooms more responsive to diversity. *American Educational Research Journal, 34*(1), 174–206.

Fuligni, A., & Eccles, J. (1993). Perceived parent-child relationships and early adolescents' orientation toward peers. *Developmental Psychology, 29*(4), 622–632.

Furth, H. G. (1970). *Piaget for teachers.* Englewood Cliffs, NJ: Prentice-Hall.

Gable, R. A., & Warren, S. F. (Ed.).(1993). *Strategies for teaching students with mild to severe mental retardation.* Baltimore, MD: Paul H. Brookes.

Gaffney, J. S., & Anderson, R. C. (1991). Two-tiered scaffolding: Congruent processes of teaching and learning. In E. H. Hiebert (Ed.), *Literacy in a diverse society: Perspectives, practices, and policies* (pp. 141–156). New York: Teachers College Press.

Gage, N. L. (1984). What do we know about teaching effectiveness? *Phi Delta Kappan, 66*(2), 87–93.

Gagné, E. D., Yekovich, C. W., & Yekovich, F. R. (1993). *The cognitive psychology of school learning* (2nd ed.). New York: HarperCollins.

Gall, M. D., Gall, J. P, Jacobsen, D. R., & Bullock, T. L. (1990). *Tools for learning: A guide to teaching study skills.* Alexandria, VA: Association for Supervision and Curriculum Development.

Gallagher, J. J., & Gallagher, S. A. (1994). *Teaching the gifted child.* (4th ed.). Boston: Allyn and Bacon.

Gallagher, P. A. (1995). *Teaching students with behavior disorders: Techniques and activities for classroom instruction.* (2nd ed.). Denver: Love.

Gallimore, R., & Tharp, R. (1990). Teaching mind in society: Teaching, schooling, and literate discourse. In L. C. Moll (Ed.), *Vygotsky and education: Instructional implications and applications of sociohistorical psychology.* Cambridge: Cambridge University Press.

Gan, S. (1999). Motivating at-risk students through computer-based cooperative learning activities. *Educational Horizons, 77*(3), 151–156.

Gantner, M. W. (1997). Lessons learned from my students in the barrio. *Educational Leadership, 54*(7), 44–45.

García, E. (1999). *Student cultural diversity: Understanding and meeting the challenge* (2nd ed.). Boston: Houghton Mifflin.

Garcia, J. (1993). The changing image of ethnic groups in textbooks. *Phi Delta Kappan, 75*(1), 29–35.

Gardner, H. (1983). *Frames of mind: The theory of multiple intelligences.* New York: Basic Books.

Gardner, H. (1991). *The unschooled mind: How children think and how schools should teach.* New York: Basic Books.

Gardner, H., & Hatch, T. (1989). Multiple intelligences go to school. *Educational Researcher, 18*(8), 4–10.

Garland, A. F., & Zigler, E. (1993). Adolescent suicide prevention: Current research and social policy implications. *American Psychologist, 48*(2), 169–182.

Garner, R. (1987). *Metacognition and reading comprehension.* Norwood, NJ: Ablex.

Garrison, J. W. (1997). *Dewey and eros: Wisdom and desire in the art of teaching.* New York: Teachers College Press.

Garrod, A. (Ed.).(1993). *Approaches to moral development: New research and emerging themes.* New York: Teachers College Press.

Gelman, R. (1994). Constructivism and supporting environments. In D. Tirosh (Ed.), *Implicit and explicit knowledge: An educational approach*. Norwood, NJ: Ablex.

Gelman, R., & Baillargeon, E. E. (1983). A review of some Piagetian concepts. In J. H. Flavell & E. M. Markman (Eds.) *Handbook of child development: Vol. 3: Cognitive development* (4th ed.). New York: Wiley.

Genesee, F., & Cloud, N. (1998). Multilingualism *is* basic. *Educational Leadership, 55*(6), 62–65.

Georgi, D., & Crowe, J. (1998). Digital portfolios: A confluence of assessment and technology. *Teacher Education Quarterly, 25*(1), 73–84.

Gersten, R. (1999). The changing face of bilingual education. *Educational Leadership, 56*(7), 41–45.

Gersten, R., & Brengelman, S. U. (1996). The quest to translate research into classroom practice: The emerging knowledge base. *Remedial and Special Education, 17*(2), 67–74.

Gick, M. L. (1986). Problem-solving strategies. *Educational Psychologist, 21*(1,2), 99–120.

Gilligan, C. (1979). Women's place in man's life cycle. *Harvard Educational Review, 49*(4), 431–446.

Gilligan, C. (1982). *In a different voice: Psychological theory and women's development*. Cambridge, MA: Harvard University Press.

Gilligan, C. (1987). Adolescent development reconsidered. In C. E. Irwin, Jr. (Ed.), *Adolescent social behavior and health*. San Francisco: Jossey-Bass.

Gilligan, C. (1988). Exit-voice dilemmas in adolescent development. In C. Gilligan, J. Ward, J. Taylor, & B. Bardige (Eds.), *Mapping the moral domain: A contribution of women's thinking to psychological theory and education*. Cambridge, MA: Harvard University Press.

Ginott, H. (1965). *Between parent and child*. New York: Macmillan.

Ginott, H. (1972). *Teacher and child*. New York: Macmillan.

Ginsburg, H. P., & Opper, S. (1988). *Piaget's theory of intellectual development* (3d ed.). Englewood Cliffs, NJ: Prentice-Hall.

Gipson, J. (1997). Girls and computer technology: Barrier or Key? *Educational Technology, 37*(2), 41–43.

Glasgow, N. J. (1997). Keep up the good work! Part II: Using multimedia to build reading fluency and enjoyment. *Learning and Leading with Technology, 24*(5), 22–25.

Glasser, W. (1986). *Control theory in the classroom*. New York: Harper & Row.

Glasser, W. (1990). *The quality school*. New York: Harper & Row.

Gleason, M. M. (1995). Using direct instruction to integrate reading and writing for students with learning disabilities. *Reading and Writing Quarterly, 11*(1), 91–108.

Gold, M., & Petronio, R. J. (1980). Delinquent behavior in adolescence. In J. Adelson (Ed.), *Handbook of adolescent psychology*. New York: Wiley.

Goldstein, A. P., & Conoley, J. C. (Eds.). (1997). *School violence intervention: A practical handbook*. New York: Guilford Press.

Gollnick, D. A., & Chinn, P. C. (1998). *Multicultural education in a pluralistic society* (5th ed.). Upper Saddle River, NJ: Merrill.

Golub, J. N. (1994). *Activities for the interactive classroom*. Urbana, IL: National Council of Teachers of English.

Gomez, L. M., Fishman, B. J., & Pea, R. D. (1998). The CoVis project: Building a large scale science education testbed. *Interactive Learning Environments, 6*(1–2), 59–92.

Gonzalez, V., Brusca-Vega, R., & Yawkey, T. (1997). *Assessment and instruction of culturally and linguistically diverse students with or at-risk of learning problems: From research to practice*. Boston: Allyn & Bacon.

Good, T. (1982). *Classroom research: What we know and what we need to know* (R&D Rep. No. 9018). Austin: University of Texas, Research and Development Center for Teacher Education.

Good, T. L., & Brophy, J. (1995). *Contemporary educational psychology* (5th ed.). New York: Longman.

Goodlad, J. I. (1984). *A place called school*. New York: McGraw-Hill.

Goodrich, H. (1996/1997). Understanding rubrics. *Educational Leadership, 54*(4), 14–17.

Gordon, S., & Gilgun, J. F. (1987). Adolescent sexuality. In V. B. van Hasselt & M. Hersen (Eds.), *Handbook of adolescent psychology*. New York: Pergamon Press.

Gordon, T. (1974). *TET: Teacher effectiveness training*. New York: McKay.

Gottfried, A. E., Fleming, J. S., & Gottfried, A. W. (2001). Continuity of academic intrinsic motivation from childhood through late adolescence: A longitudinal study. *Journal of Educational Psychology, 93*(1), 3–13.

Gough, P. B. (1987). The key to improving schools: An interview with William Glasser. *Phi Delta Kappan, 69*(9), 656–662.

Gould, S. J. (1981). *The mismeasure of man*. New York: Norton.

Grabe, M., & Grabe, C. (2001). *Integrating technology for meaningful learning* (3rd ed.). Boston: Houghton Mifflin.

Graham, S. (1997). Using attribution theory to understand social and academic motivation in African American youth. *Educational Psychologist, 32*(1), 21–34.

Graham, S., & Weiner, B. (1993). Attributional applications in the classroom. In T. M.Tomlinson (Ed.), *Motivating students to learn: Overcoming barriers to high achievement* (pp. 179–195). Berkeley, CA: McCutchan.

Gray, B. A. (1991). Using instructional technology with at-risk youth: A primer. *Tech Trends, 36*(5), 61–63.

Gredler, G. R. (1997). Intervention programs for young children with learning disabilities. *Psychology in the Schools, 34*(2), 161–169.

Green, K. E., & Stager, S. F (1986–1987). Testing: Coursework, attitudes, and practices. *Educational Research Quarterly, 11*(2), 48–55.

Greenberg, E. R., Canzoneri, C., & Joe, A. (2000). *2000 AMA survey on workplace testing: Basic skills, job skills, psychological measurement*. Retrieved January 2, 2002, from www.amanet.org/research/pdfs/psych.pdf

Greenwald, E. A., Persky, H. R., Campbell, J. R., & Mazzeo, J. (1999). *The NAEP 1998 writing. Report card for the nation and the states*. Washington, DC: National Center for Educational Statistics. Retrieved January 2, 2002, from nces.ed.gov/pubsearch/pubsinfo.asp?pubid=1999462

Gresham, F. M., & MacMillan, D. L. (1997). Social competence and affective characteristics of students with mild disabilities. *Review of Educational Research, 67*(4), 377–415.

Groeben, N. (1994). Humanistic models of human development. In T. Husen & T. N. Postlewhaite (Eds.), *International encyclopedia of education* (2nd ed., Vol. 5, pp. 2689–2692). New York: Pergamon.

Gronlund, N. E. (1959). *Sociometry in the classroom*. New York: Harper & Row.

Gronlund, N. E. (1998). *Assessment of student achievement* (6th ed.). Boston: Allyn & Bacon.

Gronlund, N. E. (2000). *How to write and use instructional objectives* (6th ed.).Upper Saddle River, NJ: Merrill.

Gropper, N., & Froschl, M. (2000). The role of gender in young children's teasing and bullying. *Equity and Excellence in Education, 33*(1), 48–56.

Gruber, E., & Vonèche, J. J. (Eds.). (1977). *The essential Piaget: An interpretive reference and guide*. New York: Basic Books.

Guild, P. (1994). The culture/learning style connection. *Educational Leadership, 51*(8), 16–21.

Guralnick, M. J. (1986). The peer relations of young handicapped and nonhandicapped children. In P. S. Strain, M. J. Guralnick, & H. M. Walker (Eds.), *Children's social behavior: Development, assessment, and modification*. Orlando, FL: Academic Press.

Gutek, G. L. (1992). *Education and schooling in America* (3rd ed.). Boston: Allyn & Bacon.

Haberman, M., & Dill, V. (1993). The knowledge base on retention vs. teacher ideology: Implications for teacher preparation. *Journal of Teacher Education, 44*(5), 352–360.

Hadwin, A. F., Winne, P. H., Stockley, D. B., Nesbit, J. C., & Woszczyna, C. (2001). Context moderates students' self-reports about how they study. *Journal of Educational Psychology, 93*(3), 477–487.

Hakuta, K., & Garcia, E. E. (1989). Bilingualism and education. *American Psychologist, 44*(2), 374–379.

Hakuta, G., & Gould, L. J. (1987). Synthesis of research on bilingual education. *Educational Leadership, 44*(6), 38–45.

Haladyna, T. (1999). *A complete guide to student grading*. Boston: Allyn & Bacon.

Hall, G. S. (1904). *Adolescence: Its psychology and its relations to physiology, anthropology, sociology, sex, crime, religion, and education* (2 vols.). New York: Appleton.

Hallinan, M. T. (1994). Tracking: From theory to practice. *Sociology of Education, 67*(2), 79–91.

Halmi, K. A. (1987). Anorexia nervosa and bulimia. In V. B. Van Hasselt & M. Hersen (Eds.), *Handbook of adolescent psychology*. New York: Pergamon Press.

Halpern, D. F. (1997). Sex differences in intelligence: Implications for education. *American Psychologist, 52*(10), 1091–1102.

Halpern, D. F. (1998). Teaching critical thinking for transfer across domains. *American Psychologist, 53*(4), 449–455.

Halpern, D. F., & LaMay, M. L. (2000). The smarter sex: A critical review of sex differences in intelligence. *Educational Psychology Review, 12*(2), 229–246.

Hamilton, R., & Ghatala, E. (1994). *Learning and instruction*. New York: McGraw-Hill.

Han, E. P. (1995). Reflection is essential in teacher education. *Childhood Education, 71*(4), 228–230.

Haney, W. M., Madaus, G. F., & Lyons, R. (1993). *The fractured marketplace for standardized testing*. Boston: Kluwer.

Hansgen, R. D. (1991). Can education become a science? *Phi Delta Kappan, 72*(9), 689–694.

Harasim, L., Hiltz, S. R., Teles, L., & Turoff, M., (1995). *Learning networks: A field guide to teaching and learning online*. Cambridge, MA: MIT Press

Harding, C. G., & Snyder, K. (1991). Tom, Huck, and Oliver Stone as advocates in Kohlberg's just community: Theory-based strategies for moral-based education. *Adolescence, 26*(102), 319–330.

Harper, G. F., Maheady, L., & Mallette, B. (1999). Peer tutoring and the minority child with disabilities. *Preventing School Failure, 43*(2), 45–51.

Harris, J. (1997). Content and intent shape function: Designs for web-based educational telecomputing activities. *Learning and Leading with Technology, 24*(5), 17–20.

Harter, S. (1988). Developmental processes in the construction of the self. In T. D. Yawkey & J. E. Johnson (Eds.), *Integrative processes and socialization: Early to middle childhood* (pp. 45–78). Hillsdale, NJ: Erlbaum.

Harter, S. (1990). Self and identity development. In S. S. Feldman & G. R. Elliot (Eds.), *At the threshold: The developing adolescent* (pp. 352–387). Cambridge, MA: Harvard University Press.

Harter, S., Waters, P. L., & Whitesell, N. R., (1997). Lack of voice as a manifestation of false self-behavior among adolescents: The school setting as a stage upon which the drama of authenticity is enacted. *Educational Psychologist, 32*(3), 153–174.

Hartshorne, H., & May, M. A. (1929). *Studies in service and self-control*. New York: Macmillan.

Hartshorne, H., & May, M. A. (1930a). *Studies in deceit*. New York: Macmillan.

Hartshorne, H., & May, M. A. (1930b). *Studies in the organization of character*. New York: Macmillan.

Hartup, W. W. (1989). Social relationships and their developmental significance. *American Psychologist, 44*(2), 120–126.

Haskell, R. E. (2001). *Transfer of learning: Cognition, instruction, and reasoning*. San Diego, CA: Academic Press.

Hatch, T. (1997). Getting specific about multiple intelligences. *Educational Leadership, 54*(6), 26–29.

Hattie, J., Biggs, J., & Purdie, N. (1996). Effects of learning skills interventions on student learning: A meta-analysis. *Review of Educational Research, 66*(2), 99–136.

Hatton, N., & Smith, D. (1995). Reflection in teacher education: Towards definition and implementation. *Teaching and teacher education, 11*(1), 33–49.

Hauser, J., & Malouf, D. B. (1996). A federal perspective on special education technology. *Journal of Learning Disabilities, 29*(5), 504–511.

Hawley, C. L., & Duffy, T. M. (1997, March). *Student-teacher interaction in "The Chelsea Bank" simulation*. Paper presented at the Annual Meeting of the American Educational Research Association, Chicago.

Heath, I. A. (1996). The social studies video project: A holistic approach for teaching linguistically and culturally diverse students. *Social Studies, 87*(3), 106–112.

Hebert, E. A. (1998). Lessons learned about student portfolios. *Phi Delta Kappan, 79*(8), 583–585.

Heidemann, S., & Hewitt, D. (1992). *Pathways to play*. St. Paul, MN: Redleaf Press.

Henderson, V. L., & Dweck, C. S. (1990). Motivation and achievement. In S. S. Feldman & G. R. Elliott (Eds.), *At the threshold: The developing adolescent* (pp. 308–329). Cambridge, MA: Harvard University Press.

Herman, J. L., Gearhart, M., & Baker, E. L. (1993). Assessing writing portfolios: Issues in the validity and meaning of scores. *Educational Assessment, 1*(3), 201–224.

Hersh, R. H., Paolitto, D. P., & Reimer, J. (1979). *Promoting moral growth: From Piaget to Kohlberg*. New York: Longman.

Hetherington, E. M., & Parke, R. D. (1993). *Child psychology: A contemporary viewpoint* (4th ed.). New York: McGraw-Hill.

Heubert, J. P., & Hauser, R. M. (1999). *High stakes: Testing for tracking, promotion, and graduation*. Washington, DC: National Academy Press.

Heward, W. L. (2000). *Exceptional children: An introduction to special education* (6th ed.). Upper Saddle River, NJ: Merrill Prentice Hall.

Hidi, S. (2000). An interest researcher's perspective: The effects of extrinsic and intrinsic factors on motivation. In C. Sansone & J. M. Harackiewicz (Eds.), *Intrinsic and extrinsic motivation: The search for optimal motivation and performance* (pp. 309–339). San Diego, CA: Academic Press.

Hidi, S., & Harackiewicz, J. M. (2000). Motivating the academically unmotivated: A critical issue for the 21st century. *Review of Educational Research, 70*(2), 151–179.

Higbee, K. L. (1979). Recent research on visual mnemonics: Historical roots and educational fruits. *Review of Educational Research, 49*(4), 611–630.

Higgins, K., Boone, R., & Lovitt, T. C. (1996). Hypertext support for remedial students and students with learning disabilities. *Journal of Learning Disabilities, 29*(4), 402–412.

Hill, J. P. (1987). Research on adolescents and their families: Past and prospect. In C. E. Irwin, Jr. (Ed.), *Adolescent social behavior and health*. San Francisco: Jossey-Bass.

Hills, J. R. (1991). Apathy concerning grading and testing. *Phi Delta Kappan, 72*(7), 540–545.

Hirtle, J. S. (1996). Constructing a collaborative classroom (Part 2). *Learning and Leading with Technology, 23*(8), 27–30.

Ho, B. (1995). Using lesson plans as a means of reflection. *ELT Journal, 49*(1), 66–70.

Hoffer, T. B. (1992). Middle school ability grouping and student achievement in science and mathematics. *Educational Evaluation and Policy Analysis, 14*(3), 205–227.

Hoffman, M. L. (1980). Moral development in adolescence. In J. Adelson (Ed.), *Handbook of adolescent psychology*. New York: Wiley.

Hogan, K., & Pressley, M. (Eds.).(1997). *Scaffolding student learning: Instructional approaches and issues*. Cambridge, MA: Brookline Books.

Hoge, R. D., & Renzulli, J. S. (1993). Exploring the link between giftedness and self-concept. *Review of Educational Research, 63*(4), 449–465.

Holder-Brown, L., & Parette, Jr., H. P. (1992). Children with disabilities who use assistive technology: Ethical considerations. *Young Children, 47*(6), 73–77.

Hole, S., & McEntee, G. H. (1999). Reflection is at the heart of practice. *Educational Leadership, 56*(8), 34–37.

Holman, L. J. (1997). Meeting the needs of Hispanic immigrants. *Educational Leadership, 54*(7), 37–38.

Holmes, C. T. (1989). Grade level retention effects: A meta-analysis of research studies. In L. A. Shepard & M. L. Smith (Eds), *Flunking grades: Research and policies on retention*. London: Falmer Press.

Holzberg, C. S. (1995). Classroom management at your fingertips. *Learning, 23*(4), 57–59.

Hood, S. (1998). Culturally responsive performance-based assessment: Conceptual and psychometric considerations. *Journal of Negro Education, 67*(3), 187–196.

Horowitz, F., & O'Brien, M. (1986). Gifted and talented children: State of knowledge and directions for research. *American Psychologist, 41*(10), 1147–1152.

Houston, W. R., & Williamson, J. L. (1992–1993). Perceptions of their preparation by 42 Texas elementary school teachers compared with their responses as student teachers. *Teacher Education and Practice, 8*(2), 27–42.

Howard, E. R. (1981). School climate improvement—Rationale and process. *Illinois School Research and Development, 18*(1), 8–12.

Howe, C. K. (1994). Improving the achievement of Hispanic students. *Educational Leadership, 51*(8), 42–44.

Howell, R. (1996). Technological aids for inclusive classrooms. *Theory into Practice, 35*(1), 58–65.

Huenecke, D. (1992). An artistic criticism of writing to read, a computer-based program for beginning readers. *Journal of Curriculum and Supervision, 7*(2), 170–179.

Hughes, F. P. (1991). *Children, play, and development*. Boston: Allyn & Bacon.

Hughes, F. P., & Noppe, L. D. (1991). *Human development across the life span*. New York: Macmillan.

Hughes, J. E., Packard, B. W-L., & Pearson, P. D. (2000). The role of hypermedia cases on preservice teachers' views on reading instruction. *Action in Teacher Education, 22*(2A), 24–38.

Hunt, N., & Marshall, K. (1999). *Exceptional children and youth* (2nd ed.). Boston: Houghton Mifflin.

Hurst, B., Wilson, C., & Cramer, G. (1998). Professional teaching portfolios: Tools for reflection, growth, and advancement. *Phi Delta Kappan, 79*(8), 578–582.

Huyvaert, S. (1995). *Reports from the classroom: Cases for reflection*. Boston: Allyn & Bacon.

Hyde, J. S. (1986). Gender differences in aggression. In J. S. Hyde & M. C. Linn (Eds.), *The psychology of gender.* Baltimore: Johns Hopkins University Press.

Impara, J. C., & Plake, B. S. (Eds.). (1998). *The thirteenth mental measurements yearbook*. Lincoln, NE: Buros Institute of Mental Measurements.

International Society for Technology in Education. (1998). *National Educational Technology Standards (NETS)*. Retrieved January 2, 2002, from http://cnets.iste.org/

Jackson, A. W., & Davis, G. A. (2000). *Turning points 2000: Educating adolescents in the 21st century*. New York: Teachers College Press.

Jackson, J. F. (1999). What are the real risk factors for African American children? *Phi Delta Kappan, 81*(4), 308–312.

Jackson, S., & Bosma, H. (1990). Coping and self in adolescence. In H. Bosma & S. Jackson (Eds.), *Coping and self-concept in adolescence*. New York: Springer-Verlag.

James, W. (1899). *Talks to teachers on psychology: And to students on some of life's ideals*. New York: Holt.

Janzen, R. (1994). Melting pot or mosaic? *Educational Leadership, 51*(8), 9–11.

Jeweler, S., & Barnes-Robinson, L. (1999). Curriculum from a conflict-resolution perspective. *Kappa Delta Pi Record, 35*(3), 112–114.

Johnson, D. W., & Johnson, R. T. (1995). Cooperative learning and nonacademic outcomes of schooling: The other side of the report card. In J. E. Pedersen & A. D. Digby (Eds.), *Secondary schools and cooperative learning* (pp. 81–150). New York: Garland.

Johnson, D. W., & Johnson, R. T. (1996). Conflict resolution and peer mediation programs in elementary and secondary schools: A review of the research. *Review of Educational Research, 66*(4), 459–506.

Johnson, D. W., & Johnson, R. T. (1998). Cultural diversity and cooperative learning. In J. W. Putnam (Ed.), *Cooperative learning and strategies for inclusion* (2nd ed.). Baltimore, MD: Brookes Publishing.

Johnson, D. W., Johnson, R. T., & Holubec, E. J. (1994). *The new circles of learning: Cooperation in the classroom and school*. Alexandria, VA: Association for Supervision and Curriculum Development.

Johnson, D. W., Johnson, R. T., & Smith, K. A. (1995). Cooperative learning and individual student achievement in secondary schools. In J. E. Pedersen & A. D. Digby (Eds.), *Secondary schools and cooperative learning* (pp. 3–54). New York: Garland.

Johnson, L., & O'Neill-Jones, P. (1999). Innovative mathematical learning environments: Using multimedia to solve real-world problems. *Educational Technology, 39*(5), 16–18.

Johnson, R. E. (1975). Meaning in complex learning. *Review of Educational Research, 45*(3), 425–460.

Jones, A., & Selby, C. (1997). The use of computers for self-expression and communication. *Journal of Computing in Childhood Education, 8*(2/3), 199–214.

Jones, M. C. (1957). The later careers of boys who were early- or late-maturing. *Child Development, 28*(1), 113–128.

Jones, M. C. (1965). Psychological correlates of somatic development. *Child Development, 36*(4), 899–911.

Jonassen, D. H. (2000). *Computers as mindtools for schools: Engaging critical thinking* (2nd ed.). Upper Saddle River, NJ: Merrill Prentice-Hall.

Jovanovic, J., & King, S. S. (1998). Boys and girls in the performance-based science classroom: Who's doing the performing? *American Educational Research Journal, 35*(3), 477–496.

Joyce, B., & Weil, M. (2000). *Models of teaching* (6th ed.). Boston: Allyn & Bacon.

Judge, S. L. (2001). Computer applications in programs for young children with disabilities: Current status and future directions. *Journal of Special Education Technology, 16* (1), 29–40.

Juvonen, J. (2000). The social functions of attributional face-saving tactics among early adolescents. *Educational Psychology Review, 12*(1), 15–32.

Kagan, D. M. (1990). How schools alienate students at risk: A model for examining proximal classroom variables. *Educational Psychologist, 25*(2), 102–125.

Kagan, J. (1964a). *Developmental studies of reflection and analysis*. Cambridge, MA: Harvard University Press.

Kagan, J. (1964b). Impulsive and reflective children. In J. D. Krumbolz (Ed.), *Learning and the educational process*. Chicago: Rand McNally.

Kail, R. V. (1990). *The development of memory in children* (3rd ed.). San Francisco: Freeman.

Kail, R. V. (1998). *Children and their development*. Upper Saddle River, NJ: Prentice-Hall.

Kalbaugh, P., & Haviland, J. M. (1991). Formal operational thinking and identity. In R. M. Lerner, A. C. Peterson, & J. Brooks-Gunn (Eds.), *Encyclopedia of adolescence*. New York: Garland.

Kalyuga, S., Chandler, P., Tuovinen, J., & Sweller, J. (2001). When problem solving is superior to studying worked examples. *Journal of Educational Psychology, 93*(3), 579–588.

Kameenui, E. J., & Carnine, D. W. (1998). *Effective teaching strategies that accommodate diverse learners*. Upper Saddle River, NJ: Merrill Prentice Hall.

Kamii, C. (1984). Autonomy: The aim of education envisioned by Piaget. *Phi Delta Kappan, 65*(6), 410–415.

Kamii, C. (2000). *Young children reinvent arithmetic: Implications of Piaget's theory* (2nd ed.). New York: Teachers College Press.

Kamps, D., Kravitz, T., Stolze, J., & Swaggart, B. (1999). Prevention strategies for at-risk students with EBD in urban elementary schools. *Journal of Emotional and Behavioral Disorders, 7*(3), 178–188.

Kaplan, J. S. (1991). *Beyond behavior modification: A cognitive-behavioral approach to behavior management in the school* (2d ed.). Austin, TX: Pro-Ed.

Karpov, Y. V., & Bransford, J. D. (1995). L. S. Vygotsky and the doctrine of empirical and theoretical learning. *Educational Psychologist, 30*(2), 61–66.

Karpov, Y. V., & Haywood, H. C. (1998). Two ways to elaborate Vygotsky's concept of mediation. *American Psychologist, 53*(1), 27–36.

Kashihara, A., Uji'i, H., & Toyoda, J. (1999). Reflection support for learning in hyperspace. *Educational Technology, 39*(5), 19–22.

Katayama, A. D., & Robinson, D. H. (2000). Getting students "partially" involved in note-taking using graphic organizers. *Journal of Experimental Education, 68*(2), 119–133.

Katz, L. G., & Chard, S. C. (2000). *Engaging children's minds: The project approach* (2nd ed.). Stamford, CT: Ablex.

Kaufman, P., Chen, X., Choy, S. P., Ruddy, S. A., Miller, A. K., Fleury, J. K., Chandler, K. A., Rand, M. R., Klaus, P., & Planty, M. G. (2000). *Indicators of school crime and safety, 2000*. Washington, DC: U.S. Departments of Education and Justice. NCES2001-017/NCJ-184176. Retrieved January 2, 2002, from nces.ed.gov/pubsearch/pubsinfo.asp?pubid=2001017

Kauffman, J. M. (2001). *Characteristics of emotional and behavioral disorders of children and youth* (7th ed.).Upper Saddle River, NJ: Merrill Prentice Hall.

Kauffman, J. M., Lloyd, J. W., Baker, J., & Reidel, T. M. (1995). Inclusion of all students with emotional or behavioral disorders? Let's think again. *Phi Delta Kappan, 76*(7), 542–546.

Keeler, C. M. (1996). Networked instructional computers in the elementary classroom and their effect on the learning environment: A qualitative evaluation. *Journal of Research on Computing in Education, 28*(3), 329–345.

Keller, J. (1990). Characteristics of LOGO instruction promoting transfer of learning: A research review. *Journal of Research on Computing in Education, 23*(1), 55–71.

Kelley, M. L., & Carper, L. B. (1988). Home-based reinforcement procedures. In J. C. Witt, S. N. Elliott, & F. M. Gresham (Eds.), *Handbook of behavior therapy in education*. New York: Plenum Press.

Kellogg, R. T. (1989). Idea processors: Computer aids for planning and composing text. In B. K. Britton & S. M. Glynn (Eds.), *Computer writing environments: Theory, research, and design* (pp. 57–92). Hillsdale, NJ: Erlbaum.

Kennedy, M. M. (1999). A test of some common contentions about educational research. *American Educational Research Journal, 36*(3), 511–541.

Kentucky Department of Education. (2000). *Commonwealth accountability testing system*. Retrieved January 2, 2002, from www.kde.state.ky.us/comm/commrel/cats/

Kerr, M. M., & Nelson, C. M. (1998). *Strategies for managing behavior problems in the classroom* (3d ed.). Upper Saddle River, NJ: Merrill Prentice Hall.

Ketterlinus, R. D., & Lamb, M. E. (1994). *Adolescent problem behaviors: Issues and research*. Hillsdale, NJ: Erlbaum.

Keyser, D. J., & Sweetland, R. C. (Eds.). (1994). *Test critiques* (Vol. 10). Austin, TX: Pro-Ed.

Khalili, A., & Shashaani, L. (1994). The effectiveness of computer applications: A meta-analysis. *Journal of Research on Computing in Education, 27*(1), 48–61.

Khattri, N., Reeve, A. L., & Kane, M. B. (1998). *Principles and practices of performance assessment*. Mahwah, NJ: Erlbaum.

Kiewra, K. A., & DuBois, N. F. (1998). *Learning to learn: Making the transition from student to life-long learner*. Boston: Allyn & Bacon.

Kimball, L. (1995). Ten ways to make online learning groups work. *Educational Leadership, 53*(2), 54–56.

Kinard, B., & Bitter, G. G. (1997). Multicultural mathematics and technology: The Hispanic math project. *Computers in the Schools, 13*(1), 77–88.

King, A. (1992a). Comparison of self-questioning, summarizing, and notetaking-review as strategies for learning from lectures. *American Educational Research Journal, 29*(2), 303–323.

King, A. (1992b). Facilitating elaborative learning through guided student-generated questioning. *Educational Psychologist, 27*(1), 111–126.

King, A. (1994). Guiding knowledge construction in the classroom: Effects of teaching children how to question and how to explain. *American Educational Research Journal, 31*(2), 338–368.

King, A. (1998). Transactive peer tutoring: Distributing cognition and metacognition. *Educational Psychology Review, 10*(1), 57–74.

Kirk, S. A., Gallagher, J. J., & Anastasiow, N. J. (2000). *Educating exceptional children* (9th ed.). Boston: Houghton Mifflin.

Kirschenbaum, H., & Simon, S. B. (Eds.). (1973). *Readings in values clarification*. Minneapolis: Winston.

Klauer, K. (1984). Intentional and incidental learning with instructional texts: A meta-analysis for 1970–1980. *American Educational Research Journal, 21*(2), 323–339.

Knapp, M. S., & Shields, P. M. (1990). Reconceiving Academic Instruction for the children of poverty. *Phi Delta Kappan, 71*(10), 753–758.

Knapp, M. S., Shields, P. M., & Turnbull, B. J. (1995). Academic challenge in high-poverty classrooms. *Phi Delta Kappan, 76*(10), 770–776.

Koch, M. (1994). No girls allowed. *Technos, 3*(3), 14–19.

Kochendorfer, L. (1994). *Becoming a reflective teacher*. Washington, DC: National Education Association.

Koedinger, K. R., & Anderson, J. R. (1993). Reifying implicit planning in geometry: Guidelines for model-based intelligent tutoring system design. In S. Lajoie & S. Derry (Eds.), *Computers as cognitive tools* (pp. 15–45). Hillsdale, NJ: Erlbaum.

Kohlberg, L. (1963). The development of children's orientations toward a moral order: 1. Sequence in the development of moral thought. *Vita Humana, 6*(1–2), 11–33.

Kohlberg, L. (1969). Stage and sequence: The cognitive-developmental approach to socialization. In D. A. Goslin (Ed.), *Handbook of socialization theory and research*. Chicago: Rand McNally.

Kohlberg, L. (1976). Moral stages and moralization: The cognitive-developmental approach. In T. Lickona (Ed.), *Moral development and behavior: Theory, research, and social issues*. New York: Holt, Rinehart & Winston.

Kohlberg, L. (1978). Revisions in the theory and practice of moral development. In W. Damon (Ed.), *New directions for child development: Moral development* (No.2). San Francisco: Jossey-Bass.

Kohn, A. (1993). Rewards versus learning: A response to Paul Chance. *Phi Delta Kappan, 74*(10), 783–787.

Kohn, A. (1994). The truth about self-esteem. *Phi Delta Kappan, 76*(4), 272–283.

Kohn, A. (2000). Burnt at the high stakes. *Journal of Teacher Education, 51*(4), 315–327.

Kontos, G., & Mizell, A. P. (1997). Global village classroom: The changing roles of teachers and students through technology. *TechTrends, 42*(5), 17–22.

Kounin, J. S. (1970). *Discipline and group management in classrooms*. New York: Holt, Rinehart & Winston.

Kozma, R. B. (1987). The implications of cognitive psychology for computer-based learning tools. *Educational Technology, 27*(11), 20–25.

Kozma, R. B. (1991). Learning with media. *Review of Educational Research, 61*(2), 179–212.

Kozulin, A., & Presseisen, B. Z. (1995). Mediated learning experience and psychological tools: Vygotsky's and Feuerstein's perspectives in a study of student learning. *Educational Psychologist, 30*(2), 57–75.

Krashen, S. (1999). What the research really says about structured English immersion: A reply to Keith Baker. *Phi Delta Kappan, 80* (9), 705–706.

Krathwohl, D. R., Bloom, B. S., & Masia, B. B. (1964). *Taxonomy of educational objectives. Handbook II: Affective domain*. New York: McKay.

Kroger, J. (1996). *Identity and adolescence: The balance between self and other* (2nd ed). New York: Routledge.

Krulik, S., & Rudnick, J. A. (1993). *Reasoning and problem solving: A handbook for elementary school teachers*. Boston: Allyn & Bacon.

Kubiszyn, T., & Borich, G. (2000). *Educational testing and measurement: Classroom application and practice* (6th ed.). New York: Wiley.

Kuhn, D. (1997). Constraints or guideposts? Developmental psychology and science education. *Review of Educational Research, 67*(1), 141–150.

Kuhn, D. (1999). A developmental model of critical thinking. *Educational Researcher, 28* (2), 16–26, 46.

Kulik, J. A., & Kulik, C-L. (1984). Effects of accelerated instruction on students. *Review of Educational Research, 54*(3), 409–426.

Kulik, J. A., & Kulik, C.-L. C. (1991). Ability grouping and gifted students. In N. Colangelo & G. A. Davis (Eds.), *Handbook of gifted education*. Boston: Allyn & Bacon.

Kulik, J. A., Kulik, C-L., & Bangert-Drowns, R. L. (1985). Effectiveness of computer-based education in elementary schools. *Computers in Human Behavior, 1*(1), 59–74.

Kulik, C-L., Kulik, J. A., & Bangert-Drowns, R. L. (1990). Effectiveness of mastery learning programs. *Review of Educational Research, 60*(2), 265–299.

Kumar, D. D., & Helgeson, S. L. (1995). Trends in computer applications in science assessment. *Journal of Science Education and Technology, 4*(1), 29–36.

Kumar, D., & Wilson, C. L. (1997). Computer technology, science education, and students with learning disabilities. *Journal of Science Education and Technology, 6*(2), 155–160.

Kyllonen, P. C. (1996). Is working memory capacity Spearman's g? In I. Dennis & P. Tapsfield (Eds.), *Human abilities: Their nature and measurement*. Mahwah, NJ: Erlbaum.

Labbo, L. D., Murray, B. A., & Phillips, M. (1995–1996). Writing to read: From inheritance to innovation and invitation. *Reading Teacher, 49*(4), 314–321.

LaBoskey, V. K. (2000). Portfolios here, portfolios there . . . Searching for the essence of 'educational portfolios.' *Phi Delta Kappan, 81*(8), 590–595.

Ladson-Billings, G. (1994). What we can learn from multicultural education research. *Educational Leadership, 51*(8), 22–26.

Lambert, B. G., & Mounce, N. B. (1987). Career planning. In V. B. van Hasselt & M. Hersen (Eds.), *Handbook of adolescent psychology*. New York: Pergamon Press.

Lampert, M. (1995). Managing the tensions in connecting students' inquiry with learning mathematics in school. In D. N. Perkins, J. L. Schwartz, M. M. West, & S. Wiske (Eds.), *Software goes to school: Teaching for understanding with new technologies* (pp. 213–232). New York: Oxford University Press.

Lantieri, L. (1995). Waging peace in our schools: Beginning with the children. *Phi Delta Kappan, 76*(5), 386–388.

Lantieri, L. (1999). Hooked on altruism: Developing social responsibility in at-risk youth. *Reclaiming Children and Youth, 8*(2), 83–87.

Larsen, S. (1995). What is "quality" in the use of technology for children with learning disabilities? *Learning Disability Quarterly, 18*(2), 118–130.

Lavigne, N., & Lajoie, W. (1996). Communicating performance criteria to students through technology. *The Mathematics Teacher, 89*(1), 66–69.

Lazear, D. G. (1992). *Teaching for multiple intelligences*. Bloomington, IN: Phi Delta Kappa Educational Foundation.

Leadbeater, B. (1991). Relativistic thinking in adolescence. In R. M. Lerner, A. C. Peterson, & J. Brooks-Gunn (Eds.), *Encyclopedia of adolescence*. New York: Garland.

Leaver, B. L. (1998). *Teaching the whole class* (5th ed.). Dubuque, IA: Kendall/Hunt.

Lee, C. D. (1998). Culturally responsive pedagogy and performance-based assessment. *Journal of Negro Education, 67*(3), 268–279.

Lee, F-L., & Heyworth, R. M. (2000). Electronic homework. *Journal of Educational Computing Research, 22*(2), 171–186.

Lee, W. W. (1987). Microcomputer courseware production and evaluation guidelines for students with learning disabilities. *Journal of Learning Disabilities, 20*(7), 436–438.

LeFrançois, G. (1995). *Of children: An introduction to child development* (8th ed.). Belmont, CA: Wadsworth.

Lehrer, R. (1993). Authors of knowledge: Patterns of hypermedia design. In S. Lajoie & S. Derry (Eds.), *Computers as cognitive tools* (pp. 197–227). Hillsdale, NJ: Erlbaum.

Lehrer, R., Erickson, J., & Connell, T. (1994). Learning by designing hypermedia documents. *Computers in the Schools, 10*(1/2), 227–254.

Lehrer, R., Mihwa, L., & Jeong, A. (1999). Reflective teaching of LOGO. *Journal of the Learning Sciences, 8*(2), 245–289.

Leming, J. S. (1993). In search of effective character education. *Educational Leadership, 51*(3), 63–71.

Leong, C. K. (1995). Effects of on-line reading and simultaneous DECtalk auding in helping below-average and poor readers comprehend and summarize text. *Learning Disability Quarterly, 18*(2), 101–116.

Lepper, M. R., Keavney, M., & Drake, M. (1996). Intrinsic motivation and extrinsic rewards: A commentary on Cameron and Pierce's meta-analysis. *Review of Educational Research, 66*(1), 5–32.

Lerner, J. (2000). *Learning disabilities: Theories, diagnosis, and teaching strategies* (8th ed.). Boston: Houghton Mifflin.

Lerner, J. W., Lowenthal, B., & Lerner, S. R. (1995). *Attention deficit disorders: Assessment and teaching.* Pacific Groves, CA: Brooks/Cole.

Lesar, S. (1998). Use of assistive technology with young children with disabilities: Current status and training needs. *Journal of Early Intervention, 21*(2), 146–159.

Lessow-Hurley, J. (2000). *The foundations of dual language instruction.* New York: Longman.

Levin, J., & Nolan, J. F. (2000). *Principles of classroom management: A professional decision-making model.* Boston: Allyn & Bacon.

Levin, J. A., Kim, H., & Riel, M. M. (1990). Analyzing instructional interactions on electronic message networks. In L. M. Harasim (Ed.), *Online education: Perspectives on a new environment* (pp. 185–213). New York: Praeger.

Levin, J. R. (1982). Pictures as prose-learning devices. In A. Flammer & W. Kintsch (Eds.), *Advances in psychology: Vol. 8. Discourse processing.* Amsterdam: North-Holland.

Levine, D. U., & Levine, R. F. (1996). *Society and education* (9th ed.). Boston: Allyn & Bacon.

Lewis, L., Parsad, B., Carey, N., Bartafi, N., Farris, E., & Smerdon, B. (1999, January). *Teacher quality: A report on the preparation and qualifications of public school teachers.* Washington, DC: U.S. Department of Education, National Center for Education Statistics. Retrieved January 2, 2002, from nces.ed.gov/pubsearch/pubsinfo.asp?=1999080

Leyser, Y., Frankiewicz, L. E., & Vaughn, R. (1992). Problems faced by first-year teachers: A survey of regular and special educators. *Teacher Educator, 28*(1), 36–45.

Liao, Y-K. (1992). Effects of computer-assisted instruction on cognitive outcomes: A meta-analysis. *Journal of Research on Computing in Education, 24*(3), 367–380.

Libsch, M., & Breslow, M. (2000). Students' use of computers for schoolwork and other activities. *NASSP Bulletin, 84*(613), 86–89.

Lickona, T. (1976). Research on Piaget's theory of moral development. In T. Lickona (Ed.), *Moral development and behavior: Theory, research, and social issues.* New York: Holt, Rinehart & Winston.

Lickona, T. (1998). A more complex analysis is needed. *Phi Delta Kappan, 79*(6), 449–454.

Lindholm, K. J., & Fairchild, H. H. (1990). Evaluation of an elementary school bilingual immersion program. In A. M. Padilla, H. F. Fairchild, & C. M. Valadez (Eds.), *Bilingual education: Issues and strategies.* Newbury Park, CA: Sage.

Linn, M C. (1992). Science education reform: Building on the research base. *Journal of Research in Science Teaching, 29*(8), 821–840.

Linn, M. C. (1997). The role of the laboratory in science learning. *Elementary School Journal, 97*(4), 401–417.

Linn, M. C., Lewis, C., Tsuchida, I., & Songer, N. B. (2000). Beyond fourth-grade science: Why do U.S. and Japanese students diverge? *Educational Researcher, 29*(3), 4–14.

Linn, R. L. (1994). Performance assessment: Policy promises and technical measurement standards. *Educational Researcher, 23*(9), 4–14.

Linn, R. L. (2000). Assessments and accountability. *Educational Researcher, 29*(2), 4–16.

Linn, R. L., & Gronlund, N. E. (2000). *Measurement and assessment in teaching* (8th ed.). Upper Saddle River, NJ: Merrill Prentice-Hall.

Lipka, R. R., Hurford, D. P., & Litten, M. J. (1992). Self in school: Age and school experience effects. In R. P. Lipka & T. M Brinthaupt (Eds.), *Self-perspectives across the life span* (pp. 93–115). Albany: State University of New York Press.

Liu, M. (1994). Hypermedia assisted instruction and second language learning: A semantic-network-based approach. *Computers in the Schools, 10*(3/4), 293–312.

Livingston, C., & Borko, H. (1989). Expert-novice differences in teaching: A cognitive analysis and implications for teacher education. *Journal of Teacher Education, 40*(4), 36–42.

Livson, N., & Peskin, H. (1980). Perspectives on adolescence from longitudinal research. In J. Adelson (Ed.), *Handbook of adolescent psychology.* New York: Wiley.

Lloyd, L. (1999). Multi-age classes and high ability students. *Review of Educational Research, 69*(2), 187–212.

Lockwood, A. (1978). The effects of values clarification and moral development curricula on school age subjects: A critical review of recent research. *Review of Educational Research, 48*(3), 325–364.

Loftus, E. F., & Loftus, G. R. (1980). On the permanence of stored information in the brain. *American Psychologist, 35*(5), 409–420.

Lonoff, S. (1997). Using videotape to talk about teaching. *ADE Bulletin, 118,* 10–14.

Lorayne, H., & Lucas, J. (1974). *The memory book.* New York: Ballantine Books.

Losey, K. M. (1995). Mexican American students and classroom interaction: An overview and critique. *Review of Educational Research, 65*(3), 283–318.

Lou, Y., Abrami, P. C., Spence, J. C., Poulsen, C., Chambers, B., & d'Apollonia, S. (1996). Within-class grouping: A meta-analysis. *Review of Educational Research, 66*(4), 423–458.

Loveless, T. (1998). The tracking and ability grouping debate. *Fordham Report, 2*(8). Retrieved January 2, 2002, from www.edexcellence.net/library/track.html

Loveless, T. (1999). Will tracking reform promote social equity? *Educational Leadership, 56*(7), 28–32.

Lowry, R., Sleet, D., Duncan, C., Powell, K, & Kolbe, L. (1995). Adolescents at risk for violence. *Educational Psychology Review, 7*(1), 7–39.

Lundeberg, M. A., & Fox, P. W. (1991). Do laboratory findings on test expectancy generalize to classroom outcomes? *Review of Educational Research, 61*(1), 94–106.

Luria, A. R. (1968). *The mind of a mnemonist: A little book about a vast memory.* New York: Ballantine Books.

Lyman, L., Foyle, H. C., & Azwell, T. S. (1993). *Cooperative learning in the elementary classroom.* Washington, DC: National Education Association.

Lyons, N. (1999). How portfolios can shape emerging practice. *Educational Leadership, 56*(8), 63–65.

Mabry, L. (1999). Writing to the rubric: Lingering effects of traditional standardized testing on direct writing assessment. *Phi Delta Kappan, 80*(9), 673–679.

MacArthur, C. (1994). Peers + word processing + strategies = a powerful combination for revising student writing. *Teaching Exceptional Children, 27*(1), 24–29.

MacArthur, C. A. (1996). Using technology to enhance the writing processes of students with learning disabilities. *Journal of Learning Disabilities, 29*(4), 344–354.

MacArthur, C. A. (1998a). Word processing with speech synthesis and word prediction: Effects on the dialogue journal writing of students with learning disabilities. *Learning Disability Quarterly, 21*(2), 151–166.

MacArthur, C. A. (1998b). From illegible to understandable: How word prediction and speech synthesis can help. *Teaching Exceptional Children, 30*(6), 66–71.

MacArthur, C. A., & Haynes, J. B. (1995). Student assistant for learning from text (SALT): A hypermedia reading aid. *Journal of Learning Disabilities, 28*(3), 150–159.

Macedo, D. (2000). The illiteracy of English-only literacy. *Educational Leadership, 57*(4), 62–67.

MacKay, A. P., Fingerhut, L. A., & Duran, C. R. *Health, United States, 2000.* (2000). *Adolescent health chartbook.* Hyattsville, MD:

National Center for Health Statistics Retrieved January 2, 2002, from www.cdc.gov/nchs/data/hus/hus00chT.pdf

MacMillan, D. L., Gresham, F. M., & Forness, S. R. (1996). Full inclusion: An empirical perspective. *Behavioral Disorders, 21*(2), 145–159.

Madaus, G. F., & O'Dwyer, L. M. (1999). A short history of performance assessment: Lessons learned. *Phi Delta Kappan, 80*(9), 688–695.

Maehr, M. L., & Meyer, H. A. (1997). Understanding motivation and schooling: Where we've been, where we are, and where we need to go. *Educational Psychology Review, 9*(4), 371–409.

Mager, R. F. (1962). *Preparing instructional objectives*. Palo Alto, CA: Fearon.

Mager, R. F. (1997). *Preparing instructional objectives* (3d ed.). Atlanta, GA: Center for Effective Performance.

Magnusson, S. J. (1996). Complexities of learning with computer-based tools: A case of inquiry about sound and music in elementary school. *Journal of Science Education and Technology, 5*(4), 297–309.

Maker, C. J., & Nielson, A. B. (1996). *Curriculum development and teaching strategies for gifted learners* (2d ed.). Austin, TX: Pro-Ed.

Marcia, J. E. (1966). Development and validation of ego identity status. *Journal of Personality and Social Psychology, 3*(5), 551–558.

Marcia, J. E. (1967). Ego identity status: Relationship to change in self-esteem, "general adjustment," and authoritarianism. *Journal of Personality, 35*(1), 119–133.

Marcia, J. E. (1980). Identity in adolescence. In J. Adelson (Ed.), *Handbook of adolescent psychology*. New York: Wiley.

Marcia, J. E. (1991). Identity and self-development. In R. M. Lerner, A. C. Peterson, & J. Brooks-Gunn (Eds.), *Encyclopedia of adolescence*. New York: Garland.

Mariage, T. V. (1995). Why students learn: The nature of teacher talk during reading. *Learning Disability Quarterly, 18*(3), 214–234.

Marr, P. M. (2000). Grouping students at the computer to enhance the study of British literature. *English Journal, 90*(2), 120–125.

Marsh, H. W., Byrne, B. M., & Shavelson, R. J. (1992). A multidimensional, hierarchical self-concept. In T. M Brinthaupt & R. P. Lipka (Eds.), *The self: Definitional and methodological issues* (pp. 44–95). Albany: State University of New York Press.

Marsh, H. W., Chessor, D., Craven, R., & Roche, L. (1995). The effects of gifted and talented programs on academic self-concept: The big fish strikes again. *American Educational Research Journal, 32*(2), 285–319.

Marsh, R. S., & Raywid, M. A. (1994). How to make detracking work. *Phi Delta Kappan, 76*(4), 314–317.

Marsh, H. W., & Yeung, A. S. (1998). Longitudinal structural equation models of academic self-concept and achievement: Gender differences in the development of math and English contructs. *American Educational Research Journal, 35*(4), 705–738.

Martin, C. D., Heller, R. S., & Mahmoud, E. (1992). American and Soviet children's attitudes toward computers. *Journal of Educational Computing Research, 8*(2), 155–185.

Martin, G., & Pear, J. (1999). *Behavior modification: What it is and how to do it* (6th ed.). Upper Saddle River, NJ: Prentice Hall.

Martin, K. A. (1996). *Puberty, sexuality, and the self: Boys and girls at adolescence.* New York: Routledge.

Martinez, M. E. (1998). What is problem solving? *Phi Delta Kappan, 79*(8), 605–609.

Martinez, M. E. (1999). Cognition and the question of test item format. *Educational Psychologist, 34*(1), 207–218.

Marx, R. W., Blumenfeld, P. C., Krajcik, J. S., & Soloway, E. (1997). Enacting project-based science. *Elementary School Journal, 97*(4), 341–358.

Marx, R. W., & Winne, P. H. (1987). The best tool teachers have—their students' thinking. In D. C. Berliner & B. V. Rosenshine (Eds.), *Talks to teachers*. New York: Random House.

Maryland State Department of Education. (2001). *Maryland School Performance assessment program*. Retrieved January 2, 2002, from www.msde.state.md.us/mspap/default2.htm

Marzano, R. J. (2000). *Transforming classroom grading*. Alexandria, VA: Association for Supervision and Curriculum Development.

Maslow, A. H. (1943). A theory of human motivation. *Psychological Review, 50*(4), 370–396.

Maslow, A. H. (1968). *Toward a psychology of being* (2d ed.). Princeton, NJ: Van Nostrand.

Maslow, A. H. (1987). *Motivation and personality* (3d ed.). New York: Harper & Row.

Mastropieri, M. A., Sweda, J., & Scruggs, T. E. (2000). Putting mnemonic strategies to work in an inclusive classroom. *Learning Disabilities Research and Practice, 15*(2), 69–74.

Matthews, C. E., Binkley, W., Crisp, A., & Gregg, K. (1998). Challenging gender bias in fifth grade. *Educational Leadership, 55*(4), 54–57.

Mayer, R. E. (1987). Learnable aspects of problem solving: Some examples. In D. E. Berger, K. Pezdek, & W. P. Banks (Eds.), *Applications of cognitive psychology: Problem solving, education, and computing.* Hillsdale, NJ: Erlbaum.

Mayer, R. E. (1996). Learners as information processors: Legacies and limitations of educational psychology's second metaphor. *Educational Psychologist, 31*(3/4), 151–161.

McCaslin, M., & Good, T. L. (1992). Compliant cognition: The misalliance of management and instructional goals in current school reform. *Educational Researcher, 21*(3), 4–17.

McCollum, K. (1998). How a computer program learns to grade essays. *Chronicle of Higher Education, 45*(2), 37–38.

McColskey, W., & McMunn, N. (2000). Strategies for dealing with high-stakes tests. *Phi Delta Kappan, 82*(2), 115–120.

McConnell, S. R., & Odom, S. L. (1986). Sociometrics: Peer-referenced measures and the assessment of social competence. In P. S. Strain, M. J. Guralnick, & H. M. Walker (Eds.), *Children's social behavior: Development, assessment, and modification.* Orlando, FL: Academic Press.

McLaughlin, T. F., & Williams, R. L. (1988). The token economy. In J. C. Witt, S. N. Elliott, & F. M. Gresham (Eds.), *Handbook of behavior therapy in education.* New York: Plenum Press.

McLellan, H. (1996a). "Being digital": Implications for education. *Educational Technology, 36*(6), 5–20.

McLellan, H. (1996b). Virtual realities. In D. Jonassen (Ed.), *Handbook for Research on Education Communications and Technology* (pp. 457–487). Boston: Kluwer-Nijhoff.

McLeskey, J., & Waldron, N. L. (1996). Responses to questions teachers and administrators frequently ask about inclusive school programs. *Phi Delta Kappan, 78*(2), 150–156.

McLoyd, V. C. (1998). Socioeconomic disadvantage and child development. *American Psychologist, 53*(2), 185–204.

McNally, L., & Etchison, C. (2000). Streamlining classroom management. *Learning and Leading with Technology, 28*(2), 6–9, 12.

McPartland, J., Jordan, W., Legters, N., & Balfanz, R. (1997). Finding safety in small numbers. *Educational Leadership, 55*(2), 14–17.

McTighe, J. (1996/1997). What happens between assessments? *Educational Leadership, 54*(4), 6–12.

McTighe, J., & Ferrara, S. (1998). *Assessing learning in the classroom*. Washington, DC: National Education Association.

Meagher, M. E. (1995). Learning English on the Internet. *Educational Leadership International, 53*(2), 88–90.

Means, B., & Knapp, M. S. (1991). Introduction: Rethinking teaching for disadvantaged students. In B. Means, C. Chelemer, & M. S. Knapp (Eds.), *Teaching advanced skills to at-risk students*. San Francisco: Jossey-Bass.

Meier, N. (1999). A fabric of half-truths: A response to Keith Baker on structured English immersion. *Phi Delta Kappan, 80*(9), 704–706.

Meijer, R. R., & Nering, M. L. (1999). Computerized adaptive testing: Overview and introduction. *Applied psychological measurement, 23*(3), 187–194.

Meisels, S. J., & Liaw, F-R. (1993). Failure in grade: Do retained students catch up? *Journal of Educational Research, 87*(2), 69–77.

Melton, R. F. (1978). Resolution of conflicting claims concerning the effect of behavioral objectives on student learning. *Review of Educational Research, 48*, 291–302.

Mendoza, J. I. (1994). On being a Mexican American. *Phi Delta Kappan, 76*(4), 293–295.

Mercer, C. D. (1997). *Students with learning disabilities* (5th ed.). Upper Saddle River, NJ: Merrill Prentice Hall.

Mercer, C. D., & Mercer, A. R. (2001). *Teaching students with learning problems* (6th ed.). Upper Saddle River, NJ: Merrill Prentice Hall.

Mergendoller, J. R. (1996). Moving from technological possibility to richer student learning: Revitalized infrastructure and reconstructed pedagogy. *Educational Researcher, 25*(8), 43–46.

Merrow, J. (2001). Undermining standards. *Phi Delta Kappan, 82*(9), 653–659.

Meskill, C. (1996). Listening skills development through multimedia. *Journal of Educational Multimedia and Hypermedia, 5*(2), 179–201.

Messerer, J. (1997). Adaptive technology. *Learning and Leading with Technology, 24*(5), 50–53.

Messick, S. (1989). Meaning and values in test validation: The science and ethics of assessment. *Educational Researcher, 18*(2), 5–11.

Metcalfe, J., & Shimamura, A. P. (1994). *Metacognition: Knowing about knowing*. Cambridge, MA: MIT Press.

Metz, K. E. (1995). Reassessment of developmental constraints on children's science instruction. *Review of Educational Research, 65*(2), 93–127.

Metzger, M. (1996). Maintaining a life. *Phi Delta Kappan, 77*(5), 346–351.

Metzger, M. (1998). Teaching reading: Beyond the plot. *Phi Delta Kappan, 80* (3), 240–246, 256.

Mevarech, Z., & Susak, Z. (1993). Effects of learning with cooperative-mastery method on elementary students. *Journal of Educational Research, 86*(4), 197–205.

Meyer, C. A. (1992). What's the difference between authentic and performance assessment? *Educational Leadership, 49*(8), 39–40.

Midgley, C., & Edelin, K. C. (1998). Middle school reform and early adolescent well-being: The good news and the bad. *Educational Psychologist, 33*(4), 195–206.

Milgram, J. (1992). A portrait of diversity: The middle level student. In J. L. Irvin (Ed.), *Transforming middle level education*. Boston: Allyn & Bacon.

Miller, D. (1993). Making the connection with language. *Arithmetic Teacher, 40*(6), 311–316.

Miller, L. K. (1989). *Musical savants: Exceptional skill in the mentally retarded*. Hillsdale, NJ: Erlbaum.

Miller, P. H. (1993). *Theories of developmental psychology* (3rd ed.). New York: Freeman.

Miller, P Y., & Simon, W. (1980). The development of sexuality in adolescence. In J. Adelson (Ed.), *Handbook of adolescent psychology*. New York: Wiley.

Mitchell, J. J. (1990). *Human growth and development: The childhood years*. Calgary, Alberta: Detselig Enterprises Ltd.

Mitchell, J. V., Jr. (Ed.). (1985). *Ninth mental measurements yearbook*. Highland Park, NJ: Gryphon Press.

Mitchell, P. R. (1996). Stop the world—west Georgia is getting on. *Technos, 5*(3), 14–15, 19–20.

Moely, B. E., Hart, S. S., Leal, L., Santulli, K. A., Rao, N., Johnson, T., & Hamilton, L. B. (1992). The teacher's role in facilitating memory and study strategy development in the elementary school classroom. *Child Development, 63*(3), 653–672.

Moersch, C., & Fisher III, L. M. (1995). Electronic portfolios—some pivotal questions. *Learning and Leading with Technology, 23*(2), 10–14.

Mohnsen, B. (1997). Stretching bodies and minds through technology. *Educational Leadership, 55*(3), 46–48.

Mohnsen, B., & Mendon, K. (1997). Electronic portfolios in physical education. *Strategies, 11*(2), 13–16.

Moll, L. C. (Ed.).(1990). *Vygotsky and education: Instructional implications and applications of sociohistorical psychology*. New York: Cambridge University Press.

Montgomery, K. (2000). Classroom rubrics: Systematizing what teachers do naturally. *Clearing House, 73*(6), 324–328.

Morgan, H. (1997). *Cognitive styles and classroom learning*. Westport, CT: Praeger.

Morrell, K., Marchionini, G., & Neuman, D. (1993). Sailing Perseus: Instructional strategies for hypermedia in the classics. *Journal of Educational Multimedia and Hypermedia, 2*(4), 337–353.

Morris, P. (1977). Practical strategies for human learning and remembering. In M. J. A. Howe (Ed.), *Adult learning*. New York: Wiley.

Mueller, C. M., & Dweck, C. S. (1998). Praise for intelligence can undermine children's motivation and performance. *Journal of Personality and Social Psychology, 75*(1), 33–52.

Mullis, I. V. S., Martin, M. O., Gonzalez, E., O'Connor, K. M., Chrostowski, S. J., Gregory, K. D., Garden, R. A., & Smith, T. A. (2001). *Mathematics benchmarking report TIMSS 1999—eighth grade*. Chestnut Hill, MA: Boston College. Retrieved January 2, 2002, from www.timss.org/timss1999b/publications.html

Murdick, K. (1996). Short-term sales forecasting. *Mathematics Teacher, 89*(1), 48–52.

Murphy, D. F. (1988). The just community at Birch Meadow Elementary School. *Phi Delta Kappan, 69*(6), 427–428.

Murphy, J. (1987). Educational influences. In V. B. van Hasselt & M. Hersen (Eds.), *Handbook of adolescent psychology*. New York: Pergamon Press.

Mussen, P. H., & Jones, M. C. (1957). Self-conceptions, motivations, and interpersonal attitudes of late- and early-maturing boys. *Child Development, 28*(2), 243–256.

Nagy, P., & Griffiths, A. K. (1982). Limitations of recent research relating Piaget's theory to adolescent thought. *Review of Educational Research, 52*(4), 513–556.

Nakhleh, M. B. (1994). A review of microcomputer-based labs: How have they affected science learning? *Journal of Computers in Mathematics and Science Teaching, 13*(4), 368–381.

Nastasi, B. K., & Clements, D. H. (1993). Motivational and social outcomes of cooperative computer education environments. *Journal of Computing in Childhood Education, 4*(1), 15–43.

Nastasi, B. K., & Clements, D. H. (1994). Effectance motivation, perceived scholastic competence, and higher-order thinking in two cooperative computer environments. *Journal of Educational Computing Research, 10*(3), 249–275.

National Board for Professional Teaching Standards. (1994). *What teachers should know and be able to do*. Southfield, MI: Author.

National Center for Health Statistics (1999). *Healthy people 2000 review, 1998–1999*. Hyattsville, MD: Public Health Service.

Retrieved January 2, 2002, from www.cdc.gov/nchs/products/pubs/pubd/hp2k/review/review.htm

National Coalition to Abolish Corporal Punishment in Schools. (2001). *Facts about corporal punishment.* Retrieved January 2, 2002, from www.stophitting.com/NCACPS/index.html

National Commission on Excellence in Education. (1983). *A nation at risk: The imperative for educational reform.* Washington, DC: U.S. Department of Education.

National Institute of Mental Health (1999). *Suicide facts.* Retrieved January 2, 2002, from www.nimh.nih.gov/research/suifact.htm

National Research Council. (1996). *National science education standards.* Washington, DC: National Academy Press.

Naughton, C. C., & McLaughlin, T. F. (1995). The use of a token economy system for students with behaviour disorders. *B. C. Journal of Special Education, 19*(2/3), 29–38.

Nave, B., Miech, E., & Mosteller, F. (2000). A lapse on standards: Linking standards-based reform with student achievement. *Phi Delta Kappan, 82*(2), 128–132.

Neisser, U. (1976). *Cognition and reality.* San Francisco: Freeman

Neisser, U. (1982). *Memory observed.* San Francisco: Freeman.

Nelson, J. R. (1996). Effects of direct instruction, cooperative learning, and independent learning practices on the classroom behavior of students with behavioral disorders: A comparative analysis. *Journal of Emotional and Behavioral Disorders, 4*(1), 53–62.

Nelson, W., & Palumbo, D. B. (1992). Learning, instruction, and hypermedia. *Journal of Educational Multimedia and Hypermedia, 1*(3), 287–299.

Neuwirth, C. M., & Wojahn, P. G. (1996). Learning to write: Computer support for a cooperative process. In T. Koschmann (Ed.), *CSCL: Theory and practice* (pp. 147–170). Mahwah, NJ: Erlbaum.

Newman, B. M., & Newman, P. R. (1991). *Development through life: A psychosocial approach* (5th ed.). Pacific Grove, CA: Brooks/Cole.

Newman, F., & Holzman, L. (1993). *Lev Vygotsky: Revolutionary scientist.* London: Routledge.

Newman, J. M. (1991). *Interwoven conversations: Learning and teaching through critical reflection.* Toronto, Canada: Ontario Institute for Studies in Education.

Nicholls, J. G. (1979). Quality and inequality in intellectual development: The role of motivation in education. *American Psychologist, 34*(11), 1071–1084.

Nicholson, J., Gelpi, A., Young, S., & Sulzby, E. (1998). Influences of gender and open-ended software on first graders' collaborative composing activities on computers. *Journal of Computing in Childhood Education, 9*(1), 3–42.

Nickerson, R. S. (1994). The teaching of thinking and problem solving. In R. J. Sternberg (Ed.), *Thinking and problem solving.* San Diego, CA: Academic Press.

Nickerson, R. S. (1995). Can technology help teach for understanding? In D. N. Perkins, J. H. Schwartz, M. M. West, & M. S. Wiske (Eds.), *Software goes to school: Teaching for understanding with new technologies.* New York: Oxford University Press.

Nicol, M. P. (1997). How one physics teacher changed his algebraic thinking. *Mathematics Teacher, 90*(2), 86–89.

Nieto, S. (2000). *Affirming diversity: The sociopolitical context of multicultural education* (3rd ed.). New York: Addison Wesley Longman.

Niguidula, D. (1997). Picturing performance with digital portfolios. *Educational Leadership, 55*(3), 26–29.

Norman, D. A., & Rumelhart, D. E. (1970). A system for perception and memory. In D. A. Norman (Ed.), *Models of human memory.* New York: Academic Press.

North Central Regional Educational Laboratory. (1999). *Critical issue: Using technology to improve student achievement.* Retrieved January 2, 2002, from www.ncrel.org/sdrs/areas/issues/methods/technlgy/te800.htm

Novak, J. D. (1990). Concept mapping: A useful tool for science education. *Journal of Research in Science Teaching, 27*(10), 937–949.

Novak, J. D. (1998). *Learning, creating, and using knowledge: Concept maps as facilitative tools in schools and corporations.* Mahwah, NJ: Erlbaum.

Novak, M. (1971). Rise of unmeltable ethnics. In M. Friedman (Ed.), *Overcoming middle class rage.* Philadelphia: Westminster Press.

Nye, R. D. (1979). *What is B. F. Skinner really saying?* Englewood Cliffs, NJ: Prentice-Hall.

Oakes, C. (1996). First grade online. *Learning and Leading with Technology, 24*(1), 37–39.

Oakes, J. (1985). *Keeping track: How schools structure inequality.* New Haven, CT: Yale University Press.

Oakes, J., & Lipton, M. (1992). Detracking schools: Early lessons from the field. *Phi Delta Kappan, 73*(6), 448–454.

Oakes, J., & Wells, A. S. (1998). Detracking for high student achievement. *Educational Leadership, 55*(6), 38–41.

Ochse, R., & Plug, C. (1986). Cross-cultural investigation of the validity of Erikson's theory of personality development. *Journal of Personality and Social Psychology, 50*(6), 1240–1252.

Offer, D., & Offer, J. B. (1975). *From teenage to young manhood: A psychological study.* New York: Basic Books.

Office of the Federal Register. (1994). *Code of Federal Regulations 34. Parts 300 to 399.* Washington, DC: Author.

Office of Juvenile Justice and Delinquency Prevention. (2000, December). Juvenile arrests 1999. *OJJDP Juvenile Justice Bulletin.* Retrieved January 2, 2002, from www.ncjrs.org/pdffiles1/ojjdp/185236.pdf

Ogbu, J. U. (1992). Understanding cultural diversity and learning. *Educational Researcher, 21*(8), 5–14.

Ohanian, S. (2001). News from the test resistance trail. *Phi Delta Kappan, 82*(5), 363–366.

Okagaki, L., & Sternberg, R. J. (1990). Teaching thinking skills: We're getting the context wrong. In D. Kuhn (Ed.), *Developmental perspectives on teaching and learning thinking skills.* Basel, Switzerland: S. Karger.

Okagaki, L., & Sternberg, R. J. (Eds.).(1991). *Directors of development: Influences on the development of children's thinking.* Hillsdale, NJ: Erlbaum.

Okey, J. R. (1995). Performance assessment and science learning: Rationale for computers. *Journal of Science Education and Technology, 4*(1), 81–87.

O'Lone, D. J. (1997). Student information system software: Are you getting what you expected? *NASSP Bulletin, 81*(585), 86–93.

Olson, A. (2000). Computerized testing. *American School Board Journal, 187*(3) (Suppl.).

Olson, D. R., & Torrance, N. (Eds.).(1996). *Handbook of education and human development.* Cambridge, MA: Blackwell.

O'Neil, J. (1992). Putting performance assessment to the test. *Educational Leadership, 49*(8), 14–19.

Ormrod, J. E. (1999). *Human learning* (3d ed.). Upper Saddle River, NJ: Merrill.

Ornstein, A. C., & Levine, D. U. (2000). *Foundations of education* (7th ed.). Boston: Houghton Mifflin.

Osgood, C. E. (1949). The similarity paradox in human learning: A resolution. *Psychological Review, 56*(3), 132–143.

Oshima, J., Scardamalia, M., & Bereiter, C. (1996). Collaborative learning processes associated with high and low conceptual progress. *Instructional Science, 24*(1), 125–155.

white students. *Phi Delta Kappan, 80*(1), 9–15.
Singletary, T. J., & Jordan, J. R. (1996). Exploring the globe. *Science Teacher, 63*(3), 36–39.
Singley, M. K., & Taft, H. L. (1995). Open-ended approaches to science assessment using computers. *Journal of Science Education and Technology, 4*(1), 7–20.
Sipe, R. B. (2000). Virtually being there: Creating authentic experiences through interactive exchanges. *English Journal, 90*(2), 104–111.
Skinner, B. F. (1948). *Walden two.* New York: Macmillan.
Skinner, B. F. (1968). *The technology of teaching.* New York: Appleton-Century-Crofts.
Skinner, B. F. (1976). *Particulars of my life.* New York: Knopf.
Skinner, B. F. (1979). *The shaping of a behaviorist.* New York: Knopf.
Skinner, B. F. (1983). *A matter of consequences.* New York: Knopf.
Skinner, B. F. (1984). The shame of American education. *American Psychologist, 39*(9), 947–954.
Skinner, B. F. (1986). Programmed instruction revisited. *Phi Delta Kappan, 68*(2), 103–110.
Skinner, L., Gillespie, P., & Balkam, L. (1997). Waysiders in America's classrooms. *Technos, 6*(1), 29–31.
Skrtic, T. M., Sailor, W., & Gee, K. (1996). Voice, collaboration, and inclusion. *Remedial and special education, 17*(3), 142–157.
Slavin, R. E. (1989). PET and the pendulum: Faddism in education and how to stop it. *Phi Delta Kappan, 79*(10), 752–758.
Slavin, R. E. (1990a). IBM's writing to read: Is it right for reading? *Phi Delta Kappan, 72*(3), 214–216.
Slavin, R. E. (1990b). Achievement effects of ability grouping in secondary schools: A best-evidence synthesis. *Review of Educational Research, 60*(3), 471–500.
Slavin, R. E. (1994). Student teams-achievement divisions. In S. Sharan (Ed.), *Handbook of cooperative learning methods* (pp. 3–19). Westport, CT: Greenwood Press.
Slavin, R. E. (1995). *Cooperative learning: Theory, research, and practice* (2nd ed.). Boston: Allyn & Bacon.
Slavin, R. E., Madden, N. A., Dolan, L., & Wasik, B. (1996). *Every child, every school: Success for All.* Newbury Park, CA: Corwin Press.
Slavin, R. E., Madden, N. A., Karweit, N., Dolan, L, & Wasik, B. (1992). *Success for All: A relentless approach to prevention and early intervention in elementary schools.* Arlington, VA: Educational Research Service.
Sleeter, C. E., & Grant, C. A. (1999). *Making choices for multicultural education* (3rd ed.). Upper Saddle River, NJ: Merrill.
Smelter, R. W., Rasch, B. W., & Yudewitz, G. J. (1994). Thinking of inclusion for all special needs students? Better think again. *Phi Delta Kappan, 76*(1), 35–38.
Smilansky, S. (1968). *The effects of sociodramatic play on disadvantaged preschool children.* New York: Wiley.
Smith, D. D. (2001). *Introduction to special education* (4th ed.). Boston: Allyn & Bacon.
Smith, K., Johnson, D. W., & Johnson, R. T. (1981). Can conflict be constructive? Controversy versus concurrence seeking in learning groups. *Journal of Educational Psychology, 73*(5), 651–663.
Smith, M. L., & Fey, P. (2000). Validity and accountability in high-stakes testing. *Journal of Teacher Education, 51*(5), 334–344.
Snider, S. L., & Badgett, T. L. (1995). "I have this computer, what do I do now?" Using technology to enhance every child's learning. *Early Childhood Education Journal, 23*(2), 101–105.
Snir, J., Smith, C., & Grosslight, L. (1993). Conceptually enhanced simulations: A computer tool for science teaching. *Journal of Science Education and Technology, 2*(2), 373–388.
Snow, R. E. (1986). Individual differences and the design of educational programs. *American Psychologist, 41*(10), 1029–1039.
Snow, R. E. (1992). Aptitude testing: Yesterday, today, and tomorrow. *Educational Psychologist, 27*(1), 5–32.
Snowman, J. (1986). Learning tactics and strategies. In G. D. Phye & T. Andre (Eds.), *Cognitive classroom learning: Understanding, thinking, and problem solving.* New York: Academic Press.
Snowman, J. (1987, October). *The keys to strategic learning.* Paper presented at the annual meeting of the Mid-Western Educational Research Association, Chicago.
Soldier, L. L. (1989). Cooperative learning and the Native American student. *Phi Delta Kappan, 71*(2), 161–163.
Soldier, L. L. (1997). Is there an "Indian" in your classroom? Working successfully with urban Native American students. *Phi Delta Kappan, 78*(8), 650–653.
Songer, N.B. (1998). Can technology bring students closer to science? In K. Tobin & B. Fraser (Eds.), *The International Handbook of Science Education.* The Netherlands: Kluwer.
Spalding, E. (2000). Performance assessment and the new standards project: A story of serendipitous success. *Phi Delta Kappan, 81*(10), 758–764.
Spear, N. E., & Riccio, D. C. (1994). *Memory: Phenomena and principles.* Boston: Allyn & Bacon.
Spear, R. C. (1992). Appropriate grouping practices for middle level students. In J. L. Irvin (Ed.), *Transforming middle level education.* Boston: Allyn & Bacon.
Spear-Swerling, L., & Sternberg, R. J. (1998). Curing our "epidemic" of learning disabilities. *Phi Delta Kappan, 79*(5), 397–401.
Spector, J. E. (1995) Phonemic awareness training: Application of principles of direct instruction. *Reading and Writing Quarterly, 11*(1), 37–51.
Spiro, R. J., Feltovich, P. J., Jacobson, M. J., & Coulson, R. L. (1991). Knowledge representation, content specification, and the development of skill in situation-specific knowledge assembly: Some constructivist issues as they relate to cognitive flexibility theory and hypertext. *Educational Technology, 31*(9), 22–25.
Sprinthall, N. A., & Sprinthall, R. C. (1987). *Educational psychology: A developmental approach* (4th ed.). New York: Random House.
Sprinthall, N. A., Sprinthall, R. C., & Oja, S. N. (1998). *Educational psychology: A developmental approach* (7th ed.). New York: McGraw-Hill.
Stader, D., & Gagnepain, F. G. (2000). Mentoring: The power of peers. *American Secondary Education, 28*(3), 28–32.
Standing, L. (1973). Learning 10,000 pictures. *Quarterly Journal of Experimental Psychology, 25*(2), 207–222.
Standing, L., Conezio, J., & Haber, R. (1970). Perception and memory for pictures: Single trial learning of 2500 visual stimuli. *Psychonomic Science, 19*(2), 73–74.
Staub, D., & Peck, C. A. (1994/1995). What are the outcomes for nondisabled students? *Educational Leadership, 52*(4), 36–40.
Steffe, L. P., & Gale, J. (Eds.).(1995). *Constructivism in education.* Hillsdale, NJ: Erlbaum.
Steinberg, L. (1999). *Adolescence* (5th ed.). Boston: McGraw-Hill.
Stephen, J., Fraser, E., & Marcia, J. E. (1992). Moratorium-achievement (Mama) cycles in lifespan identity development: Value orientations and reasoning system correlates. *Journal of Adolescence, 15*(3), 283–300.
Stephens, L., Leavell, J. A., & Fabris, M. E. (1999). Producing video-cases that enhance instruction. *Journal of Technology and Teacher Education, 7*(4), 291–301.
Sternberg, R. J. (1985). *Beyond IQ: A triarchic theory of human intelligence.* New York: Cambridge University Press.

Sternberg, R. J. (1994). Allowing for thinking styles. *Educational Leadership, 52*(3), 36–40.

Sternberg, R. J. (1996a). Myths, countermyths, and truths about intelligence. *Educational Researcher, 25*(2), 11–16.

Sternberg, R. J. (1996b). Matching abilities, instruction, and assessment: Reawakening the sleeping giant of ATI. In I. Dennis & P. Tapsfield (Eds.), *Human abilities: Their nature and measurement* (pp. 167–181). Mahwah, NJ: Erlbaum.

Sternberg, R. J. (1997a). What does it mean to be smart? *Educational Leadership, 54*(6), 20–24.

Sternberg, R. J. (1997b). *Thinking styles.* New York: Cambridge University Press.

Sternberg, R. J. (1997c). Technology changes intelligence: Societal implications and soaring IQ's. *Technos, 6*(2), 12–14.

Sternberg, R. J. (1998). Abilities are forms of developing expertise. *Educational Researcher, 27*(3), 11–20.

Sternberg, R. J., Ferrari, M., Clinkenbeard, P., & Grigorenko, E. L. (1996). Identification, instruction, and assessment of gifted children: A construct validation of a triarchic model. *Gifted Child Quarterly, 40*(3), 129–137.

Sternberg, R. J., & Horvath, J. A. (1995). A prototype view of expert teaching. *Educational Researcher, 24*(6), 9–17.

Sternberg, R. J., & Spear-Swerling, L. (1996). *Teaching for thinking.* Washington, DC: American Psychological Association.

Sternberg, R. J., Torff, B., & Grigorenko, E. (1998). Teaching for successful intelligence raises school achievement. *Phi Delta Kappan, 79*(9), 667–671.

Stevens, R. J., & Slavin, R. E. (1995), the cooperative elementary school: Effects on students' achievement, attitudes, and social relations. *American Educational Research Journal, 32*(2), 321–351.

Stiggins, R. J. (2001). *Student-centered classroom assessment* (3rd ed.). Upper Saddle River, NJ: Merrill Prentice-Hall.

Stipek, D. J. (1998). *Motivation to learn: From theory to practice* (3rd ed.). Boston: Allyn & Bacon.

Stitt, B. A. (1988). *Building gender fairness in schools.* Carbondale, IL: Southern Illinois University Press.

Streib, L. Y. (1993. Visiting and revisiting the trees. In M. Cochran-Smith & S. L. Lytle (Eds.), *Inside/outside: Teacher research and knowledge.* New York: Teachers College Press.

Strother, D. B. (1986). Suicide among the young. *Phi Delta Kappan, 67*(10), 756–759.

Suomala, J., & Shaughnessy, M. F. (2000). An interview with Richard E. Mayer: About technology. *Educational Psychology Review, 12*(4), 477–483.

Supovitz, J. A. (1998). Gender and racial/ethnic differences on alternative science assessments. *Journal of Women and Minorities in Science and Engineering, 4*(2 & 3), 129–140.

Supovitz, J. A., & Brennan, R. T. (1997). Mirror, mirror on the wall, which is the fairest test of all? An examination of the equitability of portfolio assessment relative to standardized tests. *Harvard Educational Review, 67*(3), 472–506.

Susman, E. J. (1991). Stress and the adolescent. In R. M. Lerner, A. C. Peterson, & J. Brooks-Gunn (Eds.), *Encyclopedia of adolescence.* New York: Garland.

Svensson, A-K. (2000). Computers in school: Socially isolating or a tool to promote collaboration? *Journal of Educational Computing Research, 22*(4), 437–453.

Swanson, H. L., & Hoskyn, M. (1998). Experimental intervention research on students with learning disabilities: A meta-analysis of treatment outcomes. *Review of Educational Research, 68*(3), 277–321.

Sweller, J., van Merrienboer, J. J. G., & Paas, F. G. W. C. (1998). Cognitive architecture and instructional design. *Educational Psychology Review, 10*(3), 251–296.

Sylwester, R. (1999). In search of the roots of adolescent aggression. *Educational Leadership, 57*(1), 65–69.

Tanner, J. M. (1972). Sequence, tempo, and individual variation in growth and development of boys and girls aged twelve to sixteen. In J. Kagan & R. Coles (Eds.), *Twelve to sixteen: Early adolescence.* New York: Norton.

Tappan, M. B. (1998). Sociocultural psychology and caring pedagogy: Exploring Vygotsky's "hidden curriculum." *Educational Psychologist, 33*(1), 23–33.

Task Force on Education of Young Adolescents. (1989). *Turning points: Preparing American youth for the 21st century.* New York: Carnegie Council on Adolescent Development.

Tauber, R. T., & Mester, C. S. (1994). *Acting lessons for teachers: Using performance skills in the classroom.* Westport, CT: Praeger.

Taylor, C. A. (1989). *Guidebook to multicultural resources 1989–1990 edition.* Madison, Wl: Praxis Publications.

Teles, L. (1993). Cognitive apprenticeship on global networks. In L. M. Harasim (Ed.), *Global networks: Computers and international communications.* Cambridge, MA: MIT Press.

Templeton, S. (1995). *Children's literacy: Contexts for meaningful learning.* Boston: Houghton Mifflin.

Terwilliger, J. (1997). Semantics, psychometrics, and assessment reforms: A close look at "authentic" assessment. *Educational Researcher, 26*(8), 24–27.

Thoma, S. J. (1986). Estimating gender differences in the comprehension and preference of moral issues. *Developmental Review, 6*(2), 165–180.

Thomas, W. P., & Collier, V. P. (1997/1998). Two languages are better than one. *Educational Leadership, 55*(4), 23–26.

Thomas, W. P., & Collier, V. P. (1999). Accelerated schooling for English language learners. *Educational Leadership, 56*(7), 46–49.

Thompson, C. P., Cowan, T. M., & Frieman, J. (1993). *Memory search by a memorist.* Hillsdale, NJ: Erlbaum.

Thompson, S. (2001). The authentic standards movement and its evil twin. *Phi Delta Kappan, 82*(5), 358–362.

Thorndike, E. L., & Woodworth, R. S. (1901). The influence of improvement in one mental function upon the efficiency of other functions. *Psychological Review, 8*, 247–261.

Thurston, C. O., Secaras, E. D., & Levin, J. A. (1997). Teaching telapprenticeships: An innovative model for integrating technology into teacher education. *Journal of Research on Computing in Education, 29*(4), 385–391.

Tidwell, R. (1989). Academic success and the school dropout: A minority perspective. In G. L. Berry & J. K. Asamen (Eds.), *Black students: Psychosocial issues and academic achievement.* Newbury Park, CA: Sage.

Tinker, R., & Haavind, S. (1996). Netcourses and netseminars: Current practice and new designs. *Journal of Science Education and Technology, 5*(3), 217–223.

Tollefson, N. (2000). Classroom applications of cognitive theories of motivation. *Educational Psychology Review, 12*(1), 63–83.

Tomchin, E. M., & Impara, J. C. (1992). Unraveling teachers' beliefs about grade retention. *American Educational Research Journal, 29*(1), 199–223.

Tomlinson, C. A. (1999). Mapping a route toward differentiated instruction. *Educational Leadership, 57*(1), 12–16.

Tomlinson, T. M. (Ed.).(1993). *Motivating students to learn: Overcoming barriers to high achievement.* Berkeley, CA: McCutchan.

Toomey, R., & Ketterer, K. (1995). Using multimedia as a cognitive tool. *Journal of Research on Computing in Education, 27*(4), 472–482.

Torgesen, J. K., & Barker, T. A. (1995). Computers as aids in the prevention and remediation of reading disabilities. *Learning Disability Quarterly, 18*(2), 76–87.

Trentin, G. (1997). Computerized adaptive tests and formative assessment. *Journal of Educational Multimedia and Hypermedia, 6* (2), 201–220.

Triandis, H. C. (1986). Toward pluralism in education. In S. Modgil, G. K. Verma, K. Mallick, & C. Modgil (Eds.), *Multicultural education: The interminable debate*. London: Falmer.

Tsangaridou, N., & O'Sullivan, M. (1994). Using pedagogical reflective strategies to enhance reflection among preservice physical education teachers. *Journal of Teaching in Physical Education, 14*(1), 13–33.

Tudge, J. R. H., & Rogoff, B. (1989). Peer influences on cognitive development: Piagetian and Vygotskian perspectives. In M. H. Bornstein & J. S. Bruner (Eds.), *Interaction in human development*. Hillsdale, NJ: Erlbaum.

Tudge, J. R. H., & Winterhoff, P. A. (1993). Vygotsky, Piaget, and Bandura: Perspectives on the relations between the social world and cognitive development. *Human Development, 36*(2), 61–81.

Tulving, E., & Pearlstone, Z. (1966). Availability vs. accessibility of information in memory for words. *Journal of Verbal Learning and Verbal Behavior, 5*(4), 381–391.

Tuttle, H. G. (1997). Electronic portfolios tell a personal story. *MultiMedia Schools, 4*(1), 32–37.

Tyler, D. K., & Vasu, E. S. (1995). Locus of control, self-esteem, achievement motivation, and problem-solving ability: LogoWriter and simulations in the fifth-grade classroom. *Journal of Research on Computing in Education, 28*(1), 98–121.

Udrey, J. R. (1990). Hormonal and social determinants of adolescent sexual initiation. In J. Bancroft & J. M. Reinisch (Eds.), *Adolescence and puberty*. New York: Oxford University Press.

Underwood, J., Cavendish, S., Dowling, S., Fogelman, K., & Lawson, T. (1996). Are integrated learning systems effective learning support tools? In M. R. Kibby & J. R. Hartley (Eds.), *Computer assisted learning: Selected contributions for the CAL 95 symposium*. Oxford, UK: Elsevier Science.

U.S. Bureau of the Census. (2000a). *Fertility in American women*. Retrieved January 2, 2002, from www.census.gov/population/socdemo/fertility/

U.S. Bureau of the Census (2000b). *National population projections I. Summary Files: Projections of the total resident population by 5-year age groups, race, and Hispanic origin with special age categories*. Retrieved January 2, 2002, from www.census.gov/population/www/projections/natsum-T3.html

U.S. Bureau of the Census. (2000c). *Poverty in the United States: 1999*. Retrieved January 2, 2002, from www.census.gov/hhes/www/povty99.html

U.S. Department of Education. (2000a). *E-learning: Putting a world-class education at the fingertips of all children*. Retrieved January 2, 2002, from /www.ed.gov/Technology/elearning/e-learning.pdf

U.S. Department of Education. (2000b). *To assure the free appropriate public education of all children with disabilities, Twenty-second annual report to Congress on the implementation of the Individuals with Disabilities Education Act*. Retrieved January 2, 2002, from www.ed.gov/offices/OSERS/OSEP/Products/OSEP2000AnlRpt/index.html

U.S. Department of Education. (2001). *The condition of education 2001*. Washington, DC: U.S. Government Printing Office. Retrieved January 2, 2002, from http://nces.ed.gov/pubsearch/pubsinfo.asp?pubid=2001072

U.S. Department of Justice. (2000). *1998 statistical yearbook of the immigration and naturalization service*. Washington, DC: U.S. Government Printing Office. Retrieved January 2, 2002, from www.ins.usdoj.gov/graphics/aboutins/statistics/1998yb.pdf

U. S. Department of Labor. (2000). *Report on the youth labor force*. Washington, DC: Author. Retrieved January 2, 2002, from www.bls.gov/opub/rylf/pdf/rylf2000.pdf

Urdan, T., Midgley, C., & Anderman, E. M. (1998). The role of classroom goal structure in students' use of self-handicapping strategies. *American Educational Research Journal, 35*(1), 101–122.

Vallecorsa, A. L., deBettencourt, L. U., & Zigmond, N. (2000). *Students with mild disabilities in general education settings*. Upper Saddle River, NJ: Merrill Prentice Hall.

Valli, L.(1993). Teaching before and after professional preparation: The story of a high school mathematics teacher. *Journal of Teacher Education, 44*(2), 107–118.

van der Voort, T. H. A. (1986). *Television violence: A child's-eye view*. Amsterdam: North-Holland.

Van Dusen, L. M., & Worthen, B. R. (1995). Can integrated instructional technology transform the classroom? *Educational Leadership, 53*(2), 28–33.

van Laar, C. (2000). The paradox of low academic achievement but high self-esteem in African American students: An attributional account. *Educational Psychology Review, 12*(1), 33–62.

Van Wagenen, L., & Hibbard, K. M. (1998). Building teacher portfolios. *Educational Leadership, 55*(5), 26–29.

Vasquez, J. A. (1990). Teaching to the distinctive traits of minority students. *Clearing House, 63*(7), 299–304.

Ventura, S. J., Martin, J. A., Curtin, S. C., Menacker, F., & Hamilton, B. E. (2001). Births: Final data for 1999. *National Vital Statistics Reports, 49*(1). Hyattsville, MD: National Center for Health Statistics. Retrieved January 2, 2002, from www.cdc.gov/nchs/data/nvsr/nvsr49/nvsr49_01.pdf

Vermont Department of Education. (2000). *Vermont's framework of standards and learning opportunities*. Retrieved January 2, 2002, from www.state.vt.us/educ/stand/framework.htm

Vitz, P C. (1990). The use of stories in moral development: New psychological reasons for an old educational method. *American Psychologist, 45*(6), 709–720.

Vockell, E. L., & Fiore, D. J. (1993). Electronic gradebooks: What current programs can do for teachers. *Clearing House, 66*(3), 141–145.

Vondracek, F. W., Schulenberg, J., Skorikov, V., Gillespie, L. K., & Wahlheim, C. (1995). The relationship of identity status to career indecision during adolescence. *Journal of Adolescence, 18*(1), 17–30.

Vye, N. J., Goldman, S. R., Voss, J. F., Hmelo, C., Williams, S., & Cognition and Technology Group at Vanderbilt. (1997). Complex mathematical problem solving by individuals and dyads. *Cognition and Instruction, 15*(4), 435–484.

Vygotsky, L. S. (1986). *Thought and language* (A. Kozulin, Trans.). Cambridge, MA: MIT Press. (Original work published 1934)

Wadsworth, B. J. (1996). *Piaget's theory of cognitive and affective development* (5th ed.). White Plains, NY: Longman.

Wainryb, C., & Turiel, E. (1993). Conceptual and informational features in moral decision making. *Educational Psychologist, 28*(3), 205–218.

Walberg, H. J. (1990). Productive teaching and instruction: Assessing the knowledge base. *Phi Delta Kappan, 71*(6), 470–478.

Walker, J. E., & Shea, T. M. (1999). *Behavior management: A practical approach for educators* (7th ed.). Upper Saddle River, NJ: Merrill.

Wallace-Broscious, A., Serafica, F. C., & Osipow S. H. (1994). Adolescent career development: Relationships to self-concept and identity status. *Journal of Research on Adolescence, 4*(1), 127–149.

Walsh, W. B., & Betz, N. E. (2001). *Tests and assessment* (4th ed.). Upper Saddle River, NJ: Prentice-Hall.

Wang, M. C., Haertel, G. D., & Walberg, H. J. (1993). Toward a knowledge base for school learning. *Review of Educational Research, 63*(3), 249–294.

Wasserman, S. (1999). Shazam! you're a teacher: Facing the illusory quest for certainty in classroom practice. *Phi Delta Kappan, 80*(6), 464–468.

Waterman, A. S. (1988). Identity status theory and Erikson's theory: Communalities and differences. *Developmental Review, 8*(2), 185–208.

Waterman, A. S., & Archer, S. L. (1990). A life-span perspective on identity formation: Developments in form, function, and process. In P. B. Baltes, D. L. Featherman, & R. M. Lerner (Eds.), *Life-span development and behavior* (Vol. 10, pp. 30–57). Hillsdale, NJ: Erlbaum.

Watson, J. B. (1913). Psychology as the behaviorist views it. *Psychological Review, 20*, 158–177.

Watson, M. F., & Protinsky, H. (1991). Identity status of black adolescents: An empirical investigation. *Adolescence, 26*(104), 963–966.

Weah, W., Simmons, V. C., & Hall, M. (2000). Service-learning and multicultural/multiethnic perspectives: From diversity to equity. *Phi Delta Kappan, 81*(9), 673–675.

Webb, N. M., Nemer, K. M., Chizhik, A. W., & Sugrue, B. (1998). Equity issues in collaborative group assessment: Group composition and performance. *American Educational Research Journal, 35*(4), 607–651.

Wechsler, D. (1975). Intelligence defined and undefined: A relativistic appraisal. *American Psychologist, 30*(2), 135–139.

Wechsler, D. (1981).*Wechsler adult intelligence scale—revised*. New York: Psychological Corporation.

Wechsler, D. (1991). *Wechsler intelligence scale for children—III*. New York: Psychological Corporation.

Wedman, J. M., Espinosa, L. M., & Laffey, J. M. (1999). A process for understanding how a field-based course influences teachers' beliefs and practices. *Teacher Educator, 34*(3), 189–214.

Weiner, I. B. (1975). Depression in adolescence. In F. F. Flach & S. C. Draghi (Eds.), *The nature and treatment of depression*. New York: Wiley.

Weinstein, C. S., & Mignano, A. J., Jr. (1997). *Elementary classroom management: Lessons from research and practice* (2d ed.). New York: McGraw-Hill.

Wellesley College Center for Research on Women. (1992). *How schools shortchange girls*. Washington, DC: American Association of University Women Educational Foundation, National Education Association.

Wellman, H. M., & Gelman, S. A. (1992). Cognitive development: Foundational theories of core domains. In M.R. Rosenzweig & L. W. Porter (Eds.), *Annual review of psychology* (Vol. 43, pp. 337–375). Palo Alto, CA: Annual Reviews, Inc.

Wertsch, J. V. (1998). *Mind as action*. New York: Oxford University Press.

Wertsch, J. V., & Tulviste, P. (1996). L. S. Vygotsky and contemporary development psychology. In H. Daniels (Ed.), *An introduction to Vygotsky*. New York: Routledge.

Westerman, D. A. (1991). Expert and novice teacher decision making. *Journal of Teacher Education, 42*(4), 292–305.

Wheatley, G. H. (1991). Constructivist perspectives on science and mathematics learning. *Science Education, 75*(1), 9–21.

Wheelock, A. (1992). *Crossing the tracks: How "untracking" can save America's schools*. New York: New Press.

Wheelock, A. (1994). *Alternatives to tracking and ability grouping*. Arlington, VA: American Association of School Administrators.

Whimbey, A., & Lochhead, J. (1999). *Problem solving and comprehension* (6th ed.). Mahwah, NJ: Erlbaum.

White, B. L., & Watts, J. C. (1973). *Experience and environment: Major influences on the development of the young child*. Englewood Cliffs, NJ: Prentice-Hall.

Wicks-Nelson, R., & Israel, A. C. (2000). *Behavior disorders of childhood* (4th ed.). Upper Saddle River, NJ: Prentice-Hall.

Wiedmer, T. L. (1998). Digital portfolios: Capturing and demonstrating skills and levels of performance. *Phi Delta Kappan, 79*(8), 586–589.

Wiggins, G. (1993). Assessment: Authenticity, context, and validity. *Phi Delta Kappan, 75*(3), 200–214.

Wiles, J., & Bondi, J. (2001). *The new American middle school* (3rd ed.). Upper Saddle River, NJ: Merrill Prentice-Hall.

Willig, A. C. (1985). A meta-analysis of selected studies on the effectiveness of bilingual education. *Review of Educational Research, 55*(3), 269–318.

Winebrenner, S. (2000). Gifted students need an education, too. *Educational Leadership, 58*(1), 52–56.

Winne, P. H., & Jamieson-Noel, D. (2001, April). *Self-regulating studying by objectives for learning: Students' reports compared to a theoretical model*. Paper presented at the annual meeting of the American Educational Research Association, Seattle, WA.

Winner, E. (1997). Exceptionally high intelligence and schooling. *American Psychologist, 52*(10), 1070–1081.

Witkin, H. A., Moore, C. A., Goodenough, D. R., & Cox, P. W. (1977). Field-dependent and field-independent cognitive styles and their educational implications. *Review of Educational Research, 47*(1), 64.

Wittrock, M. W. (Ed.).(1986). *Handbook of research on teaching* (3d ed.). New York: Macmillan.

Wlodkowski, R. J. (1978). *Motivation and teaching: A practical guide*. Washington, DC: National Education Association.

Wlodkowski, R. J., & Ginsberg, M. B., (1995a). A framework for culturally responsive teaching. *Educational Leadership, 53*(1), 17–21.

Wlodkowski, R. J., & Ginsberg, M. B. (1995b). *Diversity and motivation: Culturally responsive teaching*. San Francisco: Jossey-Bass.

Woditsch, G. A. (1991). *The thoughtful teacher's guide to thinking skills*. Hillsdale, NJ: Erlbaum.

Wong, B. Y. L. (1985). Self-questioning instructional research: A review. *Review of Educational Research, 55*(2), 227–268.

Wood, F. W., & Zabel, R. H. (1978). Making sense of reports on the incidence of behavior disorders/emotional disturbance in school-aged populations. *Psychology in the Schools, 15*(1), 45–51.

Woodring, P. (1957). *A fourth of a nation*. New York: McGraw-Hill.

Woods, P. (1996). *Researching the art of teaching: Ethnography for educational use*. New York: Routledge.

Woodul, III, C. E., Vitale, M. R., & Scott, B. J. (2000). Using a cooperative multimedia learning environment to enhance learning and affective self-perceptions of at-risk students in grade 8. *Journal of Educational Technology Systems, 28*(3), 239–252.

Woolsey, K., & Bellamy, R. (1997). Science education and technology: Opportunities to enhance student learning. *Elementary School Journal, 97*(4), 385–399.

Worthen, B. R. (1993). Critical issues that will determine the future of alternative assessment. *Phi Delta Kappan, 74*(6), 444–454.

Wynn, R. L., & Fletcher, C. (1987). Sex role development and early educational experiences. In D. B. Carter (Ed.), *Current conceptions of sex roles and sex typing*. New York: Praeger.

Xin, F., Glaser, C. W., & Rieth, H. (1996). Multimedia reading: Using anchored instruction and video technology in vocabulary lessons. *Teaching Exceptional Children, 29*(2), 45–49.

Yates, F A. (1966). *The art of memory*. London: Routledge & Kegan Paul.

Yusuf, M. (1995). The effects of LOGO-based instruction. *Journal of Educational Computing Research, 12*(4), 335–362

Ysseldyke, J. E., & Algozzine, B., & Thurlow,

M. L. (2000). *Critical issues in special education.* (3rd ed.). Boston: Houghton Mifflin.

Zehavi, N. (1997). Diagnostic learning activities using DERIVE. *Journal of Computers in Mathematics and Science Teaching, 16*(1), 37–59.

Zeichner, K. M., & Liston, D. P. (1996). *Reflective teaching: An introduction.* Mahwah, NJ: Erlbaum.

Zeldin, A.L., & Pajares, F. (2000). Against the odds: Self-efficacy beliefs of women in mathematical, scientific, and technological careers. *American Educational Research Journal, 37*(1), 215–246.

Zellermayer, M., Salomon, G., Globerson, T., & Givon, H. (1991). Enhancing writing-related metacognitions through a computerized writing partner. *American Educational Research Journal, 28*, 373–391.

Zigmond, N., Jenkins, J., Fuchs, L. S., Deno, S., Fuchs, D., Baker, J. N., Jenkins, L., & Couthino, M. (1995). Special education in restructured schools: Findings from three multi-year studies. *Phi Delta Kappan, 76*(7), 531–540.

Zwier, G., & Vaughan, G. M. (1984). Three ideological orientations in school vandalism research. *Review of Educational Research, 54*(2), 263–292.

Author/Source Index

Subject Index

Credits

Text Credits

p. 10 *Case in Print:* "Special Young Teacher Wins a $1,500 Apple" by Carolyn Bower, *St. Louis Post-Dispatch,* September 7, 1996. Reprinted with permission of the *St. Louis Post-Dispatch,* Copyright 1996; **p. 19** *Table 1.1:* Adapted with permission from *National Educational Technology Standards for Students—Connecting Curriculum and Technology,* Copyright © 2000, ISTE (International Society for Technology in Education), 800.336.5191 (U.S. & Canada) or 541.302.3777 (Int'l); **p. 52** *Case in Print:* "Return of the One-Room Schoolhouse?," by Renee Stovsky, *St. Louis Post-Dispatch,* October 15, 1996. Reprinted with permission of the *St. Louis Post-Dispatch,* Copyright 1996; **p. 61** *Table 2.3:* Lickona, Thomas, (1998). A more complex analysis is needed. Phi Delta Kappan, 79(6), 449-454. Reprinted by permission of Phi Delta Kappa International and the author; **p. 92** *Case in Print:* "Middle School Rings in a New Level of Parenting for a Mom" by Debra-Lynn B. Hook, *St. Louis Post-Dispatch,* September 24, 2000. Reprinted with permission of the *St. Louis Post-Dispatch,* Copyright 2000; **p. 136** *Case in Print:* "Girl-Powered" by Carolyn Bower, *St. Louis Post-Dispatch,* December 1, 2000. Reprinted with permission of the *St. Louis Post-Dispatch,* Copyright 2000; **p. 124** *Table 4.2:* Sternberg, R. J., "What Does It Mean to be Smart?" *Educational Leadership,* 54, 6:22, Figure 1. Used by permission of the Association for Supervision and Curriculum Development. Copyright © 1997 by ASCD. All rights reserved; **p. 168** *Case in Print:* "Students Embrace Chance to Talk Out Frustrations" by Philip Dine, *St. Louis Post-Dispatch,* May 21, 1995. Reprinted with permission of the *St. Louis Post-Dispatch,* Copyright 1995; **p. 202** *Case in Print:* "Helping Kids Gain Social Skills," by Renee Stovsky, *St. Louis Post-Dispatch,* September 25, 1996. Reprinted with permission of the *St. Louis Post-Dispatch,* Copyright 1996; **p. 240** *Case in Print:* "Studying's Rewards" by Sacha Pfeiffer, the *Boston Globe,* January 3, 1996. Reprinted with permission of the author; **p. 272** *Case in Print:* " 'Memory' Can Play Tricks, Researchers Discover Here" by John G. Carlton, *St. Louis Post-Dispatch,* November 8, 1998. Reprinted with permission of the *St. Louis Post-Dispatch,* Copyright 1998; **p. 267** *Figure 8.2:* From G. H. Bower, M.C. Clark, A.M. Lesgold, and D. Winzenz, "Hierarchical Retrieval Schemes in Recall of Categorized Word Lists." *Journal of Verbal Learning and Verbal Behavior,* 1969, 8, 323–343. Copyright 1969 by Academic Press. Reproduced by permission of the publisher and the authors; **p. 281** *Table 8.2:* From King A. (1992), "Facilitating elaborative learning through guided student-generated questioning." *Educational Psychologist,* 27 (1), 111–126. Reprinted by permission of Lawrence Erlbaum Associates, Inc.; **p. 308** *Case in Print:* "All-USA Teacher Team: Changing Lives One Class at a Time" by Tracey Wong Briggs, *USA Today,* October 14, 1999. Copyright 1999, *USA Today.* Reprinted with permission; **p. 324** *Flow Diagram:* "Solution Using Flow Diagram," adapted from A. Whimbey and J. Lochhead, *Problem Solving and Comprehension,* Fifth Edition, ©1991, p. 126. (Hillsdale, NJ: Lawrence Erlbaum Associates, Inc., Publishers). Reprinted by permission; **p. 323** *Venn Diagram:* "Solution Using Venn Diagram," adapted from A. Whimbey and J. Lochhead, *Problem Solving and Comprehension,* Fifth Edition, ©1991, p. 272. (Hillsdale, NJ: Lawrence Erlbaum Associates, Inc., Publishers). Reprinted by permission; **p. 362** *Case in Print:* "Teachers Spin a World Wide Web of Virtual Voyages" by Christina Pino-Martin, *USA Today,* September, 1998. Copyright 1998, *USA Today.* Reprinted with permission; **p. 354** *Figure 10.1:* Source: Novak, J. D. & Gowin, D. B. (1984). *Learning How to Learn.* Cambridge, England: Cambridge University Press. Reprinted by permission; **p. 402** *Case in Print:* "Instituting Efficacy: Self-Esteem Principles May Be Tested at Burke High" by Esther Shein, the *Boston Sunday Globe,* June 18, 1995, pp. 89, 95. Reprinted with permission of the author; **p. 407** *Table 11.2:* Jere Brophy. "Teacher Praise: A Functional Analysis," *Review of Educational Research,* 51, No. 1 (1981), 532. Copyright © 1981. American Educational Research Association, Washington, D.C. Used with permission; **p. 446** *Case in Print:* "Pathways to Peace" by Mickey Baca, *Merrimack Valley Sunday,* Amesbury, MA, March 5, 1995; **p. 466** *Case in Print:* "Teachers Look for New Ways to Measure Learning" by Dale Singer, *St. Louis Post-Dispatch,* January 26, 1998. Reprinted with permission of the *St. Louis Post-Dispatch,* Copyright 1998; **p. 461** *Figure 13.1:* Parke, C.S. and Lane, S., "Learning from Performance Assessments in Math." *Educational Leadership,* 54, 4: 28, Figure 3. Used by permission of the Association for Supervision and Curriculum Development. Copyright © 1997 by ASCD. All rights reserved; **p. 463** *Table 13.1: The Clearing House,* 73(6), 324–328, 2000. Reprinted with permission of the Helen Dwight Reid Educational Foundation. Published by Heldref Publications, 1319 Eighteenth St., NW, Washington, DC 20036-1802. Copyright © 2000; **p. 504** *Case in Print:* "Students Await Standardized Tests" by Holly K. Hacker, *St. Louis Post-Dispatch,* April 2, 2001. Reprinted with permission of the *St. Louis Post-Dispatch,* Copyright 2001; **p. 509** *Figure 14.4:* Shepard, L. A. & Bliem, C. L.

(1995). Parents' Thinking about Standardized Tests and Performance Assessments. *Educational Researcher,* 24(8), 25–32. Copyright (1995) American Educational Research Association. Reprinted with permission; **p. 528** *Case in Print:* "Portfolios Give Prospective Teachers an Edge When They Interview for Jobs" by Valerie Schremp, *St. Louis Post-Dispatch*, December 14, 1997. Reprinted with permission of the *St. Louis Post-Dispatch*, Copyright 1997; **p. 520** *Figure 15.1:* Source: Don J. Cosgrove, "Diagnostic Rating of a Teacher Performance," *Journal of Educational Psychology,* 1959, 50, p. 202.

Photo Credits

Chapter 1: p. 3, Esbin-Anderson/The Image Works; **p. 8,** Elizabeth Crews; **p. 12,** Bill Bachman/PhotoEdit; **p. 14,** Index Stock Imagery/Frank Siteman; **p. 16,** Flash!Light/Stock Boston.

Part I Opener: p. 23, Flash!Light/Stock Boston.

Chapter 2: p. 32, Bob Daemmrich; **p. 36,** Bob Daemmrich/Stock Boston; **p. 42,** Flash!Light/Stock Boston; **p. 50,** David Young Wolff/PhotoEdit; **p. 57,** David Young-Wolff/PhotoEdit; **p. 65,** Index Stock Imagery/Kindra Cineff.

Chapter 3: p. 77, Index Stock Imagery/K.B. Kaplan; **p. 85,** Geoffrey Biddle; **p. 87 left,** David M. Grossman/Photo Researchers, Inc.; **p. 87, right,** Junebug Clark/Photo Reseachers, Inc.; **p. 90,** David Young-Wolff/PhotoEdit; **p. 95,** Richard Lord/The Image Works; **p. 98,** Elizabeth Crews; **p. 101,** John Curtis/D. Donne Bryant Stock; **p. 104,** Richard Hutchings/PhotoEdit.

Chapter 4: p. 117, Ray Scott/The Image Works; **p. 119,** Cleve Bryant/PhotoEdit; **p. 123 left,** David Young Wolff/PhotoEdit; **p. 123 right,** Laura Druskis/Stock Boston; **p. 127 left,** Susie Fitzhugh; **p. 127 right,** Erika Stone; **p. 134,** Ray Ellis/Photo Researcher, Inc.

Chapter 5: p. 151, Bob Daemmrich/Stock Boston; **p. 160,** John Elk III/Stock Boston; **p. 161,** David Young-Wolff/PhotoEdit; **p. 163,** Diane Graham-Henry/Stone/Getty Images; **p. 170,** David Young-Wolff/PhotoEdit; **p. 177,** Bob Daemmrich/Stock Boston.

Chapter 6: p. 186, Don and Pat Valenti/Stone/Getty Images; **p. 191,** Ellen B. Senisi/The Image Works; **p. 195,** Bodham Hrynewych/Stock Boston; **p. 201,** Laura Dwight; **p. 208,** Frank Siteman/Stock Boston; **p. 213,** Bob Daemmrich/The Image Works.

Part II Opener: p. 225, C. Bachmann/The Image Works.

Chapter 7: p. 229, Lawrence Migdale/Stock Boston; **p. 231,** Bob Daemmrich/The Image Works; **p. 234,** Lawrence Migdale; **p. 239,** Jim Pickerell/Stock Boston; **p. 243,** Laura Dwight;**p. 250,** Aaron Haupt/Stock Boston.

Chapter 8: p. 265, Elizabeth Crews; **p. 268,** Andrew M. Levine/Photo Researchers, Inc.; **p. 270,** Jeffry W. Myers/Stock Boston; **p. 274,** Elizabeth Crews; **p. 283,** Rick Friedman/Black Star; **p. 290,** Rhoda Sidney/Stock Boston.

Chapter 9: p. 305 left, Joel Gordon; **p. 305 right,** Will & Deni McIntyre/Photo Researchers, Inc.; **p. 315,** Seth Resnick/Stock Boston; **p. 319,** Bob Daemmrich/Stock Boston; **p. 327,** Bob Daemmrich/Stone/Getty Images.

Chapter 10: p. 342 (both), Index Stock Imagery/Robert Finken; **p. 344,** Bob Daemmrich; **p. 348,** Bob Daemmrich/Stock Boston; **p. 353,** Michael Newman/PhotoEdit; **p. 361,** Spencer Grant/PhotoEdit; **p. 371,** Bob Daemmrich/The Image Works.

Part III Opener: p. 381, Bill Bachmann/Stock Boston.

Chapter 11: p. 384, Will Hart/PhotoEdit; **p. 388,** Blair Seitz/Photo Researchers, Inc.; **p. 394,** John Lei/Stock Boston; **p. 397,** M. Greenlar/The Image Works; **p. 413,** Richard Hutchings/PhotoEdit.

Chapter 12: p. 420, Bob Daemmrich/The Image Works; **p. 425,** David Young-Wolff/PhotoEdit; **p. 432,** Junebug Clark/Photo Researchers, Inc.; **p. 438,** Lawrence Migdale/Photo Researchers, Inc.; **p. 443,** Bob Daemmrich/Stock Boston; **p, 445,** Elizabeth Crews.

Part IV Opener: p. 451, Bob Daemmrich.

Chapter 13: p. 454, Mary Kate Denny/PhotoEdit; **p. 456,** Jean-Claude LeJeune; **p. 459,** David Young-Wolff/PhotoEdit; **p. 469,** Bob Daemmrich; **p. 480,** Laura Dwight; **p. 483,** Bob Daemmrich.

Chapter 14: p. 491, Index Stock Imagery/Don Stevenson; **p. 493,** Jim Pickerell/Stock Boston; **p. 501,** Bob Daemmrich/The Image Works; **p. 505,** Jim Harrison/Stock Boston; **p. 508,** Flash!Light/Stock Boston.

Chapter 15: p. 521, Mary Kate Denny/PhotoEdit; **p. 525,** Michael Newman/PhotoEdit.

Suggestions for Teaching

Over 30 percent of the text is devoted to extensive Suggestions for Teaching in Your Classroom—concrete examples and discussion of how to apply psychological research to the classroom.

Index to Suggestions for Teaching in Your Classroom

Ultimately, because classical music has stayed the course. Over history, it has provided generations (dozens of generations, to push the point) with pleasure, joy, inspiration, and solace. So they have said, repeatedly. It can do the same for us today.

It's important to acknowledge the "otherness" of people in history, the differences between them and people today. Nonetheless, we relate to them; they are unquestionably *us,* as we can tell from their diaries and their poems, their portraits, their political aspirations and indeed also from their philosophical reflections, if we are prepared to give them the time it takes to really grasp them. We treasure our Declaration of Independence, written more than two hundred years ago, and it will be a bad day when we lose touch with the Constitution. There is a case to be made for also staying in touch with the poetry, art, and music of what one historian has called the "usable past."

On one level, music serves as entertainment, of course, and is none the worse for that. On another level, it provides a kind of knowledge or, at least, insight into human experience and feeling and time. How music manages to do this is a famous philosophical puzzle. The best short hypothesis is that music, which on a basic level is a strange and wonderful way of filling up time, vividly represents the way time feels as we actually live through it.

Music and History

The era of Classical music extends over more than a thousand years. Naturally, music changed vastly over that time—not only in its sound but also in its function and its institutions in society, its basic support system. Classical music is not monolithic. Another trip to the Virgin Megastore will reveal that many categories exist within the Classical sanctum. In addition to one big untitled section organized by composer, the store has smaller sections labeled Early Music and Contemporary. In this book, indeed, Early Music is set apart as an optional topic of study. We should try to explain why.

In sociological terms (very quickly, now!), Western musical history can be said to fall into three great phases. The later phases overlap, as forces underlying the earlier phases decay over long periods of time and others take their place.

- In the first millennium C.E., European culture was the culture of Christianity. All musicians (or at least all musicians that we know about) were churchmen, and all their music was sung in churches, abbeys, and cathedrals. The function of church music was to stimulate and enhance worship, to make prayer more fervent, and to make services more solemn and impressive.

- Around 1100, music composed for princely courts begins to appear in richly illuminated manuscripts. Slowly the church was yielding power to kings and nobles. Courts furnished the locale for instrumental and vocal music for many centuries. Music was now entertainment for court society, and indeed there were some famous monarchs who were keen musicians: Henry VIII of England and Frederick the Great of Prussia are two examples. But also, and increasingly with time, the function of court music was to glorify kings and princes.

Music at court, 1550: King Henry VIII of England playing the harp, posing as a modern King David. Only his court jester Will Sommers was allowed to pull long faces about this.

Listening Charts Listening Charts that focus listening are another integral feature of this text. Look at the portion of Listening Chart 5 below to see how they work (the complete chart is found on page 136). After choosing the appropriate musical selection, begin by finding the logo for your recording set at the top right corner of the chart. The numeral inside the logo tells you *which number CD* to choose from the set. The numeral below the logo tells you *which track* to play. For long selections with multiple CD tracks, small boxes running down the left side show where each new track begins. In these boxes, track numbers from discs in the 6-CD set are printed in green, those from the 3-CD set in black.

In essence this Listening Chart is a table of the main musical events in Bach's *Brandenburg* Concerto ("Ritornello," "Solo," and so on) with brief explanatory notes where needed. As you listen, follow down this list with the timing figures. To the *left* of the vertical line are the CD timings that you will see on your display, starting anew with each track. The timings to the *right* of the line give the total time from the beginning of the composition.

Refer to the logo that corresponds to your recordings package. The number in the center tells you which CD to play. The numbers beneath the logo are track numbers.

Track number reminders. The upper number is the track number for this piece in the 6-CD set; the lower number is the track number for the 3-CD set.

6-CD set 3-CD set

2 1

1-5 5-9

LISTENING CHART 5

Bach, *Brandenburg* Concerto No. 5, first movement

Ritornello form. 9 min., 56 sec.

Track		Time	Section	Description
1 / 5		0:00	**Ritornello**	Complete ritornello is played by the orchestra, forte: bright and emphatic.
		0:21	**Solo**	Harpsichord, flute, and violin in a contrapuntal texture (often in trio style). Includes faster rhythms; the soloists play new themes and also play some of the motives from the ritornello.
		0:46	**Ritornello (first phrase)**	Orchestra, *f*
		0:51	**Solo**	Similar material to that of the first solo
		1:12	**Ritornello (middle phrase)**	Orchestra, *f*
		1:18	**Solo**	Similar solo material
		1:40	**Ritornello (middle phrase)**	Orchestra, *f;* minor mode
		1:45	**Solo**	Similar solo material at first, then fast harpsichord runs are introduced.
2 / 6		2:28	**Ritornello (middle phrase)**	Orchestra, *f*
	0:06	2:34	**Solo**	This solo leads directly into the central solo.

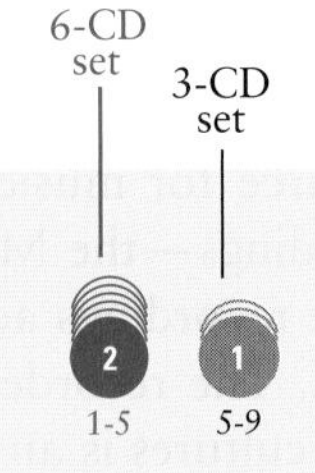

This left-hand column of timings gives you the time elapsed since the start of the current CD track.

The right-hand column of timings gives you the total time elapsed since the start of the piece.

For the benefit of those who are able to read music, the charts include a few brief notations of the main themes, directly across from the timing indications and the reference to the musical event. They are an extra; it is not necessary to read musical notation or even follow it in a general way to use these charts. Even people who think they are tone deaf (there's no such condition) can follow the music with the help of the timings.

Study Guide CD-ROM The Listening Charts are also available in an interactive format on the Study Guide CD-ROM in the back of this book and on the companion Web site at <bedfordstmartins.com/listen>. The interactive charts work in conjunction with the recordings, indicating when each new section of a piece begins and allowing you to play back specific themes or motives with a single mouse click.

The user guide for the CD-ROM can be found on the page facing the CD-ROM envelope. In addition to all the Listening Charts in an interactive format, the disk contains recordings of the listening examples in Unit I, "Fundamentals." This is the place you will go for live examples of the concepts introduced in this unit and to test your hearing of them. A logo and track numbers indicate specific recordings on the Study Guide CD-ROM.

1-3

J. K.

G. T.

About the Authors

Joseph Kerman and Gary Tomlinson are leading musicologists and music educators. Kerman, who with his wife, Vivian Kerman, was *Listen*'s original author, served for two terms as chair of the Music Department at the University of California at Berkeley, and Tomlinson has done the same at the University of Pennsylvania. Both are known as inspirational and wide-ranging teachers; between them, their course offerings encompass harmony and ear training, opera, world music, interdisciplinary studies, seminars in music history and criticism, and—many times—Introduction to Music for nonmajor students.

Kerman's books include *Opera as Drama* (second edition, 1988), *Contemplating Music* (1985), and studies of Beethoven and William Byrd. His lectures as Charles Eliot Norton Professor of Poetry at Harvard in 1997–1998 have been published as *Concerto Conversations* (1999). Tomlinson, a former MacArthur Fellow, is the author of *Monteverdi and the End of the Renaissance* (1987), *Music in Renaissance Magic* (1993), and *Metaphysical Song: An Essay on Opera* (1999). He has also published on jazz and native music of Latin America.

Contents in Brief

Global Perspectives

Maps

Listening Charts

Contents

UNIT I

Fundamentals

Unit I, the introductory unit in this book, covers music fundamentals and their standard terminology. We start right away with a piece of music, the Fantastic *Symphony by the nineteenth-century French composer Hector Berlioz. Chapter 1 presents the basic concepts of sound and time—pitch, dynamics, tone color, and duration—and introduces the terms used by musicians for these phenomena. Chapter 2 explains how, in music, time is organized into rhythm and meter, and how pitch is deployed in scales. Then Chapter 3 deals with melody and harmony in Western music, and other combinations of the basic elements that have already been treated. Chapter 4 carries the discussion one stage further, to a consideration of musical form and style. Our "Interludes" treat musical instruments and musical notation.*

Listening

The basic activity that leads to the love of music and to its understanding—to what is sometimes called "music appreciation"—is listening to particular pieces of music again and again. Such, at least, is the premise of this book. Its pages are filled mostly with discussions of musical compositions—symphonies, concertos, operas, and the like—that people have found more and more rewarding as they have listened to them repeatedly. These discussions are meant to introduce you to the contents of these works and their aesthetic qualities: what goes on in the music, and how it affects us.

The kind of hands-on knowledge of music that is necessary for a music professional—for a composer or a performer—is of no special use to you as a nonprofessional listener. But an acquaintance with musical concepts and musical terms can be useful, by helping you grasp more clearly what you already hear in music. Analyzing things, pinpointing things, even simply using the right names for things all make us more actively aware of them. Sometimes, too, this process of analyzing, pinpointing, and naming can actually assist listening. We become more alert, as it were, to aspects of music when they have been pointed out. And sharper awareness contributes to greater appreciation of music, and of the other arts as well.

Since our emphasis is on music, this is where we start—with an actual listening experience, our "overture" to this book. It will exemplify in a general way some of the concepts introduced in the following chapters, and make understanding the terminology of music, when we come to explain it, seem less abstract and mysterious, more immediate and alive.

OVERTURE

A March by Hector Berlioz

Listen, then, to what we are calling our overture, which is the fourth movement, a march, from one of the most famous of all symphonies, the *Fantastic* Symphony by the French composer Hector Berlioz. An overture is the orchestral music played prior to a play, ballet, or opera, or (stretching the point a little) a book. A movement is a section of a multisectional work such as a symphony, sonata, or concerto.

We study the whole of the *Fantastic* Symphony in Chapter 16, which also provides a short biography of the composer with a work list. For now we need only say that Berlioz was one of a galaxy of great composers born in the early 1800s, and one of the first Romantics in music. He was a near-contemporary of the American Edgar Allan Poe, a poet-storyteller with a mindset not so far from that of Berlioz, at least as manifested in the *Fantastic* Symphony. The symphony was Berlioz's first major composition, a wild success at its premiere in Paris in 1830 and a turning point in the history of music. And it is still popular today. When last tallied, the *Fantastic* Symphony was available in more than fifty CD recordings.

Listen to the movement in one or, preferably, all of three ways: (1) cold, (2) while at the same time following the prose discussion below, and (3) while following the Listening Chart on page 4. (For directions on working with Listening Charts, see page xvi.) In the discussion, we mention and cross-reference a few of the terms that will be introduced officially later and employed throughout this book. The idea is not to learn these terms at the present stage, just to get a feel for their use in the context of an actual piece of music, movement 4 of the Berlioz *Fantastic* Symphony.

Preliminaries A great deal of music of all kinds begins not with the main "song," or tune, or other main material, but with preliminaries to establish a background, usually some kind of pulse, in preparation for the material to come. (For an example from Africa, see page 108.) In our symphony, drums and low instruments set up a pulse consisting of a *beat,* an arrangement of beats (called the *meter:* duple meter in this case, ONE *two*|ONE *two*|ONE *two*), and a *tempo* or speed of the beats—a solid march tempo.

After a short time the music surges up into the first *theme.*

beat, page 10
meter, page 11
tempo, page 14
theme, page 26

The sheer loudness of Berlioz's music (though not all of it is as loud as the March to the Scaffold) shocked the Parisian public and inspired many cartoons.

Scale Theme Think of a theme in music as analogous to the theme of a political speech: the main subject matter that is going to be laid out and developed. A theme can be a tune, or merely a rhythm, or, as in this case, a downward scale. (Those with musical background will recognize it as a *minor* scale, changing in some of its repetitions to the *major*.) What makes an abstract entity like a scale into a theme is the distinctive *rhythm* given to it: DA-**DA**-DA da da-DA-DA-**DA**-DA da da DA-**DA** . . . Looks simple on paper, but the rhythm really invigorates that simple scale.

major and **minor,** page 32

rhythm, page 10

To be sure nobody fails to recognize the scale as something significant, something that will function as a theme, Berlioz plays it five times in succession. The second time a different melody is played simultaneously—in *counterpoint* with the Scale Theme, to use the technical term—by a lively low wind instrument. (Lively and somewhat grotesque; this is one characteristic sound of a *bassoon*). The combination of two melodies in counterpoint—or for that matter, the same melody in more than one instrument or voice, as in a round like "Row, row, row your boat"—is a musical resource of great importance. At the third appearance of the Scale Theme, the counterpoint shifts to low *stringed instruments,* or *strings*. Later the bassoon returns.

counterpoint, page 29

instruments:
bassoon, page 39

strings, page 36

In between playings of the theme there are excited flare-ups in various instruments of the orchestra. This music sits on a powder keg. It soon explodes.

LISTENING CHART 1

SG 1-3

Berlioz, *Fantastic* Symphony, fourth movement, March to the Scaffold

4 min., 45 sec.

1	0:00	Preliminaries: Drums and low instruments establish the beat, meter, and tempo	
	0:27	**A** Scale Theme (theme 1)—five times	
	0:38	+ Counterpoint in the bassoon	
	0:51	+ Counterpoint in low string instruments	Abrupt flare-up
	1:04	+ Counterpoint in low string instruments	
	1:16	+ Counterpoint in the bassoon	Bassoon tapers off
2	1:36	**B** March Theme (theme 2)	Band instruments
0:31	2:07	Theme 1 in "broken" orchestration	
		Repetition, but with extra instruments added:	
0:42	2:18	March Theme (theme 2)	
1:12	2:48	Theme 1 in "broken" orchestration	
1:20	2:56	Build-up to a climax: ***crescendo***	
	3:10	**A′** Scale Theme *fortissimo*	
3	3:21	Modulation	
0:02	3:23	Inversion of the Scale Theme	
0:14	3:35	Cadential section (the music sounds as though it is ending)	
0:48	4:09	**C**	

March The Scale Theme counts as the first theme in this piece; the second theme, a positively manic March, contrasts with it strongly. Here the composer uses wind instruments alone, with *trumpets* and *trombones* prominent, like a marching band. But into the very noisy, blatant music of theme 2 a bizarre version of theme 1 intrudes, broken up almost note by note among different instruments. Berlioz is famous for his innovations in *orchestration,* the art of combining and juxtaposing the sounds of orchestral instruments in effective and imaginative ways. Here is an arresting example.

instruments:
trombone, page 39
trumpet, page 39

(Perhaps this intricately "broken" version of theme 1 serves as compensation for the extreme simplicity of the original scale. Berlioz lets us hear it twice.)

Crescendo We have not said much up to now about the volume of sound in this movement, its loudness, or *dynamics.* After the March the music swells up in volume, getting louder and louder in expectation of some major event. This effect is called a *crescendo.* (*Crescendo* means "growing," in Italian. The opposite is *diminuendo,* diminishing.)

dynamics, page 7
crescendo and **diminuendo,** page 8

Scale Theme The Scale Theme returns in a mighty climax. Dynamics reach a peak; all the instruments are going at full tilt. Berlioz writes *ff* on the score, short for *fortissimo,* the musicians' conventional term for "very loud."

fortissimo, page 7

At track 3 all the instruments play a sudden new note forcibly, in unison: that is, all playing the same note. The new note seems almost to strike the music and knock it off base. This is a change of *key,* or *modulation,* a powerful and important effect in music of Berlioz's time. Modulation is hard to explain but (often) easy to hear. Typically it gives music a special spurt of energy, over and above what increased dynamics, different instrumentation, and other factors can do.

key, page 32
modulation, page 32

And then Berlioz gets a magnificent lift by *inverting* the Scale Theme, going up the scale instead of down. He trumps the immediately preceding climax.

inversion, page 140

The music has worked up to an almost superhuman level and needs to wind down—a long process as Berlioz does it, and exuberant as ever, but from now on, after the inversion of theme 1, he gives us the distinct feeling that things are coming to a close. *Cadence* is the term for a moment or passage that concludes and settles a piece of music or a section. It takes half a minute here to make a cadence and achieve closure.

cadence, page 25

Surprise But we should say "comes to the point of making a cadence," for after all the buildup the whole thing suddenly collapses. And what is *this*—the fragment of a hitherto unheard slow, quiet, even plaintive melody without any accompaniment whatsoever? It too collapses, crushed by a military drum roll and a final great blare.

Go to page 266 for the answer. We'll only tell you two things at this point. First, this final section was not part of the original music. It was added when Berlioz revisited an earlier piece and changed it to fit into his *Fantastic* Symphony as one of the movements. And second, he now gave this movement a title. It is not just a march, it is a "March to the Scaffold."

In retrospect, the main elements we have heard in this thrilling movement (there's no other word) are the Scale Theme, five times, followed by the contrasting March, leading to the Scale Theme again—not as many times as before, but now reconstituted as a formidable climax. Then comes the utterly surprising ending section. Putting together the whole experience, we can represent those main elements as **A B A′ C**. This is a letter diagram of a kind conventionally used for the *form* of music; *musical form* is a subject treated at some length in this book.

musical form, page 46

CHAPTER 1

Music, Sound, and Time

Music is the art of sound in time. We start with an outline of the basic properties of sound when it is produced, each of which corresponds to an effect that we experience when sound is heard. The scientific terms for sound all have their analogues in the terminology of music.

It has always seemed to me more important for the listener to be sensitive to the musical tone than to know the number of vibrations that produce the tone. . . . What the composer desires above all is to encourage you to become as completely conscious and wide-awake a listener as possible.

From what is still one of the best books on "music appreciation," *What to Listen For in Music* by composer Aaron Copland, 1939 (see page 363)

1 Sound Vibrations

As everyone who has taken a course in elementary physics knows, sound is produced by vibrations that occur when objects are struck, plucked, stroked, or agitated in some other way. The vibrations are transmitted through the air, or another medium, and picked up by our ears.

For the production of sound in general, almost anything will do—the single rusted hinge on a creaky door as well as the great air masses of a thunderstorm. For the production of musical sounds, the usual objects are taut strings and membranes, columns of air enclosed in pipes of various kinds, and silicon chips. These produce relatively simple vibrations, which translate into clearly focused or, as we say, "musical" sounds. Often the membranes are alive: They are called vocal cords.

Sound-producing vibrations are very fast; the range of sound that can be heard extends from around 20 to 20,000 cycles (that is, our vocal cords warble close to that many times every second). The vibrations are also very small. Look inside a piano while it is being played: You will not detect any movement in the strings, except possibly for some blurring of the very longest ones. To be heard, sound vibrations often need to be *amplified,* either electronically or with the aid of something physical that echoes or *resonates* along with the vibrating body. In a piano, this is the whole big wooden soundboard. The resonator in a guitar is the hollow box that the strings are stretched across.

Early musical instruments often have resonators found in nature: *above,* gourds in a pair of Mexican maracas; *on page 7,* a tortoise shell in the ancient Greek lyre, a small harplike instrument.

Pitch (Frequency)

The term for the rate of sound vibration is **frequency.** Frequency is measured in cycles (per second). On the level of perception, our ears respond differently to sounds of high and low frequencies, and to very fine gradations in between.

Indeed, people speak about "high" and "low" sounds quite unselfconsciously, as though they know that the latter actually have a low frequency—relatively few cycles—and the former a high frequency.

The musical term for this quality of sound, which is recognized so instinctively, is **pitch.** Low pitches (low frequencies) result from *long* vibrating elements, high pitches from *short* ones—a trombone sounds lower than a flute. Tap on a (tall) glass of water as you fill it up, and the pitch gets higher as the column of vibrating air gets shorter.

Noises, with their complex, unfocused vibrations, do not have pitch. And the totality of musical sounds, as distinct from noises, serves as a kind of quarry from which musicians of every age and every culture carve the exact building blocks they want for their music. We hear this totality in the sliding scale of a siren, starting low and going higher and higher until it is out of earshot.

But musicians never (or virtually never) use the full range of pitches. Instead a limited number of fixed pitches is selected from the sound continuum. These pitches are calibrated scientifically (European-style orchestras these days tune to a pitch with a frequency of 440 cycles), given names (that pitch is labeled A), and collected in *scales.* Scales are discussed in Chapter 2.

The experience of pitch is gained very early; babies only a few hours old respond to human voices, and they soon distinguish between high and low ones. They seem to prefer higher pitches, naturally—those in their mothers' pitch range. At the other end of life, it is the highest frequencies that older people find they are losing. The range of pitches that strike us as "normal," those that can be sung by most men and women, is shown to the right. (If you are not familiar with the notation for pitch, consult pages 20–22.)

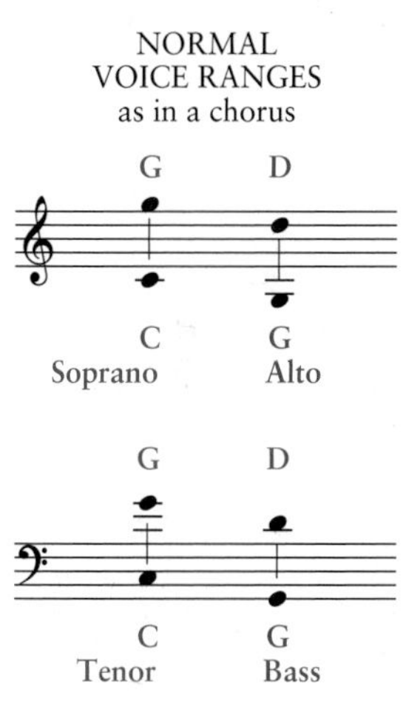

2 Dynamics (Amplitude)

In scientific terminology, *amplitude* is the level of strength of sound vibrations—more precisely, the amount of energy they contain and convey. As anyone who has been near a big guitar amplifier knows, very small string vibrations can be amplified until the energy in the air transmitting them rattles the eardrums. Amplitude is measured in *decibels.*

In musical terminology, the level of sound is called its **dynamics.** Musicians use very subtle dynamic gradations from very soft to very loud, but they have never worked out a calibrated scale of dynamics, as they have for pitch. The terms used are only approximate. Because all European music looked to Italy when this terminology first came into use, the terms used for dynamics are in Italian.

The main categories are simply loud and soft, **forte** (pronounced fórteh) and **piano,** which may be qualified by expanding to "very loud" or "very soft" and by adding the Italian word for "medium," **mezzo** (medzo):

pianissimo	*piano*	*mezzo piano*	*mezzo forte*	*forte*	*fortissimo*
pp	***p***	***mp***	***mf***	***f***	***ff***
very soft	soft	medium soft	medium loud	loud	very loud

Other terms are **più forte** and **meno forte,** "more loud" and "less loud" (pyōō, méhno). Changes in dynamics can be sudden (*subito*), or they can be

LISTEN for pitch and dynamics

4

For explanation of this icon, see page xvii.

In Unit I of this book, we will illustrate the concepts that are introduced with listening examples drawn from the enclosed CD-ROM. Follow the timings on these LISTEN charts, which are simplified versions of the Listening Charts provided for complete compositions. The charts are explained on page xvi.

High and low ***pitch*** and loud and soft ***dynamics*** are heard so instinctively that they hardly need illustration. Listen, however, to the vivid way they are deployed in one of the most famous of classical compositions, the "Unfinished" Symphony by Franz Schubert. Symphonies consist of four separate big segments, called movements; musicologists are still baffled as to why Schubert wrote two superb movements for this work and started but never finished the rest.

		PITCH	DYNAMIC
4 0:00	Quiet and mysterious	Low range	*pp*
0:15	Rustling sounds	Middle range	
0:22	Wind instruments	High	
0:35	Single sharp accent		*sf*
0:47	Gets louder	Higher instruments added	Long ***crescendo,*** leading to *f,* then *ff,* more accents
1:07	Sudden collapse		***piano*** followed by ***diminuendo***
1:15	New tune	First low, then high	(Marked ***pp*** by Schubert, but usually played ***p*** or ***mp***.)
1:52	Cuts off sharply; big sound		*ff,* more accents
	(Similar pitch and dynamic effects for the rest of the excerpt)		
3:07	Sinking passage	Individual pitches, lower and lower	
3:45	Ominous	Lowest pitch of all	*pp*

gradual—a soft passage swells into a loud one, or a powerful blare fades into quietness. Below are the terms for changing dynamics and their notational signs (sometimes called "hairpins"):

crescendo (**cresc.**)	*decrescendo* (**decresc.**), *or diminuendo* (**dim.**)
<	>
gradually getting louder	gradually getting softer

3 Tone Color: Overtones

At whatever pitch, and whether loud or soft, musical sounds differ in their general *quality,* depending on the instruments or voices that produce them. **Tone color** and **timbre** are the terms for this quality.

Tone color is produced in a more complex way (and a more astonishing way, it must seem, the first time you learn about it) than pitch and dynamics. Piano strings and other sound-producing bodies vibrate not only along their total length, but also simultaneously in half-lengths, quarters, eighths, and so on.

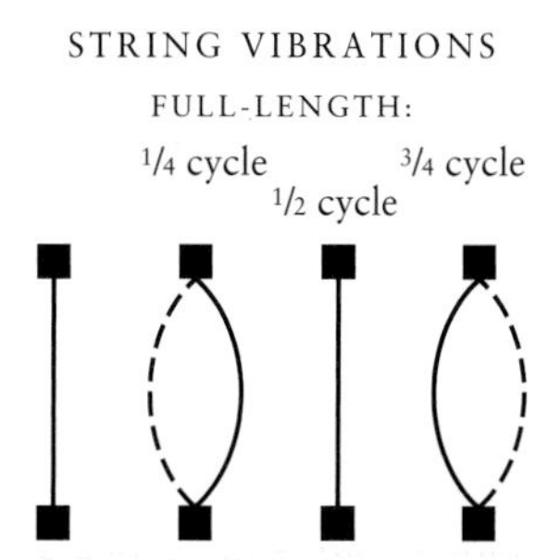

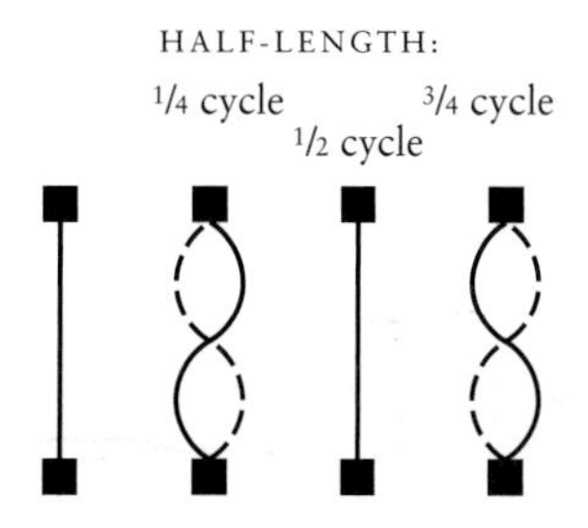

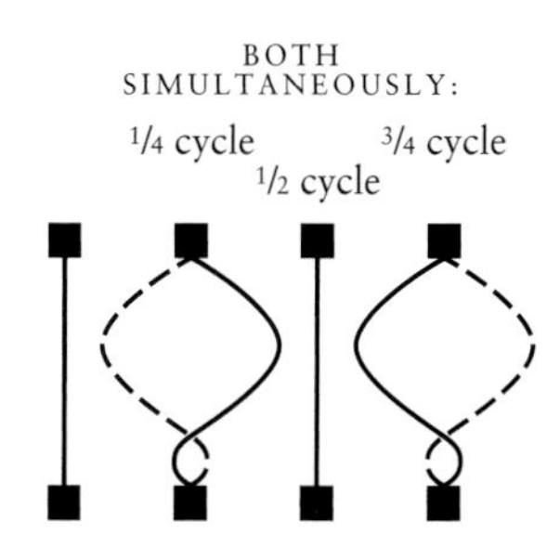

The diagrams above attempt to illustrate this. The amplitudes of these fractional vibrations, called **partials** by scientists, **overtones** by musicians, are much lower than the amplitude of the main vibration. Indeed, overtones are not heard as distinct pitches, but as part of the string's basic or fundamental pitch. The amount and proportion of overtones are what give a sound its characteristic tone color. A flute has few overtones. Luciano Pavarotti has many.

Musicians make no attempt to tally or describe tone colors; about the best one can do is apply imprecise adjectives such as *bright, warm, ringing, hollow,* or *brassy.* Yet tone color is surely the most easily recognized of all musical elements. Even people who cannot identify instruments by name can distinguish between the smooth, rich sound of violins playing together, the bright sound of trumpets, and the thump of drums.

Listen to orchestral tone colors with the Listening Chart on page 52, after following the discussion of European musical instruments in Interlude B (pages 36–45). Look forward to hearing many more non-European instruments in connection with the Global Perspectives sections of this text. The variety of devices invented for the different tone colors that people have desired for their music, in all societies, is almost unbelievable.

The most distinctive tone color of all, however, belongs to the first, most beautiful, and most universal of all the sources of music—the human voice.

4 Duration

Sound exists in time, and any sound we hear has its **duration**—the length of time we hear it in minutes, seconds, or microseconds. Though duration is not an actual property of sound, like frequency, amplitude, and other of sound's attributes that are taught in physics courses, it is obviously of central importance for music, which is the art of sounds in time. The broad term for the time aspect of music is **rhythm.**

The primacy of rhythm in the experience of music is practically an act of faith in our culture—and in most other cultures as well. However, there is some music in which rhythm counts for less than, say, tone color; such a piece will be studied in Chapter 22, *Lux aeterna* by the contemporary composer György Ligeti. Think also of New Age music. But rhythm is the main driving force in music both popular and classical, music of all ages and all cultures, and rhythm is where we will begin our discussion of the elements of music in Chapter 2.

The singing voice, "the first, most beautiful, and most universal of all the sources of music": Renée Fleming, a star in the opera world of the 2000s.

Web: *To test your understanding of music, sound, and time, take an online quiz at* **<bedfordstmartins.com/listen>**.

CHAPTER 2

Rhythm and Pitch

We start this chapter by discussing *rhythm,* the way musical time is organized by the use of durations of various magnitudes. We then go on to the organization of pitch into *scales* and *intervals.*

Music has four essential elements: rhythm, melody, harmony, and tone color. These four ingredients are the composer's materials. He works with them in the same way that any other artisan works with his materials.

Aaron Copland, *What to Listen For in Music*

1 Rhythm

As we have seen, the term **rhythm** in its broadest sense refers to the time aspect of music. In a more specific sense, "*a* rhythm" refers to the actual arrangement of durations—long and short notes—in a particular melody or some other musical passage. Of course, the term is also used in other contexts, about golfers, quarterbacks, poems, and even paintings. But no sport and no other art handles rhythm with such precision and refinement as does music.

The term *rhythmic* is often used to describe music that features simple patterns, such as ONE *two*|ONE *two,* repeating over and over again, but that is not really correct (think about what a golfer or tennis player means by rhythm). Such patterns should be described as *metrical,* or strongly metrical, not rhythmic. See the section "Rhythm and Meter" on page 12.

Beat

The basic unit for measuring time in music is the **beat.** When listening to a marching band, to take a clear example, we surely sense a regular recurrence of short durational units. These units serve as a steady, vigorous background for other, more complicated durational patterns that we discern at the same time. We can't help beating time to the music, waving a hand or tapping a foot, following the motion of the drum major's baton and the big-drum players' drumsticks. The simple durational pattern that is being signaled by waving, tapping, or thumping is the music's beat.

Accent

Beats provide the basic unit of measurement for time; if ordinary clock time is measured in seconds, musical time is measured in beats. There is, however, an all-important difference between a clock ticking and a drum beating time. Mechan-

The beat: There are times when the drummers in a band do little more than bang it out.

ically produced ticks all sound exactly the same, but it is virtually impossible to beat time without making some beats more emphatic than others. This is called giving certain beats an **accent.**

And accents are really what enable us to beat time, since the simplest way to do this is to alternate accented ("strong") and unaccented ("weak") beats in patterns such as ONE *two*|ONE *two*|ONE *two* . . . or ONE *two three*|ONE *two three*|ONE *two three*. . . . To beat time, then, is not only to measure time but also to organize it, at least into these simple two- and three-beat patterns. That is why a drum is a musical instrument and a clock is not.

Accents are not usually indicated in musical notation, since in most types of music they are simply taken for granted. When composers want a particularly strong accent—something out of the ordinary—they put the sign > above or below a note. Thus a pattern of alternating very strong and weak beats is indicated as shown to the right. An even stronger accent is indicated by the mark ***sfz*** or ***sf***, short for *sforzando*, the Italian word for "forcing."

Meter

Any recurring pattern of strong and weak beats, such as the ONE *two* and ONE *two three* we have referred to and illustrated above, is called a **meter**. Meter is a strong/weak pattern repeated again and again.

Each occurrence of this repeated pattern, consisting of a principal strong beat and one or more weaker beats, is called a **measure,** or **bar.** In musical notation, measures are indicated by vertical lines called **bar lines.** The meter indicated schematically in the margin above is notated as shown to the right.

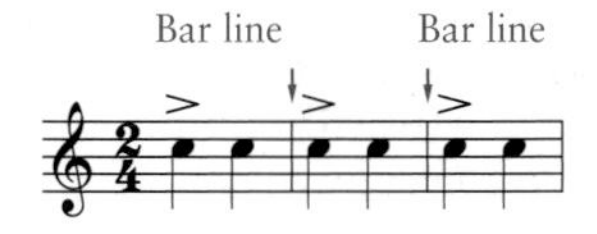

In Western music there are only two basic kinds of meter, called **simple meters:** duple meter and triple meter, plus a third, **compound meter,** which involves a subdivision of one of the simple meters.

In duple meter the beats are grouped in twos (ONE *two*|ONE *two*). Duple meter is instantly familiar from marches—such as "Yankee Doodle"—which tend always to use it in deference to the human anatomy (LEFT *right,* LEFT *right,* LEFT *right*).

In triple meter the beats are grouped in threes (ONE *two three*|ONE *two three*). As it happens, our national songs "The Star-Spangled Banner" and "My Country, 'Tis of Thee" are in triple meter. "My Country, 'Tis of Thee" starts on the strong beat ONE of the triple meter; "The Star-Spangled Banner" starts on the weak beat *three.*

Not infrequently, there is a clearly marked subdivision of the main beats into threes, resulting in *compound meters* with six or nine beats:

ONE	*two*	ONE	*two*	*three*
ONE *two three*	FOUR *five six*	ONE *two three*	FOUR *five six*	SEVEN *eight nine*

Compound meters are really best thought of as subtypes of duple and triple meter. The round "Row, row, row your boat" is in compound meter, **6/8**, but while the first voice is moving at a fast six-beat clip at the words "Merrily, merrily," the second voice comes in pounding out the basic duple meter, "Row, *row,* row":

first voice:

Row,	row,	row your	boat	gently	down the	stream,		Merrily,	merrily,	merrily,	merrily,
1 2 3	4 5 6	1 2 3	4 5 6	1 2 3	4 5 6	1 2 3	4 5 6	**1 2 3**	**4 5 6**	**1 2 3**	**4 5 6**
ONE	*two*	ONE	*two*	ONE	*two*	ONE	*two*	ONE	*two*	ONE	*two*
						second voice:		Row,	row,	row . . .	
								ONE	***two***	ONE	***two***

Meters with five beats, seven beats, and so on have never been used widely in Western music, though they are found frequently enough in some other musical cultures. It was an unusual tour de force for Chaikovsky to have provided his popular Sixth Symphony with a very convincing waltzlike movement in *quintuple* meter (five beats to a bar).

Chaikovsky, Symphony No. 6

Rhythm and Meter

We have already seen that *rhythm* in the most general sense refers to the entire time aspect of music and, more specifically, that *a* rhythm refers to the particular arrangements of long and short notes in a musical passage. In most Western music, duple or triple *meter* serves as the regular background against which we perceive music's actual rhythms.

As the rhythm now coincides with the meter, then cuts across it independently, then even contradicts it, all kinds of variety, tension, and excitement can result. Meter is background; rhythm is foreground.

The most exciting rhythms seem unexpected and complex, the most beautiful melodies simple and inevitable.

Poet W. H. Auden, 1962

Musical notation has developed a conventional system of signs (see pages 20–21) to indicate relative durations; combining various signs is the way of indicating rhythms. Following are examples of well-known tunes in duple and triple meters. Notice from the shading (even better, sing the tunes to yourself and *hear*) how the rhythm sometimes corresponds with the meter and sometimes departs from it. The shading indicates passages of rhythm-meter correspondence:

The above diagrams should not be taken to imply that meter is always emphasized behind music's rhythms. Often the meter is not explicitly beaten out at all. It does not need to be, for the listener can almost always sense it under the surface. People will even imagine they hear a duple or triple meter behind the steady dripping of a faucet or the ticking of a clock.

Naturally, meter is strongly stressed in music designed to stimulate regular body movements, such as marches, dances, and much popular music. The connection between strongly metrical music and sex is acknowledged by the uninhibited gesturing of rock stars and the explicit imagery of MTV.

At the other extreme, there is *nonmetrical* music. The meandering, nonmetrical rhythms of Gregorian chant contribute to the cool, unworldly, and spiritual quality that devotees of this music cherish. Sometimes these two different kinds of rhythmic organization are joined together. In the classical music of India, for example, most performances begin with a long section of nonmetrical music, and then proceed to music with a clearly defined meter. See page 219.

Rhythm might be described as, to the world of sound, what light is to the world of sight. It shapes and gives new meaning.

Edith Sitwell, poet and critic, 1965

Syncopation

One way of obtaining interesting, striking effects in music is to displace the accents in a foreground *rhythm* away from their normal position on the beats of the background *meter.* This is called **syncopation.** In duple meter, accents can be displaced so they go *one* TWO|*one* TWO instead of ONE *two*|ONE *two*. Or the syncopation can occur in between beats ONE and *two,* as in this Christmas ballad:

Ru*dolf* __ the red - nosed rein - deer ____________
ONE *two* | ONE *two* | ONE *two* | ONE *two*

If you know the George M. Cohan classic "Give my regards to Broadway," you know that it starts with the same syncopation as in "Rudolf," and has another syncopation in its second line:

Give ***my*** __ re- gards to Broad - - - way, Re - member me to Her*ald* ___ Square
ONE *two* | ONE *two* | ONE *two* | ONE *two* | ONE *two* | ONE *two* ONE

The consistent use of syncopation is the hallmark of African American–derived popular music, from jazz to world beat. See Chapter 23.

Tempo

Our discussion so far has referred to the *relative* duration of sounds—all beats are equal; some notes are twice as long as others, and so on—but nothing has been said yet about their *absolute* duration in fractions of a second. The term for the speed of music is **tempo**; in metrical music, the tempo is the rate at which the basic, regular beats of the meter follow one another.

Tempo can be expressed quantitatively by such indications as ♩ = 60, meaning 60 quarter-note beats per minute. These indications are called **metronome marks**, after the metronome, a mechanical or electrical device that ticks out beats at any desired tempo.

An early metronome owned by Beethoven, who was a friend of the inventor, Johannes Maelzel. A clockwork mechanism made the bar swing back and forth, ticking, at a rate determined by a little movable weight on the bar.

When composers give directions for tempo, however, they usually prefer general terms. Rather than freezing the music's speed by means of a metronome mark, they prefer to leave some latitude for different performers, different acoustical conditions in concert halls, and other factors. Like the indications for dynamics, the conventional terms for tempo are Italian:

COMMON TEMPO INDICATIONS		LESS COMMON TEMPO INDICATIONS	
adagio:	slow	*largo, lento, grave:*	slow, very slow
andante:	on the slow side, but not too slow	*larghetto:*	somewhat faster than *largo*
moderato:	moderate tempo	*andantino:*	somewhat faster than *andante*
allegretto:	on the fast side, but not too fast	*vivace, vivo:*	lively
allegro:	fast	*molto allegro:*	faster than *allegro*
presto:	very fast	*prestissimo:*	very fast indeed

In their original meaning, many of these Italian words refer not to speed itself but rather to a mood, action, or quality that can be associated with tempo only in a general way. Thus, *vivace* is close to our "vivacious," *allegro* means "cheerful," and *andante,* derived from the Italian word for "go," might be translated as "moving along steadily."

Other terms indicate irregularities of tempo and tempo changes:

accelerando (acheleráhndo) (accel.)	gradually getting faster
ritardando (rit.) or *rallentando (rall.)*	gradually getting slower
più lento, più allegro	slower, faster
𝄐 (fermata symbol)	a hold of indefinite length on a certain note or rest, which in effect suspends the tempo
a tempo	back to the main tempo

The most important terms to remember are those listed under "common tempo indications" above. When they appear at the top of a symphony movement or the like, they usually constitute its only heading. People refer to the "Andante" of Beethoven's Fifth Symphony, meaning a certain movement of the symphony (the second), which is played at an *andante* tempo.

2 Pitch

Music, as we noted in Chapter 1, generally does not use the total continuous range of musical sounds. Instead, it draws on only a limited number of fixed pitches. These pitches can be assembled in a collection called a **scale.** In effect, a scale is the pool of pitches available for making music.

Which exact pitches constitute a scale differ from culture to culture. Twelve basic pitches have been fixed for most of the music we know—and so people tend to think of the Western scale as "natural." This is a mistake. Five pitches were once used in Japan, as many as twenty-four have been used in Near Eastern countries, and Western Europe itself originally used seven.

LISTEN for rhythm, meter, and tempo

1, 4-14, 17

For samples of ***duple, triple,*** and ***compound meters,*** listen to tracks on the Study Guide CD-ROM that we are also using in Unit 1 to illustrate more complex concepts. (With duple meter, it is often hard to hear whether the music is in **2/4** or **4/4.** If the performer doesn't distinguish the beats clearly enough, ONE *two* THREE *four* in **4/4** is going to sound very much like ONE *two*|ONE *two* in **2/4.**)

Tracks	Meter	Count
1, 5, 7, 9, 10	Duple meter **2/4** or **2/2**	Count ONE *two*|ONE *two* . . . etc., for about half a minute.
12, 13	Duple meter **4/4** or **4/8**	Count ONE *two* THREE *four*|ONE *two* THREE *four* . . . etc.
4, 14, 17	Triple meter **3/4**	Count ONE *two three*|ONE *two* three . . . etc. In track 4, count nine beats (three bars) in the tenth note from the beginning. In track 14, note several ***fermatas.***
11	Compound meter **6/8**	Count ONE *two three* FOUR *five six* . . . etc.

6, 7 ***Tempo*** is best illustrated when tempo changes, as at 0:48 in track 7 (and, for a more extended example, several times in track 6).

5 ***Syncopation*** is at its most insistent and most delightful in rags, such as Scott Joplin's signature "Maple Leaf Rag." See page 391. Listen to the piano left hand, with its steady ONE *two*|ONE *two* beat in duple meter; the right hand cuts across it with syncopations in almost every measure.

For a more leisurely experience of different meters (and tempos), and syncopation effects of different kinds, listen to the *Rhapsody on a Theme by Paganini* for piano and orchestra, by the great twentieth-century pianist-composer Sergei Rachmaninov (1873–1943). The example on our CD-ROM is only a segment of this lengthy work.

The example contains several subunits, around a minute or two each, in different meters and tempos. If you note a family likeness between the subunits, that is because they are all variations on a single theme. (See page 187.)

6

0:00	Piano starts in ***duple meter.*** The loud orchestral interruptions are ***syncopated.*** (After the interruptions the meter is somewhat obscured, but it gets clearer.)
0:33	Clear duple meter by this time; then the music comes to a stop.
0:49	No meter. The piano seems to be engaged in a meditative improvisation, as though dreaming up the music to come.
1:45	Orchestral instruments suggest a slow ***duple meter***? Not for long.
2:24	Slow ***triple meter***
3:40	***Ritardando*** (getting slower)
3:56	Fast ***triple meter,*** marchlike (note one or two syncopated notes)
4:26	Faster ***triple meter***

Intervals (I): The Octave

The difference, or distance, between any two pitches is called an **interval.** Of the many different intervals used in music, one has a special character that makes it particularly important. This is the **octave.**

If a series of successive pitches is sounded, one after another—say, running up the white keys on a keyboard—there comes a point at which the pitch seems in some sense to "duplicate" an earlier pitch, but at a higher level. This

Choral singing, the route by which millions of people come to know and love music.

new pitch does not sound identical to the old one, but somehow the two sounds are very similar. They blend extremely well; they almost seem to melt into each other.

What causes the phenomenon of octaves? Recall from Chapter 1 that when strings vibrate to produce sound they vibrate in partials, that is, not only along their full length but also in halves and other fractions (page 9). A vibrating string that is exactly half as long as another will *reinforce* the longer one's strongest partial. This reinforcement causes the duplication effect of octaves.

As strings go, so go vocal cords: When men and women sing along together, they automatically sing in octaves, duplicating each other's singing an octave or two apart. If you ask them, they will say they are singing "the same tune"—not many will think of adding "at different octave levels."

As a result of the phenomenon of octaves, the full continuous range of pitches that exists in nature (and that is covered, for example, by a siren starting low and going up higher and higher) falls into a series of "duplicating" segments. Human ears are able to detect about ten of these octave segments. Two or three octaves is a normal range for most voices and instruments. A large pipe organ covers all ten and a piano covers about seven. Two octaves are shown on our next diagram.

The Diatonic Scale

The set of seven pitches originally used in Western music is called the **diatonic scale.** Dating from ancient Greek times, it is still in use today. When the first of the seven pitches is repeated at a higher duplicating pitch, the total is eight—hence the name *octave,* meaning "eight span."

Anyone who knows the series *do re mi fa sol la ti do* is at home with the diatonic scale. You can count out the octave for yourself starting with the first *do* as *one* and ending with the second *do* as *eight.* The set of white keys on the piano (or other) keyboard constitutes this scale. Shown below is a keyboard and diatonic scale notes running through two octaves, marked with their conventional letter names (see page 21).

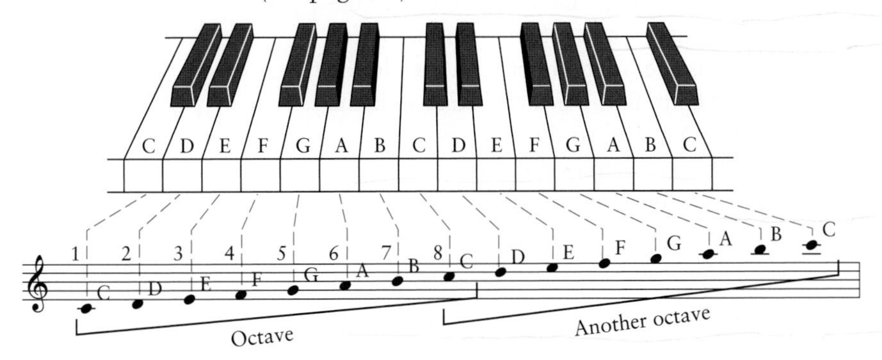

The Chromatic Scale

The diatonic scale was the original, basic scale of Western music. At a later period, five more pitches were added between certain of the seven pitches of the diatonic scale, making a total of twelve. This is the **chromatic scale,** represented by the complete set of white and black keys on a keyboard.

However, the chromatic scale did not make the diatonic scale obsolete. For centuries Western composers used the chromatic scale freely while favoring the diatonic scale that is embedded in it; in fact, most composers still do this today. Our keyboards reflect this practice, with their chromatic notes colored differently from the diatonic ones, set back and thinner. (On medieval church organs, designed to accommodate the diatonic scale only, the keyboards had no "black notes," or at most just one.)

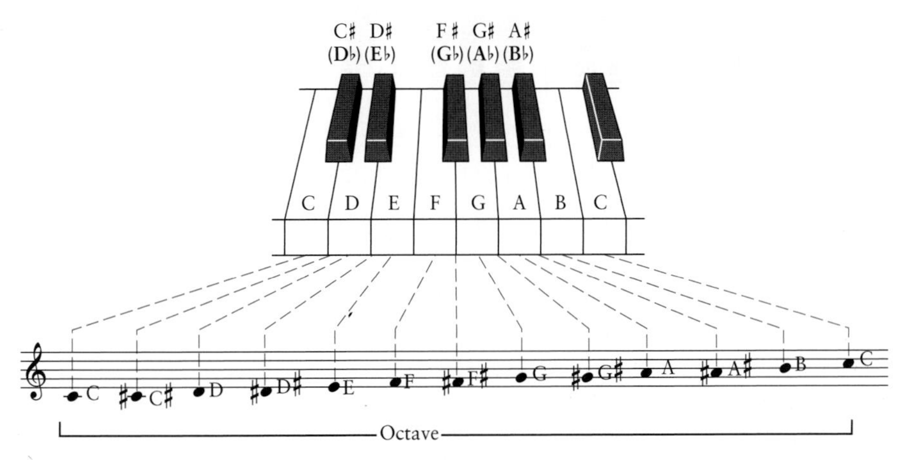

These extra pitches caused a problem for musical notation. The pitches of the diatonic scale are indicated on the lines and spaces of the staff; there are no positions in between, so symbols such as those shown to the right were introduced. B♭ stands for **B flat,** the pitch inserted between A and B; C♯ stands for C **sharp,** the pitch between C and D, and so on.

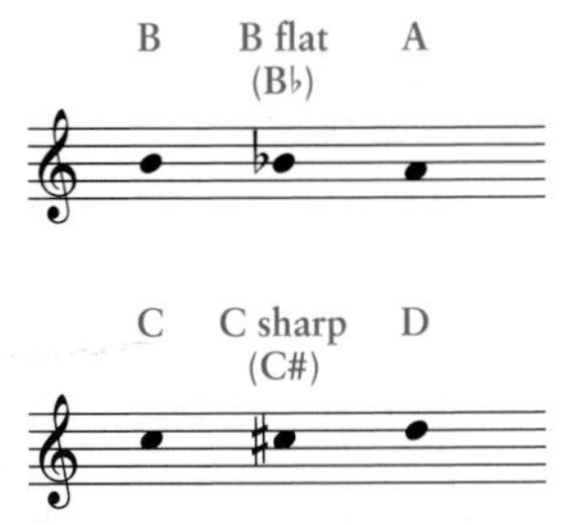

Intervals (II): Half Steps and Whole Steps

As previously noted, the difference, or distance, between any two pitches is called the interval between them. Look at the chromatic scale in the diagram above. Besides the C-to-C octave interval marked with a bracket, eleven other kinds of intervals exist between C and the other notes of the scale.

For our purposes, only two additional interval types need be considered:

The smallest interval is the **half step,** or semitone, which is the distance between any two successive notes of the chromatic scale. ("Step" is a name for small intervals.) On a keyboard, a half step is the interval between the closest adjacent notes, white or black. The distance from E to F is a half step; so is the distance from F to F sharp (F♯), G to A flat (A♭), and so on.

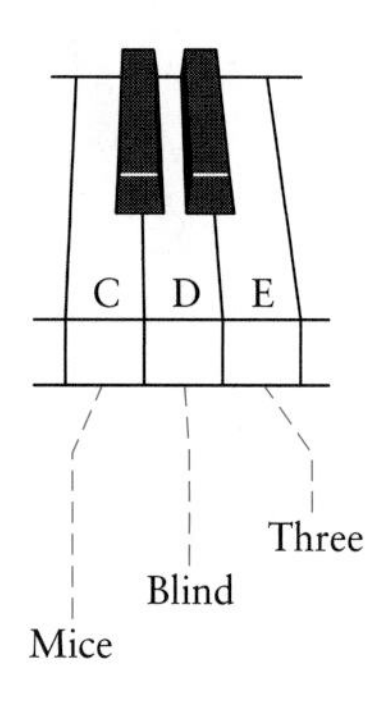

As the smallest interval in regular use, the half step is also the smallest that most people can "hear" easily and identify. Many tunes, such as "The Battle Hymn of the Republic," end with two half steps, one half step going down and then the same one going up again ("His truth is *march-ing on*").

The **whole step,** or whole tone, is equivalent to two half steps: D to E, E to F♯, F♯ to G♯, and so on. "Three Blind Mice" starts with two whole steps, going down.

The chromatic scale consists exclusively of half steps. Therefore, this scale can be described as "symmetrical," in the sense that one can start on any of its pitches and sing up or down the scale by half steps with exactly the same effect as if one started anywhere else. The diatonic scale is *not* symmetrical in this sense. It includes both half steps and whole steps. Between B and C and between E and F, the interval is a half step, but between the other pairs of adjacent notes the interval is twice as big—a whole step.

Music is made out of these scales, and the diatonic and chromatic scales differ in the intervals between their constituent pitches—hence the importance of intervals. In the diagram below, the two scales are lined up in order to show the differences in their interval structure.

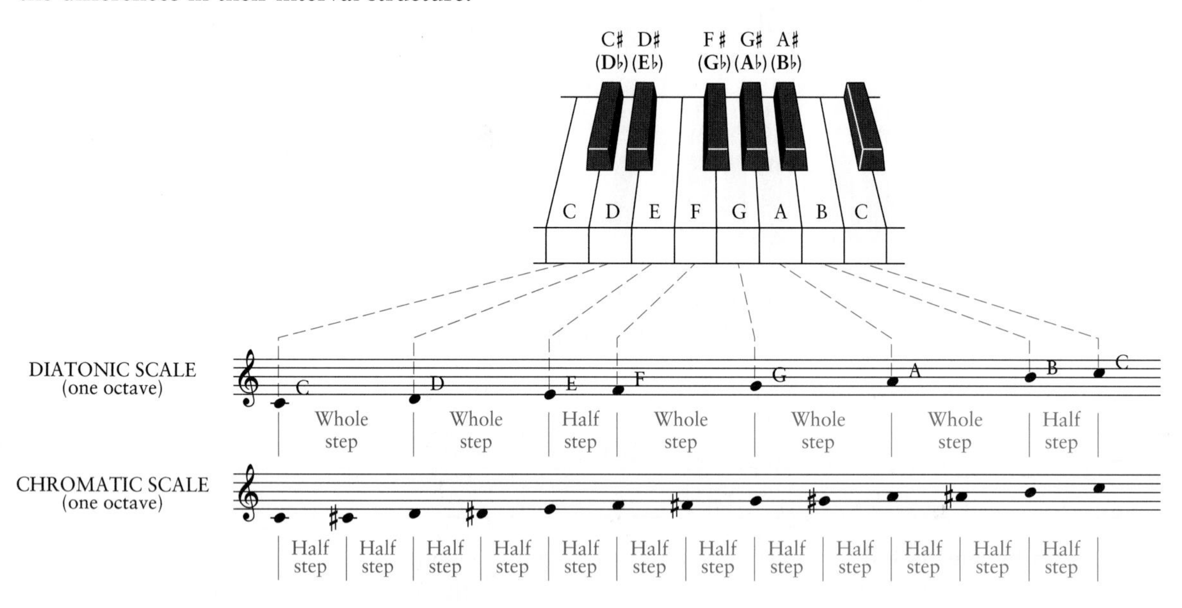

Scales and Instruments

Until fairly recently, Western music used the twelve pitches of the chromatic scale, duplicated through all the octaves, and in principle no other pitches. Features of many instruments are designed to produce these particular pitches exactly: frets on guitars, carefully measured holes in flutes, and the tuned sets of strings of harps and pianos.

Other instruments, such as the violin and the slide trombone, have a more continuous range of pitches available to them (as does a police siren or the human voice). In mastering these instruments, one of the first tasks is learning

A pioneer of modern design, the German-American painter Josef Albers (1888–1976) produced twenty-seven of these wonderful treble clefs, all in different color combinations.

to pick out exactly the right pitches. This is called *playing in tune*; singing in tune is a big concern for vocalists, too.

It is true that many instrumentalists and all singers regularly perform certain notes slightly out of tune for important and legitimate artistic effects. "Blue" notes in jazz are an example. However, these "off" pitches are only small, temporary deviations from the main pitches of the scale—the same twelve pitches that, on instruments such as the piano, are absolutely fixed.

Web: *To test your understanding of rhythm and pitch, take an online quiz at* **<bedfordstmartins.com/listen>.**

INTERLUDE A: Musical Notation

Many cultures around the world employ different notations for writing their music down. It is never necessary, obviously, to read these notations in order to understand the music or to love it; indeed, many cultures have no notation at all. However, written music examples can help clarify many points about musical style—even ones not written down by their creators—and it will help if you learn to follow the music examples in this book in an approximate way. The following brief survey of Western musical notation can be used for study or review or reference.

As we have seen in our discussion of musical elements, *time* and *pitch* are really the only ones that can be specified (and therefore notated) with any precision. Think of pitch and time as coordinates of a graph on which music is going to be plotted. The resulting pitch/time grid is quite close to actual musical notation, as shown in the diagrams below.

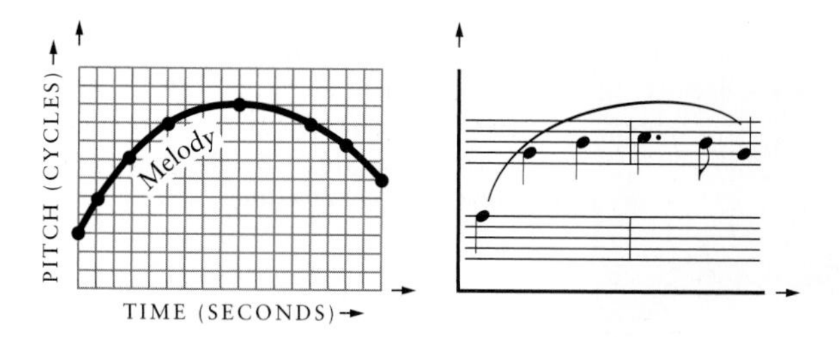

Notes and Rests

The longest note in common use is the *whole note:* 𝅝 (we are dealing here with proportional lengths; how long a whole note lasts in absolute time depends on the tempo: see page 14). A half note (𝅗𝅥) lasts for half the time of a whole note, a quarter note (♩) lasts for a quarter of the time, an eighth note (♪) for an eighth, a sixteenth (𝅘𝅥𝅯) for a sixteenth, and so on.

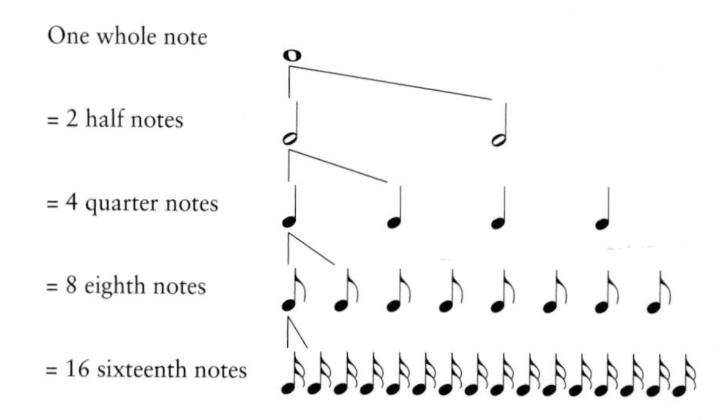

When the shorter notes come in groups, they can also be notated as shown at the top of the next column.

The "flags"—they look more like pennants—at the sides of the note "stems" have been "starched" up into horizontal "beams," for easier reading:

Rests To make rhythms, composers use not only sounds but also short silences called **rests.** The diagram below shows the relation between rests, which are equivalent in duration to their corresponding notes. (Compare the whole- and half-note rests, which are slugs beneath or atop one of the lines of the staff.)

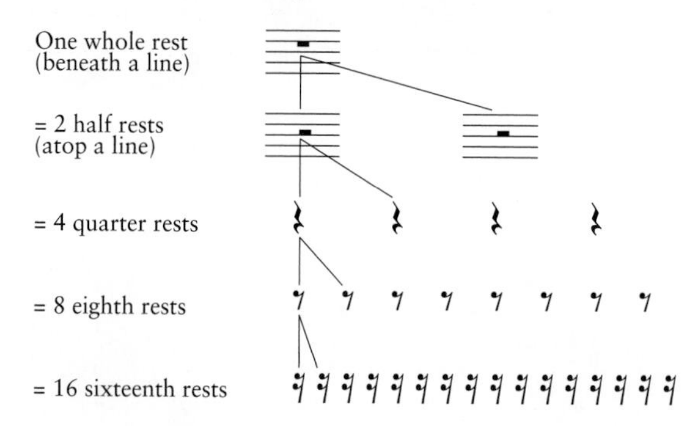

The shorter rests have their own sort of flags. As with notes, more flags can be added to rests, with each flag cutting the time value in half. Thus, three flags on a rest (𝅀) make it a thirty-second rest.

Rhythmic Notation

Beyond the notation of basic notes and rests, a number of other conventions are necessary to indicate the combining of notes and rests into actual rhythms.

Dotted Notes and Dotted Rhythms A dot placed after a note or rest lengthens its duration by 50 percent. Thus a dotted half note lasts as long as a half note plus a quarter note: 𝅗𝅥. = 𝅗𝅥 + ♩ And a dotted quarter-note rest equals a quarter plus an eighth: 𝄽. = 𝄽 + 𝄾 Even simple tunes, such as "America," make use of the dot convention.

A *dotted rhythm* is one consisting of dotted (long) notes alternating with short ones:

Ties Two notes of the same pitch can be connected by means of a curved line called a *tie.* This means they are played continuously, as though they were one note of the combined duration. Any number of notes of the same pitch can be tied together, so that this notational device can serve to indicate a pitch of very long duration.

Beware: The same sort of curved line is also used to connect notes that are *not* of the same pitch. In this case it means that they are to be played smoothly, one following the next without the slightest break (*legato* or "bound" playing). These curved lines are called *slurs.*

To indicate that notes are to be played in a detached fashion (*staccato*), dots are placed above or below them.

Triplets Three notes bracketed together and marked with a 3 (♩ ♩ ♩ with a bracketed 3) are called a *triplet.* This indicates that the three notes take exactly the same time that would normally be taken by two. A quarter-note triplet has the same duration as two ordinary quarter notes: ♩ ♩ ♩ (3) = ♩ ♩ (2)

The convention is occasionally extended to groups of five notes, seven notes, etc. For an example, see page 260.

Meter: Measures and Bar Lines A *measure* (or *bar*) is the basic time unit chosen for a piece of music, corresponding to the meter of the piece (see page 11). Measures are marked in musical notation by vertical *bar lines.* Each measure covers the same time span. In the following example, the time span covered by each measure is one whole note, equivalent to two half notes (measure 1), or four quarter notes (measure 2), or eight eighth notes (measures 3, 4).

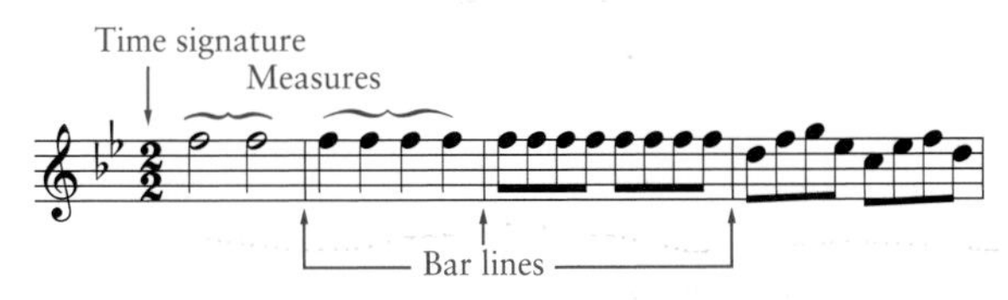

Time Signatures In the example above, the meter is indicated by means of a *time signature.* Time signatures are printed on the staffs at the beginning of all pieces of music; they are not repeated on later staffs.

In spite of appearances, time signatures are not fractions. The top digit shows *how many beats* are in each measure, and the bottom digit shows *what kind of note* represents a beat. If the bottom digit is 2, the beat is represented by a half note; if 4, by a quarter note, and so on.

In our example, the 2 at the top indicates there are two beats in each measure (duple meter), and the 2 at the bottom indicates that the beats are half-note beats. This time signature is often indicated by the sign ¢.

Pitch Notation

The letter names A B C D E F G are assigned to the original seven pitches of the diatonic scale. Then the letters are used over and over again for pitches in the duplicating octaves. Octaves are distinguished by numbers (c^1, c^2) or prime marks (A′, A″); so-called "middle C" (c^1) is the comfortable note that virtually any man, woman, or child can sing and that can be played by the great majority of instruments. On a keyboard, middle C sits in the middle, right under the maker's name—Casio, Yamaha, Steinway.

The Staff: Ledger Lines For the notation of pitch, notes are placed on a set of five parallel lines called a staff. The notes can be put on the lines of the staff, in the spaces between them, or right at the top or bottom of the staff:

Above and below the regular five lines of the staff, short extra lines can be added to accommodate a few higher and lower notes. These are called *ledger lines.*

Clefs Nothing has been said so far about which pitch each position on the staff represents. To clue us in to precise pitches, signs called *clefs* (French for "key" or "clue") are placed at the beginning of each staff. Clefs calibrate the staff: that is, they connect one of the five lines of the staff to a specific pitch.

Thus in the treble clef or G clef (𝄞), the spiral in the middle of this antique capital G curves around line 2, counting up from the bottom of the staff. Line 2, then, is the line for the pitch G—the first G above middle C. In the bass clef or F clef (𝄢), the two dots straddle the fourth line up. The pitch F goes on this line—the first F below middle C.

Adjacent lines and spaces on the staff have adjacent letter names, so we can place all the other pitches on the staff in relation to the fixed points marked by the clefs:

There are other clefs, but these two are the most common. Used in conjunction, they accommodate the maximum span of pitches without overlapping. The treble and bass clef staffs fit together as shown in Figure 1 below.

The notation of six A's, covering five octaves, requires two staffs and seven ledger lines (see Figure 2).

Sharps and Flats; Naturals The pitches produced by the black keys on the piano are not given letter names of their own. (This is a consequence of the way they arose in history; see page 17.) Nor do they get their own individual lines or spaces on the staffs. The pitch in between A and B is called A sharp (or A♯, using the conventional sign for a sharp), meaning "higher than A." It can also be called B flat (B♭), meaning "lower than B." In musical notation, the signs ♯ and ♭ are placed on the staff just *before* the note that is to be sharped or flatted.

Which of these two terms is used depends partly on convenience, partly on convention, and partly on theoretical considerations that do not concern us here. In the example below, the third note, A♯, sounds just like the B♭ later in the measure, but for technical reasons the composer (Béla Bartók) notated it differently.

The original pitches of the diatonic scale, played on the white keys of the piano, are called "natural." If it is necessary to cancel a sharp or a flat within a measure and to indicate that the natural note should be played instead, the natural sign is placed before a note (♮♩) or after a letter (A♮) to show this. The following example shows A sharp and G sharp being canceled by natural signs:

Key Signatures In musical notation, it is a convention that a sharp or flat placed before a note will also affect any later appearance of that same note *in the same measure*—but not in the next measure.

There is also a way of specifying that certain sharps or flats are to be applied throughout an entire piece, in every measure, and in every octave. Such sharps and flats appear on the staffs at the very beginning of the piece, even prior to the time signature, and at the beginning of each staff thereafter. They constitute the *key signature:*

is equivalent to:

Scores

Music for a melody instrument such as a violin or a trumpet is written on one staff; keyboard instruments require two—one staff for the right hand, another staff for the left hand. Music for two or more voices or instruments, choirs, bands, and orchestras is written in *scores.* In scores, each instrument and voice that has its own independent music gets one staff. Simultaneously sounding notes and measure lines are aligned vertically. In general, high-sounding instruments go on top, the low ones on the bottom.

Shown on page 23 is a page from Mozart's "Jupiter" Symphony, with arrows pointing to the various details of notation that have been explained above.

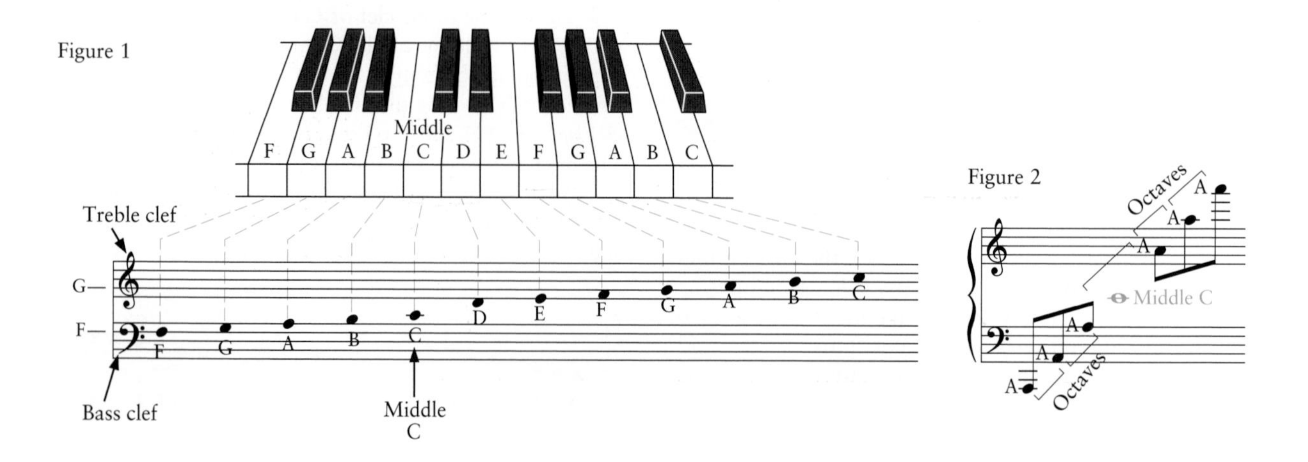

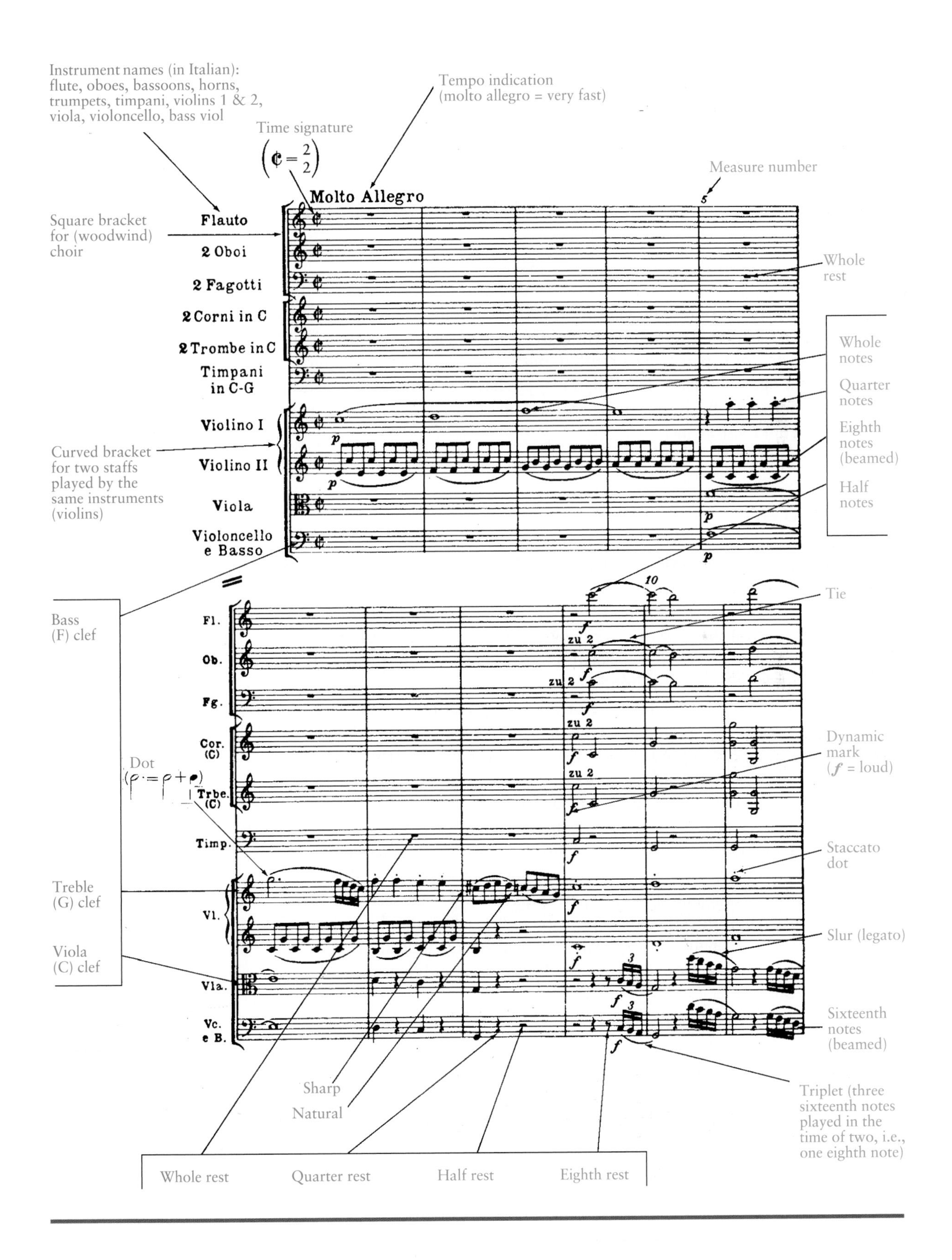

Instrument names (in Italian): flute, oboes, bassoons, horns, trumpets, timpani, violins 1 & 2, viola, violoncello, bass viol
Tempo indication (molto allegro = very fast)
Time signature
Measure number
Molto Allegro
Flauto
2 Oboi
2 Fagotti
2 Corni in C
2 Trombe in C
Timpani in C-G
Violino I
Violino II
Viola
Violoncello e Basso
Square bracket for (woodwind) choir
Whole rest
Whole notes
Quarter notes
Eighth notes (beamed)
Half notes
Curved bracket for two staffs played by the same instruments (violins)
Bass (F) clef
Tie
Fl.
Ob.
Fg.
Cor. (C)
Trbe. (C)
Timp.
Vl.
Vla.
Vc. e B.
zu 2
Dot
Dynamic mark (f = loud)
Staccato dot
Treble (G) clef
Slur (legato)
Viola (C) clef
Sixteenth notes (beamed)
Sharp
Natural
Triplet (three sixteenth notes played in the time of two, i.e., one eighth note)
Whole rest
Quarter rest
Half rest
Eighth rest

CHAPTER 3

The Structures of Music

In this chapter we take up musical concepts that combine the basic elements discussed in Chapters 1 and 2. Listening to an actual piece of music, it's obvious that we do not experience its rhythm, pitch, tone color, and dynamics in isolation from one another. Indeed, rhythms, pitches, and the rest are seldom experienced one at a time. Rather, music consists of simple and complex "structures" built from these elements.

Always remember that in listening to a piece of music you must hang on to the melodic line. It may disappear momentarily, withdrawn by the composer, in order to make its presence more powerfully felt when it reappears. But reappear it surely will . . .

Aaron Copland, *What to Listen For in Music*

1 Melody

A **melody** is an organized series of pitches. Think for a moment, if you can, of pitch and time as the two coordinates of a graph on which music is going to be plotted. A series of single pitches played in a certain rhythm will appear as dots, high or low, on the pitch/time grid, and the dots can be connected by a line (see the marginal diagram). Musicians commonly speak of "melodic line" (or simply "line") in this connection.

Just as an actual line in a painting or a drawing can possess character—can strike the viewer as forceful, graceful, or tentative—so can a melodic line. A melody in which each note is higher than the last can seem to soar; a low note can feel like a setback; a long series of repeated notes on the same pitch can seem to wait ominously. The listener develops a real interest in how the line of a satisfactory melody is going to come out.

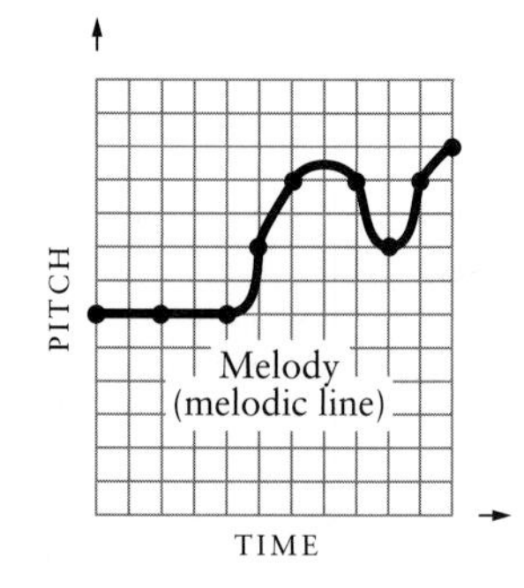

In such a melody, the succession of notes seems to hold together in a meaningful, interesting way—interesting, and also emotional. Of all music's structures, melody is the one that moves people the most, that seems to evoke human sentiment most directly. Familiar melodies "register" simple qualities of feeling instantly and strongly. These qualities vary widely: romantic in "Yesterday," martial in "Dixie," mournful in "St. Louis Blues," extroverted and cheerful in "Happy Birthday to You."

Tunes

These are the most familiar of melodies in Western music. A simple, easily singable, catchy melody such as a folk song, or a dance, or a Christmas carol is a **tune.** A tune is a special kind of melody. *Melody* is a term that includes tunes, but also much else.

"The Star-Spangled Banner," which everyone knows, can be used to illustrate the general characteristics of tunes. See the box on the next page.

Characteristics of Tunes

The best way to grasp the characteristics of tunes is by singing one you know, either out loud or "in your head."

Division into Phrases Tunes fall naturally into smaller sections, called **phrases.** This is, in fact, true of all melodies, but with tunes the division into phrases is particularly clear and sharp.

In tunes with words (that is, songs), phrases tend to coincide with poetic lines. Most lines in a song lyric end with a rhyming word and a punctuation mark such as a comma. These features clarify the musical phrase divisions:

> And the rockets' red ***glare,***
> The bombs bursting in ***air***

Singing a song, one has to breathe—and one tends to breathe at the end of phrases. You may not need to breathe after phrase 1 of our national anthem, but you'd better not wait any longer than phrase 2:

Balance between Phrases In many tunes, all the phrases are 2, 4, or 8 measures long. (The *measure* or bar is the basic time unit of music; see page 11.) Blues tunes, for example, usually consist of three four-measure phrases; hence the term *twelve-bar blues.*

Most phrases of "The Star-Spangled Banner" are two measures long (see phrase 1 and phrase 2, above). But one phrase broadens out to four measures, with a fine effect: "Oh say, does that star-spangled banner yet wave." Try not to breathe in the middle of this long phrase.

Other phrase lengths—three measures, five, and others—can certainly occur in a tune and make for welcome contrast. For a good tune, the main requirement is that we sense a balance between the phrases, in terms of phrase lengths and in other terms, too, so that taken together the phrases add up to a well-proportioned whole.

Parallelism and Contrast Balance between phrases can be strengthened by means of *parallelism.* For example, phrases can be exactly parallel except for the words ("Oh, say can you see," "Whose broad stripes and bright stars"). Others have the same rhythm but different pitches ("Oh say can you see," "By the dawn's early light").

Sometimes phrases have the same general *pattern of pitches,* but one phrase is slightly higher or lower than the other ("And the rockets' red glare," "The bombs bursting in air"). Such duplication of a phrase at two or more different pitch levels, called **sequence,** occurs frequently in music, and is a hallmark of certain musical styles.

Composers also take care to make certain phrases *contrast* with their neighbors—one phrase short, another long, or one phrase low, another high (perhaps even *too* high, at "O'er the land of the *free*"). A tune with some parallel and some contrasting phrases will seem to have logic, or coherence, and yet will avoid monotony.

Climax and Cadence A good tune has *form:* a clear, purposeful beginning, a feeling of action in the middle, and a firm sense of winding down at the end.

Many tunes have a distinct high point, or **climax,** which their earlier portions seem to be heading toward. A melodic climax is always an emotional climax; feelings rise as voices soar. The climax of our national anthem highlights what was felt to be the really crucial word in it—"free." Patriot Francis Scott Key put that word in that place (Key wrote the words of "The Star-Spangled Banner"—the words only, adapted to an old melody).

Then the later part of the tune relaxes from this climax, until it reaches a solid stopping place at the end. Emotionally, this is a point of relaxation and satisfaction. In a less definite way, the music also stops at earlier points in the tune—or, if it does not fully stop, at least seems to pause. The term for these interim stopping or pausing places is **cadence.**

Composers can write cadences with all possible shades of finality. "And the home of the brave" is a very final-sounding cadence; "That our flag was still there" has an interim feeling. The art of making cadences is one of the most subtle and basic processes in musical composition.

LISTEN for melody and tune

7

Division into phrases, parallelism and ***contrast*** between phrases, ***sequence, climax, cadence:*** These are some characteristics of tunes that we have observed in "The Star-Spangled Banner." They are not just inert characteristics—they are what make the tune work. They are at work in tunes of all kinds.

Our example is a depression-era song, "Who Cares?" by George Gershwin, a show tune from the musical comedy *Of Thee I Sing* (1932). In "The Star-Spangled Banner" the *climax* matches the text perfectly at "free." Here "jubilee" makes a good match for the climax, and a melodic *sequence* fits the words "I care for you/you care for me" neatly.

Show tunes usually have an introduction, called the *verse,* in effect another, less striking tune with more words. On our recording, by the great jazz singer Ella Fitzgerald, the band begins "Who Cares?" when she sings it a second time (with slightly different words).

7	0:12	**Verse** Let it rain and thunder . . . (eight more lines)	Includes a long (six-fold) ***sequence***
	0:48		Tempo changes
	0:57	**Tune** Who cares if the sky cares to fall in the sea?	
		Who cares what banks fail in Yonkers?	***Contrasting*** phrase
		Long as you've got a kiss that conquers.	***Parallel*** phrase—starts like the preceding, ends higher
		Why should I care? Life is one long jubilee,	Three-fold ***sequence*** ("should I care/life is one/jubilee") ***Climax*** on "jubilee"
		So long as I care for you and you care for me.	Free ***sequence*** ("I care for you"/ "You care for me")—***cadence***
	1:55	**Tune**	Begun by the band

Motives and Themes

Tunes are relatively short; longer pieces, such as symphonies, may have tunes embedded in them, but they also contain other musical material. Two terms are frequently encountered in connection with melody in longer pieces of music.

The first is **motive.** A motive is a distinctive fragment of melody, distinctive enough so that it will be easily recognized when it returns again and again within a long composition. Motives are shorter than tunes, shorter even than phrases of tunes; they can be as short as two notes. Probably the most famous motive in all music is the four-note *da da da DA* motive in Beethoven's Fifth Symphony.

The second term, **theme,** is the most general term for the basic subject matter of longer pieces of music. *Theme* is another name for "topic": The themes or topics of a political speech are the main points that the politician announces, repeats, develops, and hammers home. The composer of a symphony or a fugue treats musical themes in much the same way.

Since the term *theme* refers to the *function,* not the *nature,* of musical material, in principle almost anything can serve as a theme. A melody can perform this function, or a phrase, a motive, even a distinctive tone color. It depends on the kind of music. The theme of the last movement of Beethoven's Ninth Symphony is the tune we will hear several times on the CD-ROM, track 8 (see page 30).

The theme of Beethoven's Fifth Symphony consists of the *da da da DA* motive played twice in sequence. Many of the themes of Richard Wagner's operas are closely identified with a particular tone color and instrument (the trombone, in the excerpt discussed on page 286).

Melody and harmony: a folk-singer playing the Appalachian dulcimer.

2 Harmony

A single melodic "line" in time is enough to qualify as music: sometimes, indeed, as great music. When people sing in the shower and when parents sing to their babies they are producing melody, and that is all, to everyone's full satisfaction. The same was true of the early Christian Church, whose music, Gregorian chant, consisted of over two thousand subtly differentiated melodies, sung without instruments or any kind of "harmonizing."

Today, however—and this is the outcome of a long and complicated historical development—it seems very natural to us to hear melodies together with other sounds, which we call "accompaniments." A folk singer singing and playing a guitar is performing a song and its accompaniment. The congregation sings hymns in church; the organist plays the accompaniment.

The folk singer uses a number of standard groupings of simultaneous pitches, or **chords,** that practice has shown are sure to work well in combination. Imaginative players will also discover nonstandard chords and unexpected successions of chords in order to enrich their accompaniments. The song is said to be **harmonized;** the continuous matrix of changing chords provides a sort of constantly shifting sound-background for the song.

Any melody can be harmonized in different ways using different chords, and the overall effect of the music depends to a great extent on the nature of these chords, or the **harmony** in general. We can instinctively sense the difference in harmony between Mozart and Wagner or Debussy, or between New Orleans jazz and rock. However, to characterize the differences requires technical language, and we shall not make the attempt in this book.

Consonance and Dissonance

A pair of terms used in discussions of harmony is **consonance** and **dissonance,** meaning (roughly speaking) chords that sound at rest and those that sound tense, respectively. *Discord* is another term for dissonance. These qualities depend on the kinds of intervals (see pages 15–18) that are sounding simultaneously to make up these chords. Octaves are the most consonant of intervals. Half steps are among the most dissonant.

Medicine, to produce health, must know disease; music, to produce harmony, must know discord.

Plutarch, c. 46–120 C.E.

In everyday language, "discord" implies something unpleasant; discordant human relationships are to be avoided. But music does not avoid dissonance in its technical meaning, for a little discord supplies the subtle tensions that are essential to make music flow along. A dissonant chord leaves the listener with a feeling of expectation; it requires a consonant chord following it to complete the gesture and to make the music come to a point of stability. This is called *resolution;* the dissonance is said to be **resolved.** Without dissonance, music would be like food without salt or spices.

Important cadences—say, at the ends of pieces of music—are almost always helped by the use of dissonance. Movement from tension (dissonance) to rest (consonance) contributes centrally to a sense of finality and satisfaction.

3 Texture

Texture is the term used to refer to the blend of the various sounds and melodic lines occurring simultaneously in music. The word is adopted from textiles, where it refers to the weave of the various threads—loose or tight, even or mixed. A cloth such as tweed, for instance, leaves the different threads clearly visible. In fine silk or percale, the weave is so tight and smooth that the constituent threads can be impossible to detect.

Thinking again of the pitch/time graph on page 24, we can see that it is possible to plot more than one pitch for every time slot. Melody exists in the "horizontal" dimension, texture in the "vertical" dimension. For the moment, we leave the lower dots (below the melody) unconnected.

Monophony

This is the term for the simplest texture, a single unaccompanied melody: Gregorian chant; singing in the shower; "Row, Row, Row Your Boat" before the second person comes in:

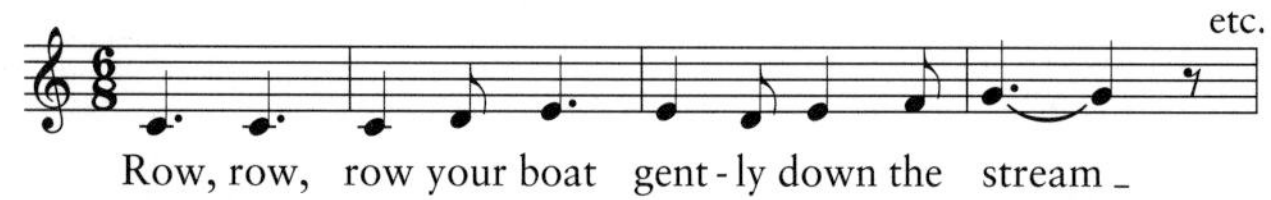

Simple as this texture is, some very beautiful and sophisticated **monophonic** music has been composed, just as artists have done wonderful things with line drawings: See page 334.

Heterophony

A special kind of monophonic texture, not much used in the European classical tradition but more prominent elsewhere, is called **heterophony.** This is a texture in which subtly different versions of a single melody are presented simultaneously. We will hear several examples of heterophony in the non-European musics discussed throughout this book.

Homophony

When there is only one melody of real interest and it is combined with other sounds, the texture is called **homophonic.** A harmonized melody is an example of homophonic texture: for instance, one person singing the tune of "Row, Row, Row Your Boat" while playing chords on a guitar:

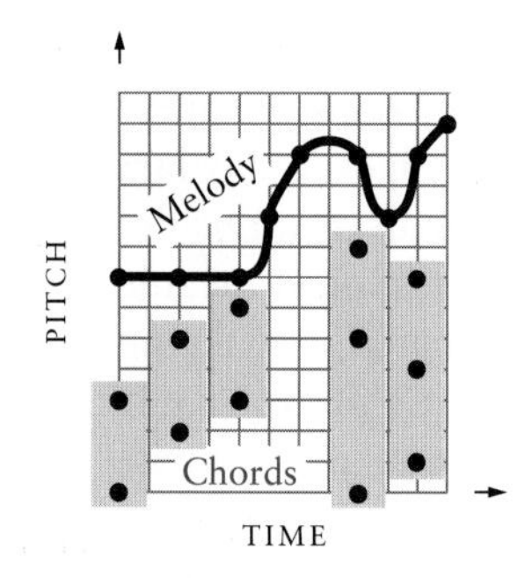

We might indicate a chord on the pitch/time graph by a vertical box enclosing the dots. The sum of these boxes represents the harmony. Homophony can be thought of as a tight, smooth texture—like silk, among the textiles.

Polyphony

When two or more melodies are played or sung simultaneously, the texture is described as **polyphonic.** In polyphony, the melodies are felt to be independent and of approximately equal interest. The whole is more than the sum of the parts, however: the way the melodies play off against one another makes for the possibility of greater richness and interest than if they were played singly. In the textile analogy, polyphony would be compared to a rough texture where the strands are all perceptible, such as tweed.

It is also important to recognize that polyphonic music automatically has harmony. For at every moment in time, on every beat, the multiple horizontal melodies create vertical chords; those chords make harmony.

A word often used for polyphonic texture is *contrapuntal,* which comes from the word **counterpoint,** the technique of writing two or more melodies that fit together. Strictly speaking, polyphony refers to the texture and counterpoint to the technique of producing that texture—one *writes* counterpoint to *produce* polyphony—but in practice the two terms are used interchangeably.

Imitation

In fact polyphonic texture, like so many other musical elements, cannot be categorized with any precision. It is impossible to distinguish all the kinds of polyphony found in Western music, to say nothing of the enormously intricate kinds in non-Western musics.

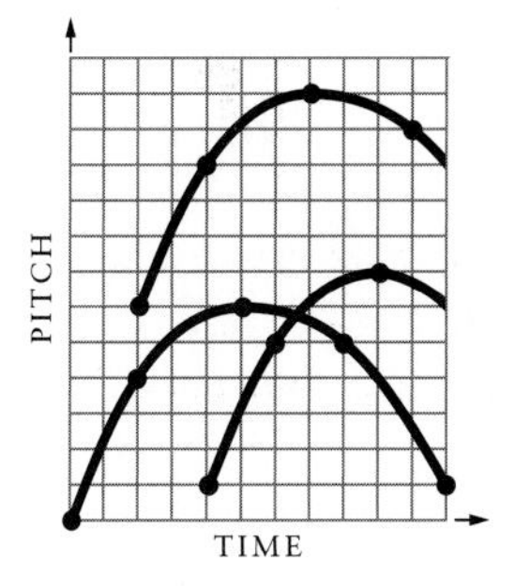

One useful and important distinction, however, is between *imitative polyphony* and *non-imitative polyphony.* **Imitative polyphony** results when the various lines sounding together use the same or fairly similar melodies, with one coming in shortly after another. The simplest example of imitative polyphony is a round, such as "Row, Row, Row Your Boat" or "Frère Jacques"; the richest kind is a fugue (see Chapter 8). When people sing a round, by singing the same tune at staggered time intervals, the result is imitative polyphony:

FIRST VOICE
Row, row, row your boat gently down the stream, Merrily, merrily, merrily, merrily, life is but a dream.
SECOND VOICE
Row, row, row your boat gently down the stream, Merrily, merrily, merrily, merrily,
THIRD VOICE
Row, row, row your boat gently down the stream,

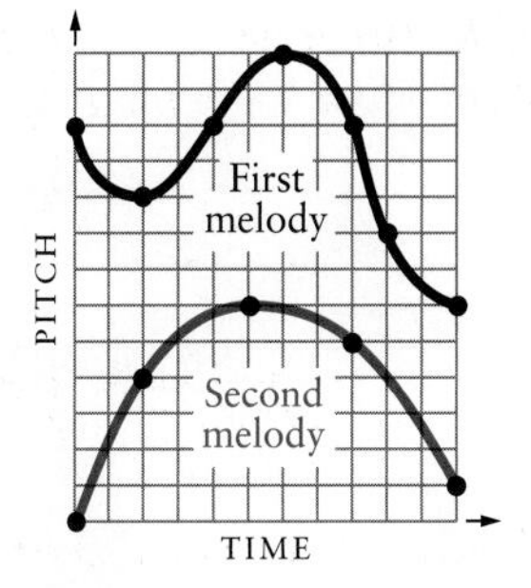

Non-imitative polyphony occurs when the melodies are essentially different from one another. An example that many will know is the typical texture of a New Orleans jazz band, with the trumpet playing the main tune flanked top and bottom by the clarinet and the trombone playing exhilarating melodies of their own. Here is a made-up example of non-imitative polyphony, with a new melody added to the tune of "Row, Row, Row Your Boat":

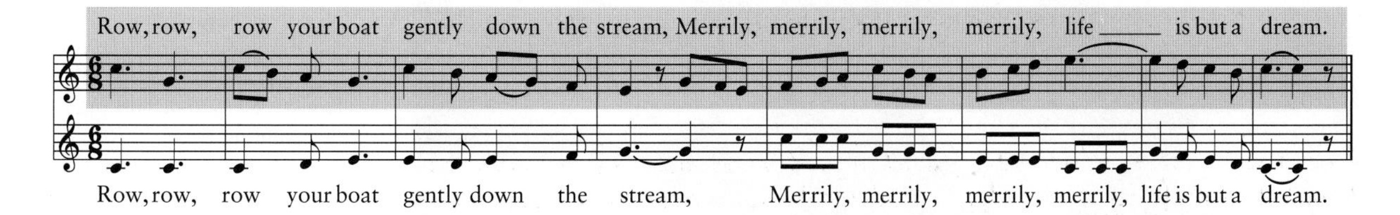

LISTEN for texture

8, 9

A famous passage from Beethoven furnishes a clear example of ***monophonic, polyphonic,*** and ***homophonic textures***—the initial presentation of the so-called Joy Theme in Symphony No. 9, the "Choral" Symphony. The theme, a tune known around the world, takes its name from the words it is set to, an enthusiastic ode to the joy that comes from human freedom, companionship, and reverence for the Deity. The words are sung by soloists and a chorus.

But before anyone sings, the theme is played several times by the orchestra, in a way that suggests that joy is emerging out of nothingness into its full realization. Beginning with utterly simple *monophony,* and growing successively higher and louder, it is enriched by *polyphony* and then reaches its grand climax in *homophony.*

8	0:00	Joy Theme	Low register	***Monophony:*** a single melodic line; cellos and double basses playing together, with no accompaniment whatsoever
	0:49	Theme	An octave higher	***Polyphony, non-imitative:*** the theme with two lines of ***counterpoint,*** in low strings (cello) and a mellow wind instrument (bassoon)
	1:36	Theme	Two octaves higher	
	2:21	Theme	Three octaves higher	***Homophony:*** full orchestra with trumpets prominent

Our example of ***imitative polyphony*** comes from the *Symphony of Psalms,* another symphony with chorus, a major work by the twentieth-century composer Igor Stravinsky. For brief characterizations of the instruments that play the contrapuntal lines, see Interlude B on pages 38–39.

9	0:00	A slow, winding melody, unaccompanied, played by a wind instrument (oboe)
	0:25	The same melody enters in another instrument (flute), as the oboe continues with new material; this produces two-part ***imitative counterpoint.***
	0:58	Third entry, second flute plays in a lower register —three-part counterpoint
	1:19	Fourth entry, second oboe —four-part counterpoint

This imaginative portrayal of imitative counterpoint is like our first pitch/time graph on page 24, at least in principle. Paul Klee (1879–1940) titled this painting *Fugue in Red*; a fugue is the supreme example of imitative texture, as we shall see.

4 Tonality and Modality

Tonality and modality are aspects of harmony, and as such they could logically have been taken up at an earlier point in this chapter. We have deferred them till last because, more than the other basic structures of music, these require careful explanation.

Tonality

We start with a basic fact about melodies and tunes: Melodies nearly always give a sense of focusing around a single "home" pitch that feels more important than do all the other members of the scale. Usually this is ***do*** in the *do re mi fa sol la ti do* scale. This pitch feels fundamental, and on it the melody seems to come to rest most naturally. The other notes in the melody all sound close or remote, dissonant or consonant, in reference to the fundamental note, and some of them may actually seem to "lean" or "lead" toward it.

This homing instinct that we sense in melodies can be referred to in the broadest terms as the feeling of **tonality.** The music in question is described as **tonal.** The "home" pitch (*do*) is called the *tonic pitch,* or simply the **tonic.**

The easy way to identify the tonic is to sing the whole melody through, because the last note is almost invariably *it.* Thus "The Star-Spangled Banner" ends on its tonic, *do.* (It also includes the tonic pitch in two different octaves as its first two accented notes: "Oh, *say* can you *see.*") An entire piece of music, as well as just a short melody, can give this feeling of focusing on a home pitch and wanting to end there.

The difficulty of describing the facts of tonality is not the difficulty of describing red to the color-blind. It is the difficulty of describing red to anybody; you can only point to red things and hope that other people see them as you do. It is even more like trying to describe the taste of a peach. . . .

Sir Donald Tovey, pianist, conductor, and educator, 1935

Modality: Major and Minor

Turn back to page 17 and the diagram of the diatonic scale, the basic scale of Western music. We have been speaking of melodies in the *do re mi fa sol la ti do* segment of this scale focusing on *do* as their tonic. But there is another important class of melodies that focus on *la* as tonic. The term for these different ways of centering or organizing the diatonic scale is **modality**; the different "home" pitches are said to determine different **modes** of music.

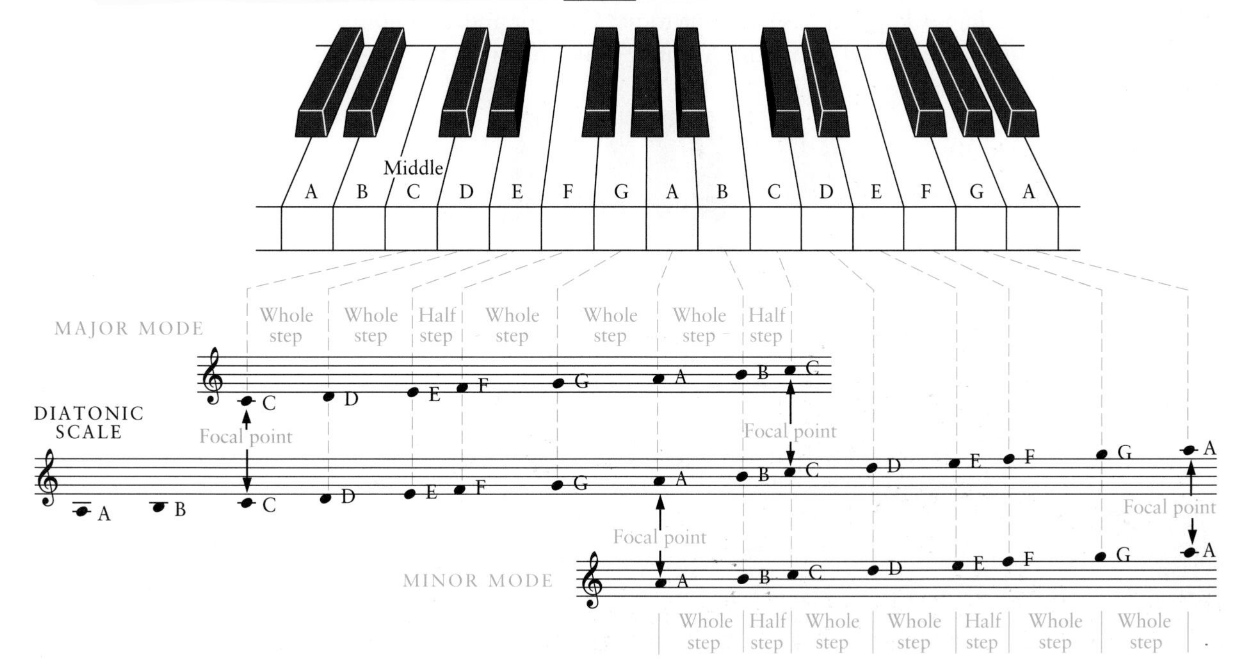

We will get to the actual listening experience of the modes in a moment. Music with the *do* center is in the **major mode**. Music with the *la* orientation is in the **minor mode**.

Keys

Mode and key are concepts that are often confused. Let us see if we can clarify them.

We have just seen how the two modes, the major with its "tonic" or home note on C and the minor on A, are derived from the diatonic scale (and this was the way it happened in history). At the piano, if you try to play a scale starting with any other note of the diatonic scale—D, E, F, or B—you will find that in each case, if you stick to the white notes, the arrangement of intervals is different from that of either the major or the minor mode. The scales you play will sound wrong.

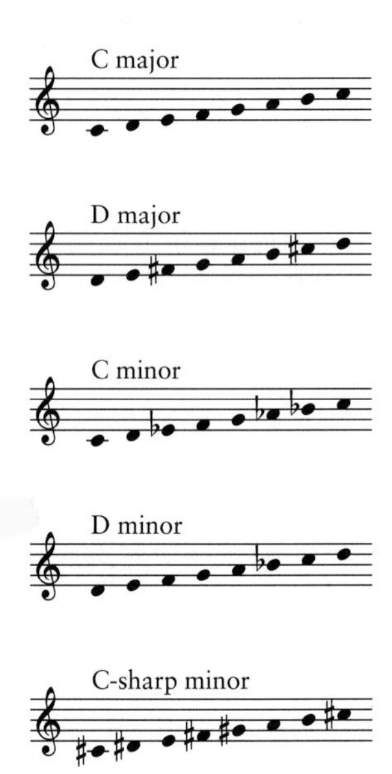

However, if you avail yourself of all the twelve notes of the *chromatic* scale, the black notes as well as the white, you can construct both the major and the minor modes starting from any note at all. Whichever note you choose as tonic, starting from there you can pick out the correct sequence of half steps and whole steps. (This is because the chromatic scale is "symmetrical"—it includes all possible half steps and whole steps.) If C is the starting point, the major mode comes out all on the white notes; if the same mode is started from D, two black notes are required, and so on.

Thanks to the chromatic scale, then, many positions are possible for the major and minor modes. These different positions are called **keys.** If the major mode is positioned on C, the music is said to be in the key of C major, or just "in C"; positioned on D, the key is D major. Likewise we have the keys of C minor, D minor, and—since there are twelve pitches in the chromatic scale—a grand total of twenty-four different major and minor keys.

This already hints at an important resource available to composers: the possibility of changing (or moving) from one key to another. Changing keys in the course of a composition is called **modulation.**

Hearing the Major and Minor Modes

On paper, it is easiest to show the difference between major and minor if we compare a major and minor key that has the same tonic: C major and C minor. We therefore *modulate* (see above!) from the A-minor scale shown in the previous diagram to C minor:

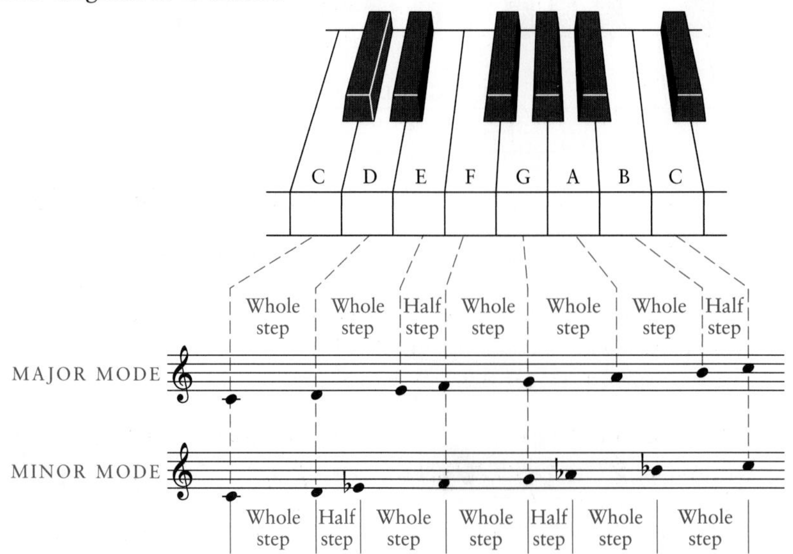

Is it fair to represent the major and minor modes by comedy and tragedy masks? Yes, but only in a very general sense—there are many "delicate nuances," as Schumann put it.

The difference between the modes is easy to see: Three of the scale degrees are lower in the minor (hence the term "minor," of course). This means that the arrangement of intervals is not the same when you sing up the scale, and this in turn makes a great difference in the "feel" of the modes.

Easy to see—but *hearing* the difference is another matter. This comes easily to some listeners, less easily to others. As a result of the three lower scale degrees, music in the minor mode tends to sound more subdued, more clouded than music in the major. It is often said that major sounds cheerful and minor sounds sad, and this is true enough in a general way; but there are many exceptions, and in any case people can have different ideas about what constitutes "sadness" and "cheerfulness" in music.

Learning to distinguish the major and minor modes requires comparative listening. Listen especially for the third scale degree up from the tonic. "Joshua Fit the Battle of Jericho," "Summertime," and "We Three Kings of Orient Are" are all in the minor mode. Singing them through, we come to recognize the characteristic minor-mode sound involving the third scale degree at the final cadence.

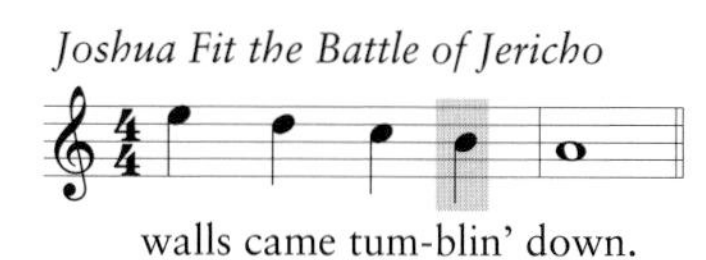

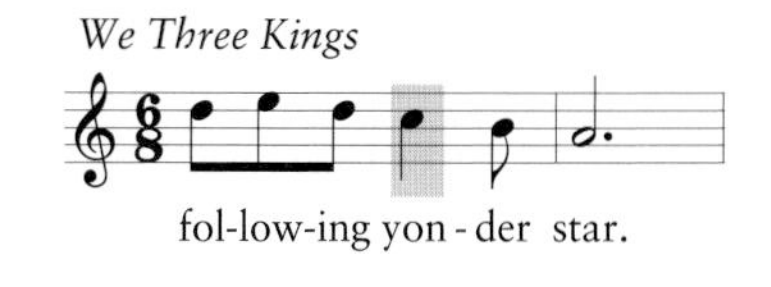

Compare this with the third note up from the tonic at the end of major-mode songs such as "Happy Birthday to You," "Row, Row, Row Your Boat," "The Star-Spangled Banner," and many others. It sounds brighter, more positive.

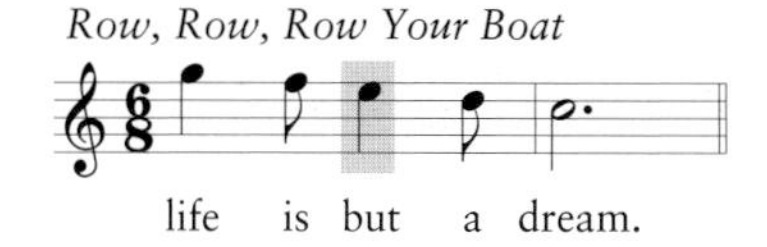

And here is the whole of "Row, Row, Row Your Boat" one more time—but this time in an altered version, with the mode switched from major to minor. Can you sing it?

Hearing Keys and Modulation

The major and minor modes can be said to differ from one another "intrinsically," for in each mode the pitches form their own special set of intervals and interval relationships. As we have seen, C major and C minor, while sharing the same central or tonic note, have their own individual arrangements of half- and whole-step intervals.

Different keys, however, merely entail the same set of intervals moved to a new position within the pitch continuum. This is a significant difference, but not an "intrinsic" one. First base is different from second base, but only because the same sort of bag, intrinsically, has been put in a significant new place.

As for actually *hearing* keys—that is, recognizing the different keys and the modulations between them—for some listeners this presents an even greater problem than hearing modality, though to others it comes more easily. The latter are the fortunate ones born with perfect pitch, the innate faculty of identifying pitches the way most people can identify colors.

However, this is not the great boon of nature it is sometimes believed to be. The important thing is not to be able to identify keys in themselves, but rather to be able to hear when keys change. For modulating or changing the key of music changes its mood or the way it feels; generations of composers have used this resource for some of their most powerful effects, as we shall see. And in large compositions we can hear *changes* of tonality, that is, changes of the tonic or "home" note, whether or not we were born with perfect pitch.

Indeed, we hear such changes instinctively in shorter compositions. If you know "The Twelve Days of Christmas," you will remember the modulation at the words "Five gold rings." (Try singing this cumulative carol all the way through leaving out the fifth gift with its modulation—the result is utter monotony.) In another Christmas carol, "Deck the Halls," modulation causes an agreeable little lift at the end of the third line, "Don we now our gay apparel, *Fa-la la, la-la la, la la la.*"

At hard-fought baseball and basketball games the organist plays a little musical figure over and over, higher and higher, louder and louder. This is brute-force modulation, and like all modulations, it changes the mood and the way you feel—it makes you feel *excited.*

The "Structures of Music" we have discussed in this chapter apply particularly to Western classical music. Two points need to be made regarding other musical traditions, outside of the European orbit.

First, questions of melody, texture, harmony, and tonality are fully as important in understanding most of these other musics as they are in understanding music closer to home. This will be clear from our discussions in the Global Perspectives sections throughout the book. But second, each musical tradition tends to have its own characteristic ways of approaching the structures of music. What counts as a tune, which textures are preferred above others, how tonality is asserted, even which combinations of pitches are considered conso-

LISTEN for mode and key

10, 11, 12

The difference between the ***major*** and ***minor modes*** is most obvious, perhaps, when a distinctive musical fragment in one mode is repeated in the other mode—soon enough so that both can be kept clearly in mind. This happens at the end of a very short piano piece by Schubert, Moment Musical in F Minor ("Musical Moment"—not Schubert's title, but his publisher's).

The phrases in this Moment Musical are in two different ***keys:*** the first in a minor key (the F minor of the title), the second in a major key, with the third starting in minor and ending in major.

Track	Time	Section	Description
10	0:00		***p:*** Introduction
	0:02	**Phrase 1 (played twice)**	Begins and ends in ***minor*** mode
	0:26	**Phrase 2 (twice)**	New key: begins and ends in the ***major***
	0:49	**Phrase 3 (twice)**	***f:*** Begins in the key of phrase 1 (***minor***) and ends in the key of phrase 2 (***major***)
	1:14	**Phrase 1 returns, once**	***pp:*** (original minor key) New continuation—repeated cadences, using fragments of phrase 1
	1:36		Turns to the ***major*** mode

For a series of fast ***modulations,*** turn to a passage from Beethoven's Piano Concerto No. 5, the "Emperor" Concerto. Here key changes are easy to hear because the modulations are carried out so brusquely—a Beethoven specialty—and also because the music in between them is harmonically very simple.

Track	Time	Description
11	0:00	Lively music for the piano, ***f,*** followed by a ***f*** response from the orchestra
	0:28	Modulation (French horns)
		New key: here similar music for piano is heard, ***pp,*** and the same orchestral response, ***f***
	1:03	Similar modulation
		New key: piano, ***p,*** and orchestra, ***f,*** as before
	1:36	The piano bursts in, ***f,*** in the same key but in the ***minor mode;*** begins modulating to further new keys in a more complicated way than before

The example that follows won't mean much to you unless you know the venerable round "Frère Jacques" ("Are you sleeping"). Gustav Mahler, in his Symphony No. 1, writes a bizarre, slow version of "Frère Jacques" ***in the minor mode.*** This is vivid evidence of how music's mood changes when the mode changes.

Track	Time	Description
12	0:00	Drum beat
	0:07	"Frère Jacques" melody enters in the minor
	0:27	Melody repeated by various instruments, as in a round: This is low-lying *imitative polyphony.*

nant or dissonant—all these differ widely from tradition to tradition. They may even differ from style to style within a single tradition.

As a result, the vocabulary we develop here for Western music cannot, in its most specific form, encompass all this variety. But the general issues raised in this vocabulary are issues you will meet also in musics from around the world.

Web: *To test your understanding of the structures of music, take an online quiz at* **<bedfordstmartins.com/listen>.**

INTERLUDE B: Musical Instruments

17-22

Different voices and different instruments produce different tone colors, or timbres. Over the course of history and over the entire world, an enormous number of devices have been invented for making music, and the range of tone colors they can produce is almost endless.

This interlude will discuss and illustrate the instruments of Western music that make up the orchestra, and a few others. Later, in our Global Perspectives sections, we will meet many instruments from other musical traditions.

Musical instruments can be categorized into four groups: *stringed instruments* or *strings, woodwinds, brass,* and *percussion.* Musical sound, as we know, is caused by rapid vibrations. Each of the four groups of instruments produces sound vibrations in its own distinct way.

Stringed Instruments

These are instruments that have their sound produced by taut strings. The strings are always attached to a "sound box," a hollow box containing a body of air that resonates (that is, vibrates along with the strings) to amplify the string sound.

The strings themselves can be played with a bow, as with the violin and other orchestral strings; the *bow* is strung tightly with horsehair, which is coated with a substance called rosin, so that the bow grips the strings. Or else the strings can be plucked or strummed, as on the guitar or the harp, using the fingers or a small pick.

Strings can be plucked on bowed instruments, too, for special effects. This is called **pizzicato.**

Listen to The Young Person's Guide to the Orchestra, *by Benjamin Britten: See page 53.*

The Violin and Its Family The **violin** is often called the most beautiful instrument used in Western music. Also one of the most versatile of instruments, its large range covers alto and soprano registers and many much higher pitches. As a solo instrument, it can play forcefully or delicately, and it excels in both brilliant and songlike music. Violinists also play chords by bowing two or more of the four strings at once, or nearly so.

As in a guitar, the (four) violin strings are stopped with a finger—that is, pressed down on the "neck" of the violin under the strings—to shorten the string length and get different pitches (see the illustrations below). Unlike a guitar, a violin has no frets, so the player has to feel for the exact places to press.

The violin is an excellent ensemble instrument, and it blends especially well with other violins. An orchestra violin section, made up of ten or more instruments playing together, can produce a strong, yet sensitive, flexible tone. Hence the orchestra has traditionally relied on strings as a solid foundation for its composite sound.

Like most instruments, violins come in *families,* that is, in several sizes with different pitch ranges. Three members of the violin family are basic to the orchestra.

The **viola** is the tenor-range instrument, larger than a violin by several inches. It has a throaty quality in its lowest range, from middle C down an octave; yet it fits especially smoothly into accompaniment textures. The viola's highest register is powerful and intense.

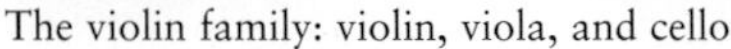

The violin family: violin, viola, and cello

Violin ➤

𝄾 The **cello,** short for *violoncello,* is the bass of the violin family. This large instrument is played between the legs. Unlike the viola, the cello has a rich, gorgeous sound in its low register. It is a favorite solo instrument, as well as an indispensable member of the orchestra.

Bass Viol Also called **string bass, double bass,** or just **bass,** this deep instrument is used to back up the violin family in the orchestra. (However, in various details of construction the bass viol differs from members of the violin family; the bass viol actually belongs to another, older stringed instrument family, the *viol* family.)

Played with a bow, the bass viol provides a splendid deep support for orchestral sound. The bass viol is often (in jazz, nearly always) plucked to give an especially vibrant kind of accent and to emphasize the meter.

Harp **Harps** are plucked stringed instruments with one string for each pitch available. The modern orchestral harp is a large instrument with forty-seven strings covering a range of six and a half octaves. A pedal mechanism allows the playing of chromatic (black-key) as well as diatonic (white-key) pitches.

In most orchestral music, the swishing, watery quality of the harp is treated as a striking occasional effect rather than as a regular timbre.

Woodwind Instruments

As the name indicates, woodwind instruments were formerly made of wood, and some still are; but today certain woodwinds are made of metal. Sound in these instru-

Cellist Yo-Yo Ma—perhaps this country's preeminent instrumentalist, certainly the most versatile and most honored.

◄Orchestral harp

Orchestras usually have two or three *oboes:* See page 39.

Flutist James Galway

Clarinetist Sabine Meyer

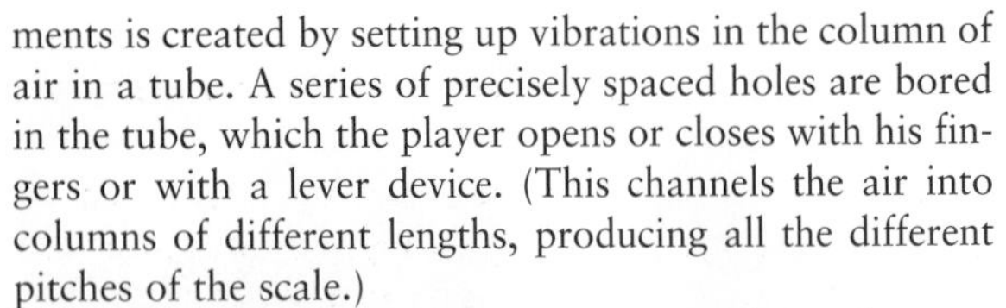

ments is created by setting up vibrations in the column of air in a tube. A series of precisely spaced holes are bored in the tube, which the player opens or closes with his fingers or with a lever device. (This channels the air into columns of different lengths, producing all the different pitches of the scale.)

Of the main woodwind instruments, *flutes, clarinets,* and *oboes* have approximately the same range. All three are used in the orchestra because each has a quite distinct tone quality, and composers can obtain a variety of effects from them. It is not hard to learn to recognize and appreciate the different sounds of these woodwinds.

The Flute and Its Family The **flute** is a long cylinder, held horizontally; the player sets the air vibrating by blowing through a side hole. The flute is the most agile of the woodwind instruments and also the gentlest. It nonetheless stands out clearly in the orchestra when played in its high register.

The **piccolo,** the small, highest member of the flute family, adds special sparkle to band and orchestral music.

The **alto flute** and **bass flute**—larger flutes—are less frequently employed.

The **recorder,** a different variety of flute, is blown not at the side of the tube but through a mouthpiece at the end. Used in older orchestral music, the recorder was superseded by the horizontal, or "transverse," flute because the latter was more agile and stronger.

In the late twentieth century recorders made a comeback for modern performances of old music using reconstructed period instruments. The instrument is also popular (in various family sizes) among musical amateurs today. It is easy to learn and fun to play.

Clarinet The **clarinet** is a slightly conical tube made, usually, of ebony (a dark wood). The air column is not made to vibrate directly by blowing into the tube, as with the flute. The way the player gets sound is by blowing on a reed—a small piece of cane fixed at one end—in much the same way as one can blow on a blade of grass held taut between the fingers. The vibrating reed vibrates the air within the clarinet tube itself.

Compared to the flute, clarinet sound is richer and more flexible, more like the human voice. The clarinet is capable of warm, mellow tones and strident, shrill ones; it has an especially intriguing quality in its low register, below middle C.

The small **E-flat clarinet** and the large **bass clarinet** are family members with a place in the modern orchestra. The tube of the bass clarinet is so long that it has to be bent back, like a thin black saxophone.

Oboe The **oboe,** pictured on page 37, also uses a reed, like the clarinet, but it is a double reed—two reeds lashed together so that the air must be forced between them. This kind of reed gives the oboe its clearly focused, crisply clean, and sometimes plaintive sound.

The **English horn** is a larger, lower oboe, descending into the viola range. (Scores often give the French equivalent, *cor anglais;* in either language, the name is wildly deceptive, since the instrument is not a horn but an oboe, and it has nothing to do with England.)

Bassoon The **bassoon** is a low (cello-range) instrument with a double reed and other characteristics similar to the oboe's. It looks somewhat bizarre: The long tube is bent double, and the reed has to be linked to the instrument by a long, narrow pipe made of metal. Of all the double-reed woodwinds, the bassoon is the most varied in expression, ranging from the mournful to the comical.

Bassoon (with a clarinet in the background)

The **contrabassoon** or **double bassoon** is a very large member of the bassoon family, in the bass viol range.

Saxophone The **saxophone** is the outstanding case in the history of music of the successful invention of a new instrument family. Its inventor, the Belgian instrument maker Adolphe Sax, also developed saxhorns and other instruments. First used around 1840 in military bands, the saxophone (or "sax") is sometimes included in the modern orchestra, but it really came into its own in jazz.

Saxophones are close to clarinets in the way they produce sound. Both use single reeds. Since the saxophone tube is wider and made of brass, its tone is even mellower than that of the clarinet, yet at the same time more forceful. The long saxophone tube has a characteristic bent shape and a flaring "bell," as its opening is called.

Most common are the **alto saxophone** and the **tenor saxophone.** But the big family also includes *bass, baritone, soprano,* and even *contrabass* (very low) and *sopranino* (very high) members. An alto saxophone is illustrated across from page 1.

Brass Instruments

The brass instruments are the loudest of all the wind instruments because of the rather remarkable way their sound is produced. The player blows into a small cup-shaped mouthpiece of metal, and this actually sets the player's lips vibrating. The lip vibration activates vibration of the air within the brass tube.

All brass instruments have long tubes, and these are almost always coiled in one way or another—something that is easy to do with the soft metal they are made from.

Trumpet The **trumpet,** highest of the main brass instruments, has a bright, strong, piercing tone that provides the ultimate excitement in band and orchestral music alike. Pitch is controlled by three pistons or valves that connect auxiliary tubes with the main tube or disconnect them, so as to lengthen or shorten the vibrating air column.

French Horn The **French horn** has a lower, mellower, "thicker" tone than the trumpet. It is capable of mysterious, romantic sounds when played softly; played loudly, it can sound like a trombone. Chords played by several French horns in harmony have a rich, sumptuous tone.

Trombone The **tenor trombone** and the **bass trombone** are also pitched lower than the trumpet. The pitch is controlled by a sliding mechanism (thus the term "slide trombone") rather than a valve or piston, as in the trumpet and French horn.

French horn and timpani

Less bright and martial in tone than the trumpet, the trombone can produce a surprising variety of sounds, ranging from an almost vocal quality in its high register to a hard, powerful blare in the low register.

Tuba The **bass tuba** is typically used as a foundation for the trombone group in an orchestra. It is less flexible than other brass instruments. And like most other deep bass instruments, it is not favored for solo work.

Other Brass Instruments All the brass instruments described so far are staples of both the orchestra and the band. Many other brass instruments (and even whole families of instruments) have been invented for use in marching bands and have then sometimes found their way into the orchestra.

Among these are the *cornet* and the *flügelhorn,* which resemble the trumpet, the *euphonium, baritone horn,* and *saxhorn,* which are somewhere between the French horn and the tuba, and the *sousaphone,* a handsome type of bass tuba named after the great American bandmaster and march composer, John Philip Sousa.

Finally there is the *bugle.* This simple trumpetlike instrument is very limited in the pitches it can play because it has no piston or valve mechanism. Buglers play "Taps" and military fanfares and not much else.

The way buglers get different pitches is by "overblowing," that is, by blowing harder into the mouthpiece so as to get strong partials (see page 9). Overblowing is, indeed, a basic, important resource of all wind instruments.

Percussion Instruments

Instruments in this category produce sound by being struck (or sometimes rattled, as with the South American maraca). Some percussion instruments, such as drums and gongs, have no fixed pitch, just a striking tone color. Other percussion instruments, such as the vibraphone, have whole sets of wooden or metal elements tuned to regular scales.

Timpani The **timpani** (or *kettledrums*) are large hemispherical drums that can be tuned precisely to certain low pitches. They are used in groups of two or more. As with most drums, players can obtain different sounds by using different kinds of drumsticks, tapping at different places on the drumhead, and so on.

Timpani are tuned by tightening the drumhead by means of screws set around the rim. During a concert, one can often see the timpani player, when there are rests in the music, leaning over the drums, tapping them quietly to hear whether the tuning is just right. Also available is a pedal mechanism to retune the timpani instantaneously.

Since they are tuned to precise pitches, timpani are the most widely used percussion instruments in the orchestra. They have the effect of "cementing" loud sounds when the whole orchestra plays.

Pitched Percussion Instruments These are all "scale" instruments, capable of playing melodies and consisting of whole sets of metal or wooden bars or plates struck with sticks or hammers. While they add unforgettable special sound effects to many compositions, they are not usually

The trombones with their horizontal slides, sousaphones with their dramatic bells: a striking Navy Band picture.

heard consistently throughout a piece, as the timpani are. They differ in their materials:

- The **glockenspiel** has small steel bars. It is a high instrument with a bright, penetrating sound.
- The **xylophone** has hardwood plates or slats. It plays as high as the glockenspiel but also lower, and it has a drier, sharper tone.
- The **marimba,** an instrument of African and South American origins, is a xylophone with tubular resonators under each wooden slat, making the tone much mellower.

Drum kit with cymbals

- The **vibraphone** has metal plates, like a glockenspiel with a large range, and is furnished with a controllable electric resonating device. This gives the "vibes" a flexible, funky quality unlike that of any other instrument.
- Like the glockenspiel, the **celesta** has steel bars, but its sound is more delicate and silvery. This instrument, unlike the others in this section, is not played directly by a percussionist wielding hammers or sticks. The hammers are activated from a keyboard; a celesta looks like a miniature upright piano.
- **Tubular bells** or **chimes** are hanging tubes that are struck with a big mallet. They sound like church bells.

Unpitched Percussion Instruments In the category of percussion instruments without a fixed pitch, the following are the most frequently found in the orchestra:

- **Cymbals** are concave metal plates, from a few inches to several feet in diameter. In orchestral music, pairs of large cymbals are clapped together to support climactic moments in the music with a grand clashing sound.
- The **triangle**—a simple metal triangle—gives out a bright tinkle when struck.
- The **tam-tam** is a large unpitched gong with a low, often sinister quality.
- The **snare drum, tenor drum,** and **bass drum** are among the unpitched drums used in the orchestra.

ORCHESTRAL SEATING PLAN

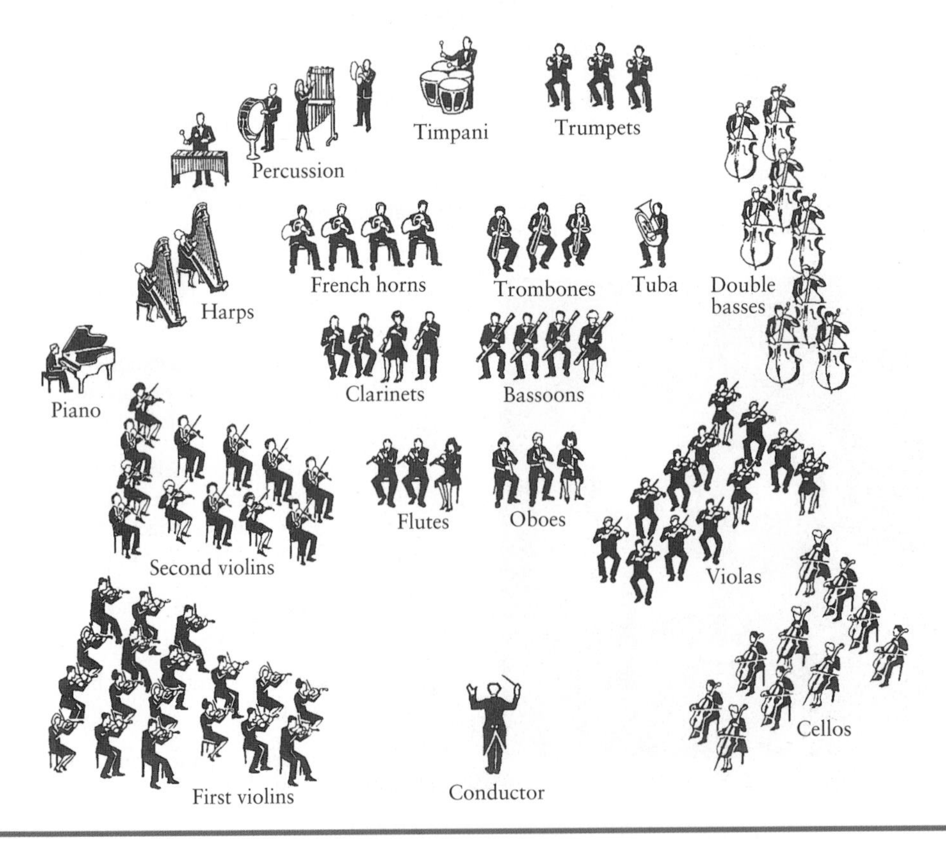

The Orchestra

The orchestra has changed over the centuries just as greatly as orchestral music has. Bach's orchestra in the early 1700s was about a fifth of the size of the orchestra required by ambitious composers today. (See pages 123, 173, and 244 for charts showing the makeup of the orchestra at various historical periods.)

So today's symphony orchestra is a fluid group. Eighty musicians or more will be on the regular roster, but some of them sit out some of the pieces on almost every program. And freelancers have to be engaged for many special compositions in which composers have imaginatively expanded the orchestra for their own expressive purposes. A typical large orchestra today includes the following sections or *choirs:*

- *Strings:* about thirty to thirty-six violinists, twelve violists, ten to twelve cellists, and eight double basses.
- *Woodwinds:* two flutes and a piccolo, two clarinets and a bass clarinet, two oboes and an English horn, two bassoons and a contrabassoon.
- *Brass:* at least two trumpets, four French horns, two trombones, and one tuba.
- *Percussion:* one to four players, who between them manage the timpani and all the other percussion instruments, moving from one to the other. For unlike the violins, for example, the percussion instruments seldom have to be played continuously throughout a piece. If a composition uses a great deal of percussion—and many modern compositions do—more players will be needed.

There are several seating plans for orchestras; which is chosen depends on at least two factors. The conductor judges which arrangement makes the best sound in the particular hall. And some conductors feel they can control the orchestra better with one arrangement, some with another. One such seating plan is shown opposite.

Keyboard Instruments

Though most orchestras today include a pianist, the piano is a relatively new addition to the symphony orchestra. In earlier times, the orchestra regularly included another keyboard instrument, the harpsichord.

The great advantage of keyboard instruments, of course, is that they can play chords and full harmony as well as melodies. One can play a whole piece on a keyboard instrument without requiring any other musicians at all. Consequently the solo music that has been written for piano, harpsichord, and organ is much more extensive than (accompanied) solo music for other instruments—more extensive, and ultimately more important.

Piano The tuned strings of a **piano** are struck by felt-covered hammers, activated from a keyboard. Much technological ingenuity has been devoted to the activating mechanism, or *action.*

A fantastically ornamented Victorian square piano

An elaborately painted eighteenth-century harpsichord

The hammers must strike the string and then fall back at once, while a damping device made of felt touches the string to stop the sound instantly. All this must be done so fast that the pianist can play repeated notes as fast as the hand can move. Also, all possible shades of loudness and softness must lie ready under the player's fingers. This dynamic capability is what gave the piano its name: "piano" is short for *pianoforte,* meaning "soft-loud."

In the nineteenth century, the piano became *the* solo instrument. The list of great virtuoso pianists who were also major composers extends from Frédéric Chopin to Sergei Rachmaninov. At the same time, every middle-class household had a piano. Obligatory piano lessons served and still serve for millions of young people as a magical introduction to the world of music (we hope).

Harpsichord The **harpsichord** is an ancient keyboard instrument that has enjoyed a healthy revival in recent years for the playing of Baroque music, in particular.

Like the piano, the harpsichord has a set of tuned strings activated from a keyboard. The action is much simpler, however. There is no damping, and instead of hammers striking the strings, little bars flip up with quills that pluck them. This means, first, that the tone is brittle and ping-y. Second, it means that the player cannot vary dynamics; when a string is plucked in this way, it always sounds the same.

Harpsichord makers had to compensate for this limitation in dynamics by adding one or two extra full sets of strings, controlled by an extra keyboard. One keyboard could be soft, the other loud. A mechanism allowed the keyboards to be coupled together for the loudest sound of all.

In spite of its brittle tone and its lack of flexibility in dynamics, the harpsichord can be a wonderfully expressive instrument. Good harpsichord playing requires, first and foremost, great rhythmic subtlety.

Clavichord Another ancient keyboard instrument, the **clavichord,** was strictly for private use. Small and relatively inexpensive, its strings (only one set) are struck by simple metal levers. The clavichord has a very sensitive but also very quiet sound—it cannot be heard across a large room, let alone a concert hall.

A five-manual organ. The player pulls out *stops* (or *stop knobs*) to change the sets of pipes that sound.

Artists loved to paint lutes and lutenists: This is *A Young Man Playing a Lute* by the great early Baroque painter Michelangelo Merisi da Caravaggio (1573–1610).

Organ The **pipe organ** has a great many sets of tuned pipes through which a complex wind system blows air, again activated from a keyboard. The pipes have different tone colors; a large organ is capable of an almost orchestral variety of sound. Most organs have more than one keyboard to control different sets of the pipes. There is also a pedal board—a big keyboard on the floor, played with the feet—to control the lowest-sounding pipes.

Each set of tuned pipes is called a *stop;* a moderate-sized organ has forty to fifty stops, but much bigger ones exist. (The biggest organ on record, at Atlantic City, has 1477 stops, for a total of 33,112 pipes.) Called "the king of instruments," the pipe organ is certainly the largest of them. Organs need their size and power in order to provide enough sound to fill the large spaces of churches and cathedrals on a suitably grand scale.

The organ is not a member of the orchestra; but since the grandest occasions call for orchestra, chorus, vocal soloists, and organ combined (e.g., the *Messiah* at Christmastime: see page 156), a major symphony hall has to have its organ—usually an imposing sight.

Electronic Keyboard Instruments Today "keyboard" or "organ" generally means an electronic instrument. Synthesizers simulate the sound of organs, pianos, and harpsichords. Electronic pianos look like acoustic ones and sound quite like them, though the "feel" is different. They cost a great deal less.

Modern concert music, from the 1960s on, has occasionally used electronic keyboards. On the whole, however, synthesizers have been used more to compose concert music than to play it.

Plucked Stringed Instruments

Plucked stringed instruments figure much less in art music of the West than in Asian countries such as India and Japan, as we shall see. One exception is the orchestral harp: See page 37. The acoustic **guitar** and the **mandolin** are used very widely in Western popular music, but only occasionally in orchestras.

However, a now-obsolete plucked instrument, the **lute,** was of major importance in earlier times. One of the most beautiful-looking of instruments, the lute sounds rather like a gentle guitar. It differs in its rounded sound box, and in the way its pegboard is set nearly perpendicular to the neck. Large members of the lute family were the **theorbo** and the **archlute.**

Like keyboard instruments, plucked stringed instruments have been revolutionized by electronic technology. The **electric guitars** of rock music have rarely found their way into concert music.

Web: *Listen to individual instruments of the orchestra at* **<bedfordstmartins.com/listen>.**

CHAPTER 4

Musical Form and Musical Style

Form is a general word with a long list of dictionary definitions. As applied to the arts, **form** is an important concept that refers to the shape, arrangement, relationship, or organization of the various elements. In poetry, for example, the elements of form are words, phrases, meters, rhymes, and stanzas; in painting, they are lines, colors, shapes, and space.

Keep two things in mind, then. Remember the general outlines of the [outer form], and remember that the content of the composer's thought forces him to use that formal mold in a particular and personal way—in a way that belongs only to the particular piece that he is writing.

Aaron Copland, *What to Listen For in Music*

1 Form in Music

In music, the elements of form and organization are those we have already discussed: rhythm, pitch and melody, dynamics, tone color, and texture. A musical work, whether a simple song or a symphony, is formed or organized by means of repetitions of some of these elements, and by contrasts among them. The repetitions may be strict or free (that is, exact or with some variation). The contrasts may be of many different kinds—the possibilities are virtually limitless—conveying many different kinds of feeling.

Over the centuries and all over the world, musicians have learned to create longer and more impressive pieces in this way: symphonies, operas, works for the Javanese gamelan or Japanese gagaku orchestras, and more. Each piece is a specific sound experience in a definite time span, with a beginning, middle, and end, and often with subtle routes between. Everyone knows that music can make a nice effect for a minute or two. But how does music extend itself—and hold the listener's interest—for ten minutes, or half an hour, or three whole hours?

This is one of the main functions of musical form. Form is the relationship that connects those beginnings, middles, and ends.

Music: an art of sound in time that expresses ideas and emotions *in significant forms* through the elements of rhythm, melody, harmony, and dynamics.

Webster's College Dictionary, 1991 (our italics)

Form and Feeling

Form in art also has a good deal to do with its emotional quality; it is a mistake to consider form as a merely structural or intellectual matter. Think of the little (or big) emotional "click" we get at the end of a limerick, or a sonnet, where the accumulated meanings of the words are summed up with the final rhyme. This is an effect to which form—limerick form or sonnet form—contributes. Similarly, when at the end of a symphony a previously heard melody comes back, with new orchestration and new harmonies, the special feeling this gives us emerges from a flood of memory; we remember the melody from before, in its earlier version. That effect, too, is created by musical form.

Form in Poetry

Fleas:
Adam
Had 'em.

Poet Ogden Nash creates rhyme and meter to add a little lift, and a smile, to the prose observation "Adam had fleas" (or "Ever since Adam, we've all suffered").

How easy is it, actually, to perceive form in music and to experience the feelings associated with form? Easy enough with a short tune, such as "The Star-Spangled Banner"—that's what our analysis on page 25 was all about. The various phrases of this tune, with their repetitions, parallel features, contrasts, and climax, provide a microcosm of musical form in longer pieces. A large-scale composition like a symphony is something like a greatly expanded tune, and its form is experienced in basically the same way.

To be sure, a symphony requires more from the listener—more time and more attention—than a tune does. Aware of the potential problem here, composers scale their musical effects accordingly. The larger the piece, the more strongly the composer is likely to help the memory along by emphasizing the repetitions and contrasts that determine the musical form.

Form and Forms

Like the word *rhythm* (see page 10), the word *form* has its general meaning and also a more specific one. "Form" in general refers to the organization of elements in a musical work, but "*a* form" refers to one of many standardized formal patterns that composers have used over the centuries.

Form in Painting

A Madonna by Raphael Sanzio (1483–1520), built out of two cunningly nested triangles. To balance the boys at the left, the Virgin faces slightly to the right, her extended foot "echoing" their bare flesh. On a larger scale, the activity at the left is matched by a steeper landscape.

Forms in this latter sense can be referred to as "outer" forms; the ones treated later in this book are listed in the margin. In most periods, artists in all media have tended to employ such outer forms. The fixed elements in them provide a welcome source of orientation for listeners, but they are always general enough to allow composers endless possibilities on the detailed level. The quality and feeling of works in the same outer form can therefore vary greatly. Or, to put it another way, any work adhering to a common "outer form" can also have an individual "inner form" of its own.

Musical forms, as standardized patterns, are conventionally expressed by letter diagrams, such as **A B A** or **a b a** (small letters tend to be used for shorter sections of music). More complicated forms come about through "nesting":

A	B	A
a b a	c d c	a b a

Two basic factors create musical form: *repetition* and *contrast.* In **A B A** form, one of the simplest and most familiar, the element of repetition is **A** and the element of contrast is **B**. Some sort of tune or theme or other musical section is presented at the beginning (**A**), then another section (**B**) that contrasts with the first, and then the first one again (**A**). If **A** returns with significant modification, a prime mark can be added: **A′**.

But this tells us only so much. With any particular work, what about the inner form: Is **B** in a different mode? A different key? Does it present material that contrasts in rhythm, texture, or tone color—or does it work its contrast by ringing changes on the original material, on **A**? The returns in **A B A′** form, too, can convey very different feelings. One return can sound exciting, another tricky, while yet another provides a sense of relief.

So identifying "outer forms"—getting the letters right—is just a preliminary step in musical appreciation. The real point about great music is the way composers refine, modify, and personalize outer forms for their own expressive purposes.

The Main Musical Forms

Form in Architecture

The central, contrasting unit of this building seems almost to flow into the unit at the right. The musical analogy would be to an interesting **A B A′** form, in which **A** comes back after **B** in an expanded version (**A′**), and that version includes some new rhythm or instrument that we first heard during **B.**

LISTEN for musical form

13, 14-16

"The Star-Spangled Banner" is in one of simplest possible forms, **a a b.** See page 25. "Oh, say can you see . . . twilight's last gleaming" is **a,** "Whose broad stripes . . . gallantly streaming" is the second **a,** and the rest of the anthem is **b.** Section **b** makes a definitive contrast with **a** by means of its new melody and higher range.

When sections of music are not identical but considered essentially parallel, they are labeled **a, a′, a″,** etc., with prime marks. Small sections can be nested in larger ones that are marked with capital letters: **A A′.** Our example comes from *The Nutcracker* by Pyotr Ilych Chaikovsky, said to be America's favorite piece of classical music. Thousands attend performances of this childhood ballet every year, as a Christmas ritual.

Act II includes a set of delightful little dances, in contrasting styles. The first of these is the Dance of the Sugar-Plum Fairy (a sugar plum is a hard candy). Chaikovsky used this dance essentially to show off the celesta, a rare instrument hardly ever featured in this way (see page 41). The piece is in **A B A′** form, breaking down into **a a′ b b a a′.**

Track	Time	Section	Description
13	0:00		Introduction—the **2/4** meter is previewed by low string instruments.
	0:08	**A a**	Solo for celesta with comments by a bass clarinet
	0:23	**a′**	Like **a**—only the ending is different, on a new pitch and harmony
	0:37	**B b**	Contrasts with **a**
	0:44	**b**	
	0:51		Transition—the music has a preparatory quality
	1:07	**A′ a**	Celesta an octave higher—a very striking new sound—with a quiet new click in the violins
	1:22	**a′**	

This **A B A′** form gets its prime mark from the new orchestration, not from changes in melody or harmony, as is often the case. (More strictly, we could mark this form as **a a′ b b** ***transition*** **a″ a‴**, but these letter diagrams are only used to show broad outlines.)

For a longer example, listen to the whole third movement of Beethoven's Fifth Symphony. It's now necessary to listen on a much longer time scale, passing by the phrases to experience larger spans of music. Section **A,** for example, includes two very different themes and other material. And here section **A′** is very different from **A,** abbreviated and reorchestrated much more radically than in *The Nutcracker.* See page 231.

Track	Time	Section	Description
14	0:00	**A**	Includes two different themes: one *p* (string instruments), one *f* (brass instruments)
15	0:00	**B**	**B** contrasts radically with **A;** starting with the tone color of the double basses, virtually all of the musical elements differ—melody, rhythm, texture, and more—except for the **3/4** meter.
	1:03	***Transition***	
16	0:00	**A′**	Another radical contrast—a shortened version of **A,** with the motives and themes of **A** played very quietly and with different tone colors: *pizzicato* (plucked) strings, bassoon, and oboe instead of bowed strings and loud French horns
	1:16		The movement is over; another passage of transition to the next movement begins.

Musical Genres

One often hears symphonies, sonatas, and operas referred to as "forms" of music. Actually this is loose terminology, best avoided in the interests of clarity, because symphonies and other works can be composed in completely different forms ("outer forms")—that is, their internal orders or organizations can be of quite different kinds. Thus, the last movement of Joseph Haydn's Symphony No. 95 is in rondo form, whereas the last movement of Hector Berlioz's *Fantastic* Symphony follows no standard form whatsoever.

The best term for these general categories of music is *genre* (jáhn-ruh), borrowed from French. A genre can be defined by its text (a madrigal has Italian verses of a specific kind), or by its function (a Mass is written for a Roman Catholic service), or by the performing forces (a quartet is for four singers or instrumentalists). The main genres of Western music are listed in the margin. Other genres from other musical traditions will be encountered in the Global Perspectives sections.

The Main Musical Genres	*page*
overture	144
Baroque concerto	129
concerto grosso	129
suite	104, 143
French overture	144
oratorio	155
church cantata	159
organ chorale	162
symphony	178
sonata	197
Classical concerto	200
string quartet	204
lied	249
song cycle	253
program symphony	265
symphonic poem	290
opera	97, 149
subtypes of opera:	
opera seria	150
opera buffa	207
music drama	279

Early Music Genres	*page*
Gregorian chant genres:	
antiphon	60
sequence	61
hymn	75
organum	65
motet	67, 85
Mass	77
madrigal	85
pavane, galliard	88
passacaglia	106

2 Musical Style

Style, like *form,* is another of those broad, general words—general but very necessary. The style of a tennis player is the particular way he or she reaches up for the serve, swings, follows through on the forehand, hits the ball deep or short, and so on. A lifestyle means the whole combination of things one does and doesn't do: the food one eats, the way one dresses and talks, one's habits of thought and feeling.

The style of a work of art, similarly, is the combination of qualities that make it distinctive. One composer's style may favor jagged rhythms, simple harmonies, and tunes to the exclusion of other types of melody. Another may prefer certain kinds of tone color; still another may concentrate on a particular form. The type of emotional expression a composer cultivates is also an important determinant of musical style.

One can speak of the lifestyle of a generation as well as the lifestyle of a particular person. Similarly, a distinction can be made between the style of a particular composer and the style of a historical period. For example, to a large extent George Frideric Handel's manner of writing falls within the parameters of the Baroque style of his day. But some features of Handel's style are unique, and perhaps it is those features that embody his musical genius.

Musical Style and Lifestyle

In any historical period or place, the musical style bears some relation to the lifestyle in general; this seems self-evident. Perhaps the point is clearest of all with popular music, where distinct (and distinctly different) worlds are evoked by rock, rap, and country music, to say nothing of earlier styles such as 1950s rhythm and blues or 1930s swing.

Older styles of music, too, relate to total cultural situations, though how this works in detail is not fully understood. We can, however, at least suggest some of these musical-cultural relationships for music of the various historical periods. For each period, we will sketch certain aspects of the culture, history, and lifestyle of the time. We will then briefly outline the musical style and, wherever possible, suggest correlations. Then the musical style will be examined in more detail through individual composers and individual pieces of their music.

Even *where* people listen to music reflects their lifestyle. The Hollywood Bowl, which has been known to hold 26,000 people, flaunts both the superb topography of Los Angeles and also the blockbuster mentality that is the hallmark of the movie industry.

These individual pieces are our principal concern—not history, or culture, or concepts of musical style in the abstract. Learning the basic concepts of music (as we have tried to do in this unit) is useful only insofar as it focuses and sharpens the process of listening to actual music. This book is called *Listen,* and it rests on the belief that the love of music depends first and foremost on careful listening to particular pieces. But such listening never happens in a cultural vacuum. It always takes place in a vivid, experienced context of some kind. The general information we present here on history, culture, styles, and genres is intended to remake, in some small way, our own listening contexts—and hence reshape our listening experiences.

Coming to the end of Unit I, after a lot of prose and a number of hasty musical excerpts, we should listen to a whole composition at some length. A convenient one at this point is *The Young Person's Guide to the Orchestra,* by the English composer Benjamin Britten (1913–1976).

This is *the* ideal piece for learning the tone colors of the Western orchestra. Britten, who wrote a lot of music for children, undertook this *Guide* as a pedagogical responsibility—and as a challenge to his ingenuity—but he also set out to create a coherent and interesting musical composition. Listen to it primarily to come to know instrumental sounds, but also as a review of several concepts introduced in Unit I.

The work uses one basic theme—a short, rather bouncy tune by an earlier English composer, Henry Purcell (see page 102). After first displaying the grand sound of the full orchestra playing this tune, Britten has each of the four orchestral choirs play it: woodwinds, brass, strings . . . but he knew he had to cheat with the percussion. It was clever, then, to prepare for the not-very-thematic percussion statement at 1:21 by freeing up the theme a little in the preceding brass and stringed statements, and afterwards to remind us of the original tune, played by the full orchestra again. (Britten makes up for his cheat by a particularly brilliant percussion episode later.)

17

theme, page 26

tune, page 24

orchestral choirs, page 43

So far everything has been in the minor mode and in triple meter. But next comes a series of *variations* on the theme—versions of the theme varied in melody, rhythm, texture, mode, tempo, everything. We study variation form on page 132. The first section of the piece has given us a theme in the minor mode and its repetitions, but the first variations already switch to the major mode. Variation 3, in a swinging triple meter, is followed at once by a variation in duple meter. Many variations—variations 1, 3, and 4, to begin with—involve a great deal of repetition of a single motive. There are variations in fast tempo that last for hardly more than half a minute, and others in slow tempo that take nearly three times as long.

major and minor mode, page 32

duple and triple meter, pages 11–12

motive, page 26

tempo, page 14

In variation form, variety is the order of the day. This central, variation section of the *Guide* offers, in addition to the catalogue of instrumental sounds, an equally dazzling catalogue of the endlessly varied moods that can be represented in music. Some variations are hardly more than half a minute long, others are slowed down to nearly three minutes.

At the end, Britten writes an extremely vigorous *fugue,* based on yet another version of the Purcell tune. We study fugue on page 105. For now, notice that this section of the *Guide* provides an excellent example of imitative polyphony.

polyphony, page 28

And our virtuoso composer has still one more trick up his sleeve: He brings the tune back triumphantly just before the end, unvaried, while the fugue is still going on. Both can be heard simultaneously. This is non-imitative polyphony. The return of the tune wraps up the whole long piece very happily as a unique variety of **A B A′** form.

form, page 46

Web: *To test your understanding of musical form and style, take an online quiz at* **<bedfordstmartins.com/listen>.**

LISTENING CHART 2

SG 17-22

Britten, *The Young Person's Guide to the Orchestra*

17 min., 13 sec.

Track	Time	Section	Instruments	Comments
17	0:00	**THEME**	Full orchestra	Note the prominent ***sequence*** in the middle of the Purcell tune. You will hear snatches of this in some of the variations.
	0:19	Transition		***Diminuendo*** (getting softer). Further transitions occurring between thematic statements and variations will not be indicated on this chart.
	0:23	Theme	WOODWIND choir	
	0:45	Theme	BRASS choir	Ending is changed.
	1:04	Theme	STRING choir	Theme is changed further.
	1:21		PERCUSSION	"Theme" only in principle; only some rhythms remain
	1:36	**THEME**	Full orchestra	Same as the first time
18	1:55	Variation 1	Flutes and piccolo	(harp accompaniment)
0:11	2:06			Piccolo and flute play in thirds.
0:35	2:30	Variation 2	Oboes	Beginning of the tune transformed into a slow, romantic melody in oboe 1; oboe 2 joins in two-part ***polyphony.***
1:42	3:37	Variation 3	Clarinet family	Solos for bass clarinet (1:42), clarinet (1:57), and E-flat clarinet (1:46)
2:21	4:16	Variation 4	Bassoon	Typical qualities of the bassoon: ***staccato*** (comic effect) and ***legato*** (melodious)
19	5:15	Variation 5	Violins	With chordal accompaniment—particularly clear ***homophonic*** texture
0:33	5:48	Variation 6	Violas	Slower
1:53	7:08	Variation 7	Cellos	Another slow, romantic melody: falls into a a′ form (clarinet in the background)
2:53	8:08	Variation 8	Double bass	Solo—humorous
3:47	9:02	Variation 9	Harp	In the background is a string ***tremolo,*** caused by bowing a single note extremely rapidly, so that it sounds like a single "trembling" note.
20	10:01	Variation 10	French horns	
0:51	10:52	Variation 11	Trumpets	With snare drum, suggesting a fast military march
1:22	11:23	Variation 12	Trombones, tuba	Typical qualities of the trombone: humorously pompous, and mysterious chords
21	12:33	Variation 13	PERCUSSION	Timpani and bass drum (heard throughout the variation), cymbals (0:15), tambourine (0:26), triangle (0:29), snare drum (0:38), Chinese block (0:42), xylophone (0:48), castanets (1:00), gong (1:06), whip (1:14), marimba and triangle (1:40) *Percussion instruments are described on page 40.*
22	14:28	FUGUE		***Imitative polyphony*** starts with flutes, then oboe, clarinet (same order as above!).
1:53	16:21	THEME		Climax: slower than before. The TUNE is superimposed on the fugue.

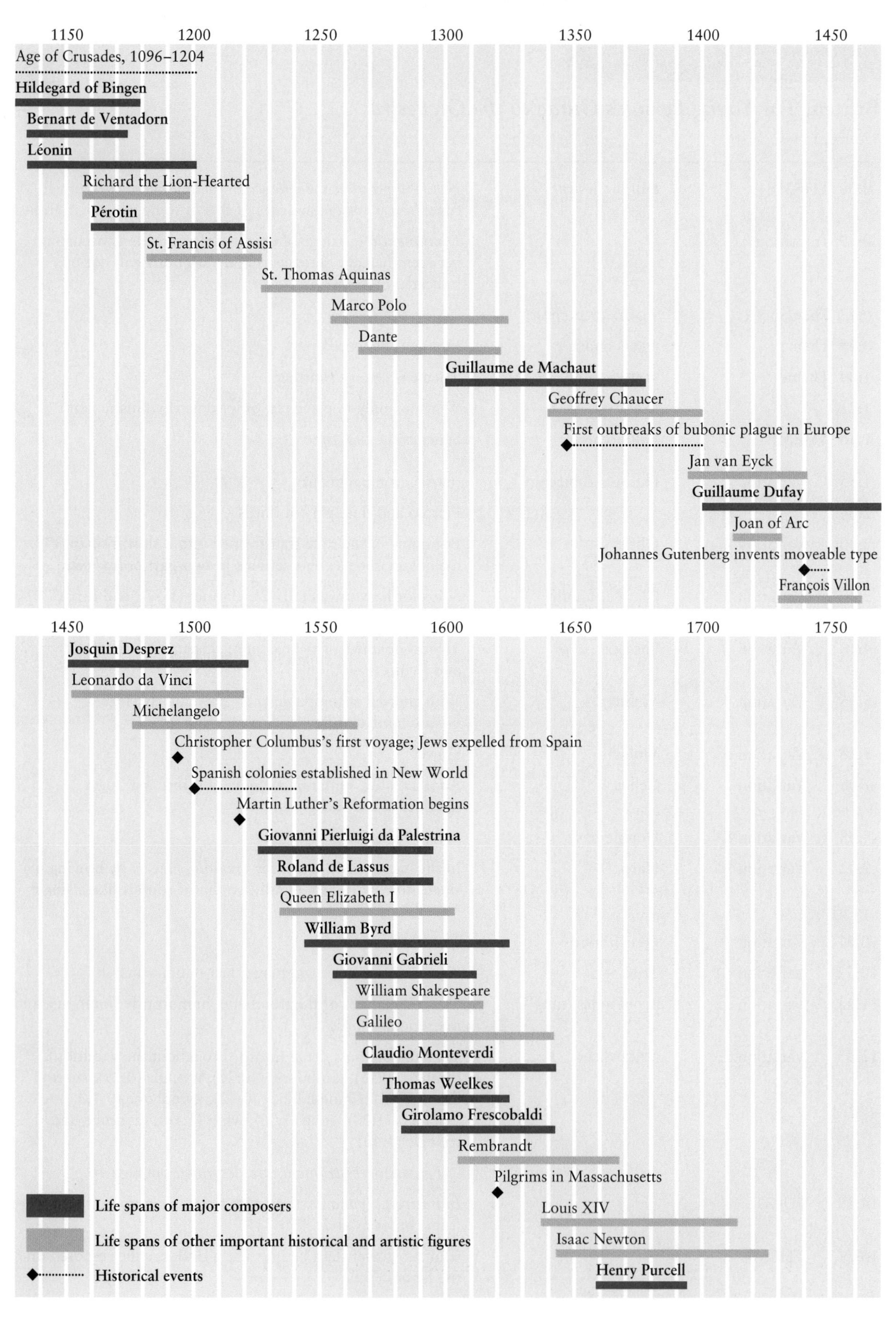

1150
1200
1250
1300
1350
1400
1450
Age of Crusades, 1096–1204
Hildegard of Bingen
Bernart de Ventadorn
Léonin
Richard the Lion-Hearted
Pérotin
St. Francis of Assisi
St. Thomas Aquinas
Marco Polo
Dante
Guillaume de Machaut
Geoffrey Chaucer
First outbreaks of bubonic plague in Europe
Jan van Eyck
Guillaume Dufay
Joan of Arc
Johannes Gutenberg invents moveable type
François Villon
1450
1500
1550
1600
1650
1700
1750
Josquin Desprez
Leonardo da Vinci
Michelangelo
Christopher Columbus's first voyage; Jews expelled from Spain
Spanish colonies established in New World
Martin Luther's Reformation begins
Giovanni Pierluigi da Palestrina
Roland de Lassus
Queen Elizabeth I
William Byrd
Giovanni Gabrieli
William Shakespeare
Galileo
Claudio Monteverdi
Thomas Weelkes
Girolamo Frescobaldi
Rembrandt
Pilgrims in Massachusetts
Louis XIV
Isaac Newton
Henry Purcell
Life spans of major composers
Life spans of other important historical and artistic figures
Historical events

UNIT II

Early Music: An Overview

Western art music extends from the great repertory of Gregorian chant, assembled around the year 600 C.E., to electronic compositions that were programmed yesterday and today. One does not have to be a specialist to have some feeling for the sheer scope, variety, and bewildering richness of all this music. Some of it was developed to maintain Christianity through centuries of barbarism, some to glorify great monarchs such as Queen Elizabeth I of England or Louis XIV of France. Some of it is being produced in today's recording studios for the enjoyment, mainly, of connoisseurs. The field ranges from music attributed to the shadowy figures Léonin and Pérotin in the twelfth century, through compositions by familiar masters such as Bach and Beethoven, to work in progress saved on the hard drives at computer music centers in Paris or Berkeley, California. All of this music has fascinated, moved, and inspired its listeners.

Certainly there is too much here to cover in a single semester or quarter course—too much, that is, if one is going to do more than skim the music, picking up a few frantic facts and figures about it without really listening. It cannot be said often enough that listening to particular pieces again and again is the basic activity that leads to the love of music and to its understanding. A hurried survey does justice to none of the world's significant music; we have to make choices. We have: The essential coverage of this book begins in the eighteenth century, with Unit III and the music of Bach and Handel, who are the first composers with a long-standing place in the "standard repertory" of concert music. This phrase refers to a large but not limitless body of music from which concert artists and conductors usually draw their programs.

As an optional introduction to all of this, Unit II presents a brief overview of music before the eighteenth century. So-called Early Music was forgotten for centuries, and is still seldom performed at standard concerts. But in today's music world, less attuned to concerts than to recordings, Early Music has become familiar. It has its own musical institutions, its own specialist performers, and its own devotees, and through recordings it has also found its way into the musical mainstream.

CHAPTER 5

The Middle Ages

"The Middle Ages" is a catch-all term for nearly a thousand years of European history, extending from the collapse of the Roman Empire in the fifth century C.E. to the advent of new learning, technology, and political organization in the age of Columbus. Even though life and culture changed slowly in those days, this is obviously too broad a span of time to mean much as a single "period."

Nowhere is this clearer than in music. Music changed radically from the beginning to the end of the medieval era, more than in any other historical period. Two of the central principles of later Western music, *tune* and *polyphony*, originated around the middle of this long period.

Medieval musicians: The boy appears to be tuning his *vihuela*—a Spanish plucked stringed instrument—to the pitch being played by the older man (his teacher?).

1 Music and the Church: Plainchant

The early history of Western music was determined by the Christian Church to an extent that is not easy for us to grasp today. The church cultivated, supported, and directed music as it did art, architecture, poetry, and learning. All composers were in holy orders, and all musicians got their training as church choirboys. (Exception must be made for popular musicians—called minstrels and **jongleurs**—but we know next to nothing about their lives or their music. The only people who wrote music down were monks and other clerics, who could not have cared less about preserving popular music.)

The music cultivated by the church was the singing or chanting of sacred words in services, and we might pause for a moment to ask why singing was so important for Christian worship. One could point to traditions of singing in older religions from which Christianity borrowed much—especially the singing of psalms in the ancient Jewish synagogue. But this merely shifts the question: Why did ancient worshipers *sing* at all?

Singing is, first of all, a way of uttering words that sets them apart from ordinary speech. Words denote concepts, and singing words gives concepts in prayer or doctrine a special status, a step above merely speaking them. Music provides words with special emphasis, force, mystery, credibility, and even magic. Throughout human history, this heightening by music has served the basic aim of religion: to bring humans into beneficial contact with unseen spirits, with deities, or with a single God.

All the largest world religions—Islam, Hinduism, and Buddhism as well as Christianity and Judaism—possess and prize old and complex systems of chant. Most other, smaller religions do, too. (See Global Perspectives 1, pages 70–72.)

Music and Church Services

Sacred texts were sung at church services—and the life of the church centered in its services. The music that has come down to us was sung in monasteries and cathedrals, not humble parish churches; the services were conducted by and for the higher ranks of Christendom: monks, nuns, and cathedral clergy. And monks and nuns spent an amazing amount of their time in prayer. Besides the Mass, a lengthy ceremony that might happen more than once a day, there were no fewer than eight other services through the day and night, known collectively as the Divine Office. Large portions of these services were sung.

A psalm is the work of the Angels, the incense of the Spirit. Oh, how wise was that Teacher who found a way for us to sing psalms and at the same time learn worthwhile things, so that in some mysterious way doctrine is more deeply impressed upon the mind!

St. Basil, fourth century C.E.

Though each service had its standard format, many details in the verbal texts for them changed according to the church calendar (Christmas, Easter, various saints' days, and so on). As a result, there were literally thousands of religious texts specified for the Mass and the Office throughout the year.

All these texts required music, but providing such music was less a matter of free invention than of small additions and adjustments to a sacrosanct, traditional prototype. And listening to it was not so much listening as worshiping, while allowing music to expand the devotional experience. Hearing Gregorian chant or later medieval music today, one feels less like a "listener" in the modern sense than like a privileged eavesdropper, someone who has been allowed to attend a select occasion that is partly musical, but mainly spiritual. The experience is an intimate and tranquil one, cool and, to some listeners, especially satisfying.

Plainchant

The official music of the Catholic Church in the Middle Ages, and far beyond the Middle Ages, was a great repertory of melodies designated for the many religious texts to be sung at services throughout the year. This is the system of **plainchant** (or plainsong), widely known as Gregorian chant.

Clerics singing plainchant, depicted within an illuminated initial letter C in a late medieval manuscript. The whimsical little viol player is definitely outside the C, for instrumental music was taboo in church.

It is called "plain" because it is unaccompanied, monophonic (one-line) music for voices, without fixed rhythm or meter. And it is called "Gregorian" after the famous pope and church father Gregory I (c. 540–604); Gregory is reputed to have assembled and standardized all the basic chants required for the church services of his time. Many medieval plainchants were composed later, however, and so cannot strictly speaking be called "Gregorian." And even with truly Gregorian chant, we only know it by extrapolating backwards from later manuscripts. Notation for music of the Middle Ages did not begin to develop until around the ninth century C.E., long after Gregory.

Characteristics of Plainchant

Plainchant has many genres, differing widely in melodic style, depending on their religious function. Some plainchants consist of simple recitation on a monotone, with only slight deviations from that single pitch; in monasteries, the entire set of 150 psalms had to be sung in this fashion every week. Other chants are intricate songs with hundreds of notes ranging well over an octave. And still others count as the first real tunes that are known in Western music.

In whatever style or genre, all plainchants share two characteristic features. First, they are *nonmetrical;* they have no clearly established meter, and therefore the rhythm is free. Not only is a distinctive beat lacking in this music, but rhythms may change from one performance (rather, one service) to the next.

Second, plainchant is not construed in the major/minor system, but according to one of the **medieval modes.** As discussed in Unit I, the original scale of Western music was the diatonic scale—the "white-note" scale on the piano—and this is still the basic scale today. We use this scale oriented around the pitches C or A as "home" or tonic (see pages 31–32). Oriented around C, the music is said to be in the major mode, oriented around A, in the minor mode.

Musicians of the Middle Ages organized the scale differently—not around C or A, but around D, E, F, or G. The result was music in other modes, different from the modern major or minor. These modes were given numbers or Greek names (since medieval scholars traced them back to the modes of ancient Greek music, as discussed by Plato and others). The medieval modes are these:

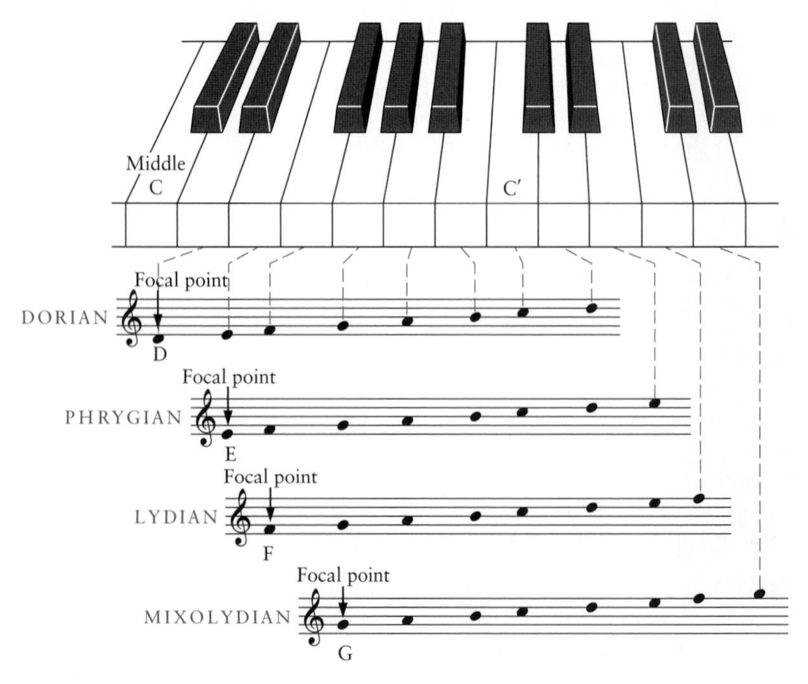

Multicultural medieval music: At a time when half of Spain was in Arab (Moorish) hands, a Moor and a Spaniard are shown playing large vihuelas together. Plucked stringed instruments like the vihuela were an important novelty brought to medieval Europe from Arab countries.

The essential difference between the modern major and minor modes comes in the different arrangement of half steps and whole steps in their scales. The medieval modes provide four other arrangements. (Compare the preceding diagram with the one on page 31.) In this respect, then, medieval plainchant is actually richer and more subtle than music in the major/minor system. The artistic effect of plainchant—music without harmony or definite rhythm—is concentrated in melody, melody built on this rich and subtle modal system.

Gregorian Recitation

As we have said, the huge repertory of Gregorian chant ranges from simple recitation on a single pitch, with scarcely any variation, to long melodies that can make one dizzy by their endless, ecstatic twists and turns. Recitation was used for texts considered fairly routine in the services, such as lengthy readings from the Bible. Melody was used on more significant occasions, such as solemn church processions. (We will see an example of this use later.)

In Gregorian recitation, the pitch on which the text is sung, called the **reciting tone,** is held except for small, formulaic variations at beginnings and ends of phrases. These punctuate the text and make it easier to understand (and sing, since they give the singers time for a breath).

ANONYMOUS
Preface for Mass on Whit Sunday, "Vere dignum"

Our example is the music for a relatively minor text in the Mass, the Preface, which serves to introduce a much more important element in the service.* This

*The preface introduces the Elevation of the Host, where the priest celebrating Mass displays the bread and wine that is or represents the body and blood of Christ. By tasting these things, the faithful reaffirm their communion with Christ—the basic purpose of this service.

text consists of three sentences, recited in the same way. Each sentence is divided into three or four phrases, and the last of them changes to a new, second reciting tone, lower than the one at the start of the sentence. All the phrases have a little opening formula sliding up to the reciting tone—launching it, as it were—and a closing formula sinking down again. These are indicated only approximately on the chart below.

LISTEN **Preface for Mass on Whit Sunday, "Vere dignum"**

1

1

The three sentences of the Preface text, each containing three or four phrases (a, b, c, d), are printed with their pitches roughly indicated by different levels. The **reciting tone** is shown in regular type, the opening and closing formulas in *italic.*

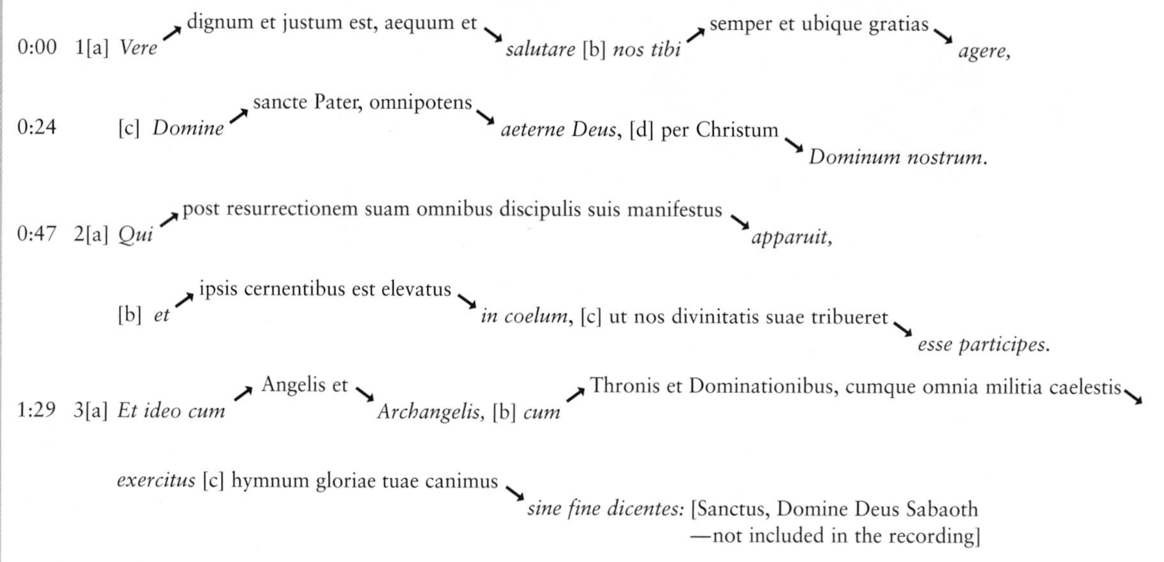

1. It is truly meet and just, right and for our salvation, that we should at all times and in all places give thanks to Thee, O Lord, holy Father, almighty and eternal God, through Christ our Lord.

2. Who after His resurrection appeared openly to all His disciples, and while they looked on, was raised up into heaven, so that He might let us share in His own divinity.

3. And therefore with the Angels and Archangels, with the Thrones and Dominations, and with all the hosts of the heavenly army, we sing the hymn of Thy glory evermore, saying: ["Holy, holy, holy, Lord God of Sabaoth"]

Gregorian Melody

In addition to recitation, melody abounds in many different genres of plainchant. We will look first at one of the simplest genres, the **antiphon.**

ANONYMOUS
Gregorian antiphon, "In paradisum"

In the liturgy for the dead, this antiphon is sung in procession on the way from the final blessing of the corpse in church to the graveyard where burial takes place. "In paradisum" is in the Mixolydian (G) mode. Modal cadences are heard in lines 4 and 5, "Chorus Ange*lo*rum" and "quondam pau*pere.*"

The way to experience "In paradisum" is to place track 2 on repeat, and imagine yourself a medieval monk or nun who has lost a brother or sister. Candles have all been extinguished in the church after the Requiem Mass (so called because you have prayed for the soul's eternal rest—in Latin, *requiem aeternam*). As the coffin is lifted up, the priest begins "In paradisum," and then the entire religious community joins in. You sing this brief antiphon again and again, for as long as it takes the slow procession to reach the graveyard.

Notice that the beginning of "In paradisum" reveals its ultimate derivation from recitation; afterwards the music grows more and more melodic. The melodic highpoint comes in line 5, where the text refers to Lazarus, the poor man raised up from the grave by Christ—a point of identification for the humble mourners. This haunting melodic figure was etched in the memory of the Middle Ages through an endless succession of last rites.

LISTEN **Gregorian antiphon, "In paradisum"**

2
2

0:00	**In paradisum deducant te Angeli:** **in tuo adventu suscipiant te Martyres,** **et perducant te in civitatem sanctam Jerusalem.**	May the Angels lead you to paradise, and the Martyrs, when you arrive, escort you to the holy city of Jerusalem.
0:39	**Chorus Angelorum te suscipiat,** **et cum Lazaro quondam paupere** **aeternam habeas requiem.**	May the Angel choir sustain you, and with Lazarus, who was once poor, may you be granted eternal rest.

A miniature illustration of Hildegard, in one of her manuscripts, shows the miracle by which fire came down from heaven to engulf and inspire her.

HILDEGARD OF BINGEN (1098–1179)
Plainchant sequence, "Columba aspexit"

Abbess Hildegard of the little convent of Bingen, in western Germany, was one of the most remarkable figures of the Middle Ages. Most famous for her book relating her religious visions, she also wrote on natural history and medicine; she gained such renown that popes and emperors sought her counsel.

Five hundred years after Gregory I, the first compiler of Gregorian chants, Hildegard composed plainchant melodies in her own highly individual style to go with poems that she wrote for special services. "Columba aspexit" honored one of the many minor saints venerated in those days, Saint Maximinus. It belongs to a late medieval plainchant genre called the **sequence.**

The sequence is a much more elaborate kind of melody than the antiphon. It consists of a series of short tunes sung twice, with some variation (and an extra unit at the end: **A A′ B B′ C C′ . . . N**). A soloist sings **A**, the choir **A′**, and so on. "Modal" cadences—Mixolydian, once again—at the beginning of the melody ("fe*ne*strae," "*e*ius") give it a deceptively humble quality that contrasts with its ecstatic soaring later.

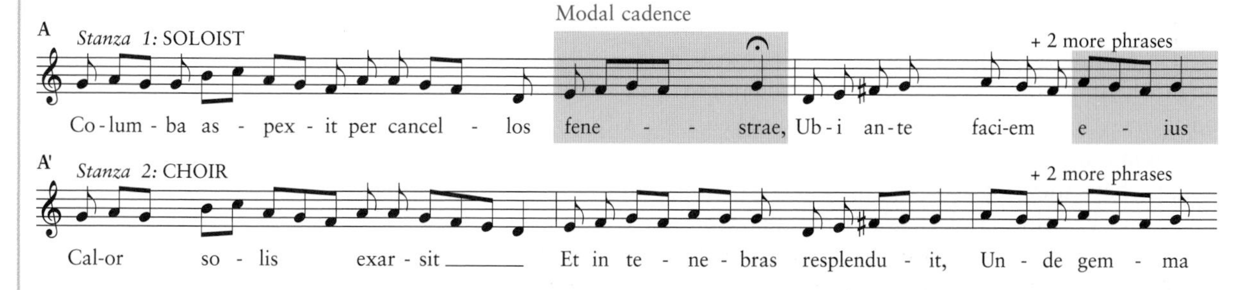

Our recording includes an instrumental *drone*—a single two-note chord running continuously. Drones are known from music around the world as well as from European folk music, and there is evidence that drones were used to accompany plainchant, although medieval manuscripts do not confirm this. The drone, the mystical words of Hildegard's poem, and the free, surging rhythm of her music work together to produce a feeling of serene yet intense spirituality.

LISTEN Hildegard of Bingen, "Columba aspexit"

3

0:02	A	Columba aspexit Per cancellos fenestrae Ubi ante faciem eius Sudando sudavit balsamum De lucido Maximino.	The dove entered Through the lattices of the window, Where, before its face, Balm emanated From incandescent Maximinus.
0:28	A′	Calor solis exarsit Et in tenebras resplenduit; Unde gemma surrexit In edificatione templi Purissimi cordis benevoli.	The heat of the sun burned And dazzled into the gloom, Whence a jewel sprang forth In the building of the temple Of the most pure loving heart.
0:56	B	Iste turis . . .	He is the high tower of Lebanon . . .
1:29	B′	Ipse velox . . .	The swift hart sped to the fountain . . .
2:03	C	O pigmentarii . . .	O you makers of incense . . .
3:15	D	O Maximine . . .	O Maximinus . . .
			(two more stanzas)

2 Music at Court

Over the long span of the Middle Ages, kings and barons gained political power at the expense of the church. They also gradually assumed leadership in artistic matters. In the later Middle Ages, the princely courts joined the monasteries and cathedrals as major supporters of music.

Troubadour and Trouvère Songs

Large groups of court songs have been preserved from the twelfth and thirteenth centuries, the Age of Chivalry. The noble poet-composers of these songs—who, we are told, also performed the songs themselves—were called **troubadours** in the south of France, **trouvères** in the north, and **Minnesingers** in Germany (*Minne* means ideal or chivalric love). Among them were knights and princes, even kings—such as the most famous of all chivalric heroes, Richard I of England, "the Lion-Hearted." Troubadour society (but not trouvère society) also allowed for women troubadours, such as Countess Beatriz of Dia, Maria di Ventadorn, and others.

My love and I keep state
In bower,
In flower,
Till the watchman on the
tower
Cry:
"Up! Thou rascal, Rise,
I see the white
Light
And the night
Flies."
—Troubadour alba

Perhaps some of these noble songwriters penned the words only, leaving the music to be composed by *jongleurs,* the popular musicians of the time. The music is relatively simple—just a tune, in most cases, with no indication of any accompaniment. We hear of jongleurs playing instruments while the trouvères sang; perhaps they improvised some kind of accompaniment, or played a drone, such as we heard in Hildegard's "Columba aspexit."

There are some very beautiful troubadour poems—crusaders' songs, laments for dead princes, and especially songs in praise of the poets' ladies, or complaints of their ladies' coldness. One interesting poetic type was the *alba,* the "dawn song" of a knight's loyal companion who has kept watch all night and now warns him to leave his lady's bed before the castle awakes. Another was the *pastourelle,* a (typically unsuccessful) seduction dialogue between a knight on horseback and a country maid.

Left: More than a hundred German Minnesingers, from around 1200, are pictured in a later manuscript. The jongleurs directed by Heinrich Frauenlob (Henry Praiselady) play medieval equivalents of a drum, flute, oboe, viola, violin, harp, and bagpipe (left to right). The illustration on the right shows the Countess of Dia, one of a small number of women troubadours.

How Did Early Music Sound?

There is a special problem about old music, a problem that is less troublesome with music of more recent times: Although we have the scores of Early Music, often we do not have a clear idea of how it actually sounded.

One reason for this is that musical instruments have changed greatly over the centuries. Obsolete instruments have survived in an imperfect condition, and we can try to reconstruct them; but figuring out how they were actually played is much more speculative. As for singing, who can guess what a cathedral choir sounded like in the late Middle Ages, to take just one example? Since then, language itself has changed so much that it is hard enough to read a fourteenth-century poet such as Geoffrey Chaucer, let alone imagine how the words that he wrote were pronounced—or sung.

Composers of Early Music never indicated the tempo and rarely specified the instrumental or vocal forces that they anticipated for their music. With vocal pieces, they did not say whether a single singer or a whole choir was to sing. It has taken generations of patient research and experiment to "reconstruct," as it were, the probable sounds of Early Music.

The earliest music taken up in this book, Gregorian chant, is usually sung today in a performance style that was thought to be "historical" in the nineteenth century—this was the first of all Early-Music "reconstructions," in fact. Our recording of the antiphon "In paradisum" (page 60) adopts this familiar style.

In recent years, however, scholar-musicians have taken another look at history and proposed a different style—austere, less refined, and closer to other traditions of religious chanting that go back as far as Gregorian chant, such as the Qur'anic chanting discussed on pages 70–71. We hear this new "reconstruction" in the Preface "Vere dignum" (page 59).

BERNART DE VENTADORN (c. 1135–1194)
Troubadour song, "La dousa votz"

Bernart was one of the finest troubadour poets and probably the most important musically; other troubadour and trouvère songs were derived from some of his pieces. Originally of humble background, he came to serve the powerful Queen Eleanor of Aquitaine, wife of Henry II of England.

Like hymns and folk songs, troubadour songs set all their stanzas to the same melody, resulting in what is called *strophic* form (**A A A . . .**); often each stanza is in **a a′ b** form. "La dousa votz" is in the G (Mixolydian) mode:

The performance on the recording stresses "secular" aspects of Bernart's song, including an imaginative reconstruction of a possible instrumental accompaniment to it. It sounds far removed indeed from the spiritual atmosphere of Hildegard of Bingen.

The language the troubadours spoke and wrote was Provençal, now almost extinct. It combines elements from Old French and Old Spanish.

LISTEN **Bernart de Ventadorn, "La dousa votz"**

4

4 0:07	*St. 1:* La dousa votz ai auzida Del rosinholet sauvatge Et es m'insel cor salhida Si que tot lo cosirer E'ls mals traihz qu'amors me dona, M'adousa e m'asazona. Et auria'm be mester L'autrui joi al meu damnatge.	I have heard the sweet voice Of the woodland nightingale And my heart springs up So that all the cares And the grievous betrayals love has given me Are softened and sweetened; And I would thus be rewarded, In my ordeal, by the joys of others.
0:48	*St. 2:* Ben es totz om d'avol vida C'ab joi non a son estatge . . .	In truth, every man leads a base life Who does not dwell in the land of joy . . .
1:28	*St. 3:* Una fausa deschauzida Trairitz de mal linhage M'a trait, et es traida . . .	One who is false, deceitful, Of low breeding, a traitress Has betrayed me, and betrayed herself . . .

The Estampie

There also survive a few—a very few—dances from the same court circles that produced the chivalric trouvère repertory. Called **estampies,** they are unassuming one-line pieces in which the same or similar musical phrases are repeated many times in varied forms. (This suggests that these estampies may have been written-down jongleur improvisations.) Estampies are marked by lively and insistent rhythms in triple meter. Modern performers often add a touch of spice with the help of percussion instruments.

This is a modest beginning to the long and important history of European dance music. We shall pick it up again in the next chapter.

3 The Evolution of Polyphony

Polyphony—the simultaneous combination of two or more melodies—must have arisen in early Europe because people took pleasure in the sensuous quality of music, in the rich sounds of intertwining melodic lines with their resulting harmony. Many cultures all over the world have developed some kind of improvised polyphony, polyphony that is made up on the spot without the aid of written scores. (If you and someone you know can "sing in thirds" together, that is improvised polyphony.) Some other cultures, also, have traditions of complex, preplanned polyphony involving little or no improvisation.

We know about early European polyphony only from its uses within the church (for, once again, all we know about very early music comes from the writing of monks and other clerics). And within the church, the sensuous aspect of polyphony had to be rationalized away. Polyphony was seen as a way of embellishing Gregorian chants—that is, as yet another way of enhancing the all-important services.

More scenes of medieval music making. These and other miniatures in this chapter are from *Songs of the Virgin Mary,* written (or perhaps compiled) by King Alphonso X of Spain, "The Wise" (1252–1284), renowned for his support of learning and the arts.

Organum

The earliest type of polyphony is called **organum** (plural *organa*). First described theoretically in treatises around 900 C.E., actual organum has survived in musical notation from around 1000. Organum consists of a traditional plainchant melody to which a composer/singer/improviser has added another melody in counterpoint, sung simultaneously to the same words.

The history of organum between about 1000 and 1200 C.E. provides a fascinating record of growing artistic ambition and technical invention. We can trace a number of steps:

- Originally, each note of the chant was accompanied by another single note in the added melody (referred to as "the counterpoint"); the two melodies moved along with the same distance, or interval, between them. The rhythm of this early, so-called "parallel" organum was the free rhythm of Gregorian chant.

- Soon the counterpoint was treated more independently—it would sometimes go up when the chant went down, and vice versa.

- Next, the counterpoint began to include several notes at the same time as each single chant note. The embellishment process was growing richer. As more and more notes were crowded in, making richer and richer added melodies, the single chant notes were slowed down to surprising lengths, sounding finally like long drones.

- The next step was a radical one. Two counterpoints were added to the chant—which required much more skill from the composer, since the second counterpoint had to fit both the chant and also the first counterpoint.

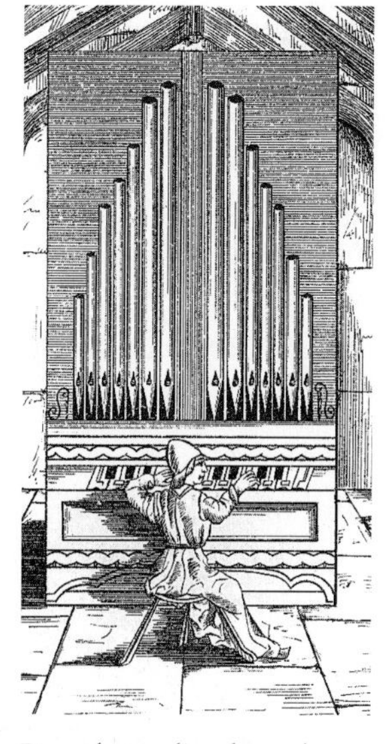

Does the medieval word *organum* imply that early polyphony was accompanied by the organ? We do not know; but churches of the time certainly had organs. The keyboard of this medieval organ seems to have heavy levers rather than keys.

Notre Dame Cathedral in Paris. Flying buttresses—the great medieval engineering feat that made such high buildings possible—support the main structure (the nave). With its lofty front towers and its spire, Notre Dame seems to reach up to heaven itself.

7 Equally radical was the idea of introducing definite rhythms controlled by meter. First the counterpoints and then the chant itself were set in lively rhythms. Fragments of the chant, too, were sometimes isolated and repeated many times, one after another.

Organum of these last, highly developed kinds flourished at the Cathedral of Notre Dame in Paris, which was built slowly over the period 1163–1235. The names of two composers of the so-called Notre Dame school are recorded: Master Léonin and his follower Pérotin (called "the Great"). Pérotin astonished thirteenth-century Paris by creating impressive organa for as many as four simultaneous voices.

PÉROTIN (c. 1200)
Organum, "Alleluia. Diffusa est gratia"

Many organa were composed for services devoted to the Virgin Mary, the patron saint of Notre Dame Cathedral. Our example is added to a chant for the Mass, "Alleluia. Diffusa est gratia." The music was probably written by Pérotin, though we cannot be certain.

At first the chant is sung—in the usual Gregorian way:

The whole chant is much longer, but this opening "Alleluia" section is the most important part—it comes back twice before the chant is over—and the most beautiful. The joyful exclamation "alleluia" is often set to **melismas,** passages of pure vocalism with many notes to a single syllable. The melisma on the syllable *-lu* rouses itself and then springs up still higher; then this melodic climax is balanced by a quiet, sinking "low climax" in phrase 3. After this (relative) excitement, phrase 4 stays within a calm range of four notes. This alleluia is a beautiful example of the characteristics of tunes discussed in Unit I: See page 25.

Then the organum starts. The voices begin with a strange, static harmony—which starts to sway, as it were, when the upper voices intertwine in various (triple-time) rhythms of the kind shown in the right margin of this page. They are singing long melismas on the syllables *Dif- fu- sa,* and so on.

Underneath, the lowest voice is singing the rest of the chant—but no longer in the characteristic free rhythm of Gregorian chanting. Sometimes the chant plods along in a stiff, regular rhythm (as at 1:21). Sometimes it is slowed down enormously (at 0:37, 1:07, and 1:33); at these points the chant is unrecognizable—it has been reduced to a series of lengthy drones. The plainchant has become a sort of musical scaffolding. Singers of organum need not attempt to bring out the chant voice. No longer perceivable as a melody, it is simply a constructive element supporting the ecstatic upper-voice melodies, which are the main focus of interest in this music.

Our recording takes a cut in this lengthy organum (the section indicated by italics below). It ends with a huge melisma on *de-* and a sort of shudder on the final syllable *-us.* Then plain, monophonic chanting is resumed, as the original "Alleluia" music returns with new words, *in aeternum* (with another big melisma on *-um*). The melody is then repeated for the word *Alleluia.*

LISTEN **Pérotin, "Alleluia. Diffusa est gratia"** 1 5

5 0:00	**Chant**	ALLELUIA, ALLELUIA——	Hallelujah.
0:37	**Organum**	Diffusa est gratia in labiis tuis; *propterea benedixit te* deus	Grace has been poured out upon your lips; therefore, God has blessed you
2:36	**Chant**	in aeternum.	eternally.
3:05		ALLELUIA, ALLELUIA——	

4 Later Medieval Polyphony

After 1200 C.E. the most significant development in polyphonic music was its gradual distancing from church services. Music's foundation was still Gregorian chant; to this extent, the church still ruled. But the chant was now handled more abstractly. Composers had already made up new rhythms for the plainchants they were using; they now set only fragments of the chants, and often repeated these fragments.

In another radical development, the upper lines were now given their own words. This sort of polyphony is no longer an organum but a **motet**, from the French word *mot* ("word"). At first, motets were set to sacred poems in Latin, then to sacred poems in French. Later motets began to use love poems or political satires for their texts. It is clear that by now a church genre had been taken over by the courts; some motets even included bits of actual trouvère songs. But almost all motets still used a fragment of Gregorian chant for the notes of their bottom line.

Ars Nova

After 1300 the technical development of polyphony reached new heights of sophistication. Composers and music theorists of the time began to speak of an *ars nova,* a "new art," or "new technique." The organum and motets of the Notre Dame composers were now regarded as "ancient art," *ars antiqua.*

Some historians have compared the fourteenth century with the twentieth, for it was a time of the breakup of traditions—an age of anxiety, corruption, and worse. Bubonic plague, the "Black Death," carried away an estimated 75 million people, at a time when the papacy had been thrown out of Rome and two rival popes claimed the allegiance of European Christendom. The motet grew increasingly secular, intricate, and even convoluted, like the painting, architecture, and poetry of the time.

The new intricacy of the motet was mainly in the area of rhythm. The *ars antiqua* composers had introduced fixed rhythms and meter into organum and the motet, as we have seen; the composers of the *ars nova* carried their innovations much further. Rhythm seems to have obsessed them. They superimposed complex rhythmic patterns in the various voices so as to produce extraordinary combinations. Rhythms of such complexity are standard in much African music, but in Europe we have to go all the way up to 1950 to find anything like the dizzy rhythms of the advanced "new music" of 1400.

The leading composers, Philippe de Vitry (1291–1361) and Guillaume de Machaut (c. 1300–1377), were both churchmen—Vitry ended his life as a bishop—but they were political churchmen serving the courts of France and Luxembourg. Machaut was also the greatest French poet of his time, admired (and imitated) by his younger English contemporary, Geoffrey Chaucer.

Of instruments of strings in accord
Heard I so play a ravishing sweetnéss
That God, that Maker is of all, and Lord,
Ne heard never better, as I guess.
—Geoffrey Chaucer, 1375

GUILLAUME DE MACHAUT (c. 1300–1377)
Motet, "Quant en moi"

Following tradition, Machaut based this motet on a repeated fragment of plainchant, taken from the Eastertide services. On the recording, it is played on a viol, an early bowed stringed instrument.

Above this, he wrote two faster counterpoints set to love poetry (very artificial and elegant poetry, in both form and content: see opposite page). To the medieval mind, there was nothing sacrilegious about combining these sacred and secular elements. Notice the exceedingly complicated rhythm of these upper voices, the nervous, hyperelegant way in which they utter the words, and the spiky harmonies they produce in combination:

As the voices stop abruptly, rest, and start up again, they create an intriguing texture—perforated, sparkling, asymmetrical. To make things even more intricate, the two singers actually sing two different poems simultaneously.

Each of these poems contains several stanzas with the same syllable counts and rhyme schemes, but Machaut (unlike a troubadour composer such as Bernart) does not repeat the same melodies for each stanza. A more esoteric system of repetition is at work. Successive stanzas are set to entirely different melodies in each voice—but these melodies have basically *the same overall rhythms,* complex patterns of over eighty notes in the soprano, forty notes in the tenor.

This technique of writing successive lengthy passages in identical rhythms but with distinct melodies is called **isorhythm.** Isorhythm represents the height of late medieval ingenuity and artifice, and it is hard to know whether anyone was ever expected to hear such purely rhythmic repetitions.

There are fast echoes between the soprano's two words in line 7 of her poem and the tenor's two words in line 2 of his, thus: "doubter—espoir—celer—d'avoir." This amusing device is called **hocket** (compare our word *hiccup*). Isorhythmic repetitions of rhythmic patterns are easiest to hear at hocket points.

Hocket is a cut-up song, composed for two or more voices. This kind of song is pleasing to the hot-tempered and to young men on account of its fluidity and speed.

From a fourteenth-century treatise on music

LISTEN Guillaume de Machaut, "Quant en moi"

6

(The soprano's poem and the tenor's poem start together, and are sung simultaneously, stanza by stanza.)

6

0:00	STANZA 1: SOPRANO	
	Quant en moi vint premierement	When I was first visited by
	Amours, si tres doucettement	Love, he so very sweetly
	Me vost mon cuer enamourer	Enamored my heart;
	Que d'un regart me fist present,	A glance is what he gave me as a gift,
	Et tres amoureus sentiment	And along with amorous sentiments
	Me donna avuec doulz penser,	He presented me with this delightful idea:
0:19	Espoir d'avoir	To hope to have
	Merci sans refuser.	Grace, and no rejections.
	Mais onques en tout mon vivant	But never in my whole life
	Hardement ne me vost donner.	Was boldness a gift he meant for me.
	TENOR	
	Amour et biauté parfaite	*Thanks to love and consummate beauty,*
	Doubter, celer	*Fearing, feigning*
	Me font parfaitement.	*Are what consume me entirely.*
0:33	STANZA 2: SOPRANO	
	E si me fait en desirant	And if, in my passion,
	Penser si amoureusement	He makes me think so amorously
	Que, par force de desirer,	That, thanks to desire
	Ma joie convient en tourment	My joy turns into torment—
	Muer, se je n'ay hardement.	Must turn, since I am not bold.
	Las! et je n'en puis recouvrer,	Alas! I cannot save myself—
0:51	Qu'amours secours	For Love no help
	Ne me vuet nul prester,	Will lend me—
	Qui en ses las si durement	Love, who holds me so tightly
	Me tient que n'en puis eschaper.	In his grasp that I cannot escape.
	TENOR	
	Et vrais desirs, qui m'a fait	*And true desire, that has made me*
	De vous, cuer doulz	*Love you, dear heart,*
	Amer sans finement,	*For ever and ever,*
1:05	STANZA 3: SOPRANO	
	Ne je me weil, qu'en attendant	Nor do I wish to escape, but awaiting
	Sa grace se weil humblement	Your mercy, I humbly
	Toutes ces dolours endurer.	Endure all these sorrows.
	Je says de vrai . . .	I know, in truth . . .
	TENOR	
	Et quant j'aime si finement,	*And since I love you so perfectly,*
	Merci vous pris . . .	*For mercy I pray you . . .*
1:38	STANZA 4: SOPRANO	
	Mais elle attend . . .	
	TENOR	
	Sans votre honeur . . .	

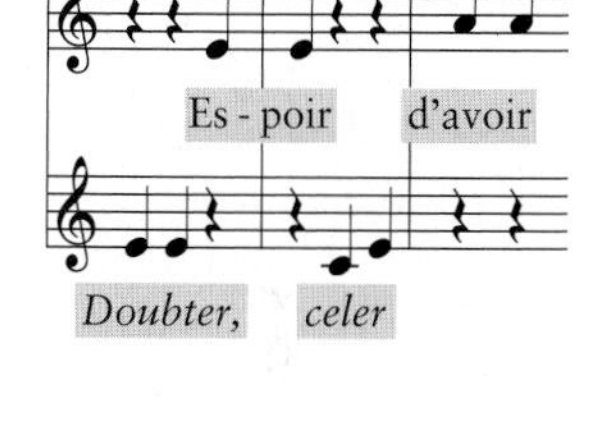

Web: *Research and test your understanding of music in the Middle Ages at* **<bedfordstmartins.com/listen>.**

GLOBAL PERSPECTIVES 1

Sacred Chant

28, 29

40

The vast number of cultures that exist or that have existed in this world all generated their own music—or, as we say, their own different "musics." Often they are very different indeed; the first time South African Zulus heard Christian hymn-singing they were amazed, just as much as the missionaries were when they first heard Zulu music. Yet for all their diversity, the musics of the world do show some parallels, as we are going to see in the Global Perspectives sections of this book. There are parallels of musical function in society, there are parallels of musical technique, and sometimes there are parallels of both together.

Often these parallels come about as the result of influences of one culture on another—but influences are never accepted without modification and the blending of a foreign music with music that is indigenous. At other times parallels appear in musics that have nothing whatsoever to do with one another. Considering all these parallels, we have to believe that certain basic functions for music and certain basic technical principles are virtually universal in humankind.

One of these near-universal features—and one of the most fundamental—is the role of music in the service of religion. Singing serves across the world as an essential means of marking off the rituals of worship, signaling their special status and their difference from other, secular, pursuits. The repertory of Gregorian chant developed in the Christian Church of the Middle Ages (see pages 56–62) is only one of many traditions of monophonic religious chant, albeit one of the more elaborate.

A muezzin high in a minaret calls the faithful to prayer in Cairo, Egypt.

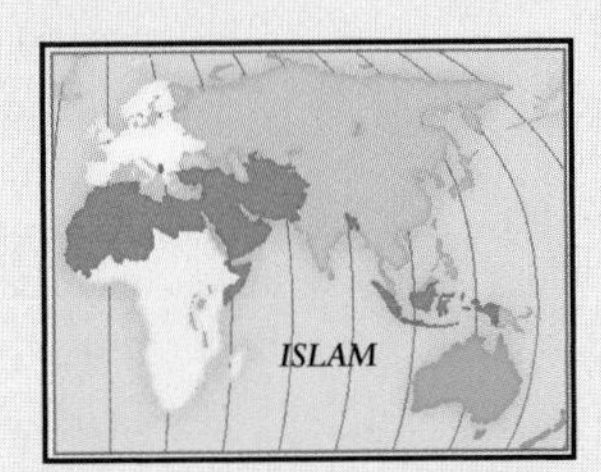

Islam: Reciting the Qur'an

Another highly elaborate tradition of chant is found in Islam, practiced today by about a fifth of the world's population, and the dominant religion in some fifty nations. Across all of Islam, the revelations of the prophet Muhammad gathered in the Qur'an (or Koran) are chanted or sung in Arabic. Muhammad himself is said to have enjoyed this melodic recitation.

Usually **Qur'anic recitation** is rigorously distinguished from all types of secular music making. It is thought of as "reading" the sacred text aloud, not "singing" it; it is not even considered to be the same sort of activity as secular singing or playing instruments. These nonreligious activities might be referred to as "music" (*musiqi*), but reading the Qur'an is not.

Given these distinctions, it is not surprising that Qur'anic recitation, like Gregorian chant, is monophonic, nonmetric, and does not involve instruments. It aims, above all else, to convey the Qur'anic text in a clearly comprehensible manner. Unlike plainchant, it has been passed along in oral tradition down to the present day. It has resisted the written notation that came to be a part of the Gregorian tradition already in the Middle Ages. To this day, great Islamic chanters sing the whole 114-chapter Qur'an from memory.

Ya Sin

Our excerpt is the beginning of a long recitation of one of the most highly revered chapters from the Qur'an. It is titled "Ya Sin" and is recited in times of adversity, illness, and death. A skilled reciter, Hafíz Kadir Konya, "reads" the verses in a style midway between heightened speech and rhapsodic melody. His phrases correspond to lines of the sacred text, and he pauses after every one. He begins:

> In the name of Allah, the Beneficent, the Merciful.
> Ya Sin.
> By the wise Qur'an,
> Lo! thou art of those sent
> On a straight path,
> A revelation of the Mighty, the Merciful,
> That thou mayst warn a folk whose fathers were not warned, so they are heedless.
> Already hath the word proved true of most of them, for they believe not.

In his first phrases, Konya begins at a low tonic and gradually expands his range to explore pitches around it. By 0:38, he reaches a pitch central to his melody, a fifth above the tonic. The succeeding phrases circle around this pitch, reciting words on it and decorating it with ornamental melodic formulas of varying intricacy. In this regard, it is a bit like the Gregorian reciting tone we studied before (page 59), only more elaborate in its melodies.

The Azan

Like Gregorian chant, Islamic chanting has developed a wide variety of approaches and styles. The best-known type of Islamic chant employs a style related to recitation, though it does not take its words from the Qur'an: the singing of the *adhan* or **azan.** This is a call to worship issued five times daily by a special singer called *mu'adhdhin* or *muezzin.* That an entire society comes to a stop five times a day for prayer reveals the tremendous force of Islamic religion.

The muezzin traditionally delivers his azan from the minaret, a tower attached to the mosque, and later inside the mosque to begin the prayers. In Islamic cities today, the azan is often broadcast over loudspeakers to enable it to sound over modern urban noises.

Hawai'ian Chant

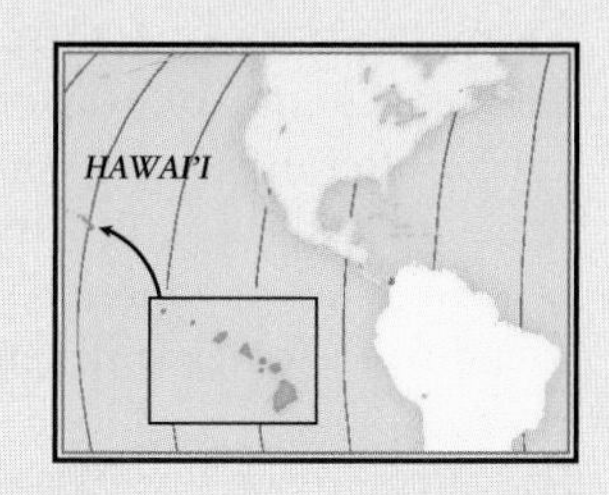

We should not be too surprised to find certain broad similarities between Qur'anic and Gregorian chant. Both Islam and Christianity emerged from the same region, the Middle East, and Muhammad drew on elements of Christian doctrine in forming his new religion. He counted Jesus Christ as one of the Islamic prophets.

It is more surprising to find some of the same features in religious chant from halfway around the globe, in Polynesia—in Hawai'ian prayer songs, or **mele pule** (mél-eh póol-eh). By reciting these prayers, Hawai'ians intended to bring to life images of their gods fashioned of wood, stone, or feathers, animating them with divine powers.

Our brief example shows a style similar in some general ways to our Gregorian Preface and Qur'anic recitation. It is monophonic, like all traditional Hawai'ian song. It is also almost monotonal, with only one prominent pitch other than the central reciting tone. In this it contrasts with more active melodic styles used in

Three Hawai'ian singers. They strike large, resonant gourds on the ground to accompany their song.

other Hawai'ian genres of song—especially love songs and *mele hula,* or hula-dance songs.

The mele pule takes its rhythms from the words and shows little trace of meter. Though nearly monotonal, it is ornamented subtly with various shifts of vocal delivery and divergences from its reciting tone. The most prominent of these is a clear, pulsating, almost sobbing *vibrato,* or wavering pitch, that the singer, Kau'i Zuttermeister, introduces on long syllables. This technique, called *i'i,* is a stylistic feature much prized in many types of traditional Hawai'ian song. It is felt to endow melodies with special, deep emotion.

A Navajo Song

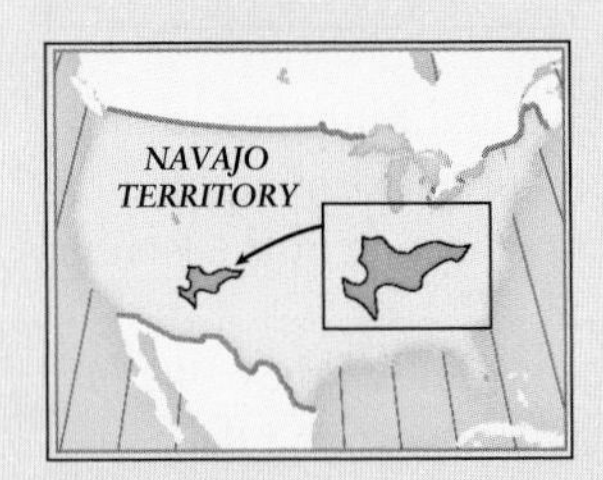

One more example of chant comes to us from Native American traditions. In these, too, singing is closely allied with the sacred. It plays a role in healing, hunting, social rituals, and—embracing all these activities—in human relations with gods, spirits, and ancestors. Most Native North American song is monophonic, like the Hawai'ian, Arabic, and Western chants we have heard. Unlike them, it is usually accompanied by drums or rattles of one sort or another.

Our example comes from the Navajo nation of the Four Corners area of the American Southwest. It is called "K'adnikini'ya'," which means "I'm leaving," and it dates from the late nineteenth century.

Just as individual Gregorian chants have their assigned places in Catholic services, so this chant has its own special role. It is sung near the end of the Enemy Way ceremony, a central event of Navajo spiritual life. In this solemn ceremony, warriors who have come in contact with the ghosts of their enemies are purified and fortified. Such purification is still performed today, sometimes for the benefit of U.S. veterans of Vietnam or other wars.

"K'adnikini'ya'" falls into a group of Navajo sacred songs known as *ho'zho'ni* songs, and you will hear the related word *ho'zhon'go* ("beautiful," "holy") sung alongside *"k'adnikini'ya'"* to end each of the seven central phrases of the song. Every phrase of the song begins with the syllables "hé-yuh-eh, yáng-a-ang-a." These are *vocables,* syllables having no precise meaning. Vocables are sometimes called "nonsense syllables" and likened to the "tra-la-las" and "hey-diddle-diddles" of European nursery rhymes. But they are hardly nonsensical. Instead, as scholars have gradually realized, they can carry secret, venerable, and even mystical significance.

At a powwow in British Columbia

The melody of "K'adnikini'ya'," like the other chants we have examined, is organized around a prominent reciting tone (the pitch of "he-yuh-eh"); each phrase turns upward at its end (on "k'adnikini'ya'"). The song's meter, given the regular drumstrokes, is more pronounced than in any of our earlier examples. The formal plan consists of a refrain at the beginning and end, with a group of parallel phrases in between.

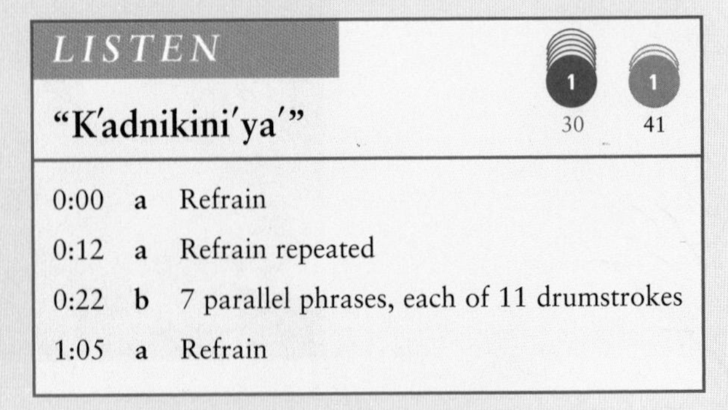

LISTEN

"K'adnikini'ya'" 1 30 1 41

0:00	a	Refrain
0:12	a	Refrain repeated
0:22	b	7 parallel phrases, each of 11 drumstrokes
1:05	a	Refrain

CHAPTER 6

The Renaissance

Renaissance ("rebirth") is the name given to a complex current of thought that worked deep changes in Europe from the fourteenth to the sixteenth century. It began in Italy. By rediscovering and imitating their ancient Greco-Roman civilization, Italians hoped they could bring about the rebirth of their glorious past. It was a somewhat confused dream, which came to nothing in political terms. Instead of becoming a new Roman empire, Italy at the end of the Renaissance consisted of the same pack of warring city-states that had been at each other's throats all through the Middle Ages.

However, the revival of Greek and Roman culture provided a powerful model for new values, both in Italy and in the rest of Europe. In the words of a famous nineteenth-century historian, the Renaissance involved "the discovery of the world and of man." This was the age of Columbus and Magellan, Leonardo da Vinci, Copernicus, and Shakespeare. Medieval society was stable, conservative, authoritarian, and oriented toward God. The Renaissance laid the groundwork for the dynamic world we know today, a world in which human beings and nature, rather than God, have become the measure in philosophy, science, art, and sometimes even religion.

Accordingly, Renaissance artists strove to make their work more relevant to people's needs and desires. They began to reinterpret the world around them—the architect's world of space and stone, the painter's world of images, the musician's world of sound—in new ways to meet these ambitions.

The church singers in these famous panels by Florentine sculptor Luca della Robbia (1400–1482) are handsome boys who seem to be taking the same sensuous pleasure in their singing as Luca did in sculpting them.

1 New Attitudes

A good indication of the Renaissance mindset, in the early fifteenth century, was a new way of treating plainchant in polyphonic compositions. Medieval composers writing organum or isorhythmic motets seem to have felt that so long as they used a traditional plainchant, there was nothing wrong with distorting it. They lengthened its notes enormously underneath the added counterpoints. They recast the meterless chant into fixed, arbitrary rhythms.

Music is a thing which delighteth all ages and beseemeth all states; a thing as seasonable in grief as in joy. The reason hereof is an admirable facility which music hath to express and represent the very standing, rising, and falling, the very steps and inflections every way, the turns and varieties of all passions.

Anglican bishop and theologian Richard Hooker, 1593

Renaissance composers no longer felt obliged always to use plainchants; but when they did they tended to treat them as melodies to listen to, not as rock-solid foundations for polyphonic structures. They embellished chants with extra notes, set them in graceful rhythms, and smoothed out passages that struck them as awkward or antiquated. This procedure is known as **paraphrase.** A fifteenth-century plainchant paraphrase is shown below; dashed lines mark the notes taken directly from the chant (shown above the paraphrase):

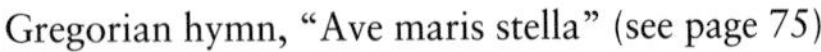

The emphasis was on the sonorous, sensuous aspect of the chant rather than on its function as structure and control—its authoritarian function, one might say. (Sonority means either tone color or, more loosely, rich tone color.) A new sensitivity to sonority and melody was perhaps the first sign of Renaissance attitudes toward music.

Having transformed plainchants into "modern" melodies with a more attractive profile, composers put them not at the bottom of the polyphony but on top, in the soprano, where they could be heard most clearly. And the soprano voice was probably already considered the most beautiful.

Early Homophony

The fifteenth century also saw the beginning of composed *homophony*—that is, music in a harmonic texture (see page 28). In the simpler plainchant paraphrases of the time, the melody is often highlighted by an accompaniment that does not really sound polyphonic. Though there are still several polyphonic voices, most of the time their independence vanishes because they move along together and form simple chords.

The result is a plainchant harmonization. Once again the emphasis is on sensuous effect, that of homophony, rather than on the more intellectual process of polyphony.

Guillaume Dufay (c. 1400–1474)

Guillaume Dufay (or Du Fay) was born and bred in the north of France near modern Belgium, a region that supplied the whole of Europe with musicians for many generations. For over twenty-five years he worked in Italy, where he

"Ave maris stella": The Virgin Mary was the subject of special veneration in the late Middle Ages and the early Renaissance. Countless plainchants, motets, paintings, and sculptures were created to honor her. Lost in her own thoughts, this serene, childlike Virgin by the German artist Stefan Lochner (1400–1451) seems oblivious to Jesus, even to God—and no doubt to the music played for her by the baby angels.

came to know artists and thinkers of the Renaissance and (equally important!) the princely patrons who supported them. His later years were spent in a glow of celebrity at the important French cathedral of Cambrai.

GUILLAUME DUFAY
Harmonized hymn, "Ave maris stella"

This is a homophonic setting of a Gregorian **hymn**, one of the most tuneful of plainchant genres. A Gregorian hymn consists of a short tune sung through many stanzas, followed by an Amen—much like a modern hymn, in fact. One of the loveliest of these hymns, "Ave maris stella," was also one of the best known, because it was addressed to the Virgin Mary and sung on all of the many special feasts in her honor, and on most Saturdays, too. Note how line 1 contains the words AVE MARI(*s stell*)A.

"Ave maris stella" is in the D (Dorian) mode. You may be able to hear at once that the third note in the tune (the sixth note of the scale) is higher than would be normal in the minor mode. The hymn itself has six or seven stanzas, but Dufay set only the even-numbered ones to his own music, leaving the others

to be sung Gregorian-style in alternation. This makes it fairly easy to hear how he embellished the plainchant.

His music for stanzas 2, 4, and 6 is the same each time—almost entirely homophonic and quite suave. The top voice sings a paraphrased, somewhat longer version of the hymn tune, as shown on page 75. The embellishment consists of a few extra notes and extensions, with the free rhythm of Gregorian chant channeled into a graceful triple meter.

LISTEN Dufay, "Ave maris stella"

7

0:00	STANZA 1: Plainchant	
	Ave maris stella, Dei Mater alma, Atque semper Virgo, Felix coeli porta.	Hail, star of the ocean, Kind Mother of God, And also still a virgin, Our blessed port to heaven.
	STANZA 2: Dufay's paraphrase	
0:22	Sumens illud Ave Gabrielis ore, Funda nos in pace, Mutans Hevae nomen.	May that blessed "Ave" From Angel Gabriel's mouth Grant us peace, Reversing the name "Eva."
	STANZA 3: Plainchant	
1:12	Solve vincla reis . . .	
	STANZA 4: Paraphrase	
1:34	Monstra te esse matrem . . .	
	STANZA 5: Plainchant	
2:26	Virgo singularis . . .	
	STANZA 6: Paraphrase	
2:48	Sit laus Deo Patri, Summo Christo decus, Spiritui Sancto, Tribus honor unus. Amen.	Praise be to God the Father, To Christ on high, To the Holy Spirit: Three honored as one. Amen.

There does not exist a single piece of music, not composed within the last forty years, that is regarded by the learned as worth hearing. Yet at this present time there flourish countless composers who glory in having studied the divine art under John Dunstable, Gilles Binchois, and Guillaume Dufay, recently deceased.

Composer and music theorist Johannes Tinctoris, 1477

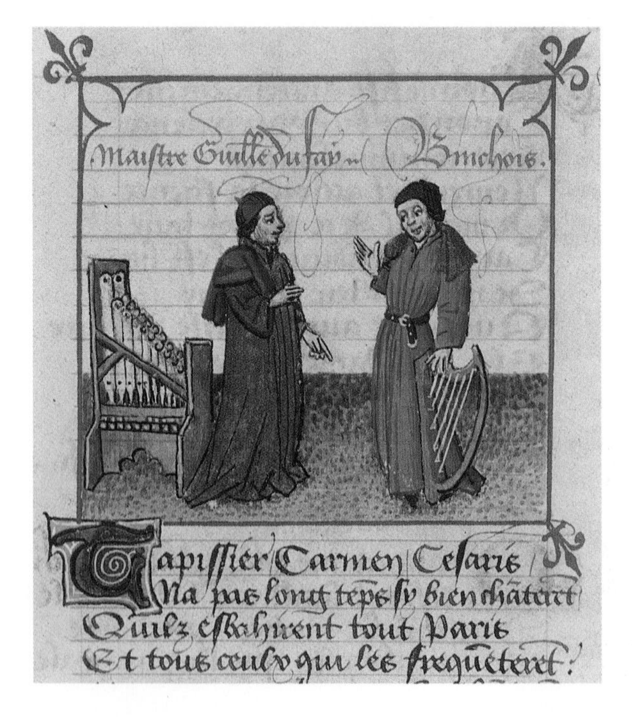

Dufay and another fifteenth-century composer, Gilles Binchois (c. 1400–1460). Portable small organs (called *portatives*) were in use at the time.

This counts as a rather simple composition for Dufay, whose fame was and is based on longer, more elaborate pieces; he wrote some of the first polyphonic Masses, for example. Still, plainsong harmonizations make up an appreciable proportion of his output, and they show the new Renaissance attitudes with particular clarity.

The Mass

The new treatment of traditional plainchant, as in the technique of paraphrase, shows Renaissance composers taking a relaxed attitude toward medieval authority. The same can be said of their reaction to medieval intricacy, as represented by that most intellectual of musical devices, isorhythm. Fourteenth-century composers such as Machaut had used isorhythm even when writing love songs. Composers now cultivated a much simpler style for their polyphonic songs, or **chansons:** simpler, gentler, and more supple. The modest style of these new chansons was sometimes used for sacred texts, including portions of the Mass.

The rejection of isorhythm did not mean, however, that composers abandoned the technical development of their craft, which had taken such impressive strides from the early days of organum. Rather, such efforts were focused on large-scale musical construction. For the first time, compositions were written to last—and to make sense—over twenty or thirty minutes.

The problem of large-scale construction that fascinated fifteenth-century composers was how to write music that would in some sense unify the **Mass.** As the largest and most important of all church services, the Mass included some twenty musical items, originally sung in plainchant. By around 1450, composers settled on these five items for their polyphonic settings:

<table>
<tr><td>Kyrie</td><td>a simple prayer:</td><td>“Lord have mercy, Christ have mercy”</td></tr>
<tr><td>Gloria</td><td>a long hymn, beginning:</td><td>“Glory to God in the highest”</td></tr>
<tr><td>Credo</td><td>a recital of the Christian’s list of beliefs, beginning:</td><td>“I believe in one God, the Father almighty”</td></tr>
<tr><td>Sanctus</td><td>another, shorter hymn:</td><td>“Holy, holy, holy, Lord God of hosts”</td></tr>
<tr><td>Agnus Dei</td><td>another simple prayer:</td><td>“Lamb of God . . . have mercy on us”</td></tr>
</table>

The polyphonic Mass thus was standardized into a five-section form, and the Mass has retained this form down to the present day, in settings by Palestrina, Bach, Mozart, Liszt, Stravinsky, and many others.

The five sections of the Mass are very different in the lengths of their texts, they serve different liturgical functions, and they come at widely separated times in the actual service. Various musical schemes were invented to unify the sections. Similar music could be used to signal the beginning of all five movements, for example. Or all the movements could paraphrase the same Gregorian chant.

So large and complex a structure presented composers with a challenge, and they took this up in a spirit of inventiveness and ambition characteristic of the Renaissance. What the symphony was to nineteenth-century composers and their audiences, the Mass was to their fifteenth-century counterparts: a brilliant, monumental test of artistic prowess.

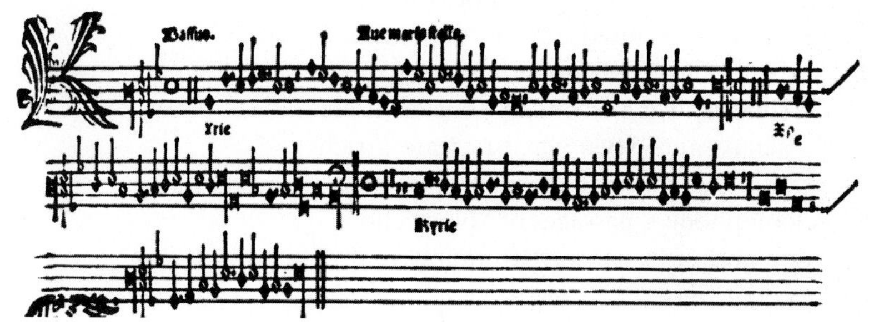

Functional, commercial: Compare this Mass printed around 1500 with the manuscript on page 79. The circulation of music (as of books, maps, images, and data in general) skyrocketed with the great Renaissance invention of the printing press.

2 The "High Renaissance" Style

Around 1500 a new style emerged for Masses, motets, and chansons that would hold sway for much of the sixteenth century. The chief characteristic of this "High Renaissance" musical style was a careful blend of two vocal techniques, *imitative counterpoint* and *homophony* (see pages 28–29).

Imitation

Most polyphony at the beginning of the fifteenth century was non-imitative; most polyphony at the end of the century was imitative. This remarkable change is due partly to the fact that imitative polyphony, or imitation, reflects the ideals of moderation and balance that also characterize the visual arts of the High Renaissance. In the Raphael Madonna on page 47, the calm, dignified repose expressed by the figures and faces is as striking as the beautiful balance among all the pictorial elements.

By its very nature, imitative texture depends on a carefully controlled balance among multiple voice parts. A first voice begins with a motive (see page 26) designed to fit the words being set. Soon other voices enter, one by one, singing the same motive and words, but at different pitch levels; meanwhile the earlier voices continue with new melodies that complement the later voices without swamping them. Each voice has a genuinely melodic quality, and all the melodies are drawn from a single source. None is mere accompaniment or "filler," and none predominates for very long.

We can get an impression of the equilibrium of imitative polyphony from its look on the page, even without reading the music exactly. The following excerpt is from the score of Josquin Desprez's *Pange lingua* Mass:

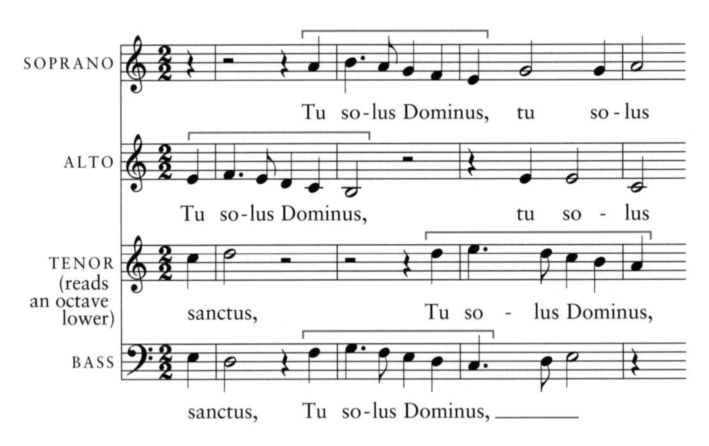

Compare two Madonnas shown in this book: One (page 75) is a late medieval masterpiece from Northern Europe, the other from the new world of Renaissance Italy (page 47; painted only fifty years later). Uncrowned, uncluttered, a mother holds her child, smiles, the children play . . . God and His angels do not encircle this Madonna by Raphael as they do Lochner's.

Homophony

Almost all polyphony involves some chords, as a product of its simultaneously sounding melodies. But in the music of Machaut, for example, the chords are more of a by-product. Late medieval composers concentrated on the "horizontal" aspects of texture at the expense of "vertical" ones, delighting in the separateness of their different voice parts. Chordal sonority was a secondary consideration.

A major achievement of the High Renaissance style was to create a rich chordal quality out of polyphonic lines that still maintain a quiet sense of independence. Composers also used pure homophony—passages of "block chord" writing. They learned to use homophony both as a contrast to imitative texture and as an expressive resource in its own right.

Other Characteristics

The ideal tone color at this time, especially for sacred music, becomes *a cappella* performance—that is, performance by voices alone. Tempo and dynamics change little in the course of a piece. The rhythm is fluid, without any sharp accents, and shifting unobtrusively all the time, so that the meter is often obscured. The melodies never go very high or very low in any one voice; the ups and downs are carefully balanced. This music rarely settles into the easy swing of a dance rhythm or into the clear patterns of an actual tune.

Music in the High Renaissance style can sometimes strike modern listeners as vague, but if we listen more closely—and always listen to the words as well as the music—its flexibility, sensitivity, and rich expressive potential may come clear. Does it remind us of a wonderfully musical and subtle speaking voice? The sixteenth century would have been pleased to think so.

Josquin Desprez (c. 1450–1521)

Josquin Desprez

The first master of the High Renaissance style was Josquin Desprez. Like Dufay, he was born in the north of France, and like Dufay and many other of his countrymen, in early life he traveled to Italy. The list of Josquin's patrons reads like a Renaissance *Who's Who:* Pope Alexander VI, the notorious Sforza family of Milan, the Estes of Ferrara, Louis XII of France.

An amazingly imaginative composer, Josquin brought the fifteenth-century Mass to a brilliant climax and pioneered whole new expressive genres, such as the sixteenth-century chanson and motet. He was famous both for his technical

A Kyrie (one voice part) from a dazzling illuminated manuscript book of Mass music. Did singers actually sing from such precious books? The man who commissioned it is shown here praying with the help of an angel, who also (below) seems to be giving a seal of approval to the family coat of arms.

prowess and for his expressive innovations—for the childlike serenity of his motet "Ave Maria," as well as the grief-stricken accents of "Planxit autem David," a setting of King David's lament for his dead son Absalom.

JOSQUIN DESPREZ
Pange lingua Mass (c. 1510)

Josquin wrote eighteen different settings of the Mass—all large pieces in the standard five-section form. The *Pange lingua* Mass, one of his masterpieces, derives its melodic material largely from a hymn called "Pange lingua." This is a Gregorian hymn of the same kind as "Ave maris stella," which we have heard in Dufay's harmonized setting. "Pange lingua" (and hence Josquin's Mass) is designed for Corpus Christi, a feast celebrating the Holy Eucharist.

This is a four-part Mass (that is, a Mass for a choir with four separate voice parts). In Josquin's day, boys sang the high parts and men the lower ones; Josquin probably started his musical career as a choirboy. Today women usually substitute for boys in music of this period.

We shall examine the first two sections of Josquin's *Pange lingua* Mass.

Kyrie The men in the choir sing line 1 of the hymn "Pange lingua" before the first section of the *Pange lingua* Mass. This first section, the Kyrie, is an elemental prayer consisting of three subsections:

Kyrie I:	Kyrie eleison.	Lord have mercy.
Christe:	Christe eleison.	Christ have mercy.
Kyrie II:	Kyrie eleison.	Lord have mercy.

For Kyrie I, Josquin wrote a **point of imitation**—a brief passage of imitative polyphony covering one short phrase of a composition's verbal text, and using a single musical motive. This motive, which enters many times, is a paraphrase (see page 74) of line 1 of the hymn:

(The order of the voice entries is tenor, bass, *wait,* soprano, alto, *wait,* bass, tenor, soprano.) Josquin did not invent this motive—it was derived from the plainchant hymn, as shown above—but his paraphrase is very beautiful, especially at the end.

The Christe has two points of imitation, also derived from the hymn, for the words *Christe* and *eleison;* the motives of these points are rhythmically similar. Kyrie II has a new point of imitation for the words "Kyrie eleison," followed by free (that is, nonhymn) material—a descending sequence and, prior to the drawn-out final cadence, a powerful oscillating passage.

Plainsong hymn, "Pange lingua"

Pan-ge lin-gua _ glo-ri - o - si

Cor - po-ris mys-te - ri-um, _

San-gui-nis-que pre-ti - o - si,

Quem in mun-di pre-ti - um _

Fruc-tus ven-tris gen-ne-ro-si

Rex ef-fu-dit _ gen - ti-um.

LISTEN Josquin, *Pange lingua* Mass, Kyrie

8	0:08	Kyrie eleison	Lord have mercy.
	0:53	Christe eleison	Christ have mercy.
	2:10	Kyrie eleison	Lord have mercy.

Gloria The four remaining sections of the Mass—the Gloria, Credo, Sanctus, and Agnus Dei—introduce countless new points of imitation, which are interspersed with occasional text phrases set in homophony.

In the second subsection of the Gloria, beginning with the words *Qui tollis,* polyphony and homophony are contrasted in a highly expressive way. At the beginning, we can almost envisage one or two persons timidly invoking Him "who takes away the sins of the world" (polyphony), and then the whole congregation—or, symbolically, the whole of Christendom—urgently responding together with a plea for mercy and relief: "have mercy" (homophony). This music gives a dramatic sense of communal worship.

The "Qui tollis" as a whole includes eight points of imitation and four homophonic or nearly homophonic phrases. (The point for "Tu solus Dominus" is illustrated on page 78.) In the imitative phrases, the vocal lines fit together smoothly into chords, and while the sequence of these chords seems hard to predict, at least for modern ears, it does not seem arbitrary. The remarkable mood of Josquin's music—at once sober, quietly energetic, and reverential—owes much to its Phrygian (E) mode. Like the hymn "Pange lingua," the *Pange lingua* Mass is in this mode.

Throughout the motet ["Planxit autem David," by Josquin] there is preserved what befits the mourner, who at first is inclined to cry out constantly, then murmur to himself, then quiet down or—as passion breaks out anew—raise his voice again in a loud cry. All these things we see most beautifully observed in this composition.

An admirer of Josquin, writing a quarter century after his death

LISTEN **Josquin, *Pange lingua* Mass, from the Gloria**

1 9

(Capital letters indicate phrases sung in homophony.)

9 0:00	Qui tollis peccata mundi,	You who take away the sins of the world,
	MISERERE NOBIS.	have mercy upon us.
0:34	Qui tollis peccata mundi,	You who take away the sins of the world,
	SUSCIPE DEPRECATIONEM NOSTRAM.	hear our prayer.
	Qui sedes ad dexteram Patris,	You who sit at the right hand of the Father,
	miserere nobis.	have mercy upon us.
1:18	Quoniam tu solus sanctus,	For you alone are holy,
	tu solus Dominus,	you alone are the Lord,
	tu solus altissimus,	you alone are the most high,
	Jesu Christe,	Jesus Christ,
	cum sancto spiritu,	With the Holy Spirit,
	in gloria Dei Patris.	in the glory of God the Father.
	AMEN.	Amen.

3 Music as Expression

In parts of Josquin's *Pange lingua* Mass, as we have just seen, the music does not merely enhance the service in a general way, but seems to address specific phrases of the Mass text and the sentiments behind them. Music can be said to "illustrate" certain words and to "express" certain feelings. The exploration of music's power to express human feelings was a precious contribution by musicians to the Renaissance "discovery of the world and of man."

Renaissance composers derived inspiration for this exploration from reports of the music of ancient Greece, just as artists, architects, and writers of the time were also looking to ancient Greece and Rome for inspiration. Philosophers such as Plato had testified that music was capable of arousing emotions in a very powerful way. In the Bible, David cures Saul when he is troubled by an "evil spirit" by playing on his harp; there are similar stories in Greek myth and Greek history. How modern music could recapture its ancient powers was much discussed by music theorists after the time of Josquin.

They reasoned somewhat as follows. If poets wish to arouse feelings, they do so by writing about them—by describing, depicting, expressing feelings in words. By doing this poets can arouse similar feelings in their readers. What is the analogy in music? How is it possible for composers to arouse feelings in their listeners?

The Renaissance answer was that this could be done indirectly, by illustrating or otherwise enhancing words. If words can express feelings and music can illustrate words, then music can express feelings and also arouse them, in conjunction with a text. Through this new link to the world of human emotions, Renaissance music sought to gain new relevance to humanity.

Devotion to the ideal of musical expression, by way of a text, was one of the main guiding ideas for composers of the later Renaissance. This led them to a new sensitivity to the words they were setting, which manifested itself in two important developments.

- First, composers wanted the words of their compositions to be clearly heard. They strove for accurate **declamation**—that is, they made sure that words were sung to rhythms and melodies that approximated normal speech.

This may seem elementary and obvious, but it is simply not true of most medieval organum and motets (or of many plainchants). The pronunciation of words set to music mattered less than the structure of the music. The Renaissance was the first era when words were set to music naturally, clearly, and vividly. The little example below shows this (try singing it).

- Second, composers began matching their music to the *meaning* of the words that were being set. The term **word painting** is used for this musical illustration of the text. Words such as "fly" and "glitter" were set to rapid notes, "up" and "heaven" to high ones, and so on:

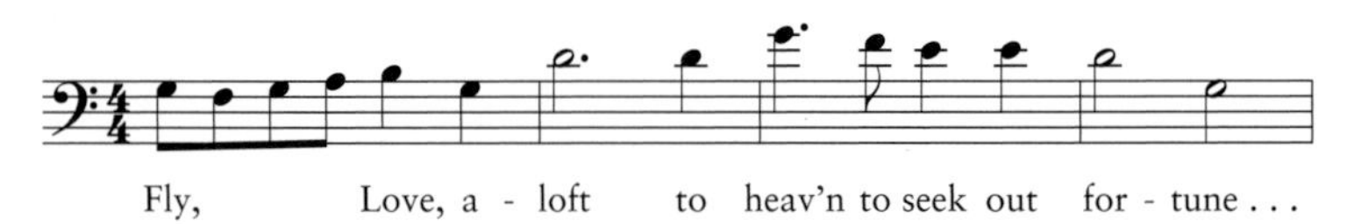

Sigh was typically set by a motive including a rest, as though the singers have been interrupted by sighing. *Grief, cruel, torment, harsh,* and exclamations such as *alas*—words found all the time in the language of Renaissance love poetry—prompted composers to write dissonant or chromatic harmony.

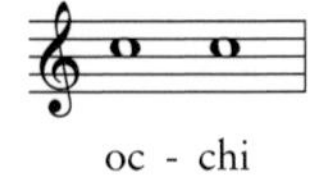

Word painting could become mechanical and silly—as for example, when the Italian word for "eyes," *occhi,* was set to two whole notes. But when used sensitively, it could intensify the emotion inherent in words and phrases in a striking way, as Renaissance doctrine demanded. First developed seriously in the sixteenth century, word painting has remained an important expressive resource of all later vocal music. For examples from the Baroque period, when it was especially important, see pages 101, 104, 157, and 161.

4 Late Renaissance Music

As we noted above, the High Renaissance style established by the generation of Josquin Desprez proved remarkably stable. Yet it was also flexible enough so that composers were able to do new things with it all the way up to the end of the sixteenth century. While its use was clearest in the church music of the time, important new secular genres also made use of this style, in a modified form.

My Lord, if in our century there is any more excellent music than that of Orlande Lassus, I leave that judgment to masters of that art. I will say only this: that Plato, who liked so much to teach political harmony through musical proportions, would have taken his examples from Orlande had they lived at the same time.

Publisher's dedication (like a jacket blurb) in a Lassus edition, 1575

Music at court: singers of the Bavarian Court Chapel in 1565, under Roland de Lassus. Each man and boy is carefully and solemnly depicted. With this imposing picture (and another, of an equally large group of court instrumentalists), the Duke showed off the size and distinction of his retinue—a reflection, of course, of his own glory.

The universality of the style is symbolized by the geographical spread of its four most famous masters, Palestrina, Lassus, Victoria, and Byrd. ***Giovanni Pierluigi da Palestrina*** (c. 1525–1594) was born just outside Rome and worked in the Holy City all his life. ***Roland de Lassus*** (c. 1532–1594), also known as Orlando di Lasso, was a worldly and much-traveled Netherlander who settled at the court of Munich. His output was enormous. ***Tomás Luis de Victoria*** (c. 1548–1611), a Spanish priest, spent many years in Rome working for the Jesuits but ended up in Madrid. ***William Byrd*** (1543–1623) was organist of England's Chapel Royal under Queen Elizabeth I but also a member of the English dissident Catholic minority, who wrote Masses for illegal and highly dangerous services held in secret in barns and attics.

GIOVANNI PIERLUIGI DA PALESTRINA (c. 1525–1594)
Pope Marcellus Mass (1557)

Palestrina was a singer in, or choirmaster of, many of Rome's most famous churches and chapels, including the Sistine (Papal) Chapel. He lived in the repressive atmosphere of the Counter-Reformation movement, which was launched by the papacy in 1545 to combat the threat of the Reformation. Palestrina wrote secular compositions in his youth, some of which were widely popular, but later he recanted and apologized for them. He wrote over a hundred Masses and published his first examples with a highly symbolic frontispiece, which shows the kneeling composer presenting the pope with a special papal Mass.

Because singing is so powerful a force in religion, as we noted on page 56, societies have felt a need to control it carefully. Christianity has witnessed periodic reforms to prune church services of musical features that were seen as abuses. The Counter-Reformation staged just such a reform. Palestrina's most famous composition, the *Pope Marcellus* Mass, was supposed to have convinced the pope and his council that composers of complicated polyphonic church music could still set the sacred words clearly, with clear enough declamation so that the congregation could hear them. Partly because of this legend, and partly because of the particular calmness and purity of his musical style, Palestrina became the most revered Renaissance composer for later centuries. His works are still treasured by Catholic choir directors today.

The frontispiece of Palestrina's *First Book of Masses*, 1554, announces to all the world that this music has the Pope's blessing. The page is open to the papal Mass *Ecce Sacerdos magnus* ("Behold the great priest").

Gloria A part of the Gloria of the *Pope Marcellus* Mass, the "Qui tollis," shows how the High Renaissance *a cappella* style changed after the time of Josquin. Compared with Josquin's setting of these same words in his *Pange lingua* Mass (see page 81), Palestrina's setting employs much more homophony. Apart from some fuzziness on a few individual words, only the last, climactic line of Palestrina's composition uses polyphony.

Beyond this, we will notice at once that vocal sonority is of major importance in Palestrina's setting. He uses a larger and richer choir than Josquin—six vocal parts, rather than four—and keeps alternating between one choral group, or semichoir, drawn from the total choir, to another. Thus the first phrase, in high voices, is answered by the second, in low voices, and so on. The total choir does not sing all together until the word *suscipe.*

What matters most to Palestrina are the rich, shifting tone colors and harmonies, which he uses to produce a generalized spiritual aura, sometimes ethereal, sometimes ecstatic. And with the dictates of the Counter-Reformation in mind, he is certainly careful to declaim the words very clearly.

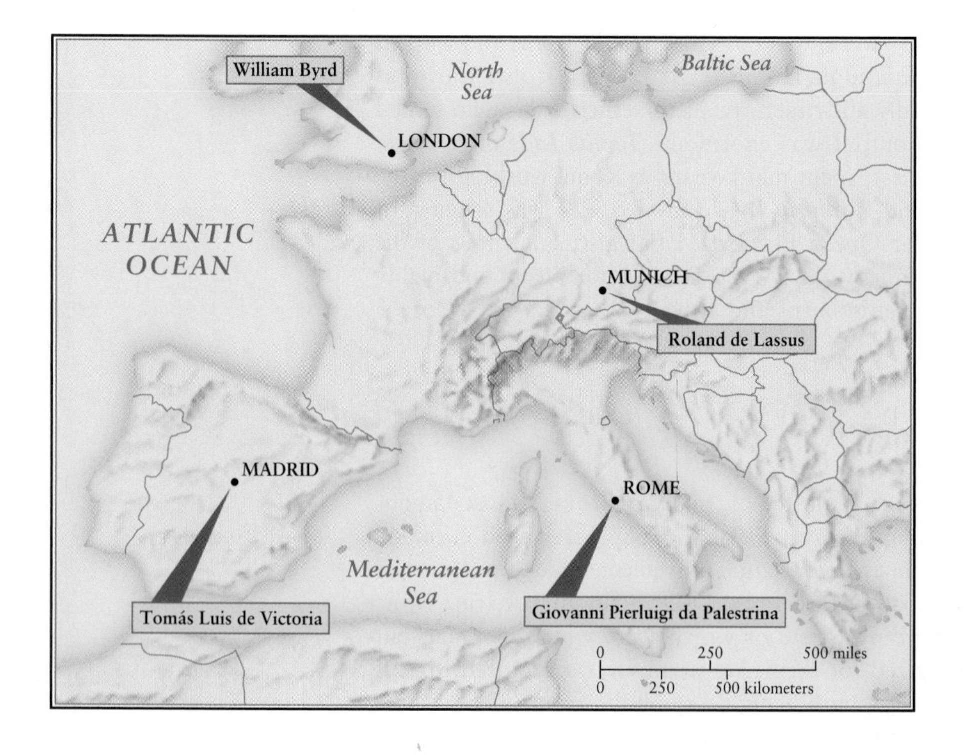

The dispersion of the High Renaissance style across Europe.

LISTEN Palestrina, *Pope Marcellus* Mass, from the Gloria

10

10 *(Capital letters indicate phrases sung in homophony.)*

0:00	QUI TOLLIS PECCATA MUNDI, MISERERE NOBIS.	You who take away the sins of the world, have mercy upon us.
	QUI TOLLIS PECCATA MUNDI, Suscipe DEPRECATIONEM NOSTRAM.	You who take away the sins of the world, hear our prayer.
1:23	QUI SEDES AD DEXTERAM PATRIS, MISERERE NOBIS.	You who sit at the right hand of the Father, have mercy upon us.
2:00	QUONIAM TU SOLUS SANCTUS, TU SOLUS DOMINUS, TU SOLUS ALTISSIMUS, JESU CHRISTE,	For you alone are holy, you alone are the Lord, you alone are the most high, Jesus Christ,
2:36	CUM SANCTO SPIRITU, in gloria Dei Patris. Amen.	With the Holy Spirit, in the glory of God the Father. Amen.

The Motet

The term *motet* has been applied to very different kinds of music over the ages; thus motets by Palestrina or Byrd have little in common with motets by Machaut or even Dufay. The sixteenth-century **motet** is a relatively short composition to Latin words made up of short sections in the homophony and imitative polyphony that were the staples of the High Renaissance style. The words are nearly always religious, taken from a variety of sources—sometimes directly from the Bible. Thus, as compared with the Mass of the same time, the motet is basically similar in *musical style,* but different in *scope* and, of course, in text.

It was the variety of the text possibilities in the motet, as contrasted to the invariable Mass, that recommended it to sixteenth-century composers. By providing them with new words to express, motets allowed church composers to convey religious messages in their music with more verve and power than ever before.

The Italian Madrigal

It was in the secular field, however, that the Renaissance ideal of music as expression made the greatest inroads. This took place principally in an important new Italian genre, after around 1530, called the **madrigal.**

The madrigal is a short composition set to a one-stanza poem—typically a love poem, with a rapid turnover of ideas and images. Ideally it is sung by one singer per part, in an intimate setting. The music consists of a sometimes equally rapid turnover of sections in imitative polyphony or homophony. Essentially, then, the plan is the same as that in High Renaissance sacred works such as Masses and motets.

But with secular words came a decisive change of emphasis. The points of imitation were shorter, and the imitation itself less strict; there was generally much more homophony; and the words assumed more and more importance. Both declamation and word painting were developed with great subtlety. For three generations a line of Italian madrigal composers, or *madrigalists,* pioneered an amazing variety of techniques to make words more vivid and to illustrate and illuminate them by musical means.

If therefore you will compose madrigals, you must possess yourself of an amorous humor, so that you must be wavering like the wind, sometimes wanton, sometimes drooping, sometimes grave and staid, otherwhile effeminate; and show the very uttermost of your variety, and the more variety you show the better shall you please.

From a music textbook by madrigal composer Thomas Morley, 1597

The English Madrigal

Queen Elizabeth I playing the lute. This miniature portrait is reproduced at almost exactly its original size.

A genre like the madrigal, tied so closely to its words—Italian words—would seem difficult to transplant. All the same, Italian madrigals became all the rage in Elizabethan England and led to the composition of madrigals in English. This popularity may well have reflected the taste and interests of Queen Elizabeth I herself. The Virgin Queen not only maintained a splendid musical establishment, like all other ambitious monarchs and nobles of the time, but she was also an accomplished musician in her own right.

In 1601, twenty-three English composers contributed madrigals to a patriotic anthology in her honor, called *The Triumphs of Oriana*. All the poems end with the same refrain: "Then sang the shepherds and nymphs of Diana: Long live fair Oriana!" Oriana was a pseudonym for Elizabeth, and the nymphs and shepherds of Diana—the goddess of virginity—were her subjects. The *Triumphs* was obviously a court-inspired project, and as such it reminds us vividly of one of the main functions of court music of all times: flattery.

THOMAS WEELKES (c. 1575–1623)
Madrigal, "As Vesta Was from Latmos Hill Descending" (1601)

11

Thomas Weelkes never rose beyond the position of provincial cathedral organist-choirmaster; in fact, he had trouble keeping even that post in later life, when the cathedral records assert that he became "noted and found for a common drunckard and notorious swearer and blasphemer." Although he is not a major figure, as are the other composers treated in this unit, he is one of the best composers of madrigals in English.

Written in better days, Weelkes's contribution to *The Triumphs of Oriana* is a fine example of a madrigal of the lighter kind. (Weelkes also wrote serious and melancholy madrigals.) After listening to the music of Josquin and Palestrina, our first impression of "Vesta" is of the sheer exuberant brightness of the musical style. Simple rhythms, clear harmonies, crisp melodic motives—all look forward to music of the Baroque era and beyond. This music has a modern feel about it.

The next thing likely to impress the listener is the elegance and liveliness with which the words are declaimed. We have already stressed the importance of declamation in the Renaissance composers' program of attention to verbal texts. Weelkes nearly always has his words sung in rhythms that would seem quite natural if the words were spoken, as shown at the right (where – stands for a long syllable, ⌣ for a short one). The declamation is never less than accurate, and it is sometimes expressive: The rhythms make the words seem imposing in the second phrase shown, dainty in the third.

Leav-ing their God-dess all a-lone

Then sang the shep-herds and nymphs of Di-a-na

To whom Di-a-na's dar-lings

As for the word painting, that can be shown in a tabular form:

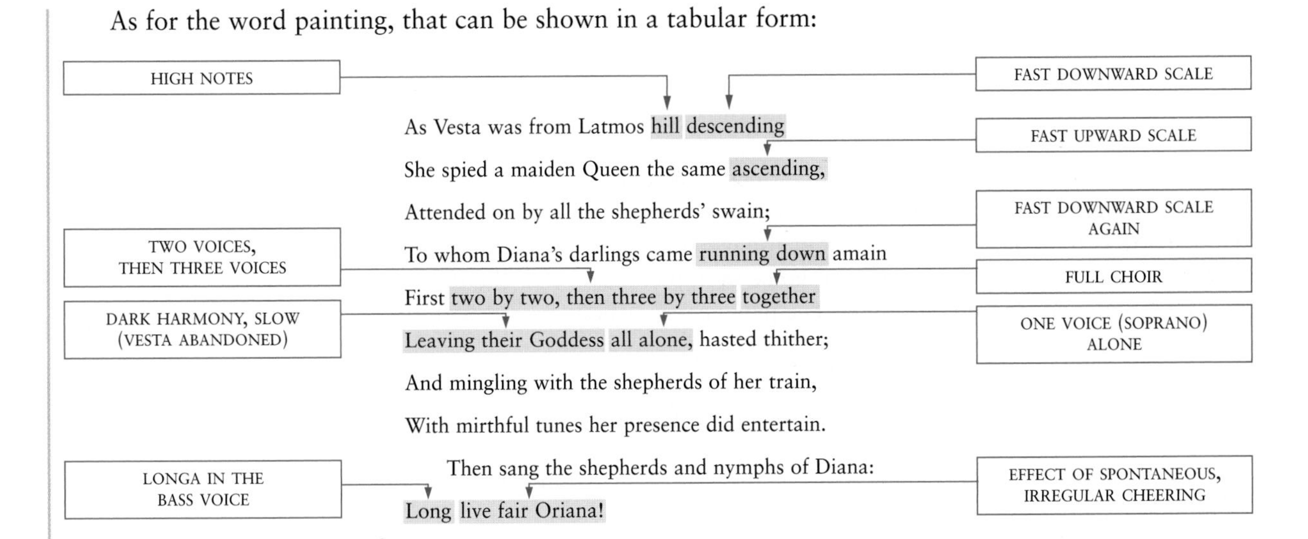

(The "maiden Queen" is Elizabeth, and "Diana's darlings" are the Vestal Virgins, priestesses of Vesta, the Roman goddess of hearth and home. The archaic word *amain* means "at full speed.")

This brilliant six-part madrigal uses two sopranos, alto, two tenors, and bass. Weelkes makes particularly good use of this group in his extended imitative setting of the poem's last line. Here we can easily imagine many more than six loyal voices endlessly cheering their Queen in a spontaneous, irregular way, one after another. Shakespeare and his contemporaries, Weelkes among them, were very fond of puns. Weelkes has the word "long" sung by the bass voice on a note four times the duration of a whole note—a note whose Latin name was *longa*. So this madrigal has its esoteric, in-joke side for musicians, as well as its public, political side for Elizabeth's subjects.

5 Instrumental Music: Early Developments

The best sixteenth-century composers concentrated almost entirely on vocal genres, on music with words. Except for the English master William Byrd, none of them devoted much attention to music for instruments alone. We have spoken above of the Renaissance preoccupation with expression in music, expression through the association of music with words.

Nevertheless, instruments and music for instruments developed significantly during this period. The first violins and harpsichords date from the sixteenth century; also perfected were the lute—a guitar-like instrument, originally from the Near East, that was perhaps the most popular of all at the time—and many other instruments. Instrumental music was to become one of the great glories of the Baroque era, and the basis for this was laid in the Renaissance.

Around 1500, hardly any music was written specifically for instruments. Instrumentalists would either play along with singers in vocal music, or else play motets, chansons, and other vocal genres by themselves, without words. The principal vocal genre after 1550, however, the madrigal, would not have made much sense performed without its words. By this time, in any case, new genres had been developed for instrumental performance.

Renaissance Dances

The most widespread of Renaissance instrumental genres was the dance, a reflection of the great popularity of dancing at the time.

Many dance types are described in detail in sixteenth-century instruction books—the steps themselves, and also their order or sequence. (In this regard, old dances were closer to square dances than to some modern social dancing, where there is no fixed order for steps or movements.) One of the most popular was the **pavane** (paván), a solemn dance in duple meter, with the participants stepping and stopping formally. The pavane was usually paired with the triple-meter **galliard.**

Simpler, less formal Renaissance dance types include the Italian *saltarello,* the Irish *jig,* known also in Scotland and the north of England, and the French *bransle*—whose name is related to our word *brawl.* The Renaissance also saw elaborately choreographed ballets, court dances in which kings and nobles could participate.

Conforming to the dance steps, dance music was written in easy-to-follow phrases, almost always four to eight bars long. Ending with especially clear cadences, the phrases were each played twice in succession to produce forms such as **a a b b** or **a a b b c c.**

ANONYMOUS
Galliard, "Daphne"

The title of this melodious Elizabethan dance suggests that originally it may have been a song. But if so, at some point the song was pressed into galliard form, **a a b b c c,** and this is the only way it has survived.

Played in our recording by an early violin ensemble, "Daphne" is mainly homophonic. The meter is kept very clear, and the distinct quality of the phrases ending **a, b,** and **c** makes it easy for the dancers to remember the place in the dance step sequence. The first violin provides extensive ornamentations at the second playing.

ANONYMOUS
"Kemp's Jig"

Will Kemp was an Elizabethan actor, comedian, and song-and-dance man, immortalized for having created comic roles in Shakespeare, such as Dogberry the Constable in *Much Ado About Nothing.* Kemp specialized in a type of popular dance number, called a jig, that was regularly presented in Elizabethan theaters after the main play. He accompanied himself with pipe and tabor—a type of simple flute, blown like a recorder, and a snare drum.

Dance Stylization

"Kemp's Jig" can lead us to an important topic that extends past the Renaissance. An oddity of this particular dance is that in phrase **a**, the cadence—a stopping place (see page 25)—comes in the fourth bar, whereas in phrase **b**, a cadence comes in the fifth. Though the motion does not stop at this point, the tonic is reached in a very solid way in measure 9. Another cadence comes three bars later, in measure 12. A dancer might be confused, even thrown off by this.

A listener, on the other hand, might well enjoy the interesting effect caused by this irregularity in the cadences. If we like to think that this little dance puts us in touch with true "folk music," we must also suspect that a musician of some sophistication has been tinkering with it.

"Kemp's Jig" is not as simple as it seems, then. It illustrates a tendency that will gain more and more importance later: the tendency to make dance music more and more elaborate and "artistic." Composers (and performers making it up on the spot) provided dance music with elements of a more strictly musical interest over and above the dancers' basic needs. Such elements are irregular cadences, as in "Kemp's Jig," subtle phrase lengths, unusual harmonies, and even counterpoint.

This was the first stage of a process that we can call the *stylization* of dance music. Already well established in the sixteenth century, dance stylization was to attain new heights in the dance suites by Bach and the symphony minuets of Haydn and Mozart. In the twentieth century, fox-trot tunes were (and sometimes still are) "stylized" into jazz numbers. Louis Armstrong and Charlie Parker did not expect that people who came to listen to them were going to dance to such stylized versions.

Not Will Kemp of Kemp's Jig, but another famous comic of Shakespeare's time: Richard Tarleton, with the traditional tools of his trade, the pipe and tabor.

"Kemp's Jig" is a lively—perhaps "perky" is the right word—and seemingly simple dance tune in **a a b** form. It is played several times on our recording, first by a recorder and then by a viol, an early string instrument in the cello range; ornaments are piled on, first to the repeated phrase **a** and then to all the repetitions. A lute accompanies.

Web: *Research and test your understanding of Renaissance music at* **<bedfordstmartins.com/listen>.**

CHAPTER 7

The Early Baroque Period

At the end of the sixteenth century, music was undergoing rapid changes at the sophisticated courts and churches of northern Italy. Composers began to write motets, madrigals, and other pieces more directly for effect—with a new simplicity, in some respects, but also with the use of exciting new resources. A new style, the style of the early Baroque period, took hold rapidly all over Italy and in most of the rest of Europe.

1 From Renaissance to Baroque

As we have seen, the madrigal was the most "advanced" form in late Renaissance music. Toward the end of the sixteenth century, the thirst for expression led madrigal composers to increasingly esoteric kinds of word painting. Extreme dissonances and rhythmic contrasts were explored in order to illustrate emotional texts in a more and more exaggerated fashion.

Why cause words to be sung by four or five voices so that they cannot be distinguished, when the ancient Greeks aroused the strongest passions by means of a single voice supported by a lyre? We must renounce counterpoint and the use of different kinds of instruments and return to simplicity!

A Florentine critic, 1581

At the same time, a reaction set in *against* the madrigal. In Florence, an influential group of intellectuals mounted an attack on the madrigalists' favorite technique, word painting. Word painting was artificial and childish, they said, and the many voices of a madrigal ensemble could not focus feeling or express it strongly. Whatever the madrigalists thought, a choir singing counterpoint could only dilute strong emotions, not concentrate them.

True emotionality could be projected only by a single human agent, an individual, a singer who would learn from great actors and orators how to move an audience to laughter, anger, or tears. A new style of solo singing was developed, *recitative,* that was half music, half recitation. This led inevitably to the stage and, as we shall see, to opera. Invented in Florence around 1600, opera became one of the greatest and most characteristic products of the Baroque imagination.

Music in Venice

Meanwhile, there were important developments in Venice, the city of canals. The "Serene Republic," as Venice called itself, cultivated especially brilliant styles in all the arts—matched, it seems, to the city's dazzling physical appearance. Wealthy and cosmopolitan, Venice produced architects whose flamboyant,

Venice, the most colorful of European cities, and one of the most musical. Several major painters made a speciality of Venetian scenes, which were very popular; this one, of the Rialto Bridge over the Grand Canal, is by Francesco Guardi (1712–1793).

varied buildings were built out of multicolored materials, and painters—the Bellinis, Titian, Tintoretto—who specialized in warm, rich hues. Perhaps, then, it is more than a play on words to describe Venetian music as "colorful."

From the time of Palestrina's *Pope Marcellus* Mass, sixteenth-century composers had often subdivided their choirs into low and high "semichoirs" of three or four voice parts each. The semichoirs would alternate and answer or echo each other. Expanding this technique, Venetian composers would now alternate two, three, or more whole choirs. Homophony crowded out polyphony as full choirs answered one another stereophonically, seeming to compete throughout entire motets and Masses, then joining together for climactic sections of glorious massed sound.

The resources of sonority were exploited even further when sometimes the "choirs" were designated for singers on some parts and instruments on others. Or else whole choirs would be made up of instruments. As the sonorous combinations of Venetian music grew more and more colorful, the stately decorum of the High Renaissance style was forgotten (or left to musical conservatives). Magnificence and extravagance became the new ideals, well suited to the pomp and ceremony for which Venice was famous.

Extravagance and Control

Wherever they looked, knowledgeable travelers to Italy around 1600 would have seen music bursting out of its traditional forms, styles, and genres. Freedom was the order of the day. But they might have been puzzled to notice an opposite tendency as well: In some ways musical form was becoming more rigorously controlled and systematic. As composers sought to make music more untrammeled in one respect, they found they had to organize it more strictly in another so that listeners would not lose track of what was happening.

The control composers exercised over Baroque form, in other words, was an appropriate response to Baroque extravagance, exaggeration, and emotionality. We shall see similar forces and counterforces at other points in musical history later in this book.

GIOVANNI GABRIELI (c. 1555–1612)
Motet, "O magnum mysterium" (published 1615)

The most important composers in Venice were two Gabrielis, Andrea and his nephew Giovanni. (Andrea's dates are c. 1510–1586). As organists of St. Mark's Cathedral, both of them exploited the special acoustics of that extraordinary building, which still impress tourists today. By placing choirs of singers and instrumentalists in different choir lofts, they obtained brilliant echo effects that even modern audio equipment cannot duplicate.

Giovanni's "O magnum mysterium," the second part of a longer motet, was written for the Christmas season. The text marvels that lowly animals—the ox and the ass—were the first to see the newborn Jesus.

And the music marvels along with the text. Quite in the manner of a madrigal, the exclamation, "O" is repeated like a gasp of astonishment. Then lush chord progressions positively make the head spin, as the words *O magnum mysterium* are repeated to the same music, but pitched higher (that is to say, in sequence: see page 25). A momentary change in the meter, which slips from duple (2/2) into triple (3/2), provides a new feeling of majesty, as much as astonishment:

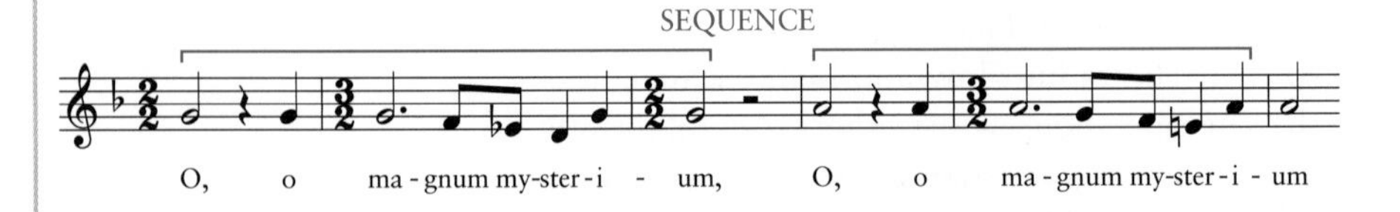

Gabrieli uses two "choirs," each with three voice parts and four instrumental parts, plus organ, though at first all we hear is a sumptuous blend of brass instruments and voices. Solo voices emerge at the word *sacramentum.* First solo tenors, then boy sopranos echo one another during the line *iacentem in presepio,* where a new rapid figure bounces back and forth from tenors to sopranos to brass.

Gabrieli really unleashes his musical resources at the choral *alleluia* section. The music moves in quick triple meter, matching the jubilation of repeated *alleluias,* and the two choirs echo back and forth across the sound space:

	FAST—triple meter									SLOW—duple meter		
	1 2 3	1 2 3	1 2 3	1 2 3	1 2 3	1 2 3	1 2 3	1 2 3	1 2 3	1 2 3 4	1 2 3 4	1
CHOIR 1	Al-le-	lu-ia,	al-le-lu-	ia;			al-le-lu-	ia,	al-le-lu-	ia: [Al - - le-	lu------	ia
CHOIR 2				Al-le-	lu-ia,	al-le-lu-	ia,	al-le-lu-	ia,	[Al - - le-	lu------	ia

To make a grand conclusion, the choirs come together again. There is another wash of voice-and-brass sonority as the tempo slows and the meter changes to duple for a climactic *alleluia.* For yet another *alleluia,* the music adds a solemn extra beat, the meter changing once again:

And for still more emphasis, Gabrieli repeats the entire *alleluia* section, comprising the fast triple-time alternations and the massive slow ending.

Notice that there are certain parallels between the beginning and the end of "O magnum mysterium." These include the tempo and meter (slow, changing from 2/2 to 3/2), the texture (massed choirs), and the musical technique (sequence). Gabrieli has imposed a kind of organization and control on the flamboyant chords and the solo rhapsodies. This is an example of the combination of extravagance and control in early Baroque music that we discussed above.

LISTEN **Giovanni Gabrieli, "O magnum mysterium"**

14

14 0:00	O magnum mysterium,	O, what a great mystery,
0:30	et admirabile sacramentum	and what a wonderful sacrament—
0:53	ut animalia viderunt Dominum natum	that animals should see the Lord new born
1:18	iacentem in presepio:	lying in the manger.
1:56	Alleluia, alleluia.	Hallelujah, hallelujah.

2 Style Features of Early Baroque Music

Music from the period of approximately 1600 to 1750 is usually referred to as "baroque," a term that captures its excess and extravagance. (It was originally a jeweler's term for large pearls of irregular shape.) A number of broad stylistic features unify the music of this long period.

Rhythm and Meter

Rhythms become more definite, regular, and insistent in Baroque music; a single rhythm or similar rhythms can be heard throughout a piece or a major segment of a piece. Compare the subtle, floating rhythms of Renaissance music, changing section by section as the motives for the imitative polyphony change. (Renaissance dance music is an exception, and in the area of dance music there is a direct line from the Renaissance to the Baroque.)

Related to this new regularity of rhythm is a new acceptance of meter. One technical feature tells the story: Bar lines begin to be used for the first time in music history. This means that music's meter is systematically in evidence, rather than being downplayed as it was in the Renaissance. The strong beats are emphasized by certain instruments, playing in a clear, decisive way. All this is conspicuous enough in Gabrieli's motet "O magnum mysterium."

Texture: Basso Continuo

Some early Baroque music is homophonic and some is polyphonic, but both textures are enriched by a feature unique to the period, the **basso continuo.**

As in a Renaissance score, in a Baroque score the bass line is performed by bass voices or low instruments such as cellos or bassoons. But the bass part in Baroque music is also played by an organ, harpsichord, or other chord instrument. This instrument not only reinforces the bass line, it also adds chords continuously (hence the term *continuo*) to go with it. The basso continuo—or just "continuo"—has the double effect of clarifying the harmony and of making the texture bind or jell.

One can see how this device responds to the growing reliance of Baroque music on harmony (already clear from Gabrieli's motet). In the early days, the continuo was simply the bass line of the polyphony reinforced by chords; but later the continuo with its chords was mapped out first, and the polyphony adjusted to it. Baroque polyphony, in other words, has systematic harmonic underpinnings.

This fact is dramatized by a musical form that is characteristically Baroque, the **ground bass.** This is music constructed literally from the bottom up. In ground bass form, the bass instruments play a single short figure many times, generating the same set of repeated harmonies (played by the continuo chord instruments). Above this ground bass, upper instruments or voices play (or improvise) different melodies or virtuoso passages, all adjusted to the harmonies determined by the bass.

A ground bass (the Pachelbel Canon)

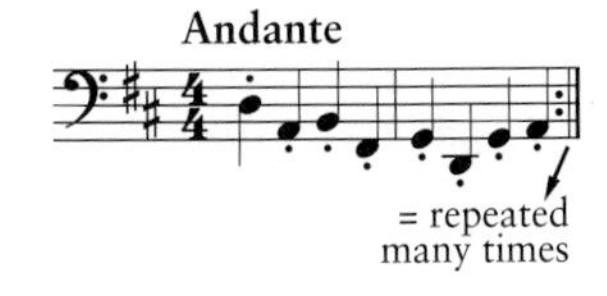

Baroque ground-bass compositions discussed in this book are "Dido's Lament" from the opera *Dido and Aeneas* by Henry Purcell (page 102), a passacaglia by Girolamo Frescobaldi (page 106), and Vivaldi's Violin Concerto in G, Op. 4, No. 12 (page 130).

Another name for the ground bass comes from Baroque Italian musicians: **basso ostinato,** meaning "persistent" or "obstinate" bass. By extension, the term *ostinato* is also used to refer to any short musical gesture repeated over and over again, in the bass or anywhere else, especially one used as a building block for a piece of music. Ostinatos are found in most of the world's musical traditions (see page 108). This is not surprising, since the formal principle they embody is so very fundamental: Set up a repeating pattern and then pit contrasting musical elements against it.

Functional Harmony

Inevitably, in view of these new techniques, the art of harmony evolved rapidly at this time. Whereas Renaissance music had still used the medieval modes, although with important modifications, Baroque musicians developed the modern major/minor system which we discussed on pages 31–34. Chords became standardized, and the sense of tonality—the feeling of centrality around a tonic or "home" pitch—grew much stronger.

Music is a roaring-meg against melancholy, to rear and revive the languishing soul; affecting not only the ears, but the very arteries, the vital and animal spirits, it erects the mind and makes it nimble.

Robert Burton, 1621

A torchlight concert in a German town square. The harpsichord continuo is at the center of the action. Notice the big music stands or racks, and the two timpani sunk in a panel, like a double sink.

Composers also developed a new way of handling the chords so that their interrelation was felt to be more logical, or at least more coherent. Each chord now assumed a special role, or function, in relation to the tonic chord (the chord on the "home" pitch). Thus when one chord follows another in Baroque music, it does so in a newly predictable and purposeful way. "Functional" harmony, in this sense, could also be used as a way of organizing large-scale pieces of music, as we will see later.

In a Baroque composition, as compared with one from the Renaissance, the chords seem to be going where we expect them to—and we feel they are determining the sense or the direction of the piece as a whole. Harmonies no longer seem to wander, detour, hesitate, or evaporate. With the introduction of the important resource of functional harmony, Baroque music brings us firmly to the familiar, to the threshold of modern music.

3 Opera

Opera—drama presented in music, with the characters singing instead of speaking—is often called the most characteristic art form of the Baroque period. For Baroque opera combined many different arts: not only music, drama, and poetry, but also dancing, highly elaborate scene design, and spectacular special effects. Incredibly ingenious machines were contrived to portray gods descending to

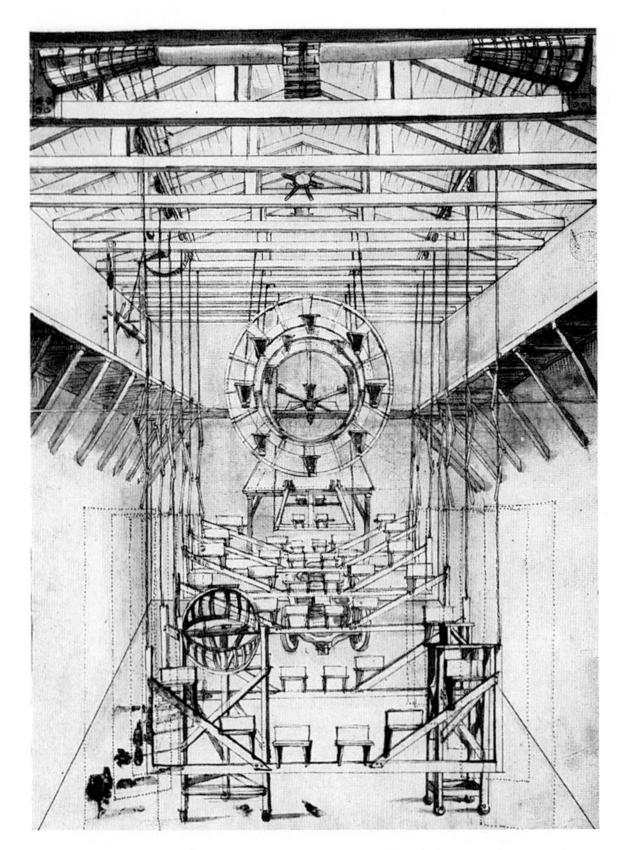

Stage designers of Baroque opera specialized in rapidly moving scenery for their most dazzling effects. Shown here is the machinery for one such set and a drawing of the intended realization.

earth, shipwrecks, volcanos, and all kinds of natural and supernatural phenomena. Scene designers often received top billing, ahead of the composers.

The early Florentine operas were court entertainments put on to celebrate royal weddings and the like. But an important step was taken in 1637 with the opening of the first public opera theater. First in Venice and then in the whole of Italy, opera soon became the leading form of entertainment. By the end of the century, seven opera houses in Venice fulfilled much the same function as movie theaters in a comparable modern city (around 145,000 people).

Opera was a perfect answer to the general desire in the early Baroque era for individual emotionalism. For opera provided a stage on which the single individual could step forward to express his or her feelings in the most direct and powerful fashion. Indeed, composers felt a need to relieve the constant emotional pressure exerted on their characters by the ever-changing dramatic action. They had to contrive moments of relaxation, moments when the characters could stop and reflect. This led to a standard dualism that has been with opera ever since: *recitative* and *aria*. This dualism between tension and repose reflects that other Baroque dualism, between freedom and strictness, extravagance and control.

Recitative

Recitative (re-si-ta-téev), from the Italian word for "recitation," is the technique of declaiming words musically in a heightened, theatrical manner. The singing voice closely follows the free rhythm of highly emotional speech; it mirrors and exaggerates the natural ups and downs that occur as an actor raises his or her voice at a question, lowers it in an "aside," or cries out in distress. The accompaniment is usually kept to a minimum. This allows the singer-actor to interpret the dialogue or the action as spontaneously as possible, and also ensures all the words can be heard clearly.

Recitative—the "free" side of the operatic dualism—is used for plot action, dialogue, and other situations in the drama where it is particularly important for the words to be brought out. On the other hand, where spoken drama would call for soliloquies or meditations, opera uses arias.

Aria

An **aria** is an extended piece for solo singer that has much more musical elaboration and coherence than a passage of recitative. The vocal part is more melodic, the rhythm is more consistent, and typically the accompaniment includes the entire orchestra. Here the singer-actor mulls over his or her feelings at some leisure, instead of reacting moment by moment, as in recitative. Emotion is controlled and "frozen" into a tableau. Paradoxically, when the music gets more elaborate, the emotion stands still.

Recitative required great singing actors, and arias required artists who could convert the notes of a score into these tableaus of furious, sensuous, or tragic expression. Opera houses in the seventeenth century became showcases of vocal virtuosity—as they still are today. Ever since the Baroque era, musical drama and vocal display have vied with one another as the driving force of opera.

Claudio Monteverdi (1567–1643)

One figure stood out above all others in music around 1600, just as Josquin Desprez had around 1500. Claudio Monteverdi, an enormously imaginative and innovative composer, also has the dubious distinction of being the first great composer whose music was attacked publicly for being too radical. Radical it was. Monteverdi has aptly been called "the last great madrigalist and the first great opera composer"; indeed, while his earliest madrigals are close enough in style to those of Thomas Weelkes, some of his later ones are more like small opera scenes.

Monteverdi first worked at the music-loving court of Mantua, in northern Italy. There he wrote his first stage work, *Orfeo* (1607), famous in music history as the first masterpiece of opera. He was then appointed choirmaster of St. Mark's Cathedral in Venice, the most prestigious musical position in Europe. At the end of his life, in the 1640s, he helped inaugurate public opera, Venice's greatest contribution to the history of music.

CLAUDIO MONTEVERDI
The Coronation of Poppea (1642)

After his first opera, *Orfeo,* none of Monteverdi's operas were printed, and some have been completely lost—a grievous loss indeed. All we have left of his *Arianna* is the heroine's big lament, one of the greatest hits of the day, which Monteverdi published by itself in several different arrangements. Fortunately, two late masterpieces have survived: *The Return of Ulysses* and *The Coronation of Poppea.* After slumbering for three hundred years, *Poppea* has recently proved to be a "sleeper" in opera houses around the world.

CLAVDIO MONTEVERDE

FIORI POETICI
Raccolti nel Funerale
DEL MOLTO ILLVSTRE;
E Molto Reuerendo
SIGNOR CLAVDIO
Monte verde
Maeſtro di Cappella della Du-
cale di S. Marco .
Conſecrati
DA D. GIO: BATTISTA
Marinoni, detto Gioue :
Maeſtro di Cappella del Do-
mo di Padoua
ALL' ILLVSTRISSIMI
& Eccellentiſſimi
SIG. PROCVRATORI
Di Chieſa di S. Marco .

In VENETIA, Preſſo Franceſco Miloco.
Con Lic. de Sup. MDCXLIV.

Monteverdi as a young man, and as pictured on a commemorative edition of poems honoring him, published in Venice ("in VENETIA") just after his death. The design includes a fine collection of old instruments, including four lutes, shown in front and back views.

Background Even today, the story of *The Coronation of Poppea* can shock by its startling and cynical dramatic realism. Poppea, mistress of the notorious Roman Emperor Nero, schemes to get his wife, Ottavia, deposed and his eminent adviser, Seneca, put to death. She succeeds in both. In a counterplot, Ottavia blackmails Ottone, Poppea's rejected lover, into an attempt on Poppea's life. He tries but fails. The counterplotters are all exiled. As an added cynical touch, Poppea's ruthless maneuvering to be crowned empress of Rome is shown to be aided by the God of Love and the Goddess of Fortune.

After a prologue sung by the mythological characters, Act I begins with Ottone arriving at Poppea's house at daybreak, and retreating in dismay after he sees Nero's guards outside it. In an ironic alba (see page 62), the guards curse military life and exchange scurrilous gossip about Poppea's scheming. This is a vivid prelude to the first of the opera's several steamy love scenes.

Recitative Enter Nero and Poppea, who tries to wheedle Nero into staying with her. Delaying his departure as long as possible, she makes him promise to return. Accompanied by a lute as continuo instrument—a voluptuous sound, in this context—she repeats the question "*Tornerai?*" ("Won't you return?") in increasingly seductive accents until Nero stops evading the issue and agrees: "*Tornerò*" ("Yes, I will return"). Notice how the vocal line does not form itself into real melodies, but goes up or down or speeds or slows, following the words in speechlike fragments.

Many men's roles in early opera were written for castrati, male soprano singers (see page 152). On our recording, Nero is sung by a female mezzo-soprano, Della Jones, whose lower, more "focused" voice contrasts with that of the soprano singing Poppea.

Nero's most extended evasion is a short aria-like fragment, called an arioso. Then the recitative resumes. On the final *addios*—some of them melting, others breathless—the singers say goodbye, improvising delicate vocal ornaments.

Aria As soon as Nero leaves, Poppea shows her true colors in a jubilant aria, a sort of victory dance. It is accompanied by a small orchestra, and contains three short sections. The first is an orchestral tune (strings and recorder) to which Poppea sings her first two lines of text:

Allegro

POPPEA (with strings, recorder)

Note that a moment of uncertainty ("a mantle that is . . . illusory") is marked by a momentary lapse into recitative. Her mood becomes harder and more determined in the aria's second section. Finally, in section 3, she sings lighthearted, fast military fanfares—this is word painting in the madrigal tradition—as she crows that the gods are fighting on her behalf.

Mercurial, manipulative, fearless, dangerously sensual: Poppea has been characterized unforgettably by Monteverdi's music in this scene.

LISTEN Monteverdi, *The Coronation of Poppea,* from Act I

1
15-16

(*Italics indicate repeated words and lines. For a word about singing Italian,* *see page 102.*)

		RECITATIVE		
15	0:00	**Poppea:**	Tornerai?	Won't you return?
		Nero:	Se ben io vò,	Though I am leaving you,
			Pur teco io stò, *pur teco stò* . . .	I am in truth still here . . .
		Poppea:	Tornerai?	Won't you return?
		Nero:	Il cor dalle tue stelle	My heart can never, never be torn away
			Mai mai non si disvelle . . .	from your fair eyes . . .
		Poppea:	Tornerai?	Won't you return?
		ARIOSO		
	0:24	**Nero:**	Io non posso da te, *non posso da te, da te* viver disgiunto	I cannot live apart from you
			Se non si smembra l'unita del punto . . .	Unless unity itself can be divided . . .
		RECITATIVE		
	0:56	**Poppea:**	Tornerai?	Won't you return?
		Nero:	Tornerò.	I will return.
		Poppea:	Quando?	When?
		Nero:	Ben tosto.	Soon.
		Poppea:	Ben tosto, me'l prometti?	Very soon—you promise?
		Nero:	Te'l giuro.	I swear it!
		Poppea:	*E me l'osserverai?*	And will you keep your promise?
		Nero:	*E s'a te non verrò, tu a me verrai!*	If I do not come, you'll come to me!
	1:23	**Poppea:**	Addio . . .	Farewell . . .
		Nero:	Addio . . .	
		Poppea:	Nerone, Nerone, addio . . .	
		Nero:	Poppea, Poppea, addio . . .	
		Poppea:	Addio, Nerone, addio!	Farewell, Nero, farewell!
		Nero:	Addio, Poppea, ben mio.	Farewell, Poppea, my love.
16	2:25	ARIA	(Section 1)	
0:10	2:35	**Poppea:**	Speranza, tu mi vai	O hope, you
			Il core accarezzando;	Caress my heart;
			Speranza, tu mi vai il genio lusingando;	O hope, you entice my mind;
			E mi circondi intanto	As you cloak me
			Di regio si, ma immaginario manto.	In a mantle that is royal, yes, but illusory.
			(Section 2)	
0:46	3:11		No no, non temo, no, *no no, non temo, no* di noia alcuna:	No, no! I fear no adversity:
			(Section 3)	
1:03	3:28		Per me guerreggia, *guerreggia,*	I have fighting for me,
			Per me guerreggia Amor, *guerreggia Amor* e la Fortuna, *e la Fortuna.*	I have fighting for me Love and Fortune.

Singing Italian

The Coronation of Poppea is the first of many Italian texts printed in this book. To follow the recordings, it will help to know a few simple rules about Italian pronunciation and singing conventions.

- The consonants *c* and *g* are soft (pronounced "ch" and "j") when followed by *e* or *i* (cello, Genoa, cappuccino, DiMaggio). They are hard when followed by other letters, including *h* (Galileo, spaghetti con Chianti).
- In poems, when an Italian word *ending* with a vowel is followed by another word *beginning* with a vowel, the two vowels are elided, run together as one.
- In Italian (and German) *z* is pronounced *dz* or *tz* (pizza, Mozart).

Lines from our selection from *The Coronation of Poppea* are sung as indicated below:

3	Pur **teco** io stò	= Pur téc'yo stó
18	**tu a** me verrai	= tw'a méh verrah-ee
26	Il core accarezzando	= Il cór'accaretzándo
28	E mi **circondi** intanto	= E mi chircónd'intánto
33	Per me **guerreggia** Amor	= Per méh gwerréj'Amór

Henry Purcell (1659–1695)

Italy was the undisputed leader in music throughout the seventeenth century. However, music also flourished in France, Germany (or what is now Germany), and other countries, always under Italian influence.

The greatest English composer of the Baroque era, Henry Purcell, was the organist at Westminster Abbey and a member of the Chapel Royal, like several other members of his family. In his short lifetime he wrote sacred, instrumental, and theater music, as well as twenty-nine "Welcome Songs" for his royal masters. Purcell combined a respect for native traditions, represented by the music of William Byrd, Thomas Weelkes, and others, with a lively interest in the more adventurous French and Italian music of his own time. He wrote and published the first English examples of a new Italian genre, the sonata.

HENRY PURCELL
Dido and Aeneas (1689)

Though Purcell wrote a good deal of music for the London theater, his one true opera, *Dido and Aeneas,* was performed at a girls' school (though there may have been an earlier performance at court). The whole thing lasts little more than an hour and contains no virtuoso singing roles at all. *Dido and Aeneas* is an exceptional work, then, and a miniature. But it is also a work of rare beauty and dramatic power—and rarer still, it is a great opera in English, perhaps the only great opera in English prior to the twentieth century.

Background Purcell's source was the *Aeneid,* the noblest of all Latin epic poems, written by Virgil to celebrate the glory of Rome and the Roman Empire. It tells the story of the city's foundation by the Trojan prince Aeneas, who escapes from Troy when the Greeks capture it with their wooden horse. After many adventures and travels, Aeneas finally reaches Italy, guided by the firm hand of Jove, king of the gods.

In one of the *Aeneid*'s most famous episodes, Aeneas and the widowed Queen Dido of Carthage fall deeply in love. But Jove tells the prince to stop dallying and get on with his important journey. Regretfully he leaves, and Dido kills herself—an agonizing suicide, as Virgil describes it.

Henry Purcell

In Acts I and II of the opera, Dido expresses apprehension about her feelings for Aeneas, even though her courtiers keep encouraging the match in chorus after chorus. Next we see the plotting of some witches—a highly un-Virgilian touch, but ever since Shakespeare's *Macbeth*, witches had been popular with English theatergoers, perhaps especially with school-age ones. For malicious reasons of their own, these witches make Aeneas believe that Jove is ordering his departure.

In Act III, Aeneas tries feebly to excuse himself. Dido spurns him in a furious recitative. As he leaves, deserting her, she prepares for her suicide.

Our Songs and our Musick
Let's still dedicate
To *Purcell*, to *Purcell*,
The Son of *Apollo*,
'Till another, another,
Another as Great
In the Heav'nly Science
Of Musick shall follow.

—Poet Thomas d'Urfey, seventeenth century (Apollo was the Greek god of music.)

Recitative Dido addresses this regal, somber recitative to her confidante, Belinda. Notice the imperious tone as she tells Belinda to take her hand, and the ominous setting of the word *darkness*. Purcell even contrives to suggest a kind of tragic irony when Dido's melodic line turns to the major mode on the word *welcome* in "Death is now a welcome guest."

Aria The opera's final aria, usually known as "Dido's Lament," is built over a slow ground bass or ostinato (see page 96), a descending bass line with chromatic semitones repeated a dozen times. The bass line sounds mournful even without accompaniment, as in measures 1–4. Violins in the string orchestra imitate this line while Dido is singing, and especially after she has stopped.

As often happens in arias, the words are repeated a number of times; Dido has little to say but much to feel, and the music needs time to convey the emotional message. We experience an extended emotional tableau. Whereas recitative makes little sense unless the listener understands the exact words, with arias a general impression of them may be enough. Indeed, even that is unnecessary when the song is as poignant as Purcell's is here.

The most heartbreaking place comes (twice) on the exclamation "ah," where the bass note D, harmonized with a major-mode chord during the first six appearances of the ground bass, is shadowed by a new minor chord:

Dec. 6, 1665. *Here the best company for musique I ever was in, in my life, and I wish I could live and die in it, both for the musique and the face of Mrs. Pierce, and my wife, and Mrs. Knipp, who is pretty enough and sings the noblest that ever I heard in my life.*

London civil servant Samuel Pepys, from his diary (first published in 1825)

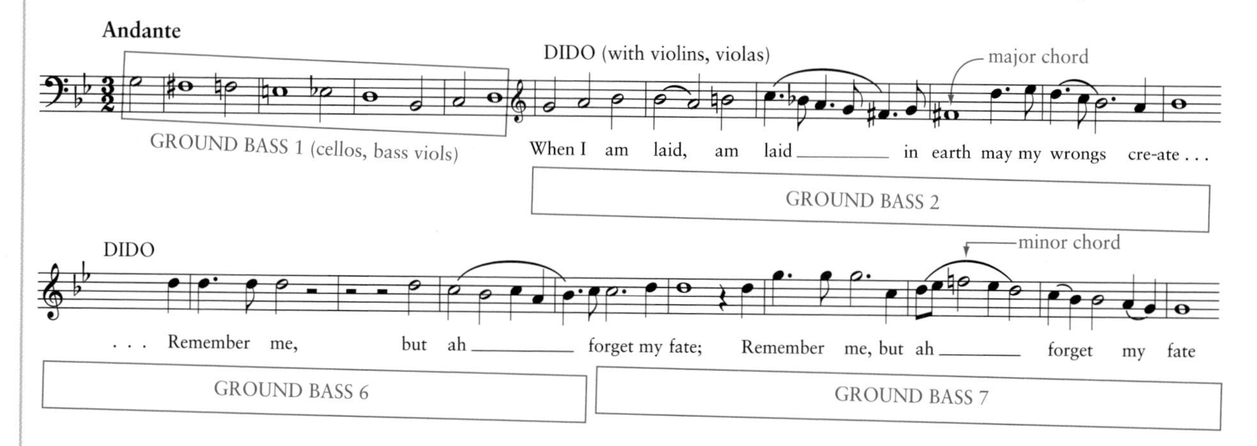

Chorus The last notes of this great aria run into a wonderful final chorus. We are to imagine a slow dance, as groups of sorrowful cupids (first-graders, perhaps) file past the bier. Now Dido's personal grief and agony is transmuted into a communal sense of mourning. In the context of the whole opera, this chorus seems even more meaningful, because the courtiers who sing it have matured so much since the time when they thoughtlessly and cheerfully urged Dido to give in to her love.

The general style of the music is that of the madrigal—imitative polyphony and homophony, with some word painting. (The first three lines are mostly imitative, the last one homophonic.) But Purcell's style clearly shows the inroads of functional harmony and of the definite, unified rhythms that had been developing in the seventeenth century. There is no mistaking this touching chorus for an actual Renaissance madrigal.

Like "Dido's Lament," "With drooping wings" is another emotional tableau, and this time the emotion spills over to the opera audience. As the courtiers grieve for Dido, we join them in responding to Dido's tragedy.

LISTEN **Purcell, *Dido and Aeneas,* Act III, final scene**

17-18

(Italics indicate repeated words and lines.)

RECITATIVE

17 0:00 **Dido:** Thy hand, Belinda! Darkness shades me;
On thy bosom let me rest.
More I would—but death invades me:
Death is now a welcome guest.

ARIA

0:58 **Dido:** When I am laid, *am laid* in earth
May my wrongs create
No trouble, *no trouble* in thy breast; *(repeated)*
Remember me . . . *remember me,* but ah, forget my fate;

2:17 *Remember me, but ah, forget my fate.*
(stabs herself)

CHORUS

18 4:01 **Courtiers:** With drooping wings, ye cupids come
(words repeated)
And scatter roses, *scatter, scatter roses* on her tomb.
Soft, soft and gentle as her heart.

1:30 5:31 Keep here, *here* your watch;
Keep here, here, keep here your watch,
and never, *never, never,* part.

Colored type indicates words treated with word painting.

4 The Rise of Instrumental Music

The development of instrumental music—music without words, music that does not depend on words—counts as one of the most far-reaching contributions of composers in the early Baroque period. Broadly speaking, we can trace instrumental music to three main sources.

Dance, the first of these sources, is one we have already discussed. In the Baroque period dance received a special impetus from opera, the genre that most fascinated people at the time. The reason is that opera was firmly linked to ballet, as we have seen in *Dido and Aeneas.* Musicians, especially in France, the center of ballet at the time, would put together sets of dances selected from operas or ballets. These dance **suites,** as they were called—groups of dances—could then be played by an orchestra and enjoyed apart from an actual stage performance.

Composers also wrote many dances and suites for harpsichord. These are "stylized" dances (see page 89), pieces written in the style or the form of dance music but intended for listening rather than dancing, for mental rather than physical pleasure.

- *Virtuosity* was the second source from which composers of instrumental music drew. As long as instruments have existed there have surely been virtuoso players ready to show them off—and audiences ready to applaud the show. But the art of early virtuosos was improvised and scarcely ever written down; only in the sixteenth and seventeenth centuries was some of their art incorporated systematically into written-out compositions. Even then, not all the virtuosity on which the compositions depended for their effect was notated. Much was left to be improvised, and so modern performers often have to play a good deal more than what appears in the old scores.

Even that vulgar and tavern music, which makes one man merry, another mad, strikes in me a deep fit of devotion, and a profound contemplation of the first Composer; there is something in it of divinity more than the ear discovers.

Physician-author Sir Thomas Browne, 1642

- *Vocal music* was the third source for instrumental music. More specifically, the principal technique of vocal music, imitative polyphony (imitation), was transferred to the instrumental medium. In fact, this happened already in the Renaissance, which developed several instrumental genres by modeling on vocal music in this way. Each genre consists of a series of points of imitation (see pages 78, 80) built on different motives, like a motet or a madrigal.

From these genres developed the characteristic polyphonic genre of the Baroque era, the **fugue.** A typical fugue uses only one theme throughout—like a single gigantic point of imitation—and often treats that theme with a considerable display of contrapuntal ingenuity and learning. The art of improvising and writing fugues was practiced especially by keyboard players: organists and harpsichordists. We will discuss fugue more fully in Chapter 9.

Vocal music influenced instrumental music in another way as well. It gave instrumentalists a fund of materials they could use as the basis for sets of **variations**—that is, sectional pieces in which each section repeats certain musical elements while others change around them.

Girolamo Frescobaldi (1583–1643)

The three main sources of instrumental music are all evident in the keyboard works of Girolamo Frescobaldi. Frescobaldi was the foremost organ virtuoso of the early seventeenth century, famed through much of Europe for his expressive and even extravagant improvising and composition. Organist of St. Peter's in Rome, he was an influential teacher, and his influence reached far beyond his own pupils. A century later Johann Sebastian Bach—keyboard virtuoso in his own right and composer of an immense body of organ and harpsichord works—carefully studied Frescobaldi's music.

We will hear Frescobaldi's music on an organ specially modeled on an instrument of his own time. The player employs four different *registrations,* that is, different combinations of the organ's many sets of pipes: See page 44. Frescobaldi's works represent several distinct genres:

- **Toccatas,** free-formed pieces meant to capture the spirit of Frescobaldi's own improvisation (*toccata* means "touched" in Italian, as in the touching of keys);

- **Canzonas,** more rigorously organized works emphasizing imitative texture—the ancestors of later fugues;

- Stylized dances, formed of two phrases each, one or both of them repeated to yield the pattern **a a b** or **a a b b** (for similar Renaissance patterns, see page 88); these dances are sometimes grouped together in small suites; and

- Sets of variations on melodic or harmonic patterns borrowed from vocal music.

Girolamo Frescobaldi

GIROLAMO FRESCOBALDI
Suite (Canzona, Balletto, Corrente, and Passacaglia) (1627–1637)

19-22

LISTEN

Frescobaldi, Suite

0:00 **Canzona**
0:27 new theme

0:00 **Balletto a**
0:08 **a**
0:16 (0:30) **b b**

0:00 **Corrente a**
0:10 **a**
0:21 (0:36) **b b**

0:00 **Passacaglia**
0:14 Variation 2
1:37 Variation 14

Frescobaldi's Balletto, Corrente, and Passacaglia is a miniature suite made up of two short dance movements followed by a set of variations. We introduce it, as Frescobaldi himself might have done, with the opening section of one of his canzonas.

19 *Canzona* This piece opens with a point of imitation (see page 80) using a theme that begins with long leaps followed by running sixteenth notes:

After four entries of this theme the music comes to a cadence. Then a new theme enters at the top of the texture, this one marked by three repeated notes at its start. Frescobaldi immediately combines the second theme in counterpoint with the first, pitting the two against each other until he brings the music to a solid cadence.

20, 21 *Balletto and Corrente* Each of these dance movements consists of two phrases, both of which are repeated: **a a b b.** Careful listening reveals that the two dances are related, especially by their bass lines:

While sharing a bass line, however, the dances also contrast strongly in their meters, the first duple, the second triple. Such metrical contrast from one dance to the next was a basic principle of suites from the late Renaissance on. (Compare the pavane and galliard on page 88.)

22 *Passacaglia* This mellifluous term (pronounced *pas-sa-cáhl-ya*) refers to a set of variations on a brief series of chords and also the bass line associated with the chords. Both the harmonies and the bass line were at first associated with vocal music. Because of their repeating bass lines, **passacaglias** bear a close kinship to slower ostinato pieces like "Dido's Lament." But usually the bass line of a passacaglia is repeated less strictly than is the ostinato of Purcell's work; it can even disappear entirely, leaving only the general chord progression to mark the variations. New at the time of Frescobaldi, the passacaglia remained popular a century later in the age of Bach and Handel.

The bass line of this passacaglia (and many others) runs in its simplest form something like the example to the right. Its length determines the length of each variation: four measures of fairly quick triple meter. (Get used to the main beat of the piece and then count **1** 2 3|**2** 2 3|**3** 2 3|**4** 2 3.) You can hear the bass line in its original, descending form in the first four measures, the theme, and many times more thereafter. Already in the second variation, however, and several times later, Frescobaldi plays a trick on the listener, composing an *ascending* bass line instead of the descending one while maintaining essentially the same progression of harmonies.

Violins are varnished and sun dried in Cremona, a little town in northern Italy famous for its violin makers since the 1600s. Violinist-composers such as Vivaldi (see page 132) wrote for instruments by Antonio Stradivarius and other master craftsmen. See page 128.

Frescobaldi seems able to milk endless variety from this simple material; this facility is the essence of skillful composing of variations. He is especially fond of coloring his music with piquant flashes of unexpected half steps, or **chromaticism** (especially piquant on this historical organ). At the same time he devises many different rhythmic patterns, some with fast running notes, others slower, some even and flowing, some dotted and jaunty.

Listen also for one more clever twist near the end of the movement: Frescobaldi changes key, or modulates, and at the same time shifts from major to minor mode. There are eighteen quick variations in all; the last five of them take place in this new key.

The instrumental music of the early seventeenth century was the quiet precursor to an explosion of new instrumental styles and genres in the late Baroque era. We go on to discuss this in Unit III, after an introductory "Prelude" chapter dealing with aspects of the history and culture of the time.

Web: *Research and test your understanding of early Baroque music at* **<bedfordstmartins.com/listen>.**

GLOBAL PERSPECTIVES 3

Ostinato Forms

32, 33

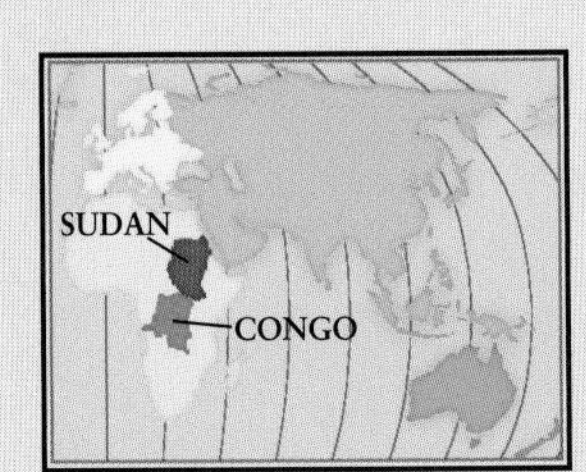

Though we borrow the term *ostinato* from Italian Baroque music, the technique is much older than the seventeenth century and is dispersed around the globe. The organizational principle at stake is, indeed, basic: Set up a brief repeating musical unit and use it as the foundation for other more varied melodies and harmonies.

Musical forms built according to this principle come in a wide variety of shapes and patterns. We have already begun to appreciate this variety in comparing "Dido's Lament" by Purcell with Frescobaldi's Passacaglia: The first presents a free-flowing melody over an unchanging bass line, while the second rings changes on an underlying harmonic pattern.

African Ostinatos

Nowhere in the world is ostinato form more prominent, or practiced with a richer array of techniques, genres, and instruments, than in Africa. From northern African nations, with their traditions of troubadour-like singers accompanying themselves on a single instrument, all the way to South Africa, with its electrified, rock'n'roll–derived Township Jive—up and down the continent, ostinato forms multiply in fascinating variety. (Rock itself is a great repository of ostinato forms.)

A Sudanese lyre (compare with the ancient Greek lyre on page 7).

On our CD we hear two examples of African ostinato form, one from the Sudan, a nation lying along the Nile River to the south of Egypt, and the other from the Mbuti pygmies of the rainforests of Congo in central Africa.

A Minstrel's Song In the first, Sudanese excerpt we hear a virtuosic singer-reciter named Doogus Idris accompanying himself on a plucked-string instrument called a *jangar,* a type of lyre. Two upright bars extend from a resonating sound box and are fastened to a crossbar at the top; five strings are stretched between the crossbar and the bottom of the sound box. Traditions of solo song accompanied by the lyre reach back very far in history in the cultures around the Mediterranean Sea, whether in Europe, the Middle East, or Africa. Homer's *Iliad* and *Odyssey* were sung to the lyre, but for some reason in most of Europe the lyre has not survived to the present day.

In Africa, the singers in these traditions fulfill a wide variety of social roles. They sing the praises of powerful leaders, narrate historical or legendary events, contribute to social rituals such as weddings, or simply provide informal entertainment. In all these functions they are not so different from the troubadours and trouvères of medieval France (see page 62).

In our example, the singer declaims in lively fashion a song about a young man and woman in love and the dowry he must pay to have her as his bride:

Doia, ben uli Kana	Kana, he comes!
Kaya ba cuzon nabore	Kaya desires her brown lover;
turi koleth Ebasel gnalek	she admired the knife on his shoulder.
bungur ley agamat ben	When he arrived at the house, he said:
ering-ei-yama kol mal.	"I need a large goat."

To accompany himself the singer plays a brief ostinato on the jangar. He alters it at times from a chordal strumming to a more melodic presentation—treating it, in other words, with the same freedom

Frescobaldi used in altering the bass line and texture of his Passacaglia. But the ostinato never loses its clear, repetitious identity.

Over this rigid scaffolding, Doogus Idris sings a relatively free melody. He presents the same stanza of words twice, repeating many individual words along the way: Listen at 0:53 on track 32 when, after a brief break for the jangar alone, he begins the whole text over again. Through each stanza his melody gradually and gracefully falls from the high pitches at its beginning to the low cadence at its end.

Pygmy Polyphony Since it was first recorded in the 1950s, Mbuti communal singing has become famous for its delicate and complex polyphony. You may recognize the style, even if you have not heard recordings of pygmies before, since it has often been imitated by pop and world-beat singers such as Madonna and the group Zap Mama.

Pygmy polyphony is created in improvised group singing, sometimes in rituals central to the society, sometimes to accompany work, sometimes for simple pleasure and relaxation. It involves a technique common to many kinds of African music: *interlocking ostinatos.* In a pygmy chorus, various voices form an intricate, repetitive texture by singing over and over again their own short melodic lines—often only one or two notes—in quick alternation. (This technique may remind us of the *hocket* we encountered in the isorhythmic motet of the Middle Ages; see page 69.) The overall effect is of a multistranded, hypnotically recycling ostinato. This choral ostinato can be savored on its own or else, as in our example, used as the foundation for freer melodies of lead singers.

A Hunting Song for Chorus Two exclamations for the whole chorus announce the beginning of a song describing the bravery and daring of an elephant hunt. At first, we hear no clear ostinato. Instead, the two lead singers alternate prominent melodic phrases while, underneath them, we can hear the chorus singing softly—almost murmuring—an indistinct, ostinatolike melody.

Then something marvelous happens: At about 0:47 on track 33 the individual melodic motives of a polyphonic ostinato begin to crystallize in the chorus. We hear the polyphony taking shape. (How many distinct components of the ostinato can you make out?) By 1:30 the choral ostinato is fully formed and clearly articulated; it continues through to the end of the song (not heard here) underneath the soloists.

The singing is underlaid throughout by the simplest of instrumental accompaniments: two sticks struck together to mark the beat. The Mbuti rarely employ more elaborate instruments in their choral singing, though in other, individual contexts they regularly play on drums, flutes, musical bows, and other instruments.

This song was recorded in the mid-1950s by Colin Turnbull, a British anthropologist who was among the first to study the pygmies. He described their society poetically and lovingly in a book still read today, *The Forest People,* but he didn't give the names of the singers of this song.

Mbuti villagers, singing and dancing to tall drums

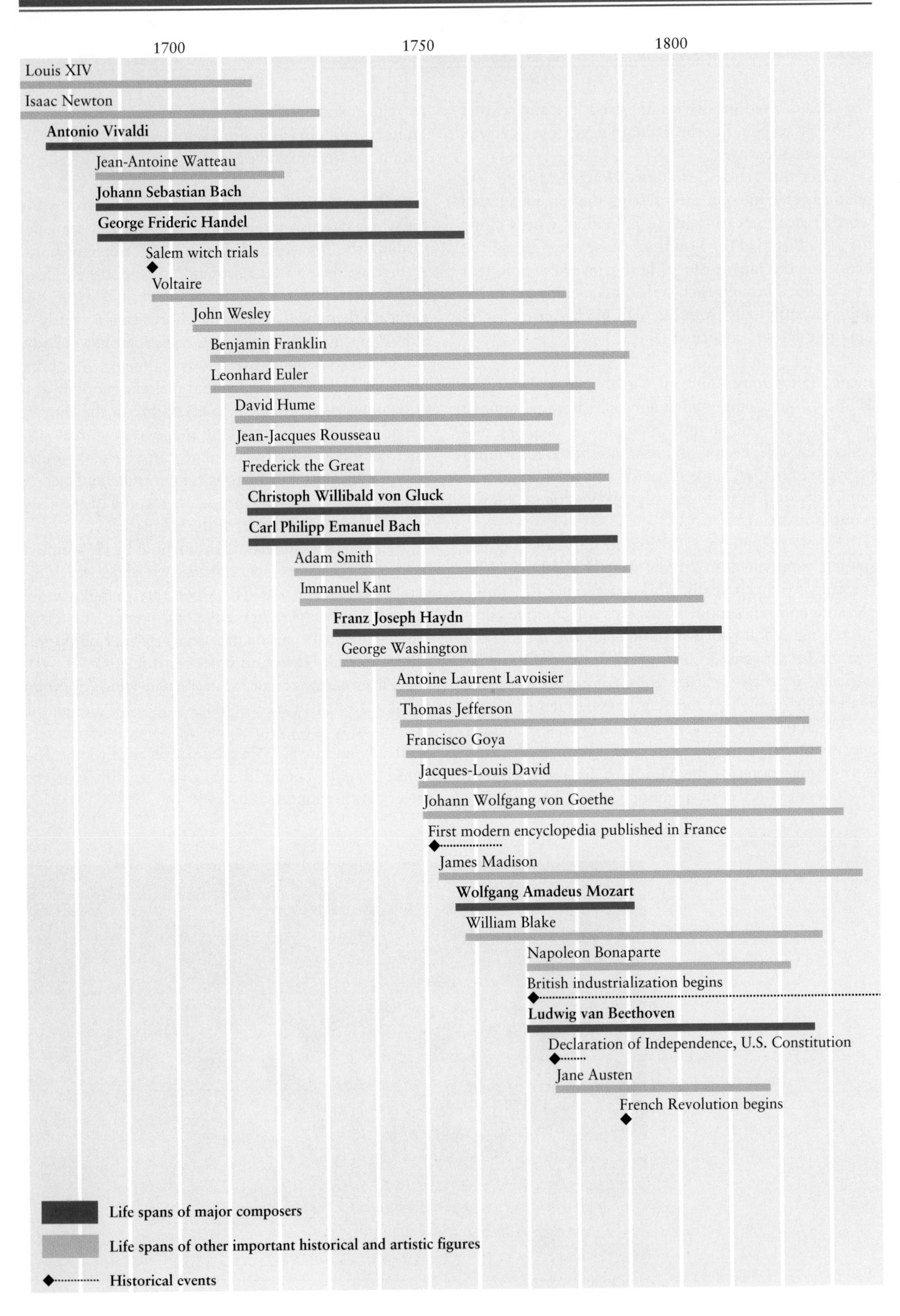
1700
1750
1800
Louis XIV
Isaac Newton
Antonio Vivaldi
Jean-Antoine Watteau
Johann Sebastian Bach
George Frideric Handel
Salem witch trials
Voltaire
John Wesley
Benjamin Franklin
Leonhard Euler
David Hume
Jean-Jacques Rousseau
Frederick the Great
Christoph Willibald von Gluck
Carl Philipp Emanuel Bach
Adam Smith
Immanuel Kant
Franz Joseph Haydn
George Washington
Antoine Laurent Lavoisier
Thomas Jefferson
Francisco Goya
Jacques-Louis David
Johann Wolfgang von Goethe
First modern encyclopedia published in France
James Madison
Wolfgang Amadeus Mozart
William Blake
Napoleon Bonaparte
British industrialization begins
Ludwig van Beethoven
Declaration of Independence, U.S. Constitution
Jane Austen
French Revolution begins
Life spans of major composers
Life spans of other important historical and artistic figures
Historical events

UNIT III

The Eighteenth Century

The first body of music this book takes up in some detail is the music of the eighteenth century, the earliest music we hear regularly in concerts and on the radio. The eighteenth century in music covers two very different style periods: the late Baroque era and the era of Viennese Classicism. In the following pages we will need to clarify the differences between these periods and their music.

In spite of these differences, the music of the eighteenth century can be thought of as a unit. The reason is not a matter of musical style, at least not directly, important as style may be. Rather, it has to do with a certain quality of musical expression, a certain objectivity in the feelings this music seems to express or depict. Even when it is powerful and moving, it keeps its distance from the listener. Music of the nineteenth century is more demonstrative, more personal, more obviously intense; this music is called "romantic." In drawing the broadest distinctions, then, it is fair to put Baroque and Classical music on one side, Romantic music on the other. Romantic music often seems to want to share—even impose—feelings. Eighteenth-century music seems rather to demonstrate feelings.

A fair distinction, and also a functional one, it seems. In one large American metropolitan area, not long ago, two radio stations used to broadcast what they called "good music" around the clock; and most of the time, eighteenth-century music was played on one of the stations, nineteenth-century music on the other. On some basic level, there must be a distinction between the music of these two centuries; these stations, their advertisers, and their audiences were responding to it. Some listeners are temperamentally attuned to one kind of music, some to the other. Probably still other listeners punch buttons on the car radio depending on their mood of the moment.

The social and economic conditions under which the music was originally produced are behind this broad distinction in expressive quality. In our "Prelude" chapters, Chapters 8 and 11, we look at the cultural background and the social setting of eighteenth-century music, and suggest how these factors influenced musical style and expression. The other chapters in this unit look into specific works by the leading late Baroque composers Bach, Handel, and Vivaldi, and the Classical composers Haydn and Mozart.

CHAPTER 8

Prelude The Late Baroque Period

Music from the period of approximately 1600 to 1750 is usually referred to as "baroque," a term borrowed from art history. Art historians themselves borrowed the term from seventeenth-century jewelers, who applied it to large pearls of irregular shape. At one time, then, Baroque art was considered imperfect, bizarre, or at least erratic. With changing taste over the centuries, however, what was originally a negative implication has turned positive.

And over the last fifty years, with the help of recordings, Baroque music has grown more and more popular. Instruments of the period have been revived to play it, among them the harpsichord, the recorder, and a special high-pitched trumpet without valves. (Some of these instruments were discussed on pages 38–45.) Most of the Baroque music heard today dates from the eighteenth century—from around 1700 to 1750, a subperiod sometimes classified as the "late Baroque." Johann Sebastian Bach and George Frideric Handel were the greatest composers of this period, and among their most important contemporaries were Alessandro Scarlatti and Antonio Vivaldi in Italy, François Couperin and Jean Philippe Rameau in France, Domenico Scarlatti (the son of Alessandro) in Spain, and Georg Philipp Telemann in Germany.

1 Absolutism and the Age of Science

"Baroque" is a period term used by art historians and musicologists. Historians are more likely to speak of the period from 1600 to 1750 as the Age of Absolutism, a time when the doctrine of the "divine right of kings" ensured the absolute rule of "God-chosen" monarchs. This was the time when Louis XIV of France became the most powerful monarch in all of European history, and also one of the most ruthless. The pomp and splendor of his court were emulated by a host of lesser kings and nobles.

Students of the history of ideas, on the other hand, speak of this as the Age of Science. In this era, the telescope and the microscope revealed their first secrets; Newton and Leibniz invented calculus; Newton developed his laws of

Louis XIV's palace of Versailles, with a procession of carriages arriving in the great courtyard. Note the formal gardens and canal.

mechanics and the theory of gravity. These discoveries stimulated both technology and philosophy—not only the formal philosophy of the great empiricist thinkers Descartes, Locke, and Hume, but also philosophy in a more informal sense. People began to think about ordinary matters in a new way, affected by the newly acquired habits of scientific experimentation and proof. The mental climate stimulated by science significantly affected the music and the art we call Baroque.

Absolutism and science were two of the most vital currents that defined life in the seventeenth and early eighteenth centuries. The result was an interesting dualism that can be traced throughout Baroque art: pomp and extravagance on the one hand, system and calculation on the other. The same dualism can be traced in Baroque music.

Art in the service of royalty: a *very* idealized portrait of Louis XIV by the greatest sculptor of the day, Gianlorenzo Bernini (1598–1680).

Art and Absolutism

Though there had always been royalty in Europe who practiced the arts of peace as well as the arts of war, sponsorship of the arts rose to new heights in the Baroque era. In earlier years, the artistic glories of the Renaissance were supported by powerful merchant-princes, such as the Medici family in Florence, who were determined to add luster to the city-states they ruled. But never before the seventeenth century did one state loom so large in Europe as did France under Louis XIV (1638–1715), the so-called Sun King.

Design for an opera stage set by G. G. Bibiena. This astonishing scene was intended for an opera at the court of Dresden in Germany.

All of French life orbited around the royal court, like planets, comets, and cosmic dust in the solar system. Pomp and ceremony were carried to extreme lengths: The king's *levée*—his getting-up-in-the-morning rite—involved dozens of functionaries and routines lasting two hours. Artists of all kinds were supported lavishly, so long as their work symbolized the majesty of the state (and the state, in Louis's famous remark, "is me"—"*l'état, c'est moi*").

The influence of this monarch and his image extended far beyond France, for other European princes and dukes envied his absolute rule and did everything they could to match it. Especially in Germany—which was not a united country, like France, but a patchwork of several hundred political units—rulers vied with one another in supporting artists who built, painted, and sang to their glory. Artistic life in Europe was kept alive for many generations by this sort of patronage, and the brilliance and grandeur of much Baroque art derives from its political function.

Art was to impress, even to stupefy. Thus Louis XIV built the most enormous palace in history, Versailles, with over three hundred rooms, including an eighty-yard-long Hall of Mirrors, and great formal gardens extending for miles. Many nobles and prelates built little imitation-Versailles palaces, among them the archbishop of Würzburg, whose magnificent residence was built in Bach's lifetime. The rooms were decorated by the Venetian artist Giovanni Battista Tiepolo (1696–1770), a master of Baroque ceiling painting.

Looking up at the ceiling shown on page 115, and trying to imagine its true dimensions, we are dazzled by figures in excited motion, caught up in great gusts of wind that whirl them out of the architectural space. Ceiling painting provides a vivid example of the extravagant side of the Baroque dualism.

The Music of Absolutism

Just as painting and architecture could glorify rulers through color and designs extending through space, music could glorify by sound extending through time. The nobility demanded horn players for their ceremonial hunts, trumpeters for their battles, and orchestras for balls and entertainments. They required smaller groups of musicians for *Tafelmusik* ("table music"), background music for their lengthy banquets. A special "celebratory" or "festive" orchestra featuring military instruments—trumpets and drums—was used to pay homage to kings and princes; by extension, it also glorified God, the "King of Kings," as he is called in Handel's "Hallelujah" Chorus. The words sung by the chorus in this famous work praise God, but the accompanying orchestra with its trumpets also pays splendid homage to King George II of England (see pages 158–59).

The main musical vehicle of Baroque absolutism was opera. Opera today is an expensive entertainment in which a drama is presented with music and elaborate stage spectacle. So it was in the Baroque era. The stage set shown opposite was created by a member of the Bibiena family, the foremost set designers of the time. It conveys the majestic heights and distances of an ideal Baroque palace by means of perspective, though the stage was actually quite shallow. The figures gesture grandly, but they are dwarfed by pasteboard architecture that seems to whirl as dizzily as does the painted architecture on Tiepolo's ceiling.

Baroque grandeur: a ceiling painting by Giovanni Battista Tiepolo (1696–1770). The oval measures 30 feet by 60 feet.

One aspect of Baroque opera is unlike opera today: The stories were allegorical tributes to the glory and supposed virtue of those who paid for them. For example, one favorite Baroque opera story tells of the Roman Emperor Titus, who survives a complicated plot on his life and then magnanimously forgives the plotters. This story was set to music by dozens of different court composers. It told courtiers that if they opposed their king, he might well excuse them out of the godlike goodness of his heart (for he claimed to rule by divine right). But it also reminded them that he was an absolute ruler—a modern Roman tyrant—who could do exactly the reverse if he pleased. Operas flattered princes while at the same time stressing their power and, not incidentally, their wealth.

Art and Theatricality

Opera was invented in Italy around the year 1600. Indeed, opera counts as Italy's great contribution to the seventeenth century's golden age of the theater. This century saw Shakespeare and his followers in England, Corneille and Racine in France, and Lope de Vega and Calderón in Spain.

The very term *theatrical* suggests some of the extravagance and exaggeration we associate with the Baroque. But the theater is first and foremost a place where strong emotion is on display, and it was this more than anything else that fueled the Baroque fascination with the theater. The emotionality that we generally sense in Baroque art has a theatrical quality; this is true even of much Baroque painting. Compare Raphael's calm Renaissance Madonna on page 47 with the early Baroque Madonna by Guercino. Jesus seems to be falling out of the picture as he twists toward his mother; she gestures in theatrical fashion, clenching with one hand while pointing delicately with the other; and the stagey lighting contrasts bright patches of flesh with dark shadows.

Madonna and Child with the Young St. John the Baptist, by Giovanni Francesco Barbieri (1591–1666), known as Il Guercino.

View of Delft, by Jan Vermeer (1632–1675)

Science and the Arts

All this may seem some distance away from the observatories of Galileo and Kepler, and the laboratories where Harvey discovered the circulation of the blood and Leeuwenhoek first viewed microorganisms through a microscope. And indeed, the scientific spirit of the time had its most obvious effect on artists who were outside the realm of absolutism. The Dutch were citizens of free cities, not subjects of despotic kings. In Jan Vermeer's painting of his own city, Delft, the incredibly precise depiction of detail reflects the new interest in scientific observation. The painter's analysis of light is worthy of Huygens and Newton, fathers of the science of optics. There is something scientific, too, in the serene objectivity of this scene.

Man's control over nature is also symbolized by Baroque formal gardens. Today, landscape architecture is not usually regarded as one of the major arts, but it was very important in the age of the Baroque palace. Baroque gardens regulate nature strictly according to geometrical plans. Bushes are clipped, lawns tailored, and streams channeled, all under the watchful eye of big statues of Venus, Apollo, Hercules, and the rest, lined up in rows. Such gardens spell out the new vision of nature brought to heel by human reason and calculation.

Below the surface, furthermore, science is at work in even the most grandiose and dazzling of Baroque artistic efforts. The perspective of Tiepolo's ceiling painting or Bibiena's stage set depends on the use of very sophisticated geometry. (Bibiena published a manual detailing the mathematics behind his scene designs.) This dual influence of extravagance and scientism, of the splendid and the schematic, can also be traced in Baroque music.

The Age of Absolutism and the Age of Science converge: Louis XIV founding the Academy of Sciences.

Science and Music

Various aspects of Baroque music reflect the new scientific attitudes that developed in the seventeenth century. Scales were tuned, or "tempered," more precisely than ever before, so that for the first time all the twenty-four major and minor keys were available to composers. Their interest in exploring this resource is evident from collections such as Bach's *The Well-Tempered Clavier,* containing preludes and fugues in every key. Harmony was systematized so that chords followed one another in a logical and functional way.

Regularity became the ideal in rhythm, and in musical form—the distribution of sections of music in time—we find a tendency toward clearly ordered, even schematic plans. Whether consciously or not, composers seem to have viewed musical time in a quasi-scientific way. They divided it up and filled it systematically, almost in the spirit of the landscape architects who devised Baroque formal gardens.

In the important matter of musical expression, too, science was a powerful influence. Starting with the philosopher-mathematician René Descartes, thinkers applied the new rational methods to the analysis and classification of human emotions. It had always been felt that music has a special power to express and arouse emotions. Now it seemed that there was a basis for systematizing—and hence maximizing—this power.

Thus scientifically inclined music theorists compiled checklists of musical devices and techniques corresponding to each of the emotions. Grief, for example, was projected with a specific kind of melodic motive and a specific kind of rhythm—even with a specific key. By working steadily with these devices and saturating their pieces with them, composers believed they could achieve the maximum musical expressivity.

The emotions of Hope and Fear, as represented in a Baroque scientific treatise. Like composers of the time, the artist felt that feelings could be isolated and depicted in the abstract.

2 Musical Life in the Early Eighteenth Century

The eighteenth century was a great age for the crafts—the age of Chippendale in furniture, Paul Revere in silver, Stradivarius in violin making, to name just a few. Though attitudes were changing, composing music was also regarded as a craft. The Romantic idea of the composer—the lonely genius working over each masterpiece as a long labor of love expressing an individual personality—was still far in the future. Baroque composers were more likely to think of themselves as servants with masters to satisfy. They were artisans with jobs, rather than artists with a calling, and they produced music on demand to fill a particular requirement.

This is why many Baroque pieces seem relatively anonymous, as it were. They are not so much unique masterpieces as satisfactory examples of their style and genre, of which there are many other equally satisfactory examples.

There were three main institutions where composers could make a living by practicing their craft. In order of increasing glamour, these were the church, the court, and the opera house.

The church. In the cathedrals, monasteries, and town churches of the Baroque era, the general assumption was that the organists or choirmasters would compose their own music, then play and conduct it. Organists had to improvise or write out music to accompany especially solemn places in the church services. They played long pieces to see the congregation out when the service was over.

At large institutions, important occasions called for elaborate music scored for chorus, soloists, and instruments: a Catholic Mass for the installation of an archbishop, or a Lutheran Church cantata for the anniversary of the Reformation. Church musicians were also responsible for training the boys who sang in their choirs, often in special choir schools.

The court. Under the patronage of kings or members of the lesser nobility, a musician was employed on the same terms as a court painter, a master of the hunt, or a head chef. Though musicians had to work entirely at the whim of their masters, they could nevertheless count on a fairly secure existence, a steady demand for their services, and a pension.

Naturally, conditions varied from court to court, depending on the ruler's taste. For some, music was a good deal less interesting than hunting or banqueting. Others could not have enough of it. Frederick the Great of Prussia was a very keen flutist, so at his court concertos and sonatas for flute were composed at an especially healthy rate (see page xiv). He wrote many himself.

Court musicians kept in better touch with musical developments than church musicians, since they were required to travel with their employers. There were extended trips to major cities, where diplomacy was eased along by music they composed for the occasion.

The opera house. Although many opera houses were attached to courts, others were maintained by entrepreneurs in major cities. (The public opera house existed before the public concert hall; in the Baroque era, public concerts were not a regular feature of musical life.) Audiences were alert to the most exciting new singers, and it was part of the composer's job to keep the singers well supplied with music that showed off their talents. Composers traditionally conducted their own operas, sitting at the harpsichord.

The revival of an older opera—usually because a favorite singer liked his or her part in it—was nearly always the occasion for massive recomposition, because another singer might want *her* part redone, too. If the opera's original

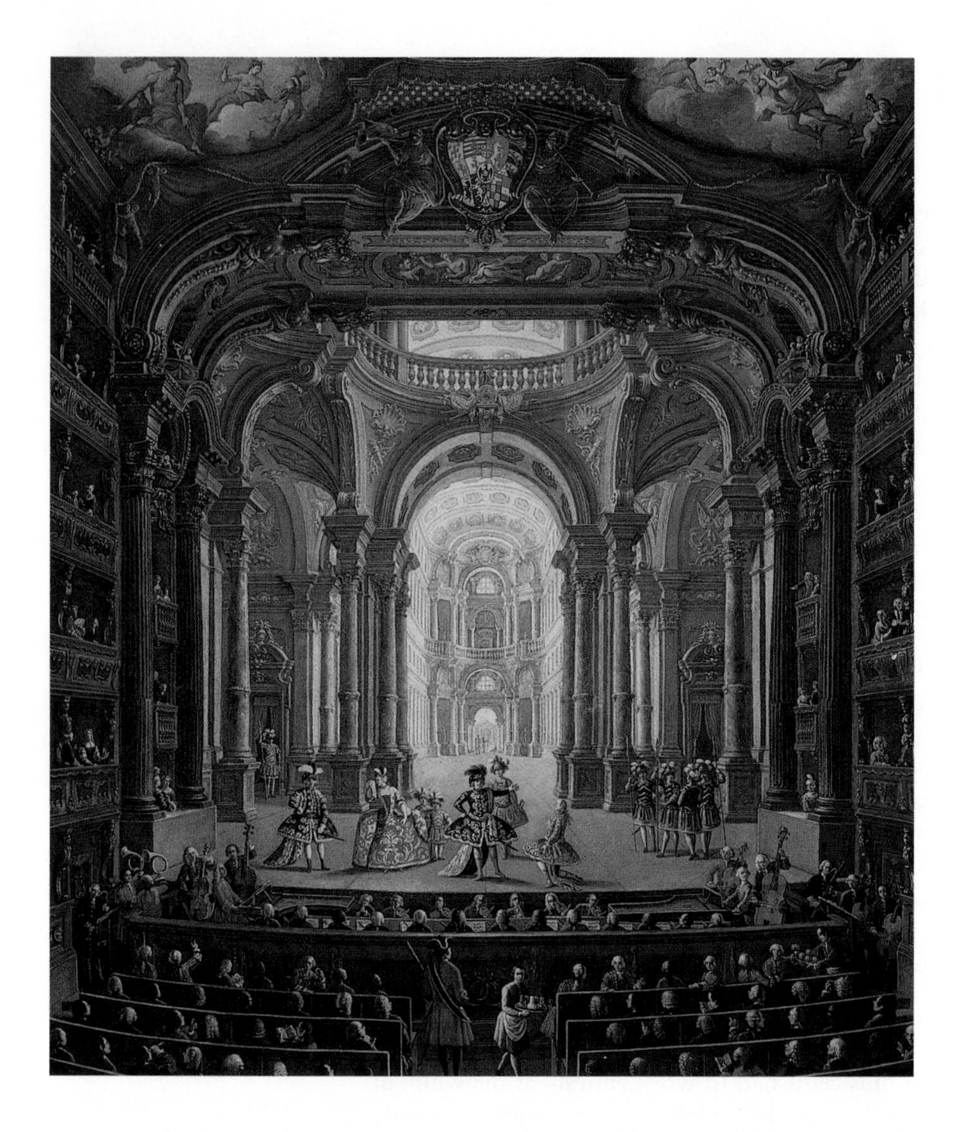

A Baroque opera performance (Turin, 1740). The stage set represents a great palace hall; the characters are striking various extravagant attitudes. Note the orchestra, a boy selling oranges, and a security guard.

composer had moved to the next town, other musicians would have no hesitation about rewriting (or replacing) some of the music. It was an exciting, unpredictable life, promising great rewards as well as humiliating reverses.

The life stories of the two greatest composers of the late Baroque period show a good deal about the interaction between musicians, the patrons who supported them, and the institutions that required music. Johann Sebastian Bach labored as a church organist, a court musician, and then a major composer-administrator for the Lutheran Church. George Frideric Handel, who also had a court position, became an independent opera composer and opera promoter. Their biographies are given on pages 138 and 155.

3 Style Features of Late Baroque Music

If any one characteristic can be singled out as central to the music of the late Baroque period, it would be its thorough, methodical quality. After listening to a short Baroque piece, or to one section of a longer piece, we may be surprised to realize, first, how soon all the basic material is set forth, and second, how much of the music after that consists of inspired repetition and variation.

It is as though the composers had set out to draw their material out to the maximum extent and wring it dry, as it were.

Indeed, the shorter pieces we will be examining in Chapters 9 and 10—pieces like Contrapunctus 4 from Bach's *The Art of Fugue* and the aria "La giustizia" from Handel's opera *Julius Caesar*—contain little if any notable contrast in rhythm, dynamics, melody, texture, or tone color (see pages 141 and 153). Baroque composers preferred thoroughness and homogeneity.

With longer pieces, Baroque composers tended to break them up into blocks of music that contrast with one another in obvious ways, but are still homogeneous in themselves. This is the case with Bach's *Brandenburg* Concerto No. 5, for example, where the orchestral and solo sections contrast clearly enough. Within each orchestral or solo section, however, things are usually quite regular (page 135).

Rhythm

Baroque music is brimming with energy, and this energy is channeled into a highly regular, determined sort of motion. Like jazz and other popular music, Baroque music gets its rhythmic vitality by playing off distinctive rhythms against a very steady beat. The meter nearly always stands out, emphasized by certain instruments in the ensemble. Most characteristic of these "marking-time" instruments is the busy, crisp harpsichord.

Another common feature that hammers home the beat is the so-called **walking bass,** a bass part that moves in absolutely even notes, usually eighths or quarters. In the Air from Bach's Suite No. 3 in D (see page 146), the bass keeps going for 138 "walking" eighth notes, plus 8 sixteenth notes and one half note (at the final cadence, of course). Rhythmic variety in the upper instruments is heard in reference to absolute regularity below.

Attentive listening will also reveal another aspect of regularity in the steady *harmonic rhythm*—that is, a Baroque piece tends to change chords at every measure or at some other set interval. (This must not be taken absolutely literally, but it is the tendency, and it is often the case.)

Dynamics

Another steady feature of Baroque music is dynamics. Composers rarely used loud and soft indications (*f* and *p*) in their scores, and once a dynamic was chosen or set, it remained at about the same level for the whole section—sometimes even for the whole composition.

Neither in the Baroque period nor in any other, however, have performers played or sung music at an absolutely even level of dynamics. Instrumentalists made expressive changes in dynamics to bring out rhythmic accents, and singers certainly sang high notes louder than low ones. But composers did not go much beyond natural variations of these kinds. Gradual buildups from soft to loud, and the like, were rarely used.

Abrupt dynamic contrasts were preferred—again, between fairly large sections of a longer piece, or whole movements. A clear *forte/piano* contrast is built into the concerto genre, with its alternating blocks of music for the full orchestra and for one or more quieter solo instruments. When, exceptionally, a Baroque composer changed dynamics in the middle of a section or a phrase of music, he could count on the great surprise—even the amazement—of his listeners. A famous sudden *forte* in Handel's "Hallelujah" Chorus has been known to electrify the audience, to bring them to their feet (page 158).

We spoke earlier of a characteristic dualism between extravagance and order that can be detected in various aspects of Baroque culture (page 113). The methodical, regular quality of Baroque musical style that we are tracing here clearly reflects the orderly, quasi-scientific side of this dualism. But Baroque music can also be highly dramatic, bizarre, or stupendous—a reflection of the other side of the dualism. Indeed, the magnificent momentary effects that occur occasionally in Handel and Bach are all the stronger because of the regular music around them.

Tone Color

Tone color in Baroque music presents something of a contradiction. On the one hand, the early part of the period evinced a new interest in sonority, and the end of it echoed with some very sophisticated sounds: Handel's imaginative orchestration in his operas, Bach's notably sensitive writing for the flute, and the refined harpsichord textures developed by several generations of composers in France. There are distinctive and attractive "Baroque sounds" that we do not hear in other periods: the harpsichord, the bright Baroque organ, the virtuoso recorder, and what we will call the "festive" Baroque orchestra, featuring high trumpets and drums.

On the other hand, a significant amount of music was written to allow for multiple or alternative performing forces. Thus it was a regular practice to designate music for harpsichord *or* organ, for violin *or* oboe *or* flute. Bach wrote a sonata for two flutes and rewrote it as a sonata for viola da gamba (a cello-like instrument) and harpsichord. Handel took solo arias and duets and rewrote them as choruses for his oratorio *Messiah*. In the last analysis, then, it seems the original tone color was often not critical.

The Baroque Orchestra

The core of the Baroque orchestra was a group of instruments of the violin family. The famous orchestra maintained by Louis XIV in the late seventeenth century was called "The Twenty-Four Violins of the King"; it consisted of six violins, twelve violas, and six cellos. A great deal of Baroque music was written for such an orchestra or a similar one—what would today be called a "string orchestra": violins, violas, cellos, and one or two bass viols.

To this was added a keyboard instrument as continuo (see page 124)—usually a harpsichord in secular music and an organ in church music.

Woodwinds and brass instruments were sometimes added to the string orchestra, too, but there was no fixed complement, as was to be the case later. For special occasions of a festive nature—music celebrating a

Eighteenth-century instruments: flute, violin, lute (back view), and *cornetto*—a wooden instrument played with a trumpet-like mouthpiece, with the pitch controlled by finger holes, as in a flute.

military victory, for example, or Christmas music ordered for a great cathedral—composers augmented the "basic Baroque orchestra" with trumpets or French horns, timpani, bassoons, and oboes and/or flutes. This "festive orchestra" has a particularly grand, open, and brilliant sound.

THE BASIC BAROQUE ORCHESTRA
as in Vivaldi's Concerto in G (page 130)

STRINGS	KEYBOARD
Violins (divided into two groups, called violins 1 and violins 2) Violas Cellos Bass viol (playing the same music as the cellos an octave lower)	Harpsichord or organ

THE FESTIVE BAROQUE ORCHESTRA
as in Bach's Orchestral Suite in D (page 145)

STRINGS	WOODWINDS	BRASS	PERCUSSION	KEYBOARD
Violins 1 Violins 2 Violas Cellos Bass viol	2 Oboes 1 Bassoon	3 Trumpets	2 Timpani (kettledrums)	Harpsichord or organ

Melody

Baroque melody tends toward complexity. Composers liked to push melodies to the very limits of ornateness and luxuriance. As a rule, the range of Baroque melodies is extended; they use many different rhythmic note values; they twist and turn in an intricate way as they reach high and low. It can be maintained that in the European classical tradition, the art of melody reached a high point in the late Baroque era, a point that has never been equaled since.

These long, intricate melodies, with their wealth of "decorations" added to the main direction of the line, are not easy to sing, however. They hardly ever fall into any simple pattern resembling a tune; even their appearance on the page seems to tell the story:

One easily recognized feature of Baroque melodies is their frequent use of sequence (see page 25; a sequence is shaded on the melody above). Baroque melodies repeatedly catch hold of a motive or some longer section of music and play it again and again at several pitch levels. Sequences provide Baroque music with one of its most effective means of forward motion.

Ornamentation

Not all melodies of the time are as ornate as the one shown above, however, and some, such as the simpler Baroque dances, are exceptions to the rule. On the other hand, the most highly prized art of the elite musicians of the era, opera singers, was improvising melodic extras in the arias they sang night after night in the theater. This practice is called **ornamentation.**

Before the present era of sound amplification, when volume does much of the work, audiences thrilled to brilliant, fast, very high (or very low) music played and especially improvised by singers and instrumentalists. This is still very much the case with jazz. In the Baroque era, enough improvisations were written down, as guides for musicians who were not the most imaginative, to give us some idea of the art of the great virtuosos—such as the singers Bordoni and Cuzzoni (page 157) and the violinist-composer Vivaldi (page 132). They

There is nothing uniquely Baroque about musical ornamentation. If you heard Mariah Carey at Superbowl XXXVI, you heard "The Star-Spangled Banner" sung with ornaments added, not absolutely "straight."

would spontaneously add all kinds of ornaments (jazz players would call them "riffs" or "licks") to whatever scores composers placed before them. Artists today have re-created Baroque ornamentation, or something like it; for a superb example, listen to Handel's aria "La giustizia," page 153.

Texture

The standard texture of Baroque music is polyphonic (or contrapuntal). Even many Baroque pieces that consist of just melody and bass count as contrapuntal because of the independent melodic quality of the bass. And large-scale pieces spin a web of contrapuntal lines filling every nook and cranny of musical spacetime. While cellos, bass viols, bassoons, and organ pedals play the lowest line, the other string instruments stake out their places in the middle, with oboes and flutes above them and the trumpets piercing their way up into the very highest reaches of the sound universe. The density achieved in this way is doubly impressive because the sounds feel alive—alive because they are all in motion, because they are all parts of moving contrapuntal lines.

Again, some exceptions should be noted to the standard polyphonic texture of Baroque music. Such are the homophonic orchestra sections (the *ritornellos*) in the concerto, and Bach's highly expressive harmonizations of old German hymns (chorales: see page 160). But it is no accident that these textures appear *within pieces that feature polyphony elsewhere.* The ritornello in Bach's *Brandenburg* Concerto No. 5 alternates with polyphony played by the solo flute, violin, and harpsichord (see page 135). The harmonized hymn in his Cantata No. 4 comes at the very end, where it has the effect of calming or settling the complex polyphony of the preceding music (see page 161).

The Continuo

Yet all this polyphony is supported by a solid scaffold of harmony. The central importance of harmony in Baroque music appears in the universal practice of the *basso continuo,* or just **continuo.**

The continuo is a bass part (the lowest part in polyphonic music) that is always linked to a series of chords. These chords are played by a harpsichord, organ, or lute as support or accompaniment for the important melodies in the other instruments. Indeed, we might say "mere accompaniment," for composers did not bother to write the chords out in detail, but only notated them in an abstract way by a numerical shorthand below the bass part.

This left continuo players with a good deal to do, even though their role was considered subsidiary. By reading the basso continuo part, the harpsichordist or organist would play along with the cellos or bassoons—this with the left hand, which "doubles" the bass line. But the right-hand chords could be played in many ways: high or low, widely or closely spaced, smoothly connected or not. A certain amount of quick, on-the-spot improvisation was (and still is) required to "realize" a continuo, that is, to derive actual chords from abstract numbers. Another name for continuo, **figured bass,** derives from this numerical shorthand.

Continuo part, as written: cello and harpsichord, left hand

Simple "realization" of chords: harpsichord

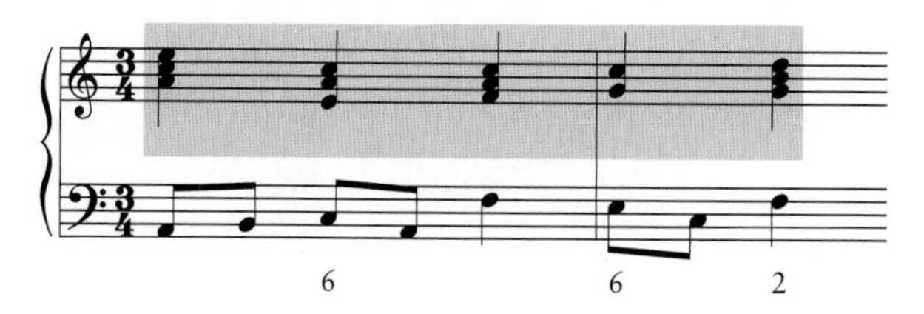

More ornate "realization": harpsichord

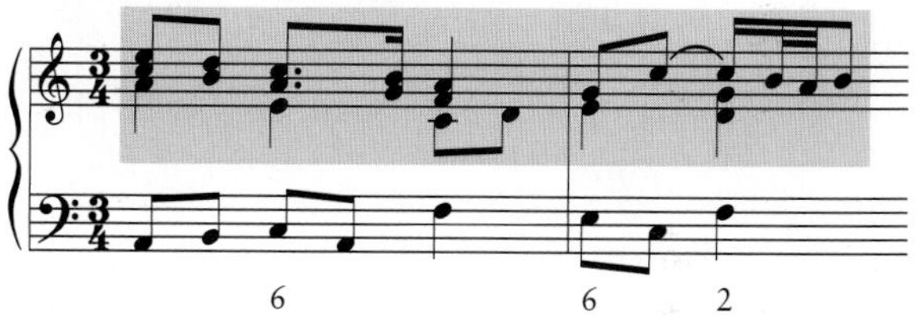

Continuo chords provide the basic harmonic framework against which the contrapuntal lines of Baroque music trace their airy patterns. Under the influence of the continuo, Baroque texture may be described as "polarized"—a "polarity of voices" between a strong bass and a clear, high (soprano) range, the domain of the melody. Less clearly defined is a middle space containing the improvised chords. In Baroque works on the largest scale, this space is also filled in by polyphonic lines drawn from the median range of the orchestra and chorus, such as violas, tenors, and altos. In more modest works a characteristic texture is a hollow one: one or two high instruments (violins, flutes) or voices, a bass instrument, and subsidiary chord improvisation in the middle.

Baroque music is usually easily identified by the presence of the continuo—by the continuous but discreet sound of the harpsichord or organ playing continuo chords in the background. Indeed, the Baroque era in music was once called the "basso continuo" era, not a bad name for it.

Musical Form

Musical forms are clearer and more regular in the Baroque period than in most other historical periods. Two factors that appear to have contributed to this, one of them social, the other intellectual, were mentioned earlier.

The social factor is the patronage system, whereby the court and the church demanded a large amount of music and expected it to be produced in a hurry, almost as soon as it was ordered. Therefore composers needed to rely on formulas that could be applied quickly and efficiently. What is amazing about the church cantatas that Bach wrote at Leipzig, one a week, is how imaginatively he varied the standard forms for the various components of a cantata. But it was very helpful—in fact, it was absolutely necessary—for him to have those standard forms in place as a point of departure.

The other factor is the scientific spirit of the age, which affected composers only indirectly, but affected them nonetheless. One can detect the composer's ambition to "map" the whole range of a piece of music and to fill it in systematically in an orderly, logical, quasi-scientific way. This ambition seems to have

In a typical Baroque texture, singers and violins in the upper register are supported by the *continuo,* played by three musicians in this performance. A cello plays the bass, and the middle range is filled in by two chord-playing instruments (harpsichord and lute).

been based on the conviction that musical time could be encompassed and controlled at man's will, an attitude similar to that of scientists, philosophers, and craftsmen of the time.

The music of Bach, in particular, shows this tendency on various levels. Look, for example, at the symmetrical arrangement of the seven sections of his Cantata No. 4, diagrammed on page 161. The last fugue in his *Art of Fugue* (he died before finishing it) is a more famous example. An ordinary fugue, as we shall see, is a polyphonic composition that deals exclusively with a single theme. This fugue deals with *four* themes, one after another, in four sections; then in the last section all four themes combine in four-part counterpoint. Theme No. 4 spells "Bach" in a musical code (!). A simpler Bach fugue may still have a ground-plan that is highly symmetrical (see page 140).

4 The Emotional World of Baroque Music

All music, it seems safe to say, is deeply involved with emotion. But in the music of different cultures, and also in the music of different historical eras within a single culture, the nature of that involvement can be very different. The emotional effect of Baroque music strikes the modern listener as very powerful and yet, in a curious way, also impersonal. Baroque composers believed firmly that music could and should mirror a wide range of human feelings, or "affects," such as had been analyzed and classified by the scientifically oriented psychology of the day. Composers did not believe, however, that it was their task to mirror feelings of their own. Rather, they tried to isolate and analyze emotions in general and then depict them consistently.

The exhaustiveness of their musical technique made for a similar exhaustiveness of emotional effect. A single movement or aria was usually restricted to depicting one specific emotion, feeling, or mood. As the rhythms and themes are repeated, the music intensifies and magnifies a single strong feeling. Sadness in Baroque music is presented as the deepest gloom, calmness as profound quiet, brightness as pomp and splendor, happiness as jubilation.

These are extreme sentiments; the people who can be imagined to experience them would have to be almost larger than life. All this fits perfectly into place with the Baroque fascination with the theater. The Baroque theater concentrated on grand gestures and high passion, on ideal emotions expressed by ideal human beings. Kings and queens were shown performing noble actions or vile ones, experiencing intense feelings, delivering thunderous speeches, and taking part in lavish stage displays. How these personages looked and postured can be seen in the picture on page 120.

Theatrical emotion has the virtues of intensity, clarity, and focus; it has to have, if it is to get past the footlights and reach its audience. Actors analyze the emotion they are asked to depict, shape it and probably exaggerate it, and then methodically project it by means of their acting technique. It is not their personal emotion, though for the moment they *make* it their own. We may come to feel that Baroque composers worked in a similar way, not only in their operas—actual stage works set to music—but also in their oratorios and church cantatas, and even in their instrumental concertos and sonatas.

Web: *Research and test your understanding of late Baroque music at* **<bedfordstmartins.com/listen>.**

CHAPTER 9

Baroque Instrumental Music

In most cultures, music with words is the norm; strictly instrumental music is less common or less important. So it is with popular music today, and so it was with the early music of Europe. In the Middle Ages, Gregorian chant was sung by monks and nuns to texts for the church services, and later some of these same texts were set to new polyphonic music for cathedral choirs and royal chapels. Troubadours set their love poems as solo songs. In the Renaissance, love poetry was set to music as madrigals, intricate part-music for a few solo singers. Vocal music was still very important in the late Baroque era, as we shall see in Chapter 10.

But part of the importance of the Baroque era was that for the first time, listeners and musicians began to take instrumental music much more seriously. A momentous change was set in motion, and the reasons for it are not entirely clear. It can hardly be a coincidence, however, that the rise of instrumental music took place at the same time as a similar development in the technology of instrument making. The name of Antonio Stradivarius (1644–1737) is known to many because of auctions where prices soar into the millions for one of his violins, unmatched after three hundred years. (They rarely come on the market. "Strad" cellos are even rarer.) Instruments by other master builders of the era, less well known, can still sound glorious: the organs of Gottfried Silbermann, the harpsichords of François Étienne Blanchet, the viols of Barak Norman (a viola da gamba is pictured on page 133 and also to the right).

In any case, the rise of instrumental music meant that there had to be a basic understanding between composers and audiences about instrumental forms and genres. To pose the most basic question: When the music starts, how long should the composer keep going, and what should the listener expect? With vocal music, the answer was (roughly speaking): until the words end—when the sense of the sentence, paragraph, or total text is completed with a punctuation mark, a summing-up, or a concluding passage. For instrumental music, there was no such "sense." Conventional forms and genres had to supply it.

In this chapter we shall look at the most important instrumental forms and genres established, developed, and refined in the Baroque era. Baroque vocal music will be treated in Chapter 10.

An early instrument that has now been revived, the viola da gamba is like a cello, with a quieter but also a rather husky sound. The beautiful viols by the Baroque maker Barak Norman have elaborately carved pegboards.

1 Concerto and Concerto Grosso

The **concerto** and the **concerto grosso** (plural: concerti grossi) are the most important orchestral genres of the Baroque era. The basic idea underlying these genres is contrast between an orchestra and a soloist (in the concerto) or a small group of soloists (in the concerto grosso). Indeed, the word *concerto* comes from the Latin word *concertare,* to contend—an origin that accurately indicates a sort of contest between solo and orchestra.

This contest pits the brilliance of the soloist or soloists—and brilliance often involves improvisation—against the relative power and stability of the orchestra. Contrast comes to these genres naturally, then; a good deal of Baroque music is more uniform, as we shall see. But people soon tire of music that stays more or less the same. Composers who wanted to develop large-scale forms had to find ways of bringing contrast into their music; they wanted large-scale forms because audiences, then as now, were more impressed by extended compositions than by short ones.

Movements

One way to extend a composition was and is to lay it out in several movements (or, to put it another way, join together several movements as a single composite work). A **movement** is a self-contained section of music that is part of a larger work; movements can be compared to chapters in a book. Movements in a multimovement work will always show some variety in tempo, meter, key, mood, and musical form.

The typical late Baroque concerto has three movements. The *first* movement is a bright, extroverted piece in a fast tempo. After this, the *second* movement strikes an obvious contrast: It is quieter, slower, and more emotional. The *third* movement is fast again—if anything, faster than the first. In the first concerto we study, Vivaldi's Violin Concerto in G, the first and last movements are in ritornello form, the second movement in ground bass form.

Ritornello Form

Many concerto movements are in *ritornello form,* from **ritornello,** the name for the orchestral music that typically starts the movement off. Contrast is basic to the concerto, and ritornello form focuses on contrast between two musical ideas, or groups of ideas—one belonging to the orchestra and the other to the soloist. The orchestral material (the ritornello) tends to be solid and forceful, the solo material faster and more brilliant.

Ritorno, the Italian word for "return," tells us that the function of the ritornello in ritornello form is to return many times as a stable element of the form. Usually it returns only in part, and usually it is played in different keys as the movement proceeds. As for the "musical ideas" for the solo, sometimes these are virtuoso passages, sometimes themes, sometimes larger sections including themes and other material. To end the movement, the orchestral ritornello returns in the tonic key and, often, at full length.

If the first movement [of a concerto] takes five minutes, the Adagio five to six, and the last movement three to four, the whole is of the proper length. And it is in general better if listeners find a piece too short rather than too long.

J. J. Quantz (1697–1773), court composer to Frederick the Great, 1752

Ritornello form can be diagrammed as shown at the top of page 130, where RIT stands for the entire ritornello, [RIT] for any part of the ritornello, and Solo 1, 2, 3, etc. for the solo sections.

We need not worry too much about the exact number of ritornello fragments, the keys, and other details shown in such form diagrams. More important is

RIT	Solo 1	[RIT]	Solo 2	[RIT]	Solo 3	[RIT]	Solo 4	RIT
Tonic key	Other keys							Tonic key

the general impression that the form gives: the sense of a sturdy, reliable support in the orchestra for rapid and sometimes fantastic flights by the solo or solo group. As a condition for the quasi-improvisational freedom of the solo instruments, the ritornello is always there, ready to bring them back down to earth and remind us of the original point of departure.

ANTONIO VIVALDI (1678–1741)
Violin Concerto in G, *La stravaganza,* Op. 4, No. 12 (1712–13)

The undisputed champion of the concerto was the Venetian composer Antonio Vivaldi. Vivaldi wrote hundreds of concertos, but published relatively few of them, in sets of six or twelve; each set was given a work number (*opus* is Latin for "work"). To some opuses he gave titles which evoke the "extravagant" side of the Baroque dualism (see page 113), such as "Harmonic Whims" (*L'estro armonico,* opus 3) and "Extravagance" (*La stravaganza,* opus 4). This Concerto in G is the last and one of the best of his opus 4.

Archlute, heard in the Vivaldi slow movement

It is a concerto for solo violin and the "basic" Baroque orchestra of strings and continuo (see page 123); on our recording the continuo chords are played by a large lute (an *archlute*). The orchestra is quite small. In the age of Antonio Stradivarius, violin-maker supreme, a great deal of music was composed at least partly to show off this favorite instrument. The violin's brilliance was especially prized, as was its ability to play expressively.

The Concerto in G begins and ends with movements in ritornello form.

First Movement (Spiritoso e non presto) Read the following material about the first movement, checking the various points with the entries in Listening Chart 3. Then listen to the music, following along with the Listening Chart—see page xvi if anything about the chart (or the icons) is not clear. Read again, listen again.

"Spirited, not too fast" writes Vivaldi at the start of this triple-meter movement. The first and second violins of the orchestra echo one another brightly. The opening ritornello—with its typical loud, extroverted sound—consists of three parts. The first begins with a couple of loud chords to catch the audience's attention and set the tempo (**a**); then comes a central section with sequences (**b**), and then a cadential section featuring loud/soft echoes (**c**):

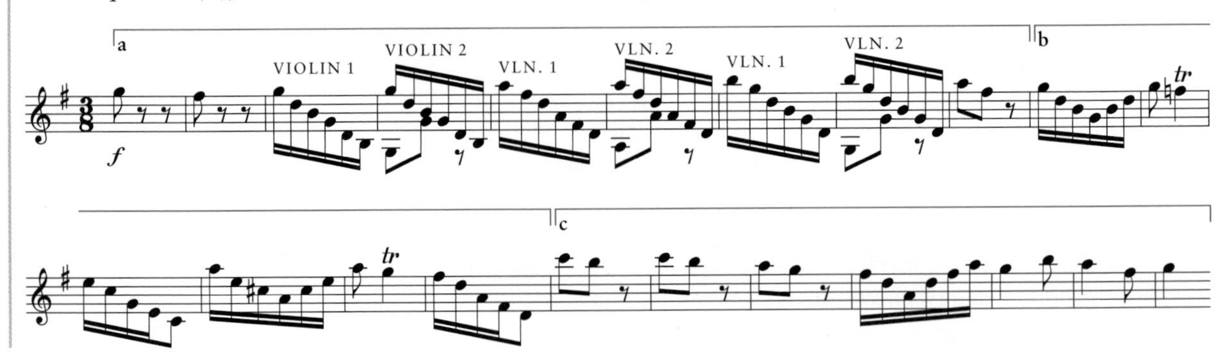

LISTENING CHART 3

1 23 1 3

Vivaldi, Violin Concerto in G, first movement

Ritornello form. 2 min., 46 sec.

0:00	**Ritornello**	a
0:11		b
0:18		c
0:26	**Solo 1**	Contrasting solo violin music
0:41	**Ritornello 2**	c
0:49	**Solo 2**	Virtuoso solo violin music; several different sections
		Continuo drops out for a short time
1:18	**Ritornello 3**	Part of this is derived from **b** and **c**; the rest is free.
		CADENCE in a minor key
1:34	**Solo 3**	More expressive
1:52	**Ritornello 4**	Even freer than Ritornello 3
2:11	**Solo 4**	Very fast
2:24	**Ritornello 5**	**b c**

Once the ritornello ends with a very solid cadence (another typical feature of Baroque ritornellos), the solo violin enters, first with music moving at about the same speed as the ritornello, but soon speeding up. Virtuosity for the Baroque violinist meant jumping from the high strings to the low, executing fast scales, in fact any and all kinds of fast playing.

Ritornello 2 is an exact repetition of **c**. The second solo has several subsections, which makes it much longer than any of the others; in one section the continuo drops out entirely. Ritornello 3 begins with derivatives of **b** and **c** but then wanders off freely and ends in a minor key. This provides a springboard for some expressive playing in the next solo. Ritornello 4 is freer still; it takes just enough from the original ritornello (part **b**) so that it seems to fit in with it and, indeed, to grow out of it spontaneously.

Vivaldi seems to have wanted his first four ritornellos to feel freer and freer, before he finally pulls the piece back in line. After the last solo (following Ritornello 4) cuts in very energetically, he ends the movement with a literal statement of **b** and **c**. (Absent is **a**, perhaps because its "wake-up" function is no longer needed.) Compare the "inner form" of this movement with the standard "outer form" shown in the previous diagram.

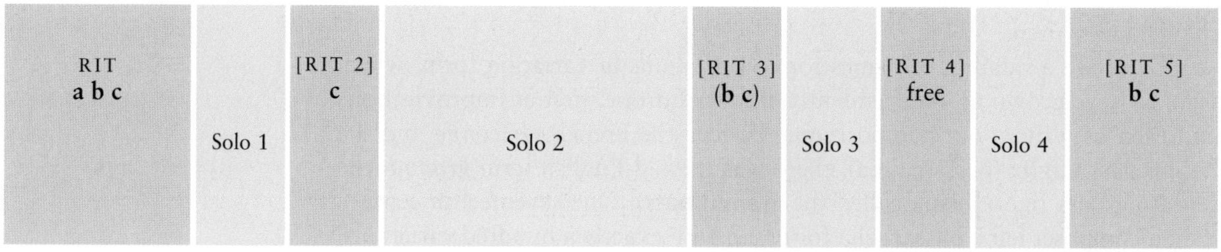

RIT **a b c**	Solo 1	[RIT 2] **c**	Solo 2	[RIT 3] **(b c)**	Solo 3	[RIT 4] free	Solo 4	[RIT 5] **b c**

Antonio Vivaldi (1678–1741)

The son of a Venetian violinist, Antonio Vivaldi was destined to follow in his father's footsteps. He entered the priesthood—where his bright red hair earned him the nickname of the "Red Priest"—and in 1703 became a music teacher at the Seminario Musicale dell'Ospedale della Pietà, a Venetian orphanage for girls. The Ospedale was one of several such institutions in Venice that were famous for the attention they paid to the musical training of their students. A large proportion of Vivaldi's works were composed for the school, whose concerts were a great tourist attraction.

The Ospedale allowed him frequent leaves of absence, so Vivaldi toured a good deal, but the composer's contract specified that he should write two concertos a month for the pupils and rehearse them if he was in town. Near the end of his life, Vivaldi left Venice permanently to settle in Vienna.

Internationally renowned as a virtuoso violinist, Vivaldi is remembered today chiefly for his brilliant concertos. He wrote more than four hundred of these, including concertos for harp, mandolin, bassoon, and various instrumental combinations; we know of more than 250 solo violin concertos, including our Concerto in G from *La stravaganza.* Critics of the day complained that Vivaldi's music was thin and flashy and that the composer was always playing for cheap effects. But the young Bach, before writing his *Brandenburg* Concertos, carefully copied out pieces by Vivaldi as a way of learning how to write concertos himself.

Vivaldi's most famous work—it has been recorded well over a hundred times—is also one of his most unusual: *The Four Seasons,* a set of four violin concertos which illustrate, in one way or another, spring (bird songs, gentle breezes, and so on), summer (a nap in the sun), fall (a tipsy peasant dance at a harvest festival), and winter ("the horrible wind," says the score). Baroque composers were fond of musical illustration, especially with the words of vocal music, as we shall see; but they seldom pursued it this far.

Since no reliable portrait seems to exist of Vivaldi, we show a contemporary caricature.

Chief Works: Solo concertos for many different instruments, including the very famous *Four Seasons* ■ Concerti grossi for various instruments ■ 21 extant operas; oratorios; cantatas

Encore: After the Violin Concerto in G, listen to *The Four Seasons;* Concerto for Two Violins in A Minor, Op. 3, No. 8.

Baroque Variation Form: The Ground Bass

Variation forms are among the simplest and most characteristic of Baroque forms. Although they are not as common as other forms, they project the Baroque desire for systematic, thorough structures in a very direct way. This is because **variation form** entails the successive, uninterrupted repetition of one clearly defined melodic unit, with changes that rouse the listener's interest without ever losing touch with the original unit, or theme.

That theme may be a complete melody in the soprano range or a shorter melodic phrase in the bass. Given the emphasis in the Baroque era on the basso continuo, it is not surprising that Baroque variations tend to occur above stable bass patterns; a name for such patterns is **basso ostinato,** meaning "persistent" or "obstinate" bass. Sometimes the bass itself is slightly varied—though never in such a way as to hide its distinctive quality. Dynamics, tone color, and some harmonies are often changed in variations. Tempo, key, and mode are changed less often.

There are a number of names for compositions in variation form, which seem to have grown up independently all over Europe, first as improvisations and then as written-out compositions. Besides the French *chaconne* and the Italian *passacaglia* (passa-cáhlia), there was the old English term *ground* (the repeating bass figure being called the **ground bass**). One seventeenth-century Italian composer left a passacaglia for organ with exactly a hundred variations.

As this child appears to be finding out, music lessons can often serve as a cover for lessons in something else—a fact which helps explain the popularity of "music lesson" pictures.

More compact examples of variation form sometimes appear as one movement in a larger Baroque genre, such as a concerto.*

Note that the term *ostinato* is also used to refer to any short musical unit repeated many times, in the bass or anywhere else, especially one used as a building block for a piece of music. Ostinatos are by no means unique to European music of the Baroque; in some form they are found in almost all musical traditions (see, for example, pages 108 and 217).

ANTONIO VIVALDI
Violin Concerto in G, *La stravaganza,* Op. 4, No. 12 (1712–13)

Second Movement (Largo) As is typical, Vivaldi's Concerto in G has three contrasting movements—the first vigorous and brilliant, the second gentle and slow. This slow movement is in variation (ground bass) form.

Our first impression of this music is probably of its texture—the gentle throbbing, the ingenious weaving in and out of the orchestral violins and the solo violin, and the delicate, subsidiary continuo sounds. There is, however, not much melody to listen to in the violin's music. There is less, in fact, as the movement goes along and the texture changes.

Sooner or later we notice that the only real melody is in the bass, where a solemn, quiet theme (the ground bass) is heard repeatedly in the cellos and bass viol. The theme sinks down and down, ending with a strong cadence:

*We examine earlier examples of variation (ground bass) form on pages 103 and 106: Dido's Lament, from *Dido and Aeneas* by Henry Purcell, and a Passacaglia by Girolamo Frescobaldi.

LISTENING CHART 5

Bach, *Brandenburg* Concerto No. 5, first movement

Ritornello form. 9 min., 56 sec.

Track		Time	Section	Description
1 5		0:00	**Ritornello**	Complete ritornello is played by the orchestra, forte: bright and emphatic. 
		0:21	**Solo**	Harpsichord, flute, and violin in a contrapuntal texture (often in trio style). Includes faster rhythms; the soloists play new themes and also play some of the motives from the ritornello. 
		0:46	**Ritornello** (first phrase)	Orchestra, *f*
		0:51	**Solo**	Similar material to that of the first solo
		1:12	**Ritornello** (middle phrase)	Orchestra, *f*
		1:18	**Solo**	Similar solo material
		1:40	**Ritornello** (middle phrase)	Orchestra, *f;* minor mode
		1:45	**Solo**	Similar solo material at first, then fast harpsichord runs are introduced.
2 6		2:28	**Ritornello** (middle phrase)	Orchestra, *f*
	0:06	2:34	**Solo**	This solo leads directly into the central solo.
	0:32	3:00	Central solo	Quiet flute and violin dialogue (accompanied by the orchestra, *p*) is largely in the minor mode. The music is less motivic, and the harmonies change less rapidly than before. 
	0:58	3:26		Detached notes in cello, flute, and violin; sequence
	1:35	4:03		Long high notes prepare for the return of the ritornello.
3 7		4:18	**Ritornello** (first phrase)	Orchestra, *f*
	0:04	4:22	**Solo**	
	0:50	5:08	**Ritornello** (first and second phrases)	Orchestra, *f;* this ritornello section feels especially solid because it is longer than the others and in the tonic key.
	1:02	5:20	**Solo**	
	1:30	5:48	**Ritornello** (middle phrase)	Orchestra, *f*
	1:37	5:55	**Solo**	Fast harpsichord run leads into the cadenza.
4 8		6:33	Harpsichord cadenza	*Section 1:* a lengthy passage developing motives from the solo sections
	1:56	8:29		*Section 2:* very fast and brilliant
	2:15	8:48		*Section 3:* long preparation for the anticipated return of the ritornello
5 9		9:30	**Ritornello**	Orchestra, *f,* plays the complete ritornello.

This painting is thought to depict Bach and three of his musician sons. It is a symbolic painting: The kindly, soberly dressed father is shown holding a cello—a basso continuo instrument—ready to support the treble lines of the boys, who are decked out in the frothy costumes of a later generation.

They introduce new motives and new patterns of figuration, take over some motives from the ritornello, and toss all these musical ideas back and forth between them. Every so often, the orchestra breaks in again, always with clear fragments of the ritornello, in various keys. All this has a very, very different effect from that of Vivaldi's Violin Concerto in G, not only because of the sheer length of the movement and its elaborate form, but because of the richness of the counterpoint and the harmony.

During a particularly striking solo section in the minor mode, the soloists abandon their motivic style and play Baroque mood music, with even richer harmonies and intriguing, special textures. After this, you may be able to hear that all the solos are closely related to solos heard before the minor-mode section—all, that is, except the very last. Here the harpsichord gradually outpaces the violin and the flute, until finally it seizes the stage and plays a lengthy virtuoso passage, while the other instruments wait silently.

An improvised or improvisatory solo passage of this kind within a larger piece is called a **cadenza.** Cadenzas are a feature of concertos in all eras; the biggest cadenza always comes near the end of the first movement, as in *Brandenburg* Concerto No. 5.

In this cadenza, the harpsichord breaks out of the regular eighth-note rhythms that have dominated this long movement. Its swirling, unexpectedly powerful patterns prepare inexorably for the final entrance of the orchestra. The whole ritornello is played, exactly as at the beginning; at last we hear it as a complete and solid entity, not in fragments.

Second Movement (Affettuoso) After the forceful first movement, a change is needed: something quieter, slower, and more emotional (*affettuoso* means just that, *emotional*). As often in concertos, this slow movement is in the minor mode, contrasting with the first and last, which are in the major.

Johann Sebastian Bach (1685–1750)

During the Baroque era, crafts were handed down in family clans, and in music the Bach clan was one of the biggest, providing the region of Thuringia in central Germany with musicians for many generations. Most of the Bachs were lowly town musicians or Lutheran Church organists; only a few of them gained court positions. Johann Sebastian, who was himself taught by several of his relatives, trained four sons who became leading composers of the next generation.

Before he was twenty, Bach took his first position as a church organist in a little town called Arnstadt, then moved to a bigger town called Mühlhausen. Then he worked his way up to a court position with the Duke of Weimar. As a church organist, Bach had to compose organ music and sacred choral pieces, and at Weimar he was still required to write church music for the ducal chapel, as well as sonatas and concertos for performance in the palace.

The way his Weimar position terminated tells us something about the working conditions of court musicians. When Bach tried to leave Weimar for another court, Cöthen, the duke balked and threw him in jail for several weeks before letting him go. At Cöthen the prince happened to be a keen amateur musician who was not in favor of elaborate church music, so Bach concentrated on instrumental music.

In 1723 Bach was appointed cantor of St. Thomas's Church in Leipzig, a center of Lutheran church music in Germany. He not only had to compose and perform, but also organize music for all four churches in town. Teaching in the choir school was another of his responsibilities. Almost every week, in his first years at Leipzig, Bach composed, had copied, rehearsed, and performed a new cantata—a religious work for soloists, choir, and orchestra containing several movements and lasting from fifteen to thirty minutes.

Bach chafed under bureaucratic restrictions and political decisions by town and church authorities. The truth is he was never appreciated in Leipzig. Furthermore, at the end of his life he was regarded as old-fashioned by modern musicians, and one critic pained Bach by saying so in print. Indeed, after his death Bach's music was neglected by the musical public at large, though it was admired by composers such as Mozart and Beethoven.

Bach had twenty children—seven with his first wife, a cousin, and thirteen with his second, a singer, for whom he prepared a little home-music anthology, *The Note-Book of Anna Magdalena Bach.* The children were taught music as a matter of course, and also taught how to copy music; the performance parts of many of the weekly cantatas that Bach composed are written in their hands. From his musical response to the sacred words of these cantatas, and other works, it is clear that Bach thought deeply about religious matters. Works such as his Passions and his Mass in B Minor emanate a spirituality that many listeners find unmatched in any other composer.

Bach seldom traveled, except to consult on organ construction contracts (for which the customary fee was often a cord of wood or a barrel of wine). Blind in his last years, he continued to compose by dictation. He had already begun to assemble his compositions in orderly sets: organ chorale preludes, organ fugues, preludes and fugues for harpsichord. He also clearly set out to produce works that would summarize his final thoughts about Baroque forms and genres; such works are the Mass in B Minor, the thirty-three *Goldberg* Variations for harpsichord, and *The Art of Fugue,* an exemplary collection of fugues all on the same subject, left unfinished at his death.

Bach was writing for himself, for his small devoted circle of students, perhaps for posterity. It is a concept that would have greatly surprised the craftsmen musicians who were his forebears.

Chief Works: More than 200 sacred and secular cantatas; two Passions, with words from the gospels of St. Matthew and St. John; *Christmas Oratorio;* Mass in B Minor; *Magnificat;* motets ▪ *The Well-Tempered Clavier,* consisting of 48 preludes and fugues in all major and minor keys for harpsichord or clavichord ▪ Three sets of suites (six each) for harpsichord—the French and English Suites and the Partitas; *Goldberg* Variations ▪ Organ works: many fugues (including the *St. Anne* Fugue) and chorale preludes ▪ *Brandenburg* Concertos, other concertos, orchestral suites, sonatas ▪ Late composite works: *A Musical Offering* and *The Art of Fugue* ▪ Chorale (hymn) harmonizations

Encore: After *Brandenburg* Concerto No. 5, listen to the Concerto for Two Violins; Mass in B Minor (Gloria section).

Bach's musical handwriting—the most beautiful and intricate of any composer's.

Baroque composers had a simple way of reducing volume: They could omit many or even all of the orchestra instruments. So here Bach employs only the three solo instruments—flute, violin, and harpsichord—plus the orchestra cello playing the continuo bass.

Third Movement (Allegro) The full orchestra returns in the last movement, which, however, begins with a lengthy passage for the three soloists in fugal style (see below). The lively compound meter with its triple component—ONE two three *four* five six—provides a welcome contrast to the duple meter of the two earlier movements.

2 Fugue

Fugue is one of the most impressive and characteristic achievements of Baroque music, indeed of Baroque culture altogether. In broad, general terms, fugue can be thought of as systematized imitative polyphony (see page 29). Composers of the Middle Ages first glimpsed imitative polyphony, and Renaissance composers developed it; Baroque composers, living in an age of science, systematized it. The thorough, methodical quality that we pointed to in Baroque music is nowhere more evident than in fugue.

A **fugue** is a polyphonic composition for a fixed number of instrumental lines or voices—usually three or four—built on a single principal theme. This theme, called the fugue **subject,** appears again and again in each of the instrumental or vocal lines.

The term *fugue* itself comes from the Latin word *fuga,* which means "running away"; imagine the fugue subject being chased from one instrument to another. Listening to a fugue, we follow that chase. The subject stays the same, but it takes on endless new shadings as it turns corners and surrounds itself with different melodic and rhythmic ideas.

Fugal Exposition

A fugue begins with an **exposition** in which all the voices present the subject in an orderly, standardized way. (The contrapuntal lines in fugues are referred to as *voices,* even when the fugue is written for instruments. We shall be speaking of the lines in a Bach fugue for strings as the *soprano, alto, tenor,* and *bass.*)

First of all, the subject is announced in the most prominent fashion possible: It enters in a single voice without any accompaniment (usually), while the other voices wait. Any voice can begin; in the diagram below, we follow the regular order of the example on our CD (soprano, alto, tenor, bass), but any order is possible. After leading off, voice 1 continues with new material of its own while the subject enters in voice 2. Next, the subject arrives in voice 3—with 1 and 2 continuing in counterpoint with it (and with each other), using more new material, and so on. This section of a fugue, the exposition, is over when all the voices have stated the subject.

SOPRANO	Subject — New material ——————→			
ALTO		Subject — New material —————→		
TENOR			Subject — New material ————→	
BASS				Subject — New material ———→

After the exposition, the subject enters at intervals, spaced out by passages of other music. It may come at the top of the texture (in the soprano), the bottom (bass), or else half hidden away in the middle; see the diagram below. Some of these later **subject entries** come in different keys. Although the modulations to these other keys may not be very obvious—less so than in music of the Classical era, for example—without them the music would be dull and stodgy.

The passages of music separating the later subject entries are called **episodes.** They provide a contrast to the subject entries. This is true even though their material is often derived from the subject: In such cases, the episodes sound less distinct and solid than the subject entries, and so stand apart from them. A regular feature of fugal episodes is the use of sequences (see page 25).

After the exposition, the form of a fugue falls into an alternating pattern: Episodes of various lengths come between subject entries in various keys. Here is a diagram of a typical short fugue:

Exposition	Episode	Entry	Episode	Entry	Longer Episode	Entry
Subject						Subject
Subject		Subject				
Subject				Subject		
Subject						
TONIC KEY		ANOTHER KEY		ANOTHER KEY		TONIC KEY

Fugues, Free and Learned

Fugue is a somewhat complicated concept. We need to think of fugue not always as a genre ("*a* fugue"), but also as a style or a procedure (just "fugue," or fugal style), which is not always used strictly over the full length of a composition.

For in fact, full-scale fugues were very seldom written for public performance, at concerts (of which there were few in the Baroque era, anyway) or courts. Fugues occur as parts of French overtures—curtain-raisers for operas—but such fugues are invariably "free," in that the individual voice lines are not maintained all the way through, as in virtually all of Bach's freestanding fugues. Since Bach is unquestionably the greatest master of fugue, there is a tendency to think of strict fugues as the main kind.

Nonetheless, "free" fugues are the more common and important. They can be free in the sense that they take up only part of a composition, not the whole of it (sometimes called *fugato*). They can be free by constantly slipping out of polyphony—the true texture of fugue—into homophony and then back again.

As for Bach, his greatest fugues are keyboard works written for study purposes, not for public performance: Such are *The Well-Tempered Clavier,* his very famous collection of preludes and fugues in each of the twelve major and twelve minor keys, and *The Art of Fugue.*

And in the study context, fugues developed technical refinements, showing off the composers' contrapuntal skill and treating the subject in various learned, seemingly intellectual ways. Some of these *fugal devices* are:

- ***countersubject*** The name given to the "new material" in the diagram on page 139 when it sticks with the subject, accompanying it one way or another throughout the fugue (i.e., the countersubject is the melodic line in voice 1 that is heard while the subject enters in voice 2).
- ***stretto*** One subject entry overlaps another entry in time, with the second jumping in before the first is complete.
- ***augmentation, diminution*** All note lengths in the subject are multiplied or divided (usually by two): A half note becomes a whole note, etc.
- ***inversion*** All intervals in the subject are reversed: Steps up become steps down, and so on.

Sometimes these fugal devices sound as academic and dry as their descriptions, but the Baroque masters of fugue could make wonderful music out of such technical procedures. *The Well-Tempered Clavier* includes "learned" fugues that are moving and serene, airy and even comical. Some sound very much like dance music.

Contrapunctus 4 from *The Art of Fugue*, from the first edition of 1751. The fugue subject can be seen entering on lines 1, 2, 3, and 8.

JOHANN SEBASTIAN BACH (1685–1750)
The Art of Fugue, Contrapunctus 4 (published 1751)

Bach wrote *The Art of Fugue* at the end of his life, as a testament to his astonishing skill in writing fugues of all kinds, and with all shades of feeling. This huge work consists of twenty different canons and fugues—Bach uses the archaic and slightly pompous term *contrapunctus*—all on the same fugue subject. The number is not quite certain; Bach did not finish *The Art of Fugue*, and the heirs made something of a muddle when they published whatever they could find, soon after his death.

The bearer, Monsieur *J. C. Dorn, student of music, has requested the undersigned to give him a testimonial to his knowledge* in musicis . . . *As his years increase it may well be expected that with his good native talent he will develop into a quite able musician.*

JOH. SEB. BACH (a tough grader)

As a demonstration of his "art of fugue," Bach showed off the fugal devices mentioned in the box on page 140 in most of the fugues. But in Contrapunctus 4, one of the most melodious, he seems more interested in the long, smooth, and attractive episodes that come between the subject entries. These episodes are derived mainly from two sources, one from art—the rapid ending of the fugue subject, marked *x* on the music below—and the other from nature, it seems: a cuckoo figure, used repeatedly yet never sounding silly.

By comparison, the subject itself sounds restrained and serious, and it is presented in a very orderly way. The exposition brings the voices in a regular order from high to low (soprano, alto, tenor, bass). After an episode, four more entries follow the same order, modulating to a major key. After another episode, another four entries arrive in the reverse order, which is more climactic—and meanwhile the pitch range of the subject is expanded, as shown below:

LISTENING CHART 6

1 26-27

Bach, *The Art of Fugue*, Contrapunctus 4

Fugue form. 3 min., 30 sec.

CD		Time	Section	Description
			Exposition	*Fugue subject in:*
26		0:00		S (soprano; violin 1)
		0:06		A (alto; violin 2)
		0:15		T (tenor; viola)
		0:21		B (bass; cello)
		0:28	Episode	Uses a cuckoo figure, in sequence, then motive *x*, going up and down
		0:39	Subject Entries	S Major mode
		0:45		A Major
		0:51		T Minor mode
		0:56		B Minor
		1:03	Long Episode	Similar material, plus lead-up to the cadence →
				CADENCE minor mode Similar material
27		1:34	Entries	B Climactic: expanded form of the fugue subject, modulating
	0:06	1:39		T
	0:17	1:51		A
	0:23	1:57		S
	0:29	2:03	Long Episode	
	0:38	2:12		CADENCE major mode (different key) Similar material, plus lead-up to the cadence →
	1:01	2:35		CADENCE minor mode (different key) Similar material
	1:08	2:42	Entries	T
	1:13	2:47		A (with a very close *stretto* in the S)
	1:19	2:53	Episode	Episode material becomes more and more fluid.
	1:40	3:14	Final Entries	T Expanded form of subject
	1:46	3:20		A

cuckoo

x

This automatically makes the subject sound more intense, and also lets the music modulate naturally, increasing the intensity even more. This climax is recalled by the fugue's imposing conclusion.

The Art of Fugue was written for harpsichord, but it is often played by an instrumental group of some kind, which allows the individual voices to be heard more clearly. Mozart and Beethoven both arranged Bach fugues for string ensembles. We use an arrangement for string quartet by the English composer Robert Simpson (1921–1997).

3 The Dance Suite

Dance music was popular in the Baroque era, as has been true in every era, including of course our own. Dance music also inspired the greatest composers of the time to some of their best efforts.

The custom was to group a collection of miscellaneous dances together in a genre called the **suite.** Composers usually wrote "stylized" dances, that is, their music was intended for listening rather than dancing. Compared with music written for the actual dance floor, stylized dances naturally allowed for more musical elaboration and refinement, while still retaining some of the special features of the various dances.

Suites were written for orchestra, for chamber music combinations, or even for solo instruments such as the harpsichord or lute. Harpsichord suites are some of the very finest. Which dances occurred in a suite was not subject to any general rule, nor was there any specified order. All the dances in a suite were kept in the same key, and the last of them was always fast—frequently a **gigue,** a dance in compound meter that may have been derived from the Irish jig. Otherwise there was no standard overall structure to a suite.

Baroque Dances

Many different dances existed in the Baroque era. What distinguished them were features originally associated with the dance steps—a certain meter, a distinctive tempo, and some rhythmic attributes. The dance called the *gavotte,* for example, always begins with a double *upbeat,* two weak beats preceding the first strong beat (the *downbeat*) of a measure.

These are the main Baroque dances and their distinguishing features:

Dance	Usual Meter	Tempo	Some Rhythmic Characteristics
Allemande	4/4	Moderate	Upbeat sixteenth note; flowing motion
Courante	3/2	Moderate	Occasional substitution of 6/4 measures
Sarabande	3/4	Slow	Often a secondary accent on beat 2 (no upbeat)
Minuet	3/4	Moderate	Rather plain in rhythm (upbeat optional)
Gavotte	4/4	Moderate	Double upbeat of two quarter notes
Bourrée	2/2	Rather fast	Short upbeat
Siciliana	12/8	Moderate	Gently moving uneven rhythms; minor mode
Gigue	6/8	Fast	Short upbeat; uneven rhythms; lively movement

Baroque Dance Form

Although the number, type, and arrangement of dances in a suite varied widely, the *form* of dances was standardized. The same simple form was applied to all types, and it is an easily recognized feature of Baroque dance music.

A Baroque dance has two sections, **a** and **b.** Each ends with a strong cadence coming to a complete stop, after which the section is immediately repeated. Both sections tend to include the same motives, cadences, and other such musical details, and this makes for a sense of symmetry between them, even though **b** is nearly always longer than **a.** In the Baroque era there is usually no full-scale, clear repeat of the whole of **a** after **b,** as we shall see happen in later dances.

Hence Baroque dance form is diagrammed

a a b b *abbreviated as:* |: **a** :||: **b** :|

Royals perform a Baroque court dance.

where the signs |: and :| indicate that everything between them is to be repeated. This form is also called **binary form.**

Trio With shorter dances, composers tended to group them in pairs of the same type, with the first coming back after the second. The result was a large-scale **ABA** form. The **B** dance in such a pair was called the **trio,** because in seventeenth-century orchestral music it had often been scored for only three instruments.

This made for a simple, agreeable contrast with the full orchestration of the **A** dance. Even when the trio is scored for full orchestra, the idea of contrast between the two dances was always kept; the second is quieter than the first, or it changes mode. (As for the term *trio,* to indicate a contrasting, subsidiary section, that was still used in the waltzes of Johann Strauss and the marches of John Philip Sousa.)

Thus a Baroque minuet and trio, to choose this dance as an example, consists of one minuet followed by a second, quieter minuet, after which the first is heard again. This time, however, the repeats are normally omitted:

	MINUET	TRIO	MINUET
	A	B	A
	a a b b	c c d d	a b
abbreviated as:	|: a :||: b :|	|: c :||: d :|	a b

The French Overture

A dance suite begins not with the first dance but with a special preparatory number called a **French overture.** *Overture* is of course a general term for any substantial piece of music introducing a play, opera, or ballet. The French overture was a special type developed by the court orchestra of Louis XIV, de-

Concerts began late in the Baroque era. They were sometimes given in parks, where music accompanied gossip, flirtation, and food.

signed to symbolize the pomp and majesty of his court. Even after the French overture style had become antiquated, it was kept alive for the benefit of lesser rulers outside of France who aped everything associated with the Sun King.

The French overture consists of two sharply contrasted sections, an **A** section and a faster **B** section. They are typically arranged in an **A B A′** pattern, where **A′** stands for a variant—often an abbreviated variant—of **A.**

The slow **A** section is the one that is distinctively "French"; dotted rhythms (see page 20), sweeping scales and heavy accents, and other such features give it a majestic, pompous gravity that is easily recognized (and was easily imitated). This section was often labeled with the French word *Grave* (*grahv*).

The fast **B** section is in imitative polyphony. In some overtures this section amounts to a full-scale fugue.

JOHANN SEBASTIAN BACH
Orchestral Suite No. 3 in D (c. 1730)

It is thought that Bach wrote this suite for the Collegium Musicum of the University of Leipzig, a student music organization that seems to have provided a congenial outlet for his later work. The Suite in D is scored for the "festive" Baroque orchestra diagrammed on page 123: strings, two oboes, three trumpets, two timpani, and harpsichord. Bach carefully varied the orchestration from number to number.

This suite, like others written all over Europe, uses French titles as an acknowledgment of French leadership in ballet and the dance. After the overture, its movements are cast in the Baroque dance form described above.

Ouverture The French overture that starts the suite is scored for all the instruments, and in fact it is the only movement in which the oboes have (slightly) independent parts that do not always double the violins. What is more, a solo violin emerges unexpectedly to dominate two passages during the **B** part of the overture, which is a full-scale fugue.

The form of this overture is **A B A′**. Shown below are the beginning of the **A** section, the "Grave," with its arresting drum roll and the obligatory "French" dotted rhythms, and part of the fugal exposition in **B**:

The episodes in this fugue are played by the solo violin. Indeed, this **B** part of the movement can be understood in two ways: as a fugue with solo violin episodes, or as a Baroque concerto with a fugal ritornello.

Following the overture come four pieces in dance form. Three of them follow the Baroque pattern |: **a** :||: **b** :|. Notice the "full stop" effect after each playing of all the **a**'s and **b**'s. Only the gavotte, the second of the dances, has a trio and so falls into **A B A** (gavotte and trio) form.

Air *Air* is the French word for "aria"—and Bach composed this "instrumental song" in dance form, since it has to take its place in a dance suite. It is perhaps Bach's most famous and beloved melody. Only the strings and continuo play, as the quiet melody in the first violins is accompanied by a regular,

Eighteenth-century debates on the merits of French and Italian music could become catty. In this French cartoon, Italy's greatest composers—each playing the instrument he was famous for—join "Le chat de Caffarelli" in an aria (Caffarelli was a leading castrato).

downward-moving, soothing bass line in the cellos and bass viols (a **walking bass**: See page 121). And there are subsidiary but highly expressive counterpoints in the second violins and violas.

The exquisite fluidity of this melody is a function of its rhythmic variety—variety that is set off by the regularity of the "walking" bass. Most of the basic two-beat (half-measure) units in the melody have rhythms not duplicated elsewhere. Therefore when measures 13–14 do repeat a rhythmic figure several times, they gain a special kind of climactic intensity. This intensity is underpinned by quiet *upward* motion in the bass, which had generally been moving downward, and by a newly prominent second violin part.

Anticipated by some melodic figures in **a,** the figures in **b** keep reaching ever upward, in a wonderfully spontaneous way. This sense of aspiration is balanced by the graceful falling cadences ending **a** and **b.**

To counteract all the rhythmic and melodic variety, Bach puts in several beautiful sequences, whose repetitive quality ensures a sense of organization: See measures 3–4, 13–14, and 15–16.

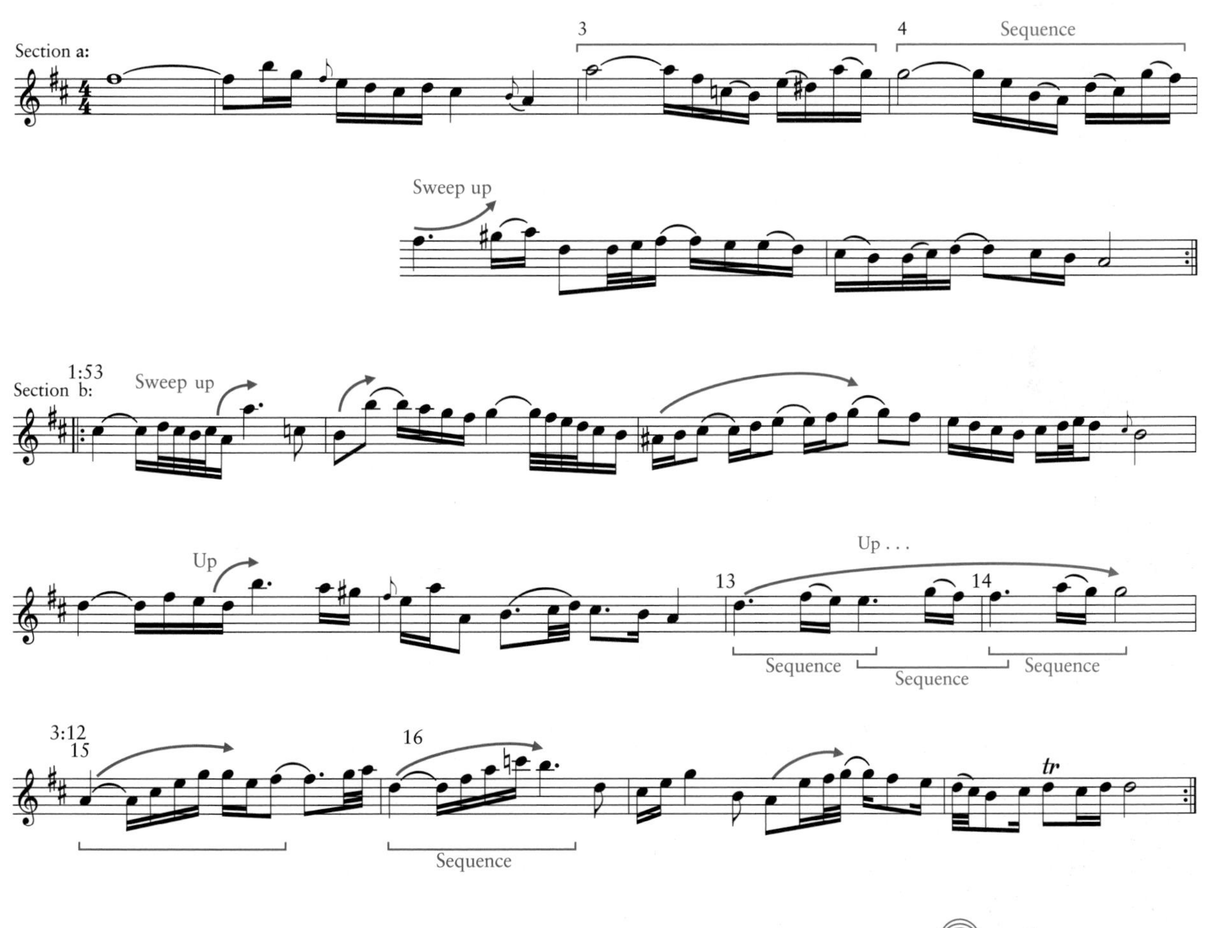

Gavotte The wind instruments and timpani return in this number; the trumpets make this dance sound more like a march, as the festive orchestra evokes the military conquests that formed the basis of Baroque princely power. Trumpets deliver the strong two-quarter-note upbeat that characterizes the gavotte (see page 143). Then Bach inverts the bold opening melody of **a**

to obtain the opening of **b.** This inversion may *look* academic—a technical trick to be appreciated by the Collegium Musicum connoisseurs—but it *sounds* fresh and natural, another product of Bach's endlessly fertile melodic imagination:

The trio, or second gavotte, also fully orchestrated, sounds even more military than the first. Strings and oboes play fanfares to begin both **c** and **d.**

LISTEN

Bach, Suite No. 3 in D, Gavotte

0:00 Gavotte (**A**): **a**
0:15 **a** *repeated*
0:30 **b**
0:56 **b** *repeated*
1:21 Trio (**B**): **c c**
2:10 **d d**
3:02 **A** (**a b**)

Bourrée The lightest dance in this suite, a bourrée, is scored for full orchestra; the wind instruments and timpani are used mainly to underscore the sharp, exhilarating rhythms.

Gigue Another drum roll (as in the French overture) launches this vigorous gigue, the most common dance for the last movement in a suite. The violins, doubled by the oboes, play almost continuous eighth notes in **6/8** time.

Web: *Research and test your understanding of Baroque instrumental music at* **<bedfordstmartins.com/listen>.**

CHAPTER 10

Baroque Vocal Music

Vocal music—music for solo voices, choruses, or both—formed a major part of the output of virtually all Baroque composers. We have seen that composers were supported by three main institutions: the church, the opera house, and the court. Each of these demanded vocal music. Indeed, of the three, only the court was a major source of instrumental music—and every court had its chapel, for which the court composers were also required to provide vocal music. Courts had their own opera theaters, too.

Words and Music

Theories of musical expression in the Baroque era were touched on in Chapter 8 (page 118). It was believed at the time that emotions could be isolated, categorized, and listed in a fairly simple way, and that music could enhance or even arouse each emotion by means of certain musical devices applied consistently, even single-mindedly, throughout a piece. Theorists developed checklists of musical devices corresponding to each of the "affects," as they called emotions conceived in this way.

It was particularly in vocal music—where the words that are sung define or suggest a specific emotion—that this musical "vocabulary of the emotions" was applied most consistently. If a text refers to "rejoicing," for example, a Baroque composer would match this with fast, lively runs; a mention of "victory" would probably require trumpets and drums to evoke battle music. More literally, when a text speaks of "high" or "low," a setting in high or low voices was likely, and so on.

1 Opera

The principal genre of secular vocal music of the Baroque era was opera. Introduced around the year 1600, opera flourished mightily all over Europe, and soon became the most glamorous and probably the most adventurous and influential artistic genre of the Baroque era.

In characterizing the emotional world of Baroque art (see page 116), we stressed its theatrical quality. The Baroque was fascinated by the theater, and especially by opera—the ultimate multimedia experience of its day, combining

A German opera house of the Baroque era. Notice that the best seats were actually on the stage.

poetry, drama, music, vocal virtuosity, scenic splendor, dance, and more. Spectacular singing was of the essence in Baroque opera, and so was spectacular stage architecture, featuring amazing transformation scenes and the like. Systems of pulleys and counterweights could rapidly change the set from a palace to a magic garden, with gods and goddesses descending from the heavens in a fiery chariot. Opera offered a wealth of satisfactions, then—most obviously, no doubt, for the vocal connoisseurs of the day, the fans of great singers. They are said to have gossiped and played cards in the boxes while waiting for their favorites to sing their special arias.

But opera's ability to project emotion was the real basis of its appeal. First and foremost, opera erected a stage on which individual singers could step forward to express feelings in the most direct and powerful fashion. Since the singers were portraying actual characters in a drama, they were repeatedly thrown into situations which made it natural for them to experience (and express) intense emotions.

Such emotions were intensified, of course, by music. Emotion could be intensified by great vocal virtuosity, too. The most obvious kind of vocal virtuosity is *coloratura* singing—fast brilliant runs, scales, high notes, vocal cadenzas, and so on, stressing technique for its own sake. But the legendary singers of old moved their audiences not only by singing faster than anyone else, but by singing more beautifully, more delicately, and more emotionally.

Italian Opera Seria

The principal type of Italian Baroque opera was **opera seria,** or serious opera. The plots—mostly derived from ancient history, with all kinds of alterations and additions—were designed to stir up powerful emotions, such as passion, rage, grief, and triumph. Such plots gave the singers many opportunities to excel in one kind of expression or another. Opera seria consists mainly of solo singing by sopranos and mezzo-sopranos, including castrati (see page 152). Tenors and basses play subordinate roles; there are few duets or choruses.

The text of an opera is called the *libretto* ("little book"), and the author of the text is the *librettist.* Librettists had to build up the drama as a whole from a series of texts, alternating with one another, for *recitatives* and *arias.*

Recitative

Recitative (resita-téev), from the Italian word for "recite," is a technique of declaiming words musically in a heightened, theatrical manner. There is always an instrumental accompaniment. The singing voice closely follows the free rhythm of emotional speech; it mirrors and indeed exaggerates the natural ups and downs that occur as an actor raises his or her voice at a question, lowers it in "asides," or cries out angrily. The composer makes no effort to organize these speechlike utterances into real melodies.

Recitative was used for plot action, dialogue, and other places in the drama where it is particularly important for the words to be brought out. Text phrases and individual words are not ordinarily repeated, of course, any more than they would be in speech.

Most of the time, recitative accompaniment was kept to a minimum—basso continuo (cello and harpsichord) alone—so that the singer could interpret

A much more informal picture of a Baroque opera performance—evidently during a recitative, to judge from the interaction of the characters on stage and the inattention of the audience. (The painting is perhaps by Antonio Longhi, 1702–1785.)

The Castrato

Intimately tied up with Italian opera seria was the castrato singer (plural: *castrati*). The starring male roles in opera were hardly ever sung by tenors or basses but rather by men who had submitted to castration as young boys in order to preserve their voices in the soprano or alto range. At its best, the castrato voice was a prized virtuoso instrument, more powerful and brilliant than a woman's soprano.

This practice seems an outrage to us today, as it did to everybody outside Italy at the time (and to many in Italy itself). It has been pointed out that for an intelligent peasant boy, the classic way to avoid a lifetime of labor in the fields was to enter the priesthood, with its vow of chastity, and that becoming a castrato provided another, similar option.

In any case, in Italy and all over Europe—though France was a notable exception—castrati were gladly accepted because of their wonderful singing and given top billing, along with women prima donnas. But the presence of frankly unnatural men in the main opera roles, which were of course usually romantic roles, made it hard to believe in the ideal of opera as serious drama in music. Often it was closer to "concert in costume." Contributing to the side-show quality, it was common for male characters to disguise themselves as women (and vice versa). The male soprano voice was used for female impersonation.

Farinelli

The most famous castrati were international stage figures. Some were pampered stars and objects of ridicule at the same time, such as Caffarelli (see page 146), who was once jailed for indecent gestures during an opera performance. Others were serious artists. Carlo Broschi, whose stage name was Farinelli, the most famous of all, was also a composer and later in life an influential figure at the court of Spain.

Many more castrati worked out of the limelight, in Italian churches. The last known castrato, a member of the Sistine Choir in Rome, made a recording in 1902; the voice has been described as "penetrating and curiously disembodied."

For a 1995 film about Farinelli, a virtual castrato voice was invented by digital wizardry.

the dialogue or the action as spontaneously as possible. A name for recitative with continuo accompaniment is **secco recitative,** from the Italian word *secco,* meaning "dry" (think of the sound of the harpsichord).

In every opera, however, one or two of the most excited, emotion-filled recitatives were provided with orchestral accompaniment of one kind or another. This type is called **accompanied recitative.**

Aria

An **aria** is a set piece for solo singer that has much more musical elaboration and coherence than a passage of recitative. The vocal part is more melodic, and ordinarily the accompaniment includes the orchestra, not just the continuo, as in secco recitative. Here the singer-actor is mulling over his or her emotions at some leisure, "getting his feelings out," instead of reacting moment by moment, as in recitative. Consequently in arias the repetition of poetic phrases or words is common and, in principle, appropriate.

The standard form for the Baroque Italian opera aria is **da capo** form, **A B A** (less usual is free da capo form, **A B A′**). Both the words and music of **A** are repeated after **B**; *da capo* ("from the head") is a direction on scores meaning repeat from the beginning. The composer wrote the music for **A** and **B** only, leaving the performers to do the rest. Indeed, the singer would do more than just repeat **A**. He or she would also ornament the music with improvised runs, cadenzas, and so on, so as to create an exciting enhanced effect the second time around.

If we can neither get [the famous castrato] Senesino, nor Carestini, then Mr. Handel desires to have a man soprano and a woman contralto, and the price (for both) must not exceed 1100 guineas, and that the persons must set out for London the latter end of August, and that no engagement must be made with one without a certainty of getting the other.

Letter from one of Handel's agents, 1730

For connoisseurs of the day, a great deal depended on the **A** repeats, since it was there that the singers really dazzled their audiences. Many modern singers have relearned the lost improvisational art of the Baroque era, and we can recapture some of the original excitement on recordings.

GEORGE FRIDERIC HANDEL
Julius Caesar (*Giulio Cesare in Egitto*) (1724)

As a young man, Handel wrote a few German operas for the Hamburg opera company (most of the music is lost) and a few Italian operas for theaters in Florence and Venice; in his maturity he wrote as many as forty Italian operas for London. Probably the most famous of them is *Julius Caesar,* one of a trio of Handel masterpieces written in the years 1724–25, the others being *Rodelinda* and *Tamerlano.*

Background Like most opera seria plots of the late Baroque era, *Julius Caesar* draws on Roman history. Cleopatra, the unprincipled Queen of Egypt, applied her formidable charms to Julius Caesar and then, after Caesar's assassination, also to his successor Mark Antony. Shakespeare deals with the second of these famous affairs in *Antony and Cleopatra;* Handel tackles the first.

But Handel's librettist added a great deal of nonhistorical plot material that Shakespeare would have shaken his head at. History tells that Pompey—who comes into the story because he waged war on Caesar and lost and fled to Egypt—was murdered by his centurion, but in the opera the murderer is Cleopatra's brother Ptolemy. Pompey's widow Cornelia is thrown into Ptolemy's harem and has to resist his advances (among others'). Her son Sextus rattles around the opera swearing vengeance on Ptolemy and finally kills him. In actuality Ptolemy was poisoned by Cleopatra, but her character is whitewashed, and she gets to sing some of the opera's most ravishing music, seductive indeed, while she is disguised as her maid.

Although the role of Sextus, for mezzo soprano, was presumably meant for a castrato, at the first performance it was sung by a woman singer who was one of Handel's regulars.

Aria, "La giustizia" Sextus promises revenge on Ptolemy, not for the first time, in the aria "La giustizia" (Justice). This aria is preceded or, rather, set up by a recitative (as usual). Since it makes more sense to study recitative when the words are in English, we leave that discussion until we get to Handel's *Messiah.*

The aria starts with a ritornello played by the string orchestra, establishing the mood right away:

The "affect" Handel means to covey by this strenuous, vigorous music is anger, and Sextus starts up with the same music. We will hear this ritornello three more times, abbreviated one time, prior to the second **A** section.

Apart from this abbreviation, "La giustizia" is in strict **A B A** (da capo) form. In the **A** section Handel goes through the words three times, with short ritornellos in between to allow the singer to catch her breath. (These short spacers are not marked on the Listening Chart.) Notice how the music tends to explode angrily on certain key words, principally by the use of *coloratura* (fast scales and turns), as on "ven-*det*-ta" (vengeance) and "tradi-*tor*" (traitor). Even more vivid are the sudden high notes on "pu-*ni*-re" (punish) and a suspense-making long note on "tradi-*tor*."

Lorraine Hunt Lieberson in another Handel opera role

There is a flamboyant effect typical of the Baroque near the end of **A**, where Sextus pauses dramatically for effect. After a breathless fermata (see page 14), he moves on to make a very forceful final cadence. Revenge is nigh!

The aria's **B** section introduces some new keys for contrast; otherwise it is brief and seems rather subdued—the strings drop out, leaving only the continuo as accompaniment. What the audience is waiting for is the da capo of **A**, where we can forget about Sextus and get to admire a display of vocal virtuosity. Lorraine Hunt Lieberson, the singer on our recording, adds brilliant improvised flourishes to the high notes on "pu-*ni*-re" and the long note on "tradi-*tor*." When she gets to the fermata in **A** she fills it in with a cadenza, and her (ornamented) final cadence sweeps us away. Anyone who can carry off a feat like this, the aria seems to say, will be more than a match for Ptolemy.

Vocal cadenzas at the time were short, because they were supposed to be sung in a single breath—thus showing off virtuoso breath control as well as vocal technique and inventiveness.

LISTEN **Handel, *Julius Caesar,* Aria "La giustizia"**

8

0:00	A	RITORNELLO		
0:16		*St. 1:* first time	La giustizia ha già sull' arco Pronto strale alla vendetta Per punire un traditor	Justice now has in its bow The arrow primed for vengeance To castigate a traitor!
0:50		*St. 1:* second time	*La giustizia . . . etc.*	
1:10		*St. 1:* third time	*La giustizia . . . etc.*	
1:31		RITORNELLO		
1:47	B	*St. 2:*	Quanto è tarda la saetta Tanto più crudele aspetta La sua pena un empio cor.	The later the arrow is shot The crueler is the pain suffered By a dastardly heart!
2:15	A	RITORNELLO		
2:22		(abbreviated)	*La giustizia . . . etc.*	Justice . . . etc.

For a note on Italian pronunciation, see page 102: "La joostidzia (ah) jah sool arco."

2 Oratorio

Sacred, or religious, vocal music of the Baroque era exhibits considerable diversity in style and form. Most of it was written directly for church services, and so its style and form depend first of all on whether those services were of the Roman Catholic, Lutheran, or Anglican rite. Every service has places where music is appropriate, even if they are not actually specified by the liturgy. In principle, each place gives rise to a different musical genre.

There are, however, two general factors that are important for all Baroque sacred-music genres—oratorio and passion, cantata, Mass, and motet. One of these factors is traditional in origin; the other is specific to the Baroque era.

𝄿 The traditional factor is the participation of the choir. Choral music has had a functional place in the religious music of virtually all rites and ages. For

George Frideric Handel (1685–1759)

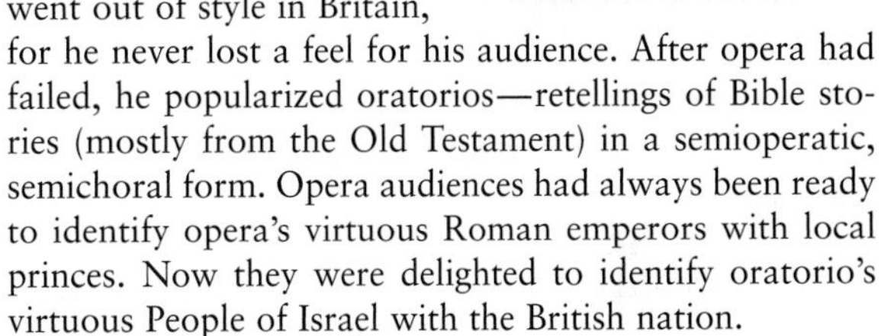

Georg Friedrich Händel—he anglicized his name to George Frideric Handel after settling in England—was one of the few composers of early days who did not come from a family of musicians. His father was a barber-surgeon and a valet at a court near Leipzig. He disapproved of music, and the boy is said to have studied music secretly at night, by candlelight. In deference to his father's wishes, Handel studied law for a year at Halle, one of Germany's major universities, before finally joining the orchestra at Hamburg, Germany's leading center of opera.

From then on, it was an exciting, glamorous life. Still in his teens, Handel fought a duel with another Hamburg musician about which was to get top billing. In 1706 he journeyed to the homeland of opera and scored big successes in Venice, Florence, and Rome. Though he became a court musician for the Elector of Hanover, in northern Germany, he kept requesting (and extending) leaves to pursue his career in London, a city that was then beginning to rival Paris as the world capital.

Here Handel continued to produce Italian operas, again with great success. He also wrote a flattering birthday ode for Queen Anne and some big pieces to celebrate a major peace treaty; for this he was awarded an annuity. In 1717, after the Elector of Hanover had become George I of England, Handel got back into his good graces by composing music to be played on boats in a royal aquatic fete on the River Thames—the famous *Water Music* (two suites for the Baroque festive orchestra).

As an opera composer, Handel had learned to gauge the taste of the public and also to flatter singers, writing music for them that showed off their voices to the best advantage. He now became an opera impresario—today we would call him a promoter—recruiting singers and negotiating their contracts, planning whole seasons of opera, and all the while composing the main attractions himself: an opera, every year, on average, between 1721 and 1743. He also had to deal with backers—English aristocrats and wealthy merchants who supported his opera companies, and persuaded their friends to take out subscriptions for boxes.

Handel made and lost several fortunes, but he always landed on his feet, even when Italian opera went out of style in Britain, for he never lost a feel for his audience. After opera had failed, he popularized oratorios—retellings of Bible stories (mostly from the Old Testament) in a semioperatic, semichoral form. Opera audiences had always been ready to identify opera's virtuous Roman emperors with local princes. Now they were delighted to identify oratorio's virtuous People of Israel with the British nation.

Handel was a big, vigorous man, hot-tempered but quick to forget, humorous and resourceful. When a particularly temperamental prima donna had a tantrum, he calmed her down by threatening to throw her out the window. At the end of his life he became blind—the same surgeon operated (unsuccessfully) on both him and Bach—but he continued to play the organ brilliantly and composed by dictating to a secretary.

Chief Works: 40 Italian operas, including *Giulio Cesare* (Julius Caesar) ▪ Near-operatic works in English: *Semele* and *Acis and Galatea* ▪ Oratorios, including *Messiah, Israel in Egypt, Samson,* and *Saul* ▪ Concerti grossi and organ concertos ▪ *Water Music,* written for an aquatic fete on the River Thames, and *Royal Fireworks Music,* celebrating the end of the War of the Austrian Succession, in 1747 ▪ Sonatas for various instruments; variations ("The Harmonious Blacksmith") for harpsichord

Encore: After *Messiah,* listen to the *Royal Fireworks Music;* Concerto Grosso in B-flat, Op. 6, No. 7.

when one person utters a religious text, he or she speaks as an individual, but when a choir does so, it speaks as a united community. A church choir can be said to speak for the whole church, even for the whole of Christianity.

The other important fact about Baroque sacred vocal music is its strong tendency to borrow from secular vocal music—which is to say, from opera. In an era fascinated by the theater, the church grew more and more theatrical. Arias inspired by Italian opera seria appear even in Baroque settings of the Catholic Mass. Solo singers could display their vocal prowess at the same time as they were presenting parts of the divine service.

The most operatic of all religious genres was oratorio, which existed in Catholic and Protestant countries alike. An **oratorio** is basically an opera on a religious subject, such as an Old Testament story or the life of a saint. It has a narrative plot in several acts, real characters, and implied action—even though oratorios were not staged, but presented in concert form, that is, without scenery, costumes, or gestures. Oratorio takes over such operatic features as recitatives and arias. On the other hand, it also makes much use of the chorus—a major difference from Italian opera of the time.

Unlike most other religious genres, an oratorio was not actually part of a church service. Indeed, in opera-crazed Italy, the oratorio was prized as an entertainment substituting for opera during Lent, a season of abstinence from opera as well as other worldly diversions.

In England, the oratorio was also a substitute for opera, though in a different sense. Thanks largely to Handel, Italian opera became very popular in London for a quarter of a century, but finally audiences tired of it. At that point, Handel, already in his mid fifties, began composing oratorios, and these turned out to be even more popular yet, the pinnacle of his long career.

On Tuesday the 2nd day of May will be performed, the Sacred Story of Esther, an Oratorio in English. Formerly composed by Mr. Handel, and now revised by him, with several Additions . . . N.B. There will be no Action on the Stage . . .

London newspaper announcement, 1731

GEORGE FRIDERIC HANDEL
Messiah (1742)

Handel's oratorio *Messiah,* his most famous work, is also one of the most famous in the whole of Western music. It is the only composition of its time that has been performed continuously—and frequently—since its first appearance. Today it is sung at Christmas and Easter in hundreds of churches around the world, as well as at symphony concerts and "*Messiah* sings," where people get together just to sing along with the Hallelujah Chorus and the other well-known choral numbers, and listen to the well-loved arias.

Unlike most oratorios, *Messiah* does not have actual characters acting out a biblical story in recitative and arias, although its text is taken from the Bible. In a more typical Handel oratorio, such as *Samson,* for example, Samson sings an aria about his blindness and argues with Delilah in recitative, while choruses represent the People of Israel and the Philistines. Instead, *Messiah* works with a group of anonymous narrators, relating episodes from the life of Jesus in recitative. The narration is interrupted by anonymous commentators who react to each of the episodes by singing recitatives and arias.

All this is similar in many ways to opera in concert form (that is, not staged); but in addition, the chorus has a large and varied role to play. On one occasion, it speaks for a group of angels that actually speaks in the Bible. Sometimes it comments on the story, like the soloists. And often the choristers raise their voices to praise the Lord in Handel's uniquely magnificent manner.

We shall first examine two numbers in *Messiah* covering the favorite Christmas story about the announcement of Christ's birth to the shepherds in the fields. Included are a recitative in four brief sections and a chorus.

Recitative *Part 1 (secco)* Sung by a boy soprano narrator accompanied by continuo (cello and organ), this recitative has the natural, "proselike" flow typical of all recitatives. Words that would be naturally stressed in ordinary speech are brought out by longer durations, higher pitches, and pauses: "*shep*-herds," "*field,*" "*flock,*" and "*night.*" No words are repeated.

Part 2 (accompanied) Accompanied recitative is used for "special effects" in operas and oratorios—here the miraculous appearance of angels. The slowly pulsing high-string background furnishes the angel with a sort of musical halo. It is also a signal for more vigorous declamation: The words *lo, Lord,* and *glory*

Women in Music

Before the twentieth century, opportunities for women were limited. Though some women worked as teachers, nurses, and laborers, society viewed women's primary role as that of wife and mother. Occasionally accidents of royal succession placed a woman in a position of great power, and the eighteenth century saw two amazingly long-lasting cases: Catherine the Great, empress of Russia, who ruled from 1762 to 1796, and Maria Theresa, de facto empress of the Austrian Empire from 1740 to 1780. But what we now think of as "careers" were simply not open to women, with few exceptions.

Bordoni

Music provided one of those exceptions. It did so by way of the theater, because an opera singer, like an actress or a ballet dancer, could attain fame and fortune and the opportunity to develop her talents in the same way as men in those same fields. Indeed, opera depended on women singers; without them the genre could never have developed or survived.

The names—although not, alas, the voices—of opera's legendary prima donnas have come down to us, along with those of opera's great composers: from **Anna Renzi** (c. 1620–c. 1660), who sang in Monteverdi's *Poppea* (see page 99), to the notorious rival sopranos **Faustina Bordoni** (1700–1781) and **Francesca Cuzzoni** (1698–1770) in the age of Handel, and beyond. Cuzzoni sang in the star-studded premiere of Handel's *Julius Caesar* (see page 153).

Cuzzoni

Women of the theater paid a price for their career opportunities, of course. They were displaying themselves—their legs or their voices—for the enjoyment of, mainly, men, who paid for the privilege. There was always a question about the respectability and marriageability of opera singers.

While women opera singers were a fixture in the musical workplace of the Baroque, women instrumentalists were much rarer. Women composers were simply flukes. We noted on page 138 that Baroque music was often the product of clans, like the Bachs; but next to none of these clans ever thought to make one of its daughters into a composer.

One that did was the Jacquet family, harpsichord makers in Paris for at least four generations. **Elizabeth-Claude Jacquet** (1667–1729) was a Mozart-style prodigy who was sponsored by Louis XIV himself. Famous as a harpsichordist, she composed music of all kinds, including an opera which was put on at the forerunner of the Paris Opéra—then as now the grandest venue for opera in Europe.

There was no respectability problem with Elizabeth-Claude Jacquet; by the time she was seventeen she was married to an organist, one Marin de la Guerre, whose name is usually hyphenated with hers.

are brought out with increasing emphasis. The end of this brief accompanied recitative is heavily punctuated by a standard cadence formula, played by the continuo. This formula is an easily recognized feature of recitatives.

Part 3 (secco) Notice that the angel speaks in a more urgent style than the narrator. And in *Part 4 (accompanied),* the excited, faster pulsations in the high strings depict the beating wings, perhaps, of the great crowd of angels. When Handel gets to what they will be "saying," he brings the music to a triumphant high point, once again over the standard recitative cadence.

Chorus, "Glory to God" "Glory to God! Glory to God in the *highest!*" sing the angels—the *high* voices of the choir, in a bright marchlike rhythm. They are accompanied by the orchestra, with the trumpets prominent. The *low* voices alone add "and peace on *earth,*" much more slowly. Fast string runs following "Glory to God" and slower reiterated chords following "and peace on earth" recall the fast and slow string passages in the two preceding accompanied recitatives.

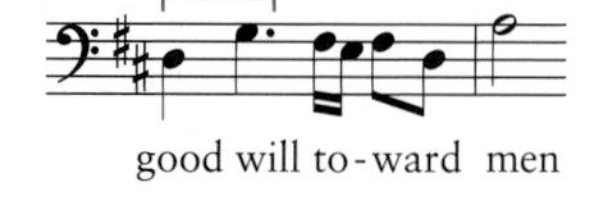

After these phrases are sung and played again, leading to another key, the full chorus sings the phrase "good will toward men" in a fugal style. The

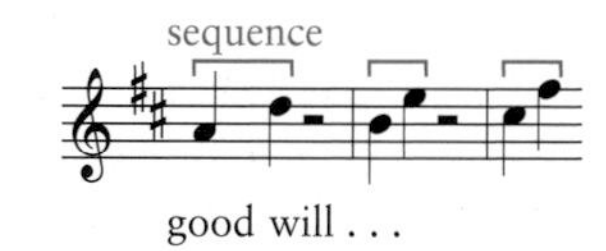

important words are *good will,* and their two-note motive is happily sung (in imitation) again and again by all the voices of the angel choir. To conclude, the "good will" motive is singled out in an enthusiastic ascending sequence.

The whole chorus is quite concise, even dramatic; the angels do not stay long. At the very end, the orchestra gets quieter and quieter—a rare effect in Baroque music, here indicating the disappearance of the shepherds' vision.

LISTEN **Handel, *Messiah,* Recitative "There were shepherds" and Chorus, "Glory to God"**

9

11

*(**Bold italic type** indicates accented words or syllables. Italics indicate phrases of text that are repeated.)*

	RECITATIVE PART 1 (secco)	
0:01	There were ***shep***herds abiding in the ***field,*** keeping ***watch*** over their ***flock*** by ***night.***	
	PART 2 (accompanied)	
0:13	And ***lo!*** the angel of the ***Lord*** came upon them, and the ***glo***ry of the Lord shone round about them; and they were sore afraid.	Standard cadence
	PART 3 (secco)	
0:34	And the angel said unto ***them: Fear*** not, for be***hold,*** I bring you good ***ti***dings of great ***joy,*** which shall ***be to all peo***ple.	Standard cadence
	For unto you is born this ***day*** in the city of ***Da***vid a ***Sa***viour, which is ***Christ*** the ***Lord.***	Standard cadence
	PART 4 (accompanied)	
1:08	And ***sud***denly there was with the ***an***gel a ***mul***titude of the heavenly ***host,*** praising ***God, and saying:***	Standard cadence
	CHORUS	
1:20	Glory to God, *glory to God,* in the highest, and peace on earth,	
2:02	good will toward men *good will*	
2:21	*Glory to God*	

Hallelujah Chorus This famous chorus brings Act II of *Messiah* to a resounding close. Like "Glory to God," "Hallelujah" makes marvelous use of monophony ("King of Kings"), homophony (the opening "Hallelujah"), and polyphony ("And he shall reign for ever and ever"): almost a textbook example of musical textures. Compare "And peace on earth," "Glory to God," and "Good will toward men" in the earlier chorus.

In a passage beloved by chorus singers, Handel sets "The Kingdom of this world is become" on a low descending scale, *piano,* swelling suddenly into a similar scale in a higher register, *forte,* for "the Kingdom of our Lord, and of his Christ"—a perfect representation of one thing becoming another thing, similar but newly radiant. Later the sopranos (cheered on by the trumpets) solemnly utter the words "King of Kings" on higher and higher long notes as the other voices keep repeating their answer, "for ever, Hallelujah!"

George II of England, attending the first London performance of *Messiah,* was so moved by this chorus that he stood up in his box—prompting everyone else to stand in honor of the King of Kings, no doubt, but also reminding everyone of his own majesty, which was being acclaimed by the typical Baroque festive orchestra. Audiences still sometimes stand during the "Hallelujah" Chorus.

An oratorio performance, caught by the satirical pen of Handel's contemporary William Hogarth (1697–1764). Note the words. Is nothing sacred?

LISTEN **Handel, *Messiah*, Hallelujah Chorus**

10

12

(Italics indicate phrases of text that are repeated.)

0:07 Hallelujah, *Hallelujah!*
0:26 For the Lord God omnipotent reigneth. *Hallelujah!*
For the Lord God omnipotent reigneth.
1:17 The Kingdom of this world is become the kingdom
of our Lord and *of his Christ.*
1:35 And He shall reign for ever and ever, *and he shall reign for ever and ever.*
1:58 KING OF KINGS *for ever and ever, Hallelujah!*
AND LORD OF LORDS *for ever and ever, Hallelujah!*

3 The Church Cantata

Second in importance to oratorio among Baroque sacred-music genres is the **church cantata.** *Cantata* is a general name for a piece of moderate length for voices and instruments, and in Germany church cantatas were written to be performed during Lutheran Church services. Lutheran Churches had (and still have today) fixed readings and hymns specified for every Sunday of the year, as well as for special occasions such as Easter and Christmas. The words of cantatas addressed the religious content of the day in question. Sung before the sermon, the cantata was in effect a second, musicalized sermon.

As cantor, or music director, of Leipzig's biggest church (the Thomaskirche), Bach was required to produce cantatas for the entire year—a stupendous task that kept him very busy indeed for years after he was appointed. Over two hundred cantatas by Bach have survived, each of them with several movements, including some secular cantatas written for court or civic celebrations.

The Lutheran Chorale

The content and structure of the church cantata were quite various. One kind, for example, has singers who represent Hope, Fear, the Soul, and so on, discussing Christian issues in operatic arias and recitatives, like a short scene from an oratorio. A special feature of nearly all Lutheran cantatas is their use of traditional congregational hymns. Lutheran hymns are called **chorales** (coráhls), from the German word for hymn (*Choral*).

I have always been very fond of music. Whoever is proficient in this art is a good man, fit for all other things. Hence it is absolutely necessary to have it taught in the schools. A schoolmaster must know how to sing or I shan't tolerate him.

Martin Luther, 1538

Martin Luther, the father of the Protestant Reformation, placed special emphasis on hymn singing when he decided on the format of Lutheran services. Two hundred years later, in Bach's time, a large body of chorales served as the foundation for Lutheran worship, both in church services and also at informal pious devotions in the home. Everybody knew the words and music of these chorales. You learned them as a small child and sang them in church all your life. Consequently when composers introduced chorale tunes into cantatas (and other sacred-music genres), they were drawing on a rich source of association.

Just how were tunes "introduced"? There were many ways. The last movement of a Bach cantata is usually a single hymn stanza sung straight through, in much the same simple way as the congregation would sing it, but with the orchestra playing.

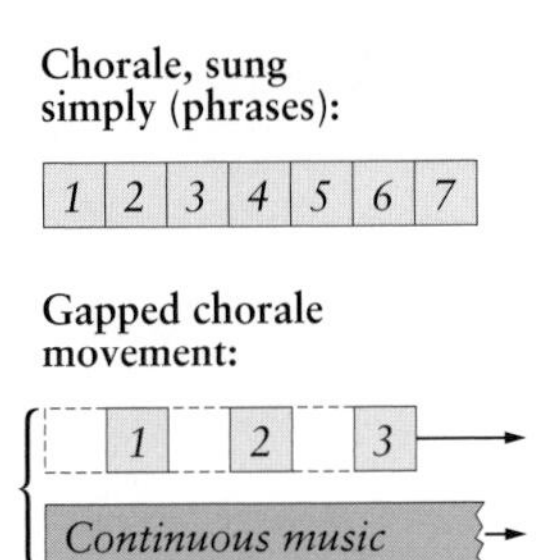

Longer cantata movements present the individual lines or phrases of the chorale one by one, with gaps in between them, while other music runs on continuously, both during the chorale phrases (that is, in counterpoint with them) and during the gaps. In a **gapped chorale**, the chorale melody is delivered in spurts. It can be sung, or it can be played by one prominent instrument—an oboe, say, or a trumpet—while the continuous music goes along in the other instruments and/or voices.

JOHANN SEBASTIAN BACH (1685–1750)
Cantata No. 4, "Christ lag in Todesbanden" (Christ Lay in Death's Dark Prison) (1707)

In his posts as an organist and cantor, Bach made multiple settings of many hymns, both in cantatas and also as chorale preludes for organ (see page 162). We shall study just a few of his settings of the Easter chorale "Christ lag in Todesbanden" (Christ Lay in Death's Dark Prison).

This rugged old tune had been fitted with even more rugged words by Martin Luther himself, in 1524. The seven stanzas of the chorale, each ending with "Hallelujah!," tell in vivid language of mankind's struggle with Death and the victory achieved through Christ's sacrifice. The fact that this hymn is in the minor mode throws a tough, sober shadow over all the rejoicing; the mood is unforgettable.

We cannot recapture the associations that Bach's contemporaries would have brought to this tune, but we can begin to learn it by singing the first stanza:

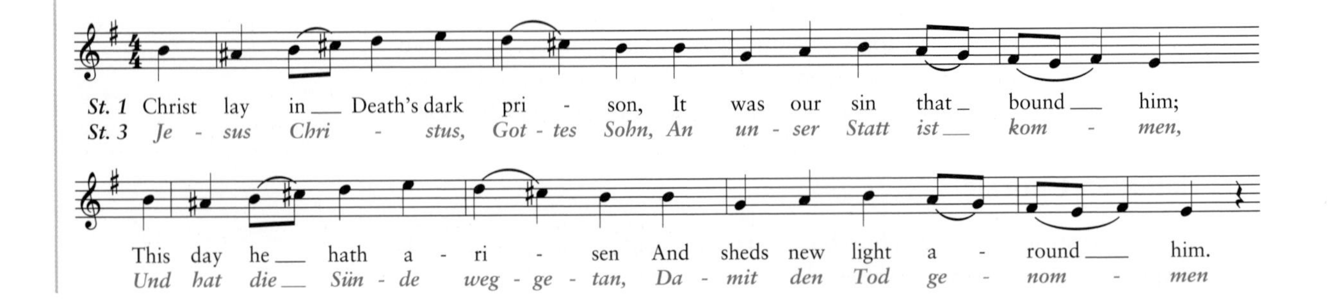

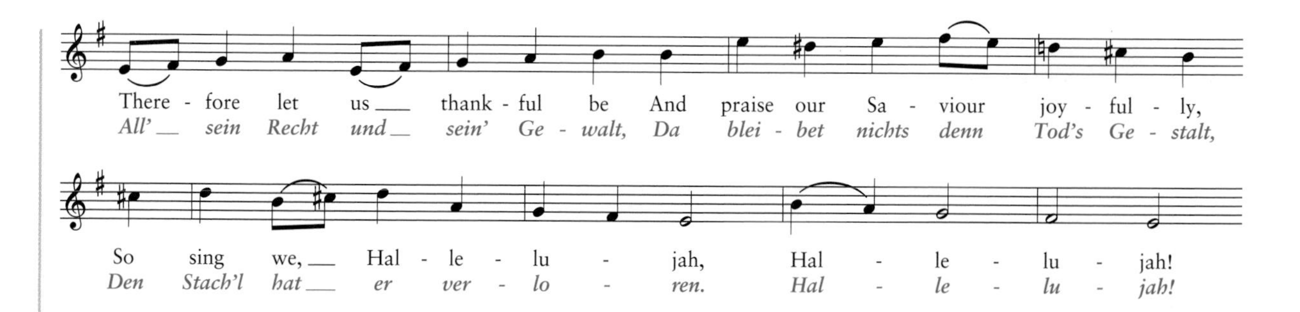

The cantata based on "Christ lag in Todesbanden" is one of Bach's earliest. It employs simple forces: voices and a string orchestra, with continuo.* The words of the seven movements are the words of the seven stanzas of the famous Easter chorale.

Bach set these seven stanzas with a sharp eye (or ear) for symmetry. Not all of the voices sing in all of the stanzas; the diagram below tallies the voices that sing in each one:

SINFONIA	STANZA 1	2	3	4	5	6	7
Orchestra	Soprano	S		S		S	S
	Alto	A		A			A
	Tenor		T	T		T	T
	Bass			B	B		B

Color shading indicates which voice sings the chorale melody. (In stanza 6, it is divided between two voices.)

A Leipzig church service

After a short orchestral prelude—Bach calls it "sinfonia"—all the stanzas except the last are set as "gapped" chorales of some sort.

Stanza 3 The tenor sings the "gapped" chorale tune; follow him along with the music, above. Accompanied by the continuo (played on the organ), a violin plays an urgent melody at both ends of the piece and in the gaps between the lines. At the word *nichts* ("nothing") the music comes to a wrenching stop and a slowdown, a quite astonishing effect. Then the violin starts up again as though nothing had happened. The sudden absence of music tells us what is left of Death's power: *nichts,* zilch!

Stanza 4 Here it is the alto (doubled by an organ stop) that sings the gapped chorale tune, more slowly than the tenor of stanza 3. The "continuous" music is assigned to other voices singing faster imitative polyphony to the same words, always using fragments of the chorale melody. (Compare the music to the right with the chorale melody.) Perhaps all this busy imitative polyphony makes a good illustration of the warfare described with such gusto in this stanza. Perhaps, too, the jaunty rhythm at *ein Spott* can indeed be heard as mocking Death who has lost his sting.

Stanza 7 No longer gapped, this is a straightforward presentation of the hymn as it might be sung by the congregation. Bach's rich harmonies below the soprano melody are sung by the lower voices, doubled by the instruments. The cantata comes to a restful conclusion at last, as the text turns from battles to the confidence of faith. Even "hallelujah" can now be uttered simply.

STANZA 4

*When Bach wrote Cantata No. 4 he was a young small-town organist, and probably could not count on more than one singer to a part, as on our recording—which compensates, however, by adding reverberation to suggest an echoing church.

LISTEN Bach, "Christ lag in Todesbanden"

11-13

11	*Stanza 3:* Jesus Christus, Gottes Sohn, An unser Statt ist kommen, Und hat die Sünde weggetan, Damit den Tod genommen All' sein Recht und sein' Gewalt; Da bleibet *nichts*—denn Tod's Gestalt; Den Stach'l hat er verloren. Hallelujah!	Jesus Christ, the Son of God, Has come on our behalf, And has done away with our sins, Thereby robbing Death Of all his power and might; There remains nothing but Death's image; He has lost his sting. Hallelujah!
12	*Stanza 4:* Es war ein wunderlicher Krieg, Da Tod und Leben rungen; Das Leben da behielt das Sieg, Es hat den Tod verschlungen. Die Schrift hat verkündiget das Wie ein Tod den andern frass; Ein Spott aus dem Tod ist worden. Hallelujah!	It was a marvelous war Where Death and Life battled. Life gained the victory; It swallowed up Death. Scripture has proclaimed How one Death gobbled up the other; Death became a mockery. Hallelujah!
13	*Stanza 7:* Wir essen und leben wohl Im rechten Osterfladen. Der alter Sauerteig nicht soll Sein bei dem Wort der Gnaden. Christus will die Koste sein Und speisen die Seel' allein, Der Glaub' will keins andern leben. Hallelujah!	We eat and live fitly On the true unleavened bread of Passover; The old yeast shall not Contaminate the word of grace. Christ alone will be the food To feed the soul: Faith will live on nothing else. Hallelujah!

4 The Organ Chorale

German churches took special pride in their organs, both in their appearance and their acoustic quality. Organ technology developed prodigiously in the Baroque era. The **chorale prelude** or *organ chorale,* an important genre of keyboard music at the time, is an organ composition incorporating a hymn (chorale) tune.

Like cantatas, organ chorales incorporated hymn tunes in many ways. The "gapped" method (see page 160) was common. Played on the organ, the tune could also be ornamented with scales, trills, and so on, for expressive purposes—much the same technique as was applied to opera melodies.

In religious terms, the effect of an organ chorale was probably not very different from a sung one. Lutherans knew their hymns by heart, so the tune on the organ would automatically bring to mind the hymn text and its message or lesson.

When Bach seated himself at the organ, he used to choose some theme and treat it in all the various forms of organ composition. First, he used this theme for a prelude and fugue, with the full organ. Then he showed his art of using the stops for a trio, quartet, etc., on the same theme. Afterwards followed a chorale, the melody of which was playfully surrounded by the same theme in three or four contrapuntal parts . . .

From the first biography of Bach, 1802

JOHANN SEBASTIAN BACH
Chorale Prelude, "Christ lag in Todesbanden" (Christ Lay in Death's Dark Prison) (1715)

14

At certain points in a Lutheran service, the organist would play chorale preludes based on seasonal hymns. On Easter Sunday, Bach might well have played this organ prelude on "Christ lag in Todesbanden."

The music is powerful and triumphant—a wordless hallelujah for the miracle of Easter. The chorale tune can be heard on the high organ pipes, played without any gaps, but with a vigorous faster motive accompanying it, a motive that clatters away splendidly in the organ pedals. The rich harmonies are formed

Lavishly decorated in Baroque style, the splendid organ of St. John's Church in Lüneburg, northern Germany, may have been played by the young Bach; Bach is thought to have studied with its organist, Georg Böhm. Böhm was an important composer of organ music.

by dense counterpoint. Perhaps next in the service the hymn would have been sung by the congregation.

This piece comes from the *Orgelbüchlein*, a "Little Organ Book" of 162 short chorale preludes that Bach planned for use in different services throughout the entire church year. This not-so-little collection bears witness to both sides of Bach's temperament: encyclopedic on the one hand and on the other strictly practical.

Web: *Research and test your understanding of Baroque vocal music at* **<bedfordstmartins.com/listen>.**

CHAPTER 11

Prelude Music and the Enlightenment

In the second part of the eighteenth century, a new musical style emerged in Europe. Called the Classical style, it had important pioneers in Italy and northern Germany; one of them was Carl Philipp Emanuel Bach, a son of Johann Sebastian. But the Classical style was developed particularly by several great composers active in Vienna, capital of Austria. Here conditions seem to have been ideal for music. Geographically, Austria stands at the crossroads of four other musical nations—Germany, Bohemia (now the Czech Republic), Hungary, and Italy—and Vienna was also central in political terms. As the capital of the powerful Hapsburg empire, Vienna was plunged into every European conflict of the time and exposed to every new cultural and intellectual current.

Vienna's golden years were from 1780 to 1790, during the reign of Emperor Joseph II, the most enlightened of the long line of Hapsburg monarchs. Joseph emancipated the peasantry, furthered education, and reduced the power of the clergy; he supported music and literature with his patronage and encouraged a free press. In a city of only 150,000 people, there were three hundred newspapers and journals during Joseph's reign, representing every shade of opinion.

In this liberal atmosphere, Franz Joseph Haydn of nearby Eisenstadt became recognized as the principal composer of Europe; his symphonies were commissioned from far-off Paris and London. The young Wolfgang Amadeus Mozart was drawn to the capital in 1781 from Salzburg, a hundred miles to the west, to spend his brilliant last decade there. And in 1792 a young musician from the other end of Germany, who had composed a long cantata mourning Emperor Joseph's death, decided to come to this great musical center to launch his career. His name was Ludwig van Beethoven.

1 The Enlightenment and Music

Emperor Joseph II

To describe Joseph II as an "enlightened" ruler is both to commend him and also to locate him in European intellectual history. Like a number of other rulers of the time, Joseph II derived his principles of governance from an important intellectual movement of the eighteenth century known as the Enlightenment, a movement that also helped to define the music that flourished under his reign.

Centered in France, the Enlightenment had strong roots in English philosophy and strong offshoots in Germany and Austria. Its original source was the faith in reason that led to the great scientific discoveries of the Baroque period. Now, however, the emphasis veered away from the purely intellectual and scientific toward the social sphere. People were less intent on controlling natural forces by science than on turning these forces to human benefit. People also began to apply the same intelligence that solved scientific problems to problems of public morality, education, and politics.

Social injustice came under especially strong fire in the eighteenth century; so did established religion. For the first time in European history, religion ceased to be an overriding force in many people's minds. There were currents

The phrase "Viennese Classical style" brings to mind Haydn, Mozart, and Beethoven; each of them came to the capital city from other, smaller centers.

of agnosticism and even outright atheism—to the outrage of the English poet and mystic William Blake:

> Mock on, mock on, Voltaire, Rousseau:
> Mock on, mock on, 'tis all in vain!
> You throw the sand against the wind,
> And the wind blows it back again.

The two French philosophers named by Blake are always mentioned in connection with the Enlightenment: François Marie Arouet, whose pen name was Voltaire (1694–1778), tireless satirist and campaigner for justice and reason, and the younger, more radical, more disturbing Jean-Jacques Rousseau (1712–1778). Rousseau is one of the few major figures of European philosophy who had a direct effect on the history of music, as we shall see.

Voltaire, by Jean-Antoine Houdon (1740–1828), master sculptor of the neo-Roman busts that were much favored at the time. (All the other portrait busts in this chapter are also by Houdon.)

"The Pursuit of Happiness"

The Enlightenment was also the occasion for the first great contribution to Western civilization from America. In colonial days, the austere Puritan spirit was hardly in step with the growing secularization of European society, but the Declaration of Independence and the Federalist Papers proved to be the finest flowers of Enlightenment idealism. The notion that a new state could be founded on rational principles, set down on a piece of paper, and agreed to by men of good will and intelligence—this could only have emerged under the influence of the political and philosophical writings of the eighteenth century.

"Life, liberty, and the pursuit of happiness": The last of these three famous rights, too, was very much of its time. One can imagine the medieval barons who forced King John to accept the Magna Carta insisting on life and liberty, of a sort, but it would never have occurred to them to demand happiness as a self-evident right for all. Voltaire and Rousseau fought passionately for social justice so that people might live good lives according to their own convictions.

In the Classical era, lighter entertainments took over the stage, in place of the heavy drama characteristic of the Baroque. Compare this picture (a London ballet of 1791) with the opera seria shown on page 120.

A French Rococo ceramic plaque

The eighteenth century was an age of good living, then, an age that valued intelligence, wit, and sensitivity. The age cultivated elegant conversation, the social arts, and hedonism. One of its inventions was the salon—half party, half seminar: a regular gathering in a fashionable lady's home where notables would discuss books, music, art, and ideas. Another innovation of the time was the coffee house. Another was the public concert.

Art and Entertainment

Entertainment, for most people, contributes to the good life—though certainly Thomas Jefferson was thinking of more than entertainment when he wrote of "the pursuit of happiness." However, the pursuit of entertainment was not something that the eighteenth century looked down upon at all. The arts were expected to *please* rather than to instruct, impress, or even express, as had been the case in the Baroque era. The result of this attitude is evident in the style of all the arts in the eighteenth century.

Thomas Jefferson

For a time at midcentury a light and often frothy style known as *Rococo* was fashionable in painting, decoration, furniture and jewelry design, and so on. Our illustration—a ceramic plaque—catches the spirit of this entertainment art with special charm. Wreathed in leaves that fit in with the border, two well-dressed court gentlemen cavort in an ideal countryside; one plays the flute while the other dances. The subject, the feathery designs on the frame, even the pretty rim itself, are all characteristic of the light art of the Rococo.

Music at midcentury, just before the formation of the Viennese Classical style, was also very light—charming at best, but often frivolous and empty. A genre that was typical of the time was the **divertimento,** a piece designed to divert, amuse, and entertain. Elegant figurines of musicians and ornamented music boxes, playing little tunes, were extremely popular (see page 176).

The Viennese Classical music of Haydn and Mozart is far from this light style, yet these composers never put pen to paper without every expectation that their audiences were going to be "pleased." Every historical era, of course, has had its entertainment music. But only in the Classical era was great music of the highest quality put forth quite frankly and plainly as entertainment.

Jean-Jacques Rousseau

Jean-Jacques Rousseau and Opera

Rousseau is remembered today as Europe's first "alienated" intellectual. Whatever his subject, he always came around to blasting the social institutions of his day as stifling to the individual. Passionately devoted to nature and to personal feeling, he disseminated the very influential idea of "natural man," born good but corrupted by civilization. This interest, incidentally, caused Rousseau to think hard and sympathetically about the so-called primitive peoples in the Americas, peoples whom Europeans had colonized and enslaved for over two hundred years.

To the great French *Encyclopédie* of 1751–65, which was the bible of Enlightenment thought, Rousseau contributed articles on two subjects: politics and music. For Rousseau was also a self-taught composer, who made his living for years as a professional music copyist.

Both by means of his fiery writings and by actual example, Rousseau launched a devastating attack on the aristocratic opera of the late Baroque era. And to attack opera—the most important, extended, and glamorous musical genre of the time—was to throw Baroque music itself into question. For Rousseau, the complicated plots of Baroque operas were as impossibly artificial as their complicated music. He demanded a kind of opera that would portray real people in actual life—simple people, close to nature, singing "natural" music.

Thus Rousseau acclaimed a famous Italian comic opera of the time that played in Paris, Giovanni Battista Pergolesi's *La serva padrona* ("The Maid as Mistress," 1733). The music is lively and catchy, with no elaborate coloratura singing, rich harmonies, or exaggerated emotional outpourings. And the story could scarcely be more down-to-earth or rudimentary: A servant girl uses a simple ruse to trick a rich old bachelor into marriage.

Thanks to Pergolesi and Rousseau—and to Mozart—comic opera became the most progressive operatic form of the later part of the century. It dealt not with Roman emperors and their idealized noble sentiments, but with contemporary middle- and lower-class figures expressing everyday feelings in a relatively vivid and natural way. *Opera buffa,* as Italian comic opera was called, will be discussed on pages 206 and 207.

Rousseau himself composed a very successful opera of the uncomplicated kind he recommended. Pictured are the shepherdess Colette, with sheep, and her lover Colin from Rousseau's *Le Devin du village (The Village Soothsayer),* 1752.

The Novel

In its ideals, this new kind of opera was comparable to the most important new literary genre that grew up at the same time. This was the novel, which—together with the symphony—counts as the Enlightenment's greatest artistic legacy to the nineteenth and twentieth centuries.

Precursors of the novel go back to ancient Rome, but the genre did not really capture the European imagination until around 1750. Among the best-known early novels are Henry Fielding's *Tom Jones,* the tale of a rather ordinary young man and his adventures in town and country, and Samuel Richardson's *Pamela,* a domestic drama that manages to be sexually explicit, sentimental, and moralistic all at the same time. Just before the end of the century, Jane Austen began her subtle explorations of the social forces at work on the hearts of her very

A late eighteenth-century court musician surrounded by the tools of his trade. However, he is depicted not in a palace of the era, but in a sober imitation classical temple—amusing testimony to the Neoclassical enthusiasms and aspirations of the time.

sensitive (and sensible) characters in novels such as *Pride and Prejudice, Emma, Persuasion,* and others. These novels still provide plots for Hollywood films today.

Sharp, realistic observation of contemporary life, and sensitive depiction of feeling—these are the ideals shared by late eighteenth-century opera and the novel. It is no accident that within a few years of their publication, both *Tom Jones* and *Pamela* were turned into major operas, one French, the other Italian.

In Mozart, opera buffa found a master comparable to Jane Austen in the sensitive response to feeling and action. In his opera *Don Giovanni,* for example, the three women romantically involved with the hero—the coquettish country girl, Zerlina, the steely aristocrat, Donna Anna, and the sentimental Donna Elvira—are depicted in music with the greatest human sympathy and psychological acumen. One can come to feel that the same qualities are reflected in Mozart's symphonies and concertos.

Neoclassicism

It is from the standpoint of "the natural," that great rallying cry of the Enlightenment, that we should understand Neoclassicism, an important movement in the visual arts at this time influenced by the Greek and Roman classics. The classics have meant many things to many eras; to the eighteenth century, they meant a return to simple, natural values. They meant a rejection of the complex solemnities of the Baroque on the one hand, and of the pleasant frivolities of the Rococo on the other. Shown throughout this chapter, the portrait busts (modeled on Roman busts) by Jean-Antoine Houdon are prime examples of eighteenth-century Neoclassical art.

Christoph Willibald von Gluck

Christoph Willibald von Gluck (1714–1787), an important composer active in both Vienna and Paris, used austere classical subjects in a determined effort to "reform" (that is, simplify and ennoble) eighteenth-century opera. His *Orfeo ed Euridice* (1762) is based on the Greek myth of Orpheus, his *Alceste* (1767) on a classical Greek drama. When *Alceste* reached Paris, it was greeted enthusiastically by the aging Rousseau.

Apart from the operas of Gluck, however, Neoclassical art has little direct connection with music in what is traditionally called the Classical style. One can perhaps see that a taste inclined toward moderation, simplicity, and balance would also appreciate the order and clarity of late eighteenth-century music, but the traditional label is not a very happy one. "Classicism" was a label coined in the nineteenth century to distinguish the music of Haydn and Mozart from the "Romanticism" that came after it.

2 The Rise of Concerts

A far-reaching development in the sociology and economics of music was the rise of public concerts. Occasional concerts had been put on before, in taverns, private homes, palaces, and theaters, but it was only in the middle of the eighteenth century that they became a significant force in musical life. Concert series, financed by subscription, were put on by the forerunners of today's promoters. Concerts for the benefit of charity were set up on a regular basis as major society events.

In 1748 Europe's first hall designed especially for concerts was built in a college town, Oxford. Still in use, the Holywell Music Room holds about 150 people.

Music of all kinds was presented at these new public concerts; one major series—the Parisian *Concert spirituel,* founded in 1725—originally concentrated on sacred vocal music. But orchestral music was the staple. The importance of concerts lay mainly in the impetus they gave to the composition of orchestral music—symphonies and concertos. For there were, after all, other public forums for church music (churches) and opera (opera houses). Now purely orchestral music, too, moved into the public domain, and its importance and prestige grew rapidly.

However, the livelihood of musicians still depended principally on court patronage, the opera house, and the church (see page 119). Concerts were certainly a factor in the careers of both of the masters of Classical style already mentioned: Haydn wrote his last symphonies, the "London" symphonies, for concerts on two celebrity tours to that city, and Mozart wrote most of his

For the Benefit of Mr. F L A G G.
This Evening,
A public CONCERT of
Vocal and Inſtrumental MUSIC,
Will be performed at Concert Hall in Queen-ſtreet.
The Vocal part to be performed by Four Voices, and to conclude with the BRITISH GRENADIERS.—N. B. *TICKETS* to be had at the Printers, or at the London Book-ſtore, at *HALF a DOLLAR* each.—To begin preciſely at half after ſeven.
***** The laſt Concert this Seaſon.**

The rise of concerts: With only around 15,000 inhabitants, pre-revolutionary Boston already had a concert hall and a concert promoter (bandmaster Josiah Flagg). This advertisement is from the *Boston Chronicle* of 1769.

piano concertos—among his greatest works—for concerts he himself put on in Vienna. But concerts were a resource that Haydn did not draw upon significantly until the end of his long life, and they were not an adequate resource, alas, to sustain Mozart.

3 Style Features of Classical Music

In discussing the musical style of the late Baroque period, we started with a single guiding concept. There is a thorough, even rigorous quality in the ways early eighteenth-century composers treated almost all aspects of music, and this quality seems to underpin the expressive gestures of grandeur and overstatement that are characteristic of the Baroque.

Classical music cannot be discussed quite as easily as this. We have to keep two concepts in mind for its understanding, concepts that were constantly on the lips of men and women of the time. One was "natural," and the other was "pleasing variety." In the late eighteenth century, it was taken for granted that these two artistic ideals went hand in hand and provided mutual support.

Today we can see that sometimes they pulled in opposite directions. For although "variety" was invoked as a guard against boredom, it was also an invitation to complexity, and complexity would seem to run counter to "natural" simplicity and clarity. In any case, in Classical music one or the other—and sometimes both—of these qualities can be traced in all the elements of musical technique: in rhythm, dynamics, tone color, melody, texture, and form. A new expressive quality developed in this music as a result of its new technique.

Rhythm

Perhaps the most striking change in music between the Baroque and the Classical periods came in rhythm. In this area the artistic ideal of "pleasing variety" reigned supreme. The unvarying rhythms of Baroque music came to be regarded as dreary, obvious, and boring.

Classical music is highly flexible in rhythm. Throughout a single movement, the tempo and meter remain constant, but the rhythms of the various themes tend to differ in both obvious and subtle ways. In the first movement of Mozart's Symphony in G Minor, for example, the first theme moves almost entirely in eighth notes and quarters, whereas the second theme is marked by longer notes and shorter ones—dotted half notes and sixteenths.

Audiences wanted variety in music; composers responded by refining the rhythmic differences between themes and other musical sections, so that the differences sound like more than differences—they sound like real contrasts. The music may gradually increase or decrease its rhythmic energy, stop suddenly, press forward by fits and starts, or glide by smoothly. All this gives the sense that Classical music is moving in a less predictable, more interesting, and often more exciting way than Baroque music does.

Dynamics

Variety and flexibility were also introduced into dynamics. Passages were now conceived more specifically than before as loud, soft, very loud, and so on, and marked ***f, p, ff, mf*** by composers accordingly. Again, concern for variety went along with a new sensitivity to contrast. By insisting on the contrast between

Domestic music making in the eighteenth century: a group portrait by Johann Zoffany (1733–1810), one of many fashionable painters in Britain (and British India). It was not uncommon for members of the gentry—including, here, an earl—to order pictures showing off their musical accomplishments.

loud and soft, soft and very soft, composers made variety in dynamics clearly perceptible and, we must suppose, "pleasing."

Furthermore, instead of using the steady dynamics of the previous period, composers now worked extensively with gradations of volume. The words for growing louder (*crescendo*) and growing softer (*diminuendo*) first came into general use in the Classical period. Orchestras of the mid-eighteenth century were the first to practice long crescendos, which, we are told, caused audiences to rise up from their seats in excitement.

The clearest sign of the new flexibility in dynamics was the rise in popularity of the piano, at the expense of the ever-present harpsichord of the Baroque era. The older instrument could manage only one sound level, or at best a few sound levels, thanks to its two or three separate sets of strings. The new pianoforte could produce a continuous range of dynamics from soft to loud (the name, in fact, means "soft-loud" in Italian). It attracted composers because they wished their keyboard instruments to have the same flexibility in dynamics that they were teaching to their orchestras.

Tone Color: The Orchestra

Classical composers also devoted increasing attention to tone color. The clearest sign of this was the emergence of the Classical orchestra. The orchestra standardized in this period formed the basis of the symphony orchestra of later times.

The heart of the Classical orchestra was still (as in the Baroque orchestra) a group of stringed instruments: violins, divided into two groups, first violins and second violins; violas; and cellos, with a few basses playing the same music as the cellos an octave lower. As we saw on page 123, there was a "basic" Baroque orchestra consisting of just these instruments, plus the continuo, and various other possibilities, including the "festive" Baroque orchestra:

THE BASIC BAROQUE ORCHESTRA

STRINGS	KEYBOARD
Violins (divided into two groups, called violins 1 and violins 2) Violas Cellos Bass viol (playing the same music as the cellos, an octave lower)	Harpsichord or organ

THE FESTIVE BAROQUE ORCHESTRA

STRINGS	WOODWINDS	BRASS	PERCUSSION	KEYBOARD
Violins 1 Violins 2 Violas Cellos Bass viol	2 Oboes 1 Bassoon	3 Trumpets	2 Timpani (kettledrums)	Harpsichord or organ

In the Classical orchestra, however, the woodwind and brass instruments were given clearly defined, regular roles. With the strings as a framework, woodwind instruments were added: in the high range, pairs of flutes, oboes, and (a bit later) clarinets; in the low, bassoons. These instruments provided "pleasing variety" by playing certain melodies and other passages; each of the woodwinds contributed its own characteristic tone color or timbre. They also strengthened the strings in loud sections.

THE CLASSICAL ORCHESTRA

STRINGS	WOODWINDS	BRASS	PERCUSSION
Violins 1	2 Flutes	2 French horns	2 Timpani
Violins 2	2 Oboes	2 Trumpets*	
Violas	2 Clarinets*		
Cellos	2 Bassoons		
Bass viols		*Optional	

Brass instruments were added in the middle range. The function of French horns and trumpets was mainly to provide solid support for the main harmonies, especially at points such as cadences when the harmonies needed to be made particularly clear. The only regular percussion instruments used were two timpani, which generally played along with the brass.

The great advance in the orchestra from the Baroque to the Classical era was in flexibility—flexibility in tone color and also in rhythm and dynamics. The orchestra now became the most subtle and versatile musical resource that composers could employ, as well as the grandest.

Melody: Tunes

The Enlightenment ideal of "pleasing variety" was a secondary issue with Classical melody. Rather the demand was for simplicity and clarity, for relief from the complex, richly ornamented lines of the Baroque period. When people at the time demanded "natural" melodies, what they meant were tunes: uncomplicated, singable melodies with clear phrases (and not too many of them), melodies with easily grasped parallelisms and balances.

Confronted with a Baroque work such as Bach's Suite No. 3 in D (see page 145), a late eighteenth-century audience might have tolerated the fairly straightforward Gavotte, but would have been unmoved by the beautiful Air.

Its elegant winding lines and the mere fact of its great length would have struck them as completely "unnatural":

In their move toward melodic simplicity, composers of the Classical period moved much closer to popular music, and some varieties of folk music, than their Baroque predecessors had. There is an unmistakable popular lilt in Haydn's music that people have traced to the Croatian folk melodies he heard in childhood. Short tunes—or, more often, attractive little phrases that sound as though they might easily grow into tunes—are heard again and again in Classical symphonies, quartets, and other pieces. Tunes are not the only melodic material to be heard in these works, as we shall see in a moment. Nonetheless, by comparison with a Baroque concerto, a Classical symphony leaves listeners with a good deal more to hum or whistle as they leave the concert.

Often entire tunes were worked into larger compositions. For example, variation form (theme and variations) grew popular both for separate pieces improvised by virtuosos and for movements in multimovement genres. Haydn wrote variations on the Austrian national anthem (he also wrote the tune), and Mozart wrote variations on "Twinkle, Twinkle, Little Star," in its original French version, "Ah vous dirai-je, maman" ("Oh mama, I must tell you"). Occasionally, popular songs were even introduced into symphonies. There is a contemporary opera tune in Mozart's *Jupiter* Symphony, the last he composed.

Texture: Homophony

The predominant texture of Classical music is homophonic. In Classical compositions, melodies are regularly heard with a straightforward harmonic accompaniment in chords, without counterpoint and without even a melodic-sounding bass line. Again, this was thought (not unreasonably) to be a more "natural," clearer way of presenting a melody than polyphony.

All this made, and still makes, for easy listening. The opening of Mozart's famous Symphony No. 40 in G Minor proclaims the new sonorous world of the late eighteenth century:

A single quiet chord regrouped and repeated by the violas, the plainest sort of bass support below, and above them all a plaintive melody in the violins—this simple, sharply polarized texture becomes typical of the new style.

Homophony or melody with harmony was not, however, merely a negative reaction to what people of the time saw as the heavy, pedantic complexities of Baroque counterpoint. It was also a positive move in the direction of sensitivity. When composers found that they were not always occupied in fitting contrapuntal parts to their melodies, they also discovered that they could handle other elements of music with more "pleasing variety." In particular, a new sensitivity developed to harmony for its own sake.

One aspect of this development was a desire to specify harmonies more precisely than in the Baroque era. The first thing to go was the continuo, which had spread its unrelenting and unspecified (because improvised) chord patterns over nearly all Baroque music. Classical composers, newly alert to the sonorous quality of a particular chord, wanted it "spaced" and distributed among various instruments in just one way. They refused to allow a continuo player to obscure the chord with unpredictable extra notes and rhythms.

It may seem paradoxical, then, but the thrust toward simplicity in texture and melody led through the back door to increased subtlety in other areas, notably in rhythm and in harmony.

Classical Counterpoint

The rise of homophony in the Classical period represents a major turnaround in musical technique. For although Baroque composers did write some homophonic pieces, as we have seen, the predominant texture of music at that time was polyphonic. This turning point was, in fact, one of the most decisive in all of musical history, for polyphony had monopolized music since the Middle Ages.

Yet it is not the way of history to abandon important resources of the past completely, even when the past is discredited. Classical composers rejected Baroque music, but they cautiously retained the basic principle of counterpoint. They were able to do this by refining it into a more delicate, unobtrusive kind of counterpoint than that of the Baroque era. And there was a sharper awareness now of counterpoint's expressive possibilities. In a texture that was mostly "natural" and homophonic, counterpoint attracted special attention; this texture could be used to create the impression of tension, of one line rubbing against another. The more intense, "artificial" texture of polyphony stood out against "natural" homophonic texture.

Hence, as we shall see in the next chapter, the section in Classical sonata form called the development section, whose basic function is to build up tension, typically involves contrapuntal textures. Sonata form was the most important musical form of the time, and so counterpoint was often heard.

4 Form in Classical Music

How can a piece of music be extended through a considerable span of time when listeners expect everything to be "natural," simple, and easily understood? This was the problem of musical form that faced composers of the Viennese Classical era. They arrived at a solution of considerable elegance and power, involving several elements.

Repetitions and Cadences

First, themes in Classical music tend to be *repeated* immediately after their first appearance, so that listeners can easily get to know them. (In earlier music, this happened only in dance music, as a general rule.) Later in the piece, those same themes will be repeated again.

Porcelain musicians, c. 1770

Second, themes are *led into* in a very distinctive manner. The music features prominent transitional passages that do not have much melodic profile, only a sense of urgency about arriving someplace—the place where the real theme will be presented (and probably presented twice).

Third, after themes have been played, they are typically *closed off* just as distinctively. Often there are quite long passages consisting of cadences repeated two, three, or more times, as though to make it clear that one musical idea is over and another, presumably, is coming up. Composers would devise little cadential phrases, often with minimal melodic interest, that could be repeated and thus allow for such multiple cadences.

Multiple cadences are a characteristic and easily recognizable feature of Classical music, particularly, of course, at the very ends of movements. Two clear examples come from our CD set.

Haydn, Symphony No. 95 in C Minor, second movement: This is rather formal-sounding, deliberate music, so repeated cadences at the end sound even a little pompous. It is as though each of the instruments of the Classical orchestra wants to make sure the movement ends properly: first the violins, playing ornamented cadences (thirty-second notes) with bassoons in the background; then the French horns alone; then the rest of the orchestra. For the dynamics at the very end (*pp* and *ff*), see page 189.

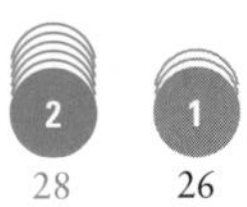

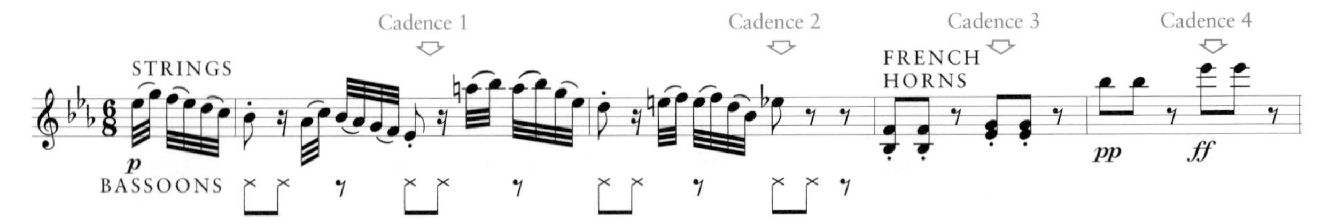

Aria "Ho capito" from Don Giovanni: Near the end of this aria (1:11), the singer sings much the same cadence over and over again. (A few seconds later, the orchestra has its cadence, and the whole piece is over.) The situation is explained on page 209: Sputtering with rage at Zerlina, Masetto keeps reiterating his sarcastic taunts until he is finally chased away. This cadence, then, is even more solid than it needed to be—for Mozart, a comical effect:

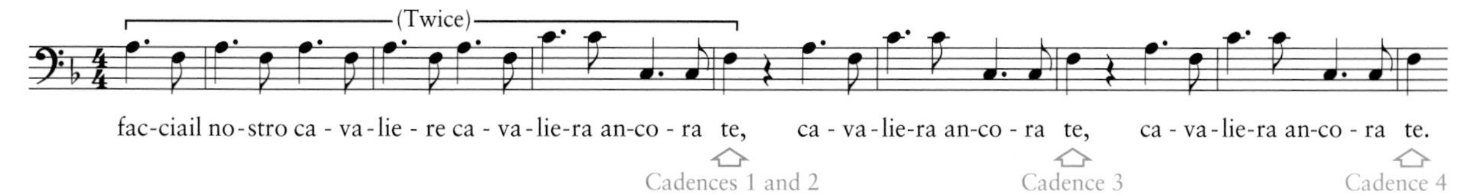

Classical Forms

A third feature designed to cope with the problem of musical form in Classical music is perhaps the most far-reaching. Composers and their audiences came to rely on a limited number of "forms," or standard formal patterns, the most important of which are *sonata form, minuet form, rondo,* and *theme and variations form.*

These provided a commonly understood frame of reference for composing music and appreciating it. Broadly speaking, after listening for just a short time to some new piece, an eighteenth-century music lover could always tell what sort of themes and keys it would include, when they would return, and about how long the piece would last. This frame of reference is not so obvious today, so the four Classical forms just mentioned will be taken up in some detail in Chapter 12.

Houdon's most unclassical portrait bust—of his wife

The repetitions, self-conscious transitions, and emphatic cadences that are so characteristic of the Classical style all help clarify the forms. And the forms themselves were a special necessity at a time when composers were filling their compositions with contrasts of all kinds. It is a mark of the aesthetic success of Classical music that the contrasts don't sound too drastic, because the forms control and, in effect, tame them. The seemingly inexhaustible emotional range of Classical music is directly proportional to the extent of those contrasts, on the one hand, and, on the other, to the elegance of their control by musical form.

Web: *Research and test your understanding of music during the Enlightenment at* **<bedfordstmartins.com/listen>.**

CHAPTER 12

The Symphony

The genres of music that arose in the Classical period, replacing those of the Baroque era, continued to hold their own in the nineteenth century. Indeed, they are still in use today, at least in the sense that their names are still encountered. Not surprisingly, the style, the number of movements, and the forms employed today will bear little relation to norms from two hundred and more years ago. But it is still true that if you compose a large, impressive concert piece for orchestra, the best way to convey that fact to conductors, musicians, and audiences is to name it a **symphony.**

One reason for the prominence of the symphony in the Classical era is its close association with a crucial development in the sociology of music, discussed in Chapter 11: the growth of public concerts. As concerts became more and more frequent, people felt a need for some genre that would make an effective, substantial focus for these occasions. Symphonies filled the bill—and in turn, required more variety and flexibility of sound than anything orchestras of the early eighteenth century could provide. The symphony spurred a major technical development within music, the evolution of the Classical orchestra (see page 173).

The symphony, then, is rightly viewed as the crowning achievement of Viennese Classical music—but when any musician acknowledges this, he or she wants to add a plea in the same breath: Please don't forget the other genres that grew up alongside the symphony, for these genres accommodate music that you will find just as beautiful, and that has become for us, sometimes, just as precious. In Chapter 13 we shall study the sonata, the Classical concerto, the string quartet, and—in the field of opera—Italian *opera buffa.*

Movements of the Symphony

Opening Movement
tempo: fast/moderate
form: sonata form (sometimes preceded by a slow **Introduction**)

Slow Movement
tempo: slow/very slow
form: sonata form, variations, rondo, other

Minuet (with Trio)
tempo: moderate
form: minuet form

Closing Movement
tempo: fast/very fast
form: sonata form or rondo form

1 The Movements of the Symphony

As with Baroque genres, works in the Classical period consist of several movements, which contrast in tempo and are composed in different musical forms. The outline in the margin of this page gives the particulars for the four movements of a typical symphony. Compare the following brief description with the description given on page 129 for the Baroque concerto:

The *first* opening movement of a symphony is a substantial piece in fast or moderate tempo, written in the most important new form of the time: sonata form (which we will study in the next section). Sometimes this fast music is preceded by a short but solemn *introduction* in a slower tempo.

- The *second* movement strikes an obvious contrast with the first by its slow tempo and its quiet mood.

- The *third* movement contrasts in another way, by its persistent dance rhythms: It is always a minuet and trio. A minuet is a moderately paced dance in triple meter: See page 143.

- The *fourth,* closing movement is fast again—if anything, faster than the first. It may also be in sonata form, like the first movement.

If we compare the symphony table shown on the previous page with a parallel table for the Baroque concerto, on the right, we see many differences, but also certain similarities. The forms used for the movements are entirely different, and there is the extra minuet. However, in the broadest terms, the sequence from *fast/complex* to *slow/quiet* to *fast/brilliant* is the same.

A word of caution: The symphony table on page 178 represents the norm, but there are always exceptions. Some famous ones are Mozart's *Prague* Symphony, lacking a minuet, and Haydn's *Farewell* Symphony with an extra slow movement—five movements in all. (Likewise, Bach's First *Brandenburg* Concerto has two dance movements added to the "normal" three for the concerto.)

Movements of the Baroque Concerto

Opening Movement
tempo: fast/moderate
form: ritornello form

Slow Movement
tempo: slow/very slow
form: no standard form

Closing Movement
tempo: fast/very fast
form: ritornello form

2 Sonata Form

A new form developed at this time, called **sonata form,** is closely associated with the symphony—even though it turns up in much other music of the time. The opening movement of every symphony is in sonata form, and this movement counts as the intellectual and emotional core of the whole work. Many Classical works have two or even three movements in this same form.

The reason for this wide use, perhaps, was that more than any other form, sonata form exploited what was the overriding interest of Classical composers. This was an interest in contrasts of every kind—especially contrast of thematic material and contrast of key, or tonality. In any case, whatever the reason, composers found sonata form particularly rich and flexible in its expressive application. It was something they could use for forceful, brilliant, pathetic, even tragic opening movements, gentle or dreamy slow movements, and lively, often humorous closing movements.

Viewed on the highest level, sonata form is simple enough—a very large-scale example of **A B A′** form, usually with repetitions: |: **A** :||: **B A′** :| or |: **A** :|| **B A′**. What is less simple, and what makes sonata form different from other **A B A** forms, is the nature and the function of the musical material in each letter-section. This is implied by the special terms that are used for them: **A** is called the *exposition,* **B** the *development,* and **A′** the *recapitulation.* We need to look more closely at what each of these terms entails.

Exposition (A)

The **exposition** of a sonata-form movement is a large, diverse section of music in which the basic material of the movement is presented (or "exposed"). The material always consists of the following elements:

To begin, a main theme is presented in the first key, the tonic key (see page 31; this key is the key of the piece as a whole—in Mozart's Symphony in G Minor, the tonic is G minor). This **first theme** may be a tune, a group of small phrases that sound as though they are about to grow into a tune, or just a motive or two (see page 26) with a memorable rhythmic character.

After the first theme is firmly established, often with the help of a repetition, there is a change in key, or *modulation.* The subsection of the exposition that accomplishes the change is called the **bridge,** or the *transition.*

The modulation in the bridge is an essential feature (even *the* essential feature) that gives sonata form its sense of dynamic forward movement. With a little experience, it is not hard to hear the contrast of key and sense the dynamism, for the idea is not to make the crucial modulation sound too smooth. There has to be a sense of tension in the way the new themes, now to be introduced, "set" in the new key.

Next comes a group of themes or other musical ideas in the new key, called the **second group.** At least some of these new themes contrast with the first theme in melody, rhythm, dynamics, and so on, as well as in key. Usually one new theme stands out by its melodious quality; this is called the **second theme.**

The last theme in the second group, the **cadence theme,** or *closing theme,* is constructed so as to make a solid ending prior to a full stop and the big repeat. The very end of the exposition is marked by a loud series of repeated cadences, as though the composer wanted listeners to know exactly where they are in the form. This **A** (exposition) section is almost always repeated.

Development (B)

The following section, the **development,** heightens the tonal-thematic tension set up by the contrasting themes and keys of the exposition. The themes are "developed" by being broken up, recombined, reorchestrated, extended, and in general shown in unexpected and often exciting new contexts.

Eighteenth-century English spinet, a type of small harpsichord. Especially away from the main musical centers, the harpsichord continued in use along with the piano.

Most development sections use counterpoint to create a sense of breakup and turmoil. This section moves around restlessly from key to key; there are frequent modulations that can easily be heard. The music sounds unstable.

After considerable tension has been built up in this way, the last modulation of the development section returns to the first key. The passage that accomplishes this, called the **retransition,** has the function of discharging the tension and preparing for the recapitulation to come. Classical composers were amazingly inventive in devising ways to make this crucial juncture of the form seem both fresh and inevitable.

Recapitulation (A′)

With a real sense of relief or resolution, we now hear the first theme again, followed by all the other themes and other elements of the exposition. There may be minor changes, but in principle everything comes back in its original order. Hence the name for this section—the **recapitulation** (meaning a step-by-step review).

But there is an important difference: The music now remains in the same key, the tonic key. (In practical terms, this means that the whole second group is relocated in the tonic. To allow for this, the bridge has to be rewritten—often in a very interesting way.) Stability of key in the recapitulation is especially welcome after the instability of the development section. Basically, as we have said, sonata form depends on a strong feeling of balance between exposition and recapitulation (**A B A′**). But it is a weighted balance, because **A′** has achieved a new solidity.

I compare a symphony with a novel in which the themes are the characters. We follow their evolution, the unfolding of their psychology. . . . Some of these characters arouse feelings of sympathy, others repel us. They are set off against one another or they join hands; they make love; they marry or they fight.

Swiss composer Arthur Honegger, 1951

The entire **B A′** sequence may be repeated. Whether this happens or not, another section in the tonic is often added at the end, a post mortem or wrap-up for the main action. This optional section is called the **coda** (coda is a general term for a concluding section in any musical form).

In the following schematic diagram for sonata form, changes of key (tonality) are shown on a continuous band. Notice the tonal stability of the recapitulation, where the steady horizontal band contrasts dramatically with the fluctuations of the exposition and development sections.

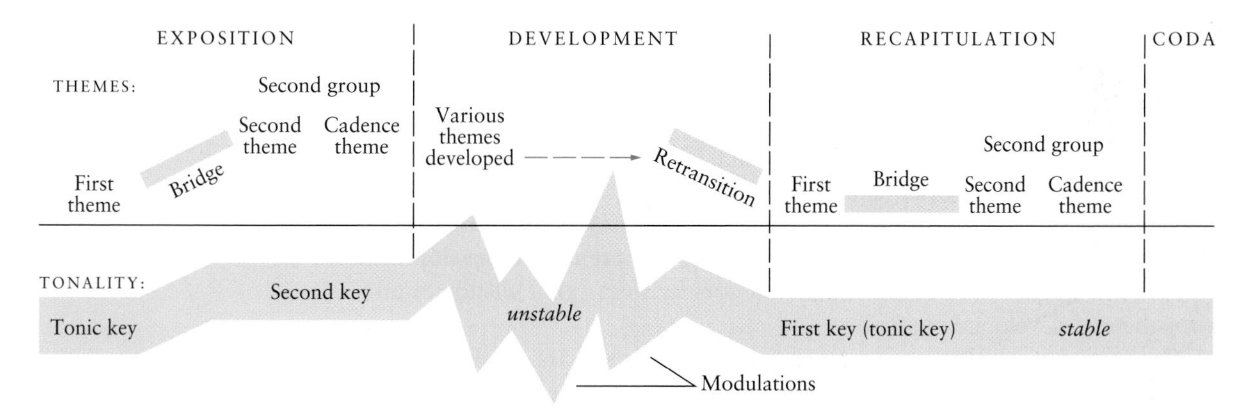

It may not be accidental that the terms used in discussing sonata form resemble those used in discussions of drama. We speak of the "exposition" of a play, where the initial situation is set forth, and of the "development" of the plot. Indeed, sonata form has a "dramatic" quality compared with the more "architectural" quality of Baroque music such as a fugue. In a Classical symphony, the themes seem almost like characters in a play or a novel to whom things are happening. They seem to change, take part in various actions, and react to other themes and musical processes.

WOLFGANG AMADEUS MOZART (1756–1791)
Symphony No. 40 in G Minor, K. 550* (1788)

Mozart's Symphony in G Minor is one of the most famous and admired of all his works. The opening movement, with its sharp contrasts and clear demarcations, makes an arresting introduction to sonata form.

Not many Classical compositions convey as dark and uneasy a mood as does this symphony. (Not many Classical symphonies are in the minor mode.) It suggests some kind of muted struggle against inescapable restraints. Mozart's themes alone would not have created this effect; expressive as they are in themselves, they only attain their full effect in their setting. Mozart needed sonata form to manage these expressive themes—in a sense, to give them something to struggle against.

First movement (Molto allegro) We have already cited this movement's opening texture—melody with a strictly homophonic accompaniment—as characteristic of the Viennese Classical style (see page 174). So also are the delicate dynamic changes toward the end of the theme and the loud repeated cadences that terminate it. The unique nervous energy of this theme, a blend of refinement and subdued agitation, stamps the first movement unforgettably.

Exposition The first theme is played twice. The second playing already begins the modulation to the exposition's second key, and a forceful bridge passage completes this process, after which the music comes to an abrupt stop. Such stops will come again and again in this movement.

The second theme, in the major mode, is divided up, measure by measure or phrase by phrase, between the strings and the woodwinds:

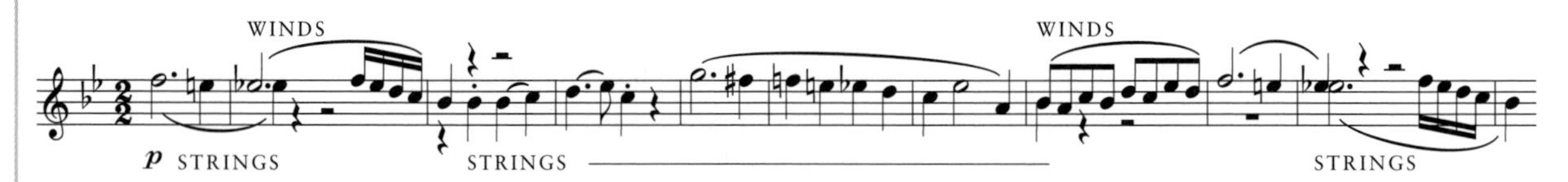

Then it is repeated with the role of the instruments reversed, the strings taking the notes originally played by the winds, and vice versa. These instrumental alterations contribute something absolutely essential to the character of the theme, and show Mozart's fine ear for tone color.

The second appearance of the second theme does not come to a cadence, but runs into a series of new ideas which make up the rest of the second group. Since all of them are so brief, and leave so little impression on the rest of the movement, it is best not to consider them actual "themes." One of these ideas begins to develop the motive of the first theme—a premature development process, one might think; but once again, it goes by so fast that we do not take it for the real development section.

A short cadence theme, *forte,* and a very insistent series of repeated cadences bring the exposition to a complete stop. (We still hear the rhythm of theme 1.) After one dramatic chord, wrenching us back from major to the original minor key, the whole exposition is repeated.

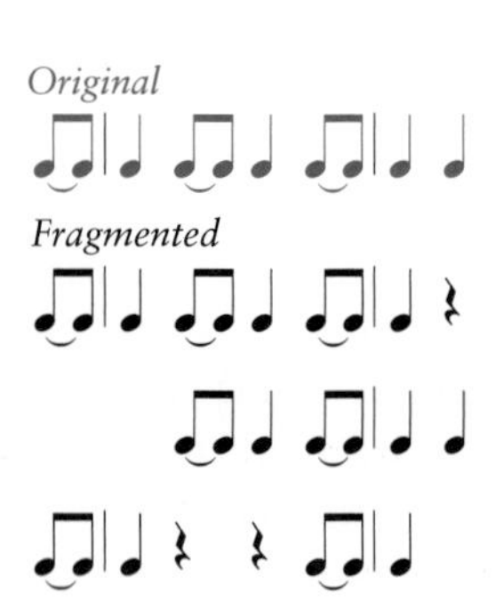

Development Two more dramatic chords—and then the development section starts quietly. The first theme is accompanied as before. It modulates at

*Mozart's works are identified by K numbers, after the chronological catalog of his works compiled by Ludwig von Köchel. The first edition (1862) listed 626 works composed by Mozart in his short lifetime; later editions add many more that may have come to light since then.

Freemasonry in the eighteenth century was a high-minded society of intellectuals and aristocrats, promulgating ideas that were often radical. "Enlightened" Emperor Joseph II tolerated them, barely. Mozart joined the group and wrote a good deal of music for their secret meetings; this extraordinary painting shows him at the far right.

once, and seems to be losing itself in grief, until the rest of the orchestra bursts in with a furious contrapuntal treatment of that tender, nervous melody.

The music seems to exhaust itself, and comes to another stop. But in the following ***piano*** passage, the modulations continue, with orchestral echoes based on smaller and smaller portions of the melody, as shown at the bottom of page 182. Breaking up a theme in this way is called *fragmentation.*

Passion breaks out anew in another ***forte*** passage; but the modulations, we notice, have finally ceased. The fragmentation reaches its final stage, as shown. At last the harmony seems to be waiting or preparing for something, rather than shifting all the time. This passage is the *retransition.*

Recapitulation After its fragmentation in the development section, the first theme somehow conveys new pathos when it returns in its original form, and in the original tonic key. The bassoon has a beautiful new descending line.

And pathos deepens when the second theme and all the other ideas in the second group—originally heard in a major-mode key—are now recapitulated in the tonic key, which is minor. The result is a great many small alterations of the exposition material—small, but they change the mood decisively. There should be no problem hearing that the recapitulation is more stable than the exposition, because both the first and second groups are now in the same mode (minor), as well as in the same key. The bridge theme, much expanded, also hammers away at the minor mode, recalling the contrapuntal outburst of the development section. It is a passage of great power.

Coda In a very short coda, Mozart refers one last time to the first theme. It sounds utterly disheartened, and then battered by the usual repeated cadences.

The Mozart children as prodigies. Both seem to have been great talents, but—inevitably for that time—it was the boy who went ahead. Nannerl grew up to be a rather straitlaced woman, married, and took care of her father in his old age.

Wolfgang Amadeus Mozart (1756–1791)

Mozart was born in Salzburg, a charming town in central Austria, which today is famous for its music festivals. His father, Leopold, was a court musician and composer who also wrote an important book on violin playing. Mozart showed extraordinary talent at a very early age. He and his older sister, Nannerl, were trotted all over Europe as infant prodigies; between the ages of six and seventeen, Wolfgang never spent more than ten successive months at home. His first symphony was played (at a London concert) when he was only eight years old.

But mostly Wolfgang was displayed at courts and salons, and in a somewhat depressing way, this whole period of his career symbolizes the frivolous love of entertainment that reigned at midcentury. The future Queen Marie Antoinette of France was one of those for whose amusement the six-year-old prodigy would name the keys of compositions played to him, and sight-read music at the piano with a cloth over his hands.

It was much harder for Mozart to make his way as a young adult musician. As usual in those days, he followed in his father's footsteps as a musician at the court of Salzburg, which was ruled by an archbishop. (Incidentally, one of their colleagues was Joseph Haydn's brother Michael.) But the archbishop was a disagreeable autocrat with no patience for independent-minded underlings. Mozart hated working for him. In 1781, he extricated himself from his court position, not without a humiliating scene, and set himself up as a freelance musician in Vienna.

It seems clear that another reason for Mozart's move was to get away from his father, who had masterminded the boy's career and now seemed to grow more and more possessive as the young man sought his independence. Leopold disapproved of Wolfgang's marriage around this time to Constanze Weber, a singer. (Mozart had been in love with her older sister, Aloysia—a more famous singer—but she rejected him.)

Mozart wrote his greatest operas in Vienna, but only the last of them, *The Magic Flute,* had the success it deserved. Everyone sensed that he was a genius, but his music seemed too difficult—and he was a somewhat "difficult" personality, too. He relied for his living on teaching and on the relatively new institution of concerts. Every year he set up a concert at which he introduced one of his piano concertos. In addition, the program might contain arias, a solo improvisation, and an overture by somebody else.

But as happens with popular musicians today, Mozart seems (for some unknown reason) to have suddenly dropped out of fashion. After 1787, his life was a struggle, though he did receive a minor court appointment and the promise of a church position, and finally scored a really solid hit with *The Magic Flute.* When it seemed that financially he was finally getting out of the woods, he died suddenly at the age of thirty-five.

He died under somewhat macabre circumstances. He was composing a Requiem Mass, that is, a Mass for the dead, commissioned by a patron who insisted on remaining anonymous. Mozart became ill and began to think he was writing for his own demise. When he died, the Requiem still unfinished, a rumor started that he had been poisoned by the composer Antonio Salieri.

Unlike Haydn, the other great master of the Viennese Classical style, Mozart allowed a note of disquiet, even passion, to emerge in some of his compositions (such as the Symphony in G Minor). The Romantics correctly perceived this as a forecast of their own work. Once we recognize this, it is hard not to sense something enigmatic beneath the intelligence, wit, and sheer beauty of all Mozart's music.

Chief Works: The comic operas *The Marriage of Figaro, Don Giovanni, Così fan tutte* (That's What They All Do), and *The Magic Flute* ▪ *Idomeneo,* an *opera seria* ▪ Church music: many Masses, and a Requiem (Mass for the Dead) left unfinished at his death ▪ Symphonies, including the *Prague,* the G minor, and the *Jupiter* ▪ String quartets and four superb string quintets; a quintet for clarinet and strings; a quartet for oboe and strings ▪ Concertos: nearly twenty much-loved concertos for piano; also ones for French horn, violin, and clarinet ▪ Piano sonatas; violin sonatas ▪ Lighter pieces (such as divertimentos, etc.), including the famous *Eine kleine Nachtmusik*

Encore: After Symphony No. 40, listen to the Clarinet Quintet and *The Marriage of Figaro* (Act I).

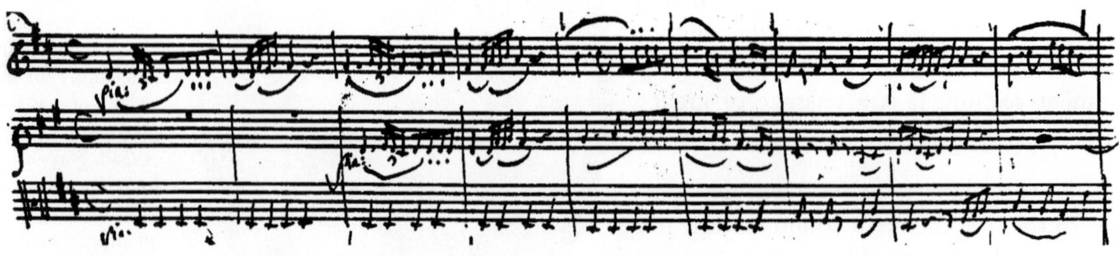

Mozart's musical handwriting

LISTENING CHART 7

15-20

1

13-18

Mozart, Symphony No. 40 in G Minor, first movement

Sonata form. 8 min., 16 sec.

Track / time	Time	Section	Description
15 13		**EXPOSITION**	
	0:01	**Theme 1 (main theme)**	Theme 1, *p,* minor key (G minor); repeated cadences *f*
	0:25		Theme 1 repeats and begins the modulation to a new key.
	0:34	**Bridge**	Bridge theme, *f,* confirms the modulation.
			CADENCE Abrupt stop
		Second Group	
16 14	0:53	**Theme 2**	Theme 2, *p,* in major key; phrases divided between woodwinds and strings
0:11	1:04		Theme 2 again, division of phrases is reversed
0:29	1:22		Other shorter ideas, *f,* and *p:* echoes of theme 1 motive
0:55	1:48	**Cadence theme**	Cadence theme, *f,* downward scales followed by repeated cadences
			CADENCE Abrupt stop
1:11	2:03	*Exposition repeated*	
		DEVELOPMENT	
17 15	4:10	**Theme 1 developed**	Theme 1, *p,* modulating
0:16	4:26	**Contrapuntal passage**	Sudden *f:* contrapuntal treatment by the full orchestra of theme 1
0:44	4:54	**Fragmentation**	Sudden *p:* beginning of theme 1 echoes between strings and woodwinds; theme fragmented from to and finally to
1:01	5:11		Retransition *f* (full orchestra), *p* (woodwinds), which leads into the recapitulation
18 16		**RECAPITULATION**	
	5:26	**Theme 1**	Theme 1, *p,* G minor, as before
0:24	5:50		Theme 1, modulating differently than before
0:33	5:59	**Bridge**	Bridge, *f,* longer than before
			CADENCE Abrupt stop
		Second Group	
19 17	6:41	**Theme 2**	Theme 2, *p,* this time in the minor mode (G minor)
			All the other second-group themes are in the tonic key (minor mode); otherwise much the same as before
1:00	7:41	**Cadence theme**	Scale part of the cadence theme, *f*
20 18		**CODA**	
	7:54		New imitative passage, *p,* strings; based on theme 1 motive
0:10	8:03		Repeated cadences, *f*
			Stop, this time "confirmed" by three solid chords

3 Classical Variation Form

Variation form, as we saw on page 132, entails the successive, uninterrupted repetition of a clearly defined melodic unit, the *theme,* with various changes at each repetition. In the Baroque era, the theme was usually a bass pattern (sometimes called a ground bass). The same basic principle is at work in Classical variation form, but now the theme is a tune in the upper register.

We can understand why the Baroque era, which developed the idea of the basso continuo supporting harmonies from below, would have cultivated variations on a bass pattern, whereas the Classical era, with its emphasis on simple melody, preferred variations on short tunes in the upper register.

The point of variations is to create many contrasting moods with the same theme, which is transformed but always somehow discernible under the transformations. Nothing distracts from this process, at least until the end, where composers usually add a coda. There are no contrasting themes, modulations, transitions, cadence sections, or development sections, as there are in sonata form movements (and in many rondos).

© Jasper Johns/VAGA, NY, NY.

Variations in the visual arts: three monotypes (from a total of seventeen) by the contemporary American artist Jasper Johns. While the variations all differ from the "theme"—an actual coffee can with paint brushes, all bronzed—they never lose it entirely.

A Classical **theme and variations** movement begins with a theme that is typically in |: **a** :||: **b** :| or |: **a** :||: **ba** :| or |: **a** :||: **b′** :| form. This miniform "nests" within the larger variation form:

Theme	Variation 1	Variation 2 . . .	Coda
|: a :||: b :|	|: a^1 :||: b^1 :|	|: a^2 :||: b^2 :|	(free)

Variations were part of the stock-in-trade of virtuosos of the Classical era. At a musical soirée, someone might suggest a popular opera tune, and the pianist would improvise variations on the spot, for as long as his or her imagination held out. Twelve was a common number for these variations when they were published; virtuosos piled them up for maximum effect.

In symphonies and concertos, theme and variations movements are less extended, since they have to fit into a time scale with all the other movements. For our example we turn to Joseph Haydn, since tuneful, witty variations movements in symphonies were a specialty of his.

FRANZ JOSEPH HAYDN (1732–1809)
Symphony No. 95 in C Minor (1791)

During the last twenty years of his active career, from around 1780 to 1800, Joseph Haydn averaged better than one symphony a year, nearly all of them masterpieces.

The most famous of them are the last twelve, written for concerts in London, where Haydn enjoyed enormous success on two tours after his retirement from the court of the Esterházy princes. Symphony No. 95 is one of these "London" symphonies, composed on the first tour in 1791.

First movement (Allegro moderato) Symphonies always begin with movements in sonata form, and since we have already worked on this form with Mozart's Symphony in G Minor, we will not go through Haydn's movement in the same detail. (Follow the mini–Listening Chart at the right.) The music starts in the minor mode, in a rather somber mood, but this all clears up when it turns cheerfully to the major, for good, in the recapitulation. Compare Mozart's first movement, which ends in the minor. In lighter moods, Haydn is every bit the equal of Mozart, but in his late years, at least, he avoids the beautiful shadows that occasionally—and unforgettably—darken Mozart's music, as in the G-minor Symphony.

Coming out of a long, eventful development section, Haydn slips into the expanded recapitulation before we even notice. Where Mozart's recapitulation mostly mirrors the exposition, Haydn's is more like an imaginative rewrite, treating the exposition material quite freely.

Second movement (Andante) The second movement of a symphony is the slow movement—a restful episode to contrast with the vigorous first movement. There is no standardized form for slow movements (in symphonies or in other genres, such as sonatas or concertos). Mozart, in his late symphonies, preferred sonata form or some derivative of sonata form. Haydn favored his own version of variation form.

In Symphony No. 95 the variation theme is a graceful tune in |: **a** :||: **b** :| form. Whereas **a** is rather simple, the melody of **b** melts into counterpoint for a time, before ending peacefully in the low register.

Haydn, Movements of Symphony No. 95

Opening Movement
tempo: fast
form: sonata form

Slow Movement
tempo: slow
form: variations

Minuet (with Trio)
tempo: moderate
form: minuet form

Closing Movement
tempo: fast
form: rondo

LISTEN  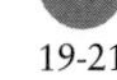

Haydn, 21-23 19-21
Symphony No. 95,
first movement

EXPOSITION
0:00 Theme 1: minor
0:49 Theme 2, etc.: major
1:44 ***Repeated***

DEVELOPMENT
0:00 Uses theme 1
0:42 Uses theme 2
0:59 Back to theme 1

RECAPITULATION
0:00 Theme 1: minor
0:42 Theme 2, etc. major
End expanded: major

Now the variations start; the music example on page 189 shows the key melody notes that each of them preserves, while much else is varied. The normal expectation would be the scheme shown in the margin, as discussed on page 187. Haydn wrote dozens of variation movements like this—though not, interestingly, in symphonies. He seems to have felt it would be boring for a concert audience, and he needed to do something freer and more interesting. For example, instead of repeating the **a** and **b** phrases in the variations exactly, he sometimes writes "variations within variations," as indicated by prime marks on the chart below:

THEME	|: a :||: b :|
Variation 1	|: a_1 :||: b_1 :|
Variation 2	|: a_2 :||: b_2 :|
Variation 3	|: a_3 :||: b_3 :|

	"NORMAL" VARIATIONS	HAYDN, SYMPHONY NO. 95	
THEME	a a b b	a a b b	
Variation 1	a_1 a_1 b_1 b_1	a_1 a_1' b_1 b_1	
Variation 2	a_2 a_2 b_2 b_2	a_2 b_2 b_2'	—— transition ——→
Variation 3	a_3 a_3 b_3 b_3	a_3 a_3' b_3	

Variation 1 starts with a cello solo that stays very close to the theme itself, with new material in the other strings above. It is as though the composer wants to remind us of the original **a**, one more time, before varying it in $\mathbf{a_1'}$.

Esterháza, where Haydn spent most of his life—a huge palace built by Esterházy princes in imitation of Versailles. It cannot compare with the real item, however: See page 113.

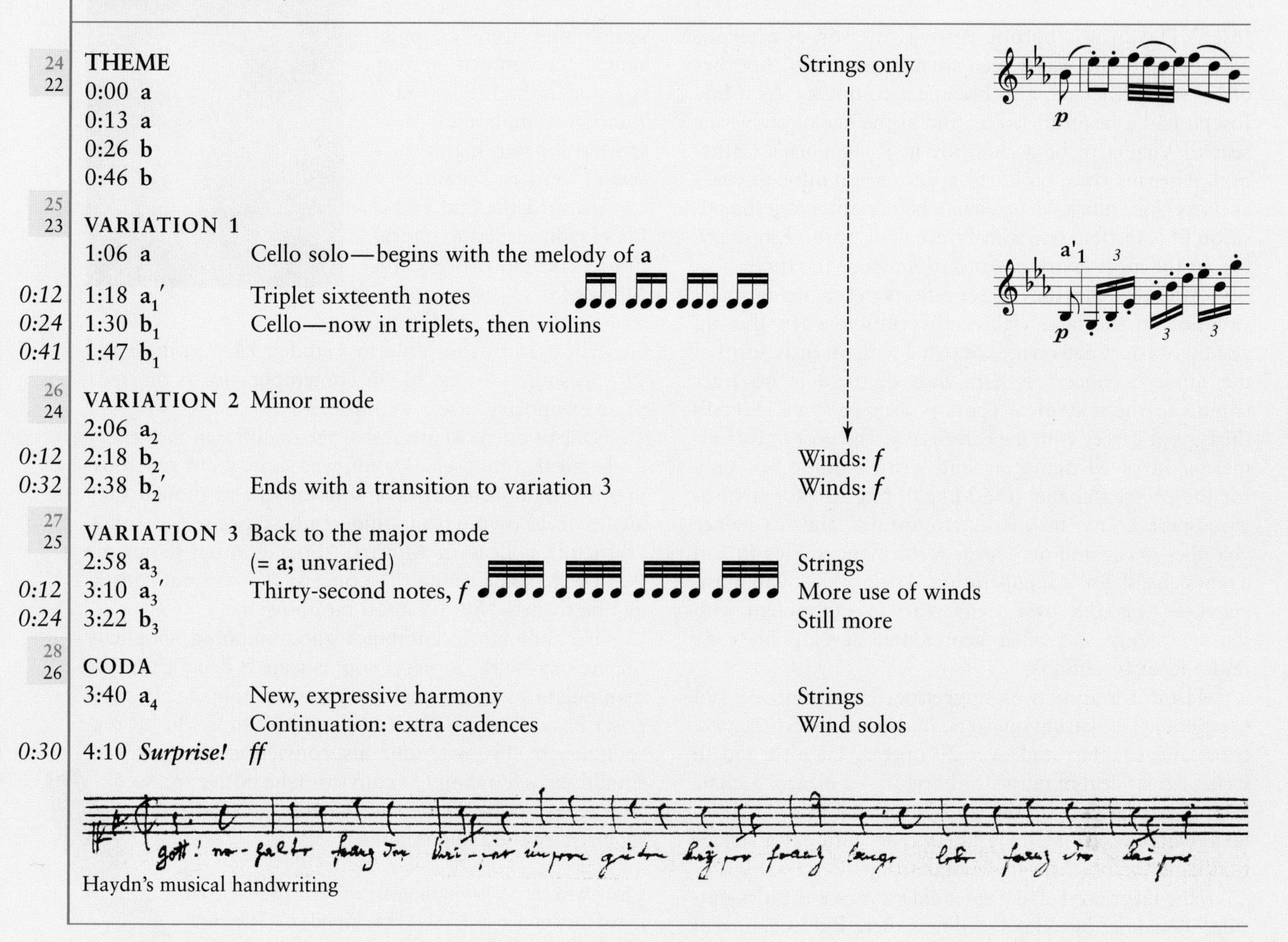

LISTENING CHART 8

Haydn, Symphony No. 95, second movement (Andante cantabile)

Variation form. 4 min., 17 sec.

Track	Time	Section	Description	Instrumentation
24 / 22		**THEME**		Strings only
	0:00	a		
	0:13	a		
	0:26	b		
	0:46	b		
25 / 23		**VARIATION 1**		
	1:06	a	Cello solo—begins with the melody of a	
0:12	1:18	a_1'	Triplet sixteenth notes	
0:24	1:30	b_1	Cello—now in triplets, then violins	
0:41	1:47	b_1		
26 / 24		**VARIATION 2**	Minor mode	
	2:06	a_2		
0:12	2:18	b_2		Winds: *f*
0:32	2:38	b_2'	Ends with a transition to variation 3	Winds: *f*
27 / 25		**VARIATION 3**	Back to the major mode	
	2:58	a_3	(= a; unvaried)	Strings
0:12	3:10	a_3'	Thirty-second notes, *f*	More use of winds
0:24	3:22	b_3		Still more
28 / 26		**CODA**		
	3:40	a_4	New, expressive harmony	Strings
			Continuation: extra cadences	Wind solos
0:30	4:10	*Surprise!*	*ff*	

Haydn's musical handwriting

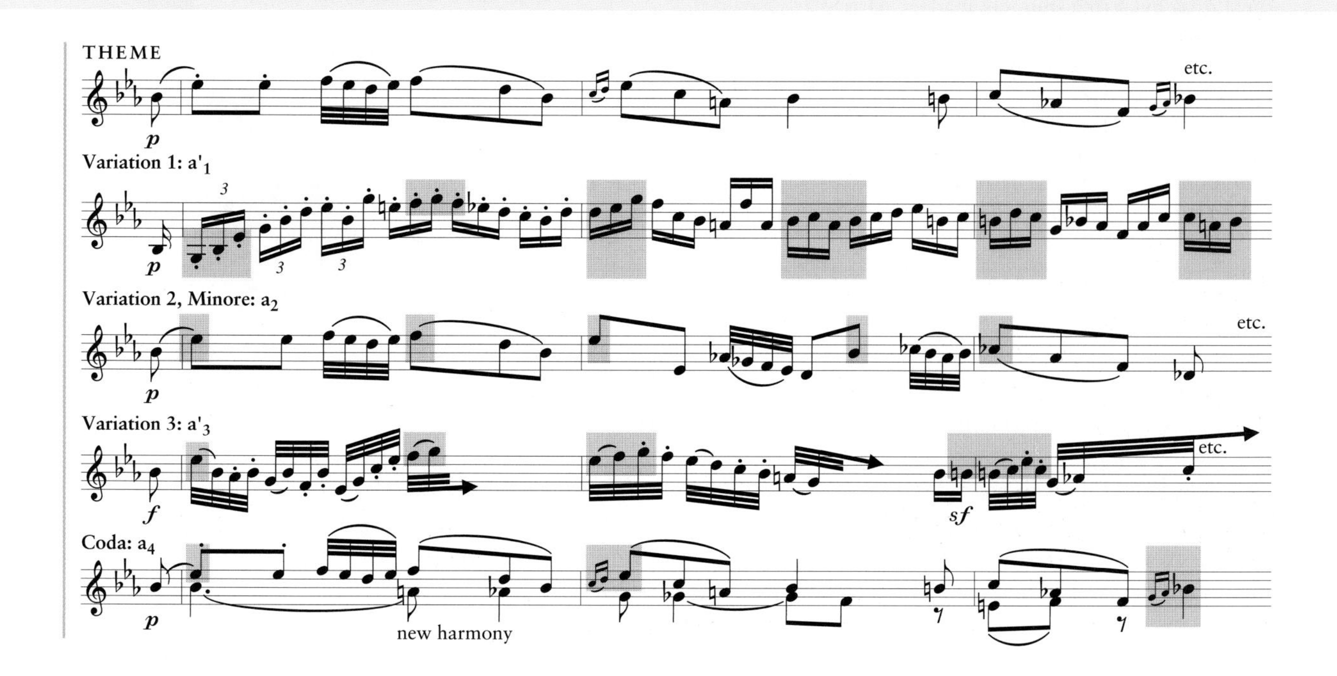

Franz Joseph Haydn (1732–1809)

Joseph Haydn was born in Austria, the son of a village wheelwright who was a keen amateur musician. Another of his sons, Michael, also became a composer. As a boy Joseph had a beautiful voice, and at the age of eight was sent to Vienna to be a choirboy in St. Stephen's Cathedral. After his voice broke, he spent several difficult years as a freelance musician in Vienna before obtaining the position of Kapellmeister with Prince Paul Anton Esterházy, one of the most lavish patrons of music at the time.

After this, Haydn's career reflects the changing social situation in the later eighteenth century, when the old system of court patronage coexisted with an early form of the modern concert system. Indeed, there is no finer tribute to the system of court patronage than Haydn's thirty-year career with the Esterházys. The post of Kapellmeister involved managing and writing music not only for the prince's chapel (the *Kapell*), but also for his private opera house, his marionette theater, and for palace chamber music and orchestral performances. Haydn had a good head for administration. Hiring his own musicians, he was able over many years to experiment with the symphony and other genres and develop his style under ideal conditions.

Haydn's output was staggering. He composed 104 symphonies, 83 string quartets, numerous divertimentos, trios, and sonatas, and over 20 operas. He also had to write a great deal of music for baryton—a bizarre archaic instrument fancied by the next Esterházy prince, Nikolaus, which was something like a cello with extra strings that could be plucked, like guitar strings.

The Esterházys had a splendid estate some miles outside of Vienna, but Haydn's duties there did not prevent him from spending a good deal of time in the capital. In the 1770s his string quartets made a particularly strong impression in the metropolis. In the 1780s he befriended Mozart, and the two actually played together in an amateur string quartet.

Meanwhile the spread of Haydn's international fame was accelerated by the growth of public concerts. At first his symphonies were picked up by French concert organizers (who paid Haydn nothing). Then in the 1780s his six *Paris* symphonies were commissioned for concerts in that city, and in the 1790s twelve *London* symphonies were written for two highly successful tours to Britain.

Toward the end of his life Haydn turned to choral music: six impressive Latin Masses for soloists, chorus, and orchestra, and two German oratorios inspired by Handel, *The Creation* and *The Seasons,* admired by his contemporaries as the apex of an exemplary career in music.

One of the most attractive personalities in the gallery of the great composers, Haydn was shrewd but generous-minded, humorous, always honorable, and though fully aware of his own worth, quite ready to praise his young, "difficult" colleague, Mozart. "Friends often flatter me that I have some genius," he once said—without contradicting them—"but he stood far above me."

Haydn's music combines good-humored simplicity of melody with a very sophisticated delight in the manipulations of musical form and technique. No composer has ever enjoyed a (musical) joke more. In his reasonableness, his wit, and his conviction that his art should serve humanity (a conviction he both expressed and acted upon), Haydn is the true musical representative of the Enlightenment.

Chief Works: 104 symphonies; the last twelve, composed for London in 1791–1795, include the *Surprise, Clock, Drum Roll,* and "London" symphonies ▪ A cello concerto and a delightful trumpet concerto ▪ Over 80 string quartets; piano trios and piano sonatas ▪ Choral music in his late years: six Masses and the oratorios *The Creation* and *The Seasons*

Encore: After Symphony No. 95, listen to Symphony No. 102; Trumpet Concerto.

Baryton

In $\mathbf{a}_1'$ and the two $\mathbf{b}_1$ phrases, the variation is supplied by fast-moving violins that effectively swamp the melody. Still, the melody's phrases and its harmonic pattern are clear.

Variation 2 goes to the minor mode; the mood shifts from melancholy (in $\mathbf{a}_2$) to blustering and then apprehensive (in $\mathbf{b}_2$). Perhaps we need a moment to recover from all this, before returning to the major mode and the original feeling. Haydn provided a short transition passage to ease the way.

Variation 3 begins with a_3, equivalent to **a** in its original, unvaried form—another reminder of the fundamental source of all the variations. Then a_3' and b_3 sound like a more intense version of Variation 1, with the violins moving faster. There is a hush, and a lovely new harmonization of **a** suggests the arrival of another variation. But instead of continuing with the theme, repeated cadences marked *p* and *pp* begin guiding the music to its close. It is an utter surprise, then, when the very last chords are jolted by a sudden *ff.*

Haydn used this kind of effect on more than one occasion. Is he making fun of the repeated cadences, which do sound a bit heavy-handed, or is the joke on this whole elegant movement—or even on the whole Classical style itself? Haydn can write serious, profound music, yet there are times when he seems to make a point of not taking himself too seriously.

Notice that at first this slow movement is scored for strings alone, and that the wind instruments play a larger and larger role, until they solo in the coda.

The admirable and matchless HAYDN! *From whose productions I have received more pleasure late in my life, when tired of most Music, than I ever received in the ignorant and rapturous part of my youth.*

English music historian Charles Burney, 1776

4 Minuet Form (Classical Dance Form)

Stylized dances—music of considerable elaboration in the style and form of dances, but intended for listening rather than dancing—reached a state of high development in the Baroque era. In Chapter 9 we saw how various dance types such as the gavotte and the bourrée were assembled into suites. Unlike the Baroque era, which developed a single genre made up of different dances, the Classical era brought a single stylized dance into many different genres.

The sole dance type from the Baroque suite to survive in the multimovement genres of the Classical period was the **minuet.** One reason for its endurance was simply that the dance itself, originally popularized at the court of Louis XIV in the seventeenth century, continued as one of the major fashionable social dances during the eighteenth. The minuet movement of a symphony was always a reminder of the aristocratic courts which had originally established orchestras.

Another reason was more technical. As a moderately paced piece in triple meter, the minuet makes an excellent contrast to the quick duple meter that was by far the most common meter in the opening and closing movements of Classical symphonies, quartets, and the like.

Works with four movements—symphonies and string quartets—always included a minuet, usually as a light contrast after the slow movement. Mozart even managed to fit a minuet into some of his piano concertos, though traditionally the concerto, as a three-movement genre, did not leave room for one.

Baroque and Classical Dance Form

A Baroque minuet consists of two sections; each comes to a complete stop and is immediately repeated (|: **a** :||: **b** :|). See page 144. Minuets tend to come in pairs, alternating in an **A B A** pattern. The second dance, **B**, is called the **trio,** because in early days it was often played by only three instruments.

A Baroque minuet movement can be diagrammed as follows. (Remember that |: :| means repeat, and that in the second **A** the parts are not repeated.)

MINUET	TRIO	MINUET
A	**B**	**A**
|: **a** :||: **b** :|	|: **c** :||: **d** :|	**a b**

Classical composers extended the internal form of minuets (and trios) by developing internal **a b a** structures according to one of the following schemes:

MINUET	TRIO	MINUET		MINUET	TRIO	MINUET
A	**B**	**A**	or (more often)	**A**	**B**	**A**
|: a :||: b a :|	|: c :||: d c :|	a b a		|: a :||: b a′ :|	|: c :||: d c′ :|	a b a′

Prime marks (**a′** and **c′**) indicate significant changes or extensions to the original **a** and **c** sections. It is easy to see why Classical dance form is sometimes called **ternary form.**

And indeed, changes of this kind were a major element in the dance "stylization" of this time. Haydn and Mozart could fashion a microcosm of the art of Classical music out of the basic elements of minuet form, always remaining within earshot of the ballroom with its easy, regular dance beat. (Mozart makes particularly creative use of minuet form in his Symphony in G Minor.)

Be assured, my D. H., that among all your numerous admirers NO ONE *has listened with more* PROFOUND *attention, and no one can have such veneration for your* MOST BRILLIANT TALENTS *as I have. Indeed, my D. H., no tongue* CAN EXPRESS *the gratitude I* FEEL *for the infinite pleasure your Music has given me . . .*

Letter to Haydn from another, more intimate English admirer, 1792

FRANZ JOSEPH HAYDN
Symphony No. 95 in C Minor, third movement (Menuetto)

The minuet movement of Symphony No. 95 takes a small mental journey from the ballroom to the countryside, and then back again. Perhaps it is not a real countryside but a "stylized" one, like the one shown on page 167.

LISTENING CHART 9

Haydn, Symphony No. 95, third movement (Menuetto)

Minuet form. 4 min., 56 sec.

Track		Time		
29 / 27		**MINUET (A)**		
		0:00	a	Theme
		0:09		Theme again, moving to the major mode
		0:25	a	*Repetition*
		0:50	b	(Picks up a motive introduced for the previous cadence)
		1:00	a′	Theme (back in the minor)
		1:13		Unexpected pause, with fermata 𝄐
		1:20		Strong return to the minor
		1:30	b a′	*Repetition*
30 / 28		**TRIO (B)**		
		2:12	c	Slower tempo, major mode: cello solo
	0:13	2:25	c	*Repetition*
	0:26	2:38	d	
	0:39	2:51	c′	
	0:46	2:58		Violins
	0:59	3:11	d c′	*Repetition*
31 / 29		**MINUET (A)**		
		3:46		*Repetition of* a b a′

CELLO *p*

Minuet Although the minuet starts with a quiet and weakly accented theme, it soon switches into the easy, energetic swing of a real ballroom dance, as a switches from the original minor to the major mode.

If you count the triple-meter bars, you will find almost all of them fit into the four- and eight-bar phrases that are necessary for the dance floor, if the dancers are to keep going. However, this is a stylized minuet, ripe for one of Haydn's jokes, and in phrase a′ he suddenly puts in a long rest, with a fermata. The music starts up again coolly, with a mysterious harmony, and goes on to a solid conclusion, but any in-the-flesh dancers would be thrown off completely.

Trio As happens quite often in Haydn, this trio sounds less like a court dance, even of a muscular kind, than like some sort of country dance, with a suggestion of none-too-competent peasant musicians. The tempo slows, the mode changes from minor to major, and a somewhat awkward tune, all in even eighth notes, is played by a solo cello (who also starred, we remember, in the slow movement). Haydn knew that London audiences liked solo turns in symphonies.

Phrase c′ is another joke: The cello player seems to forget how to go on, and has to be given his cue by the violins. Then he apparently has to play for time by repeating the cue over and over again, before finding a way to the cadence.

Minuet The minuet returns unchanged, except for omission of the repeats. But coming after the quiet trio, there is an interesting new feel to the minuet's quiet opening.

Unlike a recapitulation in a sonata-form movement, the return of **A** after the trio in minuet form does not give the impression of emerging out of previous musical events and completing them. Minuet returns are more formal than organic. We probably listen to them less reflectively than to recapitulations, remembering their origin in the ballroom, where dances are played as many times as the dancers need them and are always gratefully received.

Informal pencil drawing of Haydn, which he once singled out as the best likeness he had ever seen: not the choice of a vain man. Compare page 190.

The minuet movement of Mozart's Symphony in G Minor—another "stylized" minuet—is not on our CD set, but it is easy to find and fascinating to compare with the minuet from Haydn's Symphony No. 95. There are no jokes in Mozart, and if there is anything rustic about his trio, the quality is laced with nostalgia, even romanticism.

The minuet itself is even more highly stylized than Haydn's. Full of raging music in three-bar phrases with grating counterpoint—both features guaranteed to confuse ballroom dancers—it never modulates so as to depart from the gloom of the minor mode (beyond four bars of major at the start of the **b** section). In this extraordinary minuet, the mood of Mozart's symphony intensifies, from nervous agitation and distress in the first movement to near-tragedy in the third.

5 Rondo Form

The **rondo** is a relatively simple form with popular leanings. In the symphonies and other multimovement genres of the Classical era, it was used mainly for closing movements, which tend to be relatively light.

The basic principle of the rondo is simply repetition, repetition of a full-fledged tune. The main tune (**A**) recurs again and again after *episodes* that serve as spacers between its appearances. If **A** falls into the favorite |: **a** :||: **b a′** :| pattern of the time, the recurrences of **A** may present only **a b a′** or **a b**, or **a**, but there is always enough of the tune for one to recognize.

In the simplest rondos, the episodes are little tunes much like **A**; we shall see such a rondo in Mozart's Piano Sonata in B-flat, on page 198. In more elaborate works such as symphonies, the episodes may contain transitions to new themes, cadence formulas, and even sonata-form style developments. (Rondos of these kinds are sometimes called *sonata rondos.*) Various schemes are possible; often a coda is added. Whatever the specific structure, the regular return of the main tune **A** is the critical feature of rondo form.*

Rondo schemes:

A B A C A coda
A B A C A B A
A B A C A D A
—and others

Symphony No 95:
A B A B C A coda

*In some ways, rondo form resembles ritornello form (see page 129), but the differences are worth noting. Ritornello form usually brings back its ritornello in fragments and in different keys; rondo form usually brings back its theme complete and in the same key.

LISTENING CHART 10

Haydn, Symphony No. 95, fourth movement (Finale. Vivace)

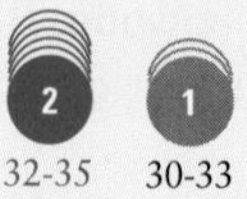

Rondo. 3 min., 41 sec.

Track		Time	Section			Dynamic
32 30		0:00	A (Tune)	a	Dynamic is *p*	
		0:08		a		
		0:15		b		
		0:22		c	Long extension (winds)	
		0:36		b c		
33 31		0:58	B (Episode 1)	Fugal exposition, *f*:	First subject entry	
	0:06	1:04			Second entry (rapid counterpoint in the bassoons)	
	0:10	1:08			Third entry (stretto)	
	0:14	1:12		Further material: many new, non-fugal ideas		
	0:19	1:17		Seems to head for a big cadence; trumpets		
	0:40	1:38		Fugue resumes:	Subject entry	
	0:48	1:46			Final entry—in the bass	
	1:04	2:02		Expectant STOP		
34 32		2:05	A	a b c 𝄐		*p*
	0:28	2:33	B (Episode 2)	Fugue starts up again, *f*: seems to almost *reach* a cadence		
	0:41	2:46	C	***Surprise! sudden stormy section in the minor mode, ff***		
	1:00	3:05		Transition (in several short stages)		
35 33		3:14	A	a New, expressive harmony		*p*
	0:12	3:26	Coda	Brass fanfares		*f*

FRANZ JOSEPH HAYDN

Symphony No. 95 in C Minor, fourth movement (Finale. Vivace)

The rondo theme, **A,** starts out as a rather delicate, airy tune played by the strings. The form could be diagrammed |: **a** :||: **b** :|, but |: **a** :||: **b c** :| better represents what we actually hear. Phrases **a, a,** and **b** are played by the strings alone. Then, when **b** seems to have answered **a** and rounded it off with a full cadence, the wind instruments enter much less delicately, adding **c** as a lively appendage lasting as long as **a** and **b** together. A three-note figure ♩♩♩𝄽 appears in **a** and **c** and *under* **b.**

The first episode, **B**, starts with a bang right on the last note of **A**. It is a fugue on a subject derived from **A** (the beginning of **a** played in sequence):

We spoke earlier of free and learned fugues (page 140). This one is *very* free; once the exposition of only three (instrumental) voices is over, the polyphonic texture changes to homophony and even monophony, in sweeping downward scales.

Theme **A** returns, this time without the repeats, and the next episode starts much like **B**, that is, with the same fugue—which turns out to be a feint. After a few bars the mode changes suddenly from major to minor and the dynamic rises from *f* to *ff* for a passage of furious, stormy music that would have jolted—and also delighted—the London audience during Haydn's first triumphant tour.

They would have been delighted because they would have recognized it as another of Haydn's jokes, similar in spirit to the sudden fortissimo ending of this symphony's slow movement (see page 191). For the music here is not just noisy and furious, it is disproportionately noisy and furious, a manic explosion that rattles the orderly Classical style of the rest of the finale.

The harmony soon turns to the major mode and the storm subsides (the audience knew this would happen, too). We touch base on **A** one more time, with its **a** phrase in a newly harmonized version, and the piece comes quickly to a close.

Thinking back on Haydn's Symphony No. 95, we might ask if there is any aesthetic quality that derives from the combination of the particular four movements we have heard. Is the whole greater than the sum of the parts?

If so, this is not something that musicians or musicologists have been able to elucidate with any consistency. It seems, rather, that Classical composers wrote symphony movements to fit together only in a general way, without thinking very much about connections between them, or any greater whole. This is as true of Mozart's agitated G-minor Symphony as of Haydn's more cheerful Symphony No. 95.

Indeed, the question only comes up because later, nineteenth-century symphonies often *do* make such connections. Symphony No. 5 by Ludwig van Beethoven seems to trace a psychological process from turmoil to triumph. The *Fantastic* Symphony by Hector Berlioz literally traces a story line written by the composer. See pages 227 and 265.

Haydn's most famous composition is a simple Austrian patriotic song:

It appears with variations in his *Emperor* Quartet, Op. 76 No. 3 (1797). The tune was adopted for the German national anthem, "Deutschland über Alles," and for the hymn "Glorious Things of Thee Are Spoken."

Web: *Research and test your understanding of the symphony at* **<bedfordstmartins.com/listen>.**

CHAPTER 13

Other Classical Genres

In Chapter 12 we examined the symphony as exemplified by Haydn's Symphony No. 95 in C Minor and the first movement of Mozart's Symphony No. 40 in G Minor. We go on in this chapter to examine the other main genres of music in the Viennese Classical era: the sonata, the Classical concerto, the string quartet, and opera buffa, the name for Italian comic opera of the time.

It would be impractical to spend the same amount of detail on each of these genres as on the symphony, and also somewhat redundant, for many features of the symphony are duplicated in these other genres. Indeed, for Classical instrumental music, the symphony can be used as a sort of prototype. With this use in mind, the symphony outline given on page 178 is reprinted on this page.

In the following pages we select a sonata, a concerto, and a string quartet and then discuss a single movement in each (using recordings and Listening Charts, as usual). The discussions will emphasize generic specificity—that is, the specific features that differentiate the music in question from the symphony. In the case of opera buffa, two numbers will serve as samples of the whole.

Movements of the Symphony

Opening Movement
tempo: fast/moderate
form: sonata form (sometimes preceded by a slow **Introduction**)

Slow Movement
tempo: slow/very slow
form: sonata form, variations, rondo, other

Minuet (with Trio)
tempo: moderate
form: minuet form

Closing Movement
tempo: fast/very fast
form: sonata form or rondo form

1 The Sonata

The term **sonata** has multiple meanings. We know its adjectival use in the term "sonata form," the scheme employed in the first movements of Classical overtures, symphonies, quartets, and also (as it happens) most sonatas. As a noun, *sonata* refers to a piece for a small number of instruments or a single one. And whereas in the Baroque period there were trio sonatas and solo sonatas—solo plus continuo, usually—in the Classical period the term was restricted to compositions for one or two instruments only.

Sonatas were not designed for concerts, which in any case were still rare at this time, but for private performance, often by amateurs. The symphony is a public genre, the sonata a domestic one. Given their destination in social life, some (not all!) sonatas are easy to play and may be limited in expression.

Piano sonatas were composed for solo piano, the favorite new instrument of the time, and *violin sonatas* were composed for violin and piano. In Classical

The sonata was said by a German critic to be intended by its earliest writers to show in the first movement what they could do, in the second what they could feel, and in the last how glad they were to have finished.

Philadelphia musician
P. H. Goepp, 1897

sonatas with violin or (less frequently) another instrument, the piano is not a mere accompaniment but an equal partner; it holds its own in such combinations in a way that the earlier harpsichord did not.

Compare the movement plan for the sonata, shown to the right, with the symphony prototype on the previous page. But also note that sonatas are much less uniform than symphonies, concertos, or quartets. In Mozart's sonatas, for example, only 65 percent follow the plan, leaving many exceptions. None of them has more than three movements, however, and the movements are always shorter than those of a symphony.

Movements of the Sonata

Opening Movement
tempo: fast/moderate
form: sonata form

Slow Movement
tempo: slow/very slow
form: sonata form, variations, rondo, other

Closing Movement
tempo: fast/very fast
form: often rondo

WOLFGANG AMADEUS MOZART (1756–1791)
Piano Sonata in B-flat, K. 570 (1787)

This sonata finds Mozart in a sunny mood—a more frequent mood for him than the sometimes painful agitation that we recall from Symphony No. 40. The first movement, a lively work in the major mode, is in sonata form. The second is in simple rondo form (see page 194), and the third in an irregular, compressed form similar to a rondo.

First Movement (Allegro) As is usual with Mozart's movements in sonata form, all the formal articulations—bridges, cadences, and the like—are signaled clearly, in fact almost flaunted. There is one novelty, however. After a long bridge that clearly announces the second key, the "second theme" turns out to be the first theme in the left hand with a faster counterpoint in the right:

As always, the recapitulation remains in the tonic key, rather than moving to a new one. Otherwise it stays very close to the exposition (closer than in either of the symphony first movements we have heard). There is no coda.

From the late eighteenth century on, musical accomplishment was regarded as a highly desirable social asset for women worldwide: for a French princess (painted by Elizabeth Vigée-Lebrun, a fashionable court painter, 1755–1842) or an American First Lady—Louise C. (Mrs. John Quincy) Adams—at a later period.

LISTENING CHART 11

Mozart, Piano Sonata in B-flat, third movement (Allegro)

A B C A form. 3 min., 35 sec.

2 36-38

36	0:00	A	a	
	0:14		b	
	0:24		a	
	0:38	B	c	
	0:52	(Episode 1)	c	*Repetition*
	1:06		d	
	1:14		c′	
	1:28		d c′	*Repetition*
	1:50			Short transition
37	1:54	C	e	In a new key
		(Episode 2)	e	*Repetition*
0:13	2:07		f	
0:20	2:14		e′	
0:27	2:21		f e′	*Repetition*
0:40	2:34			Short transition = end of **b**
38	2:45	A	a	Back in the tonic key
0:13	2:58	Coda		Refers to **d** (or **c**), then **f**
0:34	3:19			CADENCE Trill and strong cadence New cadence motive

Second Movement (Adagio) Mozart is at his most melodious in this lovely slow movement. The first rondo episode, **B,** in the minor mode, offers a whiff of agitation that may recall the G-minor Symphony. The coda looks back nostalgically to **C** and **f.** The rondo form can be diagrammed as follows:

A	B	short	A	C	short	A	Coda
|: a :||: b a :|	|: c :||: d c′ :|	transition	a′	|: e :||: f :|	transition	a′	

Third Movement (Allegretto) There is a sharp edge, almost a bite, to this movement; one thing that contributes to this is the set of tart little syncopations (see page 13) within the **a** and **b** phrases of the main tune, **A.**

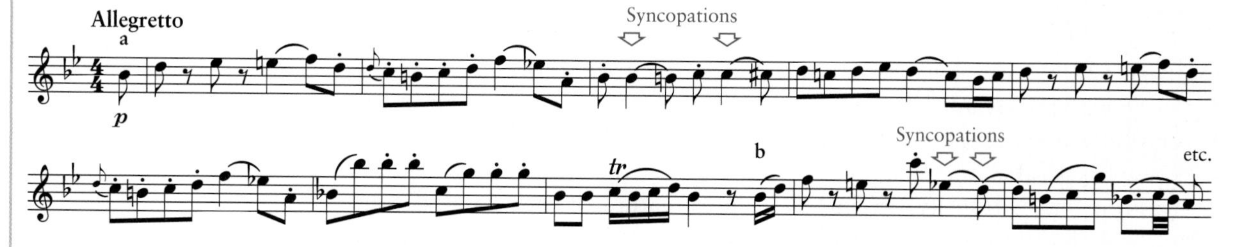

Syncopations are also heard in the first episode, **B,** together with a repeated-note figure in the left hand, which Mozart takes over for the beginning of the second episode, **C.** This rather simple-minded repeated-note figure, originally meant for a routine accompaniment function, is soon combined with spiky

Mozart's fortepiano, the eighteenth-century version of a pianoforte—smaller than today's instrument, with strings strung less tightly because iron was not used in the frame. Hence the volume was lower, but the fortepiano made up for this by its responsive touch and delicate tone. Compare the sound of a fortepiano in our recording of this sonata with the modern piano in Mozart's A-major Concerto, page 202.

counterpoints (in phrase **f**). Some charming little ornaments in the last **A** are not written in the score—they were improvised by the pianist in our recording.

The coda makes witty references to both episodes, and arrives at its cadence with a small flourish and a trill—except that this is not quite the end: Mozart adds a new motive for a doubly emphatic, self-satisfied conclusion.

The form has the feel of a simple rondo because of the structure of the main tune and of the episodes: Compare the Adagio. But there is no central **A**:

A	B	short	C	short	A	Coda
a b a	|: c :||: d c′ :|	transition	|: e :||: f e′ :|	transition	a	

2 The Classical Concerto

On page 129 we discussed the Baroque concerto and concerto grosso at the time of Bach and Vivaldi in terms of the basic concerto idea—the contest between soloist and orchestra. This basic idea was refined and sharpened by the Viennese Classical composers.

Instrumental virtuosity remained a central feature of the Classical concerto. At the same time, the orchestra was growing. With its well-coordinated string, woodwind, and brass groups, the Classical orchestra was much more flexible than the Baroque concerto orchestra could ever be.

So the balance between the two contesting forces—soloist and orchestra—presented a real problem, a problem that Mozart worked out in a series of seventeen superb piano concertos written during his years in Vienna, mostly for his own concert use. He pitted the soloist's greater agility, brilliance, and expressive capability against the orchestra's increased power and variety of tone color. The contestants are perfectly matched; neither one can ever emerge as the definite winner.

Compare the movement plan for the Classical concerto with the symphony prototype in the margin of page 197. Concertos have long opening movements—see below—and no minuet movements.

Movements of the Classical Concerto

Opening Movement
tempo: fast/moderate
form: double-exposition sonata form
cadenza near the end

Slow Movement
tempo: slow/very slow
form: sonata form, variations, rondo, other

Closing Movement
tempo: fast/very fast
form: rondo form (occasionally variation form)

Double-Exposition Form

For the first movements of concertos, Mozart developed a special form to capitalize on the contest that is basic to the genre. Though the diagram for **double-exposition form** may look rather cluttered, it is in fact simply an extended variant of sonata form. Compare the sonata-form diagram, page 181:

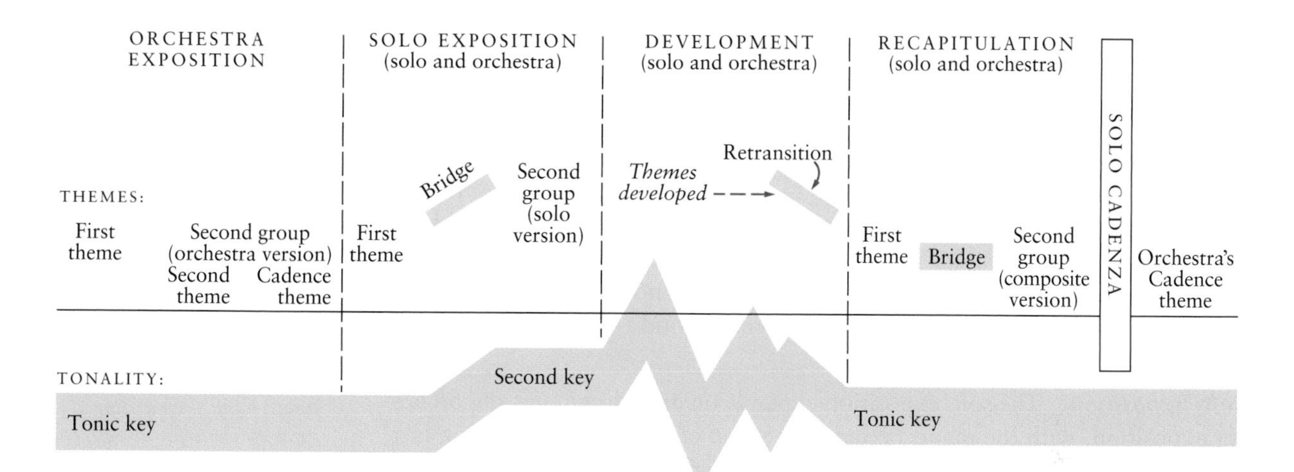

In sonata form, the exposition is repeated; here each of the competing forces presents the thematic material in its own somewhat different version. Note that unlike the exposition in a symphony, in a concerto the **orchestra exposition** does not modulate—an important difference. The point is to save the change of key (which counts for so much in all sonata-form compositions) until the **solo exposition.** The listener senses that the orchestra can't modulate and the soloist can—evidence of the soloist's superior range and mobility. This is demonstrated spectacularly by the soloist playing scales, arpeggios, and other brilliant material, making the solo exposition longer than the orchestral one.

The recapitulation in double-exposition form amounts to a composite of the orchestral and solo versions of the exposition. Typically the orchestra's cadence theme, which has been crowded out of the solo exposition to make room for virtuoso activity, returns at the end to make a very satisfactory final cadence.* Shortly before the end, there is a big, formal pause for the soloist's **cadenza** (see page 137). The soloist was supposed to improvise at this point—to show his or her skill and flair by working out new thematic developments on the spot, and also by carrying off brilliant feats of virtuosity.

*Double-exposition form, like sonata form, may also have a coda—a feature exploited by Beethoven more than Mozart and Haydn.

WOLFGANG AMADEUS MOZART (1756–1791)
Piano Concerto in A, K. 488 (1786)

This favorite Mozart concerto proceeds from one of his most gentle and songful first movements to a second movement that is almost tragic followed by an exuberant, sunny finale. The first movement might almost have been intended as a demonstration piece for double-exposition form, except for one unique feature: a new theme introduced halfway through.

These piano concertos are a happy medium between too easy and too difficult; they are very brilliant, pleasing to the ear, and natural, without being simple-minded. There are passages here and there which only connoisseurs will be able to appreciate, but less learned listeners will like them too, without knowing why.

Letter from Mozart to his father, 1782

First Movement (Allegro) No fewer than four themes in this movement could be described as gentle and songful—though always alert. For a work of this character, Mozart uses a reduced orchestra, keeping the mellow clarinets but omitting the sharper-sounding oboes as well as trumpets and timpani.

Orchestra Exposition Theme 1, played ***piano*** by the strings and repeated by the woodwinds, is answered by a vigorous ***forte*** passage in the full orchestra.

This "response" idea returns many times, balancing the quiet themes, and often leading to something new—here, theme 2, another quiet melody, full of feeling. A somewhat agitated passage interrupts, touching on two different minor keys, but this is only a momentary deflection from the basic tonality of this section. It is all in the major tonic key, without any actual modulation. The cadence theme that ends the section maintains the gentle mood.

Richter, the piano virtuoso, is giving six Saturday concerts . . . The nobility subscribed, but remarked that they really did not care much about going unless I played too. So Richter asked me to do so. I promised to play three times—and then arranged three concerts for myself, to which they all subscribed.

Letter from Mozart to his father, 1784

Solo Exposition The solo exposition expands on and illuminates the orchestra exposition, with the piano taking over some of it, while also adding fast-moving scales or other figuration of its own. The main difference comes at the bridge; the modulation, needed to give the music a lift, is engineered by the piano. The orchestral second theme sounds especially intimate and lovely when played on the piano—as Mozart planned. And at the end, instead of the gentle cadence theme, the piano has a moment of brilliant passage work, culminating in a drawn-out, triumphal cadence with a long trill.

Showy cadences of this kind are a regular feature of Classical concertos; the orchestra always answers with loud music of its own, like a cheer. Here it is the orchestra's "response" passage again. But this time it stops in mid-course, as though the music has suddenly remembered something intimate and a little serious. A new theme in the orchestra (yet another quiet, gentle melody, this time with a thoughtful character) appears out of nowhere:

After the orchestra plays the new theme, the solo repeats it in an elaborated version, and we slip into the development section.

Development The basic idea behind concertos, the contest between orchestra and soloist, is brought out wonderfully here. Mozart sets up a rapid-fire dialogue between the two contestants; fragments of the new theme in the wood-

LISTENING CHART 12

Mozart, Piano Concerto in A, K. 488, first movement

Double-exposition form. 11 min., 16 sec.

3 1-5

On this chart, the column arrangement distinguishes the main orchestra and solo sections.

Track		Time			
1			**ORCHESTRA EXPOSITION**		
		0:00	Theme 1, *p*	Orchestra	Strings; woodwinds for the second playing
		0:33	*f* response		
		0:56	Theme 2, *p*		
		1:26	"Deflection" passage		Two minor-mode keys are suggested
		1:57	Cadence theme, *p*		
2			**SOLO EXPOSITION**		
		2:06	Theme 1		SOLO: melody is increasingly ornamented
	0:29	2:35	*f* response	Orchestra, with SOLO cutting in	
	0:37	2:43	Bridge—modulates		
	0:59	3:05	Theme 2		
	1:28	3:34	"Deflection" passage		
	1:57	4:03	Solo virtuoso passage		
3		4:17	*f* response, leads to		
	0:12	4:29	*new theme*	Orchestra	
	0:23	4:40			SOLO *ornaments* the new theme
			DEVELOPMENT		
	0:36	4:53		Orchestra and SOLO: *dialogue* around the new theme; modulations	
	1:18	5:35	Retransition		
	1:38	5:55	Short cadenza		in free time; ends with a fermata
4			**RECAPITULATION**		
		6:12	Theme 1, *p*	Orchestra, with SOLO cutting in for the second playing	
	0:29	6:41	*f* response	Orchestra, with SOLO cutting in again	
	0:37	6:49	Bridge		
	0:57	7:09	Theme 2		
	1:27	7:39	"Deflection" passage		
5		8:12	*New theme* (longer virtuoso passage)		(the first time the SOLO plays it without ornaments)
	0:42	8:54	*f* response, leads to		
	0:54	9:06	*new theme*		
	1:11	9:23	Main CADENZA		SOLO free, improvised passage
	2:30	10:42	*f* response	Orchestra	
	2:45	10:56	Cadence theme, *p*		
	2:52	11:04	Brief ending *f* ⟶ *p*		

p

p

Cadence theme

p

Doodle on a Mozart concerto score

winds seem to discuss or argue with the piano, as the music modulates to minor-mode keys and the material is developed. (A changeable upbeat attaches itself to the new theme: See the music example on page 202).

The new theme turns unexpectedly anxious in the retransition (see the music in the margin, to the right). Finally, with a brief cadenza, the piano pulls out of the dialogue and steers the way to the recapitulation.

Recapitulation At the start of the movement, the songful first theme was claimed in turn by the orchestra and the solo in their respective expositions. In the recapitulation, a composite of the two expositions, they share it.

The recapitulation resembles the solo exposition, though the bridge is altered so that the whole remains in the tonic key. There is a beautiful extension at the end, and when the "response" passage comes again, it leads to a heavy stop, with a fermata—the standard way for the orchestra to bow out, after preparing for the soloists's grand re-entrance for the main cadenza. Compared to the cadenza in Bach's *Brandenburg* Concerto—see page 135—this one is much more varied. Written out by Mozart himself, it includes mild improvisatory moments as well as brilliant ones.

The solo's showy cadence after the cadenza is cheered along once again by the orchestra's "response" passage, which we have heard so many times before. This time it leads to something we have *not* heard many times—only once, nine minutes back: the quiet cadence theme of the orchestra exposition. Do you remember it? It makes a perfect ending for the whole movement, with an extra twist: a little flare-up to *forte* that subsides almost at once.

3 The String Quartet

Developed in the Classical era, the **string quartet** is a genre for four instruments: two violins, a viola, and a cello. ("String quartet" is also the name for a group of four musicians who work together playing quartets.) The plan for a string quartet, with its four movements, is close to that of the symphony; compare page 197. Indeed, next to the symphony the quartet counts as the most important genre of Classical music.

Movements of the String Quartet

Opening Movement
tempo: fast/moderate
form: sonata form

Slow Movement
tempo: slow/very slow
form: sonata form, variations, rondo, other

Minuet (with Trio)
tempo: moderate
form: minuet form

Closing Movement
tempo: fast/very fast
form: sonata form or rondo form

The quartet may have as many movements as the symphony, but of course it doesn't have as many instruments, and it cannot match the symphony's range of volume and tone color. This can disappoint listeners today. For the eighteenth century, however, volume was no issue, because quartets were never intended for concert listening. They were intended primarily for the performers, with small, informal audiences—or none at all.

As for range of tone color, the quartet compensates for this by its own special qualities: nuance, delicacy, and subtlety. Without any conductor, the quartet players are partners responding to one another as only old, close associates can. As developed by Haydn, the four instruments of the quartet grow more and more similar in their actual musical material, and more and more interdependent. There is a fine interplay as they each react to musical gestures by the others, sometimes supporting them, sometimes countering.

This interplay has been aptly compared to the art of cultivated conversation—witty, sensitive, always ready with a perfectly turned phrase—that was especially prized in eighteenth-century salons (page 167).

There are dozens of wonderful string quartets by Haydn and ten, equally wonderful, by Mozart. We could have chosen any one of these for the example

String quartets, then and now (left, below, and next page). Nineteenth-century quartets were often led by celebrated violin soloists; shown here is a group led by a virtuosa of the time, Wilma Norman-Néruda (1838–1911). From left to right: two violins, viola (slightly larger), and cello.

on our CD set. However, since Haydn and Mozart are already well represented in this book, we will use an example by a somewhat later composer. If you like, jump ahead to page 232 for Ludwig van Beethoven's String Quartet in F, Op. 135.

Chamber Music

The string quartet was the main but not the only genre developed at this time for small forces in relatively intimate circumstances. **Chamber music** is a term for music designed to be played in a room (a chamber)—in a palace drawing room or in a small hall. Chamber music can be taken as encompassing compositions for from two to nine players. Other types are the piano trio (violin, cello, piano: a favorite of Haydn) and string quintets (string quartet plus another low instrument; Mozart wrote four superb quintets with two violas, and one of Schubert's great masterpieces is a quintet with two cellos).

The Juilliard Quartet, perhaps the leading American quartet, was formed at the Juilliard School in New York in 1946 and is still active. Two violins, cello, and viola.

The Kronos Quartet, based in San Francisco, plays almost exclusively contemporary music, including jazz arrangements and other "crossover" items. They have commissioned more than 400 new works in their 25-year history. Two violins, viola, and cello.

Broadly speaking, what has been said above about the intimate character of the quartet applies to all chamber music, though it is probably obvious that a string octet must be less subtle and more "orchestral" than a string trio.

4 Opera Buffa

In the late eighteenth century, comic opera grew to equal in importance the serious opera that was a hallmark of the Baroque era (see page 150). Roman emperors and their courtly confidants gave way to contemporary peasant girls and soldiers; castratos were edged aside by basses specializing in comical diatribes and exasperated "slow burns," the so-called *buffo* basses (*buffone* is

In an opera buffa ensemble, characters register different feelings musically, by singing contrasting melodies. In this production of a Haydn opera buffa, they also do so visually—by their contrasting grimaces and gestures.

Italian for "buffoon"). Happy endings were the result of pranks, rather than issuing from the decrees of magnanimous princes.

Comic opera stars had to be funny; they had to act, not just sing. The new flexibility of the Classical style was perfectly suited to the casual, swift, lifelike effects that are the essence of comedy. As much as its humor, it was this "natural," lifelike quality of comedy that appealed to audiences of the Enlightenment. Enlightened monarch Joseph II of Austria actively promoted comic opera.

Italian comic opera was the most important, though there were also parallel developments in Germany, France, and England. Serious Italian opera was called *opera seria;* comic Italian opera was called **opera buffa.** Just as Italian opera seria was very popular in London in Handel's time, so Italian opera buffa was in Vienna at the time of Haydn and Mozart. Thus Haydn, whose court duties with the Esterházys included running their opera house, wrote twelve comic operas—all in Italian. Mozart in his mature years wrote six comic operas, three in German (one is a one-acter) and three in Italian.

Chamber music never sounds as well as when one is close to it. Probably the ideal place is directly in the middle of the players. Retreat forty feet, and at once the thing begins to be thin and wheezy. Go back sixty feet, and one may as well leave the place altogether.

H. L. Mencken, famously skeptical American critic, 1930

The Ensemble

Baroque opera seria, as we have seen (page 151), employs two elements in alternation: recitatives for the dialogue and the action, and numbers that are fully musical—almost always arias—for static meditation and "tableaus" of emotional expression. Classical opera buffa works with the same elements, except that the fully musical numbers include *ensembles* as well as solo arias.

An **ensemble** is a number sung by two or more people. And given the Classical composers' skill in incorporating contrast into their music, they were able to make their ensembles depict the different sentiments of the participating characters simultaneously. This meant that sentiments could be presented much more swiftly and vividly: swiftly, because we don't have to wait for the characters to sing whole arias to find out what they are feeling, and vividly, because the sentiments stand out in sharp relief one against the other.

The music also depicts these sentiments in flux. For in the course of an ensemble, the action proceeds and the situation changes. This is usually projected by means of new musical sections with different tempos, keys, and themes. A Classical opera ensemble, then, is a sectional number for several characters in which the later sections represent new plot action and the characters' new reactions to it.

In short, whereas the aria was essentially a static number, the ensemble was a dynamic one. At the end of a Baroque da capo aria (see page 152), the return of the opening music tells us that the dramatic situation is just where it was when the aria started. But at the end of a Classical ensemble, the drama has moved ahead by one notch or more, and the music, too, has moved on to something different. The ensemble transformed opera into a much more dramatic genre than had been possible within the Baroque aesthetic.

On Monday the 29th the Italian opera company gave the eagerly awaited opera by Maestro Mozard, Don Giovanni, or The Stone Guest. *Connoisseurs and musicians say that Prague had never heard the like. Herr Mozard conducted in person; when he entered the orchestra he was received by three-fold cheers, as also happened when he left. The opera is extremely difficult to perform . . .*

Prague newspaper, 1787

WOLFGANG AMADEUS MOZART
Don Giovanni (1787)

Mozart wrote *Don Giovanni* in 1787 for Prague, the second largest city of the Austrian empire, where his music was enjoying a temporary spurt in popularity. While technically it counts as an opera buffa, *Don Giovanni* is neither a wholly comic drama nor wholly tragic. A somewhat enigmatic mixture of both—what might be called today a "dark comedy"—it seems to convey

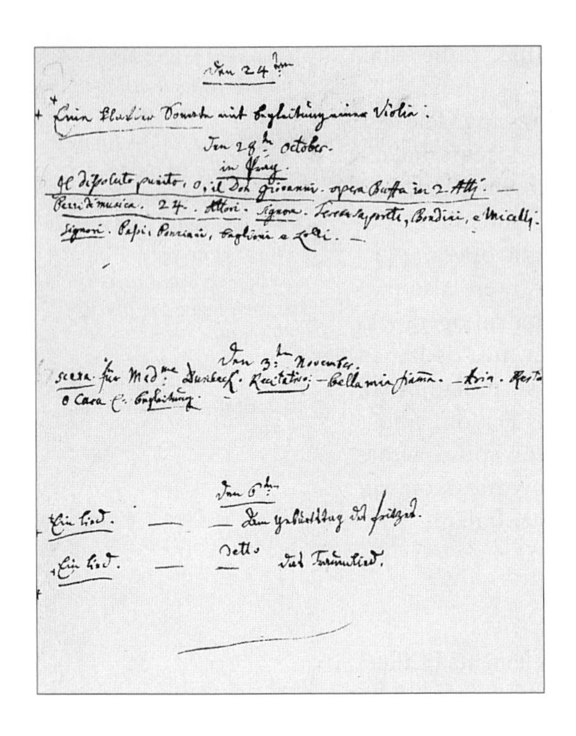

24th [of August, 1787]
A Piano Sonata with accompanying violin

28th of October
in Prague
The Reprobate Punished, or Don Giovanni: opera buffa in 2 acts. 24 musical numbers. Actors. Ladies: Teresa Saporitti, Bondini, and Micelli. Gentlemen: Papi, Ponziani, Taglioni and Lolli.

3rd of November
Scena [operatic scene] for Mad.me Dušek. Recitative: "My lovely flame." Aria: "Stay, dearest." Accompaniment:

6th
A Song — — "Little Frederick's Birthday"
ditto
A Song — — "The Phantom"

Mozart's feeling that events have both comical and serious dimensions, and that life's experiences cannot be pigeonholed.

Background Don Giovanni is the Italian name for Don Juan, the legendary Spanish libertine. The tale of his endless escapades and conquests is meant to stir up incredulous laughter, usually with a bawdy undertone. Certainly a subject of this kind belongs to opera buffa.

But in his compulsive, completely selfish pursuit of women, Don Giovanni ignores the rules of society, morality, and God. Hence the serious undertone of the story. He commits crimes and mortal sins—and not only against the women he seduces. He kills the father of one of his victims, the Commandant, who surprises Giovanni struggling with his daughter.

This action finally brings Don Giovanni down. Once, when he is hiding from his pursuers in a graveyard—and joking blasphemously—he is reproached by the marble statue that has been erected over the Commandant's tomb. He arrogantly invites the statue home for dinner. The statue comes, and when Giovanni refuses to mend his ways drags him off to *its* home, which is hell. The somber music associated with the statue was planted ahead of time by Mozart in the orchestral overture to *Don Giovanni,* before the curtain rises.

Thanks to Mozart's music, our righteous satisfaction at Don Giovanni's end is mixed with a good deal of sympathy for his verve and high spirits, his bravery, and his determination to live by his own rules, not those of society, even if this dooms him. The other characters in the opera, too, awaken ambivalent feelings. They amuse us and move us at the same time.

Act I, scene iii The opera's third scene begins with a chorus of peasants, celebrating the betrothal of Masetto and Zerlina. Don Giovanni enters with his manservant Leporello and immediately takes a fancy to Zerlina. He promises Masetto various favors, and then tells him to leave—and tells Leporello to take him away by force if necessary.

From the scary final scene of *Don Giovanni:*
"Repent, tell me you will live a new life: this is your last chance!"
"No, never, let me alone!"
"Repent, villain!"
"Never, old fool!"

Mozart kept a little notebook in which he entered every new composition when it was finished. On the right-hand page he wrote the first few measures of the music, and on the left the title and date. The pages shown include *Don Giovanni* (under its subtitle *The Reprobate Punished*) and an operatic scene for a soprano named Josefa Dušek.

Mozart first met Dušek in the 1770s, before moving to Vienna, and may have been involved with her in the 1780s.

Aria, "Ho capito" This opera buffa aria, sung by Masetto, shows how vividly (and rapidly!) Mozart could define character in music. Singing almost entirely in very short phrases, Masetto almost insolently tells Don Giovanni that he will leave only because he has to, because great lords can always bully peasants. Then he rails at Zerlina in furious, fast asides; she has always been his ruin. He sings a very sarcastic little tune when he promises her that Don Giovanni is going to make her into a fine lady:

Toward the end of the aria he forgets Don Giovanni and the opening music he used to address him, and thinks only of Zerlina, repeating his furious words to her and their sarcastic tune. He gets more and more worked up as he sings repeated cadences, so characteristic of the Classical style. A variation of the tune, played by the orchestra, ends this tiny aria in an angry rush.

The total effect is of a simple man (judging from the music he sings) who nonetheless feels deeply and is ready to express his anger. There is also a clear undercurrent of class conflict: Masetto the peasant versus Don Giovanni the aristocrat. Mozart was no political radical, but he had indeed rebelled against court authority; and the previous opera he had written, *The Marriage of Figaro,* was based on a notorious French play that had been banned because of its anti-aristocratic sentiments. Two years after *Don Giovanni* was composed, the French Revolution broke out in Paris.

17 MAY 1788. *To the Opera.* Don Giovanni. *Mozart's music is agreeable and very varied.*

Diary of a Viennese opera buff, Count Zinzendorf

Recitative Next comes an amusing secco recitative, sung with just continuo accompaniment, as in Baroque opera (see page 151). Giovanni invites Zerlina up to his villa, promising to marry her and make her into a fine lady, just as Masetto had ironically predicted.

Duet, "Là ci darem la mano" Operas depend on memorable tunes, as well as on musical drama. The best opera composers are able to write melodies that are not only beautiful in themselves, but also further the drama at the same time. Such a one is the most famous tune in *Don Giovanni,* in the following **duet** (an ensemble for two singers) between Don Giovanni and Zerlina.

Section 1 (Andante) Don Giovanni sings his first stanza to a simple, unforgettable tune that combines seductiveness with a delicate sense of banter. When Zerlina sings the same tune to *her* first stanza, we know she is playing along, even though she hesitates (notice her tiny rhythmic changes, and her reluctance to finish the tune in eight measures—she delays for two more).

In stanza 3, as Don Giovanni presses more and more ardently, yet always gently, Zerlina keeps drawing back. Her reiterated "non son più forte" ("I'm weakening") makes her sound very sorry for herself, but also coy. When the main tune comes back—section 1 of the ensemble falls into a **A A′ B A″ coda** form—Giovanni grows more insistent, Zerlina more coquettish. The words they sing (from stanzas 1–3) are closer together than before, and even simultaneous. The stage director will place them physically closer together, too.

Don Giovanni and Zerlina, in an early engraving; page 211, a modern production.

Section 2 (Allegro) Zerlina falls happily into Don Giovanni's arms, echoing his "andiam" ("let us go"). The "innocent love" they now mean to celebrate is depicted by a little rustic melody (Zerlina is a peasant girl, remember) in a faster tempo. But a not-so-innocent sensuous note is added by the orchestra after the singers' first phrase in this section.

How neatly and charmingly an ensemble can project dramatic action; the whole duet leads us step by step through Don Giovanni's successful "technique." By portraying these people through characteristic action or behavior—Don Giovanni winning another woman, Zerlina playing her own coy game—Mozart exposes their personalities as convincingly as any novelist or playwright.

LISTEN **Mozart, *Don Giovanni:* from Act I, scene iii**

2
39-41

(Italics indicate phrases of the text that are repeated.)

39 ARIA: "Ho capito"

0:03	**Masetto:**	Ho capito, *signor, sì!*	I understand you, *yes sir!*
	(to Don Giovanni)	Chino il capo, e me ne vò	I touch my cap and off I go;
		Ghiacche piace a voi così	Since that's what you want
		Altre repliche *non fò. . . .*	I have nothing else to say.
		Cavalier voi siete già,	After all, you're a lord,
		Dubitar non posso affè,	And I couldn't suspect you, oh no!
		Me lo dice la bontà,	You've told me of the favors
		Che volete *aver per me.*	You mean to do for me!
0:30	*(aside, to Zerlina)*	(Briconaccia! malandrina!	(You wretch! you witch!
		Fosti ognor la mia ruina!)	You have always been my ruin!)
	(to Leporello)	Vengo, vengo!	Yes, I'm coming—
	(to Zerlina)	(Resta, resta!	(Stay, why don't you?
		È una cosa molto onesta;	A very innocent affair!
0:45		Faccia il nostro cavaliere	No doubt this fine lord
		cavaliera ancora te.)	Will make you his fine lady, too!)

(last seven lines repeated)

RECITATIVE (with continuo only)

	Time	Character		Italian	English
40	1:32	**Giovanni:**		Alfin siam liberati,	At last, we're free,
				Zerlinetta gentil, da quel scoccione.	My darling Zerlinetta, of that clown.
				Che ne dite, mio ben, so far pulito?	Tell me, my dear, don't I manage things well?
		Zerlina:		Ma signore, io gli diedi	But sir, I gave him
				Parola di sposarlo.	My word that we would be married.
		Giovanni:		Tal parola	That word
				Non vale un zero! voi non siete fata	Is worth nothing! You were not made
				Per esser paesana. Un'altra sorte	To be a peasant girl. A different fate
				Vi procuran quegli occhi bricconcelli,	Is called for by those roguish eyes,
				Quei labretti sì belli,	Those beautiful little lips,
				Quelle dituccie candide e odorose,	These slender white, perfumed fingers,
				Parmi toccar giuncata, e fiutar rose.	So soft to the touch, scented with roses.
		Zerlina:		Ah, non vorrei—	Ah, I don't want to—
		Giovanni:		Che non voreste?	What don't you want?
		Zerlina:		Alfine	To end up
				Ingannata restar! Io so che raro	Deceived! I know it's not often
				Colle donne voi altri cavalieri	That with women you great gentlemen
				siete onesti e sinceri.	Are honest and sincere.
		Giovanni:		È un' impostura	A slander
				Della gente plebea! La nobiltà	Of the lower classes! The nobility
				Ha dipinta negli occhi l'onestà.	Is honest to the tips of its toes.
				Orsù non perdiam tempo; in quest'istante	Let's lose no time; this very instant
				Io vi voglio sposar.	I wish to marry you.
		Zerlina:		Voi?	You?
		Giovanni:		Certo io.	Certainly, me;
				Quel casinetto è mio, soli saremo;	There's my little place; we'll be alone—
				E là, gioella mio, ci sposeremo.	And there, my precious, we'll be married.

DUET "Là ci darem la mano"

SECTION 1 Andante, **2/4** meter

	Time	Character		Italian	English
41	3:17	**Giovanni:**	A	Là ci darem la mano	There *[in the villa]* you'll give me your hand,
				Là mi dirai di si!	There you'll tell me yes!
				Vedi, non è lontano;	You see, it isn't far—
				Partiam, ben mio, da qui!	Let's go there, my dear!
		Zerlina:	A′	Vorrei, e non vorrei;	I want to, yet I don't want to;
				Mi tremo un poco il cor.	My heart is trembling a little;
				Felice, è ver, sarei,	It's true, I would be happy,
				Ma può burlarmi ancor.	But he could be joking with me.
0:40	3:57	**Giovanni:**	B	Vieni, mio bel diletto!	Come, my darling!
		Zerlina:		Mi fa pietà Masetto . . .	I'm sorry for Masetto . . .
		Giovanni:		Io cangierò tua sorte!	I shall change your lot!
		Zerlina:		Presto non son più forte . . .	All of a sudden I'm weakening . . .

(repetition of phrases [both verbal and musical] from stanzas 1–3)

	Time	Character		Italian
1:01	4:18	**Giovanni:**	A″	Vieni, vieni! Là ci darem la mano
		Zerlina:		Vorrei, e non vorrei . . .
		Giovanni:		Là mi dirai di si!
		Zerlina:		Mi trema un poco il cor.
		Giovanni:		Partiam, ben mio, da qui!
		Zerlina:		Ma può burlarmi ancor.
1:28	4:45	**Giovanni:**	coda	Vieni, mio bel diletto!
		Zerlina:		Mi fa pietà Masetto . . .
		Giovanni:		Io cangierò tua sorte!
		Zerlina:		Presto *non son più forte* . . .
		Both:		Andiam!

SECTION 2 Allegro, **6/8** meter

	Time	Character	Italian	English
1:57	5:14	**Both:**	Andiam, andiam, mio bene,	Let us go, my dear,
			A ristorar le pene	And relieve the pangs
			D'un innocente amor.	Of an innocent love.

(words and music repeated)

Web: ***Research and test your understanding of Classical music genres at <bedfordstmartins.com/listen>.***

GLOBAL PERSPECTIVES 4

Musical Form: Three Case Studies from Asia

As we have seen, musical forms in the Classical style become quite elaborate. It is certainly no accident that these intricate designs emerged across the eighteenth century, just when independent instrumental music was gaining unprecedented prestige in the Western classical tradition. Instrumental music often seems to require such complexities. It is as if the removal of other determinants of form—a poem set to music, a specific religious ritual, or a pattern of dance steps—calls for a different, more abstract musical organization.

If we take the broadest view of these complex forms, however, we can see that they work changes through a simple process. Composers state a tune and then repeat it throughout a movement, joining with it contrasting elements that might be either more complex (sonata form, first-movement concerto form) or simpler (minuet and trio, most rondos and slow movements). Such a basic concept may be realized in myriad ways, according to the imagination and inclination of the composer, resulting in an unlimited array of individual styles.

Many other traditions of instrumental music around the world also start from this simple idea and elaborate it, building intricate forms. In this segment we will take a historical snapshot of three Asian instrumental traditions, from Japan, Indonesia, and India, and then examine music from each.

The togaku orchestra: *kakko, biwa, sho,* and *hichiriki* (back left).

1. *Japan*

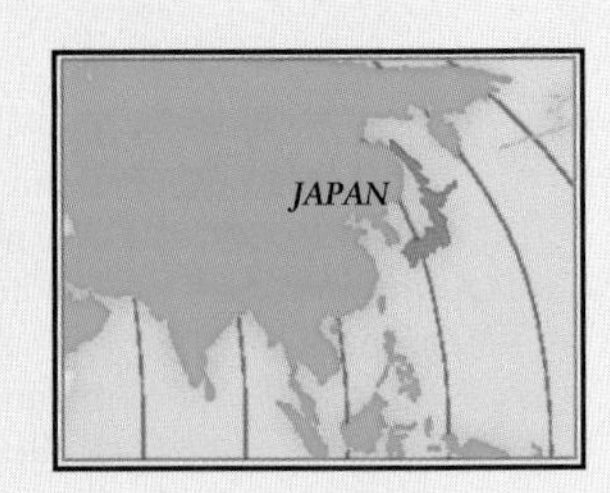

The European symphony orchestra as we know it emerged in the seventeenth century as a reflection of the power and splendor of various courts (see page 122). In Japan, a court orchestra had been established a thousand years earlier. This was the period in Japanese history, from the sixth century C.E. to the eighth, when the first centralized government of the islands was created. The new Japanese central government, many of its institutions, and even its newly constructed capital city of Nara were modeled on the greatest empire in Asia, China. In the process, many elements of Chinese culture were imported to Japan—most importantly Buddhism, which had in turn been imported to China from India centuries before.

The new Japanese court also imported various musical styles from continental Asia. These were altered and developed into an independent Japanese tradition, which came to play an important role in the court's ceremony and ritual. Altogether, these styles are known as **gagaku** (gáh-gáh-koo), from Chinese characters meaning "elegant music," though their sources are more than just Chinese.

The gagaku repertory is divided into two parts. One, known as *togaku* (tóh-gáh-koo), consists of music derived from Chinese styles (with ingredients from India and Southeast Asia as well). The other, *komagaku* (ko-máh-gáh-koo), is made up of works of Korean and Manchurian origin. Further distinctions are made when gagaku accompanies dance, which is often the case, just as with European Baroque orchestral music.

The Japanese Togaku Orchestra The togaku orchestra is so distinctive, and so different from any European orchestra, that we should spend a moment getting to know the various instruments. While European orchestras are dominated by strings, all gagaku orchestras feature wind instruments. The instruments all have specific functions:

- The sliding, wailing double-reed *hichiriki* (héechee-ree-kée) carries the main melody. Several are heard on our recording, playing together.

The togaku orchestra: *tsuridaiko* suspended on the large stand, back right, and, in the foreground, *gakuso, ryuteki,* and a small suspended gong not heard on our recording, called *shoko.*

The side-blown flute called *ryuteki* (ree-óo-taykée) is the first instrument heard. It plays the melody along with the hichirikis, though in a slightly different version. Thus it produces a *heterophonic* texture with the hichirikis (see page 28); heterophony is an important feature in many non-Western musics.

The *sho,* a mouth reed-organ with seventeen pipes, plays chordal clusters of tones derived from the main melody. This unusual instrument contributes a haunting background of harmonic haze to the texture.

The *kakko,* a two-headed barrel drum played with sticks, is used for single strokes or short rolls. It is the first drum heard.

A deep, larger barrel drum *tsuridaiko* (tzóo-reedíe-koh; its first beat is heard at 0:13) marks off long phrases of the melody with two successive strokes, the first soft and the second louder.

A *biwa* or four-stringed lute (bée-wah, first plucked at 1:11) strums across several strings quickly, punctuating the melody.

A *gakuso,* a zither with thirteen strings (gáh-kóo-so, first heard at 1:31), plays short motives, mainly of three notes related, again, to the melody. Both the biwa and the gakuso take a more active role as this performance proceeds, finally even playing some of the main melody.

Etenraku *Etenraku* is the most famous piece for the togaku orchestra. Its name means "music of divinity," and it emanates a deep, powerful calm associated with Buddhist contemplation. This is the oldest music on our CD set; its origins reach back almost to the origins of gagaku itself.

The musical form of this piece exhibits three characteristics of gagaku music. *First,* the piece as a whole is constructed from a single melody, according to a predetermined plan and without improvisation. The melody is played through by some of the instruments and punctuated by others, as described above. It consists of three phrases, labeled **a, b,** and **c** in the musical example and Listening Chart on page 214. Each phrase is 32 beats long. The beats move by slowly at first, so slowly that the phrases can be hard to discern; but as you get used to the melody you will be able to follow their repetitions.

Second, the instruments of the orchestra are introduced gradually and in a predetermined order as they fulfill their various functions.

Third, the beat quickens, the meter is more clearly marked, and the general musical activity increases as the performance proceeds. At first, while the flute alone carries the melody, the beats are very slow and flexible—the music seems almost to have no meter at

Sho

LISTENING CHART 13

Etenraku 8 min., 4 sec.

0:00	**a**	Ryuteki, kakko, tsuridaiko only
0:51		Sho and hichirikis enter.
1:11	**a**	Biwa enters.
1:31		Gakuso enters, completing the orchestra.
2:18	**b**	
3:15	**b**	
4:04	**c**	Paired beats of tsuridaiko every 8 beats
4:46	**c**	Gakuso and biwa gradually play more and more fragments of main melody, joining in heterophony of hichirikis and ryuteki.
5:25	**a**	
6:02	**a**	
6:37	**b**	
7:11	**b**	After the phrase is completed (at 7:55), biwa and gakuso end the piece with a brief coda.

all. (Each pair of beats on the tsuridaiko drum, however, coming 16 very slow beats after the last, provides a certain sense of regularity and meter.) When the double-reed hichirikis enter, they play the melody along with the flute to a more prominent beat. Then, at the **c** phrases of the melody, the tsuridaiko doubles its pace, beating twice every 8 beats instead of every 16.

Meanwhile the tempo gradually quickens: At the outset the beats come every 2–3 seconds (*very* slow!), while at the close they move by at about one per second.

Even at this relatively quick tempo, the music never loses its sense of restraint. Virtuosic playing is strictly avoided. *Etenraku*'s aura of quiet, inward-looking Buddhist contemplation characterizes the gagaku repertory as a whole.

2. *Indonesia*

The Southeast Asian Republic of Indonesia consists of some six thousand islands in all, half of them inhabited. The central island is Java. Across Indonesia, ensembles playing traditional musics thrive—alongside, these days, many kinds of pop, rock, and world beat ensembles, especially in large urban centers such as Jakarta. A traditional musical ensemble in Indonesia is called a **gamelan.**

The Indonesian Orchestra: Gamelan Gamelans assume a wide, even bewildering variety of shapes and sizes, as we might expect of musical traditions that extend back many centuries and that have served an

array of religious, political, and social functions. Gamelans may involve three or four musicians or they may involve dozens. They may or may not include singers. They frequently accompany drama or dance: sacred temple dances, danced dramas, or the famous Indonesian shadow-puppet plays enacting stories from Hindu epics. The music gamelans play may have been passed down over hundreds of years or it may be recently composed.

At the heart of gamelan music stands a great variety of gongs and **metallophones** (instruments like a xylophone, with metal keys). These make Indonesia the home of the most highly developed of the so-called gong-chime musical cultures prominent throughout Southeast Asia. Indeed the word *gong* itself comes to us from Java, where it names (and also evokes the sound of) the largest gamelan instrument.

Balinese Gamelans Nowhere in Indonesia are gamelans more prevalent than on Bali, a good-sized island to the east of Java. In 1980 it was estimated that there was a gamelan for every 350 inhabitants of the island—a staggering number, in a population of around two million!

Gamelans seem to have come to Bali in the sixteenth century, brought from Java by aristocratic refugees when their Hindu kingdom fell to Islamic invaders from the Asian mainland. Balinese gamelans, at least the elaborate ones with many instruments, were associated especially with temples and princely courts. When Bali came under colonial control of the Netherlands, in 1906, the courts declined, but their traditions of gamelan music did not simply disappear. Instead they were taken over more and more by village gamelan clubs, and these comprise the main venue in which Balinese gamelan music thrives today.

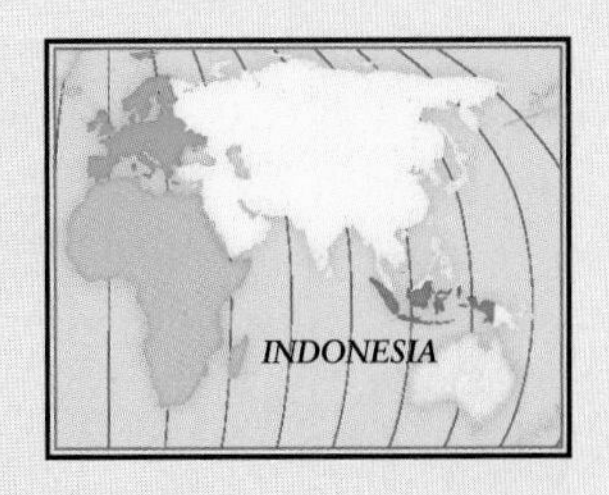

Gamelan Pelegongan *Gamelan pelegongan,* heard on our recording, is a type of Balinese orchestra used primarily to accompany elaborate dance-dramas. It takes its name from this dance, called *legong*. The primary instruments in gamelan pelegongan are:

- two hand-beaten drums; the drummers direct the ensemble in the manner of a Western orchestra conductor.
- several gongs of varying sizes
- a large group of metallophones, some low-pitched, some high. Most of these have five metal keys each, with a range of a single octave, while some have thirteen keys and a wider range. The sounds, construction,

Gamelan pelegongan, with floor gongs, drum, gangsas, and, in the rear, large suspended gongs.

A *legong* dancer and part of the *gamelan pelegongan*: a drum, a small floor gong, and a thirteen-key gangsa are prominent.

and names of these metallophones vary, but all of them can be called by the umbrella term *gangsa,* "bronze."

- one or two bamboo flutes. What Western ears might hear as "out of tune-ness" in their playing is a quality recognized and prized by Balinese musicians.

Form in Gamelan Music A traditional piece for gamelan is usually organized around the repetition of a long, symmetrical melody. This melody is made up of smaller, equal phrases, generally 8 or 16 beats long, so that the whole melody will last a multiple of these numbers, especially 64 or 128 beats. A central group of instruments in the gamelan presents this nuclear melody. At the same time it may be played by other instruments in a simpler version, mainly in even note values, creating a heterophonic presentation.

At the end of each statement of the melody, the largest, deepest gong in the orchestra sounds. The unit between one gongstroke and the next, known as a *gongan,* is considered the basic structural unit for the piece. The gongan is divided into smaller units by other instruments in the gamelan: first into two units by a higher-sounding gong, then into four by other gongs, then into eight, and so forth. A 64-beat melody, for example, breaks down audibly into units of 32 beats, 16 beats, 8 beats, 4 beats, and so on.

This process of division continues right through the rhythmic level of the main melody, so that certain instruments elaborate upon its pitches twice as fast, four times as fast, and perhaps even eight times as fast.

The whole texture, then, is an elaborately *stratified* polyphony, with rhythmic layers ranging from the gongan itself all the way down to subdivisions of individual beats. Each instrument or group of instruments plays a single role, occupying one of these rhythmic strata. In the midst of it all is the nuclear melody, presented in one version or simultaneously in distinct versions.

Bopong The piece on our recording, *Bopong,* is not a full dance piece but instead a sort of brief overture, played before the dancing begins. It was composed by I Lotring, a famous Balinese master musician born about 1900 and involved in many stylistic innovations of the 1920s and 1930s.

The 64-beat melody is played through three times; this is the traditional heart of the piece. Before it we hear introductory material, partly based on the main melody. After it comes a lengthy, separate section with an ostinato (see page 132), and then a new concluding melody played by the whole gamelan.

As you listen to the first statement of the nuclear melody itself, from 0:29 to 1:19, *count* the beats,

LISTENING CHART 14

I Lotring, *Bopong* 4 min., 33 sec. 3 27

0:00	Introduction: a few gangsas alone
0:04	Gong; introduction continues with fast gangsa figuration
0:29	Gong; ***first*** statement of melody begins
1:19	Gong; ***second*** statement of melody
2:06	Gong; ***third*** statement of melody
2:38	Melody truncated
2:41	Ostinato begins (fourteen times through); gong every eight beats
4:04	Syncopated, unison closing melody
4:20	Final gongstroke

A gamelan at a Balinese funeral. The large array of gongs in the foreground is not found in *gamelan pelegongan.*

counting slightly faster than one beat per second. The melody is 64 beats long and composed of four phrases of 16 beats each. The large gong sounds at the end of the 64-beat cycle.

The core melody, the most prominent melody you hear, is played by some of the gangsas and by two flutes, one high-pitched and one lower and less easy to hear. At the same time other gangsas play a simpler, unadorned version of this melody in slow notes. They are omitted from the beginning of the melody; listen for them starting at 0:42.

Around this melody is woven faster figuration, dividing each beat you count into four, played by a group of brittle-sounding gangsas. They fall silent at the start of each statement of the melody. Then they enter, softly at first, finally asserting themselves with a clamorous outburst (listen for the first instance at 0:58). Such outbursts are a famous hallmark of the newer, post-court styles of Balinese gamelan music.

The third statement of the melody speeds up toward the end but does not quite finish. An entirely new melodic phrase breaks in to start a different section or "movement" of the piece. Beginning at 2:41, some of the gangsas play a single, eight-beat ostinato, repeated many times; other gangsas and the flutes play along with a slightly elaborated version. Meanwhile the brittle-sounding gangsas contribute spectacular figuration, moving eight times as fast as the main beat. The large gong, sounding at the end of every ostinato—hence every eight beats instead of every 64—adds to the feeling of rhythmic climax.

Finally, all this rhythmic energy is channeled into a single closing melody with striking syncopations (see page 13), played in unison by most of the gamelan.

3. *India*

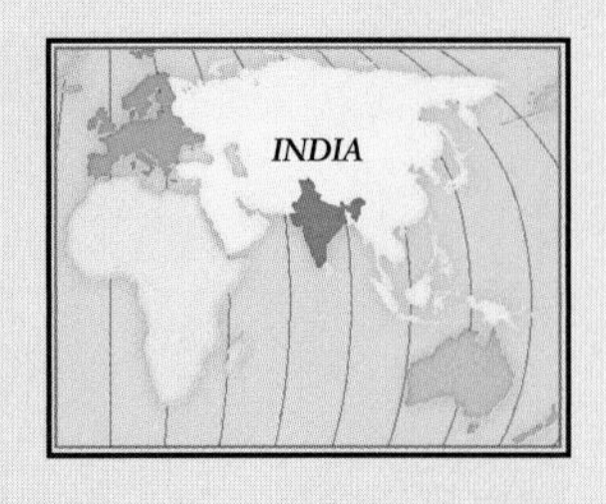

The classical music of India finds its ancient origins in the singing of the Vedas, sacred writings in Sanskrit from two thousand years ago. Here is another example, along with Christian plainchant and Qur'anic recitation, of sacred chant and its fundamental importance all over the globe (see pages 57 and 70).

Two traditions of Indian music emerged, and diverged, beginning in the thirteenth century: one Hindustani, associated with the Muslim and Hindu regions of north India, and the other Karnatak (or Carnatic), practiced in the mainly Hindu south. Though distinct in many ways, they share many features, the most important of which are *improvisation* and the *rag*. Improvising music—making it up on the spot according to certain prescribed guidelines—is something we know well from jazz but hear less often in Western classical music. (Remember, however, the improvised cadenzas and ornaments of Bach, Mozart, and others.) Improvisation has no place in Japanese gagaku and plays a limited role in Indonesian gamelan music. There is none to speak of in our gamelan pelegongan example. In India, however, it is basic to both classical traditions.

Melody: The Rag Indian melody is based on the concept of <u>rag</u> (or *raga* or *ragam*). A rag is something like a Western scale, only much more: It is really a comprehensive kit or set of guidelines for producing melody. Each rag specifies not only a scale, but also a hierarchy of more and less important pitches, certain melodic gestures associated with those pitches, ways of ascending and descending the scale, characteristic patterns of ornamentation, and even snatches of melody used to improvise variations.

Rags carry broader implications also. They are felt to express particular emotional states and are associated with specific times of the day or seasons of the year. Indian musicians spend years mastering both the subtleties of technique and the "character" of rags. The best of them can improvise complex, beautiful, appropriate, and distinct melodies out of dozens of different rags.

The texture of Indian classical music is in principle monophonic. But a simple notion of monophony hardly does justice to what we hear in this music. In the first place, several resonant, continuous drone pitches sound against the melody. Second, the melody might be simultaneously presented by two instruments, or voice and instrument, in a loosely synchronized fashion; this creates a heterophonic texture. In addition, the melody unfolds most of the time in carefully prescribed interaction with complicated metrical patterns played by a drummer.

A Hindustani Ensemble The typical north Indian performance ensemble consists of one instrument that carries the main melody—on our recording the most famous Indian melodic instrument today, the *sitar,* a long-necked lute with a characteristic buzzing, almost

The joy of dueling sitars: Ravi Shankar plays with his daughter Anoushka.

metallic resonance. (A lute is a plucked stringed instrument something like a guitar; see page 45.)

A second melodic instrument, as we have noted, may interact with the first in constructing the melody. In our performance this is the *sarod,* another lutelike instrument sounding less metallic than the sitar and a bit closer to an acoustic guitar. Yet another type of lute, a *tambura,* plays no melody but supplies the drone pitches.

Finally, a drummer plays *tabla,* two small, hand-beaten drums. These have very different sounds: one rather like a bongo drum, the other deep, with a sliding *whoop* to its tone.

LISTENING CHART 15

Rag *Mauj-Khammaj* 7 min., 15 sec. 28, 29

First excerpt

0:00	**Alap:** tambura, then sarod, then sitar
3:15	Rhythms quicken as the alap ends.
3:32	**First gat:** tune played by sitar and sarod in heterophony; tabla enter.

Second excerpt

0:23	Tempo quickens as **second gat** begins.
0:35	Tune from the first gat returns, faster.

***A Performance of Rag* Mauj-Khammaj** In the most famous and esteemed instrumental performances of rags, the musicians start from a tune, like the European, Japanese, and Indonesian musicians we have studied. The tune may be relatively fixed and unimprovised or freer, depending on the rag. Our rag, named *Mauj-Khammaj,* has a fixed melody.

Around this tune, the instrumentalists spin out a long, continuous performance that falls into several connected "movements" marked by different styles and tempos. The movements always involve much improvisation, but at the same time they develop according to broad outlines. (Vocalists perform several different genres of song based on rags, also according to elaborate guidelines.) Knowledgeable listeners savor the skill of the musicians for their adherence to the features of the particular rag performed, for their virtuosic elaborations of them, and for their gradual and skillful presentation of this multimovement form.

A performance such as this can last as long as an hour. We choose two excerpts from a condensed rag performance, excerpts that will help us understand the rag's multimovement format. The rag is played, in a spirit of friendly, virtuosic rivalry, by two of the most renowned Indian musicians of the twentieth century, Ravi Shankar on sitar and Ali Akhbar Khan on sarod. They are accompanied by tambura and tabla.

Excerpt 1 An **alap**—the first movement—opens the performance, without any clear meter. The drums do not play at all. The sarod and sitar begin to alternate phrases in a free, dreamy exploration of the rag's pitches and associated melodic gestures. Toward the end of the alap, the rhythmic activity quickens, but there is still no clear meter. (In a full performance, this leads to subsections of the alap, each quicker than the last and each announcing to the audience another stage of the musical form.) Finally, at 3:32, the sitar begins a metrical melody and the sarod joins in. Quickly, the tabla player begins as well, marking a regular beat with complex rhythmic patterns.

This shift to metrical music marks the beginning of the second movement, the first **gat** (pronounced *gut*). In a moderate tempo, the first gat now introduces the basic tune of *Mauj-Khammaj.* Free variations on the tune follow, improvised according to the rag guidelines.

Excerpt 2 Our second excerpt picks up near the end of the first gat. At 0:23 the tempo quickens slightly, marking the beginning of the second gat, always faster than the first. If you listen closely, you will hear that the second gat begins with an up-tempo version of the melody that began the first. The tune basic to the rag introduces both metered movements. The quicker tempo results in especially dazzling improvisations by the sitar and sarod as well as the tabla. The pace continues to speed up through the second gat, bringing the performance, which ends after our excerpt, to a spectacular close.

One more, general point: We saw this same gradual quickening of tempo in Japanese gagaku, but without the flashy spirit of the Indian performance. If we think about it, indeed, this tendency to move faster and faster across a lengthy work applies to the European Classical genres we have studied: All save the fastest for last. There is, apparently, something deeply ingrained and satisfying about speeding up across a performance; perhaps it is the release of energy involved for both listeners and performers. It is a trait of countless musical repertories across the globe.

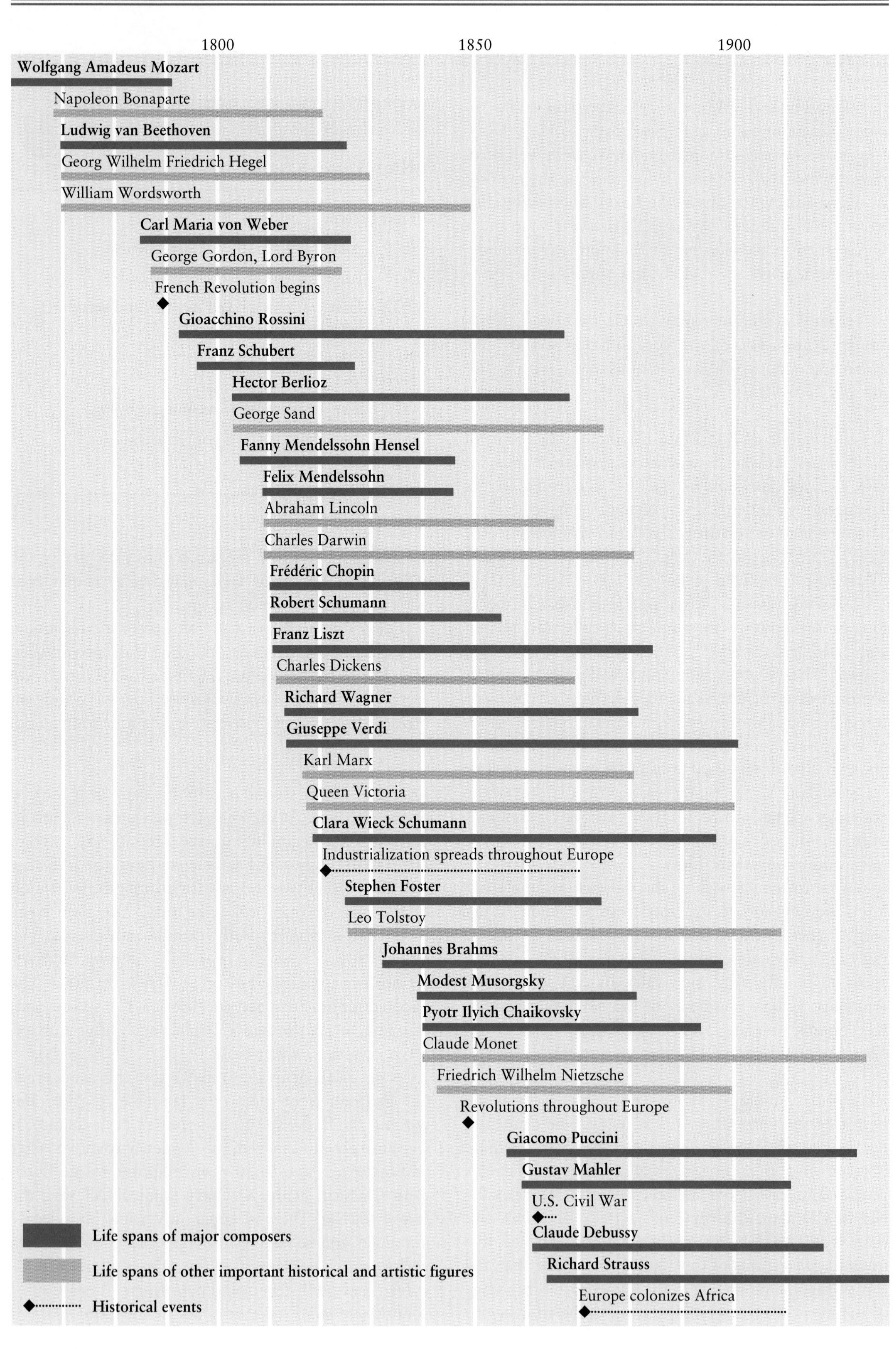
1800
1850
1900
Wolfgang Amadeus Mozart
Napoleon Bonaparte
Ludwig van Beethoven
Georg Wilhelm Friedrich Hegel
William Wordsworth
Carl Maria von Weber
George Gordon, Lord Byron
French Revolution begins
Gioacchino Rossini
Franz Schubert
Hector Berlioz
George Sand
Fanny Mendelssohn Hensel
Felix Mendelssohn
Abraham Lincoln
Charles Darwin
Frédéric Chopin
Robert Schumann
Franz Liszt
Charles Dickens
Richard Wagner
Giuseppe Verdi
Karl Marx
Queen Victoria
Clara Wieck Schumann
Industrialization spreads throughout Europe
Stephen Foster
Leo Tolstoy
Johannes Brahms
Modest Musorgsky
Pyotr Ilyich Chaikovsky
Claude Monet
Friedrich Wilhelm Nietzsche
Revolutions throughout Europe
Giacomo Puccini
Gustav Mahler
U.S. Civil War
Claude Debussy
Richard Strauss
Europe colonizes Africa
Life spans of major composers
Life spans of other important historical and artistic figures
Historical events

UNIT IV

The Nineteenth Century

In Unit IV we take up music of the nineteenth century. Starting with the towering figure of Beethoven in the first quarter of the century, famous names now crowd the history of music: Schubert, Schumann, Chopin, Wagner, Verdi, Brahms, Chaikovsky, Mahler, and others. Nearly everyone, whether conscious of it or not, knows a fair amount of music by these masters, or at least some of their melodies. These tend to turn up as background music to movies and television; some of them are metamorphosed into pop tunes and advertising sound tracks.

The appeal of this music today in the symphony hall and the opera house, the classroom and the teaching studio, seems to rest on much the same grounds as those governing its great success a hundred years ago and more. It is important to realize, first of all, that nineteenth-century music was a great success story. For the first time in European history, music was taken entirely seriously as an art on the highest level. Composers were accorded a new, exalted role, to which they responded magnificently, writing music that sounds important and impressive; and listeners ever since have been thoroughly impressed.

Music and Individual Emotion

Music's prestige, in the Romantic scheme of things, derived first and foremost from the belief that music more than any other art mirrors one's inner emotional life. Music, then, should have a unique power to convey individual feeling. Again, composers rose to the challenge. Nineteenth-century music is more direct and unrestrained in emotional quality than the music of any earlier time. And for most audiences, full-blooded emotion in music—even exaggerated emotion—seems never to lose its powerful attraction.

The individuality of all artists, including composers, was accorded special value in the nineteenth century. Composers produced music with much more pronounced personal attributes than in the late Baroque period or the Classical period (when many pieces by Haydn and Mozart, for example, sounded rather similar in character). It is therefore a natural tendency to think of the history of nineteenth-century music in terms of great names, such as those in the list given above. The prospect of getting to know all these distinct, unusual, and probably fascinating characters—meeting them, as it were, under the emotional conditions of Romantic music—surely contributes to the appeal of this particular body of music. And since the Romantic composers have such strong distinct personalities, it is not only natural but inevitable to find oneself drawn to certain of these individuals, and put off by others. There are music lovers who recoil from Wagner. Others cherish Schubert above even Beethoven and Bach.

Like eighteenth-century music, music of the nineteenth century is not stylistically homogeneous, yet it can still be regarded as a larger historical unit. We shall take up the Romantic style, usually dated from the 1820s, after discussing the music of Beethoven, who was born in 1770 and as a young man traveled twice to Vienna, the city of Classicism—first to meet Mozart and then to study with Haydn.

But while in technique Beethoven was clearly a child of the eighteenth century, in his emotionalism, his artistic ambition, and his insistence on individuality he was a true inhabitant of the nineteenth. Indeed, Beethoven was the model, either direct or indirect, for many of the great nineteenth-century composers who came after him. Understanding Beethoven is the key to understanding Romantic music.

CHAPTER 14

Beethoven

If any single composer deserves a special chapter in the history of music, that composer is Ludwig van Beethoven (1770–1827). Probably no other figure in the arts meets with such a strong universal response. People may pity van Gogh, respect Michelangelo and Shakespeare, and admire Leonardo da Vinci, but Beethoven instantly summons up a powerful, positive image: that of the tough, ugly, angry genius staring down adversity and delivering himself of one deeply expressive masterpiece after another. Beethoven's music has enjoyed broad-based, uninterrupted popularity from his own day to the present. Today its place is equally secure with unsophisticated listeners and with the most learned musicians.

There is much to be done on earth, do it soon!
I cannot carry on the everyday life I am living; art demands this sacrifice too. Rest, diversion, amusement—only so that I can function more powerfully in my art.

From Beethoven's journal, 1814

There is a sense, furthermore, in which music may be said to have come of age with Beethoven. For despite the great music that came before him—that of Bach, Mozart, and many other composers we know—the art of music was never taken so seriously until Beethoven's symphonies and sonatas struck listeners of his time as a revelation. They were almost equally impressed by the facts of his life, in particular his deafness, the affliction that caused him to retire from a career as a performing musician and become solely a composer.

A new concept of artistic genius was evolving at the time, and Beethoven crystallized this concept powerfully for his own age. He still exemplifies it today. No longer a mere craftsman, the artist suffers and creates; endowed not just with greater talent but with a greater soul than ordinary mortals, the artist suffers and creates for humanity. Music is no longer merely a function of bodily parts like the ear or the fingers. It exists in the highest reaches of the artist's spirit.

1 Between Classicism and Romanticism

Beethoven is special in another sense, in the unique position he occupies between the eighteenth-century Viennese Classical style and nineteenth-century Romanticism. Beethoven's roots were firmly Classical. He was a student of Haydn when the latter was at the height of his fame. Beethoven remained committed to the principles of the Classical style until the end of his life.

Beethoven was committed to the *principles* of Classicism—but not to every one of its manifestations, and certainly not to the mood behind it. There is almost always a sense of excitement, urgency, and striving in Beethoven's music that makes it instantly distinguishable from that of Haydn and Mozart. These qualities emerged in response to Romantic stirrings that are the subject of our next chapter.

The French Revolution

Romanticism, as we shall see, was originally a literary movement. Though well under way by the beginning of the nineteenth century, it was not yet influential in Vienna; and, in any case, Beethoven did not have a very literary sensibility. At the root of Romanticism, however, there lay one great political event that made an enormous impact on the composer's generation. This was the French Revolution. Beethoven was one of many artists who felt compelled to proclaim their sympathy with the ideal of freedom symbolized by that cataclysmic event.

When the Parisian crowd stormed the Bastille in 1789, Beethoven was a highly impressionable eighteen-year-old, already grounded in liberal and humanistic ideals. More than a decade later, Beethoven's admiration for Napoleon Bonaparte as hero of the revolution led him to an extravagant and unprecedented gesture—writing a descriptive symphony called *Bonaparte*. Retitled the *Eroica* (Heroic) Symphony, it was the decisive "breakthrough" work of Beethoven's maturity, the first work to show his full individual freedom as an artist.

Before Beethoven could send the symphony to Paris, Napoleon crowned himself Emperor of France. Liberal Europe saw this as a betrayal of the revolution, and Beethoven scratched out the title in a fury. But idealism dies hard. To Beethoven, and to many of his contemporaries, the French Revolution still stood for an ideal of perfectibility—not so much of human society (as

Storming the Bastille, a contemporary engraving of the most famous event of the French Revolution.

The revolution betrayed: Napoleon's coronation as Emperor of France in 1803, as portrayed by Jacques-Louis David (1748–1825), the greatest practitioner of Neoclassical art (see page 169). Today this huge (20 by 30 feet) and pompous painting repels some viewers as much as the actual event it depicts enraged Beethoven.

Beethoven himself acknowledged by deleting Napoleon's name) as of human aspiration. That ideal, too, is what Beethoven realized by his own triumph over his deafness. The point was not lost on those of his contemporaries who were swept away by his music.

And that is what listeners have responded to ever since. Listening to the *Eroica* Symphony, we sense that it has less to do with Napoleon than with the composer's own self-image. The quality of heroic striving and inner triumph is what emerges so magnificently in Beethoven's most famous compositions.

2 Beethoven and the Symphony

As we have said, what sets Beethoven instantly apart from Haydn or Mozart is his mood of excitement and urgency. This he achieved by maximizing virtually all musical elements. Higher and lower registers, sharper syncopations, stronger accents, harsher dissonances yielding to more profound resolutions—all of these are found in Beethoven's music. He made new demands on instruments, expanded the orchestra, and stretched Classical forms to their limits.

Given all this, it is not surprising that this composer should be especially associated with the symphony, the most "public" of Classical genres, with the greatest range of expression, variety, and sheer volume. In fact, Beethoven wrote fewer symphonies (nine) than piano sonatas (thirty-two) or string quartets

His clothes were very ordinary and not in the least in the customary style of those days, especially in our circles. . . . He was very proud; I have seen Countess Thun, the mother of Princess Lichnowsky, on her knees before him begging him to play something—and he would not. But then, Countess Thun was a very eccentric woman.

An old lady remembers the young Beethoven (1867)

Ludwig van Beethoven (1770–1827)

Beethoven, like Mozart, followed his father as a court musician; the Beethovens served the archbishop-elector of Bonn in West Germany. But Ludwig's father—unlike Wolfgang's—was a failure and an alcoholic who beat the boy to make him practice. A trip to Vienna to make contacts (he hoped to study with Mozart) was cut short by the death of his mother. Still in his teens, Beethoven had to take charge of his family because of his father's drinking.

Nonetheless, Bonn was an "enlightened" court, ruled by the brother of the liberal Emperor Joseph II of Austria. The talented young musician had an opportunity to mix with aristocrats and intellectuals. The idealism that is so evident in Beethoven's later works—such as his Ninth Symphony, ending with a choral hymn to universal brotherhood—can be traced to this early environment.

Compared to Mozart, Beethoven was a slow developer, but by the age of twenty-two he had made enough of an impression to receive a sort of fellowship to return to Vienna, this time to study with Haydn. He was soon acclaimed as a powerful virtuoso pianist, playing his own compositions and improvising brilliantly at the palaces of the music-loving aristocracy of that city. He remained in Vienna until his death.

After the age of thirty, he became progressively deaf—a devastating fate for a musician, which kept him from making a living in the traditional manner, by performing. The crisis that this caused in Beethoven's life is reflected by a strange, moving document (called the "Heiligenstadt Testament," after the town where it was written, in 1802) that is half a proclamation of artistic ideals, half suicide note. But Beethoven overcame his depression and in 1803 wrote the first of his truly powerful and individual symphonies, the Third (*Eroica*).

Beethoven all but demanded support from the nobility in Vienna, who were awed by his extraordinarily forceful and original music as well as by his uncompromising character. An alarmingly brusque and strong-willed person, he suffered deeply and seemed to live for his art alone. His domestic life was chaotic; one anecdote has him pouring water over himself to cool off in summer and being asked by his landlord to leave. (He changed lodgings an average of once a year.) By the end of his life he was well known in Vienna as an eccentric, teased by street boys.

Probably the first musician to make a career solely from composing, Beethoven was regarded as a genius even in his lifetime. He had an immense need to receive and to give affection, yet he never married, despite various love affairs. After he died, passionate letters to a woman identified only as his "Immortal Beloved" were found; we now know she was the wife of a Frankfurt merchant, both members of Beethoven's circle. In his later years Beethoven adopted his own orphan nephew, but his attitude was so overprotective and his love so smothering that the boy could not stand it and attempted suicide.

Beethoven had always lived with ill health, and the shock of this new family crisis hastened his death. Twenty thousand attended his funeral; his eulogy was written, and delivered at the funeral, by Vienna's leading poet.

Taste in many matters has changed many times since Beethoven's lifetime, but his music has always reigned supreme with audiences and critics. The originality and expressive power of his work seem never to fade.

Chief Works: Nine symphonies, the most famous being the Third *(Eroica)*, Fifth, Sixth *(Pastoral)*, Seventh, and Ninth *(Choral)* ▪ The opera *Fidelio* (originally called *Leonore*), for which he wrote four different overtures; overtures to the plays *Egmont*, by Goethe, and *Coriolanus* ▪ Violin Concerto and five piano concertos, including the *Emperor* (No. 5) ▪ 16 string quartets ▪ 32 piano sonatas, including the *Pathétique, Waldstein, Appassionata,* and the late-period *Hammerklavier* Sonata ▪ Mass in D *(Missa solemnis)*

Encore: After Symphony No. 5, listen to the "Moonlight" Sonata; Sonata in A-flat, Op. 110; Symphonies No. 6 and 9.

(sixteen)—and no musician would rank these works any lower than the symphonies. But at the height of his career, from around 1800 to 1810, even many of his piano sonatas and string quartets sound like symphonies. The torrents of sound Beethoven summoned up in these works demanded whole new techniques of piano and string playing.

We can approach Beethoven's "symphonic ideal" through his Fifth Symphony, written in 1808. Three main features of this work have impressed generations of listeners: its rhythmic drive, its motivic consistency or unity, and the sense it gives of a definite psychological progression. The first feature is apprehended at once, the second by the end of the opening movement, and the third only after we have experienced all four of the symphony's movements.

- *Rhythmic drive.* Immediately apparent is the drive and blunt power of the rhythmic style. Beethoven hammers the meter, piles accent upon accent, and calculates long time spans with special power: a far cry from the elegance and wit of the Classical style.
- *Motivic consistency.* During the first movement of the Fifth Symphony, a single motive is heard constantly, in many different forms. They are not random forms; the motive becomes more and more vivid and significant as the work proceeds. People have marveled at the "organic" quality of such music, which seems to them to grow like a plant's leaves out of a simple seed.

- *Psychological progression.* Over the course of the Fifth Symphony's four movements, Beethoven seems to trace a coherent and dramatic psychological progression in several stages. "There Fate knocks at the door!" he is supposed to have said about the first movement—but after two eventful middle stages, Fate is nullified in the last movement, trampled under by a military march.

In Beethoven's hands, the multimovement symphony seems to trace an inspirational life process, one so basic and universal that it leaves few listeners unmoved. This was, perhaps, the greatest of all his forward-looking innovations.

The Scherzo

Another of Beethoven's technical innovations should also be mentioned. On the whole, Beethoven continued to use Classical forms for his symphonies and other multimovement works. As early as his Second Symphony, however, he substituted another kind of movement for the traditional minuet.

This was the **scherzo** (*scairtzo*), a fast, rushing movement in triple meter—inherited from the minuet—and in the basic minuet-and-trio form, **A B A.** With their fast tempo, Beethoven's scherzos sometimes need more repetitions to make their point; **A B A** is sometimes extended to **A B A B A.**

The word *scherzo* means "joke" in Italian. Beethoven's brand of humor is very different from, say, Haydn's: It is broad, brusque, jocular, even violent. Originally associated with the court of Louis XIV, the minuet at the time of the French Revolution still stood for eighteenth-century formality and elegance; one can see why Beethoven rejected it. The scherzo became an ideal vehicle for Beethoven's characteristic rhythmic drive. See page 234.

LUDWIG VAN BEETHOVEN (1770–1827)
Symphony No. 5 in C Minor, Op. 67 (1808)

Beethoven composed his Fifth Symphony together with his Sixth *(Pastoral)* for one of the rare concerts in which he showcased his own works. This concert, in December 1808, was a huge success, even though it lasted for five hours and the heating in the hall failed.

First Movement (Allegro con brio) Motivic consistency, as we have said, is a special feature of Beethoven's work. The first movement of the Fifth Symphony is dominated by a single rhythmic motive, ♪♪♪𝅗𝅥 . This motive forms the first theme in the exposition; it initiates the bridge; it appears as a subdued

Beethoven striding through Vienna: a caricature by one of his contemporaries.

background to the lyrical, contrasting second theme; and it emerges again in the cadence material:

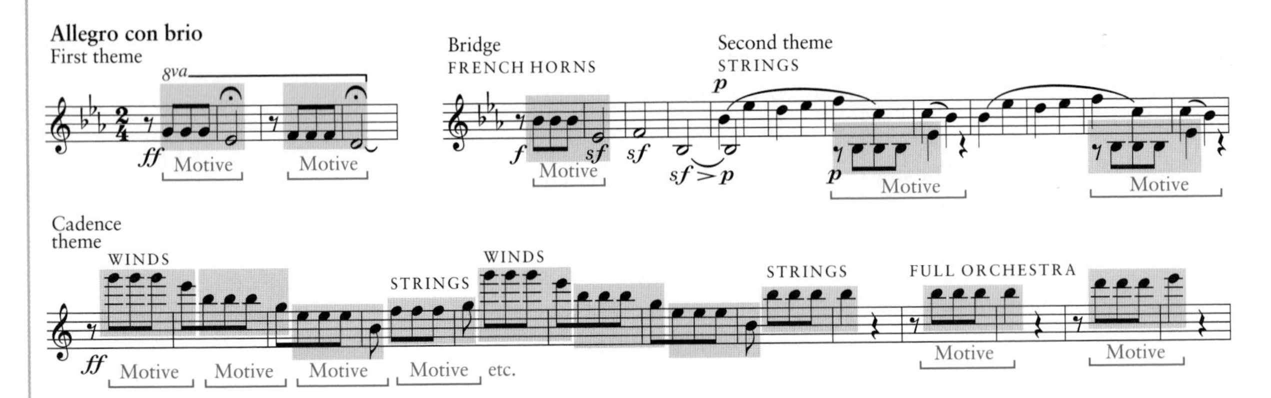

The motive then expands further in the development section and continues growing in the long coda.

How is this different from Classical motivic technique? In such works as Mozart's Symphony No. 40, a single motive is likewise developed with consistency and a sense of growth. But Beethoven's use of the same device—the use of a Classical device for non-Classical ends—gives the Fifth Symphony its particular gripping urgency. The difference is not in the basic technique but in the way it is being used—in the expressive intensity it is made to serve. Let us see how this works.

Went to a German charitable concert [the American premiere of Beethoven's Fifth Symphony]. . . . The music was good, very well selected and excellently well performed, as far as I could judge. The crack piece, though, was the last, Beethoven's Sinfonia in C minor. It was generally unintelligible to me, except the Andante.

Diary of a New York music lover, 1841

Exposition The movement begins with an arresting presentation of the first theme, in the key of C minor (shown above). The meter is disrupted by two fermatas (see page 14), which give the music an improvisational, primal quality, like a great shout. Even after the theme rushes on and seems to be picking up momentum, it is halted by a new fermata, making three fermatas in all.

The horn-call bridge (see above) performs the usual function of a bridge in an unusually dramatic way. That function is to cement the new key—a major key—firmly and usher in the second theme with power and authority.

The second theme introduces a new gentle mood, despite the main motive rumbling away below it. But this mood soon fades—Beethoven seems to brush it aside impatiently. The main motive bursts out again in a stormy cadence passage, which comes to a satisfying, complete stop. The exposition is repeated.

Development The development section starts with a new shout, as the first theme makes an immediate modulation, a modulation back to the minor mode. There is yet another fermata. It sounds like the crack of doom.

For a time the first theme (or, rather, its continuation) is developed, leading to a climax when the ♪♪♪𝅗𝅥 rhythm multiplies itself furiously, as shown to the right. Next comes the bridge theme, modulating through one key after another. Suddenly the *two middle pitches* of the bridge theme are extracted and echoed between high wind instruments and lower strings. This process is called **fragmentation** (for an example from Mozart, see page 183). The two-note figure breaks apart, and the echoing process focuses on just one note:

LISTENING CHART 16

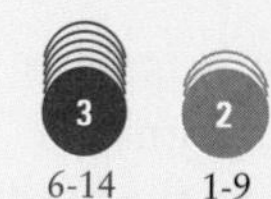

Beethoven, Symphony No. 5 in C Minor, first movement

Sonata form. 7 min., 18 sec.

Track		Time		
			EXPOSITION	
6 / 1		0:00	**Theme 1**	Main theme with *two fermatas,* followed by the *first continuation* (based on ♪♪♪ 𝅗𝅥); *another fermata (the third)*
		0:20		Main motive (♪♪♪ 𝅗𝅥), *ff,* is followed by a *second continuation:* timpani, crescendo
7 / 2		0:46	**Bridge theme**	French horn, *f*
			Second Group	
	0:02	0:48	**Theme 2**	Major mode, *p,* strings and woodwinds (♪♪♪ 𝅗𝅥 in background)
8 / 3		1:17	**Cadence theme**	Based on ♪♪♪ 𝅗𝅥 motive
	0:05	1:22		CADENCE
	0:09	1:26	***Exposition repeated***	
9 / 4			**DEVELOPMENT**	
		2:52		First modulation, using ♪♪♪ 𝅗𝅥 motive; French horns, *ff;* minor mode
	0:05	2:57		Development of *first continuation* of theme 1
	0:29	3:21		Climactic passage of powerful reiterations: ♪♪♪ | ♪♪♪♪ | ♪♪♪♪ | 𝅗𝅥
	0:36	3:28		Development of bridge theme
10 / 5		3:39		Fragmentation of bridge theme to two notes, alternating between strings and winds
	0:09	3:48		Fragmentation of bridge theme to one note, alternating between strings and winds, *p*
	0:29	4:08	**Retransition**	Based on ♪♪♪ 𝅗𝅥, *ff,* runs directly into the recapitulation
			RECAPITULATION	
11 / 6		4:13	**Theme 1**	Harmonized; *two fermatas. First continuation* of theme; woodwind background
	0:18	4:31		*Slow oboe cadenza in place of the third fermata*
	0:33	4:46		*Second continuation of* theme 1
	0:53	5:06	**Bridge theme**	Bassoons, *f*
12 / 7			**Second Group**	
		5:09	**Theme 2**	Strings and winds, *p* (♪♪♪ 𝅗𝅥 in timpani); major mode
	0:33	5:42	**Cadence theme**	This time it does not stop.
13 / 8			**CODA**	
		5:49		Another climax of reiterations (as in the development)
	0:15	6:04		Returns to the minor mode. New expanded version of bridge theme, in counterpoint with new scale figure
	0:30	6:19		New marchlike theme, brass; winds and strings build up
14 / 9		6:51		Theme 1: climactic presentation in brass. *Last fermatas*
	0:08	6:59		*First continuation* of theme 1, with a pathetic coloration; oboe and bassoon figures
	0:13	7:04		Strong conclusion on ♪♪♪ 𝅗𝅥

FRENCH HORN

Adagio OBOE

Beethoven is famous for the tension he builds up in retransitions, the sections in sonata form that prepare for the recapitulations (see page 181). In the Fifth Symphony, the hush at this point becomes almost unbearable. Finally the whole orchestra seems to grab and shake the listener by the lapels, shouting the main motive again and again until the first theme settles out in the original tonic key.

I expected to enjoy that Symphony [Beethoven's Fifth], but I did not suppose it possible that it could be the transcendent affair it is. I've heard it twice before, and how I could have passed by unnoticed so many magnificent points—appreciate the spirit of the composition so feebly and unworthily—I can't imagine.

Diary of the same New Yorker, 1844

Recapitulation The exposition version of the main theme was jolted by three fermatas. Now, in the recapitulation, the third fermata is filled by a slow, expressive passage for solo oboe, a sort of cadenza in free rhythm. This extraordinary moment provides a brief rest from the incessant rhythmic drive. Otherwise the recapitulation stays very close to the exposition—a clear testimony to Beethoven's Classical allegiance.

Coda On the other hand, the action-packed coda that follows is an equally clear testimony to Beethoven's freedom from Classical formulas.

In the exposition, we recall, the stormy cadence passage had been defused by a satisfying "Classical" cadence and a complete stop. At the end of the recapitulation, the parallel passage seems to reject any such easy solution. Instead, after a violent climax reminiscent of the development section, a new contrapuntal idea appears:

Compare the bottom contrapuntal line of this example with the first theme, as shown on page 228. Here the four main-theme *pitches* (G E♭ F D) are played in the bridge *rhythm* (♪♪♪| 𝅗𝅥 𝅗𝅥 | 𝅗𝅥), so that GGG–E♭ FFF–D becomes GGG–E♭ F D. Then the two middle notes E♭ and F—the common ground between the themes—are emphasized by a long downward sequence.

The sequence evolves into a sort of grim minor-mode march—a moment of respite from the endless thematic evolutions of the main motive. A final appearance of the original theme leads this time to continuations that are unexpectedly poignant. But the very end of the movement consists of affirmative, defiant-sounding cadences, built once again out of the main motive.

The Remaining Movements The defiant-sounding final cadence of the first movement feels like a standoff at the end of a heroic struggle. Beethoven now builds on this feeling to give the impression of a dramatic psychological progression, another characteristic feature of his symphonic writing.

The later movements of the Fifth Symphony feel like responses to—and, ultimately, a resolution of—all the tension Beethoven had summoned up in the first movement. We are never allowed to forget the first movement and its mood, not until the very end of the symphony, mainly because a form of the first movement's rhythmic *motive,* ♪♪♪𝅗𝅥 , is heard in each of the later movements. This motive always stirs uneasy recollections. Furthermore, the later movements all refer to the *key* of the first movement. Whenever this key returns in its original minor mode (C minor), it inevitably recalls the struggle that Beethoven associated with "Fate knocking at the door." When it returns in the major mode (C major), it signifies (or foretells) the ultimate resolution of all that tension—the triumph over Fate.

A New Year's card from Beethoven to Baroness Ertmann, one of many women with whom his name has been romantically linked.

You need not worry about recognizing C major or distinguishing it from any other major-mode key. Almost any time you hear a very loud, triumphant theme in the later movements, it is in the key of C major. As important as the melody of those themes and their orchestration (often with brass) is the fact that they come in C major, thus negating the first movement's struggle.

A special abbreviated Listening Chart for the entire symphony is provided on page 233. All the C-major sections are indicated.

Second Movement (Andante con moto) The first hint of Beethoven's master plan comes early in the slow movement, after the cellos have begun with a graceful theme, which is rounded off by repeated cadences. A second placid theme commences, but is soon derailed by a grinding modulation—to C major, where the second theme starts again, blared out by the trumpets, *ff*.

This shattering fanfare or near-fanfare fades almost immediately into a mysterious passage where the ♪♪♪𝅗𝅥 rhythm of the first movement sounds quietly. Beethoven is not ready to resolve the C-minor turmoil of the first movement just yet. Variations of the first theme follow (one is in the minor mode), but there is something aimless about them. What stays in the memory from this movement are two more enormous brass fanfares in C major.

Third Movement (Allegro) This movement, in **3/4** time, is one of Beethoven's greatest scherzos (though the composer did not label it as such, probably because its form is so free). There are two features of the smooth, quiet opening theme (**a**) that immediately recall the mood of the first movement—but in a more muted, apprehensive form. One is the key, C minor. The other is the interruption of the meter by fermatas.

First movement:

Third movement (**b**):

Then a very forceful second theme (**b**), played by the French horns, recalls in its turn the first movement's rhythmic motive. The two themes alternate and modulate restlessly, until the second makes a final-sounding cadence.

When now a bustling and somewhat humorous fugal section starts in the major mode—in C major—we may recognize a vestige of the old minuet and trio form, **A B A** (though the **A** section, with its two sharply contrasted themes **a** and **b**, has nothing in common with a minuet beyond its triple meter). **B**, the major-mode "trio," is in the traditional |: **c** :| |: **d c′** :| form, but with an important modification. The second **d c′** is reorchestrated, becoming quieter and quieter.

After this, the opening minor-mode music, **A′**, returns quietly—almost stealthily—with the tone color transformed. Hushed *pizzicato* (plucked) strings for **a** and a brittle-sounding oboe for **b** replace the smooth and forceful sounds heard before. Everything now breathes a quite unexpected mood of mystery.

Fourth Movement (Allegro) The point of this reorchestration appears when the section does not reach a cadence but runs into a doubly mysterious transition passage, with timpani tapping out the rhythm of **b** over a strange harmony. The music grows louder and clearer until a forceful military march erupts—in the key, needless to say, of C major.

Minor cedes to major, ***pp*** to ***ff***, mystery to clarity; the arrival of this symphony's last movement has the literal effect of triumph over some sort of adversity. This last movement brings in three trombones for the first time in the symphony. (They must have really awakened the freezing listeners at that original 1808 concert.)

The march turns out to be the first theme of a sonata-form movement; the second theme includes a speeded-up version of the ♪♪♪𝅗𝅥 rhythm, with a slower, upward-stepping bass which will drive the development section. The bridge and the cadence theme are wonderfully gutsy. The end of the development offers another example of Beethoven's inspired manipulation of musical form. The second theme (**b**) of the previous movement, the scherzo, comes back quietly once again, a complete surprise in these surroundings (there is even a change from the **4/4** meter of the march back to **3/4**). This theme now sounds neither forceful nor mysterious, as it did in the scherzo, but rather like a dim memory. Perhaps it has come back to remind us that the battle has been won.

All that remains is a great C-major celebration, in the recapitulation and then later in a huge accelerating coda. "There Fate knocks at the door"—but fate and terror alike yield to Beethoven's optimistic major-mode vision.

A modern impression of Beethoven in his later years. The artist has captured both the famous scowl of defiance, and also the chaotic state of Beethoven's household—the broken piano strings, the sheets of musical sketches all over the place, and the useless ear trumpets.

3 Beethoven's "Third Period"

Beethoven's output is traditionally divided into three style periods. The first period (until 1800, in round numbers) covers music building on the style of Haydn and Mozart. The middle period contains characteristically "heroic" works like the *Eroica* and Fifth Symphonies.

In the third period (from around 1818 to 1827) Beethoven's music loses much of its earlier tone of heroism. It becomes more abstract, introspective, and serene, and tends to come framed in more intimate genres than the symphony, such as the piano sonata and the string quartet. (However, Beethoven's mightiest symphony, the Ninth, also dates from this period.) His control of contrast and musical flow becomes more potent than ever, and a new freedom of form leads to a range of expression that can only be called miraculous. All the strength of his earlier music seems to be encompassed together with a new gentleness and spirituality.

While disruption was always a feature of Beethoven's music—think of the fermatas in the first movement of the Fifth Symphony, and the C-major trumpets in the second—now the breaks and breaches in the musical fabric can be almost frightening. At any rate, they proved incomprehensible in his own time and for many years thereafter. Today these features seem if anything to increase the power of Beethoven's late music.

LUDWIG VAN BEETHOVEN
String Quartet in F, Op. 135, second movement (Vivace) (1826)

Three blind mice, see how they run. The tiny and very quiet **a** phrase in this extraordinary movement skitters through the pitches A (three), G (blind), and F (mice) nearly thirty times before the piece is over.

Phrase **b**, consisting of just two pitches, is even simpler. Pitch-wise, it contrasts with **a**, but resembles it in its constant use of syncopation (see the

LISTENING CHART 17

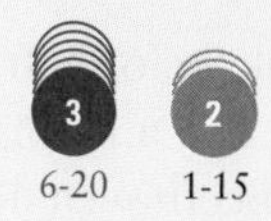

6-20 1-15

Beethoven, Symphony No. 5 in C Minor (complete work)

31 min., 31 sec.

Track	Time	Section	Description	Key
		FIRST MOVEMENT (Allegro con brio, 2/4; sonata form)		C minor, *ff*
		See Listening Chart 16.		
15 / 10		**SECOND MOVEMENT (Andante, 3/8; variations)**		A♭ major, *p*
	0:00	Theme 1	Ends with repeated cadences	
	1:03	Theme 2	Played by clarinets and bassoons	
	1:26		Trumpets enter	(goes to C MAJOR, *ff*)
	2:12	Theme 1	Variation 1, played by strings	
	3:06	Theme 2	Clarinets and bassoons	
	3:29		Trumpets enter	(goes to C MAJOR, *ff*)
	4:16	Theme 1	Variations 2–4 (without repeated cadences), ending *f*; then a long, quiet transition: woodwinds	
	6:13	Theme 2	Trumpets	C MAJOR, *ff*
16 / 11	6:59	Theme 1	Variations 5 (minor; woodwinds) and 6 (full orchestra); cadences	
1:30	8:29	Coda		A♭ major
		THIRD MOVEMENT (Allegro, 3/4; A B A′)		C minor, *pp*
		Scherzo (A)		
17 / 12	0:00	a b		
	0:40	a′ b′		
	1:21	a″ b″	Ends with a loud cadence built from **b**	
18 / 13		Trio (B)		C MAJOR, *ff*
	1:52	‖: c :‖	Fugal	
0:33	2:25	d c′		
1:03	2:55	d c′	*Reorchestrated, p;* runs into scherzo	(goes back to C minor, *pp*)
		Scherzo (A′)		
1:37	3:29		Scherzo repeated, shorter and ***reorchestrated, pp***	
2:54	4:46	Transition	Timpani; leads directly into the fourth movement	(goes to C MAJOR, *ff*)
		FOURTH MOVEMENT (Allegro, 2/2; sonata form)		C MAJOR, *ff*
		Exposition		
19 / 14	0:00	Theme 1	March theme	
	0:34	Bridge theme	Low horns and bassoons	
	1:00	Theme 2		
	1:27	Cadence theme		
		Development		
	1:57		Development begins; modulation	
	2:02		Theme 2 and its bass developed	
20 / 15	3:31	Retransition	Recall of the scherzo (A′, 3/4 meter)	(recall of C minor, *pp*)
		Recapitulation		C MAJOR *ff*
0:32	4:03	Theme 1		
1:07	4:38	Bridge theme		
1:36	5:07	Theme 2		
2:02	5:33	Cadence theme		
		Coda		
2:30	6:01		Coda; three sections, accelerating; uses parts of the bridge, cadence theme, and theme 1	C MAJOR, *ff*

ff

p

f TRUMPETS

a CELLOS *p*

b FRENCH HORNS *f*

c DOUBLE BASSES *f* fugue subject

with TROMBONES *ff*

ff

bass:

music example below). It is this rhythmic feature, syncopation, that makes the motion seem like a strange skittering, rather than just running fast.

Though Beethoven did not label this movement a scherzo (his heading was simply Vivace, meaning vivacious), that is what it is: a fast triple-meter movement, full of surprises, jolts, and even violent shocks, in **A B A** form. *Scherzo,* as we have seen, means "joke," and this scherzo is all smiles at first. Later, however, it taps into a level of ferocity that not even this composer had scarcely touched before.

For he appears to have determined to carry the traditional contrast between minuet and trio to the breaking point. Whereas section **A** uses only a few adjacent pitches, as we have seen, at least up to the cadential **c** segment, **B** takes off like a rocket. Scales shoot up through the octaves, starting—significantly!—first from F, then from G, then from A. In **B** the traditional |: **a** :||: **b a** :|-type form of **A** is thrown overboard—nothing like |: **c** :||: **d c** :| happens here. After each of the upward scales has started with a ***forte*** jolt (Beethoven writes ***fp,*** meaning ***f*** followed directly by ***p***), the dynamic swells up to an almost insane ***ff*** explosion, as the instruments get stuck sawing away at repeated figures. The beat is relentless, counteracting all the syncopation that came before.

This episode of turmoil, or terror, depending on how you react, could hardly make a greater contrast to **A.** As though to make the point, **A** now comes back without change—"vivacious," very quiet, smiling through its syncopations as though nothing has happened. But a brief coda ends with one final ***f*** jolt.

LISTEN

Beethoven,
String Quartet in F, Op. 135: Vivace

3 21

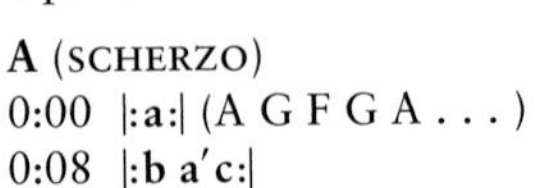

A (SCHERZO)
0:00 |:**a**:| (A G F G A . . .)
0:08 |:**b a′ c**:|

B (TRIO)
0:56 ***fp*** scales up from F
1:10 . . . from G, then A
1:31 ***ff*** explosion
1:55 ***ppp*** A G F G A

A (SCHERZO)
1:58 ***pp*** **a** |:**b a′ c**:| **coda**

We have not said anything yet about the string quartet as a medium, and its special sounds and textures. The subtlety and variety of these should be evident after listening to Beethoven's Vivace movement. For example, take first of all the delicate counterpoint of the various instruments in **a,** which allows the original bass line in the cello *below* "Three blind mice" to rise and shine later *above* it in the two violins (at the end of **a′**):

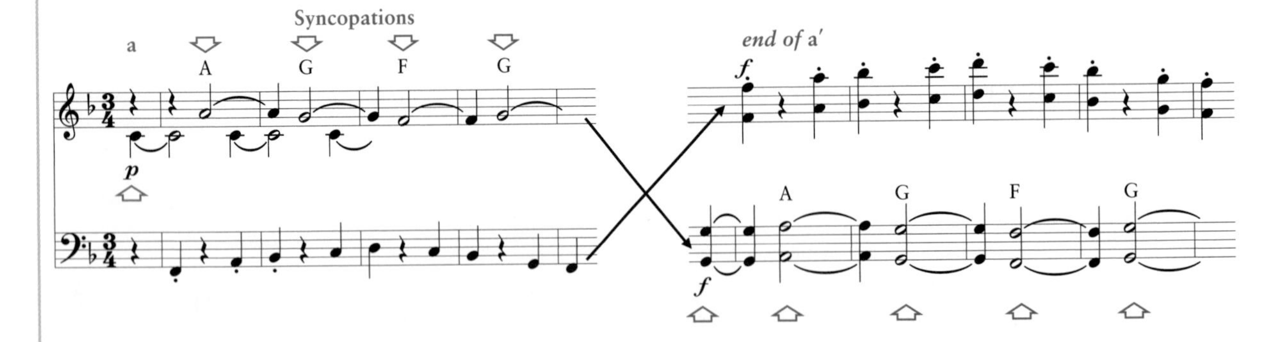

Only now are we really sure of the beat. In **c** and in the first of **B**'s scale passages, notice the interplay between high and low, the two violins answered back and forth by the cello and viola. The retching sound of the ***ff*** explosion passage in **B**—Beethoven's prediction of Heavy Metal—fades into ghostly syncopated octaves, with all four instruments playing the same pitches (which are A, G, and F, once again) in the unusual dynamic ***ppp.***

Web: *Research and test your knowledge of the works of Beethoven at* **<bedfordstmartins.com/listen>.**

CHAPTER 15

Prelude Music after Beethoven: Romanticism

Baroque, as a designation for an historical style period in music, was adopted by musicologists from the field of art history many years after the period in question. The term *Romantic* was adopted from literature—and it was adopted by the literary Romantics themselves. When the first Romantic composers began their careers in the 1820s, their literary contemporaries were already excitedly talking about "Romantic" music.

This may seem like just one more footnote to history, but it tells us two important things about music after the time of Beethoven. One is that largely thanks to Beethoven, people had become highly aware of music as a major art. Music was treated with a new respect in cultivated circles; it was taken seriously in a way it never had been before.

The other is that it seemed quite natural for observers of the time to link up developments in music with parallel developments in literature. From Homer and Virgil to Shakespeare and Milton, literature had always been considered the most important and most convincing of the arts. The prestige and power of literature were now freely extended to music.

This fact is illustrated in a highly Romantic—not to say romanticized—painting that was popular at midcentury, showing a group of celebrities of the time listening to Franz Liszt at the piano (page 236). Their expressions tell us how profoundly the music moves them; their aesthetic experience is very different, clearly, from the casual enjoyment of eighteenth-century listeners pictured on page 145. For the nineteenth century, Beethoven's symphonies had been a revelation of music's profundity. It is no accident, then, that in the Liszt painting a larger-than-life bust of Beethoven rests on the piano, and that Liszt gazes on it so soulfully.

1 Romanticism

Romantic literature and literary theory flourished particularly in and around the first two decades of the nineteenth century. In England, this was a great age of poetry: Wordsworth, Coleridge, Shelley, Keats, and Byron. There was also a brilliant outpouring of German Romantic literature during the same period,

The power of Romantic music: Liszt as the inspiration for novelists Alexandre Dumas, Victor Hugo, George Sand, Daniel Stern (on the floor), legendary violinist Niccolò Paganini, and opera composer Gioacchino Rossini. Daniel Stern was the pseudonym of the Countess d'Agoult (see page 263).

though the names of its writers are less familiar in the English-speaking world: Tieck, Novalis, Kleist, Hölderlin, and E. T. A. Hoffmann.

For us, the word *romantic* refers to love; this usage dates from the nineteenth century and derives from the literary movement. But the glorification of love was only one of the many themes of Romantic literature, themes that were also central to the music of the nineteenth century.

The Cult of Individual Feeling

Striving for a better, higher, ideal state of being was at the heart of the Romantic movement. Everyday life, to the Romantics, seemed harsh, dull, and meaningless; it could be transcended only through the free exercise of individual will and passion. The rule of feeling, unconstrained by convention, religion, or social taboo (or anyone else's feelings, often enough)—this became the highest good, and emotional expression became the highest artistic goal. "Bohemians," as they were disparagingly called at the time, proclaimed romantic love, led irregular lives, and wore odd clothes. We have the Romantics to thank for one familiar image of the artist that is still around today.

These attitudes may be laid at the door of Jean-Jacques Rousseau—the same Enlightenment philosopher who had spoken up in the mid-eighteenth century for "natural" human feelings, as opposed to the artificial constraints imposed by society. Hailed as the ideological father of the French Revolution, Rousseau provided the Romantics with the ideal of individual, as well as political, freedom and fulfillment. (We have also seen Rousseau as a proponent of a "natural" music, and indeed his own music was still being played at French revolutionary rallies and pageants.)

But there was more than philosophy behind the new attitudes. The Industrial Revolution had already begun its inexorable course, and increasingly as the nineteenth century went on, people felt their helplessness in the face of the factories, slag heaps, and inhumane working conditions of developing capitalism. The smokestacks of what William Blake called "these dark, Satanic mills" now loomed over the European landscape. Understandably there was an element of escapism in Romantic striving.

Romanticism and Revolt

In the wake of the Industrial Revolution came actual revolution—the central fact in the politics of the age. It began with our own American Revolution. The French Revolution of 1789 rocked Europe as deeply in the nineteenth century as did the Russian Revolution of 1917 in the twentieth. It was followed by a whole set of aftershocks up to 1848, a year of major traumatic upheavals in France, Germany, Austria, and Italy.

The Romantics were inevitably cast in the role of rebels against the established order. Many musicians (like many poets and painters) associated themselves with libertarian politics, starting with Beethoven, who wrote a symphony named *Bonaparte* (which he renamed the *Eroica:* See page 224). In a later generation, Liszt briefly espoused a strange half-communistic, half-religious movement founded by a French priest, Father Felicité Lamennais. Giuseppe Verdi's name became an acronym for the Italian liberation movement. Richard Wagner was thrown out of Germany in 1849 for inflammatory speeches he made from the revolutionary barricades in the town of Dresden.

Along with political revolution went social revolution. The barriers of hereditary nobility were breached, and the lower and middle classes assumed more social mobility. Thus Franz Liszt, who was the son of an estate foreman, could conduct glamorous liaisons—one stormy, the other stable—with a French countess and a Russian princess. The importance of this was not lost on Liszt's contemporaries; the countess is another of the celebrities included in the picture of Liszt at the piano (though the artist tactfully hid her face).

La Marseillaise, the great rallying song of the French Revolution.

Music and the Supernatural

The supernatural—often linked to the macabre—loomed large in the Romantic firmament, as we might expect of a movement so intent on transcending the ordinary. In *Nightmare,* a weird picture by the early Romantic painter Henry Fuseli, dream is made concrete, visible, and public in the figure of a horrible incubus (see page 238). Faust pledging his soul to the Devil for a single moment of transcendent happiness

In their use of standard forms or form-types, nineteenth-century composers broke with classical norms. To return to a distinction made earlier, on page 48, the Romantics wanted each work of art to express its own individual "inner form"; they distrusted "outer forms" as dry and conventional. Even when they followed forms such as sonata form, rondo, and so on, they tended to follow them so loosely that it becomes a matter of opinion whether they are doing so at all. Themes tend to blend into one another, and there is much less of the neat, clear cadencing of Classical music.

Some Romantic compositions deliberately break down the boundary between music and nonmusical silence. Robert Schumann's song "Im wunderschönen Monat Mai" (page 254) begins hesitantly, as though already in the middle of a transition; we feel we have just begun hearing music that started long ago. Instead of ending with a decisive cadence, the song comes to a questioning dissonance, then—silence. The vague, atmospheric quality at the start, and the suggestion of "infinity" at the end—again, these are typically Romantic.

Yet the music had to avoid real formlessness if it was to hold the attention of an audience. Once again, for romantic composers the problem was how to create the impression of spontaneous form while at the same time giving the listener some means of following the music. They developed a number of interesting and characteristic solutions.

"Miniature" Compositions

While many Romantic compositions last for about as long as works from the eighteenth century, special classes of music arose with quite different dimensions.

First of all, composers cultivated what we will call **miniatures**, pieces lasting only a few minutes. Mostly songs and short piano pieces, these were designed to convey a particularly pointed emotion, momentary and undeveloped. In this way the composer could commune with the listener intensely but intimately, as though giving him or her a single short, meaningful glance. The meaning might well be hinted at by a programmatic title.

Though short pieces were also written in earlier times, of course—think of minuet movements in classical symphonies—usually they were components of larger units, where their effect was balanced by other, longer movements.

The man has put down his violin to sit with the woman at the piano; we can imagine the four-hand music they are playing, perhaps, but we cannot see their faces. This picture catches both the intimacy and privacy of the Romantic "miniature" and also its characteristic location, the middle-class living room.

Romantic "miniatures," though they were often published in sets, as we will see, nevertheless were composed so as to stand out as individuals in their own right, apart from their sets. Miniatures for piano were sometimes given general titles, such as Schubert's Impromptus (Improvisations) and Brahms's Capriccios (Whims). Sometimes they masqueraded as dances, like Chopin's Mazurkas (a Polish dance). Often they were given more suggestive, "programmatic" titles: *Years of Pilgrimage* by Franz Liszt, *Spring Song* by Felix Mendelssohn, *To a Wild Rose* by Edward MacDowell, America's leading late Romantic composer. Schumann was something of a specialist in such titles: *The Poet Speaks, Confession, The Bird as Prophet,* and—*Why?*

As for the problem of musical form, in such pieces this was not so much solved as bypassed. They are over before the listener begins to wonder where the music is going, what the next effect will be, and why.

"Grandiose" Compositions

Another Romantic tendency was diametrically opposed to the "miniatures." Many composers wrote "grandiose" compositions—larger and larger symphonies, cantatas, and so on, with more and more movements, increased performing forces, and a longer (sometimes much longer) total time span. For example, Hector Berlioz's "dramatic symphony" *Romeo and Juliet* of 1839 lasts for nearly an hour and a half. (Haydn's Symphony No. 95 lasts twenty minutes.) Starting with an augmented symphony orchestra, Berlioz added soloists and a chorus in certain of the movements and a narrator between them, and then threw in an off-stage chorus for still other movements.

In the field of opera, Richard Wagner's *The Ring of the Nibelung* is an opera that goes on for four evenings with a huge orchestra including specially invented instruments, a cast of thirty, and fifteen separate stage sets (see page 283). The total effect of these "grandiose" compositions was laced with poetry, philosophical or religious ideas, and (in operas) dramatic action. Listeners were impressed, even stupefied, by a combination of opulent sounds, great thoughts, powerful emotions, and sheer length.

These works met what we have called the problem of musical form in their own way. The bigger the work, the bigger the problem, but to help solve it com-

The "grandiose" compositions of the nineteenth century occasioned many cartoons—amusing enough, but not in the last analysis friendly to the advanced music of the time.

posers could draw on extramusical factors—on the text of a vocal work, or the program of an instrumental one. Music could add emotional conviction to ideas or stories; in return these extramusical factors could supply a rhyme and reason for the sequence of musical events, that is, for the musical form.

The Principle of Thematic Unity

An important general principle developed by Romantic composers was that of thematic unity. There was an increasing tendency to maintain some of the same thematic material throughout whole works, even (or especially) when these works were in many movements.

In nineteenth-century symphonies and other such works, several different levels of thematic unity can be distinguished:

- Most obviously, themes from one movement may come back literally and quite clearly in other movements. We have already heard this happen in Beethoven's Fifth Symphony, when the scherzo theme returns in the last movement.

- In other compositions, new *versions* of a single theme are used at important new points in the music, either later in the same movement or in later movements. While these new versions are really nothing more than variations of the original theme, this procedure differs fundamentally from Classical theme-and-variations form (see page 187). In Classical variation form, the "theme" is an entire tune, and the variations follow one another directly. In the new Romantic procedure, the theme is (generally) much more fragmentary than a tune, and the new versions of the theme appear at irregular intervals.

  The term **thematic transformation** is used for this variationlike procedure in Romantic music, whereby short themes are freely varied at relatively wide and unpredictable intervals of time. A precedent for it can be traced to works such as Beethoven's Fifth Symphony, where the ♪♪♪𝅗𝅥 motive of the first movement is evoked freely in each of the later ones.

- In still other nineteenth-century pieces, we hear themes with even looser relationships among them. Clearly different, they nonetheless seem to exhibit mysterious inner similarities—similarities that seem to help unify the music, though they are too shadowy to count as transformations in the Romantic definition, let alone as variations in the Classical style. Wagner's operas are famous for such themes. In the Prelude to *Tristan und Isolde,* for example, the family resemblance between some of the motives can't be missed—yet it can scarcely be pinned down, either (see page 283).

Of all the levels of thematic unity employed by nineteenth-century composers, this last is the most typical of all. Vague similarity rather than clear likeness, suggestion rather than outright statement, atmosphere rather than discourse, feeling rather than form: All these go to the heart of Romanticism. We cannot appreciate Romantic music fully if we approach it in too literal a frame of mind. In much of this music, the "inner form"—the special spontaneous form of the individual piece, as distinct from standard "outer forms" such as sonata form and rondo—is tied to the principle of thematic unity. Listening to Romantic music requires ears that are not only attentive but also imaginative, exploratory, and more than a little fanciful.

Web: *Research and test your understanding of Romanticism at* **<bedfordstmartins.com/listen>.**

CHAPTER 16

The Early Romantics

Perhaps the most brilliant generation of composers in the entire history of music was that of the early Romantics. Franz Schubert was born in Vienna in 1797; then the ten-year period between 1803 and 1813 saw the birth of Robert Schumann, Frédéric Chopin, Felix Mendelssohn, Franz Liszt, Hector Berlioz, Richard Wagner, and Giuseppe Verdi. It was a brilliant generation, but not a long-lived one. Only the last four of these composers survived to continue their major work into the second half of the century.

Two general points are worth making about this early Romantic galaxy. First, Beethoven's music had a profound effect on them, though this was naturally felt more strongly by German composers than by non-Germans. Schubert, who lived in Vienna under Beethoven's shadow, was influenced by the older master much more directly than Chopin, a Pole who lived in Paris.

The second important point is that these composers were deeply influenced by literary Romanticism, which had flourished some decades before their time. Schubert wrote many songs to texts by Romantic poets such as Goethe, Novalis, and Friedrich Schlegel, and Schumann's enthusiasm for the German Romantic novelist Jean Paul Richter was reflected in his music, as well as in his own prose writings. We have mentioned that Shakespeare was particularly admired by the Romantics; nearly all the composers mentioned here wrote music associated with Shakespeare's plays.

1 The Lied

The ordinary German word for song is *Lied* (plural, *Lieder*—pronounced "leader"). The word also has a special application: the **lied** is a particular type of German song that evolved in the late eighteenth century and flourished in the nineteenth. As such, the lied is one of the most important "miniature" genres of Romanticism.

Though one cannot generalize about the melodies of these songs—some consist of little more than a tune, others are melodically much more complex—they share certain other characteristic features.

Accompaniment. A lied is nearly always accompanied by piano, and the accompaniment contributes significantly to the artistic effect. Indeed, the pianist becomes more of a discreet partner to the singer than a mere accompanist.

Beethoven: a late Romantic view. The awesome, ideal figure—nude, and carved in marble, like a Greek statue—sits, kinglike, on a superb throne. He seems to be both reigning over and deploring the music that was written after his own time.

Poetry. The text of a lied is usually a Romantic poem of some merit (at least in the composer's estimation). Hence, although we need to understand the words of almost any vocal music, with the lied we should also try to appreciate how the poem's words and meanings fit together as poetry. The art of the lied depends on the sensitivity of the composer's response to the poetic imagery and feeling.

Mood. A third characteristic, harder to explain, is the intimacy of expression that is captured by these pieces. The singer and the pianist seem to be sharing an emotional insight with just you, rather than with an entire audience; words and music are uttered softly, inwardly. Composers intended lieder for the intimacy of a living room, not a formal concert hall, and that is where they are best heard.

Is not music the mysterious language of a distant realm of spirits, whose lovely sounds re-echo in our soul and awaken a higher, more intensive life? All the passions, arrayed in shining armor, vie with each other, and ultimately merge in an indescribable longing that fills our breast.

Arch-Romantic novelist, critic, and composer E. T. A. Hoffmann, 1816

FRANZ SCHUBERT
"Erlkönig" ("The Erlking") (1815)

The earliest and (for most musicians) greatest master of the lied is Franz Schubert. He wrote close to seven hundred songs in his short lifetime. In his eighteenth year, 1815, he averaged better than a song every two days! Many of these are quite short tunes with simple piano accompaniments, but Schubert's tunes are like nobody else's; he was a wonderfully spontaneous melodist. Later in life his melodies became richer but no less beautiful, and taken together with their poems, the songs often show remarkable psychological penetration.

One of those songs from 1815 was an instant hit: "The Erlking," published as the composer's opus 1, and still today Schubert's best-known lied. In those early years, Schubert wrote a considerable number of long, narrative songs, though this one stands out from the others in its dramatic intensity.

Franz Schubert (1797–1828)

Schubert was the son of a lower-middle-class Viennese schoolmaster. There was always music in the home, and the boy received a solid musical education in the training school for Viennese court singers. His talent amazed his teachers and also a number of his schoolmates, who remained devoted to him throughout his career. Schubert began by following in his father's footsteps as a schoolteacher, without much enthusiasm, but soon gave up teaching to devote all his time to music.

Schubert was an endearing but shy and unspectacular individual who led an unspectacular life. However, it was the sort of life that would have been impossible before the Romantic era. Schubert never married—he was probably gay—and never held a regular job. He was sustained by odd fees for teaching and publications and by contributions from a circle of friends who called themselves the Schubertians—young musicians, artists, writers, and music lovers. One of the Schubertians, Moritz von Schwind, who became an important painter, has left us many charming pictures of the group at parties, on trips to the country, and so on.

It was an atmosphere especially conducive to an intimate musical genre such as the lied. Schubert wrote nearly seven hundred lieder and many choral songs. For a time he roomed with a poet, Johann Mayrhofer, who provided him with gloomy texts for about fifty of them.

It is unfortunate that Schubert's wonderful songs have tended to overshadow his symphonies, sonatas, and chamber music. Starting out with Classical genres, Schubert in his very short lifetime transformed them under the influence of Romanticism. He never introduced himself to Beethoven, even though they lived in the same city; perhaps he instinctively felt he needed to keep his distance from the overpowering older master. It speaks much for Schubert that he was able to write such original and powerful works as the "Unfinished" Symphony, the so-called *Great* Symphony in C, and others, right under Beethoven's shadow.

A few of Schubert's instrumental works include melodies taken from his own songs: the popular *Trout* Quintet, the String Quartet in D Minor (*Death and the Maiden*), and the *Wanderer* Fantasy for piano.

Schubert died in a typhoid fever epidemic when he was only thirty-one. He never heard a performance of his late symphonies, and much of his music came to light only after his death.

Our portrait shows Schubert around the time he wrote *The Erlking.*

Chief Works: Lieder, including the song cycles *Die schöne Müllerin, Winterreise,* and *Schwanengesang,* "The Erlking," "Gretchen at the Spinning Wheel," "Hedgerose," "Death and the Maiden," "The Trout," and hundreds of others ▪ "Character" pieces for piano; waltzes ▪ Symphonies, including the "Unfinished"—Schubert completed only two movements and sketches for a scherzo—and the *Great* Symphony in C ▪ Many piano sonatas—five (plus an "Unfinished Sonata") in his mature years; *Wanderer* Fantasy for piano ▪ Four mature string quartets; a string quintet; the genial *Trout* Quintet for piano and strings (including double bass)

Encore: After "The Erlking," listen to the "Unfinished" Symphony and songs from *Winterreise.*

The poem is by Johann Wilhelm von Goethe, the greatest literary figure of the day—by turns a Romantic and a Classic poet, novelist, playwright, naturalist, philosopher, and a favorite source of texts for many generations of lied composers. Cast in the old ballad form, which enjoyed a vogue in the Romantic era, and dealing with death and the supernatural, the poem is famous in its own right.

Though Goethe's ballad poem consists of eight parallel stanzas, they are not set to the same music. Schubert provided the later stanzas with different or modified music; such a song is said to be **through-composed.** (A song that uses the same music for all its stanzas is called **strophic:** See page 64.) In mood, the poem changes so much as it goes along that it almost demands this kind of musical setting. A father rides furiously through the night with a child who is presumably running a high fever, for he claims to see and hear a murderous demon. The Erlking first beckons the child, then cajoles him, then threatens and assaults him. The father—uncomprehending, even impatient—tries to quiet the boy, but by the time they reach home the boy is—dead!

Title page of the first edition of "The Erlking" (1821). Note the stunted tree; the literal meaning of "Erlkönig" is King of the Alders, or birches—in effect, a forest troll.

The opening piano introduction sets the mood of dark, tense excitement. The right hand hammers away at harsh repeated notes in triplets, representing the horse's hooves, while the left hand has an agitated motive:

Schubert invented different music for the poem's three characters (and also the narrator). Each "voice" characterizes the speaker in contrast to the others. The father is low, stiff, and gruff, the boy high and frantic. Marked ***ppp,*** and inaudible to the father, the ominously quiet and sweet little tunes crooned by the Erlking, offering his "schöne Spiele," add a chilling note.

The triplet accompaniment keeps the whole song alive and gives it more unity, as it were; yet one could wish that Herr Schubert had occasionally transferred it to the left hand; for the ceaseless striking of one and the same note in triplets tires the hand, if the piece is to be played at the rapid pace demanded by Herr Schubert.

Review of "Erlkönig," 1821

Schubert playing at an evening with the Schubertians. To the left is Johann Vogel, an older singer, one of his main supporters. Their friend Moritz von Schwind started this picture but didn't quite finish it.

Two things help hold this long song together as an artistic unity. First, the piano's triplet rhythm continues ceaselessly, until the very last line, where recitative style lets us know that the ride is over. (The triplets are muffled during the Erlking's speeches—because the child is hearing him in a feverish daze?) Second, there are some telling musical repetitions: the agitated riding motive (stanzas 1–2 and 7–8), and a desperately strained phrase sung higher and higher as the boy appeals to his father (stanzas 4, 6, and 7).

LISTEN **Schubert, "Erlkönig"**

22

34

0:22	Wer reitet so spät, durch Nacht und Wind? Es ist der Vater mit seinem Kind; Er hat den Knaben wohl in dem Arm, Er fasst ihn sicher, er hält ihn warm.	Who rides so late through the night and wind? It is the father with his child. He holds the youngster tight in his arm, Grasps him securely, keeps him warm.
0:55	"Mein sohn, was birgst du so bang dein Gesicht?" "Siehst, Vater, du den Erlkönig nicht? Den Erlenkönig mit Kron' und Schweif?" "Mein Sohn, est ist ein Nebelstreif."	"Son, what makes you afraid to look?" "Don't you see, Father, the Erlking there? The King of the forest with his crown and train?" "Son, it's only a streak of mist."
1:28	"Du liebes Kind, komm, geh mit mir! Gar schöne Spiele spiel' ich mit dir; Manch' bunte Blumen sind an dem Strand; Meine Mutter hat manch' gülden Gewand."	*"Darling child, come away with me! I will play some lovely games with you; Many bright flowers grow by the shore; My mother has many golden robes."*
1:52	"Mein Vater, mein Vater, und hörest du nicht Was Erlenkönig mir leise verspricht?" "Sei ruhig, bleibe ruhig, mein Kind: In dürren Blättern säuselt der Wind."	"Father, Father, do you not hear What the Erlking is softly promising me?" "Calm yourself, be calm, my son: The dry leaves are rustling in the wind."
2:14	"Willst, feiner Knabe, du mit mir gehn? Meine Töchter sollen dich warten schön; Meine Töchter führen den nächtlichen Reihn Und wiegen und tanzen und singen dich ein."	*"Well, you fine boy, won't you come with me? My daughters are ready to wait on you. My daughters lead the nightly round, They will rock you, dance for you, sing you to sleep!"*
2:31	"Mein Vater, mein Vater, und siehst du nich dort Erlkönigs Töchter am düstern Ort?" "Mein Sohn, mein sohn, ich seh es genau: Es scheinen die alten Weiden so grau."	"Father, Father, do you not see The Erlking's daughters there in the dark?" "Son, my son, I see only too well: It is the gray gleam in the old willow trees."
3:01	"Ich liebe dich, mich reizt deine schöne Gestalt, Und bist du nicht willig, so brauch' ich Gewalt." "Mein Vater, mein Vater, jetzt fasst er mich an! Erlkönig hat mit ein Leids getan!"	*"I love you, your beauty allures me, And if you're not willing, then I shall use force."* "Father, Father, he is seizing me now! The Erlking has hurt me!"
3:26	Dem Vater grauset's, er reitet geschwind, Er hält in Armen das ächzende Kind, Erreicht den Hof mit Müh and Not; In seinen Armen das Kind war tot.	Fear grips the father, he rides like the wind, He holds in his arms the moaning child; He reaches the house hard put, worn out; In his arms the child was—dead!

The Song Cycle

A song cycle is a group of songs with a common poetic theme or an actual story connecting all the poems. Composers would either find whole coherent groups of poems to set, or else make their own selections from a larger collection of a poet's work. Schubert, who wrote two great song cycles relatively late in his career, was able to use ready-made groups of poems published by a minor Romantic poet named Wilhelm Müller: *Die schöne Müllerin* ("The Fair Maid of the Mill") and *Winterreise* ("Winter Journey").

The advantage of the song cycle was that it extended the rather fragile expression of the lied into a larger, more comprehensive, and hence more impressive unit. It was, in a sense, an effort to get beyond "miniaturism." The "unity" of such larger units, however, is always loose, even when the songs are related by melodic or rhythmic means, as occasionally happens. The individual songs can often be sung separately, as well as in sequence with the rest of the cycle.

ROBERT SCHUMANN (1810–1856)
Dichterliebe ("A Poet's Love") (1840)

"Schubert died. Cried all night," wrote the eighteen-year-old Robert Schumann in his diary under a date in 1828. Yet living in Zwickau, Germany, far from Schubert's Vienna, Schumann did not know many of the older composer's best-known works, his lieder. He loved Schubert's piano music, and indeed, for the first ten years of his own career as a composer, Schumann wrote only piano music.

To cast light into the depths of the human heart—the artist's mission!

Robert Schumann

Then in 1840, the year of his marriage, he suddenly started pouring out lieder. Given this history, it is not surprising that in Schumann's songs the piano is given a more complex role than in Schubert's. This is particularly true of his most famous song cycle, *Dichterliebe,* the first and last songs of which (nos. 1 and 16) we shall examine here. *Dichterliebe* has no real story; its series of love poems traces a psychological progression from cautious optimism to disillusionment and despair. They are the work of another great German poet, Heinrich Heine, a man who reacted with bitter irony against Romanticism, while acknowledging his own hopeless commitment to its ideals.

"Im wunderschönen Monat Mai" ("In the wonderfully lovely month of May") The song begins with a piano introduction, halting and ruminative in quality—which seems at first to be a curious response to the "wonderfully lovely" month of May. The piano part winds its way in and out of the vocal line, ebbing and flowing rhythmically and sometimes dwelling on quiet but piercing dissonant harmonies.

What Schumann noticed was the hint of unrequited longing in Heine's very last line, and he ended the song with the piano part hanging in midair, without a true cadence, as though in a state of reaching or yearning: a truly Romantic effect. Technically, the last sound is a dissonance that requires resolution into a consonance but does not get it (until the next song).

In this song, both stanzas of the poem are set to identical music. As mentioned earlier, such a song is called *strophic;* strophic setting is of course familiar from folk songs, hymns, popular songs, and many other kinds of music. For Schumann, this kind of setting had the advantage of underlining the similarity in the text of the song's two stanzas, both in meaning and in actual words. Certainly his music deepens the tentative, sensitive, hope-against-hope quality of Heine's understated confession of love.

The qualities of intimacy and spontaneity that are so important to Romantic miniatures can be inhibited by studio recording. Our recording of Schumann's song was made at a concert (you will hear applause as the artists enter).

LISTEN **Schumann, "Im wunderschönen Monat Mai"**

23

35

0:28	Im wunderschönen Monat Mai, Als alle Knospen sprangen, Da ist in meinem Herzen Die Liebe aufgegangen.	In the wonderfully lovely month of May, When all the buds were bursting, Then it was that in my heart Love broke through.
1:05	Im wunderschönen Monat Mai, Als alle Vögel sangen, Da hab' ich ihr gestanden Mein Sehnen und Verlangen.	In the wonderfully lovely month of May, When all the birds were singing, Then it was I confessed to her My longing and desire.

"Die alten, bösen Lieder" ("The hateful songs of times past") After many heart-wrenching episodes, the final song in the *Dichterliebe* cycle begins strongly. The very insistent rhythm in the piano part sounds a little hectic and forced, like the black humor of Heine's poem. Although basically this is a through-composed song, there are musical parallels between many of the stanzas, and the music of stanza 1 comes back even more forcefully in stanza 5.

But there is a sudden reversal of mood in stanza 6, as the poet suddenly offers to tell us what this morbid action is about. In the music, first the accompaniment disintegrates and then the rhythm. All the poet's self-dramatization vanishes when he speaks of his grief in recitative-like accents; the end of the song would be a whimper if Schumann at the piano were not quietly and firmly in control. In a lovely meditative piano solo, music takes over from words. The composer comments on and comforts the frantic poet.

Not only does the composer interpret the poet's words with great art, both in the hectic early stanzas and the self-pitying final one, but he adds something entirely his own in the final solo. The sixteen vignettes by Heine and Schumann in *Dichterliebe* add up to a memorable anthology of the endless pains and pleasures of love celebrated by the Romantics.

During the night of October 17, 1833, I suddenly had the most frightful thought a human being can possibly have: "What if you were no longer able to think?" Clara, anyone who has been crushed like that knows no worse suffering, or despair.

Letter from Robert Schumann, 1838

LISTEN **Schumann, "Die alten, bösen Lieder"**

24

0:05	Die alten, bösen Lieder, Die Träume bös' und arg, Die lasst uns jetzt begraben: Holt einen grossen Sarg.	The hateful songs of times past, The hateful, brutal dreams, Let's now have them buried; Fetch up a great coffin.
0:23	Hinein leg' ich gar Manches, Doch sag' ich noch nicht, was. Der Sarg muss sein noch grösser Wie's Heidelberger Fass.	I've a lot to put in it— Just what, I won't yet say; The coffin must be even bigger Than the Great Cask of Heidelberg.
0:41	Und holt eine Todtenbahre Und Bretter fest und dick, Auch muss sie sein noch länger Als wie zu Mainz die Brück'.	And fetch a bier, Boards that are strong and thick; They too must be longer Than the river bridge at Mainz.
0:59	Und holt mir auch zwölf Riesen, Die mussen noch stärker sein Als wie der starke Christoph Im Dom zu Köln am Rhein.	And fetch me, too, twelve giants Who must be stronger Than St. Christopher, the great statue At the Cathedral of Cologne on the Rhine.
1:17	Die sollen den Sarg forttragen Und senken in's Meer hinab, Denn solchem grossen Sarge Gebührt ein grosses Grab.	It's they that must haul the coffin And sink it in the sea, For a great coffin like that Deserves a great grave.
1:49	Wisst ihr, warum der Sarg wohl So gross und schwer mag sein? Ich senkt' auch meine Liebe Und meinen Schmerz hinein.	Do you know why the coffin really Has to be so huge and heavy? Because I sank all my love in it, And all of my grief.

Robert Schumann (1810–1856)

Robert Schumann's father, a bookseller and writer, encouraged the boy's musical talent and started him studying the piano at the age of six. When his father died, his mother wanted him to go into law; he attended the University of Leipzig, but finally persuaded her to let him pursue the career of a piano virtuoso. He had to give this up, however, after an injury sustained when he tried to strengthen his fingers with a mechanical device.

Besides his musical talent, Schumann had a great flair for literature, no doubt inherited from his father. When he was only twenty-three, Schumann founded a magazine to campaign for a higher level of music, *Die Neue Zeitschrift für Musik* ("The New Music Journal"—it is still being published). For several years he wrote regular music criticism, often couched in a fanciful romantic prose style. For example, he signed some of his reviews with the names "Florestan" or "Eusebius," representing the opposite (but both thoroughly romantic) sides of his character—the impetuous side and the tender, dreamy side. He encouraged fledgling composers such as Chopin and (later) Brahms.

Schumann's piano works—among his most important music—are mostly "character pieces," often with imaginative titles, and occasionally signed "Eu." or "Fl." at the end. They are arranged in loosely organized sets, with titles such as *Butterflies, Kreisleriana* (after a character in a Romantic novel), *Scenes from Childhood,* and *Carnaval.*

Schumann fell in love with Clara Wieck, the daughter of his piano teacher; at the age of fifteen she was already a famous pianist. Thanks to her father's fanatical opposition—he did not think Robert was a very savory character—they had to wait until she was twenty-one (minus one day) before getting married, in 1840. A charming outcome of the marriage was that Robert, whose early compositions were almost entirely for the piano, suddenly started to write love songs for Clara. Nearly 150 songs were composed in this "song year."

A little later, he also turned to the composition of larger works: concertos, symphonies, chamber music, choral music, and one opera. Thereafter he worked as a teacher and conductor, but his withdrawn personality made him less than successful. Schumann suffered from mood swings and had experienced breakdowns in his youth, and now he began to show tragic signs of insanity. In 1854, tormented by voices, hallucinations, and loss of memory, he tried to drown himself in the River Rhine and was committed to an asylum. He died two years later.

Chief Works: Sets of "miniatures" for piano, among them *Scenes from Childhood, Album for the Young, Papillons* (Butterflies), and *Carnaval* ▪ Songs (lieder) and song cycles: *Woman's Life and Love, Dichterliebe* ▪ Piano Fantasy (a free sonata); Piano Concerto and the first important concerto for cello; four symphonies ▪ Chamber music: a quintet and a quartet for piano and strings ▪ An opera, *Genoveva;* incidental music to Byron's *Manfred* and Goethe's *Faust;* choral works

Encore: After *Dichterliebe* and *Carnaval,* listen to the Piano Concerto in A Minor.

CLARA SCHUMANN
"Der Mond kommt still gegangen" ("The moon has risen softly") (1843)

This lied is another perfect Romantic miniature, in spite of the cliché-filled poem, with its moonlight, its dreams of love, and its downhearted lover. Both melody and piano accompaniment are very plain, but the slightly unusual chords chosen by Schumann create a unique pensive mood. The form, too, is simple: modified strophic form, **A A A′**. Some modification, however slight, had to occur in stanza 3, where the poem's speaker, catching sight of the lit-up windows in the house, registers his excitement by crowding his poetic lines with extra words and extra syllables—which require extra notes.

There is an obvious, banal way of setting such crowded lines: See page 259, in the margin. But instead Schumann very skillfully pulls the words out of phase with the musical phrases, achieving beautiful rhythmic matches for some of the extra words: slower for *drunten* (down), livelier for *funkeln* (light—literally, sparkle), and very slow for *still* (silently):

Clara Wieck (Clara Schumann) (1819–1896)

Clara Wieck was the eldest child (she had two younger brothers) of a highly ambitious music teacher named Friedrich Wieck (pronounced *Veek*). Wieck had his own piano method, and he determined to make Clara a leading pianist. By the age of fifteen she was widely known as a prodigy. Like most virtuosos of the time, she also composed music to play at her own concerts: variations on popular opera arias, waltzes, a piano concerto.

Robert and Clara Schumann figure in what must be music's greatest love story. Still, there seems to have been just a little friction between them because she was so much better a pianist; she, on her part, felt diffident about composing under his shadow, though he did encourage her to some extent, and they published one song cycle jointly, containing music by both of them. Clara often wrote songs to give Robert on his birthdays. The last of these is dated 1853, the year before he was committed to an insane asylum.

Even before that, Robert's depression and instability made life difficult for Clara. She continued her career as best she could, but more and more, she had to take care of the family. During the 1848 revolution in Leipzig, for example, it was up to her to get the five Schumann children out of town (three more were born later).

Things were difficult in another way when Robert died. At the age of thirty-seven, after losing the husband whom she loved and revered, Clara found herself more than half in love with his twenty-two-year-old protégé Johannes Brahms (see page 298). It is not known which of them withdrew from the relationship. They remained close friends; Brahms was a lifelong bachelor, and she did not remarry.

Today we tend to regret that Clara decided to give up composing, for she left enough good pieces to make us wish there were more of them. But she knew it would have been an uphill battle, given the all too common nineteenth-century view that great music couldn't be written by a woman. With so many children to support, she can hardly be blamed for concentrating instead on activities that had already earned her admiration and respect—and a good living: playing and teaching.

Clara Schumann went on to further establish herself as one of Europe's leading pianists and a much-sought-after pedagogue. She concertized and toured widely. Brahms (who always asked her to critique his new compositions) was just one in the eminent circle of her friends and associates. Outliving Robert by forty years, Clara became a major force in late nineteenth-century music.

Chief Works: Miniatures for piano, with names such as *Romances* and *Soirées musicales* ("Musical Evenings"); songs ▪ A piano concerto and a trio for piano, violin, and cello ▪ *Piano Variations on a Theme by Robert Schumann* (Brahms wrote a set of variations on the same theme)

Encore: After "Der Mond," listen to *Romances* for piano and the Piano Concerto.

Three things help make the climactic word *Liebchens* (loved one) radiant: the new long high note, the new harmony, and the expansive phrase (five bars in place of four). Schumann's piano postlude adds a wistful minor-mode aftertaste. As with many great lieder, music here far transcends the words.

An amazing nineteenth-century score of Schumann lieder. The poems are given in ornate calligraphy and illustrated in the richest, most opulent Romantic style. The picture might well be for Clara Schumann's "The Moon Has Risen Softly" (page 256; actually, it is for Robert's similar song "Moonlit Night").

LISTEN Clara Schumann, "Der Mond kommt still gegangen"

25 36

0:03	*St. 1:* [1]Der Mond kommt still gegangen [2]Mit seinen goldn'en Schein, [3]Da Schläft in holdem Prangen [4]Die müde Erde ein.	The moon has risen softly With gleaming rays of gold, Beneath its shining splendor The weary earth's at rest.
0:30	*St. 2:* [1]Und auf den Lüften schwanken [2]Aus manchem treuen Sinn [3]Viel tausend Liebesgedanken [4]Über die Schläfer hin.	And on the drifting breezes From many faithful minds Endearing thoughts by the thousand Waft down on those who sleep.
0:58	*St. 3:* [1]Und drunten im Tale, da funkeln [2]Die Fenster von Liebchens Haus; [3]Ich aber blikke im Dunkeln [4]Still in die Welt hinaus.	And down in the valley, a light can Be seen in my loved one's house; But I keep staring, in darkness, Silently out to the world.

Obvious (i.e., unmodified strophic) setting:

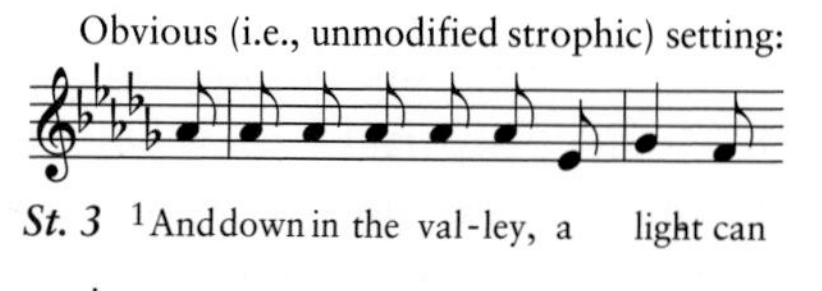

2 The "Character Piece" for Piano

Besides the lied, the other chief type of Romantic miniature composition was the short piano piece. Such pieces were written in great profusion in the nineteenth century, and they appeared under many names. Frédéric Chopin preferred simple genre titles such as Nocturne, Waltz, Scherzo, or **Étude** (study). Robert Schumann preferred descriptive titles. Piano miniatures were composed at all levels of difficulty, ranging from virtuoso tours de force, which hardly anyone but their composers could negotiate, to unassuming pieces playable (and enjoyable) by beginning students.

A good general name for these short Romantic piano pieces (one sometimes used by the Romantics themselves) is **character pieces,** for the essential point about them is that each portrays some definite mood or character. In principle, at least, this is as true of the brilliant virtuoso works as of the simple ones. Each conveys an intense, distinct emotion—an emotion often hinted at by an imaginative title supplied by the composer.

This explains why the Romantic character piece can be thought of as analogous to the Romantic song, or lied, though without its poem. Indeed, six books of such piano pieces by Felix Mendelssohn—pieces that were very popular in Victorian times—are entitled *Songs Without Words.* Some of them have subtitles that stress still further their similarity to lieder: "Spinning Song," "Venetian Boat Song," and the famous "Spring Song."

FRANZ SCHUBERT
Moment Musical No. 2 in A-flat (1827?)

Creative publishers gave Franz Schubert's piano miniatures their titles: "Momens musicals" (spelled wrong) and "Impromptus" (improvisations—Johannes Brahms would later call some of *his* miniatures "caprices"). We heard No. 3 from the published set of "musical moments" on the CD-ROM for Unit I (page 35). No. 2 is the most romantic of its companions.

The main idea, **A,** is a gentle rocking figure, with a nostalgic mood characteristic of Schubert. The mood deepens when **A′** is provided with a relatively long coda, which seems reluctant ever to let go. In between comes **B,** a sad melody in the minor mode; the piano texture changes from cloudy chords in **A** to plain melody with a steady moving accompaniment in **B.** As usual in piano miniatures, the form is simple, at least on the surface: **A B A′ B′ A″.**

LISTEN

Schubert, Moment Musical No. 2

1

A
0:00 **a,** ***p***
0:35 **a′**
B
1:20 **b:** minor, ***p***
A′
2:23 **a″** (longer)
3:17 **coda**
B′
3:57 **b′**: minor, ***ff***
Turns to the major
A″
4:54 **a‴**, ***p***
5:36 coda

But in fact this is an excellent example of how much these impersonal form diagrams can hide. After **A B A′**, especially with its coda, and after four minutes, we think that the piece must be over—except, perhaps, for a hint when the piano moves to an unusually high register at the coda's final cadence. And indeed **B** returns—***fortissimo,*** in the high register, no longer sad but terribly anguished, a cry of pain. In the wake of this climax, there is a momentary switch from the minor mode to the major, a Schubert fingerprint we also noted in Moment Musical No. 3. Does this change heal the pain? By the end of A″ the high register no longer hints at anything. It simply hovers at the border of hearing, a Romantic evocation of the ineffable.

ROBERT SCHUMANN
Carnaval (1833–35)

2-3 38-39

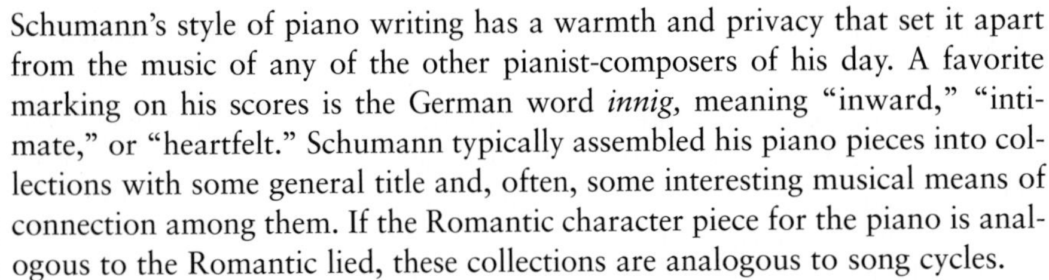

Schumann's style of piano writing has a warmth and privacy that set it apart from the music of any of the other pianist-composers of his day. A favorite marking on his scores is the German word *innig,* meaning "inward," "intimate," or "heartfelt." Schumann typically assembled his piano pieces into collections with some general title and, often, some interesting musical means of connection among them. If the Romantic character piece for the piano is analogous to the Romantic lied, these collections are analogous to song cycles.

Such a collection is *Carnaval,* a set of twenty short character pieces that really *are* characters—musical portraits of masked guests at a Mardi Gras ball. After the band strikes up an introduction, the sad clown Pierrot arrives, followed by the pantomime figures Harlequin and Columbine, Schumann himself, two of his girlfriends masquerading under the names Estrella and Chiarina, a Coquette, and even the composers Paganini and Chopin. This diverse gallery provided Schumann with an outlet for his whimsy and humor, as well as all his Romantic melancholy and passion.

Eusebius: "In sculpture, the actor's art becomes fixed. The actor transforms the sculptor's forms into living art. The painter turns a poem into a painting. The musician sets a picture to music." Florestan: "The aesthetic principle is the same in every art; only the material differs."

Robert Schumann, 1833

"Eusebius" "Eusebius" was Schumann's pen name for his tender, dreamy self, and this little piece presents him at his most introspective. In the passage below, the yearning effect of the high notes (shaded) is compounded by the vague, languorous rhythm:

The right-hand triplets and quintuplets blur with the left-hand quarter notes, especially when played with Romantic rubato. The somewhat unusual form is **aa ba b′a′ ba**, in which **b′a′** stands out although it differs from **ba** only in its much thicker chords and its use of the pedal.

"Florestan" After "Eusebius" ends very tentatively, Schumann's impetuous other self makes his entrance. "Florestan" is built out of a single explosive motive; the piece moves in fits and starts. It gets faster and faster, almost madly, ending completely up in the air. This non-cadence is resolved only in the next number.

Frédéric Chopin (1810–1849)

Chopin was born near Warsaw, where his father, a Frenchman who had emigrated to Poland and married a Polish lady, ran a private school for young gentlemen. In this atmosphere Fryderyk—later he adopted the French form Frédéric—acquired his lifelong taste for life in high society. Provided with the best teachers available, he became an extraordinary pianist. There are many reports of the exquisite delicacy of his playing, and his miraculous ability, as it seemed at the time, to draw romantic sounds out of the piano.

Furthermore, his set of variations on Mozart's "Là ci darem la mano" (see page 210), written when he was seventeen, was already an impressive enough composition to earn a rave review from Robert Schumann.

Chopin settled in Paris, where he found ready acceptance from society people and from other artists and intellectuals, such as the novelist Honoré de Balzac and the painter Eugène Delacroix, who produced a famous portrait of the composer. Chopin made his way as a highly fashionable piano teacher and by selling his music to publishers. The facts that he was Polish and that Poland was being overrun by Russia at that time seem to have made him even more glamorous to the French. Among Chopin's piano miniatures are over fifty Mazurkas and sixteen Polonaises, which are stylized Polish dances.

Chopin was a frail and fastidious personality. Though he sometimes played in public, he truly disliked the hurly-burly of concert life and preferred to perform for select audiences in great houses. More than any other of the great composers, he restricted his work to music for *his* instrument, the piano. Even his works for piano and orchestra—two concertos and a few other works—were all from his pre-Paris days.

The major event of his personal life was his ten-year romance with Madame Aurore Dudevant, an early feminist and a famous novelist under the pen name George Sand. (They were introduced by Liszt, who wrote an admiring book about Chopin after his death.) The relationship was a rocky one; Sand sketched some unkind scenes from their life together in one of her novels. After the affair broke up in 1847, Chopin's health declined with his spirits. He toured England and Scotland unhappily in 1848 and died the next year, aged thirty-nine, of tuberculosis, a major killer in the nineteenth century.

Chief Works: Character pieces for piano: Preludes (including the "Raindrop" prelude), Nocturnes, Études, Ballades, Waltzes (including the "Minute" waltz), and Polish Mazurkas and Polonaises ▪ Three piano sonatas, including one with a famous funeral march as the slow movement ▪ Two piano concertos ▪ A cello sonata; a few Polish songs

Encore: Listen to some other Chopin Nocturnes, the Fantasy-Impromptu, and Ballade in G Minor.

"Chiarina" As we are probably meant to guess from the letters in the name, this is a musical portrait of then sixteen-year-old Clara Wieck. The heading is "Passionato," and by the end the dynamic has risen to *fortissimo*. Robert did not see his future wife as a shrinking violet.

FRÉDÉRIC CHOPIN
Nocturne in F-sharp, Op. 15, No. 2 (1831)

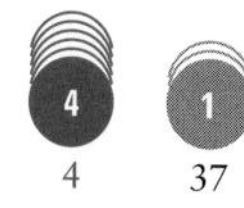

4 37

LISTEN

Chopin, Nocturne in F-sharp

0:00 **a**
0:27 **a′** ornamented
0:58 **b**
1:28 **c**
2:13 **a″**
2:55 **coda**

Chopin's twenty-one **nocturnes,** meaning "night pieces," written throughout his career, are as different as twenty-one different nights. But each features a particularly striking tune—a languid serenade, for example, or a dark, secret lament. Something else is usually heard or overheard in the night, too, such as a distant procession, a passionate encounter, or even a fragment of a dance or a folk song.

The opening tune in Chopin's Nocturne in F-sharp has an elegance unique to the composer—an elegance that stems partly from the wonderfully graceful rhythm, partly from the Romantic turns of harmony, and partly from the pianistic decorations of the melodic line. We have seen decorated melodies before,

Was this striking painting, by a minor late nineteenth-century artist, done with Chopin's nocturnes in mind? Called *Notturno,* its cool elegance, faint sensuality, and vaguely apprehensive quality might suggest so.

but Chopin's have an almost liquid quality, caused partly by chromaticism—by the free use of all the notes of the chromatic scale, as in this fragment:

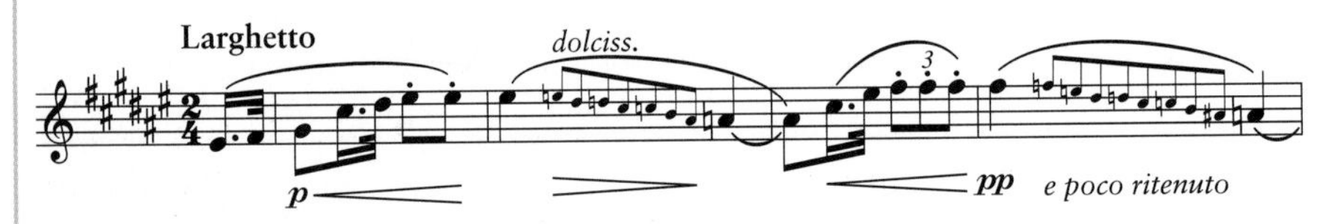

Romantic form contributes to the Romantic effect. Chopin avoids sharp demarcations and literal returns; the music seems to grow spontaneously, in an almost improvisational way. The main tune, **A** (**a a′ b**), does not really end; it is interrupted by plaintive sounds emerging out of nowhere, which surge up to a moment of real passion. Then the return of the tune (**a″**) is fragmentary, though in a way more intense, and the whole is capped by an unexpected little coda: delicious right-hand arpeggios over a bolero rhythm in the left. Free rhythm in the performance (rubato) mirrors the freedom of form.

"That's not your own fingering, is it?" he asked, in his melodious little voice. "No, Liszt's" I said. "Ah, that one has ideas, I tell you!" And Chopin began to try this fingering. "But one could go down the whole keyboard this way like a crayfish scuttling back to his stream. It is perfect, your fingering! I shall use it!"

Reminiscence by a student of Chopin, 1859

3 Early Romantic Program Music

The lied and the character piece for piano—the two main forms of early Romantic miniature compositions—were intimately tied up with nonmusical, usually poetic, ideas. Furthermore, in a work such as Schumann's *Carnaval,* the various piano portraits are juxtaposed in such a way as to hint at their interaction—hint, that is, at a shadowy story line. Poems, stories, and nonmusical ideas in general were also associated with large-scale instrumental pieces.

Liszt's phenomenal virtuosity as a pianist inspired many a cartoonist. The sword here refers to his many decorations; he has a halo because he had turned to religion and become an unordained priest. "The Abbé Liszt" was known to break, if not pianos, piano strings, and this helped ruin one Viennese piano maker (Graf).

Liszt was the greatest piano virtuoso of the nineteenth century; greatest in the twentieth century was the Russian-American pianist Vladimir Horowitz (1904–1989).

Franz Liszt (1811–1886)

There are some important composers whose music we unfortunately have to pass over in this book, because of space limits. In this box and the one on page 264 we give the biographies of three of them, together with some account of their roles in the history of Romantic music.

Franz Liszt learned music from his father on the Hungarian estate of the princes Esterházy, whom Haydn had once served. At age eleven, the boy gave his first piano concert in Vienna, where he met Beethoven. He later settled in Paris, home of another great pianist-composer, Chopin.

Liszt's dashing looks and personality and his liaisons with married noblewomen—Countess d'Agoult and, later, Princess Sayn-Wittgenstein—dazzled Europe as much as his incredible pianistic technique. No one had heard such virtuosity. He drew crowds like a modern rock star and cultivated a lifestyle to match.

After his relationship with d'Agoult came to a stormy end in 1839, Liszt spent a few years giving sensational concerts all over Europe. Tiring of concert life, he then took a position as conductor and director of the theater at Weimar, in Germany, where there was still a court that supported the arts in the eighteenth-century manner. There he wrote his most radical and influential music.

Like many other Romantic composers, Liszt was a writer of note, as well as a musician. He was a strong advocate of the music of Richard Wagner; the two men learned from each other. Both friend and foe linked Wagner's "music dramas" with Liszt's symphonic poems as "Music of the Future." In his personality, however, Liszt was as generous as Wagner was self-centered and devious.

Liszt really had two major careers. The first, at Paris, his career as a fantastic piano virtuoso, underpins a musical ideal that was still alive and well in the 1997 movie *Shine*. It left a mass of fiercely difficult piano music, including the *Transcendental Études* (the name says it all!) and the popular *Hungarian Rhapsodies*—important early products of nationalism in music (see page 292).

Liszt's second career, at Weimar, focused on orchestral music: program symphonies and symphonic poems. We will take up these genres on pages 265 and 290.

Felix Mendelssohn (1809–1847)

Felix Mendelssohn may be the only great composer who has ever come from an upper-class family, a family of converted Jews who were in banking. Their home was a meeting place for artists and intellectuals over generations. Felix and his sister Fanny were brought up with music and every other advantage that came with a life of privilege. (Felix also became a fine amateur painter.)

By the time he was fifteen Felix was conducting the family orchestra in his own music. He went on to a stellar career, not only as an enormously successful composer, but as a pianist, organist, conductor, educator—he founded the Leipzig Conservatory of Music—and even as a musicologist. His performance of Bach's *St. Matthew Passion* was a landmark in the revival of "early music."

This action was typical, for from the start Mendelssohn showed a great respect for, even deference toward, the classics. His music never goes as far as, say, Schumann or Chopin in acceding to Romantic tendencies, but always keeps a firm foundation of Classical technique.

One of Mendelssohn's most significant fields of activity was the concert overture, an early **genre** of Romantic program music; see below. In his lifetime he was admired even more for his oratorios *St. Paul* and *Elijah,* and for popular sets of piano miniatures he called *Songs Without Words*. His Violin Concerto is a special favorite.

Fanny Mendelssohn (1805–1847)

Fanny Mendelssohn, Felix's older sister, was also a highly prolific composer. The siblings were always very close; music was one of their bonds, for Fanny showed as much talent as her brother. Married to a painter named Wilhelm Hensel, she devoted herself to weekly concerts at the Mendelssohn home in Berlin, for which she composed music of all kinds, including even oratorios.

However, Fanny's music did not pass beyond the threshold of the Mendelssohn mansion. Only a small percentage of it found its way into print, at the end of her short life. Fanny is often seen as a victim of patriarchal society and of the general refusal in the past to take women composers seriously. Like Mozart's sister Nannerl, she watched as her younger brother built a great career while she was expected—indeed, conditioned—to put motherhood and family first, music second. But we should remember that unlike other successful women composers of the nineteenth century—from Louise Farrenc (1804–1875) to Clara Schumann (1819–1896) to Cécile Chaminade (1857–1944) and Ethel Smythe (1858–1944)—Fanny Mendelssohn belonged to the upper class. Few members of this class, male or female, had ever pursued public careers in the arts. They didn't need the rat race. Workaholic Felix was an exception.

Fanny's sudden death at age forty-one devastated Felix, and hastened his own death six months later.

As we have seen, *program music* is a term used for instrumental compositions associated with poems, stories, and the like. Program music grew up naturally in opera overtures, for even in the eighteenth century it was seen that an overture might gain special interest if it referred to moods or ideas in the opera to come by citing (or, rather, forecasting) some of its themes.

This happens in Mozart's *Don Giovanni,* in which the next-to-last scene has Don Giovanni carried off to hell by the statue of the murdered Commandant (see page 208). The somber music associated with the Statue is first heard in the opera's overture, even before the curtain has gone up. Lively, effervescent music follows; but the half-serious, half-comical mood of Mozart's opera is already manifest in the overture.

The Concert Overture: Felix Mendelssohn

A further step, conceptually, was the **concert overture,** never intended to be followed by a stage play or an opera—never intended, indeed, for the theater. Robert Schumann wrote an overture to *Hermann und Dorothea,* by Goethe, which is not a play but an epic poem. Hector Berlioz wrote overtures to literary works of various kinds: plays (Shakespeare's *King Lear*), long poems (*The Corsair* by Lord Byron, a special hero for the Romantics), and novels (*Waverly* by Sir Walter Scott).

Probably the best-known and best-loved concert overtures are by Felix Mendelssohn. His concert overture to *A Midsummer Night's Dream* was written at the age of seventeen; the play was a special favorite with both Felix and Fanny. He had no theatrical occasion in mind, though years later the overture was indeed used in productions of the Shakespeare play. At that time Mendelssohn also added other music, and a suite derived from this piece (see page 143) has become a popular concert number.

A work in sonata form, following Classical models quite clearly, the overture to *A Midsummer Night's Dream* nonetheless includes some representational features. Music illustrates the delicate, fluttering fairies in the service of King Oberon and Queen Titania, the sleep induced by Puck's magic flower, and even the braying of Bottom the Weaver when he is turned into a donkey.

Another fine example by Mendelssohn is the *Hebrides* Overture, an evocative, moody depiction of lonely Scottish islands rich in romantic associations. Surging string music suggests the swell and the spray of waves; woodwind fanfares suggest seabird calls, perhaps, or romanticized foghorns. This is evidently program music, but what makes it an overture? Nothing more than the fact that it follows the standard scheme for overtures at the time—namely, a single movement in sonata form.

The Mendelssohns

The Program Symphony: Hector Berlioz

> PROGRAM OF THE SYMPHONY: A young musician of unhealthy sensibility and passionate imagination poisons himself with opium in a fit of lovesick despair. Too weak to kill him, the dose of the drug plunges him into a heavy sleep attended by the strangest visions, during which his sensations, emotions, and memories are transformed in his diseased mind into musical thoughts and images. Even the woman he loves becomes a melody to him, an *idée fixe* [an obsession], as it were, that he finds and hears everywhere.

So begins a long pamphlet that the French Romantic composer Hector Berlioz distributed at performances of his first symphony—a symphony which he could justifiably call *Fantastic,* and which to this day remains his most famous work. It certainly represents a more radical approach to program music than that of the concert overture. Berlioz, too, had written several concert overtures, but he now felt the need for a broader canvas. In his **program symphonies**—entire symphonies with programs, spelled out movement by movement, in this case—Berlioz set the tone for the "grandiose" compositions that were to become as characteristic of Romanticism as its musical miniatures.

HECTOR BERLIOZ
Fantastic Symphony: Episodes in the Life of an Artist (1830)

Clearly Berlioz had a gift for public relations, for the program of his *Fantastic* Symphony was not a familiar play or novel, but an autobiographical fantasy of the most lurid sort. Here was music that encouraged listeners to think it had been written under the influence of opium, the drug of choice among the Romantics, which shocked society at large. What is more, half of Paris knew that Berlioz was madly in love (from afar) with an Irish actress, Harriet Smithson, who had taken the city by storm with her Shakespearean roles.

Audiences have never been quite sure how seriously to take it all, but they continue to be bowled over by Berlioz's effects of tone color. He demanded an orchestra of unprecedented size, which he used in incredibly original and imaginative ways. Also highly original was the notion of having a single theme recur in all the movements as a representation of the musician's beloved—his **idée fixe.**

Love or music—which power can uplift man to the sublimest heights? It is a large question; yet it seems to me one should answer it in this way: Love cannot give an idea of music; music can give an idea of love. But why separate them? They are the two wings of the soul . . .

From the *Memoirs of Hector Berlioz,* 1869

Here is the *idée fixe* theme as it first appears:

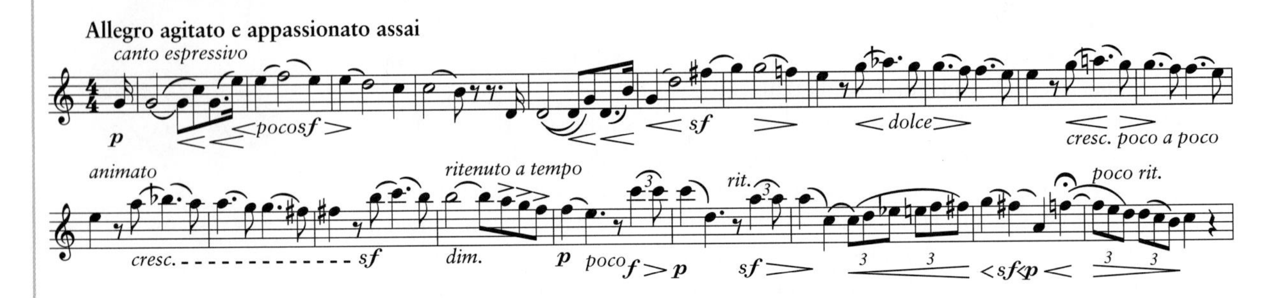

This typically Romantic melody seems like a passionate struggle to inch higher and higher up the scale: E–F (measure 2), F♯–G (measure 7), G–A♭, G–A♮, A–B♭, B♮–C. Near the end, measure 19 provides a positive shudder of emotion. Notice how many dynamic, rubato, and other marks Berlioz has supplied, to ensure just the right expressive quality from moment to moment.*

To illustrate his drastic mood swings, Berlioz subjects the *idée fixe* to thematic transformation (see page 248) for all its other appearances in the opium dream. The last movement, for example, has a grotesque parody of the theme; its new jerky rhythm and squeaky orchestration (using the small E-flat clarinet) thoroughly undermine the original Romantic mood.

First Movement: Reveries, Passions (Largo—Allegro agitato e appassionato assai) We first hear a short, quiet run-in—a typically Romantic touch suggesting that the music has grown up imperceptibly out of silence. Then the "soul-sickness" mentioned in the program is depicted by a halting, passionate melody. A faster section begins with the *idée fixe,* and the music picks up energy (the "volcanic love" of the program).

THE PROGRAM CONTINUES: First he recalls the soul-sickness, the aimless passions, the baseless depressions and elations that he felt before first seeing his loved one; then the volcanic love that she instantly inspired in him; his jealous furies; his return to tenderness; his religious consolations.

This fast section follows sonata form, but only very loosely indeed. The *idée fixe* is the main theme, and a second theme is simply a derivative of the first. Some of the finest strokes in this movement run counter to Classical principles—for example, the arresting up-and-down harmonized chromatic scale that arrives in the development section without any logical connection to anything else. The recapitulation, too, is extended in a very un-Classical fashion; it actually includes a whole new melody for the oboe.

Near the end, beginning an outsized coda, the *idée fixe* returns noisily at a faster tempo—the first of its many transformations. At the very end, slower music depicts the program's "religious consolations."

Second Movement: A Ball (Allegro non troppo) A symphony needs the simplicity and easy swing of a dance movement, and this ballroom episode of the opium dream conveniently provided one. The dance in question is not a minuet or a scherzo, but a waltz, the most popular ballroom dance of the nineteenth

He encounters his beloved at a ball, in the midst of a noisy, brilliant party.

*The music example has been simplified to facilitate reading. *Canto espressivo* = expressive song; *dolce* = sweetly; *poco* = somewhat; *poco a poco* = bit by bit; *animato* = animated; *ritenuto* = slowed down (ritardando); *a tempo* = back to the original tempo.

century. The *idée fixe,* transformed into a lilting triple meter, first appears in the position of the trio (**B** in the **A B A** form) and then returns hauntingly in a coda.

On a summer evening in the country, he hears two shepherds piping in dialogue. The pastoral duet, the location, the light rustling of trees stirred gently by the wind, some newly conceived grounds for hope—all this gives him a feeling of unaccustomed calm. But *she* appears again . . . what if she is deceiving him?

Third Movement: Scene in the Country (Adagio) Invoking nature to reflect human emotions was a favorite Romantic procedure. The "pastoral duet" is played by an English horn and an offstage oboe (boy and girl, perhaps?). At the end, the English horn returns to the accompaniment of distant thunder sounds, played on four differently tuned timpani. Significantly, the oboe can no longer be heard.

In this movement the *idée fixe* returns in a new, strangely agitated transformation. It is interrupted by angry sounds swelling to a climax, indicative of the anxieties chronicled in the program.

He dreams he has killed his beloved, that he is condemned to death and led to execution. A march accompanies the procession, now gloomy and wild, now brilliant and grand. Finally the *idée fixe* appears for a moment, to be cut off by the fall of the axe.

Fourth Movement: March to the Scaffold (Allegretto non troppo) This movement is the exciting march that you (may) have heard as the Overture to this book. See Listening Chart 1, on page 4. Adding a fifth movement to the traditional four of the Classical symphony was a typical Berlioz innovation (though it can be traced back to the Beethoven he so much admired).

SG 1-3

There are two main themes: a long downward scale ("gloomy and wild") and a blaring, ominous military march ("brilliant and grand"). Later the scale theme appears divided up in its orchestration between plucked and bowed strings, woodwinds, brass, and percussion—a memorable instance of Berlioz's novel imagination for tone color. The scale theme also appears in a truly shattering inverted form (that is, moving up instead of down).

As we noted on page 5, Berlioz had written the march itself or something like it several years earlier. As he revised it to go into the *Fantastic* Symphony, he added a coda that uses the *idée fixe* and therefore only makes sense in terms of the symphony's program. The final fall of the axe is illustrated musically by the sound of a guillotine chop and a military snare-drum roll, right after bars 1–2 of the *idée fixe.* "Berlioz tells it like it is," conductor Leonard Bernstein once remarked. "You take a trip and you end up screaming at your own funeral."

Fifth Movement: Dream of a Witches' Sabbath (Larghetto—Allegro) Now the element of parody is added to the astonishing orchestral effects pioneered

Witches' Sabbath (detail), by Francisco Goya (1746–1828)

Take great pains with the contrast between the two levels! The lower one is gloomy, with stark colors, bathed in a grey-green light; the temple [above] glows with light, warm colors.

Columns will serve very well to mask the lighting mechanism, which should preferably be gas jets.

Verdi on the visuals in *Aida*

Recitative The scene opens with quiet, ominous music in the strings—already, in its understated way, a forecast of doom. The first singing consists of three short passages of recitative. Each follows the same general plan. In each recitative passage, simple declamatory singing (with very light orchestral accompaniment) leads to an intense moment of genuine melody, with rich harmonic and orchestral support.

Radames begins singing on a lengthy monotone, but works up some emotion when he thinks of Aida and hopes she will be spared knowledge of his fate. Then his more excited second speech is still fragmentary, up to the point when he discovers that Aida has hidden in his tomb to see him once again and die with him. He cries out "You, in this tomb!" on a high note, picking up from an anguished downward scale in the orchestra.

The third recitative passage, Aida's reply, begins simply, over a knell-like orchestral accompaniment. It melts into a beautiful and sensuously harmonized melodic phrase when she tells him she wants to die in his arms.

Ariosos There follow two concise tunelike sections, or *ariosos* (see page 100). In the first of them, sung by Radames, notice the subdued, subservient role of the orchestra. The next arioso is more tuneful yet, with Aida's phrases falling into an almost Classical **a a′ b a′ c** pattern. The harmony is fully Romantic, however, especially in phrase **b.**

Duet (with Chorus) Then Verdi mounts his impressive final scene. At the top level of the stage, priests and priestesses move slowly as they sing a hymn with an exotic, Near Eastern flavor. They are invoking the great god Ptah:

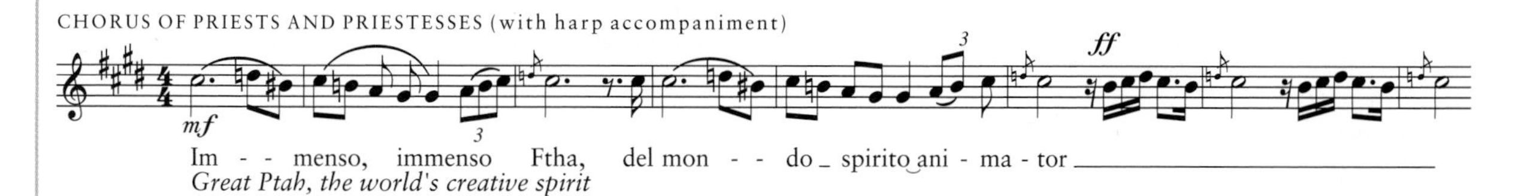

At the bottom level, Aida and Radames begin their final duet, a farewell to the sorrows of earth and a welcome to eternity. It is a famous instance of Verdi's simple and yet expansive melodic style:

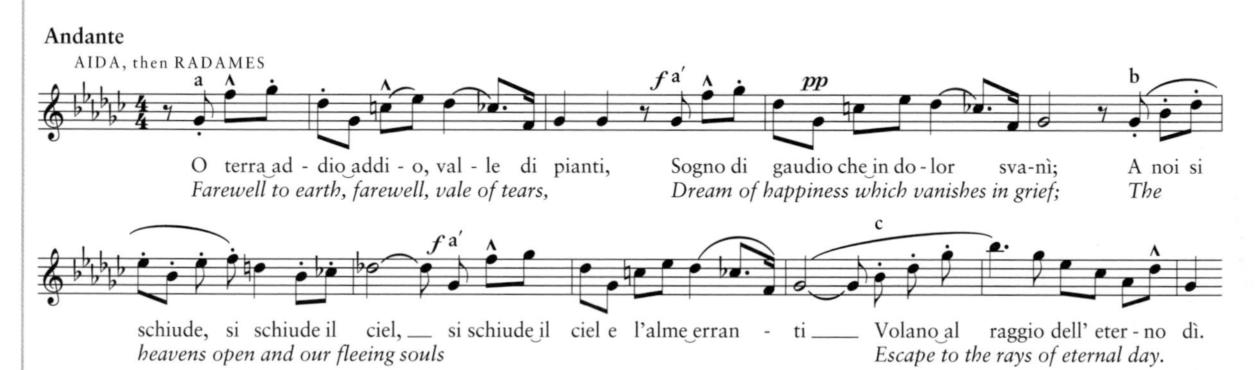

There is an exquisite Romantic harmony at the climax of the melody, in **c** of the **a a′ b a′ c** form—and the final climax, on nearly the highest note in the tenor's range, has to be sung very softly. This gives the melody a uniquely ethereal effect, as befits a couple who are about to die from lack of oxygen.

Other features reinforce this effect: the melodic line that focuses on just a few notes (high and low G♭ and D♭), and the high accompanying haze of string instruments that later swell up ecstatically. We sense that Aida and Radames are already far out of this world, perfectly attuned to each other (they sing the same tune in octaves) in a love that transcends death itself.

LISTEN Verdi, *Aida*, Tomb Scene, Act IV, scene ii

12-15

23-26

RECITATIVE: Radames alone, then Aida

Part 1: Radames reflects *Quiet orchestral introduction (strings) sets the mournful mood. Radames sings his first three lines on a monotone. Accompaniment: slow and halting.*

12 23	0:26	**Radames:**	La fatal pietra sopra me si chiuse;	The fatal stone closes over me;
			Ecco la tomba mia.	This is my tomb.
			Del dì la luce più non vedro . . .	The light of day I'll never see again.
			Non rivedrò più Aida.	I'll never see Aida.
			Aida, dove sei tu? possa tu almeno	Aida, where are you?
	1:51		Viver felice, e la mia sorte orrenda	Live happily, and never know
			Sempre ignorar!	Of my terrible death.

Part 2: Radames hears a sound *Accompaniment: the rhythm picks up*

2:04	**Radames:**	Qual gemito—una larva—un vision . . .	What sound was that? a ghost? a vision?
		No! forma umana è questa . . . Ciel, Aida!	No, a human form . . . Aida!
	Aida:	Son io . . .	Yes . . .
	Radames:	Tu, in questa tomba!	You, in this tomb!

Part 3: Aida explains *Accompaniment: mournful low notes*

Time	Singer	Italian	English
2:41	**Aida:**	Presago il core della tua condanna, In questa tomba che per te s'appriva Io penetrai furtiva, E qui lontana da ogni umano sguardo Nelle tue braccia desiai morire.	A presentiment of my heart foretold your sentence; This tomb awaited you— I hid secretly in it, And here, far from any human gaze, I wanted to die in your arms.

ARIOSO I

13 / 24 **Radames reacts in despair** *"Con passione"—passionately*

Time	Singer	Italian	English
3:33	**Radames:**	Morir! si pura e bella! Morir per me d'amore, Degli anni tuoi nel fiore, *degli anni tuoi nel fiore* fuggir la vita! T'avea in cielo per l'amor creata, Ed io t'uccido per averti amata! No, non morrai, troppo t'amai, troppo sei bella!	Dying, so innocent and beautiful, Dying, for love of me! So young, so young to give up life! You were made in heaven for love And I have killed you by loving you! You cannot die! I love you too much, you are too beautiful!

ARIOSO II

Aida, "almost in a trance" *Ethereal high strings*

Track	Time	Singer	Italian	English
14 / 25	4:50	**Aida:**	Vedi? di morte l'angelo Radiante a noi s'appressa, Ne adduce a eterni gaudii Sovra i suoi vanni d'or. Già veggo il ciel dischiudersi; Ivi ogni affano cessa,	See, the angel of death Approaches us in radiance, Leading to eternal joys On his golden wings. I see the heavens open; Here pain ceases,
0:40	5:30		Ivi *commincia l'estasi* *D'un immortal amor.*	Here begins the ecstasy Of immortal love.

CHORUS (on the upper stage) with interjections by Radames and Aida
Modal harmonies, harp, and flute

Track	Time	Singer	Italian	English	Chorus *(simultaneously):*
1:13	6:03	**Aida:**	Triste canto!	Mournful chant!	Immenso Ftha,
		Radames:	Il tripudio dei sacerdoti . . .	The priestly rites . . .	del mondo spirito animator,
		Aida:	Il nostro inno di morte.	Our funeral hymn.	noi *t'invocchiamo.*
		Radames:	Nè le mie forti braccia Smuovere ti potranno, o fatal pietra!	All of my strength cannot Move that fatal stone!	
		Aida:	Invan—tutto e finito Sulla terra per noi.	In vain—all is finished For us on earth.	Great Ptah, the world's creative spirit,
		Radames:	È vero, è vero!	True, it is true.	we invoke thee.

15 / 26 DUET: First Aida, then Radames with Aida *With quiet high strings*

Time	Singer	Italian	English
6:44	**Aida and Radames:**	O terra, addio, addio, valle di pianti, Sogno di gaudio che in dolor svanì, A noi *si schiude* il ciel, si schiude il ciel e l'alme erranti Volano al raggio dell'eterno dì.	Farewell to earth, vale of tears, Dream of happiness which vanishes in grief; The heavens open, And our fleeing souls Escape to the rays of eternal day.

CHORUS (on the upper stage) singing with Aida and Radames
DUET continues: Aida and Radames together (same music) with Amneris and the Chorus

Track	Time	Singer	Italian	English	Chorus *(simultaneously):*
2:39	9:23	**Aida and Radames:**	O terra addio, addio valle di pianti, Sogno di gaudio che in dolor svanì, A noi *si schiude* il ciel, si schiude il ciel e l'alme erranti Volano al raggio dell'eterno dì.		Immenso Ftha, del mondo spirito animator, noi *t'invocchiamo.*
4:18	11:02	**Amneris:**	Pace t'imploro, salma adorata, Isi placata, *Isi placata* ti schiuda il ciel,	Rest in peace, I pray, beloved spirit; May Isis, placated, welcome you to	Great Ptah, the world's creative spirit,
4:34	11:18		*pace t'imploro, pace . . .*	heaven . . . peace, peace . . .	we invoke thee.

Ends with violins playing the "O terra" tune, Amneris singing "Pace, pace," and the Chorus repeating "Immenso Ftha!"

Conclusion Before the final curtain, a figure in mourning enters the temple above the tomb to pray. Drained of all the emotion that she poured out in earlier scenes, Amneris can only whisper on a monotone, "Peace, rest in peace, I pray" *(Pace t'imploro)*. The different psychic states of the characters are made more vivid by simultaneous contrast, a principle we saw at work in Mozart's opera buffa ensembles (see page 206). Amneris's grief is set directly against the ecstatic, otherworldly togetherness of Radames and Aida.

High violins take over the duet melody; one can almost visualize the souls of Aida and Radames ascending to "eternal day." And by giving the last words to the priests—the judges of Radames and the proponents of Egypt's wars—Verdi hands them the ultimate responsibility for the threefold tragedy.

2 Wagner and "Music Drama"

Richard Wagner was, after Beethoven, the most influential of all nineteenth-century composers. His strictly musical innovations, in harmony and orchestration, revolutionized instrumental music as well as opera. In terms of opera, Wagner is famous for his novel concept of the "complete work of art" (*Gesamtkunstwerk;* see below) and his development of a special operatic technique, that of the "guiding motive" (leitmotiv).

Unlike earlier innovative composers, it seems Wagner could not just compose; he had to develop elaborate theories announcing what art, music, and opera ought to be like. (Indeed, he also theorized about politics and philosophy, with very unhappy results.) Wagner's extreme self-consciousness as an artist was prophetic of attitudes toward art of a much later period.

His theory of opera had its positive and negative sides. First, Wagner wanted to do away with all the conventions of earlier opera, especially the French and Italian varieties. Opera, he complained, had degenerated from its original form as serious drama in music—Wagner was thinking of ancient Greek drama, which he knew had been sung or at least chanted—into a mere "concert in costume." He particularly condemned arias, which were certainly at the heart of Italian opera, as hopelessly artificial. Why should the dramatic action keep stopping to allow for stretches of pretty but undramatic singing?

The "Total Work of Art"

The positive side of Wagner's program was the development of a new kind of opera in the 1850s, for which he reserved a special name: **music drama.** Music, in these works, shares the honors with poetry, drama, and philosophy—all furnished by Wagner himself—as well as the stage design and acting. Wagner coined the word **Gesamtkunstwerk,** meaning "total work of art," for this powerful concept. He always insisted on the distinction between music drama and ordinary "opera."

Since words and ideas are so important in the *Gesamtkunstwerk,* the music is very closely matched to the words. Yet it is also unrelievedly emotional and intense, as Romantic doctrine required. The dramas themselves deal with weighty philosophical issues, or so at least Wagner and his admirers believed, and they do so under the symbolic cover of medieval German myths and legends.

This use of myths was another Romantic feature, one that strikingly anticipated Freud, with his emphasis on myths (for example, the myth of Oedipus)

Richard Wagner (1813–1883)

Wagner was born in Leipzig during the turmoil of the Napoleonic wars; his father died soon afterward. His stepfather was a fascinating actor and writer, and the boy turned into a decided intellectual. Wagner's early interests, literature and music (his idols were Shakespeare and Beethoven), later expanded to include philosophy, mythology, and religion.

As a young man he worked as an opera conductor, and he spent an unhappy year in Paris trying to get one of his works produced at the very important opera house there. The virulent anti-French sentiments in his later writings stemmed from this experience. Back in Germany, he produced the first of his impressive operas, *The Flying Dutchman* and *Tannhäuser,* and wrote *Lohengrin.* Though these works basically adhere to the early Romantic opera style of Carl Maria von Weber, they already hint at the revolutionary ideal for opera that Wagner was pondering.

This he finally formulated after being exiled from Germany (and from a job) as a result of his part in the revolution of 1848–49. He wrote endless articles and books expounding his ideas—ideas that were better known than his later operas, for these were extremely difficult to stage. His book *Opera and Drama* set up the principles for his "music drama" *The Rhinegold,* the first segment of the extraordinary four-evening opera *The Ring of the Nibelung.* He also published a vicious essay attacking Felix Mendelssohn, who had just died, and other Jews in music. Fifty years after Wagner's death, his anti-Semitic writings (and his operas) were taken up by the Nazis.

Wagner, Cosima, and their son Siegfried, who followed Cosima as director of the Wagner festivals at Bayreuth.

Wagner's exile lasted thirteen years. His fortunes changed dramatically when he gained the support of the young, unstable, and finally mad King Ludwig II of Bavaria. Thanks to Ludwig, Wagner's mature music dramas were at last produced (*The Rhinegold*, completed in 1854, was not produced until 1869). Wagner then promoted the building of a special opera house in Bayreuth, Germany, solely for his music dramas—an amazing concept! These grandiose, slow-moving works are based on myths, and characterized by high-flown poetry of his own, a powerful orchestral style, and the use of *leitmotivs* (guiding or leading motives). To this day the opera house in Bayreuth performs only Wagner, and tickets are almost impossible to get.

A hypnotic personality, Wagner was able to spirit money out of many pockets and command the loyalty and affection of many distinguished men and women. His first marriage, to a singer, ended in divorce. His great operatic hymn to love, *Tristan und Isolde,* was created partly in response to his love affair with the wife of one of his patrons. His second wife, Cosima, daughter of Franz Liszt, had been married to an important conductor, Hans von Bülow, who nonetheless remained one of Wagner's strongest supporters. Cosima's diaries tell us about Wagner's moods, dreams, thoughts, and musical decisions, all of which he shared with her. After the death of "the Master," Cosima ruled Bayreuth with an iron hand.

Half con man and half visionary, bad poet and very good musician, Wagner created a storm of controversy in his lifetime that has not died down to this day. He was a major figure in the intellectual life of his time, a thinker whose ideas were highly influential not only in music but also in other arts. In this sense, at least, Wagner was the most important of the Romantic composers.

Chief Works: Early operas: *The Flying Dutchman, Tannhäuser,* and *Lohengrin* ▪ Mature "music dramas": *Tristan und Isolde, The Mastersingers of Nuremberg* (a brilliant comedy), *Parsifal,* and *The Ring of the Nibelung,* a four-opera cycle consisting of *The Rhinegold, The Valkyrie, Siegfried,* and *The Twilight of the Gods* ▪ *Siegfried Idyll,* for small orchestra (based on themes from *Siegfried;* a surprise birthday present for Cosima after the birth of their son, also named Siegfried)

Encore: After selections from *Tristan,* listen to "Wotan's Farewell" from *Die Walküre* (Act III); *Siegfried Idyll.*

as embodiments of the deepest unconscious truths. Wagner employed the old romance of Tristan and Iseult, the saga of the Nordic god Wotan, and the Arthurian tale of Sir Perceval to present his views on love, political power, and religion, respectively. Wagner's glorification of Germanic myths in particular made him the semiofficial voice of German nationalism, paving the way for Hitler.

One of the first great conductors and a superb orchestrator, Wagner raised the orchestra to new importance in opera, giving it a role modeled on Beethoven's symphonies with their motivic development. Leitmotivs (see below) were among the motives he used for this "symphonic" continuity. The orchestra was no longer used essentially as a support for the singers (which was still the situation, really, even in Verdi); it was now the orchestra that carried the opera along. Instead of the alternation of recitatives, arias, and ensembles in traditional opera, "music drama" consisted of one long orchestral web, cunningly woven in with the singing.

Leitmotivs

A **leitmotiv** (guiding, or leading, motive) is a musical motive associated with some person, thing, idea, or symbol in the drama. By presenting and developing leitmotivs, Wagner's orchestra guides the listener through the story.

Leitmotivs are easy to ridicule when they are used mechanically—when, for example, the orchestra obligingly sounds the Sword motive every time the hero reaches for his weapon. On the other hand, leitmotivs can suggest with considerable subtlety what the hero is thinking or feeling even when he is saying something else. Wagner also became very skillful in thematic transformation—the characteristic variation-like technique of the Romantic composers (see page 248). By transforming the appropriate motives, he could show a person or an idea developing and changing under the impact of dramatic action.

And since, for the Romantics, music was the undisputed language of emotion, leitmotivs—being music—could state or suggest ideas in *emotional* terms, over and above the intellectual terms provided by mere words. This was Wagner's theory, a logical outcome of Romantic doctrine about music. Furthermore, the complex web of leitmotivs provided his long music dramas with the thematic unity that Romantic composers sought. On both counts, psychological and technical, leitmotivs were guaranteed to impress audiences of the nineteenth century.

RICHARD WAGNER
Tristan und Isolde (1859)

Two major life experiences helped inspire Wagner's first completed music drama, *Tristan und Isolde*. One was his discovery of the Romantic philosophy of Arthur Schopenhauer, and the other was his love affair with Mathilde Wesendonck, the wife of one of his wealthy patrons.

Mathilde Wesendonck

Schopenhauer had made his own philosophical formulation of the Romantic insight into the central importance of music in emotional life. All human experience, said Schopenhauer, consists either of emotions and drives—which he called "the Will"—or of ideas, morals, and reason, which he downgraded by the term "Appearance." He insisted that the Will always dominates Appearance, and that our only direct, unencumbered sense of it comes through music.

For the philosopher, the inevitable domination of the Will was a source of profound pessimism. But a composer could read another message in Schopen-

In Act II of Wagner's opera, Isolde signals Tristan that all is clear for their fatal meeting.

hauer's work. It reinforced Wagner's conviction that music was specially privileged for emotional representation, that the deepest truths—those to do with the Will—could indeed be plumbed by music, in a music drama. And what would exemplify the Will better than the most exciting human drive that is known, sexual love? As usual, the story itself would be taken from a medieval legend.

Music never expresses outer phenomena, but only mankind's inner nature, the "in-itself" of all phenomena: the Will itself.

Philosopher Arthur Schopenhauer, 1818

Tristan und Isolde is not just a great love story, then, but something more. It is a drama that presents love as the dominant force in life, one that transcends every aspect of worldly Appearance. Many love stories hint at such transcendence, perhaps, but Wagner's story makes it explicit, on the basis of an actual philosophy that the composer espoused.

Background Written by Wagner himself, though derived from a medieval legend, the story of *Tristan und Isolde* shows step by step the growing power of love. In Act I, when Tristan and Isolde fall in love by accidentally drinking a love potion, the Will overpowers Isolde's fierce pride, which had previously made her scorn Tristan as her blood enemy. It also dissolves Tristan's heretofore perfect chivalry, the machismo of the medieval knight, which had demanded that he escort her safely to her marriage to King Mark of Cornwall, his uncle and liege lord.

In Act II, love overcomes the marriage itself when the two meet adulterously (in the longest unconsummated love scene in all of opera). The lovers' tryst is discovered, and Tristan is mortally wounded—but love seems to overcome the wound, too. In Act III he simply cannot or will not die until Isolde comes to him from over the seas. Then, after Isolde comes and he dies in her arms, she herself sinks down in rapture and expires also. For both of them, death is not a defeat but an ecstatic expression of love.

At this point (if not earlier) the plot passes the bounds of reality—which was exactly Wagner's point. Tristan and Isolde, representing Schopenhauer's

Will, move in a realm where conventional attitudes, the rules of society, and even life and death have lost their powers. Transcendence is a recurring theme of Romanticism; here love becomes the ultimate transcendent experience, beyond reality. Indeed, the opera's transcendental quality brings it close to mystical experience.

Incidentally, Wagner and Mathilde did not live up to their operatic ideals. After a while, Wesendonck—the King Mark in this triangle—put his foot down and the affair came to an end.

Prelude Given Wagner's emphasis on the orchestra in his music dramas, it is not surprising that the strictly orchestral Prelude (or Overture) to *Tristan und Isolde* is already a magnificent depiction of romantic love. Or at least one aspect of romantic love: not the joys of love, but love's yearning.

The Prelude opens with a very slow motive whose harmonies create a remarkably sultry, sensual, yearning feeling. The motive is actually made up of two fragments in counterpoint, easily heard because *x* is played by the cellos

Wagner's *Ring of the Nibelung*

Four evenings long and nearly thirty years in the making, Richard Wagner's mega-opera *The Ring of the Nibelung* is one of the towering artworks of all time, comparable to the Taj Mahal, the *Iliad* and the *Odyssey,* and Michelangelo's Sistine Chapel (comparisons which the megalomaniac Wagner would have enjoyed). Its story, of epic scope, spans many generations. It relates a myth originating in the Middle Ages, one with powerful resonance for Wagner's own time and ours, too—as witness its clear echoes in *Star Wars* and *Lord of the Rings.* Wotan, King of the Gods, has attained absolute power by subterfuge. But as the price, he has lost—along with an eye—the golden ring that ultimately dooms his kin and his enemies and brings down his empire. First, though, they and he experience fantastic adventures.

Water spirits and the Earth mother, giants and dwarfs, dragons, toads, and prophetic birds, magic swords and magic potions mix it up with some of the most psychologically complex characters in all of opera. The music of the *Ring* paints a wide range of emotions: innocence, spite, rage, regret, love at first sight, passion, sympathy, exuberance, and wonder. In its leitmotivs, matched flexibly with people and events in the drama, it also paved the way for the composers of today's sound tracks.

See the *Ring* on DVD, in the Bayreuth production conducted by Pierre Boulez.

Medieval themes on a monumental, mythic scale were a specialty of Wagner and remain a staple of recent epic films. Shown here are a stage set from 1893 for the castle of the gods in Wagner's *Ring* and the Argonauth, statues of ancient kings, from *Lord of the Rings* (2001).

and *y* by an oboe. Fragment *x* includes four *descending* notes of the chromatic scale. Fragment *y* consists of four *ascending* chromatic notes.

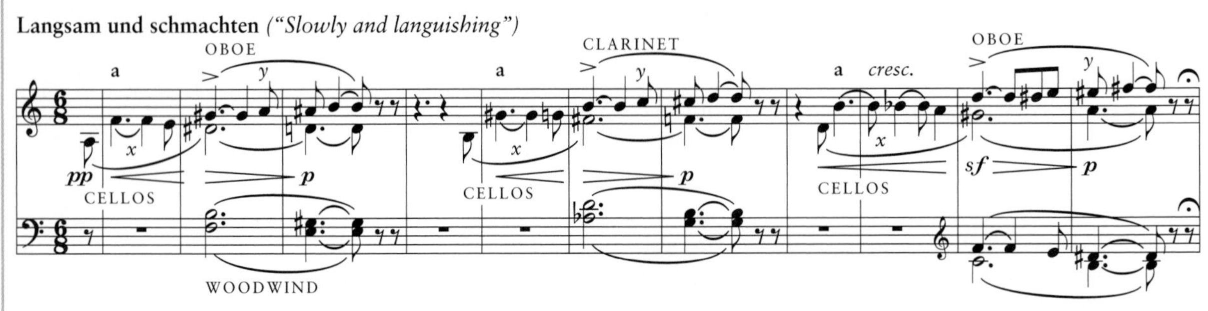

Often treated (as here) in a threefold sequence (see page 25), motive **a** turns out to be the opera's chief leitmotiv. It becomes associated with a rich compound of meaning, including passion, yearning, and release in death. At the risk of oversimplification, we can label it the Love-Death Motive.

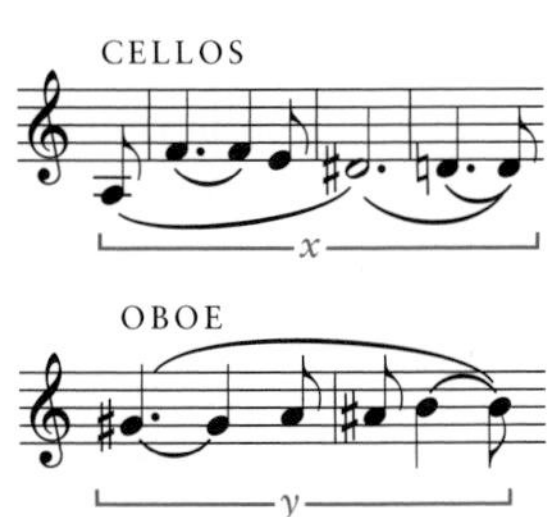

This Love-Death Motive is an example of a Romantic theme that derives its essential character from harmony, rather than from melody or rhythm. The harmony is dissonant and complex: It does not feel at rest, and we expect it to proceed to some other harmony. After the slow opening sequence, the music stretches up and up—still very slowly!—but when the dissonance finally resolves, it resolves in the "wrong" place and still sounds decidedly uneasy.

In other words, the cadence has been undercut; instead of the chord we expect (because it has been clearly prepared by the upward motion), we hear a different chord. This is called a *deceptive cadence.* Deceptive cadences were not new with Wagner, of course; we have heard many of them in works studied in this book. But Wagner used them continuously in order to keep his music surging ahead. When the music stops, it stops "deceptively" at an unexpected place. Those places sound unstable, and so they motivate further surging.

Here, near the beginning of the Prelude, a flowing melodic theme follows, played by the cellos. This passionate theme is heard again and again:

As new themes emerge—yet are they new, or are they subtle transformations of earlier themes?—we realize that Wagner is never going to let the music rest. A marvelous dark churning of emotion is produced by the many sequences, by Wagner's orchestration, and by his characteristic way of avoiding true cadences in favor of deceptive cadences. The music constantly shifts in key (modulates); every time it seems ready to stop, it starts moving forward restlessly.

In form, the total Prelude amounts to a gradual, irregular crescendo, reaching a climax with a *fortissimo* return of the original threefold sequence on the Love-Death Motive. (Nineteenth-century listeners heard this as climactic in another sense, but they did not say so in print.) Then there is a hush. The motive is heard again in brooding new versions, growing quieter, so that when the curtain goes up the orchestra has fallen entirely silent, without ever having come to a cadence.

It is not easy to make a Listening Chart for music that sets out to create the sense of formless waves of emotion, as this Prelude does. In addition to motive **a** and the surging cello theme **B**, we are using the symbol **d/c** to refer to specially prominent deceptive cadences.

LISTENING CHART 19

16-20

Wagner, Prelude to *Tristan und Isolde*

10 min., 31 sec.

(Note: **d/c** *stands for deceptive cadence.)*

	Time	Event	Description
16	**MAIN THEMATIC GROUP** (a d/c B): dynamics *pp*, surge to *f*, back to *p*		
	0:00	a in threefold sequence	With fermatas (long gaps)
	1:33	d/c	Deceptive cadence, *f:* French horn
17	1:37	B	B followed by extension: cellos
0:46	2:23	C	Descending sequence
1:04	2:41		Somber trombone motive
18	**B WITH NEW EXTENSIONS**		
	3:06	B	B followed by extension: woodwinds
0:23	3:29		Quieter material; strings answered by strings and woodwinds
1:05	4:10	d/c	
1:10	4:16	C	Descending sequence: woodwinds, horn
1:21	4:27		Trombone motive, louder now
1:32	4:38		Big surge begins
2:03	5:09	B	
19	**RETRANSITION PASSAGE** (bass is more static)		
	5:54		New, yearning string music
0:15	6:09	*y*, 4 times	(*y* is first heard in the oboe)
0:51	6:45	d/c - B overlaps	Louder and louder: *ff*
20	7:17	*x*, played twice ⟶	Climactic horn calls, in preparation for:
		ENTIRE THEMATIC GROUP	Dynamics *ff*, then down to *p* and *pp*
0:11	7:26	a in threefold sequence	Varied, and with the gaps filled in
1:23	8:38	d/c	Deceptive cadence, as at first, but *p*
1:27	8:42	B fragments	Varied; minor-mode coloration. Drum roll
2:07	9:24	a in twofold sequence	Varied (English horn) ⟶ curtain goes up

OBOE a y x CELLOS

B CELLOS

C VIOLAS

"Philter" Scene from Act I A short segment from *Tristan und Isolde* will show how Wagnerian music drama works, and how it makes dramatic use of previously introduced leitmotivs—in this case, the Love-Death Motive and its threefold sequence, featured in the opera's Prelude. In Act I, a bleak shipboard scene, Isolde is being escorted by Tristan to Cornwall, the kingdom of King Mark. To her maid and confidante, Brangaene, Isolde furiously denounces Tristan, bewails her coming marriage to King Mark, and mutters something about a loveless marriage.

The "Philter" Scene has three subsections:

Brangaene's Song "Loveless?" answers Brangaene. "But anyone would love you; and if he doesn't, we have our magic potions."

First, we hear a short solo passage that is about as close as Wagner got to writing a clear-cut aria, at least in his later years. The music is seductive and

Never in my life having enjoyed the true happiness of love, I shall build a monument to this most beautiful of dreams, in which love will for once find utter, complete fulfillment, from first to last. I have devised in my mind a Tristan und Isolde . . .

Letter from Wagner to his friend Liszt, 1854

sweet, but though Brangaene certainly sings rich melodic phrases, they do not fall together into a tune. Her melody follows the words closely, without word repetitions. Such repetition, which was taken for granted in all Baroque and Classical arias and ensembles, and most Romantic ones, Wagner would have called an "artificial" feature. The orchestra develops its own seductive motive more freely and more consistently than does the singer.

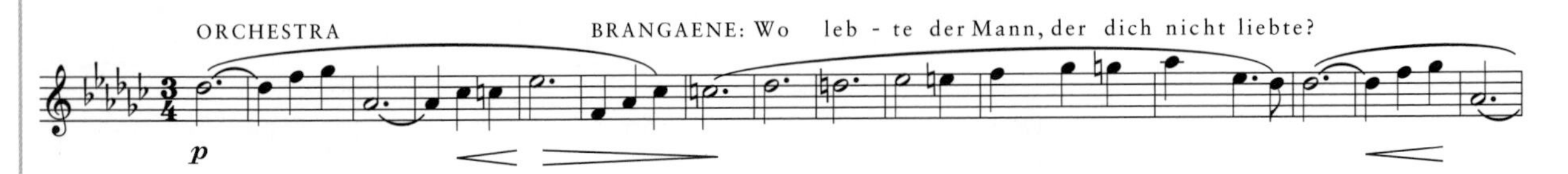

Dialogue Lowering her voice, and glancing meaningfully at Isolde, Brangaene asks her if she has forgotten the golden chest containing her mother's magic love potion. (Isolde's mother was a famous sorceress.) Here her singing line is like heightened recitative. In the orchestra the Love-Death Motive sounds three times, in a sequence, as in the Prelude. Through the orchestra, then, Brangaene is hinting about the love potion.

Isolde answers her by imitating or parodying her recitative: No, she has not forgotten her mother's magic; and the Love-Death Motive sounds again. But whatever Brangaene was hinting about, Isolde in her despair is thinking instead of the "death philter," a poison. She recalls a special philter that she marked for just such an occasion as this. At the thought (not even the mention!) of death, a sinister new Death Motive emerges in the trombones. And when Isolde actually *mentions* the death philter and Brangaene realizes that she means to kill herself, the orchestra practically explodes. A harsh, intense passage paints Brangaene's horror.

Wagner's time scale is often enormously slow, as we recall from the Prelude. He can, however, move fast enough when he chooses. Before Brangaene can fully absorb the enormity of the situation, she is cut off by a rousing sailors' sea chantey announcing that land is in sight—the Cornwall so hated and feared by Isolde. The women's moody talk is dramatically interrupted.

Kurvenal's Song Tristan's squire, Kurvenal, enters and tells them roughly to get ready for landing. Again, this passage for Kurvenal is not really a song or an aria. Exactly the same points can be made about it as about Brangaene's speech. Though Kurvenal's song is melodious enough, the main musical idea is an orchestral motive, not the singer's melody; no one will leave the theater humming Kurvenal's music. Yet its bluff accents characterize the man sharply, especially by comparison with the more sensitive, more impassioned women.

Isolde's suicide never takes place, of course. Brangaene switches the philters, and Isolde and Tristan drink the aphrodisiac, setting the opera's slow, inexorable action into motion.

Sept. 27 1878 R. *had a restless night, he dreamed of a clarinet that played by itself. . . . Toward the end of the evening, he sits down at the piano and plays* Tristan; *he does this so beautifully, in a way so far above the ordinary bounds of beauty, that I feel the sounds I am hearing will bless me when I die.*

From Cosima Wagner's diary

Web: *Research and test your understanding of Romantic opera at* **<bedfordstmartins.com/listen>.**

LISTEN Wagner, *Tristan und Isolde,* "Philter" Scene, from Act I

21-23

(Note: The English translation attempts to reproduce the "antique" quality of Wagner's poetry.)

Track				German	English	
			BRANGAENE'S SONG			
21		0:10	**Brangaene:**	Wo lebte der Mann, Der dich nicht liebte? Der Isolden säh' Und Isolden selig nicht ganz verging'? Doch, der dich erkoren, wär' er so kalt, Zög ihn von dir ein Zauber ab, Den Bösen wüsst' ich bald zu binden Ihn bannte der Minne Macht.	Where lives a man Who does not love you? Who sees you And sinks not into bondage blest? And, if any bound to you were cold, If any magic drew him from thee, I could soon draw the villain back And bind him in links of love.	ORCHESTRA  
			DIALOGUE		*(Secretly and confidentially)*	
22		1:26		Kennst du der Mutter Künste nicht? Wähnst du, die alles klug erwägt, Ohne Rath in fremdes Land Hätt' sie mit dir mich entsandt?	Mind'st thou not thy mother's arts? Do you think that she, the all-wise, Helpless in distant lands Would she have sent me with you?	Love-Death Motive, three times: 
	0:46	2:08	**Isolde:**	Der Mutter Rath gemahnt mich recht; Willkommen preis' ich ihre Kunst; Rache für den Verrath, Ruh' in der Noth dem Herzen! Den Schrein dort bring' mir her!	My mother's counsel I mind aright; And highly her magic arts I hold: Vengeance for treachery, Rest for the broken heart! Yon casket hither bear!	Love-Death Motive, three times: 
	1:34	2:56	**Brangaene:**	Er birgt was heil dir frommt,	It holds a balm for thee: *(Brings out a golden medicine chest)*	
				So reihte sie die Mutter, Die mächt'gen Zaubertränke: Für Weh' und Wunden Balsam hier, Für böse Gifte Gegengift; Den hehrsten Trank, ich halt' ihn hier.	Your mother filled it with The most potent magic philters; For pain and wounds there's salve, For poisons, antidotes; The noblest draught is this one— *(Takes out a flask)*	
	2:51	4:13	**Isolde:**	Du irrst, ich kenn' ihn besser; Ein starkes Zeichen schnitt ich ihm ein. Der Trank ist's, der mir taugt!	Not so, you err: I know a better; I made a mark to know it again: Here's the drink that will serve me! *(Seizes another flask)*	New, ominous motive–Death Motive TROMBONE
	3:26	4:48	**Brangaene:**	Der Todestrank!	The death philter! 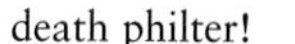	
	3:32	4:54	**Sailors** *(offstage):*	*Ho, he, am Untermast! Die Segel ein! Ho, he!*	*Ho, heave ho! Watch the lower mast! The mainsail in! Heave ho!*	*ff* Ho! he! ho! he!
			Isolde:	Das deute schnelle Fahrt. Weh' mir, Nahe das Land!	They tell of a swift journey; Woe's me! Near to the land!	
			KURVENAL'S SONG		*(Kurvenal enters, boisterous and insolent)*	
23		5:17	**Kurvenal:**	Auf, auf, ihr Frauen! Frisch und froh! Rasch gerüstet! Fertig nun, hurtig und flink! Und Frau Isolden, sollt' ich sagen Von Held Tristan, meinem Herrn: Vom Mast der Freude Flagge Sie wehe lustig ins Land; In Marke's Königschlosse Mach' sie ihr Nahen bekannt. Drum Frau Isolde bät' er eilen, Für's Land sich zu bereiten Dass er sie könnt' geleiten.	Up, up, ye ladies! Look lively, now! Bestir you! Be ready, and quick, prepare! Dame Isolde, I'm told to tell you, By Tristan our hero, my master: The mast is flying the joyful flag; It waveth landwards aloft; From King Mark's royal castle It makes our approach be seen. So, Dame Isolde, he bids you hasten For land to prepare you, So that he may there conduct you.	

CHAPTER 18

The Late Romantics

The year 1848 in Europe was a year of failed revolutions in France, Italy, and in various of the German states. Political freedom, which for the Romantics went hand in hand with freedom of personal expression in life and art, seemed further away than ever. While not all the early Romantics lived in free societies, at least by today's standards, freedom was an ideal they could take seriously as a hope for the future. We recall Beethoven's enthusiasm for Napoleon as a revolutionary hero, reflected in the *Eroica* Symphony of 1803, one of the landmarks of nineteenth-century music. In the 1820s, artists and intellectuals thrilled to the personal role of one of them—Lord Byron, a poet—in the struggle for Greek independence. Then they lamented his death near the field of battle.

But the failure of the revolutions of 1848 symbolized the failure of so many Romantic aspirations. In truth, those aspirations had had little to nourish them since the days of Napoleon. Romanticism lived on, but it lived on as nostalgia.

The year 1848 is also a convenient one to demarcate the history of nineteenth-century music. Some of the greatest early Romantic composers—Mendelssohn, Chopin, and Schumann—died between the years 1847and 1856. By a remarkable coincidence of history, too, the 1848 revolution transformed the career of Richard Wagner. Exiled from Germany for revolutionary activity, he had no opera house to compose for. Instead he turned inward and—after a long period of philosophical and musical reflection—worked out his revolutionary musical ideas. Wagner's music dramas, written from the 1850s on, came to dominate the imagination of musicians in the second part of the century, much as Beethoven's symphonies had in the first part.

Romanticism and Realism

European literature and art from the 1850s on was marked not by continuing Romanticism, but by realism. The novel, the principal literary form of the time, grew more realistic from Dickens to Trollope and George Eliot in Britain, and from Balzac to Flaubert and Zola in France. In French painting, there was an important realistic school led by Gustave Courbet. Thomas Eakins was a realist painter in America; William Dean Howells was our leading realist novelist.

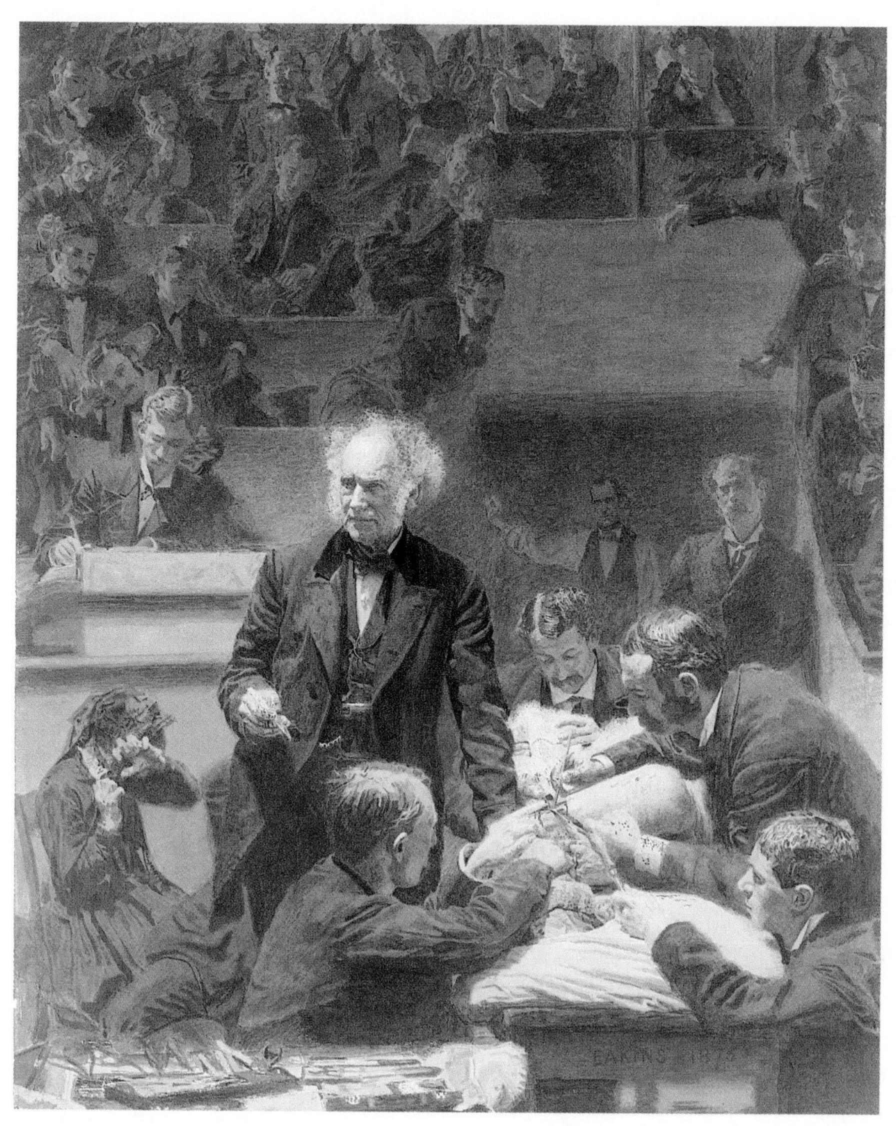

Realists in the arts of the nineteenth century tended toward glum or grim subject matter. The Philadelphia artist Thomas Eakins was so fascinated by surgery that he painted himself in among the students attending a class by a famous medical professor, Dr. S. D. Gross *(The Gross Clinic,* 1875).

Even more important as regards realism in the visual arts, no doubt, was that powerful new invention, the camera.

There was a move toward realism in opera at the end of the nineteenth century, in France as well as in Italy. On the other hand, the myth-drenched music dramas of Wagner were as unrealistic as could be. And what would "realism" in orchestral music be like? Given music's nature, it was perhaps inevitable that late nineteenth-century music assumed a sort of inspirational and emotional escape function—an escape from political, economic, and social situations that were not romantic in the least.

Perhaps, too, music serves a similar function for many listeners of the late twentieth century. Significantly, concert life as we know it today, with its emphasis on great masterpieces of the past, was formed for the first time in the late nineteenth century.

1 Late Romantic Program Music

Late Romantic program music took its impetus from an important series of works called "symphonic poems," composed in the 1850s by Franz Liszt. A **symphonic poem** is a one-movement orchestral composition with a program, in a free musical form. By using the word "poem," Liszt insisted on the music's programmatic nature.

It is not often that a great virtuoso pianist such as Liszt, who started out composing études and other miniatures of the kind cultivated by Chopin and Schumann, turns himself into a major composer of large-scale orchestral works. Liszt's formula was simply to write a one-movement piece for orchestra associated in one way or another with a famous poem, play, or narrative poem. Though obviously inspired by the earlier genres of program music (see page 262), Liszt departed from them in musical form, as well as in style. Unlike a Berlioz program symphony, a symphonic poem was in one movement. Unlike a Mendelssohn concert overture, it was not written in sonata form or some clear derivation of sonata form. Although the term failed to gain universal acceptance, symphonic poems under that or some other name became very popular in the later nineteenth century.

Among Liszt's symphonic poems are *Hamlet, Orpheus, Prometheus,* and *Les Préludes,* the latter loosely connected with a poem by the French Romantic poet Alphonse de Lamartine. But except for *Les Préludes,* these works are heard less often today than other symphonic poems written by composers influenced by Liszt's example. The most popular of later symphonic poems are those by Pyotr Ilyich Chaikovsky and Richard Strauss (see page 353).

PYOTR ILYICH CHAIKOVSKY
Overture-Fantasy, *Romeo and Juliet* (1869, revised 1880)

Chaikovsky wrote several symphonic poems, including one on a subject already used by Liszt and Berlioz, Shakespeare's *Hamlet.* Rather than "symphonic poem," he preferred the descriptions "symphonic fantasia" or "overture-fantasy" for these works. They are lengthy pieces in one movement, with free forms adopting some features from sonata form, rondo, and so on.

In his *Romeo and Juliet,* Chaikovsky followed the outlines of the original play only in a very general way, but one can easily identify his main themes with elements in Shakespeare's drama. The surging, romantic string melody clearly stands for the love of Romeo and Juliet. The angry, agitated theme suggests the vendetta between their families, the Capulets and the Montagues. More generally, it suggests the fate that dooms the two "star-cross'd lovers," as Shakespeare calls them. The hymnlike theme heard at the very beginning of the piece (later it sounds more marchlike) seems to denote the kindly Friar Laurence, who devises a plan to help the lovers that goes fatally wrong.

The kernel of a new work usually appears suddenly, in the most unexpected fashion . . . All the rest takes care of itself. I could never put into words the joy that seizes me when the main idea has come and when it begins to assume definite shape. You forget everything, you become a madman for all practical purposes, your insides quiver . . .

Chaikovsky writes to Mme. von Meck about his composing, 1878

Slow Introduction The slow introduction of *Romeo and Juliet* is already heavy with drama. As low clarinets and bassoons play the sober Hymn theme, the strings answer with an anguished-sounding passage forecasting an unhappy outcome. The wind instruments utter a series of solemn announcements, interspersed by strumming on the harp, as though someone (Friar Laurence?) was preparing to tell the tale. This sequence of events is repeated, with some variation, and then both the woodwind and string themes are briefly worked up to a climax over a dramatic drum roll.

Pyotr Ilyich Chaikovsky (1840–1893)

The composer's name is usually spelled Tchaikovsky, but it is time to retire this French spelling, which exists only because "ch" sounds like "sh" in that language. We spell it "ch," as in Chekhov the author, Chernobyl the nuclear site, Chomsky the linguist, etc.

Chaikovsky was born in the Russian countryside, the son of a mining inspector, but the family moved to St. Petersburg when he was eight. In nineteenth-century Russia, a serious musical education and a musical career were not accorded the social approval they received in Germany, France, or Italy. Many of the famous Russian composers began in other careers and only turned to music in their mature years, when driven by inner necessity.

Chaikovsky was fortunate in this respect, for after working as a government clerk for only a few years, he was able to enter the brand-new St. Petersburg Conservatory, founded by another Russian composer, Anton Rubinstein. At the age of twenty-six he was made a professor at the Moscow Conservatory. Once Chaikovsky got started, after abandoning the civil service, he composed prolifically—six symphonies, eleven operas, symphonic poems, chamber music, songs, and some of the most famous of all ballet scores: *Swan Lake, Sleeping Beauty,* and *The Nutcracker.*

Though his pieces may sometimes sound "Russian" to us, he was not a devoted nationalist like some other major Russian composers of the time (see page 295). Of all the nineteenth-century Russian composers, indeed, Chaikovsky had the greatest success in concert halls around the world. His famous Piano Concerto No. 1 was premiered in 1875 in Boston, and he toured America as a conductor in 1891.

Chaikovsky was a depressive personality who more than once attempted suicide. He had been an extremely delicate and hypersensitive child, and as an adult he worried that his homosexuality would be discovered and exposed. In an attempt to raise himself above suspicion, he married a highly unstable young musician who was in love with him. The marriage was a fiasco; in a matter of weeks, Chaikovsky fled and never saw his wife again. She died in an asylum.

For many years Chaikovsky was subsidized by a remarkable woman, Nadezhda von Meck, a wealthy widow and a recluse. She not only commissioned compositions from him but actually granted him an annuity. By mutual agreement, they never met; nevertheless, they exchanged letters regularly over the thirteen years of their friendship. This strange arrangement was terminated, without explanation, by Madame von Meck.

By this time Chaikovsky's position was assured, and his music widely admired. By a tragic mishap, he died after drinking unboiled water during a cholera epidemic.

Chief Works: Symphonies No. 4, 5, and 6 *(Pathétique);* Violin Concerto; piano concertos ▪ Operas: *The Queen of Spades* and *Eugene Onegin,* based on works by the Russian Romantic poet Aleksandr Pushkin ▪ Symphonic poems: *Romeo and Juliet, Hamlet, Francesca da Rimini, Overture 1812* (about Napoleon's retreat from Russia in that year) ▪ Ballet scores: *Swan Lake, Sleeping Beauty, The Nutcracker*

Encore: After *Romeo and Juliet,* listen to the *Nutcracker* Suite; Symphony No. 4; Violin Concerto.

Allegro The tempo changes to allegro, and we hear the Vendetta or Fate theme. It is made up of a number of short, vigorous rhythmic motives, which Chaikovsky at once begins to develop. Then the Vendetta theme returns in a climax punctuated by cymbal claps.

The highly romantic Love theme (illustrated on page 243) is first played only in part, by the English horn and violas—a mellow sound. It is halted by a curious but affecting passage built out of a little sighing figure:

The Love theme, now played at full length by the French horn, is made doubly emotional by a new two-note accompaniment derived from the sighing motive (marked with a bracket above).

A famous Juliet of Chaikovsky's time: Mrs. Patrick Campbell in an 1895 London production of Shakespeare's play.

After the Love theme dies down at some length, a lively development section begins (a feature suggesting sonata form). Confronted by various motives from the Vendetta theme, the Hymn theme takes on a marchlike character. We may get the impression of a battle between the forces of good and evil.

The Vendetta theme returns in its original form (suggesting a sonata-form recapitulation). The sighing motive and the lengthy Love theme also return, but the end of the latter is now broken up and interrupted—a clear reference to the tragic outcome of the drama. At one last appearance, the Vendetta theme is joined more explicitly than before with the Hymn theme.

Coda (slow) A fragment of the Love theme appears in a broken version over funeral drum taps in the timpani. This seems to depict the pathos of Romeo's final speeches, where he refers to his love before taking poison. A new, slow theme in the woodwinds is really a transformation of the sighing motive heard earlier.

But the mood is not entirely gloomy; as the harp strumming is resumed, the storyteller seems to derive solace and inspiration from his tale. Parts of the Love theme return for the last time in a beautiful new cadential version, surging enthusiastically upward in a way that is very typical of Chaikovsky. Doesn't this ecstatic surge suggest that even though Romeo and Juliet are dead, their love is timeless—that their love transcends death? The influence of Wagner's *Tristan und Isolde* was felt here as everywhere in the later nineteenth century.

2 Nationalism

One legacy of Romanticism's passion for freedom played itself out all through the nineteenth century: the struggle for national independence. The Greeks struggled against the Turks, the Poles rose up against Russia, the Czechs revolted against Austria, and Norway broke free of Sweden.

As people all over Europe became more conscious of their national character, they also came to prize their distinctive artistic heritages more and more.

LISTENING CHART 20

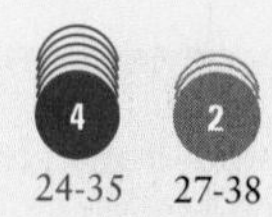

Chaikovsky, Overture-Fantasy, *Romeo and Juliet*

18 min., 39 sec.

Track	Time	Section	Description
		INTRODUCTION (Andante)	
24 27	0:00	Hymn theme	Low woodwinds, *pp*
	0:34	String motives	Anguished quality; contrapuntal
	1:26	Strumming harp	With "announcements" in the high woodwinds
25 28	2:07	Hymn theme	High woodwinds with pizzicato strings. Followed by the string motives and harp; the "announcements" are now in the strings.
1:50	3:57	Buildup	Ends with drum roll, *f*
26 29	4:32	Preparation	Prepares for the main section; *p*, then *crescendo*
		MAIN SECTION (Allegro)	
27 30	5:01	Vendetta theme	Full orchestra, *f*
0:22	5:23		Development of the Vendetta theme; contrapuntal
0:46	5:47		Reaches a climax: cymbals
0:58	5:59	Vendetta theme	Full orchestra, *ff*
1:17	6:18		Relaxes, in a long slowdown
1:57	6:58		Prefatory statement of Love theme (English horn): phrase **a**
28 31	7:13		"Sighing" theme; muted strings, *pp*
29 32	7:52	Love theme	Form is **a b a**, in woodwinds, with the sighing motive played by the French horn.
0:58	8:50		Harp. Cadences; the music dies down and nearly stops.
30 33		**DEVELOPMENT**	
	9:53	Developmental combination	Vendetta theme fragments are combined with the Hymn theme, which now sounds more like a march than a hymn.
31 34	11:07		This works up to a climax, marked by a cymbal clash.
0:23	11:30	Hymn theme	Played by trumpets; syncopated rhythm in the cymbals
32 35		**FREE RECAPITULATION (abbreviated)**	
	11:58	Vendetta theme	Full orchestra, *ff*
0:22	12:20		Sighing theme
1:00	12:58	Love theme	**a b a**; ecstatically in the strings, with the sighing motive again in the French horn; the last **a** is *ff*.
33 36	14:01		Fragments of the Love theme
0:25	14:26	(Love theme)	Sounds like another ecstatic statement, but is interrupted.
0:35	14:36		Interruption by the Vendetta theme: conflict! Cymbals
0:49	14:50	Developmental combination	Vendetta theme fragments combined with the Hymn theme Builds up to *fff*
1:21	15:22		Then dies down, rather unwillingly; ends on drum roll, *f*
34 37		**CODA (Moderato)**	
	15:59	Love theme	A broken version of the Love theme, with muffled funeral drums. The music seems to be ending.
35 38	16:37	New theme	Woodwinds; ends with a transformation of the sighing motive
1:05	17:43	Love theme	Section **a** in a slow cadential "transcendent" version. The strumming harp of the slow introduction has returned.
1:40	18:17		Final cadences; a drum roll and solemn ending gestures

CYMBALS

Nationalism: Finnish myths inspired both the composer Jean Sibelius and his compatriot the painter Akseli Gallen-Kallela. The wounded hero Lemminkaïnen is tended by his mother, who sends bees to fetch a healing balm from a magic fountain.

This gave rise to a musical movement, **nationalism** in music. The characteristic feature of this movement is simply the incorporation of national folk music into concert pieces, songs, and operas. Symphonic poems or operas were based on programs or librettos that took up national themes—a hero of history such as Russia's Prince Igor; a national literary treasure such as the Finnish Lemminkaïnen legends; or a beloved river such as the Vltava (Moldau) in Bohemia. Such national themes were reinforced by actual musical themes taken from folk song. The result was music that stirred strong emotions at home, and often made an effective ambassador abroad.

The art of music is above all other arts the expression of the soul of a nation. The composer must love the tunes of his country and they must become an integral part of him.

Nationalist composer Ralph Vaughan Williams

Although in the nineteenth century political nationalism was certainly a major factor all over Europe, composers in Germany, Italy, and France are not categorized with the musical nationalists. For musical nationalism also strove to make local music independent of Europe's traditional cultural leaders. Nationalist composers often deliberately broke the traditional rules of harmony, form, and so on. They did this both in a spirit of defiance and also in an effort to develop new, genuinely local musical styles.

Exoticism

Audiences came to enjoy hearing folk music at symphony concerts, whether it was their own folk music or somebody else's. We have seen that Verdi wrote Egyptian music, in the priest's hymn in *Aida*. French composers wrote Spanish music, Russians wrote Italian music, and Czechs wrote American music (George Bizet's opera *Carmen*, Chaikovsky's orchestra piece *Capriccio Italien*, and Antonín Dvořák's famous *New World* Symphony, with its reference to spirituals). Such music cannot be called nationalistic, since its aim was not national self-definition. Perhaps the best name for it is "exotic."

Yet even this nonpolitical, exotic music had the effect of emphasizing the unique qualities of nations. In the later nineteenth century, Romantic individuality had become a national ideal as much as a personal one.

Modest Musorgsky (1839–1881)

Musorgsky (pronounced MOO-sorgsky) was the son of a well-to-do landowner. The social class into which he was born dictated that he become an officer in the Russian Imperial Guard. Musorgsky duly went to cadet school and joined a regiment after graduation, but he could not long ignore his deep-seated desire to become a composer.

In the meantime, the emancipation of the serfs and other political-economic changes in Russia caused the liquidation of his family estate. For a time Musorgsky tried to help run the family affairs, but in his twenties he was obliged to work at a clerical job. Meanwhile, he experimented with musical composition, struggling to master the technique of an art that he had come to late in life. It was around this time that he joined the circle of Russian nationalist composers that was dubbed the *kuchka* (the Group).

Musorgsky never felt secure in his technique, and relied on his skillful *kuchka* friend, Nikolai Rimsky-Korsakov, to criticize his work. But his intense nationalism formed his vision of what he wanted his work to be—truly Russian music. His masterpiece, the opera *Boris Godunov,* is based on the story of the sixteenth-century tsar as told by the great Russian poet Alexander Pushkin. It hardly had the success it deserved when it was finally revised and put on in St. Petersburg. Indeed, this and other works by Musorgsky only succeeded some time later, after their orchestration had been touched up (some say glamorized) by Rimsky-Korsakov.

Musorgsky led a rather grim life; his was a personality filled with doubts, and his instability was a constant concern to his friends. He became an alcoholic early in life. Musorgsky died of alcoholism and epilepsy in an army hospital at the age of forty-two.

Chief Works: Operas: *Boris Godunov* and *Khovanschina* ▪ Orchestral program compositions: *Pictures at an Exhibition* (originally for piano) and *Night on Bald Mountain* ▪ Songs, including the very impressive song cycles *The Nursery* and *Songs and Dances of Death*

Encore: After *Pictures,* listen to *Boris Godunov,* Coronation Scene (scene ii).

The Russian *Kuchka*

A close group of five Russian nationalist composers were nicknamed (by one of their critic friends) the *kuchka*—sometimes translated as the "Mighty Five," but actually meaning a group or clique. They were an interesting and exceptionally talented group—even though they included only one trained musician, Mily Balakirev (1837–1910). Alexander Borodin (1833–1887) was a distinguished chemist, César Cui (1835–1918) an engineer, Nikolai Rimsky-Korsakov (1844–1908) a navy man, and Modest Musorgsky (1839–1881) an officer in the Russian Imperial Guard.

What held this group together were their determination to make Russian music "Russian," their deep interest in collecting folk song, and their commitment to self-improvement as composers, relatively late in life.

MODEST MUSORGSKY
Pictures at an Exhibition (1874)

1-4

1-4

The title of this interesting work refers to a memorial exhibit of pictures by a friend of Musorgsky's who had recently died, the Russian painter Victor Hartmann. Like Musorgsky, Hartmann cared deeply about getting Russian themes into his work. *Pictures at an Exhibition* was originally written for piano solo, as a series of piano miniatures joined in a set, like Robert Schumann's *Carnaval.* In 1922 the set was orchestrated by the French composer Maurice Ravel, and this is the form in which it has since become popular.

Promenade [1] To provide some overall thread or unity to a set of ten different musical pieces, Musorgsky hit upon a plan that is as simple and effective as it is ingenious. The first number, "Promenade," does not refer to a picture, but depicts the composer strolling around the picture gallery. The same music returns several times in free variations, to show the promenader's changes of mood as he contemplates Hartmann's varied works.

The promenade theme recalls a Russian folk song:

Ravel orchestrated this forceful theme first for brass instruments, later for woodwinds and strings. Quintuple meter (**5/4:** measures 1, 3, and 5) is a distinct rarity, and having this meter alternate with **6/4** (measures 2, 4, and 6) rarer still. The metrical anomaly gives the impression of blunt, unsophisticated folk music—and perhaps also of walking back and forth without any particular destination, as one does in a gallery.

Gnomus "Gnomus" is a drawing of a Russian folk-art nutcracker. The gnome's heavy jaws crack the nut when his legs (the handles) are pulled together; the same grotesque figure, which could frighten a little child, comes to life and dances in Chaikovsky's well-known Christmas ballet *The Nutcracker.* Musorgsky writes music that sounds suitably macabre, with a lurching rhythm to illustrate the gnome's clumsy walk on his handle-legs, and striking dissonant harmonies.

The lurching rhythms and dissonance of "Gnomus" and the **5/4** meter of "Promenade" are among the features of Musorgsky's music that break with the norms of traditional European art music, in a self-consciously nationalistic spirit.

Promenade [2] Quieter now, the promenade music suggests that the spectator is musing as he moves along . . . and we can exercise our stroller's prerogative and skip past a number of Hartmann's pictures, pictures that are not nationalistic in a Russian sense. Some do refer to other peoples, and Musorgsky follows suit, writing music we would call "exotic": "Bydlo," which is the name of a Polish cattle-cart, and "Il Vecchio Castello," Hartmann's Italian title for a conventional painting of a medieval castle, complete with a troubadour serenading his lady.

The Great Gate at Kiev The last and longest number is also the climactic one. It illustrates—or, rather, spins a fantasy inspired by—a fabulous architectural design by Hartmann that was never executed.

Musorgsky summons up in the imagination a solemn procession with clashing cymbals, clanging bells, and chanting Russian priests. The Promenade theme is now at last incorporated into one of the musical "pictures"; the promenader himself has become a part of it and has joined the inspiring parade. In addition, two real Russian melodies appear:

The ending is very grandiose, for grandiosity forms an integral part of the national self-image of Russia—and, unfortunately, of many other nations.

The Great Gate at Kiev

Other Nationalists

Nationalism enjoyed new life after the turn of the century. Some of the most impressive nationalists were also among the earliest modernists, among them Béla Bartók in Hungary and Charles Ives in the United States. We shall examine this "new nationalism" in Chapters 20 and 21, restricting ourselves here to a listing of some of the main nationalists outside of Russia.

Bohemia Bohemia, as the Czech Republic was then called, produced two eminent national composers: Bedřich Smetana (1824–1884), who wrote the symphonic poem *Vltava* (The Moldau) and the delightful folk opera *The Bartered Bride,* and Antonín Dvořák (1841–1904), composer of the popular *Slavonic Dances* as well as important symphonies and other large-scale works.

Scandinavia The Norwegian composer Edvard Grieg (1843–1907) wrote sets of piano miniatures with titles such as *Norwegian Mountain Tunes,* which were very popular at the time; also a well-known suite of music for *Peer Gynt,* the great drama by the Norwegian playwright Henrik Ibsen.

Jean Sibelius (1865–1957), a powerful late-Romantic symphonist, produced a series of symphonic poems on the folklore of his native Finland: *The Swan of Tuonela, Finlandia,* and others.

Spain Among Spanish nationalists were Enrique Granados (1867–1916), Joaquín Turina (1882–1949), and Manuel de Falla (1876–1946), best known for his *Nights in the Gardens of Spain* for piano and orchestra. Spain was a favorite locale for "exotic" composition with a Spanish flavor written by Frenchmen—among them Bizet's opera *Carmen* and orchestral pieces by Emmanuel Chabrier *(España),* Claude Debussy *(Iberia),* and Maurice Ravel *(Boléro).*

Great Britain The major English nationalist in music was Ralph Vaughan Williams (1872–1958). His *Fantasia on a Theme by Thomas Tallis* is a loving meditation on a psalm tune that was written by a major composer from Britain's national heritage at the time of Queen Elizabeth I.

Less well known is Irish composer Sir Charles Villiers Stanford (1852–1924), who wrote *Irish Ballads* for orchestra and the opera *Shamus O'Brien.*

Johannes Brahms (1833–1897)

The son of an orchestral musician in Hamburg, Brahms was given piano lessons at an early age. By the time he was seven, he was studying with one of Hamburg's finest music teachers. A little later he was playing the piano at dockside taverns and writing popular tunes.

A turning point in Brahms's life came at the age of twenty when he met Robert and Clara Schumann. These two eminent musicians befriended and encouraged the young man and took him into their household. Robert wrote an enthusiastic article praising his music. But soon afterward, Schumann was committed to an insane asylum—a time during which Brahms and Clara (who was fourteen years his senior) became very close. In later life Brahms always sent Clara his compositions to get her comments.

With another musician friend, Joseph Joachim, who was to become one of the great violinists of his time, the young Brahms signed a foolish manifesto condemning the advanced music of Liszt and Wagner. Thereafter he passed an uneventful bachelor existence, steadily turning out music—chamber music, songs, and piano pieces, but no program music or operas. Indeed, he was forty-three before his first symphony appeared, many years after its beginnings at his desk; it seemed that he was hesitating to invoke comparison with Beethoven, whose symphonies constituted a standard for the genre. In fact, this symphony's last movement contains a near-quotation from Beethoven's Ninth Symphony that is more like a challenge. When people pointed out the similarity, Brahms snarled, "Any jackass can see that," implying that it was the differences between the two works that mattered, not their superficial similarities.

Brahms would eventually write four symphonies, all harking back to forms used by Beethoven and even Bach, but thoroughly Romantic in their expressive effect.

For a time Brahms conducted a chorus, and he wrote much choral music, including *A German Requiem,* a setting of sober texts from the Bible. As a conductor, he indulged his traditionalism by reviving music of Bach and even earlier composers, but he also enjoyed the popular music of his day. He wrote waltzes (Johann Strauss, the "Waltz King," was a valued friend), folk song arrangements, and the well-known *Hungarian Dances.*

Chief Works: Four symphonies, *Tragic* Overture, and a rather comical *Academic Festival* Overture ▪ Violin concerto and two piano concertos ▪ Much chamber music, including a beautiful quintet for clarinet and strings, a trio for French horn, violin, and piano, as well as string quartets, quintets, and sextets ▪ Piano music and many songs ▪ Choral music, including *A German Requiem* and *Alto Rhapsody* ▪ Waltzes, *Hungarian Dances*

Encore: After the Violin Concerto, listen to the Clarinet Quintet; Symphony No. 3.

3 Responses to Romanticism

At the beginning of this chapter, we remarked that European art and literature after the 1850s were marked not by continuing Romanticism, but by realism, which was in fact a reaction against Romanticism. In music, an art that can hardly be realistic in the usual sense, the anti-Romantic reaction came later—at a time when realism was no longer an ideal in the other arts.

After 1850, music continued to develop along Romantic lines, but it seemed oddly out of phase with a no-nonsense world increasingly devoted to industrialization and commerce. In the world of Victorian morality, people devoted to the work ethic denied themselves and others the heady emotion that the Romantics had insisted on conveying in their art. There is probably some truth to the contention that late nineteenth-century music assumed the function of a sort of never-never land of feeling. Music was an emotional fantasy-world for a society that placed a premium on the suppression of feeling in real life.

The work of the two greatest late nineteenth-century German composers can be viewed in terms of their responses to this situation. Johannes Brahms, a devoted young friend of Robert Schumann, one of the most Romantic of composers, nonetheless turned back to the Classicism of the Viennese masters.

Evidently he saw this as a way of tempering the unbridled emotionalism of Romanticism, which he expressed only in a mood of restraint and resignation.

A younger man, Gustav Mahler, reacted differently. Lament was his mode, rather than resignation; his music expresses an intense, bittersweet nostalgia for a Romanticism that seems to have lost its innocence, even its credibility. The lament for this loss is almost clamorous in Mahler's songs and symphonies.

The Renewal of Classicism: Brahms

Born in the dour industrial port city of Hamburg, Johannes Brahms gravitated to Vienna, the city of Haydn, Mozart, and Beethoven. The move seems symbolic. For Brahms rejected many of the innovations of the early Romantics and went back to Classical genres, forms, and, to some extent, even Classical style.

Brahms, without giving up on beauty and emotion, proved to be a progressive in a field that had not been cultivated in half a century [i.e., the Classical tradition]. He would have been a pioneer if he had simply returned to Mozart. But he did not live on inherited wealth; he made a fortune of his own.

Modernist composer Arnold Schoenberg, 1947

Brahms devoted his major effort to traditional genres such as string quartets and other chamber music works, symphonies, and concertos. In these works, he employed and indeed found new life in the Classical forms—sonata form, theme and variations, and rondo. The only typical Romantic genre he cultivated was the "miniature"—the lied and the characteristic piano piece; he never contemplated "grandiose" works such as philosophical program symphonies or mythological operas. Almost alone among the important composers of his time, he made no special effort to pioneer new harmonies or tone colors.

What impels a great composer—and Brahms *was* a great composer, not a timid traditionalist—to turn back the clock in this way? One can only speculate that he could not find it in himself to copy or continue the enthusiastic, open-ended striving of the early Romantics. In the late nineteenth century, this type of response no longer rang true, and Brahms recognized it.

On the other hand, the nobility and power of Beethoven inspired him with a lifelong model. Seen in this way, Brahms's effort was a heroic one: to temper the new richness and variety of Romantic emotion with the traditional strength and poise of Classicism.

Violinist Joseph Joachim, for whom Brahms wrote his Violin Concerto, playing with another Brahms friend, Clara Schumann (see page 257).

JOHANNES BRAHMS
Violin Concerto in D, Op. 77 (1878)

Concertos are always written to show off great virtuosos—who are often the composers themselves, as with Mozart, Chopin, and Liszt. Brahms wrote his one violin concerto for a close friend, Joseph Joachim, a leading violinist of the time and also a composer. Even this late in life—Brahms was then forty-five—he accepted advice about certain details of the composition from Joachim, and Joachim wrote the soloist's cadenza for the first movement.

We can appreciate Brahms's traditionalism as far as the Classical forms are concerned by referring to the standard movement plan for the Classical concerto, on page 201. Like Mozart, Brahms wrote his first movement in double-exposition sonata form; this must have seemed extremely stuffy to the many writers of Romantic concertos who had developed new and freer forms. Also, Brahms's last movement is a rondo—the most common Classical way to end a concerto. If it is a relatively simple movement, by Brahms's standards, that is because the last movements of Classical concertos were typically the lightest and least demanding on the listener.

Third Movement (Allegro giocoso, ma non troppo vivace) *Giocoso* means "jolly"; the first theme in this rondo, **A,** has a lilt recalling the spirited gypsy fiddling that was popular in nineteenth-century Vienna. Imitating gypsy music in this work and others counts as an "exotic" feature in Brahms's music (see page 294).

The solo violin plays the theme (and much else in the movement) in *double stops,* that is, in chords produced by bowing two violin strings simultaneously. Hard to do well, this makes a brilliant effect when done by a virtuoso.

The theme falls into a traditional **a a b a′** form; in Brahms's hands, however, this becomes something quite subtle. Since the second **a** is identical to the first,

Brahms was a serious man; this is one of the few pictures of him smiling. He is sketched with some bachelor friends at his favorite Vienna tavern, the Red Hedgehog.

LISTENING CHART 21

5

5-10

Brahms, Violin Concerto, third movement

Rondo. 7 min., 43 sec.

	Time	Section	Description
5	0:00	A (Tune)	The entire tune is presented.
	0:00	a	Solo violin, with double stops
	0:11	a	Orchestra
	0:22	b	Solo violin
	0:35	a′	Orchestra
	0:46		The solo violin begins the cadences ending the tune, which lead into a transition.
	1:05		Fast scales prepare for B.
6	1:14	B (Episode 1)	Melody (emphatic upward scale) in the violin, with inverted motive below it, in the orchestra
0:21	1:35		Melody in the orchestra, with inverted motive above it
0:36	1:50		Cadential passage (orchestra), *f*
7	2:00	A′	
	2:00	a	Solo
0:11	2:11	a″	Orchestra
0:20	2:20		Transition (orchestra and solo), *p*
8	2:38	C (Episode 2)	Lyrical tune (solo and orchestra), *p*
0:33	3:11		Expressive climactic section, solo
0:44	3:22		Orchestra interrupts, *f*.
0:48	3:26		Scales prepare for B.
0:57	3:35	B	
9	4:23	A″	Starts with b′ (solo)
0:20	4:43	a‴	In orchestra, extended; the real feeling of "return" comes only at this point.
0:45	5:08	Short cadenza	Solo, double stops again; orchestra soon enters.
1:02	5:25		Solo trills and scales; motive
1:31	5:54		Passage of preparation: motive in low French horns
10	6:09	Short cadenza	
0:11	6:20	Coda	Mostly in 6/8 time. Starts with a marchlike transformation of phrase a (solo), over a drum beat.
0:35	6:44		References to B
1:07	7:16		Final-sounding cadences
1:19	7:28		The music dies down and ends with three loud chords.

From Brahms's score of his Violin Concerto

except in instrumentation, the last **a** (**a′**) might be dull unless it were varied in an interesting way. Brahms extends it and yet also makes it compressed and exciting by free diminutions of the basic rhythmic figure:

Such "cross-rhythms"—**3/8** fitted in for a moment within **2/4**—are a characteristic fingerprint of Brahms's style. There are other examples in this movement.

The first rondo episode, **B,** a theme with a fine Romantic sweep about it, begins with an emphatic upward scale played by the solo violin (high double stops in octaves). This is answered by a *downward* scale in the orchestra in a lower range. When the orchestra has its turn to play **B,** timpani are added; the upward scale is transferred down to the low register, and the downward scale up to the high register.

The second rondo episode, **C,** involves another rhythmic change; this charming melody—which, however, soon evaporates—is in **3/4** time:

The coda presents a version of the **a** phrase of the main theme in **6/8** time, in a swinging march tempo. Again the timpani are prominent. Most of the transitions in this movement are rapid virtuoso scale passages by the soloist, who is also given two short cadenzas prior to the coda.

Romantic Nostalgia: Mahler

If, like Brahms, Gustav Mahler felt ambivalent about the Romantic tradition, he expressed this ambivalence very differently. He eagerly embraced all the excesses of Romanticism that Brahms had shrunk from, writing huge program symphonies (though he vacillated on the question of distributing the programs to his audiences) and symphonies with solo and choral singing. Mahler once said that a symphony is "an entire world." Again and again his works set out to encode seemingly profound metaphysical or spiritual messages.

Yet it would appear that Mahler felt unable to enter freely into this Romantic fantasy world. There is an uneasy quality to his music that sets it apart from other late Romantic music. For while we may feel that the emotion expressed in Chaikovsky's music, for example, is exaggerated, we do not feel that Chaikovsky himself thought so. Mahler's exaggeration, on the other hand, seems deliberate and self-conscious.

A symphony must be like the world, it must embrace everything.

Famous dictum of Gustav Mahler

Exaggeration spills over into another characteristic feature, distortion. Mahler tends to make more or less slight distortions of melody, motive, and harmony. Sometimes these distortions put a uniquely bittersweet touch on the musical material; sometimes they amount to all-out parody. The parody does not seem harsh, however, but affectionate, nostalgic, and ultimately melancholy. Distortion for Mahler was a way of acknowledging his inability—and the inability of his generation—to recapture the lost freshness of Romantic music.

Mahler's Symphony No. 8, called "Symphony of a Thousand," represents a peak in the nineteenth-century tradition of "grandiose" compositions (see page 247). One early performance (in Philadelphia) did indeed reach 1,069 orchestral players, chorus singers, and soloists.

To give an example: The slow movement of his Symphony No. 1 quotes the cheerful children's round, "Frère Jacques," strangely distorted so as to sound like a funeral march. Mahler explained that this march was inspired by a well-known nursery picture of the time, *The Huntsman's Funeral Procession,* showing forest animals shedding crocodile tears around the hearse of a hunter. But an innocent children's song was not distorted in this way in order to mock childhood or childish things. If anything, Mahler used it to lament his own lost innocence, and that of his time.

GUSTAV MAHLER
Symphony No. 1 (1888)

Mahler's first symphony started out as a symphonic poem in one movement, grew to a five-movement symphony, and was finally revised into four movements. As is also true of several of his other symphonies, Symphony No. 1 includes fragments from a number of earlier songs by Mahler, songs about lost love. The program that Mahler once published for the whole symphony, but then withdrew, concerns the disillusion and distress of disappointed love, ending with the hero pulling himself together again.

An important general feature of Mahler's style is a special kind of counterpoint closely tied up with his very individual style of orchestration. He picks instruments out of the orchestra to play momentary solos, which are heard in counterpoint with other lines played by other "solo" instruments. The changing combinations can create a fascinating kaleidoscopic effect, for the various bright strands are not made to blend, as in most Romantic orchestration, but rather to stand out in sharp contrast to one another.

The Huntsman's Funeral Procession, inspiration for the slow movement of Mahler's Symphony No. 1.

Third Movement (Feierlich und gemessen, ohne zu schleppen—"With a solemn, measured gait; do not hurry") This ironic funeral march is also a personal lament, for its trio is taken from an earlier song by Mahler about lost love. (Though the musical form of the movement is quite original, it is based on march and trio form, analogous to the Classical minuet and trio.)

Section 1 Mahler had the extraordinary idea of making his parody funeral march out of the French round "Frère Jacques," as we have said. He distorts the familiar tune by playing it in the minor mode at a slow tempo:

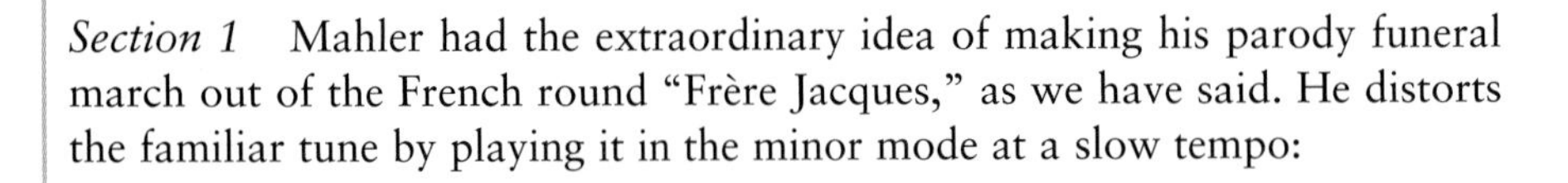

The mournful, monotonous drumbeat that accompanies the march is derived from the ending of the tune. (Note that Mahler slightly changed that ending of "Frère Jacques" as he transformed it into his march—he wanted only so much monotony.)

The slow march itself is played first by a single muted double bass playing in its high register—a bizarre, deliberately clumsy sonority. An additional figure that Mahler appends to his version of "Frère Jacques," played by the oboe, fits so naturally that we almost accept it as part of the traditional tune. The music dies out on the drumbeat figure (played by the harp), then on a single repeated note.

Section 2 This section is a study in frustration, as fragmentary dance-music phrases that sound distorted, parodistic, and even vulgar, give way to equally fragmentary recollections of the funeral march. One dance starts up in band instruments, with a faster beat provided by pizzicato strings; notice the exaggerated way in which its opening upbeat is slowed down. It is cut short by a new dance phrase—louder, more vulgar yet, scored with bass drum and cymbals. "With Parody," Mahler wrote on the score at this point:

This phrase, too, is cut short, and a varied repetition of the material introduced so far does not proceed much further. Instead, a long, grieving cadential passage is heard over the funeral-march drumbeat. Other fragments of "Frère Jacques" are recalled. Mourning gives way to utter exhaustion.

Section 3 A note of consolation is sounded by this contrasting "trio," beginning with warm major-mode sounds and a triplet accompaniment on the harp. (The funeral-march beat dissolves into a faster but gentler throb.) The melody introduced is the one that belonged originally to a nostalgic song about lost love. Played first by muted strings, then the oboe and solo violins, the song melody soon turns bittersweet.

The rhythm is halted by quiet but dramatic gong strokes. Flutes play a few strangely momentous new phrases, also taken from the song.

Section 4 The final section combines elements from both sections 1 and 2. Soon after the "Frère Jacques" round commences, in a strange key, a new counterpoint joins it in the trumpets—another parodistic, almost whining sound:

Mahler and his daughter: an informal photo.

Gustav Mahler (1860–1911)

Mahler's early life was not a happy one. Born in Bohemia to an abusive father, five of his brothers and sisters died of diphtheria, and others ended their lives in suicide or mental illness. The family lived near a military barracks, and the many marches incorporated into Mahler's music—often distorted marches—have been traced to his childhood recollections of parade music.

After studying for a time at the Vienna Conservatory, Mahler began a rising career as a conductor. His uncompromising standards and his authoritarian attitude toward the orchestra musicians led to frequent disputes with the authorities. What is more, Mahler was Jewish, and Vienna at that time was rife with anti-Semitism. Nonetheless, he was acknowledged as one of the great conductors of his day and also as a very effective musical administrator. After positions at Prague, Budapest, Hamburg, and elsewhere, he came to head such organizations as the Vienna Opera and the New York Philharmonic.

It was only in the summers that Mahler had time to compose, so it is not surprising that he produced fewer pieces (though they are very long pieces) than any other important composer. Ten symphonies, the last of them unfinished, and six song cycles for voice and orchestra are almost all he wrote. The song cycle *The Song of the Earth* of 1910, based on translated Chinese poems, is often called Mahler's greatest masterpiece.

He married a famous Viennese beauty, Alma Schindler, who after his death went on to marry the great architect Walter Gropius and later the novelist Franz Werfel and then wrote fascinating memoirs of her life with the composer. By a tragic irony, Gustav and Alma's young daughter died of scarlet fever shortly after Mahler had written his grim orchestral song cycle *Songs on the Death of Children.*

Mahler's life was clouded by psychological turmoil, and he once consulted his famous Viennese contemporary, Sigmund Freud. It has been said that his disputes with the New York Philharmonic directors, which discouraged him profoundly, may have contributed to his early death.

Chief Works: Ten lengthy symphonies, several with chorus, of which the best known are the First, Fourth, and Fifth ▪ Orchestral song cycles: *The Song of the Earth, Songs of a Wayfarer, The Youth's Magic Horn* (for piano or orchestra), *Songs on the Death of Children*

Encore: After Symphony No. 1, listen to the Adagietto from Symphony No. 5; *Songs of a Wayfarer.*

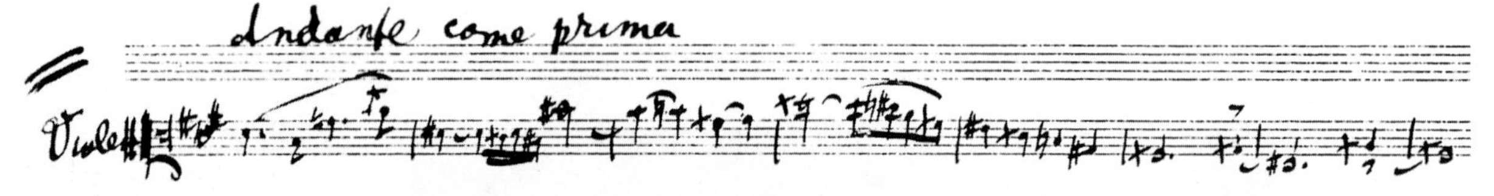

From the score Mahler was working on at his death—the unfinished Symphony No. 10.

One of the dance phrases from section 2 interrupts, picking up the tempo; and when "Frère Jacques" and the trumpet tune return, the tempo picks up even more for a wild moment of near chaos. But the mourning passage that ended section 2 returns, with its constant somber drumbeat. The movement ends after another series of gong strokes.

Web: *Research and test your understanding of late Romantic music at* **<bedfordstmartins.com/listen>.**

LISTENING CHART 22

11-18 5-12

Mahler, Symphony No. 1, third movement, Funeral March

10 min., 20 sec.

Track	Time		Description
	SECTION 1		
11 / 5	0:00	**Funeral March**	Drum beat, then four main entries of the round "Frère Jacques" (minor mode), which is the march theme.
	0:07		Entry 1: Double bass, muted
	0:28		Entry 2: Bassoon (a subsidiary entry follows: cellos)
	0:48		Entry 3: Tuba
	1:02		("Additional" fragment: oboe)
	1:15		Entry 4: Flute in low register
	1:35		("Additional" fragment). The march gradually dies away; the drum beat finally stops.
	SECTION 2		
12 / 6	2:09	**Dance-Band Phrases**	**a** Oboes, *p,* repeated (trumpets in counterpoint); pizzicato string beat
0:30	2:39		**b** Faster, ***mf;*** high (E-flat) clarinets, bass drum, and cymbals
13 / 7	2:53		**a** Strings, with varied repeat (trumpets in counterpoint)
0:31	3:24		**b′** With new continuation
0:48	3:41	**Conclusion**	Descending cadential passage, a little slower, based on **a**
1:19	4:12	**Return to Funeral-March Motives**	The funeral-march drumbeat, which entered during the previous passage, continues in the background. The march dies away; the drumbeat almost stops.
	SECTION 3		
2:00	4:53	**Trio (Song)**	The rhythm gradually picks up: a gentle triplet accompaniment with a throbbing background
14 / 8	5:09		A songlike melody starts in muted strings, then moves to the flute, two solo violins, clarinet, and oboe.
1:16	6:25		The trio dies away (violins).
15 / 9	6:43		Gong strokes
0:07	6:50		Flutes play two new phrases, as though waiting.
	SECTION 4		
16 / 10	7:02	**March**	Drumbeat, faster, in a new key: march ("Frère Jacques")
0:16	7:18		("Additional" fragment: E-flat clarinet, strings, flute)
17 / 11	7:36		March theme with new, parodistic counterpoint: trumpets
0:23	7:59		Dance-band phrase **b:** clarinets, cymbals, drums
18 / 12	8:17		March theme with new trumpet counterpoint; new sudden speedup: clarinets, ***ff***
0:19	8:36	**Conclusion**	Descending cadential passage, based on **a,** with drumbeat as in section 2; slower
1:21	9:38		("Additional" fragment, in low range: bassoon)
1:36	9:53		The music dies down; gong strokes

GLOBAL PERSPECTIVES 5

Musical Drama Worldwide

We saw earlier (page 56) that most religious traditions make substantial use of singing of one sort or another. Likewise, most traditions of drama worldwide do not consist of plain speech and little else, but instead incorporate chanting, singing, instrumental music, and dance. In this way they resemble the European opera we have studied and other kinds of Western drama, from ancient Greek tragedy and comedy to today's megamusicals on Broadway.

Perhaps, in fact, this connection of music and drama is related at a very deep level to the connection of singing and religion. Just as the heightening of prayer in song seems to give readier access to invisible divinity, so music seems somehow compatible with the illusory, real-and-yet-unreal enactment of actions and events onstage.

Whatever the reason, from the ancient beginnings of drama down to the present day, music has been joined with acting more often than not. The operatic notion of singing a play is more in line with world traditions than the purely spoken rendition of Shakespeare or Ibsen or Tom Stoppard. And where would the movies be without music?

Japanese Drama

Asia has developed particularly rich traditions of musical drama. These include the shadow plays of Indonesia, accompanied by gamelan music and relating stories from lengthy epic poems by means of the shadows of puppets cast on a screen (see page 215). In India, religious dance-dramas reach back hundreds of years. Today the main form of musical drama is on screen: Movie musicals are the staple of the huge and lucrative Indian film industry. China, meanwhile, offers hundreds of regional styles of music theater, the most famous of which, Beijing (or Peking) opera, we will study on page 310.

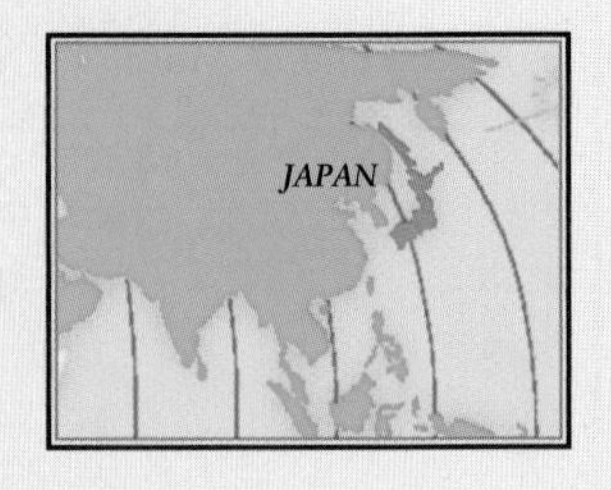

In Japan, the main traditions of musical drama are these:

- **Noh** dramas emerged in the fourteenth and fifteenth centuries and were particularly prized in the elite shogun and samurai culture of the time. Noh dramas are steeped in Zen Buddhist philosophy. Their stage action consists of highly restrained, stylized, and symbolic gestures and movements. They involve singing (both by the actors and a chorus), dance, and complex, carefully predetermined instrumental accompaniment by a strictly limited ensemble: three percussion players and a flutist.
- **Bunraku** (bóon-ráh-koo) is a puppet theater, like the Indonesian shadow plays, but instead of casting shadows on a screen, large puppets are skillfully manipulated onstage, each by three puppeteers. Meanwhile one singer

Inside a kabuki theater, c. 1745

provides narration and the different voices for each of the puppets. He is accompanied by a single three-stringed Japanese lute called *shamisen* (shah-mée-sen).

Kabuki (kah-bóo-kee) theater arose in the seventeenth century and adopted features from both noh and bunraku. Kabuki played to an audience different from the samurai class that prized noh. It used more modern stories and appealed to a new public made up of members of the urban merchant class that was emerging in Japan at this time. In a strikingly similar way, Baroque opera in Europe evolved from its aristocratic origins to become a cherished entertainment of new, upper-middle-class audiences (see page 98).

Kabuki. Behind the elaborately costumed actors are the stage musicians: the four noh players (lower row) and the chorus and shamisen players (upper row).

Performing Kabuki Theater Kabuki was first performed by women and young boys, but before long both of these types of performance were banned because of their associations with prostitution. Until recently, only men sang kabuki. Female roles were played by special female impersonators.

The musical forces in kabuki are particularly complex. In addition to the singing actors, they can involve three other musical groups. Onstage, the main group sits behind the actors and accompanies their dialogue and dances. This group consists of a chorus, a number of shamisen players, and the three percussionists and flute player of the noh orchestra.

A second orchestra is hidden in a room to the left of the stage. Its makeup is variable, and it performs many functions. It can create musical sound effects, provide appropriate "mood" music and musical interludes, accompany certain onstage actions, and even suggest unspoken thoughts of the actors onstage.

Finally, the singer-narrator and shamisen player of bunraku may also be present. They sit to the right of the stage.

Nagauta Music from **Dojoji** The most famous genre of music involved in kabuki is the **nagauta** (náh-gah-óo-ta), or "long song," which usually accompanies dance. It is an extended piece for a singer (or singers in unison) and the onstage orchestra of shamisens, percussion, and flute. Sometimes the offstage orchestra takes part too.

We hear part of a nagauta from the kabuki play *Dojoji*. The singer and shamisens carry the main melody in a free and complex heterophony—you will hear the voice lagging behind or running ahead of the same pitches played by the shamisens. The flute contributes either its own version of the main melody or, in the most striking fashion, an independent melody in the style of noh music that is often not even in the same tonality as the main melody.

Meanwhile the drummers play either rhythmic patterns synchronized with the shamisens and voice or independent, "out-of-sync" patterns, derived from noh music.

LISTEN

Nagauta Music from the Kabuki Play *Dojoji* 3 min., 30 sec.

44

0:02	Part 1	Instrumental: shamisens play the main melody, accompanied by drums and a bell-like gong. Flute plays an independent melody. Exclamations by percussionists can also be heard.
0:55	Part 2	Main melody in heterophony (singer, shamisens, flute), supported by percussion
1:55	Part 3	Singer pauses; main melody in shamisens and flute
2:12	Part 4	Main melody (singer, shamisens); flute plays independent melody.
3:07	Part 5	Free heterophony for singer and shamisen alone

Chinese Opera

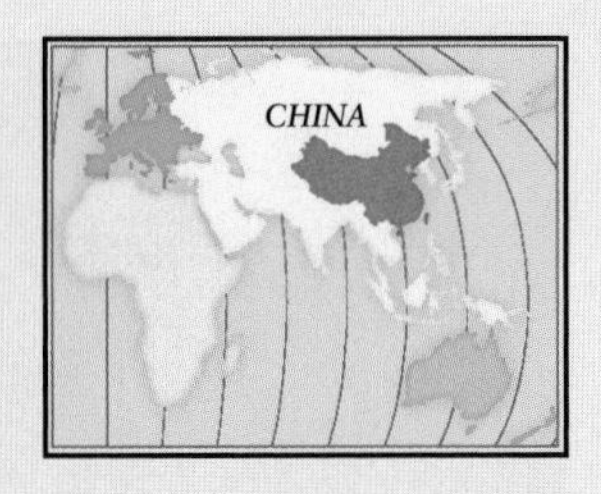

What we know as Beijing opera, the most famous variety of Chinese musical drama, is in China called **jingju** (chéeng-chu), meaning "theater of the capital." It is one of more than three hundred different local varieties of traditional Chinese musical drama, each identified by the province or district of its origin. Beijing opera is a rich amalgam of song, spoken dialogue, instrumental music, dance, elaborate costume, and martial arts. In a nation of vast size and immense cultural diversity, the "theater of the capital" comes closest to being a national tradition of musical drama.

Beijing opera is a relatively recent product of a long, complex history. Some of its stylistic features were introduced to the capital by provincial theater troupes at the end of the eighteenth century, while others developed through much of the nineteenth. Only by the late 1800s did Beijing opera assume the form we know today, and even that form has more recently undergone striking changes, especially during the Communist period of the last half-century.

Voice Types in Beijing Opera In European opera, different voice types have been habitually associated with specific character types. In Romantic opera, tenors usually play young, vital, and amorous characters (for example, Radames in Verdi's *Aida*), and sopranos play their female counterparts (Aida herself); most often the two are star-crossed lovers. The lower female voice is often reserved for a character who conspires against the soprano and tenor (Amneris), while the low male voices, baritone and bass, can variously have fatherly, comic, or evil associations.

Beijing opera: a female character and a *jing*

Such conventional connections of voice and character type are highly developed in Beijing opera, too—but the voice types are different. Young men of romantic, dreamy inclination sing in a high register and usually in falsetto. Older, bearded men, trusted and loyal advisors of one sort or another, sing in the high baritone range. Warriors sing with a forced, throaty voice; in addition they must be skilled acrobats in order to enact lively, athletic battle scenes.

Two other special male roles are the male comic, who speaks more than he sings, and the *jing* or face-painted role, who may be a warrior, a dashing bandit, or even a god. His face is painted more elaborately than those of the other actors, with patterns whose colors symbolically reveal much about his character. The *jing* sings in a loud, hoarse manner that takes years to master, like the other voice types here—and like the equally artificial voice types of European opera.

The female roles in Beijing opera were, until the Communist era, almost always sung by male impersonators. They include a mature, virtuous woman, sung in a refined, delicate falsetto (when women sing these roles today, they imitate that male falsetto). A younger woman, lively and flirtatious, is sung in a suggestive, innuendo-laden falsetto. There is also an acrobatic female warrior.

The Orchestra The small orchestra of Beijing opera consists of a group of drums, gongs, and cymbals, a few wind instruments, and a group of bowed and plucked stringed instruments. These are all played by a handful of versatile musicians who switch from one instrument to another during the performance.

The percussion group is associated especially with martial music, accompanying battle scenes. But it also fulfills many other roles: It can introduce scenes, provide special sound effects, use conventional drum patterns to announce the entrances and social status of different characters, and play along with the frequent songs. The most important function of the stringed instruments is to introduce and accompany the songs.

Beijing Opera Songs In a way that is somewhat akin to the Western contrast of recitative and aria, Beijing opera shows a wide range of vocal styles, from full-fledged song through more declamatory song to heightened, stylized speech and even, for comic and

A Beijing opera orchestra: The player in front holds the banjo-like *yueqin;* behind him are an *erhu* player and, standing, percussion players.

minor characters, normal speech. In general, the songs of Beijing opera are like the arias of Italian opera. They are the musical heart of the drama, marked off from the other singing around them by their lyrical style. The songs suggest the feelings and internal psychological states of their singers.

Unlike Italian opera, however, these Chinese arias are not composed anew for each new opera. Instead, their music is chosen from a stock collection of melodies and percussion patterns and fitted to the song-texts of each new libretto added to the repertory. Sometimes whole songs are fitted to new texts in standard poetic forms; at other times, looser musical patterns are taken over and adapted to texts of freer poetry. The crucial concern in this fashioning of arias is to choose melodies and rhythms that convey effectively the emotional situation of a particular song-text.

The Prince Who Changed into a Cat

5
45

Our recording presents the beginning of a scene from *The Prince Who Changed into a Cat,* one of the most famous of Beijing operas. The story concerns an Empress who is banished from Beijing through the machinations of one of the Emperor's other wives. (Her newborn son, the prince of the title, is stolen from his cradle and replaced by a cat.) The present scene takes place many years later, when a wise and just Prime Minister meets the Empress and determines to restore her to her rightful position.

First the percussion plays, and then the string instruments, along with a wooden clapper, introduce an aria sung by the Prime Minister (0:25). There are only three strings: a high-pitched two-string fiddle played with a bow called a *jinghu* (chéeng-hoo), a similar but lower-pitched fiddle called *erhu* (ár-hoo), and a plucked lute called *yueqin* (yuéh-chin). All three play the same melody, the erhu doubling the jinghu an octave below while the yueqin adds characteristic repeated notes created by the quick, banjo-like strumming of a string.

Finally, the singer enters (0:41). He sings the same melody as the stringed instruments, though he pauses frequently while they continue uninterrupted. This heterophonic texture (see page 28) is typical of Beijing opera arias. The Prime Minister is a bearded old-man role and sings in the appropriate high baritone range.

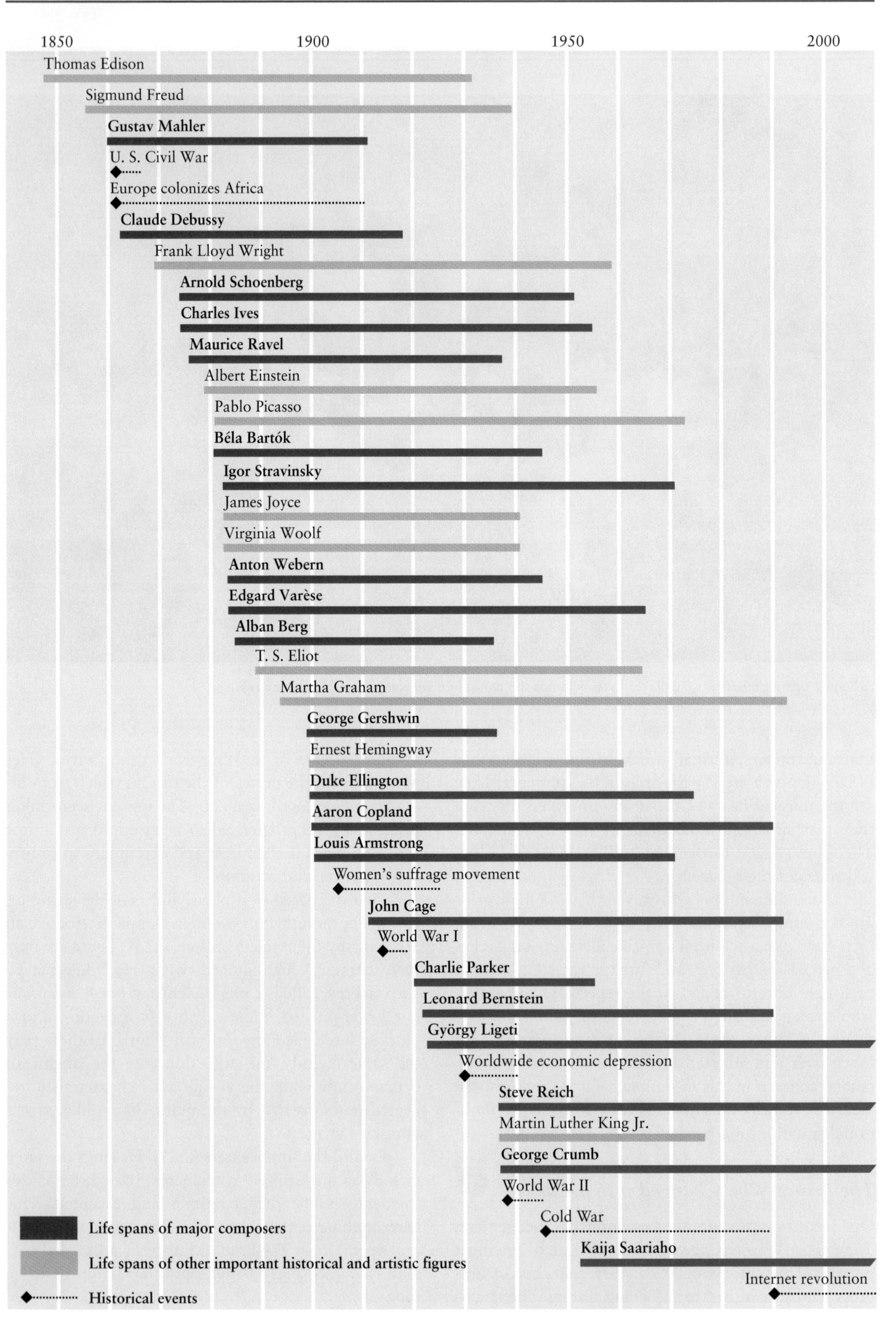

1850
1900
1950
2000
Thomas Edison
Sigmund Freud
Gustav Mahler
U. S. Civil War
Europe colonizes Africa
Claude Debussy
Frank Lloyd Wright
Arnold Schoenberg
Charles Ives
Maurice Ravel
Albert Einstein
Pablo Picasso
Béla Bartók
Igor Stravinsky
James Joyce
Virginia Woolf
Anton Webern
Edgard Varèse
Alban Berg
T. S. Eliot
Martha Graham
George Gershwin
Ernest Hemingway
Duke Ellington
Aaron Copland
Louis Armstrong
Women's suffrage movement
John Cage
World War I
Charlie Parker
Leonard Bernstein
György Ligeti
Worldwide economic depression
Steve Reich
Martin Luther King Jr.
George Crumb
World War II
Cold War
Kaija Saariaho
Internet revolution
Life spans of major composers
Life spans of other important historical and artistic figures
Historical events

UNIT V

The Twentieth Century

This unit, which deals with music from around 1900 on, brings our survey up to the present. Looking back to the year 1900, we can recognize today's culture in an early form. Large cities, industrialization, inoculation against disease, advertising, processed food, the first automobiles, telephones, movies, and phonographs—all were in place by the beginning of the twentieth century.

Hence many of the phenomena treated in this unit will strike us as fairly familiar, compared to those of earlier centuries. For one thing, the wide availability of art to mass audiences—not just to the various select groups, as in the past—is something we take for granted. The new mass audience emerged because of sociological factors, as mobility between social classes became easier and more common, along with technological factors—the amazing development of the phonograph, radio, television, and more. We also take for granted the split that has occurred between classical music and popular music. A rift that had widened in the nineteenth century became a prime factor of musical life in the twentieth.

We are also aware of the force of American popular music—music whose characteristic features emerged around the year 1900, once again. With the evolution of ragtime and early jazz, a vital rhythmic spring derived from African-American sources was brought into the general American consciousness. This led to a long series of developments: swing, bebop, rhythm and blues, rock, rap. After World War II, when the United States began to play a commanding political role in the world at large, our popular music became a world language.

Modernism and Traditionalism

What was classical music like in this same period? Classical music itself experienced a split. On the one hand there was music that we shall call "modernist," on the other hand, music of a more traditional nature.

The term modernist *requires a word of explanation. It is not the same as* contemporary *or* modern, *terms that refer to anything at all that happens to take place in the present; the* -ist *at the end of the word* modern *gives it an extra twist. The modernists of 1900 were artists and intellectuals who insisted on their modernity—that is, their anti-traditionalism—and who formed a specific cultural movement marked by radical experimentation. Though its roots go back earlier, this movement peaked during the years 1890 to 1918—a period of breakthrough works by such novelists, poets, and painters as Marcel Proust and James Joyce, Ezra Pound and T. S. Eliot, Pablo Picasso and Henri Matisse.*

The chief composers associated with the modernist movement were Claude Debussy, Arnold Schoenberg, and Igor Stravinsky. Sometimes they are referred to as members of the "avant-garde"; **avant-garde**—*"vanguard"—is a military or at least a militant term that has long been embraced by radical artists and intellectuals to denote the forefront of their activity.*

At the same time, some twentieth-century artists and composers resisted modernism, and some artists, after some experiments, turned back from it. They found they could comfortably continue in the general spirit of late Romanticism, or even look back to earlier styles. Though the avant-gardists often claimed that the old principles of art had been "used up," there was still plenty of potential left in more traditional methods.

In this unit we shall study the music of modernism and also the reaction against modernism. Our final chapter deals with America's characteristic music, jazz, and some of its consequences.

CHAPTER 19

Prelude
Music and Modernism

Modernism in art, literature, and music flourished especially from around 1890 to 1918, the end of World War I. It was an unusually brilliant movement. A sharp reaction to late nineteenth-century culture, especially to the accepted rules of art within that culture, modernism found amazing resources within the materials of the arts themselves. It is probably the case that the arts of Europe and the West had never before gone through such revolutionary developments together.

1 Industrialization and Progress

Industrialization is one of two overriding historical facts of the nineteenth century. The other one, the emergence of the modern nation-state, we spoke of earlier; see pages 292–94. Ever since the first so-called age of science in the seventeenth century, technological discoveries had come faster and faster, and industry was transformed. The harnessing of steam power in the eighteenth century was matched by the capturing of electricity in the nineteenth. Europe and America were crisscrossed with railroads, built for the benefit of industry and commerce. By the early twentieth century, automobile and air travel were in their early stages of development, as were telephones, movies, and sound recordings.

What had been essentially rural societies, controlled by stable aristocracies, turned into modern nations, dominated by urban societies and run by self-made entrepreneurs. These changes occurred at breakneck speed, as people saw at the time. Yet no one could have forecast how the stresses caused by such social changes would lead on the one hand to the disturbing artistic-intellectual movement known as modernism, and on the other to the catastrophe of World War I.

For at the heart of "official" nineteenth-century culture was a sense of confidence in progress. Progress in science and technology, it was thought, would be matched in due time by progress in human affairs. And although anyone could see evidence to the contrary—for example, in the appalling conditions of the new industrial poor, as exposed by the novels of Charles Dickens—this evidence was easily ignored by the rich and powerful who were profiting from technology's advances.

Another, dark side of progress became evident in the development of weaponry. The deadly novelty of the American Civil War was the rifle, effective over five times the range of previous shoulder weapons. In World War I, tanks, submarines, and chemical weapons showed technology's terrible potential for destruction: an estimated forty million military and civilian dead from war, famine, and epidemic, and twenty million wounded. With World War I, modern nation-states came into their own, pitting themselves against one another. Nineteenth-century confidence in progress—a response to the successes of technology—was thrown into question by technology itself.

Science and Uncertainty

By this time, however, the groundwork for such loss in confidence had already been laid by science in other areas. Men and women were shaken in their most basic assumptions about life by ominous advances in physics, biology, and psychology.

The impact of Einstein's theory of relativity (which later in the century made its own contributions to the technology of weaponry) was at first more philosophical than practical in nature. The idea that things depend on the standpoint of the observer, and cannot be counted on according to the "objective" rules of Newtonian physics, rocked people's sense of certainty.

For many, this uncertainty deepened a crisis in religion that the Victorians had already experienced as a result of scientific theories of evolution. Here the key figure was Charles Darwin. Were human beings created by God in God's image, as the Bible teaches, or did they evolve by an impersonal process from animals? The disturbance that this idea caused in people's sense of stability is still reflected in today's disputes about creationism and "creation science."

Meanwhile the psychological theories of Sigmund Freud suggested that in spite of what people thought they were doing or feeling, they were in fact controlled by unconscious drives. The idea of men and women in the grip of irrational forces of their own (or their parents') making was, again, very disturbing. At the same time, the prospect of "working out" one's problems through psychotherapy gave the new century its paradigm for personality change.

2 The Response of Modernism

If the traditional laws of physics, biblical authority, and psychological certainty could no longer be accepted, it seemed a small enough step to question the rules, assumptions, and prohibitions surrounding the arts.

One such assumption was that visual art had to represent something from the external world. Once this idea was questioned, and then abandoned, the materials of painting and the other arts could be used for themselves—and a whole world of abstract (or nonrepresentational) painting opened up. This general category includes cubism, abstract expressionism, op art, and other such subcategories.

Cubism was one of the earliest forms of abstract or near-abstract art, developed around the time of World War I by Pablo Picasso, Georges Braque, and others. In this painting by Braque, one can discern a guitar and the score of *Socrate,* by a leading modernist composer, Erik Satie.

In literature, the basic assumption was that poets and novelists would use ordinary sentence structure, syntax, and grammar. Freedom from these conditions opened up a whole new sphere of suggestion. Using the so-called stream-of-consciousness method, James Joyce ended his novel *Ulysses* of 1922 with a famous long section—forty pages, without punctuation or paragraphs—tracking the miscellaneous but not-so-idle thoughts of a character who hadn't even spoken until then, Molly Bloom, as she lies in bed.

In music, the basic assumptions were melody and its close associates harmony and tonality. These assumptions, too, were thrown into doubt. Arnold Schoenberg's song cycle *Pierrot lunaire* ("Moonstruck Pierrot") of 1912 traumatized the world of music by employing a kind of half-speaking, half-singing style that the composer called *Sprechstimme* (speech-song; see page 340) throughout all twenty-one of its numbers. Ranging from a throaty whisper to a near-hysterical shriek, *Sprechstimme* was an explicit—indeed aggressive—denial of melody.

New Languages for Art

Avant-garde artists developed whole new languages for art—for example, the "language" of cubism, shown in the painting by Georges Braque, above. If we take the word *language* literally, the most dramatic case is that of James Joyce whose last novel, *Finnegans Wake,* makes use of a language that is half English and half a construction of words he invented.

Schoenberg, once again, provides a striking analogue in music. His twelve-tone method, or **serialism,** developed in the 1920s, replaced the old "language" for music based on tonality (see page 326). By arranging the twelve notes of the chromatic scale into fixed patterns, and manipulating those patterns by means of mathematical operations, Schoenberg arrived at a radical new way of composing music—and hearing it, too. His experiments were continued with great energy after World War II, as we shall see in Chapter 22.

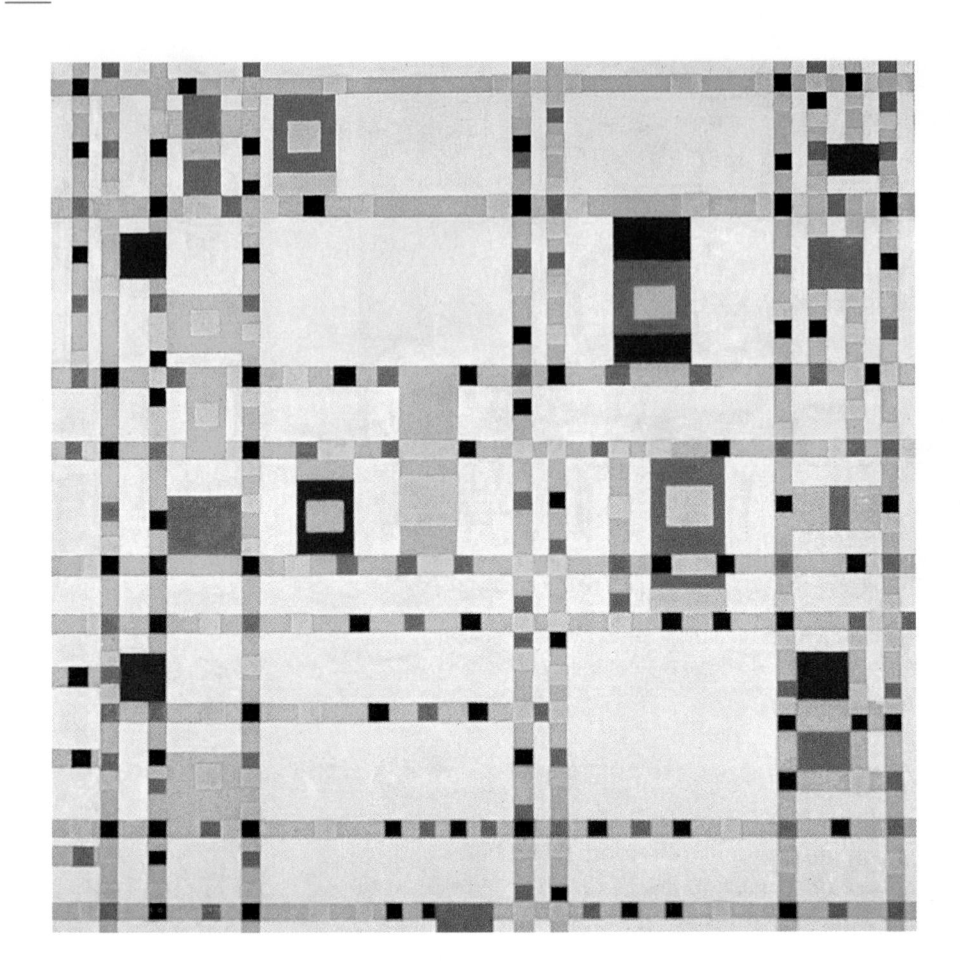

Broadway Boogie-Woogie by Piet Mondrian—a tribute to the "mechanical" rhythms of jazz (as he perceived them) by a premier abstract painter.

Art and Objectivity

The "new languages" for art were unquestionably (and unapologetically) difficult. To this day, few people understand *Finnegans Wake*. Few can follow Schoenberg's serial compositions. Avant-garde art became detached from music's ordinary public, and hence abstracted from a base in society.

At the same time, the modernists' concentration on artistic materials led to abstraction of another kind, the abstraction of technique from expression. This emphasis on technique was welcomed by some as a relief from the overheated emotionality of late Romantic music of Chaikovsky, Mahler, and the like. Especially in the 1920s, "objectivity" was an ideal espoused by many artists. Only too often, their works struck the public as "abstract" in a cold, dry sense.

Characteristic of this phase of the avant-garde were various experiments with schematic, even mathematical devices in the arts. The Dutch painter Piet Mondrian made pictures out of straight lines at right angles to one another, and juxtaposed planes of bright color. Among composers, Igor Stravinsky was known for his provocative statements extolling objectivity and attacking Romantic music—and certainly the brisk, mechanistic rhythms that characterize Stravinsky's style are diametrically opposed to rubato (see page 242), the rhythmic "stretching" that contributes so much to nineteenth-century music's emotionality.

Several lesser composers, fascinated by "machine" rhythms, even tried to evoke machinery in their works: the American George Antheil *(Ballet mécanique)*, the Russian A. V. Mosolov *(The Iron Foundry)*, and the Swiss Arthur Honegger (*Pacific 231*—a locomotive).

Cover for *The Blue Rider,* a magazine that promulgated modernist art and music.

3 Literature and Art before World War I

There was a tendency around this time for artists of various kinds to gravitate together in formal or informal groups, both for mutual encouragement and for the exchange of ideas. Thus Claude Debussy was friends with several avant-garde poets. Schoenberg, himself a painter as well as a musician, associated with a group of artists who set forth their ideas in *The Blue Rider,* a magazine named after a picture by the pioneer nonrepresentational painter Wassily Kandinsky (see page 323). Stravinsky and Maurice Ravel belonged to a group who called themselves the Apaches. With all this interchange, it is not surprising that one can sometimes detect similar tendencies in music and the other arts.

Impressionists and Symbolists

As we have already remarked, modernism got its start in the late nineteenth century and then peaked in the twentieth. The best-known modernist movement, **impressionism,** dates from the 1870s, when people were astonished by the flickering network of color patches used by impressionist painters to render simple scenes from everyday life (as in Edouard Manet's *In the Boat;* see page 320). These painters claimed that they had to develop such a technique to catch the actual, perceived quality of light. They proudly called themselves "realists," in reaction to the idealized and overemotional art of Romanticism.

With pure nails brightly
flashing their onyx
Anguish at midnight
holds up (Lucifer!)
A multitude of dreams
burnt by the Phoenix
A mortuary urn
cannot recover
On credence table,
in empty hall: . . .

Opening of a symbolist sonnet (Stéphane Mallarmé)

Symbolism, a consciously *un*realistic movement, followed soon after impressionism. Symbolist poets revolted against the "realism" of words being

In the Boat, an impressionist painting by Edouard Manet (1832–1883).

Does nature imitate art? This snapshot of Debussy (second from the left) and some friends is startlingly similar in mood to the (earlier) impressionist painting by Manet shown above.

used for reference—for the purpose of exact definition or denoting. They wanted words to perform their symbolizing or signifying function as freely as possible, without having to fit into phrases or sentences. The meaning of a cluster of words might be vague and ambiguous, even esoteric—but also rich, "musical," and endlessly suggestive.

"Musical" was exactly what the symbolists called it. They were fascinated by the music dramas of Richard Wagner, where again musical symbols—Wagner's leitmotivs—refer to elements in his dramas in a complex, ambivalent, multi-layered fashion. All poets use musical devices such as rhythm and rhyme, but the symbolists were prepared to go so far as to break down grammar, syntax, and conventional thought sequence to approach the elusive nonreferential quality of music.

Claude Debussy is often called an impressionist in music, because his fragmentary motives and little flashes of tone color seem to recall the impressionists' painting technique. Debussy can also—and more accurately—be called a symbolist, since suggestion, rather than outright statement, is at the heart of his aesthetic. Famous symbolist texts inspired two famous Debussy works: the orchestral *Prelude to "The Afternoon of a Faun"* (a poem by Stéphane Mallarmé), and the opera *Pelléas et Mélisande* (a play by Maurice Maeterlinck), where Debussy's elusive musical symbols and Maeterlinck's elusive verbal ones combine to produce an unforgettable effect of mysterious suggestion.

Expressionists and Fauves

Symbolism is also the force behind powerful images in the work of Vincent van Gogh. In his *Thatched Roofs at Cordeville*, the distorted rooftop and the almost liquid trees are not there to represent objects, but to symbolize the artist's disturbing vision of the universe.

But even in van Gogh's most extreme works, the trees are still recognizably trees. In Paris and Vienna—artistic centers which were also centers of avant-

Thatched Roofs at Cordeville, by Vincent van Gogh, 1890.

Horses and riders, painted by Wassily Kandinsky over a four-year period, show his path toward nonrepresentational painting. In the first picture, the figures are quite clear; in the last, they could be missed entirely. Top left: *Couple on Horseback* (1907); top right: *Blue Mountain* (1909); bottom: *Romantic Landscape* (1911).

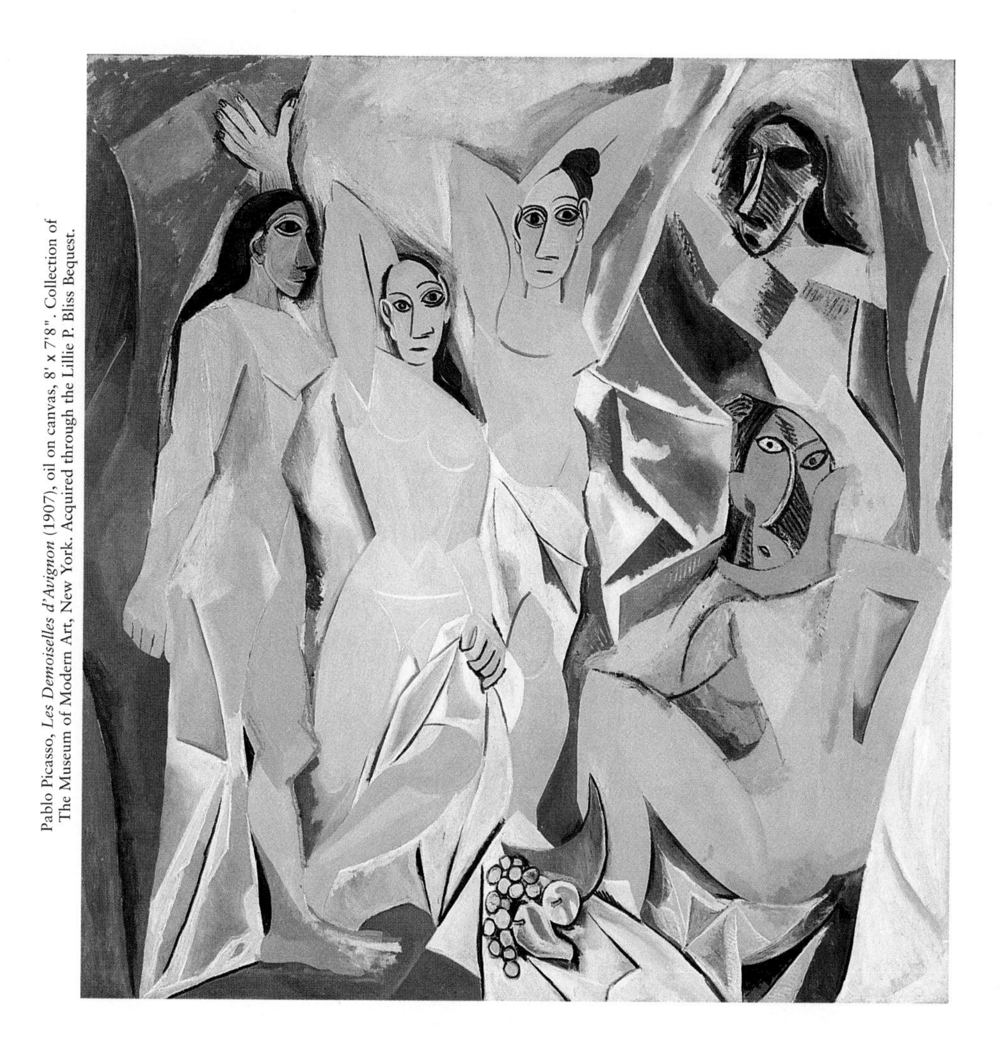

Pablo Picasso, *Les Demoiselles d'Avignon* (1907), oil on canvas, 8' x 7'8". Collection of The Museum of Modern Art, New York. Acquired through the Lillie P. Bliss Bequest.

Picasso's famous shocker *Les Demoiselles d'Avignon* (1907). Picasso and other abstract painters designed sets for the Diaghilev Ballets Russes, sponsor of Stravinsky and other modernist composers.

garde music—two émigré artists pursued separate but parallel paths toward completely abstract painting.

Our horse-and-rider pictures on page 322 by the Russian-born Wassily Kandinsky (1866–1944) show step by step how the process was accomplished. (Where does the *Blue Rider* picture fit in?) Kandinsky belonged to a German movement in the arts called **expressionism**—not to be confused with impressionism—which sought to express the most extreme human feelings by divorcing art from everyday literalness. Anguish, even hysteria, could be conveyed by the harsh clashing of strong colors, irregular shapes, and jagged lines. What seems to be conveyed is not something external but the artist's inner turbulence—most violently in the last Kandinsky picture, *Romantic Landscape,* which is almost entirely abstracted from the outer world.

Parallel to the expressionists was a short-lived group in Paris dubbed *Les fauves,* "the wild beasts." The fauves experimented with distorted images bordering on the grotesque; they also employed motifs from what they called "primitive" art as though in defiance of a decadent European culture. In Pablo Picasso's famous painting *Les Demoiselles d'Avignon* of 1907 (Avignon is a street in the red-light district of Barcelona), the quality of abstraction is evident in the angular bodies and the African-mask-like heads—a complete break with the conventional rules of human portrayal. Picasso took a further step toward abstraction a little later when he turned to cubism (see page 317).

There is violence in both Kandinsky's and Picasso's work of this period. Certainly that is how it struck a generation used to the nonthreatening art of the impressionists—painters of flickering summer landscapes, soft-edged nudes, and diaphanous action pictures of the ballet. Composers, too, courted violence in their music. The Hungarian composer Béla Bartók wrote a "barbarous" piano piece entitled *Allegro barbaro*. Stravinsky, in his ballet *The Rite of Spring*, depicted human sacrifice in the fertility ceremonies of primitive Slavic tribes.

4 Music before World War I

The art of music never enjoyed (or suffered) a link to the tangible world that was comparable to representation in painting, or to reference in poetry. But it did have its own stable, generally accepted set of principles, its own traditional "internal logic." This rested upon elements that we have discussed many times in this book: tune, motive, harmony, tonality, tone color, and rhythm.

The music of Bach, Beethoven, and Brahms was based on this "logic," and so was the entire stream of Western European folk songs, popular songs, dances, military marches, and the rest. Avant-garde music moved away from this norm.

Music by Gustav Klimt, the leading modernist painter in Vienna in the years around 1900.

Like abstract, nonrepresentational painting, music worked out new principles based on the materials of the art itself.

With European music before World War I, we can lay our main emphasis on developments in melody, harmony, and tonality, for on the whole, these features were the main preoccupations of avant-garde composers in that period. Developments in tone color and rhythm—or, more broadly, musical sonority and musical time—dominated music after World War II.

Experiment and Transformation: Melody

Melody, harmony, and tonality all work closely together. In historical terms, harmony arose as a way of supporting and adorning melody, and tonality first arose as a means of clarifying both melody and harmony; later tonality functioned as a more general way of organizing music. Each of these functions was transformed in the early twentieth century.

We have seen the Viennese Classical composers bring tunes to the fore in their music, and the Romantics capitalize on tunes as the most emphatic means of conveying powerful emotion. Yet Wagner, despite the melodic quality of many of his leitmotivs, was criticized for the confusing quality of his singing lines, and Mahler's audiences were puzzled and irritated by the bittersweet distortions that he applied to folklike melodies. In his later works, such as his immense Ninth Symphony of 1909, Mahler wrote increasingly intricate and difficult melodic lines. The long melodies surge, swoop, and yearn in a strange, almost painful manner.

And by that time another Viennese composer, Arnold Schoenberg, was writing even more complex melodies that simply made no sense to contemporary listeners. The intense rhythms and the anguished intervals of Romanticism were there, but the actual notes did not appear to fit together at all.

Outside of Vienna, the disintegration of traditional melody was accomplished in other ways. In many (not all) of his works, Claude Debussy used only the most shadowy motives—a constant suggestion of melody without clear tunes. A little later Igor Stravinsky, writing in Paris, seized upon Russian folk songs but whittled them down (or abstracted them) into brief, utterly simple fragments, blank and "objective," as his theories demanded.

New Horizons, New Scales

We have mentioned the influence of African masks on Picasso's *Demoiselles*. Non-Western musics, too, began to make inroads into Western classical music. At a World's Fair that fascinated Paris in 1889—the fair for which the Eiffel Tower was built—Debussy heard his first non-Western music played by native musicians, under simulated native conditions. He tried to recapture the sounds of the Indonesian gamelan (see page 214) in a number of his compositions, even taking a Balinese melody for the theme of a concerto finale.

Debussy sensed a resonance between his own music and the unique timbres of the gamelan, and also the scales used in Indonesian music. The traditional diatonic scale had served as the foundation of Western music for so long that

Schoenberg and Serialism

Arnold Schoenberg at forty, by Egon Schiele. Schoenberg was fifty before he developed the twelve-tone system.

Of all early twentieth-century composers, Arnold Schoenberg (1874–1951) was the most keenly aware of the problem caused by ever-broadening dissonance and atonality. The problem, to put it simply, was the clear and present danger of chaos. In the early 1920s Schoenberg found a way that he felt would impose order or control over the newly "emancipated" elements of music.

This resulted in the **twelve-tone system,** defined by Schoenberg as a "method of composing with the twelve tones solely in relation to one another"—that is, *not* in relation to a central pitch, or tonic, which is no longer the point of reference for music. This method became known as **serialism.** Serialism can be regarded as a systematization of the chromaticism developed by Romantic composers, especially Richard Wagner (see pages 244, 328).

Schoenberg's "Twelve-Tone System"

Schoenberg developed a way of composing with the twelve pitches of the chromatic scale held to a *fixed ordering.* An ordered sequence of the twelve pitches is called a **twelve-tone row** or **series:** hence the term *serialism.* For any composition, he would determine a series ahead of time and maintain it (the next piece would have a different series).

What does "maintain" mean in this context? It means that Schoenberg composed by writing notes only in the order of the work's series, *or of certain carefully prescribed other versions of the series* (see below). As a general rule, he always went through the entire series without any repetitions or backtracking before starting over again. The pitches can, however, appear in any octave, high or low. They can stand out as melody notes or blend into the harmony. They can assume any rhythm.

And what are those "versions" of the series? The series can be used not only in its original form, but also

- *transposed,* that is, the same note ordering can start from any note in the chromatic scale: a series beginning A B D D♯ can appear as D E G G♯, or G A C C♯, or in nine other transposed forms.
- *inverted,* with the intervals between notes turned upside down:
  A B D becomes A G E
- used in *retrograde,* played backwards:
  A B D D♯ E F♯ C♯ G♯ A♯ C F G becomes G F C A♯, etc.

The basic idea of serialism may seem to impose order with a vengeance, putting very severe limits on what a composer can do. But once the versions are taken into consideration, an enormous number of options becomes available, especially since transposition and inversion can both occur at the same time (A B D becoming G F D, and so on).

Serialism and Unity

Part of the point of twelve-tone composition is that each piece has its own special "sound world" determined by its series. This permeates the whole piece. The next piece has a new series and a new sound world.

Indeed, serialism can be regarded as the end result of an important tendency in nineteenth-century music, the search for ever stronger means of unity within individual compositions. We have traced the "principle of thematic unity" in music by Berlioz, Wagner, and others, and mentioned the different "levels" on which it operated—actual recurring themes, thematic transformations, and subtler similarities between motives (see page 248).

A serial composition is, in a sense, totally unified, since every measure of it shares the same unique sound world. Thus, on its own special terms, Schoenberg's serialism seemed to realize the Romantic composers' ideal of unity.

Phrase of a Schoenberg melody using a twelve-tone series.

it was almost regarded as a fact of nature. But now composers were beginning to reconsider the basic sound materials of music. Notable among these experimenters was Charles Ives, in America (see page 348). New scales were employed for themes or even whole movements, first among them the **pentatonic scale,** a five-note scale playable on the black notes of the keyboard. Imported from folk song and Asian music, this scale was tried in all the usual genres, not only (as before) in nationalist or other folk-derived compositions.

Incidentally, Debussy was also intrigued by another "exotic" music: ragtime and a dance associated with it, the cakewalk, precursors of American jazz (see page 350). In a simple piano piece he dedicated to his young daughter, Debussy wrote a cakewalk up front and contrasted it with a little spoof of Wagner's *Tristan und Isolde*—a pretty clear pronouncement on the direction he saw music taking.

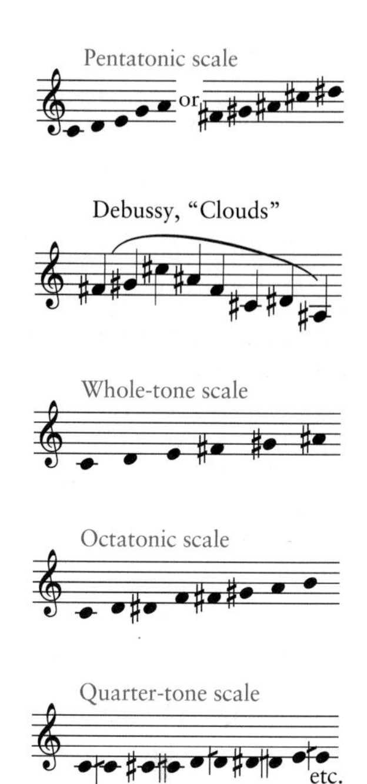

Three other new scales introduced at this time are (significantly enough) abstract constructions, which anyone can figure out by systematically analyzing the total chromatic scale. The **whole-tone scale** divides the octave into six equal parts—all of its intervals are whole steps; again, Debussy worked with this resource in many pieces. The **octatonic scale**—a specialty with Stravinsky—fits eight pitches into the octave by alternating whole and half steps.

Less used, the **quarter-tone scale** employs all the pitches of the chromatic scale plus the pitches that come halfway between each pair of them.

More important as a means of composition than the use of any of these scales was serialism, the "new language" for music invented in the 1920s by Arnold Schoenberg. As is explained in the box on the opposite page, serialism in effect creates something like a special scale for every serial composition.

"The Emancipation of Dissonance"

As melody grew more complex, more fragmentary, or more vague, harmony grew more and more dissonant. The concepts of consonance and dissonance, as we noted on page 27, rest on the fact that certain chords (consonant chords) sound stable and at rest, whereas others (dissonant chords) sound tense and need to resolve to consonant ones. In a famous phrase, Schoenberg spoke of "the emancipation of dissonance," meaning emancipation from that need to resolve. Dissonance was to be free from the "rule" that says it must always be followed by the appropriate consonance.

To be sure, dissonance and consonance are relative matters; there are mild dissonances (play A on the piano together with the G above it) and more tense, strident dissonances (play A and G and all the nine notes between them simultaneously). As early twentieth-century composers explored higher and higher levels of dissonance, they discovered that a kind of resolution could be obtained by proceeding not from dissonance to consonance, but from a harsh dissonance to a milder one. Slowly listeners began hearing this, too.

Tonality and Atonality

Tonality is the feeling of centrality, focus, or "homing" toward a particular pitch that we get from simple tunes and much other music. As melody grew more complex or fragmented, and harmony grew more dissonant and chromatic, tonality grew more indistinct. Finally, some music reached a point at which no tonal center could be detected at all. This is **atonal** music.

However, just as consonance and dissonance are not open-and-shut concepts, neither are tonality or atonality. Most Baroque music sounds firmly rooted in its key, for example, whereas certain Romantic music seems rather to hover around a general key area. Much early twentieth-century music that was once criticized as "atonal" can be heard on careful listening to have a subtle sense of tonality after all.

Wagner, as we recall, went further than other Romantic composers in the direction of *chromaticism,* the free use of all twelve pitches of the chromatic scale. For example, there are as many as ten different chromatic notes in this prominent phrase from his opera *Tristan und Isolde* (see page 284).

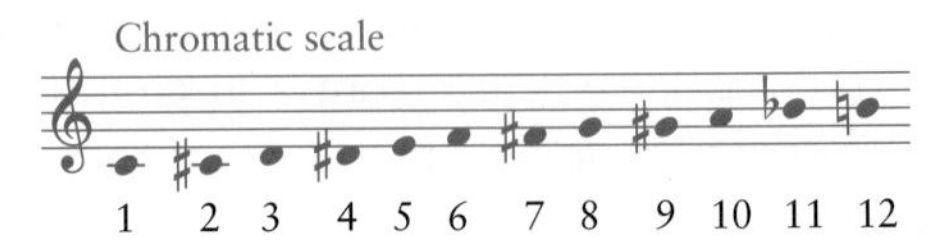

Since tonality depends on one pitch standing out from the others in the ordinary diatonic scale (for example, C in the C-major scale C D E F G A B), when all twelve chromatic pitches are used freely, the centrality of any single one is automatically diluted. Wagner's technique of chromaticism was a significant forecast of atonality, which was realized most systematically by Schoenberg's development of serialism.

Melody, harmony, tonality: All are closely related. Beleagured conservatives around 1900 referred to them jokingly as the "holy trinity" of music. The "emancipation" of melody, harmony, and tonality all went together. This joint emancipation counts as the central style characteristic of the first phase of twentieth-century avant-garde music.

Web: *Research and test your understanding of music and modernism at* **<bedfordstmartins.com/listen>.**

CHAPTER 20

The Twentieth Century: Early Modernism

The first major phase of avant-garde music—what we now call modernist music—took place in Paris and Vienna from around 1890 to 1914. Claude Debussy, Igor Stravinsky (a young Russian working in Paris), and Arnold Schoenberg were the leading figures in this brilliant era. And there were strong modernist rumblings in Russia, Hungary, Italy, and the United States.

It was a period of rapid development in all the arts, as we have seen, in which the basic tenets of nineteenth-century art were everywhere challenged. In particular, nineteenth-century ideas of melody, harmony, and tonality came under attack. Developments in tone color and rhythm—or, more broadly, musical sonority and musical time—dominated the second phase of modernism, which followed after World War II.

To be sure, musical elements such as melody, harmony, rhythm, and sonority affect each other intimately, and composers hardly ever think of them in isolation. Debussy, Stravinsky, and Schoenberg were all noted for their novel treatment of tone color and rhythm. In terms of historical impact, however, Stravinsky's rhythm, though widely imitated, really worked for him alone, and Debussy's concept of tone color was not fully absorbed until the post–World War II period. It was the revolution in tonality—which went along with a radical reconsideration of melody and harmony—that caught the imagination of the early twentieth century.

1 Debussy and Impressionism

Claude Debussy occupies the border area between late nineteenth- and early twentieth-century styles. His investigation of sensuous new tone colors for orchestra and for piano, his development of new rich harmonies, and his search for new ways to express emotion in music—all remind us of the Romantics. Yet while in some ways his work seems tied to Romanticism, in others it represents a direct reaction against it.

(. . . Sounds and perfumes sway in the evening air)

Title of a Debussy "miniature" for piano; the parentheses and dots are his.

Debussy's tone colors avoid the heavy sonorities that were usual in late Romantic music, merging instead into subtle, mysterious shades of sound. His

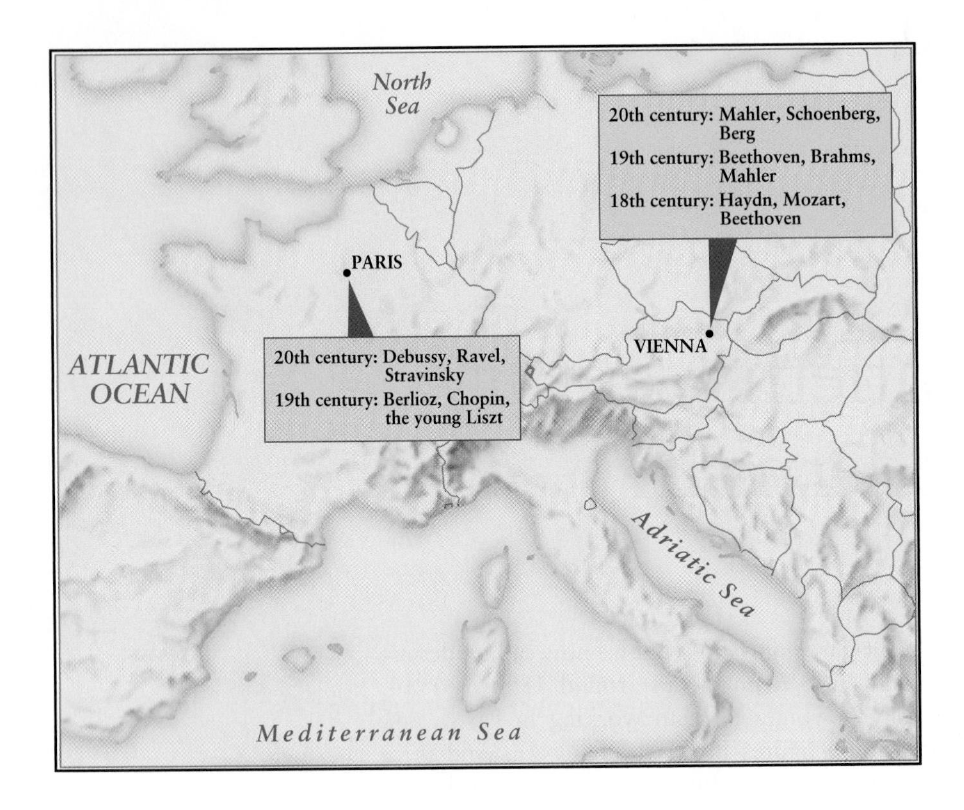

Paris and Vienna as musical centers.

themes and motives are usually fragmentary and tentative, his harmonies sound strangely vague, and the tonality of his music is often clouded. His themes often draw on the vague-sounding new scales mentioned in Chapter 19.

Debussy's orchestral sound differs sharply from that of his contemporary, Gustav Mahler, another great innovator in orchestration. Mahler treated the orchestra more and more contrapuntally; each instrument tends to stand out from the others like a Romantic hero striving for his own say in the world. Debussy's orchestra is more often a single, delicately pulsing totality to which individual instruments contribute momentary gleams of color. One thinks of an impressionist picture, in which small, separate areas of color, visible close up, merge into unified color fields as the viewer stands back and takes in the painting as a whole.

CLAUDE DEBUSSY
Three Nocturnes (1899)

Debussy's Three Nocturnes, like most of his orchestral works, might be described as impressionist symphonic poems, though without narrative programs. They evoke various scenes without attempting to illustrate them literally.

The title "nocturne" evokes a night-time scene, the great examples before Debussy being the piano nocturnes of Chopin (see page 261). But in fact Debussy's reference was to famous atmospheric paintings by an artist who was close to the impressionists, James McNeill Whistler (see page 331). The first of the nocturnes, *Clouds,* is a pure nature picture, the least nocturnal of the three. The second, *Festivals,* depicts mysterious night-time fairs and parades. The third Nocturne, *Sirens,* includes a women's chorus along with the orchestra, singing not words but just vowels, like an extra orchestral "choir" (see page 43). The women's voices evoke the legendary maidens of the title, who tempt lonely sailors and pull them into the deep.

The title "Nocturnes" should be taken here in a more general and especially in a more decorative sense. . . . Clouds: *the unchanging aspect of the sky, the slow, melancholy motion of the clouds, fading away into agonized grey tones, gently tinged with white.*

Claude Debussy

Nocturne—Grey and Gold by James McNeill Whistler (1834–1903). The American-born expatriate artist painted many more "Nocturnes" and other pictures with musical titles: "Symphony," "Harmony," and "Variations."

Clouds We first hear a quiet series of chords, played by clarinets and bassoons, that circles back on itself repeatedly. They seem to suggest great cumulus clouds, moving slowly and silently across the sky.

As a "theme," however, these chords do not function conventionally. They make no strong declarations and lead nowhere definitive. This is also true of the next motive, introduced by the English horn—a haunting motive that occurs many times in *Clouds,* with hardly any change. (It is built on an octatonic scale: See page 327.) Yet even this muted gesture, with its vague rhythm and its fading conclusion, seems sufficient to exhaust the composition and bring it to a near halt, over a barely audible drum roll:

After this near stop, the "cloud" music begins again, leading this time to a downward passage of remarkably gentle, murmuring chords in the strings—chords all of the same structure (major ninth chords):

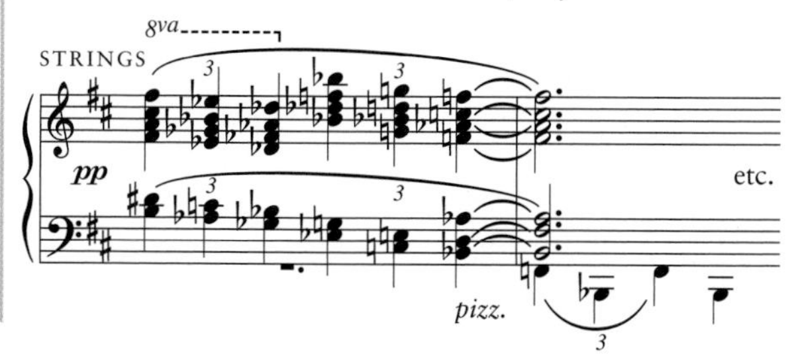

Claude Debussy (1862–1918)

Claude Debussy went through the strict curriculum of the famous Paris Conservatory of Music, which he entered at the age of ten. He did not do well in the piano exams, or at least not well enough, but won various awards in theory and composition. He was finally awarded the coveted Grand Prix (Top Prize)—a three-year fellowship to study in Rome.

Before this, Debussy took a job with Madame von Meck, the eccentric patron of Chaikovsky, playing in a trio at her house in Moscow. Russian music (music of the *kuchka:* see page 295) was one of several vivid influences on the young composer; another was the Indonesian gamelan (see page 214), which he encountered at the World's Fair in Paris in 1889. Visits to Bayreuth, the shrine of Wagner's music dramas, afforded another, even stronger influence. But Debussy soon turned against Wagner and German music in general. He felt it was a stifling influence on modern music in France.

Debussy settled into Parisian café life, becoming a familiar bearded figure in his broad-brimmed hat and flowing cape. A long-term relationship with a mistress came to a bad end, as did Debussy's first marriage, when he eloped with a married woman, who later became his wife. They had a daughter—Debussy wrote the well-known *Children's Corner* Suite for her before she was old enough to play the piano.

In his early thirties Debussy seems to have rather suddenly crystallized his musical style, reflecting the influences of the French symbolist poets and impressionist painters. One remarkable work after another was given its premiere, greeted with a flurry of controversy, and then generally accepted by the critics and the public. His one opera, *Pelléas et Mélisande* (1902), written directly to the words of a play by the prominent symbolist Maurice Maeterlinck, exasperated the author. But today Maeterlinck's play is remembered mainly on account of Debussy's opera.

Debussy is famous for his innovations in orchestration and in piano writing; his Preludes and Études for the piano are the most impressive "miniatures" since the time of the early Romantics. Some would say the same for his songs. One of his later works, music for the ballet *Jeux* (Games), dissolves melody, theme, and rhythm so far that it was taken up as a model by the avant-garde after World War II.

For a short time Debussy wrote music criticism, in which he expressed in pungent prose the anti-German attitudes that were already manifest in his music. Debussy died of cancer in Paris during World War I, during a bombardment of his city by the Germans he hated.

Chief Works: For orchestra, *Prelude to "The Afternoon of a Faun"* (a famous poem by the French symbolist poet Mallarmé), Three Nocturnes, *La Mer* (The Sea), *Iberia, Jeux* (Games) ▪ The opera *Pelléas et Mélisande* ▪ For piano: Preludes and Études, *Children's Corner* Suite, and *Suite bergamasque,* including "Clair de lune" ▪ Songs to poems by Baudelaire, Verlaine, and Mallarmé ▪ A string quartet and other chamber music ▪ *Syrinx* for solo flute

Encore: After *Clouds,* listen to *Fêtes* (Festivals), *Prelude to "The Afternoon of a Faun,"* "Clair de lune."

These rich chords slip by without establishing a clear sense of tonality; gorgeous in themselves, they are not "functionally" significant. This use of parallel chords is one of Debussy's finest and most famous innovations.

Clouds might be said to fall into an **A B A′** form—but only in a very general way. Debussy shrinks from clear formal outlines; the musical form here is much more fluid than that of **A B A** structures observed in earlier music. This fluidity is something to bear in mind when following *Clouds* and other avant-garde music with Listening Charts. By design, avant-garde composers break down the sharp and (to them) oversimple divisions of older musical styles. If they avail themselves of form types such as rondo, sonata form, and so on, they do so in very free, imaginative ways.

In the **A** section of *Clouds,* the return of the "cloud" theme after a more active, restless passage suggests an internal **a b a′** pattern as well. The next idea, **B,** sounds at first like a meditative epilogue to **A;** it is built on a pentatonic scale (see page 327, again). But when the little pentatonic tune is repeated

LISTENING CHART 23

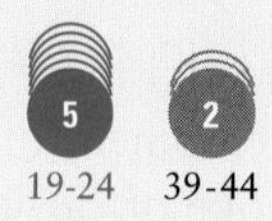

Debussy, *Clouds*

7 min., 0 sec.

Track		Time			
19 39		0:00	A	a	Cloud theme: clarinets and bassoons
		0:15			English-horn motive
		0:20			Quiet timpani roll—music almost stops
		0:34			Cloud theme: high strings
20 40		0:47			Downward chord passage
	0:15	1:02			Further development: strings
	0:34	1:21			English-horn motive, with a new echo in the French horn
	1:02	1:49			Downward chord passage
21 41		2:10		b	Rising section, more restless: woodwinds added
	0:30	2:40			Brief climax
	0:38	2:48			English-horn motive (with new even-note rhythm accompaniment) is repeated several times, until it dies away.
22 42		3:38		a′	Cloud theme, with new solo viola counterpoint
	0:16	3:54			Downward chord passage
23 43		4:12	B		A new tune enters tentatively, but then repeats itself; flute and harp
	0:27	4:39			Tune in strings and solo violin
	0:44	4:56			Tune in flute and harp
			(A′)		*Not a real "return" of* **A**, *only of selected elements standing in for* **A**
24 44		5:19			English-horn motive, with its echo
	0:31	5:50			Quiet timpani and low strings—prominent until the end
					Recollection of thematic fragments:
	0:54	6:13			Cloud theme: bassoons, then cellos
	1:13	6:32			**B** tune
	1:21	6:40			French-horn echo to the English-horn motive

ENGLISH HORN

FLUTE

several times, it begins to feel like a substantial section of contrast. The "return," **A′**, is really just a reference to some of **A**'s material, notably the English-horn figure. Then at the end the bassoons play a dim, disturbed fragment of the cloud theme; the flute hovers for a moment on the **B** tune; and the drum roll is extended—so as to suggest distant thunder, perhaps.

2 Stravinsky: The Primacy of Rhythm

Stravinsky's earliest work followed from that of his teacher, the nationalist composer Rimsky-Korsakov. But in three famous ballet scores written for the Ballets Russes in Paris, Stravinsky rapidly developed his own powerful, hard-edged avant-garde style, a style that can be compared to the contemporary fauve style in French painting (see page 323). These ballets reveal a fascinating progression toward a more and more abstract use of folk material. Compare the development of abstraction in art by Kandinsky and Picasso, which we spoke of earlier.

The first ballet, *The Firebird* (1910), spins a romantic fairy tale about the magical Firebird, the ogre Kastchei, and Prince Ivan Tsarevitch, son of the tsar. Its rich, half-Asian setting is matched by beautifully colored folk music and orchestral sound worthy of Debussy himself. But in the next ballet, Stravinsky moved from the steppes to the urban marketplace, to Mardi Gras in St. Petersburg. *Petrushka* (1911), the story of a carnival barker and his puppet, encouraged him to put a hard, satirical edge on his folk material. Then in *The Rite of Spring* (1913), Stravinsky boldly and brutally depicted the fertility cults of prehistoric Slavic tribes. Here Russian folk music, broken down into repeated, fragmentary motives, is treated as the source of primitive rhythmic and sexual energy, rather than picture-postcard charm.

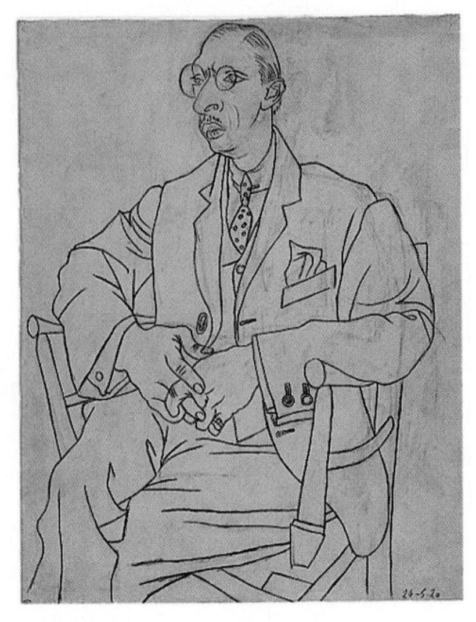
Stravinsky, drawn by Picasso during the period when they were associated at the Ballets Russes.

The musical style that Stravinsky brought to a head in the *Rite* has many features that struck listeners of the time as "barbaric," apart from its use of deliberately crude folk-tune fragments. The music was "abstract" in the sense that it sounded utterly unemotional, by Romantic standards. It was grindingly dissonant. It emphasized meter in a very heavy, exciting way, and the rhythms themselves were dazzling and unpredictable. Finally, the score is enormously loud: It demands a colossal orchestra, as though the composer wanted to show how he could control—and transform—the chief powerhouse of musical Romanticism.

IGOR STRAVINSKY
The Rite of Spring (1913): Part I, "The Adoration of the Earth"

The first performance of *The Rite of Spring* caused a riot; the audience was shocked and infuriated by the violent, dissonant sounds in the pit and the provocative choreography on the stage, suggesting rape and ritual murder.

The ballet has no real story, and Stravinsky even said that he preferred to think of the music as an abstract concert piece. However, inscriptions on the score specify a series of ancient fertility rites of various kinds, culminating in the ceremonial choice of a virgin for sacrifice. After this she is evidently danced to death in the ballet's second part, entitled "The Sacrifice."

My idea was that the Prelude should represent the awakening of nature, the scratching, gnawing, wiggling of birds and beasts.

Igor Stravinsky, reminiscing in 1960 about *The Rite of Spring*

Introduction The halting opening theme is played by a bassoon at the very top of its normal register. Avant-garde composers strained all the elements of music, including the ordinary capabilities of instruments. The bleating bassoon is joined by odd hootings on other woodwinds, gradually building up an extraordinary texture that is highly dissonant. The instrumental parts sound rather like a static series of preliminary fanfares (or perhaps like the calls of prehistoric wildlife?).

"Omens of Spring"—"Dance of the Adolescents" After a brief introduction, in which the dancers presumably "register" an awareness of spring's awakening, the "Dance of the Adolescents" commences with a famous instance of Stravinskian rhythmic irregularity. (Probably the original audience started their catcalls at this point.) A single very dissonant chord is repeated thirty-two times in even eighth notes—but with heavy accents reinforced by short, fat chords played by eight (!) French horns on the most unexpected beats:

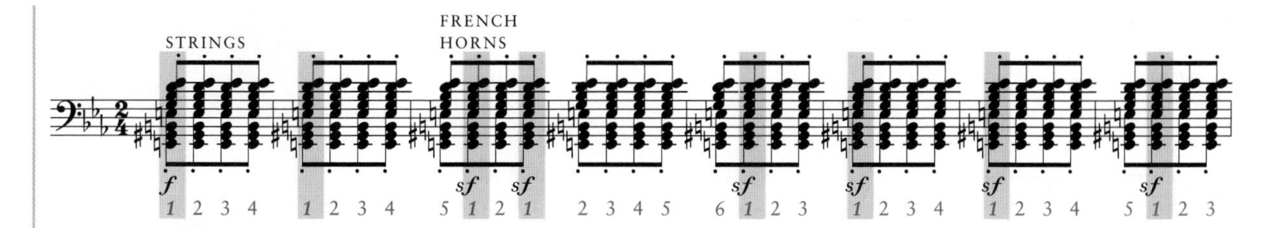

These accents completely upset ordinary meter. Instead of eight standard measures of four eighth notes— **1** *2 3 4,* **1** *2 3 4,* etc.—Stravinsky makes us hear **1** *2 3 4,* **1** *2 3 4 5,* **1** *2,* **1** *2 3 4 5 6,* **1** *2 3,* **1** *2 3 4,* **1** *2 3 4 5,* **1** *2 3.* (For a truly bewildering experience, try beating time to this passage.) Yet these irregular rhythms are also exhilarating, and they certainly drive the music forward in a unique way.

The repeating chords are now overlaid with new motives, derived from Russian folk song. The motives are repeated with slightly different rhythms and at slightly different lengths. This is Stravinsky's distinctive type of ostinato, a technique we have met with in many other kinds of music (pages 96, 108, 132); the ostinato is indicated by brackets on the example below. Like Debussy, Stravinsky tends to concentrate on small melodic fragments, but whereas Debussy soon abandons his fragments, Stravinsky keeps repeating his in this irregular, almost obsessive way.

"The Game of Abduction" New violence is introduced with this section, a whirlwind of brilliant rhythms, with much frantic pounding on the timpani.

The climax of *The Rite of Spring*

Igor Stravinsky (1882–1971)

The son of an important opera singer, Igor Stravinsky studied law and did not turn seriously to music until he was nineteen. He was fortunate to be able to study with Nikolai Rimsky-Korsakov, a survivor of the nationalist *kuchka* (see page 295) who was still composing actively.

Rimsky's brand of nationalism served young Stravinsky well in the famous (and still outstandingly popular) ballet scores *The Firebird, Petrushka,* and *The Rite of Spring,* which he wrote for the Ballets Russes, a Russian company centered in Paris. This enormously dynamic organization, run by a brilliant producer and man-about-the-arts named Sergei Diaghilev, astonished the blasé Parisian public with its exotic spectacles combining the newest and the most sensational in dance, music, scenery, and costume design. Among Diaghilev's dancers were Vaslav Nijinsky and George Balanchine; among his designers were Pablo Picasso and Henri Matisse.

After World War I Stravinsky composed more ballets for Diaghilev, as well as other works in a dazzling variety of styles, forms, and genres. One of the first classical composers, along with Debussy, to be interested in jazz, Stravinsky wrote *Piano Ragtime* in 1917 (and, much later, *Ebony Concerto* for clarinetist Woody Herman's jazz band). He became an outspoken advocate of "objectivity" in music, which meant to him the rejection of Romantic emotionality. For many years he modeled his music on pre-Romantic composers such as Bach, Handel, and Mozart, transforming the music by his own unique rhythmic and harmonic style.

His final work in this vein, called **Neoclassicism,** was an opera, *The Rake's Progress,* which is a modern transformation of Mozart's *Don Giovanni.* This was written in America (to English words), where Stravinsky moved in 1939. After World War II his music grew more abstract and formal in style. During the last twenty years of his life, Stravinsky had as his protégé the young American conductor and critic Robert Craft, who helped to manage his affairs, conducted and promoted his music, and introduced him to the music of Schoenberg and Anton Webern.

For a quarter of a century people had regarded Stravinsky (and he regarded himself) as the leading Neoclassical composer in the French orbit, at the opposite pole from Schoenberg and the Viennese serialists. So he created yet another sensation when, in his seventies, he produced a remarkable group of late compositions employing serial technique.

After some scary stays in American hospitals, on which the composer's comments were particularly sardonic, Stravinsky died at his home in New York in 1971. He is buried in Venice, near the grave of Diaghilev.

Chief Works: Ballet scores, including *The Firebird, Petrushka, The Rite of Spring, The Wedding, Orpheus, Agon* ▪ *The Soldier's Tale,* an unusual chamber-music piece with narrator ▪ An "opera-oratorio," *Oedipus the King; The Rake's Progress,* an opera in English (words by the poet W. H. Auden) ▪ Two symphonies; concertos; *Symphony of Psalms* for orchestra and chorus ▪ Other religious works: a Mass, *Requiem Canticles, Threni* (settings from the Lamentations of Jeremiah)

Encore: After *The Rite of Spring,* listen to *Petrushka* and *Symphony of Psalms.* Read *Conversations with Stravinsky* by Robert Craft.

"Round Dances of Spring" After a moment of respite, a short, quiet introduction conveys a remarkably desolate, empty feeling, partly as a result of its novel orchestration: a high (E♭) clarinet and low (alto) flute playing two octaves apart. Then a slow dragging dance emerges, built out of the third folk-tune fragment from the "Dance of the Adolescents."

The strong downbeat makes the meter hypnotic—but one or two added or skipped beats have a powerful animating effect. The dance reaches a relentless climax with glissando (sliding) trombones, gong, cymbals, and big drum. After a sudden fast coda, the primordial introduction returns to conclude the section.

Four more sections follow our selection in Part I of *The Rite of Spring.* The dynamic "Games of the Rival Tribes" introduces two more folk-tune fragments. A huge masked figure is borne aloft by the male dancers in a slower section, the "Procession of the Sage"; the Sage then performs a brief ceremony,

LISTENING CHART 24

5 25-31 3 13-19

Stravinsky, *The Rite of Spring,* from Part I

Ballet score. 10 min., 41 sec.

Track	Time	Total	Section	Description
25 13		0:00	**Introduction**	Bassoon "fanfare," *p,* twice interrupted by English horn
		1:04		Fanfares in oboe, high (E♭) clarinet, bass clarinet
		1:41		Buildup
26 14		2:04		New motive in the oboe and E♭ clarinet
	0:29	2:33		Stop; return of the bassoon fanfare, *p*
	0:37	2:41	**Omens of Spring**	Dance of the Adolescents is foreshadowed; the music stops and starts, ending with a high violin chord.
	0:58	3:02		Tempo is established; trill, ♩♩♩♩ rhythm introduced
27 15		3:08	**Dance of the Adolescents**	Loud rhythmic passage with irregular accents (French horns); various motives are introduced
	0:36	3:44		Rhythmic passage again
28 16		3:53		Folk-song fragment no. 1—bassoons and contrabassoon, etc.
	0:28	4:21		Abrupt interruption of the regular rhythm
	0:37	4:30		Return of the introductory "Omens" music
	0:53	4:46		Folk-song fragment no. 2—French horn, flutes
	1:27	5:20		Folk-song fragment no. 3—trumpets (triangle)
	1:50	5:43		Folk-song fragment no. 2—piccolos; big buildup
29 17		6:16	**The Game of Abduction**	Faster; frantic rhythms. Brass is prominent; sliding horn calls
	0:55	7:11		Ending passage: alternation between scurrying figures in the winds and heavy booms in the drums
30 18		7:33	**Round Dances of Spring**	Slower; introduction: flute trills, clarinet melody
	0:34	8:07		The main slow dance rhythm is introduced; woodwind motive
31 19		8:45		Folk-song fragment no. 3 (slower than before)—violas, *mf*
	0:54	9:39		Folk-song fragment no. 3, *ff,* with cymbals
	1:15	10:00		Climactic passage—brass
	1:33	10:18		Short coda: faster, with violent rhythmic interjections
	1:49	10:34		Brief return of the slow introduction, *p*

Very fast *ff*

Slow *mf*

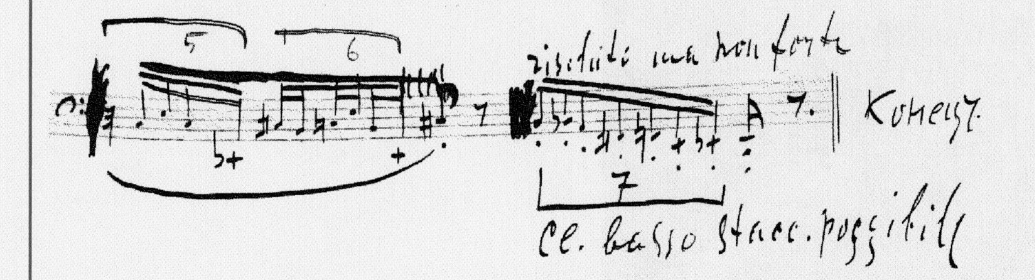

Musical sketches for *The Rite of Spring*

"Adoration of the Earth." The concluding orgiastic "Dance of the Earth" is built on a fast and furious ostinato.

What is conspicuously absent from any of this is emotionality. Tough, precise, and barbaric, it is as far from old-line Romantic sentiment as it is from the delicate, shadowy vision of Debussy. In Stravinsky's later works the barbarism was tamed, but the dry, precise quality remained, and so did the exhilarating irregular rhythms. Throughout his long career they provided him with a powerful strategy for movement, unlike that of any other composer. It was the primacy of rhythm that produced Stravinsky's "new language" for music.

3 Expressionism

In Paris during the first decades of the twentieth century, Debussy's shifting musical shadows and Stravinsky's extroverted gestures were on display nightly at the Ballets Russes. Some analogies can be drawn between these composers in stylistic terms, but primarily what they had in common was their rejection, in their different ways, of the steamy emotions of late Romanticism.

In Austria and Germany, however, composers pressed forward with music that was increasingly emotional and complex. As though intent on taking Romantic fervor to its ultimate conclusion, they found themselves exploiting

Nightmarish images recur in expressionist art. Perhaps the most famous expressionist image is *The Scream,* by the Norwegian artist Edvard Munch (1863–1944).

Arnold Schoenberg (1874–1951)

The most conscious and self-conscious member of music's avant-garde was Arnold Schoenberg, who grew up in Europe's most intense musical environment, the Vienna of Johannes Brahms and Gustav Mahler. He was largely self-taught in music, though he found a mentor in the conductor and composer Alexander von Zemlinsky, whose sister became Schoenberg's first wife. (His second wife, also had a musical brother, the leader of an important string quartet—a quartet that featured Schoenberg's music.) A man of unusual versatility, Schoenberg produced important books on music theory, painted (and gave exhibitions of) pictures in expressionist style, and wrote the literary texts for many of his compositions.

His early music—notably *Transfigured Night* of 1899, still his best-known work—followed from the late Romantic tradition of Brahms and Mahler. But Schoenberg soon came to feel that he was destined to carry this tradition through to its logical modern development, by way of increasing chromaticism and atonality. Listeners felt otherwise, and Schoenberg's revolutionary compositions of the 1900s probably met with more hostility than any other works in the entire history of music. At the same time, they attracted the sympathetic interest of Mahler and Richard Strauss, and drew a coterie of brilliant young students to Schoenberg.

Schoenberg's music grew progressively more and more atonal, but he was nearly fifty before he developed the twelve-tone (or serial) system. Of all the "new languages" for music attempted by the early avant-garde composers, serialism was the most radical and also the most fruitful. After World War II, even though some leading radicals rejected Schoenberg's music, they still used his fundamental idea of a serial language for music.

As a Jew, Schoenberg was forced to leave Germany when the Nazis came to power, and he spent the rest of his life in Los Angeles, becoming a U.S. citizen in 1941. His unfinished opera *Moses and Aaron* of 1933 is both a Judaic epic and an allegory of the problem of modernist communication with the public. *A Survivor from Warsaw* was written in memory of the slaughter that occurred in Warsaw's Jewish quarter when the Nazis crushed the uprising there in 1943.

Arnold Schoenberg was a strange personality: gloomy, uncompromising, inordinately proud, and also highly superstitious. Of all the major composers, he was the first great teacher since Bach; besides his close associates of the Second Viennese School, he strongly influenced many other musicians who sought him out as a teacher. At the end of his life he taught at UCLA. Though only some of his music has won popular approval, musicologists (and many musicians) regard Schoenberg as the most significant composer of the twentieth century.

Chief Works: An early "symphonic poem" for string sextet, *Transfigured Night;* Five Orchestral Pieces; two chamber symphonies, a piano concerto and a violin concerto ▪ *Erwartung* ("Anticipation"), an expressionist monodrama for one singer and orchestra; the unfinished opera *Moses and Aaron* ▪ Choral works, including *Gurrelieder,* the unfinished oratorio *Jacob's Ladder,* and *A Survivor from Warsaw* ▪ Songs, including *The Book of the Hanging Gardens,* to texts by the German symbolist poet Stefan George; *Pierrot lunaire* ("Moonstruck Pierrot"), a chamber-music piece with *Sprechstimme* singer ▪ Four string quartets and other chamber music

Encore: After *Pierrot lunaire,* listen to *Verklärte Nacht* ("Transfigured Night") and Five Orchestral Pieces.

extreme states, extending all the way to hysteria, nightmare, even insanity. This movement, *expressionism,* shares its name with important parallel movements in art and literature (see page 323).

These years also saw the publication of the first works of Sigmund Freud, with their bold new analysis of the power of unconscious drives, the significance of dreams, and the central role of sexuality. Psychoanalytic theory had a clear impact on German expressionism; a vivid example is *Erwartung* (Anticipation), a monologue for soprano and orchestra written by Arnold Schoenberg in 1909. In it, a woman comes to meet her lover in a dark wood and spills out all her terrors, shrieking as she stumbles upon a dead body she believes to be his. One cannot tell whether *Erwartung* represents an actual scene of hysteria, an allegory, or a Freudian dream fantasy.

Schoenberg was the leading expressionist in music. He pioneered in the "emancipation of dissonance" and the breakdown of tonality, and shortly after

World War I he developed the revolutionary technique of serialism (see page 326). Even before the war, Schoenberg attracted two brilliant Viennese students who were only about ten years his junior, and who shared almost equally in his path-breaking innovations. Schoenberg, Anton Webern, and Alban Berg are often referred to as the Second Viennese School, by analogy with the earlier Viennese triumvirate of Haydn, Mozart, and Beethoven.

5
32-33

ARNOLD SCHOENBERG
Pierrot lunaire (1912)

This highly influential song cycle sets text by a minor symbolist poet, Albert Giraud. Like many artists of the time—poets as well as composers—Giraud is not easy to figure out at once. Pierrot is the eternal sad clown, and hence perhaps also the alienated artist; but why is he called "lunar"? In poems that are dotted with Freudian imagery, we hear about his obsession with the moon, his amorous frustrations, his nightmarish hallucinations, his pranks and his adventures.

To match all this, Schoenberg wrote music which utterly lacks the tunes that one might expect to find in a set of songs. The soprano does not exactly sing or exactly speak, but performs in an in-between style of Schoenberg's invention called *Sprechstimme* ("speech-song"). **Sprechstimme** is an extreme example of the avant-garde composers' search through the most basic artistic materials—here, sound that is not even fully organized into pitches—for new

An expressionist Pierrot by Georges Rouault (1871–1958).

expressive means. Through *Sprechstimme,* Giraud's strange moonstruck poems are somehow magnified, distorted, parodied, and haunted all at the same time.

Pierrot lunaire calls for five instruments: flute, clarinet, violin, cello, piano. Three of their players double on other instruments; that is, the flutist sometimes switches to piccolo, the clarinetist to bass clarinet, and the violinist to viola. Not all the songs involve all the players, so nearly every song has its own unique accompaniment, ranging from a single flute in No. 7 to all eight instruments in No. 21 (the players switching within this one). Schoenberg's dazzling variety of instrumental effects compensates for the inherent sameness of the *Sprechstimme.*

We will examine two songs vastly different in expressive tone—both unsettling in their distinctive ways.

I only know that on the two occasions I heard Pierrot lunaire *I was conscious of the most profound impression I have ever experienced from a work of art, and that the enigmatic power of these pieces has left* permanent *traces on my innermost being. But when I look at the score it still remains completely mysterious. . . .*

Letter to Schoenberg from student Alban Berg, 1914

32 ***No. 8: "Night"*** (voice, piano, bass clarinet, cello) The poem presents the nightmarish aspect of expressionism; we could easily imagine the screaming figure of Edvard Munch's famous painting (see page 338) responding to a vision of this sort:

Finstre, schwarze Riesenfalter	Sinister giant black butterflies
Töteten der Sonne Glanz.	Eclipse the blazing disk of sun.
Ein geschlossnes Zauberbuch,	Like a sealed-up book of wizard's spells
Ruht der Horizont—verschwiegen.	Sleeps the horizon—secret silent.
Aus dem Qualm verlorner Tiefen	From dank forgotten depths of Lethe
Steigt ein Duft, Erinnrung mordend!	A scent floats up, to murder memory.
Finstre, schwarze Riesenfalter	Sinister giant black butterflies
Töteten der Sonne Glanz.	Eclipse the blazing disk of sun.
Und vom Himmel erdenwarts	And from heaven downward dropping
Senken sich mit schweren Schwingen	To the earth in leaden circles,
Unsichtbar die Ungetüme	Invisible, the monstrous swarm
Auf die Menschenherzen nieder...	Descends upon the hearts of men,
Finstre, schwarze Riesenfalter.	Sinister giant black butterflies.

Schoenberg used the lowest instruments of his ensemble to depict these ominous insects, weighty in a way utterly unlike real butterflies. Through the last section of the poem we can hear their swarm settling heavily downwards, blotting out the light of day and bringing on artificial night.

Schoenberg called this song a *passacaglia,* recalling a type of ostinato piece from the Baroque period (see page 106). If you listen closely you will hear that his music is dominated by the three-note ostinato shown in the margin.

The ostinato is announced at the very beginning by the piano, then taken up by the cello and bass clarinet; and is also the last thing you hear at the end of the song. Throughout, the instrumental accompaniment is largely constructed from overlapping versions of it, moved freely to various pitch levels. The soprano is even asked to sing it, at the eerie bottom of her range, on the word *verschwiegen* (secret silent)—the only moment in the entire song cycle when Schoenberg has her abandon *Sprechstimme* for conventional song.

Note, however, that the ostinato is chromatic in essence, its last pitch set a half-step below its first. From such simple materials, Schoenberg can both unsettle conventional tonality and match the scary tone of Giraud's words.

33 ***No. 18: "The Moonfleck"*** (voice, piano, piccolo, clarinet, violin, cello) The piano plays a short introduction, or transition from the previous number. Listen to this piano passage several times. Dense, dissonant, atonal, and alarmingly intense in its motivic insistence, the passage gives us Schoenberg's uncom-

promising version of musical modernism in a nutshell. It also seems devised to recall the loudest, scariest moments of "Night," one of many such musical connections across Schoenberg's cycle.

In the song itself, the tone shifts abruptly from this intensity; now it is not horror but the nagging bother of an obsession. Pierrot can neither forget nor bear the moonfleck that has soiled his tuxedo:

Einen weissen Fleck des hellen Mondes Auf dem Rücken seines schwarzen Rockes, So spaziert Pierrot im lauen Abend, Aufzusuchen Glück und Abenteuer.	With a fleck of white—bright patch of moonlight— On the back of his black jacket, Pierrot strolls about in the mild evening air On his night-time hunt for fun and good pickings.
Plötzlich stört ihn was an seinem Anzug, Er beschaut sich rings und findet richtig— Einen weissen Fleck des hellen Mondes Auf dem Rücken seines schwarzen Rockes.	Suddenly something strikes him as wrong, He checks his clothes over and sure enough finds A fleck of white—bright patch of moonlight— On the back of his black jacket.
Warte! denkt er: das ist so ein Gipsfleck! Wischt und wischt, doch— bringt ihn nicht herunter!	Damn! he thinks, There's a spot of plaster! Rubs and rubs, but can't get rid of it.
Und so geht er, giftgeschwollen, weiter, Reibt und reibt bis an den frühen Morgen— Einen weissen Fleck des hellen Mondes.	So goes on his way, his pleasure poisoned, Rubbing and rubbing till dawn comes up— At a fleck of white, a bright patch of moonlight!

In his setting Schoenberg explores timbres completely different from those of "Night." He uses high-pitched, quicksilver motives, scattered through the whole ensemble, to depict flickering moonlight. Simultaneous fugues and canons are at work, but what the listener perceives is a fantastic lacework of sounds, with hardly a hint of tonality, as Pierrot frantically but in vain brushes at himself. "The Moonfleck" uses extremely complicated technical means to achieve a unique sonorous effect.

ALBAN BERG (1885–1935)
Wozzeck (1923)

After Schoenberg, the most powerful exponent of expressionism in music was his student Alban Berg. Berg's opera *Wozzeck,* first conceived during World War I, was completed in 1923. In general plan, this opera can be described as Wagnerian, in that it depends on musical continuity carried by the orchestra. It uses leitmotivs, and contains no arias. Its musical style owes much to Schoenberg's *Pierrot lunaire.*

Background Berg set a remarkable fragmentary play by the German dramatist Georg Büchner, a half-legible draft that was discovered after his death in 1837. In a series of brief, savage scenes spoken in the plainest vernacular, Büchner presents an almost paranoid vision of the helpless poor oppressed by society. Berg's music for the play's dialogue is all highly intense, and he kept the tension up by writing continuous orchestral interludes during the blackouts between all the scenes, five in each of the opera's three acts.

Franz Wozzeck is an inarticulate and impoverished soldier, the lowest cog in the military machine. He is troubled by visions and tormented for no apparent reason by his captain and by the regimental doctor, who pays him a pittance for serving as a human guinea pig in bizarre experiments. Wozzeck's lover, Marie, sleeps with a drum major, who beats Wozzeck up when he makes some objection. Finally Wozzeck murders Marie, goes mad, and drowns himself.

Act III; Interlude after Scene ii Scene ii is the murder scene. When Wozzeck stabs Marie, she screams, and all the leitmotivs associated with her blare away in the orchestra. It is said that all the events of our lifetime flash before our eyes at the moment of dying.

A blackout follows, and the stark interlude between the scenes consists of a single pitch played by the orchestra in two gut-bursting crescendos. Don't turn the sound down if this passage hurts your ears—it is supposed to. (It is also pretty hard on the stagehands, who have less than half a minute for the scene change.)

Scene iii The lights snap on again. In a sordid tavern, Wozzeck gulps a drink and seeks consolation with Marie's friend Margret. Berg's idea of a ragtime piano opens the scene—one of many signs that European music of the 1920s had woken up to American influences. But it is a distorted, utterly dissonant ragtime, heard through the ears of someone on the verge of a breakdown.

The music is disjointed, confused, shocking. When Margret gets up on the piano and sings a song, her song is distorted, too:

Suddenly she notices blood on Wozzeck's hand. It smells like human blood, she says. In a dreadful climax to the scene, the apprentices and street girls in the inn come out of the shadows and close in on Wozzeck. He manages to escape during another blackout, as a new orchestral interlude surges frantically and furiously.

An earlier scene from *Wozzeck*

The Second Viennese School

This is a phrase often applied to Schoenberg and his two closest associates, Anton von Webern and Alban Berg. Both studied with him in Vienna before World War I, and both followed him in adopting serialism in the 1920s. They were very different in musical personality, and serialism did not really draw them together; rather it seems to have accentuated the unique qualities of each composer.

But both Webern's vision of musical abstraction and his brilliant use of serialism made him a natural link between the first phase of modernism, around World War I, and the second. Though he died in 1945, shot in error by a member of the American occupying forces in Austria, his forward-looking compositions caught the imagination of an entire generation of composers after World War II.

Anton von Webern (1883–1945), who later dropped the aristocratic von, was an unspectacular individual whose life revolved around his strangely fragile artistic accomplishment. Despite his aristocratic background, he became a devoted conductor of the Vienna Workers' Chorus, as well as holding other rather low-profile conducting positions.

From the start, Webern reacted against the grandiose side of Romanticism, as represented by the works of Richard Strauss and Gustav Mahler. He turned his music about-face, toward abstraction, atomization, and quiet: so quiet, that listening to his music, one listens to the rests almost as much as to the notes themselves. His compositions are all extremely brief and concentrated (we will discuss one of them on page 370). Webern's entire musical output can be fitted on three CDs.

Alban Berg (1885–1935), in contrast, looked back; more than Schoenberg and certainly more than Webern, he kept lines of communication open to the Romantic tradition by way of Mahler. Berg's first opera, *Wozzeck,* was an immediate success on a scale never enjoyed by the other "Second Viennese" composers. His second opera *Lulu* (1935) is now also a classic, though it made its way slowly—Berg had only partly orchestrated Act III when he died, and both operas were banned by the Nazis.

Berg died at the age of 50 as a result of an infected insect bite. After his death, it came out that he had been secretly in love with a married woman, and had employed a musical code to refer to her and even to address her in his compositions—among them a very moving Violin Concerto (1935), his last work, which also refers to two other women.

The whole of scene iii is built on a single short rhythm, repeated over and over again with only slight modifications—*but presented in many different tempos.* This twitching "master rhythm" is marked above the two previous examples, first at a fast tempo, then at a slow one; we first heard it in the timpani in the interlude between scenes ii and iii. Another obvious instance comes when Margret first notices the blood:

Here is yet another kind of ostinato—very different from Stravinsky's kind (see page 335). Even though this master rhythm may elude the listener in a good many of its appearances, its hypnotic effect contributes powerfully to the sense of nightmare and fixation.

Scene iv Fatefully, Wozzeck returns to the pond where he murdered Marie. The orchestra engages in some nature illustration, making strange macabre

For once, a composer picture that's different: Alban Berg looks out over a lifesized portrait of himself painted by Arnold Schoenberg.

sounds (so different from the nature illustration in Debussy's *Clouds*!). Wozzeck's mind has quite cracked. He shrieks for the knife (in powerful *Sprechstimme* reminiscent of *Pierrot lunaire:* see page 340), discovers the corpse, and sees the blood-red moon and the pond, too, seemingly filled with blood. He walks into the water, saying that he has to wash himself.

At this point, his principal tormenters walk by. The Captain and the Doctor hear the vivid orchestral gurgles and understand that someone is drowning, but like people watching a mugging on a crowded city street, they make no move to help. "Let's get away! Come quickly!" says the terrified Captain—in plain, naturalistic speech, rather than the *Sprechstimme* used by Wozzeck.

In the blackout after this scene, emotional music wells up in the orchestra, mourning for Wozzeck, Marie, and humanity at large. Here Berg adopts and even surpasses the late Romantic style of Gustav Mahler. Our recording fades after a few minutes of this great lament.

Scene v Berg (following Büchner) has yet another turn of the knife waiting for us in the opera's final scene. Some children who are playing with Wozzeck's little son run off to view his mother's newly discovered corpse. Uncomprehending, he follows them. The icy sweetness of the music here is as stunning as the violent music of the tavern scene and the weird pond music. In turning Büchner's visionary play fragment into an expressionist opera, Berg created one of the great modernist theater pieces of the twentieth century.

LISTEN Berg, *Wozzeck,* Act III, scenes iii and iv

34-38

SCENE iii: A tavern

Track	Time	Character	German	English
34	0:29	**Wozzeck:**	Tanzt Alle; tanzt nur zu, springt, schwitzt und stinkt, es holt Euch doch noch einmal der Teufel!	Dance, everyone! Go on, dance, sweat and stink, the devil will get you in the end.
				(Gulps down a glass of wine) *(Shouts above the pianist:)*
			Es ritten drei Reiter wohl an den Rhein, Bei einer Frau Wirtin da kehrten sie ein. Mein Wein ist gut, mein Bier ist klar, Mein Töchterlein liegt auf der . . .	*Three horsemen rode along the Rhine, They came to an inn and they asked for wine. The wine was fine, the beer was clear, The innkeeper's daughter . . .*
			Verdammt! Komm, Margret!	Hell! Come on, Margret! *(Dances with her)*
			Komm, setzt dich her, Margret! Margret, Du bist so heiss. . . . Wart' nur, wirst auch kalt werden! Kannst nicht singen?	Come and sit down, Margret! Margret, you're hot! Wait, you too will be cold! Can't you sing?
				(She sings:)
	1:43	**Margret:**	*In's Schwabenland, da mag ich nit, Und lange Kleider trag ich nit. Denn lange Kleider, spitze Schuh, Die kommen keiner Dienstmagd zu.*	*But Swabia will never be The land that I shall want to choose, For silken dresses, spike-heeled shoes, Are not for servant girls like me.*
		Wozzeck:	Nein! keine Schuh, man kann auch blossfüssig in die Höll' geh'n! Ich möcht heut raufen, raufen. . . .	No shoes! You can go to hell just as well barefoot! I'm feeling like a fight today!
35	2:29	**Margret:**	Aber was hast Du an der Hand?	But what's that on your hand?
		Wozzeck:	Ich? Ich?	Me? My hand?
		Margret:	Rot! Blut!	Red! Blood!
		Wozzeck:	Blut? Blut?	Blood? Blood? *(People gather around)*
		Margret:	Freilich . . . Blut!	Yes, it is blood!
		Wozzeck:	Ich glaub', ich hab' mich geschnitten, da an der rechten Hand. . . .	I think I cut myself, on my hand. . . .
		Margret:	Wie kommt's denn zum Ellenbogen?	How'd it get right up to the elbow, then?
		Wozzeck:	Ich hab's daran abgewischt.	I wiped it off there. . . .
		Apprentices:	Mit der rechten Hand am rechten Arm?	Your right hand on your right arm?
		Wozzeck:	Was wollt Ihr? Was geht's Euch an?	What do you want? What's it to you?
		Margret:	Puh! Puh! Da stinkt's nach Menschenblut!	Gross! It stinks like human blood! *(curtain)*

Confusion. The people in the Inn crowd around Wozzeck, accusing him. Wozzeck shouts back at them and escapes.

SCENE iv: A pond in a wood

Track	Time	Character	German	English
36	3:41	**Wozzeck:**	Das Messer? Wo ist das Messer? Ich hab's dagelassen . . . Näher, noch näher. Mir graut's! Da regt sich was. Still! Alles still und tod . . . Mörder! Mörder! Ha! Da ruft's! Nein, ich selbst.	The knife! Where is the knife? I left it there, around here somewhere. I'm scared! Something's moving. Silence. Everything silent and dead . . . Murderer! Murderer! Ah, someone called! No, it was just me.
			Marie! Marie! Was hast Du für eine rote Schnur um den Hals? Hast Dir das rote Halsband verdient, wie die Ohrringlein, mit Deiner Sünde? Was hangen Dir die schwartzen Haare so wild?	Marie, Marie! What's that red cord around your neck? A red necklace, payment for your sins, like the earrings? Why is your dark hair so wild?

	Time	Speaker	German	English
1:03	4:44		Mörder! Mörder! Sie werden nach mir suchen. . . . Das Messer verrät mich! Da, da ist's!	Murderer! Murderer! They will come look for me. . . . The knife will betray me! Here, here it is.
			So! da hinunter! Es taucht ins dunkle Wasser wie ein Stein. Aber der Mond verrät mich . . . der Mond ist blutig. Will denn die ganze Welt es ausplaudern?!— Das Messer, es liegt zu weit vorn, sie finden's beim Baden oder wenn sie nach Muscheln tauchen.	There! Sink to the bottom! It plunges into the dark water like a stone. But the moon will betray me. . . . The moon is bloody. Is the whole world going to betray me? The knife is too near the edge— they'll find it when they're swimming or gathering mussels.
			Ich find's nicht . . . Aber ich muss mich waschen. Ich bin blutig. Da ein Fleck . . . und noch einer.	I can't find it. But I have to get washed. There's blood on me. Here's one spot . . . here's another. . . .
			Weh! Weh! Ich wasche mich mit Blut! Das Wasser ist Blut . . . Blut. . . .	Oh, woe! I am washing myself in blood! The water *is* blood . . . blood. . . . *(drowns)*
37	6:21	**Captain:**	Halt!	Wait!
		Doctor:	Hören Sie? Dort!	Don't you hear? There!
		Captain:	Jesus! Das war ein Ton!	Jesus! What a sound!
		Doctor:	Ja, dort.	Yes, there.
		Captain:	Es ist das Wasser im Teich. Das Wasser ruft. Es ist schon lange Niemand entrunken. Kommen Sie, Doktor! Es ist nicht gut zu hören.	It's the water in the pond, the water is calling. It's been a long time since anyone drowned. Come away, Doctor! This is not good to hear.
		Doctor:	Das stöhnt . . . als stürbe ein Mensch. Da ertrinkt Jemand!	There's a groan, as though someone were dying. Somebody's drowning!
		Captain:	Unheimlich! Der Mond rot und die Nebel grau. Hören Sie? . . . Jetzt wieder das Achzen.	It's weird! the red moon, the gray mist. Now do you hear? . . . That moaning again.
		Doctor:	Stiller, . . . jetzt ganz still.	It's getting quieter—now it's stopped.
		Captain:	Kommen Sie! Kommen Sie schnell!	Let's get away! Come quickly! *(curtain)*
38	7:53	ORCHESTRAL MUSIC (LAMENT)		

4 Modernism in America: Ives

I remember, when I was a boy—at the outdoor Camp Meeting services in Redding (Conn.), all the farmers, their families and field hands, for miles around, would come afoot or in their farm wagons. I remember how the great waves of sound used to come through the trees . . . There was power and exaltation in those great conclaves of sound from humanity.

Charles Ives

As we have seen, Paris and Vienna, centers of intense activity in all the arts, were also the first centers of modernist music. Echoes of modernism, some loud, some soft, were heard elsewhere in Europe: in Italy, where there was a short-lived movement called Futurism, and in Germany, Russia, Hungary, and England. We will discuss the case of two important modernist composers, Béla Bartók and Richard Strauss, in Chapter 21.

It is still amazing, however, that a major modernist composer should have emerged in the United States as early as around 1900; for at that time America had no rich tradition of classical music, and what we did have was resolutely conservative. "Emerged" is not quite the word, for what also amazes is that Charles Ives worked in isolation, composing in his spare time. His music was scarcely performed until the 1950s.

Many of Ives's compositions have American subjects, such as *Central Park in the Dark* and *Some Southpaw Pitching*. His *Holidays* Symphony includes

Ravel with the legendary dancer Vaclav Nijinsky, the star of his ballet *Daphnis and Chloé* in 1912. A year later Nijinsky was responsible for the riot-inducing choreography of Stravinsky's *Rite of Spring.*

1 Maurice Ravel

Of the many impressive composers active in the first half of the twentieth century, several have maintained and even increased their hold on audiences up to the present day. One is the opera composer Giacomo Puccini (1858–1924), discussed on page 353. The surprise Broadway hit of 2002 was Puccini's opera *La Bohème,* sung in its original language with English supertitles, over a hundred years after its premiere in Turin, Italy.

Two other composers were Russians who fled the Russian Revolution of 1917: Sergei Rachmaninov (1873–1943), who went to Switzerland and then to the United States, and Sergei Prokofiev (1891–1953), who relocated to Paris, but later returned home to a hard life in the Soviet Union under Stalin. Rachmaninov, one of the greatest pianists of all time, wrote extraordinarily popular piano concertos.* Prokofiev is known for a wider range of works—operas, including one based on *War and Peace* by Tolstoy, film scores, concertos, and his famous ballet *Romeo and Juliet.*

Maurice Ravel, born in 1875 in the south of France, was also attracted to Paris. From the very start, his music was marked by refinement, hyper-elegance, and a certain coolness; musicians admire him for his superb workmanship and high style. As Debussy occupied the middle ground between Romanticism and modernism, Ravel carved out a place for himself between impressionism and Neoclassicism. While his harmonies and chord progressions often remind us of Debussy, he favored clarity, precision, and instant communication, qualities he found in earlier musical forms and styles.

Few composers have ranged as widely in imagination as Ravel. In his music he visited Spain, Madagascar, Asia, ancient Greece, America, and—again and again—the world of childhood. He even evoked Vienna, in a bitter anti-German parody of waltz music, *La Valse.*

SG 6

*There is a section from Rachmaninov's *Rhapsody on a Theme by Paganini,* a concerto-like work for piano and orchestra, on our Student Guide CD-ROM.

MAURICE RAVEL
Piano Concerto in G (1931)

A light-hearted piece for piano and small orchestra, the Piano Concerto in G is Ravel's tribute to jazz (his most outspoken tribute, but not his first; like Debussy and Stravinsky, Ravel was fascinated by jazz long before he came to the United States in 1928 and haunted night-spots in Harlem). Americans like George Gershwin and Aaron Copland incorporate jazz accents in their compositions in a fairly direct way (see page 404). With Ravel everything is slightly skewed, as through a special filter, with a delicacy and elegance that we think of as characteristically French, perhaps, and that Ravel projects more clearly than any other composer.

First Movement (Allegramente) The first theme is *not* jazzy. A long, lively, folk-like tune is presented in the sort of fabulous orchestration that is this composer's hallmark: After a whiplash—literally—a piccolo plays the tune with syncopated *pizzicato* (plucked) string chords and the piano shimmering in the background. But the tune really belongs to a special high trumpet (trumpet in C), with the syncopated chords barked out by the other brass.

PICCOLO

Maurice Ravel (1875–1937)

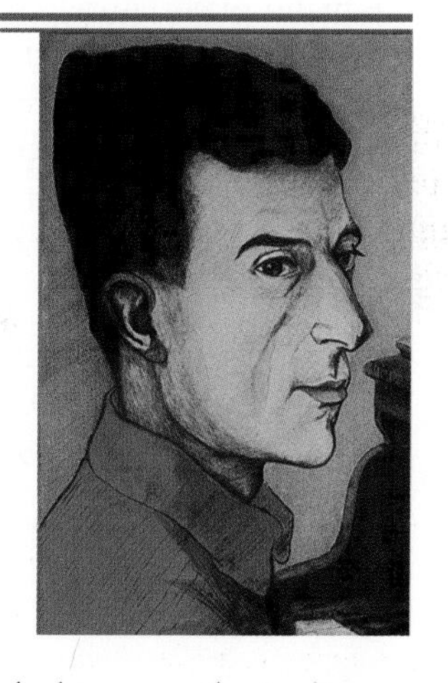

Maurice Ravel was born in a little town in the south of France, two miles from the Spanish border, and was brought to Paris at an early age. His mother came from the Basque region of Spain, and many of his compositions have "exotic" Spanish resonances—*Boléro,* most famously, also *Habanera, The Spanish Hour,* and others.

Ravel spent no fewer than sixteen lackluster years at the Paris Conservatory, the gateway to French musical life in those days, while his older contemporary Claude Debussy emerged as a leader in the music of modernism. When Debussy died in 1918, Ravel was acknowledged as the leading composer of war-ravaged France. Ravel despised Germany and German music, and he was young enough to volunteer for military service against the Germans in World War I, despite his frail and retiring personality.

From the time of his first major success, with the impressionistic piano piece *Jeux d'eau* (*Fountains;* 1901), it was clear Ravel had an amazing ear for sonority, and the magical sound of his music for piano or orchestra is unmatched. In the following years he belonged to a group of modernist artists and writers who called themselves the Apaches (a name with fauve overtones: see page 323), but he never really warmed to the modernist spirit. He was the most meticulous and exquisite of composers, and his aim was for clarity above all. Some of his most famous compositions make use of classical forms, such as the *Sonatine* for Piano and the Piano Concerto in G.

Ravel never married, seems to have had no close relationships, and lived an uneventful life at his home in Paris. His one big trip, in 1928, was to America; here he met George Gershwin (and Charlie Chaplin) and came back with a small fortune. In 1932, Ravel succumbed to a rare brain disease; he died five years later. The Piano Concerto in G of 1931 was his last work but one.

Chief Works: Orchestral works: *Mother Goose Suite, La Valse,* two piano concertos, the ballet scores *Boléro* and *Daphnis and Chloé* ■ One-act operas: *L'Heure espagnole* (The Spanish Hour) and *L'Enfant et les sortilèges* (The Child Bewitched), a delightful childhood fantasy ■ *Gaspard de la nuit,* one of the hardest pieces ever written for piano; *Jeux d'eau;* and a charming piano *Sonatine* ■ Songs; a string quartet ■ Many arrangements for orchestra, including Musorgsky's *Pictures at an Exhibition* (see page 295)

Encore: After the first movement of the Piano Concerto in G, listen to the second movement; *Boléro; Sonatine* for Piano.

The piano now introduces a second theme that recalls the blues—not directly, but clearly enough. A third theme suggests romantic torch songs of the 1930s. Typical of early jazz is Ravel's use of short *breaks,* instrumental interludes between lines of a song lasting just one or two measures (see page 390). He catches this device perfectly with the high clarinet (E-flat clarinet) and a muted trumpet cutting into theme 2, with swishing sounds from the piano and the harp.

At a later point, the harp plays theme 2 itself, in a dreamlike episode that brings this busy movement to a state of near suspension.

After the piano and orchestra have presented themes 2 and 3, the piano engages in vigorous, propulsive music of the sort that often leads to cadences in concertos (see page 202). A new syncopated motive strongly implies that a cadence is coming, though the actual resolution is disguised.

Ravel uses the classical form for a concerto first movement (see page 201), but in the freest possible way. He skips both the orchestra exposition and the development section entirely. A passage that he labels "cadenza" resembles a true cadenza in that it comes near the end of a concerto first movement and the piano plays entirely solo, yet it feels nothing like a free improvisation; in fact, the unaccompanied piano plays theme 3. Ravel drew on classical tradition but at the same time invented his own super-clear and listener-friendly form for the Piano Concerto in G.

(At the very end of the first movement, Ravel borrows a favorite device invented by Debussy, a long series of parallel chords. The effect could hardly be more different: Debussy's chords—in *Clouds,* for example; see page 331—are *piano,* legato, silky, vague, and atmospheric; Ravel's are *fortissimo* and staccato, crisp and clear.)

2 Béla Bartók

Growing up in Hungary in the 1890s, the young Béla Bartók was first swept away by the international avant-garde leaders Debussy and especially Richard Strauss. Later in his career he was also influenced by his close contemporary Stravinsky. Bartók was, however, a man of multiple careers—pianist, educator, and musicologist as well as composer. His deep commitment to folk music—much deeper than Stravinsky's—and his professional involvement with it had a decisive impact on his music. Many would say that Bartók was more successful in integrating folk music into classical music than any other composer.

The right type of peasant music is most perfect and varied in its forms. Its expressive power is amazing, and at the same time it is devoid of all sentimentality and superfluous ornaments. It is simple, sometimes primitive, but never silly. . . . A composer in search of new ways cannot be led by a better master.

Béla Bartók

Folk music assured that Bartók's music would never (or seldom) become as abstract as much modernist music was. There is always an earthy feel to it; even at its most dissonant, there will be an infectious folk-dance swing or a touch of peasant melody. This is true even in works of his most modernist period, around 1925–1935. The austere String Quartet No. 4 of 1928 is often regarded as Bartók's masterpiece.

LISTENING CHART 26

5
39-43

Ravel, Piano Concerto in G, first movement

Free sonata form. 8 min., 12 sec.

Track		Time	
39			**EXPOSITION**
		0:00	**Theme 1,** piccolo, syncopated strings *pizzicato*
		0:24	**Theme 1,** trumpet, syncopated brass
		0:36	Sudden modulation
			Second group
		0:44	**Theme 2,** piano: slower; interrupted by the "break"
40		1:40	**Theme 3,** piano
	0:37	2:17	**Theme 3,** orchestra—bassoon, trumpet
	0:55	2:35	Vigorous, driving music for the piano
	1:14	2:54	Break
	1:48	3:28	Approach to a cadence
41		3:36	**Retransition:** upward scales in the piano
			RECAPITULATION
	0:09	3:45	**Theme 1,** piano, *ff;* returns to the tonic key
	0:21	3:57	Sudden modulation
			Second group
	0:29	4:05	**Theme 2:** piano—with gong
42		4:30	Dreamlike episode: **theme 2,** harp
	0:38	5:08	Break; melody continues in the French horn
	1:15	5:45	"Cadenza": **theme 3,** with extensive trills
	2:04	6:34	**theme 3:** piano and orchestra
	2:35	7:05	Piano: vigorous, brilliant
	3:07	7:37	Approach to a cadence
			CODA
43		7:42	Orchestra (trumpet), *f,* in the original tonic key, with motives derived from **theme 1**
	0:17	7:59	*ff*

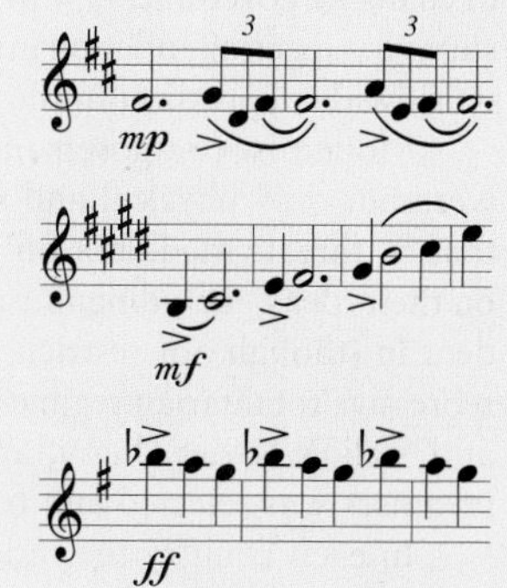

After that time Bartók's music gradually became more accessible, and the references to folk songs in it became more mellow and, often, more poignant. He now used established forms such as sonata form and rondo; this made his music easier to follow for listeners already accustomed to these forms from eighteenth- and nineteenth-century music. And many of his last works include passages reminiscent of Romanticism: Violin Concerto No. 2, the popular Concerto for Orchestra, and Quartet No. 6 of 1939—another good candidate for Bartók's greatest composition.

Music and Totalitarianism

European composers of the early twentieth century found their lives profoundly affected by the economic, political, and military upheavals of the time. Besides the sheer threat of annihilation in a time of war, other, more subtle difficulties loomed. Many institutions that composers' careers depended on—orchestras, opera companies, and the like—disappeared or fell into disarray. Some were victims of changing governments with new priorities. Others did not survive staggering inflation in parts of Europe in the 1920s, worldwide depression in the 1930s, or war in the 1940s.

Modernist composers in particular faced threats that were not only physical and social but also *ideological*—that is, threats made not on their lives or livelihoods but on their ideas, including musical ideas. This was most evident in (though not restricted to) the two most powerful repressive totalitarian regimes of the era. In Nazi Germany and Stalin's Soviet Union, artistic modernism in most of its guises was rejected and banned.

In each country the rationale for repression was the same distorted outgrowth of nineteenth-century nationalism: Art ought to speak straightforwardly to the national "folk" and give voice to its aspirations and history. This tenet was foreign to modernist art's emphasis on originality and individualism, its formal intricacies, and its questioning of the fundamental bases of artistic expression—its elitism, as the culture czars in Russia and Germany saw it. For Nazis and Stalinists alike, modernist art had no right to exist.

Nazi Germany

Hitler's regime promoted music of the great German masters; Beethoven and Wagner were special favorites. But it banned explicitly modernist music, supporting instead the latter-day romanticism of the aging Richard Strauss, for example (see page 353). Meanwhile Jewish composers and other musicians faced extermination. Those who could fled to countries all over the world, many of them to the United States. Arnold Schoenberg is the best known of these refugees (see page 339), but there were many others, including Kurt Weill, composer of "Mack the Knife," who established a second career on Broadway. Béla Bartók, who was not Jewish, but who also decided to emigrate when his native Hungary finally joined with Hitler, had a harder time (see page 359).

The Soviet Union

Perhaps the most famous victim of ideological muzzling was the greatest Russian composer after Stravinsky, Dmitri Shostakovich (1906–1975; Shostakóvitch). Growing up under Communism, he originally followed the dictates of the state without question. Shostakovich was certainly no radical modernist of the Schoenberg sort; but his music did show novel tendencies, including especially strong dissonant harmonies. A darling of the regime in the early 1930s, he nevertheless walked a perilous path.

With his opera *Lady Macbeth of the Mtsensky Region* of 1934, when he was twenty-eight, he went over the edge. Subject matter and music were equally shocking. The worldwide clamorous success of this work brought Stalin himself to see it. Two days later the official government newspaper *Pravda* condemned the work and issued a scarcely veiled threat to the composer: "The power of good music to affect the masses has been sacrificed to a petty-bourgeois, formalist attempt to create originality through cheap clowning. It is a game of clever ingenuity *that may end very badly.*"

In fact, Shostakovich was rehabilitated a year after the *Pravda* broadside. But his troubles were not over; he was condemned again ten years later—only to be rehabilitated once more when Stalin died. To what extent Shostakovich accommodated the regime, or criticized it by means of half-secret musical signals in his later compositions—signals recognized by his audiences—is a fascinating question still under debate.

Dmitri Shostakovich, on one of his rare trips to the West (1962). Looming over him is the Communist Party functionary who came along.

Bartók collecting folk songs: He was using recording equipment just a few years after commercial records began coming out. Around 1906, these rural Hungarians seem less amazed by the primitive phonograph than by the camera.

BÉLA BARTÓK (1881–1945)
Music for Strings, Percussion, and Celesta (1936)

This interesting composition can be thought of as an informal symphony in the usual four substantial movements, composed for a specially constituted small orchestra. Much of the time the instruments are divided into two sections that answer one another back and forth.* Besides strings, Bartók includes piano, harp, celesta (see pages 37 and 41), timpani—very important—and other percussion. We do not learn this all at once, however. The celesta makes its first entrance with an exquisite effect halfway through the first movement. The piano and harp arrive in the second, and the xylophone only in the third.

We've rehearsed a lot . . . the conductor and orchestra have all worked with me showing the greatest affection and devotion; they claim to be very enthusiastic about the work (I am too!). A couple of spots sound more beautiful and startling than I had imagined. There are some very unusual sounds in it!

Bartók writes to his wife about rehearsals for the premiere of Music for Strings, Percussion, and Celesta

Second Movement (Allegro) The music bubbles over with variety, an exhilarating rush of little melodic tags, rhythms, folk-dance fragments, and novel percussion sounds. It is all held together by sonata form.

A "preface" played by *pizzicato* (plucked) strings precedes theme 1:

The preface, theme 1, and the contrapuntal bridge passage—all are energized by motive **a.** One thinks of Beethoven's Fifth Symphony. This motive works especially well in the timpani, which play a powerful role in this movement.

*This is a principle that goes back at least as far as Giovanni Gabrieli in the early Baroque era: See page 94.

Béla Bartók (1881–1945)

Béla Bartók showed unusual talent as a pianist and composer at an early age. Music was the avocation of his father, who was principal of an agricultural school in Hungary; after his death Bartók's mother worked as a piano teacher, tirelessly promoting her son's career.

Few musicians have ever had as varied a career as Bartók. He was a prolific composer and a fine pianist, as was his second wife; they appeared as a two-piano team. (Both of his wives had been his students.) In conjunction with another important Hungarian composer, Zoltán Kodály, he directed the Budapest Academy of Music, where the two men tried out new ideas in music teaching. An outcome of this side of Bartók's career is his *Mikrokosmos,* a series of 153 graded piano pieces starting with the very easiest. Well known to most piano students today, the *Mikrokosmos* has probably done more than any other work to introduce modernism to large numbers of musicians in their impressionable years.

Also with Kodály, Bartók undertook a large-scale investigation of Hungarian (and other) folk music, writing several standard books in the field of ethnomusicology, which is the scholarly study of folk music and the music of non-Western cultures. He published many folk-song and folk-dance arrangements, and his other compositions are saturated with folk elements such as rhythms, modes, and melodic turns. The outstanding nationalist composer of the twentieth century, Bartók left a body of work that equals or surpasses that of any nineteenth-century nationalist.

Bartók was strongly opposed to the Nazis. After they came to power in Germany, he refused to concertize there and switched away from his German publisher. And his liberal views caused him a good deal of trouble from right-wingers in Hungary. In 1940, after the outbreak of World War II, Bartók came to America, but he was not well known here and there was little interest in his music. His last years were a struggle to complete his Third Piano Concerto and the Viola Concerto. Ironically, his important works earned a wide, enthusiastic audience shortly after his death.

Chief Works: Concerto for Orchestra, 3 piano concertos, Violin Concerto, Music for Strings, Percussion, and Celesta (for small orchestra) ▪ Six string quartets; a fascinating Sonata for Two Pianos and Percussion ▪ An opera, *Bluebeard's Castle,* and a ballet, *The Miraculous Mandarin* ▪ *Cantata profana,* for chorus, soloists, and orchestra ▪ *Mikrokosmos* and other works for piano ▪ Many folk-song arrangements for various ensembles, including Six Rumanian Dances

Encore: After Music for Strings, Percussion, and Celesta, listen to the Violin Concerto and Quartet No. 6.

There is a full stop after the bridge, so self-conscious that one wonders if Bartók is making fun of sonata-form conventions. The second theme group contains at least three very short themes. Theme 3 has a folk-dance lilt about it:

Suddenly the piano enters with a theme containing odd note-repetitions. Since the pianist has hardly played at all up to this point, this new theme feels more like a beginning than like a conclusion. Still, it functions as a cadence theme; very soon the exposition ends with another exaggerated cadence.

The timpani introduce the ***development section.*** Motive **b,** played *pizzicato,* comes in for an extensive workout. After a moment the strings drop down into an accompaniment for an amazing passage for piano, snare drum, and xylophone,

LISTENING CHART 27

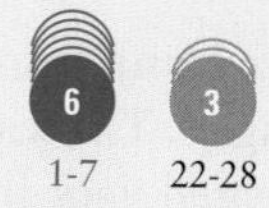

Bartók, Music for Strings, Percussion, and Celesta, second movement (Allegro)

Sonata form. 6 min., 59 sec.

Track		Time	Section	Description
			EXPOSITION	
1 / 22		0:00	Theme 1	With pizzicato "preface"
		0:23		Held note, drum
		0:26	Bridge	
				CADENCE Big stop, after drum beat
2 / 23			**Second group**	
		0:56	Theme 2	
	0:14	1:10	Theme 3	Folklike tune, strong beat
				Developmental
	0:36	1:32	Theme 4	Over a string trill
	1:08	2:04	Cadence theme	Piano
				CADENCE Exaggerated cadence; drum beat
			DEVELOPMENT	
3 / 24		2:24	Section 1	Irregular rhythms: piano and percussion, leading to the Stravinskian passage (see below)
	0:49	3:13	Section 2	Pizzicato scales, from the "preface"
4 / 25		3:34		New folklike tune
				Drum prepares:
	0:31	4:05	Section 3	Crescendo
	1:21	4:55	(retransition)	Drum grows insistent; slowdown ⟶
			RECAPITULATION	
5 / 26		5:10	Theme 1	With timpani; meter change
	0:18	5:28	Bridge	
6 / 27			**Second group**	
		5:40	Theme 2	Transformation: triple meter
	0:11	5:51		New continuations
	0:24	6:04	Theme 4	Transformation: triple meter
	0:44	6:24	Cadence theme	Piano, as before
			CODA	
7 / 28		6:32		New fast dialogue on theme 1

punching out syncopated notes. This must have been inspired by the riot-producing "Dance of the Adolescents" in Stravinsky's *The Rite of Spring* (see page 334).

Next, pizzicato string scales in imitative polyphony weave endless new knots and tangles. The scales blend into another folklike tune, similar to theme 3, which is repeated very freely. Introduced by the timpani, a fugue starts up in the lowest register, preparing for the recapitulation. The fugue subject is derived from theme 1, with the meter askew.

And when the ***recapitulation*** comes, after much signaling from the timpani, and after an expectant slowdown, the meter is changed throughout. Theme 1 vacillates between duple and triple meter, and the second group tips the balance: themes 2 and 4 each return in swinging triple meter (as shown in the examples on page 360). Theme 3 returns more freely. It takes the piano's odd "cadence theme" to bring us back to the solid duple meter of the start. As a *coda,* Bartók stages a fast, intense dialogue on theme 1.

What I like about music is its ability to be convincing, to carry an argument through to the finish, though the terms of the argument remain unknown quantities.

Poet John Ashbery, 1976

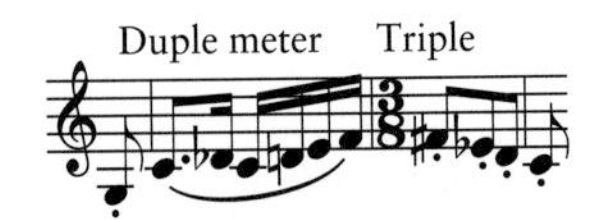

3 Aaron Copland

America's leading composer of the generation after Charles Ives was Aaron Copland. (Ives was active from around 1895 to 1920; Copland wrote his main works from 1925 to 1950.) Young composers after World War I found many more options open to them than Ives had around 1900. The musical climate was much more favorable to new ideas, partly because the United States had been growing more aware of all things European, including European new music. Like important American writers who lived abroad—Gertrude Stein, T. S. Eliot, Edith Wharton, Ernest Hemingway—composers now associated themselves with European modernism in a way that their predecessors never did.

The chief modernist influence on Copland was Stravinsky, and one of Copland's most impressive works is a strenuous set of twenty Variations for Piano (1930) that reflects Stravinsky's dry rhythmic style and his "objective"

It bothers me not at all to realize that my range as a composer includes both accessible and problematic works. To have confined myself to a single compositional approach would have enhanced my reputation for consistency, no doubt, but would have afforded me less pleasure as a creator.

Aaron Copland, 1941

Ben Shahn, *Trio*, 1955. © Estate of Ben Shahn/VAGA, NY, NY

A worker, a farmer, and a boss are shown "harmonizing": a political allegory by New York painter Ben Shahn (1898–1969), a friend of Copland.

Aaron Copland (1900–1990)

Aaron Copland was the son of Russian-Jewish immigrants living in Brooklyn. After a solid musical education at home, he went abroad to study in Paris. Like many other overseas students, Copland was fortunate to be able to work with a remarkable musician named Nadia Boulanger (1887–1979). For fifty years Boulanger was a revered teacher and mentor of composers, even though she gave up composition herself in deference to the talent of her sister Lili, also a composer, when Lili died tragically at the age of twenty-four. Boulanger encouraged Copland's interest in Stravinsky, whose avant-garde style influenced him greatly.

Back in America, Copland tirelessly promoted American music. He organized an important series of concerts (with another composer, Roger Sessions) to showcase new American scores, wrote articles and books, and formed a Composer's Alliance. Like many artists and writers of the 1930s, he was attracted by leftist ideology and the idea that art should "serve the people." Many works drawing on American folk materials stem from this period of Copland's career, as does his high-school opera *The Second Hurricane.* During World War II he wrote *A Lincoln Portrait* and *Fanfare for the Common Man,* patriotic works, and *Appalachian Spring,* a celebration of traditional American values.

After 1940 Copland headed up the composition faculty at the important summer school at Tanglewood, Massachusetts, in association with the Boston Symphony Orchestra, but his output as a composer decreased. Among his students was Leonard Bernstein. Devoid of the egoism characteristic of so many artists, Copland was one of the most beloved figures of modern American music.

Chief Works: For orchestra: 3 symphonies, *A Lincoln Portrait* (with a speaker), *El salón México* (incorporating South American jazz) ▪ Film scores: *Of Mice and Men* and *The Red Pony* (by John Steinbeck), *Our Town* (Thornton Wilder) ▪ Clarinet Concerto, written for jazzman Benny Goodman ▪ Operas: *The Second Hurricane* and *The Tender Land;* ballet scores *Billy the Kid, Rodeo, Appalachian Spring* ▪ For piano: Variations (Copland's outstanding modernist work; 1930), a sonata, Piano Fantasy (a fine late work; 1957) ▪ A song cycle to poems by Emily Dickinson

Encore: After *Appalachian Spring,* listen to *El salón México* and Clarinet Concerto.

aesthetic. But after this, Copland's music grew more traditional. Like Strauss, Bartók, and most other composers of the time, he held back from the most extreme manifestations of modernism and forged his own style using such elements of modernism as he needed.

Music for Americans

Again like Bartók, Copland adopted a nationalist agenda. From the start he felt that as an American, he should write music that would speak to his fellow Americans. Unlike Bartók, however, and unlike Ives, he did not focus on the music of his own immediate tradition—in the one case, Hungarian folk song and dance, and in the other, hymns and popular songs known in New England. Copland reached out for American music of all kinds, regions, and ages.

He first turned to jazz, in orchestral pieces called *Music for the Theater* and *El salón México.* Later he incorporated cowboy songs in the ballets *Rodeo* and *Billy the Kid,* an old Shaker melody in *Appalachian Spring,* and square dancing in *The Tender Land,* an opera about growing up in the corn belt. Old hymns make an appearance in his song cycle *Twelve Poems of Emily Dickinson.* In this eclectic attitude we can perhaps again trace the influence of Stravinsky, who over his long career also tapped many musical sources, from Russian folk song to Bach, Chaikovsky, and Schoenberg.

AARON COPLAND
Appalachian Spring (1945)

8-11 29-31

The ballet *Appalachian Spring* was choreographed and danced by Martha Graham, a towering figure in American modern dance. She conceived of "a pioneer celebration in spring around a newly built farmhouse in the Pennsylvania hills in the early part of the last century." From his ballet music, Copland arranged a concert suite in six continuous sections. Our recording is conducted by the composer.

'Tis the gift to be simple,
'tis the gift to be free,
'Tis the gift to come down
where you ought to be,
And when we find ourselves
in the place just right
'Twill be in the valley of
love and delight. . . .
When true simplicity is
gained
To bow and to bend we
shan't be ashamed,
Turn, turn will be our
delight,
Till by turning, turning
we come round right.

"Simple Gifts"

8
29

Section 1 The ballet begins with a very still, clear, static passage of a kind that Copland made very much his own. It seems to catch the spirit of a vast silent landscape at dawn, perhaps, or just before dawn. Solo instruments play meditative figures in counterpoint; an occasional solemn pulse is heard in the harp.

9
30

Section 2 Here "the bride-to-be and the young farmer husband enact the emotions, joyful and apprehensive, their new domestic partnership invited." The celebration of their new house starts with a lively square dance. Soon a new slower melody—something like a hymn—looms up in counterpoint to the dance figures, first in the wind instruments and then in the strings:

After a section of irregular rhythm, reminiscent of Stravinsky, the music dies down into a prayerful version of the hymn. We also hear little fragments of the dance.

Sections 3 and 4 The next two sections pick up the tempo: Section 3 evokes another whirling square dance and section 4 is a danced sermon by a revivalist and his followers. Both sections include quiet statements of the hymn.

LISTEN

Copland, *Appalachian Spring* SECTION 5

0:00	5:14	**Theme**
0:37	5:51	**Variation 1**
1:05	6:19	**Variation 2**
1:51	7:05	**Variation 3**
2:31	7:45	**Variation 4**

10
31

Section 5 The next dance is choreographed to a set of variations on a Shaker song, "Simple Gifts." The Shakers, a religious sect adhering to celibacy and common ownership of property, founded scattered communities from New York to Kentucky in the late eighteenth century.

The four variations are little more, really, than playings of the tune or part of the tune by different instruments, in different keys, and in different tempos. Sometimes melodic phrases are heard in imitation.

11 *Section 6* Finally, after some music that the program says is "like a prayer," the hymn and the landscape music return once again. We realize that Copland has ingeniously made one grow out of the other. The ballet concludes very quietly. Perhaps the housewarming celebrations have gone on all night, and we are now experiencing another clear gray dawn, a reminder of the many lonely dawns the pioneer couple will face together in the years to come.

Web: *Research and test your understanding of alternatives to modernism at* **<bedfordstmartins.com/listen>.**

Modern dance is, with jazz, one of the great American art forms. Martha Graham (1894–1991), who commissioned and choreographed Copland's *Appalachian Spring,* was one of the legendary group of women who created modern dance in the early twentieth century.

CHAPTER 22

The Late Twentieth Century

Only twenty-one years, from 1918 to 1939, separated the two cataclysmic wars of the twentieth century. It was an uneasy period. The terrible devastation of World War I had stunned artists as well as everybody else, and the sorts of extravagant experimentation that had marked the prewar period no longer seemed appropriate. There was a new tendency toward abstraction, and also a search for standards and norms. At the time, Schoenberg's serialism and Stravinsky's Neoclassicism were seen as two different efforts to achieve some kind of consolidation, organization, and order.

But these efforts were undercut by a new round of devastating events. First came the economic depression, worldwide and protracted, that began in the late 1920s. Then, in the 1930s, the ominous rise of Hitler and the unbelievable (and, by many, disbelieved) tyranny of Stalin led to a second world war. With the attack on Pearl Harbor at the end of 1941, the United States was thrown into this war to an extent that made our involvement in World War I seem minor. The occupation of France, the siege of Leningrad, the bombings of London, Dresden, and Tokyo, the mass murders in the concentration camps, the detonation of atom bombs over Hiroshima and Nagasaki—these events were virtually impossible for human beings (including artists) to take in. History seemed to be showing that all human conceptions or representations of the world were illusory.

In the postwar world, artists in any medium faced greater uncertainties than ever before. One response to this among composers was to move toward a kind of absolute freedom. While some of them continued to write music according to models of the past, a radical generation of avant-garde composers invented new systems—or entertained the idea of destroying all systems.

1 Modernism in Music: The Second Phase

Modernism reemerged as the driving force in music during the third quarter of the twentieth century, but it was modernism in a new, more extreme phase. It was a fascinating phase—and no less fascinating because two of its main tendencies can seem almost contradictory.

First of all, highly intellectual constructive tendencies came to the fore, inspired by Schoenberg's serialism, but going far beyond it. There were even efforts to "serialize" rhythm, sonority, and dynamics—that is, to set up predetermined series of note durations or tone colors and compose with them in a fixed order. Never before had such complex mathematical theories been advanced to compose and explain music.

Meanwhile, other composers moved in the opposite direction, relinquishing control over some elements of musical construction and leaving them to chance. (We have already discussed an early anticipation of this move, *The Unanswered Question* by the ever-original Ives.) Some of these same composers also worked toward an extreme simplification of musical materials, offering a stark alternative to the cerebral complexities of post–World War II "total serialism."

It may seem strange to find composers who followed such different paths grouped together under the same general rubric of avant-garde modernism. However, both groups, the complex constructivists and the chance composers, pursued the same goal: They all wanted to question the most general premises that had guided music composition before them. Debussy might have blurred the identity of melodic themes, Stravinsky might have undermined the regularity of musical meter, and Schoenberg might have dispensed altogether with tonality. But mainstream modernism after 1945 questioned every one of these features of the musical tradition at once and others as well—to the point of even questioning the composer's role in structuring a work at all.

New Sound Materials

In this light another general tendency of modernist composers after World War II is not at all surprising: their demand for new sound materials. The ordinary orchestra, even as expanded by Debussy, Stravinsky, and others, now struck them as stiff and antiquated. They explored amazing new sonorities—nonmusical noises, unexpected new sounds squeezed out of old instruments, and an infinite range of musical materials produced not by instruments at all, but by electronics.

The search for new sonorities began when composers made new demands of the standard sources of music. Singers were instructed to lace their singing with hisses, grunts, clicks, and other "nonmusical" noises. Pianists had to stand up, lean over the piano, and pluck the strings or hit them with mallets. Using a special kind of breath pressure, clarinetists learned to play chords called *multiphonics*—weird-sounding chords by conventional standards but fascinating to those attuned to the new sound universe.

Western orchestras and chamber music groups had always been weak in percussion, as compared to their counterparts in many non-Western cultures, notably the gamelans of Indonesia, as we have seen (page 214). Even more to the point, Western art music had been weak in this respect as compared to jazz. Marimbas, xylophones, gongs, bells, and cymbals of many kinds—percussion instruments that had been used only occasionally in the art music of earlier times—became standard in the postwar era.

However, the truly exciting prospect for new sonorities in music emerged out of technology developed during the war: the production of music by electronic means.

Electronic Music

Recording equipment can *reproduce* sounds of any sort—music, speech, and all the sounds and noises of life. Electronic sound generators can *generate* sounds from scratch—in principle, any sounds that can be imagined, or calculated using formulas derived from the science of acoustics.

The Pianist by Pablo Picasso

A technological breakthrough during World War II, the development of magnetic tape, made the storing and handling of sound much easier. It also opened up exciting possibilities for modifying it by manipulating the tape: making tape loops, changing speed, cutting and splicing, and so on. Across the second half of the twentieth century, we can discern three stages in the evolution of electronic music, each of them defined by new technological possibilities:

- *Musique concrète* Shortly after World War II composers began incorporating the sounds of life into their compositions. This they called "concrete" music because it used actual sound, as contrasted to the "abstract" products of electronic sound generators. Sounds (traffic noise was a favorite) were recorded, painstakingly manipulated in ways such as those mentioned above, and then (usually) put on phonograph discs.

  Musique concrète lives on, in a sense, in *sampling,* now that technology has made it easy for anything that is recorded—traffic noise, commercial records, special effects—to be put under keyboard control for easy combination.

- *Synthesizers* In the early postwar period electronic sound-generation was unbelievably clumsy, requiring whole rooms full of radio equipment and complicated machinery to carry out tape manipulations. Only after the advent of transistors (silicon chips were still in the future) could viable equipment be envisaged. In the 1960s various *synthesizers* appeared, apparatus designed specifically for music, with arrays of sound-producing modules connected by "patch cords" to create complex sounds.

  At first they worked one note at a time. Still, they allowed many composers to produce taped music, and also to combine music on tape with performed live music. It was still difficult to produce "customized" sound in real time.

Electronic music: from a synthesizer of the 1960s to a mixing board of the 2000s. Violinist Chee-Yun, left, and pianist Akira Eguchi, right, stand in front of the board.

Computer music The amazing evolution of computers over the last twenty years has allowed for an equally amazing evolution in music. Today electronic music can be produced on a home computer, using sequencer software to record, edit, and reproduce digital sounds in patterns and sequences at will. Advanced synthesizers now produce their stuff in real time (as the simpler synthesizers of popular music have been doing for years). They can interact via computer with live musicians as they perform to produce today's cutting-edge interactive computer music.

On the Boundaries of Time

Sonority is one of two areas in which avant-garde music in its second postwar phase made the greatest breakthroughs. The other area was time and rhythm.

To understand one aspect of this development, let us try to contrast two radically different pieces of music. One is a tiny piece by Schoenberg's student and friend Anton Webern, the fourth of his Five Orchestral Pieces of 1913 (see page 344). The whole piece—it is all of six measures long—can be shown on one line of music:

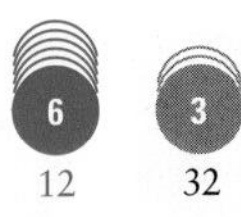

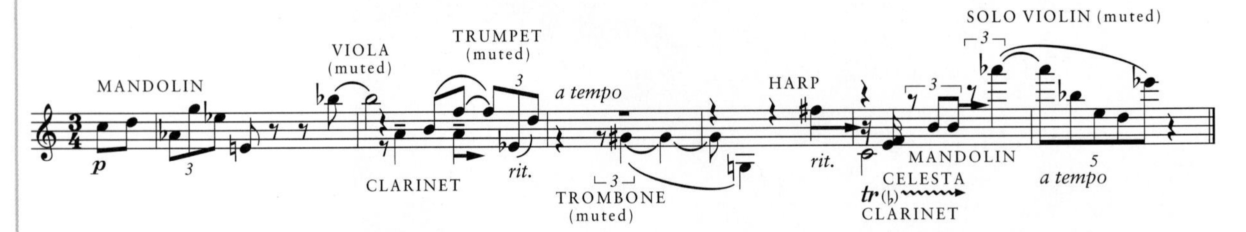

Listen to it several times: The music feels exceptionally concentrated, because the relationship between the notes is so strained by the "atomized" orchestration and the complex network of pitches and rhythms. Each note somehow becomes a separate little source of tremendous energy. This might be described as a *very short* time segment of *very high* intensity.

Contrast this with *In C,* a famous avant-garde work from the 1960s by the American composer Terry Riley. *In C* lasts for about forty-five minutes. During this time the instruments repeat over and over again a set of fifty-three tiny melodic figures that spell out only three harmonies—three harmonies drawn out over the music's total span. The pitches and rhythms are simple, indeed deliberately soothing. This might be described as a *very long* time segment of *very low* intensity.

With both Webern and Riley, we measure time (because we have no other way) in the same units: minutes and seconds. Yet the *feeling* of time is very different in the two. It is like the difference between one minute at the end of a tied basketball game and one minute in the middle of an all-night truck run across South Dakota. Such contrasting perceptions of time were now widely explored and exploited by musicians of the avant-garde.

Webern's unique vision of time made him a major influence in the postwar years, even though he died at the end of World War II. Composers were fascinated by his intense, seemingly disconnected note patterns, with their flickering instrumental sounds and their highly complex rhythms. Riley's *In C* and works like it became prophetic of a later development in music which gathered force in the 1970s and 1980s, *minimalism* (see page 380).

Chance Music

In playing his fragmentary melodies, the instrumentalists in Riley's *In C* interacted with each other in ways largely unspecified by the composer. *In C* thus exemplifies the **chance music** we mentioned earlier. (It was also called *aleatoric music,* from *alea,* Latin for "dice.") This term covers a great variety of music in which certain elements are not precisely specified by the composer, but left to chance—in a way that usually *is* specified by the composer.

In an extreme case, a chance composer would work out a way of throwing dice so as to determine which instruments, which pitches, and so on were to be used in his or her music. In a less extreme case, a performer getting to a certain place in a piece would be told to play anything at all, so long as it was (for example) loud and fast. Strictly speaking, what would be heard would be determined by chance, but the composer could count on a type of controlled chaos for a limited span of time, a span situated between two passages of fully written-out music.

Whereas earlier modernists had questioned traditional assumptions about melody and dissonance, chance composers questioned even more basic assumptions about musical time. The musical forms we have studied throughout this book tend to mark off time as a clear linear progress and even make it goal-directed: Think of the recapitulation of a Beethoven sonata form. More generally, time is conventionally plotted on a graph in the same way that distance is—see page 20—and a "timer" tells us when to get things done.

Is time always (chance composers would ask: is it *ever*) actually experienced in this way? Must music convey such an experience? Could it instead mark time as a random sequence of events, or even as "timeless," like the suspended consciousness we experience in certain kinds of meditation? Such questions, and a passive sense of time that cuts against our goal-directed culture, lie at the root of chance music.

2 The Postwar Avant-Garde

After World War II, exciting composers seemed to appear like magic from almost every corner of the globe. Among the leaders from France, Germany, and Italy were Olivier Messiaen (1908–1994), Pierre Boulez (b. 1925), Karlheinz Stockhausen (b. 1928), and Luciano Berio (1925–2003). They were joined by the Poles Witold Lutosławski (1913–1994) and Krzysztof Penderecki (b. 1933), the Hungarian György Ligeti (b. 1923), the Greek Iannis Xenakis (1922–2001), the Americans Milton Babbitt (b. 1916), John Cage (1912–1992), and Elliott Carter (b. 1908), and the Japanese Tōru Takemitsu (1930–1996).

Many of these composers are still composing actively—and interestingly—fifty years later, in the new millennium. But fifty years later, it cannot be said that their music has gained a firm place in the musical repertory or in the hearts of most music listeners (at least, as far as the United States goes). Modernism's first phase—the phase just before World War I—produced works that now count as "classics": Berg's *Wozzeck,* a fixture in the opera house; Bartók's string quartets, played by every professional string quartet; and Stravinsky's *Rite of Spring,* an all-time favorite in the CD catalog, with more than fifty listings. For acknowledged masterpieces written after World War II, however—such as Boulez's fascinating song cycle *Le Marteau sans maître,* or Berio's moving and powerful *Sinfonia*—similar acceptance has been slow in coming.

György Ligeti (b. 1923)

György Ligeti studied at the Budapest Academy of Music, and as a young man was appointed professor there. Unable to pursue his unique sound visions under the Communist restrictions prevailing in Hungary, he left for the West in 1956. Ligeti was past thirty before his advanced music became known.

Ligeti typifies both the search for new sonorities that occupied the postwar avant-garde and also their new attitudes toward time. Some of his music uses no clear pitches, or chords; or, more accurately, while he may start with pitches and chords, he soon adds so many more pitches that all sense of consonance, dissonance, and even the quality of pitch itself is lost. What remain

Violet, Black, Orange, Yellow on White and Red, by the American painter Mark Rothko (1903–1973). The overwhelming yet placid sheets of color merging into one another recall the musical technique in compositions such as Ligeti's *Lux aeterna.*

are "sound complexes" that can be experienced better than they can be described, sound complexes that slowly change with time.

And in the time dimension, there is no discernible meter or rhythm. Rather there is a sense of gradual, almost glacial surging of the sound complexes, followed by a sense of receding—all the while revealing incredibly diverse new tone colors.

My idea was that instead of tension-resolution, dissonance-consonance, and other such pairs of opposition in traditional tonal music, I would contrast "mistiness" with passages of "clearing up." "Mistiness" usually means a contrapuntal texture, a micropolyphonic cobweb technique . . .

From an interview with György Ligeti, 1978

GYÖRGY LIGETI
Lux aeterna (1966)

Ligeti's *Lux aeterna* is written for sixteen solo singers and chorus; often they sing chords that include all twelve pitches of the chromatic scale. We need a new vocabulary even to talk about music such as this, and some new diagrams—our pitch-time graph on page 20, which indicated melodies by lines, doesn't work for Ligeti's sound complexes. To represent them and show how they develop over time, we have to use nonmusical figures:

"expand" up and down

"expand" upward

"expand" downward

"contract" upward

"contract" downward

"focus"

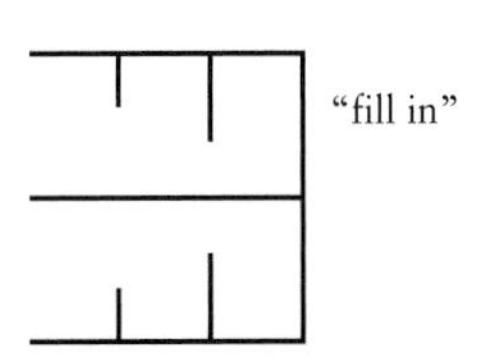

"fill in"

Lux aeterna starts with a single pitch, which Ligeti "expands" both upward and downward by slowly adding a dense mix of pitches above and below it. At other times he starts with a single pitch and expands it upward (adding mainly higher pitches) or downward (adding lower ones). Starting with a full-range sound, Ligeti can "contract" it: either downward (by removing notes till only a single low pitch remains), or upward, or to some pitch in the middle—an effect that can be called "focusing," on the analogy of a camera lens.

György Ligeti

The interest of this music, as we have said, is in the astonishing rich sonorities that are revealed by the slow ebbing and flowing of the sound complexes. Once we have accustomed our ears to this, we can appreciate that the musical form of *Lux aeterna* is simplicity itself. Of the four lengthy sound surges that constitute the piece, No. 1 (going up) seems to be "resolved" by No. 4 (going down). Nos. 1 and 4 are parallel, too, in that a high pitch is added halfway through—in this music, a very dramatic effect.

The words of *Lux aeterna* are taken from the Requiem Mass, but they can scarcely be heard and understood; the piece is a study in sheer vocal sonority. Ligeti wrote other "sound complex" pieces employing other forces, such as *Atmosphères* for full orchestra; *Lux aeterna* is his most famous work, thanks to its use in the 1968 Stanley Kubrick film *2001: A Space Odyssey.*

In the years since, Ligeti has written music in different styles. With Luciano Berio, he now stands out as one of the most active and impressive figures of the brilliant postwar generation.

Lux aeterna luceat eis, Domine, cum sanctis tuis in aeternum, quia pius es. . . .

May everlasting radiance shine upon them, O Lord, with thy saints in eternity: for you are merciful. . . .

LISTENING CHART 28

6
13-16

Ligeti, *Lux aeterna*
7 min., 52 sec.

13	0:00	WOMEN'S VOICES	Single pitch, high voices *(Lu)* The sound "expands," *up and down.*
	1:39		A high pitch is added softly: SOPRANO.
	2:02 2:22		The sound "contracts" *upward,* ending in . . . a single pitch (octave).
14	2:28	MEN'S VOICES	The high pitch stops, replaced by a chord (*Domine*). in the high men's voices.
0:08	2:36		The sound expands *downward.*
0:36	3:04		More lower voices; higher men's voices drop out; the sound slowly "focuses" to . . .
1:30	3:58		a held, dissonant chord.
15	4:03	MEN AND WOMEN	Complex sound, *f* (with a clear high, low, middle)
			The sound "contracts" *downward* to a lengthy focus,
1:30	5:33		ultimately to a single pitch.
16	5:45		Complex sound—low voices *(Domine)* Sound expands, *up.*
0:28	6:13		A high note is added: SOPRANO.
0:58	6:43		The high note is dropped, replaced by a very low note: BASS. Sound contracts *downward* to . . .
1:45	7:30		a two-note dissonant chord.

Edgard Varèse (1883–1965)

Edgard Varèse

Edgard Varèse is an older composer who bridged both phases of modernism in twentieth-century music. Though he had started his career in France before World War I, he emigrated to America in 1915, and it was here that he found his voice (late in life, like Haydn).

The music Varèse wrote in the 1920s was among the most radical in the world at that time. He developed an approach to rhythm and especially to sonority that surpassed anything the other early avant-garde composers had attempted. *Hyperprism* is scored for seven wind instruments and seven percussion, and *Ionisation* is for percussion alone—thirteen percussionists playing forty-five instruments, including a siren. The manipulation of what had been thought of as "noise" into coherent musical patterns was a heady forecast of modernist music of the post–World War II era.

EDGARD VARÈSE
Poème électronique (1958)

17

Indeed, it was after World War II that this veteran of many a modernist battle really came into his own. Around 1930, Varèse had unsuccessfully tried to persuade the Bell Telephone Company to set up a research center for electrically produced music. Now the introduction of electronic composing equipment was a vindication of his vision. His *Déserts* (1950–54), for instruments and tape, was one of the most ambitious early essays in electronic music. And his entirely electronic *Poème électronique* is recognized as one of the masterpieces of the genre.

***Poème électronique* (1958)** (ending) As we stroll within earshot of *Poème électronique* (see below), a heavy electronic crash is followed by various seemingly random rustles. Then a brilliant section displays a veritable anthology of electronic effects: low sliding groans, rattles, bell-like noises, and watery sounds. Suddenly something human joins these space-age sounds—a short vocal hum. This tells us that Varèse makes use of *musique concrète* in *Poème:* that is, he uses prerecorded sounds from real life, such as humming, singing, bells, and train noises, as well as material that is generated electronically.

The rhythm has been highly irregular. Now it slows down, and a sustained chord appears quietly, grows almost unbearably loud, and then fades. Varèse introduces isolated pitches that appear to be arbitrary, though in fact they merge into another sustained chord. We hear drum rhythms, too, and a *musique concrète* snare drum (remember Varèse's affection for percussion instruments).

Humanity seems to reassert itself in the form of a soprano solo—but this is manipulated electronically so as to shriek its way out of hearing in the high register. Sharp, explosive punctuations decimate the men's voices that follow. A mournful three-note motive (also heard earlier in *Poème*) is played twice with the notes sliding into one another. Then a momentous-sounding siren moves up, falters, and moves up again until it becomes a violent noise, which ceases abruptly and mechanically.

So ends the Varèse *Poème électronique:* for some, on a strange note of unspecified disquiet.

Modernist Music and Architecture

The *Poème électronique* of Edgard Varèse was just one part of an extraordinary multimedia experience. It was written for an exhibit at the 1958 Brussels World Fair by the Philips Radio Corporation, held in a pavilion designed by the famous modernist architect Le Corbusier (1887–1965). Corbu, as he was called, also designed a sequence of colored lights and images to be projected while Varèse's three-track tape was played from 425 speakers.

Here is another example of modernist artists of various kinds working in tandem (see page 319). Le Corbusier himself had been a painter in his youth.

As visitors entered the pavilion and walked around, the music came at them from various angles. Likewise, as they kept turning corners they kept seeing different parts of the superb building and of the light show. All this was very new at that time.

There was obviously an element of chance in the way one got to experience *Poème électronique*—an element that the composer of course encouraged. John Cage would have concurred enthusiastically. So it is quite in Varèse's spirit for us to take a quick tour of the pavilion, as it were, and happen to hear just the last few minutes of this music, rather than the entirety.

John Cage (1912–1992)

John Cage

The most consistent radical figure of postwar music was John Cage, the father of chance music (Charles Ives has to count as the grandfather). He studied with Schoenberg, among others—when Schoenberg was teaching in California, Cage's home state—and early developed an almost bewildering variety of interests. Cage exhibited specially prepared prints, toured as music director of avant-garde dancer Merce Cunningham's dance company, and was a recognized mycologist (mushroom authority). In the 1950s, his study of Zen led him to a fresh attitude toward music, time, and indeed all experience.

Cage posed questions that challenge all the assumptions on which traditional music rests. Why should music be different from the sounds of life? Why compose with "musical" sounds, rather than noises? Why work out music according to melodies, climaxes, twelve-tone series, or anything else that gives the impression of one thing following another in a purposeful order? Why not leave it to chance? The basic message that Cage has conveyed is that we should open our ears to every possible kind of sound and every possible sound conjunction.

JOHN CAGE
4' 33" (1952)

Often, indeed, the actual sounds Cage produced were less crucial than the "statement" he was making about sound by means of his music. This is the case with *4'33"*, perhaps his most celebrated work (or statement). Any number of players can perform it. They sit silently on the stage for 4 minutes and 33 seconds.

When you get right down to it, a composer is simply someone who tells other people what to do. I find this an unattractive way of getting things done.

John Cage

Is this just an exasperating hoax? What Cage is saying is that silence is an entity, too, as well as sound. When did you last really concentrate on silence? (Try it.) In fact, *4'33"* consists not of silence but of little bits of random audience noise, sounds from outside the hall, and the thump of the irate listener's heartbeat. And how does the experience of concentrating on near silence for exactly 4 minutes and 33 seconds compare with concentrating for exactly three minutes, or exactly five?

We seldom really analyze our experience freshly; life is unpredictable and full of surprises. Music should be, too. This is the philosophy represented by Cage and his music. It has had a major impact on avant-garde composers all over the world, and on some innovators in popular music, also (see page 416).

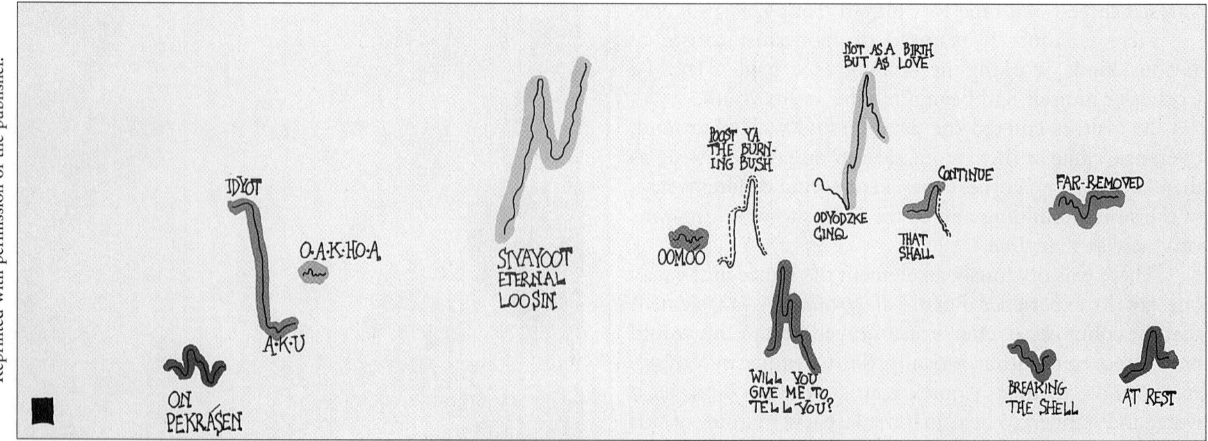

Score for a multilingual solo vocal work by John Cage, *Aria* (1958). Much is left to the singer's imagination!

John Cage, *Aria*: ©1960 by Henmar Press, Inc., N.Y. Reprinted with permission of the publisher.

3 Music at the End of the Century

I think composers are everything they've ever experienced, everything they've ever read, all the music they've ever heard. All these things come together in odd combinations in their psyche, where they choose and make forms from all their memories and their imaginings.

George Crumb, 1988

It is not easy to characterize the confused, multivalent, multicultural music of our own time, at the beginning of the twenty-first century. A date comes to mind, 1971—not because anything as complex as music changes in a year, but because an event in it can symbolize a complex historical process. When Stravinsky died in 1971, at the age of eighty-eight, classical music lost its last great master, and a figure whose role in music history was uniquely comprehensive.

His first, Russian works were wholehearted essays in late nineteenth-century nationalism. Then works for Paris such as *The Rite of Spring* were prime monuments of modernism in its first, early twentieth-century phase. In Los Angeles, Stravinsky remained a major player in modernism in its second phase, the extreme phase following World War II.

Since the 1970s modernism has mellowed. The trauma of atonality is now a thing of the past. Not all composers relinquished tonal music with its clear harmonies and melodies, as we have seen in Chapter 21, and now it has returned gradually into the music of modernism. Works that we will now study absorb modernist ideas and ideals but also show more concern for communication than did music of the immediate postwar period.

George Crumb (b. 1929)

George Crumb, 1988

A later representative of the American postwar avant-garde is George Crumb, a professor at the University of Pennsylvania. Unlike Cage, he is not a "chance" composer, and unlike Varèse or his followers, he does not write electronic or computer music—though he makes powerful use of amplification effects, as we shall see. Instead he has devised new ways of playing all kinds of standard and nonstandard instruments. In *Black Angels* he asks string quartet players to do things to their instruments that would make a traditional violin teacher turn pale. By such means Crumb obtains a predominantly violent, grotesque quality that could not be achieved in any other way.

In other works (and occasionally in this one), Crumb achieves remarkably delicate effects—quiet, precise, a controlled musical kaleidoscope of fascinating elegance. Like many American composers today, he has been much influenced by Asian music; thanks to such composers, Western music has for the first time employed large groups of percussion instruments with something of the subtlety known to East Asia.

GEORGE CRUMB
Black Angels, for Electric String Quartet (1970)

18-22

Subtitled "Thirteen Images from the Dark Land," *Black Angels* was inspired by the Vietnam War, if not directly, at least by way of the anguished mood that the war instigated. "There were terrifying things in the air," the composer has said recently. "They found their way into *Black Angels*."

This highly unconventional string quartet consists of thirteen short (often very short) sections arranged in three groups, of which we will hear the first. A sense of doom is conveyed partly by the titles—*threnody* means a funeral lamentation song—and partly by various quotations of earlier music with lethal associations. But of course it is the quality of the music itself that conveys the sense of stress most powerfully.

18 ***No. 1 Threnody I: Night of the Electric Insects*** The skittery, amplified string playing suggests some sort of menacing insect life. A loud clatter alternates with quiet scratching. Against this, the high violins play fast glissandos, or scooping effects. Crumb marks them *piangendo,* "crying."

The scores of Nos. 1, 3, and 4 of *Black Angels* are not written with barlines, and the music has no discernible meter. In contrast, Nos. 2 and 5 project dance rhythms quite clearly, and in No. 2, at least, one can often beat out a regular meter.

19 ***No. 2 Sounds of Bones and Flutes*** This section evokes Asian music. The players click their tongues and chant "Ka-to-ko to-ko" to illustrate the rattling of bones, and somehow imitate a flute by bowing their strings with the back of the bow, that is, with the wood *(col legno).*

20 ***No. 3 Lost Bells*** This duo for violin and cello mimics the mournful, bell-like noises characteristic of electronic music. Fragmentary melodies at the end remind us of the "flute" in No. 2.

21 ***No. 4 Devil-music*** An extremely vehement solo for the first violin is accompanied by the other players, one of whom also strikes a gong. The violinist produces what can only be called retching sounds; then the cellist, followed by the other players, rasps or grates by dragging the bow very slowly over the strings while applying maximum pressure. Toward the end there are some siren effects, and the electric insects put in another appearance.

22 ***No. 5 Danse Macabre*** Rhythmic energy picks up again, as the players tap on the wood of their instruments and jiggle maracas. Crumb borrowed the title for this section from a nineteenth-century concert piece by the French composer Camille Saint-Saëns, and he quotes bits of Saint-Saëns's music as well as *Dies irae,* from the Mass for the dead (see page 268). Isolated phrases of this plainchant appear high in the violin; they are vaguely reminiscent of the "flute" in No. 2 and the ending melodic fragments of No. 3.

The players end up with some mysterious chanting (actually, they count from one to seven in Hungarian).

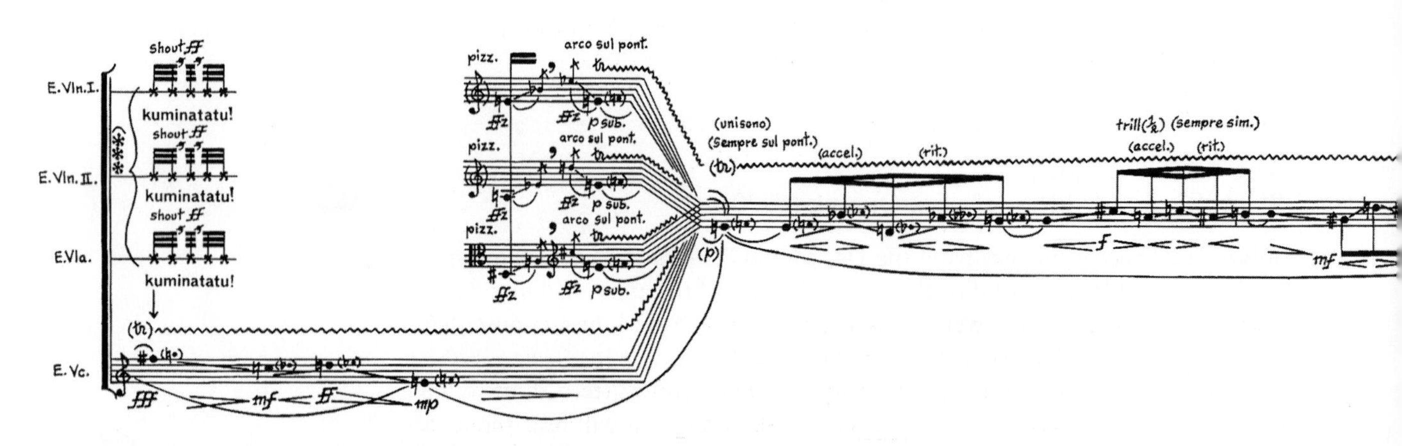

Avant-garde music has made obsolete the old "pitch–time" graph that forms the basis of traditional musical notation (see page 20). Composers often invent their own notations: George Crumb, above, and John Cage, page 376.

Kaija Saariaho (b. 1952)

The Finnish composer Kaija Saariaho is representative of a generation of European composers born after World War II who have carried on the experiments of earlier modernism. She regularly combines live performers with electronic and computer music, often working at IRCAM, a famous center for electronic music composition in Paris. While her long list of compositions exploits a wide variety of performing forces, her special interest is vocal music, and more specifically, the soprano voice. A major work, the opera *L'Amour de loin* (*Love from Afar*), received its U.S. premiere in 2002.

Kaija Saariaho

KAIJA SAARIAHO
From the Grammar of Dreams (1988)

From the Grammar of Dreams is a cycle of five songs for two unaccompanied sopranos. The songs set words of Sylvia Plath, a moving American poet who struggled with depression and took her own life at an early age in 1963. The words of the songs bring together prose excerpts from Plath's most famous work, the novel *The Bell Jar,* and a multistanza poem entitled "Paralytic." The poem recounts the impressions and sensations of a polio patient lying in an iron lung. (This was a huge medical machine, all too common in the years before vaccinations, that pumped air in and out of the lungs of patients paralyzed by polio.)

Saariaho departs in a number of ways from a conventional musical setting of these words. First, she scatters the stanzas of the poem unevenly across her five songs. Songs 1 and 3, which we will consider here, set stanzas 1–4 and 8, respectively. Second, Saariaho often superimposes two different texts sung simultaneously, a treatment rarely encountered in songs. (For one genre that did it as a matter of course, see the isorhythmic motet of the late Middle Ages, page 68.) Finally and most strikingly, Saariaho employs her restricted performing forces with great versatility, presenting a miniature catalogue of unorthodox—and highly expressive—vocal techniques.

Song 1 The more active soprano here sings stanzas 1–2 of "Paralytic" to a violent, leaping, swooping melody. At first she tears apart the words, as in some sort of bizarre verbal dissection, delivering the sounds of individual letters and word fragments with distorted emphasis: *huh—huh—appp—enzzzzzzz* for "happens," and so on. Meanwhile the other soprano unfolds a gentler line in counterpoint, filled with warbling trills, in which we gradually come to hear words from *The Bell Jar:* "A bad dream. I remembered everything." Is she casting the experience of the paralytic as a nightmare, and nothing more?

Finally, at about 1:20, the violent soprano begins to shift to her partner's more lyrical style (stanza 3). In the end, each soprano is reduced in turn to deliberate, monotonal speech, accompanied by a lingering trill from the other singer.

Song 3 This is the lyrical and emotional heart of the cycle—and also its most conventional song. Its words, the last stanza of "Paralytic," are sung by both voices. The singers, like the poetic image of their words, seem to convey a calm, quiet renunciation (of struggle against the iron lung? of the attempt to touch an unreachable world?)—perhaps even a renunciation of life altogether. The song is organized around an arch of shifting pitch levels, as the voices gradually rise to a climax (at 1:35), then fall back to their starting places.

It is organized also by a technique we have heard often since the Renaissance: imitative polyphony. Listen for this especially in the half-step motives at the beginning and end, which wind together like the clawed tree roots and branches alluded to in the poem, or at the repeated word *magnolia* starting at 1:01.

Song 4 Here images from *The Bell Jar* eerily summon up Plath's own suicidal thoughts, only to turn to the life force of a beating heart. We can hear this song as a free **A B A′** form, with the **A** section formed of harsh, impassioned panting. The longer, fully sung **B** section (starting at 0:19) rises steadily to an ecstatic, almost unbearable climax on "I am I am I am"; along the way, the panting from **A**, now sung, returns. An abrupt collapse (at 1:25) ushers in **A′**, made up of fading, panting repetitions of "I am" in heartbeat-like rhythms. Song 4 seems to affirm that the renunciation of life, desire, and self hinted at in Song 3 does not come without struggle.

LISTEN Kaija Saariaho, *From the Grammar of Dreams*

23-25

33-35

23 / 33
SONG 1

Soprano 1 ("Paralytic," stanzas 1–4)

It happens. Will it go on? —
My mind a rock,
No fingers to grip, no tongue,
My god the iron lung
That loves me, pumps
My two
Dust bags in and out,
Will not
Let me relapse
While the day outside glides by like ticker tape.
The night brings violets,
Tapestries of eyes,
Lights,
The soft anonymous
Talkers: "You all right?"
The starched, inaccessible breast.

Soprano 2 (from *The Bell Jar;* sung simultaneously with soprano 1)

A bad dream.
I remembered everything.

24 / 34
SONG 3

Sopranos 1 and 2 ("Paralytic," stanza 8—the last stanza)

The claw
Of the magnolia,
Drunk on its own scents,
Asks nothing of life.

25 / 35
SONG 4

Soprano 1 (*The Bell Jar*)

I thought I would swim out
until I was too tired to swim back.
As I paddled on, my heartbeat
boomed like a dull motor in my ears.
I am I am I am

Soprano 2 (*The Bell Jar*)

I took a deep breath and listened
to the old brag of my heart.
I am I am I am

Minimalism

One of the most interesting new musical styles to develop in the last thirty years is called **minimalism.** A sharp reaction to the complexities of modernist composition, minimalist music uses very simple melodies, motives, and harmonies repeated many, many times. Terry Riley's *In C*, mentioned on page 370, is an ancestor of minimalism (some say, the first great example of it).

Minimalism has proved to be an unusually successful style for American opera: a scene from *Nixon in China* (1987) by John Adams.

This style has worked wonders for American opera, which has become the success story of modern music since *Einstein on the Beach* (1976) by a leading minimalist composer, Philip Glass (b. 1937). Later works by Glass, *Satyagraha* and *Akhnaten,* and *Nixon in China* and *The Death of Klinghoffer* by John Adams (b. 1947) have been performed again and again in this country and abroad, all of them in spectacular productions.

STEVE REICH (b. 1936)
Tehillim (1981)

Steve Reich, a philosophy major at Cornell, studied music subsequently and has become the acknowledged old master of the minimalist style. A keyboardist, he has performed his work with his own special group—a procedure that a number of other contemporary composers follow, including Philip Glass. Reich has written operas—*The Cave* (1998) and *Three Tales* (2002)—with his wife, video artist Beryl Korot.

Steve Reich

Tehillim (tehéelim) is the Hebrew word for "psalms," and in Reich's composition, verses from several biblical psalms are sung by a women's choir accompanied by a small instrumental group. There are four sections, running into one another. The first two are fast, the third slow, and the climactic fourth section is fast again, so the piece amounts to a sort of minimalist "symphony of psalms."

The text for the last movement comes from Psalm 150, "Praise ye the Lord," the last in the Book of Psalms. And the very last *word* in this psalm, "hallelujah," has echoed down through the ages at the heart of worship. The word is the same in Hebrew, Latin, English, and German (see pages 66, 95, 158, and 161).

Section 4 (Psalm 150: "Haleluhu") To begin, the full text of "Haleluhu" is sung to a sprightly melody backed by an insistent beat on tambourines. The text, with its reiterations of "haleluhu" and "haleluyah," seems perfectly suited to Reich's repetitious musical technique.

1	Haleluhu betof umachol, Haleluhu beminim ve-ugav;	a	Praise the Lord with tambourines and dancing, praise him with flute and strings;
2	Haleluhu betzil-tzilay shamah, Haleluhu betzil-tzilay teruah;	b	praise him with the clash of cymbals, praise him with triumphant cymbals;
3	Kol hanshamah tehalail Yah, Haleluyah.	c	let everything that has breath praise the Lord! Hallelujah.
	Kol hanshamah tehalail Yah, Haleluyah.	c′	*Let everything that has breath praise the Lord! Hallelujah.*

Each syllable gets a single note, and these notes are arranged in lively irregular rhythms—we show the climactic last phrases, **c** and **c′**:

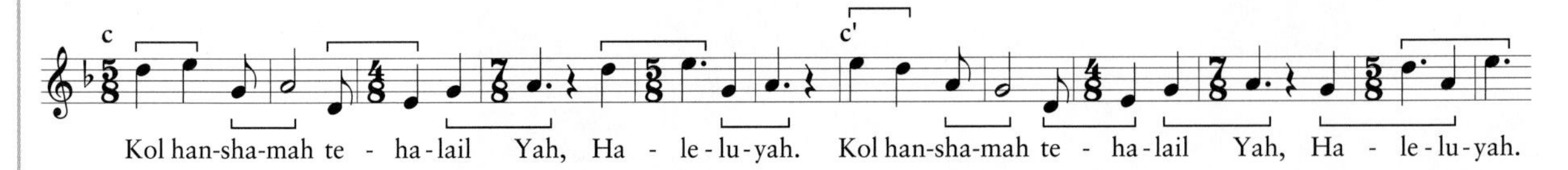

The melody falls into an **a b c c′** form, though this is not easy to hear, since there is so much repetition of tiny melodic cells within the phrases. The phrases shown above are built entirely out of the steps D–E (or E–D) and G–A. Repetitions *within* the melody, combined with the many repetitions *of* the melody, give this music its feeling of incantation, both static and ecstatic, always changing yet always the same.

Behind the singing, a few chords are played by the orchestral strings and then sustained—a solemn counterpoint to the sprightly melody. These strange,

Minimalism in music and art: *Chant II* by Bridget Riley (b. 1931).

LISTENING CHART 29

26-30

Reich, *Tehillim,* fourth section

6 min., 44 sec.

Track	Time	Section	Description
26	0:00	Transition from part 3—accelerates to a new steady beat	
	0:14	**Theme: a b c c′:**	Two sopranos in harmony with irregularly placed chords accompanying the singing
27	0:43	**Variation 1**	Two-part canon **a b c c′**
0:28	1:11	**Variation 2**	Four-part canon—**a** repeated many times
1:11	1:54		After a brief punctuation, **b** (starts with voices alone)
1:36	2:19		After a brief punctuation, **c** (starts with voices alone)
28	2:54	**Variation 3**	Two voices with clarinets, drums
0:47	3:41	**Instrumental interlude**	Background chords continue
29	4:17	**Variation 4**	
0:55	5:12		Climactic high note
30	5:28	**Coda**	on the word "Hallelujah" only; electric organ, bells
1:13	6:41		Abrupt stop

a
Haleluhu betof . . .

b
Haleluhu betzil . . .

c
Kol hanshamah . . .

irregularly placed chords continue through nearly the whole of the movement, including the orchestral interlude.

Section 4 of *Tehillim* is a type of free variation movement: The instrumentation changes with each variation. After the theme has been sung by two sopranos in harmony, they sing it in variation 1 as a round, one starting several beats after the other. The constant melodic intertwining adds new energy and charm. In variation 2, the longest and most complicated variation, four sopranos sing the melody as a four-part round—and what is more, each phrase is sung several times before the next is heard. In variation 3, the melody is slowed down and altered so as to include several exhilarating high notes for the soprano. Step by step, the psalm singing grows more intense.

After an orchestral interlude, the chords in the stringed instruments grow more intense too. Variation 4 follows, with the melody varied even further, but something like the original "Hallelujah" melody is heard again at the end of **c**, with the highest soprano note yet.

In an enthusiastic *coda,* extra instruments pile in—a vibraphone, two organs, and bells. United in their joyous ritual, the voices cry out "Hallelujah" again and again. The piece ends—after a particularly emphatic "Hallelujah"—without the feeling of finality we would expect from a traditional cadence. After all the mounting excitement, the music simply *ceases,* as though someone has switched off the current.

Web: *Research and test your understanding of late twentieth-century music at* **<bedfordstmartins.com/listen>.**

CHAPTER 23

Music in America: Jazz and Beyond

As we have observed a number of times in this book, in the nineteenth century a rift opened up between popular music and the music we now call "classical." Nowhere has this rift been more apparent than in the United States of America, the most populist of all nations. And nowhere else have such strenuous efforts been made to close the rift. We can see this if we think back to the various American composers discussed in the last few chapters, from the unlikely modernist Charles Ives, who quoted marches, ragtime, and hymns in his symphonic music, to the minimalist Steve Reich, American pioneer in a worldwide movement. It is not accidental that we have seen more than one of these composers working with popular as well as "classical" music sources—and that in this chapter we shall see more.

"Popular" and "classical" are fuzzy terms; think of the *popularity* of the Three Tenors, singing opera excerpts in stadiums around the world; think how broad the application of *classical* and the related *classic* can be, from the "classical antiquity" of Greece and Rome to "classic rock." For music in America, the terms "cultivated" and "vernacular" have proven to be more illuminating. To "cultivate" means to nurture, as microorganisms are cultivated in a petri dish in a laboratory, or orchids in a greenhouse. "Vernacular," on the other hand, refers to one's native language, as opposed to some other that may be in use, such as the Latin used, long after people stopped speaking it every day, in the church, universities, and law courts of the Middle Ages. **Cultivated music**, then, is music that has been brought to this country and consciously developed, fostered at concerts, and taught in conservatories. **Vernacular music** is music we sing and hear as naturally as we speak our native argot.

There is a bitter twist to this terminology as applied to American music. The word *vernacular* comes from the Latin word *vernaculus*, which is itself derived from *verna:* and "verna" means a family slave. The heritage of African American music was and is central to the story of American music.

1 Early American Music: An Overview

Long before European settlers and African slaves arrived here, Native Americans had their own musical styles. (We touched on one of these in discussing sacred chant; see page 72.) As Native Americans were pushed farther and farther west, however, their music played little role in the development of European American and African American music.

The history of music among the early European settlers and their descendants is not a rich one. The Puritans disapproved of music; they thought it was frivolous, except for its supporting role in religion. In Puritan church services, rhyming versions of the psalms were sung like hymns, but when the words of the psalms were printed in the *Bay Psalm Book* of 1640—the first book ever printed in North America—the music was not included, because just a few tunes, known to everyone, were used for all 150 psalms. In succeeding years, much of the energy of early American musicians was devoted to the composition of new psalm and hymn tunes, and to the teaching and improvement of church singing.

William Billings (1746–1800) of Boston is often mentioned as our first composer. He wrote hymns and **fuguing tunes,** which are simple anthems based on hymns, with a little counterpoint. (An anthem is a choral piece in the vernacular for use in Protestant services.) When sung with spirit, fuguing tunes sound enthusiastic, rough, and gutsy.

Billings's more secular-minded contemporaries enjoyed the Classical music of the era. Benjamin Franklin, who tried his hand at most everything, also tried composing. But without well-established musical institutions, there was not much support for native composers outside the church. The problem in those years is hardly that of distinguishing between cultivated and vernacular music. The problem is finding written music to listen to and talk about at all.

"Cultivated" music in America: a scene from Philadelphia society of the 1890s, *The Concert Singer,* by Thomas Eakins.

A concert at New York's Castle Garden in 1850, in a print issued by Currier & Ives. Their hand-colored lithographs are famous for vividly illustrating nineteenth-century America.

The "Cultivated" Tradition

After the United States won its independence, things changed. As cities grew, first on the East coast and then progressively to the West, more and more concerts appeared, and with them inveterate concertgoers. One such was a New York lawyer and civic leader named George Templeton Strong, who left a four-and-a-half-million-word diary discussing (among other things) all the symphonies, oratorios, and organ music he heard, in unending enthusiastic detail.* By the mid-1800s, all our major cities had their concert halls and opera organizations and amateur choral societies. The 1860s saw the foundation of our first conservatories of music, in Boston, Cincinnati, and elsewhere.

Americans eagerly bought tickets to hear traveling celebrities from Europe, and skilled native composers and performers began to appear. The first American musicians to gain worldwide reputations were the immigrant German composer Anthony Philip Heinrich (1781–1861), a quirky early Romantic, and the Louisiana piano virtuoso Louis Moreau Gottschalk (1829–1869).

On the whole, however, Americans were content to look to Italy for opera and to Germany for instrumental music. That the cultivated tradition in American music was essentially German in orientation is not surprising. Ever since the time of Mozart and Beethoven, German music had achieved wonders and had earned enormous prestige all over Europe. The mid-nineteenth-century immi-

- *Vivaldi's concertos in parts*
- *Bach's songs 2nd collection*
- *Handel's Coronation anthems*
- *Heck's art of playing the harpsichord*
- *Hayden's [sic] cantatas...*

In 1783 Thomas Jefferson's music library contained these and a hundred other items.

*Bits of Strong's diary are cited on pages 228 and 230.

gration from Germany brought us many musicians who labored long and hard for the cause of music in this country. We can hardly blame them for their German bias.

There were significant native composers at the end of the nineteenth century: John Knowles Paine, Arthur Foote, and Henry Chadwick of the so-called Boston School, and Edward MacDowell of New York. They wrote symphonies, piano "miniatures," and so on, in a competent but conservative German Romantic style. Time has not been kind to their work, despite recent efforts to revive it.

The music of Amy Beach (1867–1944), in particular, has stirred interest in recent years. Active as both a composer and a pianist, she made her debut with the Boston Symphony Orchestra at the age of seventeen. "Mrs. H. H. A. Beach" (as she always signed her works) contributed to many traditional genres, such as the piano concerto, the piano quintet, and the symphony. Her *Gaelic* Symphony of 1896 was the first symphonic work ever composed by an American woman.

Louis Moreau Gottschalk

The emergence of Charles Ives in the midst of this conservative tradition seems like a miracle of music history (see page 348). Yet Ives profited more than he sometimes cared to admit from the grounding in European concert music he received from his German-trained professor, Horatio Parker.

Music in the Vernacular

We might well count the psalms and hymns mentioned above as vernacular music, for in colonial days everybody who could carry a tune sang them at church and in the home, and later they were widely sung at revival meetings and the like. Nineteenth-century America was also rich in secular popular

Hymn singing at home in Revolutionary times, an engraving by Paul Revere (Psalm 23, "The Lord is my shepherd").

music. Our two most famous composers wrote timeless tunes and ever-popular marches, respectively: Stephen Collins Foster (1826–1864) and John Philip Sousa (1854–1932).

Foster, it is sad to say, led a dispiriting life. Even in those days, song writing was closely tied to the music business; Foster was dependent on Christie's Minstrels, the leading traveling theater troupe of the time. They had exclusive rights to his songs and helped popularize them—indeed, some of them soon achieved the status of folk songs. But Foster had a hard time making ends meet. His marriage broke up. He turned to drink and died at the age of thirty-eight.

John Philip Sousa, son of Spanish and German immigrant parents, was a Marine Corps bandmaster who later formed a wildly successful touring band of his own. Every American knows his masterpiece *The Stars and Stripes Forever* (even if they don't all know its name). Leonard Bernstein once said that his greatest regret as a musician was that he hadn't composed that march.

African American Music

Foster excelled in sentimental ballads, such as "Jeanie with the Light Brown Hair" and "Beautiful Dreamer." But his most notable songs have to do with the black slaves of his time. There are sentimental "plantation songs" such as "Swanee River" ("The Old Folks at Home") and "Old Black Joe," and comic minstrel songs such as "Oh, Susanna!" and "Camptown Races." The **minstrel show**, performed by white actors in blackface, was very popular at mid-century; it consisted of comedy routines, "Ethiopian" songs, dances, and solos on the banjo (an instrument with African roots). Though today this kind of entertainment strikes us as an ugly parody of black speech and character, it was also an acknowledgment of the vitality of the slaves' music. From at least the time of Foster, African American music has had a profound effect on the music of America at large.

Original illustration accompanying a song by Stephen Foster (1862).

What was the slaves' music like? This is hard to say, for there were no devoted folk-song collectors to write it down, as in Europe (Bártok is a case in point; see page 356). Nonetheless, by studying somewhat later black American music and comparing it with today's African music, scholars have been able to show how much the slaves preserved of their native musical cultures.

For example, a musical procedure known as **call and response** is common in West Africa. Phrases sung by a leader—a soloist—are answered or echoed again and again by a chorus. This procedure is preserved in black American church music, when the congregation answers the preacher's "call," as well as in spirituals, work songs, and "field hollers," by which the slaves tried to lighten their labors. It is also an important feature in blues and in jazz, as we shall see.

Spiritual is a term for a religious folk song that came into being outside an established church (white or black). Moving "Negro spirituals," such as "Nobody Knows the Trouble I've Seen," "Go Down, Moses," and others, were the first black American music to gain the admiration of the white world. After Emancipation, black colleges formed touring choirs. To be sure, spirituals in their concert versions were considerably removed from folk music.

The singing was accompanied by a certain ecstasy of motion, clapping of hands, tossing of heads, which would continue without cessation for about half an hour. One would lead off in a kind of recitative style, others joining in the chorus.

A former slave recalls call-and-response singing, 1881

The music of African Americans got a powerful boost from the first major European composer to spend time in America, Antonín Dvořák. This highly respected Bohemian musician, head of New York's National Conservatory of Music (ancestor of the Juilliard School) in the 1890s, announced his special admiration for spirituals, advised his American colleagues to make use of them in their concert music, and showed the way himself. He incorporated the essence

Negro spirituals were first popularized after the Civil War by groups like the Fisk Singers. In 1871, this group of former slaves toured to raise funds for Fisk, one of the earliest African American colleges.

of spirituals so skillfully in his ever-popular *New World* Symphony that one of his own tunes was later adapted to made-up "folk song" words, "Goin' Home." This is the first of several examples we shall see of the conscious effort to narrow the gap between America's vernacular and cultivated styles.

2 Jazz: The First Fifty Years

But if Dvořák and his contemporaries could have been whisked for a moment into the twenty-first century, they would have been astonished to see and hear what actually happened. With little help from the cultivated tradition, a strictly vernacular type of music emerged from African American communities. It was called—at first contemptuously—**jazz.** From the most modest beginnings, this music developed prodigiously. It produced a whole series of new musical styles, performers of the greatest artistry, and composers of genius.

Jazz developed into America's most distinctive—many would say greatest—contribution to the arts worldwide. And if our time-travelers were to find it hard to believe their ears, there would be something else to amaze them. All this music was actually preserved—preserved on acetate discs by means of a revolutionary new technology, sound recording.

Jazz is a performance style that grew up among black musicians around 1910 and has since gone through a series of extraordinary developments. Its first key feature is *improvisation.* When jazz musicians play a song, they do not play it the way they hear it or see it on paper; they always improvise *around* a song. They add ornaments and sometimes also short interludes, called **breaks;** in effect, they are always playing variations on whatever tunes they are working with.

The second key feature of jazz is a special rhythmic style involving highly developed *syncopation* (see below). Notice that jazz is not so much a kind of music—the music it is based on usually consists of popular songs, blues, or abstract chord-series called "changes"—but a special, highly charged way of performing that music.

Jazz Syncopation

Syncopation occurs when some of the accents in music are moved away from the main beats, the beats that are normally accented (see page 13). For example, in **2/2** meter, instead of the normal ONE *two* ONE *two,* the accent can be displaced from beat 1 to beat 2—*one* TWO *one* TWO. This is called a "back beat" in jazz parlance.

Some syncopation occurs in all Western music. In jazz, there is much more of it. Syncopation becomes a regular principle, so much so that we can speak of at least two rhythmic "levels" in a jazz piece. One rhythmic level is a simple one—the **rhythm section** of percussion (drums, cymbals), piano, string bass, and sometimes other instruments, emphasizes the meter forcefully, and continuously. A second, more complex rhythmic level is produced by the melody instruments—trumpet, clarinet, trombone, piano, and the saxophones that were so brilliantly developed in jazz. They play a constantly syncopating music that always cuts across the rhythm section.

In addition, jazz developed syncopation of a more subtle kind, sometimes called **beat syncopation.** Derived from African drumming (see page 398), this technique can also be traced in earlier black American music. In beat syncopation, accents are moved *just a fraction of a beat* ahead of the metrical points. When this happens in just the right way, the music is said to "swing."

The Blues

The **blues** is a special category of black folk song whose subject is loneliness, trouble, and depression of every shade. Indeed, the blues is more than song, more than music: It is an essential expression of the African American experience. Though gloom and dejection are at the heart of the blues, not infrequently blues lyrics also convey humor, banter, and especially hope and resilience.

Emerging around 1900, the blues was a major influence on early jazz—and has remained a major force in American music ever since.

A blues melody consists typically of stanzas made up of three four-measure phrases ("twelve-bar blues"), repeated again and again as the blues singer develops a thought by improvising more stanzas. The stanzas are just two lines long, with the first line of words repeated and with the ends of the lines rhyming. Each line is sung to one of the three phrases of the twelve-bar pattern. Here are stanzas 1 and 4 of *"If You Ever Been Down" Blues:*

STANZA 1 *a* If you ever been down, you know just how I feel,
a *If you ever been down, you know just how I feel,*
b Like a tramp on the railroad ain't got a decent meal.

STANZA 4 *a* Yes, one thing, papa, I've decided to do,
a *Oh pretty daddy, I've decided to do,*
b I'm going to find another papa, then I can't use you.

I'd like to think that when I sing a song, I can let you know all about the heartbreak, struggle, lies, and kicks in the ass I've gotten over the years for being black and everything else, without actually saying a word about it.

Blues, gospel, and soul singer Ray Charles, 1970

Ragtime: Scott Joplin (1868–1917)

5

Ragtime, a precursor of jazz, was a style of piano playing developed by black musicians playing in bars, dives, and brothels. The music resembled march music, but while the left hand played strictly on the beat, the right hand syncopated the rhythm in a crisp, cheerful way. "To rag" meant to play in a syncopated style; "ragging" evolved into jazz syncopation.

In the early 1900s, when phonographs were still new and most music in the home was played on the piano, ragtime became enormously popular throughout America by means of sheet music and piano rolls for mechanical ("player") pianos. The term ragtime could also be applied to nonpiano music: witness the famous song *Alexander's Ragtime Band* of 1911 by Irving Berlin.

Scott Joplin was the leading rag composer. Frustratingly little is known about his early life. The son of an ex-slave, he grew up in Texarkana and worked as a pianist and band musician in many midwestern towns. "Maple Leaf Rag," named after the Maple Leaf Club in Sedalia, Missouri, where Joplin played, was published in 1899. It quickly sold a million copies. You can hear this famous rag on your Study Guide CD-ROM; see also page 15.

Joplin followed "Maple Leaf" with "The Entertainer" and many other rags. They stand out for an elegance that might not have been expected in this simple and commercial genre. In *Solace: A Mexican Serenade* Joplin mixed ragtime with Latin American dance styles in a work of nostalgic sophistication. He even published a small treatise on the playing of ragtime, warning those who would race through his pieces: "Never play ragtime fast at any time." And to those who saw ragtime as a style too lowbrow for their tastes, he wrote: "Syncopations are no indication of light or trashy music, and to shy (i.e., throw) bricks at 'hateful ragtime' no longer passes for musical culture."

Joplin's evident desire to break into cultivated musical circles was not realized. After he moved to New York in 1907 he gradually faded from the limelight. He wrote two operas, the second of which, *Treemonisha,* received a single unstaged, unsuccessful performance in 1915. His death in 1917 was noted by few.

There was a strong new surge of interest in ragtime in the 1960s. At last, in 1972, *Treemonisha* was fully staged and recorded. In 1975 Joplin was posthumously awarded the Pulitzer Prize in composition.

Composed blues—for example, W. C. Handy's famous *St. Louis Blues*—can be more complicated than this one, but the ***a a b*** poetic scheme is basic for the blues.

Blues melodies (and especially the bass lines under blues melodies) provided jazz musicians with powerfully emotional patterns for improvisation. But more than that, blues also provided jazz with a sonorous model. Jazz instrumental playing has an astonishing vocal quality, as though in imitation of the blues. The trumpet, saxophone, and trombone sound infinitely more flexible and "human" played in jazz style than when played in military band or symphonic style. Jazz instruments seem to have absorbed the vibrant accents of black singing. (This is another feature that jazz passed on to rock, where the electric guitar is the instrument that powerfully imitates the voice.)

SIPPIE WALLACE
"If You Ever Been Down" Blues (1927) (Composed by G. W. Thomas)

Here is an example of unvarnished blues singing, by one of the legendary woman blues singers who dominated the earliest recordings. Sippie Wallace is not as renowned as Mamie Smith, Ma Rainey, or the great Bessie Smith, but she poured her heart out with the best of them in response to the eternal themes of the blues:

STANZA 2 I'm a real good woman but my man don't treat me right,
He takes all my money and stays out all night.

31 36

LISTEN

Thomas, *"If You Ever Been Down" Blues*

0:10 **Stanza 1**
0:45 **Stanza 2**
1:19 **Trumpet**
1:51 **Stanza 3**
2:24 **Stanza 4**

STANZA 3 I'm down today but I won't be down always,
'Cause the sun's going to shine in my back door some day.

Wallace accompanies herself on the piano. The recording adds two jazz musicians, but she would have sung just about the same way if she had been performing alone. One of the musicians is the outstanding genius of early jazz, Louis Armstrong.

After a brief instrumental introduction, Wallace sings two blues stanzas from the piano bench. The instruments play short breaks in between her lines—the trumpet (Armstrong) in stanza 1, the clarinet (the little-known Artie Starks) in stanza 2. Sympathetic respondents to her "call," they deepen the melancholy of her song and nuance it:

Perhaps the essential sound of jazz is Louis Armstrong improvising the breaks in the blues sung by [famous blues-singer] Bessie Smith. . . . In the break we have the origin of the instrument imitating the voice, the very soil in which jazz grows.

Composer Leonard Bernstein, 1955

Then Armstrong plays a solo section—an entire twelve-bar blues stanza. He does not play the blues melody note by note, but improvises around the melody and its bass. Armstrong has a wonderful way of speeding up the dragging blues rhythm, and his rich, almost vocal tone quality echoes and complements the singer's bleak sound. The clarinet joins him; this is a simple example of improvised jazz polyphony.

Wallace, too, joins in quietly during this instrumental chorus; she too, no doubt, was singing on impulse. She then sings two more stanzas, with instrumental breaks as before.

It's necessary to listen to this recording in a different spirit from that in which we approach the other recordings of Western music accompanying this book. The scratchy sound on these old discs cannot be helped by digital remastering, and the music itself is not "composed," of course. It lies somewhere in between true folk music and jazz, a fascinating juxtaposition of the direct, powerful simplicity of Sippie Wallace and the artistry of Armstrong. With a little imagination, one can virtually hear history happening in this recording: Jazz is evolving from the blues.

Sippie Wallace (1898–1986)—her nickname is said to derive from a childhood lisp—was equally known for gospel music and for the blues. And indeed **gospel** music—ecstatic choral singing associated with black American church services—grew up at the same time as ragtime and the blues. Wallace was also a pianist and songwriter, who usually sang her own compositions, and published a good many of them. Her long performing career began at little churches in Houston and ended with a concert at Lincoln Center, the sprawling New York music facility that houses the New York Philharmonic Orchestra and the Metropolitan Opera.

Sippie Wallace

New Orleans Jazz

Early jazz was local entertainment for black audiences, an informal, low-budget, and even a somewhat casual art. Small bands, usually of six to eight players, typically featured three melody instruments to do the "swinging"—trumpet, clarinet, and trombone. The rhythm section could include piano, banjo, string bass, or even tuba, along with drums and other percussion.

Louis Armstrong (1901–1971)

Louis Armstrong was born into abject poverty in New Orleans. He learned to play the cornet in the Colored Waifs' Home, where he had been placed as a juvenile delinquent. Determined to become a musician, Armstrong played in seedy clubs and on riverboats, which were floating dance halls that traveled from town to town on the Mississippi every summer. Riverboats became a cradle of early jazz, importing it up the river from New Orleans to Kansas City and other centers.

Soon Armstrong was playing in the pioneering jazz bands led by King Oliver (see page 394) and Fletcher Henderson. He rapidly emerged as a more exciting artist than any of his colleagues. His sophisticated, flowing rhythms, his imaginative "breaks" and variations, and the power and beauty of his trumpet tone—all these were unique at the time. A famous series of records he made in the 1920s, playing with small New Orleans–style bands, drew jazz to the serious attention of musicians all over the world.

In the 1930s the popularity of jazz led to a great deal of commercialization, and to the cheapening and stereotyping that always seem to result from this process. Armstrong went right along, while often contributing moments of breathtaking beauty to records that were "listenable virtually only when Louis is playing," according to one jazz critic of the time. Armstrong became a nationally loved star, familiar from his appearances in nearly twenty movies. The State Department sponsored him on so many international tours that people called him "Ambassador Satch" ("Satchmo," his nickname, was derived from "satchel-mouth").

However, the more successful Armstrong became in the world of popular music, the more he drifted away from true jazz, to the distress of jazz enthusiasts. His last hit record was *Hello, Dolly!,* the title song of a 1964 Broadway musical; in this number he sang (with his famous raspy delivery) more than he played the trumpet.

Encore: Listen to *West Side Blues, Heebie Jeebies, Hotter Than That, St. Louis Blues* (with Bessie Smith).

Early jazz players developed the art of collective improvisation, or "jamming." They learned to improvise simultaneously, each developing the special resources of his instrument—bright melodic spurts for the trumpet, fast running passages from low register to high for the clarinet, forceful slides for the trombone. They also acquired a sort of sixth sense for fitting in with the other improvisers. The nonimitative polyphony produced in this way is the hallmark of early jazz.

The first important center of jazz was New Orleans, home of the greatest early jazzman, Louis Armstrong, who played cornet and trumpet. Armstrong and his colleagues developed wonderfully imaginative and individual performance styles; aficionados can recognize any player after hearing just a few measures of a jazz record. With players of this quality, it is not surprising that solo sections soon became a regular feature in early jazz, along with collective improvisation.

Recording technology was already crucial in the dissemination of jazz. As popular records in those days were all just three minutes long, the jazz that has survived from that era is all slimmed down into three-minute segments. (If not for this, Sippie Wallace and Louis Armstrong would have given us many more blues stanzas.) Originally issued on labels that appealed to black audiences—

Jazz in the early 1920s: Louis Armstrong (center) in his first important band, Joe ("King") Oliver's Creole Jazz Band. The pianist, Lil Hardin—also a bandleader and songwriter—later married Armstrong and is credited with directing his early career.

coldly categorized as "race records" by the music business—Armstrong's discs of the late 1920s and 1930s not only attracted white listeners, but also excited the admiration of a new breed of jazz musicologists and critics.

Swing

Around 1930, jazz gained significantly in popularity, thanks in part to Armstrong's recordings. With popularity came changes, not all of them to the good. Jazz now had to reach bigger audiences in ballrooms and roadhouses. This meant **big bands,** with ten to twenty-five players—and such large numbers required carefully written out arrangements of the songs played. Improvisation, which was really the rationale behind jazz, was necessarily limited under these conditions.

However, big-band jazz—called **swing**—compensated for some of its lost spontaneity by variety of tone color and instrumental effects. A novel style of band orchestration was developed, based on the contrast between brass (trumpets and trombones) and "reed" (mainly saxophone) groups. Soloists cut in and out of the full-band sounds. Jazz "arrangers," who arranged current songs for the bands, treated this style with the greatest technical ingenuity and verve; they deserve the name of composers. Sometimes they contrived to allow for some improvisation within their arrangements.

Swing in the late 1930s: one of the most famous of the "big bands" (Glenn Miller)—brass to the left, reeds to the right. Miller's sideman Bobby Hackett (cornet) was one of many white musicians inspired by Louis Armstrong.

With popularity, too, came white musicians and managers, who moved in on what had previously been a relatively small black operation. Not only were black jazzmen marginalized in the mass market, but their art was watered down to suit the growing audience. The big swing bands that were commercial successes were white, and their leaders—Benny Goodman, Glenn Miller, Artie Shaw—were household names in the 1930s and 1940s. But the best of the big bands were black: those led by Count Basie (1904–1984), Jimmie Lunceford (1902–1947), Chick Webb (1909–1939), and Duke Ellington.

DUKE ELLINGTON (1899–1974)
Conga Brava (1940)

32

37

The tune used in *Conga Brava* was written by Ellington together with his Puerto Rican sideman Juan Tizol. (A conga is a dance of Afro-Cuban origin, named after the *conga* drum.) In it, the characteristic beat of Latin American music is appropriated by jazz—a mild tit-for-tat on behalf of a musical style that had given up much more to the nonblack world.

Only the beginning of this unusual tune—the **a a** section of the **a a b** form—has a Latin beat. Played by trombonist Tizol, the first **a** is presented with a minimal and mysterious accompaniment; but after this ends with a fancy

Duke Ellington (1899–1974)

Edward Kennedy Ellington was born in Washington, D.C., son of a butler who occasionally worked at the White House. The young Ellington considered a career as an artist, but he started playing the piano in jazz bands—ragtime was a major influence—and soon organized his own. He learned arranging too, and became an almost unique phenomenon: a major bandleader who was also its composer and its arranger.

He was called "Duke" because of a certain aristocratic bearing—and he was fastidious about his music, too. Ellington held fast to his own high standards of innovation and stylishness. And although his band never "went commercial," it did as well as any black band could in the 1930s and 1940s. "Duke Ellington and His Famous Orchestra" were renowned as the backup to sumptuous revues put on at the Cotton Club, an upscale Harlem night spot that catered to white audiences. Their recordings from around 1930 to 1940 constitute Ellington's major legacy.

After World War II, Ellington went his own imperturbable way, keeping his big band at a time when such organizations were regarded as jazz dinosaurs. He had experimented with long, symphonic-style jazz compositions as a young man, and now wrote more of these, as well as movie scores, a ballet, and an opera. The Ellington band, which had toured Europe twice in the 1930s, now toured all over the world, including the Soviet Union.

Ellington was finally recognized for what he was, just about America's most eminent composer, and he received the Presidential Medal of Freedom and other tributes. His last creative phase found him writing lengthy religious pieces, called *Sacred Concerts,* for the Ellington band with a Swedish soprano, Alice Babs, who was not really a jazz singer at all.

Ellington's *Sacred Concerts* would have been impossible without Babs—but the same is true of his earlier, better-known music and the musicians of his early bands. These individual soloists, or *sidemen,* as they are called—among them Barney Bigard (clarinet), Cootie Williams (trumpet), Johnny Hodges (alto saxophone), and Juan Tizol, who is featured on valve trombone in *Conga Brava* (below)—were vital to Ellington's art in a way singers or instrumentalists very rarely are in classical music. He molded his music so closely to their sometimes eccentric styles of playing that we cannot conceive of his music without them.

Ellington's sidemen can be regarded as co-composers of his music—or, better, as its *material,* like the songs and the blues that were transformed by Ellington's magic.

Chief Works: Very many songs—one estimate is 2,000—and jazz arrangements ▪ Large-scale jazz compositions, including *Creole Fantasy* and *Black, Brown, and Beige* ▪ Musical comedies, ballets, an incomplete opera *(Boola)* and other stage music ▪ Five film scores; *Sacred Concerts*

Encore: Listen to *Mood Indigo, Harlem Airshaft, Saddest Tale, Concerto for Cootie, Ko-ko, Don't Get Around Much Anymore, Sophisticated Lady.*

clarinet break, the second **a** includes brilliant interjections from the muted brass (an Ellington specialty). From now on things change rapidly. The brass choir plays **b,** with a speedy low clarinet cutting in. The rhythm section switches from a Latin beat to a typical jazz back-beat duple meter. The music begins to swing hard, as the trumpets remove their mutes.

The second appearance of the tune is a dazzling free improvisation by tenor sax player Ben Webster. He sounds genuinely spontaneous; he probably never again improvised around this melody in just this way. After he has gone through **a** and **a,** the muted brass come in again with a lively variation of **b.**

Webster has strayed far from the tune, so it is good to hear the third appearance of the tune in its original form (more or less), now on the reed choir (saxophones). This time the brilliant interpolations are by sideman Rex Stewart on trumpet. And this time, after a single **a,** there comes an extraordinary brass-choir version of **b,** with wildly syncopated rhythms. The coordination of the brass instruments is breathtaking, and the sheer verve of their variation makes this the high point of the composition.

LISTEN

Ellington, *Conga Brava*

0:03	a a	Trombone
0:45	b	Brass and alto sax
0:59	a a	Sax
1:39	b	Muted brass
1:46	a	Reed Choir (with trumpet)
2:07	b′	Brass Choir
2:32	a	Trombone

My band is my instrument.

Duke Ellington

Jazzmen as listeners: Duke Ellington and (behind him to the right) Benny Goodman listen to Ella Fitzgerald, one of the greatest vocalists of the jazz era. You can hear her sing "Who Cares?" on the Study Guide CD-ROM.

7

At the piano, Duke gives a quiet signal for this brass episode before it starts; he also plays a single, hardly audible note in the middle of the episode, as though to remind us who is in charge. The piece ends as it started, with the tune played by Tizol, but it fades halfway through.

How strange to be back to the rather mournful and still conga melody, with its Latin beat! The listener to *Conga Brava* can end up feeling a bit mystified. All that exhilarating jazz activity that blew up so suddenly and has now been cut off—was it some kind of dream? Only a master of musical form like Ellington could make you think of such questions, make you feel that way about a piece of music.

GLOBAL PERSPECTIVES 6

African Drumming

38 41

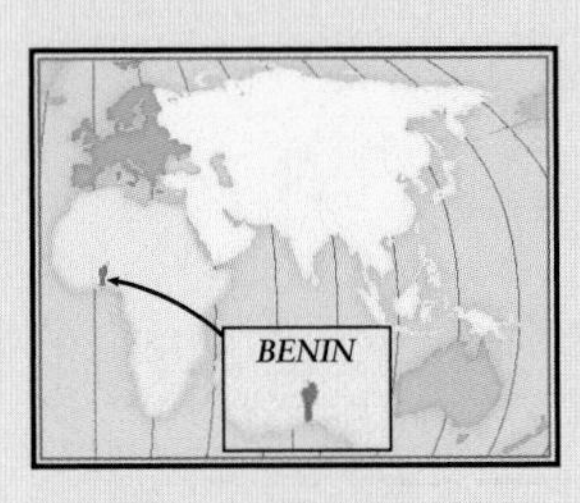

We said before that the syncopated rhythms of ragtime, blues, and jazz derived from traditional African music, particularly drumming. We don't know enough about African or African American music in the nineteenth century to detail this connection in all its stages, but we can surmise that the rhythmic complexities of modern jazz and today's African drumming are connected in a history that reaches back centuries.

Listen now to our recording of a drum ensemble from Benin, a small West African nation situated between Ghana and Nigeria. This music is used in the worship of ancestral spirits among the Yoruba people—one of a wide variety of religious and nonreligious uses of drumming in the region.

Syncopation and Polyrhythms

The rhythms of this music cannot be said to *swing* precisely in the manner of jazz, but they show a complexity and vitality related to jazz rhythms and not found in the European classical music tradition through the nineteenth century.

These rhythms are related to what we have termed "beat syncopation" in jazz (see page 390). A single drum lays down a basic, fast, four-plus-four pulse;

A drumming club in Ghana

each group of four feels like a beat, and two groups of four take about a second. (This quick pulse is heard all the way through the recording, except for three brief moments: This drummer speeds up momentarily at 1:09, 1:46, and 2:33, with stunning, energizing effect, fitting six strokes into the space usually taken up by four.)

Against the main drum's consistent pulse, the other drums play a variety of different rhythms. Sometimes they underscore the main drum's even pulse, or even duplicate it. Often, however, they play off it with more complicated and varied rhythms, including extensive syncopation within the groups of four (or beats), and occasionally they boldly contradict it.

Such overlapping of varied patterns with the main pulse is essential in West African drumming. Since several rhythmic formulas can be heard at once, it is sometimes called *polyrhythm.* From its polyrhythms the musical whole gains an extraordinary richness of rhythmic profile. And from the syncopations within the beat it derives its irresistible vitality (irresistible also to the ancestral spirits invoked).

A Closer Look

For those who wish to study this recording more closely, here are a few clear polyrhythmic interactions to listen for:

- One drummer aligns a regular syncopated formula against the main pulse, in this manner:

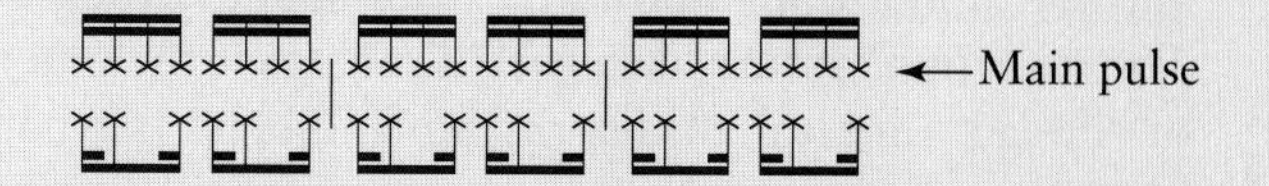

Listen for this four times in the recording, at 0:23–0:29, 0:50–0:53, 1:23–1:28, and 2:13–2:19.

- Another drummer plays an even 3 + 3 pulse against the main 4 + 4, seeming to contradict its duple meter with a triple orientation. This occurs prominently twice, at 0:41–0:44 and again at 2:22–2:26.

- One drummer in particular departs freely from the main pulse all the way through this recording. He is the soloist, so to speak, improvising against the more regular and predictable playing of his ensemble-mates. His drum is recognizable by its wooden, clickety-clack timbre and by the fact that it plays two distinct pitches (the higher pitch is more wooden-sounding than the lower).

One good way to listen for his distinctive, irregular syncopations is to clap along with the main pulse as you listen, once every four strokes. You will be clapping about twice a second. Then compare the regularity of your own clapping with the seemingly free fantasy of the clickety-clack drum.

3 Later Jazz

After World War II the popularity of the big bands collapsed suddenly. They were too expensive to run; furthermore, styles in entertainment had changed, and the smooth, high-powered band sound struck people as cold and slick. The mass market turned to rock'n'roll, itself the outcome of a vital new genre of African American music, rhythm and blues (see page 411). Even during the war, this collapse had been forecast by a revolutionary new movement within jazz called *bebop*.

Bebop

During the early 1940s, young black jazz musicians found it harder to get work than white players in big bands. When they did get jobs, the setup discouraged free improvisation, the life and soul of jazz; the big bands seemed to have co-opted and distorted a style grown out of black experience. These musicians got together in small groups after work for jam sessions at clubs in Harlem. There they developed a new style that would later be called **bebop.** Contrasting sharply with the big bands, the typical bebop combo (combination) was just trumpet and saxophone, with a rhythm section including piano.

Bebop was a determined return to improvisation, then—but improvisation of a new technical virtuosity. "That horn ain't supposed to sound that fast," an elder musician is said to have complained to bebop saxophonist Charlie Parker. In addition to unprecedented velocity, Parker and leading bebop trumpeter Dizzy Gillespie (1917–1993) cultivated hard, percussive sounds and sharp, snap rhythms (one derivation of the term "bebop").

Playing bop is like playing Scrabble with all the vowels missing.

Duke Ellington, 1954

Equally radical was the treatment of harmony in bebop. New Orleans jazz used simple, in fact naïve, harmonies. The swing arrangers used much more sophisticated ones. Bebop musicians took these complex harmonies and improvised around them in a more and more "far out" fashion. In long stretches of their playing, even the tonality of the music was obscured. Bebop melodies grew truly fantastic; the chord "changes" became harder and harder to follow.

CHARLIE PARKER (1920–1955) and MILES DAVIS (1926–1991)
Out of Nowhere (1948)

33

38

The life of Charlie ("Bird") Parker, bebop's greatest genius, reads like a modern-day version of a persistent Romantic myth—the myth of the artist who is driven by the demon of his creativity, finding fulfillment only in his art. Parker was on drugs from the age of fifteen, and in later years could not control his immoderate drinking and eating. A legend in his own lifetime, Parker died at the age of thirty-four after a suicide attempt and a period of hospitalization in a California mental institution.

Out of Nowhere is one of the many popular songs of the 1930s that were used as the basis for jazz, swing, and bebop singles. Our version of the number was recorded live in a New York nightclub, so it can give us an exact idea of what an improvised bebop number actually sounded like. Notice the informal opening—no arranged introduction as in Ellington's *Conga Brava,* or even in the Wallace-Armstrong blues number. Parker plays the attractive song fairly "straight" to begin with, but he inserts a sudden skittering passage just before the **A′** section (the song is in **A A′** form). This is a preview of things to come.

LISTEN

Parker, *Out of Nowhere*

0:00 **Tune**
0:51 **Trumpet**
1:36 **Sax**
2:26 **Piano**
2:49 **Tune**

The trumpet solo by Miles Davis has the characteristic tense, bright bebop sound, some very rapid passage work, and one or two piercing high notes. Then Parker's improvisation shows his impressive powers of melodic development. He works mainly with the opening motive of three eighth notes in the original song:

He had already expanded these three notes to many more, much shorter and faster ones, in his original presentation of the tune. Now he builds a whole series of phrases of different lengths, all starting with fast, increasingly elaborate runs derived from this basic rhythmic idea.

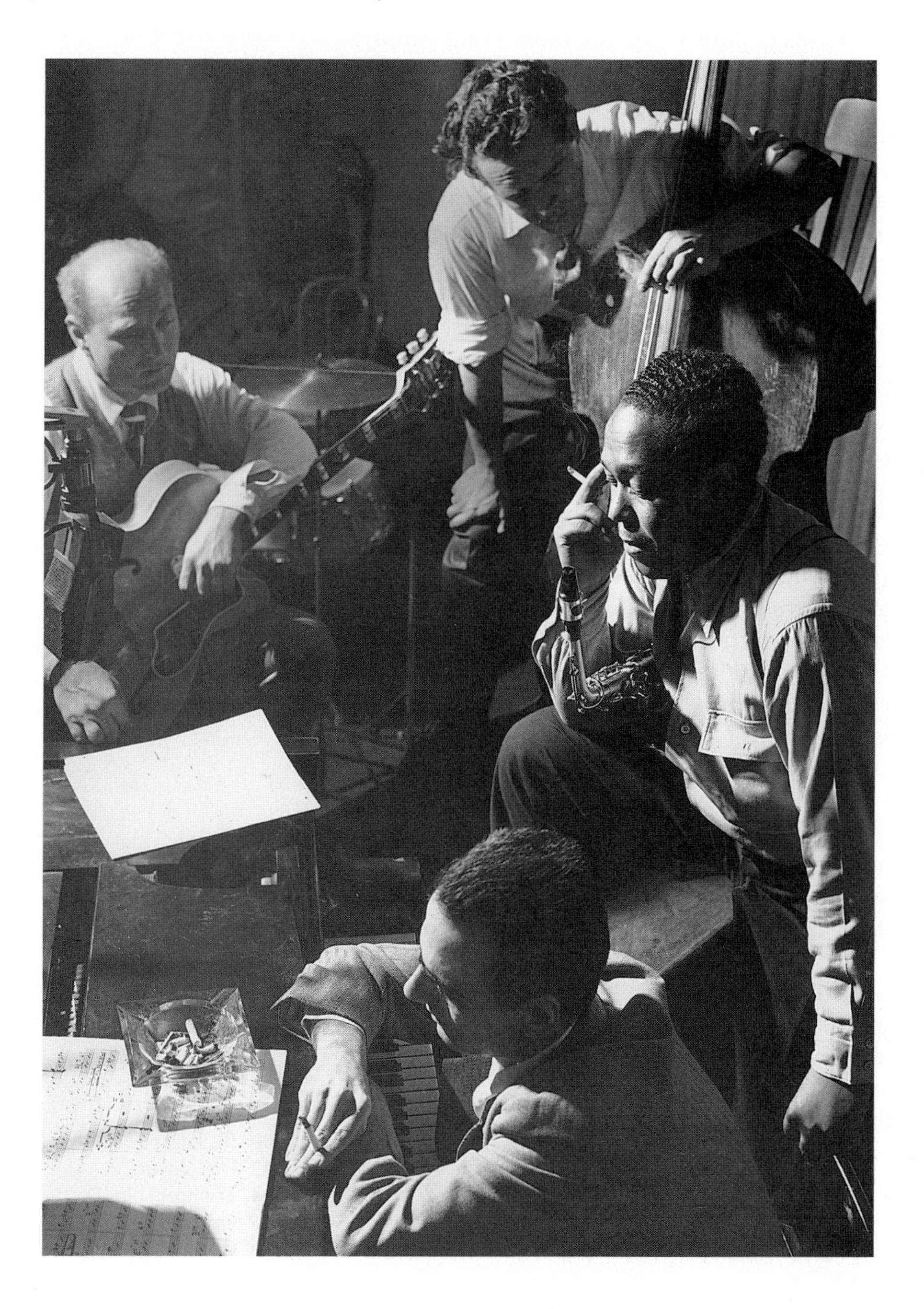

In a recording studio, Charlie Parker listens to a playback as the other musicians wait for his reaction. Will he approve this "take" of the number they are recording, or will they have to do another?

The irregular, almost discontinuous-sounding rests between Parker's phrases have their own special fascination. You may recognize an Irish jig, named "The Kerry Dancers," which seems to have popped into Parker's head right in the middle of the solo, as the outgrowth of a short melody figure he had come to. He plays the jig at a dizzying rate for just a moment, before inventing something else; fantastically, it fits right in.

At the end of his solo the nightclub audience applauds, and the pianist plays his own improvised solo on the tune's **A** section. The number ends with the **A′** section of *Out of Nowhere* played once again quite simply, except for new trumpet breaks and a new, comical ending.

Jazz after Bebop

Melody, harmony, and tonality—these were the very elements in music that had been "emancipated" by Schoenberg, Stravinsky, and other avant-gardists in the early 1900s. With the bebop movement, the avant-garde finally came to jazz.

Many new jazz styles followed after the bebop emancipation, from the 1950s to the present day. Jazz aficionados distinguish between cool jazz, free jazz, modal jazz, Afro-Cuban jazz, electric jazz, and even avant-garde jazz. Among the leaders in this diverse, exciting music were pianist Thelonious Monk (1917–1982), trumpeter Miles Davis (1926–1991), keyboardist Sun Ra (1928–1994), and saxophonists John Coltrane (1926–1967) and Ornette Coleman (b. 1930). They were the first to improvise really freely—that is, without a song or blues or any pre-existing chord changes as a basis.

The synthesizer has changed everything, whether purist musicians like it or not. It's here to stay and you can either be in it or out of it. I choose to be in it because the world has always been about change.

From Miles Davis's autobiography, 1989

MILES DAVIS (1926–1991)
Bitches Brew (1969)

34

39

Trumpeter Miles Davis, one of the most innovative figures in the whole history of jazz, started out playing with Charlie Parker and other bebop musicians, but soon realized that his own aptitude (or at least one of his main aptitudes) was for a more relaxed and tuneful kind of melody. Davis's style went through many stages—from bebop to cool jazz to modal jazz and beyond—as he worked in various groups with a veritable who's-who of modern jazz artists.

Bitches Brew, one of his biggest hits, was also one of his most original. A conscious (and controversial) attempt to blend jazz with rock, the album used a rhythm section with electric guitar, bass, and two electric keyboards in addition to regular jazz drums, acoustic bass, and augmented percussion. Instead of the traditional chord changes of jazz, this group produced repetitive, rocklike rhythms of the greatest variety and, often, delicacy. This backdrop provides an unlikely but also unforgettable setting for Davis's haunting improvisations.

Our selection covers a solo from the title track of *Bitches Brew.* Before Davis begins, the electric piano and guitar pick out rhythmic patterns against a quiet jazz drum background; mostly the electric guitar has isolated single notes and the electric piano has syncopated chords. As the piano and guitar die down, new fascinating rhythms are heard in the bass.

The trumpet solo starts with short patterns of relatively long notes, a Davis signature. The mood is meditative, almost melancholy: an evocation of the blues. A rocklike ostinato is heard in the bass. Soon Davis is employing more elaborate patterns—a string of repeated notes, scalelike passages up and

LISTEN

Davis, *Bitches Brew* (part)

0:00 **Backdrop**
0:42 **Dies down**
1:04 **Trumpet solo**
2:56 **Ostinato**
3:39 **Climax**

Miles Davis

Cuban pianist Gonzalo Rubalcaba, leading light of a new jazz generation.

down—but the effect is, in its own way, as repetitive as the backdrop. Then he explodes into a series of little snaps: a recollection of bebop. As the backdrop drives harder and harder, we realize that Davis has now arrived at a wild, free ostinato in the high register. The solo sinks down again after a climactic high trumpet squeal, another Davis hallmark.

With jazz-rock or *fusion,* Davis and others reached out for vernacular roots in American music. Still, jazz in its modern stage is usually complex and often difficult to follow. Formerly America's dominant form of truly popular music, today this music can really only be described as "popular" with loyal fans who crowd to jazz festivals from Newport, Rhode Island, to Monterey, California. These fans view with mixed emotions efforts by Washington's Smithsonian Institution and New York's Lincoln Center to cultivate jazz in a classical-concert format, led especially by the latest great jazz trumpet virtuoso, Wynton Marsalis (b. 1961). The life and soul of jazz is its spontaneity. Will spontaneity survive institutionalization?

Jazz continues to flower cumulatively, taking on and transforming the new without ever abandoning the old. It is a fugue with a life of its own, endlessly recapitulating.

Time magazine, 1976

4 The Influence of Jazz and Blues

How was jazz first received in this country's "cultivated" musical circles? Many longtime symphony and opera subscribers certainly hated it. They considered its saxophones and muted trumpets vulgar, its rhythms dangerously sexual and likely to corrupt their children. This reaction was strongly tinged with racism.

On the other hand, jazz was from the first an inspiration as well as a delight for less hidebound musicians, music students, and young composers.

The 1920s era was a confident one, and composers coming of age at that time promised a bright new day for American music. A vital, fresh musical idiom had emerged—the decade from 1920 to 1930 called itself the Jazz Age—and the idea of working jazz into concert music was both natural and exciting.

Jazz in the Concert Hall

We have already heard one example of this trend in Maurice Ravel's blues-influenced Piano Concerto in G (see page 355). Ravel heard the new African American styles when they took Paris by storm in the 1920s, making that city the first jazz center outside the United States.

In America, the composer who most successfully carried off the fusion of jazz with concert-hall music was George Gershwin (1898–1937). Born in New York, Gershwin received a sketchy musical education. He quit school at sixteen to work as a song plugger, or music publisher's agent, playing through the newest sheet music hits for potential customers and promoting them to singers and bandleaders. Soon he was writing his own songs, and he went on to compose some of the finest tunes of the 1920s—"Lady be Good," "Embraceable You," "The Man I Love," and dozens of others. He was an accomplished and original jazz pianist.

Oh sweet and lovely
Lady be good,
Oh lady be good
To me.
I'm just a lonely
Babe in the wood,
Oh lady be good
To me . . .
Gershwin song lyric

Harboring an ambition to enter the world of cultivated music, Gershwin electrified musical America with his *Rhapsody in Blue* of 1924. Billed as "An Experiment in Modern Music," this fourteen-minute work for piano and orchestra was first performed by Paul Whiteman's Orchestra, a sleek forerunner of the 1930s big bands. This music is not true jazz, but is Gershwin's translation of jazz into his own individual idiom, halfway between jazz and the concert hall's concerto.

After *Rhapsody in Blue,* Gershwin wrote more works importing jazz and blues styles into concert-hall genres: *An American in Paris,* a symphonic poem for orchestra; a piano concerto; and an opera, *Porgy and Bess*—works that have remained widely popular, known and loved by millions of Americans. Gershwin had thrown a bridge across the canyon between vernacular and cultivated music. Of course, the existence of bridges doesn't mean that the rift has gone away.

GEORGE GERSHWIN
Prelude No. 1 (1926)

35

40

Gershwin's Prelude No. 1 for piano is the first in a set of three he published in 1927. In its dimensions it looks back to Romantic piano miniatures (see page 246); its title recalls collections of such works by Chopin and Debussy that Gershwin knew well. Indeed, Gershwin originally intended a set of twenty-four preludes, just the number Chopin had published. He had the idea of calling this set *The Melting Pot,* a reference to the various cultivated and vernacular styles he would bring together in it.

Prelude No. 1 recalls Romantic miniatures also in its simple **A B A′** form. **A** and **A′** each consist of little more than a statement of the main melody of the piece:

LISTEN

Gershwin, Prelude No. 1

0:00 **A**
0:07 Left-hand syncopations begin
0:22 **B**
0:54 Beginning of **A:** buildup
1:04 **A′**

B is a longer section. It changes key frequently, employing many sequences, and is dominated by a melody that begins with repeated notes, a favorite gesture of Gershwin in his piano music.

What gives this music its distinctive appeal, however—and what makes it sound nothing like Chopin—are the elements it borrows from jazz and blues. Both the little half-step slide up that begins the main theme and the unexpected note that ends its second bar are borrowed from the so-called *blues scale*—a scale characteristic of blues singing but not of the European classical tradition. Such "blue notes" come back again and again in the melodies of the piece.

Even more distinctive is the jazzy syncopation that marks the left-hand part. Listen to the accompaniment at the beginning, before the main melody joins it, counting two fairly slow beats per measure. The beginning of each measure—the downbeat—is clearly marked by a thudding low note. The *second* beat, however, is not struck, but instead undercut by a syncopated chord that anticipates it by a fraction. Syncopated patterns like this one continue throughout the piece, playing off against the melodies to give the piece its rhythmic verve.

Constantin Alajálov, who left unforgettable pictures of the Jazz Age, sketched himself painting George Gershwin in 1932.

The American Musical

Throughout the ages and throughout the world, the theater has always provided fertile soil for the growth of popular music. America, once the Puritan spirit had subsided somewhat, proved no exception. One of the main sources of modern American popular music can be located in the thriving New York theatrical scene in the decades around 1900. Then, as now, the New York City theater district was located at, and known as, Broadway.

Broadway was first of all home of **operetta**, a very popular European genre of light opera in the nineteenth and early twentieth centuries. Operettas employ spoken dialogue (rather than recitative) between the musical numbers—light, attractive tunes and plenty of dances. Their plots are amusing, farfetched, and frothy. Typically they are set in some mythical eastern European country, where amorous, fun-loving aristocrats rub shoulders with merry, contented peasants.

Among the best European composers of operettas were Johann Strauss Jr., the "Waltz King" (*Die Fledermaus*—"The Bat": 1874), and Arthur Sullivan (*The Mikado, HMS Pinafore,* and others—these are called "Gilbert and Sullivan" operettas as a tribute to the very witty librettist, W. S. Gilbert). The most important American composer in this tradition was Victor Herbert (1859–1924). Born in Ireland and educated in Germany, Herbert produced more than forty operettas from the 1890s on; chiefly remembered today is *Babes in Toyland* (1903).

Musical Comedy and Popular Song

It was around 1910 that the American popular theater picked up its characteristic accent. It was a musical accent, and it came from jazz. Although Broadway did not employ actual jazz, it swiftly appropriated and assimilated jazz syncopation and swing. As projected by white theater bands and carried over into popular songs, this jazz accent contributed more than anything else to the appeal of a new kind of musical show.

A vaudeville team of the 1890s, the Southern Four.

Theatergoers had also begun to demand stories that were American and up to date, and so the writers of the song lyrics learned to make up smart, catchy verses full of American locutions. To distinguish them from operettas—with their Old World ambience, aristocrats, waltzes, and students' drinking songs—these new shows were called **musical comedies**, or **musicals.**

Irving just loves hits. He has no sophistication about it—he just loves hits.

Said of Irving Berlin (1888–1990), author of "Alexander's Ragtime Band," "Always," "Easter Parade," and "White Christmas," among other hits

The rise of the musical in the 1920s and thirties was closely tied to the great outpouring of popular songs in this era. It was truly a golden age for song. Not all of them were written for musicals, of course (Ellington, for example, wrote many songs that had no link to the theater). But the theater provided songwriters with an extra fee and gave songs invaluable exposure, magnified after 1926 by "talking pictures." Theater songs were popularized by the very successful movie musicals of the 1930s, as well as by radio and 78-rpm recordings.

The two principal composers of early American musical comedy were also composers of many favorite old tunes: Jerome Kern (1885–1945) and George Gershwin. Kern's masterpiece, *Show Boat* (1927), has returned to the stage again and again, and Gershwin's *Porgy and Bess* (1935), which is more like a jazz opera than a musical, occupies a solid place in the operatic repertory.

Gershwin's actual musicals are seldom heard because most of the plots now seem so silly—but there are exceptions, notably *Of Thee I Sing* (1931), a hilarious spoof of the presidential election process. There is a song from this show on our Study Guide CD-ROM.

7

The Musical after 1940

Show Boat and *Of Thee I Sing* both look forward to the new dramatic sophistication of the musical in the postwar era. From the 1940s on, the plots of musicals were worked out with more care. Instead of the plot being a mere pretext for songs and dances in the manner of a revue, musical numbers grew logically out of a plot that had interest in its own right.

Richard Rodgers (1902–1979) and his lyricist Oscar Hammerstein (1895–1960) dominated this period. Their works such as *Oklahoma!* (1943) and *The King and I* (1951) ran for thousands of performances on Broadway. They still define the golden age of the musical—perhaps especially because they offered a sentimental and innocent vision of the world as America in the postwar era wished to see it.

Other musicals tackled more challenging subjects—psychoanalysis, trade unionism, gang warfare—but these rarely rivaled the megahits of Rodgers and Hammerstein. One exception to this rule is *West Side Story,* with music by the classical composer and symphony conductor Leonard Bernstein. Here we see the cultivated tradition reaching out to the vernacular—but in a genre defined by the vernacular.

LEONARD BERNSTEIN (1918–1990)
West Side Story (1957)

Leonard Bernstein was one of the most brilliant and versatile musicians ever to come out of America, the consummate crossover artist before the term was invented. Composer of classical symphonies and hit musicals, internationally acclaimed conductor, pianist, author, and mastermind of wonderful shows in the early days of television, he won Grammys, Emmys, and a Tony.

West Side Story (1957) boasts three exceptional features—its moving story, its sophisticated score, and its superb dances, created by the great American choreographer Jerome Robbins. The musical, by turns funny, smart, tender, and enormously dynamic, gave us song classics such as "Maria" and "Tonight." Our recording of *West Side Story* is from the soundtrack to the 1961 movie version of the show.

The great thing about conducting is that you don't smoke and you breathe in great gobs of oxygen.

Chain-smoker Leonard Bernstein

Background Shakespeare's play *Romeo and Juliet* tells of young lovers frustrated and driven to their deaths by a meaningless feud between their families, the Montagues and the Capulets of Verona. *West Side Story* transplants this plot to a turf war between teenage gangs on the West Side of Manhattan. In Shakespeare, the feud is a legacy from the older generation, but in *West Side Story* the bitter enmity is the kids' own, though it has ethnic overtones. The Jets are whites, the Sharks Puerto Ricans.

Bernardo, leader of the Sharks, is livid when he learns that his sister Maria is in love with Jet Tony. As in Shakespeare, one Jet (Capulet) and one Shark (Montague) die tragically on stage, in a street fight. Tony is shot in revenge, and Maria is left distraught.

Some of the transpositions into the modern world are ingenious. Shakespeare's famous soliloquy "Romeo, Romeo, wherefore art thou Romeo?" shows the lovestruck Juliet fondly repeating her lover's name; Tony cries "Maria" over and over again in his famous song of that title. (An aria in an opera or a song in a musical is, in fact, often equivalent to a soliloquy in a play.) And whereas Shakespeare's young lovers fall in love at a Capulet masked ball, which Romeo has crashed, Bernstein's are smitten at a gym dance organized by a clueless teacher who hopes to make peace between the gangs.

Cha-cha This is the music danced to by the Puerto Rican girls—the Sharks' girlfriends—at the gym where Tony and Maria first meet. The cha-cha, a Cuban dance, was new to the United States when *West Side Story* was written.

36

West Side Story: trouble at the gym

The charm of the fragile cha-cha melody owes a good deal to Bernstein's skillful accompaniment. Melody and accompaniment seem nervously aware of each other, but they keep slipping out of sync:

LISTEN

Bernstein, "Cool"

0:14 **Riff:** "Cool"
1:13 **Fugue** begins
2:40 Fugue breaks down
3:10 Band version of "Cool"
3:39 **Jets:** "Cool"
4:08 **Countersubject**

Meeting Scene Tony and Maria catch sight of one another. The cha-cha may be continuing, but they don't hear it, so neither do we. Or at most they hear fragments of the cha-cha slowed down and made unexpectedly tender, as background for their voice-over.

And when Tony gets to sing the big romantic number, "Maria," the music is yet another transformation of the cha-cha melody, now sounding rich and enthusiastic. Thematic transformation technique, which Bernstein knew from Liszt and other Romantic composers, allowed him to show Tony's love emerging and blossoming out of that one heart-stopping moment in the gym.

"Cool" A little later in the action, the Jet leader, Riff, tries to persuade his troops to stay calm in the face of Shark provocations. The main production number of Act I, it consists of an introduction, again with voice-over; a short song by Riff; a dazzling dance; and then Riff's song again.

37

The song's introduction uses the motive of the cha-cha melody—the same motive that turns into "Maria"—in a highly charged, syncopated form:

Boy, boy, crazy boy,
Get cool, boy!
Got a rocket
In your pocket,
Keep coolly cool, boy!
Don't get hot
'Cause, man, you got
Some high times ahead.
Take it slow,
And, Daddy-o,
You can live it up
and die in bed!

After the introduction, Riff sings two stanzas of his song, in 1950s "hip" street language. There is a steady jazz percussion accompaniment.

The dance that follows, subtitled "Fugue," is accompanied throughout by the soft jazz drum beat. First played by muted trumpet, the fugue subject consists of four slow notes, with an ominous snap at the end of the last of them. Soon another theme—the fugue countersubject (see page 140)—comes in, played by flute and vibraphone, featured instruments of 1950s "cool jazz." The two themes combine in counterpoint, along with fragments of the introduction, getting louder and more intricate as the dance proceeds. Bernstein must have thought that fugue, about the most "controlled" of musical forms, would depict perfectly the Jets' effort to stay cool.

But things appear to get out of hand toward the end of the dance. The music stomps angrily and breaks into electrifying improvised drum solos. The Jets yell various words taken from the song, and the song's melody returns, orchestrated in the exuberant, brash style of a big swing band. While the brasses blare away on the tune, breaks (see page 390) are played by the reeds at the end of each line.

To conclude, the Jets sing parts of "Cool" quietly, prior to its atmospheric conclusion. The vibraphone recollects the fugue countersubject.

MUTED BRASS

Stephen Sondheim (b. 1930), who wrote the lyrics for *West Side Story,* was himself an aspiring composer. He has gone on to write words and music for a string of successful musicals with an intellectual bent: *A Little Night Music* (1972), *Sweeney Todd* (1979), and *Into the Woods* (1987). *Sweeney Todd* in particular pushed at the border between musical and opera, as Gershwin had done forty years earlier in *Porgy and Bess.*

Meanwhile the musical in the 1960s began to acknowledge the rock revolution: *Hair* (Galt MacDermott, 1967) has been described as a "plotless American tribal love-rock musical." It was as much celebrated in its time for its onstage nudity as for any noteworthy rock music. In spite of its recent revival and such follow-ups as *Rent* (Jonathan Larson, 1997), true rock musicals have never ruled Broadway. Instead it has in recent years been home to anodyne foreign musicals, especially by the English composer Sir Andrew Lloyd Webber: *Cats* (1981), *The Phantom of the Opera* (1986), and others.

Just at this moment, however, the musical in an old-fashioned guise was revitalized from an unexpected quarter. In a series of Disney full-length animated films, including *Beauty and the Beast, The Little Mermaid,* and *The Lion King,* the musical was transplanted from stage to film. Of course musicals had been filmed before—think of *The Sound of Music, My Fair Lady,* or *The Music Man.* But these Disney musicals were created expressly to be animated. In a predictable twist, one of them, *The Lion King,* has now made its way back to live action as a Broadway hit.

Today the tradition of the musical thrives in many forms. On Broadway it can go so far as to erase the distinction between vernacular and cultivated traditions, as in the 2002 production in full of Puccini's opera *La Bohème,* sung in Italian. Elsewhere it ranges from the Hollywood film *Moulin Rouge,* set in a Paris music hall from the 1800s, to the annual student revivals of Broadway hits of the past in thousands of high schools and summer camps across the country.

5 Rock: The First Fifty Years

Throughout the jazz age in the first half of the twentieth century, another, related type of vernacular music poured forth from American composers: popular songs. We have seen the beginnings of this tradition in the nineteenth century in the works of Stephen Foster (see page 388), and we have also discussed one of the best popular songwriters of the 1920s and 1930s, George Gershwin (page 404).

One thing that often happened to the best-known songs—"standards" when they became popular enough to be hummed by everyone "in the know"—was that they served as a platform for jazz improvisors. The example of Charlie Parker's *Out of Nowhere* (page 404) shows that standards could sometimes support even the most progressive jazz styles. To *become* a standard, however, such songs needed to catch on with the public through versions by the best-loved singers of the day. Vocalists like Bing Crosby and Frank Sinatra sang the sentimental, jazzy tunes to dance-hall audiences, to the ever-growing radio audience, in the movies, and—most importantly by the end of the 1940s—on records.

After World War II, the popularity of such songs began to be rivaled by another set of styles, less tame, louder, and with a driving beat that made the subtleties of jazz syncopation plainer and cruder—all in all, more brash and youthful. By the middle of the 1950s the new style took a name that captured this compelling rhythm: *rock'n'roll.* (Later, in the 1960s, the name of choice became **rock.**) Teenagers went wild. Their parents, reacting much as parents had thirty years earlier in the face of jazz, bemoaned the demise of civil culture and decent society.

Nevertheless, rock endured and evolved—indeed, it positively burgeoned. Its explosive development from 1955 to 1970 and its reinvention in the following decades have put rock on a historical par with jazz. If jazz can claim to be America's most distinctive contribution to world art from the first half of the twentieth century, rock can make similar claims for the last fifty years. Today the development of global pop, discussed in Global Perspectives 7 (page 418), depends on various styles of American-derived rock more than on any other musical idiom.

Early Rock'n'Roll

The origins and subsequent history of rock and related popular styles conform to a pattern in American vernacular music we have seen as early as the minstrel show and then in 1930s swing: the mixing of African American and white American styles. Sometimes in rock history this mix was a relatively balanced meeting of differing styles; at other times it looks more like the appropriation of African American idioms by white musicians. In either case it shows that the history of pop music, like so many other American histories, unfolded against the backdrop of white/black race relations.

With his sultry voice and sexual stage presence, Elvis Presley had a gripping effect on audiences of the 1950s.

The very earliest rock'n'roll shows this pattern, emerging after World War II from the blending of *hillbilly* or *country* music with **rhythm and blues.** Country music was a white rural style derived from southern and southwestern folk song and emphasizing acoustic guitar, fiddle, and voice. Rhythm and blues was a black urban updating of earlier blues, marked by more pronounced, driving rhythms and electric guitar accompaniment. Together they created the first rock'n'roll style, *rockabilly.*

The first superstar of rock'n'roll, Elvis Presley, continued the trend. His amazing string of hits in the late 1950s ("Heartbreak Hotel," "Love Me Tender," and many others) combined a lyrical style derived from white popular singers with the strong beat and passionate, throaty vocal delivery of rockabilly. Many of these hits (for example, "Hound Dog") were Elvis's versions of songs originally recorded by black artists—"covers," as we now call them.

Millions in white America loved Elvis's music while millions more found it threatening. Across the late 1950s a string of both white (Jerry Lee Lewis, Buddy Holly) and black musicians (Fats Domino, Little Richard, Chuck Berry) followed him up the charts—and soon it was "Rock around the Clock," as Bill Haley had declared in his 1955 hit. Radio stations and record companies alike realized there was a lasting market for the new sound.

So did Elvis's manager, Colonel Tom Parker, who shrewdly calculated the sales potential of Elvis's crossover style and advanced his stardom by securing him TV appearances and signing him to movie contracts. Parker made Elvis the first great example of manipulative rock marketing. He would not be the last.

The 1960s: Rock Comes of Age

The blending of black and white styles that resulted in early rock'n'roll lasted into the 1960s and has reappeared in various forms down to this day. At the same time, the early and mid 1960s witnessed the emergence of new styles, many of them clearly black or white in their origin and target audience. There was an explosion of new sounds, distinct from one another and gaining the allegiance of different groups of fans.

Motown, Soul, and Funk As the civil rights movement of the 1950s evolved into the Black Power movement of the late 1960s, a succession of important black styles asserted their independence from white rock. These grew out of several sources: the remnants of black rhythm and blues in the late 1950s, most notably represented by singer-pianist Ray Charles, urban doo-wop groups that spawned such hit-makers as the Drifters ("Under the Boardwalk"), and "girl groups" such as the Shirelles ("Will You Love Me Tomorrow?").

The first in this line was the *Motown* style, created by the part-time songwriter and record producer Berry Gordy Jr. of Detroit—"Motorcity" or "Motown." Gordy was the most important black entrepreneur in early rock history. The groups he sponsored, among them the Supremes ("Where Did Our Love Go?") and the Temptations ("My Girl"), evolved polished, lyrical styles and performances featuring dance steps and sequins.

A more visceral style that emerged around the same time was *soul.* Soul derived especially from southern gospel singing combined with the rhythm and blues of Ray Charles. Its leading lights were the powerful Aretha Franklin ("Respect") and James Brown, self-styled as "the hardest working man in show business"—and certainly one of the hardest singing ("I Got You (I Feel Good)"). Its most haunting vocal presence was Otis Redding, whose only number-one hit, "(Sittin' On) The Dock of the Bay," is doubly haunting since it was recorded just days before he died in a 1967 plane crash.

By the end of the 1960s, soul was evolving into *funk,* a style in which the large bands with wind instruments typical of soul gave way to a sparer, hip sound (fuzztone bass guitar ostinatos, syncopated guitar scratching). One of the early groups pointing in this direction was the Bay Area–based Sly and the Family Stone ("Thank You (Falettinme Be Mice Elf Agin)"). A decade later, in the hands of George Clinton and his band Funkadelic, funk was the source early DJs sampled to accompany the first rappers.

The British Invasion

On February 7, 1964, the Beatles landed in New York for their first American tour. The resulting Beatlemania changed the face of rock'n'roll, and in a certain sense it has never ended. More than thirty years after their disbanding, the Beatles remain one of the highest-grossing entertainment institutions in the world.

Dozens of other British rock bands followed in the wake of the Beatles' arrival, some good, some not. The best of them, cast from the first as a kind of evil-twin mirroring of the Beatles, was the Rolling Stones. What British groups had in common at the start was their emulation of American rhythm and blues and the styles of black American rockers like Chuck Berry and Little Richard. One of the most influential of these British rockers, Eric Clapton, has ranged widely in the early history of the blues for his inspiration.

The difference between the Beatles and the Rolling Stones was not merely the good/bad contrast of their carefully groomed market images. It was musical as well. The Stones, despite nods in other directions, specialized in a blues-oriented, hard-rocking style led by Mick Jagger's manic vocal presence, heard in such hits as "Satisfaction" and "Honky Tonk Woman." The Beatles, in contrast, seemed to blossom in all musical directions—reflecting the differing musical interests of John Lennon, Paul McCartney, and George Harrison that would tear the group apart by 1970. From covers of Chuck Berry ("Roll Over, Beethoven") and sneakily insightful pop/rock numbers ("She Loves You," "Help!"), they moved on to countless other approaches: lyrical

January 1969: The Beatles in their final concert, an impromptu affair on the roof of the Apple Records building. From left: Ringo, Paul, John, and George.

ballads ("Yesterday," "Blackbird"), hymnlike anthems ("Hey Jude," "Let It Be"), visionary and psychedelic rock ("A Day in the Life," "Strawberry Fields"), and irresistible pop songs harkening back to the 1930s ("When I'm Sixty-Four," "Maxwell's Silver Hammer"—surely the sweetest tune imaginable about a serial killer). And they easily returned, led by Lennon, to straight-ahead, blues-derived rock ("Revolution").

American Counteroffensives

The irony of the British groups' interest in American rhythm and blues is that their massive popularity chased dozens of American groups, black and white, off the charts and out of business. About the only American music that swam well during the highest tide of the British invasion was the surfing sound out of southern California, typified by the Beach Boys ("I Get Around," "Good Vibrations").

Meanwhile another movement looking back to the hillbilly side of rock's ancestry was gaining steam. *Folk rock* was led by Bob Dylan, whose evocative, often socially conscious lyrics ("Blowin' in the Wind," "The Times They Are A-Changin'") rivaled his music in importance. Dylan's resuscitation of white country and folk styles, building on "folkies" such as Woody Guthrie and Pete Seeger, had long-lasting consequences. The most important of these was creating a place, at the edge of the rock tradition, for the singer-songwriter using acoustic accompaniment. Dylan and the folkies inspired musicians as different

Like many singer-songwriters, Tori Amos has adopted a confessional style in her lyrics; her personal revelations have captivated audiences as much as her passionate stage presence and strong piano playing.

as Paul Simon, originally part of the folk-rock duo Simon and Garfunkel; the straight-ahead rocker Bruce Springsteen; and the unpredictable, versatile Elvis Costello. Women musicians in particular have found the singer-songwriter niche congenial. Their line extends from Joan Baez and Joni Mitchell in the 1960s down to Tori Amos, k.d. lang, and Alanis Morissette today.

In the late 1960s a broad, mainly white, stratum of American youth, espousing free love, free drugs, and ever-louder opposition to the U.S. war in Vietnam, embraced new styles. From San Francisco, a center of this counterculture, came *acid rock,* named after LSD, known as "acid." In the hands of groups like the Grateful Dead, the style involved long, jazzlike improvisations on electric guitar alongside hallucinatory images in the words; the Dead was the first great "jam band."

Other guitar virtuosos embraced the new, improvisational style and linked it back to rhythm and blues guitar playing. The most famous of them were Jimi Hendrix, a rare black musician in the midst of psychedelic acid rock ("Purple Haze"), and the Latin-influenced Carlos Santana ("Black Magic Woman"). This powerful new guitar style would find its way into groups on both sides of the Atlantic; the best were the Who (creators of the "rock opera" *Tommy*), Cream (led by Clapton; "Sunshine of Your Love"), and Led Zeppelin ("Whole Lotta Love"). The guitar work of such groups formed the roots of *heavy metal.*

After the 1960s

By 1970, many of the trends that evolved over the following decades were in place. Self-conscious *art rock* (for example, Pink Floyd's album *Dark Side of the Moon*), singer-songwriter rock, heavy metal, and funk can all be seen, retrospectively, as outgrowths of music at the end of the 1960s.

The decade of the 1970s was perhaps most influential, however, in its consolidation of the global *business* of rock. Tendencies begun in the 1960s came to exert ever greater control over the music people heard: high-tech mass-marketing, aggressive promotion of "superstars" (the word itself came into common usage at this time, alongside "supertanker" and "superpower"), and play-listed, market-researched, repetitive radio stations. In 1981 a powerful new outlet emerged to promote a small and carefully selected sample of rock music: MTV began broadcasting nonstop on cable.

In the wake of the 1970s it is wise to remember that even the music that seems to rage loudest "against the machine" is usually brought to you by a multinational communications conglomerate.

Trends since 1980: Punk, Rap, and Post-Rock

Despite—or perhaps on account of—this commercialization, rock has survived. Indeed the last twenty-five years or so have brought something of a rejuvenation. Three trends can be summarized here:

1 The youthful disaffection that set in by the end of the 1960s, as the idealistic counterculture began to sense its impotence, hardened in the next decade. Its most influential expression was the nihilistic alienation of *punk rock*. In New York City and Britain, groups like the Patti Smith Group ("Gloria"), the Ramones ("Blitzkrieg Bop"), and the Sex Pistols ("Anarchy in the UK") reacted against the commercial flashiness of much rock with what we might call an anti-aesthetic: All expression was possible, including no expression. All musical

The Jimi Hendrix Experience, on the cover of their first album, dressed in their Carnaby Street best.

Kurt Cobain

expertise was acceptable, including none. (Some of the punks knew that in this move they were following the lead of arch-modernists like John Cage; see page 376.)

The punk approach gave strong impetus to a kind of populist movement in rock, encouraging the formation of countless "garage bands" and today's *indie rock,* distributed on small, independent labels. Some punk singers also pioneered an alienated, flat vocal delivery that contrasts both with the impassioned singing of earlier rock and with the streetwise cool of rap. In these features punk looked forward to the unpolished, moving, but somehow distant style of *grunge rock,* led by Kurt Cobain (until his death in 1994) and his band Nirvana ("Lithium," "Smells Like Teen Spirit").

First emerging about the same time as punk, *hip-hop* or **rap** has compiled a quarter-century history as a primary black rhetorical and musical mode. Early on, its influence was transmitted, with stunning postmodern quickness, around the globe. Rap is now a strong undercurrent sweeping through world pop-music traditions. Its influence is heard in the vocal delivery of countless rock groups.

The early 1990s marked rap's moment of highest notoriety in the American mass media. One strain of rap—the violent, misogynist variety known as *gangsta rap*—figured centrally in the public debate, which was marked not only by some justifiable distaste at the vision of these rappers but also by unmistakable racist undertones. However, the debate tended to miss two important points: First, while rap originated as a pointed expression of black urban concerns, it was marketed successfully to affluent whites, especially suburban teens. Second, the clamor against gangsta rap ignored the wider expressive terrains that rap as a whole had traveled. Already in 1980 rap was broad enough to embrace the hip-hop dance numbers of the Sugarhill Gang ("Rapper's Delight") and the trenchant social commentary of Grandmaster Flash ("The

Message"). By the 1990s, rap could range from the black empowerment messages of Public Enemy ("Don't Believe the Hype") through sensuous love lyrics and tongue-twisting word games to Queen Latifah's assertions of women's dignity and strength ("Latifah's Had It Up 2 Here"). And the 2000s would bring Eminem, the first white superstar of rap.

Around 1990 a new, experimental rock movement began to take shape; soon it was dubbed *post-rock*. Early post-rock groups (for example, Slint: "Good Morning Captain") emerged from the indie rock movement. They typically employed rock instrumentation and technology in a style that features hypnotically repeated gestures (especially bass ostinatos), juxtaposition of contrasting plateaus of sound, slow transitions and buildups, free improvisation, and emphasis of instruments rather than voice. (When a voice is present, it often doesn't so much *sing* as recite fragments of poetry in front of the instrumental backdrop.) This thumbnail sketch alone is enough to reveal post-rock's relation to two other musical movements we have encountered: minimalism (page 380) and avant-garde jazz (page 402).

And, just as jazz and classical music purists questioned those styles, some listen to post-rock and wonder, "But is it rock'n'roll?" The question grows more pressing still in the presence of recent post-rock groups (for instance, Godspeed You Black Emperor!; "Storm") that have featured acoustic rather than electrified instruments and even avoided the foremost trait of rock: a strong beat.

Questions of style, it seems to us, are not a matter of pre-set categories but of fluid affiliations, changing always as new music develops. Rock will accommodate post-rock, just as jazz accommodated fusion and classical concert music accepted minimalism, but it will be transformed in the process. In fact, the transformation is already under way. One of the most widely noticed rock bands of the late 1990s, Britain's Radiohead, began around 2000 to expand its earlier, song-oriented style with traits of post-rock ("Pyramid Song").

Web: *Research and test your understanding of jazz and popular American music at* **<bedfordstmartins.com/listen>.**

At a rave, dancing to *techno*, one of several varieties of electronic dance music that emerged in the 1980s.

GLOBAL PERSPECTIVES 7

Global Music

We have seen in Global Perspectives 2 (page 90) that European efforts to colonize foreign lands never resulted in the simple substitution of European cultures for native ones, but rather in new, complex mixed cultures. Such is the way of all meetings of distinct cultures and distinct musics. An Andean chorus singing Catholic Church polyphony to Quechua words and accompanying itself on Inca flutes and drums is the perfect example of such mixture.

But a funny thing happened to mixed musical cultures on their way through the twentieth century: recorded sound. Around the globe, the impact on music of technologies that store and play back sound has been nothing short of revolutionary. Combined with radio and TV broadcasts, and indeed with the modern ease of travel and commerce, it has given musicians and listeners from all parts of the world access to a much wider variety of music than ever before. Nothing in the whole history of culture, probably, has ever traveled more widely and easily than certain kinds of music do today.

Complexities of Globalism

Two opposing tendencies have arisen from this situation. The first works toward the worldwide *homogenization* of musics. Huge stretches of the sonic landscape are now inhabited by styles that are similar in certain basic features: electrified instruments, especially guitars; strong percussive presence; extensive syncopation; and relatively brief song-form presentation.

These features spread out from the American and especially African American pop-music revolution that occurred in the decades after World War II. Since the 1960s the dispersion of styles such as rhythm and blues, rock, soul, and rap has been powerful. Musical currents have, to be sure, flowed in both directions. *Reggae,* to take one example, was formed in the 1960s from a merger of native Jamaican styles with American rhythm and blues and soul, but by the late 1970s it had crossed back over to exert a great influence on American rock. The global dispersion has been enabled by a recording industry that has grown increasingly

A choir—not for isicathamiya, given the many women participating—rehearses in South Africa. The beauty of the singers' costumes contrasts with the stark landscape of Soweto Township behind them.

Isicathamiya praktisa: a rehearsal at the Beatrice St. YMCA, Durban, South Africa, 1996.

rich, increasingly multinational, and increasingly influential in determining our musical tastes. It is enough to make one observer of these developments speak—with some worry—of a "universal pop aesthetic."

There is another tendency, however, opposing this move toward sameness, a move to *localize* music making. People are never willing simply to take on foreign things without in some way making them their own. Even as musicians around the world have felt the influence of American pop styles, they have combined these styles in their local musics to forge new, distinct styles. (Reggae is one example of this process.)

Pop music is now, in some general way, recognizable worldwide. We know it when we hear it, and we easily distinguish it from traditional folk musics like Andean panpipe groups or Appalachian fiddling and traditional elite musics like Japanese gagaku or European classical music. Nevertheless, what we recognize as pop music comes in an immense variety of distinct idioms derived from specific interactions of global and local tendencies.

South African Choral Song: Isicathamiya

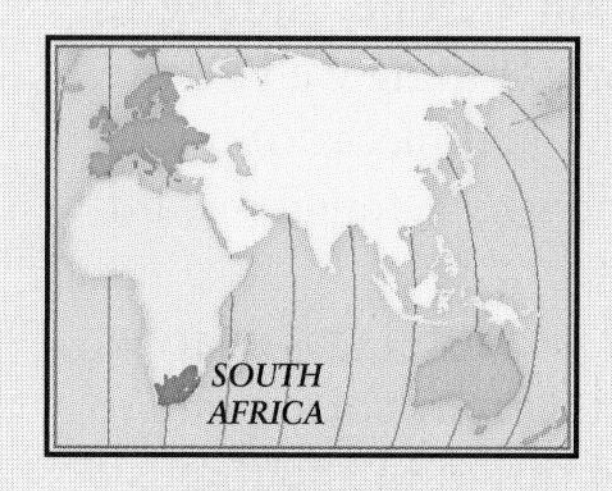

A South African musical tradition with a difficult name, *isicathamiya* (ees-ee-caht-ah-mée-ah), provides an example reaching back many decades of this diversity-within-sameness. It has become familiar to listeners worldwide through the recordings of the singing group Ladysmith Black Mambazo, famous from their participation in Paul Simon's album *Graceland* of 1986. Isicathamiya is an all-male, *a cappella* song style that arose among an impoverished class of black, mostly Zulu-speaking migrant laborers. A chief diversion in the laborers' camps were Saturday-night contests among singing groups, and for the musical styles the performers looked back to earlier, complex international roots.

Standing behind isicathamiya are traditions of choral polyphony native to the Zulus and other groups of the region. In the nineteenth century, these traditions seem to have merged readily with the four-part harmony of Christian hymn-singing brought to the area by European and American missionaries. Then another ingredient was added to the mix: American vaudeville or minstrel shows, with their syncopated, ragtime songs (see page 391 and the picture on page 406). An enormously influential African American minstrel—not a white minstrel in blackface—named Orpheus McAdoo toured South Africa extensively in the 1890s, to the great acclaim of black audiences.

By the 1930s, these musical influences were put together by the first recording stars of the local Zulu singing scene, Solomon Linda and the Evening Birds. Their greatest hit, "Mbube" or "Lion," known to most of us today as "The Lion Sleeps Tonight," was originally recorded around 1939. Then it was re-recorded by pop singers and became a top-40 hit in the 1960s. You likely know it in a more recent version from Disney's animated film *The Lion King*.

So when, not so many years back, you watched a McDonald's commercial on TV featuring this song and Disney's animation, you were participating in a rich musical and cultural convergence utterly dependent on recording and broadcast technology. You heard a song first recorded in Africa a half-century ago, remade by one multinational corporation (Disney) and exploited to sell the products of another (McDonald's), that traces its musical origins to native African choral polyphony, European hymn-singing, and ragtime styles created largely by African Americans. The modern global village may be a small place, but it is immensely complex.

"Anoku Gonda"

Solomon Linda's song "Anoku Gonda" ("You Must Understand This"), from the same period as "Mbube," combines two distinct styles that are still heard today in isicathamiya. The first is a richly-harmonized, homophonic style that recites the text freely and shows no clear or consistent sense of meter—*choral declamation,* we can call it. We hear two phrases of choral declamation, each stated and repeated in the pattern **a a b b a a.** Notable here, and frequent in isicathamiya, is the slide in all voices from high to lower pitches.

Then, after about a minute, the music takes on a clear meter. This is the second style common in isicathamiya. It is still organized in repeating phrases, but now the texture departs from the simple homophony of the recitational opening section. It uses call-and-response techniques (see page 388), pitting Linda against the rest of the group at first; later the basses in the chorus sing against the group as a whole. The call-and-response phrases alternate with a falling cadential phrase sung by the whole chorus.

LISTEN

"Anoku Gonda"

6 39

0:00	Unmetered choral declamation
0:00	a
0:13	a
0:25	b
0:30	b
0:35	a
0:47	a
0:57	Metrical call and response: Solomon Linda against the full chorus
1:26	Metrical call and response: Basses against the full chorus

6 Conclusion

Just a few words in conclusion: not so much as a conclusion to this chapter, but rather to our total effort in this book as a whole.

We might recall what was said at the end of the introductory unit, on page 51. Our basic goal has been to learn how to listen better, in order to understand and appreciate music—music of the European art tradition, mostly, but also other musics, other musical traditions. Some musical terminology has been introduced that should help clarify listening, and a somewhat rapid trip has been conducted through the history of Western music from Hildegard of Bingen to Kaija Saariaho, by way of Bach, Mozart, Beethoven, Wagner, Stravinsky, and Ellington. There have been side trips beyond Europe, gaining us perspectives on music around the globe. The most important thing we've done, by far, is *listen:* listen with some care to numerous individual pieces of music. Not all, but many of them are famous works that listeners have found rewarding over a period, in most cases, of many generations.

Rewarding is a pale, neutral term that will cover beautiful, fascinating, profound, exciting, comforting, and any other adjective that may correspond to something deep in your personal experience. Feelings of this kind about music tend to last a long time. If you have come to appreciate and love some of the music this book has introduced you to, it may be forever. Consider yourself ahead.

[Music] takes us out of the actual and whispers to us dim secrets that startle our wonder as to who we are, and for what, whence and whereto.

Ralph Waldo Emerson, 1838

Appendix Further Listening, Suggested Readings, and Recommended Web Sites

This appendix directs you to music that the authors of Listen *believe is especially attractive for further listening, and to books and Web sites that will give you further information about that music. It's probably unnecessary to note that this is a personal list, and that other musicians would undoubtedly come up with different entries.*

Further Listening

Symphonies, operas, and other "standard" items, recorded by many different artists, will be available at any college record library or can be purchased. For help in choosing among the various recordings, most record stores have the latest copies of the *Penguin Guide to Classical CDs* or the *Gramophone Classical Good CD Guide* on hand for customers to consult. Buy budget labels—Naxos is a good one—when available.

With more specialized music, however, including early music and non-Western music, particular recommended items may not be so easy to find.

The booklets included with CDs vary greatly in quality, but they will almost always be of some value as listening supplements. With vocal music, always follow along with the (translated) texts.

Early Music

Medieval The group that sings the plainchant "Vere dignum" on CD 1, Ensemble Organum, directed by Marcel Pérès, has issued many fascinating discs combining Gregorian chant and various kinds of organum. (Ask the clerk in the record store.) Other excellent groups for medieval music are Anonymous Four and Gothic Voices. The latter have issued several discs of music by Hildegard of Bingen.

Renaissance Look for CDs of Masses by Renaissance composers that are recorded along with the plainchants sung in the actual Mass service. One such is *Palestrina: Missa Viri Galilaei*, recorded by Philippe Herreweghe (Harmonia Mundi); there are also a number of such recordings of the beautiful Masses of William Byrd. English groups often record miscellaneous collections of music from Elizabethan times, bringing together favorite madrigals, songs, and instrumental music.

Early Baroque There are numerous recordings of Monteverdi's madrigals—very impressive works, but it is especially important to follow along closely with the words. Look in particular for the "Lament of the Nymph." If you want to explore another Monteverdi opera, listen to his *Orfeo* (Orpheus); the recording of John Eliot Gardiner is first-rate. Listen to the whole of Purcell's *Dido and Aeneas*, which is about fifty-five minutes long.

Global Perspectives

In this area, you need to beware of commercialized recordings that can be very far from the actual music itself. The place to start is with the recordings from which the *Listen* selections have been taken. They are worth a search in your college music library. Here they are, along with a few additional suggestions:

GP 1: *The Music of Islam,* vol. 10 (Celestial Harmonies 13150-2); *Hawaiian Drum Dance Chants: Sounds of Power in Time* (Smithsonian Folkways 40015); *Navajo Songs from Canyon de Chelly* (New World 804062)

GP 2: *Spain in the New World* (Koch 3-7451 2 H1); also, for music of seventeenth-century Mexico, listen to *Missa Mexicana* by The Harp Consort (Harmonia Mundi 907293).

GP 3: *Sudan: Music of the Blue Nile Province* (Auvidis D8073); *Mbuti Pygmies of the Ituri Rainforest* (Smithsonian Folkways 40401); for more pygmy polyphony, *Africa: The Ba-Benzélé Pygmies* (Rounder 5107)

GP 4: *Gagaku: The Imperial Court Music of Japan* (Lyrichord 7126); *Music of Bali: Gamelan Semar Pegulingan* (Lyrichord 7408); *Anthology of Indian Classical Music* (Auvidis D8270). For more gamelan music, try *Yogyakarta: Gamelan of the Kraton*

(Celestial Harmonies 7869); for more gagaku, *Gagaku: Court Music of Japan* (JVC 5354-2).

GP 5: Our kabuki performance is not available on CD; listen instead to *Japan: Kabuki and Other Traditional Music* (Nonesuch 9 72084-2); for our Beijing opera excerpt, *China: The Peking Opera* (Playasound 65197).

GP 6: *Yoruba Drums from Benin, West Africa* (Smithsonian Folkways 40440); for a different, wonderful African tradition, *Zimbabwe: The Soul of Mbira* (Nonesuch 9 72054-2).

GP 7: *Mbube Roots: Zulu Choral Music from South Africa, 1930s–1960s* (Rounder 5025); many recordings of Ladysmith Black Mambazo are also available.

Finally, two fascinating samplers of music from around the world: *Voices of Forgotten Worlds* (Ellipsis Arts 3252) and *The Secret Museum of Mankind: Ethnic Music Classics, 1925–1948* (Yazoo 7004-6, 7010, 7014)

Jazz

The famous, truly classic jazz anthology, available in every library, is the *Smithsonian Collection of Classic Jazz.* Its five CDs present expertly chosen numbers by Armstrong, Ellington, Parker, Davis, and many other jazz greats. A fine two-CD anthology is *Visions of Jazz,* selected by leading jazz critic Gary Giddens (Capitol). Many Ellington collections are available; any one will be an ear-opener.

Listen to these other artists, not featured in this book: Count Basie, Bix Beiderbecke, Ornette Coleman, John Coltrane, Ella Fitzgerald, Dizzy Gillespie, Billie Holliday, Wynton Marsalis, Thelonious Monk, Art Tatum, Lester Young, and blues singers Robert Johnson and Bessie Smith.

Major European Composers

The main works of the major composers are listed in the *Listen* biography boxes. Needless to say, we recommend them all, especially those marked in the boxes for "Encores." Here are further recommendations for selected composers:

Bach: If you like Bach, you must get to know all six *Brandenburg* Concertos (we recommend the recording by Jordi Savall).

Berg: There is a very good video of *Wozzeck* available (Kultur).

Berlioz: Listen to the whole hour-long *Fantastic* Symphony, watching page 266 for transformations of the *idée fixe.*

Brahms: Work your way into the symphonies by first hearing the shorter movements: the second movement in Symphony Nos. 1 and 2 and the third movement in Nos. 3 and 4.

Copland: The video of *Appalachian Spring* (DVD, Kultur), which presents Martha Graham's choreography, brings a whole new dimension to Copland's music.

Handel: Many selections from Handel operas are available. You can choose almost at random (we recommend recordings by Nicholas McGegan).

Mendelssohn: Listen to the *Midsummer Night's Dream* music; *Hebrides* Overture; *Italian* Symphony.

Mozart: After the Symphony in G Minor, you might go to the two very different masterpieces written with it in 1788: No. 39 in E-flat and No. 41 (*Jupiter*). View the *Don Giovanni* DVD from La Scala Opera House in Milan (Image).

Puccini: The Metropolitan Opera DVD of *La Bohème* is the perfect introduction to Puccini—indeed, to opera altogether (Pioneer).

Strauss: Listen to his symphonic poems *Don Juan* and *Till Eulenspiegel's Merry Pranks* and to his Four Last Songs.

Verdi: Watch the Metropolitan Opera DVD of *Aida,* starring Placido Domingo (DGG).

Vivaldi: A must-hear recording of *The Four Seasons* is by Fabio Biondi and L'Europa Galante (Opus 111).

Suggested Readings

The New Grove Dictionary of Music and Musicians (2nd edition, 23 volumes) is a superb reference tool, though probably more detailed than most readers will require. There are also specialized *Grove* dictionaries, in two to four volumes, devoted to American music, jazz, opera, and musical instruments. For world music, the standard reference is the illustrated *Garland Encyclopedia of World Music* (10 volumes). The standard single-volume reference works are *The Harvard Dictionary of Music* for all material except biographies, and *Baker's Biographical Dictionary of Musicians* for biographies.

Outstanding program notes by Michael Steinberg on the classical masterpieces are assembled in two books, covering symphonies and concertos. For operas, consult the two-volume *International Dictionary of Opera.* Single-volume collections of notes covering orchestral repertory are Jonathan D. Kramer, *Listen to the Music,* and D. Kern Holoman, *Evenings with the Orchestra* (Holoman has also authored a useful guide, *Writing about Music).*

Strange as it may seem, there is no good one-volume history of Western music available—none, at least, of a reasonable length (*The Concise Oxford History of Music* by Gerald Abraham runs to 968 pages). A detailed but very interesting series, *Music and Society* (8 volumes), investigates the relationship of music to society in various locations and historical periods. A book that concentrates on musical style is *A History of Musical Style* by Richard Crocker. An excellent anthology of historical readings, *Music in the Western World,* has been assembled by Piero Weiss and Richard Taruskin. Highly regarded texts on world music are Bruno Nettl, *Excursions in World Music,* and Jeff Titon, *Worlds of Music.*

For works on composers, there is quite a jump from the three or four densely packed pages in *Baker* to the thirty or forty equally packed pages in *Grove.* Check "Musical Lives" under serials on your computerized library catalogue for biographies that are concise and up-to-date. There are beautifully illustrated biographies by Christopher Hogwood on Handel and H. C. Robbins Landon on Beethoven and Mozart.

You might prefer to consult "documentary biographies," which reprint letters, notices, and all sorts of other contemporary documentation of the lives of early composers. Nobody reads these books from cover to cover, but they are fascinating to browse in: *The Bach Reader*, *The Schubert Reader*, *Mozart: A Documentary Biography. The Diary of Cosima Wagner* also makes for an astonishing browse.

Finally, a scattering of favorites with *Listen*'s authors: Hector Berlioz, *Memoirs;* Robert Craft, *Conversations with Igor Stravinsky;* Thomas Kelly, *First Nights;* Greil Marcus, *Mystery Train* (rock'n'roll); Susan McClary, *Conventional Wisdom;* Leonard Meyer, *Emotion and Meaning in Music* (musical aesthetics); Richard Powers, *The Time of Our Singing* (a novel set in the Civil Rights era); Paul Robinson, *Opera and Ideas*; John Rockwell, *All-American Music*; George Bernard Shaw, *The Perfect Wagnerite*;

Tim Taylor, *Global Pop*; Donald Francis Tovey, *Essays in Musical Analysis* (a program note collection, old but good).

Recommended Web Sites

The following sites will provide the start of an excellent Web library of reference materials relating to genres and composers we have discussed in *Listen*. Many more reference materials and additional Web site links can be found on the *Listen* Web site at **<bedfordstmartins.com/listen>**.

General Reference Web Sites for Classical and Popular Music

The Classical Music Pages
http://w3.rz-berlin.mpg.de/cmp/classmus.html
Designed by an orchestra conductor and Web wizard as a resource for "everyone from 'beginners' to the musical professional," this well-organized site provides information extracted from the *Grove Concise Dictionary of Music* on a wide variety of topics including musical periods, genres, composers, and basic theory. It also features excellent articles on select topics and a concise "History of Music" by musicologist James Zychowicz.

Women Composers
http://www.kapralova.org/DATABASE.htm
This database provides links to information on numerous women composers of various styles and genres. (The Kapralova Society)

Women in Music: Historical Women Composers
http://music.acu.edu/www/iawm/historical/historical.html
Part of the International Alliance for Women in Music web ring, this site provides links to online materials about individual women composers, special articles, historical surveys, collections, and databases. (IAWM)

Carolina Classical Connection: An Index of Classical Music Web Sites
http://classicalmus.hispeed.com/links.html
A substantial collection of links to information on composers, historical periods, instruments, genres, opera, and much more. (Charles K. Moss)

Ethnomusicology Resources on the Web
http://echarry.web.wesleyan.edu/ethno.html
Substantial database of links, the main categories cover African music and drumming, Indonesian music, Caribbean and Latin American music, South Asian music, music of Australia and Oceania, East Asian music, West Asian music, European music, and American music. (Eric Charry)

All-Music Guide
http://www.allmediaguide.com/
Enormous collection of information covering popular musical styles and artists. Features include "music maps" that trace the development of musical styles, articles, biographies, a glossary, and record reviews; also includes an "All-Classical" guide. (AEC One Stop Group, Inc.)

OperaGlass
http://opera.stanford.edu/main.html
Enormous "opera information server" with pages on opera libretti, source texts, performance histories, synopses, discographies, composers, librettists, companies, people, and more.

Unit I Web Sites

Solomon's Glossary of Technical Musical Terms
http://music.theory.home.att.net/glossary.htm
Supplementary glossary of terms. (Larry J. Solomon)

Teoría: Online Music Theory Reference
http://www.teoria.com/reference/index.htm
Basic guide to scales, intervals, and chords with audio examples. (José Rodriguez Alvira)

Unit II Web Sites

Medieval and Renaissance Music: Early Music Resources on the Web
http://www.angelfire.com/mi/spanogle/emusic.html
Directory of Internet resources. (Sharon Spanogle)

Selected Early Music Links
http://www.vanderbilt.edu/htdocs/Blair/Courses/MUSL242/earlymus.htm
Link directory. (Dr. Cynthia Cyrus, Blair School of Music, Vanderbilt University)

Welcome to the Wonderful World of Baroque Music
http://www.baroquemusic.org/
Educational page with "over two hours" of audio files, a portrait gallery, information on specific composers, and much more. (Michael Sartorius)

Chapter 5

Hildegard von Bingen: Symphony of the Harmony of Heaven
http://historymedren.about.com/gi/dynamic/offsite.htm?site=http://www.uni%2Dmainz.de/%7Ehorst/hildegard/music/music.html
Information on Hildegard of Bingen's music, including definitions of musical terms and genres, and a select discography. An icon of Hildegard hyperlinks you to the Hildegard.org page with historical and modern images of the town of Bingen on the Rhine. (Nancy Fiero)

International Machaut Society: Machaut on the Web
http://www.vanderbilt.edu/~cyrus/machaut/imslinks.htm
This helpful directory of links provides access to a variety of Machaut-related pages, including sound clips.

Troubadours, Trouvères and Minnesingers
http://www.hoasm.org/IIA/IIATroubadours.html
Overview with information on numerous songwriters of these traditions. (Chris Whent)

Chapter 6

Giovanni Pierluigi da Palestrina
http://www.npr.org/programs/specials/milestones/motm.palestrina.html
Installment of NPR's *Milestones of the Millennium* lecture series focusing on the composer, featuring Professor Tom Kelly. (National Public Radio, Washington, D.C.)

Nymphes des bois: Introduction to the music of Josquin Desprez
http://perso.wanadoo.fr/josquin.desprez/Ecouter_e.htm
MIDI transcriptions of several compositions. (Arnaud Saint-Antonin)

Webern. (Dr. Steven Kreinberg, Esther Boyer College of Music, Temple University)

Chapter 21

Copland House
http://www.coplandhouse.org/
The homepage of the Copland House, which has become "a focal point for the continuation and enhancement of his life-long advocacy of American music," this site offers information on the composer's life and works and a bibliography. (Copland House)

Chapter 22

The Official George Crumb Home Page
http://www.georgecrumb.net/
This introduction to the composer of *Black Angels* provides a thumbnail biography, an index of works with detailed information on each piece, an extensive bibliography including lectures, Web sites, dissertations, and a discography. The site also contains a fascinating essay by Crumb himself, "Music: Does It Have a Future?" (Robert Starobin)

Edgard Varèse: Father of Electronic Music
http://csunix1.lvc.edu/~snyder/em/varese.html
Essay on Varèse's influence in the area of electronic music with images and recommended listening. (Jeff Snyder)

John Cage Online
http://home.flash.net/~jronsen/cagelinks.html#interviews
Directory of links to articles, interviews, writings, paintings and visual art by Cage, sound files, discographies and filmographies, lists of works, photos, online videos, and other resources. (Josh Ronsen)

Kaija Saariaho
http://www.saariaho.org/
Biographical information, indexes of works, a discography, and a directory of links to other related sites.

Steve Reich
http://www.stevereich.com/
The official site for this innovative composer offers a biography, news, discography, a few multimedia resources, articles and interviews, a schedule of concerts, and information on new pieces.

Chapter 23

The BigBands Database Plus
http://www.nfo.net
Archive of overviews and essays on jazz and big bands in America, Canada, Britain, and Europe. Offers concise histories of jazz, Dixieland, and swing, a glossary of terms, an explanation of the etymology of *jazz*, and an index of links. (Murray Pfeffer)

What is Jazz?
http://www.town.hall.org/Archives/radio/Kennedy/Taylor/
This site contains audio files of four extensive lectures on jazz delivered by noted jazz pianist, historian, and educator Dr. Billy Taylor for the ArtsEdge program at the John F. Kennedy Center for the Performing Arts. Also offers information in the form of commentary or an audio extract from the lectures related to particular jazz artists, styles, and geographical areas. (The Internet Multicasting Service)

Louis "Satchmo" Armstrong
http://www.redhotjazz.com/louie.html
Part of the Red Hot Jazz Archive—devoted to jazz history before 1930—this page combines biographical information and real-audio samples for an extensive multimedia introduction to Armstrong. Also includes discographies for Armstrong and the many ensembles with which he played. (Scott Alexander)

Bernstein's Studio
http://www.leonardbernstein.com/
This charmingly designed site offers an intimate glimpse into Leonard Bernstein's creative world through a rich compilation of commentary, letters, audio and video files, photographs, interviews, articles, original scripts, working notes, news items, and reviews. (Leonard Bernstein.com, Inc./Primate, LLC)

The Official Miles Davis Web Site
http://www.milesdavis.com/
An excellent resource on this "trumpeter, composer, bandleader, and artist," the site provides a biography, audio and video files, a discography, images of Davis's original artworks, and related links. (Miles Davis Properties, LLC and The Estate of Miles Davis)

The Duke Ellington Society
http://museum.media.org/duke/
Dedicated to promoting appreciation of Ellington's musical creations, the homepage of this association offers an entertaining and informative collection of essays and commentary. The "Sing a Song" section also features real-audio samples of famous vocal interpreters of Ellington's art. Also features a tribute to Billy Strayhorn, Ellington's long-time collaborator and friend. (Media.org)

George and Ira Gershwin: The Official Web Site
http://www.gershwin.com/
A snazzy multimedia presentation on these brothers and creative partners, combining an historical overview and time lines, information on select films and shows featuring Gershwin music and/or lyrics, concert schedules, news items, and recommendations for further reading and listening. The real hit of this site, however, is the "jukebox" with audio clips featuring outstanding Gershwin interpreters. (Gershwin Enterprises)

Scott Joplin International Ragtime Foundation, Inc.
http://www.scottjoplin.org/
Contains an excellent biographical essay by Joplin scholar Edward A. Berlin, an online ragtime catalog, and a directory of related links.

Charlie "Yardbird" Parker: Jazz Original
http://www.cmgww.com/music/parker/
Full-service official site of this celebrated saxophonist with many multimedia features. (Estate of Charlie Parker/CMG Worldwide)

Classic Motown
http://www.motown.com/classicmotown/
Engaging multimedia tour of the history of Motown Records. Visitors navigate the timeline to the diverse resources (biography, discography, audio-video gallery, and news) on famous Motown artists from the 1960s to the 1980s. This attractive site also has a "jukebox" full of audio clips, which you can search by artist or year.

The Red Hot Jazz Archive
http://www.redhotjazz.com/
This top-notch site offers a wealth of information on jazz music and artists before 1930. Includes numerous audio files and images. (Scott Alexander)

Elvis Presley: Elvis.com
http://www.elvis.com/
The official site of "The King" presents biographical information, a list of gold and platinum records, billboard chart statistics, a filmography (including TV appearances), Elvis quotes, related writings, links to family and friends, and fan goodies. (EPE, Inc.)

The Beatles
http://www.thebeatles.com/
The deceptively simple layout of this site hides a wealth of rare audio and video clips, photos, and other resources on some of the Beatles's most popular songs. (Beatles.com)

Global Perspectives

Global Perspectives 1

Islamic Art, Music, and Architecture around the World
http://www.uga.edu/islam/IsArt.html
The music section of this site connects to a broad array of materials, including scholarly articles, multimedia presentations with audio/video files, and descriptive commentary. The homepage offers information on other Islamic topics and issues. (Dr. Alan Godlas, University of Georgia, Islamic Studies)

The Hawaiian Home Page
http://www.geocities.com/~olelo/home.html
An extraordinary resource on Hawai'ian culture, this site has an impressive directory of links on Hawai'ian music, including artists, history, lyrics, mp3 clips, and Hawai'ian radio stations, many with live stream via the Internet.

Gathering of Nations Web Site
http://www.gatheringofnations.com/
The home site of this organization, which promotes Native American culture and tradition. Features include "all-Native-music" internet radio, audio clips from powwows and other events, photographs and pictures, and artwork.

Navajo Sites
http://unr.edu/homepage/daved/natlinks.html
Directory of links to Navajo and Native American resources. (Dave DuBois)

Global Perspectives 2

Mission Music
http://www.californiamissions.com/music/index.html
Part of an extensive "California Missions" Web tour, this section contains an essay by musicologist William Summers on the history of mission music and real-audio files of music primarily from the Renaissance period that blends European and indigenous traditions.

What is Andean Music?
http://otto.cmr.fsu.edu/~cma/andes.htm
This site features an essay by CMA director and ethnomusicologist Dale A. Olsen on the music and common instruments of the central Andes and includes photographs. (Center for Music in the Americas, Florida State University)

Aztec Music
http://history.smsu.edu/jchuchiak/HST%20350—Theme%203—Aztec_music.htm
Small collection of images of Aztec instruments and sound clips. (Dr. John F. Chuchiak IV, Department of History, Southwest Missouri State University)

Global Perspectives 3

African Music
http://www.africana.com/Articles/tt_422.htm
Article presenting the history of African music, common characteristics and regional styles, African music in society, popular music, and influence of African music on music from other parts of the world.

The Mbuti of Zaire
http://www.ucc.uconn.edu/~epsadm03/mbuti.html
This brief essay on the pygmy population of the Ituri Forest in northern Zaire addresses the influence of the physical environment on their way of life, describes the traditional Molimo ritual, and discusses the effects of historical events (colonialism, war) on the Mbuti people. (Cathy Suroviak)

Pygmies of the Congo
http://www.cwu.edu/~yaegerl/pygmypage.htm
Brief essay on the pygmy population of Central Africa with a bibliography. (Lewis Yaeger)

Global Perspectives 4

Some Thoughts on the Origins of Gagaku
http://aris.ss.uci.edu/rgarfias/gagaku/gagaku.html
Created by ethnomusicologist Robert Garfias, this site offers an engaging introduction to gagaku and related topics with concise essays, colorful images, and real-audio samples.

Indonesian Music: Gamelan
http://indonesia.elga.net.id/music.html#GAMELAN
Directory of links to online information on the gamelan. (Budi Rahardjo)

Sify Carnatic Music
http://www.carnaticmusic.com/main.asp
The first Web resource to visit for in-depth information on Carnatic music, including its history, instruments, and raga and tala types. Also provides an impressive audio gallery. (Sify.com)

Fundamentals of Rag
http://www.chandrakantha.com/articles/indian_music/raga.html
This specialist-authored site offers an excellent introduction to raga, with a glossary of terms, images of instruments, audio files, and a list of recommended books and CDs. (David and Chandrakantha Courtney)

Global Perspectives 5

Kabuki for Everyone
http://www.fix.co.jp/kabuki/kabuki.html
This attractive, multimedia introduction to kabuki theater features essays on kabuki history, an online video theater, sound samples, information on and images of kabuki makeup, and links to related sites. (Matthew Johnson)

Kabuki Page
http://www.aichi-gakuin.ac.jp/~jeffreyb/kabuki.html
With sample stories of kabuki productions at the Misonoza in Nagoya, Japan, this site also provides a time line of four hundred years of kabuki theater, historic images, and links to other resources. (Jeff Blair)

The Development of Beijing Opera during the Cultural Revolution
http://home.earthlink.net/~athenart/opera/bodevelop.html
This noteworthy site contains an extensive essay on the development of Beijing opera during the Cultural Revolution, an impressive gallery of images of performers and instruments, and a small directory of links to resources on China and Chinese music. (Wendy A. Levine)

Global Perspectives 6

C.K. Ladzekpo: African Music and Drumming
http://www.cnmat.berkeley.edu/~ladzekpo/
An attractive collection of graphics, audio files, and video clips on African drums and drumming and African ethnic groups, particularly Ewe culture. (University of California, Berkeley, Music Department)

Yoruba Bata in Nigeria
http://www.batadrums.com/background/yoruba.htm
Handy assortment of resources on Yoruba culture and the bata drumming of Nigeria and Benin, including field-recording audio files. (BataDrums.Com)

Global Perspectives 7

African Voices: Traditional Culture
http://www.africanvoices.co.za/culture/culture.htm#Isicathamiya
Information on the Xhosa and Zulu people and isicathamiya.

Glossary of Musical Terms

The italicized words refer to other definitions in the glossary, which you can look up if necessary. The page numbers refer to fuller explanations in the text.

A cappella (ah kah-pél-la): Choral music for voices alone, without instruments *(79)*

Accelerando (a-chel-er-áhn-do): Getting faster *(14)*

Accent: The stressing of a note—for example, by playing it somewhat louder than the surrounding notes *(11)*

Accidentals: In musical notation, signs indicating that a note is to be played *sharp, flat,* or *natural*

Accompanied recitative: See *recitative (152)*

Adagio: Slow tempo *(14)*

Alap: In Indian music, a slow movement without meter that introduces the performance of a *rag (219)*

Alba: *Troubadour* song about a knight leaving his lady at dawn *(62)*

Allegro; allegretto: Fast; moderately fast *(14)*

Allemande: A Baroque dance in moderate *duple meter (143)*

Alto, contralto: The low female voice

Andante: A fairly slow tempo, but not too slow *(14)*

Andantino: A little faster than *andante (14)*

Antiphon: A genre of plainchant usually showing a simple melodic style with very few melismas *(60)*

Aria: A vocal number for solo singer and orchestra, generally in an opera, cantata, or oratorio *(99, 152)*

Arioso: A singing style between *recitative* and *aria (100)*

Ars antiqua, ars nova: Contemporary terms for the "old technique" of 13th-century *organum* and the new *polyphonic* music of the 14th century *(67)*

A tempo: At the original tempo *(14)*

Atonality: The absence of any feeling of *tonality (327)*

Avant-garde: In the most advanced style *(314)*

Azan: An Islamic call to worship, issued five times daily by a muezzin *(71)*

Bar: Same as *measure (11)*

Baritone: A type of adult male voice similar to the *bass,* but a little higher

Bar line: In musical notation, a vertical line through the staffs to mark the measure *(11)*

Bass (not spelled "BASE"): (1) The low adult male voice; (2) the lowest vocal or instrumental line in a piece of music

Basso continuo: See *continuo (96)*

Basso ostinato: An *ostinato* in the bass *(96, 132)*

Beam: In musical notation, the heavy stroke connecting eighth notes (two beams connect sixteenth notes, etc.) *(20)*

Beat: The regular pulse underlying most music; the lowest unit of *meter (10)*

Beat syncopation: In jazz, the fractional shifting of accents away from the beats *(390)*

Bebop: A jazz style of the 1940s *(400)*

Bel canto: A style of singing that brings out the sensuous beauty of the voice *(272)*

Bel canto opera: Term for early Romantic opera, which featured *bel canto* singing *(272)*

Big bands: The big jazz bands (10 to 20 players) of the 1930s and 1940s *(394)*

Binary form: A musical form having two different sections; **AB** form *(144)*

Biwa: A Japanese four-stringed lute; heard in *gagaku (213)*

Blue note: A note deliberately sung or played slightly off pitch, as in the *blues (19)*

Blues: A type of African American *vernacular music,* used in jazz, rhythm and blues, rock, and other styles of popular music *(390)*

Bourrée: A Baroque dance in fast *duple meter (143)*

Break: In jazz, a brief solo improvisation between song phrases *(390)*

Bridge: In *sonata form,* the section of music that comes between the first theme and the second group and makes the *modulation;* also called "transition" *(180)*

Bunraku (bóon-ráh-koo): Japanese tradition of puppet theater *(308)*

Cadence: The notes or chords (or the whole short passage) ending a section of music with a feeling of conclusiveness. The term *cadence* can be applied to phrases, sections of works, or complete works or movements *(25)*.

Cadence theme: In *sonata form,* the final conclusive theme in the *exposition (180)*

Cadenza: An improvised passage for the soloist in a concerto, or sometimes in other works. Concerto cadenzas usually come near the ends of movements *(137, 201).*

Cakewalk: Around 1900, a dance of African American origin associated with *ragtime (327, 350)*

Call and response: In African and early African American music, a style in which a phrase by a leading singer or soloist is answered by a larger group or chorus, and the process is repeated again and again *(388)*

Canon: Strict *imitative polyphony,* with the same melody appearing in each voice, at staggered intervals

Cantata: A composition in several movements for solo voice(s), instruments, and perhaps also chorus. Depending on the text, cantatas are categorized as secular or *church cantatas (159).*

Canzona: A lively, fugue-like composition, one of several sixteenth- and seventeenth-century genres of instrumental music *(105)*

Chaconne (cha-kón): Similar to *passacaglia (132)*

Chamber music: Music played by small groups, such as a string quartet or a piano trio *(205)*

Chance music: A type of contemporary music in which certain elements, such as the order of the notes or their pitches, are not specified by the composer but are left to chance *(370)*

Chanson (shahn-sohn): French for song; a genre of French secular vocal music *(77)*

Chant: A way of reciting words to music, generally in *monophony* and generally for liturgical purposes, as in *Gregorian chant (57, 70)*

Character piece: A short Romantic piano piece that portrays a particular mood *(259)*

Choir: (1) A group of singers singing together, with more than one person singing each voice part; (2) a section of the orchestra comprising instruments of a certain type, such as the string, woodwind, or brass choir

Choral declamation: Chordal recitation by a chorus with free, speech-like rhythms *(420)*

Chorale (co-ráhl): German for hymn; also used for a four-part *harmonization* of a Lutheran hymn, such as Bach composed in his Cantata No. 4 and other works *(160)*

Chorale prelude: An organ composition based on a *chorale* tune *(162)*

Chord: A grouping of pitches played and heard simultaneously *(27)*

Chromaticism: A musical style employing all or many of the twelve notes of the *chromatic scale* much of the time *(107, 244)*

Chromatic scale: The set of twelve pitches represented by all the white and black notes on the piano, within one *octave (17)*

Church cantata: A *cantata* with religious words *(159)*

Clef: In musical notation, a sign at the beginning of the *staff* indicating the pitches of the lines and spaces. The main clefs are the treble (or G) clef, 𝄞; and the bass (or F) clef, 𝄢 *(21).*

Climax: The high point of a melody or of a section of music *(25)*

Closing theme: Same as *cadence theme (180)*

Coda: The concluding section of a piece or a movement, after the main elements of the form have been presented. Codas are common in *sonata form (181).*

Coloratura: An ornate style of singing, with many notes for each syllable of the text *(150)*

Compound meter: A meter in which the main beats are subdivided into three, e.g. **6/8**—*one* two three *four* five six *(11)*

Con brio: Brilliantly, with spirit

Concerto, solo concerto: A large composition for orchestra and solo instrument *(129)*

Concerto grosso: The main early Baroque type of concerto, for a group of solo instruments and a small orchestra *(129)*

Concert overture: An early 19th-century genre resembling an opera overture—but without any following opera *(264)*

Con moto: Moving, with motion

Consonance: Intervals or chords that sound relatively stable and free of tension; as opposed to *dissonance (27)*

Continuo (basso continuo): (1) A set of chords continuously underlying the melody in a piece of Baroque music; (2) the instrument(s) playing the continuo, usually cello plus harpsichord or organ *(96, 124)*

Contralto, alto: The low female voice

Counterpoint, contrapuntal: (1) *Polyphony;* strictly speaking, the technique of writing *polyphonic* music; (2) the term *a counterpoint* is used for a melodic line that forms polyphony when played along with other lines; (3) *in counterpoint* means "forming polyphony" *(29).*

Countersubject: In a *fugue,* a subsidiary melodic line that appears regularly in *counterpoint* with the *subject (140)*

Courante (koor-ahnt): A Baroque dance in moderately slow *triple meter (143)*

Crescendo (kreh-shén-do): Getting louder *(8)*

Cultivated music: In America, genres and styles of music that were brought from Europe and subsequently nurtured here through formal training and education *(384)*

Da capo: Literally, "from the beginning"; a direction to the performer to repeat music from the beginning of the piece up to a later point *(152)*

Da capo aria: An aria in **ABA** form, i.e., one in which the **A** section is sung *da capo* at the end *(152)*

Dance suite: See *suite (104, 143)*

Declamation: The way words are set to music, in terms of rhythm, accent, etc. *(82)*

Decrescendo (dáy-kreh-shén-do): Getting softer *(8)*

Development: (1) The process of expanding themes and short motives into larger sections of music; (2) the second section of a *sonata-form* movement, which features the development process *(180)*

Diatonic scale: The set of seven pitches represented by the white notes of the piano, within one *octave (16)*

Dies irae: "Day of wrath": a section of the *Requiem Mass (268)*

Diminuendo: Getting softer *(8)*

Dissonance: Intervals or chords that sound relatively tense and unstable; in opposition to *consonance (27)*

Divertimento: An 18th-century genre of light instrumental music, designed for entertainment *(167)*

Dotted note: In musical notation, a note followed by a dot has its normal duration increased by a half *(20)*.

Dotted rhythm: A rhythm of long, dotted notes alternating with short ones *(20)*

Double-exposition form: A type of *sonata form* developed for use in concertos *(201)*

Downbeat: A strong or accented *beat*

Duet, duo: A composition for two singers or instrumentalists *(210)*

Duple meter: A meter consisting of one accented beat alternating with one unaccented beat: *one* two *one* two *(11–12)*

Duration: The length of time that a sound is heard *(9)*

Dynamics: The volume of sound, the loudness or softness of a musical passage *(7)*

Eighth note: A note one-eighth the length of a whole note *(20)*

Electronic music: Music in which some or all of the sounds are produced by electronic generators or other apparatus *(367)*

Ensemble: A musical number in an opera, cantata, or oratorio that is sung by two or more people *(207)*

Episode: In a *fugue*, a passage that does not contain any complete appearances of the fugue *subject (140)*

Erhu (áhr-hoo): A Chinese low-pitched fiddle; heard in Beijing opera *(311)*

Espressivo: Expressively

Estampie (ess-tom-pée): An instrumental dance of the Middle Ages *(64)*

Ethnomusicology: The scholarly study of music and society, usually oriented toward music outside the European classical tradition *(360)*

Étude (áy-tewd): A piece of music designed to aid technical study of a particular instrument *(259)*

Exposition: (1) The first section of a *fugue (139)*; (2) the first section of a *sonata-form* movement *(179)*

Expressionism: An early 20th-century movement in art, music, and literature in Germany and Austria *(323)*

Fermata: A hold of indefinite length on a note; the sign for such a hold in musical notation *(14)*

Festive orchestra: A brilliant-sounding Baroque orchestra with drums, trumpets, and/or French horns, used for gala occasions *(115, 123)*

Figured bass: A system of notating the *continuo* chords in Baroque music, by means of figures; sometimes also used to mean continuo *(125)*

Finale (fih-náh-lay): The last movement of a work, or the *ensemble* that concludes an act of an *opera buffa* or other opera

First theme: In *sonata form*, a *motive* or tune (or a series of them) in the *tonic* key that opens the *exposition* section *(180)*

Flag: In musical notation, a "pennant" attached to a note indicating that the length is halved (two flags indicate that it is quartered, etc.) *(20)*

Flat: In musical notation, a sign (♭) indicating that the note to which it is attached is to be played a *semitone* lower. A double flat (♭♭) is sometimes used to indicate that a note is played two semitones lower *(17)*.

Form: The "shape" of a piece of music *(46)*

Forte (fór-teh); **fortissimo**: Loud; very loud *(f; ff) (7)*

Fragmentation: The technique of reducing a theme to fragmentary *motives (228)*

French overture: A Baroque type of overture to an opera, oratorio, or suite *(144)*

Frequency: Scientific term for the rate of sound vibration, measured in cycles per second *(6)*

Fugue (fewg): A composition written systematically in *imitative polyphony*, usually with a single main theme, the fugue *subject (105, 139)*

Fuguing tune: A simple anthem based on a hymn, with a little *counterpoint (385)*

Functional harmony, functional tonality: From the Baroque period on, the system whereby all chords have a specific interrelation and function in relation to the *tonic (96)*

Gagaku (gáh-gáh-koo): A group of Japanese orchestral styles, named by the Chinese characters meaning "elegant music," which were performed in traditional court ceremonies and rituals; includes togaku (tó-gáh-koo) and komagaku (ko-má-gáh-koo) *(212)*

Gakuso: A Japanese zither with thirteen strings; heard in *gagaku (213)*

Galliard: A Renaissance court dance in *triple meter (88)*

Gamelan: A traditional Indonesian orchestra consisting of gongs, *metallophones*, and other instruments *(214)*

Gapped chorale: A setting of a *chorale* melody in which the tune is presented in phrases with "gaps" between them, during which other music continues in other voices or instruments *(160)*

Gat: In Indian music, a moderate or fast movement with clear meter in the performance of a *rag (219)*

Gavotte: A Baroque dance in *duple meter (143)*

Genre (jáhn-ruh): A general category of music determined partly by the number and kind of instruments or voices involved, and partly by its form, style, or purpose. "Opera," "symphonic poem," and "sonata" are examples of genres *(50, 264)*.

Gesamtkunstwerk (geh-záhmt-kuhnst-vairk): "Total work of art"—Wagner's term for his music dramas *(279)*

Gigue (zheeg), **jig**: A Baroque dance in a lively *compound meter (143)*

Glissando: Sliding from one note to another on an instrument such as a trombone or violin *(336)*

Gospel, gospel music: Genre of African American choral church music, associated with the *blues (392)*

Grave (grahv): Slow; the characteristic tempo of the first section of a *French overture (14)*

Gregorian chant: The type of *chant* used in the early Roman Catholic Church *(57)*

Ground bass: An *ostinato* in the bass *(96, 132)*

Half note: A note half the length of a whole note *(20)*

Half step: The *interval* between any two successive notes of the *chromatic scale;* also called a *semitone (18)*

Harmonize: To provide each note of a melody with a chord *(27)*

Harmony, harmonic: Having to do with chords, or the "vertical" aspect of musical texture *(27)*. The term *harmonic* is sometimes used to mean *homophonic.*

Heterophony: *Monophonic* texture in which subtly different versions of a single melody are presented simultaneously *(28)*

Hichiriki (hée-chee-ree-kée): A Japanese double-reed wind instrument; heard in *gagaku (212)*

Hocket: The alternation of very short melodic phrases, or single notes, between two or more voices *(69)*

Homophony, homophonic: A musical texture that involves only one melody of real interest, combined with chords or other subsidiary sounds *(28)*

Hymn: A simple religious song in several stanzas, for congregational singing in church *(75)*

Idée fixe (ee-day feex): A fixed idea, an obsession; the term used by Berlioz for a recurring theme used in all the movements of one of his program symphonies *(265)*

Imitation, imitative polyphony, imitative counterpoint: A *polyphonic* musical texture in which the various melodic lines use approximately the same themes; as opposed to *non-imitative counterpoint (29)*. See also *point of imitation.*

Impressionism: A French artistic movement of the late 19th and early 20th centuries *(319)*

Interval: The difference or distance between two pitches, measured by the number of *diatonic scale* notes between them *(15)*

Introduction: An introductory passage: the "slow introduction" before the *exposition* in a symphony, etc.; in an opera, the first number after the overture

Inversion: Reading or playing a melody or a *twelve-tone series* upside down, i.e., playing all its upward intervals downward and vice versa *(140, 326)*

Isicathamiya (ees-ee-caht-ah-mée-ah): An *a cappella* song style that is part of the South African choral song tradition *(419)*

Isorhythm: In 14th-century music, the technique of repeating the identical rhythm for each section of a composition, while the pitches are altered *(68)*

Jangar: A type of lyre played to accompany singing in the Sudan *(108)*

Jazz: A major African American performance style that has influenced all 20th-century popular music *(389)*

Jing (cheeng): A male role in *jingju*, or Beijing opera, enacting a warrior, a bandit, or a god *(310)*

Jinghu (chéeng-hoo): A Chinese high-pitched, two-string fiddle; heard in Beijing opera *(311)*

Jingju (chéeng-chu): The most famous variety of Chinese musical drama; meaning "theater of the capital," it is known in English as Beijing (or Peking) opera *(310)*

Jongleur (jawn-gler): A medieval secular musician *(56)*

Kabuki (kah-bóo-kee): A Japanese tradition of musical drama involving singing actors, chorus, and orchestra *(309)*

Kakko: A Japanese two-headed barrel drum; heard in *gagaku (213)*

Key: One of the twelve positions for the *major-* and *minor-mode* scales made possible by using all the notes of the *chromatic scale (32)*

Key signature: Sharps or flats placed at the beginning of the staffs to indicate the *key,* and applied throughout an entire piece, in every measure and in every octave *(22)*

K numbers: The numbers assigned to works by Mozart in the Köchel catalog; used instead of *opus* numbers to catalog Mozart's works *(182)*

Largo; larghetto: Very slow; somewhat less slow than largo *(14)*

Ledger lines: In music notation, short lines above or below the staff to allow for pitches that go higher or lower *(21)*

Legato (leh-gáh-toe): Playing in a smooth, connected manner; as opposed to *staccato (21)*

Leitmotiv (líte-moh-teef): "Leading motive" in Wagner's operas *(281)*

Lento: Very slow *(14)*

Libretto: The complete book of words for an opera, oratorio, cantata, etc. *(151)*

Lied (leed; pl. *Lieder*): German for "song"; also a special genre of Romantic songs with piano *(249)*

Line: Used as a term to mean a melody, or melodic line *(24)*

Madrigal: The main secular vocal genre of the Renaissance *(85)*

Major mode: One of the modes of the *diatonic scale,* oriented around C as the *tonic;* characterized by the interval between the first and third notes containing 4 *semitones,* as opposed to 3 in the *minor mode (32)*

Mass: The main Roman Catholic service; or the music written for it. The musical Mass consists of five large sections: Kyrie, Gloria, Credo, Sanctus, and Agnus Dei *(77)*.

Mazurka: A Polish dance in lively *triple meter (247)*

Measure (bar): In music, the unit of *meter,* consisting of a principal strong beat and one or more weaker ones *(11)*

Medieval modes: See *mode (58)*

Mele pule (mél-eh póol-eh): Hawai'ian prayer song *(71)*

Melisma: In vocal music, a passage of many notes sung to a single syllable *(66)*

Melody: The aspect of music having to do with the succession of pitches; also applied ("a melody") to any particular succession of pitches *(24)*

Meno: Less (as in *meno forte,* less loud) *(7)*

Metallophone: An instrument like a xylophone, but with keys of metal, not wood *(215)*

Meter: A background of stressed and unstressed beats in a simple, regular, repeating pattern *(11)*

Metronome mark: A notation of tempo, indicating the number of beats per minute as ticked out by a metronome, the mechanical or electrical device that ticks out beats at all practicable tempos *(14)*

Mezzo (mét-so): Italian for half, halfway, medium (as in *mezzo forte* or *mezzo piano*—***mf, mp***) *(7)*

Mezzo-soprano: "Halfway to soprano": a type of female voice between *contralto* and *soprano*

Miniature: A term for a short, evocative composition for piano or for piano and voice, composed in the Romantic period *(246)*

Minimalism: A late 20th-century style involving many repetitions of simple musical fragments *(380)*

Minnesingers: Poet-composers of the Middle Ages in Germany *(62)*

Minor mode: One of the modes of the *diatonic scale,* oriented around A as the *tonic;* characterized by the interval between the first and third notes containing 3 *semitones,* as opposed to 4 in the *major mode (32)*

Minstrel show: A type of variety show popular in 19th-century America, performed in blackface *(388)*

Minuet: A popular 17th- and 18th-century dance in moderate *triple meter;* also a movement in a sonata, symphony, etc., based on this dance *(143, 191)*

Mode, modality: In music since the Renaissance, one of the two types of *tonality: major mode* or *minor mode;* also, in earlier times, one of several orientations of the *diatonic scale* with D, E, F, and G as tonics *(31)*

Moderato: Moderate tempo *(14)*

Modulation: Changing key within a piece *(32)*

Molto allegro: Faster than *allegro (14)*

Monophony: A musical texture involving a single melodic line, as in *Gregorian chant;* as opposed to *polyphony (28)*

Motet: (Usually) a sacred vocal composition *(67, 85)*. Early motets were based on fragments of Gregorian chant.

Motive: A short fragment of melody or rhythm used in constructing a long section of music *(26)*

Movement: A self-contained section of a larger piece, such as a symphony or concerto grosso *(129)*

Musical comedy, musical: American development of *operetta,* involving American subjects and music influenced by jazz or rock *(406)*

Music drama: Wagner's name for his distinctive type of opera *(279)*

Musicology: The scholarly study of music history and literature

Music video: Video "dramatization" of a popular song, rock number, or rap number

Musique concrète (moo-zeek kohn-krét): Music composed with natural sounds recorded electronically *(368, 375)*

Mute: A device put on or in an instrument to muffle the tone

Nagauta (náh-gáhoo-ta): A genre of music involved in Japanese *kabuki* theater; translated as "long song," it is used especially to accompany dance *(309)*

Nationalism: A 19th-century movement promoting music built on national folk songs and dances, or associated with national subjects *(294)*

Natural: In musical notation, a sign (♮) indicating that a sharp or flat previously attached to a note is to be removed *(22)*

Neoclassicism: (1) An 18th-century movement in the arts returning to Greek and Roman models *(169)*; (2) a 20th-century movement involving a return to the style and form of older music, particularly 18th-century music *(336)*

Nocturne: "Night piece": title for Romantic "miniature" compositions for piano, etc. *(261)*

Noh: A Japanese tradition of musical drama, often based on Zen Buddhist philosophy, which includes singing, highly stylized and symbolic movement, and instrumental accompaniment by percussion and flute *(308)*

Non-imitative polyphony, counterpoint: A *polyphonic* musical texture in which the melodic lines are essentially different from one another; as opposed to *imitation (29)*

Non troppo: Not too much (as in *allegro non troppo,* not too fast)

Note: (1) A sound of a certain definite pitch and duration; (2) the written sign for such a sound in musical notation; (3) a key pressed with the finger on a piano or organ

Octatonic scale: An eight-note scale (used by Stravinsky and others) consisting of half and whole steps in alternation *(327)*

Octave: The *interval* between a pair of "duplicating" notes, eight notes apart in the *diatonic scale (15)*

Office services, Divine Office: The eight daily services, other than the Mass, specified by the Roman Catholic Church *(57)*

Opera: Drama presented in music, with the characters singing instead of speaking *(97, 149)*

Opera buffa (bóo-fa): Italian comic opera *(207)*

Opera seria: A term for the serious, heroic opera of the Baroque period in Italy *(150, 207)*

Operetta: A 19th-century type of light (often comic) opera, employing spoken dialogue in between musical numbers *(405)*

Opus: "Work"; opus numbers provide a means of cataloging a composer's compositions *(130)*.

Oratorio: Long semidramatic piece on a religious subject for soloists, chorus, and orchestra *(155)*

Orchestra: A large group of instruments playing together *(43);* at different periods of Western music *(123, 173, 244);* see *festive orchestra, gamelan, gagaku*

Orchestra exposition: In Classical concerto form, the first of two *expositions,* played by the orchestra without the soloist *(201)*

Orchestration: The technique of writing for various instruments to produce an effective total orchestral sound

Organ chorale: See *chorale prelude (162)*

Organum: The earliest genre of medieval *polyphonic* music *(65)*

Ornament, ornamentation: Addition of fast notes and vocal effects (such as *trills*) to a melody, making it more florid and expressive. Ornamentation is typically improvised in the music of all cultures, and in Western music is often written out *(123)*.

Ostinato: A motive, phrase, or theme repeated over and over again *(96, 108, 132, 335)*

Overtone: In acoustics, a secondary vibration in a sound-producing body, which contributes to the tone color; also called *partial (9)*

Overture: An orchestral piece at the start of an opera, oratorio, etc. (but see *concert overture*) *(144)*

Paraphrase: The modification and decoration of *plainchant* melodies in early Renaissance music *(74)*

Part: Used as a term for (1) a section of a piece; (2) one of the *voices* in contrapuntal music; (3) the written music for a single player in an orchestra, band, etc. (as opposed to the *score*)

Partial: Scientific term for an *overtone (9)*

Passacaglia (pas-sa-cáhl-ya): A set of variations on a short theme in the bass *(106, 132)*

Passion: A long, oratorio-like composition telling the story of Jesus' last days, according to one of the New Testament gospels

Pavane (pa-váhn): A slow, 16th-century court dance in *duple meter (88)*

Pedal board: That keyboard of an organ which is played with the feet *(45)*

Pentatonic scale: A five-note *scale* (familiar from folk music) playable on the black notes of a keyboard *(327)*

Phrase: A section of a melody or a tune *(25)*

Piano; pianissimo: Soft; very soft *(p; pp) (7)*

Piano trio: An instrumental group usually consisting of violin, cello, and piano; or a piece composed for this group; or the three players themselves

Pitch: The quality of "highness" or "lowness" of sound; also applied ("a pitch") to any particular pitch level, such as middle C *(7)*

Più: More (as in *più forte,* louder) *(7)*

Pizzicato (pit-tzih-cáh-toe): Playing a stringed instrument that is normally bowed by plucking the strings with the finger *(36)*

Plainchant, plainsong: Unaccompanied, *monophonic* music, without fixed rhythm or meter, such as *Gregorian chant (57)*

Poco: Somewhat (as in *poco adagio* or *poco forte,* somewhat slow, somewhat loud)

Point of imitation: A short passage of *imitative polyphony* based on a single theme, or on two used together *(80)*

Polonaise: A Polish court dance in a moderate *triple meter (261)*

Polyphony, polyphonic: Musical texture in which two or more melodic lines are played or sung simultaneously; as opposed to *homophony* or *monophony (28)*

Prelude: An introductory piece, leading to another, such as a fugue or an opera (however, Chopin's Preludes were not intended to lead to anything else)

Premiere: The first performance ever of a piece of music, opera, etc.

Presto; prestissimo: Very fast; very fast indeed *(14)*

Program music: A piece of instrumental music associated with a story or other extramusical idea *(245)*

Program symphony: A symphony with a program, as by Berlioz *(265)*

Quarter note: A note one-quarter the length of a whole note *(20)*

Quarter-tone scale: A 24-note scale, used in the 20th century, consisting of all the *semitones* of the *chromatic scale* and all quarter tones in between the semitones *(327)*

Quartet: A piece for four singers or players; often used to mean *string quartet*

Quintet: A piece for five singers or players

Qur'anic recitation: An Islamic tradition in which the revelations of the prophet Muhammad gathered in the Qur'an (or Koran) are chanted in Arabic *(70)*

Rag: In Indian music, a set of pitches, gestures, patterns of ornamentation, and other guidelines for producing melody *(218)*

Ragtime: A style of American popular music around 1900, usually for piano, which led to *jazz (391)*

Range: Used in music to mean "pitch range," i.e., the total span from the lowest to the highest pitch in a piece, a part, or a passage

Rap: Genre of African American popular music of the 1980s and '90s, featuring rapid recitation in rhyme *(416)*

Recapitulation: The third section of a *sonata-form* movement *(181)*

Recitative (reh-sih-ta-téev): A half-singing, half-reciting style of presenting words in opera, cantata, oratorio, etc., following speech accents and speech rhythms closely. Secco recitative is accompanied only by *continuo;* accompanied recitative is accompanied by orchestra *(98, 151, 152)*

Reciting tone: Especially in *chant,* the single note used for musical "recitation," with brief melodic formulas for beginning and ending *(59, 71)*

Reed: In certain wind instruments (oboe, clarinet), a small vibrating element made of cane or metal *(38)*

Registration: In organ music, the choice of stops with which to play a passage

Requiem Mass, Requiem: The special *Mass* celebrated when someone dies

Resolve: To proceed from *dissonant* harmony to *consonance (27)*

Rest: A momentary silence in music; in musical notation, a sign indicating momentary silence *(20)*

Retransition: In *sonata form,* the passage leading from the end of the *development* section into the beginning of the *recapitulation (181)*

Retrograde: Reading or playing a melody or twelve-tone *series* backwards *(326)*

Rhythm: The aspect of music having to do with the duration of the notes in time; also applied ("a rhythm") to any particular durational pattern *(9, 10)*

Rhythm and blues: Genre of African American music of the early 1950s, forerunner of *rock (411)*

Rhythm section: In jazz, the instrumental group used to emphasize and invigorate the meter (drums, bass, and piano) *(390)*

Ritardando: Slowing down *(14)*

Ritenuto: Held back in tempo

Ritornello: The orchestral material at the beginning of a concerto grosso, etc., which always returns later in the piece *(129)*

Ritornello form: A Baroque musical form based on recurrences of a *ritornello (129)*

Rock: The dominant popular-music style of the late 20th century *(410)*

Rondo: A musical form consisting of one main theme or tune alternating with other themes or sections (**ABACA, ABACABA,** etc.) *(194)*

Round: A simple type of sung *canon,* with all voices entering on the same note after the same time interval *(29)*

Row: Same as *series (326)*

Rubato: "Robbed" time; the free treatment of meter in performance *(242)*

Ryuteki (ree-óo-tay-kée): A Japanese side-blown flute; heard in *gagaku (213)*

Sampling: Especially in rap, the extraction, repetition, and manipulation of short excerpts from other popular songs, etc. *(368)*

Sarabande: A Baroque dance in slow *triple meter,* with a secondary accent on the second beat *(143)*

Scale: A selection of ordered pitches that provides the pitch material for music *(14)*

Scherzo (scáir-tzo): A form developed by Beethoven from the *minuet* to use for movements in larger compositions; later sometimes used alone, as by Chopin *(227)*

Score: The full musical notation for a piece involving several or many performers *(22)*

Secco recitative: See *recitative (152)*

Second group: In *sonata form,* the group of themes following the *bridge,* in the second key *(180)*

Second theme: In *sonata form,* one theme that is the most prominent among the second group of themes in the *exposition (180)*

Semitone: Same as *half step (18)*

Sequence: (1) In a melody, a series of fragments identical except for their placement at successively higher or lower pitch levels *(25)*; (2) in the Middle Ages, a type of *plainchant* in which successive phrases of text receive nearly identical melodic treatment *(61)*

Serialism, serial: The technique of composing with a *series,* generally a twelve-tone series *(317, 326)*

Series: A fixed arrangement of pitches (or rhythms) held to throughout a serial composition *(326)*

Sforzando: An especially strong accent; the mark indicating this in musical notation (*sf* or >) *(11)*

Shamisen (shah-mée-sen): A Japanese three-stringed lute; used as accompaniment in *kabuki (309)*

Sharp: In musical notation, a sign (♯) indicating that the note it precedes is to be played a *semitone* higher. A double sharp (𝄪) is occasionally used to indicate that a note is played two semitones higher *(17)*

Sho: A Japanese mouth reed-organ with seventeen pipes; heard in *gagaku (213)*

Siciliana: A Baroque dance type in *compound meter (143)*

Simple meter: A meter in which the main beats are not subdivided, or are subdivided into two, e.g., **2/4, 3/4, 4/4** *(11)*

Sixteenth note: A note one-sixteenth the length of a whole note *(20)*

Slur: In musical notation, a curved line over several notes, indicating that they are to be played smoothly, or *legato (21)*

Solo exposition: In Classical concerto form, the second of two *expositions,* played by the soloist and the orchestra *(201)*

Sonata: A chamber-music piece in several movements, typically for three main instruments plus *continuo* in the Baroque period, and for only one or two instruments since then *(197)*

Sonata form (sonata-allegro form): A form developed by the Classical composers and used in almost all the first movements of their symphonies, sonatas, etc. *(179)*

Song cycle: A group of songs connected by a general idea or story, and sometimes also by musical unifying devices *(253)*

Sonority: A general term for sound quality, either of a momentary chord, or of a whole piece or style *(74)*

Soprano: The high female (or boy's) voice

Spiritual: Religious folk song, usually among African Americans (called "Negro spiritual" in the 19th century) *(388)*

Sprechstimme: A vocal style developed by Schoenberg, in between singing and speaking *(340)*

Staccato: Played in a detached manner; as opposed to *legato (21)*

Staff (or stave): In musical notation, the group of five horizontal lines on which music is written *(21)*

Stanza: In songs or ballads, one of several similar poetic units, which are usually sung to the same tune; also called verse

Stop: An organ stop is a single set of pipes, covering the entire pitch range in a particular tone color *(45)*

Stretto: In a *fugue,* overlapping entrances of the fugue *subject* in several voices simultaneously *(140)*

String quartet: An instrumental group consisting of two violins, viola, and cello; or a piece composed for this group; or the four players themselves *(204)*

Strophic form, strophic song: A song in several *stanzas,* with the same music sung for each stanza; as opposed to *through-composed song (251)*

Structure: A term often used to mean *form*

Style: The combination of qualities that make a period of art, a composer, a group of works, or an individual work distinctive *(50)*

Subito: Suddenly (as in *subito forte* or *subito piano,* suddenly loud, suddenly soft) *(7)*

Subject: The term for the principal theme of a *fugue (139)*

Subject entries: In a *fugue,* appearances of the entire fugue *subject* after the opening *exposition (140)*

Suite: A piece consisting of a series of dances *(104, 143)*

Swing: A type of big-band jazz of the late 1930s and 1940s *(394)*

Symbolism: A late 19th-century movement in the arts that emphasized suggestion rather than precise reference *(319)*

Symphonic poem: A piece of orchestral *program music* in one long movement *(290)*

Symphony: A large orchestral piece in several movements *(178)*

Syncopation: The accenting of certain beats of the meter that are ordinarily unaccented *(13)*

Synthesizer: An electronic apparatus that generates sounds for electronic music *(45, 368)*

Tempo: The speed of music, i.e., the rate at which the accented and unaccented beats of the meter follow one another *(14)*

Tenor: The high adult male voice

Ternary form: A three-part musical form in which the last section repeats the first: **ABA** form *(192)*

Texture: The blend of the various sounds and melodic lines occurring simultaneously in a piece of music *(28)*

Thematic transformation: A variation-like procedure applied to short themes in the various sections of Romantic *symphonic poems* and other works *(248)*

Theme: The basic subject matter of a piece of music. A theme can be a phrase, a short *motive*, a full tune, etc. *(26)*.

Theme and variations: A form consisting of a tune (the theme) plus a number of variations on it *(187)*

Through-composed *(durchkomponiert)* song: A song with new music for each stanza of the poem; as opposed to *strophic song (251)*

Tie: In musical notation, a curved line joining two notes of the same pitch into a continuous sound *(20)*

Timbre (tám-bruh): Another term for *tone color (8)*

Time signature: In musical notation, the numbers on the staff at the beginning of a piece that indicate the meter *(21)*

Toccata: Especially in Baroque music, a written-out composition in improvisational style, generally for organ or harpsichord *(105)*

Tonality, tonal: The feeling of centrality of one note (and its chord) to a passage of music; as opposed to *atonality (31)*

Tone: A sound of a certain definite pitch and duration; same as *note*

Tone color: The sonorous quality of a particular instrument, voice, or combination of instruments or voices *(8)*

Tone poem: Same as *symphonic poem (290)*

Tonic (noun): In *tonal* music, the central-sounding note *(31)*

Transition: A passage whose function is to connect one section of a piece with another; see *bridge*

Transpose: To move a whole piece, or a section of a piece, or a *twelve-tone series*, from one pitch level to another *(326)*

Trill: Two adjacent notes played very rapidly in alternation

Trio: (1) A piece for three instruments or singers; (2) the second or B section of a *minuet* movement, *scherzo*, etc. *(144, 191)*

Trio sonata: A Baroque sonata for three main instruments plus the *continuo* chord instrument

Triple meter: Meter consisting of one accented beat alternating with two unaccented beats: *one* two three *one* two three *(12)*

Triplet: A group of three notes performed in the time normally taken by two *(21)*

Troubadours, trouvères: Aristocratic poet-musicians of the Middle Ages *(62)*

Tsuridaiko (tzóo-ree-díe-koh): A large Japanese barrel drum; heard in *gagaku (213)*

Tune: A simple, easily singable melody that is coherent and complete *(24)*

Twelve-tone series (or row): An ordering of all twelve notes of the *chromatic scale*, used in composing *serial* music *(326)*

Twelve-tone system: Method of composition devised by Arnold Schoenberg in which the twelve pitches of the octave are ordered and strictly manipulated *(326)*

Upbeat: A weak or unaccented beat leading to a *downbeat*

Variation form: A form in which a single melodic unit is repeated with harmonic, rhythmic, dynamic, or timbral changes *(105, 132)*

Vernacular music: Music that was developed in America outside the European concert music tradition *(384)*

Vivace, vivo: Lively *(14)*

Vocables: Sung syllables which have no precise meaning, e.g. "tra-la-la" *(72)*

Voice: (1) Throat sound; (2) a contrapuntal line—whether sung or played by instruments—in a *polyphonic* piece such as a *fugue*

Walking bass: A bass line consisting of steady equal note values, usually eighths or quarters *(121, 147)*

Waltz: A 19th-century dance in *triple meter*

Whole note: The longest note in normal use, and the basis of the duration of shorter notes (half notes, quarter notes, etc.) *(20)*

Whole step, whole tone: The interval equal to two half steps (semitones) *(18)*

Whole-tone scale: A scale, used sometimes by Debussy, comprising only six notes to the octave, each a whole tone apart (i.e., two semitones) *(327)*

Word painting: Musical illustration of the meaning of a word or a short verbal phrase *(82)*

Yueqin (yuéh-chin): A Chinese lute; heard in Beijing opera *(311)*

Music and Literary Credits

6, 10, 24, 46 Aaron Copland, brief excerpts from *What to Listen for in Music* by Aaron Copland. Copyright © 1939 by Aaron Copland. Reprinted by permission of the Aaron Copland Fund for Music, Inc., copyright owner.

26 "Who Cares?" by George Gershwin and Ira Gershwin. © 1931 (Renewed) WB Music Corp. All rights reserved. Used by permission of Warner Bros. Publications U.S. Inc., Miami, FL 33014.

33 "Happy Birthday to You," by Mildred J. Hill and Patty S. Hill © 1935 (Renewed) Summy-Birchard Music, a Division of Summy-Birchard Inc. All rights reserved. Used by permission of Warner Bros. Publications U.S. Inc., Miami, FL 33014.

321 Arnold Schoenberg. Excerpts from Piano Concerto. Used by permission of Belmont Music Publishers, Pacific Palisades, CA 90272.

334–35, 337 Igor Stravinsky. Excerpts from "The Adoration of the Earth." From *The Rite of Spring*. Copyright © 1912, 1921 by Hawkes & Son (London) Ltd. Copyright Renewed. Reprinted by permission.

341 Arnold Schoenberg. Excerpt from *Pierre lunaire*. Used by permission of Belmont Music Publishers, Pacific Palisades, CA 90272.

343–44 Alban Berg. Excerpts from *Wozzeck*. © 1931 by Universal Edition A.G. Vienna. © Renewed. All Rights Reserved. Used by permission of European American Music Distributors Corporation, sole U.S. and Canadian agent for Universal Edition A.G. Vienna.

350 Charles Ives. Excerpts from "The Rockstrewn Hills Join in the People's Outdoor Meeting," from Second Orchestral Set, No. 2. Copyright © 1971, 1978 by Peer International Corporation. Used by permission.

355–56 Maurice Ravel. Excerpts from Piano Concerto in G (1931). Courtesy Durand Music Publishing (France).

359–61 Béla Bartók. Excerpts from Music for Strings, Percussion, and Celesta from String Quartet No. 2. © 1920 by Universal Edition A.G. Vienna. © Renewed. All Rights Reserved. Used by permission of European American Music Distributors Corporation, sole U.S. and Canadian agent for Universal A.G. Vienna.

364 Aaron Copland. Excerpt from *Appalachian Spring*. Copyright © 1945 by The Aaron Copland Fund for Music, Inc. Copyright Renewed. Boosey & Hawkes, Inc., Sole Publisher and Licensee. Used by permission.

370 Anton Webern. Excerpt from Five Orchestral Pieces, Opus 10, No. 4. Copyright © 1923 by Universal Edition A.G. Vienna. © Renewed. All Rights Reserved. Used by permission of European American Music Distributors Corporation, sole U.S. and Canadian agent for Universal Edition A.G. Vienna.

370 Terry Riley. Excerpt from *In C*. © 1964 Terry Riley. Reprinted by permission of Celestial Harmonies, Tucson, AZ.

376 John Cage. *Aria*. Copyright © 1960 by C.F. Peters Corporation. On Behalf of Henmar Press, Inc. Used by permission. All rights reserved.

378 George Crumb. Excerpts from *Black Angels*. © 1971 by C.F. Peters Corporation. Used by permission. All rights reserved.

380 Sylvia Plath. Excerpts from "Paralytic" from *The Collected Poems of Sylvia Plath* by Sylvia Plath. Copyright © 1963 by Ted Hughes. Excerpts from *The Bell Jar* by Sylvia Plath. Copyright © 1971 by Harper & Row, Publishers, Inc. Reprinted by permission of HarperCollins Publishers Inc. and Faber & Faber Ltd.

382–83 Steve Reich. Excerpts from *Tehillim*. Copyright © 1981 by Hendon Music, Inc., a Boosey & Hawkes Company. Revised edition Copyright © 1994 by Hendon Music, Inc. Reprinted by permission.

401 Johnny Green and Edward Heyman. Excerpt from *Out of Nowhere*. Copyright © 1931 by Famous Music Corporation. Copyright renewed 1958 and assigned to Famous Music Corporation. Reprinted by permission.

404 Prelude No. 1, by George Gershwin. © 1927 (Renewed) WB Music Corp. All rights reserved. Used by permission of Warner Bros. Publications U.S. Inc., Miami, FL 33014.

408–09 "Maria," "Cool" from *West Side Story*, music by Leonard Bernstein, lyrics by Stephen Sondheim. Copyright © 1956, 1957 (renewed) by Leonard Bernstein and Stephen Sondheim. Boosey & Hawkes, Inc., Publisher. "Cha-cha" from *West Side Story*. Copyright © 1956, 1957, 1958, 1959 by Amberson Holdings LLC and Stephen Sondheim. Copyright Renewed. Leonard Bernstein Music Publishing company LLC, Publisher, Boosey & Hawkes, Inc., Sole Agent. Reprinted by permission.

Illustration Credits

xiii Henry VIII psalter (c. 1540), British Library, London, UK/Bridgeman Art Library

xiv Adolph von Menzel, *The Flute Concert*, 1850/52. Stattliche Museen zu Berlin—Preussischer Kulturbesitz—Nationalgalerie

xxviii Bob Krist/CORBIS

3 Copyright The Pierpont Morgan Library/Art Resource, NY

7 *top*: Richard Megna/Fundamental Photographs; *bottom*: Copyright British Museum

9 © Jack Vartoogian

11 Carol Simowitz

14 Musée de la Musique—Cité de la Musique, Paris, France/ Bridgeman Art Library

16 Bill Stanton/Image State

19 Josef Albers Museum, Bottrop

25 Bettmann/CORBIS

27 George Pickow/Photo Media

30 Private Collection, Switzerland

33 Scala/Art Resource, NY

36 *left*: © Steve J. Sherman; *right*: Boltin Picture Library

37 *top*: © Ebet Roberts; *bottom left:* © Jack Vartoogian; *bottom right*: Lebrecht Music Collection

38 *both*: © Steve J. Sherman

39 Carol Simowitz

40 Lebrecht Music Collection

41 *top*: Carol Simowitz; *bottom*: Bob Daemmrich/The Image Works

42 © Steve J. Sherman

43 Square piano by Nunn and Clark, New York, 1853. The Metropolitan Museum of Art, Gift of George Lowther, 1906. (06.1312) Photograph © 1977 The Metropolitan Museum of Art

44 *top*: Boltin Picture Library; *bottom*: Lawrence Migdale/ Photo Researchers

45 Caravaggio, *Young Man Playing a Lute*, Hermitage, St. Petersburg, Russia/Bridgeman Art Library

47 Kunsthistorisches Museum, Vienna

48 Paul Steel/CORBIS Stock Market

51 Joseph Sohm, ChromoSohm, Inc./CORBIS

55 Institut Amatller d'Art Hispànic

56 Institut Amatller d'Art Hispànic

57 Lambeth Palace Library, London, UK/Bridgeman Art Library

59 Institut Amatller d'Art Hispànic

61 Wisse der Wege, Scivias. Otto Müller Verlag, Salzburg, 8. Aufl. 1987. Photo Courtesy Abtei Sankt Hildegard

63 *left*: Grosse Heidelberger Liederhandschrift (Codex Manesse), fol. 399r. Universitätsbibliothek, Heidelberg; *right*: Bibliothèque Nationale de France, Paris

65 *tiles*: Institut Amatller d'Art Hispànic; *bottom*: Culver Pictures

66 Robert Harding Picture Library

70 Christine Osborne/CORBIS

71 William Waterfall/Pacific Stock

72 Gunter Marx/CORBIS

73 *both*: Scala/Art Resource, NY

75 Wallraf-Richartz Museum, Cologne. Photo: Rheinisches Bildarchiv, Cologne

76 Bibliothèque Nationale de France, Paris/Giraudon-Bridgeman Art Library

77 University of California at Berkeley Music Library

78 Francis G. Mayer/CORBIS

79 *top*: Bettmann/CORBIS; *bottom*: Austrian National Library, Vienna

83 Bayerische Staatsbibliothek, Munich

84 Bettmann/CORBIS

86 Berkeley Castle, Gloucestershire, UK/Bridgeman Art Library

89 Copyright British Library

90 Centre Nationale de la Recherche Scientifique

91 Museo de Arte Religioso, Cuzco, Peru

93 Canaletto, *The Rialto Bridge*. Photo: Scala/Art Resource, NY

97 Museum für Kunst und Gewerbe, Hamburg

98 *both*: Bibliothèque Nationale de France, Paris

100 *left*: Conservatory of St. Peter, Naples, Italy/Giraudon-Bridgeman Art Library; *right*: Bettmann/ CORBIS

102 By courtesy of the National Portrait Gallery, London

105 Scala/Art Resource, NY

107 David Lees/CORBIS

108 H. Rogers/TRIP

109 Giacomo Pirozzi/Panos Pictures

113 *top*: Pierre Patel, *Carriages Arriving at Versailles,* 1688. Photo: Giraudon/Art Resource, NY; *bottom*: Scala/Art Resource, NY

114 G.G. Bibiena, stage set for Metastasio's *Didone Abbandonata*. Photo: Blauel/Artothek

115 Giovanni Battista Tiepolo, Painted Ceiling, Residenz, Würzburg. Photo: Scala/Art Resource, NY

116 National Gallery of Scotland, Edinburgh/Bridgeman Art Library

117 Scala/Art Resource, NY

118 *top*: Giraudon/Art Resource, NY; *center, bottom*: from LeBrun's Conférence sur l'Expression, 1698

120 Oliviero, Performance at Teatro Reggio, Turin. Photo: Scala/Art Resource, NY

122 Munari, *Still Life with Instruments* (detail). Photo: Scala/Art Resource, NY

124 Agence France Presse

126 © Steve J. Sherman

128 *both*: Boltin Picture Library

130 Bettmann/CORBIS

132 Bettmann/CORBIS

133 Gaspar Netscher, *The Viola da Gamba Lesson*. Photo: Giraudon/Art Resource, NY

137 Private Collection

138 *top*: Bettmann/CORBIS; *bottom*: University of California at Berkeley Music Library

141 University of California at Berkeley Music Library

144 Scala/Art Resource, NY

145 Thomas Rowlandson, *Old Vauxhall Gardens*. Victoria & Albert Museum, London

146 Private Collection

150 Sächsische Landesbibliothek—Staats- und Universitätsbibliothek Dresden/Abteilung Deutsche Fotothek

151 School of Pietro Longhi, *Opera Seria*. Photo: Scala/Art Resource, NY

152 Royal College of Music, London, UK/Bridgeman Art Library

154 Carol Rosegg

155 Bettmann/CORBIS

157 *both*: Mary Evans Picture Library

159 Private Collection

161 Herbert Kratz, gouache, 1885. Photo: AKG London/Photo Researchers

163 Lüneburg Marketing GmbH

165 Archivo Iconografico, S.A./CORBIS

166 *top*: H.H. Arnason, by permission of the Comédie Française; *bottom*: Guildhall Library, Corporation of London, UK/Bridgeman Art Library

167 *top*: faïence plaque, *The Magic Flute*, Museum of Fine Arts Lille. Photo: Giraudon/Art Resource, NY; *bottom*: Jean-Antoine Houdon, bust of Thomas Jefferson, 1789, marble, Museum of Fine Arts, Boston, George Nixon Black Fund. Photograph © 2003 Museum of Fine Arts, Boston

168 *top*: Jean-Antoine Houdon, bust of Rousseau (detail). Photo H.H. Arnason, Collection of Edmond Courty; *bottom*: Bettmann/CORBIS

169 *top*: Peter Jacob Horemans, *Court Musicians with Stringed Instruments*. Photo: Blauel/Artothek; *bottom*: Jean-Antoine Houdon, statue of Gluck (detail), Stiftung Weimarer Klassik, Goethe-Nationalmuseum

170 Bettmann/CORBIS

172 Johann Zoffany (1733–1810), *George, 3rd Earl Cowper, with the Family of Charles Gore*, c. 1775 (oil on canvas). Yale Center for British Art, Paul Mellon Collection/Bridgeman Art Library

176 Scala/Art Resource, NY

177 Jean-Antoine Houdon, bust of Mme. Houdon, Louvre. Photo: Giraudon/Art Resource, NY

180 Spinet, probably by Thomas Hitchcock, English, 1742, Fenton House, Hampstead, London/Bridgeman Art Library

183 *top*: Historisches Museum der Stadt Wien, Vienna, Austria/ Bridgeman Art Library; *bottom*: Mozart Museum, Salzburg, Austria/Bridgeman Art Library

184 *top*: Ali Meyer/CORBIS; *bottom*: University of California at Berkeley Music Library

186 *top left*: Jasper Johns, Painted Bronze, 1960. Reproduced Courtesy of Universal Limited Art Editions; *top right, bottom left and right*: Monotypes #7, #16, #4 from *Jasper Johns* by Judith Goldman. Reproduced Courtesy of Universal Limited Art Editions

188 Pesci, *Esterháza Castle*, Orszagos Müemleki Felügveloség. Photo: Gabor Barca

190 *top*: John Hoppner, *Franz Joseph Haydn* (detail), 1791. The Royal Collection, copyright 2003 Her Majesty Queen Elizabeth II; *bottom*: The Metropolitan Museum of Art, The Crosby Brown Collection of Musical Instruments (89.4.1235)

192 Lebrecht Music Collection/AL

194 Bettmann/CORBIS

198 *left*: Marie-Louise-Elizabeth Vigée-LeBrun, *The Duchess of Polignac*, 1783. Waddesdon Manor, The Rothschild Collection (The National Trust); *right*: Charles Bird King, *Mrs. John Quincy Adams*, ca. 1824. Oil on canvas, 130.8 x 100.6 cm. Adams-Clement Collection, gift of Mary Louisa Adams Clement in memory of her mother, Louisa Catherine Adams Clement. Smithsonian American Art Museum, Washington, DC/Art Resource, NY

200 Mozart Museum/Archive

203 University of California at Berkeley Music Collection

205 *top*: Bettmann/CORBIS; *bottom*: © Steve J. Sherman

206 *top*: © Jack Vartoogian; *bottom*: Courtesy Holland Festival

208 *top*: University of California at Berkeley Music Library; *bottom*: Culver Pictures

209 University of California at Berkeley Music Library

210 Bettmann/CORBIS

211 Winnie Klotz/ Metropolitan Opera

212 © Jack Vartoogian

213 © Jack Vartoogian

214 © Jack Vartoogian

215 William Waterfall/Pacific Stock

216 © Jack Vartoogian

217 Roman Sorimar/CORBIS

218 © Dugowson/STM Concept/CORBIS Sygma

224 Hulton-Deutsch Collection/CORBIS

225 Jacques-Louis David, *The Coronation of Napoleon* (detail), Louvre. Photo: Giraudon/Art Resource, NY

226 Library of Congress

227 Bettmann/CORBIS

230 Beethoven-Archiv, Bonn, H.A. Bodmer Collection

232 *Beethoven Nearing the End* by Batt (plate 18, *The Oxford Companion to Music*, copyright Mrs. W.A. Barrett) is reproduced by kind permission of the copyright owner.

236 Bettmann/CORBIS

237 Private Collection/Archives Charmet/Bridgeman Art Library

238 Henry Fuseli, *The Nightmare*, 1771. Founders Society Purchase with funds from Mr. and Mrs. Bert L. Smokler and Mr. and Mrs. Lawrence H. Fleischman. Photograph © 1995 The Detroit Institute of Arts

239 J.M.W. Turner, *The Fighting Téméraire*, © National Gallery Collection. By kind permission of the Trustees of the National Gallery, London/CORBIS

240 *left*: Caspar David Friedrich, *Mountainous Landscape*, c. 1812, Kunsthistorisches Museum, Vienna. Photo: Erich Lessing/Art Resource, NY; *right*: John Martin, *The Bard*, c. 1817, oil on canvas, 50 x 40", Yale Center for British Art, Paul Mellon Collection/ Bridgeman Art Library

241 *left*: Hulton Archive/Getty Images; *right*; Carnegie Hall Archives

244 The Metropolitan Museum of Art. The Crosby Brown Collection of Musical Instruments, 1889 (89.4.1851)

245 Bettmann/CORBIS

246 Wilhelm von Lindenschmidt the Younger, *The Music Makers*, 1856. Neue Pinakothek, Munich. Photo: Blauel/Artothek

247 Bettmann/CORBIS

250 Max Klinger, *Beethoven*, bronze, marble, ivory, etc. Museum der Bildenden Künste, Leipzig/Maximilian Speck von Sternberg Stiftung

251 Kunsthistorisches Museum, Vienna, Austria/Bridgeman Art Library

252 *top*: Private Collection; *bottom*: Historisches Museum der Stadt Wien, Vienna, Austria/Bridgeman Art Library

256 Bettmann/CORBIS

257 Robert-Schumann-Haus, Zwickau

258 Archiv/Photo Researchers

261 Bettmann/CORBIS

262 Ludwig von Hofmann, *Notturno*, Neue Pinakothek, Munich. Photo: Blauel/Artothek

263 *top left*: © Steve J. Sherman; *top right, bottom*: Mary Evans Picture Library

265 *both*: Bettmann/CORBIS

267 Francisco Goya, *Witches' Sabbath* (detail). Photo: Scala/ Art Resource, NY

268 Bettmann/CORBIS

271 Deutsches Theatermuseum, Munich. Photo: Klaus Broszat

272 *left, left center, right center*: Culver Pictures; *right*: Bettmann/CORBIS

274 *top*: Museo Teatrale alla Scala, Milan; *bottom*: Bettmann/CORBIS

276 © Jack Vartoogian

280 *both*: Richard Wagner Museum Bayreuth

281 Bettmann/CORBIS

282 The Art Archive/Richard Wagner Museum Bayreuth/Dagli Orti (A)

283 *top*: Max Bruckner, scenery for Wagner's *Der Ring der Nibelungen* (Valhalla), 1896. Photo: The Art Archive/Richard Wagner Museum Bayreuth/Dagli Orti; *bottom*: The Kobal Collection/New Line/Saul Zaentz/Wing Nut

289 The Metropolitan Museum of Art, Rogers Fund, 1923. (23.94) Photograph © 1994 The Metropolitan Museum of Art

291 Bettmann/CORBIS

292 Mary Evans Picture Library

294 Akseli Gallen-Kallela, *Lemminkäinen's Mother*, 1987. Ateneum, Helsinki. Photo: The Central Art Archive

295 Private Collection/Elizabeth Harvey-Lee/Bridgeman Art Library © 2000 Artists Rights Society (ARS), New York/ADAGP, Paris

296 Royalty-Free/CORBIS

297 Novosti/Bridgeman Art Library

298 Bettmann/CORBIS

299 Archivo Iconografico, S.A./CORBIS

300 Snark/Art Resource, NY

303 © Jack Vartoogian

304 *top*: The New York Public Library, Astor, Lenox and Tilden Foundations; *bottom*: Bettmann/CORBIS

305 Austrian National Library, Vienna

306 *top*: Bettmann/CORBIS; *bottom*: University of California at Berkeley Music Library

308 Woodblock print by Okamura Masanobu (1686–1764), British Museum, London/Bridgeman Art Library

309 © Jack Vartoogian

310 © Jack Vartoogian

311 Dean Conger/CORBIS

317 Georges Braque, *Still Life with Score by Satie*, Museum of Modern Art, Paris. Photo: Scala/Art Resource, NY © 2000 Artists Rights Society (ARS), New York/ADAGP, Paris

318 Bettmann/CORBIS

319 Wassily Kandinsky, design for cover of *The Blue Rider Almanac*, Städtische Galerie im Lenbachhaus, Munich. Photo: Blauel/Artothek

320 *top*: Edouard Manet, *In the Boat*, Neue Pinakothek, Munich. Photo: Scala/Art Resource, NY; *bottom*; Debussy, Chausson, Bonheur and Mme. Chausson on the banks of the Marne. Photo: Bibliothèque Nationale de France, Paris

321 Vincent van Gogh, *Les Chaumes à Cordeville*, 1890, Jeu de Paume, Paris. Photo: Scala/Art Resource, NY

322 *left*: Wassily Kandinsky, *Couple on Horseback*, 1907, Städtische Galerie im Lenbachhaus, Munich. Photo: Blauel/Artothek; *right*: Wassily Kandinsky, *Blue Mountain*, 1908–09, oil on canvas, 41¾ x 38". The Solomon R. Guggenheim Museum. Photo: David Heald, The Solomon R. Guggenheim Foundation; *bottom*: Wassily Kandinsky, *Romantic Landscape*, 1911, Städtische Galerie im Lenbachhaus, Munich. Photo: Blauel/Artothek

323 Digital Image © The Museum of Modern Art/Licensed by Scala/Art Resource, NY © 2000 Estate of Pablo Picasso/Artists Rights Society (ARS) New York

324 Klimt, *Musik*, lithograph. Private Collection/Bridgeman Art Library

326 Bettmann/CORBIS

331 James MacNeil Whistler, *Nocturne: Grey and Gold—Canal, Holland*, Freer Gallery of Art, Smithsonian Institution, Washington, DC. Gift of Charles Lang Freer (F1902.160a-b)

332 Giraudon/Art Resource, NY

334 Pablo Picasso, *Stravinsky*, 1927. Photo: Giraudon/Art Resource, NY © 2000 Estate of Pablo Picasso/Artists Rights Society (ARS), New York

335 Robbie Jack/CORBIS

336 Sanford A. Roth/Photo Researchers

338 Bettmann/CORBIS

339 Man Ray, *Arnold Schoenberg*, 1926, gelatin-silver plate, 11⅝ x 8¾". Collection of The Museum of Modern Art, New York. Gift of James Thrall Soby. Digital Image © The Museum of Modern Art/Licensed by Scala/Art Resource, NY © 2000 Man Ray Trust/Artists Rights Society (ARS), NY/ADAGP, Paris

340 Georges Rouault (1871–1958), *Pierrot*, c. 1937, oil on paper, Private Collection. Photo: Christie's Images/Bridgeman Art Library © 2000 Artists Rights Society (ARS), New York/ADAGP, Paris

343 Beth Bergman

345 Bettmann/CORBIS

348 Bettmann/CORBIS

349 *both*: Bettmann/CORBIS

353 *left*: Archivo Iconografico, S.A./CORBIS; *left center*; Frontispiece to the score of *Madama Butterfly*, Private Collection. Photo: Bridgeman Art Library; *right center*: Austrian National Library, Vienna; *right*: Frontispiece by Lovis Corinth to the piano score of *Elektra*, British Library, London. Photo: Bridgeman Art Library

354 Bettmann/CORBIS

355 Bibliothèque Nationale de France, Paris/Trela/Bridgeman Art Library

358 G.D. Hackett/Getty Images

359 Bettmann/CORBIS

360 Bettmann/CORBIS

362 Ben Shahn, *Trio*, c. 1985. Estate of Ben Shahn/Licensed by VAGA, New York. Photo: Scala/Art Resource, NY

363 Marcos Blahove, *Portrait of Aaron Copland*, 1972. National Portrait Gallery, Smithsonian Institution. Photo: Art Resource, NY

365 Barbara Morgan, Martha Graham in *Deep Song*

368 Pablo Picasso, *The Pianist,* Cannes, 1957. Museo Picasso, Barcelona, Spain/Index/Bridgeman Art Library © 2000 Estate of Pablo Picasso/Artists Rights Society (ARS), New York

369 *top*: Bill Stanton/Image State; *bottom*: © Steve J. Sherman

372 Mark Rothko, *Violet, Black, Orange, Yellow on White and Red*, oil on canvas, 81½ x 66". The Solomon R. Guggenheim Museum, Gift of Elaine and Werner Dannheisser and the Dannheisser Foundation. Photo: David Heald, The Solomon R. Guggenheim Foundation

373 University of Louisville, Courtesy Mrs. Doris Keyes. Photo: Anderson/Schott Archive

374 Bettmann/CORBIS

375 Lucien Hervé, Paris. Research Library, Getty Research Institute, Los Angeles (2002.R.41)

376 *top*: © Jack Vartoogian

377 G. D. Hackett/Getty Images

379 Maarit Kyotohärju/FIMIC

381 *top*: Martha Swope © Time Inc.; *bottom*: © Jack Vartoogian

382 Private Collection

385 Thomas Eakins, *The Concert Singer*, 1892 (detail), The Philadelphia Museum of Art, Given by Mrs. Thomas Eakins and Miss Mary Adeline Williams

386 Nathaniel Currier, *First Appearance of Jenny Lind in America: At Castle Garden*, September 11, 1850, lithograph. Clarence J. Davies Collection, Museum of the City of New York

387 *both*: Bettmann/CORBIS

389 Culver Pictures

391 Bettmann/CORBIS

392 © Syndey Byrd

393 Bettmann/CORBIS

394 Culver Pictures

395 Underwood & Underwood/CORBIS

396 Institute of Jazz Studies, Rutgers

397 © Herman Leonard

398 Jak Kilby, Arena/Stage Image

401 © Herman Leonard

403 *left*: © Amalie R. Rothschild; *right*: David Redfern/Retna

405 Private Collection

406 Culver Pictures

407 Barton Silverman/NYT Pictures

408 Martha Swope © Time Inc.

411 Getty Images

413 © Apple Corps, Camera Press/Retna

414 Matthew Mendelsohn/CORBIS

415 Courtesy Reprise Records

416 S.I.N./CORBIS

417 Gianni Muratore, Camera Press Digital/Retna

418 Louise Gubb/The Image Works

419 Carol Muller

421 Guy Marche/Image State

Index

Listen's Study Guide CD-ROM, a Multimedia Companion

The Study Guide CD-ROM, included with each copy of *Listen,* provides the **interactive Listening Charts** designed to work with the 6-CD and 3-CD sets purchased separately. In addition, it enhances the listening experience with twelve key recordings that coordinate with six **focused listening exercises** in Unit I on music fundamentals. The CD-ROM concludes with a thirteenth recording, Benjamin Britten's *Young Person's Guide to the Orchestra.*

User Guidelines

To use this CD-ROM, simply insert the disk into your CD-ROM drive and select the "Setup" file located on the disk. Then follow the directions offered. For more assistance, select the "ReadMe" file located on the disk. You may also insert this disk into your CD player to listen to the thirteen recordings. For technical assistance, please contact our technical support team at 1-800-936-6899 or <techsupport@bfwpub.com>.

Minimum System Requirements

PC: Windows 95/98/NT4/2000/ME/XP—Intel Pentium processor or equivalent—32 MB of installed RAM—Color monitor: at least 800 x 600 with support for 16-bit color—Keyboard—Mouse—Quad-speed (4x) or faster CD-ROM drive—Browser software: Netscape 4.0 or later/Internet Explorer 4.0 or later/AOL 4.0 or later.

Macintosh: OS 8.1 or higher/PowerPC processor—32 MB of installed RAM—Color monitor: at least 800 x 600 monitor with support for 16-bit color—Keyboard—Mouse—Quad-speed (4x) or faster CD-ROM drive—Browser software: Netscape 4.0 or later/Internet Explorer 4.5 or later/AOL 4.0 or later.

The track numbers for each recording are as follows:

- 1–3 Berlioz, *Fantastic* Symphony, IV, March to the Scaffold
- 4 Schubert, from Symphony No. 8 ("Unfinished"), I
- 5 Joplin, "Maple Leaf Rag"
- 6 Rachmaninov, from *Rhapsody on a Theme by Paganini*
- 7 Gershwin, "Who Cares?"
- 8 Beethoven, "Joy Theme" from Symphony No. 9, IV
- 9 Stravinsky, from *Symphony of Psalms,* II
- 10 Schubert, Moment Musical No. 3
- 11 Beethoven, from Piano Concerto No. 5 ("Emperor"), III
- 12 Mahler, from Symphony No. 1, III
- 13 Chaikovsky, from *The Nutcracker Suite:* Dance of the Sugar-Plum Fairy
- 14–16 Beethoven, Symphony No. 5, III
- 17–22 Britten, *The Young Person's Guide to the Orchestra*

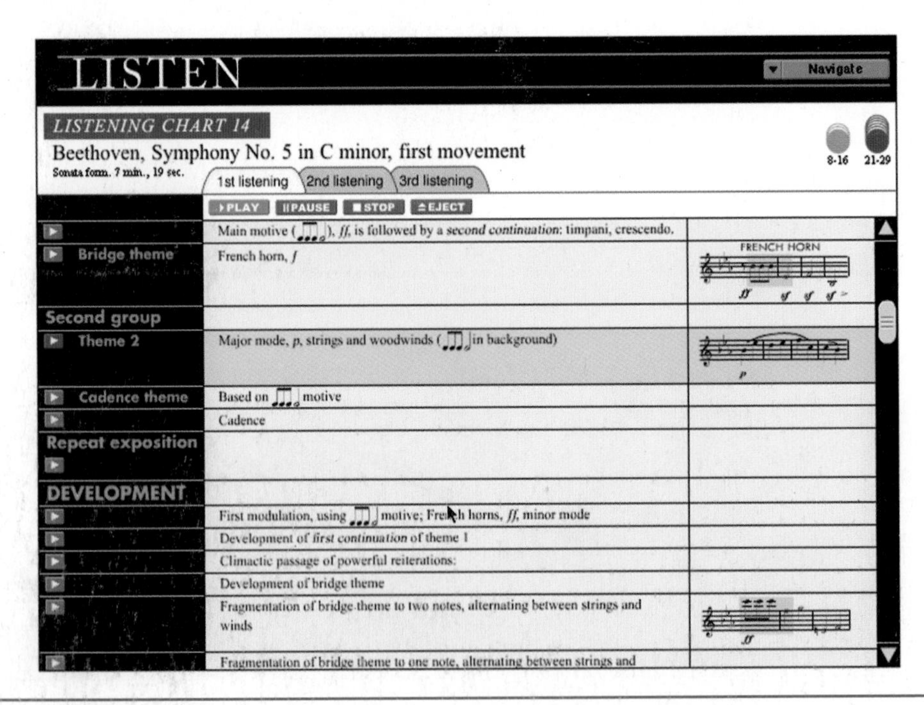